Patterns of World History

Patterns of World History

Volume 2: Since 1400

Peter von Sivers
University of Utah

Charles A. Desnoyers
La Salle University

George B. Stow
La Salle University

New York   Oxford
OXFORD UNIVERSITY PRESS

Oxford University Press, Inc., publishes works that further Oxford University's
objective of excellence in research, scholarship, and education.

Oxford   New York
Auckland   Cape Town   Dar es Salaam   Hong Kong   Karachi
Kuala Lumpur   Madrid   Melbourne   Mexico City   Nairobi
New Delhi   Shanghai   Taipei   Toronto

With offices in
Argentina   Austria   Brazil   Chile   Czech Republic   France   Greece
Guatemala   Hungary   Italy   Japan   Poland   Portugal   Singapore
South Korea   Switzerland   Thailand   Turkey   Ukraine   Vietnam

For titles covered by Section 112 of the U.S. Higher Education Opportunity Act, please
visit www.oup.com/us/he for the latest information about pricing and alternate formats.

Published by Oxford University Press, Inc.
198 Madison Avenue, New York, New York, 10016
http://www.oup.com

Library of Congress Cataloging-in-Publication Data
Von Sivers, Peter.
 Patterns of world history / Peter von Sivers, Charles A. Desnoyers, George Stow.
  v. cm.
 Includes bibliographical references and index.
 Contents: v. 1. To 1600 — v. 2. Since 1400 — [v. 3.] Since 1750.
  ISBN 978-0-19-533287-2 (combined v.: acid-free paper) — ISBN 978-0-19-533288-9
(v. 1: acid-free paper) — ISBN 978-0-19-985898-9 (v. 2: acid-free paper) — ISBN 978-
0-19-533334-3 (Since 1750: acid-free paper) 1. World history—Textbooks. I. Desnoyers,
Charles, 1952– II. Stow, George B. III. Title.
 D21.V66 2012
 909—dc23

Printing number: 9 8 7 6 5 4 3 2 1
Printed in the United States of America
on acid-free paper

Coniugi Judithae dilectissimae
—Peter von Sivers

To all my students over the years, who have taught me at least as much as I've taught them; and most of all to my wife, Jacki, beloved in all things, but especially in her infinite patience and fortitude in seeing me through the writing of this book.

—Charles A. Desnoyers

For Susan and our children, Meredith and Jonathan.

—George B. Stow

—I hear and I forget; I see and I remember; I do and I understand
(Chinese proverb) 我听见我忘记；我看见我记住；我做我了解

Brief Contents

Part 3: The Formation of Religious Civilizations
600–1450 CE

Part 4: Interactions Across the Globe
1450–1750   518

Part 5 The Origins of Modernity
1750–1900   744

Part 6 From Three Modernities to One
1914–Present   972

Contents

PART THREE
The Formation of Religious Civilizations
600–1450 CE

Chapter 15
600–1550 CE

Features:

Patterns Up Close:
Human Sacrifice and Propaganda   510

Concept Map:
Comparing Patterns of Innovation in the Americas and Eurasia, 600–1500 CE   515

PART FOUR
Interactions Across the Globe
1450–1750   518

Chapter 16
1450–1650

Chapter 17
1450–1750

Renaissance, Reformation, and the New Science in Europe
558

Chapter 18
1500–1800

New Patterns in New Worlds: Colonialism and Indigenous Responses in the Americas
598

Chapter 19
1450–1800

African Kingdoms, the Atlantic Slave Trade, and the Origins of Black America
638

Chapter 20

1400–1750

The Mughal Empire: Muslim Rulers and Hindu Subjects   674

Chapter 21

1500–1800

Regulating the "Inner" and "Outer" Domains: China and Japan   708

Chapter 27
1790–1917

Creoles and Caudillos: Latin America and the Caribbean in the Nineteenth Century

Features:

Patterns Up Close:
Slave Rebellions in
Cuba and Brazil   954

Concept Map:
Latin America in the
Nineteenth Century 969

PART SIX

From Three Modernities to One
1914–Present

Chapter 28
1900–1945

World War and Competing Visions of Modernity

Features:

Patterns Up Close:
Mapping Utopia in
Soviet Georgia   1002

Concept Map:
Three Patterns
of Modernity,
1850–1939   1018

Maps

Studying with Maps and Concept Maps

MAPS

World history cannot be fully understood without a clear comprehension of the chronologies and parameters within which different empires, states, and peoples have changed over time. Maps facilitate this understanding by illuminating the significance of time, space, and geography in shaping the patterns of world history.

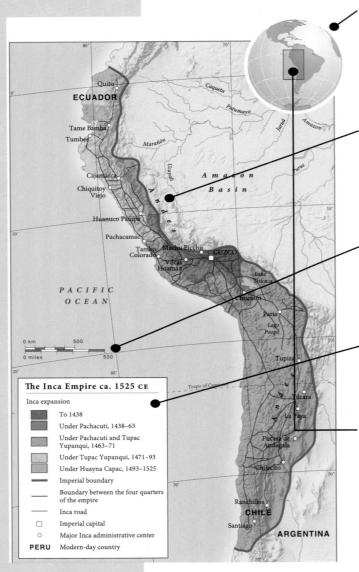

Projection

A map *projection* portrays all or part of the earth, which is spherical, on a flat surface. All maps, therefore, include some distortion. The projections in *Patterns of World History* show the earth at global, continental, regional, and local scales.

Topography

Many maps in *Patterns of World History* show *relief*—the contours of the land. Topography is an important element in studying maps because the physical terrain has played a critical role in shaping human history.

Scale Bar

Every map in *Patterns of World History* includes a *scale* that shows distances in both miles and kilometers and, in some instances, in feet as well.

Map Key

Maps use symbols to show the location of features and to convey information. Each symbol is explained in the map *key*.

Global Locator

Many of the maps in *Patterns of World History* include *global locators* that show the area being depicted in a larger context.

The Inca Empire ca. 1525 CE

Inca expansion

- To 1438
- Under Pachacuti, 1438–63
- Under Pachacuti and Tupac Yupanqui, 1463–71
- Under Tupac Yupanqui, 1471–93
- Under Huayna Capac, 1493–1525
- Imperial boundary
- Boundary between the four quarters of the empire
- Inca road
- □ Imperial capital
- ○ Major Inca administrative center
- **PERU** Modern-day country

CONCEPT MAPS

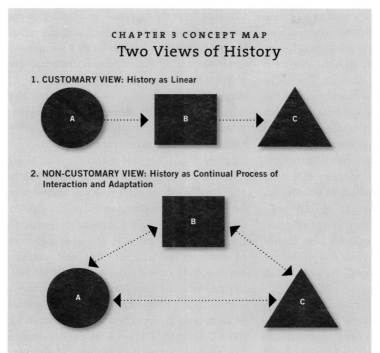

CHAPTER 3 CONCEPT MAP
Two Views of History

1. CUSTOMARY VIEW: History as Linear

2. NON-CUSTOMARY VIEW: History as Continual Process of Interaction and Adaptation

Ideas and concepts are at the center of *Patterns of World History*. Tackling these ideas and concepts—instead of simply memorizing dates and facts—is what makes history interesting. To help "see" core ideas, *concept maps* at the end of each chapter **use clear, simple, yet provocative graphics to synthesize key take-away points.**

Concept maps **employ simple, universal shapes** to symbolize ideas and processes.

Many concept maps, such as this one, use juxtaposition **to compare and contrast different ways of looking at a topic** or, in the example shown here, to **show change over time**

Clean graphics and clear colors **express big ideas simply and without fuss**—in this case, the changing dynamic between Europe, India, and China between 1500 and 1800.

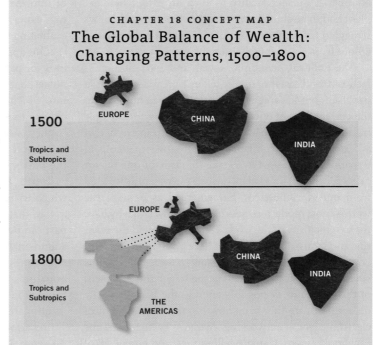

CHAPTER 18 CONCEPT MAP
The Global Balance of Wealth: Changing Patterns, 1500–1800

1500

Tropics and Subtropics

EUROPE   CHINA   INDIA

1800

Tropics and Subtropics

EUROPE   CHINA   INDIA

THE AMERICAS

Preface

It was the most violent earthquake ever to hit the islands in the 150 years during which records had been kept. On March 11, 2011, a quake measuring 8.9 on the 9-point Richter scale ripped through the northern part of the main Japanese island of Honshu. Despite Japan's long experience with earthquakes and some of the most stringent protection measures and building codes on earth, the destruction was on a colossal scale. But the damage itself was almost immediately overshadowed by the destruction wrought by the enormous tsunami generated by the quake, which hit the port city of Sendai and its surrounding vicinity within hours of the initial shocks. A 23-foot wave crushed everything in its path for miles inland and landed even giant cargo ships on the wharves. Oil refinery tanks exploded into flames, children were trapped on the roofs of their schools, and warnings of the tsunami's shockwaves were broadcast around the Pacific Rim.

Amid the vast debris fields and the hundreds of bodies washing up on the beaches, however, the most ominous part of the disaster was only beginning to unfold. The waves in their fury had wrecked the turbine of one nuclear power plant and flooded the entire Fukushima Number 2 nuclear facility to such an extent that the plant had to be shut down—but not before repair crews struggled for weeks to contain the radiation leaks and fallout from a possible meltdown.

The political, economic, social, and even cultural effects of this disaster naturally tell us a great deal about Japan itself; but in some ways they tell us even more about the current state of our modern world. How, for example, has the world come to be globalized to such an extent that an extreme disaster in Japan generates instantaneous international concern? Or, to take things back one historical step, how is it that Japan, once so purposefully isolated from outside influences, has emerged as perhaps the world's most modern society? Indeed, how and why have the vast majority of the world's nations adopted the scientific and industrial systems that have given us the oil refineries and nuclear power plants now so threatened by this epic natural disaster? What are the larger consequences of these systems in possibly altering the balance of life on earth? In another vein, how has the development of electronic "social networking" media—Twitter, YouTube, Facebook, Internet, smart cell phones, and e-mail, all of which are deeply ingrained in our lives—changed the way societies behave in the face of such events? How did human beings cope with natural or human-created disasters before the advent of these systems and devices? And, perhaps the largest question of all, what are the broad currents in human societies over the tens of thousands of years that modern humans have walked the earth that have brought us to our present state in which modernity holds such enormous promise and peril?

How all of these things and a myriad of others came to be is, in a large sense, the theme of this book. One of the hallmarks of our species is that we are historical creatures. We strive to remember the past in innumerable ways for an endless array of purposes: for cultural transmission, for moral instruction, for record keeping, to minimize risk in attempting new enterprises, to improve society or individuals, to tell entertaining or satisfying stories of ourselves. You, your family, your town or city, state, province, or country all have histories, all of them used in an endless variety of ways. As the historian G. R. Elton (1921–1994) put it, history is the only living laboratory we have of human behavior. So how is one to make sense of this bewildering, unending stream of information—especially if, as Elton would have it, the "experiments" in the "laboratory" are running and evaluating themselves?

Our approach in this book is, as the title suggests, to look for patterns in world history. We should say at the outset that we do not mean to select certain categories into which we attempt to stuff the historical events we choose to emphasize; nor do we claim that all world history is reducible to such patterns; nor do we mean to suggest that the nature of the patterns determines the outcome of historical events. We see them instead as broad, flexible, organizational frameworks around which to build the structure of a world history in such a way that the enormous sweep and content of the past can be viewed in a comprehensible narrative, with sound analysis and ample scope for debate and discussion. In this sense, we view them much like the role of armatures in clay sculptures, giving support and structure to the final figure but not necessarily preordaining its ultimate shape.

Take, for example, the role of innovation, in the broadest sense, in world history. The quest for the new and better has always been an animating spirit within the human saga—from the first wheel to the latest smart phone. Certainly, all such innovations, whether they are technological, intellectual, social, political, and so on, are vital to an understanding of human history. Our approach is to highlight the patterns we find in the development of such innovations as a way of taking a step back to make sense of them and the way that they foster change. Take the history of something from our recent past, e-mail, for example: Although electronic technology had advanced to the point in the 1960s where messages could be sent by computer, they could be sent and received only by operators using the same "server," as we would say today. What was needed, therefore, was a new system whereby messages could be sent and received by multiple servers in remote locations. The young engineer Ray Tomlinson (b. 1941), well versed in an early form of computer communication known as "ARPANET," which the American military used to share classified documents, concluded that, given the correct linkage, computers in far-flung locations could "talk" to each other. He worked out the missing piece in the form of the simple "@" sign, which he said "was used to indicate that the user was 'at' some other host rather than being local." Thus, the text message—and the e-mail address format we use today—originated through Tomlinson's interactions with other people and by means of his adapting other technologies available to him; these were then expanded exponentially by millions of others interacting with Tomlinson's breakthrough. This is but one recent example of the unfolding of a pattern of innovation; world history is full of them, and tracing their stories, effects, and implications comprises the heart of this book.

From its origins, human culture grew through interactions and adaptations on all the continents except Antarctica. A voluminous scholarship on all regions of the world has thus been accumulated, which those working in the field have to attempt to master if their explanations and arguments are to sound even remotely persuasive. The sheer volume and complexity of the sources, however, mean that even the knowledge and expertise of the best scholars are going to be incomplete. Moreover, the humility with which all historians must approach their material contains within it the realization that no historical explanation is ever fully satisfactory or final: As a driving force in the historical process, creative human agency moves this process into directions that are never fully predictable.

As we enter the second decade of the twenty-first century, world historians have long since left behind the "West plus the rest" approach that marked the field's early years, together with economic and geographical reductionism, in the search for a new balance between comprehensive cultural and institutional examinations, on the one hand, and those highlighting human agency, on the other. All too often, however, this is reflected in texts that seek broad coverage at the expense of analysis, thus resulting in a kind of "world history-lite." Our aim is therefore to simplify the study of the world—to make it accessible to the student—without making world history itself simplistic.

World History and Patterns of World History

Patterns of World History thus comes to the teaching of world history from the perspective of the relationship between continuity and change. What we advocate in this book is a distinct intellectual framework for this relationship and the role of innovation and historical change through patterns of origins, interactions, and adaptations, or as we like to call it, O-I-A. Each small or large technical or cultural innovation originated in one geographical center or independently in several different centers. As people in the centers interacted with their neighbors, the neighbors adapted to, and in many cases were transformed by, the innovations. By "adaptation" we include the entire spectrum of human responses, ranging from outright rejection to creative borrowing and, at times, forced acceptance.

Small technical innovations often went through the pattern of origin, interaction, and adaptation across the world without arousing much attention, even though they had major consequences. For example, the horse collar, which originated in ninth-century China and allowed for the replacement of oxen with stronger horses, gradually improved the productivity of agriculture in eleventh-century western Europe. More sweeping intellectual–cultural innovations, by contrast, such as the spread of universal religions like Buddhism, Christianity, and Islam and the rise of science, have often had profound consequences—in some cases leading to conflicts lasting centuries—and affect us even today.

Sometimes change was effected by commodities that to us seem rather ordinary. Take sugar, for example:

It originated in southeast Asia and was traded and grown in the Mediterranean, where its cultivation on plantations created the model for expansion into the vast slave system of the Atlantic basin from the fifteenth through the nineteenth centuries, forever altering the histories of four continents. What would our diets look like today without sugar? Its history continues to unfold as we debate its merits and health risks and it supports huge multinational agribusinesses. Or take a more obscure commodity: opium. Opium had been used medicinally for centuries in regions all over the world. But the advent of tobacco traded from the Americas to the Philippines to China created an environment in which the drug would be smoked for the first time. Enterprising rogue British merchants, eager to find a way to crack closed Chinese markets for other goods, began to smuggle it in from India. The market grew, the price went down, addiction spread, and Britain and China ultimately went to war over China's attempts to eliminate the traffic. Here, we have an example of an item generating interactions on a worldwide scale, with impacts on everything from politics to economics, culture, and even the environment. The legacies of the trade still weigh heavily on two of the rising powers of the twenty-first century: China and India. And opium and its derivatives, like morphine and heroin, continue to bring relief and suffering on a colossal scale to hundreds of millions of people.

What, then, do we gain by studying world history through the use of such patterns? First, if we consider innovation to be a driving force of history, it helps to satisfy an intrinsic human curiosity about origins—our own and others. Perhaps more importantly, seeing patterns of various kinds in historical development brings to light connections and linkages among peoples, cultures, and regions—as in the examples—that might not otherwise present themselves.

Second, such patterns can also reveal differences among cultures that other approaches to world history tend to neglect. For example, the differences between the civilizations of the Eastern and Western Hemispheres are generally highlighted in world history texts, but the broad commonalities of human groups creating agriculturally based cities and states in widely separated areas also show deep parallels in their patterns of origins, interactions, and adaptations: Such comparisons are at the center of our approach.

Third, this kind of analysis offers insights into how an individual innovation was subsequently developed and diffused across space and time—that is, the patterns by which the new eventually becomes a necessity in our daily lives. Through all of this we gain a deeper appreciation of the unfolding of global history from its origins in small, isolated areas to the vast networks of global interconnectedness in our present world—that is, how a tsunami in Japan can affect everything from early warning systems in coastal areas of distant countries to fluctuations in international bond and currency markets.

Finally, our use of a broad-based understanding of continuity, change, and innovation allows us to restore culture in all its individual and institutionalized aspects—spiritual, artistic, intellectual, scientific—to its rightful place alongside technology, environment, politics, and socioeconomic conditions. That is, understanding innovation in this way allows this text to help illuminate the full range of human ingenuity over time and space in a comprehensive, evenhanded, and open-ended fashion.

It is widely agreed that world history is more than simply the sum of all national histories. Likewise, *Patterns of World History* is more than an unbroken sequence of dates, battles, rulers, and their activities; and it is more than the study of isolated stories of change over time. Rather, in this textbook we endeavor to present in a clear and engaging way how world history "works." Instead of merely offering a narrative history of the appearance of this or that innovation, we present an analysis of the process by which an innovation in one part of the world is diffused and carried to the rest of the globe. Instead of focusing on the memorization of people, places, and events, we strive to present important facts in context and draw meaningful connections, analyzing whatever patterns we find and drawing conclusions where we can. In short, we seek to examine the interlocking mechanisms and animating forces of world history, without neglecting the human agency behind them.

Patterns of Change and Six Periods of World History

For the convenience of instructors teaching a course over two 15-week semesters, we have limited the book to 31 chapters. For the sake of continuity and to accommodate the many different ways schools divide the midpoint of their world history sequence, Chapters 15–18 overlap in both volumes; in Volume 2, Chapter

15 is given as a "prelude" to Part 4. Those using a trimester system will also find divisions made in convenient places, with Chapter 10 coming at the beginning of Part 3 and Chapter 22 at the beginning of Part 5. Finally, for those schools that offer a modern world history course that begins at approximately 1750, a volume is available that includes only the final two parts of the book.

Similarly, we have attempted to create a text that is adaptable to both chronological and thematic styles of instruction. We divide the history of the world into six major time periods and recognize for each period one or two main patterns of innovation, their spread through interaction, and their adoption by others. Obviously, lesser patterns are identified as well, many of which are of more limited regional interactive and adaptive impact. We wish to stress again that these are broad categories of analysis and that there is nothing reductive or deterministic in our aims or choices. Nevertheless, we believe the patterns we have chosen help to make the historical process more intelligible, providing a series of lenses that can help to focus the otherwise confusing facts and disparate details that comprise world history.

Part 1 (Prehistory–600 BCE): Origins of human civilization—tool making and symbol creating—in Africa as well as the origins of agriculture, urbanism, and state formation in the three agrarian centers of the Middle East, India, and China.

Part 2 (600 BCE–600 CE): Emergence of the axial age thinkers and their visions of a transcendent god or first principle in Eurasia; elevation of these visions to the status of state religions in empires, in the process forming multiethnic and multilinguistic polities.

Part 3 (600–1450): Disintegration of classical empires and formation of religious civilizations in Eurasia, with the emergence of religiously unified regions divided by commonwealths of multiple states.

Part 4 (1450–1750): Rise of new empires; interaction, both hostile and peaceful, among the religious civilizations and new empires across all continents of the world. Origins of the New Science in Europe, based on the use of mathematics for the investigation of nature.

Part 5 (1750–1900): Origins of scientific–industrial "modernity," simultaneous with the emergence of constitutional and ethnic nation-states, in the West (Europe and North America); interaction of the West with Asia and Africa, resulting in complex adaptations, both coerced as well as voluntary, on the part of the latter.

Part 6 (1900–Present): Division of early Western modernity into the three competing visions: communism, fascism, and capitalism. After two horrific world wars and the triumph of nation-state formation across the world, capitalism remains as the last surviving version of modernity. Capitalism is then reinvigorated through the "dot.com revolution," in which increasingly sophisticated software, Internet applications, and electronic communication devices lead to increasing use of social networking media in popularizing both "traditional" religious and cultural ideas and constitutional nationalism in authoritarian states.

Chapter Organization and Structure

Each part of the book addresses the role of change and innovation on a broad scale during a particular time and/or region, and each chapter contains different levels of exploration to examine the principal features of particular cultural or national areas and how each affects, and is affected by, the patterns of origins, interactions, and adaptations:

- *Geography and the Environment*: As we saw in the opening of this preface, the relationship between human beings and the geography and environment of the places they inhabit is among the most basic factors in understanding human societies. In Japan, for example, earthquakes and tsunamis have always been seen as part of the natural condition of things. Indeed, "tsunami" is a Japanese word with the tragically evocative meaning of "harbor wave." In this chapter segment, therefore, the topics under investigation involve the natural environment of a particular region and the general conditions affecting change and innovation. Climatic conditions, earthquakes, tsunamis, volcanic eruptions, outbreaks of disease, and so forth all have obvious effects on how humans react to the challenge of survival. The initial portions of chapters introducing new regions for study therefore include environmental and geographical overviews, which are revisited and expanded in later chapters as necessary. The larger issues of how decisive the impact of geography on the development of human societies is—as in the commonly asked question "Is geography destiny?"—are also examined here.

- *Political Developments*: In this segment, we ponder such questions as how rulers and their supporters wield political and military power. How do different political traditions develop in different areas? How do states expand, and why? How do different political arrangements attempt to strike a balance between the rulers and the ruled? How and why are political innovations transmitted to other societies? Why do societies accept or reject such innovations from the outside? Are there discernable patterns in the development of kingdoms or empires or nation-states?

- *Economic and Social Developments*: The relationship between economics and the structures and workings of societies has long been regarded as crucial by historians and social scientists. But what, if any, patterns emerge in how these relationships develop and function among different cultures? This segment explores such questions as the following: What role does economics play in the dynamics of change and continuity? What, for example, happens in agrarian societies when merchant classes develop? How does the accumulation of wealth lead to social hierarchy? What forms do these hierarchies take? How do societies formally and informally try to regulate wealth and poverty? How are economic conditions reflected in family life and gender relations? Are there patterns that reflect the varying social positions of men and women that are characteristic of certain economic and social institutions? How are these in turn affected by different cultural practices?

- *Intellectual, Religious, and Cultural Aspects*: Finally, we consider it vital to include an examination dealing in some depth with the way people understood their existence and life during each period. Clearly, intellectual innovation—the generation of new ideas—lies at the heart of the changes we have singled out as pivotal in the patterns of origins, interactions, and adaptations that form the heart of this text. Beyond this, those areas concerned with the search for and construction of meaning—particularly religion, the arts, philosophy, and science—not only reflect shifting perspectives but also, in many cases, play a leading role in determining the course of events within each form of society. For example, the shift to the use of mathematics as a foundation of the "scientific revolution" contributed mightily to the rationalism and empiricism of the Enlightenment—and hence to the development of the modernity that we find ourselves in today. All of these facets of intellectual life are, in turn, manifested in new perspectives and representations in the cultural life of a society.

Features

- **Seeing Patterns/Thinking Through Patterns:** Successful history teachers often employ recursive, even reiterative, techniques in the classroom to help students more clearly perceive patterns. In a similar fashion, "Seeing Patterns" and "Thinking Through Patterns" use a question–discussion format in each chapter to pose several broad questions ("Seeing Patterns") as advance organizers for key themes, which are then matched up with short essays at the end ("Thinking Through Patterns") that examine these same questions in a sophisticated yet student-friendly fashion. Designed to foster discussion, instructors who have class-tested *Patterns of World History* report that "Thinking Through Patterns" also serve as excellent models for writing short essays.

- **Patterns Up Close:** Since students frequently better apprehend macro-level patterns when they see their contours brought into sharper relief, "Patterns Up Close" essays in each chapter highlight a particular innovation that demonstrates origins, interactions, and adaptations in action. Spanning technological, social, political, intellectual, economic, and environmental developments, the "Patterns Up Close" essays combine text, visuals, and graphics to consider everything from the pepper trade to the guillotine to rock and roll.

- **Concept Maps/Putting It All Together:** To further reinforce understanding of the central ideas presented in *Patterns of World History*, each chapter concludes with a "Putting It All Together" section that includes compelling yet simple graphics, called "Concept Maps," that synthesize key take-away points. Carefully designed and field-tested with direct input from world history instructors, Concept Maps can be used to prompt classroom discussion and to help students focus on the big picture. They have been widely praised for the opportunities they offer for visual learning and critical thinking.

- **Voices and Vignettes:** In the end, history is made by people, not anonymous social forces; and while we examine large trends throughout the book, we try never to lose sight of how people in all walks of life originated, interacted, and adapted to the circumstances in which they found themselves or, in some cases, created for themselves. Thus, each chapter includes approximately four "voices"—short excerpts from people from all walks of life whose life experiences shed light on the patterns discussed in each chapter. Additionally, many different people—from contemporary figures like the female Yemeni activist Tawakkol Karman (Chapter 31) to Leo Africanus in the sixteenth century (Chapter 16) and the Chinese sage Mencius in the fourth century BCE (Chapter 9)—are featured in opening vignettes and then woven throughout the chapters to further reinforce the concept of human agency within history.
- **Photo Clusters:** In keeping with the patterns approach of the book, each chapter includes at least one and sometimes as many as three "photo clusters"—assemblages of visual sources, each of which pertains to the same topic, and all sharing a common caption.
- **Marginal Glossary:** To avoid the necessity of having to flip pages back and forth, definitions of words that the reader may not know, as well as definitions of key terms, are set directly in the margin at the point where they are first introduced.

Today, more than ever, students and instructors are confronted by a vast welter of information on every conceivable subject. Beyond the ever-expanding print media, the Internet and the Web have opened hitherto unimaginable amounts of data to us. Despite such unprecedented access, however, all of us are too frequently overwhelmed by this undifferentiated—and all too often indigestible—mass. Nowhere is this more true than in world history, by definition the field within the

historical profession with the broadest scope. Therefore, we think that an effort at synthesis—of narrative and analysis structured around a clear, accessible, widely applicable theme—is needed, an effort that seeks to explain critical patterns of the world's past behind the billions of bits of information accessible at the stroke of a key on a computer keyboard. We hope this text, in tracing the lines of transformative ideas and things that left their patterns deeply imprinted into the canvas of world history, will provide such a synthesis.

Additional Learning Resources for *Patterns of World History*

- **Instructor's Resource Manual:** Includes, for each chapter, a detailed chapter outline, suggested lecture topics, learning objectives, map quizzes, geography exercises, classroom activities, "Patterns Up Close" activities, "Seeing Patterns and Making Connections" activities, "Concept Map" exercises, biographical sketches, a correlation guide for the list of assets on the Instructor's Resource DVD, as well as suggested Web resources and digital media files. Also includes, for each chapter, approximately 40 multiple-choice, short-answer, true-or-false, and fill-in-the-blank as well as approximately 10 essay questions.
- **Instructor's Resource DVD:** Includes Power-Point slides and JPEG and PDF files for all the maps and photos in the text, an additional 400 map files from *The Oxford Atlas of World History*, as well as approximately 250 additional PowerPoint-based slides organized by theme and topic. Also includes approximately 1,500 questions that can be customized by the instructor.
- **Sources in Patterns of World History: Volume 1:** *To 1600:* Includes approximately 200 text and visual sources in world history, organized to match the chapter organization of *Patterns of World History*. Each source is accompanied by a headnote and reading questions.
- **Sources in Patterns of World History: Volume 2:** *Since 1400:* Includes approximately 200 text and visual sources in world history, organized by the chapter organization of *Patterns of World History*.

Each source is accompanied by a headnote and reading questions.

- **Mapping Patterns of World History, Volume 1: To 1600:** Includes approximately 50 full-color maps, each accompanied by a brief headnote, as well as Concept Map exercises.
- **Mapping Patterns of World History, Volume 2: Since 1400:** Includes approximately 50 full-color maps, each accompanied by a brief headnote, as well as Concept Map exercises.
- **Companion Web Site (www.oup.com/us/von sivers):** Includes quizzes, flashcards, map exercises, documents, interactive Concept Map exercises, and links to YouTube videos.
- **ClassMate for Patterns of World History:** Includes approximately 800 quizzes (25–30 per chapter) for low- or mid-stakes testing as well as an online gradebook for instructors.
- **E-book for Patterns of World History, Volumes 1 and 2:** An e-book is available for purchase at www.coursesmart.com.

Bundling Options

Patterns of World History can be bundled at a significant discount with any of the titles in the popular Very Short Introductions or Oxford World's Classics series, as well as other titles from the Higher Education division world history catalog (www.oup.com/us/catalog/he). Please contact your OUP representative for details.

Acknowledgments

Throughout the course of writing, revising, and preparing *Patterns of World History* for publication we have benefited from the guidance and professionalism accorded us by all levels of the staff at Oxford University Press. John Challice, vice president and publisher, had faith in the inherent worth of our project from the outset and provided the initial impetus to move forward. In the early stages of the editorial process, Brian Wheel and Frederick Speers provided helpful critiques and advice, saving us from textual infelicities; Meg Botteon later added a final polish. Lauren Aylward carried out the thankless task of assembling the manuscript and did so with generosity and good cheer. Picture researcher Francelle Carapetyan diligently tracked down every photo request despite the sometimes sketchy sources

we provided, Andrew Pachuta copyedited the manuscript with meticulous attention to detail, and Barbara Mathieu steered us through the intricacies of production with the stoicism of a saint.

Most of all, we owe a special debt of gratitude to Charles Cavaliere, our editor. Charles took on the daunting task of directing the literary enterprise at a critical point in the book's career. He pushed this project to its successful completion, accelerated its schedule, and used a combination of flattery and hard-nosed tactics to make sure we stayed the course. His greatest contribution, however, is in the way he refined our original vision for the book with several important adjustments that clarified its latent possibilities. From the maps to the photos to the special features, Charles's high standards and concern for detail are evident on every page.

Developing a book like *Patterns of World History* is an ambitious project, a collaborative venture in which authors and editors benefit from the feedback provided by a team of outside readers and consultants. We gratefully acknowledge the advice that the many reviewers, focus group participants, and class testers (including their students) shared with us along the way. We tried to implement all of the excellent suggestions. Of course, any errors of fact or interpretation that remain are solely our own.

Reviewers

Stephanie Ballenger, Central Washington University

Alan Baumler, Indiana University of Pennsylvania

Robert Blackey, California State University

Robert Bond, San Diego Mesa College

Mauricio Borrero, St. John's University

Linda Bregstein-Scherr, Mercer County Community College

Scott Breuninger, University of South Dakota

Paul Brians, Washington State University

Gayle K. Brunelle, California State University-Fullerton

James De Lorenzi, City University of New York, John Jay College

Jennifer Kolpacoff Deane, University of Minnesota-Morris

Andrew D. Devenney, Grand Valley State University

Francis A. Dutra, University of California, Santa Barbara

Jeffrey Dym, Sacramento State University

Jennifer C. Edwards, Manhattan College

Lisa M. Edwards, University of Massachusetts-Lowell

Charles T. Evans, Northern Virginia Community College

Christopher Ferguson, Auburn University

Scott Fritz, Western New Mexico State University

Arturo Giraldez, University of the Pacific

Candace Gregory-Abbott, California State University-Sacramento

Derek Heng, Ohio State University

Eric Hetherington, New Jersey Institute of Technology

Laura J. Hilton, Muskingum University

Elizabeth J. Houseman, State University of New York-Brockport

Hung-yok Ip, Oregon State University

Geoffrey Jensen, University of Arkansas

Roger E. Kanet, University of Miami

Kelly Kennington, Auburn University

Amelia M. Kiddle, University of Arizona

Frederic Krome, University of Cincinnati-Clermont College

Mark W. Lentz, University of Louisiana, Lafayette

Heather Lucas, Georgia Perimeter College

Susan Mattern, University of Georgia

Susan A. Maurer, Nassau Community College

Jason McCollom, University of Arkansas

Douglas T. McGetchin, Florida Atlantic University

Stephen Morillo, Wabash College

Carolyn Neel, Arkansas Tech University

Kenneth J. Orosz, Buffalo State College

Alice K. Pate, Columbus State University

Patrick M. Patterson, Honolulu Community College

Daniel Pope, University of Oregon

G. David Price, Santa Fe College

Michael Redman, University of Louisville

Leah Renold, Texas State University

Jeremy Rich, Middle Tennessee State University

Jason Ripper, Everett Community College

Chad Ross, East Carolina University

Nana Yaw B. Sapong, Southern Illinois University-Carbondale

Daniel Sarefield, Fitchburg State College

Claire Schen, State University of New York, Buffalo

Robert C. Schwaller, University of North Carolina-Charlotte

George Sochan, Bowie State University

Ramya Sreenivasan, State University of New York, Buffalo

John Stanley, Kutztown University

Vladimir Steffel, Ohio State University

Anthony J. Steinhoff, University of Tennessee-Chattanooga

Micheal Tarver, Arkansas Tech University

Shane Tomashot, Georgia State University

Kate Transchel, California State University-Chico

Melanie Tubbs, Arkansas Tech University

Andrew Wackerfuss, Georgetown University

Evan R. Ward, Brigham Young University

Joseph K. S. Yick, Texas State University-San Marcos

Focus Group Participants
San Diego, California

Robert Bond, San Diego Mesa College

Lisa Marie Edwards, University of Massachusetts-Lowell

Christine Moore, Palomar College

Elizabeth Ann Pollard, San Diego State University

Charles Romney, Whittier College

Tom Sanders, United States Naval Academy

Sharlene Sayegh-Canada, California State University-Long Beach

Micheal Tarver, Arkansas Tech University

Michael G. Vann, California State University-Sacramento

Russellville, Arkansas

Michael Cox, Rich Mountain Community College

Peter Dykema, Arkansas Tech University

Karen Franks, University of the Ozarks

Jan Jenkins, Arkansas Tech University

Alexander Mirkovic, Arkansas Tech University

Carolyn Neel, Arkansas Tech University

Micheal Tarver, Arkansas Tech University

Melanie Tubbs, Arkansas Tech University

Class Testers

Barbara Allen, La Salle University

Robert Bond, San Diego Mesa College

John A. Dempsey, Westfield State University

Candace Gregory-Abbott, California State University-Sacramento

Jeffrey Hamilton, Baylor University

Padhraig Higgins, Mercer County Community College

Lybeth Hodges, Texas Woman's University

John M. Hunt, University of North Florida

Kara Kaufman, Salem State University

Kelly Kennington, Auburn University

Mark Lentz, University of Louisiana, Lafayette

Margaret Markmann, La Salle University

Douglas T. McGetchin, Florida Atlantic University

J. Kent McGaughy, Houston Community College, Northwest

Carolyn Neel, Arkansas Tech University

Patricia O'Neill, Central Oregon Community College

David Peck, Brigham Young University

Walter D. Penrose, San Diego State University

William Pierce, Northern Virginia Community College

G. David Price, Santa Fe College

Michael Redman, University of Louisville

Jason Ripper, Everett Community College

Chad Ross, East Carolina University

Linda Rupert, University of North Carolina-Greensboro

Cliff Stratton, Washington State University-Pullman

Micheal Tarver, Arkansas Tech University

Evan R. Ward, Brigham Young University

Please let us know your experiences with *Patterns of World History* so that we may improve it in future editions. We welcome your comments and suggestions.

Peter von Sivers
pv4910@xmission.com

Charles A. Desnoyers
desnoyer@lasalle.edu

George B. Stow
gbsgeorge@aol.com

Note on Dates and Spellings

In keeping with widespread practice among world historians, we use "BCE" and "CE" to date events and the phrase "years ago" to describe developments from the remote past.

The transliteration of Middle Eastern words has been adjusted as much as possible to the English alphabet. Therefore, long vowels are not emphasized. The consonants specific to Arabic (alif, dhal, ha, sad, dad, ta, za, ayn, ghayn, and qaf) are either not indicated (except for ayn in the middle of words) or rendered with common English letters. A similar procedure is followed for Farsi. Turkish words follow the alphabet reform of 1929, which adds the following letters to the Western alphabet or modifies their pronunciation: *c* (pronounced "j"), ç (pronounced "tsh"), ğ (not pronounced, lengthening of preceding vowel), ı ("i" without dot, pronunciation close to short e), *i/İ* ("i" with dot, including in caps), ö (no English equivalent), ş ("sh"), and ü (no English equivalent). The spelling of common Middle Eastern and Islamic terms follows daily press usage (which, however, is not completely uniform). Examples are "al-Qaeda," "Quran," and "sharia."

The system used in rendering the sounds of Mandarin Chinese—the northern Chinese dialect that has become in effect the national spoken language in China and Taiwan—into English in this book is *hanyu pinyin*, usually given as simply *pinyin*. This is the official Romanization system of the People's Republic of China and has also become the standard outside of Taiwan, Republic of China. Most syllables are pronounced as they would be in English, with the exception of the letter *q*, which is given an aspirated "ch" sound; *ch* itself has a less aspirated "ch" sound. *Zh* carries a hard "j" and *j*, a soft, English-style "j." Some syllables also are pronounced—particularly in the regions around Beijing—with a retroflex *r* so that the syllable *shi*, for example, carries a pronunciation closer to "shir." Finally, the letter *r* in the *pinyin* system has no direct English equivalent, but an approximation may be had by combining the sounds of "r" and "j."

Japanese terms have been Romanized according to a modification of the Hepburn system. The letter *g* is always hard; vowels are handled as they are in Italian—*e*, for example, carries a sound like "ay." We have not, however, included diacritical markings to indicate long vowel sounds in *u* or *o*. Where necessary, these have been indicated in the pronunciation guides.

For Korean terms, we have used a variation of the McCune-Reischauer system, which remains the standard Romanization scheme for Korean words used in English academic writing, but eliminated any diacritical markings. Here again, the vowel sounds are pronounced more or less like those of Italian and the consonants, like those of English.

For Vietnamese words, we have used standard renditions based on the modern Quoc Ngu ("national language") system in use in Vietnam today. The system was developed by Jesuit missionaries and is based on the Portuguese alphabet. Once more, we have avoided diacritical marks, and the reader should follow the pronunciation guides for approximations of Vietnamese terms.

Latin American terms (Spanish, Nahua, or Quechua) generally follow local usage, including accents, except where they are Anglicized, per the *Oxford English Dictionary*. Thus, the Spanish-Quechua word "Tiahuanacu" becomes the Anglicized word "Tiwanaku."

We use the terms "Native American" and "Indian" interchangeably to refer to the peoples of the Americas in the pre-Columbian period and "Amerindian" in our coverage of Latin America since independence.

In keeping with widely recognized practice among paleontologists and other scholars of the deep past, we use the term "hominins" in Chapter 1 to emphasize their greater remoteness from apes and proximity to modern humans.

Phonetic spellings often follow the first appearance of a non-English word whose pronunciation may be unclear to the reader. We have followed the rules for capitalization per *The Chicago Manual of Style*.

About the Authors

Peter von Sivers is associate professor of Middle Eastern history at the University of Utah. He has previously taught at UCLA, Northwestern University, the University of Paris VII (Vincennes), and the University of Munich. He has also served as chair, Joint Committee of the Near and Middle East, Social Science Research Council, New York, 1982–1985; editor, *International Journal of Middle East Studies*, 1985–1989; member, Board of Directors, Middle East Studies Association of North America, 1987–1990; and chair, SAT II World History Test Development Committee of the Educational Testing Service, Princeton, NJ, 1991–1994. His publications include *Caliphate, Kingdom, and Decline: The Political Theory of Ibn Khaldun*, several edited books, and three dozen peer-reviewed chapters and articles on Middle Eastern and North African history, as well as world history. He received his Dr. Phil. from the University of Munich.

Charles A. Desnoyers is associate professor of history and director of Asian studies at La Salle University, Philadelphia. He is also past director of the Greater Philadelphia Asian Studies Consortium and president (2011–2012) of the Mid-East Region Association for Asian Studies. His scholarly publications include *A Journey to the East: Li Gui's "A New Account of a Trip Around the Globe"* (University of Michigan Press, 2004) and former coeditor of the World History Association's *Bulletin*.

George B. Stow is professor of history and director of the graduate program in history at La Salle University, Philadelphia. His teaching experience embraces a variety of undergraduate and graduate courses in ancient Greece and Rome, medieval England, and world history; and for excellence in teaching he has been awarded the Lindback Distinguished Teaching Award. Professor Stow is a member of the Medieval Academy of America and a fellow of the Royal Historical Society. He is the recipient of a National Defense Education Act Title IV Fellowship, a Woodrow Wilson Foundation Fellowship, and research grants from the American Philosophical Society and La Salle University. His publications include a critical edition of a fourteenth-century monastic chronicle, *Historia Vitae et Regni Ricardi Secundi* (University of Pennsylvania Press), as well as numerous articles and reviews in scholarly journals including *Speculum, The English Historical Review*, the *Journal of Medieval History*, the *American Historical Review*, and several others. He received his PhD from the University of Illinois.

Patterns of
World History

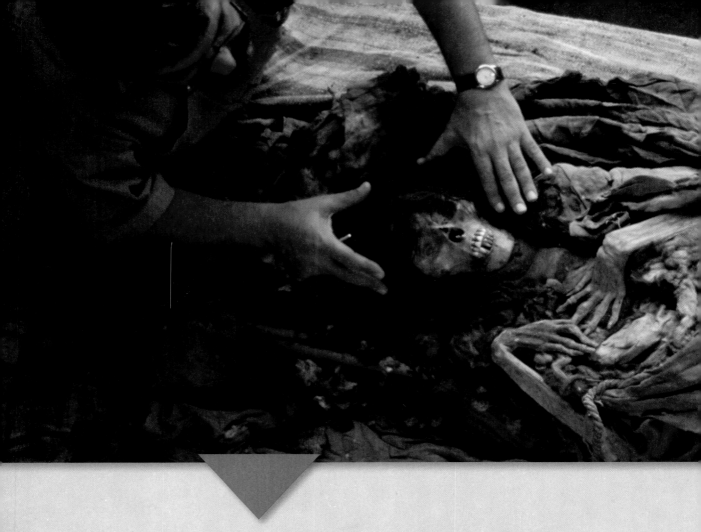

Chapter 15
The Rise of Empires in the Americas
600-1550 CE

Just outside Lima, in a sandy and dry ravine 3 miles to the east, is the shantytown of Túpac Amaru, named after the last Inca ruler, who died in 1572. People fleeing the Maoist-Marxist "Shining Path" guerillas in the highlands southeast of Lima settled here during the 1980s. Archaeologists had known for years that the site was an ancient burial place called "Puruchuco" (in Quechua "Feathered Helmet") but could not prevent the influx of settlers. By the late 1990s, the temporary shantytown had become an established settlement with masonry houses, streets, and a school. Dwellers were anxious to acquire title to their properties, introduce urban services and utilities, and clean up ground contaminated in many places

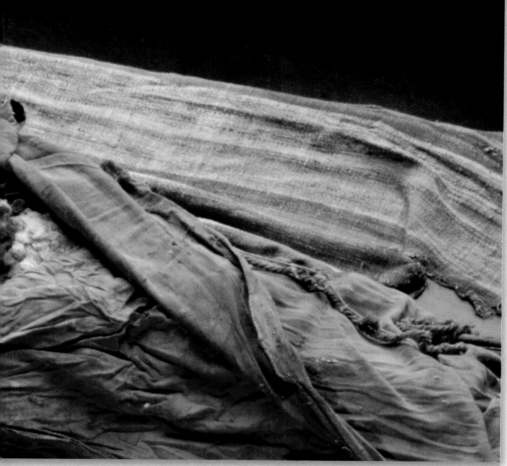

▶ Within the patterns of state formation basic to the Americas, which types of states emerged in Mesoamerica and the Andes during the period 600–1550? What characterized these states?

▶ Why did the Tiwanaku and Wari states have ruling classes but no dynasties and central bureaucracies? How were these patterns expressed in the territorial organization of these states?

▶ What patterns of urban life characterized the cities of Tenochtitlán and Cuzco, the capitals of the Aztec and Inca Empires? In which ways were these cities similar to those of Eurasia and Africa?

by raw sewage. However, residents realized that archaeologists had to be called in before the shantytown could be officially recognized. Túpac Amaru was facing an increasingly familiar dilemma in the developing world, pitting modern needs against the wish to know the past through discovering and (if possible) preserving its last traces.

During emergency excavations from 1999 to 2001, the archaeologist Guillermo Cock, together with Túpac Amaru residents hired as field assistants, unearthed one of the most astounding treasures in the history of American archaeology. The team discovered some 2,200 mummies, most of them bundled up in blankets and perfectly preserved with their hair, skin, eyes, and genitals intact. Many bundles also contained rich burial gifts, including jewelry, corn, potatoes, peanuts, peppers, and coca leaves. Forty bundles had false heads made of cotton cloth, some topped with wigs, making the bundles look like oversized persons.

One bundle, stuffed with over 300 pounds of cotton, contained the mummies of a child and a man of about 40, dubbed the "cotton king" because of his many sumptuous burial gifts. In 2004, during renewed excavations, Cock discovered the remains of 72 hastily buried bodies that had not

Excavations in Tupac Amaru in 1999–2001. During excavations in Túpac Amaru, a slum in Lima, Peru, in 1999–2001, archaeologists unearthed some 2,200 mummies. They dated them to the Inca period (1438–1533). Many mummies were surrounded by rich grave gifts of food and jewelry.

been mummified, many of which bore traces of violence. One skeleton with a hole in the skull was declared to have been the first victim of a gunshot in the Americas, fired by a Spanish conquistador in 1536 during an Inca uprising in Lima. Altogether, Cock was able to excavate about 40 percent of Puruchuco, collecting mummies, skeletons, and artifacts in numbers not previously seen in Peru.

The cemetery was once part of a larger complex, excavated in 1956, that also included what was perhaps an Inca administrative center and colony or a provincial ruler's palace. Scholars hope that in a few years, when all of the mummies will be unwrapped, answers can be given as to the social characteristics of the buried people. Were they members of an Inca colony planted into one of the empire's provinces? Or were they locals under their own lord, recognizing Inca overlordship? Were they specialized laborers, such as weavers, who produced cloth tributes for the Incas? Were children and women sacrificed to accompany the cotton king in his journey to the afterlife? Had assimilation between the conquerors and conquered begun? These questions are difficult to answer as so much about the Inca Empire that ruled the Andes from 1438 to 1533 remains unknown. Yet, the questions are exciting precisely because they could not have been posed prior to the discovery of these mummies.

The Inca Empire and its contemporary, the Aztec Empire (1427–1521), both grew out of political, economic, and cultural patterns that began to form around 600 CE in Mesoamerica and the Andes (see Chapter 5). At that time, kingdoms had emerged out of chiefdoms in two small areas of Mesoamerica, the southern Yucatán Peninsula and the Valley of Mexico. After 600, kingdom formation became more general across Mesoamerica and arose for the first time in the Andes. These kingdoms were states with military ruling classes that used new types of weapons and could conquer larger territories than was possible prior to the 600s. Military competition prepared the way for the origin of empires—multireligious, multilinguistic, and multiethnic states encompassing many thousands of miles. Even though empires arrived later in the Americas than in Eurasia, they demonstrate that humans, once they had adopted agriculture, evolved in remarkably similar patterns of social and political formation across the world.

The Legacy of Teotihuacán and the Toltecs in Mesoamerica

As discussed in Chapter 5, the city-state of Teotihuacán had dominated northern Mesoamerica from 200 BCE to the late 500s CE. It fell into ruin probably as the result of an internal uprising against an overbearing ruling class. After its collapse, the surrounding towns and villages, as well as half a dozen other cities in and around the Valley of Mexico, perpetuated the cultural legacy of Teotihuacán for centuries. Employing this legacy, the conquering state of the Toltecs unified a major part of the region for a short period from 900 to 1180. At the same time, after an internal crisis, the southern Maya kingdoms on the Yucatán Peninsula reached their late flowering, together with the northern state of Chichén Itzá.

Militarism in the Valley of Mexico

After the ruling class of Teotihuacán disintegrated at the end of the sixth century, the newly independent local lords and their supporters in the small successor states of Mesoamerica continued Teotihuacán's cultural heritage. This heritage was defined by Teotihuacán's temple style, ceramics, textiles, and religious customs, especially the cult of the feathered serpent god Quetzalcoatl [Ketz-al-CO-wa]. The Toltecs, migrants from the north, militarized the Teotihuacán legacy and transformed it into a program of conquest.

Ceremonial Centers and Chiefdoms   In the three centuries after the end of the city-state of Teotihuacán, the local population declined from some 200,000 to about 30,000. Although largely ruined, the ceremonial center continued to attract pilgrims, but other places around the Valley of Mexico and beyond rose in importance. The semiarid region to the northwest of the valley had an extensive mining industry, with many mine shafts extending a mile or more into the mountains. It produced gemstones, such as greenstone, turquoise, hematite, and cinnabar. Independent after 600, inhabitants built ceremonial centers and small states of their own, trading their gemstones to their neighbors in all directions.

To the north were the Pueblo cultures in today's southwestern United States. These cultures were based on sophisticated irrigated farming systems and are known for their distinctive painted pottery styles. They flourished between 700 and 1500 in the canyons of what are today the states of New Mexico, Arizona, southwestern Colorado, and southeastern Utah. In turn, these cultures might have been in contact with the Mississippi cultures, among which the ceremonial center and city of Cahokia (650–1400) near modern St. Louis is the best known. An obsidian scraper from the Pachuco region north of the Valley of Mexico found in Spiro Mounds, Oklahoma, attests to at least occasional contacts between Mesoamerica and the Mississippi culture (see Map 15.1).

In western Mesoamerica, ceremonial centers and chiefdoms flourished on the basis of metallurgy, which arrived through Ecuadoran seaborne merchants

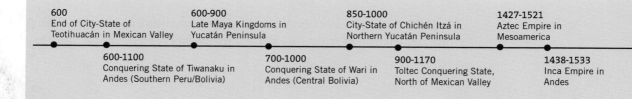

600	600–900	850–1000	1427–1521
End of City-State of Teotihuacán in Mexican Valley	Late Maya Kingdoms in Yucatán Peninsula	City-State of Chichén Itzá in Northern Yucatán Peninsula	Aztec Empire in Mesoamerica

600–1100	700–1000	900–1170	1438–1533
Conquering State of Tiwanaku in Andes (Southern Peru/Bolivia)	Conquering State of Wari in Andes (Central Bolivia)	Toltec Conquering State, North of Mexican Valley	Inca Empire in Andes

> ### A Tearful Departure
>
> "1. At Tula there stood the house of beams, there yet stands the house of plumed serpents left by Nacxitl Tolpitzin; going forth weeping, our nobles went to where he was to perish, down there at Tlapallan [mythical place on the Gulf of Mexico] . . .
>
> "4. With the falling down of mountains I wept, with the lifting up of sands I was wretched that my lord had gone.
>
> "5. At Tlapallan he was waited for, it was commanded that there he should sleep, thus being alone."
>
> —Daniel Brinton, ed. and trans. *Ancient Nahuatl Poetry*, New York: AMS Press, 1969, p. 105. Originally published 1887.

ca. 600–800. The Ecuadorans received their copper from Peru, in return for seashells found in the warm waters off their coast as well as farther north. Copper, too soft for agricultural implements or military weapons, served mostly in households and as jewelry for the rich. Smiths fashioned domestic articles such as needles and tweezers, as well as ornaments and bells, from the metal. Members of the ruling classes typically used copper earrings, pendants, and strings of bells around their ankles as markers of their elevated rank.

In the south, a number of small, fortified hilltop states flourished in the post-Teotihuacán period. Their inhabitants built moats and ramparts to protect these states. More than in other Mesoamerican states, the southern ruling classes were embroiled in fierce wars during 600–900, images of which are depicted in the stone reliefs of gruesome battle scenes. In one such relief, "bird men" and "jaguar men" are shown pitted against each other, amid flowing blood, severed heads, and disemboweled bodies. One of these groups of antagonists was possibly a band of mercenary troops, dislodged from a defeated state and seeking employment or even dominance elsewhere in the south.

The Toltec Conquering State   Early after the collapse of Teotihuacán, craftspeople and farmers migrated some 60 miles north to Tula, a place on a ridge in the highlands watered by two tributaries of a river flowing into the Gulf of Mexico. They founded a small ceremonial center and town with workshops known for the high quality of the scrapers, knives, and spear points fabricated from the local Pachuca obsidian. Around 900, new migrants arrived from northwest Mexico as well as the Gulf coast. The northerners spoke Nahuatl [Na-hua], the language of the later Aztecs, who considered Tula their ancestral city.

The integration of the new arrivals was apparently not peaceful since it resulted in the abandonment of the temple and the departure of a defeated party of Tulans. This abandonment may well have been enshrined in the myth of Tolpiltzin, a priest-king of the feathered serpent god Quetzalcoatl, who after his departure to the east would one day return to restore the cult to its rightful center. The myth later played a fateful part in the establishment of Spanish rule in the Americas.

The new Tula of 900 developed quickly into a large city with a new temple, 60,000 urban dwellers, and perhaps another 60,000 farmers on surrounding lands. It was the first city-centered state to give prominence to the sacrifice of captured warriors. The captives were apparently slaughtered on a skull altar so that the gods would be properly served with blood, the life-giving substance of humankind. As it evolved, Tula became the capital of the conquering state of the Toltecs, which imprinted its warrior culture on large parts of Mesoamerica from around 900 to 1180 (see Map 15.1).

Militarism   The Toltec innovation of a military state with a warrior class is extensively documented by sculptures. Toltec warriors, probably recruited from among

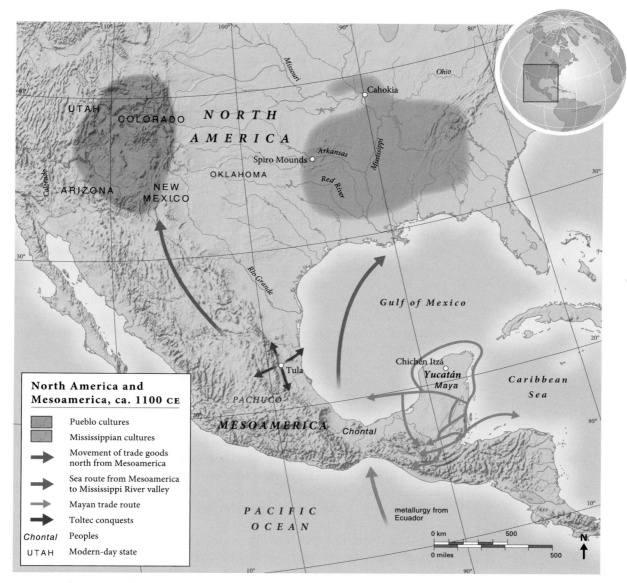

MAP 15.1 **North America and Mesoamerica, ca. 1100.**

newly arriving immigrants from northwest Mexico, were organized into regiments identified by totem animals, such as the coyote, jaguar, and eagle. Standard-bearers, displaying the totems, rallied the warriors around their officers. Wooden butterfly breastplates, worn over thick cotton shirts, also displayed totems. Helmets made of layers of cotton and festooned with bird feathers protected the heads. Shields were worn for the protection of the back. Not all warriors wore full armor, but those who did were clearly well protected.

The Toltecs introduced two innovations in weaponry that improved the effectiveness of hand-to-hand combat. First, there was the new weapon of the short (1.5-foot) sword made of hardwood with inlaid obsidian edges, which could slash as well as crush, in contrast to the obsidian-spiked clubs that had been primary weapons in earlier times. Second, warriors wore obsidian daggers with wooden handles inside a band on the left arm, replacing simpler obsidian blades, which were difficult to use as they had no handles. Traditional dart throwers and slings for stone projectiles completed the offensive armament of the warriors. Soldiers of lower rank were largely without protective armor and wore simple loincloths, their weapons limited to sticks for striking and fending off opponents. Some officers depicted in the sculptures wear nose rings or nose/ear plugs, indicating their noble status. Coming from a military culture in which status depended on performance, these officers appear to have been adopted into the lineages of the ruling elite as a result of their successes in war.

The Toltec army of 13,000–26,000 soldiers was sufficiently large to engage in battles of conquest within an area of 4 days' march (roughly 40 miles) away from Tula. Any target beyond this range was beyond their capabilities at this point, given the logistics of armor, weapons, food rations, narrow dirt roads, and uneven terrain—and, of course, Toltecs did not have the benefit of wheeled vehicles. Thus, the only way of projecting power beyond the range of 40 miles was to establish colonies and to have troops accompany traders, each of which could then supply himself by foraging or through trade along the way. As a result, the Toltec state projected its power by the prestige of its large military, rather than through a full-scale imperial program with the imposition of governors, tributes, and taxes.

Trade   Apart from demonstrating military might, the Toltecs pursued the establishment of a large trade network. Merchants parlayed Tula's obsidian production into a trade network that radiated southward into the cacao, vanilla, and bird feather production centers of Chiapas and Guatemala; to the north into gemstone mining regions; and westward into centers of metal mining. Metallurgy advanced around 1200 with the development of the technology of bronze casting. Bronze axes were stronger and more useful for working with wood than copper axes. Bronze bells produced a greater variety of sounds than those of copper. As ornamental objects, both were trade goods highly prized by the elites in Tula.

The Late Toltec Era   Toltec military power declined in the course of the twelfth century when the taxable grain yield diminished, because of either prolonged droughts or a depletion of the topsoil on the terraces, or a combination of the two. Sometime around 1180, a new wave of foraging peoples from the northwest invaded, attacking with bows and arrows and using hit-and-run tactics against Toltec communication lines. The disruptions caused an internal revolt, which brought down the ceremonial center and its palaces. By 1200, Tula was a city with a burned-out center, like Teotihuacán six centuries earlier; and Mesoamerica relapsed into a period of small-state coexistence characteristic of the pre-600 period.

Late Maya States in Yucatán

Teotihuacán's demise at the end of the sixth century was paralleled by a realignment of the balance of power among the Maya kingdoms in the southern Yucatán lowlands of Mesoamerica. This realignment, accompanied by extensive warfare, was resolved by around 650. A period of late flowering spanned the next two centuries, followed by a shift of power from the southern to the northern part of the peninsula.

The Southern Kingdoms   At its height during the fourth and fifth centuries, Teotihuacán in the Valley of Mexico had interjected itself into the delicate balance of power existing among the Maya kingdoms of southern Yucatán. Alliances among the states shifted, and prolonged wars of conquest racked the lowlands, destroying several older states. A dozen new kingdoms emerged and established a new balance of power among themselves. After a lengthy hiatus, Maya culture entered its final period (650–900).

The most striking phenomenon of the final period in the southern, rain forest–covered lowlands and adjacent highlands were massive new programs of agricultural expansion and ceremonial monument construction. Agriculture was expanded again through cutting down the rain forest on hillsides and terracing the hills for soil retention. The largest kingdoms grew to 50,000–60,000 inhabitants and reached astounding rural population densities of about 1,000 persons per square mile. (In comparison, England's most densely populated counties just prior to its agricultural expansion after 1700 were Middlesex and Surrey, with 221 and 207 persons per square mile, respectively.) Although the late Maya states were geographically small, they were administratively the most centralized polities ever created in indigenous American history.

The late Maya states did not last long. In spite of all efforts, the usually torrential downpours of the rainy season gradually washed the topsoil from the newly built hillside terraces. The topsoil, accumulating as alluvium in the flatlands, was initially quite fertile; but from around 800 onward it became more and more depleted of nutrients. In addition, in many wetlands, farmers found it difficult to prevent clay from forming over the alluvium and hardening in the process. Malnutrition resulting from the receding agricultural surface began to reduce the labor force. Ruling classes had to make do with fewer workers and smaller agricultural surpluses. In the end, even the ruling classes suffered, with members killing each other for what remained of these surpluses. By about 900, the Maya kingdoms in southern Yucatán had shriveled to the size of chiefdoms with small towns and villages.

Chichén Itzá in the North   A few small Maya states on the periphery survived. The most prominent among them was Chichén Itzá [Chee-CHEN Eat-SA] in the northern lowlands, which flourished from about 850 to 1000. At first glance the region would appear to be less than hospitable for a successful state. The climate in the north was much drier than that in the south. The surface was rocky or covered with thin topsoil, supporting mostly grass, scrub vegetation, and isolated forests. In many places, where the soil was too saline, agriculture was impossible and the production of salt was the only source of income. There were no rivers, but many sinkholes in the porous limestone underneath the soil held water. Countless cisterns to hold additional amounts of water for year-round use were cut into the limestone and plastered to prevent seepage. This water, carried in jars to the surface, supported an intensive garden agriculture, productive enough to sustain entire towns and city-states.

Chichén Itzá was founded during the phase of renewed urbanization in 650. It was built near two major sinkholes and several salt flats. The population was composed of local Maya as well as the Maya-speaking Chontal from the Gulf coast farther west. Groups among these people engaged in long-distance trade, both overland and in boats along the coast. Since trade in the most lucrative goods (such as cacao, vanilla, jade, copper, bronze, turquoise, and obsidian) required contact with

Chichén Itzá, El Caracol ("The Snail") Observatory. This domed building was aligned with the northern extreme of the path of Venus. Here, astronomers made the lengthy and systematic observations necessary to coordinate the three different calendars in use in Mesoamerica from about 500 BCE (see Chapter 6).

people well outside even the farthest political reach of either Teotihuacán or Tula, merchants (*pochtecas* [potsh-TAY-cas]) traveled in armed caravans. These merchant groups enjoyed considerable freedom and even sponsorship by the ruling classes of the states of Mesoamerica. Such was their importance that they occupied positions of high honor in ceremonies and festivities.

Chontal traders adopted Toltec culture, and when they based themselves in Chichén Itzá around 850 they superimposed their adopted culture over that of the original Maya. How the city was ruled is only vaguely understood, but there is some evidence that there were two partially integrated ruling factions, possibly descended from the Chontal and local Maya, sharing in the governance of the city. At the very end of the period of Teotihuacán, Maya, and Toltec cultural expansion, the three cultural traditions finally merged on the Yucatán Peninsula in only one geographically marginal region. This merger, however, did not last long; already at around 1000 the ruling-class factions left the city-state for unknown reasons. As a result, the city-state diminished in size and power to town level.

The Legacy of Tiwanaku and Wari in the Andes

Mesoamerica and the Andes, from the time of chiefdom formation in 2500 BCE in Caral-Supé onward, shared the tradition of regional temple pilgrimages. In the Andes, the chiefdoms remained mostly coastal, with some inland extensions along valleys of the Andes. Around 600 CE, the two conquering states of Tiwanaku in the highlands of what are today southern Peru and Bolivia, and Wari, in central Peru, emerged. Both states encompassed several tens of thousands of inhabitants and represented a major step in the formation of larger, militarily organized polities.

The Conquering State of Tiwanaku

Tiwanaku was a political and cultural power center in the south-central Andes during the period 600–1100. It began as a ceremonial center with surrounding villages and gradually developed into a state dominating the region around Lake Titicaca. At its apogee it was an expanding state, planting colonies in regions far from the lake and conveying its culture through trade to peoples even beyond the colonies.

Agriculture on the High Plain   The Andes consist of two parallel mountain chains stretching along the west coast of South America. For the most part, these chains are close together, divided by small plains, valleys, and lower mountains. In southeastern Peru and western Bolivia an intermountain plain, 12,500 feet above sea level, extends as wide as 125 miles. At its northern end lies Lake Titicaca, subdivided into a larger and deeper northern valley and a smaller, shallower, swampy, and reed-covered southern valley. Five major and 20 smaller rivers coming from the eastern

Andes chain feed the lake, which has one outlet at its southern end, a river flowing into Lake Poopó [Po-POH], a salt lake 150 miles south. The Lake Titicaca region, located above the tree line, receives winter rains sufficient for agriculture and pasture, whereas the southern plain around Lake Poopó is too dry to sustain more than steppes.

Tiwanaku, Kalassaya Gate. Within the Temple of the Sun, this gate is aligned with the sun's equinoxes and was used for festive rituals. Note the precise stone work, which the Incas later developed further.

In spite of its elevation, the region around Lake Titicaca offered everything necessary for an advanced urbanization process. The lake's freshwater supported fish and resources such as reeds from the swamps, which served for the construction of boats and roofs. Corn flourished only in the lower elevations of the Andes and had to be imported, together with the corn-derived *chicha*, a beer-like drink. Instead of corn, food staples were potatoes and quinoa. Potatoes were preserved for the harsh winter months through drying. The grasslands of the upper hills served as pastures for llama and alpaca herds. Llamas were used as transportation animals, and alpacas provided wool. The meat of both animals—preserved for winter through drying—was a major protein source. Although frost was an ever-present danger in Tiwanaku, nutrition was quite diversified.

Farmers grew their crops on hillside terraces, where runoff water could be channeled, or on raised fields close to the lake. The raised-field system, which farmers had adopted through interaction with the peoples of the Maya lowlands, consisted of a grid of narrow strips of earth, separated from each other by channels. Mud from the channels, heaped onto the strips, replenished their fertility. A wooden foot plow with perhaps a bronze blade seems to have been the main farming implement, although hard archaeological proof is still elusive. By 500, the combined sustenance from fishing, hunting, farming, and herding supported dozens of villages and, by 700, the city of Tiwanaku and its 20,000 inhabitants.

The ceremonial center of Tiwanaku consisted of a sunken courtyard dating to the pre-600 period and several temples on platforms or sets of platforms constructed later. The most sumptuous residential quarters were next to the new temples. There, elite family lineages lived in walled compounds with houses built around courtyards. Underground drainage canals with manholes at regular intervals for cleaning took care of the removal of waste. Farther away from the centers were poorer residential areas with communal kitchens, which probably served for the preparation of foods consumed at ceremonial feasts.

Coordinated with the calendar as well as life-cycle events (such as initiation rituals), ceremonial feasts brought together elite lineages and clients, or ordinary craftspeople and villagers. Elites and clients cohered through **reciprocity**, that is, communal labor for the construction of the ceremonial centers and elaborate feasting, in which elite wealth was expended for the ceremonial leveling of status differences. Until shortly before the end of the state it does not appear that this reciprocity gave way to more forcible ways of allocating labor through conscription or taxation.

Expansion and Conquest Like Tiwanaku, the core region around the southern arm of Lake Titicaca housed a set of related but competing elite–client

Reciprocity: In its basic form, an informal agreement among people according to which a gift or an invitation has to be returned after a reasonable amount of time; in the pre-Columbian Americas, an arrangement of feasts versus taxes between ruling classes and subjects in a state.

hierarchies. Ruling clans with intermediate leaders and ordinary farmers in the villages comprised a state capable of imposing military power beyond the center. But counterbalancing clans at the head of similar hierarchies prevented the rise of dynasties that would command permanent, unified central administrations and military forces. The projection of power over the northern lake, therefore, was not primarily of a military nature. Whatever the military expeditions by ruling clans outside the city, the primary form of Tiwanaku authority was the unrivaled prestige of its ceremonial center. This center attracted pilgrims not merely from the northern lake but also from more distant regions. Pilgrims partaking in Tiwanaku feasting ceremonies can be considered as extensions of the reciprocity and clientage system of the ruling classes and, hence, of Tiwanaku power.

More direct expressions of Tiwanaku influence beyond Lake Titicaca were armed trading caravans and the foundation of colonies in the western valleys of the Andes. Merchants accompanied by warriors and llama drivers crossed multiple polities in order to exchange textiles and ceramics for basalt cores in the south, metal ingots and obsidian cores in the north, and coca leaves and other psychotropic substances in the east, often hundreds of miles away. Colonies were more tangible forms of power projection, especially those established in the Moquegua [Mow-KAY-gah] valley 200 miles or 10–12 days of walking to the west. Here, at some 2,800 feet above sea level, Tiwanaku emigrants established villages, which sent their corn or beer to the capital in return for salt, as well as stone and obsidian tools. Although overall less militarily inclined than the Mesoamerican states of the same time period, Tiwanaku wielded a visible influence over southern Peru (see Map 15.2).

The Expanding City-State of Wari

Little is known about early settlements in central Peru, some 450 miles or 3–4 weeks of foot travel north from Tiwanaku. The state of Wari emerged around 600 from a number of small polities organized around ceremonial centers. Expansion to the south put Wari into direct contact with Tiwanaku. The two states came to some form of mutual accommodation, and it appears that neither embarked on an outright conquest of the other. Their military postures remained limited to their regional spheres of influence.

Origins and Expansion   Wari was centered on the Ayacucho valley, a narrow plain in the highlands of northern Peru. Here, the land between the two chains of the Andes is mountainous, interspersed with valleys and rivers flowing to the Pacific or the Amazon. The elevation of 8,000 feet in the Ayacucho valley allowed for the cultivation of potatoes as well as corn and cotton. In the course of the seventh century, Wari grew into a city of 30,000 inhabitants and brought a number of neighboring cities under its control. It also pushed for an enlargement of the agricultural base through the expansion of terrace farming for the growing of corn, fruits, peppers, and coca. Like Tiwanaku, Wari eventually became the center of a developed urbanism and a diversified agriculture.

Some local traditions that continued under the Wari elite deserve comment. One city specialized in rituals that included the smashing of heads taken as trophies from killed war captives, marking a parallel to the militarism of some of the Mesoamerican polities. Another town had tombs in which high-status women were buried with copper jewelry, ceramic vessels, and weaving tools, illustrating the function

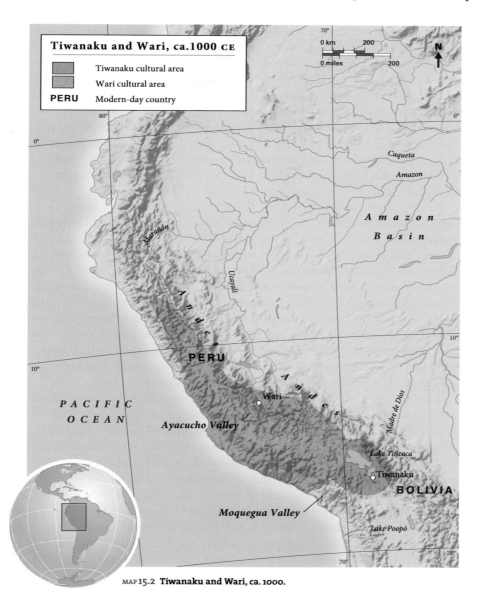

MAP 15.2 **Tiwanaku and Wari, ca. 1000.**

of women as weavers and brewers in their own right in elite society. Although American agrarian society was nearly as patriarchal as that in Eurasia, it apparently also relaxed its gender segregation for elite women.

In addition to maintaining control over the cities in its vicinity, Wari employed architects who constructed new towns. These planned centers included plazas, housing for laborers, and halls for feasting. Outside the core area, Wari elites established colonies, some of which appeared—even if only briefly around 800—in northern Peru as far as 450 miles away. It appears that Wari exercised much stronger political control over the elites of its core region than Tiwanaku and was more active in founding colonies.

The Wari–Tiwanaku Frontier   Early on, Wari established a colony upstream in the Moquegua valley on southern Peru's west coast, some 100 miles away. The settlers built extensive terraces and canals together with protective walls and settlements on mountain peaks. This building activity coincided with the Tiwanaku establishment of downstream farming colonies. It is possible that there was considerable tension with Tiwanaku during the initial period (650–800) over the division of water between the two colonies. But during 800–1000 the two agricultural communities developed closer ties, with indications that the two local elites engaged in a peaceful sharing of the water resources and common feasting activities. Very likely, the Moquegua valley was politically so far on the periphery of both states that neither had the means to impose itself on the other.

Return to Coexistence   At its origins, Wari was an expanding state very similar to Tiwanaku. Both were governed by elite clans under leaders who derived their strength from reciprocal patron–client organizations binding leaders to farmers and craftspeople. Extensive feasts strengthened the bond. Something must have happened to erode this bond, however, since there is evidence of increased internal tension after 950 in the two states. Groups arose which defaced sculptures, destroyed portals, and burned down edifices. Somehow, crowds previously happy to uphold elite control in return for participation in the lavish feasts (provided by the elites) must have become angry at these elites, their ceremonies, and the temple sculptures. Scholars have argued that it was perhaps the fragility of power based on an increasingly unequal reciprocity that caused the rift between elites and subjects.

Janusek's argument, however, provokes a deeper question: Why would elites allow reciprocity to be weakened to such a degree that it became a sham? Previous generations of scholars argued that climatic change deprived the elites of the wherewithal to throw large feasts. In the case of Tiwanaku there is evidence that a drought hit the high plain beginning in 1040, but this date is clearly a century too late for an explanation. A more convincing explanation suggests environmental degradation as the result of agricultural expansion. Land that was only marginally suitable for agriculture was exhausted and could no longer sustain a vastly increased population, as with the late Maya kingdoms. Unfortunately, there is still too little evidence to extend the environmental argument from the Maya kingdoms to the Andes highland and sierra. An ultimate explanation for the disintegration of the expanding states of Tiwanaku and Wari thus remains elusive.

American Empires: Aztec and Inca Origins and Dominance

Expanding and conquering states in the Andes and Mesoamerica gave way in the early fifteenth century to empires. At this time, demographic growth and the evolution of militarism in the Americas reached a point of transition to the pattern of imperial political formation. Conquering states had been cities with ceremonial centers, which dominated agricultural hinterlands and projected their prestige or power across regions. By contrast, the Aztec (1427–1521) and Inca (1438–1533) Empires in Mesoamerica and the Andes were states with capitals and ceremonial centers, vastly larger tributary hinterlands, and armies capable of engaging in campaigns at distances twice (or more) as far away than previous states. As in Eurasia, they were centralized multireligious, multiethnic, and multilinguistic polities: empires in every sense of the word.

The Aztec Empire of Mesoamerica

Hailing from the mountainous semidesert regions of northwest Mexico, the ancestors of the Aztecs entered history as migrants in search of a better life. They found this life as conquerors of the Valley of Mexico, the site of today's Mexico City (after the drainage of most of the valley). In the course of the fifteenth century they conquered an empire that eventually encompassed Mesoamerica from the Pacific to the Gulf of Mexico and from the middle of modern northern Mexico to the Isthmus of Panama.

Settlement in the Mexican Valley   The Aztecs traced their origins back to a founding myth. According to this myth, the first Aztec was one of seven brothers born on an island in a lake or in a mountain cave, "150 leagues" (450 miles) northwest of the Valley of Mexico. The distance, recorded by Spaniards in the sixteenth century, can be interpreted as corresponding to a mountain in the modern state of Guanajuato [Goo-wa-na-hoo-WA-to]. This Aztec ancestor and his descendants left their mythical homeland as foragers dressed in skins and lacking agriculture and urban civilization. Their hunter–warrior patron god Huitzilpochtli [Hoo-it-zil-POSHT-lee] promised to guide them to a promised land of plenty.

After settling for a while in Tula (claimed later as a place of heritage), their god urged the foragers to move on to the Valley of Mexico. Here, an eagle perched on a cactus commanded the Aztecs to settle and build a temple to their god. In this temple, they were to nourish him with the sacrificial blood of humans captured in war. Like many peoples in Eurasia as well as the contemporary Incas, the Aztecs contrasted their later empire and its glory with a myth of humble beginnings and long periods of wandering toward an eventual promised land.

The historical record in the Valley of Mexico becomes clearer in the fourteenth century. In the course of this period, the Aztecs appeared as clients of two Toltec-descended overlords in states on the southwestern shore. Here, they created the two islands of Tenochtitlán [Te-notsh-tit-LAN] and Tlatelolco [Tla-te-LOL-co], founded a city with a ceremonial center on Tenochtitlán, engaged in farming, and rendered military service to their overlords. Thanks to successes on the battlefield, Aztec leaders were able to marry into the elites of the neighboring city-states and gained the right to have their own ruler ("speaker," *tlatloani* [Tla-tlo-AH-nee]) presiding over a council of leading members of the elite and priests. Toward the end of the fourteenth century, an emerging Aztec elite was firmly integrated with the ruling classes of many of the two dozen or so city-states in and around the valley.

The Rise of the Empire   After a successful rebellion in 1428 of a triple alliance among the Aztec city-state of Tenochtitlán and two other vassal states against the reigning city-state in the Valley of Mexico, the Aztec leader Itzcóatl [Its-CO-aw] (r. 1428–1440) emerged as the dominant figure. Itzcóatl and his three successors, together with the rulers of the two allied states, expanded their city-states on the two islands and the shore through conquests into a full-fledged empire. Tenochtitlán, on one of the islands, became the capital, growing into an empire that consisted of a set of six "inner provinces" in the Valley of Mexico. Local elites were left in place, but they were required to attend ceremonies in Tenochtitlán, bring and receive gifts, leave their sons as hostages, and intermarry with the elites of the triple alliance. Commoner farmers outside the cities had to provide tributes in the form of foodstuffs and labor services, making the imperial core self-sufficient.

After the middle of the fifteenth century, the triple alliance conquered a set of 55 city-states outside the valley as "outer provinces." It created an imperial polity from the Pacific to the Gulf, from Tarasco, 200 miles to the northwest, to Oaxaca, over 500 miles to the south (see Map 15.3). This state was now far more centralized than the preceding Teotihuacán and Toltec city-states. In this empire, local ruling families with their ceremonial centers and gods were generally left in place, but commoners had to produce tributes in the form of raw materials, such as obsidian, gold, silver, copper, bronze, gemstones, cotton, and cacao, or lightweight processed and manufactured goods, such as dried peppers and fruits, feathers, rubber balls, incense, textiles, basketry, ropes, and live birds.

In some provinces, Aztec governors replaced the rulers; in most others, Aztec tribute collectors (supported by troops) held local rulers in check and supervised the transportation of the tributes by porters to the valley. Reciprocity, once of central importance in Mesoamerica, continued on a grand scale but was now clearly subordinate to military considerations.

List of Tributes Owed to the Aztecs. The list includes quantities of cotton and wool textiles, clothes, headgear with feathers, and basketry. The Aztecs did not continue the complex syllabic script of the Maya but used instead images, including persons with speech bubbles, for communication. Spanish administrators and monks who copied the Aztec manuscripts added their own explanations to keep track of Native American tributes.

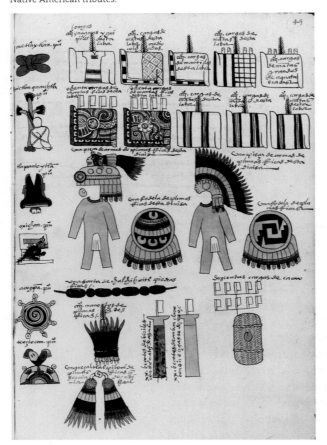

Imperial Policies The resulting multiethnic, multireligious, and multilinguistic empire of eventually some 19 million inhabitants was still a work in progress in the early sixteenth century when the Spanish arrived. Right in the middle of the empire, just 50 miles east of the Valley of Mexico, the large state of Tlaxcala [Tlash-KAH-lah], Nahuatl-speaking like the Aztecs, held out in opposition, together with multiple enemy states on the periphery. Although the ruling elites of the triple alliance did everything to expand, including even inviting enemy rulers to their festivities in order to secure their loyalty through gestures of reciprocity, pockets of anti-Aztec states survived and eventually became crucial allies of the Spanish, providing the latter's tiny military forces with a critical mass of fighters.

Some outer provinces possessed strategic importance, with Aztec colonies implanted to prepare for eventual conquest of remaining enemies outside the empire. The most relentlessly pursued policy of continued expansion of Aztec central control was the threat of warfare, for the purpose of capturing rebels or enemies as prisoners of war to be sacrificed to the gods in the ceremonial centers. Death on the battlefield was bad enough, but to have one's heart ripped out on top of the Tenochtitlán pyramid must have been outright horrifying to the enemies of the

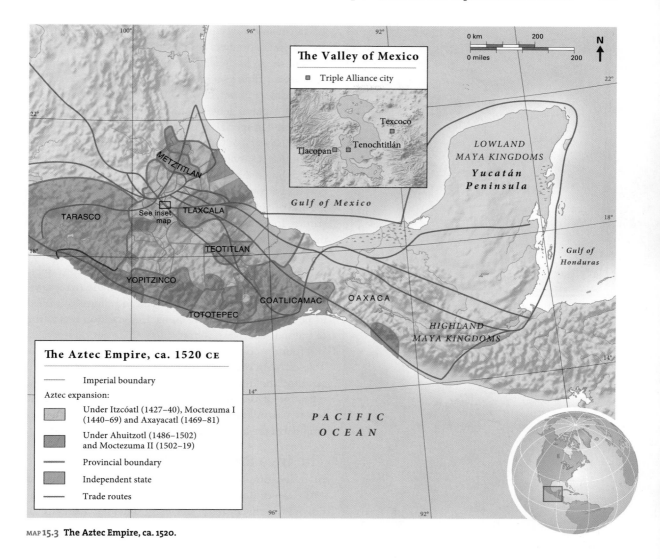

MAP 15.3 **The Aztec Empire, ca. 1520.**

Aztecs—as it was later to the Spanish. This fear-inducing tactic—or "power propaganda"—was an integral innovation in the imperialism of the Aztecs.

The Military Forces   The triple alliance ruled a Nahuatl-speaking population of some 1.5 million inhabitants in the core provinces of the Valley of Mexico. This number yielded a maximum of a quarter of a million potential soldiers, taking into consideration that most soldiers were farmers with agricultural obligations. From this large number of adult males, the Aztecs assembled units of 8,000 troops each, which they increased as the need arose. Initially, the army was recruited from among the elite of the Aztecs and their allies. But toward the middle of the fifteenth century, Aztec rulers set up a military school system for the sons of the elite plus those commoners who were to become priests. A parallel school system for the sons of commoners, aged 15–20 years, also included military training. After graduation, recruits began as porters, carrying supplies for the combat troops—an Aztec innovation

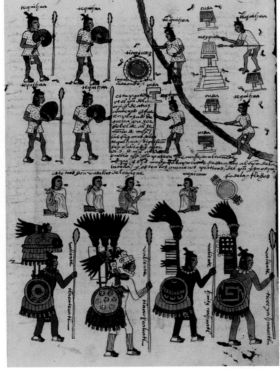

Aztec Weapons. Aztec weapons were well-crafted hardwood implements with serrated obsidian edges, capable of cutting through metal, including iron. As slashing weapons they were highly effective in close combat.

which considerably enlarged the marching range of armies on campaign. Soldiers rose in the army hierarchy on the basis of merit, particularly their success in the capture of enemies for future sacrifice. After four captures, a soldier was considered a veteran; additional captures yielded the ranks of captain, general, and commander in chief. Elite sons served in special regiments, identified by emblems of coyotes, jaguars, or eagles on their uniforms.

The Aztecs inherited the weaponry and armor of the Toltecs but also made some important innovations. The bow and arrow, which arrived from northwest Mexico at the end of Toltec rule, became a standard weapon in Aztec armies. In addition, perhaps as late as the fifteenth century, the Aztecs developed the three-foot obsidian-spiked broadsword, derived from the Toltec short sword, in order to enhance the latter's slashing force. As a result, clubs, maces, and axes declined in importance in the Aztec arsenal. Thrusting spears, dart throwers, and slings continued to be used as standard weapons. Body armor, consisting of quilted, sleeveless cotton shirts, thick cotton helmets, and round wooden or cane shields, was adopted from the Toltecs. With the arrival of the Aztecs, the Americas had acquired the heaviest infantry weaponry in their history, reflective of the intensity of militarism reached in their society—a militarism which was also typical of the earlier empires of the beginning Iron Age in the Middle East.

The Inca Empire of the Andes

After the disintegration of Tiwanaku and Wari around 1100, the central Andes returned to the traditional politics of local chiefdoms in small city-states with ceremonial centers and agricultural hinterlands. The best-known city-state was Chimú on the Peruvian coast, with its capital of Chan Chan numbering 30,000 inhabitants. Tiwanaku cultural traditions, however, remained dominant and were expressed in religious ceremonies, textile motifs, and ceramic styles.

Given the fierce competition among the pilgrimage centers, insecurity was rampant during the period 1100–1400, with particular influence granted to charismatic military leaders who could project military force and pacify the land. After a gestation period during the fourteenth century, the southern Peruvian city-state of Cuzco with its Inca elite emerged in the early fifteenth century at the head of a highly militaristic, conquering polity. Within another century, the Incas had established an empire, called "Tawantinsuyu" [Ta-wan-tin-SOO-yuh] (Quechua, "Four Regions"), symbolizing its geographical expanse. It stretched from Ecuador in the north to central Chile in the south, with extensions into the tropical upper Amazon region and western Argentinean steppes (see Map 15.4).

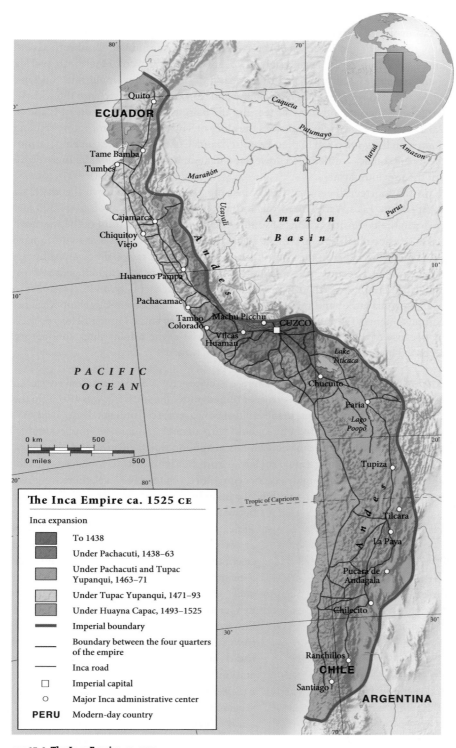

MAP 15.4 **The Inca Empire, ca. 1525.**

From Myth to History   As in the case of the Aztecs, the founding myth of the Incas involves a cave, an island, and a promised land of rich agriculture. In one version, the creator god Viracocha [Vee-rah-KOT-shah] summoned four brothers and four sisters from caves "seven leagues" (21 miles) from Cuzco to the south, pairing them as couples and promising them a land of plenty. They would find this land when a golden rod, to be used on their wanderings, would get stuck in the soil. Alternatively, the sun god Inti [IN-tee] did the pairing of the couples on an island in Lake Titicaca and thereby bestowed the glory of Tiwanaku on them, before sending them with the golden rod to their promised land. Cuzco, where the rod plunged into the fertile soil, was settled land however; and a war ensued in which the Incas drove out the previous farmers.

In the fourteenth century, Cuzco became a serious contender in the city-state competition. Like Wari, Cuzco was located at a highland elevation of 11,300 feet between the two Andes chains of southern Peru, roughly one-third of the way from Lake Titicaca north to Wari. Eight rulers (*curacas* [koo-RA-kas]) are said to have succeeded each other in the consolidation of Cuzco as a regional power. Although their names are recorded, events are hazy and dates are missing altogether. Firm historical terrain is reached with the ninth ruler, Pachacuti (r. 1438–1471), who overthrew his father and might have appropriated some of the latter's political accomplishments. The history of the Incas after 1438 is known much better, primarily because of the memories of the grandchildren of the original Inca conquerors, recorded by the Spanish who defeated them in turn.

Imperial Expansion   The system of reciprocity which characterized earlier Mesoamerican and Andean history continued under the Incas but was also, as in the case of Aztecs, decisively cast in the mold of power-enforced unilateralism. *Ayllu* [AY-yoo], the Quechua term for a household with an ancestral lineage, implied mutual obligations among groups of households, neighborhoods, villages, and city-states. To negotiate these obligations, society—from households to city-states—was divided into halves with roughly equal reciprocities. On the elite level, there were two sets of reciprocities, the first within two main branches of the elite and the second between the two branches of the elite and the subjects. The most important social expression of reciprocity remained the feast—extended celebrations with common meals and the consumption of beer fermented from corn or *molle* [MOI-yee] berries (from the Peruvian pepper tree, *molli* in Quechua). In the Incan Empire, the state collected considerably more from the subject *ayllus* than Tiwanaku and Wari had done, but whether it returned comparable amounts through feasts and celebrations was a matter of contention, often leading to armed rebellion.

The earliest conquests under Pachacuti were toward the near south around Lake Titicaca, as well as the agriculturally rich lands north of the former Wari state. Thereafter, in

---

From the Ordinances of the Inca

"We order that everyone bury their deceased in a chamber [*pucullo*], stone tomb, that the dead not be buried in their houses and that the deceased's spindle, dining service, food, drink and garments be buried with them. . . . We order that the children obey their parents, elders, grandees, and elder sons throughout the kingdom. For the first disobedience the child will be given a whipping; for the second the child will be banished to the silver and gold mines."

—Felipe Guaman Poma de Ayala. *The First New History and Chronicle of Good Government*. Translated by Roland Hamilton, p. 143. Austin: University of Texas Press, 2009.

the later fifteenth century, the Incas expanded 1,300 miles northward to southern Ecuador and 1,500 miles southward to Chile. The final provinces, added in the early sixteenth century, were in northern Ecuador as well as on the eastern slopes of the Andes, from the upper Amazon to western Argentina. The capital, Cuzco, which counted some 100,000 inhabitants in the early sixteenth century, was laid out in a cross-shaped grid of four streets leading out into the suburbs. Symbolically, the capital reached out to the four regions of the empire—coast, north, south, and Amazon rain forest.

Administration   Ethnic Inca governors administered the four regions, which were subdivided into a total of some 80 provinces, each again with an Inca sub-governor. Most provinces were composites of former city-states, which remained under their local elites but had to accept a unique decimal system of population organization imposed by the Inca rulers. According to this system, members of the local elites commanded 10,000, 1,000, 100, and 10 household or *ayllu* heads for the purpose of recruiting the manpower responsible for the *mit'a* [MIT-ah] ("to take a turn," in reference to service obligations rotating among the subjects). The services,

Inca Roads. Inca roads were paths reserved for runners and the military. They were built on beds of rocks and rubble and connected strategic points in the most direct line possible. They included staircases and suspension bridges, often over very steep and alpine terrain.

which subjects owed the empire as equivalents of taxes, were in farming, herding, manufacturing, military service, and portage. In its structure it was not unlike the Ming and Qing Chinese systems of local organization called *baojia*.

The mit'a was perhaps the single most important innovation the Incas contributed to the history of the Americas. In contrast to the Aztecs, who shipped taxes in kind to their capital by boat, the Incas had no efficient means of transportation for long distances. The only way to make use of the taxes in kind was to store them locally as provisions for visiting administrators and soldiers, apart from the traditional feasting in the villages. The Incas built tens of thousands of storehouses everywhere in their empire, requiring subjects to deliver a portion of their harvests, animal products, and domestically produced goods under mit'a obligations to the nearest storehouse in their vicinity.

The architecturally standardized storehouses, often grouped in multiples along the roads but also around cities and on state farms, contained supplies of durable food staples—corn, beer, dried potatoes, quinoa, beans, coca leaves, and dried meat called *charqui* [TSHAR-kee], from which the English term "jerky" is derived and which could last for years. Storehouses also contained raw cotton, wool, textiles, ceramics, ropes, and weapons. These supplies were available to officials and troops and enabled the Incas to conduct military campaigns far from Cuzco without the need for foraging among local farmers. In addition, it was through the mit'a that quotas of laborers were raised for the construction of inns, roads, ceremonial centers, palaces, terraces, and irrigation canals, often far away from the urban center. Finally, mit'a provided laborers for mines, quarries, state and temple farms, and colonies. No form of labor or service went untaxed.

To keep track of mit'a obligations, officials passed bundles of knotted cord (*khipu* [KEE-poo]) upward from level to level in the imperial administration. The numbers of knots on each cord in the bundles contained information on population figures and service obligations. As discussed in Chapter 5, the use of khipus was widespread in the Andes long before the Inca and can be considered as the Andean equivalent of a communication system. The only innovation contributed by the Incas seems to have been the massive scale on which these cord bundles were generated and employed. Unfortunately, all modern attempts to decipher them have so far failed, and thus, it is impossible to accurately outline the full picture of Inca service allocations.

Military Organization   Perhaps the most important mit'a obligation which subject households owed to the Inca in the conquest phase of the empire was the service of young, able-bodied men in the military. Married men 25–30 years old were foot soldiers, often accompanied by wives and children; unmarried men 18–25 years of age served as porters or messengers. As in the Aztec Empire, administrators made sure that enough laborers remained in the villages to take care of their other obligations of farming, herding, transporting, and manufacturing. Sources report armies in the range of 35,000–140,000. Intermediate commanders came from the local and regional elites, and the top commanders were members of the upper and lower Inca ruling elites, as we saw at the beginning of this chapter.

Inca weaponry was comparable to that of the Aztecs, consisting of bows and arrows, dart throwers, slings, clubs with spiked bronze heads, wooden broadswords, bronze axes, and bronze-tipped javelins. Using Bolivian tin, Inca smiths were able to make a much harder and more widely useful bronze than was possible with earlier techniques. The Incas lacked the Aztec obsidian-serrated swords but used a snare (which the Aztecs did not possess) with attached stone or bronze weights to entangle the enemy's legs. Protective armor consisted of quilted cotton shirts, copper breastplates, cane helmets, and shields. These types of weapons and armor were widely found among the Incas and their enemies. The advantage enjoyed by the Incas resulted from the sheer massiveness of their weapons and supplies, procured from craftspeople through the mit'a and stored in strategically located armories.

During the second half of the fifteenth century the Incas turned from conquest to consolidation. Faced at that time with a number of rebellions, they deemphasized the decimal draft and recruited longer-serving troops from among a smaller number of select, trusted peoples. These troops garrisoned the forts distributed throughout the empire. They also were part of the settler colonies implanted in rebellious provinces and in border regions. The fiercest resistance came from the people of the former Tiwanaku state and from the northeast Peruvian provinces, areas with long state traditions of their own. Since elite infighting also became more pronounced toward the end of the fifteenth century, personal guards recruited from non-Inca populations and numbering up to 7,000 soldiers accompanied many leading ruling-class members. The professionalization of the Inca army, however, lagged behind that of the Aztecs since the Incas did not have military academies open to subjects.

Communications   Although they lacked the military professionalization of the Aztecs, the Incas created an imperial communication and logistics structure that was unparalleled in the Americas. Early on, the Incas systematically improved on the road network which they inherited from Tiwanaku, Wari, and other states. Two parallel trunk roads extended from Cuzco nearly the entire length of the empire in both southerly and northerly directions. One followed the coast and western slopes of the western Andes chain; the other led through the mountain lands, valleys, and high plains between the western and eastern Andes chain. In numerous places, additional highways connected the two trunk roads. Suspension bridges made of thick ropes crossed gorges, while rafts were used for crossing rivers. The roads, 3–12 feet wide, crossed the terrain as directly as possible, often requiring extensive grounding, paving, staircasing, and tunneling. In many places, the 25,000-mile road network still exists today, attesting to the engineering prowess of the Incas.

The roads were reserved for troops, officials, and runners carrying messages. For their convenience, every 15 miles, or at the end of a slow 1-day journey, an inn provided accommodation. Larger armies stopped at barracks-like constructions or pitched tents on select campgrounds. Like the Romans, and despite the fact that they did not have wheeled transport, the Incas were well aware how crucial paved and well-supplied roads were for infantry soldiers.

Imperial Society and Culture

As Mesoamerica and the Andes entered their imperial age, cosmopolitan capitals with monumental ceremonial centers and palaces emerged. The sizes of both capitals and monuments were visual expressions of the exalted power which the rulers claimed. Almost daily ceremonies and rituals, accompanied by feasts, further underscore the power claims of rulers. These ceremonies and rituals expressed the shamanic and polytheistic heritage but were modified to impress on enemies and subjects alike the irresistible might of the empires.

Imperial Capitals: Tenochtitlán and Cuzco

In the fifteenth century, the Aztec and Inca capitals were among the largest cities of the world, encompassing between 100,000 and 200,000 inhabitants. Both cities maintained their high degree of urbanism through a complex command system of labor, services, and goods. Although their monumental architecture followed different artistic traditions, both emphasized platforms and sanctuaries atop large pyramid-like structures as symbols of elevated power as well as closeness to the astral gods, especially those associated with the sun and Venus.

Tenochtitlán as an Urban Metropolis

More than half of the approximately 1.5 million people living during the fifteenth century in the Valley of Mexico were urban dwellers, including elites, priests, administrators, military officers, merchants, traders, craftspeople, messengers, servants, and laborers. Tenochtitlán was among the 10 largest world cities of the fifteenth century. Such an extraordinary concentration of urban citizens was unique in the agrarian world prior to the industrialization of Europe (beginning around 1800), when cities usually held no more than 10 percent of the total population (see Map 15.5).

The center of Tenochtitlán, on the southern island, was a large platform where the Aztec settlers had driven pilings into marshy ground and heaped rocks and rubble. In an enclosure on this platform were the main pyramid, with temples to the Aztec gods on top, and a series of smaller ceremonial centers. Adjacent to this on the platform were a food market and a series of palaces of the ruling elite, which included guest quarters, administrative offices, storage facilities for tributes, kitchens, the high court for the elite and the court of appeals for commoners, the low court for civil cases, workshops for craftspeople, the prison, and councils for teachers and the military. Large numbers of Aztecs and visitors assembled each day to pay respect to the ruler and to trade in the market in preparation for assemblies and feasts.

Aqueduct from the Western Hills to Tenochtitlán. This aqueduct, still standing today, provided fresh water to the palace and mansions of the center of the island, to be used as drinking water and for washing.

In 1473, the southern island was merged with the northern island, to form a single unit. At the center of the northern island was a platform that contained the principal market of the combined islands. This daily market attracted as many as 40,000 farmers, craftspeople, traders, porters, and laborers on the main market day. Traders sold raw materials such as clay, basalt, obsidian, timber, lime, cotton, or silver to craftspeople, many of whom maintained workshops in the market where they made pottery, knives, wooden implements, or jewelry. Goods were exchanged through either barter or the use of cacao beans and copper and bronze ornaments as payment. The market also had bars, restaurants, and hotels. Itinerant hucksters dispensed water or juices, and day laborers lined up in a corner to wait for employment. Government officials saw to the observance of standardized measures and weights. Policemen hauled thieves to a courthouse at the center of the market. The sophistication of the market was comparable to that of any market in Eurasia during the fifteenth century.

A number of causeways crossed the capital and linked it with the lakeshore. People also traveled inside the city on a number of main and branch canals. Dikes with sluices on the east side regulated both the water level and the salinity of the lake water around the islands. The runoff during the summer rainy season from the southwestern mountains provided freshwater to lighten the lake's salinity, and the eastern dikes kept out salt water from the rest of the lake. Potable water arrived from the shore via an aqueduct on one of the western causeways. This aqueduct served mostly the ceremonial center and palace precinct, but branches brought potable water to a number of elite residences nearby as well. Professional water carriers took freshwater to commoners in the various quarters of the city; professional waste removers collected human waste from urban residences and took it to farmers for fertilizer. In short, Tenochtitlán possessed a fully developed urban infrastructure comparable to the best amenities found elsewhere in the world at that time.

The two city centers—the pyramid and palaces in the south and the market in the north—were surrounded by dozens of residential city quarters. Built on a layer of firm ground, many of these quarters were inhabited by craftspeople of a shared profession, such as merchants, feather workers, mat makers, and gold- and silversmiths, who practiced their crafts in their residences. As discussed earlier in this chapter, merchants occupied a privileged position between the elite and the commoners. As militarily trained organizers of large caravans of porters, the merchants also provided the Aztec capital with luxury goods. Depending on their social rank, craftspeople occupied residences of larger or smaller size, usually grouped

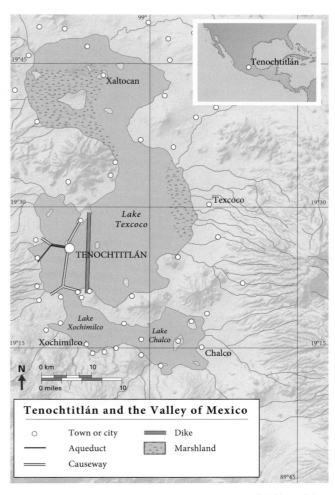

MAP **15.5 Tenochtitlán and the Valley of Mexico.**

into compounds of related families. The rooms of the houses surrounded a central patio on which most of the household activities took place—an architectural preference common to Mesoamerica and the Andes, as well as the Middle East and Mediterranean.

Farming in the Suburbs

Residents of quarters farther away from the center were farmers. In these quarters, making up nearly two-thirds of Tenochtitlán's surface, families not only produced household basics, such as pottery and textiles, but also engaged in intensive farming, which approached horticulture in its precision and complexity. Here, a grid of canals encased small, rectangular islands devoted to housing compounds and/or farming. People moved within these barrios by boat. Since the Valley of Mexico received year-round rains that were often insufficient for dry farming, a raised-field system prevailed, whereby farmers dredged the canals, heaped the fertile mud on top of the rectangular islands, and added waste from their households or brought by boat from the urban neighborhoods. In contrast to the luxurious palaces of the elite, housing for farmers consisted of plastered huts made of cane, wood, and reeds. As in all agrarian societies, farmers—subject to high taxes or rents—were among the poorest folk.

On the surface of the raised beds, or *chinampas*, farmers grew corn, beans, squash, amaranth, and peppers. These seed plants were supplemented by

Fleeting Pleasures

"For only here on earth shall the fragrant flowers last and the songs that are our bliss. Enjoy them now! One day we must go, one night we will descend into the region of mystery. Here, we only come to know ourselves; only in passing are we here on earth. In peace and pleasure let us spend our lives; come, let us enjoy ourselves."

—Anonymous poem, recorded in the early sixteenth century, expressing the near-universal farmer's attitude toward life under the weight of taxes, war, and famine. Miguel León-Portilla et al., trans. *Native Mesoamerican Spirituality*, p. 185. Mahwah, NJ: Paulist Press, 1980.

The *Chinampa*. The raised field (*chinampa*) was either a square or a rectangular strip of soil surrounded by irrigation channels. The water and mud from the channels kept the soil moist and fertile. Villagers harvested rich crops from these fields.

Cuzco Stone Masonry. Inspired by the masonry of the people of Tiwanaku, the Inca built imposing structures with much larger blocks of limestone or granite. To cut the blocks, masons used copper and bronze chisels, making use of natural fissures in the stone.

maguey [mag-AY], a large cactus related to the agave. This evergreen plant grew in poor soils; had a large root system, which helped in stabilizing the ground; and produced fiber useful for weaving and pulp useful for making *pulque* [POOL-key], a fermented drink. To plant these crops in the soft soil, a digging stick, slightly broadened at one end, was sufficient. Regular watering made multicropping of seed plants possible. Trees, planted at the edges, firmed up the islands against water erosion.

Ownership of the *chinampas* was vested in clans, which, under neighborhood leaders, were responsible for the adjudication of land allocations and disputes as well as the payment of taxes in kind to the elite. But there were also members of the elite who, as absentee owners, possessed estates and employed managers to collect rents from the farmers. Whether there was a trend from taxes to rents (that is, a central tax system to a decentralized landowner class) is unknown. Given the high productivity of raised-field farming, which was similar to that of the Eurasian agrarian–urban centers, such a trend would not have been surprising.

Cuzco as a Ceremonial-Administrative City   The site of the Inca city of Cuzco was an elongated triangle formed by the confluence of two rivers. At one end, opposite the confluence, was a hill with a number of structures, including the imperial armory, and a temple dedicated to the sun god. Enormous, zigzagging walls followed the contours of the hill. The walls were built with stone blocks weighing up to 100 tons and cut so precisely that no mortar was needed, a technique which the Incas adopted from Tiwanaku. Inside the walls today can be seen the ruins, dating from the Spanish siege in 1536, of multiple buildings which might have served religious and/or administrative purposes. No agreement exists on who resided on the hill or what the function of the heavy stone works was.

Below, on the plain leading to the confluence, the city was laid out in a grid pattern. The residents of the city, all belonging to the upper and lower Inca ruling class,

Human Sacrifice and Propaganda

Archaeologists disagree over the extent to which Paleolithic hominins or humans engaged in human sacrifices. Atapuerca in northeastern Spain is a Paleolithic site from 850,000–750,000 years ago where bone fragments suggestive of violent deaths have been found. How the victims got into the pit at the site, however, and under which circumstances, remain so far a mystery. During the Bronze Age, in Mesopotamia and in other places in Eurasia (3000–1300 BCE), children, servants, retainers, and soldiers were buried together with the kings whom they followed in death. By contrast, in the Iron Age beginning around 1000 BCE, human sacrifices declined almost everywhere in Eurasia. With the concept of transcendence emerging in the seventh century BCE, that is, of a single, invisible God or principle of truth and justice, human sacrifice was essentially abandoned.

In the first millennium CE, Mesoamerica and the Andes evolved broadly along patterns similar to those in Eurasia, from shamanic animism to polytheism, but without the conceptualization of transcendence. The animist heritage, however,

Tolland Man. Discovered in a bog in Denmark in 1950, this nearly perfectly preserved man, killed by hanging around 750 BCE, was clearly not a criminal; he was given a dignified burial after his death. Most likely, he was sacrificed to the gods.

Royal Bloodletting. Mayan kings and queens communicated with gods or ancestors through ritual bloodletting. In this example, from an early eighth-century stone relief from southern Mexico, the queen draws a spiked rope through her tongue while her husband holds a large torch above her head.

remained a strong undercurrent. Both American regions engaged in human as well as animal and agricultural sacrifices. Rulers appeased the gods also through self-sacrifice, that is, the piercing of tongue and penis, as was the case among the Olmecs (1400–400 BCE) and Mayas (600 BCE–900 CE). The feathered serpent god Quetzalcoatl was the Mesoamerican deity of self-sacrifice, revered in the city-states of Teotihuacán (200 BCE–570 CE) and Tula (ca. 900 CE). Under the Toltecs and the Aztecs, this god receded into the background, in favor of warrior gods such as Tezcatlipoca and Huitzilpochtli. The survival of animist blood rituals within polytheism was a pattern that distinguished the early American empires from their Eurasian counterparts.

Whether human sacrifices were prolific under Aztec and Inca imperialism is questionable. About the same number of human victims were excavated at the Feathered Serpent Temple of Teotihuacán and at the Templo Mayor of Tenochtitlán: 137 versus 126. These numbers are minuscule in comparison to the impression created by the Spanish conquerors and encourage doubts about the magnitude of human sacrifices in temple ceremonies. It appears that even though the Aztec and Inca ruling classes were focused on war, the ritual of human sacrifice was not as pervasive as has been widely assumed.

Could it be that there was no significant increase in human sacrifice under the Aztecs and Incas, as the self-serving Spanish conquerors alleged? Were there perhaps, instead, imperial propaganda machines in the Aztec and Inca Empires, employed in the service of conquest and consolidation—similar to those of the Assyrians and Mongols in Eurasia who sought to intimidate their enemies? In this case, the Aztec and Inca Empires would not be exceptional barbaric aberrations in world history but two typical examples of the general world-historical pattern of competitive militaristic states during the early agrarian era, using propaganda to further their imperial power.

52.

Human Sacrifice. Human sacrifice among the pre-Columbian Mesoamericans and Andeans was based on the animist concept of a shared life spirit or mind, symbolized by the life substance of blood. In the American animist-polytheistic conceptualization, the gods sacrificed their blood, or themselves altogether, during creation; rulers pierced their earlobes, tongues, or penises for blood sacrifices; and war captives lost their lives when their hearts were sacrificed.

Questions

- In examining the question of whether empires such as the Inca and the Aztec employed human sacrifice for propaganda purposes, can this practice be considered an adaptation that evolved out of earlier rituals, such as royal bloodletting?

- If the Aztec and the Inca did indeed employ human sacrifice for propaganda purposes, what does this say about the ability of these two empires to use cultural and religious practices to consolidate their power?

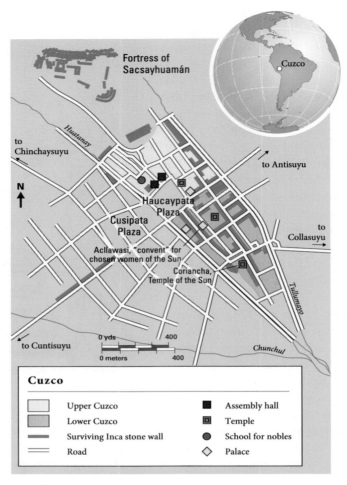

MAP 15.6 **Cuzco.**

lived in adobe houses arranged in a block and courtyard pattern similar to that of Wari. Several squares and temples within the city served as ceremonial centers. One plaza contained a platform, with the imperial throne and a pillar, placed symbolically atop what the Incas considered the earth's center or navel. The Coricancha [Co-ri-CAN-tsha], the city's main temple, stood near the confluence of the rivers. This temple was a walled compound comprised of six buildings set around a courtyard. Chambers in these buildings contained the Inca gods and goddesses as well as the divine statues or sacred objects confiscated from the provinces. Each year priests of the empire's ceremonial centers sent one such sacred object to the Coricancha, to document their obedience to the central Inca temple (see Map 15.6).

Across the rivers, in separate suburbs, were settlements for commoners with markets and storehouses. They were surrounded by fields, terraces, and irrigation canals. In the fields, interspersed stone pillars and shrines were aligned on sight lines radiating from the Coricancha, tying the countryside closely to the urban center. These alignments were reminiscent of the Nazca lines drawn half a millennium earlier in southern Peru (Chapter 9). Farther away were imperial estates with unfree laborers from outside the *mit'a* system and its feasting reciprocities. In contrast to the Aztec elite, which allowed meritorious generals to rise in the hierarchy, the Inca elite remained exclusionary, allowing no commoners to reside in Cuzco.

Power and Its Cultural Expressions

Ruling elites, as repeatedly emphasized in this chapter, put a strong emphasis on the display of their power during the period 600–1500. This was particularly true with the Aztecs and Incas during the fifteenth century. Among these displays were human sacrifices, mausoleums, and mummy burials. Although all three involved changes in social relations, these changes were accommodated in the existing overall religious culture.

Inca Ruling Class Gender Relations　The ruling classes in the Inca Empire displayed their power in several ways. Among the examples were the "Houses of Chosen Women" in Cuzco and provincial colonies. The greatest honor for Inca girls was to enter, at age 10–12, into the service of these houses. An inspector from Cuzco made regular visits to the villages of the empire to select attractive young girls for the service. The girls were marched to the capital or the colonies, where they were divided according to beauty, skills, and social standing. These houses had female instructors who provided the girls with a 4-year education in cooking, beer making, weaving, and officiating in the rituals and ceremonies of the Inca religion. After their graduation, the young women became virgin temple priestesses, were given in marriage to non-Incas honored for service to the ruler, or became palace servants, musicians, or concubines of the Inca elite. The collection of the girl tribute was separate from the reciprocity system. As such, it was an act of assigning gender roles in an emerging social hierarchy defined by power inequalities.

Traditionally, gender roles were less strictly divided than in Eurasia. The horticultural form of agriculture in Mesoamerica and the Andes gave males fewer opportunities to accumulate wealth and power than plow agriculture did in Eurasia. Hoes and foot plows distinguished men and women less from each other than plows and teams of oxen or horses did. Nevertheless, it comes as no surprise that the gradual agrarian–urban diversification of society, even if it was slower in the Americas than in Eurasia, proceeded along similar paths of increasing male power concentration in villages, ceremonial centers, temple cities, conquering states, and empires. Emphasizing gender differences, therefore, should be viewed as a characteristic phenomenon arising in imperial contexts.

Inca Mummy Veneration　Other houses in Cuzco were ghostly residences in which scores of attendants and servants catered to what were perceived as the earthly needs of deceased, mummified Inca emperors and their principal wives. During the mummification process attendants removed the cadaver's internal organs, placed them in special containers, and desiccated the bodies until they were completely mummified. Servants dressed the mummies (*mallquis* [MAY-kees]) in their finest clothing and placed them back into their residences amid their possessions, as if they had never died. The mummies received daily meals, and their retinues carried them around for visits to their mummified relatives. On special occasions, mummies were lined up according to rank on Cuzco's main plaza to participate in ceremonies and processions. In this way, they remained fully integrated in the daily life of the elite.

"Ghost residences" with mummies can be considered an outgrowth of the old Andean custom of mummification. This custom was widely practiced among the elites of the ceremonial centers, who, however, generally placed their ancestors in temple tombs, shrines, or caves. Mummies were also buried in cemeteries, sometimes collectively in bundles with "false heads" made of cotton, as we discussed in the vignette at the beginning of this chapter. Preserving the living spaces of the deceased obviously required considerable wealth—wealth provided only by imperial regimes.

As a general phenomenon in Andean society, of course, mummies were a crucial ingredient in the religious heritage, in which strong shamanic elements survived underneath the polytheistic overlay of astral gods. In the shamanic tradition, body and spirit cohabit more or less loosely. In a trance, a shaman's mind can travel, enter the minds of other people and animals, or make room for other people's minds. Similarly, in death a person's spirit, while no longer in the body, remains nearby and therefore still needs daily nourishment in order not to be driven away. Hence, even though non-Incan Andean societies removed the dead from their daily living spaces, descendants had to visit tombs regularly with food and beer or provide buried mummies with ample victuals.

The expenses for the upkeep of the mummy households were the responsibility of the deceased emperor's bloodline, headed by a surviving brother. As heirs of the emperor's estate, the members of the bloodline formed a powerful clan within the ruling class. The new emperor was excluded from this estate and had to acquire his own new one in the course of his rule, a mechanism evidently designed to intensify his imperial ambitions for conquest. In the early sixteenth century, however, when it became logistically difficult to expand much beyond the enormous territory already accumulated in the Andes, this ingenious mechanism of keeping the upper and lower rungs of the ruling class united became counterproductive. Emperors lacking resources had to contend with brothers richly endowed with inherited wealth and ready to engage in dynastic warfare—as actually occurred shortly before the arrival of the Spanish (1529–1532).

Putting It All Together

During the short time of their existence, the Aztec and Inca Empires unleashed extraordinary creative energies. Sculptors, painters, and (after the arrival of the Spanish) writers recorded the traditions as well as the innovations of the fifteenth century. Aztec painters produced codices, or illustrated manuscripts, that present the divine pantheons, myths, calendars, ceremonial activities, chants, poetry, and administrative activities of their societies in exquisite and colorful detail. They fashioned these codices, using bark paper, smoothing it with plaster, and connecting the pages accordion-style. Today, only a handful of these codices survive, preserved in Mexican and European libraries.

The most invaluable surviving work informing our understanding of Incan culture is a 1,200-page text with nearly 400 drawings that dates to 1600–1615, nearly a century

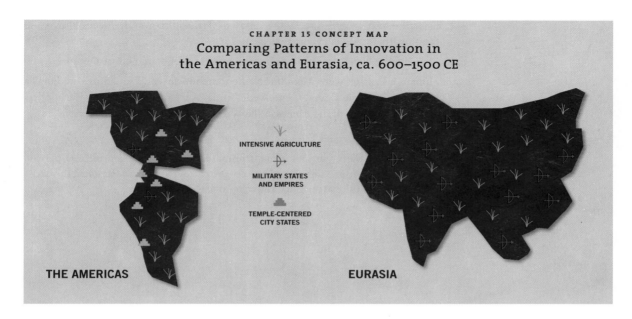

CHAPTER 15 CONCEPT MAP
Comparing Patterns of Innovation in the Americas and Eurasia, ca. 600–1500 CE

INTENSIVE AGRICULTURE

MILITARY STATES AND EMPIRES

TEMPLE-CENTERED CITY STATES

THE AMERICAS   **EURASIA**

after the Spanish conquest. Its author, Guamán Poma (ca. 1550–1616), intended this work to be a petition to the Spanish, demanding reforms in the administration, although the Spanish king never received it. The drawings are superb illustrations of life in the Inca Empire. These cultural creations make one wonder how the empires would have evolved, had they not been cut short by the Spanish conquests.

However, even if they were short-lived, the Aztec and Inca Empires were polities that illustrate how humans not in contact with the rest of the world and living within an environment that was different from Eurasia and Africa many respects developed patterns of innovation that were remarkably similar. On the basis of an agriculture that eventually produced ample surpluses, humans made the same choices as their cousins in Eurasia and Africa. Specifically, in the period 600–1500, they created temple-centered city-states, just like their Sumerian and Hindu counterparts. Their military states were not unlike the Chinese warring states. And, finally, their empires—although just beginning to flourish in the Bronze Age—were comparable to those of the New Kingdom Egyptians or Assyrians. The Americas had their own unique variations of these larger historical patterns, to be sure; but they nevertheless displayed the same humanity as found elsewhere.

Review and Respond

1. Discuss the evolution of the ruling classes in Mesoamerica and the Andes in the period 600–1100. How did militarism express itself in the states of the period 600–1100?

2. Compare indigenous American imperialism with that of Eurasia. What were the similarities? In which ways did it differ?

3. Discuss the process of militarization in Mesoamerica. Which weapons were used?

4. Describe and analyze life in the cities of Tenochtitlán and Cuzco. How were farming, trade, and crafts organized?

5. How did the Incas assure communications and supplies in their vast empire?

6. Human sacrifices were a common phenomenon in early kingdoms in Eurasia (Sumer, pharaonic Egypt, Crete, Vedic India, Ancient China, Celtic Europe), as well as the polities of the Americas. How do you explain this phenomenon?

For additional resources, including maps, primary sources, visuals, and quizzes, please go to www.oup.com/us/vonsivers. Please see the Further Resources section at the back of the book for additional readings and suggested websites.

Thinking Through Patterns

▶ **Within the patterns of states formation basic to the Americas, which types of states emerged in Meso-america and the Andes during the period 600–1550? What characterized these states?**

The basic pattern of state formation in the Americas was similar to that of Eurasia and Africa. Historically, it began with the transition from foraging to agriculture and settled village life. As the population increased, villages under elders became chiefdoms, which in turn became city-states with temples. As in Eurasia and Africa, American city-states often became conquering states, beginning with the Maya kingdoms and Teotihuacán. Both, however, remained small. Military states, in which ruling classes sought to expand regions, such as Tula and, to a lesser degree, Tiwanaku and Wari, were characteristic for the early part of the period 600–1550. The successors of these—the Aztec and Inca Empires—were multiethnic, multilinguistic, and multireligious polities that dominated Mesoamerica and the Andes for about a century, before the Spanish conquest brought them to a premature end.

The states of Tiwanaku and Wari had more or less cohesive ruling classes but no dynasties of rulers and centralized bureaucracies. These ruling classes and their subjects—corn and potato farmers—were integrated with each other through systems of reciprocity, that is, military protection in return for foodstuffs. They customarily rejuvenated the bonds of reciprocity in common feasts. After one or two centuries, however, tensions arose, either between stronger and weaker branches of the ruling classes or between rulers and subjects over questions of obligations and justice. When these tensions erupted into internal warfare, the states disintegrated, often in conjunction with environmental degradation and climate change.

▶ **Why did the Tiwanaku and Wari states have ruling classes but no dynasties and central bureaucracies? How were these patterns expressed in the territorial organization of these states?**

▶ **What patterns of urban life characterized the cities of Tenochtitlán and Cuzco, the capitals of the Aztec and Inca Empires? In which ways were these cities similar to those of Eurasia and Africa?**

Tenochtitlán and Cuzco, the capitals of the Aztec and Inca Empires, were two urban centers organized around temples and associated residences of the ruling dynasties and their priestly classes. They also contained large city quarters inhabited by craftspeople, specializing in the production of woven textiles, pottery, leather goods, and weapons. Large central markets provided for the exchange of foodstuffs, crafts, and imported luxury goods. Armed caravans of merchants and porters transported the luxury goods, such as cacao, feathers, obsidian, and turquoise, across hundreds of miles. Tenochtitlán had an aqueduct for the supply of drinking water, and Cuzco was traversed by a river. Both capitals had agricultural suburbs in which farmers used irrigation for the production of the basic food staples.

PART FOUR

Interactions Across the Globe

1450–1750

Starting around 1450, important changes can be detected in the patterns of world history. The religious civilizations that emerged in the period after 600 CE continued to evolve, but the competing states that constituted these civilizations began to give way to new empires, such as the Mughals, the Ottomans, the Safavids, and the Habsburgs. China, historically an empire, had already reconstituted itself under the Ming after the collapse of the Mongol superempire that had straddled Eurasia. Finally, on the Atlantic coast, smaller European countries, such as Portugal, Spain, the Netherlands, England, and France, were creating the first global seaborne empires. Large or small, land-based or maritime, however, all of these empires employed the vitally important innovation of firearms. In addition, many reorganized themselves as *fiscal–military states* based on money economies, centralizing bureaucracies, and professional armies. Locked into far-flung competition for resources, markets, and ideological influence, they interacted with each other with increasing intensity.

While this renewal of the drive for empire among these civilizations was a significant turning point in world history, two new phenomena appeared during the three centuries in question that would have far-reaching implications. Indeed, they would ultimately provide the basis on which our modern society would be built: the New Science (or Scientific Revolution) and the Enlightenment. Attempts to found an understanding of the universe on mathematics and experimentation would lead to the primacy of science as the chief mode of interpreting the physical realm. Attempts to apply the principles of science to understanding and improving human societies would lead to the concepts of individual rights, natural law, and popular sovereignty that would become the modern legacy of the Enlightenment. The combination of these two trends would create the foundations of the *scientific–industrial society* that now dominates our modern global culture.

The process by which this took place was, of course, extremely complex, and it is impossible for us to do more than suggest some of the larger components of it here. Moreover, because of the long-standing argument in Western historiography for European "exceptionalism"—that there was something unique in the European historical experience that preordained it to rise to dominance—we must be careful to explore the various aspects of this process without sliding into easy assumptions

1440–1897
Benin Kingdom,
West Africa

1492
Spanish Conquest of Granada,
Expulsion of Jews, and
Discovery of the Americas

ca. 1500
Beginning of
Columbian Exchange

1514
Nicolaus Copernicus
Formulates the
Heliocentric System

1453
Ottoman Capture
of Constantinople

1498
Vasco da Gama's
Circumnavigation of
Africa and Journey
to India

1511
First African
Slaves Land in
Hispaniola

1517
Beginning of
Martin Luther's
Reformation

about their inevitability. For example, one question that suggests itself is, To what extent did the societies of western Europe (what we have termed the "religious civilization" of western Christianity) part ways with the other religious civilizations of the world? Here, the aspects of the question are tantalizingly complex and, thus, have recently been the subject of considerable debate:

- On the one hand, there appears to have been no movement comparable to that of the European Renaissance or Reformation arising during this time in the other parts of the world to create a new culture similar to that of Europe. The Middle East, India, and China for the most part continued ongoing cultural patterns, although often on considerably higher levels of refinement and sophistication. Recent scholarship on neglected cultural developments in these areas from 1450 to 1750 has provided ample proof for the continuing vitality of Islamic, Hindu, Buddhist, Confucian, and Daoist cultural traditions. Thus, former assumptions of stagnation or decline no longer seem supportable.

- On the other hand, Europe, like much of the rest of the world, remained rooted in agrarian–urban patterns until the effects of the Industrial Revolution began to be felt some time after 1800. The centuries-old patterns in which the majority of the population being in agriculture in support of cities continued unchanged. Furthermore, through nearly this entire period, China and India were more populous and at least as wealthy and diversified in their economies and social structures as their European counterparts. The "great divergence," as scholars currently refer to it, happened only *after* the Western constitutional and industrial revolutions. Nonetheless, the overall wealth of European countries involved in the conquest and exploitation of the resources of the Americas and the development of global trading systems advanced immensely—as did knowledge of the globe as a whole. Thus, while India and China had possessed these resources partially or completely already for a long time, European countries were now utilizing them at an accelerating rate. This wealth and the patterns of its acquisition and distribution would soon have far-reaching consequences.

It is important to emphasize that these developments we deem crucial today were not immediately apparent to the people living at the time. Indeed, for the great majority of people, even in 1750, much seemed to go on as before. Everywhere in the world empires continued to grow and decline, religious tensions continued to erupt into warfare, and rulers continued to ground their authority not in their peoples but in the divine. Thus, for a full understanding of world history during 1450–1750 one has to carefully balance cultural, political, social, and economic factors and constantly keep in mind that although change was certainly occurring, it was often too imperceptible for contemporaries to detect.

Thinking Like a World Historian

▶ What new and different patterns characterized the development of states and empires in the period 1450–1750?

▶ How did the emergence of fiscal–military states lead to more intensive and frequent interactions among empires in the period 1450–1750? What were the consequences of this far-flung competition for new resources and markets?

▶ How did the New Science and the Enlightenment lay the foundation for the scientific–industrial society that dominates our global culture today?

▶ To what extent did the societies of western Europe part ways with the other civilizations of the world in the period 1450–1750? Why is the notion of "exceptionalism" a problematic way to examine this question?

1521, 1533
Spanish Conquest of the Aztec and Inca Empires

1577
Matteo Ricci, First Jesuit Missionary to Arrive in China

1607
Founding of Jamestown, Virginia

1720
Edo, Capital of Japan, Becomes the World's Largest City

1542–1605
Akbar, the Most Innovative of the Mughal Rulers (India)

1604
Galileo Galilei Formulates the Mathematical Law of Falling Bodies

1687
Isaac Newton Unifies Physics and Astronomy

1736–1795
Reign of Qianlong Emperor, China

Chapter 16

1450-1650

The Ottoman–Habsburg Struggle and Western European Overseas Expansion

Al-Hasan Ibn Muhammad al-Wazzan (ca. 1494–1550) was born into a family of bureaucrats in Muslim Granada soon after the Christian conquest of this kingdom in southern Iberia in 1492. Unwilling to convert to Christianity, Hasan's family emigrated to Muslim Morocco around 1499–1500 and settled in the city of Fez. Here, Hasan received a good education in religion,

Seeing Patterns

▶ What patterns characterized Christian and Muslim competition in the period 1300–1600? Which elements distinguished them from each other, and which elements were similar? How did the pattern change over time?

▶ How did the fiscal–military state in the Middle East and Europe function in the period 1450–1600? How did economics, military power, and imperial objectives interact to create the fiscal-military state?

▶ Which patterns did cultural expressions follow in the Habsburg and Ottoman Empires? Why did the ruling classes of these empires sponsor these expressions?

law, logic, and the sciences. After completing his studies, he took a position as secretary at the insane asylum of Fez but found this first job less than fulfilling. His ambition was for a more exciting life. He wanted to become a diplomat, travel, go on pilgrimage, and engage in trade. After entering the administration of the Moroccan sultan, Hasan was soon entrusted with a diplomatic mission to rulers in sub-Saharan Africa. From there, he traveled to the Middle East and performed his pilgrimage to Mecca. Along the way he traded for a variety of goods, to pay for his extended journey.

In 1517, as he was returning home from a mission to Istanbul, Christian **corsairs** kidnapped him from his ship. Like their Muslim counterparts, these corsairs roamed the Mediterranean to capture unsuspecting travelers, whom they then held for ransom or sold into slavery. For a handsome sum of money, they turned the cultivated Hasan over to Pope Leo X (1513–1521) in Rome. A member of the famed Florentine Medici family and a luxury-loving patron of the arts, architecture, and literature, Leo was delighted to add a learned Muslim world traveler to his stable of luminaries.

Leo ordered Hasan to convert to Christianity and baptized him with his own family name, Giovanni Leone di Medici. Hasan became known in

Buying Captives Their Freedom. An imperial officer in the army of Charles V places some coins in the hands of the Muslim captor of two Christian women, one of whom is accompanied by a young boy. This detail, from a tapestry, which was part of a series commissioned to celebrate the Habsburg capture of Tunis in 1535, documents the way in which individuals such as Leo Africanus became entangled in the zones of contest between empires—in this case, the Ottoman and Habsburg struggle for supremacy in the Mediterranean.

Corsairs: In the context of this chapter, Muslim and Christian pirates who boarded ships, confiscated the cargoes, and held the crews and travelers for ransom; nominally under the authority of the Ottoman sultan or the pope in Rome, but they operated independently.

Rome as Leo Africanus ("Leo the African"), in reference to his travels in sub-Saharan Africa. He stayed for 10 years in Italy, initially at the papal court, later as an independent scholar in Rome. During this time, he taught Arabic to Roman clergymen, compiled an Arabic–Hebrew–Latin dictionary, and wrote an essay on famous Arabs. His most memorable and enduring work was a travelogue, first composed in Arabic and later translated into Italian, *Description of Africa*, which was for many years the sole source of information about sub-Saharan Africa in the western Christian world.

After 1527, however, life became difficult in Rome. In this year, Charles V (r. 1516–1558), king of Spain and emperor of the Holy Roman Empire of Germany, invaded Italy and sacked the city. Hasan survived the sack of Rome but departed for Tunis sometime after 1531, seeking a better life in Muslim North Africa. Unfortunately, all traces of Hasan after his departure from Rome are lost. It is possible that he perished in 1535 when Charles V attacked and occupied Tunis (1535-1574), although it is generally assumed that he lived there until around 1550.

The world in which Hasan lived and traveled was a Muslim–Christian world composed of the Middle East, North Africa, and Europe. Muslims on the Iberian Peninsula and in the Balkans formed a bracket around this world, with the western Christians in the center. Although Muslims and Christians traveled in much of this world more or less freely—as merchants, mapmakers, adventurers, mercenaries, or corsairs—the two religious civilizations were locked in a pattern of fierce competition. For the Muslims, *jihad*, or holy war, against Christianity defined this pattern. For the western Christians the competition was twofold. On the Iberian Peninsula it expressed itself in the Reconquista (Spanish for "reconquest"), a euphemism for the conquest of the Muslim lands of Iberia and North Africa that had once been Christian. And in the Middle East this competition was defined by the Crusade for the liberation of Jerusalem from the Muslims. As much as Christians and Muslims benefited from peaceful commercial and cultural exchanges, they also suffered from immense destruction inflicted on each other in the name of their religious civilizations.

By the fifteenth century, the missions of the Reconquista and the Crusades were largely identical in the mind of the Iberian Christians, who saw the liberation of Iberia and North Africa from Muslim rule and circumventing the Muslims in the Mediterranean as stepping stones toward rebuilding the crusader kingdom of Jerusalem, which had been lost to the Muslims in 1291. Searching for a route that would take them around Africa, they hoped to defeat the Muslims in Jerusalem with an attack from the east. Driven at least in part by this search, the Christians discovered the continents of the Americas. For their part, the Muslims sought to conquer eastern and central Europe (the Balkans, Hungary, and Austria), while simultaneously shoring up their defense of North Africa and seeking to drive the Portuguese out of the Indian Ocean. After a hiatus of several centuries—when commonwealths of states characterized western Christian and Islamic civilizations—imperial polities reemerged, in the form of the Ottoman and Habsburg Empires vying for world rule.

During the climax of their battles in the sixteenth century, the Ottoman and Habsburg Empires poured gigantic resources into their military struggle, beginning a pattern of **fiscal–military state** formation by monetizing their taxation system through the use of a silver coinage. They used the money to pay professional infantry soldiers and equip them with firearms—momentous innovations that vastly enhanced state power. In this part we will see several other states—the Safavids in Persia, the Mughals in India, as well as the Ming and Qing dynasties in China—moving in a parallel direction. In the long run, however, neither the Habsburgs nor the Ottomans could sustain this gigantic war effort. The two found themselves forced to cease hostilities around 1600. Although nominally still under the rule of the two imperial dynasties, Middle Eastern Islam and western Christianity returned to competitive commonwealth politics.

The great wealth at the disposal of the two empires during their heyday also allowed for a pattern of projecting glory and cultural splendor to friend and foe alike. Rulers built palaces and embellished cities with buildings and residences, even as their battles raged. A class of wealthy aristocrats (Habsburg Empire) and administrators (Ottoman Empire) emerged who sponsored writers, painters, and architects. The sixteenth century was thus also a time of great cultural expression in the two empires, and we admire many of the literary, pictorial, and architectural achievements of the period to this day.

Fiscal–military state: Early modern conquering polity, such as the Ottoman, Habsburg, and Safavid Empires and the French, English, and Swedish kingdoms, in which the rulers raised their revenues in the form of cash and employed firearm-equipped foot soldiers for pay.

EURASIAN LAND EMPIRES, ca. 1600

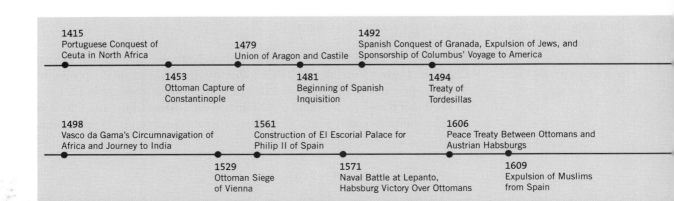

1415 Portuguese Conquest of Ceuta in North Africa		1479 Union of Aragon and Castile	1492 Spanish Conquest of Granada, Expulsion of Jews, and Sponsorship of Columbus' Voyage to America

1453 Ottoman Capture of Constantinople

1481 Beginning of Spanish Inquisition

1494 Treaty of Tordesillas

1498 Vasco da Gama's Circumnavigation of Africa and Journey to India

1561 Construction of El Escorial Palace for Philip II of Spain

1606 Peace Treaty Between Ottomans and Austrian Habsburgs

1529 Ottoman Siege of Vienna

1571 Naval Battle at Lepanto, Habsburg Victory Over Ottomans

1609 Expulsion of Muslims from Spain

The Muslim–Christian Competition in the East and West, 1450–1600

After a long period during which the Christian kings in Iberia found tributes by the Muslim emirs more profitable than war, in the second half of the fifteenth century the kings resumed the Reconquista. During the same time period, the small principality of the Ottomans took advantage of Mongol and Byzantine weakness to conquer lands in both Anatolia and the Balkans. After the Muslim conquest of Constantinople in 1453 and the western Christian conquest of Granada in 1492, the path was open for the emergence of the Ottoman and Habsburg Empires.

Iberian Christian Expansion, 1415–1498

During a revival of anti-Muslim Crusade passions in the course of the fourteenth century, Portugal resumed its Reconquista policies by expanding to North Africa in 1415. Looking for a way to circumvent the Muslims, collect West African gold along the way, and reach the Indian spice coast, Portuguese sailors and traders established fortified harbors along the African coastline. Castile and Aragon, not to be left behind, conquered Granada in 1492, occupied ports in North Africa, and sent Columbus on his way to discover an alternate route to what the Portuguese were seeking. Columbus' discovery of America did not yield Indian spices but delivered a new continent to the rulers of Castile and Aragon (see Map 16.1).

Maritime Explorations   Portugal's resumption of the Reconquista had its roots in its mastery of Atlantic seafaring. In 1277–1281, mariners of the Italian city-state of Genoa pioneered commerce by sea between the Mediterranean and northwestern Europe. One port on the route was Lisbon, where Portuguese shipwrights and their Genoese teachers teamed up to develop new ships suited for the stormy Atlantic seas. In the course of the early fifteenth century, they developed the *caravel*, a small ship with high, upward-extending fore and aft boards; a stern rudder; and square as well as triangular lateen sails. With their new ships, the Portuguese became important traders between England and the Mediterranean countries.

The sea trade now stimulated an exploration of the eastern Atlantic. By the early fifteenth century, the Portuguese had discovered the uninhabited islands of the Azores and Madeira, while the Castilians, building their own caravels, began a century-long conquest of the Canary Islands. Here, the indigenous, still Neolithic Berber inhabitants, the Guanches, put up a fierce resistance. But settlers, with the backing of Venetian investors, carved out colonies on conquered parcels of land, on which they enslaved the Guanches to work in sugarcane plantations. They thus adopted the slave labor and sugarcane plantation system from the eastern Mediterranean, where it had Byzantine and Crusader roots on the island of Cyprus, as discussed in greater detail in Chapter 18.

Apocalyptic Expectations   Parallel with the Atlantic explorations, Iberian Christians began to rethink their relationship with the Muslims on the peninsula. The loss of the crusader kingdom in Palestine to the Muslim Mamluks in 1291 was an event that stirred deep feelings of guilt among the western Christians. Efforts to organize military expeditions to reconquer Jerusalem failed to get off the ground,

Military orders: Ever since the early 1100s, the papacy encouraged the formation of monastic fighting orders, such as the Hospitalers and Templars, to combat the Muslims in the crusader kingdom of Jerusalem; similar Reconquista orders, such as the Order of Santiago and the Order of Christ, emerged in Iberia to eliminate Muslim rule.

Apocalypse: In Greek, "revelation," that is, unveiling the events at the end of history, before God's judgment; during the 1400s, expectation of the imminence of Christ's Second Coming, with precursors paving the way.

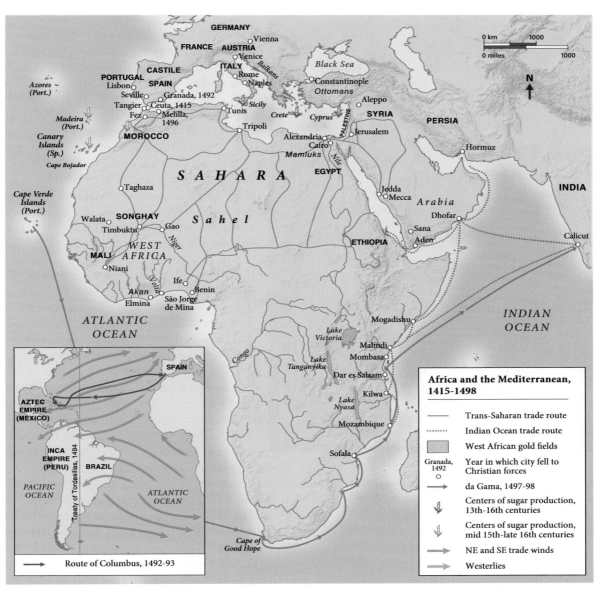

MAP **16.1 Africa and the Mediterranean, 1415–1498.**

however, mostly because rulers in Europe were now more interested in warring against each other for territorial gain. The failure did not dampen spiritual revivals, however, especially among the monks of the Franciscan and **military orders** of Iberia. These monks, often well connected with the Iberian royal courts as confessors, preachers, and educators, were believers in revelation (Greek *apocalypsis*), that is, the imminent end of the world and the Second Coming of Christ.

According to the **Apocalypse**, Christ's return could happen only in Jerusalem, which, therefore, made it urgent for the Christians to reconquer the city immediately. They widely believed that they would be aided by Prester John, an alleged Christian ruler at the head of an immense army from Ethiopia or India. In the context of the intense religious fervor of the period, Christians as well as Muslims saw

St. James the Moor-Slayer.
As the twin impulses of Reconquista and crusade surged in fifteenth-century Spain and Portugal, devotion to warrior cults increased among the Christian faithful. The cult of St. James the Moor-Slayer gained particular prominence among crusading knights during this time as the saint's miraculous appearance was believed to have helped a vastly outnumbered Christian army defeat Muslim forces in 844. Devotion to the saint (*Santiago Matatmoros*) remains high in Spain today. In 2004, authorities reversed an earlier decision to relocate an enormous statue of St. James the Moor-Slayer from the cathedral of Santiago de Compostela in northwest Spain after a storm of protest.

no contradiction between religion and military conquest. A providential God, so they believed, justified the conquest of lands and the enslavement of the conquered. The religious justification of military action, therefore, was not a pretext for more base material interests (though these would be a likely effect of such conquests) but a proud declaration by believers that God was on their side to help them convert and conquer the non-Christian world. Even today such ideas still can be found in many religious traditions; that they were very real in the minds of the Portuguese and Spanish conquistadores of the period between 1400 and 1500 is well documented as a motive for political and military action.

In Portugal, political claims in the guise of apocalyptic expectations guided the military orders in "reconquering" Ceuta, a northern port city of the Moroccan sultans. The orders argued that prior to the Berber–Arab conquest of the early eighth century CE, Ceuta had been Christian and that it was therefore lawful to undertake its Reconquista. Accordingly, a fleet under Henry the Navigator (1394–1460) succeeded in taking Ceuta in 1415, capturing there a huge stock of West African gold ready to be minted as money. Henry, a brother of the ruling Portuguese king, saw himself as a precursor in the unfolding of apocalyptic events and invested huge resources into the search for the *Rio de oro*, the West African "river of gold" thought to be the place where Muslims obtained their gold. He also instructed the explorers to look for a sea bay alleged to be in the middle of Africa that would give them access to Christian Ethiopia and Prester John. By the middle of the fifteenth century, Portuguese mariners had reached the "gold coast" of West Africa (today's Ghana), where local rulers imported gold from the interior Akan fields, near a tributary of the Niger River—the "gold river" of the Muslim merchants. The sea bay turned out to be a figment of the imagination.

Reforms in Castile   The Portuguese renewal of the Reconquista stimulated a similar revival in Castile. For a century and a half, Castile had collected tributes from Granada instead of completing the reconquest of the peninsula. The revival occurred after the dynastic union of Castile and Aragon–Catalonia under their respective monarchs Queen Isabella (r. 1474–1504) and King Ferdinand II (r. 1479–1516). The two monarchs, now joined by marriage, embarked on a political and religious reform program designed to strengthen their central administrations and used the reconquest ideology as a convenient vehicle to speed up the reforms.

Among the political reforms was the recruitment of urban militias and judges, both under royal supervision, to check the military and judicial powers of the aristocracy. Religious reform focused on improved education for the clergy and stricter enforcement of Christian doctrine in the population at large. The new institution entrusted with the enforcement of doctrine was the Spanish Inquisition, a body of clergy first appointed by Isabella and Ferdinand in 1481 to ferret out any beliefs and practices among people that were deemed to violate Christian theology and church law. With their religious innovations, the monarchs regained the initiative from the popes and laid the foundations for increased state power.

The Conquest of Granada The Reconquista culminated in a 10-year campaign (1482–1492), now fought on both sides with cannons—the military innovation also employed half a century earlier at Constantinople to batter down walls. In the end, Granada fell into Christian hands because the Ottomans, still consolidating their power in the Balkans, sent only a naval commander who stationed himself in North Africa and harassed Iberian ships. The Mamluks of Egypt, less powerful than the Ottomans, sent an embassy to Granada that merely made a feeble threat of retribution against Christians in Egypt and Syria. Abandoned by the Muslim powers, the last emir of Granada negotiated terms for an honorable surrender. According to these terms, Muslims who chose to stay as subjects of the Castilian crown were permitted to do so, practicing their faith in their own mosques.

The treaty did not apply to the Jews of Granada, however, who were forced either to convert to Christianity or to emigrate. In the 1300s, anti-Jewish preaching by the Catholic clergy and riots by Christians against Jews in Seville had substantially reduced the Jewish population of some 300,000 at its peak ca. 1050 to a mere 80,000 in 1492. Of this remainder, a majority emigrated in 1492 to North Africa and the Ottoman Empire, strengthening the urban population of the Muslims with their commercial and crafts skills. Thus, the nearly millennium and a half–long Jewish presence in "Sefarad," as Spain was called in Hebrew, ended, with an expulsion designed to strengthen the Christian unity of Iberia.

After the expulsion of the Jews, it did not take long for the Christians to violate the Muslim treaty of surrender. The church engaged in forced conversions, the burning of Arabic books, and transformations of mosques into churches, triggering an uprising of Muslims in Granada (1499–1500). Christian troops crushed the rising, and Isabella and Ferdinand took it as an excuse to abrogate the treaty of surrender. In one province after another during the early sixteenth century, Muslims were forced to either convert or emigrate. Like the family of al-Hasan al-Wazzan described at the beginning of this chapter, thousands of Muslims left for North Africa rather than convert to Christianity. The number of remaining Muslims, however, exceeded the ability of the Inquisition to enforce the conversion process. In practical terms, baptized Muslims—called *moriscos* ("Moor-like")—continued to practice Islam, even if discreetly, for another half-century.

Columbus' Journey to the Caribbean At the peak of their royal power in early 1492, Isabella and Ferdinand seized a golden opportunity to catch up quickly with the Portuguese in the Atlantic. They authorized the seasoned mariner

The Sorrows of Exile

"Time with his pointed shafts has hit my heart and split my gut, laid open my entrails, landed me a blow that will not heal, knocked me down, left me in lasting pain. Time wounded me, wasted away my flesh . . . used up my blood and fat in suffering, ground my bones to meal, and rampaged, leapt, attacked me like a lion in his rage . . ."

—Scheindlin, Raymond P., trans. "Judah Abravanel to His Sons." *Judaism* 41 (Spring 1992): 190–199. Judah Abravanel, refugee from Granada, official convert (*marrano*) to Christianity and physician to the Spanish viceroy in Naples, Italy, in a letter to his son Isaac, a *marrano* in Portugal, in 1503.

Christopher Columbus (1451–1506), the son of a Genoese wool weaver, to build two caravels and a larger carrack and sail westward across the Atlantic. Columbus promised to reach India ahead of the Portuguese, who were attempting to find a route to India by sailing around Africa. The two monarchs pledged him money for the construction of ships from Castilian and Aragonese Crusade levies collected against the Ottomans. In September, Columbus and his mariners departed from the Castilian Canary Islands, catching the favorable south Atlantic easterlies. After a voyage of a little over a month, Columbus landed on one of the Bahaman islands. From there he explored a number of Caribbean islands, mistakenly assuming that he was close to the Indian subcontinent. After a stay of 3 months, he left a small colony of settlers behind and returned to Iberia with seven captured Caribbean islanders and a small quantity of gold.

Admiral of the Sea. As a reward for his discoveries, in 1493 the Spanish crown rewarded Columbus with a coat of arms, which satisfied his obsession with status and privilege. The coat of arms depicted above reflects the modifications he made to the original crest, including a continent with islands in the bottom left quarter and golden anchors, meant to symbolize his title as "Admiral of the Sea," set in the bottom right quadrant.

Columbus was a self-educated explorer. Through voracious but indiscriminate reading, he had accumulated substantial knowledge of such diverse subjects as geography, cartography, the Crusades, and the Apocalypse. On the basis of this reading (and his own faulty calculations), he insisted that the ocean stretching between western Europe and eastern Asia was relatively narrow. Furthermore, he fervently believed that God had made him the forerunner of an Iberian apocalyptic world ruler who would recapture Jerusalem from the Muslims just prior to the Second Coming of Christ. For many years, Columbus had peddled his idea about reaching Jerusalem from the east at the Portuguese court. The Portuguese, however, while sharing Columbus' apocalyptic fervor, dismissed his Atlantic Ocean calculations as fantasies. Even in Castile, where Columbus went after his rejection in Portugal, it took many years and the victory over Granada before Queen Isabella finally listened to him. Significantly, it was at the height of their success at Granada in 1492 that Isabella and Ferdinand seized their chance to beat the Portuguese to Asia.

Although disappointed by the meager returns of Columbus' first and subsequent voyages, Isabella and Ferdinand were delighted to have acquired new islands in the Caribbean, in addition to those of the Canaries. In one blow they had drawn even with Portugal. To secure their territorial gains, Castile–Aragon had the Castilian-born pope Alexander VI draw a line at some distance west of Portuguese Cape Verde, allocating all territories beyond this line to Castile. Since the Portuguese had to sail far out into the middle of the Atlantic in order to catch the winds blowing toward South Africa, they demanded a correction. In a revision concluded in 1506, the Iberian monarchs agreed to move the line farther westward. Thereby, Portugal gained the entire Atlantic and, as it turned out, much of Brazil; in return, Castile gained what became their colonies in the Americas.

Vasco da Gama's Journey to India

Portugal redoubled its efforts after 1492 to discover the way to India around Africa. In 1498, the king appointed an important court official and member of the crusading Order of Santiago, Vasco da Gama (ca. 1469–1524), to command four caravels for the journey to India. Da Gama, an experienced mariner, made good use of the accumulated Portuguese knowledge of seafaring in the Atlantic and guidance by Arab sailors in the Indian Ocean. After a journey of 6 months, the ships arrived in Calicut, the main spice trade center on the Indian west coast.

The first Portuguese sent ashore in Calicut encountered two Iberian Muslims, who addressed him in Castilian Spanish and Italian: "The Devil take you! What brought you here?" The Portuguese replied: "We came to seek Christians and spices." When da Gama went inland to see the ruler of Calicut, he was optimistic that he had indeed found what he had come for. Ignorant of Hinduism, he mistook the Indian religion for the Christianity of Prester John. Similarly ignorant of the conventions of the India trade, he offered woolen textiles and metal goods in exchange for pepper, cinnamon, and cloves. The Muslim and Hindu merchants were uninterested in these goods designed for the African market and demanded gold or silver, which the Portuguese had only in small amounts. Rumors spread about the Muslims plotting with the Hindus against the apparently penniless Christian intruders. Prudently, da Gama lifted anchor and returned home with small quantities of spices.

After these modest beginnings, however, within a short time Portugal had mastered the India trade. The Portuguese crown organized regular journeys around Africa, and when Portuguese mariners on one such journey discovered northeast Brazil—located on their side of the Tordesillas line—they claimed it for their expanding commercial network. During the early sixteenth century, the Portuguese India fleets brought considerable amounts of spices from India back to Portugal, threatening the profits of the Egyptian and Venetian merchants who had hitherto dominated the trade. Prester John, of course, was never found; and the project of retaking Jerusalem receded into the background.

Rise of the Ottomans and Struggle with the Habsburgs for Dominance, 1300–1609

While Muslim rule disappeared in the late fifteenth century from the Iberian Peninsula, the opposite happened in the Balkans. Here, the Ottoman Turks spearheaded the expansion of Islamic rule, initially over Eastern Orthodox Christians, and eventually over western Christians. By the late sixteenth century, when the east–west conflict between the Habsburgs and Ottomans reached its peak, entire generations of Croats, Germans, and Italians lived in mortal fear of the "terrible Turk" who might conquer all of Christian Europe.

Late Byzantium and Ottoman Origins   The rise of the Ottomans was closely related to the decline of Byzantium. The emperors of Byzantium had been able to reclaim their "empire" in 1261 from its Latin rulers and Venetian troops by allying themselves with the Genoese. This empire, which during the early fourteenth century included Greece and a few domains in western Anatolia, was no more than a mid-size kingdom with modest agricultural resources. But it was still a valuable trading hub, thanks to Constantinople's strategic position as a market linking the Mediterranean with Slavic kingdoms in the Balkans and the Ukrainian–Russian principality of Kiev. Thanks to its commercial wealth, Byzantium experienced a cultural revival, which at its height featured the lively scholarly debate over Plato and Aristotle that exerted a profound influence on the western Renaissance in Italy.

Inevitably, however, both Balkan Slavs and Anatolian Turks appropriated Byzantine provinces in the late thirteenth century, further reducing the empire. One of the lost provinces was Bithynia, across the Bosporus in Anatolia. Here, in 1299, the Turkish warlord Osman (1299–1326) gathered his clan as well as a motley assembly of Islamic holy warriors (Turkish *ghazis*), including a local saint and his followers, and declared himself an independent ruler. Osman and a number of other Turkish lords in the region were nominally subject to the Seljuks, the Turkish dynasty which

Patterns Up Close | Shipbuilding

Early humans undoubtedly traveled by sea in their migrations out of Africa nearly 100,000 years ago, though no evidence of their seafaring has survived. These sea voyages, which hugged coastlines and traveled across relatively modest expanses of water, were likely made in rafts. It is not until the Bronze Age (ca. 3000–1300 BCE) that we encounter the earliest evidence of planked ships. We have records of shipwrights in Egypt constructing ships plank by plank, tying the planks together internally with ropes and cross bars. In addition, they used various types of pegs to join the planks. Side oars served for steering and square linen sails for propulsion. This "sewed" shipbuilding pattern allowed for the construction of seaworthy, flexible, relatively small boats that could be dragged through surf and pulled up on rocky shores. The pattern appeared across most of the world, either through independent invention in multiple places or by interaction and adaptation from Middle Eastern origins. The latter was certainly possible, given the diffusion of other discoveries and inventions from Mesopotamia and Egypt to India and China during the Bronze Age.

Patterns of Shipbuilding. From top: (*a*) Hellenistic-Roman roundship, (*b*) Chinese junk, (*c*) Indian Ocean dhow.

With the appearance of empires during the subsequent Iron Age, builders replaced the original sewed shipbuilding pattern with new regional traditions. Four regional but interconnected traditions—Mediterranean, Indian Ocean, Chinese Sea, and North Sea—emerged. In addition, the Pacific outrigger tradition as well as Andean and Arctic raft- and canoe-building patterns evolved separately.

In the Mediterranean, around 500 BCE, shipwrights shifted from sewed to nailed planks for their war galleys as well as cargo transports around 500 BCE, as evidenced by shipwrecks of the period. In the Roman Empire (ca. 200 BCE–500 CE), nailed planking allowed the development of the roundship (photo *a*), a large transport of 120 feet length and 400 tons of cargo transporting grain from Egypt to Italy. The roundship and its variations had double planking, multiple masts, and multiple square sails. After 100 BCE, the triangular ("lateen") sail allowed for zigzagging ("tacking") against the wind, greatly expanding shipping during a summer sailing season.

The Celtic North Sea tradition adapted to the Mediterranean patterns of the Romans. When the Roman Empire receded during the 300s CE, shipwrights in Celtic regions continued with their own innovations, shifting to frame-first construction for small boats in the 300s, three centuries before Byzantium in the Mediterranean. At the same time Norsemen, or Vikings, innovated by introducing overlapping ("clinkered") plank joining for their elegant and eminently seagoing boats. The North Sea innovations, arriving as they did at the end of the western Roman Empire, remained local for nearly half a millennium.

The evolution of China into an empire resulted in major Chinese contributions to ship construction. In the Han period (206 BCE–220 CE) there is evidence from clay models of riverboats for the transition from sewed to nailed planks. One model, dating to the first century CE, shows a central steering rudder at the end of the boat. At the same time, similar stern rudders appeared in the Roman Empire. Who adapted to whom, if at all, is still an unanswered question.

Shipbuilding innovations continued after 600 CE. In Tang China, junks, with multiple watertight compartments ("bulkheads") and multiple layers of planks appeared. The average junk was 140 feet long, had a cargo capacity of 600 tons, and could carry on its three or four decks several hundred mariners and passengers (see photo *b*). Admiral Zheng He's junk in the early 1400s, which guided Chinese fleets to southeast Asia and eastern Africa, was double the average junk size. Junks had multiple masts and trapezoid ("lug") and square sails made of matted fibers and strengthened ("battened") with poles sewed to the surface. The less innovative Middle Eastern, eastern African, and Indian *dhow* was built with sewed or nailed planks and sailed with lateen and square sails, traveling as far as southern China. It also came in many varieties, and the largest type could be as large as a small junk (see photo *c*).

In western Europe, the patterns of Mediterranean and North Sea shipbuilding merged during the thirteenth century. At that time, northern shipwrights developed the cog as the main transport for Baltic grain to ports around the North Sea. The cog was a ship of some 60 feet in length and 30 tons in cargo capacity, with square sails, flush-planking below, and clinkered planking above the water line. Northern European Crusaders traveled during 1150–1300 on cogs via the Atlantic to the Mediterranean. Builders adapted the cog's clinker technique to the roundship tradition that Muslims as well as eastern and western Christians had modified in the previous centuries. Genoese clinkered roundships pioneered the Mediterranean–North Sea trade in the early fourteenth century (see photo *d*).

Patterns of Shipbuilding. From top: (*d*) Baltic cog, and (*e*) Iberian caravel. These ships illustrate the varieties of shipbuilding traditions that developed over thousands of years.

Lisbon shipwrights in Portugal, learning from Genoese masters, borrowed from local shipbuilding traditions and Genoese roundship construction patterns for the development of the caravel around 1430. The caravel was a small and slender 60-foot-long ship with a 50-ton freight capacity, a stern rudder, square and lateen sails, and a magnetic compass (of Chinese origin). The caravel and, after 1500, the similarly built but much larger galleon were the main vessels the Portuguese, Spanish, Dutch, and English used during their oceanic voyages from the mid-fifteenth to mid-eighteenth centuries (see photo *e*).

Questions

- How does the history of shipbuilding demonstrate the ways in which innovations spread from one place to another?

- Do the adaptations in shipbuilding that flowed between cultures that were nominally in conflict with each other provide a different perspective on the way these cultures interacted?

Power Politics

"You stupid Greeks, I have known your cunning ways for long enough. The late sultan was a lenient and conscientious friend of yours. The present Sultan Mehmet is not of the same mind. If Constantinople eludes his bold and impetuous grasp it will only be because God overlooks your devious and wicked schemes."

—Doukas, Michael, *Decline and Fall of Byzantium to the Ottoman Turks: An Annotated Tranlsation of the 'Historia Byzantina-Turca.'* Trans. Harry J. Magoulias, p. 289. Detroit: Wayne State University Press, 1975. Ottoman minister (vizier) Halil Pasha addressing himself to Byzantine diplomats seeking to deflect the Ottoman threat of conquest.

had conquered Anatolia from the Byzantines two centuries earlier but by the early 1300s had disintegrated.

During the first half of the fourteenth century, Osman and his successors emerged as the most powerful emirs by conquering further Anatolian provinces from Byzantium. The Moroccan Abu Abdallah Ibn Battuta (1304–1369), famous for his journey through the Islamic world, Africa, and China, passed through western Anatolia and Constantinople during the 1330s, visiting several Turkish principalities. He was duly impressed by the rising power of the Ottomans, noting approvingly that they manned nearly 100 forts and castles and maintained pressure on the eastern Christian infidels. In 1354, the Ottomans gained their first European foothold on a peninsula about 100 miles southwest of Constantinople. Thereafter, it seemed only a question of time before the Ottomans would conquer Constantinople.

Through a skillful mixture of military defense, tribute payments, and dynastic marriages of princesses with Osman's descendants, however, the Byzantine emperors extended their rule for another century. They were also helped by Timur the Great (r. 1370–1405), a Turkish-descended ruler from central Asia who sought to rebuild the Mongol Empire. He surprised the Ottomans, who were distracted by their ongoing conquests in the Balkans, and defeated them decisively in 1402. Timur and his successors were unsuccessful with their dream of neo-Mongol world rule, but the Ottomans needed nearly two decades (1402–1421) to recover from their collapse and reconstitute their empire in the Balkans and Anatolia. Under Mehmet II, the Conqueror (r. 1451–1481), they finally assembled all their resources to lay siege to the Byzantine capital.

Siege of Constantinople, 1453. Note the soldiers on the left pulling boats on rollers and wheels over the Galata hillside. With this maneuver, Sultan Mehmet II was able to circumvent the chain spanned across the entrance to the Golden Horn (in place of the anachronistic bridge in the image). This allowed him to speed up his conquest of Constantinople by forcing the defenders to spread their forces thinly over the entire length of the walls.

From Istanbul to the Adriatic Sea   Similar to Isabella and Ferdinand's siege of Granada, Mehmet's siege and conquest of Constantinople (April 5–May 29, 1453) was one of the stirring events of world history. The Byzantines were severely undermanned and short of gunpowder, unable to defend the full length of the imposing land walls that protected the city. Although they had some help from Genoese, papal, and Aragonese forces, it was not nearly enough to make a difference. With a superiority of 11 to 1 in manpower, the Ottomans besieged and bombarded Constantinople's walls with heavy cannons. The weakest part of the Byzantine defenses was the central section of the western walls where it was relatively easy to tunnel into the soil underneath. Here, Mehmet stationed his heaviest guns to bombard the masonry and have his sappers undermine the foundations of the walls.

Another weak section was on the north side, along the harbor in the Golden Horn, where the walls were low. Here, the Byzantines had blocked off the entrance to the Golden Horn with a huge chain. In a brilliant tactical move, Mehmet circumvented the chain. He had troops drag ships on rollers over a hillside into the harbor. The soldiers massed on these ships were ready to disembark and assault the walls with the help of ladders. On the first sign of cracks in the northern walls, the Ottoman besiegers stormed the city. The last Byzantine emperor, Constantine XI, perished in the general massacre and pillage which followed the Ottoman occupation of the city.

Mehmet quickly repopulated Constantinople ("Istanbul" in Turkish, from Gr. "to the city," *istin polin*) and appointed a new patriarch at the head of the eastern Christians, to whom he promised full protection as his subjects. In quick succession, he ordered the construction of the Topkapı Palace (1459), the transfer of the administration from Edirne (which had been the capital since 1365) to Istanbul, and the resumption of expansion in the Balkans, where he succeeded in forcing the majority of rulers into submitting to vassal status (even though almost constant campaigning was necessary). One of the Balkan lords resisting the sultan was Vlad III Dracul of Wallachia, who in 1461–1462 impaled a contingent of Ottoman troops sent against him on sharpened tree trunks. Mehmet replaced Dracul with his more compliant brother, but the memory of the impalements lived on to inspire vampire folktales and, eventually, in 1897, the famous Gothic horror novel *Dracula*.

Mehmet's ongoing conquests eventually brought him to the Adriatic Sea, where one of his generals occupied Otranto on the heel of the Italian peninsula. The Ottomans were poised to launch from Otranto a full-scale invasion of Italy, when the sultan died unexpectedly. His successor evacuated Otranto, preferring to consolidate the Ottoman Empire in the Middle East, North Africa, and the Balkans before reconsidering an invasion of central and western Europe.

Imperial Apogee

Between 1500 and 1600 the Ottoman sultans succeeded magnificently in the consolidation of their empire. In 1514, with superior cavalry and infantry forces, cannons, and muskets, the Ottomans defeated the Persian Safavids in Iran, who had risen in 1501 to form a rival Shiite empire in opposition to the Sunnite Ottomans. In the southern Middle East, intermittent tensions between the Ottomans and the Mamluk Turks in Egypt, Syria, and eastern Arabia gave way to open war in 1517. The Ottomans, again due to superior firepower, defeated the Mamluks and took control of western Arabia, including the holy

Vlad Dracul in a Wall Painting (*left*) and next to Impaled Ottoman Soldiers (*right*). The woodcut depicts the alleged impalement of 1,000 Ottoman soldiers sent against Vlad Dracul, prior to Sultan Mehmet II leading a victorious campaign into Wallachia and removing Dracul from power.

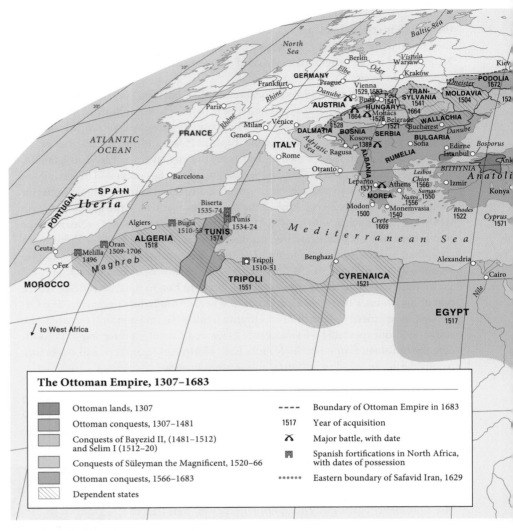

MAP **16.2** **The Ottoman Empire, 1307–1683.**

pilgrimage city of Mecca. A year later, in 1518, Sultan Süleyman I, the Magnificent (r. 1520–1566), appointed a naval commander to drive the Spanish from a series of fortifications and cities in North Africa, which the latter had conquered in the name of the Reconquista in the 1490s and early 1500s.

In the Balkans, the Ottomans completed their conquests of Serbia and Hungary with the annexation of Belgrade and Buda (of Budapest) as well as a brief siege of Vienna in 1529, begun too late in the year and eventually stopped by the approaching winter. By the second half of the sixteenth century, when the submission of most of Hungary had been secured, the Ottoman Empire was a vast multiethnic and multireligious state of some 15 million inhabitants extending from Algeria in the Maghreb to Yemen in Arabia and from Upper Egypt to the Balkans and the northern shores of the Black Sea (see Map 16.2).

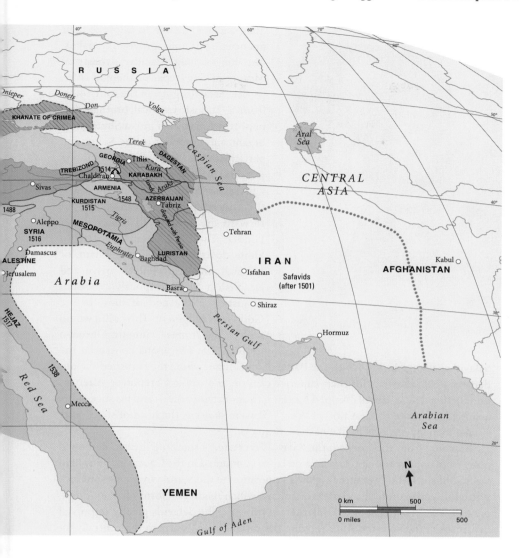

Morocco and Persia   In the early modern period 1450–1600, the two large empires of the Ottomans and Indian Mughals dominated Islamic civilization. Two smaller and more short-lived realms existed in Morocco and Persia, ruled by the Saadian (1509–1659) and Safavid (1501–1722) dynasties, respectively. The Saadian sultans defended themselves successfully against the Ottoman expansion and liberated themselves from the Portuguese occupation of Morocco's Atlantic ports which had followed the conquest of Ceuta in 1415. In 1591, after their liberation, the Saadians sent a firearm-equipped army to West Africa in order to revive the gold trade, which had dwindled to a trickle after the Portuguese arrival in Ghana. The army succeeded in destroying the West African empire of Songhay but failed to revive the gold trade. Moroccan army officers assumed power in Timbuktu, and their descendants, the Ruma, became provincial lords independent of Morocco.

Safavid Warrior's Tunic. It was customary in the Muslim world for soldiers to go into combat wearing talismanic undershirts designed to protect them from harm and to guarantee victory on the battlefield. This Safavid battle tunic, from about 1600, is embroidered with verses from the Quran that exhort the faithful to victory.

The Saadians, unable to improve their finances, split into provincial realms. The still-reigning Alaouite dynasty of Moroccan kings replaced them in 1659.

The Safavids grew in the mid-1400s from a Turkish mystical brotherhood in northwestern Iran into a Shiite *ghazi* organization (similar to the Sunni one participating in the early Ottoman expansion) that carried out raids against Christians in the Caucasus. In 1501, the leadership of the brotherhood put forward the 14-year-old Ismail as the Hidden Twelfth Imam. According to Shiite doctrine, the Hidden Imam, or Messiah, was expected to arrive and establish a Muslim apocalyptic realm of justice at the end of time, before God's Last Judgment. This realm would replace the "unjust" Sunnite Ottoman Empire. The Ottomans countered the Safavid challenge in 1514 with the Battle of Chaldiran, where they crushed the underprepared Safavids with their superior cannon and musket firepower. After his humiliating defeat, Ismail dropped his claim to apocalyptic status and his successors assumed the more modest title of "king" (Persian *shah*) as the head of state, quite similar in many respects to that of the Ottomans.

Learning from their defeat, the Safavids recruited a standing firearm-equipped army from among young Christians on lands conquered in the Caucasus. They held fast to Shiism, thereby continuing their opposition to the Sunni Ottomans, and supported the formation of a clerical hierarchy, which made this form of Islam dominant in Iran. As sponsors of construction projects, the Safavids greatly improved urbanism in the country. After moving the capital from Tabriz to the centrally located Isfahan in 1590, they built an imposing palace, administration, and mosque complex in the city. In a suburb they settled a large colony of Armenians, who held the monopoly in the production of Caspian Sea silk, a high-quality export product which the Dutch—successors of the Portuguese in the Indian Ocean trade—distributed in Europe.

As patrons of the arts, the shahs revived the ancient traditions of Persian culture to such heights that even the archrival Ottomans felt compelled to adopt Persian manners, literature, and architectural styles. Persian royal culture similarly radiated to the Mughals in India. Not everyone accepted Shiism, however. An attempt to force the religion on the Afghanis backfired badly when enraged Sunni tribes formed a coalition, defeated the Safavids, and ended their regime in 1722.

Rise of the Habsburgs   Parallel to the rise and development of the Safavid state, Castile–Aragon on the Iberian Peninsula evolved into the center of a vast empire of its own. A daughter of Isabella and Ferdinand married a member of the Habsburg dynastic family, which ruled Flanders, Burgundy, Naples, Sicily, and Austria, as well as Germany (the "Holy Roman Empire of the German Nation," as this collection of principalities was called). Their son, Charles V (r. 1516–1558), not only inherited Castile–Aragon, now merged and called "Spain," and the Habsburg territories but also became the ruler of the Aztec and Inca Empires in the Americas, which Spanish adventurers had conquered in his name between 1521 and 1536. In both Austria and the western Mediterranean the Habsburgs were direct neighbors of the Ottomans (see Map 16.3).

After a victorious battle against France in 1519, Charles V also won the title of emperor, which made him the overlord of all German principalities and supreme among the monarchs of western Christianity. Although this title did not mean much in terms of power and financial gain in either the German principalities or western Christianity as a whole, it made him the titular political head of western Christianity and thereby the direct counterpart of Sultan Süleyman in the struggle for dominance

MAP **16.3** **Europe and the Mediterranean, ca. 1560.**

Europe and the Mediterranean, ca. 1560

- ——— Boundary of the Holy Roman Empire
- Austrian Habsburg territories
- Spanish Habsburg territories
- Ottoman Empire
- Tributary to the Ottoman Empire
- Venetian territories

in the Christian–Muslim world of Europe, the Middle East and northern Africa. Both the Habsburgs and the Ottomans renewed the traditional Arab/Islamic–Christian imperialism which had characterized the period 600–950 and which had given way to the Muslim and Christian commonwealths of 950–1450.

Habsburg Distractions   Charles V faced a daunting task in his effort to prevent the Ottomans from advancing against the Christians in the Balkans and Mediterranean. Multiple problems in his European territories diverted his attention and forced him to spend far less time than he wanted on what Christians in most parts of Europe perceived as a pervasive Ottoman–Muslim threat. During the first three decades of the sixteenth century, revolts in Iberia, the Protestant Reformation in the German states, and renewed war with France for control of Burgundy and Italy commanded Charles' attention.

The emperor's distractions increased further in 1534 when, in an attempt to drive the Habsburgs out of Italy, France forged an alliance with the Ottomans. This alliance horrified western Europe. It demonstrated, however, that the Ottomans, on account of their military advances against the Christians in eastern Europe and the western Mediterranean, had become a crucial player in European politics. As fierce as the struggle between Muslims and Christians for dominance was, when the French king found himself squeezed on both sides of his kingdom by his archrival Charles V, the Ottomans became his natural allies.

Habsburg and Ottoman Losses   All these diversions seriously strained Habsburg resources against the Ottomans, who pressed relentlessly ahead on the two fronts of the Balkans and North Africa. Although Charles V deputized his younger brother Ferdinand I to the duchy of Austria in 1521 to shore up the Balkan defenses, he was able to send him significant troops only once. After a series of dramatic defeats, Austria had to pay the Ottomans tribute and, eventually, even sign a humiliating truce (1562). On the western Mediterranean front, the Habsburgs did not do well either. Even though Charles V campaigned several times in person, most garrisons on the coast of Algeria, Tunisia, and Tripoli were too exposed to withstand the Ottoman onslaught by sea and by land. In 1556, at the end of Charles V's reign, only two of eight Habsburg garrisons had survived.

A third frontier of the Muslim–Christian struggle for dominance was the Indian Ocean. After Vasco da Gama had returned from India in 1498, the Portuguese kings invested major resources into breaking into the Muslim-dominated Indian Ocean trade. In response, the Ottomans made major efforts to protect existing Muslim commercial interests in the Indian Ocean. They blocked Portuguese military support for

Ethiopia and strengthened their ally and main pepper producer the sultan of Aceh on the Indonesian island of Sumatra, by providing him with troops and weapons. War on land and on sea, directly and by proxy, raged in the Indian Ocean through most of the sixteenth century. In the long run, the Portuguese were successful at destroying the Ottoman fleets sent against them, but smaller convoys of Ottoman galleys continued to harass Portuguese shipping interests. As new research on the Ottoman "age of exploration" in the Indian Ocean has demonstrated, by 1570 the Muslims traded again as much via the Red Sea route to the Mediterranean as the Portuguese did by circumventing Africa. In addition, the Ottomans benefited from the trade of a new commodity—coffee, produced in Ethiopia and Yemen. Portugal (under Spanish rule 1580–1640) reduced its unsustainably large military presence in the Indian Ocean, followed by the Ottomans, which allowed the Netherlands in the early seventeenth century to overtake both Portugal and the Ottoman Empire in the Indian Ocean spice trade (see Map 16.4).

Habsburg–Ottoman Balance   In the 1550s, Charles V despaired of his ability to ever master the many challenges posed by the Ottomans as well as by France and the Protestants. He decided that the only way to ensure the continuation of Habsburg power would be a division of his western and eastern territories. Accordingly, he bestowed Spain, Naples, the Netherlands, and the Americas on his

MAP 16.4 **Ottoman-Portuguese Competition in the Indian Ocean, 1536-1580.**

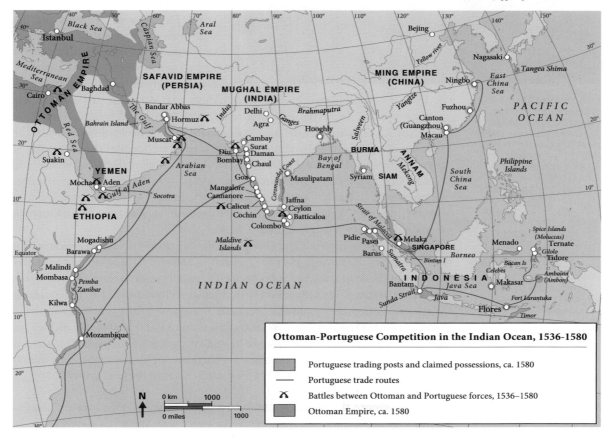

Ottoman-Portuguese Competition in the Indian Ocean, 1536-1580

▭	Portuguese trading posts and claimed possessions, ca. 1580
—	Portuguese trade routes
⚔	Battles between Ottoman and Portuguese forces, 1536–1580
▭	Ottoman Empire, ca. 1580

Paolo Veronese, The Battle of Lepanto (ca. 1572), altar painting with four saints beseeching the Virgin Mary to grant victory to the Christians. In the sixteenth century, the entire Mediterranean, from Gibraltar to Cyprus, was a naval battleground between Christians and Muslims. The Battle of Lepanto was the first major sea battle in world history to be decided by firepower: Even though Christian forces had slightly fewer ships, they had more and heavier artillery pieces. At the end of the battle "the sea was entirely covered, not just with masts, spars, oars, and broken wood, but with an innumerable quantity of blood that turned the water as red as blood."

son Philip II (r. 1556–1598). Further, Charles V had his brother Ferdinand I (r. 1558–1564) crowned Holy Roman Emperor by the pope, thereby making him overlord of the German principalities as well as ruler of the direct Habsburg possessions of Austria, Bohemia, and the remnant of Hungary not lost to the Ottomans. Together, Charles hoped, his son and his brother would cooperate and help each other militarily against the Ottomans.

When Philip took over the Spanish throne, he realized, to his concern, that most of the Habsburg military was stationed outside Spain, leaving that country vulnerable to attack. As the Ottomans had recently conquered most Spanish strongholds in North Africa, a Muslim invasion of Spain was a distinct possibility. Fearful of morisco support for an Ottoman invasion of Spain, Philip's administration and the Inquisition renewed their decrees of conversion which had lain dormant for half a century. This sparked a massive revolt among the moriscos of Granada in 1568–1570, supported by Ottoman soldiers and Moroccan arms. Philip was able to suppress the revolt only after recourse to troops and firearms from Italy. To break up the dangerously large concentrations of Granadan moriscos in the south of Spain, Philip ordered them to be dispersed throughout the peninsula. At the same time, to alleviate the Ottoman naval threat, Philip, the pope, Venice, and Genoa formed the Holy Christian League. Its task was the construction of a fleet which was to destroy Ottoman sea power in the eastern Mediterranean. The fleet succeeded in 1571 in bottling up the entire Ottoman navy at Lepanto, in Ottoman Greece, destroying it in the ensuing firefight.

The Ottomans, however, had enough resources not only to rebuild their navy but also to capture the strategic port city of Tunis in 1574 from the Spaniards. With this evening of the scores, the two sides decided to end their unsustainable naval war in the Mediterranean. The Ottomans turned their attention eastward, to the rival Safavid Empire, where they exploited a period of dynastic instability for the conquest of territories in the Caucasus (1578–1590). The staunch Catholic Philip II, on his part, was faced with the Protestant war of independence in the Netherlands. This war was so expensive that, in a desperate effort to straighten out his state finances, Philip II had to declare bankruptcy (1575) and sue for peace with the Ottomans (1580).

The Limits of Ottoman Power   After their victory over the Safavids, the Ottomans looked again to the west. While the peace with Spain was too recent to be broken, a long peace with Ferdinand I in Austria (since 1562) was ready to collapse. A series of raids and counterraids at the Austrian and Transylvanian borders had inflamed tempers, and in 1593 the Ottomans went on the attack. Austria, however, was no longer the weak state it had been a generation earlier. Had it not been for a lack of support from the Transylvanian and Hungarian Protestants, who preferred the sultan to the Catholic emperor as overlord, the Austrians might have actually prevailed over the Ottomans. However, thanks to the Protestants' support, the Ottomans drew even on the battlefield with the Austrians. In 1606, the Ottomans and Austrian Habsburgs made peace again. With minor modifications in favor of the Austrians, the two sides returned to their earlier borders. The Austrians made one more tribute payment and then let their obligation lapse. Officially, the Ottomans conceded nothing, but in practical terms Austria was no longer a vassal state.

Expulsion of the Moriscos   In the western Mediterranean, the peace between the Ottomans and Spanish Habsburgs held. But Philip and his successors remained aware of the possibility of renewed Ottoman aid to the moriscos. Even though they had been scattered after 1570, the moriscos continued to resist conversion. Among Castilians, an intense debate began about the apparent impossibility of assimilating them to Catholicism in order to create a religiously unified state. The church advocated the expulsion of the moriscos, arguing that the allegedly high Muslim birth rate in a population of 7.5 million (mostly rural) Spaniards was a serious threat. Fierce resistance against the proposed expulsion, however, rose among the Christian landowners in the southeastern province of Valencia. These landowners benefited greatly from the farming skills of the estimated 250,000 morisco tenant farmers who worked their irrigated rice and sugarcane estates. Weighing the potential Ottoman threat against the possibility of economic damage, the government decided in 1580 in favor of expulsion. Clearly, they valued Christian unity against the Ottomans more than the prosperity of a few hundred landowners in Valencia.

It took until 1609, however, before a compensation deal with the landowners in Valencia was worked out. In the following 5 years, some 300,000 moriscos were forcibly expelled from Spain, under often appalling circumstances: They had to leave all their possessions behind, including money and jewelry, taking only whatever clothes and household utensils they could carry. As in the case of the Jews a century earlier, Spain's loss was the Ottoman Empire's gain, this time mostly in the form of skilled irrigation farmers.

Fiscal-Military State: Origins and Interactions

The major technological change that occurred in the Middle East and Europe during 1250–1350 was the growing use of firearms. It took until the mid-1400s, however, before cannons and muskets were technically effective and reliable enough to make a difference in warfare. At this time, a pattern emerged whereby rulers created centralized, fiscal–military states to finance their strategic shift to firearm-bearing

Shining Fragment of a Vanished World. The expulsion of the Moriscos from Spain in 1609 marks the final demise of a culture that fused Muslim, Christian, and Jewish traditions into a brilliant synthesis. Lusterware—the process by which pottery is fired with a metallic glaze to produce an iridescent effect—was introduced into Spain from the Middle East as early as the tenth century. The region of Andalusia, in particular the city of Málaga, was the center of lusterware production in Spain, and the fame of "Málaga-ware" was so great that this luxury craft was sought after by wealthy buyers throughout all of Europe. One fifteenth-century observer commented that "the Pope himself and the cardinals and princes of the world all covet it, and are amazed that anything so amazing and noble could be made from common clay." The example shown here, from ca. 1470, is a wing-shaped vase, most likely intended to hold a bouquet of flowers, and was commissioned by one of the wealthiest and most discerning patrons of the era, Lorenzo de Medici ("the Magnificent") of Florence.

infantries. They resumed the policy of imperialism, which had lain dormant during the preceding period, when the religious civilizations of Islam and Christianity had evolved into commonwealths of many competing realms. Both the Ottomans and the Habsburgs raised immense amounts of cash in silver and gold to spend on cannons, muskets, and ships for achieving world rule.

State Transformation, Money, and Firearms

In the early stages of their realms, the kings of Iberia (1150–1400) and the Ottoman sultans (1300–1400), with little cash on hand, compensated military commanders for their service in battle with parcels of conquered land, or *land grants*. That land, farmed by villagers, generated rental income for the officers. Once the Iberian and Ottoman rulers had conquered cities and gained control over long-distance trade, however, patterns changed. Rulers began collecting taxes in cash, with which they paid regiments of personal guards to supplement the army of land-grant officers and their retainers. They created the fiscal–military state, forerunner of the absolutist state of the early seventeenth century.

The Land-Grant System   When the Ottoman *beys*, or chieftains, embarked on their conquests in the early 1300s, they created personal domains on the choice lands they had conquered. Here, they took rents in kind from the resident villagers to finance their small dynastic households. Their comrades in arms, such as members of their clan or adherents (many of whom were holy warriors and/or adventurers), received other conquered lands, from which they also collected rents. As the Ottomans conquered Byzantine cities, first in Anatolia and, in the second half of the 1300s, in the Balkans, they gained access to the **money economy**. They collected taxes in coins from the markets and tollbooths at city gates where foods and crafts goods were exchanged, as well as from the Christians and Jews responsible for the head tax (Turkish *cizye*). The taxes helped in adding luxuries to the household of the Ottoman emirs, which became a palace.

Money economy: Form of economic organization in which mutual obligations are settled in the form of monetary exchanges; in contrast, a system of land grants obliges the holders themselves to provide military service to the grantee (sultan or king).

As a consequence of the full conquest of the southern Balkans by the Ottoman Empire in the fifteenth and sixteenth centuries, both the land-grant system and the money economy expanded exponentially. An entire military ruling class of grant holders emerged, forming the backbone of the early Ottoman army and administration. The grant holders were cavalrymen who lived with their households of retainers in the villages and towns of the interior of Anatolia and the Balkans. Most of the time, they were away on campaign with the sultans, leaving managers in charge of the collection of rents from the villagers on their lands.

The main purpose of the rents was to support the grant holders as well as finance the additional numbers of horsemen (as well as their horses, infantry retainers, and baggage carriers). The grant holders were also responsible for supplying their own arms (bow and arrow, lance, and sword), armor, and foodstuffs during campaigns. At the conclusion of the rapid growth period of the Ottoman Empire toward the end of the fifteenth century, the landed ruling class of cavalrymen numbered some 80,000, constituting a vast reserve of warriors for the mobilization of troops each summer.

Janissaries: Centrally paid infantry soldiers recruited through the *devshirme*, or levy of boys, among the Christian population of the Ottoman Empire.

The Janissaries   An early indicator of the significance of the money economy in the Ottoman Empire was the military institution of the **Janissaries**—troops which received salaries from the central treasury. This institution probably appeared during the second half of the fourteenth century and is first documented for 1395. It was based on a practice (called ***devşirme***) of conscripting young boys, which palace officers carried out irregularly every few years among the empire's Christian population. For this purpose, the palace officers traveled to Christian villages, towns, and cities in the Balkans, Greece, and Anatolia. At each occasion, they selected hundreds of boys between the ages of 6 and 16 and marched them off to Istanbul, where they were converted to Islam and trained as future soldiers and administrators. The boys and young men then entered the central system of "palace slaves" under the direct orders of the sultan and his viziers or ministers.

During the time of its existence as a levy of Christian boys (c. 1380–1648), the devshirme was mostly administered in the poor, remote villages of the Adriatic mountains (opposite Italy), which could least resist it. Christian cities either negotiated their exemption or successfully resisted the levy until the administration gave up. Other communities bribed the recruiters or, occasionally, liberated child transports. During the height of the levy's administration, therefore, the great majority of Janissaries originated from a relatively small number of regions, mostly in Albania and Bosnia.

In fact, the devshirme contradicted Islamic law, which forbade the enslavement of "peoples of the Book" (Jews, Christians, and Zoroastrians). Its existence, therefore, documents the extent to which the sultans reasserted the Roman–Sasanian–Arab imperial traditions of the ruler making doctrine and law. Ruling by divine grace, the Ottomans were makers of their own law, called *kanun* (from Greek *kanon*). Muslim religious scholars, who had assumed the role of guardians of law and doctrine during the preceding commonwealth period of Islamic civilization (950–1300), had no choice but to accept sultanic imperialism and seek to adapt it to the Shari`a as best they could.

Toward the first half of the fifteenth century, the sultans equipped their Janissaries with cannons and matchlock muskets. According to reports in Arabic chronicles, firearms first appeared around 1250 in the Middle East, probably coming from China. When the Janissaries received them, firearms had therefore undergone some 150 years of experimentation and development in the Middle East and North Africa. Even though the cannons and muskets were still far from being decisive in battle, they had become sophisticated enough to make a difference. By the mid-1400s, gigantic siege cannons and slow but reliable matchlock muskets were the standard equipment of Ottoman and other armies. The sultans relied on large numbers of indigenous, rather than European, gunsmiths, as new research in Ottoman archives has revealed.

Boy Levy (*devşirme*) in a Christian Village. This miniature graphically depicts the trauma of conscription, including the wailing of the village women and the assembly of boys waiting to be taken away by implacable representatives of the sultan.

Devşirme: The levy on boys in the Ottoman Empire; that is, the obligation of the Christian population to contribute adolescent males to the military and administrative classes.

Ottoman Siege of a Christian Fortress. By the middle of the fifteenth century, cannons had revolutionized warfare. Niccolò Machiavelli, ever attuned to new developments, noted in 1519 that "no wall exists, however thick, that artillery cannot destroy in a few days." Machiavelli could have been commenting on the Ottomans, who were masters of siege warfare. Sultan Mehmet II, the conqueror of Constantinople in 1453, founded the Imperial Cannon Foundry shortly thereafter; and it would go on to make some of the biggest cannons of the period.

Revenues and Money   The maintenance of a salaried standing army of infantry soldiers and a central administration to provide the fiscal foundation would have been impossible without precious metals. Therefore, the Ottoman imperial expansion was guided by the need to acquire mineral deposits. During the fifteenth century the Ottomans captured the rich silver, lead, and iron mines of Serbia and Bosnia. Together with Anatolian copper, iron, and silver mines occupied earlier, the Balkan mines made the Ottomans the owners of the largest precious metal production centers prior to the Habsburg acquisition of the Mexican and Andean mines in the mid-1500s.

The sultans left the mining and smelting operations in the hands of preconquest Christian entrepreneurs from the autonomous Adriatic coastal city-states of Ragusa and Dubrovnik. These entrepreneurs were integrated into the Ottoman imperial money economy as tax farmers obliged to buy their right of operation from the government in return for reimbursing themselves from the mining and smelting profits. **Tax-farming** was the preferred method of producing cash revenues for the central administration. The holders of tax farms delivered the profits from the production of metals, salt, saltpeter, and other minerals to the state, minus the commission they were entitled to subtract for themselves. They also collected the head tax—payable in money—from the Jews and Christians and the profits from the sale of the agricultural dues from state domains. Thus, tax farmers were crucial members of the ruling class, responsible for the cash flow in the fiscal–military state.

The right to mint silver into the basic coin of the empire, the *akçe* [ak-TSHAY], was similarly part of the tax-farm regime, as were the market, city gate, and port duties. The tax-farm regime, of course, was crucially dependent on a strong sultan or chief minister, the grand vizier. Without close supervision, this regime could easily deteriorate into a state of decentralization, something which indeed eventually happened in the Ottoman Empire on a large scale, although not before the eighteenth century.

Süleyman's Central State   The centralized fiscal–military state of the Ottomans reached its apogee under Sultan Süleyman I, the Magnificent. At the beginning of the sultan's reign, the amount of money available for expenditures was twice that of half a century earlier. By the end of his reign, this amount had again doubled. With this money, the sultan financed a massive expansion of the military and bureaucracy. Palace, military, and bureaucracy formed a centralized state, the purpose of which was to project power and cultural splendor toward its predominantly rural subjects in the interior as well as Christian enemies outside the empire.

The bureaucrats were recruited from two population groups. Most top ministers and officers in the fifteenth and sixteenth centuries came from the devşirme among the Christians. The conscripted boys learned Turkish, received an Islamic education, and underwent intensive horsemanship or firearm training, in preparation for salaried service in the Janissary army or administration. The empire's other recruits came from colleges in Istanbul and provincial cities to which the Muslim population of the empire had access. Colleges were institutions through which ambitious villagers far from major urban centers could gain upward mobility. Graduates with law degrees found employment as clerical employees in the bureaucracy or as judges in the villages, towns, and cities. Only the judges in the upper ranks of jurisdiction, however, such as the chief judges of Anatolia and the Balkans and the supreme judge of the empire, occupied positions of influence in the administration. Muslims of Christian parentage made up the top layer of the elite, while Muslims of Islamic descent occupied the middle ranks.

Tax-farming:
Governmental auction of the right to collect taxes in a district. The tax farmer advanced these taxes to the treasury and retained a commission.

Under Süleyman, the Janissaries comprised about 18,000 soldiers, divided into 11,000 musket-equipped troopers, a cavalry of 5,000, and 2,000 gunners who formed the artillery regiments. Most were stationed in barracks in and near the Topkapı Palace in Istanbul, ready to go on campaign at the sultan's command. Other Janissaries provided service in provincial cities and border fortresses. For his campaigns, the sultan added levies from among the cavalry troops in the towns and villages of the empire. Typical campaigns involved 70,000 soldiers and required sophisticated logistics. All wages, gunpowder, and weapons and the majority of the foodstuffs were carried on wagons and barges since soldiers were not permitted to provision themselves from the belongings of the villagers, whether friend or foe. Although the fiscal–military state collected heavy taxes, it had a strong interest in not destroying the productivity of the villagers.

Ottoman Law Book. Covering the entire range of human activity—from spiritual matters, family relations, inheritance, business transactions, and crimes—the *Multaka al Abbur* (*The Confluence of the Currents*) was completed in 1517 and remained for hundreds of years the authoritative source for many of the laws in the Ottoman Empire. Written in Arabic script by the legal scholar Ibrahim Al-Halabi, later commentators added annotations in the margins and within the body of the text itself.

Charles V's Central State   The fiscal–military state began in Iberia with the political and fiscal reforms of Isabella and Ferdinand and reached the mature phase of centralization under Charles V. From the late fifteenth century onward, Castile and Aragon shared many fiscal characteristics with those of the Ottomans. The Spanish monarchs derived cash advances from tax farmers, who organized the production and sale of minerals and salt. From other tax farmers, they received advances on the taxes collected in money from the movement of goods in and out of ports, cities, and markets, as well as on taxes collected in kind from independent farmers and converted through sale on urban markets. In addition, Jews and Muslims paid head taxes in cash. Most of the money taxes were also enforced in Flanders, Burgundy, Naples, Sicily, and Austria, after Iberia's incorporation into the Habsburg domain in 1516. Together, these taxes were more substantial than those of Spain, especially in the highly urbanized Flanders, where the percentage of the urban population was about twice that of Spain.

From 1521 to 1536, the Spanish crown enlarged its money income by the one-fifth share to which it was entitled from looted Aztec and Inca gold and silver treasures. Charles V used these treasures to finance his expedition against Tunis. Thereafter, it collected a one-quarter share from the silver mines in the Americas that were brought into production beginning in 1545. Full production in the mines did not set in until the second half of the sixteenth century, but already under Charles V Habsburg imperial revenues doubled, reaching about the same level as those of the Ottomans. Thus, at the height of their struggle for dominance in the Muslim–Christian world, the Habsburgs and the Ottomans expended roughly the same amounts of resources to hurl against each other in the form of troops, cannons, muskets, and war galleys.

In one significant respect, however, the two empires differed. The cavalry ruling class of the Ottoman Empire was nonhereditary. Although land-grant holdings went in practice from father to son and then grandson, their holders had no recourse to the law if the sultans decided to replace them. By contrast, ever since the first half of the thirteenth century, when the Iberian kings were still lacking appreciable monetary resources, their landholders possessed a legal right to inheritance. The landholders met more or less regularly in parliaments (Spanish *cortes*), where they could enforce their property rights against the kings through majority decisions. When Isabella and Ferdinand embarked on state centralization, they had to wrestle with a powerful, landed aristocracy that had taken over royal jurisdiction and tax prerogatives (especially market taxes) on their often vast lands, including cities as well as towns and villages. The two monarchs took back much of the jurisdiction but were unable to do much about the taxes, thus failing in one crucial respect with their centralization effort. Although Habsburg Spain was a fully evolved fiscal–military state, it was in the end less centralized than that of the Ottomans.

The Habsburgs sought to overcome their lack of power over the aristocracy and the weakness of their Spanish tax base by squeezing as much as they could out of the Italian and Flemish cities and the American colonies. But in the long run their finances remained precarious, plentiful in some years but sparse in others. Relatively few Spanish aristocrats bothered to fulfill their traditional obligation to unpaid military service, and if they did, they forced the kings to pay them like mercenaries. As a result, in the administration and especially in the military, the kings hired as many Italians, Flemings, and Germans as possible. At times, they even had to deploy them to Spain in order to maintain peace there. Most of these foreigners were foot soldiers, equipped with muskets.

The Ottoman and Habsburg patterns of fiscal–military state formation bore similarities to patterns in the Roman and Arab Empires half a millennium earlier. At that time, however, the scale was more modest, given that the precious metals from West Africa and the Americas were not yet part of the trade network. In addition, earlier empires did not yet possess firearms, requiring an expensive infrastructure of charcoal and metal production, gunsmithing, saltpeter mining, and gunpowder manufacture. Thanks to firearms, the fiscal–military states of the period after 1450 were much more potent enterprises. They were established states, evolving into absolutist and eventually national states.

Imperial Courts, Urban Festivities, and the Arts

Habsburg kings and Ottoman sultans set aside a portion of revenues to project the splendor and glory of their states to subjects at home as well as enemies abroad. They commissioned the building of palaces, mosques, and churches and sponsored public festivities. Since the administrators, nobility, tax farmers, and merchants had considerable funds, they also patronized writers, artists, and architects. Although Christian and Muslim artists and artisans belonged to different religious and cultural traditions and expressed themselves through different media, their artistic achievements were inspired by the same impulse: to glorify their states through religious expression.

The Spanish Habsburg Empire: Popular Festivities and the Arts

The centrality of Catholicism gave the culture of the Habsburg Empire a strongly religious coloration. Both state-sponsored spectacles and popular festivities displayed devotion to the Catholic faith. More secular tendencies, however, began to appear as well, if only because new forms of literature and theater emerged outside the religious sphere as a result of the Renaissance. Originating in Italy and the Netherlands, Renaissance aesthetics emphasized pre-Christian Greek and Roman heritages, which had not been available to medieval Christian artists.

Capital and Palace   The Habsburgs focused relatively late on the typical symbols of state power and splendor, that is, a capital city and a palace. Most Spaniards lived in the northern third and along the southern and eastern rims of the Iberian Peninsula, leaving the inhospitable central high plateau, the Meseta, thinly inhabited. Catholicism was the majority religion by the sixteenth century and a powerful unifying force, but there were strong linguistic differences among the provinces of the Iberian Peninsula. Charles V resided for a while in a palace in Granada next door to the formerly Muslim Alhambra palace. Built in an Italian Renaissance-derived style and appearing overwhelming and bombastic in comparison to the outwardly unprepossessing Alhambra, Granada was too Moorish and, geographically, too far away in the south for more than a few Spanish subjects to be properly awed.

Only a few places in the river valleys traversing the Meseta were suited for the location of a central palace and administration. Philip II eventually found such a place near the city of Madrid (built on Roman-Visigothic foundations) which in the early sixteenth century had some 12,000 inhabitants. There, he had his royal architect in chief and sculptor Juan Bautista de Toledo (ca. 1515–1567), a student of Michelangelo, build the imposing Renaissance-styled palace and monastery complex of El Escorial (1563–1584). As a result, Madrid became the seat of the administration and later of the court. A large central square and broad avenue were cut across the narrow alleys of the old city, which had once been a Muslim provincial capital. People of all classes gathered in the square and avenue, to participate in public festivities and learn the latest news "about the intentions of the Grand Turk, revolutions in the

The Escorial Palace of King Philip II. Note the austere façade and the long horizontal lines of this building, representative of the Renaissance interpretation of the classical Greek-Roman architectural heritage.

Passion play: Dramatic representation of the trial, suffering, and death of Jesus Christ; passion plays are still an integral part of Holy Week in many Catholic countries today.

Netherlands, the state of things in Italy, and the latest discoveries made in the Indies."

Like its Italian paradigm, architecture of the Spanish Renaissance emphasized the Roman imperial style—itself derived from the Greeks—with long friezes, round arches, freestanding columns, and rotunda-based domes. With this style, Spanish architects departed from the preceding Gothic, stressing horizontal extension rather than height and plain rather than relief or ornament-filled surfaces. Interestingly, however, some Spanish architects incorporated the inherited traditions of the richly ornamental Gothic and Islamic styles into their Renaissance-style buildings, where these traditions appear in the so-called plateresque façades of buildings. This type of façade continued in the later Baroque style and was also transferred to the Americas (the oldest example being the monastery of San Agostín Acolman, 1560, in the outskirts of Mexico City) as well as the United States (one example, the entrance to the Hearst Castle, 1919). Plateresco is a uniquely Hispanic contribution to the architectural styles of the world.

Christian State Festivities   Given the close association between the state and the church, the Spanish crown expressed its glory through the observance of feast days of the Christian calendar. Christmas, Easter, Pentecost, Trinity Sunday, Corpus Christi, and the birthdays of numerous saints were the occasion for processions and/or **passion plays**, during which urban residents affirmed the purity of their Catholic faith. Throngs lined the streets or marched in procession, praying, singing, weeping, and exclaiming. During Holy Week preceding Easter, Catholics—wearing white robes, tall white or black pointed hats, and veils over their faces—marched through the streets, carrying heavy crosses or shouldering large floats with statues of Jesus and Mary. A variety of religious lay groups or confraternities competed to build the most elaborately decorated floats. Members of flagellant confraternities whipped themselves. The physical rigors of the Holy Week processions were collective reenactments of Jesus' suffering on the Cross.

By contrast, the Corpus Christi (Latin, meaning "body of Christ") processions that took place on the Sunday after Trinity Sunday (several weeks after Easter) were joyous celebrations. Central to these processions was a float with a canopy covering the consecrated host (bread believed to have been transfigured into the body of Jesus). Marchers dressed as giants, serpents, dragons, devils, angels, patriarchs, and saints participated in jostling and pushing contests. Others wore masks, played music, performed dances, and enacted scenes from the Bible. Being part of the crowd in the Corpus Christi processions meant partaking in a joyful anticipation of salvation.

The Auto-da-Fé   The investigation or proceeding of faith (Portuguese *auto-da-fé*, "act of faith") was a show trial in which the state, through the Spanish Inquisition, judged a person's commitment to Catholicism. Inquisitional trials were intended to display the all-important unity and purity of Counter-Reformation Catholicism.

Auto-da-Fé, Madrid. This detail from a painting showing a huge assembly in Plaza Mayor, Madrid, in 1683, captures the drama and spectacle of the auto-da-fé. In the center, below a raised platform, the accused stand in the docket waiting for their convictions to be pronounced; ecclesiastical and civil authorities follow the proceedings from huge grandstands set up for the event. On the left, an outdoor altar is visible—the celebration of mass was a common feature of the auto-da-fé, which would often last for several hours.

The Inquisition employed thousands of state-appointed church officials to investigate anonymous denunciations of individuals failing to conform to the prescribed doctrines and liturgy of the Catholic faith.

Suspected offenders, such as Jewish or Muslim converts to Catholicism or perceived deviants from Catholicism, had to appear before one of the 15 tribunals distributed over the country. In secret trials, officials determined the degree of the offense and the appropriate punishment. These trials often employed torture, such as stretching the accused on the rack, suspending them with weights, crushing hands and feet in an apparatus called "the boot," and burning them with firebrands. In contrast to the wide perception of the Inquisition as marked by pervasive cruelties, however, scholarship has emphasized that in the great majority of cases the punishments were minor or investigations did not lead to convictions.

On the other hand, whenever conviction entailed major penalties, the sentencing was a public spectacle. On the appointed day of punishment, to the accompaniment of trumpets and drums, the convicts were marched to a stage on the city square, dressed in yellow tunics and pointed fools' caps. After long sermons and solemn affirmations of Catholic doctrines, officials read the sentence. These sentences ranged from the wearing of the yellow tunic (the color of shame and the dress of Judas, who in the Christian gospels betrayed Jesus) in public for stipulated amounts of time to condemnation to hard labor as rowers on war galleys to execution. Offenders condemned to death were turned over to executioners on the outskirts of the city, who burned them at the stake. Autos-da-fé were usually scheduled to coincide with important dynastic events, such as royal accessions, weddings, and births, or to celebrate military victories, thus emphasizing the overwhelming power of the state.

Popular Festivities   *Jousts* (mock combats between contestants mounted on horseback) were secular, primarily aristocratic events, also frequently connected with dynastic occurrences. The contestants, colorfully costumed as "Muslims," "Turks," and Christians, rode their horses into the city square accompanied by trumpets and drums and led their Arabian thoroughbreds or Lusitanian warmbloods through a precise and complex series of movements. At the height of the spectacle, contestants divided into groups of three or four at each end of the square. At a signal, they galloped at full speed past each other, hurling their javelins at one another while protecting themselves with their shields. The joust evolved eventually into exhibitions of dressage ("training"), cultivated by the Austrian Habsburgs, who in 1572 founded the Spanish Court Riding School in Vienna.

Bullfights, also fought on horseback, often followed the jousts. Fighting wild animals, including bulls, in spectacles was originally a Roman custom that had evolved from older bovine sacrifices in temples around the Mediterranean. During the Middle Ages, bullfights were aristocratic occupations that drew spectators from local estates. Bullfighters, armed with detachable metal points on 3-foot-long spears, tackled several bulls in a town square, together with footmen who sought to distract the bulls by waving red capes at them. The bullfighter who stuck the largest number of points into the shoulders of the bull was the winner. The bullfight remained an encounter between mounted man and animal in Portugal. In the expanding cities of eighteenth-century Spain, slaughterhouse workers popularized the modern version of the bullfight, in which a rapier-wielding matador on foot engages in a deadly fight with a bull bred to kill.

Theater and Literature The dramatic enactments of biblical scenes in the passion plays and Corpus Christi processions were the origin of a new phenomenon in Spain, the secular theater. During earlier centuries, traveling troupes had often performed on wagons after processions. Stationary theaters with stages, main floors, balconies, and boxes appeared in the main cities of Spain during the sixteenth century. A performance typically began with a musical prelude and a prologue describing the piece, followed by the three acts of a drama or comedy. Brief sketches, humorous or earnest, filled the breaks. Plays dealt with betrayed or unrequited love, honor, justice, or peasant–nobility conflicts. Many were hugely successful, enjoying the attendance or even sponsorship of courtiers, magistrates, and merchants.

The outstanding Spanish dramatist of the second half of the sixteenth century was Félix Lope de Vega (1562–1635). His father, an embroidery shop owner, sent him to college, although he left without graduating. Lope de Vega's works, of which nearly 500 are extant, use plots, themes, and dramatic devices designed to appeal to a mass urban audience. Many of his dramas reflect his own adventurous life, which included military campaigns, countless love affairs, abductions, and several marriages. He also wrote historical plays dramatizing national events and heroic pieces based on Spanish legends. For many years, Lope de Vega lived from hand to mouth, finding aristocratic patrons only toward his later life. At the time of his death, Lope de Vega was a celebrated poet laureate of Spanish literature.

Another important writer of the period was Miguel de Cervantes (1547–1616), who wrote his masterpiece, *Don Quixote*, in the new literary form of the novel. *Don Quixote* describes the adventures of a poverty-stricken knight and his attendant, the peasant Sancho Panza, as they wander around Spain searching for the life of bygone Reconquista chivalry. Their journey includes many hilarious escapades during which they run into the reality of the early modern fiscal–military state dominated by monetary concerns. Cervantes confronts the vanished virtues of knighthood with the novel values of the life with money.

Cervantes' personal life was full of struggle. The son of a poor surgeon, he received a literary education before enlisting in the military. In the battle of Lepanto in 1571, an injury incapacitated his left arm. In 1575, Muslim corsairs from North Africa captured and imprisoned him in Algiers. Like Leo Africanus, discussed in the vignette at the beginning of this chapter, he was one of tens of thousands of kidnap victims on both the Christian and Muslim sides during the 1500s. Cervantes regained his freedom 5 years later when a Catholic religious order seeking release for captives in North Africa paid his ransom. Cervantes' early publications attracted little attention, and several times he was imprisoned for unpaid debts. Not until late in life did he receive recognition for his literary works.

Painters   The outstanding painter of Spain during Philip II's reign was El Greco (Domenikos Theotokopoulos, ca. 1546–1614), a native of the island of Crete. After early training in Crete as a painter of eastern Christian icons, El Greco went to Venice for further studies. In 1577, the Catholic hierarchy hired him to paint the altarpieces of a church in Toledo, the city in central Spain which was one of the residences of the kings prior to the construction of El Escorial in Madrid. El Greco's works reflect the spirit of Spanish Catholicism, with its emphasis on strict obedience to traditional faith and fervent personal piety. His characteristic style features elongated, pale figures surrounded by vibrant colors and represents a variation of the so-called mannerist style (with its perspective exaggerations), which succeeded the Renaissance style in Venice during the later sixteenth century.

King Philip II was not very fond of El Greco's paintings. While he approved of the latter's engagement in religion, he had more conventional Renaissance ideas about how personal piety should be represented in paintings. He preferred Titian (ca. 1490–1576), the more accessible and much sought-after Italian portraitist and painter of allegorical themes who, despite being lavished with favors by the king, never came to Spain. El Greco, nevertheless, found enough clerical patrons who supported his Toledo workshop until the end of his life.

El Greco, *View of Toledo*, ca. 1610–1614. The painting, now in the Metropolitan Museum, New York, illustrates El Greco's predilection for color contrasts and dramatic motion. Baroque and Mannierist painters rarely depicted landscapes and this particular landscape is represented in eerie green, gray, and blue colors giving the impression of a city enveloped in a mysterious natural or perhaps spiritual force.

The Ottoman Empire: Palaces, Festivities, and the Arts

Similar to the Habsburgs, the Ottomans built palaces and celebrated public feasts to demonstrate their imperial power and wealth. In Ottoman Islamic civilization, however, there were no traditions of official public art. The exception was architecture, where a veritable explosion of mosque construction occurred during the sixteenth century. High-quality pictorial artistry, in the form of portraits, book illustrations and miniatures, was found only inside the privacy of the Ottoman palace and wealthy administrative households. As in Habsburg Spain, theater and music enjoyed much support on the popular level, in defiance of official religious restrictions against these forms of entertainment.

The Topkapı Palace   When the Ottoman sultans conquered the Byzantine capital Constantinople in 1453, they took over one of the great cities of the world. Although richly endowed with Roman monuments and churches, it was dilapidated and depopulated when the Ottomans took over. The sultans initiated large construction projects, such as covered markets, and populated them with craftspeople and traders drawn from both Asian and European sides of their empire. By 1600 Istanbul was again an imposing metropolis with close to half a million inhabitants, easily the largest city in Europe at that time.

One of the construction projects was a new palace for the sultans, the Topkapı Saray or "Palace of the Gun Gate," begun in 1463. This palace is one of the world's most sumptuous urban dynastic residences, like the Forbidden City in Beijing or the Louvre in Paris. By design or circumstance, its sprawling size, with its many recesses, hidden rooms, and dark alleyways, made it an object of fear and fascination among the sultan's subjects. The Topkapı was a veritable minicity, with three courtyards, formal gardens, and forested hunting grounds. It also included the main administrative school for the training of imperial bureaucrats, barracks for the standing troops of the Janissaries, an armory, a hospital, and—most importantly—the living quarters, or harem, for the ruling family. Subjects were permitted access only through the first courtyard—reserved for imperial festivities—to submit their petitions to the sultan's council of ministers.

The institution of the harem rose to prominence toward the end of the reign of Süleyman. At that time, sultans no longer pursued marriage alliances with neighboring Islamic rulers. Instead, they chose slave concubines for the procreation of children, preferably boys. Concubines were usually from the Caucasus or other frontier regions, often Christian, and, since they were slaves, deprived of family attachments. A concubine who bore a son to the reigning sultan acquired privileges, such as influence on decisions taken by the central administration. The head eunuch of the harem guard evolved into a powerful intermediary for all manner of small and large diplomatic and military decisions between a sultan's mother, who was confined to the harem, and the ministers or generals she sought to influence. In addition, the sultan's mother arranged marriages of her daughters to members of the council of ministers and other high-ranking officials. In the strong patriarchal order of the Ottoman Empire, it might come as a surprise to see women exercise such power, but this power evidently had its roots in the tutelage exercised by mothers over sons who were potential future sultans.

Imperial Hall, Topkapı Palace. The Ottomans never forgot their nomadic roots. Topkapı Palace, completed in 1479 and expanded and redecorated several times, resembles in many ways a vast encampment, with a series of enclosed courtyards. At the center of the palace complex were the harem and the private apartments of the sultan, which included the Imperial Hall where the sultan would receive members of his family and closest advisors.

Public Festivities   As in Habsburg Spain, feasts and celebrations were events which displayed the state's largesse and benevolence. Typical festivities were the Feast of Breaking the Fast, which came at the end of the fasting month of Ramadan, and the Feast of Sacrifice, which took place a month and a half later at the end of the Meccan pilgrimage. Festive processions and fairs welcomed the return of the Meccan pilgrimage caravan. Other feasts were connected with the birthday of the Prophet Muhammad and his journey to heaven and hell. Muslims believed that the Prophet's birth was accompanied by miracles and that the angel Gabriel accompanied him on his journey, showing him the joys of heaven and the horrors of hell. Processions with banners, music, and communal meals commemorated the birthdays of local Muslim saints in many cities and towns. As in Christian Spain, these feasts attracted large crowds.

The circumcision of a prince was an occasion for joyous public celebrations in the city. The sultan and his administrators rode out from the palace to the Hippodrome, the stadium for public festivities left over from Roman–Byzantine days. There, they tossed fistfuls of coins to the crowds. From stands in the stadium, they watched lengthy processions of the crafts guilds. Members of the guilds pulled floats on which colleagues demonstrated their skills. Bakers made bread in real ovens, cooks roasted meats, florists created flower arrangements, and glassblowers made bottles. Fishermen pulled a boat on wheels, architects carried the model of a mosque, and gardeners carried an artificial hill, complete with sheep and gazelles. The Janissaries rolled along atop a wheeled tower, firing their muskets in mock volleys against the "Christians," who marched beside them. Other Janissaries paraded with giants and monsters made of papier-mâché. Costumed and masked dancers, accompanied by musicians, waltzed along. The guild of street sweepers concluded the procession, parading as they were cleaning up the mess left by their preceding colleagues.

Wrestlers, ram handlers, and horsemen performed in the Hippodrome. Elimination matches in wrestling determined the eventual champion. Ram handlers spurred their animals to gore one another with their horns. Horsemen stood upright on horses, galloping toward a mound, which they had to hit with a javelin. At the harbor of the Golden Horn, tightrope artists stood high above the water, balancing themselves on cables stretched between the masts of ships, as they performed juggling feats. Fireworks—producing a variety of effects, noises, and colors—completed the circumcision festival in the evening. Court painters recorded the procession and performance scenes in picture albums. The sultans incorporated these albums into their libraries, together with history books recording in word and image their battle victories against the Habsburgs.

Popular Theater   The evenings of the fasting month of Ramadan were filled with festive meals and a special form of entertainment, the Karagöz ("Blackeye") shadow theater. This form of theater came from Egypt, although it probably had Javanese–Chinese roots. The actors in the Karagöz theater used figures cut from thin, transparent leather, painted in primary colors, and fashioned with movable jaws and limbs. With brightly burning lamps behind them, actors manipulated the

> **A Glimpse Inside the Harem**
>
> "The number of women reached 4,000, including those in his [the Sultan's] mother's service, as well as his lover's. Although the plague often devastated such a multitude, their numbers never fell below 2,000, owing to the careful and continuous recruitment of replacements.... They wore the most expensive clothes, belts, and fasteners studded with gems, earrings, and several strings of pearls. Each mistress of the sultan had the power to free and give in marriage any slave girls who were in her service or who aroused her jealousy."
>
> —from the diary of Thomas Dallam, an English visitor to the Turkish court in 1599, from *Early Voyages and Travels in the Levant*. London: Hakluyt Society, 1893.

Ottoman Festivities, 1720. The sultan watches from a kiosk on the shore of the Golden Horn as artists perform high-wire acts, musicians and dancers perform from rowboats offshore, and high officials and foreign dignitaries view the festivities from a galleon.

figures against a cloth screen. The audience was seated on the other side of the screen, following the plays with rapt attention (or not).

The actors played burlesques, usually in four acts, narrating the slapstick encounters between Karagöz, the streetwise simpleton, and Hacivat [Ha-jee-VAT], his educated, conceited, but innocent counterpart. Other figures in the stories included a drunkard, an opium addict, a dwarf, a spendthrift, a woman of loose morals, assorted ethnic figures, monsters, and animals. The stories played on social contrasts and stereotypes, often containing political undertones. Theater companies toured the cities of the empire. Karagöz presentations by resident theaters also took place in taverns and coffeehouses. Like the Spanish theater with its dramas and comedies, the Ottoman Karagöz theater was a secular form of urban entertainment outside the religious circuit.

Among boys, a performance of the Karagöz theater accompanied the ritual of circumcision, a rite of passage from the ancient Near East adopted in Islamic civilization. It called for boys between the ages of 6 and 12 to be circumcised. Circumcision signified the passage from the nurturing care of the mother to the educational discipline of the father. Groups of newly circumcised boys were placed in beds from which they watched the antics of Karagöz and Hacivat. Supposedly, these churls distracted them from their pain.

Mosque Architecture   During the sixteenth century, the extraordinarily prolific architect Sinan (ca. 1492–1588) filled Istanbul and the earlier Ottoman capital Edirne with a number of imperial mosques, defined by their characteristic slender minarets. According to his autobiography, Sinan designed more than 300 religious and secular buildings, from mosques, colleges, and hospitals to aqueducts and bridges. Sultan Süleyman, wealthy officials, and private donors provided the funds. Sinan was able to hire as many as 25,000 laborers, enabling him to build most of his mosques in six years or less.

Sinan was a Christian-born Janissary from a Greek village in northwestern Anatolia. He entered the palace school at the comparatively late age of 19, and it was only after many years of service in the army corps of engineers before he received his first commission for a mosque in 1538. Sinan himself describes the Shehzade and Süleymaniye mosques in Istanbul and the Selimiye mosque in Edirne as his apprentice, journeyman, and master achievements. All three followed the central dome-over-a-square concept of the Hagia Sophia, which in turn is built in the tradition of Persian and Roman dome architecture. His primary, and most original, contribution to the history of architecture was the replacement of the highly visible and massive four exterior buttresses, which marked the square ground plan of the Hagia Sophia, with up to eight slender pillars as hidden internal supports of the dome. His intention with

Selimiye and Hagia Sophia. The architect Sinan elegantly melded the eight, comparatively thin columns inside the mosque (*a*) with the surrounding walls and allows for a maximum of light to enter the building. In addition, light enters through the dome (*b*). Compare this mosque with the much more heavily built, late Roman-founded Hagia Sophia (*c*).

each of these mosques was not massive monumentality but elegant spaciousness, giving the skylines of Istanbul and Edirne their unmistakable identity.

Putting It All Together

The Ottoman–Habsburg struggle can be seen as another chapter in the long history of competition that began when the Achaemenid Persian Empire expanded into the Mediterranean and was resisted by the Greeks in the middle of the first millennium BCE. Although India and China were frequently subjected to incursions from central Asia, neither of the two had to compete for long with any of its neighbors. Sooner or later the central Asians either retreated or were absorbed by their victims. The Ottomans' brief experience with Timur was on the same order. But the Middle East and Europe were always connected, and this chapter, once more, draws attention to this connectedness.

There were obvious religious and cultural differences between the Islamic and western Christian civilizations as they encountered each other during the Ottoman–Habsburg period. But their commonalities are equally, if not more, interesting. Most importantly, both Ottomans and Habsburgs were representatives of the return to imperialism, and in the pursuit of their imperial goals, both adopted the fiscal–military state with its firearm infantries and pervasive urban money economy. Both found it crucial to their existence to project their glory to the population at large and to sponsor artistic expression. In the long run, however, the imperial ambitions of the Ottomans and Habsburgs exceeded their ability to raise cash. Although firearms and a monetized urban economy made them different from previous empires, they were as unstable as all their imperial predecessors. Eventually, around 1600, they reached the limits of their conquests.

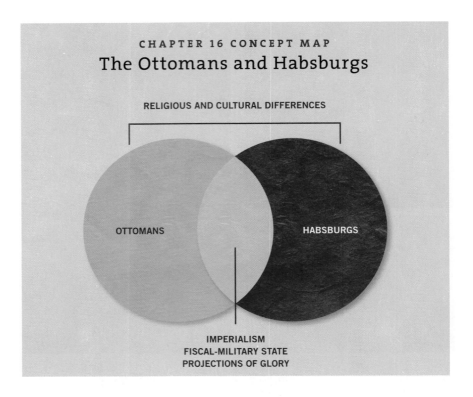

Review and Respond

1. Sketch the evolution of the Christian–Muslim struggle in Iberia. How did Portuguese and Spanish overseas explorations shape this struggle?

2. Provide an outline of the Ottoman–Habsburg struggle for dominance in Europe and the Mediterranean. What were the main theaters and stages of the struggle on land and at sea? How does the career of Leo Africanus display many of the themes that characterized this competition?

3. How were the Ottoman and Habsburg states organized? What were their economic bases? What were their social structures?

4. Who were the Janissaries, and how does the institution of the *devşirme* fit into their recruitment?

5. What was the Spanish Inquisition? What role did it play in Spanish society?

6. What were the principal cultural expressions of the Ottoman and Habsburg empires? In which ways were they similar, and in which ways were they different?

▶ For additional resources, including maps, primary sources, visuals, and quizzes, please go to www.oup.com/us/vonsivers. Please see the Further Resources section at the back of the book for additional readings and suggested websites.

Thinking Through Patterns

▶ **What patterns characterized the Christian and Muslim imperial competition in the period 1300–1600? Which elements distinguished them from each other, and which elements were similar? How did the pattern change over time?**

In 1300, the Ottomans renewed the Arab-Islamic tradition of jihad against the eastern Christian empire of Byzantium, conquering the Balkans and eventually defeating the empire with the conquest of Constantinople 1453. They also carried the war into the western Mediterranean and Indian Ocean. In western Christian Iberia, the rekindling of the reconquest after the lull of the thirteenth and fourteenth centuries was more successful. Invigorated by a merging of the concepts of the Crusade and the Reconquista, the Iberians expanded overseas to circumvent the Muslims and trade Indian spices directly. The so-called Age of Exploration, during which western Christians traveled to and settled in overseas lands, is deeply rooted in the Western traditions of war against Islamic civilization.

In the mid-1400s, the Middle East and Europe returned to the pattern of imperial state formation after a lull of several centuries, during which states had competed against each other within their respective commonwealths. The element which fueled this return was gunpowder weaponry. The use of cannons and handheld firearms became widespread during this time but required major financial outlays on the part of the states. The Ottomans and Habsburgs were the states with the most resources, and the Ottomans even built the first standing armies. To pay the musket-equipped soldiers, huge amounts of silver were necessary. The two empires became centralized fiscal–military states based on a money economy: Bureaucracies maintained centralized departments that regulated the collection of taxes and the payroll of soldiers.

▶ **How did the fiscal–military state in the Middle East and Europe function in the period 1450–1600? How did economics, military power, and imperial objectives interact to create the fiscal-military state?**

▶ **Which patterns did cultural expressions follow in the Habsburg and Ottoman Empires? Why did the ruling classes of these empires sponsor these expressions?**

The rulers of these empires were concerned to portray themselves, their military, and their bureaucracies as highly successful and just. The state had to be as visible and benevolent as possible. Rulers, therefore, were builders of palaces, churches, or mosques. They celebrated religious and secular festivities with great pomp and encouraged ministers and the nobility to do likewise. In the imperial capitals, they patronized architects, artists, and writers, resulting in a veritable explosion of intellectual and artistic creativity. In this regard, the Ottomans and the Habsburgs followed similar patterns of cultural expression.

Chapter 17

1450-1750

Renaissance, Reformation, and the New Science in Europe

URBAN POPULATION OF EUROPE IN 1700

London, Amsterdam, Paris, Naples

- Over 30%
- 25-30%
- 10-15%
- 5-10%
- 1-5%
- 0-1%
- • city with population over 200,000

Though less celebrated than her male contemporaries, one of the most remarkable scientific minds of the seventeenth century was that of Maria Cunitz (ca. 1607–1664). Under the tutorship of her father, a physician, she became accomplished in six languages (Hebrew, Greek, Latin, Italian, French, and Polish), the humanities, and the sciences. For a number of years while the Thirty Years' War (1618–1648) raged in Germany and her home province of Silesia, Cunitz and her Protestant family sought refuge in a Cistercian monastery in neighboring Catholic Poland. There,

Seeing Patterns

▶ What were the patterns of fiscal–military state formation and transformation in the period 1450–1750? How did the Protestant Reformation and religious wars modify these patterns?

▶ What are the reasons for the cultural change that began in Europe around 1750? In which ways were the patterns of cultural change during 1450–1750 different from those in the other religious civilizations of Eurasia?

▶ When and how did the New Science begin, and how did it gain popularity in northwestern Europe? Why is the popularization of the New Science important for understanding the period 1450–1750?

under difficult living conditions, she wrote *Urania propitia* (*Companion to Urania*), in praise of the Greek muse and patron of astronomy. When the family returned to Silesia after the war, Cunitz lost her scientific papers and instruments to a fire; but she continued to devote her life to the New Science through her careful astronomical observations.

Cunitz's book is a popularization of the astronomical tables of Johannes Kepler (1571–1630), the major scientific innovator remembered today for his discovery of the elliptical trajectories of the planets. Cunitz's book makes corrections in Kepler's tables and offers simplified calculations of star positions. Written in both Latin and German, she published it privately in 1650. It was generally well received, although there were a few detractors who found it hard to believe that a woman could succeed in the sciences. Whatever injustice was done to her during her lifetime, today the scientific community has made amends. A crater on Venus has been named after her, and a statue of her stands in her Silesian hometown.

Cunitz lived in a time when western Christianity had entered the age of early global interaction, from 1450 until 1750. During most of this time, Europe remained institutionally similar to the other parts of the world,

Renaissance Perspective. This 1525 print by the great German Renaissance artist Albrecht Durer is from his *Four Books on Measurement* and shows an artist and his assistant working with a *camera lucida, an* apparatus used to help convert three-dimensional objects into two-dimensional drawings, in this case, a lute. Durer was the first northern European to treat problems of perspective in a mathematical and scientific way.

especially the Middle East, India, China, and Japan. Rulers throughout Eurasia governed by divine grace. All large states followed patterns of fiscal–military organization. Their urban populations were nowhere more than 20 percent, and their economies depended on the prosperity of agriculture. As research on China, the Middle East, and India during 1450–1750 has shown, the "great divergence" in the patterns of political organization, social formation, and economic production between western Christianity and the other religious civilizations, whatever the characteristics that made each unique in other ways, did not take place until around 1800.

Culturally, however, northwestern Europe began to move in a different direction from Islamic, Hindu, Neo-Confucian, and Buddhist civilizations. The New Science and the Enlightenment of England, France, the Netherlands, and parts of Germany initiated new cultural patterns for which there was no equivalent in the other parts of Eurasia, including southern Europe. As significant as these patterns were, for almost the entire three centuries of 1450–1750 the New Science and the Enlightenment remained limited to a few hundred and later to a few thousand educated persons, largely outside the ruling classes. Their ideas and outlooks diverged substantially from those represented by the Catholic and Protestant ruling classes and resulted frequently in tensions or, in a few cases, even repression of New Scientists by the authorities. The new scientific and intellectual culture broadened into a mass movement only after 1750. The subsequent Industrial Revolution was rooted in this movement.

This chapter begins with a focus on the political pattern of fiscal–military state formation which coincided with the Protestant Reformation. The combustible mix of large armies of firearm-bearing mercenaries and fiery anti- and pro-Catholic polemics exploded in a series of religious wars lasting for a century and a half. When the religious fervor eventually died down, Europe separated into Catholic and Protestant fiscal–military states, now called "absolutist," which struggled with the challenges of economic viability. Accompanying the political–religious struggle was a pattern of rapid cultural transformations, explored in the second half of this chapter. The European Renaissance, Baroque, and New Science formed a sequence that was discontinuous with the western Christian Middle Ages and signified the search for a new cultural consensus. Cultural discontinuity, a rapid succession of different styles of cultural expression, and the absence of a consensus typified western Christianity, in contrast to the Middle East, India, and China, where cultural continuity reigned until the 1800s.

Fiscal–Military States and Religious Upheavals

The pattern of the fiscal–military state transforming the institutional structures of society was a characteristic not only in the Ottoman and Habsburg Empires during 1450–1750 but also in other countries of Europe, the Middle East, and India. The financial requirements for sustaining a fiscal–military state required everywhere a reorganization of the relationship between rulers, ruling classes, and regional as well as local forces. The Protestant Reformation and religious wars slowed the pattern of fiscal–military state formation, but once the religious fervor was spent, two types of states emerged: the French, Russian, and Prussian landed fiscal–military state and the Dutch and English naval fiscal–military state.

The Rise of Fiscal–Military Kingdoms

The shift from feudal mounted and armored knights to firearm-equipped professional infantries led to the emergence of the fiscal–military state. Rulers sought to centralize state power, collect higher taxes to subsidize their infantries, and curb the decentralizing forces of the nobility, cities, and other local institutions. Not all autonomous units (such as city-states, city-leagues, and religious orders dating to the previous period, 600–1450) were able to survive the military challenges of the rulers. A winnowing process occurred during 1450–1550, which left a few territorially coherent fiscal–military kingdoms in control of European politics.

The Demographic Curve   Following the demographic disaster of the Black Death in 1348 and its many subsequent cycles, the population of Europe expanded again after 1470. It reached its pre-1348 levels around 1550, with some 85 million inhabitants (not counting the Spanish Habsburg and Ottoman Empires). The population continued to grow until about 1600 (90 million), when it entered a half-century of stagnation during the coldest and wettest period in recorded history, the "Little Ice Age" (1550–1750).

During 1650–1750, the population rose slowly at a moderate rate from 105 to 140 million (see Figure 17.1). In 1750, France (28 million) and Russia (21 million) were the most populous countries, followed by Germany (18 million), Italy (15 million), Poland (13 million), England (7 million), and the Netherlands and Sweden (2 million each). While the population figures of the individual countries for the most part bore little resemblance to their political importance during 1450–1750, as we shall see, the overall figures for Europe demonstrate that western Christianity had risen by 1750 to a status of demographic comparability vis-à-vis the other two major religious civilizations of India (155 million) and China (225 million).

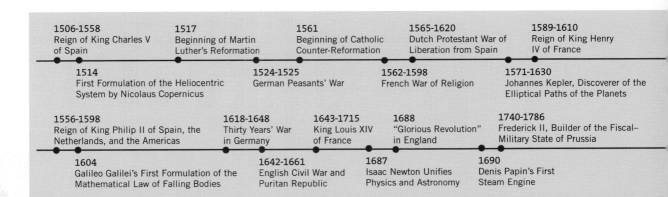

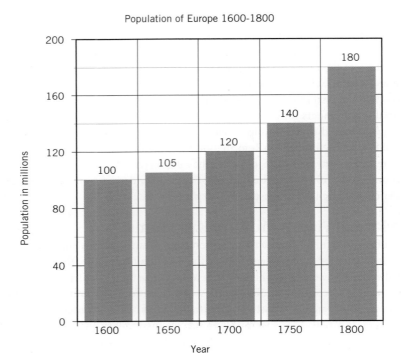

Figure 17.1 **Population of Europe 1600–1800**

Political Realignments   Bracketed between the two empires of the Ottomans and Habsburgs at either geographical end, western Christian Europe during the second half of the fifteenth century was a quilt of numerous independent or autonomous units, including the nascent fiscal–military kingdoms of France and England, the Hanseatic League of trading cities, the Catholic crusading order of Teutonic knights, and the small kingdoms of Denmark, Sweden, Norway, Poland–Lithuania, Bohemia, and Hungary. It furthermore comprised the principalities and cities of Germany, the duchy of Burgundy, the Alpine republic of Switzerland, and the city-states of Italy. At the northeastern periphery was the Grand Duchy of Moscow, representing eastern Christianity after the fall of Byzantium to the Ottomans in 1453. In this quilt, the majority of units competed vigorously with each other, seeking either to exploit the new possibilities which armies of mercenaries with firearms gave them or to survive as best as possible with just a handful.

By the first half of the sixteenth century, the competition had produced a number of winners and losers. Burgundy's dream for an independent kingdom came to an end with its defeat by and incorporation into France in 1477. France's further territorial expansion at the expense of the Italian city-states, beginning with Milan and Naples in 1499–1501, initially looked promising but eventually failed against Spain's similar aims. By the middle of the 1500s only Venice remained independent from Spain. The biggest winner was the Habsburg King Charles V of Spain (r. 1516–1558), who ended the imperial ambitions of King Francis I (r. 1515–1547) of France when the pope, handsomely bribed with Habsburg loans, bestowed the crown of the Holy Roman Empire (Germany, Austria, and the Netherlands) on Charles. Habsburg rounded off its territories in 1526 with the acquisition of Bohemia and the non-Ottoman portion of Hungary. But its lack of territorial cohesion limited its fiscal–military effectiveness.

In northern and eastern Europe, a similar sorting out occurred. England lost Calais, its last toehold on the European continent, to France in 1558. Militarily uninvolved on the Continent and with no need for a standing army, it fell behind in its evolution toward a fiscal–military state. The rising territorial kingdom of Poland–Lithuania (an elective kingdom after 1569) assumed control over a number of Baltic cities of the Hanseatic League and absorbed the lands of the Teutonic Order in 1525 as the duchy of Prussia. When united with Brandenburg in 1618, Prussia evolved into a potent fiscal–military kingdom independent from Poland. On the other side of the Baltic Sea, the union of the Scandinavian countries broke apart when Sweden, with the invasion of Danish Stockholm in 1526, declared its fiscal–military ambitions. On the eastern periphery, the Russian ruler Ivan IV, the Terrible (r. 1533–1584), took the title of emperor (*tsar*, from Latin for "caesar") in 1547 and embarked on a program of conquest which later made Russia a full-fledged fiscal–military rival of the Ottoman Empire.

Military and Administrative Capacities   The fiscal–military kingdoms which arose in the sixteenth century remained at the forefront of military innovation. In the course of the century, some kingdoms turned their mercenary troops into standing armies and stationed them in star-shaped forts, a fifteenth-century Italian innovation that made walls more resistant to artillery fire and trapped attackers in cross fires. Sweden introduced the line infantry in the mid-seventeenth century. In this strategy, three-deep lines of musketeers advanced on a broad front toward the enemy, with the front line firing, stepping back to reload, and making room for the next two lines to step forward and repeat the action. These forces underwent extensive peacetime drills and maneuvers. They wore uniforms and soon fired bayonet-equipped flintlock muskets, both introduced in the late seventeenth century in France. Pikemen, equipped with thrusting spears-cum-battle-axes for the protection of musketeers in hand-to-hand combat, were phased out with the appearance of the bayonet. By 1750, armies in the larger European countries were both more uniform and more numerous, increasing from a few thousand to hundreds of thousands of soldiers (see Map 17.1).

Musketeers. These pictures from an English illustrated drill manual demonstrate the steps by which a 17th-century musketeer "makes ready" his weapon, typically in less than 30 seconds. In battle, a sergeant would stand alongside each company of musketeers, organizing its movements and volley fire. Once a rank of musketeers had discharged its weapons it would move out of the way for another rank to fire. If combat was joined at close quarters, the musketeers would use their rifle butts as clubs.

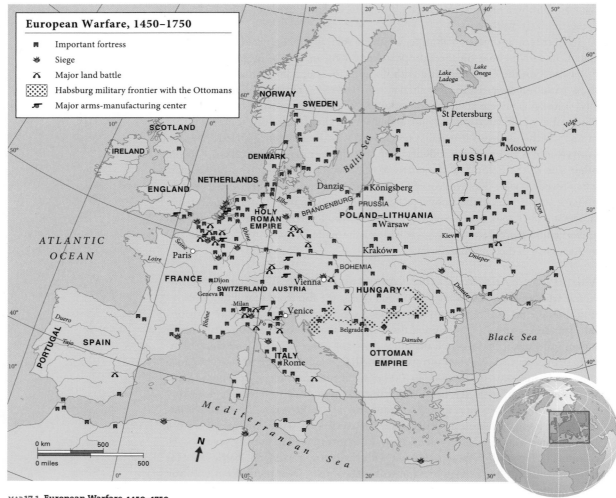

MAP **17.1** European Warfare, **1450–1750**.

The military forces devoured copious amounts of tax money. Accordingly, taxes expanded substantially during the period 1450–1550. But rulers could not raise land, head, and commerce taxes without the formal (in assemblies) or informal (based on customs and traditions) assent of the ruling classes and cities. Similarly, villagers voted with their feet when taxes became too oppressive. The taxation limits were reached in most European countries in the mid-sixteenth century, and for the next two centuries rulers could raise additional finances only to the detriment of their previously acquired central powers, such as by borrowing from merchants and selling offices. The Netherlands was an exception. Only there did the urban population rise from 10 to 20 percent, willing to pay higher taxes on expanded urban manufactures and commercial suburban farming. The Dutch government also derived substantial revenues from charters granted to armed overseas trading companies. Given the severe limits on revenue-raising measures in most of Europe, the eighteenth century saw a general deterioration of state finances, which eventually became a major contributing factor to the American and French Revolutions.

The Protestant Reformation, State Churches, and Independent Congregations

Parallel to the growing centralism of the kings, the popes restored the central role of the Vatican in the church hierarchy, after the devastating Great Schism of competing papal lines (1305–1415). Outwardly, the popes displayed this restoration through expensive Vatican construction projects that aroused considerable criticism outside Rome, especially in Germany where the leading clergy under a weak emperor was more strongly identified with Rome than elsewhere. Growing literacy and lay religiosity helped in the growth of a profound theological dissatisfaction which exploded in the **Protestant Reformation**. The Reformation began as an antipapal movement of reform in the early sixteenth century that demanded a return to the simplicity of early Christianity. The movement quickly engulfed the fiscal–military kingdoms and divided their ruling classes and populations alike. Vicious religious wars were the consequence. Although these wars eventually subsided, the divisions were never healed completely and mark the culture of many areas in Europe even today.

Background to the Reformation　　Several religious and political changes in the fifteenth century led to the Protestant Reformation. One important religious shift was the growth of popular religiosity, a consequence of the introduction of the printing press (1454/55) and the distribution of printed materials. A flood of devotional tracts catered to the spiritual interests of ordinary people. Many Christians attended mass daily, confessed, and did penance for their sins. Wealthy Christians endowed saint cults, charitable institutions, or confraternities devoted to the organization of processions and passion plays. Poor people formed lay groups or studied scripture on their own and devoted themselves to the simple life of the early Christians. More Europeans than in previous centuries had a basic, though mostly literal, understanding of Christianity.

An important political change in the fifteenth century was an increasing inability for the popes, powerful in Rome, to appoint archbishops and bishops outside Italy. The kings of France, Spain, England, and Sweden were busy transforming their kingdoms into centralized fiscal–military states, in which they reduced the influence of the popes. Only in Germany, where the powers of the emperor and the rulers in the various principalities canceled each other out, was the influence of the popes still strong. What remained to the popes was the right to collect a variety of dues in the kingdoms of Europe. They used these dues to finance their expensive and, in the eyes of many, luxuriously worldly administration and court in Rome, from which they engaged in European politics. One of the dues was the sale of **indulgences**, which, in popular understanding, were tickets to heaven. Many contemporary observers found the discrepancy between declining papal power and the remaining financial privileges disturbing and demanded reforms.

Luther's Reformation　　One such observer was Martin Luther (1483–1546), an Augustinian monk, ordained priest, and New Testament professor in northeastern Germany. Luther was imbued with deep personal piety and confessed his sins daily, doing extensive penance. After a particularly egregious sale of indulgences in his area, in 1517 he wrote his archbishop a letter with 95 theses in which he branded the indulgences and other matters as contrary to scripture. Friends translated the theses from Latin into German and made them public. What was to become the Protestant Reformation had begun.

Protestant Reformation: Broad movement to reform the Roman Catholic Church, the beginnings of which are usually associated with Martin Luther.

Indulgence: Partial remission of sins after payment of a fine. The payment would mean the forgiveness of sins by the church, but the sinner still remained responsible for his or her sins before God.

Anti-Catholic Propaganda.
This anonymous woodcut of 1520 by a German satirist depicts the devil (complete with wings and clawed feet) sitting on a letter of indulgence and holding a money collection box. The devil's mouth is filled with sinners who presumably bought letters of indulgence in good faith, thinking they had been absolved from their sins.

News of Luther's public protest traveled quickly across Europe. Sales of indulgences fell off sharply. In a series of writings, Luther spelled out the details of the church reform he envisaged. One reform proposal was the elevation of original New Testament scripture over tradition, that is, over canon law and papal decisions. Salvation was to be by faith alone; good works were irrelevant. Another reform was the declaration of the priesthood of all Christians, doing away with the privileged position of the clergy as mediators between God and believers who could forgive sins. A third reform was a call to German princes to begin church reform in their own lands through their power over clerical appointments, even if the Habsburg emperor was opposed. Finally, by translating the Bible into German, Luther made the full sacred text available to all who, by reading or listening, wanted to rely solely on scripture as the source of their faith. Luther's Bible was a monument of the emerging literary German language. A forceful and clear writer in his translation and own publications, Luther fully explicated the basics of Protestantism.

Reaction to Luther's Demands Both emperor and pope failed in their efforts to arrest Luther and suppress his call for church reform. The duke of Saxony was successful in protecting the reformer from seizure. Emperor Charles V, a devout Catholic, considered Castile's successful church reform of half a century earlier to be fully sufficient. In his mind, Luther's demands for church reform were to be resisted. Two other pressing concerns, however, diverted the emperor's attention. First, the Ottoman-led Islamic threat, in eastern Europe and the western Mediterranean, had to be met with decisive action. Second, his rivalry with the French king precluded the formation of a common Catholic front against Luther. Enthusiastic villagers and townspeople in Germany exploited Charles' divided attention and abandoned both Catholicism and secular obedience. A savage civil war, called the "Peasants' War," engulfed Germany from 1524 to 1525, killing perhaps as many as 100,000 people.

Luther and other prominent reformers were horrified by the carnage. They drew up church ordinances that regulated preaching, church services, administrative councils, education, charity, and consistories for handling disciplinary matters. In Saxony, the duke endorsed this order in 1528. He thereby created the model of Lutheran Protestantism as a state religion, in which the rulers were protectors and supervisors of the churches in their territories. A decade later, Saxony was fully Lutheran.

A minority of about half a dozen German princes and the kings of Denmark and Sweden followed suit. In England, Protestants gained strength in the wake of Henry VIII's (r. 1509–1547) break with Rome and assumption of church leadership in his kingdom (1534). Although remaining Catholic, he surrounded himself with religious reformers and proclaimed an Anglican state church whose creed and rites combined elements of Catholicism and Protestantism. A similar pattern was followed in other states in northern Europe (except for France), where upon breaking with Catholicism they established state churches (see Map 17.2).

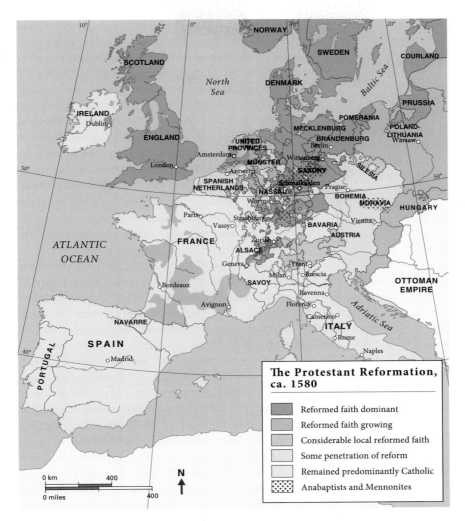

MAP **17.2** **The Protestant Reformation, ca. 1580.**

Calvinism in France   In France, as in England, the king controlled all church appointments. King Francis I, however, did not take the final step toward the creation of an independent state church. Since he competed with Charles V for dominance over the papacy in Italy, he had to appear especially loyal and devout. When a few Protestants in France went public with their demands for church reform, Francis I gave them the stark choice of exile or burning at the stake. One reformer who chose exile was the French lawyer John Calvin (1509–1564, Fr. Jean Cauvin). Calvin went to republican Switzerland, where, in the absence of a central state authority, magistrates implemented the Protestant Reformation in a number of cities.

In Geneva, the magistrates called on Calvin to help them devise a strict Protestant moral code, which they introduced in 1541. The city was under the nominal rule of the duke of Savoy (himself under the nominal rule of the Habsburgs) and not yet part of Switzerland. As expressed in Calvin's central work, *Institutes of the Christian Religion* (1536), and numerous other writings, a crucial doctrine of Calvin's was *predestination*. According to this doctrine, God has "predestined"

> ### Ignatius of Loyola on Free Will and Good Works
>
> "... [W]e ought not to speak so lengthily and emphatically about grace that we generate a poison harmful to freedom of the will. Hence one may speak about faith and grace as much as possible, with God's help, for the greater praise of his Divine Majesty; but not in such ways or manners, especially in times as dangerous as our own, that works and free will are impaired or thought worthless."
>
> —Ignatius of Loyola, *Spiritual Exercises and Selected Works*, p. 213. Translated by George E. Ganss. New York: Paulist Press, 1991.

each human prior to birth for heaven or hell. Believers could only hope, through faith alone, that sometime during a life of moral living they would receive a glimpse of their fate. In contrast to Luther, however, Calvin made the enforcement of morality through a formal moral code, administered by local authorities, part of his version of Protestantism. Calvin died in his Genevan exile, but Geneva-trained Calvinist preachers went to France and the Netherlands in the mid-1500s. Under the protection of local magistrates, they organized the first clandestine independent Calvinist congregations. Calvinist religious self-organization by independent congregations thus became a viable alternative to Lutheran state religion.

The Counter-Reformation   The rivalry between Spain and France made it initially difficult for the popes to tackle the problem of Catholic reforms in order to meet the Protestant challenge. When they finally called together the Council of Trent (1545–1563), they abolished payment for indulgences and phased out other church practices considered to be corrupt. These actions launched the **Counter-Reformation**, an effort to gain back lapsed Catholics. Supported by the kings of Spain and France, however, the popes reaffirmed the doctrines of faith together with good works, priestly mediation between believer and God, and monasticism. They even tightened church control through the revival of the papal Inquisition and a new Index of Prohibited Books. To counterbalance these punitive institutions, the popes furthered the work of the Basque priest Ignatius Loyola (1491–1556). At the head of the new order of the Society of Jesus, or "Jesuits," Loyola devoted himself tirelessly to the education of the clergy, establishment of a network of Catholic schools and colleges, and conversion of Protestants as well as non-Christians by missionaries to the Americas and eastern Asia. Thanks to Jesuit discipline, Catholics regained a semblance of self-assurance.

Counter-Reformation: Reaffirmation of the Catholic papal supremacy and the doctrine of faith together with works as preparatory to salvation; such practices as absenteeism (bishops in Rome instead of their bishoprics) and pluralism (bishops and abbots holding multiple appointments) were abolished.

Religious Wars and Political Restoration

The growth of Calvinism led to a civil war in France and to a war of liberation from Spanish Catholic rule in the Netherlands in the later sixteenth century. In England, the slow pace of reform in the Anglican Church, with which neither Calvinists nor Catholics could identify, erupted in the early seventeenth century into a civil war. In Germany, the Catholic–Protestant struggle turned into the devastating Thirty Years' War (1618–1648), which France and Sweden won at the expense of the Habsburgs. On the religious level, western Christians grudgingly accepted denominational toleration; on the political level, the fiscal–military states evolved into polities based on a combination between absolutist and decentralized administrative practices.

Civil War in France   During the mid-1500s, Calvinism in France grew to about 1,200 congregations, mostly in the western cities of the kingdom, where literate merchants and craftspeople catering to trade overseas were receptive to Protestant publications. Calvinism was essentially an urban denomination, and peasants did not join in large numbers. Some 2 million, or 10 percent of the total population of

18.5 million, were "Huguenots," as the Protestants were called in France. They continued to be persecuted, but given their numbers, it was impossible for the government to imprison and execute them all. In 1571, they even met in a kingdom-wide synod, where they ratified their congregational church order. They posed a formidable challenge to French Catholicism.

In many cities, relations between Huguenots and Catholics were uneasy. From time to time, groups of agitators crashed each other's church services. The arrival of a child king to the French throne in 1560 was an open invitation to escalate hostilities. In vain, the queen mother, Catherine de' Medici (1519–1589), who acted as the king's regent, offered a compromise. She issued a decree that legitimized Huguenot church services, provided they took place outside cities. In defiance of this decree, in 1562 a band of Catholics under the leadership of the duke of Lorraine of the Guise family slaughtered 74 Huguenots during a church service in the small town of Vassy in northeastern France. This massacre, crying out for revenge, was the first round in a cycle of destructive religious warfare in France that lasted for over a generation, from 1562 to 1598.

As in the case of the Peasants' War in Germany (1524–1525), the French war of religion was a vicious affair in which each party claimed to have God on its side. Aristocracy and commoners showed no mercy in their religious frenzy, often mutilating the bodies of massacred men, women, and children alike. The first three rounds of war ended with the victorious Huguenots achieving full freedom of religious practice and self-government in four western cities. Given this situation, Catherine de' Medici renewed her attempts at compromise. She arranged in 1572 for the marriage of her daughter to King Henry III of Navarre (later King Henry IV of France, 1589–1610), a Protestant of the Bourbon family in southwestern France. Henry had risen to the leadership of the Huguenots a few years earlier, but he detested the fanaticism that surrounded him.

The prospect of a Huguenot king drove the Catholic aristocracy into a renewed frenzy of religious persecution. On St. Bartholomew's Day (August 24, 1572), just 6 days after the wedding of the future Henry IV, they perpetrated a wholesale slaughter of thousands of Huguenots. This massacre, in response to the assassination of a French admiral, occurred with the apparent connivance of the queen. For over

Wars of Religion. The massacre of 74 Huguenots (as the Calvinists were called in France) in the town of Vassy east of Paris in 1562 was the opening salvo in the French wars of religion. The Huguenots held religious services in a barn when followers of Francis, duke of Guise, fell into a quarrel with the unarmed Calvinists and the duke was hit by a stone, inciting a bloody revenge.

a decade and a half, civil war raged, in which Spain aided the Catholics and Henry enrolled German and Swiss Protestant mercenaries.

A turning point came only in 1589 when Henry of Navarre became King Henry IV. Surviving nearly three dozen plots against his life, the new king needed 9 years and two conversions to Catholicism—"Paris is well worth a Mass," he is supposed to have quipped—before he was able to calm the religious fanaticism among the majority of French people. With the Edict of Nantes in 1598, he decreed freedom of religion for Protestants. A number of staunch Catholic adherents were deeply offended by the edict as well as the alleged antipapal policies of Henry IV. The king fell victim to an assassin in 1610. Catholic resentment continued until 1685, when King Louis XIV revoked the edict and triggered a large-scale emigration of Huguenots to the Netherlands, Germany, and England. At last, France was Catholic again.

Dutch War of Independence   In the Netherlands, the Counter-Reformation Spanish overlords were even more determined to keep the country Catholic than the French monarchs prior to Henry IV. When Charles V resigned in 1556 (effective 1558), his son Philip II (r. 1556–1598) became king of Spain and the Netherlands, consisting of the French-speaking regions of Wallonia in the south and the Dutch-speaking regions of Flanders and Holland in the north. Like his father, Philip was a staunch supporter of the Counter-Reformation. He asked the Jesuits and the Inquisition to aggressively persecute the Calvinists. For better effect, Philip subdivided the bishoprics into smaller units and recruited clergymen in place of members of the nobility. In response, in 1565 the nobility and Calvinist congregations rose in revolt. They dismantled the bishoprics and cleansed the churches of images and sculptures, thereby triggering what was to become a Protestant war of Dutch liberation from Catholic Spanish overlordship (1565–1620). Philip retaliated by sending in an army that succeeded in suppressing the liberation movement, reimposing Catholicism, and executing thousands of rebels, many of them members of the Dutch aristocracy.

Remnants of the rebellion struggled on and, in 1579, renewed the war of liberation in three of the 17 northern provinces making up the Netherlands. Later joined by four more provinces, the people in these breakaway regions called themselves members of the "United Provinces of the Dutch Republic." Spain refused to recognize the republic and kept fighting until acute Spanish financial difficulties prompted the truce of 1609–1621. But the truce collapsed at the outbreak of the Thirty Years' War, and the Netherlands were drawn into the European conflagration. Spain eventually relinquished its claims only in 1648, when the European powers ended the Thirty Years' War with the peace settlement of Westphalia.

At the head of the Dutch republic was a governor (*stadhouder*) from the House of Orange-Nassau, one of the leading aristocratic families of the Netherlands. The representative body, with which the stadhouder governed, was the States-General and the privileged religious body was the Calvinist Dutch Reformed Church. In the Netherlands, about 20 percent of the population of 1 million was Calvinist, double the percentage in France and England. But there were also sizeable groups of Catholics and other Protestants. Among the latter, the Anabaptists and Mennonites (characterized by the doctrines of adult baptism and pacifism, respectively) were prominent. The Netherlands was also a haven for Jews, who had originally arrived there after their expulsion from Spain and Portugal in 1492–1498. Gradually, the

Dutch accepted each other's doctrinal differences and the Netherlands became a model of religious tolerance.

Civil War in England

As in the Netherlands, the dominant form of Protestantism in England was Calvinism. During the sixteenth century, the Calvinists numbered about 10 percent in a kingdom in which the Anglican Church encompassed the majority of subjects in a total population of 6 million. English Catholics, who refused to recognize the king as the head of the Anglican Church, numbered 3 percent. The percentage of Calvinists was the same as in France, but the partially reformed Anglican Church was able to hold them in check. The Calvinists were, furthermore, a fractious group, encompassing moderate and radical tendencies which neutralized each other. Among the radicals were the Puritans, who demanded the abolition of the Anglican clerical hierarchy and a new church order of independent congregations. Other radicals, such as the Diggers, demanded distribution of land from the commons. In the early seventeenth century, when Anglican Church reform slowed under the Catholic successors of Elizabeth I (r. 1558–1603), the Puritan cause began to acquire traction. Realizing that these Stuart successors and their bishops were immovable, some Puritans emigrated to North America rather than continue to chafe under the Anglican yoke. Other Puritans began to agitate openly.

Along with their efforts to restrain would-be reformers, the Stuart kings were busy building their version of the fiscal–military state. They collected taxes without the approval of Parliament. Many members resented being bypassed since Parliament was the constitutional cosovereign of the kingdom. A slight majority in the House of Commons was Puritan, and the stalled church reform added to their resentment. Eventually, when all tax resources were exhausted, the king, Charles I (r. 1625–1649), had to call Parliament back together. Mutual resentment was so deep, however, that the two sides were unable to make any decisions on either financial or religious matters. The standoff erupted into civil war, which cost the king his life and ended the monarchy.

Despite the brutal fate of Charles I, the English civil war of 1642–1651 was generally less vicious than that in France. Nevertheless, because of widespread pillage and destruction of crops and houses, the indirect effects of the war were severe for the population of thousands of villages. The New Model Army, a professional body of 22,000 troops raised by the Puritan-dominated Parliament against the king, caused further upheavals by cleansing villages of their "frivolous" seasonal festivals,

Religious Toleration in the Netherlands

"The great care of this state has ever been, to favour no particular or curious Inquisition into the faith or religious principles of any peaceable man, who came to live under the protection of their laws, and to suffer no violence or oppression upon any man's conscience.... It is hardly to be imagined how all the violence and sharpness which accompanies the difference of Religion in other countries, seems to be appeased or softened here, by the general freedom which all men enjoy ..."

—Sir William Temple. *Observations upon the United Provinces of the Netherlands*, ed. Sir George Clark, pp. 103 and 106. Oxford: Oxford University Press, 1972.

Frivolous Pagan Customs. During the English Civil War, Oliver Cromwell and the New Model Army espoused many Puritan doctrines, including the need to fight "frivolous" pagan customs deeply entrenched in village culture. In this woodcut from 1653, Father Christmas finds himself caught between the two opposing sides.

deeply rooted in local pagan traditions and featuring pranks, games, dances, drunkenness, and free-wheeling behavior. A republican theocracy emerged, with preachers enforcing Calvinist morality in the population.

Republic, Restoration, and Revolution

The ruler of this theocracy, Oliver Cromwell (r. 1649–1658), was a Puritan member of the lower nobility (the gentry) and a commander in the New Model Army. After dissolving Parliament, Cromwell handpicked a new parliament but ruled for the most part without its consent. Since both Scotland and Ireland had opposed the Puritans in the civil war, Cromwell waged a brutal war of submission against the Scottish Presbyterians (Calvinists organized in a state church) and Irish Catholics. The Dutch and Spanish, also opponents of the Puritans in the civil war, were defeated in naval wars that substantially improved English shipping power in the Atlantic. But the rising fear among the gentry in Parliament of a permanent fiscal–military state led Cromwell's parliament to refuse further funds. After Cromwell's death in 1658, it took just 3 years for the restoration of the Stuart monarchy and the Anglican state church to their previous places.

The recalled kings in the Restoration of 1661–1688 resumed the policies of fiscal–military centralism and Catholicism. As before, the kings called Parliament together only sparingly and raised funds without its authorization. Their standing army of 30,000, partially stationed near London, was intended more to intimidate the parliamentarians than to actually wage war. In the "Glorious Revolution" of 1688 the defiant Parliament, dominated since the Restoration by mostly Anglican gentry, deposed the Catholic king, James II (r. 1685–1688). It feared that the recent birth of a royal son threatened the succession of the king's daughter by his first marriage, Mary, a Protestant married to William of Nassau-Orange, the *stadhouder* of the Netherlands. It offered the throne to William and Mary as joint monarchs, and the Stuarts went into exile in France.

Outbreak of the Thirty Years' War

As religious tensions were mounting in England during the early seventeenth century, they erupted into a full-blown war in Germany, the second such conflagration in a century. As we saw earlier, Lutheran Protestantism had become the state religion in a majority of the two dozen largest and most powerful princely German states. Lutheran minorities were generally free to practice their religion in the Catholic German states. Not all rulers, however, were satisfied with the status quo among the princes. One of these rulers was the Jesuit-educated Ferdinand II (r. 1619–1637), ruler of the Holy Roman Empire, who resented the century-old religious freedoms enjoyed in Bohemia by Protestants. As newly elected king of Bohemia (and before becoming emperor), he began to exclude members of the Protestant aristocracy from administrative offices in re-Catholicized cities of the Bohemian kingdom. In response, Protestant leaders in 1618 unceremoniously threw two Habsburg emissaries out of a window of the Prague castle (the "Defenestration of Prague") and made the Calvinist prince of Palatinate in the Rhineland their new king. With these events in Bohemia, open hostilities between religious groups began in Germany.

Ferdinand and the Catholic princes suppressed the Bohemian rebellion in 1619, confiscated the properties of the Protestant aristocracy, and officially converted the kingdom to Catholicism. An imperial army of over 100,000 men chased the Calvinist prince not only from Prague but also from Palatinate and advanced toward northern Germany, capturing further territories for reconversion to Catholicism. When the Danish king intervened in favor of Lutheranism, he was crushed and the Protestant cause seemed to be doomed.

Outside Powers and the Peace of Westphalia

In 1630, however, the Lutheran king Gustavus II Adolphus (r. 1611–1632) of Sweden decided to intervene. The king's main goal was the completion of a Swedish-Lutheran fiscal–military state around the Baltic Sea, a project begun before the Thirty Years' War. By aiding the German Lutherans, he hoped to consolidate or even enlarge his predominance in the region. Louis XIII (r. 1610–1643) of France granted Sweden financial subsidies since he was concerned that Ferdinand's victories would further strengthen the Habsburg Spanish–Flemish–Austrian–German–Italian grip around France. For the French, the fact that Gustavus Aldolphus was a Protestant was secondary to the intra-Catholic rivalry between the Habsburgs and France. With the politically motivated alliance between Sweden and France, the German Catholic-Protestant war turned into a war for state dominance in Europe.

Fiscal–Military States at War. German imperial troops besiege Swedish troops in the northern German city of Stralsund in 1628. The etching shows typical features of the fiscal–military state, from top to bottom: galleon-style warships (successors of the caravel); a star-shaped fort (an Italian innovation) designed to withstand artillery barrages; the medieval walls of the city; musket-equipped infantry troops; field cannons; and the colorful Baroque uniforms worn by the musketeers of the period.

At first, Swedish troops turned the situation in favor of the Protestants. Gustavus Adolphus advanced victoriously as far as Bavaria in the south. On the verge of a final victory, however, the king fell in battle and the Swedes withdrew to northern Germany. In a position of renewed strength but fearful of a French entry into the war, Ferdinand II decided to compromise with the Protestant princes of Germany. In the peace of 1635, the two sides agreed to a return to the prewar territorial division between Catholic and Protestant princes in northern Germany.

Since the French were determined to break the Habsburg grip, they now entered the war. During the next 13 years, French armies sought to cut the Habsburg supply lines from Italy to the Netherlands by occupying Habsburg Alsace. Swedish armies, exploiting the French successes against the Habsburgs, fought their way back into Germany. In the end, the Austrian–German Habsburgs, pressured on two sides, agreed in October 1648 to the Peace of Westphalia. They allowed religious freedom in Germany and ceded territories in Alsace to France and the southern side of the Baltic Sea to Sweden. The Spanish Habsburgs, however, continued their war against France until 1659, when they also bowed to superior French strength, giving up parts of Flanders and northeastern Spain. France now emerged as the strongest power in Europe (see Map 17.3).

Absolutism in France?

During its period of greatest political dominance, France came under the rule of its longest reigning monarch, King Louis XIV (1643–1715). He was of small stature—for which he compensated with high-heeled

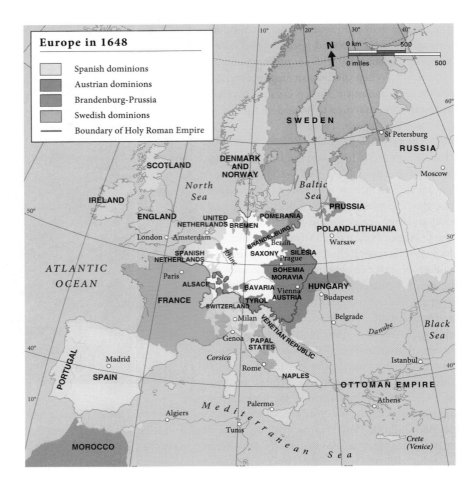

Europe in 1648

- Spanish dominions
- Austrian dominions
- Brandenburg-Prussia
- Swedish dominions
- —— Boundary of Holy Roman Empire

MAP 17.3 Europe in 1648.

shoes—but his hardy constitution and strong self-discipline helped him to dominate even the most grueling meetings with his advisors. He enjoyed pomp and circumstance and built Versailles—his gigantic palace and gardens near Paris, populated with 10,000 courtiers, attendants, and servants—into a site of almost continuous feasting, entertainment, and intrigue. It was here that Louis, the "Sun King," beamed benevolently with his "absolute" divine mandate upon his aristocracy and commoners alike. Versailles played an important role in Louis's efforts to undercut the power of the nobility. Anyone with any aspirations of attracting the king's attention had to come to the palace to attend him. By keeping both friends and potential enemies close by and forcing them to spend lavishly to stay abreast of the fashions inspired by the king and vie for his attention, he was able, like the Tokugawa shoguns in Edo, Japan, to bypass them administratively and rule through central bureaucratic institutions.

Absolutism: Theory of the state in which the unlimited power of the king under God is emphasized.

In practice, the French **absolutism** of Louis XIV and his eighteenth-century successors, as well as practitioners in other European countries, was a complex mixture of centralized and decentralized forces. On the one hand, after the end of the religious wars in 1648, mercenary armies under autonomous dukes and counts disappeared from the European scene, replaced by permanent armies or navies under the central command of fiscal–military royal or princely dynasties. The kings also no longer called their respective assemblies of nobles and notables together to have new taxes approved (in France from 1614 to 1789), and thus, many of the nobility's tax privileges disappeared.

On the other hand, the kings of the seventeenth century were acutely aware that true absolutism was possible only if centrally salaried employees collected taxes. It was physically impossible to transport tax revenues, in the form of silver money and grain, from the provinces to the capital, pay the central bureaucrats, and then cart the remaining revenues back to the provinces to pay salaried tax collectors there. A centrally paid bureaucracy would have required a central bank with provincial branches, using paper money. The failed experiment with such a bank in Paris from 1714 to 1720 demonstrates one such effort to find a solution to the central salary problem. But the bank's short life demonstrates that absolute central control was beyond the powers of the kings and princes.

Instead, the kings had to rely on subcontracting most offices and the collection of most taxes out to the highest bidders, who then helped themselves to the collection of their incomes. Under Louis XIV, a total of 46,000 administrative jobs were available for purchase in Paris and the provinces. Anyone who had money, or borrowed it from financiers, was encouraged to buy an office—from the old aristocracy of the "sword," receiving rents from the farmers on their rural estates, to ordinary merchant sons with law degrees, borrowing money from their fathers. Once in office, the government often forced these officers to grant additional loans to the crown. To retain their loyalty,

Versailles. Built between 1676 and 1708 on the outskirts of Paris, Versailles emphatically demonstrated the new centralized power of the French monarchy. The main building is a former hunting lodge that Louis XIV decorated with mythological scenes that showed him as the "Sun King." The outer wings housed government offices. Behind the palace, elaborate entertainments were held in the gardens.

the government rewarded them with first picks for retaining their offices within the family, buying landed estates, or acquiring titles of nobility to the secondary (and less prestigious) tier of the "nobility of the robe" (as opposed to the first-tier "nobility of the sword," which by the seventeenth century was demilitarized).

About the only way for Louis XIV to keep the semblance of a watchful eye on the honesty of the officeholders was to send salaried, itinerant *intendants* around the provinces to ensure that collecting taxes, rendering justice, and policing functioned properly within the allowable limits of "the venality of office," as the subcontracting system was called. Louis XIV had roughly one intendant for each province. About half of the provinces had *parlements*—appointed assemblies for the ratification of decrees from Paris—whose officeholders, drawn from the local noble, clerical, and commoner classes, frequently resisted the intendants. The Paris *parlement* even refused to accept royal writs carried by the intendants. In later years, when Louis XIV was less successful in his many wars against the rival Habsburgs and Protestant Dutch, the crown overspent and had to borrow heavily with little regard for the future. Louis's successors in the first half of the eighteenth century were saddled with crippling debts. French-inspired European "absolutism" was thus in practice a careful (or not so careful) balancing act between the forces of centralization and decentralization in the fiscal–military states of Europe.

The Rise of Russia Although France's absolutism was more theory than practice, its glorious ideological embodiment by the Versailles of Louis XIV spawned adaptations across Europe. These adaptations were most visible in eastern Europe, which was populated more thinly and had far fewer towns and cities. Since rulers in those areas did not have a large reservoir of urban commoners to aid them as administrators in adopting the fiscal–military state, they had to make do with the landowning aristocracy. As a result, the villagers who in agrarian society bore the brunt of taxation were more exposed to the absolutist aspirations of the rulers and their administrators than in western Europe.

In Russia, Tsar Peter I, the Great (r. 1682–1725), of the eastern Christian Romanov dynasty, was a towering figure who singlehandedly sought to establish the

A World Turned Upside Down.
In this popular satirical woodcut of 1766, based on a similar woodcut from the early 1700s, the mice are capturing and burying the cat: In other words, Peter the Great has turned the world upside down with his reforms.

fiscal–military state during his lifetime. At nearly 7 feet tall, Peter was an imposing, energetic ruler, controllable only by his second wife (and former mistress) Catherine, a warmhearted woman and beloved tsarina. Peter invited western European soldiers, mariners, administrators, craftspeople, scholars, and artists into his service and succeeded within just a few years in building a disciplined army and imposing navy. He built ports on the Baltic Sea and established the new capital of St. Petersburg, distinguished by many very beautiful palaces and official buildings. A typical example among thousands invited to Russia by the tsar was Peter von Sivers, a Danish mariner (and ancestor of one of the coauthors of the book) who rose to the position of vice admiral in the Baltic fleet that broke Swedish dominance in northern Europe. Since the tsar was not able to pay these advisors salaries (any more than Louis XIV could pay salaries to advisors to the French court), he gave many western guests estates with serfs in the Baltic provinces and Finland, conquered from Sweden, and made them aristocrats in his retinue.

The Russian military was completely reorganized by the tsar. After a rebellion early on, Peter savagely decimated the inherited firearm regiments and made them part of a new army recruited from the traditional Russian landed nobility. Both classes of soldiers received education at military schools and academies and were required to provide lifelong service. In order to make his soldiers look more urban, Peter decreed that they shave their traditional beards and wear European uniforms or clothes. Every twentieth peasant household had to deliver one foot soldier to conscription. A census was taken to facilitate the shift from the inherited household tax on the villagers to a new capitation tax collected by military officers. In the process, many free farmers outside the estate system of the aristocracy found themselves classified and taxed as serfs, unfree to leave their villages. The result of Peter's reforms was a powerful, expansionary fiscal–military state that played an increasingly important role among European kingdoms during the eighteenth century (see Map 17.4).

The Rise of Prussia   Similar to Russia, the principality of Prussia-Brandenburg was underurbanized. It had furthermore suffered destruction and depopulation during the Thirty Years' War. When the Lutheran Hohenzollern dynasty embarked on the construction of a fiscal–military state in the later seventeenth century, they first broke the tax privileges of the landowning aristocracy in the estates-general and raised taxes themselves. As in Russia, farmers who worked on estates held by landlords were serfs. Since there were few urban middle-class merchants and professionals, the kings enrolled members of the landlord aristocracy in the army and civilian administration.

Elevated by the Habsburg Holy Roman emperor to the status of kings in 1701, the Hohenzollern rulers systematically enlarged the army, employing it during peacetime for drainage and canal projects as well as palace construction in Berlin, the capital. Under

Prussian Military Discipline. The Prussian line infantry made full use in the mid-1700s of flintlock muskets, bayonets, and drilling. Most of the drilling concerned the rotation of the front line with the rear lines after salvos, for the purpose of reloading. The introduction of the bayonet made pikemen—infantry with long thrusting spears employed to protect the musketeers from hand-to-hand combat—obsolete.

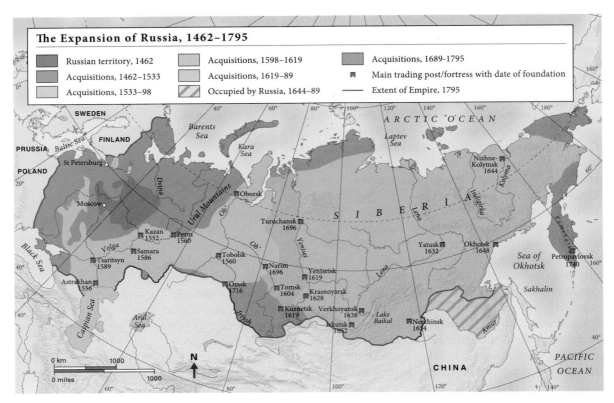

The Expansion of Russia, 1462–1795

- Russian territory, 1462
- Acquisitions, 1462–1533
- Acquisitions, 1533–98
- Acquisitions, 1598–1619
- Acquisitions, 1619–89
- Occupied by Russia, 1644–89
- Acquisitions, 1689–1795
- ⌂ Main trading post/fortress with date of foundation
- — Extent of Empire, 1795

MAP 17.4 **The Expansion of Russia, 1462–1795.**

Frederick II, the Great (1740–1786), Prussia pursued an aggressive foreign policy, capturing Silesia from the Habsburgs in a military campaign. Frederick also expended major efforts into attracting immigrants, intensifying agriculture, and establishing manufacturing enterprises. Prussia emerged as a serious competitor of the Habsburgs in the Holy Roman Empire of Germany.

English Constitutionalism   In contrast to Prussia, France, Spain, Austria, and other European states, England had since 1450 a political system ruled by a king or a queen, with a parliament composed of the aristocracy as well as representatives of towns and cities. Only in England did the interests of the nobility and the urban merchants gradually converge. Rulers on the European continent financed their early fiscal–military states through raising indirect taxes on sales, commerce, imports, and exports, affecting cities more than noble estates. In England, the cities allied with the aristocracy in resisting indirect tax increases and forcing the throne to use the less ample revenues of its royal estates to pay soldiers. Efforts of the Stuart kings to create a fiscal–military state based on firearm infantries failed. Instead, the ruling class preferred to build a naval fiscal–military state. After the Glorious Revolution of 1688, this state achieved dominance on the world's oceans.

After its victory over the Stuart kings, Parliament consolidated its fiscal–military powers through the creation of the Bank of England in 1694, two decades before a similar but ill-fated attempt in France. When first Mary and then William died without children, England continued in 1701 with a distantly related dynasty from the principality of Hannover in Germany. Under a new monarch, England and Scotland united in 1707, creating the "United Kingdom." Parliament collected higher taxes than France and, through its bank, was able to keep its debt service low. The navy grew twice as large as that of France and was staffed by a well-salaried, disciplined military, while the few land troops, deemed superfluous, were mostly low-paid Hessian-German mercenaries. A rudimentary two-party system of two aristocracy–merchant alliances came into being. The two parties were known as the Whigs and the Tories, the former more parliamentarian and the latter more royalist, with the Whigs in power for most of the first half of the eighteenth century.

Cultural Transformations: Renaissance, New Science, and Early Enlightenment

The rise of the fiscal–military state coincided with the **Renaissance**, a period of cultural formation which in the fifteenth century followed the scholastic Middle Ages in western Christianity. With state profits, rulers, courts, and merchants sponsored much of the arts and sciences that flourished during the Renaissance. In many ways, the Renaissance was an outgrowth of scholasticism, but its thinkers and artists saw themselves as people who had broken away from its precepts. They considered their period as a time of "rebirth" (which is the literal meaning of "renaissance" in French), during which they were powerfully influenced by the writings of Greek and Hellenistic-Roman authors who had been unknown during the scholastic age. In the sixteenth century, the Renaissance gave way to the Baroque in the arts and the **New Science** in astronomy and physics, which in turn produced the Enlightenment. Thus, the Renaissance was just the first of further periods of cultural formation following each other in rapid succession.

Renaissance: "Rebirth" of culture in its full sense, based on large-scale publications and translations of Greek, Hellenistic, and Roman authors whose writings were previously unknown in the West.

The Renaissance and Baroque Arts

Beginning around 1400 in Italy and spreading later through northwestern Europe, an outpouring of learning, scholarship, and art came from theologians, philosophers, writers, painters, architects, and musical composers. These thinkers and artists benefited from Greek and Hellenistic-Roman texts which scholars had discovered recently in mostly eastern Christian archives in Byzantium. In addition, in the early fifteenth century Byzantine scholars from Constantinople arrived in Italy with new texts, which exerted a profound impact. The emerging cultures of the Renaissance and Baroque were creative adaptations of those Greek and Hellenistic-Roman writings to the cultural heritage of western Christianity. Out of this vibrant mixture arose the overarching concept of **humanism**.

New Science: Changes in the practice of science inherited from the Middle Ages; the discovery of the Americas inspired Copernicus to abandon the Aristotelian theory of elements and adopt heliocentrism; Galileo then replaced Aristotelian descriptive science with mathematized science, through the law of falling bodies.

New Manuscripts and Printing   Byzantium experienced a cultural revival between its recovery in 1261 from the Latin interlude and its collapse in 1453 when the Ottomans conquered Constantinople. During this revival, for example, scholars engaged in a vigorous debate about the compatibility of Plato and Aristotle with each other. The debate made Italian scholars fully aware of how much of Greek literature was still absent from western Christianity; at the time, they possessed just two of Plato's 44 dialogues. Italians invited about a dozen eastern scholars, who brought manuscripts to Florence, Rome, and Venice to translate and to teach. Their students

Humanism: Intellectual movement focusing on human culture, in such fields as philosophy, philology, and literature, as based on the corpus of Greek and Roman texts.

Bookseller. By 1600, the increase in literacy levels combined with widespread printing of books, pamphlets, and tracts had made images like this itinerant bookseller in Italy a commonplace sight throughout much of Europe.

became fluent in Greek and translated Hesiod and Homer, the Greek tragedies and comedies, Plato and the Neo-Platonists, the remaining works of Aristotle, Hellenistic scientific texts, and the Greek church fathers. Western Christianity had finally absorbed the ancient heritage (see Table 17.1).

The work of translation was helped by the development of a more rounded, simplified Latin script, which replaced the angled, dense Gothic script used since the 1150s. In addition, the costly vellum (scraped leather) writing material on which many manuscripts had been laboriously written was replaced by cheaper paper, introduced from Islamic Spain in the early twelfth century and common in the rest of Europe by 1400, which allowed for more space on each page. Experimentation in the 1430s with movable metal typeface, arranged in frames and combined with traditional wooden presses for grape or olive crushing, resulted in the innovation of the printing press. The best known among the experimenters was the German Johannes Gutenberg (1398–1468), who printed the first Bible, still in Gothic script and with many copies in vellum, in 1454 or 1455. A half-century later, with more than 1,000 printers all over Europe and more than 8 million books in the hands of readers, a veritable printing revolution had taken place in Europe.

Table 17.1

First Appearance of Selected Ancient Greek Texts in Italy

1400	Homer, *Odyssey*; Plutarch, *Lives*; Thucydides, *History*
1402	Aristotle, *On the Soul*
1405	Plato, *Gorgias, Cratylus, Phaedo*; Ptolemy, *Geography*
1407	Aristotle, *Physics*
1415	Aristotle, *On the Parts of Animals, On the Heavens*
1416	Aristotle, *Nicomachean Ethics*
1417	Lucretius, *On the Nature of Things*
1418	Plato, *Protagoras*
1419	Aristotle (ascribed author), *Economics*
1421	Herodotus, *Histories*
1423	Plato, *Apology, Crito, Phaedrus*
1424	Plato, *The Republic*
1425	Aristotle, *Rhetoric*
1438	Aristotle, *Politics*
1440	Ptolemy, *On Astronomy*
1454	Plato, *Symposium*
1455	Aristotle, *Logic*; Euclid, *Geometry* (corrected retranslation)
1468	Archimedes, *Different Geometric Operations*; Euclid, *Elements*; Strabo, *Geography*

Philology and Political Theory   The flood of new manuscripts and the renewed examination of existing manuscripts in libraries encouraged the study of Greek, Latin, and Hebrew philology. Scholars trained in these languages edited definitive texts based on multiple manuscripts and exposed inauthentic texts. The best known among these philologists was the Dutchman Desiderius Erasmus (1466–1536), who published an edition of the Greek and Latin New Testaments in 1516. The most infamous fake text to be exposed was the so-called Donation of Constantine, which the Italian Lorenzo Valla (1407–1457) proved through textual criticism to have been a self-serving forgery favoring the papal claims to supreme authority in the Middle Ages. Critical textual research, which became central to all subsequent scholarship, can trace its foundations to the Renaissance.

Biting criticism also emerged as a central element in political thought. In *The Prince*, Niccolò Machiavelli (1469–1527) reflected on the ruthless political competition among the princes of Europe for dominance over his hopelessly disunited native Italy. What Italy needed, Machiavelli argued, was a unifier who practiced what Aristotle enumerated in Book 5 of his *Politics*, that is, an intuitive ability to take proper action when survival in power was at stake. He called this ability *virtù*, by which he meant the power instinct of a ruler to take any appropriate measure, forceful or subtle, in order to remain in control of the vicissitudes—or, in his words, the *fortuna*—of politics. The New Scientists rejected Aristotle and the majority of humanists preferred Plato over Aristotle, but Machiavelli remained faithful to Aristotle, the superior political realist—an Aristotle held in high esteem centuries later by the American founding fathers.

The Renaissance Arts   In Italy, the reception of the new texts of the fifteenth century was paralleled by a new artistic way of looking at the Roman past and the natural world. The first to adopt this perspective were the sculptor Donatello (ca. 1386–1466) and the architect Filippo Brunelleschi (1377–1446), who received their inspiration from Roman imperial statues and ruins. Donatello created the sculpture of the Apostle St. Mark (1411–1413), a freestanding, classically relaxed sculpture in a niche on the outside of the dome of Florence. In 1421, Brunelleschi began the construction of the classically and humanly dimensioned Church of San Lorenzo in Florence. Both Donatello and Brunelleschi inspired a legion of Italian artists in the fifteenth and sixteenth centuries.

The artistic triumvirate of the high Italian Renaissance included Leonardo da Vinci (1452–1519), Michelangelo (1475–1564), and Raphael (1483–1520), renowned for their paintings *The Last Supper, Mona Lisa, The Creation of Adam, The Last Judgment, Madonna del Granduca,* and *The School of Athens.* Michelangelo excelled also in sculpture, as evinced by his great *David* and the *Pietà*, as well as architecture, with the dome of St. Peter's. Inspired by the Italian creative outburst, the Renaissance flourished also in Germany, the Netherlands, and France, with such artists as Hieronymus Bosch (ca. 1450–1516), Albrecht Dürer (1471–1528), Hans Holbein the Younger (ca. 1497–1543), and Pieter Bruegel the Elder (ca. 1525–1569). With a bit of exaggeration one could conclude that sponsorship of the arts by the ruling classes became almost as competitive as victory in battle.

The earliest musical composers of the Renaissance in the first half of the fifteenth century were Platonists, who considered music a part of a well-rounded education. The difficulty, however, was that the music of the Greeks or Romans was completely unknown. A partial solution for this difficulty was found through emphasizing the

Renaissance Art. Brunelleschi's cupola for the cathedral of Florence, completed in 1436, was one of the greatest achievements of the early Renaissance (*a*). Raphael's *School of Athens* (1509–1510) depicts some 50 philosophers and scientists, with Plato (in red tunic) and Aristotle (blue) in the center of the painting (*b*). Peter Bruegel's *The Harvesters* (1565) shows peasants taking a lunch break (*c*).

relationship between the word—that is, rhetoric—and music, which coincided in the sixteenth century with the Protestant and Catholic demand for liturgical music. During this century, a huge output of hymns and masses in church music and *madrigals* (verses sung by unaccompanied voices) in secular music attests to this emphasis. The works of the Italian composer Giovanni Pierluigi da Palestrina (ca. 1525–1594) represent Renaissance music at its most exquisite. The two main characteristics of Palestrina's music were the consonant third and the development of counterpoint, that is, the development of divergent but harmonic parallel melodies—compositional elements which became foundations for the development of Western music.

The theater was a relatively late expression of the Renaissance. The popular mystery, passion, and morality plays from the centuries prior to 1400 continued in Catholic countries. In Italy, in the course of the fifteenth century, a secular popular theater, the *commedia dell'arte* emerged, often using masks and staging plays of forbidden love, jealousy, and adultery. In England during the sixteenth century the popular traveling theater troupes became stationary and professional, attracting playwrights who composed more elaborate plays. Sponsored by the aristocracy and the Elizabethan court, playwrights wrote hundreds of scripts—some 600 are still extant—beginning in the 1580s. The best known among these playwrights was William Shakespeare (1564–1616), who also acted in his tragedies and comedies. One of Shakespeare's innovations was the history play, which explored tragic flaws in rulers. Greek tragedy and comedy as well as the Italian commedia dell'arte were the English Renaissance's models, although with entirely new plots and characters suited to audiences of their own times.

The Baroque Arts   The Renaissance gave way around 1600 to the Baroque, which dominated the arts until about 1750. Two factors influenced its emergence.

First, the Protestant Reformation, Catholic Counter-Reformation, and religious wars changed the nature of patronage, on which architects, painters, and musicians depended. Many Protestant churches, opposed to imagery as incompatible with their view of early Christianity, did not sponsor artists for the adornment of their buildings with religious art. Wealthy urban merchants, often Protestant, stepped into the breach but avoided paintings with religious themes, preferring instead secular portraits, still lives, village scenes, and landscapes. The best-known representatives of these themes were Frans Hals (ca. 1580–1666), Rembrandt van Rijn (1606–1669), and Jan Vermeer (1632–1675). These painters were too creative to restrict themselves to secular themes, but they nevertheless were responsible for the rise of a nonreligious Baroque sensibility.

Second, the predilection for Renaissance measurement, balance, and restraint gave way in both Catholic and Protestant regions to greater spontaneity and dramatic effect, as visible in the paintings of the Catholics Peter Paul Rubens (1577–1640) and Diego Velázquez (1599–1660) and the Protestant Rembrandt. Even more pronounced was the parallel shift in church and palace architecture to a "baroque" voluptuousness of forms and decorations, exemplified by Bavarian and Austrian Catholic churches, the Versailles Palace, and St. Paul's Cathedral in London, all completed between 1670 and 1750. Baroque music, benefitting from ample church and palace patronage, experienced a veritable explosion of unrestrained exploration. New instruments, new forms (opera, cantata, oratorio, and concerto), and new melodic complexities characterized the Baroque style, culminating with Georg Philip Telemann (1681–1767), George Frederic Handel (1685–1759), and Johann Sebastian Bach (1685–1750). Prolific artistic creativity coincided with a tumultuous political period in Europe.

The Pioneers of the New Science

Eastern Christian scholars invited from Byzantium to Florence in Italy during the first half of the fifteenth century brought with them full sets of Platonic manuscripts, which stirred much interest among western Christian scholars. It did not take long for these scholars to realize that Plato was not fully compatible with Aristotle, whose writings had dominated the debates since the thirteenth century. Scholars also began to pay attention to other Greek authors outside the Aristotelian tradition, such as the scientist Archimedes. Eventually, three great scientific pioneers—Copernicus, Galileo, and Newton—overturned the *descriptive* science of Aristotle in the sixteenth and seventeenth centuries and replaced it with the *mathematical* New Science, which many centuries later became the basis of modern scientific–industrial society.

Copernicus Questions Aristotle   According to the scholastic heritage, based on Aristotle's physics, all objects in nature were composed of the four elements (in ascending order of lightness) of earth, water, fire, and air. In astronomy, based on Aristotle and Ptolemy, earth was in the center of the planetary universe, with planets composed of the fifth element of ether traveling around the earth in concentric circles. Both of these theories collapsed during the Renaissance, when a chorus of critics of Aristotle arose. One of the critics was Nicolaus Copernicus (1473–1543) from Torun, a German-founded city which had come under Polish rule a few years before his birth. Copernicus began his studies at the University of Kraków, the only eastern European school to offer courses in astronomy. During the years 1495–1504, he continued his studies—of canon law, medicine, astronomy, and astrology—at Italian universities. In 1500 he briefly taught mathematics in Rome and perhaps read Greek astronomical texts translated from Arabic in the library of the Vatican. Eventually, Copernicus graduated with a degree in canon law and took up an administrative position at the cathedral of Torun, which allowed him time to pursue astronomical research.

Sometime between 1507 and 1514 Copernicus became aware of the scientific significance of Columbus's discovery of the Americas. Spanish and Portuguese mariners sailing north and south from the Caribbean a few years after 1492 had realized that the Americas, with their long coastlines, were not at all islands off the coast of India, as Columbus had thought. As a result, in 1507 the German cartographer Martin Waldseemüller (ca. 1470–1520) published an early map and an accompanying updated version of Ptolemy's geography, both showing the east coast of the Americas. He was, thus, the first to describe the Americas as continents in their own right.

Copernicus saw the map soon after its publication and realized that, rather than a deep ocean, the Americas on the other side of the globe formed an entire "inhabited world" (Gr. *oikumene*). With this realization it became impossible for Copernicus to think that earth was the heaviest element: Too much earth in the form of continents was protruding from the oceans. Consequently, Copernicus rejected Aristotle's descriptive science of five elements and with it the idea that the earth was in the center of the planetary universe. He exchanged the places of the earth and sun, which described similar circles in the Ptolemaic system, and concluded that nothing much needed to be modified in the trigonometry of this system to accommodate that exchange. A century later, Johannes Kepler corrected the circles into concentric ellipses.

Waldseemüller's 1507 World Map. Although most of its features would have appeared on any Ptolemaic map of the era, this influential map is notable for one major mistake. The German map maker, Martin Waldseemüller (1470–1520), lacked any first-hand knowledge of the places he depicted on his map and he was unable to access the newly developed nautical charts of the world. Instead, he relied upon secondhand sources, including the misleading accounts of the Italian navigator, Amerigo Vespucci (1454–1512) who claimed that he, not the Portuguese, discovered the Atlantic seaboard of Brazil. As a result, instead of putting the original Portuguese name on the coast (Land of the True Cross), he placed the name of Amerigo (America). Waldseemüller soon realized his mistake, for the name America never reappeared on any of his subsequent maps.

Galileo's Mathematical Physics　During the near-century between the births of Copernicus and Galileo Galilei (1564–1642), mathematics—with its two branches of Greek geometry and Arabic algebra—improved considerably. Euclid's *Elements*, badly translated from Arabic in the late twelfth century with a garbled definition of proportions, was retranslated correctly from the Greek in 1543. In physics, the new translation in 1544 of a text on floating and sinking bodies by the Hellenistic thinker Archimedes (287–212 BCE) attracted enthusiastic attention. The text, unknown to the Arabs, had been translated from the Greek already in the thirteenth century but subsequently remained unappreciated, on account of its incompatibility with the then-prevailing Aristotelianism. All that was needed was for an anti-Aristotelian genius to bring together geometry, algebra, and Archimedian physics. In 1604, that genius came forward in the person of Galileo, who formulated his mathematical law of descending bodies (see Concept Map).

Running Afoul of the Church　Galileo was also a first-rate astronomer, one of the first to use a telescope, which had been recently invented in Flanders. On the basis of his astronomical discoveries, in 1610 he received a richly endowed appointment as chief mathematician and philosopher at the court of the Medici, rulers of Florence. But his increasing fame also attracted the enmity of the Catholic Church. As a proponent of Copernican heliocentrism, Galileo seemed to contradict the passage in the Hebrew Bible where God stopped the motion of the sun for a day, to allow the Israelites to win a battle (Joshua 10:12–13). In contrast to the more tolerant pope at the time of Copernicus, the Counter-Reformation Inquisition favored a strictly literal interpretation of this passage, which implied that the sun moves unless halted by God. In 1632 Galileo found himself condemned to house arrest and forced to make a public repudiation of heliocentrism.

The condemnation of Galileo had a chilling effect on scientists in the southern European countries where the Catholic Counter-Reformation reigned. Wealthy patrons reduced their stipends to scientists, and scientific research declined. During the seventeenth century, interest in the New Science shifted increasingly to France, Germany, the Netherlands, and England. There, no single church authority dominated, of either the Catholic or the Protestant variety, to enforce the literal understanding of scripture, as much as each would have wanted. These countries produced numerous mathematicians, physicists, and inventors, both Catholics as well as Protestants. The New Scientists in northern Europe had a certain liberty which their southern colleagues lacked. It was this intellectual freedom, not any great sympathy on the part of religious authorities for the New Science, which allowed the latter to flourish, especially in the Netherlands and England.

Isaac Newton's Mechanics　In the middle of the English dispute over the dominance of Protestant or Catholic authority, Isaac Newton (1643–1727) completed the New

> ### Copernicus Rejecting Aristotle
>
> "We should not listen to certain Peripatetics [Aristotelians] who ... say that land has emerged for a certain distance [the length of Eurasia and Africa] because, having hollow spaces inside, it does not balance everywhere with respect to weight and so the center of gravity is different from the center of magnitude. But they fall into error through the ignorance of geometry; for they do not know that there cannot be seven times more water and some parts of the land still remain dry unless the land abandon its center of gravity [the earth as center of the planetary universe] and give place to the waters as being heavier."
>
> —Nicolaus Copernicus. *On the Revolutions of the Heavenly Spheres*. Translated by Charles Glen Wallis, pp. 9–10. Philadelphia: Running Press, 2002.

Patterns Up Close | The Mathematization of Science, 1500–Present

According to Archimedes (and contrary to Aristotle), stones sink in water at the same speed, regardless of their weight. Galileo was able to prove that Archimedes was correct and that bodies descend with the same acceleration if one disregards the medium. To create the experiment, he had a craftsperson build him a 6.5-foot inclined, grooved beam, propped up at an angle, down which brass balls could be rolled. For timing, Galileo used the swings of a pendulum. After many experiments and false starts, he decided to divide the time of the ball's accelerating descent down the beam into eight equal segments. For the passing of each time segment he placed markers on the incline and carefully measured the resulting unequal distances.

As he compared these distances, he realized that their increasing lengths roughly followed the progression of the odd integers 1, 3, 5, 7, 9, 11, 13, 15, etc. On the basis of Euclid's mathematics of ratios, Galileo concluded that these distances, added together, corresponded to squares of time ($1 + 3 = 2^2$, $1 + 3 + 5 = 3^2$, $1 + 3 + 5 + 7 = 4^2$, and so forth). (Today, this lengthy number sequence is expressed in the short equation $s = t^2$, where s is distance and t is time.) Galileo concluded that, contrary to Aristotle, earthly motion—such as the accelerating motion of a body rolling down in the groove of a beam or falling from a tower—could be mathematized.

Acceleration Experiment. This nineteenth-century reconstruction of Galileo's inclined plane is located in the Museum for the History of Science in Florence, Italy. The metal gates, spaced along the grooved inclines according to Galileo's ratio of uneven integers, held bells, which helped him to measure the elapsed time segments as the balls passed through.

Galileo's math of ratios strikes us today as elementary. Several New Scientists after him, such as Descartes, Pascal, Leibniz, and Newton, created new fields of higher mathematics that enabled Newton to unify Copernican–Keplerian astronomy and Galilean physics into a single theory of a fully determined mechanical universe. Newton's concepts of atoms, forces, and planetary bodies dominated the sciences from the early eighteenth century to the early twentieth century. They became such impressively powerful tools that mathematically untrained philosophers like Auguste Comte (1798–1857) and Karl Marx (1818–1883) drew the conclusion that not only nature but also history were mechanically determined and that one could predict the future of social developments in the same way scientists predicted ballistic trajectories or astronomical constellations.

In the early twentieth century, Albert Einstein (1879–1955) formulated the theory of relativity as a replacement of Newtonianism. At the speed of light and across vast distances, space and time are no longer absolute but relative to each other, forming a single curved space–time, which in turn can be related to mass, energy, and momentum with the help of Einsteinian field equations. Newtonian planetary motions are for Einstein straight movements that appear curved because of space–time. While Newtonian mechanics can still be imagined and, therefore, mistaken as applicable to society and history, the theory of relativity is so abstract that words fail to render it comprehensible.

Between 1920 and 1930, scientists such as Nils Bohr (1885–1962) pushed scientific abstraction even further and developed quantum theory. Here, in the very small, subatomic realm of physics, as opposed to Einstein's very large space physics, scientists discovered that energy waves and subatomic particles form an indivisible duality. Paradoxical phenomena are the result: A single particle goes simultaneously through two slits, and particles at a distance from each other act instantaneously in tandem, without evidence of them being in contact, even at the speed of light. Quantum theorists assume an invisible subatomic continuum of particle waves that underlies the Einsteinian universe of space–time where relativity theory applies. The mathematics of particle waves, however, have withstood so far all efforts of unification with the mathematics of space–time, and scientists in the twenty-first century are still on the elusive hunt for what they call a "theory of everything."

Questions

• How do Galileo's experiments with falling bodies demonstrate the shift away from descriptive science to mathematical science?

• Why did the New Science lead to conflicts between thinkers like Galileo and the church?

Science of Copernicus and Galileo. As a professor at the University of Cambridge, he worked in the fields of mathematics, optics, astronomy, physics, alchemy, and theology. His main early contribution to the New Science was calculus, a new field in mathematics, which he developed at the same time as the German philosopher Gottfried Wilhelm Leibniz (1646–1716). Later in his career, Newton unified the fields of physics and astronomy, establishing the so-called Newtonian synthesis. His *Mathematical Principles of Natural Philosophy*, published in 1687, one year before the English settled their religious and constitutional disputes with the compromise of the Glorious Revolution, was the towering achievement of the New Science. It established a deterministic universe following mathematical rules and formed the basis of science until the early twentieth century.

The New Science and Its Social Impact

Scientists in the seventeenth century were in close communication with each other. They met in scientific societies or residential salons. Popularizers introduced an increasingly large public to the New Science. Scientists carried out experiments with constantly improved scientific instruments, such as telescopes, microscopes, thermometers, and barometers. Experience with barometers led technically versatile scientists and engineers to experiment with vacuum chambers and cylinders operating with condensing steam. Experimentation culminated with the invention of the steam engine in England in 1712.

New Science Societies   When the Counter-Reformation drove the New Science to northwestern Europe, the Italian-style academies gave way to chartered scientific societies, such as the Royal Society of London (1662) and the Paris Academy of Sciences (1666). Other countries, like Prussia, Russia, and Sweden, soon followed. These societies employed staffs of administrators, co-opted scientists as fellows, held regular discussion meetings, challenged their fellows to answer scientific questions, awarded prizes, and organized field trips and expeditions. They also published transactions, correspondences, and manuscripts. Many societies attracted thousands of members—famous pioneers, obscure amateurs, technically proficient tinkerers, theoretical mathematicians, daring experimenters, and flighty dreamers—representing an important cross section of the upper strata of seventeenth-century urban society in northwest Europe (see Map 17.5).

Other popularizers were textbook authors and itinerant lecturers who addressed audiences of middle-class amateurs, instrument makers, and specialized craftspeople, especially in England and the Netherlands. Many lecturers toured coffeehouses, urban residences, country estates, and provincial schools. Coffeehouses allowed the literate urban public to meet, read the daily newspapers (first published in the early seventeenth century), and exchange ideas. Coffee, introduced from Ethiopia and Yemen via the Ottoman Empire in the sixteenth century, was the preferred nonalcoholic social drink before the arrival of tea in the later eighteenth century. Male urban literacy is estimated to have exceeded 50 percent in England and the Netherlands during this period, although it remained considerably lower in France, Germany, and Italy.

Some lecturers were veritable entrepreneurs of the speaking circuit, teaching a kind of "Newtonianism-lite" for ladies and gentlemen with little time or patience for serious study. Other lecturers set up subscriptions for month-long courses. Wealthy

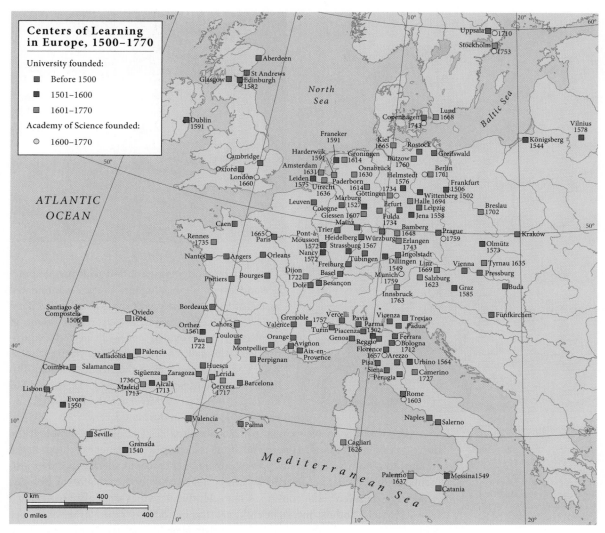

Centers of Learning in Europe, 1500–1770

University founded:
- Before 1500
- 1501–1600
- 1601–1770

Academy of Science founded:
- 1600–1770

MAP 17.5 **Centers of Learning in Europe, 1500–1770.**

businessmen endowed public lectures and supported increasingly elaborate experiments and expensive laboratory equipment. In the first half of the eighteenth century, the New Science triumphed in northwestern Europe among a large, scientifically and technically interested public of experimenters, engineers, instrument makers, artisans, business people, and lay folk.

Women and the New Science   Women formed a significant part of this public. In the fields of mathematics and astronomy, Sophie Brahe (1556–1643), sister of the Danish astronomer Tycho Brahe (1546–1601), and Maria Cunitz (see chapter-opening vignette) were the first to make contributions to the new astronomy of Copernicus and Kepler. According to estimates, in the second half of the seventeenth century some 14 percent of German astronomers were women. A dozen particularly prominent female astronomers practiced their science privately in Germany, Poland, the Netherlands, France, and England.

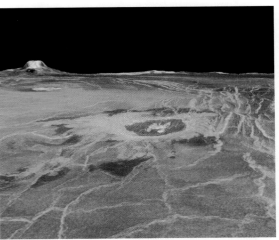

New Scientist. Maria Cunitz is honored today with a sculpture in Ratusz, Poland. Crater Cunitz is one of the larger craters (30 miles across) on the planet Venus which were named in the twentieth century to honor female scientists like Cunitz.

One later woman not content with private practice and intent on breaking into the male-dominated world of the university was the Italian Laura Bassi (1711–1778). Her father, a lawyer in Bologna in northern Italy, provided her with an early education in mathematics and physics. As a young scholar, Bassi became a member of the Academy of the Bologna Institute of Sciences and, in 1732, earned her doctorate at the city's university, the first woman to receive a doctorate in the New Science.

Bassi's lectures on Newtonian physics attracted large audiences, although the university senate refused to grant a position as a chair (a permanent member of the faculty) to a woman. Undaunted, Bassi pursued her career as a lecturer and experimenter in the new field of electricity, earning a salary higher than that of the Bologna Academy's president. She continued her scientific activities even after marrying a fellow physicist and rearing eight children. The period was a time of scholarly opportunity for a fair number of women scientists, even in Counter-Reformation Italy.

Social Salons   Another institution which helped in the popularization of the New Science was the salon. As the well-furnished, elegant living room of an urban residence, the salon was both a domestic chamber and a semipublic meeting place for the urban social elite to engage in conversations, presentations, and experiments. The culture of the salon emerged first in Paris sometime after the closure of the court-centered Palace Academy in the 1580s. Since the Catholic French universities remained committed to Aristotelianism, the emerging stratum of educated urban aristocrats and middle-class professionals turned to the salons as places to inform themselves about new scientific developments. Furthermore, French universities as well as scientific academies refused to admit women, in contrast to Italian and German institutions. The French salon, therefore, became a bastion of well-placed and respected female scholars.

One outstanding example of French salon science was Gabrielle-Emilie du Châtelet (1706–1749). In her youth, Châtelet fulfilled her marital duties to her husband, the Marquis of Châtelet. She had three children before turning to the sciences. In one of the Paris salons she met François Marie Arouet, known as Voltaire (1694–1778), the eighteenth-century Enlightenment writer, skeptic, satirist, and amateur Newtonian. Châtelet and Voltaire became intimate companions under the benevolent eyes of the Marquis at the family estate in Lorraine in northwestern France.

Voltaire had fled Paris after the publication of his Anglophile *Philosophical Letters* (1733), which angered the anti-English French court. The Châtelets offered him a refuge in exchange for Emilie being introduced to, and tutored by, the leading scientists and friends of Voltaire in Paris. The estate became a veritable intellectual center, equipped not only with a salon and laboratory but also with a theater, where Emilie Châtelet acted in plays written by Voltaire. His best known work today, however, is his satirical novel, *Candide* (1759), that mocks Leibniz' idea of theodicy, that is, the notion that history progresses and everything happens for an ultimately beneficial purpose. Voltaire uses the example of the devastating earthquake of 1750 that leveled Lisbon to argue that there is no theodicy. Humanity, in the absence of divine providence, has to remain satisfied with events as they occur. Although Voltaire published prolifically, Châtelet eventually outstripped him both in research and scientific understanding. Her lasting achievement was the translation of Newton's *Principles* into French, published in 1759.

Discovery of the Vacuum   Among the important scientific instruments of the day were telescopes, microscopes, and thermometers. It was the barometer, however, that was the crucial instrument for the exploration of the properties of the vacuum and condensing steam, eventually leading to the invention of the steam engine. The scientist laying the groundwork for the construction of this instrument was Evangelista Torricelli (1608–1647), mathematician and assistant of Galileo. In collaboration with Florentine engineers, he experimented with mercury-filled glass tubes, demonstrating the existence of atmospheric pressure in the air and of vacuums in the tubes.

Four years later, the French mathematician and philosopher Blaise Pascal (1623–1662) had his brother-in-law haul a mercury barometer up a mountain to experiment with demonstrations of lower air pressures at higher altitudes. Soon thereafter, scientists discovered the connection between changing atmospheric pressures and the weather, laying the foundations for weather forecasting. The discovery of the vacuum, the existence of which Aristotle had held to be impossible, made a deep impression on the scientific community in the seventeenth century and was an important step toward the practical application of the New Science to mechanical engineering in the eighteenth century.

Another important step in the transition from New Science to mechanics was the development of precision machining. Scientists wanted to experiment with precision instruments and gadgetry, such as air pumps and sealed vacuum chambers. The first to build a workable pump and chamber was the German Otto von Guericke (1602–1686). In the 1650s and 1660s Guericke carried out experiments with two hollow and conjoined copper hemispheres. Sealed tightly and emptied of their inside air with the help of pumps, these hemispheres held together so firmly that a team of workhorses was unable to pull them apart. Guericke and the Englishman Robert Boyle (1627–1691) were also early experimenters with electricity, which

Vacuum Power. In 1672, the New Scientist and mayor of Magdeburg, Otto von Guericke, demonstrated the experiment that made him a pioneer in the understanding of the physical properties of the vacuum. In the presence of German emperor Ferdinand III, two teams of horses were unable to pull the two sealed hemispheres apart. Guericke had created a vacuum by pumping out the air from the two sealed copper spheres.

they produced by rubbing balls of sulfur with their hands. Metal workshops in Paris and Leiden began producing air pumps, and vacuum chambers became standard equipment in laboratories.

The Steam Engine   The French Huguenot scientist and engineer Denis Papin (ca. 1647–1712) took the first crucial step from the vacuum chamber to the steam engine. Papin began his career as an assistant in English scientific laboratories, where he familiarized himself with the phenomenon of steam contracting its volume when cooled in a chamber, creating a vacuum in the process. In 1690, when he was a court engineer and professor in Germany, Papin constructed a cylinder with a piston. Weights, via a cord and two pulleys, held the piston at the top of the cylinder. When heated, water in the bottom of the cylinder turned into steam. When subsequently cooled through the injection of water, the steam condensed, forcing the piston down and lifting the weights up. Papin spent his last years (1707–1712) in London where the Royal Society of London held discussions of his papers, thereby alerting engineers, craftspeople, and entrepreneurs in England to the steam engine as a labor-saving machine. In 1712, the mechanic Thomas Newcomen built the first steam engine to pump water from coal mine shafts.

Altogether, it took a little over a century, from 1604 to 1712, for Europeans to apply the New Science to the development of the steam engine. Had it not been for the New Science, this engine—based on contracting steam—would not have been invented. (Hero of Alexandria, who invented steam-driven machines in the first century CE, made use of the expanding force of steam.) Prior to 1600, mechanical inventions—such as the wheel, the compass, the stern rudder, and the firearm—were constructed by anonymous tinkerers with a good commonsense understanding of nature. With the arrival of the New Science, Aristotelian common sense was no longer a virtue. It became a hindrance for the building of mechanical machinery. In 1700, engineers had to have at least a basic understanding of mathematics and such abstract physical phenomena as inertia, gravity, vacuums, and condensing steam if they wanted to build a steam engine or other complex machinery.

The Early Enlightenment in Northwestern Europe

The New Science engendered a pattern of radically new intellectual and religious thinking, which evolved in the course of the seventeenth and early eighteenth

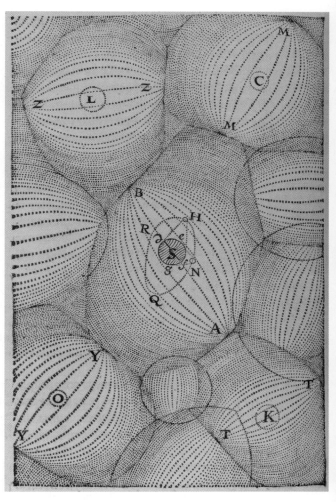

centuries. This thought, called the "Enlightenment," was deemed to be incompatible with the inherited medieval scholasticism. It eventually evolved into a powerful instrument of critique of Christian doctrine and the constitutional order of the fiscal–military states. Initially, the Enlightenment was confined to a few thinkers, but with the Glorious Revolution of 1688 in England it became a potent social force.

Descartes and Bacon　After the replacement of descriptive physics with mathematical physics, brought about by Galileo with his law of descending bodies, the question arose whether Aristotelian philosophy and Catholic theology were still adequate for the understanding of reality. New Scientists perceived the need to start philosophizing and theologizing from scratch. The first major New Scientist who, in his own judgment, started a radical reconsideration of philosophy from the ground up was the Frenchman René Descartes (1596–1650). He earned a degree in law, traveling widely after graduation. In the service of the Dutch and Bavarian courts, he bore witness to the beginning of the Thirty Years' War and its atrocities committed in the name of religious doctrines. During the war, he spent two decades in the Netherlands, studying and teaching the New Sciences. His principal innovation in mathematics was the discovery that geometry could be converted through algebra into analytic geometry.

Descartes was shocked by the condemnation of Galileo and decided to abandon all traditional propositions and doctrines of the church as well as Aristotelianism. Realizing that his common sense (that is, the five senses of seeing, hearing, touching, smelling, and tasting) were unreliable, he determined that the only reliable body of knowledge was thought, especially mathematical thought. As a person capable of thought, he concluded—bypassing his unreliable senses—that he existed: "I think, therefore I am" (*cogito ergo sum*). A further conclusion from this argument was that he was composed of two radically different substances, a material substance consisting of his senses and another immaterial substance consisting of thought. According to Descartes, body and mind, although joined through consciousness, belong to two different realms of reality.

While *Cartesian* (from Descartes) rationalism represented one road to understanding reality within the New Science, the *empirical* path of Francis Bacon (1561–1626), emphasized direct study and experimentation. In his *Novum Organum* (*New Instrument*), published in 1620, Bacon criticized current approaches to knowledge as being influenced by various kinds of common human error—"idols," as he characterized them—and argued instead for *inductive reasoning*: the close study of specific examples of phenomena from which their general principles are then *induced*. This forms the basis of what we call today the "scientific method": forming hypotheses,

A Mechanical Universe.
Descartes was also a physicist, and in *Principia philosophiae* (1644) he outlined his "mechanical universe theory" in which he described the universe as a continuously operating machine that God had set in motion. Composed of "subtle matter," it swirled in whirlpools, or vortices. In this illustration, the vortices move the planets around the Sun.

testing them through experimentation, and revising them accordingly. Thus, Bacon's "inductive method" along with Descartes' "deductive method"—reasoning from the general to the specific—have remained the twin pillars from which subsequent scientific research has proceeded.

The Philosophy of the New Science   Descartes's distinctions between body, mind, and consciousness stimulated a lively debate not only among the New Scientists but also among the growing circle of philosophers of the New Science. The Englishmen Thomas Hobbes (1588–1679) and John Locke (1632–1704) were among the latter. Hobbes, interested in the New Science since his student days, described himself as a philosopher. Locke had a basic medical education but made his contributions to the field of philosophy. Both applied Descartes's New Science philosophy to constitutional theory, making crucial contributions to the formation of constitutional nationalism in the United States, France, and Haiti at the end of the 1700s. Constitutional nationalism and its later rival, ethnic nationalism, are today the main political forces driving the patterns of world politics.

Thomas Hobbes   As a nonscientist outside the field of mathematics, astronomy, and physics—the most advanced mathematical sciences in the seventeenth and eighteenth centuries—Hobbes had little interest in Galileo's and Descartes's concept of the mind as pure mathematical thought. Therefore, it escaped him that for Descartes (as also, before him, Plato and Galileo) mathematics was the new divine: God was equivalent to mathematics; and the Mind, insofar as it could conceive of mathematics, was pure, transcendent thought.

The nonmathematician Hobbes paid attention only to consciousness; that is, the personal mind in a living body, subject to the law of motion. And since bodies are made up of corpuscles (later scientists and philosophers would speak of atoms), so, Hobbes concluded, reality is entirely material and determined by the law of motion. With Hobbes, the philosophy of materialism was born, according to which nothing but matter exists and anything mathematical, intellectual, or spiritual is dependent on matter.

Once Hobbes decided that materialism was the only possible new philosophy, the extension of materialism to political philosophy followed easily. If people are nothing but bodies, they are equal to each other with their basic bodily functions, such as their emotions and passions. Foremost among the passions, so Hobbes concluded, is selfishness. Therefore, in the natural state of humanity, which is defined as millions of atoms in motion, clashing with each other, there is "war of every man against every man."

In this general war, fear of death—another major passion—drives humans to give up their sovereignty, their "absolute" personal liberty to wage war. They do so either because they are forced by a single sovereign to do so or because they transfer their sovereignty voluntarily to a sovereign or a collective representative assembly that possesses sovereignty. Hobbes, well aware of the horrors of the recent English religious wars, preferred the alternative of the single sovereign. Thus, we can conclude that it is on the grounds of materialist philosophical thinking that Hobbes arrived at the principles of equality, rule by law, and the constitutional state. It was from the philosophy of the New Science, and specifically the concept of mathematical equality, that the theory of democracy arrived on the world historical scene.

John Locke   Locke also outlined a philosophy derived from the New Science that makes the conscious mind rigorously dependent on matter. According to Locke, the mind is a blank slate at birth on which sense perception impresses all categories of thought and reflection. Matter, in the form of atoms, impresses itself on the mind and creates consciousness. Through trial and error we overcome what Descartes considered to be the deception by the senses. Locke, in the Anglo-American philosophical tradition, became the principal figure of Enlightenment materialism.

In the political realm, Locke also took the passions as his starting point. But, for him, the basic passion was the desire of ownership—of oneself, one's labor, and property—which he considered to be inalienable rights. Self-possession excluded slavery, ownership of one's labor meant self-employment, and ownership of property included land and portable wealth. When this passion could no longer be satisfied, war would break out. But once the passions of war subsided, reason would lead humans to the establishment of a peaceful or civil government. In so doing, however, humans would not give up their liberty, as argued by Hobbes. They would merely empower the government to protect private property. Therefore, also in contrast to Hobbes, citizens retained the right to rise against an unjust government. Ironically, by default, Locke allowed for the kind of general war to which Hobbes was opposed.

The early Enlightenment was a curious mixture of a flawed philosophy of base human passions and an eventually highly successful political theory of democracy. Forgetting that Descartes held fast to the Platonic–Galilean notion of the divine as mathematics and the mind as pure mathematical thought, they developed a philosophy of consciousness as the concrete individual mind in a moving body determined by passions. A split occurred between the New Science, in which mathematics functioned as the new equivalent of religion, and the Enlightenment philosophy of materialism, in which no religion was needed, even if philosophers remained nominally Christian. This division is still unhealed today, with both scientists and the general public unaware that the equivalent of the divine in the modern age is the **transcendence** of mathematics.

The Social Contract. Hobbes believed that the "war of all against all" could only be avoided when human beings entered into a contract in which they agreed to be ruled by an absolute sovereign. The title page from his most famous work, *Leviathan*, depicts the ruler as an absolute monarch, but one whose body incorporates the many individuals of society who have consented to live in a commonwealth under his authority.

Transcendence: Realm in reality that is as real as matter; the transcendent realm is both separate and mingled with the realm of matter; the difficulty of thinking of the two as both separate and mingled has caused much confusion, beginning with Hobbes and Locke.

Putting It All Together

Prior to 1500, all religious civilizations possessed sophisticated mathematics and practiced variations of descriptive science, such as astronomy, astrology, geography, alchemy, and medicine. Only after 1550 did astronomy and physics in western

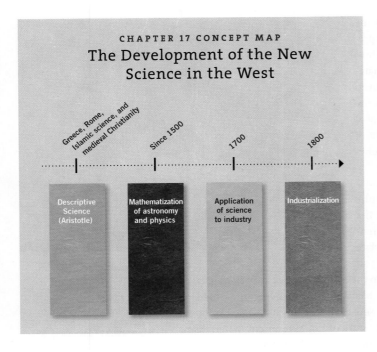

CHAPTER 17 CONCEPT MAP
The Development of the New Science in the West

Greece, Rome, Islamic science, and medieval Christianity

Since 1500

1700

1800

Descriptive Science (Aristotle)

Mathematization of astronomy and physics

Application of science to industry

Industrialization

Christianity transform themselves into mathematical science. This transformation, however, had no practical consequences prior to the invention of the steam engine in the 1700s and the subsequent industrialization of England in the 1800s. Furthermore, the mathematization of astronomy and physics did little to influence the continued prevalence of description as the chief underlying pattern of the other sciences. Astrology, alchemy, and medicine continued with what we regard today as mistaken descriptive theories well into the nineteenth century.

Most importantly, the rise of the New Science and Enlightenment should not be confused with the vast political, social, economic, and cultural changes, called "modernity" after 1750, which propelled the West on its trajectory of world dominance. Although the West began to acquire its specific scientific and philosophical identity with the introduction of mathematical science in the one hundred-year span between Copernicus and Galileo, its impact on the world became felt only after it applied science to industry. Once this process got underway, in the nineteenth century, Asia and Africa had no choice but to adapt to modern science and industrialization (see Concept Map).

Review and Respond

1. How did the Protestant Reformation originate, and who were its main representatives?

2. What were the key political and religious differences between France, Russia, Prussia, and England during the period 1450–1750?

3. What was humanism, and what role did it play in the Renaissance?

4. What are the differences between descriptive and mathematical science, and who pioneered the latter? What impact did women scientists such as Maria Cunitz have on the popularization of the New Science?

5. Discuss three inventions that illustrate the popularization of the New Science during 1450–1750.

▶ For additional resources, including maps, primary sources, visuals, and quizzes, please go to www.oup.com/us/vonsivers. Please see the Further Resources section at the back of the book for additional readings and suggested websites.

Thinking Through Patterns

▶ **What were the patterns of fiscal–military state formation and transformation in the period 1450–1750? How did the Protestant Reformation and religious wars modify these patterns?**

European kingdoms, such as France, Sweden, and Prussia, expanded their powers of taxation to the detriment of the nobility. With the accumulated funds, they hired and salaried mercenary infantries equipped with firearms, using them to conquer land from their neighbors. The religious wars of the 1500s and 1600s strengthened centralization efforts and hastened the demise of the nobility as obstacles to the fiscal–military state. In England, Parliament blocked the Stuart kings from building an infantry fiscal–military state and instead pursued the construction of a naval state, which succeeded a similar one built by the Netherlands in 1688.

Located far from the traditional agrarian-urban centers of Eurasia, western Christianity repeatedly adapted its culture (particularly theological, philosophical, scientific, and artistic forms of expression) in response to outside stimuli coming from Islamic and eastern Christian civilizations. Without these stimuli, the Renaissance, Baroque, New Science, and Enlightenment would not have developed. In contrast, the Middle East, Byzantium, India, and China, originating firmly within the traditional agrarian-urban centers, received far fewer outside stimuli prior to the scientific–industrial age.

▶ **What are the reasons for the cultural change that began in Europe around 1750? In which ways were the patterns of cultural changes during 1450–1750 different from those in the other religious civilizations of Eurasia?**

▶ **When and how did the New Science begin, and how did it gain popularity in northwestern European society? Why is the popularization of the New Science important for understanding the period 1450–1750?**

The discovery of the two new continents of the Americas prompted Nicolaus Copernicus to reject Aristotle's astronomical theory of spheres and to posit a sun-centered planetary system. It continued with Galileo Galilei's discovery of the mathematical law of falling bodies in physics and was completed with Isaac Newton unifying physics and astronomy. The New Science became popular among educated urban circles in northwestern Europe, where Catholic and Protestant church authorities were largely divided. In southern Europe, where the Catholic Counter-Reformation was powerful and rejected the New Science, no such popularization occurred. The New Science possessed practical applicability: After discovering the properties of the vacuum and condensing steam, scientists began experimenting with steam engines, which served as the principal catalyst for the launching of the scientific–industrial age.

Chapter 18

1500-1800

New Patterns in New Worlds

COLONIALISM AND INDIGENOUS RESPONSES IN THE AMERICAS

Alonso Ortíz was a deadbeat. He fled from his creditors in Zafra, Estremadura, in southwestern Spain, in the early 1770s to find a new life in the Americas. In Mexico City, with the help of borrowed money, he set up shop as a tanner. His business flourished and, with a partner, Ortíz expanded into two rented buildings. Eight Native American employees, whom he had trained, did the actual labor of stomping the hides in the vats filled with tanning acids. A black slave, belonging to his partner, was the

Seeing Patterns

▶ What is the significance of western Europeans acquiring the Americas as a warm-weather extension of their northern continent?

▶ What was the main pattern of social development in colonial America during the period 1500–1800?

▶ Why and how did European settlers in South and North America strive for self-government, and how successful were they in achieving their goals?

supervisor. Happy that he no longer had to take his shoes off to work, Ortíz concentrated on giving instructions and hustling up business.

Ortíz's situation in Mexico City was not entirely legal however. He had left his wife, Eleanor González, and children alone in Zafra, though the law required that families should be united. The authorities rarely enforced this law, but that was no guarantee for Ortíz. Furthermore, he had not yet sent his family any remittances, leaving Eleanor to rely on the largesse of her two brothers back home for survival. And then, there was still the debt. Ortíz had reasons to be afraid of the law.

To avoid prosecution, Ortíz wrote a letter to Eleanor. In this letter, he proudly described the comfortable position he had achieved. He announced that his kind business partner was sending her a sum of money sufficient to begin preparations for her departure from Spain. To his creditors, Ortíz promised to send 100 tanned hides within a year. "Your arrival would bring me great joy," he wrote to Eleanor, reneging on an original promise to be already back home in Spain. Evidently aware of her reluctance to join him in Mexico, Ortíz closed his letter with a request to grant him 4 more years

The Meeting of Moctezuma and Cortés. Antonio de Solís (1610–1686) served as the official historian of the Indies for the Spanish monarchy. In this capacity he produced his monumental work, *The History of the Conquest of Mexico by the Spaniards*. Removed by more than 150 years from the events, de Solís relied heavily on the work of previous chroniclers of the Conquest, such as Bernal Diaz del Castillo, and Cortés himself. With its artful writing style, de Solís's book was a bestseller, helping to solidify a heroic view of the Conquest that persists to this day. Shown here is the frontispiece to de Solis's book; much of what is depicted is fanciful or imaginary: Tenochtitlán is portrayed as a European-style city, and the dress of the Aztecs bears little resemblance to what they actually wore.

Chapter Outline

abroad and to do so with a notarized document from her hand. Unfortunately, we do not know her answer.

The Ortíz family drama gives a human face to European emigration and colonialism from Europe to the Americas. Like Alonso Ortíz, some 300,000 other Spaniards emigrated between 1500 and 1800. They came alone or with family, temporarily or for good, and either failed or succeeded in their new lives. A few hundred letters by emigrants exist, giving us glimpses of their lives in Mexico, Peru, and other parts of the Americas conquered by the Spanish and Portuguese in the sixteenth century. As these relatively privileged immigrants settled, they hoped to build successful enterprises using the labor of Native Americans as well as black slaves imported from Africa. As the example of Ortíz documents, even in the socially not very prestigious craft of tanning a man could achieve a measure of comfort by having people of even lower status working for him.

The Americas became an extension of Europe. European settlers extracted mineral and agricultural resources from these new lands. In Europe these resources had become increasingly expensive and impractical to produce (if they could be produced at all). A pattern emerged in which gold and silver, as well as agricultural products that could not be grown in Europe's cooler climate—such as brazilwood, sugar, tobacco, rice, cacao, indigo, and cochineal—were intensively exploited. In their role as supplementary subtropical and tropical extensions of Europe, the Americas became a crucial factor for Europe's changing position in the world. First, Europe acquired large quantities of precious metals, which its two largest competitors, India and China, lacked. Second, with its new access to warm-weather agricultural products, Europe rose to a position of agrarian autonomy similar to that of India and China. In terms of resources, compared with the principal religious civilizations of India and China, Europe grew between 1550 and 1800 from a position of inferiority to one of near parity.

The Colonial Americas: Europe's Warm-Weather Extension

The European extension into the subtropical and tropical Americas followed Columbus's pursuit of a sea route to India and its spices that would circumvent the Mediterranean and its dominance by Muslim traders. The Spaniards justified the conquest of these new continents and their Native American inhabitants with Christ's command to convert the heathen in the Spanish Habsburg world empire, the glorious final empire before Christ's return. They financed their imperial expansion as well as their wars against Ottoman and European rivals with American gold and silver, leaving little for domestic investment in productive enterprises. A pattern evolved in which Iberian settlers transformed the Americas into mineral-extracting and agrarian colonies based on either cheap or forced labor.

The Conquest of Mexico and Peru

The Spanish conquerors of the Aztec and Inca Empires, although small in number, succeeded by exploiting internal weaknesses in the empires. They swiftly eliminated the top of the power structures, paralyzing the decision-making apparatuses long enough for their conquests to succeed. Soon after the conquests, the Old World disease of smallpox—to which New World inhabitants had never been exposed and, therefore, had never developed immunity—ravaged the Native American population and dramatically reduced the indigenous labor force. To make up for this reduction, colonial authorities imported black slaves from Africa for employment in mines and in agriculture. Black Africans, who had long been in contact with Eurasia, were, similar to Europeans, less susceptible to smallpox. A three-tiered society of European immigrants, Native Americans, and black slaves emerged in the Spanish and Portuguese Americas.

From Trade Posts to Conquest   Columbus had discovered the Caribbean islands under a royal commission, which entitled him to build fortified posts and to trade with the indigenous Taínos. The Portuguese had pioneered the use of fortified trade posts in their explorations along the costs of West Africa. Friendly trade relations with the Taínos, however, quickly deteriorated into outright exploitation, with the Spaniards usurping the traditional entitlements of the Taíno chiefs to the labor of their tribesmen, who panned gold in rivers or mined it in shallow shafts. With the help of **land-labor grants** (Spanish *encomiendas*), the Spanish took over from the Taíno chiefs and, through forced labor, amassed sizeable quantities of gold. What had begun as trade post settlement turned into full-blown conquest.

Land-labor grant (*encomienda*): Land grant by the government to an entrepreneur entitling him to use forced indigenous or imported slave labor on this land for the exploitation of agricultural and mineral resources.

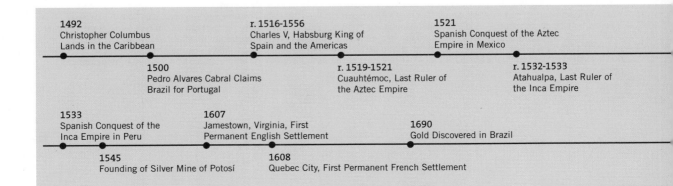

1492
Christopher Columbus
Lands in the Caribbean

r. 1516-1556
Charles V, Habsburg King of
Spain and the Americas

1521
Spanish Conquest of the Aztec
Empire in Mexico

1500
Pedro Alvares Cabral Claims
Brazil for Portugal

r. 1519-1521
Cuauhtémoc, Last Ruler of
the Aztec Empire

r. 1532-1533
Atahualpa, Last Ruler of
the Inca Empire

1533
Spanish Conquest of the
Inca Empire in Peru

1607
Jamestown, Virginia, First
Permanent English Settlement

1690
Gold Discovered in Brazil

1545
Founding of Silver Mine of Potosí

1608
Quebec City, First Permanent French Settlement

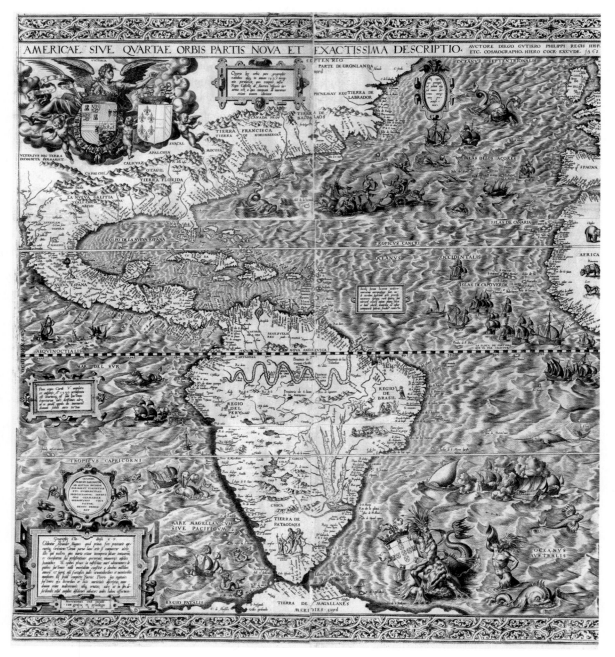

The Fourth Part of the World. "Now these [three] parts of the Earth have been extensively explored," the German cartographer Martin Waldseemüller wrote in 1507 (see Chapter 17), "but now a fourth part has been discovered by Amerigo Vespucci." This "fourth part"— America, both North and South—fired European imaginations. Drawn in 1562 by Diego Gutiérrez, the map shown here catalogs the wonders of America, as viewed through Spanish eyes. After just four decades of European exploration, the continent is already filled with place names. The course of the Amazon is accurately shown, and parrots, monkeys, cannibals, giants, and an erupting volcano speak to the riches that bedazzled the settlers. In the North Atlantic, Charles V, ruler of Spain's vast New World empire, glides across in a chariot to claim his possessions.

The Spaniards conquered the Caribbean islands not only through force. Much more severe in its consequences was the indirect conquest through disease. The Old World disease of smallpox quickly wiped out the estimated 250,000 to 1 million Taínos (estimates vary widely) on the larger northern islands as well as the less numerous Caribs on the smaller southern Caribbean islands. Isolated for more than 10,000 years from the rest of humankind, Native Americans possessed no immunity against smallpox and were similarly ravaged by other introduced diseases such as measles, diphtheria, mumps, plague, influenza, typhoid, malaria, and yellow fever.

Protests, mostly among members of the clergy, arose against both the brutal labor exploitation by the conquerors and the helplessness of the Taínos dying of disease. Unfortunately, the protesters remained a small minority, even within the clergy. The best-known among several was Bartolomé de las Casas (1474–1566), from a family of merchants in Seville. Las Casas had practiced law before emigrating to Hispaniola, where he received an *encomienda*. After becoming a priest in 1510 and later a Dominican monk, however, he became a bitter opponent of the labor grant system. He demanded nothing less than the end of this institution, something that did not come until after 1542 with the introduction of the *repartimiento* system.

First Mainland Conquests   Another early settler on Hispaniola was Hernán Cortés (1485–1547). His father was a lower-level nobleman in Estremadura, a rough, formerly Islamic frontier region in southwestern Iberia. Chosen by his parents for a career in law, Cortés learned Latin but left the university before graduation. After his arrival in the New World in 1504, he advanced quickly from governmental scribe in Hispaniola to mayor of Santiago in Cuba. Thanks to several labor grants, he became rich. When the Cuban governor asked him in the fall of 1518 to equip and lead a small preparatory expedition for trade and exploration to the Yucatán Peninsula in southeastern Mexico, Cortés enthusiastically agreed. Within a month he assembled 300 men, considerably exceeding his contract. The governor tried to stop him, but Cortés departed quickly for the American mainland.

As the Cuban governor had feared, Cortés did not bother with trade posts in Yucatán. The Spanish had previously learned of the existence of the Aztec Empire, with its immense silver and gold treasures. In a first encounter,

Cultural Intermediary. The Tabascans gave Malinche, or Dona Marina, to Hernán Cortés as a form of tribute after they were defeated by the Spanish. Malinche served Cortés as a translator and mistress, filling a central role in Cortés's eventual victory over the Aztecs. She was in many respects the principal face of the Spanish and is always depicted center stage in Native American visual accounts of the conquest.

Cortés's motley force—numbering by now about 530 Spanish men—defeated a vastly superior indigenous force at Tabasco, mostly thanks to the Spaniards' pikes, swords, daggers, plate armor, and a few matchlock muskets and horses. Their steel weapons and armor proved superior in hand-to-hand combat to the obsidian-spiked lances, wooden swords, and quilted cotton vests of the defenders. Among the gifts of submission presented by the defeated Native Americans in Tabasco was Malinche, a Nahuatl [NA-hu-wah]-speaking woman whose father, an Aztec lord, had given her as a teenager to the Tabascans. Malinche quickly learned Spanish and became the consort of Cortés, teaching him about the subtleties of Aztec culture. In her role as translator, Malinche was nearly as decisive as Cortés in shaping events. Indeed, Aztecs often used the name of Malinche when addressing Cortés, forgetting that her voice was not that of Cortés. With Tabasco conquered, Cortés quickly moved on; he was afraid that the Cuban governor, who was in pursuit, would otherwise force him to return to Cuba.

Conquest of the Aztec Empire   On the southeast coast of Mexico, Cortés founded the city of Veracruz as a base from which to move inland. In the city, he had his followers elect a town council, which made Cortés their head and chief justice, allowing Cortés to claim legitimacy for his march inland. To prevent opponents in his camp from notifying the Cuban governor of his usurpation of authority, Cortés had all ships stripped of their gear and the hulls sunk. Marching inland, the Spaniards ran into resistance from indigenous people, suffering their first losses of horses and men. Although bloodied, they continued their march with thousands of Native American allies, most notably the Tlaxcalans, traditional enemies of the Aztecs. The support from these indigenous peoples made a crucial difference when Cortés and his army reached the court of the Aztecs.

Tlaxcalan Support for Cortés

"Xicotenga [Shee-co-TEN-ga, the ruler of Tlaxcala] made many complaints about Montezuma [Moctezuma] and his allies, for they were all enemies of the Tlaxcalans and made war on them. However, they had defended themselves very well, and had meant to do the same against us. But although they had gathered against us with all their warriors three times, this had not been possible because we were invincible. Having discovered this they wished to become friends with us and vassals of our lord the Emperor for they felt certain that in our company, their wives, and their children would be guarded and protected, and freed from the danger of surprise attacks by the treacherous Mexicans [Aztecs]. Xicotenga said much else besides, and placed his people and his city at our disposal."

—Bernal Díaz del Castillo, *The Conquest of New Spain*. Translated by J. M. Cohen, pp. 167–168. London: Penguin, 1963.

When Cortés arrived at the city of Tenochtitlán on November 2, 1519, the Emperor Moctezuma II (r. 1502–1519) was in a quandary over how to deal with these invaders whose depredations neither his tributaries nor his enemies had been able to stop. To gain some time for deliberating about how to deal with Cortés, Moctezuma greeted the Spaniard in person on one of the causeways leading to the city and invited him to his palace. Cortés and his company, now numbering some 600 Spaniards, took up quarters in the palace precincts. After a week of gradually deteriorating discussions, Cortés suddenly put the incredulous emperor under house arrest and made him swear allegiance to Charles V.

Before being able to contemplate his next move, however, Cortés was diverted by the need to march back east, where troops from Cuba had arrived to arrest him. After defeating those troops, he enrolled the straggling Cuban soldiers into his own service and marched back to Tenochtitlán. During his absence, the Spaniards who had remained in Mocte-zuma's palace had massacred a number of unarmed Aztec nobles participating in a religious ceremony. An infuriated crowd of Tenochtitlán's inhabitants invaded the palace. In the melee, Moctezuma and some 200 Spaniards died. The rest of the Spanish fled for their lives, retreating east to their Tlaxcalan allies, who, fortunately, remained loyal. Here, after his return, the indomitable Cortés devised a new plan for capturing Tenochtitlán.

After 10 months of preparations, the Spaniards returned to the Aztec capital. Numbering now about 2,000 Spanish soldiers and assisted by some 50,000 Native American troops, Cortés laid siege to the city, bombarding it from ships he had built in the lake and razing buildings during forays onto land. After nearly 3 months, much of the city was in ruins, fresh water and food became scarce, and smallpox began to decimate the population of some 3–4 million inhabitants in the Valley of Mexico and 25 million in the Aztec Empire. On August 21, 1521, the Spaniards and their al-lies stormed the city and looted its gold treasury. They captured the fiercely resisting last emperor, Cuauhtémoc [Cu-aw-TAY-moc], a few days later and executed him in captivity in 1525, thus ending the Aztec Empire (see Map 18.1).

Conquest of the Inca Empire　　At about the same time, a relative of Cortés, Francisco Pizarro (ca. 1475–1541), conceived a plan to conquer the Andean empire of the Incas (which, in 1492, comprised some 9–12 million inhabitants). Pizarro, like Cortés born in Estremadura, was an illegitimate son of an infantry captain from the lower nobility. Illiterate and without education, he had come to Hispaniola as part of an expedition in 1513 that discovered Panama and the Pacific. He became mayor of Panama City, acquired some wealth, and began to hear rumors about an empire of gold and silver to the south. After a failed initial expedition, he and 13 fol-lowers captured some precious metal from an oceangoing Inca sailing raft. Since the governor of Panama opposed a new expedition, Pizarro traveled to Spain to receive direct authorization for a trade post from Charles V. He returned with his permit, four brothers, and other relatives to Panama City and, in late December 1530, de-parted south with a host of 183 men.

In a grimly fortuitous bit of luck for Pizarro, smallpox had preceded him in his ex-pedition. In the later 1520s, the disease had ravaged the Inca Empire, killing the em-peror and his heir apparent. A brutal and protracted war of succession between two surviving sons broke out. Atahualpa, in the north, sent his army south to the capital, Cuzco, where it defeated his half-brother, Huascar. When Pizarro entered the Inca Empire, Atahualpa was encamped with an army of 40,000 men near the northern town of Cajamarca, on his way south to Cuzco to install himself as emperor. Arriving at Cajamarca, Pizarro succeeded in arranging an unarmed audience with Atahualpa in the town square. On the fateful day of November 16, 1532, Atahualpa came to this audience, surrounded by several thousand unarmed retainers, while Pizarro hid his soldiers in and behind the buildings around the square. At a signal, these sol-diers rushed into the square, horses neighing, guns blazing, and swords unsheathed. Some soldiers captured Atahualpa to hold him hostage, while others charged the retainers. A bloodbath ensued, with some 1,500 panic-stricken and fleeing Inca re-tainers killed or trampled to death. When survivors reached the Inca camp, most of the encamped army panicked as well, scattering in all directions. Not one Spanish soldier was killed, and the whole massacre was over in less than an hour.

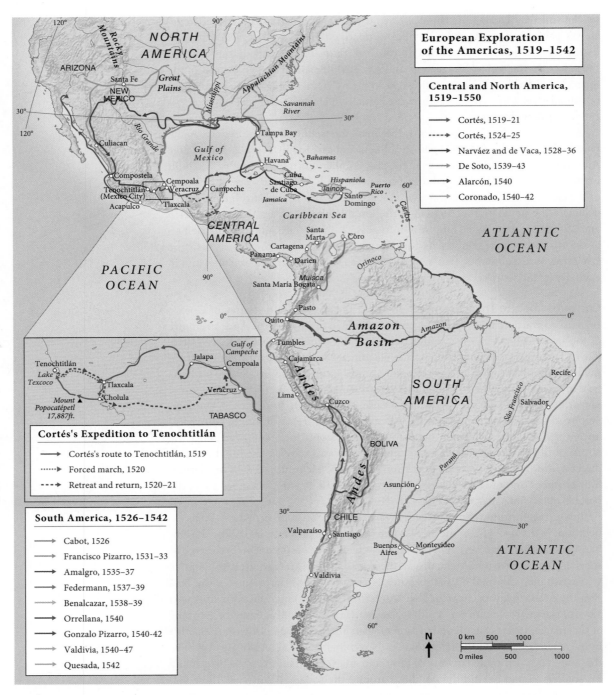

European Exploration of the Americas, 1519–1542

Central and North America, 1519–1550

→	Cortés, 1519–21
⇢	Cortés, 1524–25
→	Narváez and de Vaca, 1528–36
→	De Soto, 1539–43
→	Alarcón, 1540
→	Coronado, 1540–42

Cortés's Expedition to Tenochtitlán

→	Cortés's route to Tenochtitlán, 1519
⋯⋯▸	Forced march, 1520
⇢	Retreat and return, 1520–21

South America, 1526–1542

→	Cabot, 1526
→	Francisco Pizarro, 1531–33
→	Amalgro, 1535–37
→	Federmann, 1537–39
→	Benalcazar, 1538–39
→	Orrellana, 1540
→	Gonzalo Pizarro, 1540–42
→	Valdivia, 1540–47
→	Quesada, 1542

MAP 18.1 **The European Exploration of the Americas, 1519–1542.**

With his ambush, Pizarro succeeded in paralyzing the empire at the very top. Without their emperor Atahualpa, none of the generals in Cuzco dared to seize the initiative. Instead of ordering his captors to liberate him, Atahualpa sought to pacify their greed with a room full of gold and silver as ransom. In the following 2 months, Inca administrators delivered immense quantities of precious metals to Pizarro.

ATAHUALLPA. INCA XIIII.

Inevitably, resentment arose among the Spaniards over the distribution of the loot. When the time came to march on Cuzco, those Spaniards who felt shortchanged by the unequal distribution of loot cooled their anger by instigating the execution of the hapless Atahualpa on July 26, 1533.

The Spaniards took Cuzco 3 months later. They did so against minimal resistance, massacring the inhabitants and stripping the city of its immense gold and silver treasures. Pizarro did not stay long in the now worthless, isolated capital in the Andes. Leaving the emperor in Cuzco, in 1535 Pizarro founded a new capital, Lima, which was more conveniently located on the coast and about halfway between Cajamarca and Cuzco. As the immensity of their defeat began to sink in, the hitherto paralyzed Inca generals finally bestirred themselves. Learning from past mistakes, they avoided mass battles, focused on deadly guerilla strikes, and rebuilt a kingdom that held out until 1572. It was only then that the Spanish gained full control of the Inca Empire.

The Portuguese Conquest of Brazil

The Portuguese were not far behind the Spaniards in their pursuit of conquest. Navigators of three fleets, two Spanish and one Portuguese, sighted the Brazilian coast in 1499/1500. The Portuguese commander Pedro Alvares Cabral, on his way to India, immediately notified his king of his discovery so that the latter could claim the land as lying within the Portuguese, not Spanish, sphere of interest (see Chapter 16). Brazil's indigenous population at that time is estimated to have amounted to nearly 5 million. The great majority were tribally organized and lived in temporary or permanent villages based on agriculture, fishing, and hunting. Only a small minority in remote areas of the Amazon were pure foragers.

The Portuguese were interested initially in trade with the tribes, mostly for a type of hardwood called "brazilwood," which was ground into sawdust and used as a red dye. When French traders showed up, ignoring the Portuguese commercial treaties with the tribes, the Portuguese crown shifted from simple trade agreements to trade post settlements. This involved giving land grants to commoners and lower noblemen with the obligation to build fortified coastal villages for settlers and to engage

Conquest by Surprise. The Spanish conqueror Francisco Pizarro captured Emperor Atahualpa (top left) in an ambush (top middle). Atahualpa promised a roomful of gold in return for his release, but the Spaniards collected the gold (top right) and murdered Atahualpa (right) before generals of the Inca army could organize an armed resistance.

in agriculture and friendly trade. By the mid-sixteenth century, a handful of these villages became successful, their inhabitants intermarrying with the surrounding indigenous chieftain families and establishing sugarcane plantations.

Explanations for the Spanish Success

The slow progression of the Portuguese in tribal Brazil is readily understood. But the stupendous victories of handfuls of Spaniards over huge empires with millions of inhabitants and large cities defy easy explanation. Five factors invite consideration.

First, and most importantly, the conquistadors went straight to the top of the imperial pyramid. The emperors and their courts expected diplomatic deference by inferiors, among whom they included the minuscule band of Spaniards. Confronted, instead, with a calculated combination of arrogance and brutality, the Spaniards threw the emperors and courts off balance. Exploiting their opportunity, the conquistadors struck with deadly determination. Most importantly, as the emperors were removed from the top level, their administration immediately below fell into paralysis, unable to seize the initiative and respond in a timely fashion. There are parallels in world history for this phenomenon of administrative paralysis after the defeat of a ruler. Alexander the Great's victory over Darius III in the invasion of Achaemenid Persia in 331 BCE, Tariq ibn Ziyad's victory over Roderic in the Berber-Arab invasion of Visigothic Iberia in 711 CE, and William the Conqueror's victory over Harold Godwinson in the Norman invasion of England in 1066 come to mind as examples.

Second, both the Aztec and Inca Empires were relatively recent creations in which there were individuals and groups who contested the hierarchical power structure. The conquistadors either found allies among the subject populations or encountered a divided leadership. In either case, they were able to exploit divisions in the empires.

Third, European-introduced diseases, traveling faster than the conquerors, took a devastating toll. In both empires, smallpox hit at critical moments during or right before the Spanish invasions, causing major disruptions.

Fourth, thanks to horses and superior European steel weapons and armor, primarily pikes, swords, and breast plates, small numbers of Spaniards were able to hold large numbers of attacking Aztecs and Incas at bay in hand-to-hand combat. Contrary to widespread belief, cannons and matchlock muskets were less important since they were useless in close encounters. Firearms were still too slow and inaccurate to be decisive.

In contrast to a popular view, a fifth factor, indigenous religion, was probably of least significance. According to this interpretation, Moctezuma was immobilized by his belief in the prophecy of having to relinquish his power to the savior Quetzalcoatl returning from his mythical city of Tlapallan on the east coast (see Chapter 15). Modern scholarship provides convincing reasons, however, to declare this prophecy a postconquest legend, circulated by Cortés both to flatter Charles V and to aggrandize himself as a savior.

Spanish Steel. The Lienzo de Tlaxcala, from the middle part of the sixteenth century, is our best visual source for the conquest of Mexico. In this scene, Malinche, protected by a shield, directs the battle on the causeway leading to Tenochtitlán. The two Spanish soldiers behind her, one fully armored, brandish steel swords, which were more effective than the obsidian blades carried by the Aztec defenders (one of whom is dressed in leopard skins), shown on the left.

The Establishment of Colonial Institutions

The Spanish crown established administrative hierarchies in the Americas, similar to those of the Aztecs and Incas, with governors at the top of the hierarchy and descending through lower ranks of functionaries. A small degree of settler autonomy was permitted through town and city councils, but the crown was determined to make the Americas a territorial extension of the European pattern of fiscal–military state formation. Several hundred thousand settlers (including Alonso Ortíz) found a new life in the Americas, mostly as urban craftspeople, administrators, and professionals. By the early seventeenth century, a powerful elite of Spanish who had been born in America, called **Creoles** (Spanish *criollos*, Portuguese *crioules*, natives) was in place, first to assist and later to replace most of the administrators sent from Spain in the governance of the Americas (see Map 18.2).

Creoles: American-born descendants of European, primarily Iberian, immigrants.

From Conquest to Colonialism   The unimaginable riches of Cortés and Pizarro inspired numerous further expeditions. Adventurers struck out with small bands of followers into Central and North America, Chile, and the Amazon. Their expeditions, however, yielded only modest amounts of gold and earned more from selling captured Native Americans into slavery. One of the best-known and most infamous adventurers was Lope de Aguirre, whose exploits in the Amazon were made famous by the 1972 movie *Aguirre, the Wrath of God*. Only the fortified village chiefdoms of the 1 million Muisca, in what is today Colombia, yielded significant quantities of gold to their conquerors, in 1537. In the north, expeditions penetrated as far as Arizona, New Mexico, Texas, Oklahoma, Kansas, and Florida but encountered only villagers and the relatively poor Pueblo towns. No new golden kingdoms (the mythical El Dorado, or "golden city") beyond the Aztec and Inca Empires were discovered in the Americas.

In the mid-sixteenth century, easy looting was replaced by a search for the mines from where the precious metals came. In northern Mexico, Native Americans led a group of soldiers and missionaries in 1547 to a number of rich silver mines. In addition, explorers discovered silver in Bolivia (1545) and northern Mexico (1556), gold in Chile (1552), and mercury in Peru (1563). The conquistadors shifted from looting to the exploitation of Native American labor in mines and in agriculture.

Bureaucratic Efficiency   During the first two generations after the conquest, Spain maintained an efficient colonial administration, which delivered between 50 and 60 percent of the colonies' revenues to Spain. These revenues contributed as much as one-quarter to the Spanish crown budget. In addition, the viceroyalty of New Spain in Mexico remitted another 25 percent of its revenues to the Philippines, the Pacific province for which it was administratively responsible from 1571 onward. As in Spain, settlers in New Spain had to pay up to 40 different taxes and dues, levied on imports and exports, internal trade, mining, and sales. The only income tax was the tithe to the church, which the administration collected and, at times, used for its own budgetary purposes. Altogether, however, for the settlers the tax level was lower in the New World than in Spain, and the same was true for the English and French colonies in North America.

In the 1540s the government introduced rotating **labor assignments** (*repartimientos*) to phase out the encomiendas which powerful owners sought to perpetuate within their families. This institution of rotating labor assignments was a

Labor assignment (*repartimiento*): Obligation by villagers to send stipulated numbers of people as laborers to a contractor, who had the right to exploit a mine or other labor-intensive enterprise; the contractors paid the laborers minimal wages and bound them through debt peonage to their businesses.

continuation of the mit'a system, which the Incas had devised as a form of taxation, in the absence of money and easy transportation of crops in their empire (see Chapter 15). Rotating labor assignments meant that for fixed times a certain percentage of villagers had to provide labor to the state at low pay for road building, drainage, transportation, and mining. Private entrepreneurs could also contract for indigenous labor assignments, especially in mining regions.

In Mexico the repartimiento fell out of use in the first half of the seventeenth century as a result of the continuing Native American population decline due to recurring smallpox epidemics. It is estimated that the indigenous population in the Americas, from a height of 54 million in 1550, declined to 10 million by 1700 before recovering again. The replacement for the lost workers was wage labor. In highland Peru, where the indigenous population was less densely settled and the effects of smallpox less ravaging, the assignment system lasted to the end of the colonial period. Wage labor expanded there as well. Wages for Native Americans and blacks remained everywhere lower than for those for Creoles.

The Rise of the Creoles   Administrative and fiscal efficiency, however, did not last very long. The wars of the Spanish Habsburg Empire cost more than the crown was able to collect in revenues. King Philip II (r. 1556–1598) had to declare bankruptcy four times between 1557 and 1596. In order to make up the financial deficit, the crown began to sell offices in the Americas to the highest bidders. The first offices put on the block were elective positions in the municipal councils. By the end of the century, Creoles had purchased life appointments in city councils as well as positions as scribes, local judges, police chiefs, directors of processions and festivities, and other sinecures. In these positions, they collected fees and rents for their services. Local oligarchies emerged, effectively ending whatever elective, participatory politics existed in Spanish colonial America.

Over the course of the seventeenth century a majority of administrative positions became available for purchase. As might be imagined, the effects of the change from recruitment by merit to recruitment by wealth on the functioning of the bureaucracy were far-reaching. Creoles advanced on a broad front in the administrative positions, while fewer Spaniards found it attractive to buy their American positions from overseas. The only opportunities which European Spaniards still found enticing were the nearly 300 positions of governors and inspectors since these jobs gave their owners the right to subject the Native Americans to forced purchases of goods, yielding huge profits. For the most part, wealthy Spanish merchants delegated junior partners into these highly lucrative activities. By 1700, the consequences of the Spanish crown selling most of its American administrative offices were a decline in the competence of office holders, the emergence of a Creole elite able to bend the Spanish administration increasingly to its will, and a decentralization of the decision-making processes.

Northwest European Interference   As Spain's administrative grip on the Americas weakened during the seventeenth century, the need to defend the continents militarily against European interlopers arose. At the beginning, there were European privateers, holding royal charters, who harassed Spanish silver shipments and ports in the Caribbean. In the early seventeenth century, the French, English, and Dutch governments sent ships to occupy the smaller Caribbean islands not claimed by Spain. Privateer and contraband traders stationed on these islands engaged in further raiding and pillaging, severely damaging Spain's monopoly of shipping between Europe and the Caribbean.

Conquests of Spanish islands followed in the second half of the century. England captured Jamaica in 1655, and France colonized western Hispaniola in 1665, making it one of their most profitable sugar-producing colonies. Along the Pacific coast, depredations continued into the middle of the eighteenth century. Here, the galleons of the annual Acapulco–Manila fleet carrying silver from Mexico to China and returning with Chinese silks, porcelain, and lacquerware were the targets of English privateers. Over the course of the seventeenth century, Spain allocated one-half to two-thirds of its American revenues to the defense of its annual treasure fleets and Caribbean possessions, which continued despite limited losses to pirates and storms. Only the defense of the many islands eventually proved too difficult for the thinly stretched Spanish forces to maintain.

Bourbon Reforms   The last of the Spanish Habsburg rulers produced no heirs, and after the demise of the dynasty in 1700, the new French-descended dynasty of the Bourbons made major efforts to regain control over their American possessions. They had to begin from a discouragingly weak position as nearly 90 percent of all goods traded from Europe to the Americas were of non-Spanish origin. Fortunately, population increases among the settlers as well as the Native Americans (after having overcome their horrific losses to the epidemics) offered opportunities to Spanish manufacturers and merchants. After several false starts, in the middle of the eighteenth century the Bourbon reform program began to show results.

The reforms aimed at improved naval connections and administrative control between the mother country and the colonies. The monopolistic annual armed silver fleet was greatly reduced. Instead, the government authorized more frequent single sailings at different times of the year. Newly formed Spanish companies, receiving exclusive rights at specific ports, succeeded in reducing contraband trade. Elections took place again for municipal councils. Spanish-born salaried officials replaced scores of Creole tax and office farmers. The original two viceroyalties were subdivided into four, to improve administrative control. The sale of tobacco and brandy became state monopolies. Silver mining and cotton textile manufacturing were expanded. By the second half of the eighteenth century, Spain had regained a measure of control over its colonies.

As a result, tax receipts rose substantially. Government revenues increased more than twofold, even taking into account the inflation of the late eighteenth century. In the end, however, the reforms remained incomplete. Since the Spanish economy was not also reformed, in terms of expanding crafts production and urbanization, the changes did not diminish the English and French dominance of the import market by much. Spain failed to produce textiles, metalwares, and household goods at competitive prices for the colonies; and as a result, English and French exports to the Americas remained high.

Early Portuguese Colonialism   In contrast to the Spanish Americas, the Portuguese overseas province of Brazil remained initially confined to a broad coastal strip, which developed only slowly during the sixteenth century. The first governor-general, whose rank was equivalent to a Spanish viceroy, arrived in 1549. He and

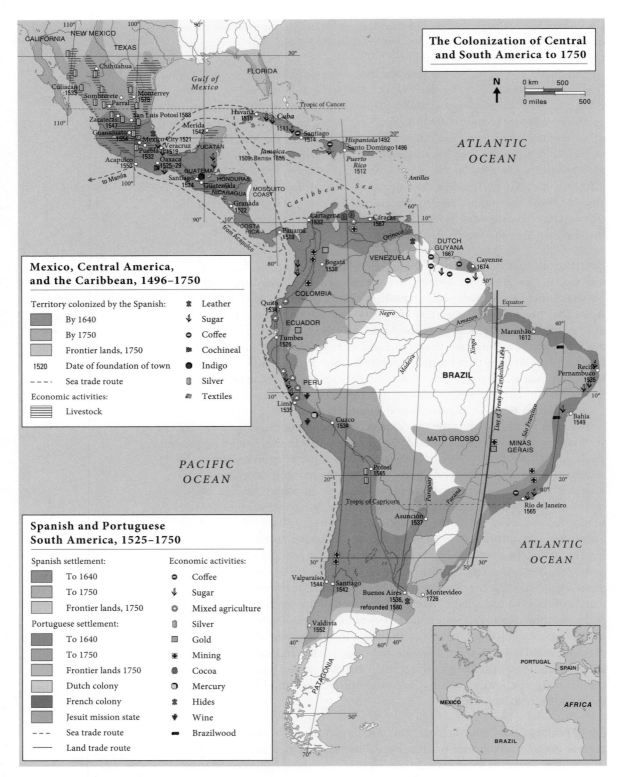

The Colonization of Central and South America to 1750

N   0 km   500

0 miles   500

Mexico, Central America, and the Caribbean, 1496–1750

Territory colonized by the Spanish:

- By 1640
- By 1750
- Frontier lands, 1750
- 1520   Date of foundation of town
- - - -   Sea trade route

Economic activities:

- Livestock

✱	Leather
⬇	Sugar
●	Coffee
🐛	Cochineal
●	Indigo
▯	Silver
▨	Textiles

Spanish and Portuguese South America, 1525–1750

Spanish settlement:

- To 1640
- To 1750
- Frontier lands, 1750

Portuguese settlement:

- To 1640
- To 1750
- Frontier lands 1750
- Dutch colony
- French colony
- Jesuit mission state
- - - -   Sea trade route
- ———   Land trade route

Economic activities:

●	Coffee
⬇	Sugar
◉	Mixed agriculture
▯	Silver
▪	Gold
✦	Mining
◉	Cocoa
◗	Mercury
✱	Hides
▼	Wine
▬	Brazilwood

MAP 18.2 The Colonization of Central and South America to 1750.

his successors were members of the high aristocracy, but their positions were salaried and
subject to term limits. As the colony grew, the
crown created a council in the capital of Lisbon
for all Brazilian appointments and established a
high court for all judicial affairs in Bahia, northern Brazil. Commoners with law degrees from
the Portuguese university of Coimbra filled
the nonmilitary colonial positions. In the early
seventeenth century, however, offices became
as open to purchase as in the Spanish colonies,
although not on the city council level, where a
complex indirect electoral process survived.

Jesuits converted the Native Americans,
whom they transported to villages that the Jesuits administered. Colonial cities and Jesuits
repeatedly clashed over the slave raids of the
"pioneers" (*bandeirantes*) in village territories.
The bandeirantes came mostly from São Paulo
in the south and roamed the interior in search
of human prey. Native American slaves were in
demand on the wheat farms and cattle ranches
of São Paulo as well as the sugar plantations of
the northeast. Although the Portuguese crown
and church had, like the Spanish, forbidden the
enslavement of Native Americans, the bandei-

Mine Workers. The discovery of gold and diamonds in Minas Gerais led to a boom, but did little to contribute to the long-term health of the Brazilian economy. With the Native American population decimated by disease, African slaves performed the back-breaking work.

rantes exploited a loophole. The law was interpreted as allowing the enslavement of
Native Americans who resisted conversion to Christianity. For a long time, Lisbon
and the Jesuits were powerless against this flagrantly self-interested interpretation.

Expansion into the Interior　In the middle of the seventeenth century, the
Jesuits and Native Americans finally succeeded in pushing many bandeirantes west
and north, where they switched from slave raiding to prospecting for gold. In the
far north, however, the raids continued until 1680, when the Portuguese administration finally prevailed and imposed an end to Native American slavery, almost
a century and a half after Spain. Ironically, it was mostly thanks to the "pioneer"
raids for slaves that Brazil expanded westward, well beyond the demarcation line of
Tordesillas agreed to with Spain, to assume the borders it has today.

As a result of gold discoveries in Minas Gerais in 1690 by bandeirantes, the European immigrant population increased rapidly, from 1 to 2 million during the 1700s.
Minas Gerais, located north of Rio de Janeiro, was the first inland region of the colony to attract settlers. By contrast, as a result of smallpox epidemics beginning in the
1650s in the Brazilian interior, the Native American population declined massively,
not to expand again until the end of the eighteenth century. To replace the loss of
labor, Brazilians imported slaves from Africa, at first to work in the sugar plantations
and, after 1690, in the mines, where their numbers increased to two-thirds of the
labor force. In contrast to Spanish mines, Brazilian mines were surface operations
requiring only minimal equipment outlays. Most blacks worked with pickaxes and

shovels. The peak of the gold boom came in the 1750s, when the importance of gold was second only to that of sugar on the list of Brazilian exports to Europe.

Early in the gold boom, the crown created a new Ministry of the Navy and Overseas Territories, which greatly expanded the administrative structure in Brazil. It established 14 regions and a second high court in Rio de Janeiro, which replaced Bahia as the capital in 1736. The ministry in Lisbon ended the sale of offices, increased the efficiency of tax collection, and encouraged Brazilian textile manufacturing to render the province more independent from English imports. By the mid-1700s, Brazil was a flourishing overseas colony of Portugal, producing brazilwood, sugar, gold, tobacco, cacao, and vanilla for export.

North American Settlements   Efforts at settlement in the less hospitable North America in the sixteenth century were unsuccessful. Only in the early part of the seventeenth century did French, English, and Dutch merchant investors succeed on the northeastern coast in establishing small communities of settlers, who grew their own food on land purchased from the local Native American villagers. These settlements were Jamestown (founded in 1607 in today's Virginia), Quebec (1608, Canada), Plymouth and Boston (1620 and 1630, respectively, New England), and New Amsterdam (1625, New York). Subsistence agriculture and fur, however, were meager ingredients for the settlements to prosper. The northerly settlements struggled through the seventeenth century, sustained either by Catholic missionary efforts or by the Protestant enthusiasm of the Puritans who had escaped persecution in England. Southern places like Jamestown survived because they adopted tobacco, a warm-weather crop, as a cash crop for export to Europe. In contrast to Mexico and Peru, the North American settlements were not followed—at least not at first—by territorial conquests (see Map 18.3).

Native Americans   Once they had settled down and established themselves agriculturally, the European arrivals in North America began supplementing agriculture with trade. They exchanged metal and glass wares, beads and seashells for furs, especially beaver pelts, with the Native American tribal groups of the interior. The more these tribal groups came into contact with the European traders, however, the more dramatic the demographic impact of the trade on them was: Smallpox, already a menace during the 1500s in North America, became devastating as contacts intensified. In New England, for example, of the ca. 144,000 estimated Native Americans in 1600, fewer than 15,000 remained in 1620. The introduction of guns contributed an additional lethal factor to trading arrangements: English, French, and Dutch traders provided their favorite Native American trading partners with flintlocks, in order to increase the yield of furs. As a result, in the course of the 1600s the Iroquois in the northeast were able to organize themselves into a heavily armed and independent-minded federation, capable of inflicting heavy losses on rival groups as well as on European traders and settlers.

Further south, in Virginia, the Jamestown settlers encountered the Powhatan confederacy. These Native Americans, living in some 200 well fortified, palisaded villages, dominated the region between the Chesapeake Bay and the Appalachian Mountains. Initially, the Powhatan supplied Jamestown with foodstuffs and sought to integrate the settlement into their confederation. When this invitation to integration failed, however, benevolence turned to hostility and the confederacy raided

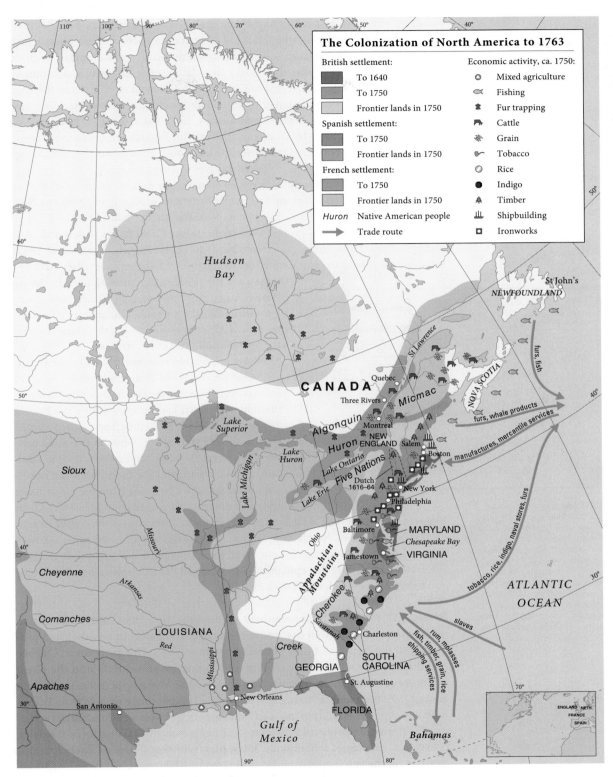

MAP 18.3 **The Colonization of North America to 1763.**

Jamestown twice in an attempt to rid their region of foreign settlers. But the latter were able to turn the tables and defeat the Powhatan in 1646, thereafter occupying their lands and reducing them to small scattered remnants. (Pocahontas, daughter of the Powhatan chief at the time of the foundation of Jamestown, was captured during one of the raids, converted to Christianity, and lived in England as the wife of a returning settler for a number of years. Her life has been the subject of many books, fireside stories, two Hollywood movies, and a video game.) The decline of the Powhatan in the later 1600s opened the way for English settlers to move westward, in contrast to New England where the Iroquois, although allied with the English against the French, de facto blocked any western expansion.

The Iroquois were fiercely determined to maintain their dominance of the fur trade and wrought havoc among the Native American groups living between New England and the Great Lakes. In the course of the second half of the 1600s they drove many smaller tribal groups westward into the Great Lakes region and Mississippi plains. Here, these groups settled as refugees. French officials and Jesuit missionaries sought to create some sort of alliance with the refugee tribes, to counterbalance the powerful Iroquois to the east. Many Native Americans converted to Christianity, creating for themselves a Creole Christianity similar to that of the Africans of Kongo and the Mexicans after the Spanish conquest of the Aztecs.

Major population movements also occurred further west on the Great Plains, where the Apaches arrived from the southwest on horses. They had captured horses which had escaped during the Pueblo uprising of 1680–1695 against Spain. The Comanches, who also arrived on horses at the same time from the Great Basin in the Rockies, had, in addition, acquired firearms. The Sioux from the northern forests and the Cheyenne from the Great Basin added to the mix of tribal federations on the Great Plains in the early 1700s. At this time, the great transformation of the Native Americans in the center of North America into horse breeders and horsemen warriors began. Smallpox epidemics did not reach the Plains until the mid 1700s while in the east the ravages of this epidemic had weakened the Iroquois so much that they concluded a peace with the French in 1701.

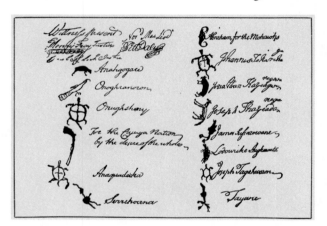

Land Sale. Signatures of the Iroquois federation leaders to a treaty with Thomas and Richard Penn in 1736. By the terms of this treaty the Iroquois sold land to the founders of the English colony of Pennsylvania. The leaders of the six nations that made up the Iroquois federation (Mohawk, Oneida, Onondaga, Cayuga, Seneca, and Tuscarora) signed with their pictograms. The names were added later.

French Canada   The involvement of the French in the Great Lakes region with refugees fleeing from the Iroquois was part and parcel of an expansion program into the center of North America, begun in 1663. The governor of Quebec had dispatched explorers, fur traders, and missionaries not only into the Great Lakes region but also the Mississippi valley and the Mississippi delta. The French government then sent farmers, craftspeople, and young single women from France with government-issued agricultural implements and livestock to establish settlements. The most successful settlement was in the subtropical district of the delta, called "La Louisianie," where some 300 settlers with 4,000 African slaves founded sugar plantations. Immigration was restricted to French subjects and excluded Protestants. Given these restrictions, Louisiana received only some 30,000 settlers by 1750, in contrast to English North America, with nearly 1.2 million settlers by the same time.

From English to British Colonies

As immigration to New England picked up, the merchant companies in Europe, which had financed the journeys of the settlers, were initially responsible for the administration of about a dozen settlement colonies. The first settlers to demand participation in the colonial administration were Virginian tobacco growers with interests in the European trade. In 1619 they deputized delegates from their villages to meet as the House of Burgesses. They thereby created an early popular assembly in North America, assisting their governor in running the colony. Using this example of self-administration as a model, the other English colonies soon followed suit, with the creation of their own assemblies. In contrast to Spain and Portugal, England—wracked by its internal Anglican–Puritan conflict—was initially uninvolved in the governance of the overseas territories.

When England eventually stepped in and took the governance of the colonies away from the charter merchants and companies in the second half of the seventeenth century, it faced entrenched settler assemblies, especially in New England. Only in New Amsterdam, conquered from the Dutch in 1664–1674 and renamed "New York," did the governor initially rule without an assembly. Many governors were deputies of wealthy aristocrats who never traveled to America but stayed in London. They were powerless to prevent the assemblies from appropriating rights to levy taxes and making appointments. The assemblies thus modeled themselves after Parliament in London. As in England, these assemblies were highly select bodies that excluded poorer settlers, who did not meet the property requirements to vote or stand for elections.

Steady immigration, also from the European mainland, encouraged land speculators in the British colonies to cast their sights beyond the Appalachian Mountains. (According to historical convention, the English are called "British" after the English–Scottish union in 1707.) In 1749, the Ohio Company of Virginia received a royal permit to develop land, together with a protective fort, south of the Ohio River. The French, however, also claimed the Ohio valley, considering it a part of their Canada–Mississippi–Louisiana territory. A few years later, tensions over the valley erupted into open hostility. Initially, the local encounters went badly for the Virginian militia and British army. In 1755, however, the British and French broadened their clash into a worldwide war for dominance in the colonies and Europe, the Seven Years' War of 1756–1763.

The Seven Years' War

Both France and Great Britain borrowed heavily to pour resources into the war. England had the superior navy and France, the superior army. Since the British navy succeeded in choking off French supplies to its increasingly isolated land troops, Britain won the war overseas. In Europe, Britain's failure to supply the troops of its ally Prussia against the Austrian–French alliance caused the war on that front to end in a draw. Overseas, the British gained most of the French holdings in India, several islands in the Caribbean, all of Canada, and all the land east of the Mississippi. The war costs and land swaps, however, proved to be unmanageable for both the vanquished and the victor. The unpaid debts became the root cause of the American, French, and Haitian constitutional revolutions that began 13 years later. Those revolutions, along with the emerging industrialization of Great Britain, signaled the beginning of the modern scientific–industrial age in world history.

The Making of American Societies: Origins and Transformations

The pattern of transforming the Americas into an extension of Europe evolved unevenly. The exploitation of both mineral resources and tropical agricultural resources, powered largely by the forced labor of Native American and black slaves, developed along different lines in the Spanish, Portuguese, French, and English colonies. Before we examine these differences, it is worth pausing for a moment to consider that the creation of new societies and economies in the Americas was made possible by the **Columbian Exchange**. The transfer of plants, animals, and diseases from the Old Word to the New and from the New World to the Old marks a major turning point in human history. Without this exchange of biota the European exploitation of the Americas cannot be fully appreciated (see Patterns Up Close).

Columbian Exchange: Exchange of plants, animals, and diseases between the Americas and the rest of the world.

Spanish exploitation of the Americas emphasized mineral extraction and focused on plantation agricultural production only at a later stage, while the Portuguese proceeded in the reverse direction. France and England, initially unable to develop either mineral or agricultural exploitation in the cold northeast, expanded southward, where they could develop plantations. Since European settlers acquired their mineral and agricultural wealth through forced labor, a social hierarchy evolved which prevented Native Americans and African slaves from rising in rebellion. Western Europe was linguistically deeply divided but ethnically relatively homogeneous. By contrast, the American colonies were linguistically largely uniform (in the upper strata) but ethnically deeply divided. In the long run, this contrast in social divisions contributed to widely divergent political paths along which Europe and the Americas embarked.

Exploitation of Mineral and Tropical Resources

The pattern of European expansion into subtropical and tropical lands began with the Spanish colonization of the Caribbean islands. When the Spanish crown ran out of gold in the Caribbean, it exported silver from Mexico and Peru in great quantities to finance a fiscal–military state that could compete with the Ottomans and European kings. By contrast, Portugal's colony of Brazil did not at first mine for precious metals, and consequently, the Portuguese crown pioneered the growing of sugar on plantations. Mining would be developed later. The North American colonies of England and France had, in comparison, little native industry at first. By moving farther south, however, they adopted the plantation system for indigo and rice and, thus, joined their Spanish and Portuguese predecessors in exploiting the subtropical–tropical agricultural potential of the Americas.

Silver Mines   When the interest of the Spaniards turned from looting to the exploitation of mineral resources, two main mining centers emerged: Potosí in southeastern Peru (today Bolivia) and Zacatecas and Guanajuato in northern Mexico. For the first 200 years after its founding in 1545, Potosí produced over half of the silver of Spanish America. In the eighteenth century, Zacatecas and Guanajuato jumped ahead of Potosí, churning out almost three times more of the precious metal. During the same century, gold-mining in Colombia and Chile rose to importance as well, making the mining of precious metals the most important economic activity in the Americas.

Innovations, such as the "patio" method, which facilitated the extraction process through the use of mercury, and the unrestrained exploitation of indigenous labor, made American silver highly competitive in the world market. Conditions among the Native Americans and blacks employed as labor were truly abominable. Entrepreneurs paid by daily quota, not by day as the law demanded. The annual rest weeks were fewer than prescribed. Loads were heavier than permitted. Day and night shifts followed each other with less rest than required. Workers had to do cleaning work overtime and use children for additional tasks, such as help in carrying loads, providing messenger services, spinning cotton, and making candles from cattle tallow. Entrepreneurs who rented the general store to mining supervisors combined the fines for labor infractions with the debts the workers owed for their purchases of coca leaves and alcohol, throwing them into permanent debt dependence. Lung diseases and mercury poisoning were endemic. Few laborers lasted through more than two forced recruitment (*repartimiento*) cycles before they were incapacitated or dead.

Given gaps in bookkeeping and high degrees of smuggling, scholars have found it extremely difficult to estimate the total production of the American mines from 1550 to 1750. The best current estimate is that Spanish America produced 150,000 tons of silver (including gold converted into silver weight). This quantity corresponded to roughly 85 percent of world production. The figures underline the extraordinary role of American silver for the money economies of Spain, Europe, the Middle East, and Asia, especially China.

The Silver Mountain of Potosí. Note the patios in the left foreground and the water-driven crushing mill in the center, which ground the silver-bearing ore into a fine sand that then was moistened, caked, and eventually amalgamated with mercury. The mine workers' insect-like shapes reinforce the dehumanizing effects of their labor.

Since the exploitation of the mines was of such central importance, for the first century and a half of New World colonization the Spanish crown organized its other provinces around the needs of the mining centers. Hispaniola and Cuba in the Caribbean were islands which had produced foodstuffs, sugar, and tobacco from the time of Columbus but only in small quantities. Their main function was to feed and protect Havana, the collection point for the Mexican and Peruvian silver and the port from where the annual Spanish fleet shipped the American silver across the Atlantic.

A second region, Argentina and Paraguay, was colonized as a bulwark to prevent the Portuguese and Dutch from cutting across the southern end of the continent and to access Peruvian silver. Once established, the two colonies produced wheat, cattle, mules, horses, cotton, textiles, and tallow to feed and supply the miners in Potosí. The subtropical crop of cotton, produced by small farmers, played a role in Europe's extension into warm-weather agriculture only toward the end of the colonial period.

Patterns Up Close | The Columbian Exchange

Few of us can imagine an Italian kitchen without tomatoes or an Irish meal without potatoes or Chinese or Indian cuisine without the piquant presence of chilies, but until fairly recently each of these foods was unknown to the Old World. Likewise, the expression, "as American as apple pie" obscures the fact that for millennia apples, as well as many other frequently consumed fruits, such as peaches, pears, plums, cherries, bananas, oranges, and lemons, were absent from the New World. It was not until the sixteenth century, when plants, animals, and microbes began to flow from one end of the planet to another, that new patterns of ecology and biology changed the course of millions of years of divergent evolution.

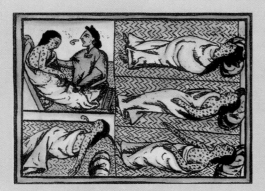

Smallpox Victims. The protracted isolation of the peoples of the Americas from the rest of the world made them vulnerable to a battery of diseases European colonists brought with them: the "breath of a Spaniard" was said to be sufficient enough to kill. These sixteenth-century illustrations, drawn by a native Mexican artist, depict smallpox victims. In the upper left panel a doctor attempts to treat his patient—undoubtedly he failed.

While the Columbian Exchange was the largest and most consequential transfer of life-forms in human history, it certainly was not the first. By 500 CE, Indonesian sailors had brought the banana to the east coast of Africa. A few hundred years later, Muslim traders facilitated the transmission of rice, oranges, lemons, sugarcane, eggplant, and cotton—all of which are indigenous to south and southeast Asia—throughout the Mediterranean and eventually to western Europe, transforming both diets and economies. Plagues, such as the Black Death of 1348–1350, also periodically swept across one end of Eurasia to another, with devastating results. Still, these intrahemispheric transfers pale in comparison to the exchange of diseases, plants, and animals between previously disconnected continents that was set in motion after 1500 (see Map 18.4).

When historians catalog the long list of life-forms that moved across the oceans in the Columbian Exchange, pride of place is usually reserved for the bigger, better-known migrants like cattle, sheep, pigs, and horses. However, as the historian Alfred Crosby pointed out in his pioneering work from over 30 years ago, the impact of European weeds and grasses on American grasslands, which made it possible for the North American prairie and the South American pampas to support livestock, should not be overlooked. By binding the soil together with their long, tough roots, these "empires of the dandelion" provided the conditions for the grazing of sheep, cattle, and horses, as well as the planting of crops like wheat.

A Beverage Fit for Kings. By 1720, when this painting was made, drinking chocolate—in a fashion similar to the manner in which the Aztecs consumed it—was a widespread habit among European elites, including King João V of Portugal, who is shown expertly pouring the luxury beverage in front of an approving audience.

The other, silent invader that accompanied the conquistadors was, of course, disease. Thousands of years of mutual isolation between the Americas and Afro-Eurasia rendered the immune systems of Native Americans vulnerable to the scourges that European colonists unwittingly brought with them. Smallpox, influenza, diphtheria, whooping cough, typhoid, chicken pox, measles, and meningitis wiped out millions of Native Americans—by some estimates, the Indian populations of Mesoamerica and the Andes plummeted by 90 percent in the period 1500–1700. In comparison, the contagion the New World was able to reciprocate upon the Old World—syphilis and tuberculosis—did not unleash nearly the same virulence, and the New World origin of these diseases is still debated.

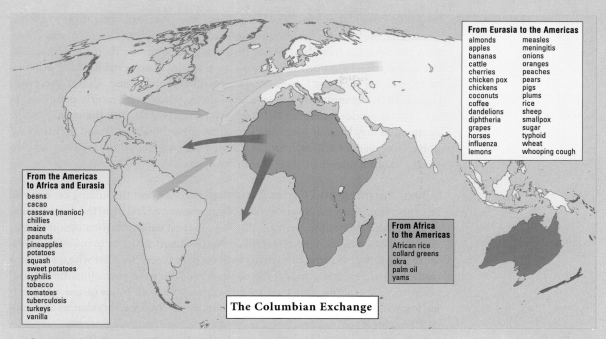

From Eurasia to the Americas

almonds	measles
apples	meningitis
bananas	onions
cattle	oranges
cherries	peaches
chicken pox	pears
chickens	pigs
coconuts	plums
coffee	rice
dandelions	sheep
diphtheria	smallpox
grapes	sugar
horses	typhoid
influenza	wheat
lemons	whooping cough

From the Americas to Africa and Eurasia

beans
cacao
cassava (manioc)
chillies
maize
peanuts
pineapples
potatoes
squash
sweet potatoes
syphilis
tobacco
tomatoes
tuberculosis
turkeys
vanilla

From Africa to the Americas

African rice
collard greens
okra
palm oil
yams

The Columbian Exchange

MAP 18.4 **The Columbian Exchange.**

It is therefore obvious that the big winner in the Columbian Exchange was western Europe, though the effects of the New World bounty took centuries to be fully discerned. While Asia and Africa also benefited from the Columbian Exchange in the forms of new foods that enriched diets, the Europeans got a continent endowed with a warm climate in which they could create new and improved versions of their homelands—what Alfred Crosby calls "Neo-Europes." Undoubtedly, Native Americans were the biggest losers: They were nearly wiped out by disease, their lands appropriated, and the survivors either enslaved or marginalized. Africans were losers as well. The precipitous drop in the population of Native Americans, combined with the tropical and semitropical climate of much of the Americas, created the necessary conditions for the Atlantic slave trade. Even though the introduction of corn and manioc from the Americas fueled population growth across Africa and more than offset population loss from slaving, overall, the traffic in slaves negatively affected African societies.

Because of the profound changes it wrought on so many societies and cultures across so many continents, few events can match the Columbian Exchange for the size and scope of its impact on the patterns of world history—something to chew on the next time you order takeout from your local pizza joint.

Questions

- Can the Columbian Exchange be considered one of the origins of the modern world? How? Why? How does the Columbian Exchange demonstrate the origins, interactions, and adaptations model that is used throughout this book?

- Weigh the positive and negative outcomes of the Columbian Exchange. Is it possible to determine whether the effects of the Columbian Exchange on human society and the natural environment were for the better or for the worse?

A third colonial region, Venezuela, began as a grain and cattle supply base for Cartagena, the port for the shipment of Colombian gold, and Panama and Porto-belo, ports for the transshipment of Peruvian silver from the Pacific to Havana. Its cocoa and tobacco exports flourished only after the Dutch established themselves in 1624 in the southern Caribbean and provided the shipping. Thus, three major regions of the Spanish overseas empire in the Americas were mostly peripheral as agricultural producers during the sixteenth century. Only after the middle of the century did they begin to specialize in tropical agricultural goods, and they were ex-porters only in the eighteenth century. By that time, the Dutch and English provided more and more shipping in the place of the Spanish.

Wheat Farming and Cattle Ranching   To support the mining centers and administrative cities, the Spanish colonial government encouraged the development of agricultural estates (*haciendas*). These estates first emerged when conquistadors used their *encomienda* rights to round up Native American labor to produce subsis-tence crops. Native American tenant farmers were forced to grow wheat and raise cattle, pigs, sheep, and goats for the conquerors, who were now agricultural entre-preneurs. In the latter part of the sixteenth century, the land grants gave way to rotat-ing forced labor as well as wage labor. Owners established their residences and built dwellings for tenant farmers on their estates. A landowner class emerged.

Like the conquistadors before, a majority of landowners produced wheat and animals for sale to urban and mining centers. Cities purchased wheat and main-tained granaries in order to provide for urban dwellers in times of harvest failure. Entrepreneurs received commissions to provide slaughterhouses with regular supplies of animals. As the Native American population declined in the seven-teenth century and the church helped in consolidating the remaining population in large villages, additional land became available for the establishment of estates. From 1631 onward, authorities granted Spanish settler families the right to main-tain their estates undivided from generation to generation. Through donations, the church also acquired considerable agricultural lands. Secular and clerical land-owning interests supported a powerful upper social stratum of Creoles from the eighteenth century onward.

Plantations and Gold Mining in Brazil   Brazil's agricultural industry began with brazilwood, followed by sugar plantations, before gold mining rose to promi-nence in the eighteenth century. A crisis hit sugar production in 1680–1700, mostly as a result of the Dutch beginning production of sugar in the Antilles. It was at that time that the gold of Minas Gerais, in the interior of Brazil, were discovered.

Gold-mining operations in Brazil during the eighteenth century were consid-erably less capital-intensive than the silver mines in Spanish America. Most min-ers were relatively small operators with sieves, pickaxes, and a few black slaves as unskilled laborers. Many entrepreneurs were indebted for their slaves to absentee capitalists, with whom they shared the profits. Since prospecting took place on the land of Native Americans, bloody encounters were frequent. Most entrepreneurs were ruthless frontiersmen who exploited their slaves and took no chances with the indigenous people. Brazil produced about 100,000 tons of gold in the eighteenth century, a welcome bonanza for Portugal at a time of low agricultural prices. Overall, minerals were just as valuable for the Portuguese as they were for the Spanish.

Plantations in Spanish and English America   The expansion of plantation farming in the Spanish colonies was a result of the Bourbon reforms. Although sugar, tobacco, and rice had been introduced early into the Caribbean and southern Mexico, it was only in the expanded plantation system of the eighteenth century that these crops (plus cactuses for cochineal, and indigo, and cacao) were produced on a large scale for export to Europe. The owners of plantations did not need expensive machinery and invested instead in African slave labor, with the result that the slave trade hit its full stride, beginning around 1750.

English North American settlements in Virginia and Carolina exported tobacco and rice beginning in the 1660s. Georgia was the thirteenth British colony, beginning in 1733 as a bulwark against Spanish Florida and a haven for poor Europeans. In 1750 it joined southern Carolina as a major plantation colony and rice and indigo producer. In the eighteenth century, even New England finally had its own export crop, in the form of timber for shipbuilding and charcoal production in Great Britain, at the amazing rate of 250 million board feet from about 1 million acres per year by the start of the nineteenth century. These timber exports illustrate an important new factor appearing in the Americas in the eighteenth century. Apart from the cheap production of precious metals and warm-weather crops, the American extension of Europe became increasingly important as a replacement for dwindling fuel resources across much of northern Europe. Altogether, it was thanks to the Americas that cold and rainy Europe rose successfully into the ranks of the wealthy, climatically balanced, and populated Indian and Chinese empires.

Shades of Skin Color: Social Strata, Castes, and Ethnic Groups

The population of settlers in the New World consisted entirely of Europeans who came from a continent that had barely emerged from its population losses to the Black Death. Although population numbers were rising again in the sixteenth century, Europe did not have masses of emigrants to the Americas to spare. Given the small settler population of the Americas, the temptation to develop a system of forced labor in agriculture and mining was irresistible. Since the Native Americans and African slaves pressed into labor were ethnically so completely different from the Europeans, however, a social system evolved in which the latter two not only were economically underprivileged but also populated the ethnically nonintegrated lowest rungs of the social ladder. A pattern of legal and customary discrimination evolved which, even though partially vitiated by the rise of ethnically mixed groups, prevented the integration of American ethnicities into settler society.

> **1543 Petition by Native Americans in Mexico to Raise Silk (from Tejupan in Southern Mexico)**
>
> "And now the Indians of that town appeared before me and reported that the time of the contract [with three Spaniards] was finished and that they wished to raise silk on their own for the profit and usefulness that (the industry) would bring them. . . . You are to allow them and to permit them to raise silk and not stop them nor allow any obstacle whatever nor that [the three Spaniards] raise silk in the said town since the contract and agreement made with the Indians of the town has expired."
>
> —Richard Boyer and Geoffrey Spurling, *eds. Colonial Lives: Documents on Latin American History, 1550–1850,* p. 9. New York: Oxford University Press, 2000.

The Social Elite   The heirs of the Spanish conquistadors and estate owners—mixed farmers, ranchers, and planters—maintained city residences and employed managers on their agricultural properties. In Brazil, cities emerged more slowly, and for a long time estate owners maintained their manor houses as small urban islands. Estate owners mixed with the Madrid- and Lisbon-appointed administrators and, during the seventeenth century, intermarried with them, creating the top tier of settler society known as Creoles. This tier, the "respectable people" (Spanish *gentes decentes*), encompassed about 4 percent of the total population. In a wider sense, the tier included also merchants, professionals, clerks, militia officers, and the clergy. They formed a relatively closed society in which descent, intermarriage, landed property, and a government position counted more than money and education.

The great majority of estate owners were mixed farmers and ranchers. In the seventeenth and eighteenth centuries, they farmed predominantly with Native American forced labor. The estates produced grain and/or cattle, legumes, cattle, sheep, and pigs for local urban markets or mining towns. In contrast to the black slave plantation estates of the Caribbean and coastal regions of Spanish and Portuguese America, the mixed farming estates did not export their goods to Europe. Madrid and Lisbon, furthermore, discouraged these mixed estates from producing olive oil, wine, or silk, to protect their home production. Nevertheless, there were Mexicans who produced silk in the second half of the sixteenth century and Peruvian and Chilean vintners who produced wine by the seventeenth century and brandy by the following century, albeit for American consumption only.

As local producers with little competition, mixed farming and ranching estate owners did not feel market pressures. Since for the most part they lived in the cities, they exploited their estates with minimal investments and usually drew profits of less than 5 percent of annual revenues. They were often heavily indebted, and as a result, there was often more glitter than substance among the *gentes decentes*.

Lower Creoles   The second tier of Creole society consisted of people like Alonzo Ortíz, the tanner introduced at the beginning of this chapter. Even though of second

Textile Production. Immigrants from Spain, like Alonso Ortíz discussed at the start of the chapter, established workshops (*obrajes*) as tanners, weavers, carpenters, or wheelwrights. As craftspeople producing simple but affordable goods for the poor, they remained competitive throughout the colonial period, in spite of increasingly large textile, utensil, and furniture imports from Europe. At the same time, indigenous textile production by native women continued as in the preconquest period, albeit under the constraints of labor services imposed by officials or clergy, as shown in these examples.

rank, these "popular people" (*gentes de pueblo*) were privileged European settlers who, as craftspeople and traders, theoretically worked with their hands. In practice, many of them were owner-operators who employed Native Americans and/or black slaves as apprentices and journeymen. Many invested in small plots of land in the vicinity of their cities. As in Spain, they were organized in guilds, which controlled prices and quality standards.

Wealthy weavers ran textile manufactures (*obrajes*), mostly concentrated in the cities of Mexico, Peru, Paraguay, and Argentina. In some of these manufactures, up to 300 Native American and black workers produced cheap, coarse woolens and a variety of cottons on dozens of looms. Men were the weavers and women, the spinners—in contrast to the pre-Columbian period, when textile manufacture was entirely a woman's job. These textiles were alternatives to the higher-quality European imports, unaffordable to most. On a smaller scale, manufactures also existed for pottery and leather goods. On the whole, the urban manufacturing activities of the popular people, serving local markets, remained vibrant until well into the nineteenth century, in spite of massive European imports.

Race, Class, and Gender in Colonial Mexico. An outraged mulatta defends herself against an aggressive Creole, with a fearful child clinging to the woman's skirt.

Mestizos and Mulattoes The mixed European–Native American and European–African population had the collective name of "caste" (*casta*), or ethnic group. The term originated in the desire of the Iberian and Creole settlers to draw distinctions among degrees of mixture in order to counterbalance as much as possible the masses of Native Americans and Africans, especially from the eighteenth century onward. The two most important castes were the *mestizos* (Spanish) or *mestiços* (Portuguese), who had Iberian fathers and Native American mothers, and *mulatos*, who had Iberian fathers and black mothers. By 1800 the castas formed the third largest population category in Latin America as a whole (20 percent), after Native Americans (40 percent) and Creoles (30 percent). In Brazil, mulattoes and black freedmen were even with Creoles (28 percent each), after black slaves (38 percent) and before Native Americans (6 percent in the settled provinces outside Amazonia). In both Spanish and Portuguese America, there was also a small percentage of people descended from Native American and black unions. Thus, most of the intermediate population groups were sizeable, playing important neutralizing roles in colonial society, as they had one foot each in the Creole and subordinate social strata (see Figure 18.1).

As such neutralizing elements, mestizos and mulattoes filled lower levels of the bureaucracy and the lay hierarchy in the church. They held skilled and supervisory positions in mines and on estates. In addition, in the armed forces mulattoes dominated the ranks of enlisted men; in the defense militias, they even held officer ranks. In Brazil, many mulattoes and black freedmen were farmers. Much of the craft production was in their hands. A wide array of laws existed to keep mestizos and mulattoes in their peculiarly intermediate social and political positions.

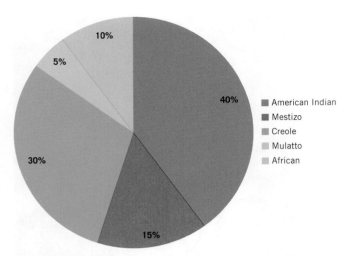

Figure 18.1 Ethnic Composition of Latin America, ca. 1800.

- American Indian — 40%
- Mestizo — 15%
- Creole — 30%
- Mulatto — 5%
- African — 10%

Women   The roles played by women depended strongly on their social position. Well-appointed elite Creole households followed the Mediterranean tradition of secluding women from men. In separate women's quarters, married women had servants for all their needs. On average, elite Creole women married three years younger than women in Spain. When they went out—seldom to anything but mass, religious festivals, or family visits—they had chaperones for protection. The public mixing of genders had to be avoided at all costs.

Within their confines of the household, elite women were persons of means and influence. They were the owners of substantial dowries and legally stipulated grooms' gifts. Often, they actively managed the investment of their assets. Outside their confines, however, even elite women lost all protection. Crimes of passion, committed by honor-obsessed fathers or husbands, went unpunished. Husbands and fathers who did not resort to violence nevertheless did not need witnesses to obtain court judgments to banish daughters or wives to convents for alleged lapses in chastity. Thus, even elite women obeyed definite limits set by a patriarchal society.

On the lower rungs of society, be it popular Creole, mestizo, mulatto, or Native American, gender separation was much less prevalent. After all, everyone in the family had to work in order to make ends meet. Men, women, and children shared labor in the fields and workshops. Girls or wives took in clothes to wash or went out to work as domestics in wealthy households. Older women dominated retail in market stalls. As in elite society, wives tended to outlive husbands. In addition, working families with few assets suffered abandonment by males. Women headed one-third of all households in Mexico City, according to an 1811 census. Among black slaves in the region of São Paulo, 70 percent of women were without formal ties to the men who

Illustration from an Indian Land Record. The Spaniards almost completely wiped out the Aztec archives after the conquest of Mexico; surviving examples of Indian manuscripts are thus extremely rare. Although the example shown here, made from the bark of a fig tree, claims to date from the early 1500s, it is part of the so-called "Techialoyan" land records created in the seventeenth century to substantiate native land claims. These "*titulos primodiales*," as they were called, were essentially municipal histories that documented in text and pictures local accounts of important events and territorial boundaries.

fathered their children. Thus, the most pronounced division in colonial society was that of a patriarchy among the Creoles and a slave society dominated by women, with frequently absent men—an unbridgeable division that persists today.

Native Americans In the immediate aftermath of the conquest, Native Americans could be found at all levels of the social scale. Some were completely marginalized in remote corners of the American continents. Others acculturated into the ranks of the working poor in the silver mines or textile manufactures. A few even formed an educated Aztec or Inca propertied upper class, exercising administrative functions in Spanish civil service. Social distinctions, however, disappeared rapidly during the first 150 years of Spanish colonialism. Smallpox reduced the Native American population by nearly 80 percent. Diseases were more virulent in humid, tropical parts of

> **Yellow Fever Arriving from Africa in 1521**
>
> "Great was the stench of the dead. After our fathers and grandfathers succumbed, half the people fled to the fields. The dogs and vultures devoured the bodies. The mortality was terrible. Your grandfathers died, and with them died the son of the king and his brothers and kinsmen. So it was that we became orphans, oh, my sons! So we became when we were young. All of us were thus. We were born to die!"
>
> —Arana Xajilá, Francisco Hernández, and Francisco Díaz Gebuto Quej. *The Annals of the Cakchiquels.* Edited and translated by Adrián Recinos and Delia Goetz, pp. 115–116. Norman: University of Oklahoma Press, 1953.

the continent than in deserts; and the epidemics took a far greater toll on dense, settled populations than they did on dispersed forager bands in dry regions. In the Caribbean and on the Brazilian coast, Native Americans disappeared altogether; in central and southern Mexico, their population shrank by two-thirds. It was only in the twentieth century that population figures reached the preconquest level again in most parts of Latin America.

Apart from European diseases, the native forager and agrarian Native Americans in the Amazon, Orinoco, and Meracaíbo rain forests were the least affected by European colonials during the period 1500–1800. Not only were their lands economically least promising, but they also defended those lands successfully with blowguns, poison darts, and bow and arrow. In many cold and hot arid or semiarid regions, such as Patagonia, southern Chile, the Argentine grasslands (*pampas*), the Paraguayan salt marshes and deserts, and northern Mexican mountains and steppes, the situation was similar. In many of these lands, the seminomadic Native Americans quickly adopted the European horse and became highly mobile warrior people in defense of their mostly independent territories. Ironically, their successful assimilation of this European import allowed them to delay their ultimate full surrender (and adaptation) to the European colonizers.

The villagers of Mexico, Yucatán, Guatemala, Colombia, Ecuador, and Peru had fewer choices. When smallpox reduced their numbers in the second half of the sixteenth century, state and church authorities razed many villages and concentrated the survivors in *pueblos de indios*. Initially, the Native Americans put up strong resistance against these resettlements, by repeatedly returning to their destroyed old settlements. From the middle of the seventeenth century, however, the pueblos were fully functional, self-administering units, with councils (*cabildos*), churches, schools, communal lands, and family parcels.

The councils were important institutions of legal training and social mobility for ordinary Native Americans. Initially, the traditional, "noble" chiefly families descending from the preconquest Aztec and Inca ruling classes were in control as administrators. The many village functions, however, for which the *cabildos* were responsible, allowed commoners to move up into auxiliary roles. In some of these roles, they had opportunities to learn the system and acquire modest wealth. Settlers constantly complained about insubordinate Native Americans pursuing lawsuits in the courts. Native American villages were closed to settlers, and the only outsiders admitted were Catholic priests. Contact with the Spanish world remained minimal, and acculturation went little beyond official conversion to Catholicism. Village notaries and scribes were instrumental in preserving the native Nahuatl in Mexico and Quechua in Peru, making them into functional, written languages. Thus, even in the heartlands of Spanish America, Native American adaptation to the rulers remained limited.

Unfortunately, however, tremendous demographic losses made the Native Americans in the pueblos vulnerable to the loss of their land. Estate owners expanded their holdings, legally and illegally, in spite of the heroic litigation efforts of the villages opposed to this expansion. When the population rebounded, many estates had grown to immense sizes. Villages began to run out of land for their inhabitants. Increasing numbers of Native Americans had to rent land from estate owners or find work on estates as farmhands. They became estranged from their villages, fell into debt peonage, and entered the ranks of the working poor in countryside or city, bearing the full brunt of colonial inequities.

In the southwestern United States, the pueblo Native Americans remained in their traditional farming villages, but estate owners subjected them first to the *encomienda* and later the *repartimiento* on their ranches. Estate farming and Native American conversion to Catholicism proceeded more slowly in this sparsely populated part of the Spanish colony. Among the indigenous people, the adaptation process to Spanish culture reached a critical point in the 1660s when priests outlawed the local masked *kachina* dances and sought to destroy masks. Tensions over these measures built, with public hangings and whippings of Native Americans convicted of sorcery. During 1680–1695, the indigenous villagers were in full revolt, killing priests, burning churches, and chasing estate owners from their lands. Spanish forces eventually suppressed this extraordinary Native American rebellion in their American colonies but ended the repartimiento system as a measure of pacification.

New England Society   For a long time in the early modern period, the small family farm where everyone had to work to eke out a precarious living remained the norm for the majority of New England's population. Family members specializing in construction, carpentry, spinning, weaving, or iron works continued to be restricted to small perimeters around their villages and towns. An acute lack of money and cheap means of transportation hampered the development of market networks in the interior well into the 1770s. The situation was better in the agriculturally more favored colonies in the Mid-Atlantic, especially in Pennsylvania. Here, farmers were able to produce marketable quantities of wheat and legumes for urban markets. The number of plantations in the south rose steadily, demanding increasing numbers of slaves (from 28,000 to 575,000 in 1700–1776), although world market fluctuations left planters vulnerable. Except for boom periods in the plantation sector, the rural areas remained largely poor.

Real changes occurred during the early eighteenth century in the urban regions. Large port cities emerged which shipped in textiles and ironwares from Europe in return for timber at relatively cheap rates. The most important were Philadelphia

(28,000 inhabitants), New York (25,000), Boston (16,000), and Newport, Rhode Island (11,000). A wealthy merchant class formed, spawning urban service strata of professionals (such as lawyers, teachers, and newspaper journalists). Primary school education was provided by municipal public schools as well as some churches, and evening schools for craftspeople existed in some measure. By the middle of the eighteenth century a majority of men could read and write, although female literacy was minimal. Finally, in contrast to Latin America, social ranks in New England were less elaborate.

The Adaptation of the Americas to European Culture

European settlers brought two distinct cultures to the Americas. In the Mid-Atlantic, Caribbean, and Central and South America, they brought with them the Counter-Reformation Catholicism of southern Europe, a culture and perspective that resisted the New Science of Galileo and the Enlightenment thought of Locke until the late eighteenth century. In the northeast, colonists implanted dissident Protestantism as well as the Anglicanism of Great Britain. The rising number of adherents of the New Science and Enlightenment in northwestern Europe had also a parallel in North America. Settlers and their locally born offspring were proud of their respective cultures, which, even though provincial, were dominant in what they prejudicially viewed as a less civilized, if not barbaric, Native American environment.

Catholic Missionary Work   From the beginning, Spanish and Portuguese monarchs relied heavily on the Catholic Church for their rule in the new American provinces. The pope granted them patronage over the organization and all appointments on the new continents. A strong motive driving many in the church as well as society at large was the belief in the imminent Second Coming of Jesus. This belief was one inspiration for the original Atlantic expansion (see Chapter 16). When the Aztec and Inca Empires fell, members of the Franciscan order, the main proponents of the belief in the imminence of the return, reinterpreted its meaning as imposing the urgent duty to convert the Native Americans to Christianity. If Jesus' kingdom was soon to come, according to this interpretation, all humans in the Americas should be Christians.

Thousands of Franciscan, Dominican, and other preaching monks, later followed by the Jesuits, fanned out among the Native Americans. They baptized them, introduced the sacraments (Eucharist, baptism, confession, confirmation, marriage, last rites, and priesthood), and taught them basic theological concepts of Christianity. The missionaries learned native languages, translated the catechism and New Testament into those languages, and taught the children of the ruling native families how to read and write. Thanks to their genuine efforts to understand the Native

Virgin of Guadalupe. There is perhaps no more potent symbol of the new patterns of religious belief that emerged out of the Spanish conquest of Mexico than the Virgin of Guadalupe. Missionary sources, written years after the fact, tell of an indigenous inhabitant of Mexico City, Juan Diego, who in 1531 had visions of the Virgin Mary on the hill of Tepeyac, which Aztec traditions associated with the mother goddess Tonantzin. By the eighteenth century, the hill attracted pilgrims throughout Mexico and the Church created books, images, and organizations devoted to her cult. To this day, the Virgin of Guadalupe remains one of the most powerful and revered symbols of Mexico.

Americans on their own terms, a good deal of preconquest Native American culture was recorded without too much distortion.

The role and function of saints as mediators between humans and God formed one element of Catholic Christianity to which Native Americans acculturated early. Good works as God-pleasing human efforts to gain salvation in the afterlife formed another. The veneration of images of the Virgin Mary and pilgrimages to the chapels and churches where they were kept constituted a third element. The best-known example of the last element is Our Lady of Guadalupe, near Mexico City, who in 1531 appeared in a vision to a Native American in the place where the native goddess Tonantzin used to be venerated. On the other hand, the Spanish Inquisition also operated in the Spanish and Portuguese colonies, seeking to limit the degree to which Catholicism, animism, and polytheism mingled. The church tread a fine line between enforcement of doctrine and leniency toward what it determined were lax or heretical believers.

Education   The Counter-Reformation expressed itself also in the organization of education. The Franciscans and Dominicans had offered general education to the children of settlers early on and, in colleges, trained graduates for missionary work. The first New World universities, such as Santo Domingo (1538), Mexico City, and Lima (both 1553) taught theology, church law, and Indian languages. Under the impact of the Jesuits, universities broadened the curriculum, offering degrees also in secular law, Aristotelian philosophy, the natural sciences, and medicine. In the seventeenth and eighteenth centuries, the number of universities grew to 26. By contrast, Brazil did not offer higher education prior to 1800. In spite of this greater breadth, however, the Counter-Reformation universities did not admit the New Sciences and Enlightenment of northwestern Europe into their curriculum prior to the independence of the colonies.

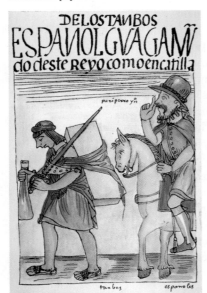

"How an Animal Is Taken from the Poor Old Man to Pay for the Tribute." Felipe Guamán Poma de Ayala, a Peruvian claiming noble Inca descent, was a colonial administrator, well educated, and an ardent Christian. He is remembered today as a biting critic of the colonial administration and the clergy, whom he accused of neglecting their duty to protect the Andean population.

Recording and Writing   As mentioned earlier, missionary monks collected and recorded Native American manuscripts and oral traditions, such as the Aztec *Anales de Tula* and the Maya *Popol Vuh*. Others wrote histories and ethnographies of the Taíno, Aztec, Maya, Inca, and Tupí peoples. Bartolomé de las Casas, Toribio Motolonía de Benavente, Bernardino de Sahagún, Diego de Landa, Bernabé Cobo, and Manoel de Nóbrega are merely a handful of noteworthy authors who wrote about the Native Americans. Many labored for years, worked with legions of informers, and produced monumental tomes.

A number of Native American and mestizo chroniclers, historians, and commentators on the early modern state and society are similarly noteworthy. Muñoz Camargo was a Tlazcaltecan; Fernando de Alva Ixtlixóchitl and Fernando Alvarado Tezózomoc were Mexican mestizos; and Juan de Santa Cruz Pachacuti Yamqui and Felipe Inca Garcilaso de la Vega were Peruvian mestizos, all writing on their native regions. Felipe Guamán Poma de Ayala (ca. 1535–1616), a native Peruvian, is of particular interest. He accompanied his 800-page manuscript, entitled *The First New Chronicle and Good Government*, with some 400 drawings of daily-life activities in the Peruvian villages. These drawings provide us with invaluable cultural details, which would be difficult to render in writing. Unfortunately, King

Philip II of Spain, a relentless proponent of the Counter-Reformation, took a dim view of authors writing on Native American society and history. In 1577 he forbade the publication of all manuscripts dealing with what he called idolatry and superstition. Many manuscripts lay hidden in archives and did not see the light of day until modern times.

Contemporary or later Creole historians wrote their own histories. They celebrated the heroic conquest and settlement of their provinces by their Spanish ancestors, the attractiveness of their cities or regions, and the moral superiority of their cities. Much of this literature is undistinguished, but it laid the foundations for the emergence of a distinct American patriotism among the Creoles by the eighteenth century. One exceptional example is Bartolomé Arzáns de Orsúa y Vela (1676–1736), whose *Tales of Potosí* are still enjoyable to read today. His chronicle of the mining city purports to be factual, although it is better described as historical fiction. It tells colorful stories of wondrous or scandalous alleged events as collected from local informants or observed personally. Arzáns is not a Cervantes, but his stories are nonetheless entertaining illustrations of Creole life in the provinces.

Theater   Stage pieces and music in Creole society were either borrowed from Iberia or composed locally in the prevalent Baroque style. On the popular level, Creole versions of religious processions, presentations, masquerades, and dances emerged. Among Native Americans and mestizos, theater had its roots in short morality plays or recreations of biblical scenes in the Catholic missions, interspersed with dances and music on indigenous instruments. Blacks appropriated this form of theater as well, and mulattoes developed it further with secular themes. Actors and musicians often came from the membership of lay religious brotherhoods responsible for processions on Christian holidays, the only institutions through which Native Americans and blacks could legitimately organize themselves in cities and towns. Thus, even though Counter-Reformation Catholicism was the religious expression of a dominant culture, variations of it became appropriated by the dominated ethnic groups.

Protestantism in New England   From the start, religious diversity was a defining cultural trait of English settlements in North America. The spectrum of Christian denominations ranged from a host of English and continental European versions of Protestantism to Anglicanism and a minority of Catholics. As if this spectrum had not been sufficiently broad, dissenters frequently split from the existing denominations, moved into new territory, and founded new settlements. Religiosity was a major characteristic of the early settlers.

An early example for religious splintering was the rise of an antinomian ("anti-law") group within Puritan-dominated Massachusetts. The Puritans dominant in this colony generally recognized the authority of the Anglican Church but strove to move it toward Protestantism from within. The preachers and settlers represented in the General Court, as their assembly was called, were committed to the Calvinist balance between "inner" personal grace obtained from God and "outer" works according to the law. The antinomian group, however, digging deep into early traditions in Christianity, advocated an exclusive commitment to inner grace through spiritual perfection. Their leader was Anne Hutchinson, an early and tireless proponent of women's rights and an inspiring preacher. She was accused of arguing that she could recognize those believers in Calvinist Protestantism who were predestined for salvation and that these believers would be saved even if they had sinned. After a power struggle with the deeply misogynistic magistrates opposed to influential women, the General Court prevailed and forced the Antinomians to move to Rhode Island in 1636.

The example is noteworthy because it led to the founding of Harvard College in 1626 by the General Court. Harvard was the first institution of higher learning in North America, devoted to teaching the "correct" balanced Calvinist Protestantism. A few years later, the college became a university and functioned as the main center for training the colony's ministers in Puritan theology and morality. In spite of its primary function as a seminary, however, Harvard did not remain closed to the New Science of Copernicus and Galileo. Copernicus's new heliocentric astronomy was part of the curriculum by 1659 at the latest. The university installed the first telescope in North America in 1672. Soon thereafter, some of Harvard's first professors published papers on astronomical subjects which caught the attention of Isaac Newton (1643–1727) at the University of Cambridge; Newton was then at work on his unification of Copernican astronomy and Galilean physics. Although Harvard was clearly provincial, it became an early outpost of the New Science.

Harvard College. The General Court of Boston founded Harvard College in 1636 as a seminary to teach "correct" Calvinism, in the face of dissenting preachers and their followers. In the second half of the 1600s, it incorporated the teaching of the New Science into its curriculum and became an important, if provincial, outpost of Copernican, Galilean, and Newtonian astronomy and physics. This engraving of 1767 is by Paul Revere.

New Science Research   As discussed in Chapter 17, the New Science had found its most hospitable home in northwestern Europe by default. The rivalry between Protestantism and Catholicism had left enough of an authority-free space for the New Science to flourish. Under similar circumstances—intense rivalry among denominations—English North America also proved hospitable to the New Science. An early practitioner was Benjamin Franklin (1706–1790), who began his career as a printer, journalist, and newspaper editor. Franklin founded the University

A Westerly View of The Colledges in Cambridge New England
A *Harvard Hall*   B *Stoughton*   C *Massachusett*   D *Hollis*   E *Holden Chapel*

of Pennsylvania (1740), the first secular university in North America, and
the American Philosophical Society
(1743), the first scientific society. This
hospitality to the New Science in North
America was quite in contrast to Latin
America, where a uniform Catholic
Counter-Reformation prevented its
rise. Here, the earliest stirrings of the
New Science date to the mid-eighteenth
century and did not include a recognition of Galileo. Thus, a multiform
Protestantism of competitive denominations allowed for a space in which the
New Scientists devoted to the pursuit
of secular knowledge could assemble
and carry out their experiments.

**The New Science in the
New World.** This painting by
Samuel Collings, *The Magnetic
Dispensary* (1790), shows
how men and women, of lay
background, participated in
scientific experiments in the
English colonies of North
America, similar to educated
middle-class people in western
Europe at the same time.

Under the impact of the New Science, seventeenth-century northern European philosophers had begun the task of replacing Aristotelianism, the dominant
medieval form of philosophy, with new forms of thought. Among the early New
Science–influenced philosophers in England were James Harrington (1611–1677)
and John Locke (1632–1704). Both wrote constitutional treatises influenced by the
experience of the New World. Harrington's *Oceanea* (1656) and Locke's political
thought, later published as *Two Treatises on Civil Government* (1690), inspired the
founders of Carolina (1664) and Pennsylvania (1681) in their experiments of colonialism. Thus, the tradition of American secular intellectual as well as political constitutionalism was born and evolved parallel to the traditions of Protestant political
self-organization in the colonies.

Secular American constitutionalism, as represented later by the founding fathers,
relied on Harrington's innovative concept of a **civil theology**. The myriad religious
denominations competing in English North America, so secular constitutionalists
argued, had in common a basic set of essential theological agreements about God,
providence, and the moral order on which society is built. Hence, any commonwealth
based on the will of the people was a polity in which everyone had to agree on a minimum of religious doctrines but was otherwise free to add his or her own specific religious obligations in the congregations to which he or she belonged. Today, of course,
civil theology is understood to be the notion of a political order that relies on neither
the acceptance of God nor providence but on a universal moral order that is shared by
the members of all religious civilizations and formulated concretely in the Preamble
of the United Nations Charter.

Civil theology: Form
of thought according to
which the state supports
basic religious principles,
without espousing a
particular denomination.

Witch Hunts and Revivalism   The level of religious competitiveness and intensity remained high throughout the seventeenth century. In the last decade of the
century, religious fervor was at the root of a witchcraft frenzy which seized New England. The belief in witchcraft was a survival of the animist concept of a shared mind
or spirit which allows initiates to influence other people, either positively or negatively. Witches, male and female, were persons exerting a negative influence, or black
magic, on their victims. Legislation against black magic and sorcery is as ancient as

Hammurabi's law in the Middle East (1700 BCE) and continued in religious civilizations from India to China. In animist Africa, as discussed in the example of Dona Beatriz's early training in Angola (see Chapter 19), the distinction between benevolent and evil magic was fundamental, as it was in Native American society.

But why was there an outburst of witchcraft hysteria in Europe between 1550 and 1800? Systematic scholarship on the phenomenon of the witch craze in both Catholic and Protestant Europe during the past two decades has arrived at the consensus that it was the result of a combination of factors coming together with a rare force. In brief, Europe (and the northern hemisphere) entered the Little Ice Age of 1550–1750, a period in which temperatures fell and agriculture became more precarious. A majority of witchcraft persecutions involved villages and towns where peasants who relied on subsistence agriculture had fallen on hard times. Women, as the embodiments of fertility, were particularly vulnerable in these persecutions. At the same time, populations, increasing again after the Black Death, put pressure on the food supply. The emerging centralized states, especially the fiscal–military ones, weakened local autonomies. And finally, religious wars tore the social and economic fabric of many European countries apart. For the world historian looking at broad patterns, it is quite understandable that this combination of natural and human-made factors could persuade literal-minded or fundamentalist believers untrained in theology that evil forces were at work.

In colonial Catholic and Protestant America, not surprisingly, the fear of witches was as widespread as in Europe. The one case where it erupted into hysteria and which therefore has attracted most attention was that of Salem, Massachusetts. Here, the excitement began in 1692 with Tituba, a Native American slave from Barbados who worked in the household of a pastor. Tituba practiced voodoo, the central African–originated, part-African and part-Christian religious practice found on some Caribbean islands. A cornerstone of voodoo belief is that evil can be removed from a person and transferred somewhere else through the administration of charms (see Chapter 19). When a young daughter and niece in the pastor's household suffered from convulsions, the hysteria erupted. In a snowballing effect, 140 persons, most of them women, were accused of being witches and 20 were even executed. A new governor finally calmed the hysteria, emptied the jails, and pardoned the accused. The problem in Salem was evidently the clash between two sets of religious practices, voodoo and literal or fundamentalist Protestantism—exhibit A for the plea to set aside practice and focus on the more basic theological commonalities of civil theology.

Witch Trial. In the course of the 1600s, in the relatively autonomous English colonies of North America more witches were accused, tried, and convicted than anywhere else. Of the 140 persons coming to trial between 1620 and 1725, 86 percent were women. Three witch panics are recorded: Bermuda, 1651; Hartford, Connecticut, 1652–1665; and Salem, Massachusetts, 1692–1693. This anonymous American woodcut of the early 1600s shows one method to try someone for witchcraft: swim if innocent, or sink if guilty.

A literal understanding of Protestantism was also central in the "Great Awakening" of the 1730s and 1740s. The main impulse for this revivalist movement came from the brothers John and Charles Wesley, two Methodist preachers in England who toured Georgia in 1735. Preachers from other denominations joined, all exhorting Protestants to literally "start anew" in their relationship with God. Fire-and-brimstone sermons rained down on the pews, reminding the faithful of the absolute sovereignty of God, the depravity of humans, predestination to hell and heaven, the inner experience of election, and salvation by God's grace alone. Thus, revivalism, recurring with great regularity to the present, became a potent force in Protestant America, at opposing purposes with the civil theology of founding father constitutionalism. Even today, the United States is torn between religious commitment, with its emotional engagement for the specifics of religious practice, and the more detached view of civil theology, with its more universal principles of faith and morality.

Putting It All Together

During the period 1500–1800 the contours of a new pattern in which the Americas formed a resource-rich and warm-weather extension of Europe took shape. During this time China and India continued to be the most populous and wealthiest agrarian–urban regions of the world. Scholars have estimated China's share of the world economy during this period as comprising 40 percent. India probably did not lag much behind. In 1500, Europe was barely an upstart, forced to defend itself against the thrust of the Ottoman Empire into eastern Europe and the western Mediterranean. Yet its successful conquest of Iberia from the Muslims led to the discovery of the Americas. Possession of the Americas made Europe similar to China and India, for it now encompassed, in addition to its northerly cold climates, subtropical and tropical regions which produced rich cash crops as well as precious metals. Over the course of 300 years with the help of its American extension, Europe narrowed the gap between itself and China and India, although it was only after the beginning of industrialization, around 1800, that it eventually was able to close this gap (see Concept Map).

Narrowing the gap, of course, was not a conscious policy in Europe. Quite the contrary, because of fierce competition both with the Ottoman Empire and within itself, much of the wealth Europe gained in the Americas, especially silver, was wasted on warfare. The fiscal–military state, created in part to support war, ran into insurmountable budgetary barriers, which forced Spain into several state bankruptcies. Even mercantilism, a logical extension of the fiscal–military state, had limited effects. Its centerpiece, state support for the export of manufactures to the American colonies through shipping monopolies in return for primary goods (minerals and warm-weather cash crops), functioned unevenly. The Spanish and Portuguese governments, with weak urban infrastructures and low manufacturing capabilities, especially in textiles, were unable to enforce this state-supported trade until the eighteenth century and even then only in very limited ways. France and especially England practiced mercantilism more successfully but were able to do so in the Americas only from the late seventeenth century onward, when their plantation systems began to take shape. Although the American

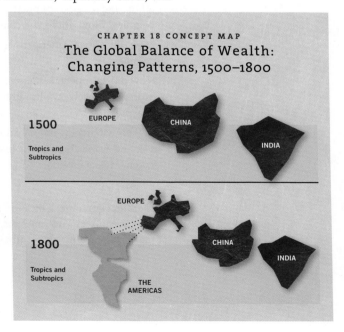

CHAPTER 18 CONCEPT MAP
The Global Balance of Wealth: Changing Patterns, 1500–1800

extension of Europe had the potential of making Europe self-sufficient, this potential was realized only partially during the colonial period.

A fierce debate has raged over the question of the degree of wealth the Americas added to that of Europe. On the one hand, considerable quantitative research has established that the British slave trade for sugar plantations added at best 1 percent to the British gross domestic product (GDP). The profits from production of sugar on the English island of Jamaica may have added another 4 percent to the British GDP. Without doubt, individual slave-trading and sugar-producing enterprises were at times immensely profitable to individuals and groups, not to mention the mining of silver through forced labor. In the larger picture, however, the profits were considerably smaller if one takes into account the immense waste of revenues on military ventures—hence, the doubts raised by scholars today about the gains made by Europe through its American colonial acquisitions.

On the other hand, the European extension to the Americas was clearly a momentous event in world history. It might have produced dubious profits for Europe, but it definitely encouraged the parting of ways between Europe and Asia and Africa as the new scientific–industrial society began to emerge around 1800.

Review and Respond

1. How did the colonial administration of the Spanish and Portuguese colonies evolve, and how do they compare with that of the English in the Americas?

2. Compare the extraction of minerals and the production of cash crops in the Americas. Which mining and agricultural enterprises did specific colonizing countries undertake? Which timelines did these economic activities follow in the various parts of the Americas?

3. American colonial societies were multitiered and complex. What were the various ethnic and religious population groups in the Latin American, English, and French colonies? How would you characterize the relations among these diverse groups?

4. How did Native Americans adapt to the new social and economic patterns of the colonies?

5. How did European settlers in the Latin American and North American colonies express themselves culturally? What were the differences between the two types of expression?

6. What is witchcraft, and why do people's concerns with its allegedly harmful effects wax and wane throughout history? Why did hysteria about witchcraft erupt in Salem, Massachusetts?

▶ For additional resources, including maps, primary sources, visuals, and quizzes, please go to www.oup.com/us/vonsivers. Please see the Further Resources section at the back of the book for additional readings and suggested websites.

Thinking Through Patterns

▶ **What is the significance of western Europeans acquiring the Americas as a warm-weather extension of their northern continent?**

In their role as supplementary subtropical and tropical extensions of Europe, the Americas became a crucial factor for Europe's changing position in the world. First, Europe acquired large quantities of precious metals, which its two largest competitors, India and China, lacked. Second, with its new access to warm-weather agricultural products, Europe rose to a position of agrarian autonomy similar to that of India and China. In terms of resources, compared with the principal religious civilizations of India and China, Europe grew between 1550 and 1800 from a position of inferiority to one of near parity.

Because the numbers of Europeans who emigrated to the Americas was low for most of the colonial period—just 300,000 Spaniards left for the New World between 1500–1800—they never exceeded the numbers of Native Americans or African slaves.The result was a highly privileged settler society that held superior positions on the top rung of the social hierarchy. In principle, given an initially large indigenous population, labor was cheap and should have become more expensive as diseases reduced the Native Americans. In fact, labor always remained cheap, in part because of the politically supported institution of forced labor and in part because of racial prejudice.

▶ **What was the main pattern of social development in colonial America during the period 1500–1800?**

▶ **Why and how did European settlers in South and North America strive for self-government, and how successful were they in achieving their goals?**

Two contrasting patterns characterized the way in which European colonies were governed. The Spanish and Portuguese crowns, primarily interested in extracting minerals and warm-weather products from the colonies, had a strong interest in exercising as much centralized control over their possessions in the Americas as they could. In contrast, the British crown granted self-government to the North American colonies from the start, in part because the colonies were initially economically far less important and in part because of a long tradition of self-rule at home. Nevertheless, even though Latin American settlers achieved only partial self-rule in their towns and cities, they destroyed central rule indirectly through the purchase of offices. After financial reforms, Spain and Portugal reestablished a degree of central rule through the appointment of officers from the home countries.

Chapter 19

1450-1800

African Kingdoms, the Atlantic Slave Trade, and the Origins of Black America

THE ATLANTIC WORLD, 1500–1800

The Capuchin Catholic monks of the kingdom of Kongo had just denounced as a heretical abomination the claim of Dona Beatriz Vita Kimpa (1684–1706) to have died and been reborn as St. Anthony of Padua. For many subjects of the kingdom, however, this claim was perfectly reasonable as part of an African Christian spirituality in which a gifted person

What was the pattern of kingdom and empire formation in Africa during the period 1500–1800?

How did patterns of plantation slavery evolve in the Atlantic and the Americas?

What are the historic origins of modern racism?

could enter other people's minds and assume their identity. But the monks prevailed. One of the claimants to the throne of the kingdom of Kongo had Dona Beatriz condemned after a trial and burned at the stake.

Dona Beatriz was intellectually precocious. In her childhood, her family had her initiated in a *Kimpasi* enclosure as a *nganga marinda* (Kikongo word derived from "knowledge" or "skill"). Such enclosures at the edges of towns and cities contained altars with crosses and censers (for burning incense). Other paraphernalia included statues believed to be capable of recognizing evildoers, animal claws to grab them, horns to mark the line between the worlds of nature and the spirit, and animal tails symbolizing power. In a ceremony, the head woman of the enclosure put Dona Beatriz into a trance that enabled her to recognize and repel all the troubling forces that disturbed a person or the community. People in Kongo were very much aware, however, that not all *ngangas* were benevolent. Some *ngangas* were thought to misuse their spiritual powers for witchcraft. Missionary Capuchin monks, preaching orthodox Counter-Reformation Catholicism, made every effort to denounce all *ngangas* as witches. Whether the young

New Patterns in Africa. In the wake of the Portuguese arrival in the kingdom of Kongo in 1483, Capuchin monks converted the royal dynasty as well as large numbers of subjects to Catholicism. Since the church did not have enough monks and clergy, it commissioned lay assistants to convert the populace and appointed schoolmasters for instruction in reading, writing, and the Catholic faith. Here, a Capuchin monk and lay assistants are moving in procession. The watercolor was drawn by the Capuchin monk Antonio Cavazzi, who served in Kongo and Angola in the second half of the 1600s.

Dona Beatriz was intimidated by these denunciations or not, she renounced her initiation, married, and pursued the domestic life of any other young woman in Kongo society.

But the spirit did not cease to move Dona Beatriz. In 1704, she had again deep spiritual experiences in which she died, only to be reborn as St. Anthony of Padua (1195–1231). St. Anthony, a Portuguese Franciscan monk, is one of the patron saints of Portugal. Devotees of the saint believe he blesses marriages and helps people find lost items. With her new saintly and male identity, more powerful than her earlier one as an *nganga*, Dona Beatriz preached a novel and inspiring vision: She was God's providential figure, arrived to restore the Catholic faith and reunify the kingdom, both of which she saw as having been torn asunder during nearly half a century of dynastic disunity and civil war (1665–1709).

After her supposed rebirth, Dona Beatriz immediately went to Pedro IV, king of Kongo (r. 1695–1718), and his Capuchin ally, the chief missionary Bernardo da Gallo, accusing them of being laggards in their efforts to restore the faith and unity of Kongo. Pedro temporized in his response, but Bernardo subjected Dona Beatriz to an angry interrogation about her faith and "possession." Beatriz countered with a remarkable attack on the Catholic cornerstone of sacraments. Intention or faith alone, she argued, not the sacraments of the church (such as baptism or confession), would bring salvation. Unlike the Protestant reformer Martin Luther, however, Dona Beatriz did not derive her theological convictions from the letters of St. Paul in the New Testament but from her *nganga* initiation: It was good intentions which distinguished the inspired preacher from the witch.

Initially unable to conceive of a concerted plan of action, the king and Bernardo let Beatriz go. In a journey reminiscent of that of Joan of Arc, Beatriz led a growing crowd of followers to the ruined capital of Kongo, M'banza (São Salvador). There, she trained "little Anthonies" as missionaries to convert the Kongolese to her Antonian-African Christianity. Under the protection of a rival of the king, Beatriz was at the pinnacle of her spiritual power when everything unraveled. As already at the time she was a married woman, in between her two lives as *nganga* and St. Anthony, the flesh reasserted itself. She gave birth to a child, conceived with one of her followers. She did so secretly at her ancestral home in Pedro's territory, evidently in a deep crisis about her spiritual mission. Allies of the king discovered the lovers by accident and arrested them. They brought them before Pedro, who, in the meantime, had decided to reject Beatriz's challenge and silence her. After a state trial—the church stayed out of the proceedings—Beatriz, her companion, and the baby were executed by burning at the stake.

This moving story illustrates a major pattern discussed in this chapter: the process by which Africans adapted their indigenous heritage to the western Christian challenge. Europeans arrived on the western coast of Africa in the fifteenth century as both missionaries and slave traders (at times also as slave raiders). Africans responded with their own adaptive forms of Christianity, as well as efforts—as in Kongo, Angola, and Benin—to limit the slave trade in accordance with their own existing political interests. Elsewhere, however, African kings and chiefs exploited the traditional indigenous system of household, agricultural, administrative, and military slavery to reap voluminous profits. As is now well recognized by scholars, the unprecedented, massive transfer of African slaves to the plantations and mines of the Americas brought to the new continents not only animist tribal Africans but also diverse peoples with complex and sophisticated Creole (mixed) cultures of their own, cultures that survived in the Americas under extraordinarily difficult circumstances.

Creolization can be understood as a cultural process parallel to the patterns of state formation in Africa and European colonization in the Americas during the period 1500–1800. While Islamic and Christian kingdoms continued to dominate the northern parts of sub-Saharan Africa in this period, population increases in the center and south of the region contributed to an acceleration of the transition from chiefdoms to kingdoms. In the Americas, the agricultural pattern of warm-weather cash crop production on plantations that relied on African slavery formed the basis upon which Europeans maintained political control of these continents.

African States and the Slave Trade

In the north of sub-Saharan Africa the pattern of Islamic and Christian dynastic state formation that had been ongoing for centuries continued to dominate herder and village societies in the period 1500–1800. An invasion by Muslim forces from Morocco during the sixteenth century, however, ended the trend toward empire building and strengthened the forces of decentralization. By contrast, in the savanna and Great Lakes regions of central Africa, improved agricultural wealth and intensified regional trade helped perpetuate the kingdom formation already under way. An

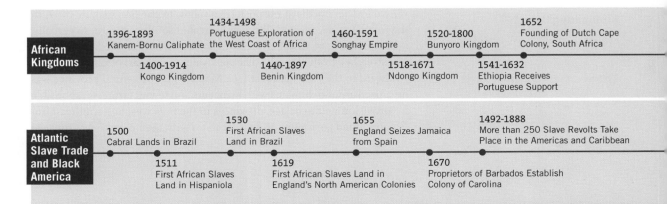

African Kingdoms

1396-1893
Kanem-Bornu Caliphate

1434-1498
Portuguese Exploration of the West Coast of Africa

1460-1591
Songhay Empire

1520-1800
Bunyoro Kingdom

1652
Founding of Dutch Cape Colony, South Africa

1400-1914
Kongo Kingdom

1440-1897
Benin Kingdom

1518-1671
Ndongo Kingdom

1541-1632
Ethiopia Receives Portuguese Support

Atlantic Slave Trade and Black America

1500
Cabral Lands in Brazil

1530
First African Slaves Land in Brazil

1655
England Seizes Jamaica from Spain

1492-1888
More than 250 Slave Revolts Take Place in the Americas and Caribbean

1511
First African Slaves Land in Hispaniola

1619
First African Slaves Land in England's North American Colonies

1670
Proprietors of Barbados Establish Colony of Carolina

important institution in the chiefdoms and states of Africa was slavery. When the Europeans inserted themselves into this institution, they profoundly altered it to benefit their own interests in the production of warm-weather cash crops on American plantations. Some African kings resisted the sale of slaves to the Europeans, while other kings and chiefs enriched themselves through slave raiding and selling.

The End of Empires in the North and the Rise of States in the Center

The Eurasian empires of the premodern world united peoples of many different religions, languages, and ethnic affiliations. Mali (1240–1460) was the first African empire that was similar to the old empires of Eurasia. Mali's successor state, the focus of this section, was the even larger Songhay Empire (1460–1591). It did not last long however.

Origins of the Songhay   Songhay was initially a tributary state of Mali. It was centered on the city of Gao downstream on the River Niger from the agricultural center of Jenné-jeno and the commercial and scholarly center of Timbuktu. Gao's origins dated to 850, when it emerged as the end point of the eastern trans-Saharan route from Tunisia and Algeria, parallel to the more heavily traveled western route from Morocco. Gao was located at the northern end of the Songhay Empire, near the Niger Bend, and was inhabited by the Songhay, an ethnic grouping composed of herders, villagers, and fishermen.

The Songhay were ethnically distinct from the Soninke of the Kingdom of Ancient Ghana and the Malinke of the Mali Empire further west. Their homeland was located to the east and southeast of the Niger Bend. At the end of the eleventh century, the leading clans of the Songhay, profiting from the trans-Saharan trade, converted to Islam. Two centuries later the warriors among them assumed positions of leadership as vassals of the *mansa*, or emperor, of Mali. By this time, tall Barbary warhorses, bred from North African stock, had become common in the steppe and savanna of West Africa, the semiarid pasture lands near the Sahara and the semiforested grasslands suitable for agriculture farther south. However, the tsetse fly, which transmits a parasite deadly to livestock, limited the range of these horses. Periodic purchases from North Africa were necessary for the Songhay to maintain their fighting strength.

The Songhay Empire   The Songhay began their imperial expansion in the mid-1400s, toward the end of the dry period in West Africa (1100–1500), during which control of the steppe region was sometimes difficult to maintain. Mali, which had its center in the much wetter savanna, lost its northern outpost, Timbuktu, to the Songhay in 1469. In the following decades, Mali slowly retreated southwestward. Eventually, it became a minor vassal of the Songhay. At its height, the Songhay Empire stretched from Hausaland in the savanna southeast of Gao all the way westward to the Atlantic coast (see Map 19.1). The central province was organized around domains with managers and tenant farmers responsible for provisioning the palace, provinces in the near west and southeast under appointed governors, and vassal states with their own kings similar to

---

A Ruthless Conqueror and Harsh Ruler

"As for the great oppressor and notorious evil-doer, Sunni Ali [the founder of the Songhay Empire, 1464–1492] . . . he was a man of great strength and colossal energy, a tyrant, a miscreant, an aggressor, a despot . . . and a butcher who killed so many human beings that only God Most High could count them. He tyrannized the scholars and holymen, killing them, insulting them, and humiliating them."

—Abd al-Rahman al-Saadi. *Timbuktu and the Songhay Empire: Al-Saʿdi's Tarikh al-Sudan down to 1613 and Other Contemporary Documents.* Translated by John O. Hunwick, p. 91. Leiden, the Netherlands: Brill, 2003.

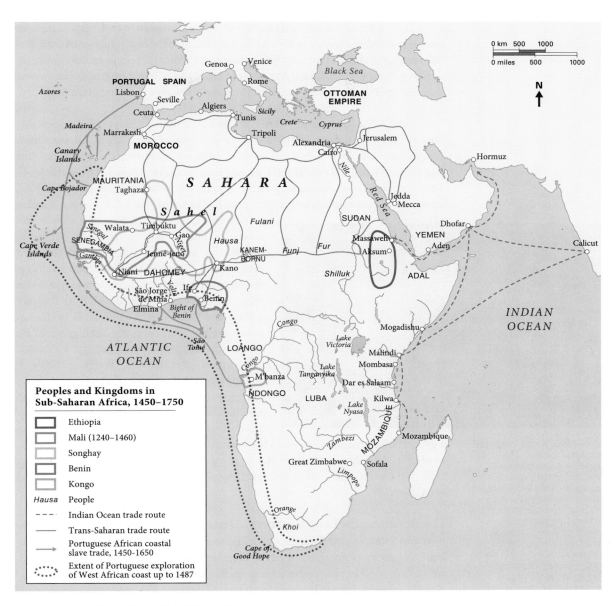

MAP **19.1** Peoples and Kingdoms in Sub-Saharan Africa, 1450–1750.

Mali. The provinces and vassal states had to provide taxes in kind, auxiliary troops, hostages, gifts, or marriage alliances, depending on the shifting abilities of Songhay rulers to enforce their authority.

As in the previous centuries under ancient Ghana and Mali, the decisive difference which elevated the Songhay emperors (*askiyas*) above their vassals was their taxation of the gold trade. The gold fields of the Upper Niger, Senegal, and Black Volta Rivers in the southern rain forest were outside the empire; but merchant clans, often accompanied by troop detachments, transported the gold to Timbuktu and Gao. Here, North African merchants exchanged their Mediterranean manufactures and salt for gold, slaves, and kola nuts. Agents of the *askiyas* in these cities collected market taxes in the form of gold, which they used for the maintenance of their central administration and troops, the production of arms and armor, and the construction of palaces and mosques. Agricultural taxes and tributes supported kingdoms; long-distance trade was needed in addition for an empire to come into being.

Songhay's Sudden End   After the initial, ruthless conquests, the Songhay Empire had little time to overcome its violent origins and consolidate on a more peaceful footing. After only a little over a century of dominance, the Songhay Empire came to a sudden end in 1591 when a Moroccan force invaded from the north. The commander was an Iberian Muslim general whose troops, consisting of a black slave infantry, were equipped with muskets and cannons. They defeated the Songhay cavalry and infantry, which fought with lances, sabers, and bows and arrows. The Moroccan sultans had successfully driven Portugal from their Atlantic coast but followed with concern the flourishing Portuguese trade for gold on the West African coast. They decided to find and occupy the West African gold fields in the rain forest, thereby depriving the Portuguese of the precious metal.

Arabic Manuscript, Timbuktu. Though undergirded by its strategic position on the caravan routes and its proximity to the gold fields, Timbuktu's key role was cultural. From the middle of the fifteenth century to the end of the eighteenth, Timbuktu was the preeminent center of Islamic learning in West Africa, with hundreds of schools, impressive mosques, and renowned libraries filled with rare manuscripts assiduously copied by hand.

However, after defeating Songhay, they were unable to march any farther, lacking necessary logistic support from Morocco through the Sahara. Although the officers turned the Niger delta and Bend initially into a Moroccan province, within a generation they assimilated into the West African royal clans. As a result, imperial politics in West Africa disintegrated, together with much of the trans-Saharan gold trade, which was siphoned off by the Portuguese on the African Gold Coast (modern Ghana).

The Eastern Sahel and Savanna   The steppe peoples between Songhay in the west and Ethiopia in the northeastern highlands near the Red Sea also possessed Islamic regimes governing moderate to large territories. Kanem-Bornu (1396–1893) was a long-lived Islamic realm, calling itself a "caliphate," with a majority of animist African subjects. Located in both the steppe and savanna, it was based on a slave and ivory trade with the Mediterranean and on agriculture and fishing for its internal organization on the south side of Lake Chad. Kanem-Bornu's imperial frontier was in the southwest, where it waged long, intermittent wars with the savanna kingdoms of Hausaland.

The Hausa kingdoms, numbering about half a dozen, had formed during the height of the Mali-dominated trans-Saharan trade as southeastern extensions of this trade into rain-forest Africa. Although they were under frequent attack by Songhay and Kanem-Bornu during the period 1500–1800, the Hausa kingdoms enjoyed periods of independence during which many of the ruling clans converted to Islam. Like their northern neighbors, they maintained cavalry forces, which—apart from military purposes—served to protect the caravans of the traders. In addition to taxing these traders, the Hausa kings collected dues from the villagers, who bred cattle and grew millet, sorghum, kola nuts, and cotton. Craftspeople in the capitals and some villages produced pottery, iron implements and utensils, cotton cloth, basketry, leather goods, and iron weapons. In other villages, miners and smiths smelted and forged copper, iron, and steel. Although more agricultural in orientation, the Hausa kingdoms closely resembled their northern neighbors in the steppe.

Farther east, in the steppe between Lake Chad and the Nile, the Fur and the Funj, cattle-breeding tribal federations, converted fully to Islam, from the royal clans down to the commoner clans. In contrast, in West Africa only the dynasties and merchants became Muslim. Their leaders adopted the title "sultan" and became Arabized in the period 1500–1800, while Christianity along the Nile disappeared completely.

Islamization and Arabization, however, reached a southern limit beyond which the two were not to penetrate until recently. This limit was located along a west–east line separating the steppe, with its cattle herders, from the savanna, which was suitable to the farming of millet, sorghum, and cotton. Most of the savanna villagers were animists who farmed and formed chiefdoms. Others also kept cattle and participated in regional trade for salt, slaves, iron, hardwood, and exotic animal skins, supporting small kingdoms with dynasties of kings as well as queens, such as the Shilluk people (*Chollo* in their own language), regionally powerful during the second half of the seventeenth and early eighteenth centuries.

South Central Africa   Most of the steppe and savanna in the northern half of sub-Saharan Africa interacted with Mediterranean Islamic civilization to some degree. They remained largely outside the sphere of the European slave trade during the period 1500–1800. On the southern side of the rain forest, the eastern part of the southern savanna and the Great Lakes area in central Africa remained similarly outside the reach of the slave trade. As a result, their population continued to grow. Large numbers of farmer and cattle herder groups, organized in chiefdoms, inhabited these regions. In the eastern savanna, the kingdom of Luba emerged precociously before 1500; and others followed at various intervals thereafter.

A steady increase in regional trade for copper, iron, salt, dried fish, beads, cloth, and palm oil enabled chieftain clans to consolidate their rule and enlarge their holdings into kingdoms. Living in enclosures and surrounded by "courts," or dense ruling-class settlements, kings maintained agricultural domains worked by slaves. Villages nearby delivered tribute in the form of foodstuffs. From the mid-seventeenth century onward, the American staples corn and cassava broadened the food supply. Tributaries at some distance delivered prestige goods, especially copper and ironware, as well as beads. At times, the kings mobilized thousands of workers to build moats and earthworks around their courts, which became centers of incipient urbanization processes.

The Great Lakes region, to the north and south of Lake Victoria, was a highly fertile eastward extension of the southern savanna with two annual crops of sorghum and sesame, as well as banana groves and herds of cattle. Traders distributed salt, iron, and dried fish in a lively regional trade. Agriculture, cattle breeding, and trade supported intense political competition in the lakes region. Small agricultural–mercantile kingdoms shared the region, but sometime in the sixteenth century cattle breeders—the Luo, relatives of the Shilluk—arrived from southern Sudan and shook up the existing political and social structures. Pronounced disparities in cattle ownership emerged on the rich pasture lands. Cattle-owning warlords rose as competitors of the kings.

North of Lake Victoria, the Bunyoro kingdom, based on agriculture and regional trade, held the cattle lords at bay, while on the south side of the lake the cattle lords created new small kingdoms. After a while cattle breeders and farmers settled into more or less unequal relations of mutual dependence. Under the colonial system in the nineteenth century, these unequal relations froze into a caste system in which the minority Tutsi cattle breeders faced off against the majority Hutu farmers. Eventually, this volatile arrangement led to the genocide committed by the Hutus against the Tutsis in 1993–1994. Farther south the pre-1500 tradition of gold-mining kingdoms, such as Great Zimbabwe, continued. But here the interaction of Africa with Portugal, to be discussed next, set the kingdoms on a different historical trajectory.

Portugal's Explorations Along the African Coast and Contacts with Ethiopia

The Portuguese expansion into North Africa and the exploration of the African coast were outgrowths of both the *Reconquista* and crusading impulses. Mixed in with these religious impulses, yet without any contradiction (as opposed to our modern views), was the practical necessity of financing the journeys of exploration through profits from trade. The combination of the two guided Portugal within one century around the African continent to India. Along the coast, the Portuguese established forts as points of protection for their merchants. In Ethiopia they supported the Christian kingdom with military aid, providing protection against the Ottomans in Yemen, just across the Red Sea.

Chartered Explorations in West Africa   Henry the Navigator (1394–1460), brother of the ruling king, a principal figure of the Portuguese *Reconquista*, and chief embodiment of the crusading zeal, occupied the Moroccan port of Ceuta in 1415. He claimed that Ceuta had been Christian, prior to the Berber-Arab conquest and subsequent Islamization of Iberia. He also wished to renew crusading for the reconquest of Jerusalem, lost to the Muslims in 1291. But the merchant wing of the Lisbon court was wary of the military expenditures. During the fifteenth century, campaigns for the military occupation of other cities of Morocco, mostly along the Atlantic coast, alternated with voyages financed by Portuguese groups of merchants and aristocrats for commerce along the West African coast.

In 1434, mariners discovered that ships could overcome adverse currents and winds and return from the West African coast by sailing out into the Atlantic, setting course for the islands of the newly discovered Canaries, Madeira, and Azores, before turning east toward Lisbon. It was the impossibility of returning along the coast from the southern part of West Africa that had doomed all previous efforts. Sailors either had to return by land, via the Sahara to the Mediterranean, or they disappeared without a trace. Thus, sailing south in the Atlantic and developing a route by which to return was a decisive step toward circumnavigating the continent.

Between 1434 and 1472, through a combination of royally chartered, private merchant–financiered as well as public state-organized expeditions, Portuguese mariners explored the coast as far east as the Bight of Benin. Trade items included European woolens and linens, in exchange for gold, cottons, and Guinea pepper (also called "malagueta pepper," not to be confused with malagueta chili pepper from South America). Small numbers of black slaves were included early on as trade items, mostly through purchases from chieftains and kings. Several uninhabited tropical islands off the coast were discovered during this time, and the Portuguese used slaves for the establishment of sugar plantations on these islands. They shipped other slaves to Europe for domestic employment, adding to the long-standing Mediterranean and trans-Saharan practice of household slavery.

Portugal and Ethiopia   By the second half of the fifteenth century, private merchant interests focused on West Africa provided few incentives for further explorations. It required the military wing of the Portuguese court to revive crusading. From 1483 through 1486 the king organized state expeditions for further expansion from the Bight of Benin south to the Congo River. Here, mariners sailed upstream in hopes of linking up with Prester John (see Chapter 16), a mythical king believed to live in Ethiopia or India. He was supposedly at the head of huge Christian armies, ready to help Portugal in the reconquest of Jerusalem. Instead of Prester John, the Portuguese mariners encountered the ruler of the powerful kingdom of Kongo, who converted to Christianity and established close relations with Portugal.

Prester John. The legend of Prester John, a Christian ruler whose lost kingdom in northeast Africa, surrounded by Muslims and pagans, captivated the European imagination from the twelfth through the seventeenth centuries. Purportedly a descendant of one of the Three Magi, Prester John (or Presbyter John) presided over a realm full of riches and fabulous creatures, and it was supposed to border the earthly paradise.

A few years later, after Christopher Columbus had discovered the Americas for Castile-Aragon in 1492, the Portuguese crown continued the search for a way to Ethiopia or India, a route presumed to lie around the southern tip of Africa. Eventually, Vasco da Gama circumnavigated the southern tip, established trade outposts in Swahili city-states of East Africa, and reached India in 1498. But Prester John was never found, and the idea of crusading receded as the Portuguese development of the Indian spice trade grew in importance.

In fact, as the Portuguese discovered in the early sixteenth century, not only did a mythically powerful king not rule Ethiopia but the kingdom was extremely weak in the face of the aggressive Muslim sultanate of Adal, on the Red Sea to the east. Until the end of the fifteenth century, Ethiopia had been a powerful Coptic Christian kingdom in the highlands of northeastern Africa. Its people practiced a productive plow-based agriculture for wheat and teff (a local cereal), and its kings controlled a rich trade of gold, ivory, animal skins, and slaves from the southern Sudan through the Rift Valley to the Red Sea. Possession of a Red Sea port for this trade, however, was a bone of contention between Ethiopia and Adal during the first half of the sixteenth century.

A Christian incursion into Muslim territory in 1529 triggered a response by Adal in the form of a furiously destructive Muslim holy war. Ethiopia would have been destroyed in this war had it not been for the timely arrival in 1541 of a Portuguese fleet with artillery and musketeers. For its part, Adal received Ottoman Muslim artillery and musketeer support from Yemen, but 2 years later, after several fierce battles, the Christians prevailed.

Ethiopia paid a high price for its victory. Adal Muslim power was destroyed, but in its place, the Ottomans took over the entire west coast of the Red Sea, mostly in order to keep out Portugal. Animist cattle breeders from the southwest occupied the Rift Valley, which separated the northern from the southern Ethiopian highlands and had been depopulated during the Christian–Muslim wars. Christians in the southern highlands were left to their own devices, surviving in small states. Small numbers of Portuguese stayed inside Ethiopia, with Jesuit missionaries threatening to dominate the Ethiopian church as well as the kings. In 1632 the Ethiopian king expelled the Jesuits and consolidated the kingdom as a shrunken power within much smaller borders.

Initially, Ethiopia continued to be culturally active under a strong court, expressed mostly through theological writings and iconic paintings. But from about 1700 Ethiopia decentralized into provincial lordships with little interest in their cultural heritage. Only in the mid-nineteenth century, in response to the Western challenge, did the kings take back their power from the provincial lords.

Coastal Africa and the Atlantic Slave Trade

After Portuguese mariners had circumnavigated Africa, they initially focused on developing their spice trade with India. Gradually, however, they also built their Atlantic slave trade, which took off in the early seventeenth century, to be followed by mariner-merchants from other European countries. To understand the pattern underlying the slave trade from 1500 to 1800 it is crucial to be aware of the importance of slavery within the African historical context. African slavery was a traditional African institution that existed in the place of landownership. The more slaves a household, chief, or king owned, to work at home or in the fields, the wealthier he was. **Household slavery**, as African slavery may also be called, existed everywhere in Africa.

Household slavery: African chiefs and kings maintained large households of retainers, such as administrators, soldiers, domestics, craftspeople, and farmers; many among these were slaves, acquired through raids and wars but also as a result of punishments for infractions of royal, chiefly, or tribal law.

Trade Forts   Early on, in the 1440s, Portuguese mariners raided the West African coast in the region defined by the Senegal and Gambia Rivers—Senegambia—for slaves. But they suffered losses in the process since their muskets were not yet superior to the precisely aimed poisoned arrows of the Africans. Furthermore, dwelling in a rain forest with its many rivers opening to the coast, West Africans possessed a well-developed tradition of boat-building and coastal navigation. Boats hollowed out from tree trunks could hold as many as 50 warriors. These warriors paddled swiftly through the estuaries and mangrove swamps along the coast and picked off the mariners from their caravels if they approached the coast too closely in a hostile manner. The Portuguese thus learned to approach the coast in a less threatening way and began what developed into a lucrative coastal fort trade in a variety of items, including slaves.

(a) **Elmina as It Appeared in a European Etching from 1562.**

(b) **Entrances to Slave Holding Cells.**

(c) **Outer Defensive Walls.**

Through treaties with local African leaders, Portugal acquired the right to build posts or forts from which to trade. Africans involved in trade in these regions produced a variety of items that were soon in demand in Europe. They wove colorful cotton cloth and wore it by the yard. A particular kind of bark or leaf cloth from central West Africa was at times highly sought in Portugal and the Caribbean. For a long time, Senegambian mats were preferred as bedcovers in Europe. In many places, Africans smelted iron and forged steel that was of higher quality than that of iron-poor Portugal. Africans paid with a currency—seashells—that resembled more closely our modern idea of abstract paper money than the silver and gold coins used by the Europeans. For adornment and celebration Africans wore bead necklaces and drank alcoholic beverages (beer from millet or sorghum, palm wine from sap, and fermented drinks from honey). Africans possessed the basic goods for a civilized and even sophisticated life on their continent.

Trade, as in most other parts in the world during the period 1500–1800, was for expensive luxury goods, not ordinary articles of daily life. Merchants had to be able to achieve high profits, while carrying comparatively little to weigh them down. African rulers purchased luxuries in order to engage in conspicuous consumption, fashion display, and lavish gift giving—all ways to enhance their status and cement power relations. They sold slaves to the Europeans, in a similar fashion, as luxuries in return for luxuries. Thus, scarcity raised demand on both sides in their respective quest for luxury items.

Elmina, in present-day Ghana, was, along with the village of São Jorge da Mina, the first Portuguese fortified trading post on the African coast, from 1482 until it passed to the Dutch in 1637. Merchants used it for storing the goods they traded and for protection in case of conflicts with Africans. It was staffed by a governor and 20–60 soldiers, a priest, surgeon, apothecary, and a variety of craftspeople. Throughout the first half of the sixteenth century Elmina was the center of Portuguese slaving activities.

African Slavery Sub-Saharan Africa—with its extended distances and few long rivers—was the one continent with the greatest hurdles to a shift in patterns from self-sufficiency to exchange agriculture and urbanization. Exchanges of food for manufactured goods over distances greater than 20 miles were prohibitively

Portuguese Traders. This brass plaque, from about the middle of the sixteenth century, decorated the palace of the Benin Obo and shows two Portuguese traders. The fact they are holding hands suggests that they could be father and son.

expensive. Human portage or donkey transport, the only available forms of moving goods, were limited to highly valuable merchandise, such as salt, copper, and iron. Everything else was manufactured within self-sufficient households, such as pottery, textiles, mats, basketry, utensils, implements, leather goods, and weapons, alongside a full range of agricultural goods.

Self-sufficiency required large households. In villages with limited outside trade, the polygamous household with the largest number of males and females employed at home and in the fields was the wealthiest. To increase his wealth further, a household master often raided neighboring villages and acquired captives, to be enslaved and put to work inside and outside the household. Not surprisingly, therefore, slave raiding and household slavery were general features in sub-Saharan African societies. The more stratified such societies were—with chiefly or royal institutions such as central administrations, armies, and juridical and fiscal offices—the more slaves rose into positions of responsibility and, frequently, autonomy. Thus, African slavery was a highly flexible institution.

Of course, slaves could always run away. In sub-Saharan Africa, they could return to freedom in their native villages, although this was difficult if these villages were still weak or destroyed altogether from the most recent raid. Running away would have been much easier if there had been walled towns or cities nearby where runaways could have sought employment in a craft. Since the urban alternative did not exist to any large degree in the interior of sub-Saharan Africa—in contrast to an urbanizing western Europe, where unfree labor in agriculture disappeared gradually after 1350—slavery, in the flexible household pattern, continued during the period 1500–1800 largely unchanged.

Limited Slave Trade from Benin   When Portugal began the slave trade for sugar plantations on West African off-coast islands, African chiefs and kings had to evaluate the comparative value of slaves for their households or for sale. The kingdom of Benin in the rain-forest region west of the Niger delta was an early example of this calculation. The ruler Ewuare (r. 1440–1473) was the first to rise to dominance over chiefs (*azuma*) and assume the title of king (*obo*). Through conquests in all directions, Ewuare acquired large numbers of slaves. A kingdom emerged on the basis of slaves employed in the army and for the construction of extensive earthworks protecting the capital, Benin City.

Early trade contacts between Portuguese mariners and Benin intensified when the successor of Ewuare granted permission to build a fort on the coast in 1487. But the king kept the exchange of palm oil, ivory, woolens, beads, malagueta pepper, and slaves for guns, powder, metalware, salt, and cottons under close control. A generation later, when the kings prohibited the sale of male slaves, the Portuguese promptly abandoned their fort. Later, a compromise was reached whereby a limited number of slaves was traded, perhaps some 30 percent of the total trade volume between Portugal and Benin, in return for firearms. The kingdom admitted missionaries and members of the dynasty acculturated to the Portuguese, making Benin an economically diversified and culturally complex African Atlantic state.

Slave exports remained restricted during the following two centuries, when Benin was a strong, centralized state. Under subsequent weak kings, decentralization set in. Provincial chiefs began to compete with each other, requiring increased numbers of firearms. To buy more weapons, toward the end of the seventeenth century a weak Benin palace lifted the restrictions on the slave trade. Even more weapons were purchased and slaves were sold during a civil war in the first half of the eighteenth century. But the kingdom reunified and the palace never lost complete control over Benin's trade with the Portuguese and, from the mid-seventeenth century onward, Dutch and British mariners and merchants. From the mid-eighteenth century, the kings even encouraged indigenous gunsmiths to make muskets to help render the country independent from imports, although apparently nothing came of this encouragement. Compared to the slave trade farther west on the West African coast, the large centralized kingdom of Benin with its high internal demand for slave labor remained a modest exporter of slaves.

The Kingdom of Kongo   Farther south, on the central West African coast, the Portuguese established trade relations with several coastal kingdoms, among which Kongo and Ndongo were the most important. These kingdoms were located south of the Congo River, with rain forest to the north and savanna to the south. Kongo, the oldest and most centralized kingdom in the region, emerged about 1400, or a century before the arrival of the Portuguese. Its capital, M'banza (São Salvador), was 20 miles inland in the fertile highlands. With 60,000 inhabitants in the sixteenth century it contained a large palace population and a royal domain, where slaves farmed sorghum, millet, and corn.

Within a radius of some 20 miles, the kings governed a region of about 300,000 independent villagers directly. To defend their rule, they relied on a standing army of 5,000 troops, including 500 musketeers, in the sixteenth century. They appointed members of the royal family as governors, who were entitled to rents but were also obliged to deliver taxes in kind to the palace. In addition, the kings collected a head tax in the form of cowrie shells, an indication that farmers engaged in a limited form of trading their agricultural surplus on markets in the capital to provide themselves with the shells for the tax. This region of direct rule was marked by a unified law and administration. Royal representatives traveled around to represent the royal writ. Farther away, vassal kings, called "dukes" (Portuguese *duque*), governed and sent tributes or gifts to the capital. They sometimes rebelled and broke away; thus, the territory of Kongo, similar to that of Songhay, shifted constantly in size.

The kings of Kongo converted to Christianity early and sent members of the ruling family to Portugal for their education. Portuguese missionaries converted the court and a number of provincial chiefs. In the ruling class, many read and wrote Portuguese and Latin fluently, impressing European aristocrats with their comportment whenever they went on missions. Muslim ethnic stereotypes against "reddish" Christians and Christian stereotypes and patronizing attitudes against dark Muslims, called "*moros*," and, by extension, blacks from sub-Saharan Africa had existed for a long time in Iberia and expressed themselves in Portugal's dealings with Kongo.

Kongolese Cross of St. Anthony.
Considered an emblem
of spiritual authority and
power, the Christian cross
was integrated into Kongo
ancestral cults and burial rituals
and was believed to contain
magical protective properties.
In Antonianism, the religious
reform movement launched by
Dona Beatriz, or Kimpa Vita, in
1704, St. Anthony of Padua, a
thirteenth-century Portuguese-
born saint, became known as
Toni Malau, or "Anthony of Good
Fortune," and was the patron
of the movement. His image
was widely incorporated into
religious objects and personal
items, such as this cross.

Kongolese royalty wore Portuguese dress, listened to church music and hymns, and drank wine imported from the Canaries. Lay assistants converted many urban and villager commoners to Catholicism, and schoolmasters instructed children at churches and chapels. The result was an African Creole culture, in which the animist veneration of territorial and ancestral spirits was combined with Catholicism. As the story of Dona Beatriz Kimpa Vita demonstrates, this Creole culture should not be viewed as a simple facsimile of European culture. Instead, it was a creative adaptation of Portuguese Catholicism to the indigenous African heritage, in the same way that East and West Africa adapted to Coptic Christianity or Islam and represented genuine variations of African culture.

Kongo began to sell slaves to Portuguese traders as early as 1502 for labor on the sugar plantations of the island of São Tomé. By the mid-1500s, the kings permitted the export of a few thousand slaves a year. But Portugal wanted more slaves, and in 1571 the crusader King Sebastião I (r. 1557–1578), who renewed Henry the Navigator's devotion to territorial conquest, chartered a member of the aristocracy with creating a colony in the adjacent kingdom of Ndongo for the mining of salt and silver by slaves. At first, this holder of the charter assisted the king of Ndongo in defeating rebels; but when his colonial aims became clear, the king turned against him and a full-scale Portuguese war of conquest and for slaves erupted.

In this war, which lasted with short interruptions from 1579 to 1657, the Portuguese allied themselves with Ibangala bands. The Ibangala were a large group of loosely organized, fierce warriors from the eastern outreaches of Kongo and Ndongo into central Africa who raided in both kingdoms for slaves. Their propaganda as well as their swift campaigns threw the population into fear and turmoil. Tales of cannibalism and the forcible recruitment of child soldiers spread by word of mouth. The Ibangala consumed large quantities of palm wine and imported Portuguese wine from the Canaries, the latter received from traders in payment for slaves. Together, a few hundred Portuguese musketeers and tens of thousands of Ibangalas raided the kingdoms of Ndongo and Kongo for slaves, often as many as 15,000 a year.

The war reduced the resourceful Queen Nzinga (r. 1624–1663) of Ndongo to a guerilla fighter. In the end, thanks to an alliance with some Ibangalas, she recreated a kingdom, greatly reduced in size, that also engaged in the slave trade. The widening conflict also spilled over into Kongo, where Portuguese and allied Ibangala troops exploited a long civil war (1665–1709) and enslaved even Catholic and Antonian Christians. The war expanded further when new entrants onto the scene, the Dutch West India Company, mistakenly assumed that the small numbers of Portuguese troops would be no match for a quick conquest of the coastal forts. Thanks to Brazilian help, however, Portugal was able to drive out the Dutch. The latter decided to return to a more peaceful trade for slaves from other fortified strongholds on the African west coast.

The Dutch in South Africa

In 1652, the Dutch built a fort on the South African coast to supply fresh water and food to ships traveling around the Cape of Good Hope. Employees of the company, working on time contracts, grew wheat on small lots and bought cattle from the Khoi, local cattle breeders. A few

African Christianity

"Even slaves dress up as if great lords, with a great escort they go to church where they hear Mass, take communion, and contract marriage according to the form of the Roman Church, then go back with great escort."

—Giovanni Francesco da Roma. *Breve relazione . . .*
(1648). Excerpt translated in Linda M. Heywood and
John K. Thornton, *Central Africans, Atlantic Creoles,
and the Foundation of the Americas, 1585–1660*, p. 174.
Cambridge: Cambridge University Press, 2007.

Queen Nzinga. In this contemporary engraving, Queen Nzinga is shown conducting negotiations with the Portuguese in 1622. She sits on a slave's back to avoid having to stand in the presence of a person beneath her rank.

wealthy landowners imported the first black slaves in 1658, from Dahomey, on the West African coast, to convert the original Dutch smallholdings into larger wheat and grape plantations. Gradually, a culturally Dutch settler society emerged, which included Protestants fleeing religious persecution in France and Germany.

The majority of these settlers were urban craftspeople and traders, while most of the actual farmers employed slaves from Mozambique, the island of Madagascar, and even as far away as Indonesia, the epicenter of Dutch colonial ambitions in the East Indies. Around 1750, there were about 10,000 *Boers* (Dutch for "farmer" [rhymes with "boars"]) in the Cape Colony, easily outnumbered by slaves. Through relentless land expansion into the interior, ranchers destroyed the Khoi, forcing their absorption into other local groups. The Boers governed themselves, following the model of Dutch representative institutions. Their descendants would one day fight the Zulu for land and the British for independence and create the system of apartheid in South Africa as they became "Afrikaaners"—as they called themselves. Today, they share political power and a troubled political legacy with their black African countrymen.

American Plantation Slavery and Atlantic Mercantilism

The pattern of African slavery was different from the pattern of American plantation slavery. While European slave traders exploited an existing African slave system, the American plantation slave system had its roots in the eastern Christian religious civilization of Byzantium. There, the Roman institution of agricultural estate slavery survived, in both law and practice. Imperial estates on the warm southern Mediterranean islands of Cyprus and Crete employed Muslim prisoners as well as captives from the Russian steppes as slaves for the expansion of such labor-intensive crops as wine and

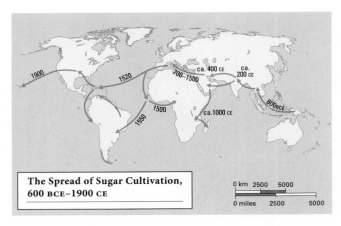

The Spread of Sugar Cultivation, 600 BCE–1900 CE

MAP 19.2 **The Spread of Sugar Cultivation, 600 BCE–1900 CE.**

olive oil. After 1191, when crusaders conquered Cyprus from Byzantium, crusader landlords and Venetian and Genoese merchants expanded into sugar production, which had been introduced in the eastern Mediterranean by Arabs in the period 800–1000. Two and a half centuries later, Venetians, Spaniards, and Portuguese established slave-based sugarcane plantations on the islands of Madeira, the Canaries, and São Tomé off the West African coast. Thus, through Byzantine, crusader, Venetian, Arab, and Iberian interaction and adaptation over the course of hundreds of years, the massive system of Atlantic–American plantation slavery came into being around 1500. About 80 percent of all slaves brought from Africa to the Americas were taken to work on sugar plantations (see Map 19.2).

The Special Case of Plantation Slavery in the Americas

In examining the rise and perpetuation for more than three centuries of the patterns of American **plantation slavery**, a number of questions arise: How many Africans were forcibly taken from Africa to the Americas? Who were they, and who were the people who exploited their labor? What institutions were created to capture, transport, supply, and work slaves? What did the labor of the African slaves help to build? And, perhaps most of all, why did this system develop the way it did—and last so long?

Plantation slavery: Economic system in which slave labor was used to grow crops such as sugar, tobacco, and cotton on large estates.

Numbers   The enslavement of Africans for labor in the Western Hemisphere constituted the largest human migration—voluntary or involuntary—in world history before the later nineteenth century. Though it is estimated that millions of Africans had earlier been taken into servitude in the Muslim world from the eighth to the fourteenth century, their numbers are dwarfed by those shipped across the Atlantic from the fifteenth through the early nineteenth century.

While the figures have been hotly debated by scholars and activists over recent decades, the latest estimates put the numbers of Africans shipped out of Africa at around 12.5 million—more than twice the number taken in the so-called Oriental slave trade to the Middle East and Indian Ocean basin during the period 700–1400. Nearly half of these slaves, 5.8 million, went to Brazil. While historical demographers and other scholars are trying to amass figures to determine how many slaves died in the process of being transferred to the African coast after their initial capture and how many more perished at sea, their conclusions are at present only tentative. However, most estimates place the numbers of slaves lost during these transfers at another 1.4 million, or 12 percent, with a total of 11 million reaching the American shores. These figures, it should be noted, exclude the numbers killed in the African slave raids and wars themselves, which will probably never be precisely known (see Map 19.3).

Chattel: Literally, an item of moveable personal property; chattel slavery is the reduction of the status of the slave to an item of personal property of the owner, to dispose of as he or she sees fit.

Chattel Slavery   By the mid-eighteenth century African slaves everywhere in the New World had been reduced to the status of **chattel**. That is, they were legally considered to be (and, in practice, were treated as) the property of their owners and

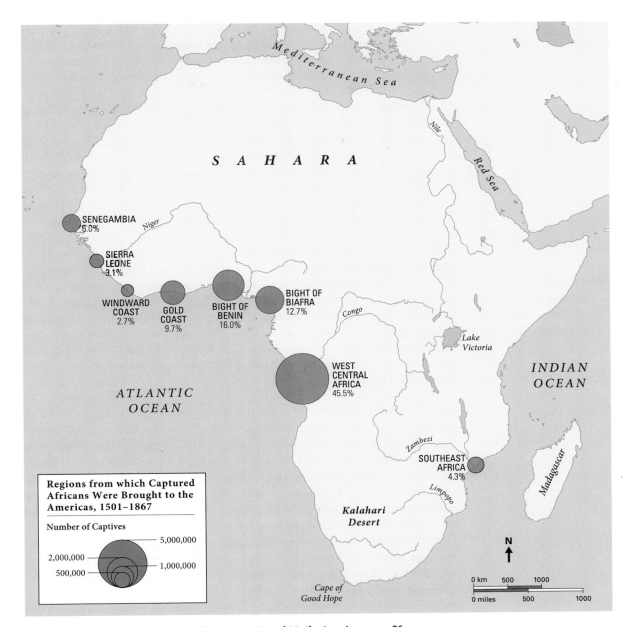

MAP **19.3** **Regions from which Captured Africans Were Brought to the Americas, 1501–1867.**

held the same status as farm animals or agricultural implements. The perfect expression of this condition may be found in the famous Dred Scott decision, handed down by the US Supreme Court a century later, in 1857. In the court's opinion, the Chief Justice, Roger B. Taney, forcefully stated that black African slaves "had no rights which a white man was bound to respect."

Within this statement we see another qualitatively different element from earlier kinds of slavery: what came to be known as the "color line." While color was sometimes not the determining factor in the early years of American slavery, it had very much come to be so by the eighteenth century. The equation of blackness with slavery prompted assumptions over time of African inferiority and created the basis for the modern expression of the phenomenon of racism, a problem that has plagued nearly all societies touched by the institutions of African slavery to this day.

The Problem of Presentism

One of the most difficult tasks historians face is to objectively determine the origins of long-term developments given the fact that they benefit from their knowledge of how things will turn out later. The progress of events becomes all too easily inevitable and can block a historian's vision from the alternatives that the people at the time might have considered. This is particularly true where the developments in question are vitally important but repugnant to our sensibilities and beliefs today. For example, how could otherwise "moral" people have deliberately created a system of slavery destined to harm or kill millions of fellow human beings? Shouldn't they have seen where their actions were ultimately leading?

Historians have long debated the role of present-day sensibilities and issues in the study of the past. The practice of looking at the past through the lens of the present is called **presentism**. Of course, everyone brings his or her own views and biases along when studying history. Historians, however, consciously try to distance themselves from these while attempting to empathetically enter the past. Nowhere is this problem more evident than in looking for the origins of the plantation system and African slavery. Here, the origins are certainly modest and distant in time and present many alternatives. But, above all, what those origins led to remains repellant to our present sensibilities.

Presentism: A bias toward present-day attitudes, especially in the interpretation of history.

Caribbean Plantations

Soon after the discovery of the Americas and the establishment of the first Spanish settlements in the Caribbean, the indigenous population of Taínos and Caribs disappeared, decimated by the European smallpox against which the native peoples were helpless. Beginning in the sixteenth century, Native Americans on the mainland were similarly decimated by smallpox. To replenish the labor force, as early as 1511, the Spanish crown authorized the importation of 50 African slaves for gold mining on the island of Hispaniola. In the following decades thousands more followed for work on newly established sugar plantations. The Africans, at this point primarily from Senegambia, shared a similar pool of disease immunities with the Europeans. They were acclimated to tropical temperatures and conditions and had no home base in the American islands to which to flee. For their European overlords, this made them ideal workers. Indeed, by the late sixteenth century African slaves outnumbered Europeans in the Spanish-controlled islands and in Mexico and Peru, where they were primarily involved in mining.

Apart from mining, plantation work for sugar is among the most arduous forms of labor. Sugar cane leaves have sharp edges and the mature stalks must be cut down with *machetes*—long, heavy knives. The stalks are then bundled, loaded into a cart, and carried to a mill. The early mills utilized horizontal rotating millstones (later versions used stone or metal rollers) turned by human, animal, or water power. Once the stalks were crushed and their juice extracted, the waste was used for animal or occasionally for slave food. The refining process involved boiling successive batches of juice, itself a hot and taxing process. The charred animal bones added to the refining were often supplemented by those of deceased slaves, thus contributing a particularly sinister element to the process.

In all, the average slave field hand on a sugar plantation was estimated to live just 5 or 6 years. Early on, the slave workforce was largely male, which meant that there were relatively few children to replenish the slave population. With the price of slaves low and the mortality rate high, it was economically more desirable to literally work slaves to death and buy more than to make the extra investments necessary to cultivate families. Not surprisingly, revolts, work slowdowns, and sabotage of equipment and cargoes were frequent, with punishments being severe and public. Slaves were flogged and branded for minor infractions and maimed, castrated, hanged, burned, and sometimes dismembered for more severe crimes.

Grinding Sugarcane. The steps in the making of refined sugar were elaborate and backbreaking. In the center, a wagon brings the harvested cane in from the fields, while slaves in the foreground sort the stalks under the watchful eyes of an overseer. The wind-powered mill uses rollers to crush the cane and extract its juice for boiling.

Mercantilism in Action in the Caribbean   With the decline of Spanish power and the rise of the North Atlantic maritime states during the seventeenth century, a profound shift of the political balance in the Caribbean took place. Portugal, Spain, the Netherlands, Great Britain, and France all followed a similar path to enrichment that came to be known as "**mercantilism**"—that is, when the wealth of the state depends on having the maximum amount of gold and silver in its treasury. Thus, states should keep their economies blocked off from competitors and import as little and export as much as possible. Colonies were seen as vital to this economic system because they supplied raw materials to the European homeland and provided safe markets for manufactured goods from the homeland.

It followed that one way to enhance your riches was to capture those of your rivals. Thus, from the late sixteenth through the early eighteenth centuries, the navies of the Dutch, English, French, Spanish, and Portuguese all attacked each others' shipping interests and maritime colonies. The Spanish, with their lucrative treasure fleets to Acapulco and through the Caribbean along the "Spanish Main," were the favorite targets of all. Moreover, all of these governments issued "letters of marque" allowing warships owned by individuals or companies called **privateers** to prey on the shipping of rival powers for a share in the prize money they obtained. Not surprisingly, a number of individuals also went into this business for themselves as pirates. Long before the motion pictures of the same name, there were a great many wildly diverse "pirates of the Caribbean."

The growing trade in plantation commodities from the Caribbean compelled Spain's European competitors to oust the Spanish from their valuable sugar islands. Thus, the rising naval power of England seized Jamaica from Spain in 1655. Jamaica's sugar production grew so valuable that the annual worth of its commodities was greater than that of all of England's North American colonies combined. The French, by the mid-seventeenth century the premier continental European power, followed a decade later in seizing the western part of Hispaniola, which came to be called Saint-Domingue.

This process was accompanied by two developments that enhanced the mercantilist economics of both powers. First, English, French, as well as Dutch merchants

Mercantilism: Political theory, according to which the wealth derived from the mining of silver and gold and the production of agricultural commodities should be restricted to each country's market, with as little as possible expended on imports from another country.

Privateers: Individuals or ships granted permission to attack enemy shipping and to keep a percentage of the prize money the captured ships brought at auction; in practice, privateers were often indistinguishable from pirates.

became involved in the African slave trade, usurping the Portuguese from their near-monopoly of the traffic. The second was that the growing demand for molasses (a syrup by-product of sugar refining) and the even greater popularity of its fermented and distilled end product, rum, pushed both sugar planting and slavery to heights that would not reach their peak until after 1750. As we will see in more detail, sugar, slaves, molasses, and rum form the vital legs of the famous triangular trade that sustained the Atlantic economic system.

The human toll, however, was appalling. Barbados, for example, was settled initially in 1627 by English planters, who grew tobacco, cotton, indigo, and ginger, employing English and Irish **indentured laborers**. In 1640, however, planters switched to the more profitable sugarcane. English and Irish indentured laborers now proved so unwilling to leave their home countries for Barbados that law courts in the home ports resorted to convicting them on trumped- up charges and sentencing them to "transportation." In addition, so many were tricked or seized by press gangs and sent there that being "barbadosed" quickly became a popular slang term for kidnapping. So great was the mortality of their African counterparts that they had to be shipped to the sugar islands at a rate of two to one in order to keep the population from declining. Thus, the pioneer of modern economics, Adam Smith (1723–1790), would note that "the profits of a sugar plantation in any of our West Indian colonies are generally much greater than those of any other cultivation that is now either in Europe or America. Yet for the slave it is, 'a more dreadful apprehension . . . than we can have of hell.'" It was a hell that they apprehended even before being led off the ship.

Indentured laborers: Poor workers enrolled in European states with the obligation to work in the Americas for 5–7 years, in return for their prepaid passage across the Atlantic.

A Vision of Hell

"The Negroes are so wilful and loth to leave their own country, that they have often leap'd out of the canoes, boat and ship, into the sea, and kept under water until they were drowned, to avoid being taken up and saved by our boats, which pursued them; they having a more dreadful apprehension of Barbadoes than we can have of hell . . ."

—Thomas Phillips. "The Voyage of the Ship *Hannibal* of London, in 1693." In: *Ships and Slaving*, ed. George Francis Dow, pp. 31–71, quote from pp. 62–63. Salem, MA: Marine Research Society, 1927. Reprint Mineola, NY: Dover, 2002.

The Sugar Empire: Brazil   The Portuguese first planted sugarcane as a crop in Brazil in the 1530s, well before Caribbean planters began to grow it and a generation after the original trade in brazilwood (a red dye) was established. Portuguese colonists turned to the production of sugar because, unlike their counterparts in the Caribbean, Mexico, and Peru, they did not find any gold or silver. Like the Spanish, the Portuguese crown repeatedly issued edicts to the colonists to refrain from enslaving indigenous people for work on the sugar plantations; these edicts were widely ignored. In addition, in the 1530s, the Portuguese trading network on the West African coast began to supply the colony with African slaves. By the end of the century, a dramatic rise in demand for sugar in Europe increased the importation of black slaves, of which the Portuguese carefully cultivated their carrying monopoly. In the next century, the insatiable demand of the sugar industry for slaves received a further boost in 1680 when enslavement of Indians was finally abolished; and in 1690 the discovery of gold in Minas Gerais, in the interior, led to a gold boom and increased demand for labor even more. Brazil ultimately became the final destination of nearly half of all the slaves transported to the Americas. Indeed, Brazil went on to be the largest slave state in the world, with about two-fifths of its entire population consisting of blacks. In the end, it was the last country in the Americas to give up the institution, in 1888 (see Map 19.4).

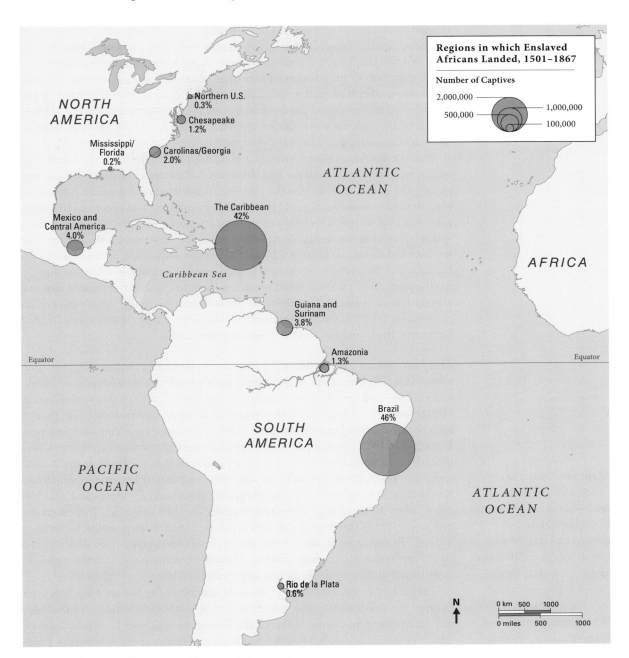

MAP **19.4** Regions in which Enslaved Africans Landed, 1501–1867.

The "Peculiar Institution" in British North America

In the 1850s a number of writers and politicians in the southern United States waxed enthusiastically about the possibility of "filibustering" expeditions to Central America, Cuba, and even Brazil to win these lands for the United States. Later, during the American Civil War, some leaders of the Confederate States even called for a great

Confederate "tropical empire," extending from Virginia in the north to the southern border of Brazil. The reason for this enthusiasm was that these men recognized a phenomenon that historians have only lately come to reexamine: that these territories, regardless of their national boundaries, shared a common economic system based on plantation agriculture producing valuable commodities for export; relied on imported manufactured goods; shared a common aristocratic culture; and relied almost totally on what was quaintly referred to in the American southern states as "the peculiar institution" of slavery to support it.

Modern historians have identified a plantation zone which, in 1750, extended unbroken from the Chesapeake Bay in England's American colonies to Brazil, embracing the entire Caribbean in the process. Such a zone represented a pattern unprecedented in world history. No system of cash cropping had ever been this large, extended over so much territory, or brought so much profit to its owners and investors. It created the largest demand for human labor yet seen, which after 1700 was satisfied almost exclusively through the African slave trade. As we noted in the beginning of this section, this in turn created a nearly immutable color line that defined a permanent underclass and identified blackness with slavery and inferiority. Though it was eventually destined to die out in the northernmost British and French possessions as well as the northern United States, legal slavery at one time extended far beyond the plantation zone into what is now Canada.

The "Sot Weed" Enterprise

As we saw in preceding chapters, the first permanent English settlements in the Americas were the for-profit enterprise at Jamestown in 1607 and the religious "errand in the wilderness" of the initial settlements in Massachusetts from 1620 on. Both would soon count Africans among them, though their descendants in Jamestown would be by far the more economically important. In August of 1619 a Dutch privateer surprised a Portuguese slaver en route to Vera Cruz, Mexico, and relieved her of 60 of her *piexas de India*—"pieces of the Indies," or African slaves. By the end of the month, the ship put in at Jamestown, which had been barely hanging on as an enterprise, and disembarked "twenty and odd Negroes," some of whom were Christians from the kingdom of Kongo. These were the first slaves sold in the English colonies of North America. They would be far from the last. Though only about 3–5 percent of the slaves shipped from Africa ended up in North America, through procreation on the continent their numbers grew to more than 4 million by the eve of the American Civil War.

Their labor, along with that of increasing numbers of indentured workers from Europe, was needed for a new enterprise that, it was hoped, would save the colonial enterprise from failure: tobacco. The Powhatan and other local peoples grew tobacco for themselves, but it was considered by the increasing numbers of European smokers to be inferior to the varieties grown in the Caribbean. The English, however, had acquired some of the Caribbean plants and begun intensive cultivation in the Chesapeake Bay region of this "sot weed," as it came to be called. Indentured labor was widely used, but those workers were bound to stay only until they had worked off the cost of their passage, usually 5–7 years. After that, they worked for wages or acquired their own land. Under these conditions, slaves came to be the preferred labor source in the colony of Virginia.

Though a surprising number of Africans earned **manumission** from their owners, gaining their freedom, acquiring land, and on occasion even starting their own

Manumission: The process by which slaves are legally given freedom; in the days of Atlantic slavery, this was most commonly done by slaves saving enough to buy themselves from their owners, by outsiders buying them and setting them free, or by owners simply granting them freedom; during the nineteenth century, abolitionists often collected money to buy the freedom of slaves or bring them north by the famous Underground Railroad.

plantations with their own slaves during the seventeenth century, the colonial authorities eventually passed laws firmly fixing the slave underclass as one based on color. For example, as if anticipating Justice Taney's ruling of 1857, the colony of Carolina's Lords Proprietors stated as early as 1669 that "freemen" were to have "absolute power and authority," over their "[N]egro slaves." Throughout the eighteenth century, slave-based tobacco-raising remained the dominant plantation activity in the upper south.

Sugar, Rice, and Indigo in the Lower South
The colony of Carolina came under the purview of the Lords Proprietors in Barbados, who began sending settlers in 1670 as a way to transport religious dissenters and to form a bulwark against the Spanish in Florida. As part of a vast pine forest running from southern Virginia to northern Florida, its position as a provider of naval stores—pitch, tar, rosin, and turpentine—as well as tall, straight tree trunks for ships' masts, was vital in the age of wooden vessels. Even today, there is a sizeable town in North Carolina named Tarboro, and the state's nickname is "The Tarheel State." Although indentured laborers and slaves were involved in these enterprises, plantation crops were destined to see the largest demand for their labor.

In the seventeenth and early eighteenth centuries, the settlers ran what was by far the most successful attempt ever to enslave Native Americans in the Carolinas. As many as 50,000 slaves labored here by the early eighteenth century. Native resistance to slaving resulted in war between the settlers and a Native American alliance in 1715–1717 that almost lost the colony for the Lords Proprietors. The settlers, angry with what they considered the mismanagement of the Lords Proprietors, appealed to the crown; and South Carolina was split off in 1719 and set up as a royal colony shortly thereafter. Deprived of Native Americans for slaves, the colonies began to import large numbers of West African slaves as the Dutch dominance of the trade gave way to the British. This initial wave of slave immigration ultimately grew to a point that made South Carolina the only North American colony, and later state, in which African Americans outnumbered Europeans.

In addition, South Carolina produced many of the same plantation commodities as Brazil and the Caribbean, along with one vitally important new addition. Sugarcane and molasses, for example, were produced in the southern lowlands and tidewater regions. Carolina rice became a vital food source and one whose production was taken up throughout the flatlands of the Deep South. Many West Africans brought with them the skills and knowledge of long-grain rice cultivation ideal for the lowlands. It was indigo, however, that was destined to become the colony's most important cash crop until the cotton boom of the nineteenth century.

The dark blue dye produced from the tropical plant *Indigofera tinctoria* had been grown

Advertisement for a Slave Auction. In this notice from 1766, potential slave buyers in Charleston, South Carolina, are informed of the time and place for the sale of a "choice cargo" of recently arrived Africans. As Charleston was undergoing a smallpox epidemic at the time, potential customers are reassured that the captives are healthy and likely to be immune to the disease.

TO BE SOLD on board the Ship *Bance-Island*, on tuesday the 6th of *May* next, at *Ashley-Ferry*; a choice cargo of about 250 fine healthy NEGROES, just arrived from the Windward & Rice Coast.—The utmost care has already been taken, and shall be continued, to keep them free from the least danger of being infected with the SMALL-POX, no boat having been on board, and all other communication with people from *Charles-Town* prevented.

Austin, Laurens, & Appleby.

N. B. Full one Half of the above Negroes have had the SMALL-POX in their own Country.

extensively throughout Asia, the ancient Mediterranean, and North and West Africa. A similar American species, *Indigofera suffruticosa*, had long been in use in Mexico and Central America. Maritime countries with Indian and East Asian connections imported vast quantities of it into Europe, while the Spanish began to cultivate the American variety. Sales in northern Europe were initially hampered because there indigo competed with the local production of dyes made from the woad plant. Restrictions on imports were gradually lifted, and South Carolina entered an indigo boom starting in the 1740s. The burgeoning need for labor in planting, stripping the leaves, fermenting, cleaning, draining, scraping, and molding the residue into balls or blocks—all accompanied by a considerable stench—drove the slave trade even further.

The final English possession in southern North America prior to 1750 was Georgia. The southern regions of what was to become the colony of Georgia had been claimed by the Spanish as early as 1526 as part of their exploration of Florida and the Gulf Coast. Attempts by the French to found a colony near Port Royal, South Carolina, and Fort Caroline (near present-day Jacksonville) in the 1560s were ultimately undone. With the expansion of the English presence in the seventeenth century and the French concentrating on their vast claims in Canada and the Mississippi valley, the territory between Carolina and the Spanish fort at St. Augustine became increasingly disputed.

Into this situation stepped James Oglethorpe (1696–1785), the only founder of an English colony in North America who lived to see it become part of the United States. Oglethorpe's vision was to set up a colony for England's poor, debtors (who would otherwise be imprisoned), and dispossessed. He obtained a royal charter for his idea and in 1733 landed with his first band of settlers at the site of the modern city of Savannah. After buying land from the local Native Americans, he began to develop the colony as a free area in which slavery was banned. The Spanish attempted to claim Georgia in 1742 but were repulsed. Pressed by settlers bringing their slaves in from South Carolina, Georgia's ban on slave labor was soon rescinded. By the end of Oglethorpe's life, which he spent in retirement in England, Georgia had developed its own slave-based plantation economy, producing rice, sugar, indigo, and, on the Sea Islands along the coast, a fine, long-fiber variety of cotton, which proved to be a harbinger of the commodity that would ensure slavery's survival in the United States until 1865.

The Fatal Triangle: The Economic Patterns of the Atlantic Slave Trade

As mentioned, the European countries that successively dominated the transportation of slaves from the West African coast moved steadily northward in a pattern that paralleled their naval and merchant marine power. That is, during the fifteenth and sixteenth centuries, Portugal had an effective monopoly on the trade from outposts in Senegambia, Elmina, and Ndongo. The success of Dutch and English privateers encouraged more concerted economic warfare and, with it, the seizure by the Dutch of Elmina in 1637. Now it was the Dutch who became the principal slave carriers, part of a pattern of aggressive colonizing that made the Netherlands the world's richest country in per capita terms through much of the seventeenth century. The rise of England's naval power at the expense of the Dutch and the fading of the Spanish and Portuguese naval presence allowed the English—and, to a lesser extent, the French—to dominate the slaving trade. By the mid-eighteenth century, as the trade approached its height, it had become the base upon which the world's most lucrative economic triangle was constructed (see Map 19.5).

Rum, Guns, and Slaves

As we have seen, England's colonies in the Americas, especially those in the Caribbean, were by the eighteenth century producing valuable crops, including sugar, tobacco, cotton, and indigo, for export to the Old World. Tobacco was raised mainly in England's North American colonies, along with some cotton for export to England, though at this point England still imported most of its cotton from India. So profitable were these exports that, in keeping with the policy of mercantilism, the crown passed a series of acts in 1651 and 1660 that produced even greater profits for merchants in the motherland. The Navigation Acts required that all goods imported to England from American colonies had to be transported only in English ships, thereby guaranteeing a virtual monopoly on trans-Atlantic trade.

British merchants acquired enormous profits from their colonial trading practices, particularly with the Atlantic colonies. We are afforded a good example of how this worked through an analysis of the Atlantic system, or the "triangular trade." In

MAP 19.5 The North Atlantic System, ca. 1750.

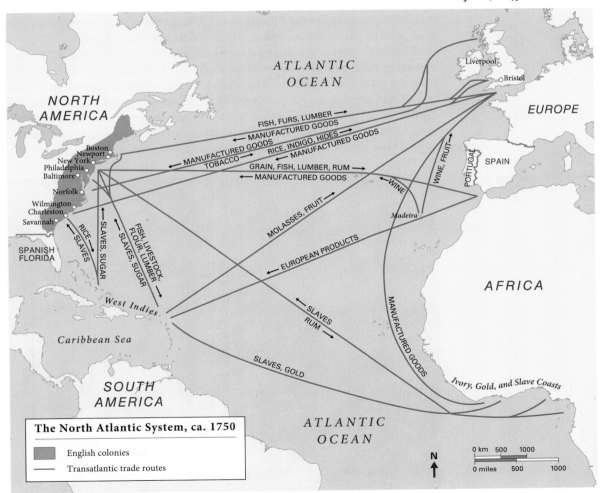

The North Atlantic System, ca. 1750

English colonies

Transatlantic trade routes

Atlantic system:
Economic system in which European ships would exchange goods for slaves in West Africa and slaves would then be brought to America and exchanged for goods that would be carried back to the home port.

general terms, British ships would leave home ports in either their North American colonies or Britain with goods of various kinds, then travel to ports along the western coast of Africa, where these goods would be exchanged for African slaves; these ships would then sail across the Atlantic, where slaves would be exchanged for goods produced in western Atlantic colonies; and finally, these goods would be carried back to the home port.

A particular pattern consisted of the following: An English ship loaded with New England rum would sail from Europe to the western coast of Africa, where the rum would be exchanged for a cargo of slaves; laden with slaves, the ship would then sail westward across the Atlantic to sugar colonies in the Caribbean, where the slaves would be exchanged for a cargo of molasses; the ship would sail to New England, where the molasses would be processed into rum. A variant pattern was the following: A British ship would leave its home port—increasingly Liverpool, the port that benefited most dramatically from the slave trade—loaded with manufactured goods, such as guns, knives, textiles, and assorted household wares. It would sail to the western coast of Africa, where these goods would be exchanged for a cargo of slaves; the ship would then sail westward across the Atlantic to the British colony of Virginia, where its human cargo would be exchanged for tobacco; the ship would then sail eastward across the Atlantic to its home port in Britain, where the tobacco would be unloaded and then sold to British and European merchants.

To a large extent, the **Atlantic system** depended upon the import of ever-increasing numbers of slaves from Africa. Beginning in the early eighteenth century, the numbers skyrocketed as the English and French imported slaves for their colonies in the Caribbean and in North America. The numbers were pushed further by the demise of Native American slavery in the Carolinas after 1719. Thus, at its height in the eighteenth century, more than half of the nearly 12 million Africans estimated to have been transported to the Americas were landed.

Bristol Docks and Quay in 1760. Up until 1750, Bristol was the largest slave-trading port in England. It supplied the majority of slaves sent to Jamaica to work in the island's booming sugar plantations. However, its small and congested harbor caused it to fall behind Liverpool as the leading British port in the Atlantic slave trade.

The Middle Passage   Following capture in Africa, prisoners were usually marched to slave markets and embarkation ports roped, chained, or ganged together by forked tree trunks. Slave lots were then wholesaled to middlemen or auctioned directly to foreign factors. From this point they would be imprisoned in fortified slave pens called "barracoons" until the next ship bound for their sale destination arrived. But it was on the voyage from Africa to the Americas, the infamous "Middle Passage," that the full horror of the slave's condition was most fully demonstrated.

Because the profits involved in transportation were so high for captains, officers, and even crewmen, they constantly experimented with ways to pack the maximum number of human beings into the holds of their ships. Because a certain percentage of mortality was expected during a voyage that lasted from a few weeks to nearly 2 months, some ship captains favored "tight packing"—deliberate overcrowding on the assumption that a few more might survive than normal. On the other hand, some captains favored the "loose pack" method, with the assumption that a higher percentage would survive if given marginally more room than normal. In either case, conditions were abominable.

Due to well-founded fears of slave mutiny, the holds of slave ships were locked and barred and the hatchways and vents covered with iron gratings. The slaves were chained to tiny bunks arranged in tiers configured to maximize the space of the hold. Food was minimal, usually corn mush, and sanitation

> ## The Middle Passage
>
> "But when a vessel arrived to conduct us away to the ship, it was a most horrible scene; there was nothing to be heard but rattling chains, smacking of whips, and the groans and cries of our fellow-men. Some would not stir from the ground, when they were lashed and beat in the most horrible manner."
>
> —Excerpt from Quobna Ottobah Cugoano, *Thoughts and Sentiments on the Evil and Wicked Traffic of the Slavery and Commerce of the Human Species*, ed. Vincent Caretta, p. 15. New York: Penguin, 1999.

Plan of a Slave Ship, 1789. This image, based on the *Brooks*, a Liverpool slave ship, was one of the first to document the horrors of the slave trade. It shows the captives laid like sardines beneath deck. In such conditions slaves perished at the rate of 10–30 percent during the Middle Passage. The engraving was widely distributed by British abolitionists, who eventually succeeded in banning the trade in 1807.

nonexistent. Small groups of captives would be brought up on deck on a rotating basis to be haphazardly washed of their vomit and feces with buckets of frigid ocean water thrown at them by the crew. They would then be "danced" for minimal exercise and sent back down, and the next group would be brought up. The dead, sick, and resistant would simply be thrown overboard. The ship and crew were also well armed to fight off attacks by competitors or pirates. On landing at their destination, the slaves were again "barracooned," cleaned up, and given better meals pending their auction to individual buyers. In the process somewhere between 5 and 20 percent of them died en route.

Culture and Identity in the African Diaspora

The original meaning of the term "diaspora" referred to the dispersal of the Jews around the Roman Empire after their revolt of the first century CE was put down. Scholars now use the term more generally for the wide dispersal by forced or voluntary migration of any large group. In the case of the **African diaspora**, in which Africans moved to nearly all parts of the Americas primarily through the slave trade, the story is far too varied and complex for us to do more than note some general patterns related to culture and identity.

African diaspora: Dispersal of African peoples throughout the world, particularly the Americas, as part of the transatlantic slave trade.

A New Society: Creolization of the Early Atlantic World

As discussed earlier in this chapter, one of the effects of the Portuguese implantation on African coasts through trade forts and colonies was the adaptation of coastal African societies to western Christianity and Portuguese culture. These societies were highly diverse. Some were tribal and peaceful, others tribal and militarily oriented; still others had transformed themselves into kingdoms, cooperating intermittently or permanently with the Portuguese and later with the Dutch, English, and French. Depending on the type or intensity of interaction, African Creole cultures emerged, that is, cultures in which an adaptation to Catholicism occurred and in which Africans appropriated cultural elements into their own heritage.

In earlier scholarship this creolization was often described as resulting in certain elements of an alien, colonizing culture uneasily grafted onto "genuine" Africanness. As in the case of Dona Beatriz and the rise of a Kongolese Catholicism, however, Creole culture has to be seen as a phenomenon in its own right. This is similarly true for black Creole cultures in the Americas. Blacks arrived either as animists with very localized animist heritages or as enslaved Creole Christians and Muslims since foreign and indigenous slave raiders penetrating inland Africa made no distinctions among their victims. Either way, African slaves adapted to their plantation life through creolization or, as African Christian or Muslim Creoles, through further creolization, a process that expressed itself in distinct languages or dialects as well as synthetic (or hybrid) religious customs. Adaptation was not imitation but a creative transformation of cultural elements to fit the conditions of life.

Recent scholarship suggests that a key formative element in the development of culture and identity of Africans in the Americas lay in the influence of the central African Creoles from Kongo and Ndongo (today's Congo and Angola) up to the middle of the seventeenth century. The Christianity of some believers and its later variants helped to nurture this religion among Africans in the new lands, especially when it was reinforced by the religious practices of the slave owners. The mix of language and terms for a multitude of objects similarly gave the early arrivals a certain degree of agency and skill in navigating the institutions of slavery as they were being established.

An example of a Creole language that has survived for centuries is Gullah, used by the somewhat isolated slaves along the coastal islands of South Carolina and Georgia and still spoken by their descendants today. In Haiti, Creole (*krayòl*) is not only the daily spoken language but also used in the media and in literary works. French is recognized as the other national language, especially in law and official pronouncements. Creole cultures typically involve not only the phenomenon of adaptation but also multiple identities—in language, religion, and culture.

Music and Food   It can justifiably be said that the roots of nearly all popular music in the Americas may be found in Africa. Regardless of where they came from in Africa, slaves brought with them a wide variety of musical instruments, songs, and chants, all of which contributed to shaping the musical tastes of their owners and society at large. The widespread use of rhythmic drumming and dance in African celebrations, funerals, and even coded communications has come down to us today as the basis for music as diverse as Brazilian samba, Cuban and Dominican rumba and meringue, New Orleans jazz funerals, and American blues, rock-and-roll, soul, and hip-hop. It is difficult to imagine American country and western music, or bluegrass, without the modern descendant of a West African stringed instrument we know today as the banjo. The chants of field hands, rhyming contests, and gospel music contributed mightily to many of these genres.

Like music, cuisine passed easily across institutional barriers. Here, the dishes that most Americans consider "southern" have in many cases deep African roots. As mentioned earlier, the earliest rice brought to the Carolinas was a variety native to the Niger inland delta in West Africa. Africans brought with them the knowledge of setting up and running an entire rice-based food system, which was established in the Carolina lowlands and Gulf Coast. The yam, the staple of West African diets, also made its way to the Americas. The heart of Louisiana Creole cooking, including rich and spicy gumbos, "dirty rice," jambalaya, and other dishes, comes from the use of the African vegetable okra and a heady mixture of African, American, and Asian spices along with rice.

Plantation Life and Resistance   Although nineteenth-century apologists for slavery frequently portrayed life under it as tranquil—"a positive good," in the words

> ## The Lord's Prayer in Gullah
>
> We fada wa dey een heaen,
> Leh ebrybody hona ya nyame.
> We pray dat soon ya gwine rule oba de wol.
> Wasoneba ting ya wahn,
> Leh um be so een dis wol
> Same like e da dey een heaben.
> Gii we de food wa we need
> Dis day yah an ebry day.
> Fagibe we fa we sin
> Same lik we fagibe dem people
> Wa do bad ta we.
> Leh we dohn hab haad test
> Wen Satan try we.
> Keep we fom ebil.
>
> —Wilbur Cross. *Gullah Culture in America*, p. 99. Westport, CT: Praeger, 2008.

Slave Culture. This ca. 1790 painting from Beaufort, South Carolina, shows the vibrancy of African American culture in the face of great hardship. Note the banjo, whose origins lie in West Africa and which would have a great impact on the development of American music.

Altar and Shrine from the Interior of the Historic Voodoo Museum in New Orleans.

One prominent pattern of world history that we have seen a number of times already is the way indigenous elements work to shape the identity of imported religions as they are taken up by their new believers. Buddhism in China and Japan, for example, adopted elements from Daoism and Chinese folk beliefs as well as spirits and demons from Shinto. Christianity added Roman and Germanic elements to its calendar of holidays, architecture, and cult of saints. Islam in Iran and India and Christianity in Africa underwent similar processes. In Kongo, for example, the African Christian cult of St. Anthony merged Portuguese Catholic and Kongolese animist spiritual traditions into a new church. This trend of interaction continues today, where we find the African Christian churches among the fastest growing in the world and increasingly sending clergy and missionaries to Europe and the United States.

In the Americas three main strains of this kind of interaction and adaptation of imported and indigenous traditions developed over time and are still widely practiced today: Santeria is found primarily in Cuba and among the Spanish-speaking Africans of the Caribbean but is now also in the larger cities of North America with communities of Caribbean immigrants; vodoun, usually written as "voodoo," developed in Haiti and old St. Domingue and is widely practiced among

of South Carolina's John C. Calhoun—for slave and master alike, the system was in fact one of constant real and implied violence. Most slaves reconciled themselves to their condition and navigated it as best they could, but the reminders of their status were constantly around them. Obviously, those who endured the Middle Passage had violence thrust upon them immediately upon capture. Even those born into slavery, however, lived in squalid shacks or cabins; ate inadequate rations, perhaps supplemented with vegetables they were allowed to grow themselves; and spent most of their waking hours at labor.

Those working as house servants had a somewhat easier life than field hands. In some cases, they were the primary guardians, midwives, wet nurses, and even confidants of their masters' families. Often, there was considerable expressed affection between the household slaves and the masters' family. But more often, this was tempered by the knowledge that one or one's family could be sold at any time, that infractions would be severely punished, and that one would be treated as a kind of unruly, temperamental child at best.

As we saw earlier, field hands led a far harder and shorter life. The price of slavery for the master was eternal vigilance; his nightmare was slave revolt. Over the

African-descended French speakers around the Caribbean and in areas of Louisiana; as well as Candomblé, whose adherents are mostly confined to Brazil.

All three are syncretic religions composed of elements that appear disconnected to outsiders but which practitioners see as part of an integrated whole. They intermingle Roman Catholic saints with West African natural and ancestral spirits and gods, see spiritual power as resident in natural things, incorporate images of objects to represent a person or thing whose power the believer wants to tap or disperse (as in the use of so-called voodoo dolls), and hold that proper ritual and sacrifices by priests and priestesses can tune into the spirits of the natural world. In some cases, they see these practices as curing sicknesses and raising the dead—the source of the famous "zombie" legends. Such innovations allowed the slaves to create a religious and cultural space in which they carried out autonomy from their masters—indeed, in which they *were* the masters. They also provided a kind of alternate set of beliefs which could be invoked alongside more mainstream Christian practices. In a real sense, they provided a precious degree of freedom for people who had almost no other form of it.

Mami Wata. Both a protector and a seducer, Mami Wata is an important spirit figure throughout much of Africa and the African Atlantic. She is usually portrayed as a mermaid, a snake charmer, or a combination of both. She embodies the essential, sacred nature of water, upon whose waves so many African Americans traveled across in their diaspora.

Questions

- How do black Christianity and voodoo religion show the new patterns of origins, interaction, and adoption that emerged after 1500?
- Can you think of more recent examples of syncretic religions? If so, which ones? Why are they syncretic?

years a variety of methods were developed to keep slaves in line and at their work. Overseers ran the work schedules and supervised punishments; drivers kept slaves at their work with a long bullwhip in hand to beat the slow or hesitant. Slaves leaving plantations on errands had to carry passes, and elaborate precautions were taken to discourage escape or even unauthorized visits to neighboring plantations. In the Carolinas, for example, owners spread tar on fence rails so that slaves attempting to climb or vault them would be marked for easy detection. Runaways were pursued with relentless determination by trackers with bloodhounds and flogged, branded, maimed, or castrated when returned.

Given these conditions, slave behaviors designed to try to manage their work on their own terms or to get back at their owners were frequent. Slaves would constantly stage work slowdowns, feign illnesses, engage in sabotage of tools and equipment, or pretend not to understand how to perform certain tasks. Kitchen slaves would sometimes spit or urinate into soups or gravies. Despite the risks involved, runaways were quite common. Later, in the United States in the 1850s, enforcement of the Fugitive Slave Act would be a prime factor driving the country toward civil war.

Punishing Slave Revolts. John Gabriel Stedman (1744–1797) was a British–Dutch soldier and writer whose years in Surinam, on the northern coast of South America, were recorded in his *The Narrative of a Five Year Expedition against the Revolted Negroes of Surinam* (1796). With its graphic depictions of slavery it became an important tract in the abolitionist cause. In this illustration, *A Negro Hung Alive by the Ribs to a Gallows*, engraved by the famous artist and romantic poet William Blake (1757–1827), Stedman shows a rebel who was hung by his ribs for two days as punishment for his crimes. Masters routinely cut off the noses of their slaves, burnt them alive, and whipped them to death with impunity.

Despite all their precautions, slave owners throughout the Americas constantly faced the prospect of slave insurrection. By some estimates, there were more than 250 slave uprisings involving 10 or more slaves during the four centuries of Atlantic slavery. In some cases, these rebellions were successful enough for the slaves to create their own isolated settlements where they could, for a time, live in freedom. These escapees were called *Maroons*, and three of the more famous instances of Maroon settlements existed in Jamaica, Columbia, and Surinam. In Brazil, slaves developed their own system of weaponless martial arts called *capoeira*, in which fighters walk on their hands and use their legs to strike. Map 19.6 lists some of the larger slave insurrections from 1500 to 1850.

Putting It All Together

Portugal, the Netherlands, England, France, and Spain built up a fully evolved pattern of trading for plantation slaves on the Atlantic coast of Africa in the course of the sixteenth and seventeenth centuries. The trade took off toward the end of the sixteenth century, with 28,000 slaves annually, and by 1700 had reached 80,000 annually, where it stayed until the early nineteenth century, when the slave trade was abolished. As for the patterns of state formation in Africa, on the whole, the more powerful a kingdom was, the fewer slaves it sold, given its own labor requirements. Conversely, the more conducive the circumstances were for the collapse of chiefly or royal rule and the emergence of raider societies such as the Imbangala, Ashante, or Dahomey, the more damaging the impact was on a given population. Thus, no global judgment is possible. Undoubtedly, in some regions of West and central Africa the effects were grave, while in

Maroon Leader and His Sons. The maroon kingdom of Esmeraldas, in present-day Colombia, remained virtually independent from the late sixteenth century until the early nineteenth century. Its leader, Don Francisco Arrove, and his two sons were painted in 1599 to commemorate a peace treaty with the Spanish. The sumptuous clothing and ornamentation of the maroons blends Spanish, Native American, and African styles.

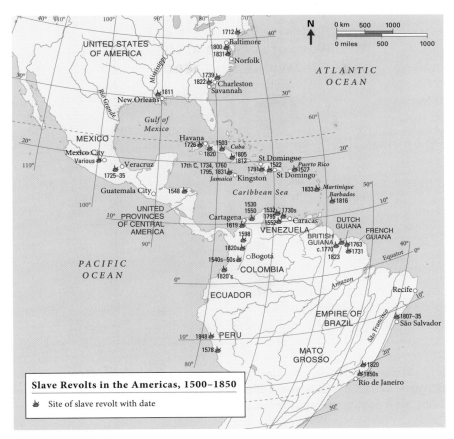

MAP **19.6 Slave Revolts in the Americas, 1500–1850.**

others, often directly adjacent, the impact was less decisive. Nonetheless, the period marked a profound transformation, with many areas depopulated by the slave trade, some enhanced through the trade and the introduction of new food crops like maize and cassava, and others undergoing creolization to some degree.

The interaction and adaptation patterns of Europeans and Africans in Africa and Europeans, Africans, and Native Americans in the Caribbean and Americas over the course of three centuries (1500–1800) created not just a new, two-hemisphere world system of trade but a new kind of society as well (see Concept Map). The Atlantic slave trade was the foundation on which the mass production of cash crops and commodities, the first world pattern of its kind, was brought into being. This economic sphere was by far the richest of its kind in the world, but with it came the creation of an enduring social underclass and the foundation of modern racism.

Yet even in the 1750s, one finds the origins of the abolition movement—the international movement to end first the slave trade and ultimately slavery itself. Among the leaders of Europe's Enlightenment, thinkers were already calling for the end of the trade and institution. Within a few decades, works like the memoirs of the former slave and abolitionist Olaudah Equiano (ca. 1745–1797) would push the movement forward, as would the work of England's William Wilberforce (1759–1833), who actually lived to see the outlawing of the trade and of English slavery itself. Elsewhere,

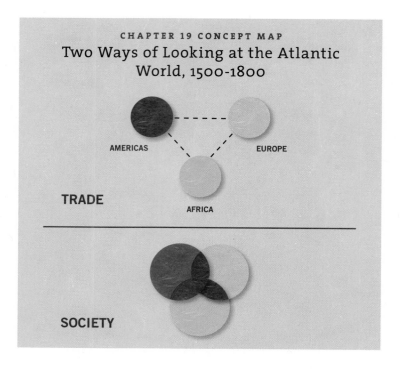

it would take a revolution, as in Haiti, or a civil war, as in the United States, for abolition to occur. In the Atlantic world, the "peculiar institution" finally ended in Brazil in 1888. But it persists informally in India, Africa, and the Middle East even today.

Review and Respond

1. What is the significance of the Songhay Empire for West African history? How did it originate, and how did it fall?

2. What impact did the Portuguese have on Ethiopia? How did this country evolve during the period 1500–1800?

3. How did the Portuguese arrive and progress along the West African coast? Describe their role and impact.

4. How was the kingdom of Kongo organized, and what role did Catholicism play in its society?

5. How did the Middle Passage function, and what role did it play within the triangular trade in the Atlantic?

6. What is Creole culture, and what forms did creolization take?

7. How did plantation slavery evolve in North America? What were the origins of African American culture, and how did that culture evolve through interaction and adaptation?

For additional resources, including maps, primary sources, visuals, and quizzes, please go to www.oup.com/us/vonsivers. Please see the Further Resources section at the back of the book for additional readings and suggested websites.

Thinking Through Patterns

▶ **On what was the pattern of kingdom and empire formation in Africa based during the period 1500–1800?**

What is remarkable about Africa during these 300 years is that it continued its pattern of kingdom and empire formation and actually did so on an accelerated pace, on the basis of increased intra-African trade. The half-dozen examples analyzed in this chapter could be applied to another dozen states. In the interior of Africa the pattern continued in spite of the demographic effects (whatever they were in specific regions) of the Atlantic slave trade.

The pattern of plantation production evolved over several centuries before it was transplanted to the islands of the Atlantic and the Caribbean as well as the Americas. It was above all a system for growing labor-intensive cash crops—indigo, sugar, tobacco—that relied increasingly on African slave labor. By 1800, the demand for plantation commodities by Europeans and the guns, textiles, rum, and other manufactured goods that Africans took in trade for slaves pushed the system to huge proportions. In turn, the mercantilist economics of Western Europe regulated the trade within an efficient, tightly controlled, triangular system.

▶ **How did the patterns of slave trade and plantation slavery evolve in the Atlantic and the Americas?**

▶ **What are the historic roots from which modern racism evolved?**

The gradual domination of African slavery in the Americas and Caribbean over other kinds of servitude created a pattern of racism, in which blackness was permanently associated with slavery. As the economics of slavery became entrenched, the participants in the system answered the criticism of slavery on moral grounds by claiming that black Africans were inherently inferior and thus deserved to be enslaved. The argument was essentially circular: They were enslaved because they were inferior, and they were inferior because they were slaves.

In North America, long after slavery was abolished, these attitudes were preserved in law and custom in many places and reinforced during the colonization of Africa in the nineteenth century and in the practice of segregation in the United States. In Latin America—although racism is no less pervasive—racial views are more subtle. People describing themselves as *mulato*, *sambo*, or *pardo* have a better chance to be recognized as members of their own distinct ethnic groups than in the United States, where the Census classifies people simply as either black or Caucasian.

Chapter 20 | The Mughal Empire:

1400-1750 | MUSLIM RULERS AND HINDU SUBJECTS

Central Asia

Southeast Asia

MUGHAL INDIA, ca. 1700

INDIAN OCEAN

June 17, 1631, could hardly have been a less auspicious day for the family of the Mughal emperor Shah Jahan. Though he ruled over the most powerful empire in India's history and commanded unprecedented wealth, the emperor's beloved wife, Mumtaz Mahal, had just died in giving birth to their fourteenth child. The royal family was naturally plunged into mourning, a grief conveyed by the following lines read at the announcement of her death:

The world is a paradise full of delights,
Yet also a rose bush filled with thorns;

Seeing Patterns

▶ What were the strengths and weaknesses of Mughal rule?

▶ What was the Mughal policy toward religious accommodation? How did it change over time?

▶ What influences shaped culture and the arts during the Mughal era?

▶ What factors account for the Mughal decline during the eighteenth century?

▶ How did the Hindu majority adapt to Mughal rule?

He who picks the rose of happiness
Has his heart pierced by a thorn . . .

Shah Jahan himself, however, plumbed far greater depths of depression. His beard turned gray, and it was said that he wept for nearly 2 years afterward. Indeed, his eyes grew so weak from his tears that he needed to wear glasses to read his daily correspondence. Inconsolable for months on end, he finally resolved to build a magnificent tomb complex for Mumtaz Mahal over her burial site along the Jumna (or Yamuna) River near the giant fortress at Agra. At a time when monumental building projects were the order of the day for Mughal rulers, this tomb, with its balance of deceptively simple lines, harmony of proportion, and technical skill, would become the most recognized symbol of India throughout the world: the Taj Mahal.

Beyond its architectural elegance, however, the Taj Mahal also conveys a great deal of information about the circumstances of Mughal rule in India, particularly about the syncretism of Muslim rulers and Hindu subjects we first saw in Chapter 12. Like their predecessors, the Mughals discovered the difficulties of being an ethnic and religious minority ruling a huge and

The Taj Mahal. Along with the Eiffel Tower and the Great Wall of China, the Taj Mahal is perhaps the most recognizable structure in the world. Its clean lines and understated elegance mark it as the high point of an architectural synthesis of both Hindu and Muslim Indian influences and Persian classicism. It remains even today a rare symbolic triumph over the difficult history of interaction and adaptation marking India's early modern history.

Chapter Outline

Allegory: A literary, poetic, dramatic, pictorial, or architectural device in which the parts have symbolic value in depicting the meaning of the whole.

diverse population. By Shah Jahan's time, moreover, religious revival was sweeping Islamic India and past Mughal rulers were subject to criticism about their laxity in ruling according to Islamic law and the accommodations they had made with India's other religious communities. Shah Jahan therefore devoted himself anew to a study of the Quran and resolved to rule insofar as possible according to Islamic precepts. Over the coming decades, such policy changes would raise tensions between Hindus and Muslims.

For the moment, however, Shah Jahan's renewed faith found its highest expression in the design and details of the Taj. Its gleaming white stone dome and minarets are, of course, instantly identifiable as the form of a mosque. But this building is only the centerpiece of a much larger complex that is, in fact, a vision of the entrance to paradise recreated on earth. From its four large water channels, central tank, and wide main entrance down to its smallest details, like the strategic placement of appropriate quranic verses, the complex is, as one scholar put it, a vast **allegory** of Allah's judgment in paradise on the day of the resurrection.

In the end, Mughal ambition to create an empire as the earthly expression of this vision lent itself to that empire's ultimate decline. The constant drive to bring the remaining independent Indian states under Mughal control continually strained imperial resources. Dynastic succession almost always resulted in internal wars fought by rival claimants to the Mughal mantle. By the eighteenth century, prolonged rebellion and the growing power of the East India companies of the European powers would conspire to put the dynasty into a downward spiral from which it never recovered. But its most visible symbol, the Taj Mahal—literally the "Crown Palace"—remains more than ever the emblem of India's peak as a syncretic religious civilization in the modern period.

History and Political Life of the Mughals

Though we have noted previously that relations between Muslims and India's other religions were *syncretic*—that they coexisted, sometimes on difficult or hostile terms, but remained largely separate—the political and social systems created by the Mughals were in many respects a successful *synthesis*. That is, the Mughals brought with them a tradition that blended the practices of what social scientists call an "extraction state"—one that supplies itself by conquest and plunder—with several centuries of ruling more settled areas. This legacy would guide them as they struggled with a set of problems similar to those faced by rulers in other areas in creating an empire centered on one religion. Aided in their conquests by the new military technologies of cannon and small firearms, the Mughals created a flexible bureaucracy with a strict hierarchy of ranks and sophisticated separation of powers but with ultimate power concentrated in the hands of the emperors. Like those of the Chinese and Ottomans, the system was easily expanded into newly conquered areas, gave considerable scope to the ambitious, and weathered all the major political storms it encountered until its decline during the eighteenth century.

From Samarkand to Hindustan

As we have seen in earlier chapters, the rise to prominence of the Turkic-speaking members of the larger Altaic language group had taken place over the course of many centuries. From at least the time of the peoples called by the Chinese *Xiongnu*, known in western Eurasia as the Huns, these groups regularly coalesced into potent raiding and fighting forces, often putting together short-lived states such as those of the Toba in fifth- and sixth-century China, the Uighurs in the eighth and ninth centuries, and, most importantly, the Mongols in the twelfth and thirteenth centuries. But the Mongol Empire, the largest in world history, soon fell apart; and in its wake the central Asian heartland of the Turkic peoples—roughly speaking, from the Sea of Azov to the western reaches of present-day Mongolia—evolved into a patchwork of smaller states, many of whose rulers claimed descent from Genghis Khan. With the ousting of the Mongol Yuan dynasty from China in 1368, the eastern regions of this vast territory were thrown into further disarray, which set the stage for another movement toward consolidation.

The Empire of Timur   Aided by the ease of travel within the Mongol Empire, Islam had by the fourteenth century become the dominant religion among the central Asian Turkic peoples. By this time some of the Turkic groups, like the Seljuks and the Ottomans, had long since moved into the eastern Mediterranean region and Anatolia. In the interior of central Asia, however, the memory of the accomplishments of the Mongol Empire among the inhabitants of Chaghatay—the area given to Genghis Khan's son of that name—was still fresh. Their desire for a new Mongol Empire, now coupled with Islam, created opportunities for military action to unite

1336-1405	1542-1605	1618-1707	1739
Timur (Tamerlane), Founder of Timurid Line of Rulers	Akbar, Most Innovative of Mughal Rulers	Aurangzeb, Last Powerful Mughal Ruler	Invasion by Persians, Looting of Delhi, Taking of Peacock Throne

1483-1530	1627-1657	1707-1858
Babur, Founder of Timurid Line in India—the Mughals	Shah Jahan, Builder of Taj Mahal	Ebbing of Mughal Power in India, Rise of British Influence

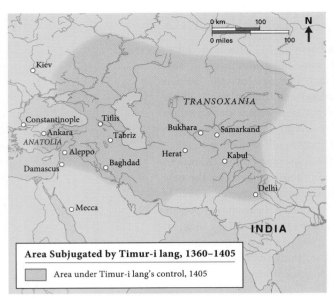

MAP 20.1 **Area Subjugated by Timur-i-lang, 1360–1405.**

Bayazid Caged at Timur's Court. Though accounts conflict regarding Bayazid's treatment as a prisoner of Timur, his imprisonment in an iron cage was routinely depicted in popular lore. In this 1680 gouache painting, the unhappy sultan languishes in his perch before his conqueror and entourage while appearing to urinate on a careless onlooker. One tradition holds that Bayazid killed himself by bashing his head against his bars, another that he took poison concealed in his ring.

the settled and nomadic tribes of Chaghatay. The result by the end of the fourteenth century was the stunning rise of Temur Gurgan (r. 1370–1405), more widely known by a variation of the Persian rendering of his name, Timur-i lang, as Timur the Lame, or Tamerlane.

What little is known about Timur's early years has been clouded by the mystique he cultivated as a ruler, which continued to grow long after his death. Though he came close to matching the conquests of Genghis Khan, his forebearers were not direct descendants of the conqueror. He therefore devised genealogies connecting him to the dominant Mongol lines to give him legitimacy as a ruler, and he even found a direct descendant of Genghis Khan to use as a figurehead for his regime. He also portrayed himself as a man whose destiny was guided by God from humble beginnings to world domination.

From 1382, when he secured the region of his homeland around the capital, the Silk Road trading center of Samarkand, until his death in 1405, Timur ranged widely through western central Asia, Afghanistan, northern India, Iran, Anatolia, and the eastern Mediterranean lands (see Map 20.1). Like his model, Genghis Khan, he proved surprisingly liberal in his treatment of certain cities that surrendered peacefully, sometimes displaying his intellectual prowess in debates with local scholars after occupation. Many more times, however, he reduced besieged cities to rubble, slaughtered the inhabitants without mercy, and erected pyramids of skulls as blunt propaganda warning others to submit. "Your sins must be great indeed for God to send me to punish you," he would tell his unfortunate opponents.

On at least one celebrated occasion, public humiliation was considered the most appropriate penalty for a conquered leader. Buoyed by his stunning victory over the cream of European knighthood at Nicopolis in 1396, the Ottoman sultan Bayazid unwisely battled Timur near Ankara in modern Turkey in 1402. After capturing Bayazid alive, Timur was said to have kept him in a small cage atop a pedestal at court for his entourage to enjoy.

At the time of his death in 1405, Timur was contemplating the invasion of Ming China. This, however, never came to pass; and Timur's empire, like that of Genghis Khan, did not long outlast him. As it fell apart, the various Chaghatay peoples largely resumed their local feuds, once again leaving the way open for a strong military force to impose order.

Babur and the Timurid Line in India   By the beginning of the sixteenth century, the region from Samarkand south into the Punjab in northern India had largely become the province of feuding Turkic tribes and clans of Afghan fighters, many of whom had migrated south to serve with the Lodi sultans of India. Into this volatile environment was born Zahir Ud-din Muhammad Babur, more commonly known as simply "Babur" (though the Turkic "Babur" means "lion," Zahir's nickname was from the Persian "Babr" for "leopard" or "tiger") in 1483. Babur's (1483–1530, r. 1526–1530) claims to legitimate rule were considerable: His father was a direct descendant of Timur, while his mother claimed the lineage of Genghis Khan. We know a considerable amount about Babur—though much of it must be seen through a lens of self-justification—through his autobiography, the *Baburnama*.

Babur's autobiography was perhaps the first by a sitting ruler. In this he set a precedent for self-chronicling that would be carried out by many of his Mughal successors. His military career began at a tender age: In the *Baburnama* he claims to have ruled over the central Asian region of Ferghana—the area of modern Uzbekistan, Tajikistan, and Kyrgystan, for centuries a fabled source of fine horses—at the age of 12.

At 14, he took Samarkand, though he was soon forced out by a competing tribe. Like Timur and Genghis Khan, his accomplishments as a youthful prodigy led him to believe that God had provided him with a special destiny to fulfill. This tended to sustain him during the next several years when, out of favor with certain powerful relatives, he roamed the border regions seeking an opportunity to return to power.

In 1504, accompanied on a campaign by his strong-willed mother, Yunus Khan, Babur moved into Afghanistan, captured Kabul, and went on to raid points farther south over the following decade. By 1519, he stepped up his raids into northern India with a view to subjugating and ruling it. As a measure of his seriousness in this endeavor, he named his son born that year "Hindal," or "Take India!" After 7 more years of campaigning, this goal was achieved in the north. In 1526, Babur's highly mobile army of approximately 12,000 met the forces of Sultan Ibrahim Lodi, whose army boasted perhaps 100,000 men and 1,000 elephants, at Panipat, near Delhi. Though the sultan enjoyed such vast numerical superiority, Babur's forces employed the new technologies of matchlock muskets and field cannon to devastating effect. In the end, the Lodi sultan was killed along with many of the Afghan tribal chiefs whose forces made up the bulk of his army, and Babur's way was now clear to consolidate his new Indian territories.

Victory at Panipat was swiftly followed by conquest of the Lodi capital of Agra and further success over the Hindu Rajputs in 1528. On the eve of his death in December 1530, Babur controlled an enormous swath of territory extending from Samarkand in the north to Gwalior in India in the south (see Map 20.2). For Babur and his successors, their ruling family would always be "The House of Timur," prompting historians to sometimes refer to the line as the "Timurids." Because of their claims to the legacy of Genghis Khan, however, they would be better known to the world as the "Mughals" (from "Mongols").

> **Babur Reflects on His Conquests (after taking and losing Samarkand, Babur paused at a mountain spring and reflected)**
>
> Many men like us have taken breath at this spring,
> And have passed away in the twinkling of an eye;
> We took the world by courage and might,
> But we could not take it with us to the grave.
>
> —*Baburnama*. Translated by Wheeler M. Thackston. New York: Oxford University Press, *1996*.

Portrait of Babur. This imagined portrait of Babur was done about sixty years after his death. He is shown receiving representatives of the Uzbeks of central Asia and the Rajputs of India in an audience dated December 18, 1528.

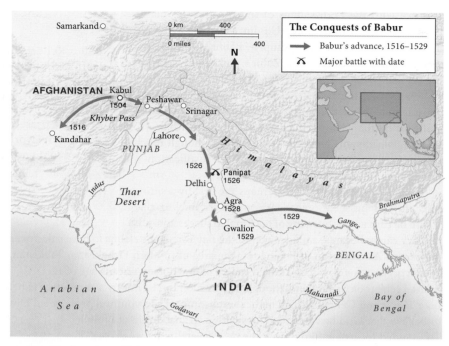

MAP 20.2 **The Conquests of Babur.**

Loss and Recovery of Empire   As had been the case so many times in the past with other newly conquered empires, the House of Timur's new rulers were now faced with the problem of consolidating, organizing, and administering Babur's vast domain. Like Timur before him, Babur had given comparatively little thought to the arts of peace. Now it fell upon his son Humayun (r. 1530–1556) to create a state. Unfortunately, Humayun's interests were geared more toward Islamic **Sufi** mysticism, poetry, astrology, and at times wine and opium than they were toward responsible leadership. Though chroniclers have generally been critical of him for losing much of Babur's legacy, he tapped a considerable reservoir of courage and determination to ultimately win it back.

A chronic problem for the long-term health of the dynasty was the **institutionalization** of traditional nomadic succession practices among the Mughal rulers. Though only one son was designated as the ruler's successor, the others were given substantial territories to govern within the empire, a situation that frequently led to conflict. In addition to such ongoing family difficulties, Humayun faced various hostile military forces still active in unconquered areas of northern India and Afghanistan. An Afghan leader named Sher Khan Sur managed to unite many of these forces and invaded the extreme eastern region of Bengal. Twice routed, Humayun fled to Persia in 1540, where, utterly humiliated, he was forced to convert to Shia Islam in a desperate bid to court the favor of the Safavid ruler, Shah Tahmasp. As distasteful as this was for him as a Sunni Muslim, he now at least had Persian backing and proceeded to move into Afghanistan and, ultimately, to Delhi. By 1555, after 15 years of exile and fighting, the dynasty was restored. For Humayun, however, the peace brought only a brief respite. In a final irony for this bookish man, he fell from the roof terrace of his palace library and died in January 1556.

Sufi: Any one of various mystical branches of Islam; Sufis have often been instrumental in spreading Islam, but they have also been viewed suspiciously by Muslim authorities.

Institutionalization: The creation of a regular system for previously improvised or ad hoc activities or things, for example, law codes to replace local customs.

Consolidation and Expansion   Because of the difficulties involved in Humayun's own accession to the throne, his death was kept secret for several weeks, while the court worked out plans for a **regency** for the emperor's son, 14-year-old Jalal Ud-Din Akbar (r. 1556–1605). The man chosen for this task, Bairam Khan, was able and attentive; and Akbar proved in many ways to be an apt pupil. His military education began quickly as Humayun's old enemy, Sher Khan Sur, sent an army to attack Delhi in 1557. In a close fight, Mughal forces finally carried the day. Over the next year and a half, they secured the eastern, southern, and western flanks of their lands, bringing them conclusively into the Mughal fold and again anchoring Islam in the former areas of its influence—"Hindustan."

Upon finally taking power in a palace coup, Akbar plunged into renewed campaigning in quest of more territory. Along the way, he seemed at once determined to master all India by any military means necessary but intolerant of cruelties practiced by his subordinates in his name. Confronting one of his commanders who had executed the surrendered garrison at Malwa, for example, an enraged Akbar threw the man from an upstairs window. On seeing he survived the fall, Akbar dragged him back upstairs and threw him out the window again, finally killing him. Despite this violent streak—or perhaps because of it—Akbar abhorred religious violence of any kind and spent much of his rule attempting to reconcile the different religious traditions of his empire. In the end his attempts, though remarkably farsighted, would prove futile and earn him the enmity of many of his fellow Muslims, who felt he had become an unbeliever.

Humayun Being Received by the Persian Shah Tahmasp. This gouache rendering of a pivotal moment in Mughal dynastic history is from a painting on a wall at Chel Soloun in Isfahan. Although all seems cordial between the two men and Humayun was treated well by the Shah, a number of accounts claim that he was threatened with execution if he did not covert to Shia Islam.

Visions of Akbar. Two very different depictions of Akbar, from 1600 (*left*) and ca. 1630 (*right*). On the left is a sketch of the emperor from life, perhaps as a preliminary drawing for a portrait painting. On the right he is depicted in all of his religious glory: surrounded by a luminous halo, surmounted by angels glorifying him and holding his crown, and graced with the holiness to make the lion lie down with the heifer.

Regency: The setting up of a guardian for an underage or incapacitated monarch to rule in his or her stead.

As a warrior Akbar was far more successful. Through the 1560s, aided by capable military advisors, Mughal armies continued to push the boundaries of the empire west, south, and east. In 1562 they subdued Malwa and in 1564, Gondwana; in 1568, the great Rajput fortress of Chitor fell. This string of victories continued into the next decade, with the long-sought conquest of Gujarat taking place in 1573. Turning eastward, Akbar set his sights on Bengal, which, along with the neighboring regions of Bihar and Orissa, fell to the Mughals by the mid-1570s. They remained, however, volatile and hostile to Mughal occupation. Both Muslim and Hindu princes in the region continued their campaigns of resistance into the following decades (see Map 20.3).

In the meantime, resistance and rebellion periodically plagued other areas of the empire. In central Asia, as early as 1564, a rebellion of Mughal Uzbek allies required a skilled combination of warfare and diplomacy to defuse. At the same time, revolts in Malwa and Gujarat required reconquest of those territories. In order to keep the old Islamic heartland of northern India—Hindustan—under firm Mughal control, the Mughals built fortresses at strategic points throughout their inner domains as well as along the frontier. Among the most important of these were Allahabad, Lahore (in modern Pakistan), Ajmer, and the largest at Agra, in its ultimate state the famous Red Fort. These remained important strong points for the remainder of the Mughal era and even during the height of British power in India.

The New City   In addition to fielding large armies—one European observer estimated that the army he accompanied on one of Akbar's campaigns surpassed

MAP 20.3 **Mughal India Under Akbar.**

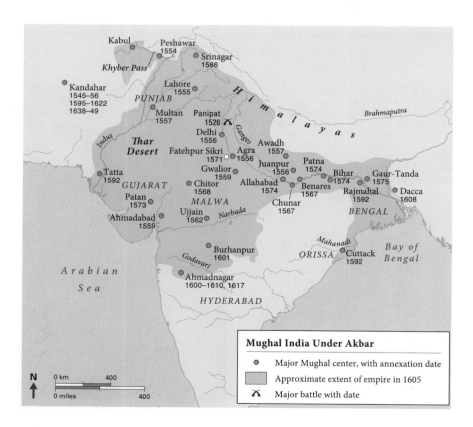

The Red Fort at Agra. While most of the early Mughal emperors lived at one point or another in the complex that came to be called "The Red Fort," it was given its final shape during the reign of Shah Jahan as part of the creation of his new city of Shahjahanabad Delhi. The fort, imperial household quarters, government buildings, and mosque were all part of an integrated complex meant to withstand attack by the most powerful cannon of the day, while demonstrating the power and stability of the state and Islam.

100,000—and huge, expensive forts, the immense revenues of the Mughal lands allowed other monumental projects to be undertaken. In an effort to show solidarity with his non-Muslim subjects, Akbar had married a Hindu Rajput princess named Manmati. Manmati had twins, who tragically died; and a distraught Akbar sought advice from a famous **Sufi** holy man named Salim Chishti. Salim told Akbar that he would ultimately have a son. When that son—named "Salim" in honor of the holy man—was born, Akbar began to build a city on the site of Salim Chishti's village of Sikri. Fatehpur Sikri, as the new city was known when it was completed in 1571, was built from the same red sandstone as the great fort at Agra, 26 miles away. As a man of many enthusiasms, Akbar's instincts for design and dynastic propaganda were everywhere evident within it. At its center was the mosque, which now housed the tomb of Salim Chishti and swiftly became an object of veneration and pilgrimage for Indian Sufis. Among the architectural innovations of Akbar's urban palace was a kind of early air-conditioning system: Reflecting pools were strategically placed to catch prevailing breezes and vent the cool moist air into the sleeping chambers of

Salim Chishti's Tomb at Fatehpur Sikri. The tomb of Sufi mystic Salim Chishti shows the sense of restrained flamboyance that marks the mature Mughal architectural style. The Chishtis had long been revered by India's Sufis and Salim's simple, elegant tomb, with its domed sarcophagus, multihued marble, and quranic inscriptions, quickly became a favorite pilgrimage site. Surrounding it is one of the red sandstone courtyards of Akbar's Fatehpur Sikri.

ازای بود یا دری زولف از ونثوان نصاری بنهم وفطرت نشان بخنایسی واست وران برم اکی کجه طراز

Akbar Presiding Over a Religious Debate. Akbar's distaste for religious orthodoxy manifested itself most dramatically in his conducting regularly scheduled debates among theologians from many of India's faiths. Here, a discussion is taking place with two Jesuit missionaries, Fathers Rudolph Aquaviva and Francis Henriquez (dressed in black) in 1578. Interestingly, the priests had unfettered access to Akbar, were free to preach, and even gave instruction to members of Akbar's family at his request.

Like their predecessors, the Mughals as Muslim rulers in India were faced with an immense array of diverse, and sometimes antagonistic, religious and cultural traditions. Amid this "religious syncretism," as we have termed it, Akbar's innovation within the world-historical pattern of religious civilizations was to create a new religion that would encompass these traditions and bind his followers directly to him as emperor and religious leader: to create an Indian "religious synthesis."

Already graced with a larger-than-life reputation for charisma and openness, he was also resistant to the strictures of Sunni Islam or any other organized religion. As a boy, he was condemned by his tutors as uneducable because he remained unable to read or write. Some scholars have suggested that he was dyslexic. Perhaps because of this, he developed an extraordinary memory for literature and poetry. Some have also suggested that his illiteracy was in emulation of the stories of the early prophets, who found illumination directly from God. In any case, his tastes within Islam centered on Sufi mysticism, which had a long tradition of tolerance and eclecticism. This openness encouraged him to study the mystical traditions of the Hindus, Parsis (Zoroastrian immigrants from Persia), and Christians. After establishing himself at Fatehpur Sikri, he sponsored regular Thursday night theological debates, mostly among Muslim scholars but gradually including Hindus, Parsis, and in 1578 Catholic missionaries. He honored many of the cultural traditions of India's various religions as well: He wore his hair long under his turban like the Hindus, coined emblems of the sun to honor the Parsis, and kept paintings of the Virgin Mary as a nod to the Christians.

During one particularly lavish and bloody hunting party in 1578, he had a sudden, intense mystical experience. Like Ashoka so long before him—of whom Akbar was completely unaware—he was now appalled by the destruction and waste in which he had participated. Out of this experience and his religious consultations, he gradually developed a personal philosophy he called *sulh-i kull*—"at peace with all." While this did not end his military campaigns, which he saw as ordained by God, it did push him to develop a new religion he called *din-i ilahi* (divine faith). Akbar shrewdly directed the movement at key courtiers, nobles, and those aspiring to gain favor from the regime. He devised elaborate rituals in which adherents swore loyalty to himself not only as emperor but as the enlightened religious master of the new sect. Borrowing heavily from Sufi mysticism, Persian court protocols, Zoroastrian sun and fire veneration, and even Muslim- and Christian-influenced **Neo-platonic** spiritualism, he sought to at once limit the power of Sunni Islamic clerics and draw followers of other religions to what he taught was a "higher" realm, one that embraced all religions and provided the elect with secret insights into their ultimate truths.

In the end, however, despite its creative merging of the needs of state and religion to overcome what had been considered deep religious and cultural divisions, Akbar's attempt must be counted as a failure. While some Hindu and Muslim courtiers embraced *din-i ilahi* enthusiastically for its perceived religious truths, many did so for opportunistic reasons and it was roundly condemned by most Sunni theologians. And while Akbar's personal magnetism was able to hold the sect together during his lifetime, his successors not only repudiated it but swung increasingly in the direction of stricter Sunni Islam.

The Virgin Mary and the Christ Child. The role of Jesus as a precursor to Muhammad is an important one in Islam, as is that of Mary as His mother. Renderings of the Madonna and Christ Child were a common theme in Mughal art, particularly during the time of Akbar. Here, Mary is portrayed in an honored position and—like some Renaissance European depictions of her—as wealthy, leisured, and sophisticated (as indicated by the open book on the pillow), as she nurses the infant Jesus.

Questions

- How does Akbar's attempt at religious syncretism demonstrate the pattern of origins–innovations–adaptations that informs the approach of this book?

- Why was Akbar's attempt to create a new divine faith doomed to failure?

Neo-Platonic/Neo-Platonism: A movement among European scholars in the fifteenth century that revived the idealist philosophy of Plato, especially the idea of an unseen reality beyond the material world.

the structure. Despite such amenities, however, the city was untenable in the long run and ultimately abandoned because there was simply not enough available water to sustain the population.

The Summer and Autumn of Empire

In a way, the saga of Fatehpur Sikri runs parallel to Mughal fortunes over the next century. The military accomplishments of the dynasty are in many ways spectacular, but they were eventually worn down by internal rebellion and succession struggles; the immense fortunes of the rulers were ultimately squeezed by the needs of defense and of ostentation to demonstrate power; and new economic and, ultimately, military competitors arrived on the scene with the coming of the Europeans.

The Revolt of the Sons   In 1585, Akbar left Fatehpur Sikri with his army for Lahore, which he would make his temporary capital for most of the rest of his life. Once again, the Afghan princes were chafing under Mughal domination and intriguing with the Uzbeks and Safavid Persians to wrest local control for themselves. For Akbar, as for his predecessors, it was vital to maintain control over these areas because of their historical connection to the Chaghatay and the need to keep control of the essential Silk Road trade. Now the key city of Kandahar, in modern Afghanistan, was in Safavid hands, disrupting Mughal control of the trade. For the next 13 years, Akbar and his generals fought a long, stubborn war to subdue the Afghans and roll back the Safavids. Though his forces were defeated on several occasions, in the end the Mughals acquired Sind and Kashmir, subdued for a time the region of Swat, and, with the defection of a Safavid commander, occupied Kandahar. By 1598, the regions in question were secure enough for Akbar to move back to Agra.

In 1600, Akbar embarked on his last great campaign against the remaining free Muslim sultanates of central India. These were reduced within a year, but Akbar was now faced with a domestic crisis. His son Salim launched a coup and occupied the fort at Agra. Salim declared himself emperor, raised his own army, and even had coins struck with his name on them. In the end, one of Akbar's wives and a group of court women were able to reconcile Akbar and Salim. Salim was confined within the palace amid intrigues that threatened to bypass him as heir in favor of his own son, Khusrau. In the end, however, he retained his position; and upon Akbar's death on October 25, 1605, Salim acceded to the throne as Jahangir (r. 1605–1627).

Renewed Expansion of the "War State"   As if to underscore the dynasty's continual problems with orderly succession, Jahangir's son, Khusrau, left the palace, quickly put a small army together, and marched on Lahore. When negotiations with his son went nowhere, Jahangir's forces swiftly defeated the insurgents. To invest his son with a special horror in what he had done, Khusrau was made to watch his comrades put to death by impalement—a punishment also used by the Ottomans and the famous Vlad "The Impaler" Dracul (Chapter 16). Sharpened posts were driven through their midsections and planted in the ground so that they would die slow, agonizing deaths suspended in the air. The doomed soldiers were made to salute Khusrau, who was forced to ride among them in a macabre military review. Undeterred, Khusrau rebelled again; and on failing this time, he was blinded and imprisoned for his efforts.

As one scholar writes, "Under Jahangir the empire continued to be a war state attuned to aggressive conquest and territorial expansion." This now meant pushing south into the Deccan and periodically resecuring Afghanistan and its adjacent regions. A move into Bengal, however, foreshadowed a major clash with a very different kind of enemy: the Shan people of southeast Asia called the "Ahoms." Southeast Asia was where the expanding cultural and political influence of China met that of Hindu and Buddhist India. In the case of the Ahoms, the territory in question was in the vicinity of Assam, along the Brahmaputra River to the north of Burma and Thailand. Though they had recently converted to Hinduism, the Ahoms had no caste system and drew upon a legacy of self-confident expansion that the Mughals had not encountered before in their opponents. With little fixed territory to defend because of their mobility, the Ahoms proved the most stubborn enemies the empire had yet encountered. Year after year, Jahangir's armies labored to secure the northeastern territories only to have the Ahoms bounce back and mount fresh offensives against them. Though both sides employed troops armed with matchlocks and cannon, neither side could obtain a clear tactical edge and their wars dragged on for decades.

More culturally and psychologically threatening to the Mughals was their relationship with the empire to their west, Safavid Persia. Both sides constantly jockeyed for position against each other and periodically went to war. There was also intense religious rivalry, with the predominantly Sunni Mughals and Shiite Safavid Persians each denouncing the other as heretical unbelievers. For the Mughals, moreover, it was particularly galling that they owed the survival of their dynasty in part to the Persian Shah Tahmasp, who had given aid to Humayun—forcing him to convert to Shiism to do so. In addition, there was a sizeable number of Persians and Shiites among the Mughal elites. Moreover, there was a pronounced feeling among these elites that Persian culture, language, and literature were superior to those of the Turks and Muslim India as a whole. In some respects, both Persians and "Persianized" Indians saw Muslim India as a kind of cultural colonial outpost, in much the same way that Chinese sophisticates viewed the high cultures of Japan, Korea, and Vietnam. This made for a highly complex set of relations between the two empires, with both vying for power in religious and cultural terms as much as in the political and military realm.

New Directions in Religious Politics   In October 1627 Jahangir died of a fever, after which his oldest son, Khurram, outmaneuvered his younger brother for the throne and reigned as Shah Jahan (r. 1627–1657). His rule coincided with perhaps the high point of Mughal cultural power and prestige, as reflected in its iconic building, the Taj Mahal. His record is less spectacular in political and military terms however. In this case, the Mughal obsession with controlling the northern trade routes coincided with the need to take back the long-contested great fort at Kandahar, Afghanistan, once again in Persian hands. Thus, Shah Jahan spent much of his reign on the ultimately fruitless drive to finally subdue the northwest. As the Mughal historian Sadiq bluntly put it, "Nothing resulted from this expedition except the shedding of blood, the killing of thirty to forty thousand people, and the expenditure of thirty-five million rupees."

As we noted earlier, the reign of Akbar and, to a considerable extent, that of Jahangir had marked a time of extraordinary religious tolerance. The attraction of both men to the Sufi school of Salim Chishti, with its mystical leanings and parallels with similar Hindu movements, created a favorable emotional community for religious pluralism. It also made Muslims for whom strict adherence to Sunni doctrine was necessary to guard against undue Persian Shia influence, apprehensive. Others, noting the ability of Hindus to incorporate the gods and beliefs of other faiths into their own, feared that the ruling Muslim minority might ultimately be assimilated to the Hindu majority.

With Shah Jahan, however, we see a definite turn toward a more legalistic tradition. Under the influence of this trend among leading Sunni theologians, Shah Jahan began to block construction and repair of non-Muslim religious buildings, instituted more direct state support for Islamic festivals, and furnished lavish subsidies for Muslim pilgrims to Mecca. The old ideal of a unified Muslim world governed by quranic law steadily gained ground at the Mughal court and would see its greatest champion in Shah Jahan's son, Aurangzeb. In the meantime, the trend lent itself to the creation of a new capital, Shajahanabad Delhi, just south of Delhi, complete with the largest mosque, college (*madrasa*), and hospital complex in India—and, of course, one of the most recognizable and beautiful buildings in the world, the Taj Mahal.

The Pinnacle of Power   The ascendancy of Aurangzeb (r. 1658–1707) was marked yet again by the now all-too-familiar pattern of princely infighting. In this case it was brought on by the extended illness of Shah Jahan in 1657. A four-way struggle broke out among the sons of Shah Jahan and his beloved Mumtaz Mahal. Although Shah Jahan soon recovered, he returned to Agra broken and depressed, while his sons fought bitterly for control. Aurangzeb outmaneuvered his older brother, surrounded the fort at Agra, and placed his father, Shah Jahan, under arrest. From this point he held the strongest position, though his brothers fought on. By 1661 they had each been defeated and assassinated, leaving Aurangzeb in control of the empire. Shah Jahan lived on in captivity until 1666.

Aurangzeb's long rule, despite its disruptive introduction, seemed to begin auspiciously enough. Renewing the Mughal bid to expand into the northeastern areas controlled by the Ahoms, his armies fought them to a standstill in the early 1660s and made them Mughal clients. When Mughal control of the area around Kabul and the Khyber Pass was threatened by a revolt of Pathan tribesmen, Aurangzeb fought several stubborn campaigns to retain control of the region and bought off other potentially troublesome groups with lavish gifts (see Map 20.4).

With these campaigns, the political power of the Mughals reached perhaps its greatest extent. But the period also marked a watershed in at least two respects: First, it saw the opening of decades-long wars with the Hindu Marathas, a federation of fiercely independent clans in west central India who speak the Mahrathi language, in which the empire's cohesion was steadily eroded. In addition, the various trading companies of the British, French, and Dutch expanded their own fortified outposts in Indian ports outside Mughal domains. As Mughal power was sapped by the revolts of the eighteenth century, the companies' armed forces became important players in regional politics.

The other watershed was Aurangzeb's bid for a more effective "Islamification" of Mughal India. As a member of the Sunni Hanafi school of Islamic law, Aurangzeb's vision for the empire was to rule by Islamic sharia law. As an Islamic state, connected to the larger commonwealth of Islamic states, he believed that Mughal rule should be primarily for the benefit of Muslims. This was an almost complete repudiation of his great-grandfather Akbar's vision of religious transcendence. While Aurangzeb stopped short of forcible conversion, he did offer multiple inducements to bring unbelievers into the faith. Elites who converted to Islam were given lavish gifts and preferential assignments, while those who did not convert found themselves isolated from the seat of power. Discriminatory tax rates were also levied on unbelievers, including a new tax on Hindu pilgrims. Zealous Muslim judges in various cities prompted protests from Hindus regarding their rulings. Moving a step beyond the actions of Shah Jahan, Aurangzeb ordered the demolition of dozens of Hindu temples that had not been constructed or repaired according to state-approved provisions. The most unpopular measure, however, was the reimposition of the hated *jiziya*, a graduated head tax on unbelievers that had been abolished by Akbar. When this was announced in 1679, massive Hindu protests broke out in several major Indian cities. In Delhi, a great crowd attempted to appeal to the emperor, who, along with his entourage, was riding an

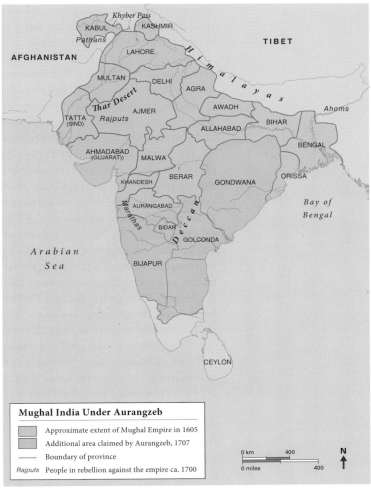

MAP 20.4 **Mughal India Under Aurangzeb.**

elephant on his way to Friday prayers. After a brief standoff, Aurangzeb ordered the elephants forward and a number of people were crushed in the chaos to clear the way. Although the intensity of the protests ultimately died down, the tax remained a sore point, even prompting some conversions simply to avoid the extra tax burden.

The new religious policies also created problems in dealing with self-governing, non-Muslim groups within the empire. The legacy of distrust of the Mughals among the Sikhs, who blended Hindu and Muslim traditions, was enhanced by Aurangzeb's heavy-handed attempts to intervene in the selection of a new Sikh guru, or religious leader, and by the destruction of some Sikh temples. When the Sikhs did not choose the candidate Aurangzeb favored, the emperor arrested the other candidate for allegedly converting Muslims and had him executed. His son and successor, Gobind Singh, would later lead a full-blown Sikh revolt. Similarly, the mostly Hindu Rajputs, who had been guaranteed representation among the nobility under previous emperors, found their position rapidly eroding under Aurangzeb's policies. Intervening in a succession struggle among the Rajputs, the emperor's attempts to put a Muslim candidate on the Rajput throne sparked yet another revolt, which, though largely suppressed by 1680, prompted continual tension among the Rajputs. Indeed, the following year, Rajput emissaries approached Aurangzeb's son to lead a palace revolt against his father. The revolt ultimately failed and, as with the Sikhs, left a legacy of mistrust toward the Mughal regime.

The Maratha Revolt   Notwithstanding these internal problems, Aurangzeb's military prowess netted him key areas that had long eluded Mughal efforts: Bijapur, Golconda, and much of the Maratha lands of the Deccan region of south central India. Yet, even here, the seeds were being cast for the rebellion that would eat away at the vitals of the empire for generations (see Map 20.4).

The Hindu Marathas, like the inhabitants of many regions bordering Mughal India, had evolved working relationships with the old Muslim sultanates that, over time, were annexed by the Timurids. For the earlier Mughal rulers, it was often enough for these small states to remit tribute and, on occasion, supply troops in order to retain their autonomy. For Aurangzeb, however, commitment to a more robust and legalistic Islam also meant political expansion of the Mughal state. This was justified on religious grounds in that the sultanates to the south had drifted from correct observance of quranic law, the lands of unbelievers were permissible to confiscate, and unbelievers would more likely convert if guided by proper Muslim rulers. Hence, Aurangzeb spent much of the last two decades of his life campaigning to bring central India under his sway.

Despite the tenacity of Maratha resistance, Aurangzeb's "carrot and stick" strategy—supporting pro-Mughal factions among the Maratha leaders, lavishing money and gifts on Maratha converts and deserters, and fielding several large armies to invest Maratha fortifications—bore fruit. In the early 1690s 11 Maratha strongholds fell to his forces. Yet prolonged fighting, with the emperor staying in the field year after year, also led to problems at court and in the interior of the empire.

The demands of constant campaigning reduced the flow of money and goods from south to north and east to west across central India. Moreover, by the early eighteenth century, the Maratha frontier, far from being steadily worn down, was actually expanding into Mughal areas. The Marathas had set up their own administrative system with its own forts and tax base and encouraged raids on Mughal caravans and pack trains. By Aurangzeb's death in 1707, the Marathas were noticeably expanding their sway at Mughal expense. With the weakening of the Mughal interior, the old enemy, Persia, took the opportunity to settle scores. The Persians sent an expeditionary force that sacked Delhi in 1739 and carried off Shah Jahan's fabled Peacock Throne—from this time forward associated with the monarchs of Persia and Iran, rather than with India and the Mughals.

The East India Companies   Within a dozen years of Vasco da Gama's first voyage to India in 1498, armed Portuguese merchant ships seized the port of Goa in 1510. Portugal's pioneering efforts in capturing the spice trade and setting up fortified bases from which to conduct business were swiftly imitated by other European maritime countries. For the English, Dutch, and French, these enterprises were conducted by royally chartered companies, which were given a monopoly over their country's trade within a certain region. Because these companies were operating thousands of miles from home in areas that were often politically chaotic, they acted much like independent states. They maintained fortified warehouses, their armed merchant ships functioned as naval forces, and they assembled their own mercenary armies.

Throughout the seventeenth century English, French, and Dutch enterprises largely supplanted Portuguese influence in the region, while the location of their trading ports outside Mughal lands allowed them considerable freedom. European naval prowess had by this time also surpassed that of any of the Indian states, and European ships controlled the sea-lanes to Indian ports. Thus, the companies grew richer and more powerful and increasingly found themselves involved in local politics. For the English, the acquisition of Bombay (Mumbai) from Portugal in the 1660s gave the company a superb harbor. In 1690, after unwisely becoming involved in a struggle with Aurangzeb, British traders were pushed down the Hugli (also Hoogli or Hooghly) River in Bengal and began building a new trading station called "Calcutta" (not to be confused with the port of Calicut, on the west coast of India). For their competitors, the French and Dutch, the ongoing Mughal wars in the Deccan were a windfall. The French station at Pondicherry, for example, supplied both Aurangzeb and the Marathas with money, goods, and even guns and gunners, while providing a haven for refugees from the war-torn interior. Aurangzeb's relations with these autonomous European enclaves remained strained however. European piracy, practiced against each other as well as on unarmed Indian merchant ships, proved a major irritant. Pirates also preyed upon vessels of pilgrims bound for Mecca, increasing religious tensions. While the companies usually paid damages to the Mughals when pressed, they continually upgraded their defenses, making it increasingly difficult for Mughal armies to successfully coerce them. By 1750, the power of the Dutch in India had been eclipsed by that of the British and French East India Companies. With the victory of the British East India Company commander, Robert Clive, at Plassey over the French forces in 1757 came British domination of Bengal and, by century's end, much of northern India.

The Dutch Trading Post at Hugli, 1665. The mid-seventeenth century was the high point of Dutch influence and trade in Asia, and the Dutch East India Company was one of the most powerful entities in the region. This fortified outpost on the Hugli River was typical of European trading establishments in the region during the late sixteenth and most of the seventeenth centuries. By the end of the century, however, the Dutch would be supplanted on the Hugli by their archrivals, the English, who would establish their own base that would swiftly grow into the great trading center of Calcutta.

Administration, Society, and Economics

One of the large patterns characteristic of the period under consideration in this section is a pronounced trend toward centralization. In a way, this phenomenon is not surprising since the creation of states and empires requires power at the center to hold the state together, assure consistent governance, provide for revenues, and maintain defense. What is noteworthy, however, is that in widely separate regions throughout Eurasia a variety of states concurrently reached a point where their governments, with armies now aided by firearms, made concerted efforts to focus more power than ever at the center. As part of this trend toward the development of fiscal–military states, some form of enforcement of approved religion or belief system legitimating the rulers was also present. As we saw in the Ottoman and Habsburg

Empires in Chapter 16 and in seventeenth-century France and other European countries in Chapter 17, the trend was toward what came to be called "absolutism," with vast powers concentrated in the person of the monarch. In China and Japan, as we will see in Chapter 21, it meant additional powers concentrated in the hands of the emperor (China) and shogun (Japan). For Mughal India, the system that attempted to coordinate and balance so many disparate and often hostile elements of society is sometimes called "autocratic centralism." While never as effective as the Chinese bureaucratic system or as tightly regulated as absolutist France, its policies and demands stretched into the lives of its inhabitants in often unexpected ways.

Mansabdars and Bureaucracy

As we mentioned earlier in this chapter, Babur and his successors found themselves forced to govern a largely settled, farming and city-dwelling society, whose traditions, habits, and (for the majority) religious affiliations were different from their own. While not unfamiliar with settled societies, the nomadic Timurids initially felt more comfortable in adapting their own institutions to their new situation and then grafting them onto the existing political and social structures. The result was a series of hybrid institutions that, given the tensions within Indian society, worked remarkably well when the empire was guided by relatively tolerant rulers but became increasingly problematic under more dogmatic ones.

Political Structure   The main early challenge faced by the Timurids was how to create a uniform administrative structure that did not rely on the unusual gifts of a particular ruler to perpetuate. It was the problem of moving from what social scientists call "charismatic leadership" (in which loyalty is invested in a leader because of his personal qualities) to "rational-legal" leadership (in which the institution itself commands primary respect and loyalty). Thus, Akbar created four principal ministries: one for army and military matters; one for taxation and revenue; one for legal and religious affairs; and one for the royal household. All of these ministries had wide latitude in their powers. The household ministry, for example, also controlled the building and maintenance of the empire's infrastructure. These primary ministries were directly responsible to the court, and the emperor reserved the right to take on responsibilities that were not directly spelled out in their respective mandates. In a departure from the practice in other Islamic states, the Mughal emperor also took direct control of the foreign affairs and diplomacy of his lands.

Below the broad central powers of these ministries, things functioned much the same on the provincial and local levels. The provincial governors held political and military power and were responsible directly to the emperor. In order to prevent their having too much power, however, the fiscal responsibility for both the civil and military affairs of the provinces were in the hands of officers who reported to the finance minister. Thus, arbitrary or rebellious behavior could, in theory at least, be checked by the separation of financial control.

Administrative Personnel   One key problem faced by the Mughals was similar to that confronting the French king Louis XIV and the Tokugawa shoguns in Japan during the following century—that is, how to impose a centralized administrative system on a state whose nobles were used to wielding power for themselves, or, in effect, acting as "emperors" in their own regions. In all three cases, the

Dealing with the Nobles

"In order to prevent the great nobles becoming insolent through the unchallenged enjoyment of power, the King [*sic*] summons them to court . . . and gives them many imperious commands, as though they were his slaves—commands, moreover, obedience to which ill suits their exalted rank and dignity."

—From Antonio Monserrate *Commentary*, quoted in Richards, *The Mughal Empire*, p. 65

solutions were remarkably similar. For the Mughals, India's vast diversity of peoples and patchwork of small states offered a large pool of potential noble recruits, and the competition among the ambitious for imperial favor was intense. The Timurid rulers were careful to avoid overt favoritism toward particular ethnic, or even religious, groups; and though most of their recruited nobility were Sunni Muslims, Hindus and even Shiite Muslims were also represented.

The primary criteria—as one would expect in a fiscal–military state—were military and administrative skills. An elaborate, graded system of official ranks was created in which the recipients, called *mansabdars*, were awarded grants of land and the revenues those working the land generated. In turn the mansabdars were responsible for remitting the correct taxes and, above a certain rank, for furnishing men and materiel for the army. Standards for horses, weapons, and physical qualities for soldiers, to which recruiters were expected to adhere, were established by the central government. The positions in the provincial governments and state ministries were filled by candidates from this new mansabdar elite chosen by the court. Thus, although the nobles retained considerable power in their own regions, they owed their positions to the court and had no hope of political advancement if they did not get court preferment.

The Mughals and Early Modern Economics

Mughal India had a vigorous trade and manufacturing economy, though, as with all agrarian-based societies, land issues and agriculture occupied the greatest part of the population. Unlike the societies of China, Japan, Korea, and Vietnam, which were influenced to a greater or lesser degree by Neo-Confucian ideas that regarded commerce as vaguely disreputable, Hindu, Muslim, Buddhist, and Jain traditions reserved an honored place for commerce and those who conducted it. Thus, Mughal economic interests routinely revolved around keeping the flow of goods moving around the empire, maintaining a vigorous import and export trade, and, as we have seen, safeguarding access to the Silk Road routes.

Agriculture and Rural Life   The basic administrative unit of rural India at the time of the Mughals was the *pargana*, a unit comprising an area usually containing a town and from a dozen to about 100 villages. It was in the pargana that the lowest levels of officialdom had met the network of clan and caste leaders of the villages under both the Hindu rajas and the Muslim sultans before the Timurids, and this pattern continued over the coming centuries. But because the earliest years of the Mughals were marked by conquest and plunder, and later by an administrative apparatus that contented itself with taxation and defense at the local level, life in the villages tended to go on much as it had before the conquest. Thus, the chief duties of the *zamindars*, as the local chiefs and headmen were called, was to channel the expansive and competitive energies among local clans, castes, and ethnic and religious groups into activities the Mughals considered productive. In border areas especially, this frequently involved clearing forests for farmland, harvesting tropical woods and products for market, and often driving off bands of foragers from the forests and hills.

Imperial Reception of Dignitaries and Diplomats. Mughal rulers held regular *durbars*—public audiences. Here, in an illustration from Akbar's biography *Akbarnama*, he receives diplomats from Badakshan at a durbar in 1561.

A Merchants' Dispute. In this whimsical gouache miniature, dated 1640, confusion ensues as a young boy attempts to undersell a group of water merchants who then come after him and attempt to drive him off. While artists generally concentrated on depicting the elites who sustained them, genre paintings of social activities, markets, and holy sites were also popular. This piece was part of a manuscript once belonging to a daughter of Emperor Aurangzeb.

Agricultural expansion went hand in hand with systematic integration of the rural and town and city economies. One enormous obstacle facing the Mughals, as it had faced previous regimes, was efficiency and equity in rural taxation. Grain and other agricultural commodities provided the bulk of Indian tax revenues, but vast differences in regional soil conditions, climate, and productivity made uniform tax rates extremely difficult to enforce. During Akbar's reign, therefore, massive surveys of local conditions were conducted to monitor harvests and grain prices over 10-year periods. These were then compiled into data tables used by local officials to calculate expected harvests and tax obligations. Imperial and local officials would sign agreements as to grain amounts to meet tax obligations over a set period. These obligations, like the Chinese "single-whip" system (see Chapter 21), would then be paid in silver or copper coin in four installments. Peasants needing loans to carry them to harvest season could obtain them from government-approved moneylenders, and the remission of vast amounts of grain and agricultural commodities at regular intervals to towns and cities contributed to their economic integration with the countryside. The system worked well through the sixteenth and seventeenth centuries, with tax rates on grain usually about one-third of the annual harvest and perhaps one-quarter of that of other agricultural commodities. Transport of bulk cargoes was eased by the excellent road system maintained by the Mughals.

The net effect of rural economic expansion was that Mughal India's growth kept pace, roughly speaking, with that of China from the mid-sixteenth century to the beginning of the nineteenth. Expansion in Bengal and northeast India of wet rice cultivation and the introduction of American crops such as maize and potatoes in dryer areas allowed for a population increase from about 150 million in 1600 to 200 million in 1800. Moreover, acreage under cultivation increased by perhaps as much as one-third over this same period. Preferential tax rates on tobacco, indigo, sugarcane, cotton, pepper, ginger, and opium ensured that supplies of these coveted trade items would be secure. India began a burgeoning silk industry during this time as well. Thus, revenues more than doubled between Akbar's and Aurangzeb's reigns, to about 333.5 million rupees a year, while the increase in population meant that the per capita tax burden actually went down.

International Trade   India had been the center of Indian Ocean trade for nearly two millennia before the rise of the Mughals, but the advent of the world trading systems being created by the Atlantic maritime states added a vastly expanded dimension to this commerce. The intense and growing competition among the English, Dutch, and French East India Companies meant that Indian commodities were now being shipped globally, while imports of American silver and food and cash crops were growing by the year. By the mid-seventeenth century, the Dutch and British dominated maritime trade in Indian spices. Between 1621 and 1670, for example, Indian exports of pepper to Europe doubled to 13.5 million pounds. An often added bonus was Indian saltpeter, a vital component of gunpowder, used as ships' ballast (see Map 20.5).

Perhaps of even more long-term importance, however, was the growth of India's textile trade. Here, French access to Bengali silk contributed immensely to French leadership in European silk products, while Indian indigo supplied European needs for this dye until slave production of it in the Americas lowered its cost still further. Most momentous of all, though, was the rapid rise of Indian cotton exports. Lighter and more comfortable than wool or linen, Indian cotton *calicoes* (named for Indian port of Calicut) proved immensely popular for underwear and summer clothing. Indeed, the familiar term "pajamas" comes from the Hindi word *pyjama*, the light-weight summer garments worn in India and popularized as sleepwear in Europe. The immense popularity of cotton can be seen by the imports of the British East India Company, which, in the 20 years from 1664 to 1684, saw its imports of Indian cotton cloth rise sevenfold to 27 million square meters. The low price and huge popularity of Indian textiles would play a central role in both the British effort to develop machine spun and woven cotton goods to compete with the Indian product and the colossal expansion of slavery in the American South to grow cotton during the first part of the nineteenth century.

Society, Family, and Gender

Though the majority of the material in this chapter describes the activities of the Muslim Timurids in Indian history and society, it must be kept in mind that the vast majority of people in all areas of India were Hindus rather than Muslims. Thus, although the laws and customs of the areas controlled by the Mughals had a considerable effect on all members of Indian society, most of the everyday living of Indians at the pargana, village, clan, and family levels went on much as it had before the arrival of the Mughals—or, for that matter, before the arrival of Islam.

Caste, Clan, and Village   As we saw in earlier chapters, the ties of family, clan, and caste were the most important for the majority of Indians (most of whom were Hindu), particularly in rural society, which comprised perhaps 90 percent of the subcontinent's population. Even after the reimposition of the tax on unbelievers by Aurangzeb and the restrictions on the building and rehabilitating of Hindu temples, Hindu life at the local level went on much as it had before. Indeed, many new converts to Islam kept up their caste and clan affiliations much as before, especially in areas in which caste affiliation was determined by language, village designation, or profession.

Attempts by the Mughals to create a uniform system of taxation and military obligation ran up against a familiar problem of minority rulers: How does one persuade the people to go along with new systems that have not grown organically out of their own institutions? In the case of local rural life in India, perhaps the most important obstacle was the clan council, whose network of village headmen connected by real or adopted blood relations conducted most of the business of the pargana. One vital source of early modern Indian social history is the archives of clan councils, and the records of their deliberations and voting provide researchers with a vital counterpoint to the carrying out of Mughal official policy. Much like their counterparts in rural Chinese society, Indian clan councils organized militias for defense, collected donations for disaster relief, and arbitrated disputes. Unlike rural Chinese society, however, there was nearly always a degree of tension between these bodies and the Mughal hierarchy of zamindars and mansabdars. While Chinese clan leaders and village headmen frequently had disagreements with individual Confucian magistrates and both Ming and Qing dynasties attempted to bypass the power of local elites with alternative schemes of village organization, there was still fundamental agreement with the system as a whole.

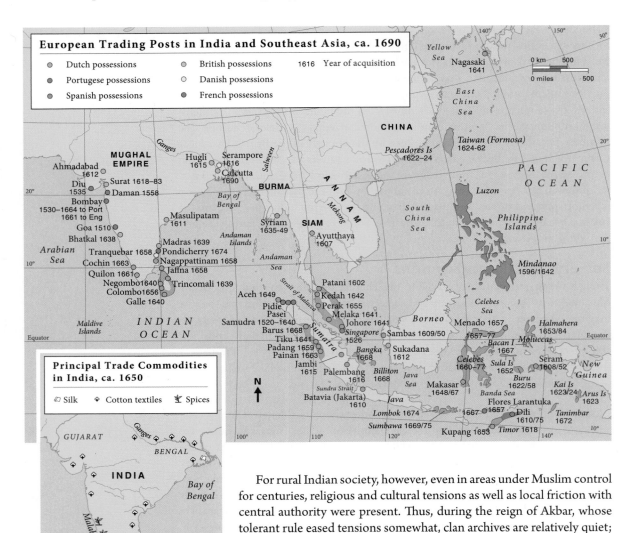

European Trading Posts in India and Southeast Asia, ca. 1690

- ◉ Dutch possessions
- ◉ Portugese possessions
- ◉ Spanish possessions
- ◉ British possessions
- ○ Danish possessions
- ◉ French possessions

1616 Year of acquisition

Principal Trade Commodities in India, ca. 1650

🧵 Silk   ✦ Cotton textiles   ⚜ Spices

MAP 20.5 **European Trading Ports in India and Southeast Asia, ca. 1690.**

For rural Indian society, however, even in areas under Muslim control for centuries, religious and cultural tensions as well as local friction with central authority were present. Thus, during the reign of Akbar, whose tolerant rule eased tensions somewhat, clan archives are relatively quiet; to the contrary, during Aurangzeb's long rule and during periods of internal conflict, these same archives bristle with militia drives and petitions for redress of assorted grievances. In areas only marginally under Mughal control, clan councils offered resources for potential rebels.

Family and Gender For the Indian elites outside the areas of Mughal control, family life of the higher castes went on largely as it had from the time of the Guptas. The "twice-born" Hindus of the brahman varna went through lengthy training and apprenticeship in the household of a trusted guru in preparation for their roles as religious and societal leaders through their various stages of life. Women, who in the pursuit of dharma it was said are "worthy of worship," nevertheless spent most of their lives in seclusion. Whether among the highest castes or the lowest, their primary duties still included the running of the household and childrearing. Among the elites, where education in literature, poetry, and basic mathematics was also available to certain women, maintaining the household accounts, supervising servants, as well as education in the arts of living and loving as depicted in the *Kama*

Sutra were also considered part of a wife's proper knowledge. In all cases, however, as in China, the "inner" world of the household and the "outer" world of business, politics, warfare, and so on were clearly defined by gender. In rural areas, the lives and work of peasant families, though generally guided by traditional gender roles, were more flexible in that large collective tasks such as planting and harvesting required the participation of both men and women.

The conquests of the Mughals brought with them a somewhat different temperament among their elites. The nomadic Turkic peoples of the Asian steppes, with their reliance on mobility and herding and organization around small groups of fiercely independent families and clans, had not developed the elaborate class, caste, and gender hierarchies of their settled neighbors. Women could, and often did, exercise a far greater degree of power and influence than even among the Hindu, Sikh, or Muslim elites in India.

Jahangir's Influential Wife, the Former Persian Princess Nur Jahan, in Her Silk Gauze Inner Court Dress.

Even after the conversion of these nomadic peoples to Islam, this tradition of female independence continued among the Timurids. As we saw earlier, for example, Babur's mother played a vital role in his rise to power, and emperors' wives, like Mumtaz Mahal, exercised a considerable degree of control in the imperial household. Moreover, since marriages played a vital role in cementing diplomatic and internal relations, women exercised a good deal of influence in terms of the extension of imperial power. Nur Jahan (d. 1645), the striking Persian princess married to Jahangir, played a leading role in court politics and in mediation during the succession wars at the end of Jahangir's reign. Indeed, Jahangir turned the running of the empire over to her on several occasions, stating that he felt quite secure that it was in her capable hands.

As the Mughals assimilated local Muslim elites, the court quickly set up the harem as an institution of seclusion and protection for court women. Yet, within the harem, women enjoyed considerable freedom, constructed their own hierarchies among the imperial wives and their attendants, and celebrated their own holidays and ceremonies surrounding marriages, births, and deaths largely insulated from the influence of men. It was in many respects a kind of alternative women's society, in which a distinct system of values was instilled in daughters and, crucially, newcomers by marriage. For women newly married into the household, navigating the harem's social relationships was of supreme importance since the inner harmony of the court—and sometimes lives—depended on it.

Science, Religion, and the Arts

While science and technology in Mughal India did not enjoy the same pace of advancement that was being set during the scientific revolution in western Europe, there were nonetheless several noteworthy developments in weaponry, mathematics, and astronomy. In terms of religion, as we have seen, the great theological differences between Hindus and Muslims persisted—and with the reign of Aurangzeb increased. Again, however, the tendency of Hinduism to assimilate other traditions and the relative compatibility of Islamic Sufi practices with other mystical traditions did sometimes decrease tensions. This, of course, was most dramatically seen with Akbar's efforts at bridging the religious gaps of his empire.

Finally, one could say that where attempts at reconciling religions failed, language, literature, art, and architecture often succeeded and left a brilliant legacy of cultural synthesis.

Science and Technology

As they had done for centuries already, Muslim scholars in India drew upon the rich scientific history of the subcontinent and merged it with their efforts at preservation, commentary on, and transmittal of the Greco-Roman and Persian achievements of the ancients. Among the most important developments in this regard, as we have seen in other chapters, was the spreading of the Indian decimal number system and the use of zero as a placeholder in mathematical computations. This had already had a profound effect on the development of European science, which forever after referred to that system as "Arabic numerals." Among the developments that directly fostered the rise of Muslim empires, none was more important than the rapid development of gunpowder weapons.

New Directions in Firearms in the Gunpowder Empires
The spread of firearms from China and the shift in emphasis among weapons developers from rockets to tubular weapons firing projectiles is an extraordinarily complex subject and one littered with claims and counterclaims for the ultimate sources of particular innovations. We can say, however, that by the beginning of the sixteenth century, the armies of the major European kingdoms, Ming China, Ottoman Turkey, and Persia had all become accustomed to employing cannons and explosive charges for besieging fortresses, were developing more convenient and effective small arms for their infantries, and were beginning to employ lighter, more portable cannons as field guns for pitched battles. The use of these weapons became so pervasive and the changes that accompanied them so important that scholars often refer to the states of the Mughals, Persians, and Ottomans as the **gunpowder empires**.

Gunpowder empires: Muslim-ruled empires of the Ottomans, Safavids, and Mughals that used cannons and small arms in their military campaigns, 1450–1750.

Given the desire on the part of all armies to expand their firepower, it is not surprising that a gifted engineer, astronomer, and philosopher named Fathullah Shirazi (ca. 1580) came up with a concept for a multibarreled gun—similar in design to that of Leonardo da Vinci—for Akbar's armies. In this case, 12–16 light cannons were mounted side by side on a gun carriage and fired by the operator in quick succession. Two other ingenious military devices sprang from Fathullah's mind as well: a large revolving "tree" apparatus powered by an ox that was designed to clean powder residue from 16 gun barrels at a time, and field and siege cannons whose barrels could be dismantled section by section for ease of transport. For his part, Akbar designed prefabricated quarters and movable buildings to support his continual campaigning.

Mathematics and Astronomy
India's long history of mathematical innovation merged with Muslim work on astronomical observation to make impressive advances in celestial calculation. A century before Akbar, Indian mathematicians had pushed their calculations of the value of pi to nine decimal places and expanded their facility with the geometric relationships surrounding sine, cosine, and tangent to the point where some of the fundamental concepts of infinite series and calculus had been worked out.

By the sixteenth century, astronomical observation was a popular activity among elites—all the Mughal emperors had observatories, and the dynamic empress Nur

Jahan had planned one for herself—and one that entailed practical utility as well. Like other agrarian peoples reliant on an accurate calendar for the yearly agricultural and ceremonial cycle, Mughal rulers had a vital interest in knowing when unusual celestial phenomena such as comets, eclipses, and meteor showers were due and in having explanations for them ready to hand. Using extremely fine calculations and careful observation, the astronomers of the Kerala school, active from the fourteenth to the sixteenth centuries, had calculated elliptical orbits for the visible planets a century in advance of Johannes Kepler and suggested systems of planetary orbits similar to those of both Tycho Brahe and Copernicus (Chapter 17).

Perhaps the most spectacular scientific and technical development of the Mughal era was the construction of 21 seamless celestial globes during the sixteenth and seventeenth centuries. Ali Kashmirir ibn Luqman of Lahore is believed to have devised a variation of the ancient "lost-wax" casting technique for these unique devices in 1589. In addition to their utility as global star maps, it was believed into the twentieth century that casting seamless globes was a technological impossibility. The rediscovery of these instruments in the 1980s added an entirely new dimension to our understanding of the technological capabilities of the Mughal period.

Religion: In Search of Balance

As scholars have often noted, Indian Islam has gone through relatively open, inclusive, and Sufi-oriented cycles—most notably in this chapter during the reigns of Babur, Humayun, and Akbar—and phases in which a more rigorous attention to orthodox Sunni practices and the desire to connect with Muslim communities beyond India prevail, such as during the reigns of Jahangir, Shah Jahan, and especially Aurangzeb. These periods, as we have already seen, had a profound effect on the relations of minority Muslim rulers with non-Muslim subjects. But they also played an important role in mandating which forms of Islam would be most influential in Mughal India and the relations of the Mughals with the Muslims of other regions.

The Position of Non-Muslims in Mughal India   As we have seen in earlier chapters, despite profound theological differences between the monotheism of Islam and the profuse polytheism of popular Hindu religious traditions, there was a degree of attraction between the adherents of one and the other. As was the case with mystical and devotional sects of both, they saw a commonality in their ways of encountering the profound mysteries of faith. Thus, as we saw with Akbar, his grounding in Islamic Sufi mysticism made him interested in and receptive to Hindu mystical traditions. For their part, in addition to the mystical elements of Islam—in any case accessible only to a relative few—far more Hindus of the lower castes were attracted to the equality before God of all Islamic believers. Thus, like Buddhism before it, Islam promised emancipation from the restrictions of the caste system and a shared brotherhood of believers without regard for ethnicity, race, job, or social position.

More generally, however, the religious divisions remained difficult to reconcile. From the time of the first territories occupied by Muslim armies in the seventh century, nonbelievers had been granted the legal status of "protected peoples" (Chapter 10). That is, they were allowed to worship as they pleased and govern according to their own religious laws. There were also inducements and penalties aimed at conversion to Islam. Unbelievers were subject to the jiziya and pilgrimage taxes, and they suffered job discrimination in official circles, all of which did not apply once

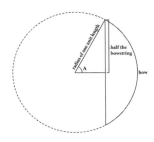

Origins of the Trigonometric Sine of an Angle as Described by Indian Mathematicians. Indian mathematicians did pioneering work in all of the fields of mathematics, particularly arithmetic and geometry. Hindu geometers knew of the trigonometric sine of an angle from at least the eighth century CE, if not earlier. In the early ninth century, the great Arabic mathematician al-Khwarizmi described the sine of an angle in his treatise on "Hindu" numbers, which was subsequently translated into Latin in the twelfth century. Through a series of mistranslations from one language to another, the original Sanskrit word for sine, *jya-ardha* ("half the bowstring") ended up being rendered as "sine" in Latin and other western European languages.

they converted. For their part, Hindus considered Muslims to be ritually "unclean" (*mleccha*), and upper-caste members underwent elaborate purification rites after coming into contact with them.

Yet the presence of a vastly larger Hindu population also meant that considerable accommodations had to be made by the rulers in order to run the empire effectively and even more to maintain order at the local level. Akbar, as we noted earlier, banned the discriminatory taxes on unbelievers. In addition, the financial skills of Hindus and Jains were increasingly sought by the court, and their status rose further when Akbar made a Hindu his finance minister and employed Hindu court astrologers. Perhaps of even more symbolic and political importance was the habit of Mughal rulers of occasionally marrying Hindu women. In order to cement good relations with the Rajputs, for example, Akbar married several Rajput princesses, including Manmati, who became the mother of the next emperor, Jahangir.

Seeing himself as emperor of all the people, Akbar also took part in Hindu festivals. The festival of *holi*, for example, in which the revelers squirt each other with red-colored water, was popular at the Mughal court; and a number of paintings depict men and women merrily engaged in it. At the same time, like his fellow monarchs, he was taken by the impulse to reform practices among both Muslims and unbelievers that he found disquieting. Like the British in the eighteenth and nineteenth centuries, he sought to ban the compulsory practice of *sati* (suttee), in which newly widowed women committed suicide by throwing themselves on the deceased's funeral pyre.

The position of Christians was similar. They, along with Jews, were considered "people of the Book" and, therefore, "protected" but still subject to the same taxes and impediments before the reign of Akbar. While the position of Christian missionaries in Mughal lands was often precarious, the reverence with which Muslims regarded the biblical prophets and Jesus also helped to smooth diplomatic relations at court. Akbar invited Jesuits to his debates, and paintings of Christian religious figures, especially the Virgin Mary, can be found in Mughal depictions of court life.

Yet this period of relative openness toward religion peaked with Akbar, and the pendulum soon shifted and picked up speed. Mughal receptiveness toward Islamic mysticism and other religions, as most dramatically displayed by Akbar's new din-i-ilahi religion, offended more orthodox Sunni Muslims. Their influence was felt at court during the reign of Jahangir and especially during that of Shah Jahan, whose love and piety came together in the form of the Taj Mahal. It reached its zenith during Aurangzeb's reign. As Mughal lands stretched to their farthest point, the austere Aurangzeb reimposed the taxes on unbelievers and purged many Hindus from his court.

One group greatly affected by all of these changes was neither Hindu nor Muslim. The Sikhs had grown during the sixteenth century into a movement seeking to transcend the religious differences between Hindus and Muslims. Though awarded the city of Amritsar, the Golden Temple of which became their religious center, Mughal repression of the Sikhs provoked a prolonged rebellion, which turned them into a fierce fighting faith. Sikh men are distinctive even today for their uncut hair piled within tall turbans, large beards, the carrying of daggers, and the adoption by many of the surname "Singh" (meaning "lion"). They established control of most of the Punjab region during the eighteenth-century decline of the Mughals. During the days of British control, the reputation of the Sikhs as fierce fighters prompted the British to employ them as colonial troops and policemen throughout their empire.

Islamic Developments   While the vast majority of India's Muslims remained adherents of the Sunni branch and Hanafi school of interpretation of Islamic law, there were also several noteworthy developments in other areas. First, as we have noted several times already, there was an influential Shiite presence in India. For centuries, Shiites had migrated into Hindu areas of southern India, where, despite being a notable minority, they generally escaped discrimination from Sunnis characteristic of the north. In addition, Mughal relations with Safavid Persia, where Shia Islam was the official state religion, meant a certain influence on the Mughal court was unavoidable. Hence, Akbar studied mystical elements of Shiism, while Jahangir married the Safavid princess Nur Jahan, probably the most powerful woman of the Mughal period.

One branch of Shiism that attained considerable influence despite its small numbers was the Ismailis. Like a number of Muslim mystical brotherhoods, the Ismailis, originally refugees from the fall of the Fatimid caliphate, blended Shiite mysticism with practices borrowed from the devotional (*bakti*) cults of Hinduism. During Aurangzeb's reign they were suppressed as part of his general drive to make Indian Islam more in accordance with Islamic law. They survived and later prospered however, and in the twentieth century, their leader, the Aga Khan, was one of the world's wealthiest men.

Of the many Sufi branches of both Sunni and Shia Islam, the one most favored during much of the Mughal era was that of Chishtis. The voluntary poverty, mystical personae, and deep piety of the Chishtis had, as we have seen, a profound effect on Humayun and Akbar and influenced the latter's ideas of religious tolerance. Some Sufi groups sought a mystical encounter with the divine through strict contemplation of the Quran and demanded absolute obedience to religious law. Other groups that developed outside the mainstream of Sunni Islam included the Maddawis, who preached the arrival of the Mahdi ("the rightly guided one"), a savior who would lead an Islamic renewal and reunite all the Islamic lands. The Maddawis preached poverty and devotion to God and the Mahdi and were severely persecuted. One final movement worth mentioning is that of the Nuqtawis. This was a heretical sect that mixed Sufi mysticism with the belief that Muhammad was not the final prophet and preached the unity of all creation. One practitioner found his way to Akbar's court in 1576 and may have influenced the emperor's insistence on "peace with all."

Literature and Art

The Mughal period was one of India's most prolific in terms of its profusion of literary genres. Moreover, literature, art, and architecture were the areas in which India's rich multicultural environment produced its most arrestingly synthetic works. In translation projects, classical Persian works, poetry in nearly all of India's languages, even treatises on law and theology, Indian writers borrowed freely and frequently from each other. In painting, realistic portraits of personages and dramatic contemporary and historical scenes were recorded; and of course, the great buildings of the era, many of which are currently on the United Nations Educational, Scientific,

The Golden Temple at Amritsar. Sikhism, founded in part as an attempt to reconcile differences between Hindus and Muslims, ended up being persecuted by both by the seventeenth century, and ultimately was transformed into a faith that aggressively defended itself. In the accompanying illustration of the most sacred Sikh shrine, the Golden Temple at Amritsar, one can see the faithful in typical postures of worship, their hair uncut and wound up under their turbans, and their beards mandated to grow untrimmed.

Life's Tragedy

Not only the laughing buds
Are always fleeing from me;
No, even the desert thorns
Draw their pricks away from me . . .
Life's tragedy lasts but two days.
I'll tell you what these two are for:
One day, to attach the heart to this
and that;
One day, to detach it again.

—Abu Talib Kalim, Diwan in Annemarie
Schimmel, *The Empire of the Great Mughals*.
(London: Reaktion Books, 2004), p. 248

and Cultural Organization (UNESCO) register of world landmarks, remain for many the "authentic" symbols of India.

New Literary Directions   As they had been for centuries in Islamic India, Arabic and Persian remained the principal literary languages. The use of both, however, was considerably enlivened by the introduction of the latest wave of Turkic terms by the Chaghatay–Turkic Mughals. Chaghatay itself remained in use among the elites until the nineteenth century, while many of its loan words, along with a considerable Persian and Arabic vocabulary, were grafted onto the base of Sanskrit grammar to form the modern languages of Hindi and Urdu. Regional languages, such as Kashmiri and Bengali, also rose to prominence for both literary and general use.

Ironically, one of the catalysts for the explosion of literary work from the mid-sixteenth to the mid-seventeenth centuries came from the Mughals' most humiliating period. The exile of Humayun to Persia in the 1540s coincided with the Persian Shah Tahmasp embarking on a program of self-denial and abstinence in response to criticism about the worldliness of his court. Writers, painters, and poets who suddenly found themselves out of favor at the Persian court attached themselves to Humayun. They followed him to India, where their talents enlivened the arts already developing there. Their classical Arab and Persian verse forms were ultimately adopted into Urdu, as seen in the classical verse forms of *qasida* and *mathnavi*. By the following century, these forms had matured with the verses of Qudsi and Abu Talib Kalim (d. 1602).

Sanskrit and Hindi poets also continued verse forms pioneered by Chandra Lor in the 1300s, and the Mughal rulers up to Aurangzeb all had Hindi court poets—in some cases, members of the same family over several generations. Perhaps of more importance in terms of cultural synthesis, however, were the efforts pioneered by Akbar and Jahangir at translations of the great works of non-Muslim Indian literature into Persian. It was here that the émigrés who traveled with Humayun made their greatest contributions. Despite the objections of the more orthodox members of his court, Akbar commissioned a complete translation of the Mahabharata, followed shortly by the Ramayana. These he had read to him, and he had the members of his cult study them as well.

Though Sunni scholarship languished somewhat under Akbar, Sufi works proliferated, many borrowing concepts and terminology from non-Islamic sources. The most famous of these was Muhammad Ghauth Gwaliori's "The Five Jewels," which tapped sources from Hindu and Muslim astrology and Jewish Kabbala traditions, as well as Sufi mysticism. By Aurangzeb's reign, the pendulum had swung back to the more "Mecca-centered, prophetic, and exclusive" strain in Indian Islam. Thus, the works tended to be more geared toward treatises on Islamic law, interpretation of *hadith*—the traditions of the Prophet—and Sunni works on science and philosophy.

Art and Painting   One of the more interesting aspects of Islam as practiced by the Mughals—as well as the Safavid Persians and Ottomans—is that, like prohibitions on wine and other intoxicants, the injunctions against depicting human beings in art were often widely ignored in the inner chambers and private rooms of the court. Of course, during Aurangzeb's long reign, there was a marked drop in artistic output because of his much more strict interpretation of proper Islamic behavior. Nonetheless, the accompanying pronouncement of Akbar might be seen as more typical of the Timurids in general.

Not surprisingly, Akbar had a direct hand in the creation of what is considered to be the first painting in the "Mughal style"—a combination of the extreme delicacy of Persian miniature work with the vibrant colors and taste for bold themes of Hindu painters. Akbar inherited two of the master painters who accompanied Humayun from Persia, and the contact they acquired with Hindu works under Akbar's patronage resulted in the first of hundreds of Mughal **gouache** works: 250 miniature illustrations of the *Tutinama* and the colossal illustrated *Hamzanama* of 1570. The Persian tradition of miniature painting flourished under the Mughals, as did larger works on a variety of backings. Charcoal sketches and especially gouache were the preferred artistic media. Illustrations of Muslim and Hindu religious themes and epics were perennial favorites, as were numerous depictions of imperial *durbars*— receptions requiring noble attendance at court. These usually included authentic portraits of key individuals and provide scholars with important clues as to the identities of courtiers and dignitaries. Mughal artists often passed their skills on within their families over generations and represented an important subset of members at the imperial court and among the entourages of regional elites.

Gouache: Watercolors with a gum base.

By the end of the sixteenth century, a new influence was moving into Mughal art: Europeans. The realistic approach of European artists and their use of vanishing point perspective began to be felt at the courts of Akbar and Jahangir. One prominent female artist, Nadira Banu, specialized in producing Flemish-style works. Some took European paintings and added "Mughal" touches—flatter backgrounds, gold leaf, and mosques in the distance. The period of Akbar's religious experiments also prompted an unparalleled interest among Mughal painters in Christian religious figures. Depictions of Christ from the gospels and from Muslim tales were popular fare, as were angels; even more so was the figure of the Virgin, a picture of whom even appears in a portrait of Jahangir. It was perhaps the most dramatic meeting of cultural influences since the era of the Gandharan Buddhas that were fashioned in the style of the Greek god Apollo.

Architecture   Nowhere was the Mughal style more in evidence than in the construction of tombs and mausoleums. The most prominent of these, the Taj Mahal, was introduced in the opening to this chapter and needs little additional discussion. The ethereal lightness of so colossal a construction and the perfection of its layout make it the most distinctive construction of its kind. Europeans sometimes assumed that its architects were influenced by French or Italian artistic trends, though this remains a subject of debate. The chief architect, Ustad Ahmad Lahori (d. 1649), also designed the famous Red Fort of Shah Jahan's city, Shahjahanabad.

The Taj Mahal is scarcely the only noteworthy mausoleum of the Mughal period. All of the emperors commissioned massive tomb complexes for themselves and loved ones. Most of these survive in some form today, though many have been stripped at various times for their marble and other valuable building materials. Two of the more noteworthy tombs include Humayun's complex near Delhi and

> ### Akbar on Painting
>
> "There are many that hate painting; but such men I dislike. It appears to me, as if a painter had quite peculiar means of recognizing God, for a painter in sketching anything that has life . . . must come to feel that he cannot bestow personality on his work, and is thus forced to think of God, the giver of life, and this increases his knowledge."
>
> —Akbar, (unattributed) quoted in Schimmel, page 270.

Durbar of Jahangir. The tradition of the durbar—lavish imperial receptions for nobles and dignitaries, including foreign ambassadors and leading merchants—lasted throughout the Mughal era and was continued by the British into the twentieth century. In this portrayal of a durbar held by Jahangir (r. 1605–1627), the realism of the faces of the participants, many of whom are identifiable to scholars, is apparent. The emperor himself sits under the pillared canopy in the top center of the painting; on the lower left one can see a black-robed Jesuit priest among the attendees.

Akbar's tomb in Sikandra, near Agra. Though neither is as elaborate as the Taj, both include most of the same elements of mausoleum, mosque, and gardens.

A less benign way of demonstrating the power of the empire was the building of forts throughout the realm. While fortifications on the frontier were fairly austere and utilitarian compared to their counterparts in the capital and major cities, their watchtowers, crenellations, and central bastions all have a kind of artistic flair and lightness to them that belie the structures' primary belligerent purpose. While highly effective against the siege techniques of the day, they seem ironically in many ways more like the tomb complexes of their sponsors. The most famous of these structures was the Red Fort at Agra. Built up over centuries from the local red sandstone, the fort housed the palaces of Babur, Humayun, Akbar, Jahangir, and Shah Jahan. Shah Jahan made it the centerpiece of his new city, Shajahanabad, and expanded it into its present size and configuration. It is said that he died in one of its towers gazing at his wife's resting place, the Taj Mahal, a mile and a half distant.

During the high point of Mughal wealth and power, several Mughal emperors built entire cities. By far the most famous of these, as we have previously seen, was Akbar's Fatehpur Sikri. Indeed, as an idealized tribute to the inclusive Sufi master Salim Chishti, with architectural influences from Hindu and Muslim sources, materials from all over India, and a quote from Jesus, as handed down in Islamic lore, over its gateway—"The world is but a bridge; cross over it but build no house upon it"—it does indeed reflect Akbar's vision of what his realm should be. Not to be outdone, of course, Shah Jahan created his own city complex at Delhi, Shahjahanabad.

As one would expect, just as they were integral to the tomb complexes of the Mughals, mosques would be among the empire's most important constructions. Many were built as shrines at holy sites or to mark significant events in the lives of holy men or martyrs. Once again, a distinctive style emerged in which the basic form of the dome symbolically covering the world and the slender arrow of the minaret pointing heavenward interacted with central Asian, Persian, and even Hindu architectural influences. The largest Mughal mosques, like the Friday Delhi Mosque in Shahjahanabad and Aurangzeb's huge Badshahi Mosque in Lahore, contain immense courtyards, surrounded by cloisters leading to small rooms for intimate gatherings, domed areas for men and women, and distinctive minarets with fluted columns and bell-shaped roofs. One mosque in Burhanpur built by Shah Jahan even has quranic verses translated into Sanskrit in it. As scholars have noted, the location of many of the largest mosques, like that of some European cathedrals, is adjacent to government buildings and forts in order to demonstrate the seamless connections of these religious civilizations.

Putting It All Together

The rise of the Turkic central Asian peoples to prominence and power in a variety of areas, from the borders of successive Chinese dynasties to Anatolia and the domains of the Ottomans, and with the Timurids or Mughals in India, is one of the most dramatic sagas of world history. In India, this latest group of outside conquerors faced what might be called the "great question" of the subcontinent: how to create a viable state out of so many long-standing religious traditions, many of which are in direct opposition to each other. Even before the coming of Islam, rulers such as Ashoka felt the need to use transcendent concepts, such as dharma, to try to bridge cultural and religious gaps. The Guptas, for their part, tried to use state-supported Hinduism. With the coming of Islam, a new religion that stood in opposition to the older Hindu pattern of assimilation of gods and favored instead the conquest and conversion of opponents, a divide was created, which persists to this day. It should be remembered that, as recent scholarship has shown, even within these dramatically opposed religious traditions, much more accommodation than previously supposed had taken place. The later development of Sikhism, as another attempt to bridge India's religious syncretism, both added to attempts at greater tolerance and at times contributed to religious tensions.

Against this backdrop the accomplishmentss of the Mughals must be weighed as significant in terms of statecraft and artistic and cultural achievement, and perhaps less so in religious areas. At its height, Mughal India was the most populous, wealthy, politically powerful, and economically vibrant empire in the world next to China. It thus allowed the Mughal rulers unprecedented wealth and financed the proliferation of monumental architecture that became forever identified with India: the Red Fort, Fatehpur Sikri, and, above all, the Taj Mahal.

Yet, for all its wealth and power, the Mughal dynasty was plagued by problems that ultimately proved insoluble. The old nomadic succession practices of the Timurids repeatedly led to palace revolts by potential heirs. These wars in turn encouraged conflict with internal and external enemies who sensed weakness at the core of the regime. Protracted conflicts in Afghanistan, with Safavid Persia, and in Bengal also bled this fiscal–military state of resources. Finally, the Maratha wars slowly wore down even the semblance of unity among the rulers following Aurangzeb.

But perhaps an equally important factor in the ultimate dissolution of the empire was that of Hindu–Muslim syncretism. Here, we have two of the world's great religions interacting with each other in prolonged and profound ways, with the added complication of Muslim rulers and Muslims in general being a small minority among the subcontinent's people. Despite the flexibility of the early rulers in trying to deemphasize the more oppressive elements of Islamic rule in Hindu India—most dramatically, Akbar through his effort to create an entirely new religion—the attempt at a stricter orthodoxy under Aurangzeb hardened Hindu–Muslim and Sikh divisions for centuries to come (see Concept Map).

Throughout the period, one other factor loomed on the horizon but became larger day by day as the dynasty went into decline. The well-financed and well-armed trading companies of the Europeans, increasingly adept at reading Indian politics, gradually moved into positions of regional power. By 1750, they were on the cusp of changing the political situation completely. Indeed, the seeds that had been planted by 1750 would soon be reaped as the first great clash of mature religious civilizations with the new industrially based societies. By 1920, all of these religious civilizations would be gone.

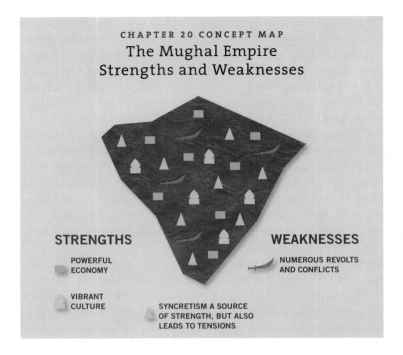

CHAPTER 20 CONCEPT MAP
The Mughal Empire
Strengths and Weaknesses

STRENGTHS

POWERFUL
ECONOMY

VIBRANT
CULTURE

WEAKNESSES

NUMEROUS REVOLTS
AND CONFLICTS

SYNCRETISM A SOURCE
OF STRENGTH, BUT ALSO
LEADS TO TENSIONS

Review and Respond

1. What do you see as the greatest strengths of the individual Mughal rulers? Their greatest weaknesses?

2. What, in your view, provides a state with more stability: unity of religion or plurality of religion? Why? How did religious differences affect the Mughals?

3. Although the Mughals often struggled with the religious aspects of their empire, they seem to have been wonderfully successful on the cultural and artistic front. Why was this so?

▶ For additional resources, including maps, primary sources, visuals, and quizzes, please go to www.oup.com/us/vonsivers. Please see the Further Resources section at the back of the book for additional readings and suggested websites.

Thinking Through Patterns

▶ **What were the strengths and weaknesses of Mughal rule?**

The weaknesses are probably more obvious than the strengths at first glance. Two things are immediately apparent: first, the position of the Mughals as an ethnic and religious minority ruling a vastly larger majority population and, second, the conflict-prone succession practices of the older central Asian Turkic leaders. The minority position of the Mughals aggravated long-existing tensions between Muslim rulers and Hindu subjects in India, of which the Mughals were to be the last line. In an age of religious civilizations, where some kind of unity of religion was the ideal, this put considerable strains on the Mughals as rulers—as it did the Ottomans in predominantly Christian lands and Catholics and Protestants in Europe. Central Asian Turkic succession practices almost always guaranteed conflict when it was time for a new ruler to accede the throne. Nearly every Mughal successor during this period ended up having to fight factions and family to gain the empire.

In some respects the strengths of Mughal rule were in reaction to these problems. Babur and Akbar, in particular, were extraordinarily tolerant rulers in terms of religion. When later rulers like Aurangzeb returned to strict Sunni Islamic policies, it prompted resistance, especially among Hindus. Also, while Mughal rulers were never able to completely free themselves from succession struggles, they succeeded in setting up a well-run fiscal–military state with the mansabdar system, largely undercutting old local and regional loyalties and tying the new loyalty to the state. Like France, the Ottomans, and the Confucian states of eastern Asia, the development of bureaucratic forms was an important earmark of the early modern era.

As we noted, Mughal rulers faced the problem confronted by nearly all "religious civilizations": Religious orthodoxy was seen, in theory, as a vital element of loyalty to the state. But for the Mughals, as for previous Muslim rulers in India, the desire for strict adherence to Muslim law was always tempered by the problem of Islam being a minority religion in India. Here, as we saw, the early Mughal rulers—Babur, Humayun, Akbar—were far less tied to strict Sunni Islam than their successors. Thus, their way of ruling was to uphold Sunni Islam as the approved state religion but to scrupulously refrain from forcing Muslim practices on other religious groups. Akbar went so far as to create a new religion and held Thursday night discussions with leaders of other religions to find ways to satisfy the desires of all. With Shah Jahan, however, the reaction building among reform-minded Sunni Muslims to this liberalization turned to enforcing more strict practices, which peaked during the long reign of Aurangzeb. By the end of Aurangzeb's reign the Sikhs were near revolt and the long Hindu Maratha revolt was in full swing. But even during this period, local religious customs remained largely intact and, indeed, often thrived.

▶ **What was the Mughal policy toward religious accommodation? How did it change?**

▶ **What factors account for the Mughal decline during the eighteenth century?**

At the beginning and for much of the eighteenth century, Mughal India was the second richest and most prosperous empire in the world, after China. But by 1750 it was already in pronounced decline. A large part of this was due to rebellions by the Sikhs, Rajputs, and especially the Marathas that raged off and on through the century. By the 1750s as well, the European trading companies with their small but well-trained armies were becoming locally powerful. Here, the great milestone would take place during the Seven Years' War (1756–1763), when the British East India Company eliminated its French competitors and in essence took over the rule of Bengal from its headquarters in Calcutta. Within 100 years it would take over all of India.

Chapter 21
1500-1800

Regulating the "Inner" and "Outer" Domains

CHINA AND JAPAN

CHINA AND JAPAN, 1500–1800

The time seemed right for a letter home. In only 2 weeks the Japanese invasion force had captured the Korean capital of Seoul, and the skill and firepower of the Japanese warriors seemed to brush their opponents aside at will. The Japanese commander, Toyotomi Hideyoshi, was a battle-hardened commoner who had risen through the ranks of his patron, Oda Nobunaga, as Oda fought to unite Japan before his assassination in 1582. Now, a decade later, Hideyoshi, as he was still known (as a commoner he had no surname and had only been given the family name "Toyotomi" by

Seeing Patterns

▶ Why did late Ming and early Qing China look inward after such a successful period of overseas exploration?

▶ How do the goals of social stability drive the policies of agrarian states? How does the history of China and Japan in this period show these policies in action?

▶ In what ways did contact with the maritime states of Europe alter the patterns of trade and politics in eastern Asia?

▶ How did Neo-Confucianism in China differ from that of Tokugawa Japan?

the imperial court in 1586) had embarked on an audacious campaign to extend his power to the Asian mainland. Six years before, he had written his mother that he contemplated nothing less than the conquest of China. Now seemed like a good time to inform her that his goal was at last within his grasp.

As if in an eerie foreshadowing of another Korean conflict to come centuries later, however, the Japanese soon faced a massive Chinese and Korean counterattack and became mired in a bloody stalemate, their guns and tactics barely enough to compensate for the determination and numbers of their enemies. After 4 more years of negotiation punctuated by bitter fighting, Hideyoshi finally withdrew to Japan. One final invasion attempt of Korea in 1597 collapsed when his death the following year set off a bloody struggle for succession, which ultimately placed in power the Tokugawa family, who would go on to rule Japan for more than 250 years.

Hideyoshi's dream of conquering China was, in a sense, a quest to claim the wellsprings of Japanese civilization as well. The episode brought together the politics, cultures, and fortunes of three of the four fiercely independent realms that together wove the primary strands of an east Asian

The Floating World. Perhaps the most popular painting style for mass consumption in Japan during the Tokugawa Shogunate was the ukiyo-e wood block print. An artist often considered the founder of the style, Hishikawa Mononobu (ca. 1625–1694), painted a variety of subjects but was especially renowned for his renderings of Japan's "floating world" (a literal translation of ukiyo-e) of the pursuit of pleasure. In this picture featuring the "blown-out" perspective of seeing behind the walls, a brothel in the capital of Edo's Yoshiwara quarter—even today the modern capital of Tokyo's most famous red light district—is depicted in which men are engaged in a variety of enjoyable pursuits with the women of the house. In the central room they talk with the proprietor [in black] in front of a screen with the kanji (Chinese) character doku—here, meaning "sole" or "alone"— and suggesting the private pleasures to be had within...

pattern of history. The fourth, Vietnam, while not involved in this particular struggle, had been subject to similar pressures of Chinese cultural and political diffusion for eighteen centuries. As we have seen in other areas, such as the Mediterranean and the expanding kingdoms of Europe, the rise of Japanese power represents a vitally important pattern of world history: A state on the periphery absorbs innovation from a cultural center, in this case China, and then becomes a vital center itself. And like the other states in the region, Japan had absorbed the structures of "religious civilizations," as we have termed them—in this case, the philosophical system of Neo-Confucianism.

Of equal importance, Hideyoshi's invasion was made possible in part by the arrival of a new factor: the appearance of the first Europeans in the region. While their arrival in the sixteenth century provided only the barest inkling of the reversals of fortune to come, by the middle of the nineteenth century their presence would create a crisis of power and acculturation for all of east Asia. For Japan, the industrializing West would then become a new center from which to draw innovation. For the present, however, European intrusions provided powerful incentives for both China and Japan to turn inward to safeguard their own security and stability.

Late Ming and Qing China to 1750

Proclaimed as a new dynasty in 1368, the Ming in its early years appears to have followed the familiar pattern of the "dynastic cycle" of previous dynasties. Having driven out the Mongol remnant, the Hongwu emperor and his immediate successors consolidated their rule, elevated the Confucian bureaucracy to its former place, and set up an administrative structure more focused on the person of the emperor than in previous dynasties. In 1382, the Grand Secretariat was created as the top governmental board below the emperor. Under the Grand Secretariat were the six boards, the governors and governors-general of the provinces, and various degrees of lower-level officials down to the district magistrate.

In this section we will also examine the question of China's greatest maritime expansion—and sudden withdrawal to concentrate on domestic matters. Why such an abrupt change in policy? What factors led to the ultimate decline of the Ming dynasty and the rise to power of the Manchus, a bordering nomadic people who drove out the Ming and created China's last imperial dynasty, the Qing [CHING]? By what means did the Manchus create a state in which, despite being a tiny ruling minority, they held their grip on power into the twentieth century? Finally, what faint hints of the dynasty's problems appeared during its time of greatest power in the mid-eighteenth century?

From Expansion to Exclusion

During the late fourteenth and early fifteenth centuries, while China was rebuilding from the war to drive out the Mongols, the more pressing problems of land distribution and tenancy had abated somewhat. As in Europe, the depopulation of some areas from fighting and banditry and the lingering effects of the Black Death (which had reduced China's population from perhaps 100 million to about 60 million) had raised the value of labor, depressed the price of land, and increased the proportional amount of money in circulation. While the problems of land tenure would recur, another period of relief from their full effects soon came, albeit indirectly, from the creation of overseas empires by the Portuguese and the Spanish in the sixteenth century. The resulting Columbian Exchange saw the circulation of a number of new food crops on a global scale that had a substantial impact on the world's agricultural productivity (see Chapter 18).

New Food Crops   In addition to new, higher-yielding rice strains coming out of southeast Asia (as they had a number of times in the past), the Chinese began to cultivate sugarcane, indigo, potatoes, sweet potatoes, maize (corn), peanuts, and tobacco that came from Africa and the Americas by way of the Spanish in the Philippines and the Portuguese at Macao. Corn and potatoes, versatile crops suitable

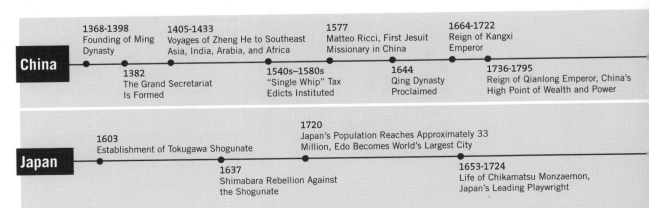

China

1368-1398
Founding of Ming Dynasty

1382
The Grand Secretariat Is Formed

1405-1433
Voyages of Zheng He to Southeast Asia, India, Arabia, and Africa

1540s–1580s
"Single Whip" Tax Edicts Instituted

1577
Matteo Ricci, First Jesuit Missionary in China

1644
Qing Dynasty Proclaimed

1664-1722
Reign of Kangxi Emperor

1736-1795
Reign of Qianlong Emperor, China's High Point of Wealth and Power

Japan

1603
Establishment of Tokugawa Shogunate

1637
Shimabara Rebellion Against the Shogunate

1720
Japan's Population Reaches Approximately 33 Million, Edo Becomes World's Largest City

1653-1724
Life of Chikamatsu Monzaemon, Japan's Leading Playwright

for cultivation in a variety of marginal environments, accounted for a considerable increase in the arable land within China. Peanuts, sugarcane, indigo, and tobacco quickly established themselves as important cash crops. Even today, cigars and tobacco products sometimes carry the characters *lusong* a transliteration of "Luzon," the island in the Philippines from which they were first obtained from the Spanish. Cotton, first cultivated in China for its fiber during the Song period, had also now become a major part of what had grown into the world's largest textile industry.

Aided by the productivity of these new crops, China's population grew from its low of perhaps 60 million at the beginning of the Ming period to an estimated 150 million by 1600. There was also a marked growth in urbanism as market towns and regional transshipment points multiplied. The efficiency of Chinese agriculture, the continued incorporation of marginal and border lands into production, and the refinement of the empire's immense internal trade all contributed to another doubling of the population to perhaps 300 million by 1800. This accelerating growth began China's movement toward what some historical demographers have called a *high-level equilibrium trap*—a condition in which the land has reached its maximum potential for feeding an increasing population; that population then (barring radical improvements in crops or technology) becomes slowly squeezed into impoverishment (see Map 21.1).

MAP **21.1 China in 1600.**

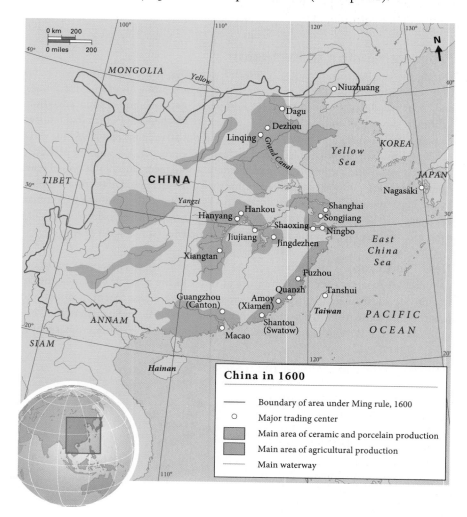

China and the World Commercial Revolution   China's rapid recovery, particularly as the sixteenth century brought new crops from the Americas, placed the late Ming and Qing Empires in the center of an increasingly extensive and complex worldwide commercial revolution (see "Patterns Up Close: The China Trade"). The competition for markets among the emerging maritime Atlantic states of Europe pushed them to develop ever-widening trade networks in the Indian Ocean, the Pacific, along the African coast, and in the Americas. In all of these regions (except the Americas) they faced stiff competition from local traders long involved in regional networks, particularly in the Indian Ocean, among the many ports of what is now Indonesia.

Among the European states, commercial, political, and religious competition resulted in policies of mercantilism (see Chapters 17 and 18), in which countries strove to control sources of raw materials and markets. Similarly, China and Japan (by the early seventeenth century) sought to tightly control imports, regulate the export trade, and keep potentially subversive foreign influences at bay. China's immense production of luxury goods, the seclusion policies of Japan and Korea, and the huge and growing demand for porcelain, tea, silk, paper, and cotton textiles made the Chinese empire the world's dominant economic engine until the productive capacity of the Industrial Revolution vaulted Great Britain into that position in the nineteenth century. Indeed, recent work by world historians has shown how extensively China's economy powered that of Eurasia and much of the world before what Kenneth Pomeranz has called "the great divergence" of Western economic ascendancy (see Map 21.2).

MAP **21.2 World Trade Networks, ca. 1770.**

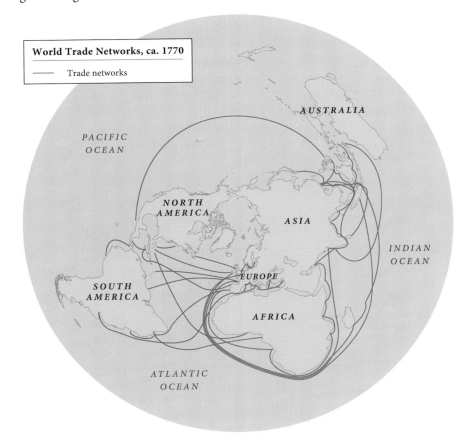

World Trade Networks, ca. 1770

——— Trade networks

AUSTRALIA

PACIFIC OCEAN

NORTH AMERICA

ASIA

INDIAN OCEAN

EUROPE

SOUTH AMERICA

AFRICA

ATLANTIC OCEAN

Patterns Up Close | The "China" Trade

Ming and Qing China may be said to be at the heart of two innovations of enormous importance to the patterns of world history. The first is one that we have tracked through all of the chapters in this book pertaining to China: the technical and aesthetic development of ceramics culminating in the creation of true porcelain during the Song period (960–1279). The early Ming period saw the elaboration of the use of kaolin white clays with what are called "flux" materials—minerals, metals, and compounds—that can fuse with the clay under extremely high temperatures to form durable glazes and striking artistic features. Thus, the Song and Yuan periods were characterized by pure white and green celadon wares, some with a purposely created "crackled" glaze on them, while by the Ming period, highly distinctive blue and white ware—the result of employing pigments with cobalt oxide imported from the areas around modern Iran and Iraq—set the world standard for elegance.

The artistic excellence of Chinese porcelain, like earlier styles of Chinese ceramics, spawned imitators throughout the Chinese periphery. By 1500, porcelain works in Korea, Japan, and Vietnam supplied a burgeoning market both at home and throughout east and southeast Asia. While these regional manufacturers for the most part followed the designs of the Chinese imperial works at Jingdezhen, some, especially the Japanese ceramicist Chojiro, preferred highly rustic, rough-hewn earthenware designs with glazes that formed spontaneous designs as the pieces were fired—the famous raku ware. Thus, there was already a highly developed regional market for what was, at the time, arguably the world's most highly developed technology.

The period from 1500 to the mid-nineteenth century brings us to the second great innovation in which China was the driving force: the world market for porcelain.

Porcelain Vase, Ming Period. Porcelain ware of the Song and Ming periods are among the most coveted Chinese art objects even today. Here we have a Ming vase showing characteristically vibrant colors and a degree of technical perfection indicative of the best Chinese pottery works, such as Jingdezhen. The motif of the grass carp on the vase is symbolic of endurance and perseverance, and thus associated with the god of literature and scholarship.

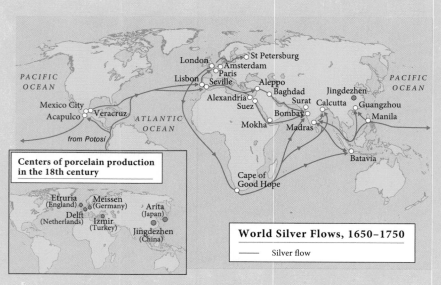

Centers of porcelain production in the 18th century

Etruria (England) · Meissen (Germany) · Arita (Japan) · Delft (Netherlands) · Izmir (Turkey) · Jingdezhen (China)

World Silver Flows, 1650–1750

—— Silver flow

MAP 21.3 **Silver Flows and Centers of Porcelain Production.**

China's wares had found customers for centuries in nearly every corner of Eurasia and North and East Africa. Shipwrecks have been found in the Straits of Malacca laden with Ming porcelain; traders in the Swahili cities along the East African coast were avid collectors, while Africans farther inland decorated their graves with Chinese bowls. All stops on the Silk Road had their precious supplies of porcelain, while the Ottoman Turks did their best to copy the blue and white Ming wares in their own factories at Izmir.

Before the sixteenth century, a trickle of Ming porcelain also made its way to Europe. With the establishment of the first European trade empires, however, the demand for porcelain skyrocketed. Portuguese, Spanish, and later Dutch, French, English, and (after 1784) American merchants all sought porcelain in ever-increasing amounts. From 1500 to 1800 it was arguably the single most important commodity in the unfolding world commercial revolution. While estimates vary, economic historians have suggested that between one-third to one-half of all the silver produced in the Americas during this time went to pay for porcelain. Incoming ships often used the bulk cargoes of porcelain as ballast, and foreign merchants sent custom orders to their Chinese counterparts for Chinese-style wares designed for use at Western tables. Such was the prominence of this "export porcelain" in the furnishings of period homes that scarcely any family of means was without it (see Map 21.3).

With the prominence of mercantilist theory and protectionism toward home markets during the seventeenth and eighteenth centuries, it is not surprising that foreign manufacturers sought to break the Chinese monopoly. During Tokugawa times, the Japanese, for example, forced a group of Korean potters to work at the famous Arita works to turn out Sino–Korean designs; the Dutch marketed "delftware" as an attempt to copy Chinese "blue willow" porcelain. It was not until German experimenters in Saxony happened upon a workable formula for hard-paste porcelain—after years of trial and error, even melting down Chinese wares for analysis—that their facility at Meissen began to produce true porcelain in 1710. Josiah Wedgwood set up his own porcelain factory in 1759 in England. But Chinese manufacturers would still drive the market until the end of the nineteenth century. And fine porcelain would forever carry the generic name of "china" regardless of its origins.

Porcelain Candlestick for the Export Market, Qing Period. By the early 1700s, luxury exports from China such as porcelain, lacquerware, and, of course, tea had become important staples of European maritime trade. Export porcelain—items either made to order by Chinese porcelain works for overseas buyers, or generic ones made to suit European and colonial tastes—had become such a big business that cheaper pieces were sometimes actually used as ship's ballast on the homeward voyages. Shown here is a candlestick for use in a European home with Chinese motifs of vessels at the top. The cobalt blue color is characteristic of the Ming and Qing designs.

Questions

- How does the development of porcelain serve as an example of Chinese leadership in technical innovations during the premodern and early modern periods?

- How did the emergence of a global trading network after 1500 affect both the demand for porcelain and its impact on consumer tastes?

In the midst of this growth, the government took steps to simplify the system of land taxation. As in previous regimes, land was assessed and classified according to its use and relative productivity. Land taxes were then combined into a single bill, payable in silver by installments over the course of the year: the so-called single-whip tax system. The installment plan allowed peasants to remain relatively solvent during planting season when their resources were depleted, thus reducing the need to borrow at high rates from moneylenders at crucial times of the yearly cycle. Significantly, the requirement that the payment be in silver also played a crucial role in the increasing monetization of the economy. *Corvée* labor—the contribution of labor as a form of tax—was effectively abolished as well.

Regulating the Outer Barbarians   By the late fifteenth century, Ming China had made considerable progress toward the goals of peace and stability long sought by Chinese regimes. In addition to the practical requirements of defending the historic avenues of invasion in China's remote interior, the view of the empire cultivated by China's elites placed it at the center of a world order defined by Neo-Confucian philosophy and supported by a host of Chinese cultural assumptions. As we will see in the following sections, like the Tokugawa shogunate in Japan in the seventeenth century, the Ming, and later the Qing, had come to view foreign influence as less "civilized" and far too often injurious to established social order. Hence, successive rulers placed severe restrictions on maritime trade and conceived of diplomatic relations primarily in commercial terms. "All the world is one family," imperial proclamations routinely claimed, and the emperor was conceived as the father, in Confucian terms, of this world-family system. "Tribute missions," a term sometimes (though somewhat misleadingly) applied to this diplomatic–commercial relationship, were sent from Korea, Vietnam, the Ryukyu Islands, and occasionally Japan to pay periodic ceremonial visits to the emperor, who then bestowed presents on the envoys and granted them permission to trade in China. This arrangement worked reasonably well within the long-standing hierarchy of the Confucian cultural sphere. By the late eighteenth century, however, it came into direct conflict with the more egalitarian system of international trade and diplomacy that had evolved in the West.

Tribute Mission. This illustration, from a popular English travel account first published in 1745, shows the retinue of the Siamese (Thailand) ambassador being escorted to an audience with the emperor inside the Forbidden City. For the Qing, these annual tribute missions had as much symbolic importance as anything diplomatic. As the "Son of Heaven," the emperor's supreme cultural authority over the lands in his "inner" domains was to be acknowledged through elaborate gift-giving and the performing of the kowtow by the ambassador—a deep bow in which one's head touches the ground.

The Ming in Decline   Despite the increased attention directed at the Mongol resurgence of the 1440s, periodic rebellions in the north and northwest punctuated the late fifteenth and sixteenth centuries. The huge commitment of Chinese troops in Korea against the forces of the Japanese leader Hideyoshi during his attempted invasion of Korea and China from 1592 to 1598 weakened the dynasty further during a crucial period that saw the rise of another regional power: the Manchus. By the turn of the seventeenth century, under the leadership of Nurhachi (r.1616–1626) and Abahai (r.1636–1643), the Manchus, an Altaic-speaking nomadic people inhabiting the northeastern section of the Ming domain, had become the prime military force of the area and dissident Chinese sought them as allies. In 1642, the Chinese general Wu Sangui invited the Manchu leader Dorgon to cross the Great Wall where it approaches the sea at Shanhaiguan. For the Chinese, this event would come to carry the same sense of finality as Caesar's crossing of the Rubicon: The Manchus soon captured Beijing and declared the founding of a new regime, the Qing, or "pure," dynasty. Like the defeated remnant of the Nationalist regime in 1949, some Ming loyalists fled to the island of Taiwan, where they expelled the Dutch (who had established a trading base there) and held on until succumbing to Qing forces in 1683.

> **Banner system:** The organizational system of the Manchus for military and taxation purposes; there were eight banners under which all military houses were arranged, and each was further divided into blocks of families required to furnish units of 300 soldiers to the Manchu government.

The Spring and Summer of Power: The Qing to 1750

Like the Toba and Mongols before them, the Manchus now found themselves in the position of having to "dismount and rule." A good deal of preparation for this had already taken place within the borderland state they had created for themselves—for a time, successfully isolated by the Ming—on the Liaodong Peninsula of south Manchuria. Long exposure to Chinese culture and Confucian administrative practices provided models that soon proved adaptable by Manchu leaders within the larger environment of China proper.

The Banner System   The **banner system**, under which the Manchus were organized for military and tax purposes, was also expanded under the Qing to provide for segregated Manchu elites and garrisons in major cities and towns. Under the banner system, the Manchu state had been divided into eight major military and ethnic (Manchu, Han Chinese, and Mongolian) divisions, each represented by a distinctive banner. Within each

division, companies were formed of 300 fighters recruited from families represented by that banner. Originally organized for a mobile warrior people, the system eventually became the chief administrative tool of the Manchu leadership. It was now introduced into China in such a way as to constitute the Manchus as a hereditary warrior class occupying its own sections of major Chinese cities. The Han, or ethnic Chinese, forces were organized into their own "Armies of the Green Standard," so named for the color of the flags they carried.

Manchu Bannermen, Canton, ca. 1872. Until the twentieth century, the Qing maintained garrisons of Manchu soldiers organized under the old "banner system" in all of China's major cities. The bannermen lived in their own quarter, often in reduced circumstances, as a check on the local Chinese population. Significantly, in terms of China's difficulties with Western imperialism in the later nineteenth century, the group pictured here was part of the guard of the British consul.

Minority Rule   Always conscious of their position as a ruling minority in China, with their numbers comprising only about 2 percent of the population, the Manchus, like the Mongols before them, sought to walk a fine line between administrative and cultural adaptation and the kind of complete assimilation that had characterized

Dyarchy: A system of administration consisting of two equal or parallel parts.

previous invaders. Thus, under what is sometimes termed the Sino–Manchu **dyarchy**, Chinese and Manchus were scrupulously recruited in equal numbers for high administrative posts; Manchu quotas in the examination system were instituted; edicts and memorials were issued in both Chinese and the Manchu written language; Qing emperors sought to control the empire's high culture; and, of course, Manchu "bannermen" of the various garrisons were kept in their own special quarters in the towns and cities. In addition, the Manchu conqueror Dorgon instituted the infamous "queue [pronounced like the letter Q] edict" in 1645: All males, regardless of ethnicity, were required on pain of death to adopt the Manchu hairstyle of shaved forehead and long pigtail in the back—the *queue*—as the outward sign of loyalty to the new order. This hairstyle can be seen in early photographs taken of Chinese men until the Qing dynasty fell in 1912. As it was put with a kind of sinister whimsy, "Keep the hair, lose the head; keep the head, lose the hair."

The results, however, were bloody and long-lasting. The queue edict provoked revolts in several cities, and the casualties caused by its suppression may have numbered in the hundreds of thousands. For the remainder of the Qing era, rebels and protestors routinely cut their queues as the first order of business; during China's Taiping Rebellion (1851–1864), perhaps the bloodiest civil war in human history, insurgents were known as "the long-haired rebels" for their immediate abandonment of the Qing hair style.

As a number of scholars have suggested, the situation of the Qing represents a curious relationship between a cultural core and its periphery, in which the conquest of the core by the periphery brings the core temporary renewal but the interests of stability loom so large for the newcomers that they become the ones who cling most tenaciously to the forms of the old order. In this view, by the end of the Qing period, when the empire was faced with foreign pressure and domestic agitation for reform, the Manchu court and nobility were willing to risk the collapse of the empire to preserve the power of their dynasty and position.

Creating the New Order

Though the Qing kept the centralized imperial system of the Ming largely intact, while importing the banner system as a kind of Manchu parallel administrative apparatus, they also made one significant addition to the uppermost level of the bureaucracy. While retaining the Ming Grand Secretariat, the emperor Kangxi's successor, Yongzheng, set up an ad hoc inner advisory body called the "Grand Council" in 1733. Over the succeeding decades the Grand Council became the supreme "inner" advisory group to the emperor, while the Grand Secretariat was relegated to handling less crucial "outer" matters of policy making and implementation.

For much of the seventeenth century, however, the pacification of the empire remained the primary task. Under the able leadership of Nurhachi's great-grandson, the Kangxi emperor (r. 1661–1722), the difficult subjugation of the south was concluded, the Revolt of the Three Feudatories (1673–1681) ultimately crushed, and the naval stronghold of the Ming pretender called "Koxinga" by the Dutch captured on Taiwan in 1683.

As had been the case in past dynasties, the Qing sought to safeguard the borders of the empire by bringing peoples on the periphery into the imperial system through a judicious application of the carrot and the stick, or, as it was known to generations of Chinese strategists, the "loose rein" and "using barbarians to check barbarians."

In practical terms, this meant a final reckoning with the Mongols in the 1720s by means of improved cannon and small arms, along with bribes and presents to friendly chieftains, and the intervention of the Qing in religious disputes regarding Tibetan Buddhism, which had also been adopted by a number of the Mongol groups. Toward this end, the Qing established a protectorate over Tibet in 1727, with the Dalai Lama ruling as the approved temporal and religious leader. To cement the relationship further, the emperor built a replica of a Tibetan stupa just outside the Manchu quarter in Beijing and a model of the Dalai Lama's Potala Palace at the emperor's summer retreat in Jehol [Yeh-hole].

The Qianlong Emperor

With the traditional threats from the borders now quashed, the reign of the Qianlong [Chien-LUNG] emperor, from 1736 to 1795, marked both the high point and the beginning of the decline of the Qing dynasty—and of imperial China itself. The period witnessed China's expansion to its greatest size during the imperial era. This was accompanied by a doubling of its population to perhaps 300 million by 1800. By almost any measure, its internal economy dwarfed that of any other country and equaled or surpassed that of Europe as a whole until the Industrial Revolution was well under way.

Tibetan Stupa and Temple, Beijing. This marble *chorten*, the Tibetan version of the Buddhist stupa, or reliquary, was built by the Qianlong emperor for the visit of the Panchen Lama in 1779, in part to cement the new Sino–Tibetan relationship growing from the establishment of a Qing protectorate over Tibet.

The Qing army, though perhaps already eclipsed in terms of efficiency and weaponry by the leading nations of Europe, was still many times larger than that of any potential competitor. Moreover, Qianlong wielded this power successfully a number of times during his reign, with expeditions against pirates and rebels on Taiwan and in punitive campaigns against Vietnam, Nepal, and Burma between 1766 and 1792 (see Map 21.4). During his long life, he also tried, with limited success, to take up the writing brush of a scholar and connoisseur, creating the collection of art that is today the core of the National Palace Museum's holdings on Taiwan. Under his direction, the state sponsored monumental literary enterprises on a scale still awesome to contemplate today. Based on the small but steady stream of information on the Qing empire circulating around Europe, it seemed to some that the Chinese had solved a number of the problems of good government and might provide practical models of statecraft for Europeans to emulate.

Early European Contacts

Ironically, it was precisely at the time that China abandoned its oceanic expeditions that tiny Portugal on the Atlantic coast surmounted its first big hurdle in pursuit of what would become a worldwide maritime trade empire (see Chapters 16, 18, 19) By the 1440s, Portuguese navigators had

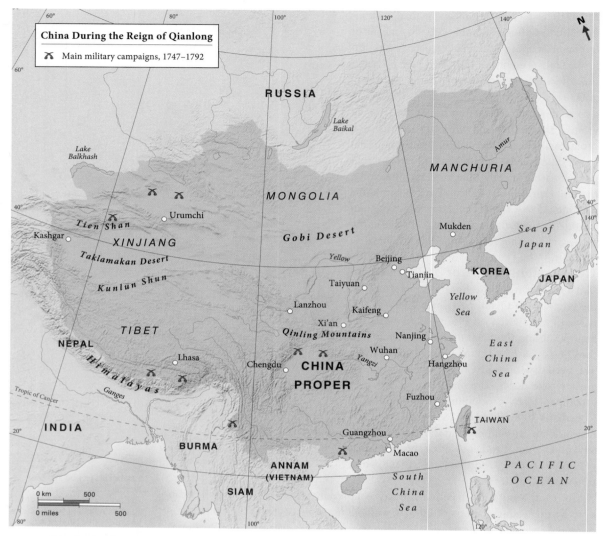

MAP 21.4 **China During the Reign of Qianlong.**

rounded the bulge of West Africa and opened commercial relations with the coastal kingdoms there. Scarcely a decade after Vasco da Gama arrived in Calicut in 1498, the first Portuguese ships appeared in Chinese waters. By 1557, these *Folangqi*—the Chinese transliteration of "Franks," a generic term for Europeans transmitted by the Arabs to Malacca, where it was transformed into *Ferenghi* [Fa-REN-gee]—had wrested the first European colony from the Chinese at Macao. It was destined to be the longest-lived European colony as well, remaining under Portuguese control until 1999. From this point on, through merchants and missionaries, the contacts would frequently be profitable—and, sometimes, disastrous. Ultimately, they provided some of the most far-reaching interactions of world history.

The first Portuguese and Spanish traders were less than impressive to the Chinese officials charged with handling commercial affairs. Confucian tradition had long maintained that merchants were generally a disreputable, if necessary, class. The outlandish appearance, disagreeable smell—from months aboard ship with primitive sanitary facilities—and aggressive behavior of these "men of the Western Ocean" only solidified this impression. Additionally, trade restrictions imposed by the Ming had only partially reduced the network of Chinese merchants long established in the ports of southeast Asia, Malaya, and the Moluccas. In these areas they often traded in contraband goods and competed for markets with Arab, Malayan, and Japanese merchants and pirates. In short, the Europeans had now entered a region of trade where the lines were quite fluid between legitimate and illegitimate enterprises, and both they and the Chinese authorities reacted accordingly.

Missionaries The arrival of the first European merchants in east Asia was followed shortly by that of the first Catholic missionaries. Although the crusading impulse was still very much alive in Christian dealings with Muslim merchants in the Indies, Christian missionaries (at first from Franciscan and Dominican orders and later from the Jesuits) were quick to realize the vast potential for faith conversions in China and Japan. The various missionary orders set up headquarters in Malacca, and in 1549 the Franciscan Francis Xavier landed in Japan. The endemic conflict among the *daimyo* (regional warlords) of Japan helped create a demand for Western goods, especially firearms; and the association of these with Christianity allowed considerable progress to be made in gaining conversions. China, however, required a vastly different strategy.

Wary of potentially disruptive foreign influences, the Ming at first refused entry to missionaries. Once admitted, the Franciscans and Dominicans, with their limited training in Chinese language and culture, made little headway. Additionally, their efforts were largely aimed at seeking conversions among the poor, which won them scant respect or influence among China's elite. The Jesuits, however, tried a different tack. Led by Matteo Ricci (1552–1610) and his successors Adam Schall Von Bell (1591–1666) and Ferdinand Verbiest (1623–1688), they immersed themselves in the classical language and high culture of the empire and gained recognition through their expertise in mathematics, astronomy, military science, and other European skills sought by the imperial court. Jesuit advisors served the last Ming emperors as court astronomers and military engineers and successfully made the transition to the new dynasty. The high point of their influence was reached during the reign of the Qing Kangxi emperor. With Schall as the official court astronomer and mathematician and an entire European-style observatory set up in Beijing, Kangxi actively considered conversion to Catholicism.

Matteo Ricci and Li Paul. The cross-cultural possibilities of sixteenth- and seventeenth-century Sino–Western contact were perhaps best exemplified by the activities of the Jesuit Matteo Ricci (1552–1610). Ricci predicated his mission in China on a respectful study of the language and classical canon of the empire coupled with a thorough knowledge of the new mathematics and astronomy of the West. Here, he is pictured with one of his most prominent converts, a literatus and veteran of the war against the Japanese in Korea, Li Yingshi. Upon his conversion in 1602, Li took the Christian name of Paul.

The papacy, however, had long considered Jesuit liturgical and doctrinal adaptations to local sensibilities problematic. In China, the Jesuits' use of tea and rice during the Eucharist instead of bread and wine set off the "rites controversy." The liturgical substitution proved unacceptable to Rome, as did Jesuit tolerance of their converts' veneration of Confucius and maintenance of ancestral shrines. After several decades of intermittent discussion, Kangxi's successor, Yongzheng, banned the order's activities in China in 1724. Christianity and missionary activity were driven underground, though the Qing would retain a Jesuit court astronomer into the nineteenth century.

China and the European Enlightenment　While the European intellectual influence on China was limited to a small circle at court, the reports of the Jesuits and other foreign observers from the empire had a considerable effect on several of the important figures of the Enlightenment and on creating an overall image of China in the West. For the *philosophes* (e.g. Voltaire, Liebnitz, Diderot, and Montesquieu) the vision of a vast, wealthy, and powerful empire governed by a highly developed bureaucracy according to a pragmatic and secular system of ethics provided much ammunition for their critiques of European regimes. A Chinese Christian convert, Hoange [HO-ahn-guh], who secured a minor position in the French government as a cataloguer of its Chinese works, provided a wealth of information to the young Montesquieu, who incorporated it into his satire of French life, *The Persian Letters*. The emphasis placed on the importance of land by Chinese officials was also reflected in the economic arguments of the physiocrats, whose chief exponent, Francois Quesnay, was sometimes called "the Confucius of Europe." Philology was also greatly enhanced by the production of the first Chinese dictionaries for use with European languages. Finally, the growing trade in luxury goods spurred both a fashion for *chinoiserie* (items manufactured in Chinese styles, real or imagined) among the elite and a desire among European manufacturers to develop domestic industries in such items as silk and porcelain. While viable silk industries were created in both France and Italy, the manufacture of true porcelain in Europe would not be seen until the innovations of Meissen and Wedgwood (see Patterns Up Close).

The Canton Trade　While China's commerce with the maritime Atlantic states grew rapidly in the eighteenth century, the Europeans had not yet been fully incorporated into the Qing diplomatic system. A century before, the expansion of Russia into Siberia and the region around the Amur River had prompted the Qing to negotiate the Treaty of Nerchinsk in 1689. Under its terms, negotiated with Kangxi's Jesuit advisors acting as interpreters and go-betweens, the Russians agreed to abandon their last forts along the Amur and were given rights to continue their lucrative caravan trade in the interior. Formal borders were established in Manchuria, and the first attempts at settling claims to the central Asian regions of Ili and Kuldjia were made. Significantly, Russian envoys were also permitted to reside in Beijing but in a residence like those used by the temporary envoys of tribute missions.

The situation among the European traders attempting to enter Chinese seaports, however, was quite different. The British East India Company, having established its base at Calcutta in 1690, soon sought to expand its operations to China. At the same time, the Qing, fresh from capturing the last Ming bastion on Taiwan and worried about Ming loyalists in other areas, sought to control contact with foreign and overseas Chinese traders as much as possible, while keeping their lucrative export trade at a sustainable level. Their solution, implemented in 1699, was to permit overseas trade only at the southern port of Guangzhou [GWANG-joe], more widely known as Canton. The local merchants' guild, or *cohong*, was granted a monopoly on the trade and was supervised by a special official from the imperial Board of Revenue. Much like the Tokugawa in seventeenth-century Japan, the Qing permitted only a small number of foreigners, mostly traders from the English, French, and Dutch East India Companies, to reside at the port. They were confined to a small compound of foreign "**factories**," were not permitted inside the city walls, and could not bring their wives or families along. Even small violations of the regulations could result in a suspension of trading privileges, and all infractions and disputes were judged according to Chinese law. Finally, since foreign affairs under these circumstances were considered a dimension of trade, all diplomatic issues were settled by local officials in Canton.

The eighteenth century proved to be a boom time for all involved in trade, and the British in particular increasingly viewed it as a valuable part of their growing commercial power. While the spread of tea drinking through Europe and its colonies meant that tea rapidly grew to challenge porcelain for trade supremacy, silk also grew in importance, as well as lacquerware, wicker and rattan furniture, and dozens of other local specialties increasingly targeted at the export market. After 1784, the United States joined the trade; but despite the growing American presence, it was the British East India Company that dominated the Canton factories. Both the cohong and foreign chartered companies carefully guarded their respective

Factory: In the sense used in this chapter, the place where various "factors" (merchants, agents, etc.) gathered to conduct business.

Canton Factories, ca. 1800. Under the "Canton system" begun in 1699, all maritime trade with the Europeans was tightly controlled and conducted through the single port of Canton, or Guangzhou. Foreign merchants were not allowed to reside within the walled city, so they constructed their own facilities along the Pearl River waterfront. Though it kept profits high for the concerned parties, the restrictiveness of the system caused nineteenth-century merchants and diplomats to push the Chinese to open more ports to trade, which proved to be a major sticking point in Sino–Western relations.

monopolies, and the system worked reasonably well in keeping competition low and profits high on all sides.

Village and Family Life

Just as the effort toward greater control and centralization was visible in the government and economy of China during the Ming and Qing, it also reverberated within the structures of Chinese village life. While much of local custom and social relations among the peasants still revolved around family, clan, and lineage—with the scholar-gentry setting the pace—new institutions perfected under the Ming and Qing had a lasting impact into the twentieth century.

Organizing the Countryside

During the sixteenth century, the administrative restructuring related to the consolidation of the tax system into the "single-whip" arrangement led to the creation of the *lijia* system. All families were placed into officially designated *li*, or "villages," for tax purposes; 10 households made up a *jia*, and 100 households comprised a *li*, whose headmen, appointed by the magistrate, were responsible for keeping tax records and labor dues.

While the lijia system was geared primarily toward more efficient tax collection and record keeping, the *baojia* (Chapter 12) system functioned as a more far-reaching arrangement of government surveillance and control. The baojia system required families to register all members and be organized into units of 10 families, with one family in each unit assuming responsibility for the other nine. Each of these responsible families were arranged in groups of 10, and a member of each was selected to be responsible for that group of 100 households, and so on up to the *bao*, or 1,000-household level. Baojia representatives at each level were to be chosen by the families in the group. These representatives were to report to the magistrate on the doings of their respective groups and held accountable for the group's behavior. The system was especially important during the Qing, when it allowed authorities to bypass potential local gentry resistance to government directives and guaranteed a network of informers at all levels of rural life. During the White Lotus Rebellion at the end of the eighteenth century and the Taiping Rebellion of the 1850s and 1860s, the government relied on this mode of organization extensively.

Glimpses of Rural Life

As with other agrarian–urban empires, much of what little we know about Chinese peasant life comes through literary sources. Most of these were compiled by the scholar-gentry, though starting in the seventeenth century a small but influential number of chronicles were also produced by Westerners traveling in China. The local histories and gazetteers, with their reliance on unusual events—famines, revolts, riots, spectacular feats, and exemplary wives—generally fit peasant experiences, when they are addressed at all, into the mold of history as Confucian morality. More authentic, though still fragmentary, pictures of village life emerge from the works of popular writers like Pu Songling in his rich depictions of folk myth and religious syncretism. Even with these limitations, however, some generalizations can still be made about rural and family life in Ming and Qing times.

First, while the introduction of new crops during the period had brought more marginal land under cultivation, allowed for a huge increase in the population, and helped lend momentum to the trend toward more commercialization of agriculture, the work, technology, and overall rhythms of peasant life had changed little over the centuries.

Second, as with gathering political tensions, some early signs of economic stress were already present toward the end of Qianlong's reign. Chief among these was the problem of absentee landlordism. This would grow increasingly acute as the vitality of the commercial networks and market towns of central and southern China increased and the gentry were drawn away from the countryside by urban opportunities and amenities. In addition, successful tea, cotton, silk, and luxury goods traders frequently

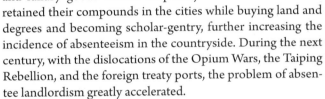

retained their compounds in the cities while buying land and degrees and becoming scholar-gentry, further increasing the incidence of absenteeism in the countryside. During the next century, with the dislocations of the Opium Wars, the Taiping Rebellion, and the foreign treaty ports, the problem of absentee landlordism greatly accelerated.

Third, as we have seen before, pressures on patterns of village life tended to be magnified in the lives of women and girls. Elite women were routinely educated to be as marriageable as possible. Study of proper Confucian decorum, writing model essays, chanting poetry, and a firm grasp of the *Xiaojing* (*Classic of Filial Piety*) were central to their lessons. As noted earlier, women were expected to be modest and obedient and were usually separated from and subordinate to men. In addition, marriage and property laws were set up to reinforce these qualities. In addition to the emphasis placed on mourning by both sexes, widows were expected to remain single and be subordinate to their oldest sons. As also noted previously, the custom of foot binding had long since become institutionalized, though in some areas—among south China's Hakka minority, for example—it never caught on. The sale of infant girls and, in extreme cases, female infanticide rose markedly in rural areas during times of war, famine, or other social stresses. It should be remembered, however, that, as in previous Chinese dynasties, the dominance of women over the "inner realm" of the family remained largely complete.

Science, Culture, and Intellectual Life

As we saw in Chapter 12, the Ming dynasty in many ways marked the high point as well as the beginning of the decline of China's preeminent place as a world technological innovator. One area in which this became painfully evident by the eighteenth and nineteenth centuries was in military matters.

Superpower   The Ming at their height have been described by some Chinese scholars as a military superpower. Perhaps most important in this regard was that

Chinese Commercial Enterprises. The growing volume and profits of the export trade encouraged further development and specialization of long-standing Chinese domestic industries during the eighteenth and nineteenth centuries. The men in the first photograph are *shroffs*, moneychangers involved in testing the quality of silver taken from foreign concerns in exchange for Chinese goods. The second picture depicts a worker and overseer running a silk reeling machine. The third illustrates women sorting tea while a foreman looks on. The packing chests for the tea are stacked in back of the sorters. The hairstyle of the men in the photos—shaved forehead with long braid called a *queue*—was mandatory for all Chinese males as a sign of submission to the Qing.

the ascendancy of the Ming in 1368 marked the beginning of what one historian has called a "military revolution" in the use of firearms. The first use of metal gun barrels in the late thirteenth century spurred the rapid development of both cannon and small arms—so much so that by the mid-fifteenth century the Ming arsenal at Junqiju [JWUN-chee-joo]was producing thousands of cannon, handguns, and "firelances" every year. By one estimate, in 1450 over half of the Ming frontier military units had cannon and one-third of all troops carried firearms. As early as the 1390s large shipborne cannon were already being installed in naval vessels. Indeed, court historians of the late Ming credited nearly all the military successes of the dynasty to the superiority of their firearms.

By the Qing period, however, following the pacification of the realm, the need for constant improvement of arms was seen as increasingly costly and unnecessary. While marginal improvements were made in the **matchlock** firing mechanisms of Chinese small arms, such improvements as were made in larger guns were largely directed by European missionary advisors to the throne.

Matchlock: An early type of gun in which the gunpowder charge is ignited by a burning taper (the "match") attached to the trigger mechanism.

Science and Literature   In geography, mathematics, and astronomy a fruitful exchange was inaugurated between European Jesuit missionaries in the seventeenth and eighteenth centuries and a small but influential group of Chinese officials. The most lasting legacy of this meeting was the European-style observatory in Beijing and a number of new maps of the world based on sixteenth- and seventeenth-century explorations. Unfortunately, by the nineteenth century these were all but forgotten, and the inadequacy of the geographical knowledge of Chinese officials in policy-making positions was soon all too apparent.

As in seventeenth-century France, the centralizing tendency of the government of China led to the exercise of considerable control in the cultural realm through patronage, monopoly, and licensing. As Manchus, the Kangxi, Yongzheng, and Qianlong emperors strove to validate their reigns by being patrons of the arts and aspiring to high levels of connoisseurship and cultivation of the best of the literati. As in the other absolutist realms, they not only set the tone in matters of aesthetics

Observatory in Beijing. One of the ways the Jesuits were able to gain favor at the imperial courts of two successive dynasties was through the new science of the West. Jesuit mathematicians, technical advisors, mapmakers, and astronomers found an eager reception among their Chinese counterparts, the fruits of which included armillary spheres pictured on the left and right foreground and the celestial globe in the center. The instruments were cast by Chinese artisans to the specifications of the Jesuit court mathematician Ferdinand Verbiest in the 1680s.

but also used mammoth cultural projects to direct the energies of scholars and officials into approved areas. At the same time, they sought to quash unorthodox views through lack of support and, more directly, through literary inquisitions. Kangxi, for example, sponsored the compilation of a huge dictionary of approved definitions of Chinese characters—still considered a primary reference work today. Under his direction, the commentaries and interpretations of Neo-Confucianism championed by the Song philosopher Zhu Xi became the approved versions. Kangxi's 13 sacred edicts, embodying maxims distilled in part from Zhu Xi's thought, became the official Qing creed from 1670 on. Anxious to legitimize themselves as culturally "Chinese," Kangxi and Qianlong sponsored huge encyclopedia projects. Qianlong's effort, at 36,000 volumes, was perhaps the most ambitious undertaking of its kind ever attempted.

Neo-Confucian Philosophy
While the urge to orthodoxy pervaded both dynasties, considerable intellectual ferment was also brewing beneath the surface of the official world. As we saw in Chapter 12, in the sixteenth century the first major new directions in Neo-Confucianism were being explored by Wang Yangming (1472–1529). While Wang's school remained a popular one, his emphasis on intuition, on a kind of enlightenment open to all, and, more and more, on a unity of opposites embracing different religious and philosophical traditions placed his more radical followers increasingly on the fringes of intellectual life. In addition, the Qing victory ushered in an era of soul-searching among Chinese literati and a wholesale questioning of the systems that had failed in the face of foreign conquest.

Two of the most important later figures in Qing philosophy were Huang Zongxi [Hwang Zung-SHEE] (1610–1695) and Gu Yanwu [Goo Yen-WOO] (1613–1682). Both men's lives spanned the Qing conquest, and like many of their fellow officials, both men concluded that the collapse of the old order was in part due to a retreat from practical politics and too much indulgence in the excesses of the radicals of the Wang Yangming school. With a group of like-minded scholars, they based themselves at the Donglin Academy, founded

---

Toward Proper Behavior: The Sacred Edict of Kangxi

1. Esteem most highly filial piety and brotherly submission, in order to give due importance to the social relations.
2. Behave with generosity toward your relatives, in order to illustrate harmony and benignity.
3. Cultivate peace and concord in your neighborhoods, in order to prevent quarrels and litigations.
4. Recognize the importance of husbandry and the culture of the mulberry tree (i.e., as food for silkworms), in order to ensure sufficient food and clothing.
5. Show that you prize moderation and economy, in order to prevent the lavish waste of your means.
6. Give weight to colleges and schools, in order to make correct the practice of the scholar.
7. Banish strange principles, in order to exalt the correct doctrine.
8. Lecture on the laws, in order to warn the ignorant and obstinate.
9. Demonstrate ceremony and deference in order to improve popular customs.
10. Labor diligently at your proper callings, in order to stabilize the will of the people.
11. Instruct sons and younger brothers, in order to prevent them from doing wrong.
12. Put a stop to false accusations, in order to preserve the honest and good.
13. Warn against sheltering deserters, in order to avoid being involved in their punishment.
14. Fully remit your taxes, in order to avoid being pressed for payment.
15. Unite in hundreds and tens [i.e., the baojia system] in order to end thefts and robbery.
16. Remove enmity and anger, in order to show the importance due to the person and life.

—Translated by Victor Mair, "Language and Ideology in the Written Popularizations of the Sacred Edict." In: *Popular Culture in Late Imperial China.* Edited by David Johnson, Andrew J. Nathan, and Evelyn S. Rawski, pp. 325–359. Berkeley: University of California Press, 1985.

Qianlong Emperor (1736–1795). One of the more interesting cross-cultural interactions during the early Qing period was that inspired by the Jesuit missionary, Giuseppe Castiglione (1688–1766). Trained as an architect and painter, Castiglione (Chinese name Lang Shining), arrived in Beijing in 1715 and served as court painter to emperors Kangxi, Yongzheng, and Qianlong. He influenced Chinese painters in the use of Western perspective and also absorbed Chinese techniques of portraiture and landscape painting. Here, the young Qianlong emperor is shown in his imperial regalia—including his robes of imperial yellow with dragon motifs—but with an authentically detailed face looking confidently full on toward the viewer.

in 1604. There, they devoted themselves to reconstituting an activist Confucianism based on rigorous self-cultivation and on remonstrating with officials and even the court. One outgrowth of this development, which shares interesting parallels with the critical textual scholarship of the European Renaissance, was the so-called Han learning movement. Convinced that centuries of Buddhism, religious Daoism, and Confucian commentaries of questionable value had diverted Confucianism from the intent of the sages, Han learning sought to recover the original meaning of classic Confucian works through exacting textual scholarship and systematic philology, or historical linguistics. The movement, though always on the fringe of approved official activities, peaked in the eighteenth century and successfully uncovered a number of fraudulent texts, while setting the tone for critical textual analysis during the remainder of the imperial era.

The Arts and Popular Culture   Although China's artists and writers clung to an amateur ideal of the "three excellences" of poetry, painting, and calligraphy, increasing official patronage ensured that approved schools and genres of art would be maintained at a consistent, if not inspired, level of quality. Here, the Qianlong emperor was perhaps the most influential force. Motivated in part by a lifelong quest to master the fine arts, he collected thousands of paintings—to which he added, in the tradition of Chinese connoisseurs, his own colophons—rare manuscripts, jade, porcelain, lacquerware, and other objets d'art. Because the force of imperial patronage was directed at conserving past models rather than creating new ones, the period is not noteworthy for stylistic innovation. One interesting exception to this, however, was the work of the Jesuit painter Giuseppe Castiglione (1688–1766). Castiglione's access to Qianlong resulted in a number of portraits of the emperor and court in a style that merged traditional Chinese subjects and media with Western perspective and technique. Evidence of this synthesis can also be seen in the Italianate and Versailles-inspired architecture at the emperor's Summer Palace just outside of Beijing.

Local Custom and Religion   Urban and village China were populated by storytellers, corner poets, spirit mediums, diviners, and a variety of other sorts of entertainers. While village social life revolved principally around clan and family functions, popular culture was also dominated by Daoism, Buddhism, and older traditions of local worship, all with their own temples, shrines, and festivals. The oldest beliefs of the countryside involving ancestral spirits, "hungry ghosts" (roaming spirits of those not properly cared for in death), fairies, and demons were enhanced over the centuries by a rich infusion of tales of Daoist adepts and "immortals," *yijing* diviners, Buddhist bodhisattvas, and underworld demons. Popular stories incorporating all of these, like *A Journey to the West* continued to be popular fare for the literate as well as for storytellers and street performers.

One of the richest glimpses into local society comes from Pu Songling's (1640–1715) *Strange Tales from the "Make-Do" Studio*, sometimes translated in English as *Strange Tales from a Chinese Studio*. Though considered a master stylist among his circle of friends, Pu never progressed beyond the provincial-level examinations and spent most of his life in genteel poverty. He traveled extensively, collecting folktales, accounts of local curiosities, and especially stories of the supernatural. Considered an unparalleled interpreter of the *pinghua* style of literary versions of popular tales, which had originated during the Song period, his stories are available to us today thanks to the foresight of his grandson, who published them in 1740. In Pu's world, "fox-fairies" appear as beautiful women, men are transformed into tigers, the young are duped into degenerate behavior—with predictable consequences—and crooked mediums and storytellers take advantage of the unwary.

The slow movement of popular literature away from the classical and toward more current, colloquial language would grow during the nineteenth century. Later, with an infusion of literature from the West and the westernizing Meiji culture of Japan, it would burst forth during the so-called literary renaissance at Peking University, from 1915 to 1921. This increasing emphasis on *baihua*, or "plain speech," would ultimately force the classical language aside. For most of the twentieth century, the great stylists of Chinese literature would be masters of the expressive power of colloquial language.

Ming and Qing China in Global Context   The trend we have noted among the Ming and Qing toward greater regulation and centralism in politics and diplomacy, economics, social institutions, and even literary pursuits may be seen more generally as part of a regional—even a global—trend during the seventeenth and eighteenth centuries. In the case of east and southeast Asia, governments emerging from internal or external conflict naturally sought to emphasize stability—even to the point of severely limiting foreign contact, banning foreign religions, and imposing new regulations aimed at limiting social mobility. As we saw in Chapter 17, many European governments, led by France under Louis XIV, came to adopt a governmental system of *absolutism*, in which the state attempts to eliminate disruptive tendencies among the nobility by creating professional armies and centralized bureaucracies as well as pursuing mercantilist economics. We have also seen this in the form of the fiscal–military state we noted among the Ottomans and Mughals. Now, however, we will examine one of the most extreme cases of these trends toward stabilizing the state, eliminating subversive influences and **hothousing** cultural traditions: that of Tokugawa Japan.

Hothousing: Carefully protecting and cultivating cultural traditions as one does with plants in a hothouse or greenhouse.

The Long War and Longer Peace: Japan, 1450–1750

As we recall from Chapter 13, the struggles by court factions in Japan's capital of Heian-Kyo (Kyoto) had ultimately resulted in the creation of the office of the *shogun*, the chief military officer of the realm, in 1185. Actual executive power gradually receded from the emperor's hands, however, into the shogun's; and by the fourteenth century the emperor had become in reality the puppet of his first officer. As we also saw, a fundamental shift occurred with the attempt by Emperor Go-Daigo to reassert his prerogatives in 1333. When his one-time supporter Ashikaga Takauji expelled him and set up his headquarters in the capital, power and prestige were pressed together once again, with profound political and cultural consequences for Japan. Courtly elegance insinuated itself into the brutal world of the warrior, while power, intrigue, and ultimately a prolonged and debilitating civil war would ravage the capital until it ended with Japan's unification.

The price for unification, however, was high. As we saw in the opening vignette of this chapter, the first of Japan's unifiers, Oda Nobunaga, was assassinated for his efforts; the invasions of Korea undertaken by his successor Hideyoshi resulted in the loss of hundreds of thousands of lives. The final custodians of Japanese unification, the Tokugawa family, created a system over several generations that they hoped would freeze Japan forever in a state of unity and seclusion. Yet over the two and a half centuries of the Tokugawa peace, forces were building that would allow Japan to vault into the modern world with unprecedented speed in the late nineteenth century.

The Struggle for Unification

As we have seen, the fundamental instability of the Ashikaga regime abetted continual contesting for the shogun's office among the more powerful *daimyo*, or regional warlords. In 1467, these factional battles finally erupted into a devastating civil war that would last off and on for more than a century. The opening phase of this struggle, the Onin War, lasted 10 years and devastated the city of Kyoto, while leaving the imperial court barely functional and the shogunate in tatters. With no real center of power, a bitter struggle of all against all among the daimyos continued into the 1570s.

Toyotomi Hideyoshi (1536–1598). Portraits of Japanese daimyo and shoguns tend to position them in similar ways, looking to the front left, with stiff, heavily starched official robes to reflect their austerity and dignity. In this 1601 portrait, done several years after his death, Hideyoshi is shown in a typical pose, with the signs of his adopted family and imperial crests around the canopy to denote his role of imperial guardian.

Oda Nobunaga and Toyotomi Hideyoshi   For the Japanese, the period was called *Gekokujo*, or "those below toppling those above." By the mid-sixteenth century, a handful of daimyo began the painful process of consolidating their power and securing allies. One important factor in deciding the outcome of these wars was the result of intrusion from the outside. By the 1540s, the first Portuguese and Spanish merchants and missionaries had arrived in southern Japan. One daimyo who was quick to use the newcomers and their improved small arms to his advantage was Oda Nobunaga, the son of a small landholder who had risen through the ranks to command. Oda employed newly converted Christian musketeers to secure the area around Kyoto and had largely succeeded in unifying the country when he was assassinated in 1582. His second in command, Hideyoshi, whom we met in the opening of this chapter, was another commoner who had risen through the ranks. Now he assumed Oda's mantle and systematically brought the remaining daimyo under his sway over the next nine years.

Hideyoshi viewed a foreign adventure at this point as an excellent way to cement the loyalties of the newly subdued daimyo. In addition, the army he had put together—battle-hardened, well trained, with perhaps the largest number of guns of any force in the world at the time—might prove dangerous to disband. Hence, as early as 1586 he announced his grandiose plans to conquer China itself. Thus, in 1592 he set out with a massive expeditionary force, which at its peak numbered over 200,000 men. Though his supply lines were harassed unmercifully by the Korean naval forces in their well-armored "turtle ships," the Japanese made good progress up the peninsula until massive Chinese counterattacks slowly eroded their gains and decimated large stretches of Korea.

Hideyoshi's adventure ended when he turned homeward to Japan with the remnants of his army in 1596. His stature as a commander and force of personality kept

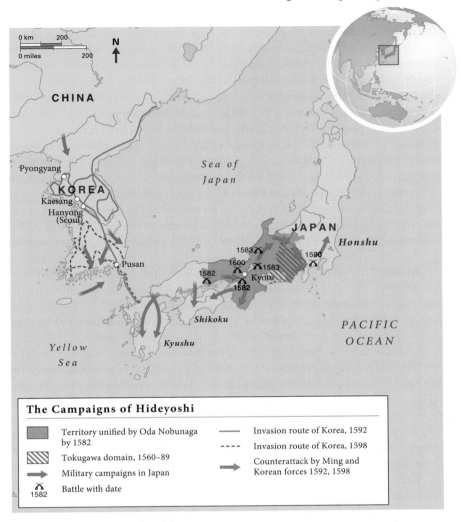

MAP 21.5 **The Campaigns of Hideyoshi.**

his coalition of daimyo together until his death during his second Korean campaign in 1598. The coalition then broke in two, and a civil war began between Tokugawa Ieyasu, charismatic leader of the eastern coalition of daimyos, and their western counterparts. In the fall of 1600, the back of the western coalition was broken by the Tokugawa victory at the Battle of Sekigahara, near Kyoto. Ieyasu, who claimed to be a descendant of the Minamoto clan, the original shoguns, laid claim to the office and was officially invested with it in 1603. His accession marked the beginning of Japan's most peaceful, most secluded, and perhaps most thoroughly regulated and policed interval in its long history. Breaking precedent, the Tokugawas would create a hereditary shogunate, organized along Chinese Neo-Confucian models of morality and government, that would last until 1867 (see Map 21.5).

The Tokugawa *Bakufu* to 1750

The realm that Tokugawa Ieyasu (1542–1616) had won at the Battle of Sekigahara was one that had been scarred by seemingly endless warfare and social disruption.

The daimyo and samurai, their armies as large as hundreds of thousands of soldiers in some cases, employed some of the most advanced military technology in the world; but their depredations had broken old loyalties and alliances. The intrusion of European missionaries and merchants, along with their converts and agents, contributed to the social ferment. The brief interlude of unity that had supported Hideyoshi's continental adventures had thoroughly unraveled and, indeed, had been a contributing cause of the civil war that had brought Ieyasu to power.

Ieyasu's assumption of the shogunate in 1603 thus began a process of unparalleled centralization and stabilization in Japan that would last until 1867. Initially, however, seclusion did not figure among its principles. In fact, under the direction of European advisors, Ieyasu and his son Hidetada (1579–1632) laid plans to build a powerful naval and merchant fleet during their first decade of rule. The most pressing order of business, however, was to erect a system within which to place all the daimyo that would at once reward the loyal and keep a watchful eye on the defeated.

"Tent Government"   The system devised under the Tokugawa *bakufu* ("tent government," referring to the shogun's official status as the emperor's mobile deputy) was called *sankin kotai*, the "rule of alternate attendance." An inner ring of daimyo holdings was annexed by the Tokugawa family and administered by their retainers. All daimyo were then given either *fudai*, or "inner" domains, if they had been allies of the Tokugawa or *tozama*, "outer" domains, if they had ultimately surrendered to Ieyasu's eastern coalition. The shogunate placed its new headquarters in the Tokugawa castle in Edo, the future city of Tokyo. In order to ensure their loyalty, all outer daimyo were required to reside in the capital in alternate years and return to their domains during the off years. Members of their families were required to stay as permanent hostages in Edo. Daimyo were also required to bring their most important retainers and their households with them during their stays. Almost from the beginning, therefore, the main roads to Edo, most famously the Tokaido, were the scene of constant daimyo processions. Like the great pilgrimage routes of Islam, Buddhism, and Christianity, these roads spurred enormous commerce and the creation of an array of services to meet the needs of the constant traffic. (And

The Tokaido Road. This scroll map, from about 1700 and painted in watercolor, shows an aerial view of the country along the route of the most famous highway in Japan—the Tokaido. Fishing villages dot the coast and Mt. Fuji looms in the background.

like the French nobility a few decades later at Versailles, the daimyo found both their power and their purses increasingly depleted).

Freezing Society   In turning the office of shogun over to his son Hidetada in 1605, Ieyasu made it legally hereditary for the first time. With the possibility of revolt always just under the surface, Ieyasu stayed on as regent and pursued further measures to enhance the stability of the regime. Under his grandson, Iemitsu (1604–1651), most of the characteristic Tokugawa policies in this regard became institutionalized. The shogunate declared that, like the jati system in India, the members of the officially recognized classes in Japan—daimyo, samurai, peasants, artisans, merchants—and their descendants would be required to stay in those classes forever. The Tokugawa adopted Neo-Confucianism as the governing ideology, thus joining the commonwealth of Confucian "religious civilizations" in the region; and its long-established precepts of filial piety, models of ethical behavior, and unswerving loyalty to the government were incorporated into the new law codes.

Significant differences, however, separated the practice of this system in Japan from similar, concurrent systems in China, Korea, and Vietnam. In China and Vietnam, a civil service had long been in place, complete with a graded system of examinations from which the best candidates would be drawn for duty. The situation in Japan was closer to that of Korea, in which the *Yangban* were already a hereditary aristocracy in the countryside and so monopolized the official classes. Japan, though, differed even further because the samurai and daimyo were now not just a hereditary class of officials but a military aristocracy as well. Not only was the low position traditionally given the military in Chinese Confucianism totally reversed, but the daimyo and samurai had absolute, unquestioned power of life and death over all commoners. Like their counterparts in China, they were expected to have mastered the classics and the refined arts of painting, poetry, and calligraphy. But official reports

---

A Code for Samurai Behavior: The Laws Governing Military Houses, 1618

1. The arts of peace and war, including archery and horsemanship, should be pursued single-mindedly.
2. Drinking parties and wanton revelry should be avoided.
3. Offenders against the law should not be harbored or hidden in any domain.
4. Great Lords [daimyo], the lesser lords, and officials should immediately expel from their domains any among their retainers or henchmen who have been charged with treason or murder.
5. Henceforth no outsider, none but the inhabitants of a particular domain, shall be permitted to reside in that domain.
6. Whenever it is intended to make repairs on a castle of one of the feudal domains, the [shogunate] authorities should be notified. The construction of any new castles is to be halted and stringently prohibited.
7. Immediate report should be made of innovations which are being planned or of factional conspiracies being formed in neighboring domains.
8. Do not enter into marriage privately [i.e., without notifying the shogunate authorities].
9. Visits of the daimyo to the capital are to be in accordance with regulations. . . . Daimyo should not be accompanied by a large number of soldiers. Twenty horsemen shall be the maximum escort of daimyo with an income of from one million to two hundred thousand *koku* of rice. For those with an income of one hundred thousand *koku* or less, the escort should be proportionate to their income. On official missions, however, they may be accompanied by an escort proportionate to their rank.
10. Restrictions on the type and quality of dress to be worn should not be transgressed.
11. Persons without rank shall not ride in palanquins [sedan chairs].
12. The samurai of the various domains shall lead a frugal and simple life.
13. The lords of the domains should select officials with a capacity for public administration.

The purport of the foregoing should be conscientiously observed.

—adapted from *Bukke Shohatto (Laws Governing Military Households). Dai Nihon shiryo (Chronological Sourcebooks of Japanese History)*, vol. 12, pt. 22, pp. 19–20. In: William T. DeBary, et al., *Sources of Japanese Tradition*, vol. 1, pp. 327–329. New York: Columbia University Press, 1964.

and popular literature are full of accounts of samurai cutting down hapless peasants who failed to bow quickly enough to daimyo processions or who committed other infractions, no matter how trivial.

Giving Up the Gun   In order to ensure that the samurai class would be free from any serious challenge, the government required them to practice the time-honored skills of swordsmanship, archery, and other forms of individual martial arts. But the rapid development of firearms and their pervasive presence in the realm remained a threat to any class whose skills were built entirely around hand-to-hand combat. Thus, in a way perhaps unique among the world's nations, the Tokugawa literally "gave up the gun." Tokugawa police conducted searches for forbidden weapons among commoners and destroyed almost the entire nation's stock of firearms. A few museum pieces were kept as curiosities, as were the bronze cannon in some of the Tokugawa seaside forts. Thus, weapons that had been among the most advanced in the world when they were cast in the 1600s were the ones that confronted the first foreign ships nearly 250 years later in 1853.

As the shogunate strove to impose peace on the daimyo and bring stability to the populace, it became increasingly anxious to weed out disruptive influences. In addition to the unsettling potential of the country's guns, therefore, they began to restrict the movements of foreigners, particularly missionaries. From the earliest days of European arrivals in Japan, subjects of competing countries and religions had brought their quarrels with them, often involving Japanese as allies or objects of intrigue. The influence of the missionaries on the growing numbers of Japanese Christians—perhaps 200,000 by the 1630s—was especially worrisome to those intent on firmly establishing Neo-Confucian beliefs and rituals among the commoners. Moreover, the bitter duel between Catholic and Protestant missionaries and merchants carried its own set of problems for social stability, especially in the ports, where the majority of such activities tended to take place.

Christian Martyrs. Beginning in 1617, and culminating in the suppression of a rebellion by impoverished Christian peasants in 1637–1638, missionaries and their converts to the foreign faith were brutally persecuted by the Tokugawa. Wholesale massacres and even crucifixions along the main roads were not uncommon, or as in this engraving, hanging criminals—in this case, Jesuits—upside down and setting them on fire.

Tokugawa Seclusion   Ultimately, therefore, missionaries were ordered to leave the country, followed by their merchants. The English and Spanish withdrew in the 1620s, while the Portuguese stayed until 1639. Ultimately, only the Dutch, Koreans, and Chinese were allowed to remain, in small, controlled numbers and subject to the pleasure of the shogunate. Further, in 1635 it was ruled that Japanese would be forbidden to leave the islands and that no oceangoing ships were to be built. Any Japanese who left would be considered traitors and executed upon return. Like the Canton system later in Qing China, foreign merchants would be permitted only in designated areas in port cities and could not bring their families with them. As the only Europeans permitted to stay, the Dutch were chosen because they appeared to be the least affected by the religious bickering that characterized their European counterparts. They were, however, restricted to a tiny island called Dejima (also known as Deshima) built on a landfill in Nagasaki harbor. In return for the privilege, they were required to make yearly reports in person to the shogun's ministers on world events. Over time, the collections of these reports found a small but willing readership among educated and cultured Japanese. This "Dutch learning" and the accounts of Chinese and Korean observers formed the basis of the Japanese view of the outside

Dutch Ships in Nagasaki Harbor, 1764. This detail from a 1764 map shows Dutch and Japanese ships in Nagasaki harbor. The Japanese ships are dwarfed by the much larger Dutch sailing vessels. The small fan-shaped area connected to the town of Nagasaki was the only place where the Dutch were allowed to disembark and trade. They were forbidden to cross the causeway into the city itself.

world for over two centuries. Like European learning in Korea and Vietnam, it also provided useful examples for reformers to use in critiquing Neo-Confucian society.

Trampling the Crucifix   Much less tolerance was meted out to Japan's Christian community. Dissatisfaction with the new Tokugawa strictures provoked a rebellion at Shimabara just outside Nagasaki in 1637 by Christian converts and disaffected samurai. As the revolt was suppressed, many of those facing the prospect of capture and execution by the Tokugawa flung themselves into the volcanic hot springs nearby. Those who were captured were subjected to what their captors understood to be appropriate European-style punishment: Instead of being burned at the stake, they were clustered together and roasted to death inside a wide ring of fire. Subsequently, remaining missionaries were sometimes crucified upside down, while suspected converts were given an opportunity to "trample the crucifix" to show they had discarded the new faith. Those who refused to convert back to approved faiths were imprisoned or executed. In the end, perhaps 37,000 people were killed. For all their attempts at suppressing the religion, however, tens of thousands continued to practice in secret until Christianity was declared legal again during the reign of Emperor Meiji (r. 1867–1912). Though foreign ships would occasionally attempt to call at Japanese ports, by the eighteenth century Europeans generally steered clear of the islands. As we will see in Chapter 24, however, by the middle decade of the nineteenth century the opening of more ports in China for trade, the growth of the whaling industry, and the quest for gold in California would all conspire to change this situation forever.

Growth and Stagnation: Economy and Society

While a number of the processes begun under earlier shogunates continued during the seventeenth and eighteenth centuries, their pace quickened immensely. Perhaps most dramatically, by 1750, Japan had become the most urbanized society on earth.

Edo itself reached a million people, making it arguably the world's largest city. Osaka and Kyoto were both approaching 400,000, and perhaps as much as 10 percent of Japan's population lived in cities with populations above 10,000 (see Map 21.6). In a way, such explosive growth is even more remarkable given that the Tokugawa placed strict curbs on travel within their realms. Commoners, for example, were not to leave their home districts without permission from the local authorities. On the other hand, as we have seen, the law of alternate attendance ensured an immense and growing traffic in and out of the major cities along the major routes into Edo. The vast array of services required to support that traffic aided urban and suburban growth and had the effect of spreading the wealth down to the urban merchants, artisans, entertainers, bathhouse proprietors, and even refuse collectors.

Population, Food, and Commerce   Perhaps a more direct cause of this urbanization may be found in the growth of the population as a whole. By various estimates, Japan may have had as many as 33 million people in 1720. The efficiency of small-scale, intensive rice and vegetable farming, aided by easy-to-operate, simple machines such as the Chinese-style "climbing stair" or "dragon chain" pump made

MAP 21.6 Urban Population and Road Major Transport Routes in Japan, ca. 1800.

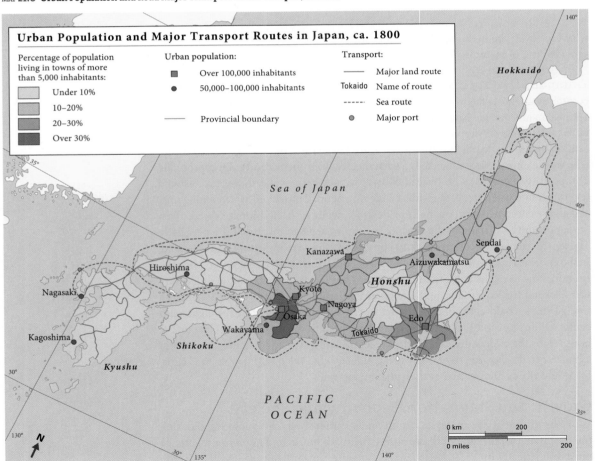

Japanese agriculture the most efficient in the preindustrial world. Such efficiencies would create one of the most densely populated rural landscapes in the world even into the twentieth century.

As we have noted, various Tokugawa policies aimed at stabilizing the country politically and socially had the unanticipated effect of spurring the economy. A number of factors contributed to this in addition to the forced movement of the daimyo and their retinues in alternate years. The Tokugawa tax structure set quotas in rice for each village, rather than for individuals and left the individual daimyos responsible for remitting these to the capital. Thus, an immense traffic in bulk rice further spurred the carrying trade along the roads and in the coastal waters. In addition to guaranteeing provisions for the cities, the need to convert rice to cash for the treasury contributed greatly to building a banking and credit infrastructure. Indeed, the practice of merchant bankers advancing credit to wholesalers against anticipated rice crops created what some scholars have called an early kind of futures market. The progress of the famous Mitsui *zaibatsu*, or cartel, of the nineteenth and twentieth centuries followed such a route, starting in 1670 as dry goods merchants and gradually moving into the position of bankers for the shogunate.

The tastes of the three largest cities—Edo, with its high concentration of the wealthy and well-connected; Kyoto, with its large retinue of the imperial household; and Osaka, the chief port—created a huge demand for ever more sophisticated consumer goods and services. Such enterprises as sake brewing, wholesaling dried and prepared foods, running bathhouses, and managing large studios of artisans all became booming businesses. Even the import and export trades, slowed to a relative trickle by government regulations, proved quite lucrative for the few engaged in them. Books, porcelains, lacquerware, and objets d'art were exchanged for Japanese hard currency. Indeed, the vibrancy of Japanese urban life and a burgeoning middle class created what scholars have sometimes called the "democratization of taste." That is, what was once the strict province of the court, daimyo, and samurai was now widely available to anyone who had the money and interest to afford it. Moreover, the new moneyed classes were also creating new directions in the arts and entertainment.

Woodblock Print of the Fish Market at the East Side of Nihonbashi (The Bridge of Japan). The Tokugawa period, with its long interlude of peace and prosperity, was Japan's first great age of urban life. The constant traffic of daimyo progressions along the main roads and the large coasting trade along the Inland Sea ensured a growing middle class of artisans, tradespeople, and merchants. The capital, Edo, had ballooned to over a million people on the eve of the American intrusion; and the bustle of the capital is illustrated in this panel depicting a famous fish market.

Rural Transformations   Life in rural areas underwent certain changes as well. As they had with the military houses, the Tokugawa promulgated Neo-Confucian rules for the comportment of families and their individual members. Like parish churches in Europe, each local Buddhist temple was to keep the registers of the villagers in its district. Weddings, funerals, travel, rents, taxes, and so forth were subject to official permission through either the village headman or the samurai holding a position equivalent to a magistrate. Within these strictures, however, and subject to the hereditary occupation laws, families, clans, and villages were relatively autonomous.

This was especially true within rural families, where men, women, and children commonly worked together on their plots. While the "inner domain," so central to Neo-Confucian thought as the strict province of women, retained a good deal of that character, there were also any number of areas that served to mitigate it. Men, for example, routinely helped in the everyday tasks of childrearing. As late as the 1860s, foreign observers reported watching rural groups of men minding infants while their wives were engaged in some collective task. Women in cities and larger villages routinely ran businesses, especially those involved in entertainment. Indeed, the women of the famous geisha houses, owned and run by women, were renowned for their skills, education, wit, and refinement. Even on a more humble level, women ran bathhouses, taverns, restaurants, and retail establishments of all sorts. Interestingly, by the eighteenth century, merchants increasingly utilized the spinning and weaving talents of rural and semirural women in parceling out the various steps in textile manufacturing to them—a Japanese version of the English "putting out system" (Chapter 23).

The Samurai in Peacetime   As time went by, the position of the samurai in rural society changed as well. Though expected to hone his military skills, his role as an official and Neo-Confucian role model gradually became paramount. Samurai existed on stipends, either directly from the Tokugawa or from their local daimyo. These, however, were no guarantee of prosperity and by the later eighteenth century the samurai living in genteel poverty had become something of a popular stereotype. In many areas, they functioned as schoolmasters and founded village academies in the local temples for the teaching of practical literacy and correct moral behavior. By the mid-nineteenth century Japan may have had the world's highest level of functional literacy. As in Korea, this proved important in popularizing new crops or agricultural techniques.

By the middle of the eighteenth century there were signs of tension among the aims of the government in ensuring peace and stability, the dynamism of the internal economy, and the boom in population. Like China a century later, some scholars contend that Japan had approached the limit of the ability of the land to support its people. In fact, Japan's population remained remarkably steady from the middle of the eighteenth century to the latter nineteenth. Repeated signs of creeping rural impoverishment and social unrest manifested themselves, however, and were often noted by commentators. Inflation in commodity prices ran ahead of efforts to increase domain revenues, squeezing those on fixed incomes and stipends. Efforts to keep rural families small enough to subsist on their plots led to an increasing frequency of infanticide. Compounding such problems were large-scale famines in 1782 and 1830. By the early nineteenth century, there was an increasing perception that the government was gradually losing its ability to care for the populace.

Hothousing "Japaneseness": Culture, Science, and Intellectual Life

As with so many elements of Japanese cultural history, existing genres of art—major styles of painting, poetry, and calligraphy—continued to flourish among the daimyo and samurai, while exerting an increasing pull on the tastes of the new middle classes. Indeed, Zen-influenced **monochrome** painting, the ideals of the tea ceremony championed by Sen Rikyu, the austere Noh theater, and the abstract principles of interior design and landscape gardening were carefully preserved and popularized until they became universally recognized as "Japanese."

Monochrome: Single color; in east Asian painting, a very austere style popular in the fourteenth and fifteenth centuries, particularly among Zen-influenced artists.

New Theater Traditions   Traditional cultural elements coexisted with new forms, with some adapting aspects of these earlier arts and others conceived as mass entertainment. Among the former was the development of *bunraku*, the elaborate puppet theater still popular in Japan today. Bunraku puppets, perhaps one-third life size, generally took three puppeteers to manipulate. Their highly facile movements and facial expressions staged against a black backdrop to conceal the actions of their handlers readily allowed the audience to suspend disbelief and proved a highly effective way to popularize the older Noh plays. But renowned playwrights soon wrote special works for these theaters as well. The most revered was Chikamatsu Monzaemon [Chick-ah-MAT-soo Mon-ZAE-mon] (1653–1724), who skillfully transferred the tragically noble sentiments of the best Noh works into contemporary themes. The fatal tension between love and social obligation, for example, made his *Love Suicide at Sonezaki* wildly popular with Edo audiences. His most famous work *The Forty-Seven Ronin*, written in 1706, is based on a 1703 incident in which the daimyo of 47 samurai was killed by a political opponent, leaving them as *ronin*—masterless. Out of loyalty to their dead daimyo the ronin kill his assassin in full knowledge that their lives will then be forfeit to the authorities, a price they then stoically go on to pay.

> **Emotional Release Through Poetry: "Old Battlefield"**
>
> Old battlefield, fresh with spring flowers again
> All that is left of the dream
> Of twice ten-thousand warriors slain.
>
> —Translated by C. H. Page in *Classic Haiku: An Anthology of Poems by Basho and His Followers*. Asataro Miyamori, ed. and trans. (Tokyo: Maruzen Co. Ltd., 1932) Dover reprint p. 80

Originally written for bunraku, *The Forty-Seven Ronin* was adapted a few decades later as a work for *kabuki*, the other great mass entertainment art of Tokugawa Japan. Originally a satirical and explicitly bawdy form of theater, the government banned women from appearing in kabuki, hoping to sever its association with prostitution. Female impersonators as actors continued its risqué reputation, however, while more serious works also drew immense crowds to the pleasure districts, to which the theaters were by law segregated. Kabuki remained by far the most popular Japanese mass entertainment, and interestingly, given the medium's off-color reputation, *The Forty-Seven Ronin* remained the most frequently performed play throughout the Tokugawa period.

The era also marked the golden age of the powerfully brief poetic form of *haiku*, the most famous practitioner of which was the renowned Matsuo Basho (1644–1694). As a poet he used a dozen pen names; he took "Basho" from the banana plant he especially liked in his yard. In poems like "Old Battlefield" the 17-syllable couplets compressed unbearable emotion and release in a way that has made them a treasured form in Japan and, more recently, in much of the world.

Two Courtesans. During the late seventeenth century, the new genre of *ukiyo-e*, "pictures of the floating world," developed and remained popular through the nineteenth century. Finely wrought woodblock prints in both monochrome and color, their name comes from the pleasure districts whose people and scenes were favorite subjects. This work is from a series by the noted artist Kitagawa Utamaro (ca. 1753–1806) on famous courtesans of "the Southern District," part of the Shinagawa section of Edo.

The visual arts found new forms of expression through the widespread use of fine woodblock printing, which allowed popular works to be widely duplicated. The new genre was called *ukiyo-e*, "pictures of the floating world," a reference to the pleasure quarters on the edge of the cities that furnished many of its subjects. Though largely scorned by the upper classes, it remained the most popular form of advertising, portraiture, and news distribution until the end of the nineteenth century, when it began to be supplanted by photography. During Tokugawa times, one of the most famous practitioners of the art was Kitagawa Utamaro (1753–1806), whose studies of women became forever associated with Japanese perceptions of female beauty. In the works of Katsushika Hokusai (1760–1849) and Ando Hiroshige (1797–1858) scenes like Hokusai's *Thirty-Six Views of Mt. Fuji*, or, like Utamaro's work, gentle snowfalls on temples, formed many of the first popular images that nineteenth-century Westerners had of Japan.

While Neo-Confucianism occupied a central place as the Tokugawa's governing orthodoxy, the eighteenth and nineteenth centuries proved to be a fertile time for critical thought both within and without the approved avenues of discussion. On the one hand, scholars such as Hirata Atsutane (1776–1843) and Honda Toshiaki (1744–1821) managed to convey their admiration for "Dutch learning," the information about the events in the outside world contained in reports to the shogun made by the representatives of the Dutch East India Company, while still managing to acknowledge the primacy of Japan. Honda, in particular, advocated Japanese expansion along the lines of what he understood to be the policies of the European countries with regard to mercantilism, colonial possessions, and the pursuit of science in his "Secret Plan for Managing the Country." His late eighteenth-century colleague, Sato Nobuhiro (1769–1850), expressed similar sentiments in his "Confidential Memoir on Social Control."

On the other hand, some writers felt that Japan's problems lay in the stifling of its true national character by the Chinese-influenced Neo-Confucian institutions of the Tokugawa. Starting as early as the late seventeenth century, this "national learning" movement, whose most famous exponent was Motoori Norinaga (1730–1801), emphasized Japan's unique governmental tradition of a single imperial line—later an important part of the Meiji-era concept of *kokutai*, or "national polity"—and advocated a return to the earliest Japanese histories, the *Kojiki* and *Nihongi*.

Perhaps most influential of all was the outwardly mainstream Mito school. Formed by a branch of the Tokugawa family and hewing to the Neo-Confucian orthodoxy of the shogunate, writers like Aizawa Seishisai (1782–1863) demanded that the government take a firm stand against any foreign intrusion. Failure to do so would be to surrender the mandate of the shogunate as the emperor's military and political arm. In the turmoil following the American Commodore Matthew Perry's visits in the nineteenth century and the opening of the first treaty ports, the Mito scholars would be at the forefront of advocating the immediate expulsion of the foreigners by any means necessary.

Putting It All Together

During the late Ming and early Qing periods, imperial China achieved social and political stability and developed the world's largest economy. Yet, by the second part of the eighteenth century, internal problems were already germinating that would come to the surface in succeeding decades. In the following century, these initial cracks in the empire's structure would continue to grow and have a profound impact on China's fortunes.

The arrival of large numbers of foreign traders who brought with them the new technologies of the first scientific–industrial societies, combined with China's profound self-confidence in its own culture and institutions, added more pressure to an already volatile internal situation and ultimately created an unprecedented challenge for China. Over the coming decades, Chinese expectations of being able to civilize and assimilate all comers would dissolve, along with the hope that a renewed faithfulness to Confucian fundamentals would produce the leaders necessary to navigate such perilous times. But at the halfway mark of the eighteenth century, the Chinese still expected that they would successfully regulate the "inner" and "outer" domains of their empire and keep pernicious foreign influences at arm's length.

Ravaged by a century of warfare and foreign intrusion, Japan also sought to regulate its inner and outer domains and minimize outside influences. As with China, however, the stability perfected by the Tokugawa shogunate in the seventeenth and eighteenth centuries would be increasingly threatened in the nineteenth by the growing commercial power of the Europeans and Americans. Before the nineteenth

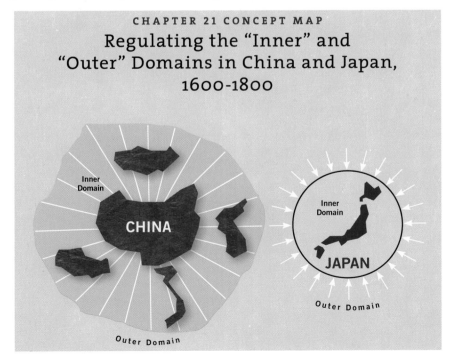

CHAPTER 21 CONCEPT MAP

Regulating the "Inner" and "Outer" Domains in China and Japan, 1600-1800

Inner Domain

CHINA

Outer Domain

Inner Domain

JAPAN

Outer Domain

century was finished, China would be rent by the bloodiest civil war in human history, while Japan would experience its own civil war and, in its aftermath, install a unified government under an emperor for the first time since the twelfth century. In the final years of the nineteenth century, Japan would once again invade Korea to attack China—this time with very different results. In the process, the relationship of more than two millennia between the two countries would be altered forever (see Concept Map).

Review and Respond

1. What innovations did the Qing bring to the governance of China?

2. What advantages did the late Ming "single-whip" tax system bring to those who had to pay it? What disadvantages did it bring?

3. Why were the Qing able to subdue the Ming in the 1640s?

4. What reasons best explain the actions of the Tokugawa in establishing a policy of seclusion?

5. Were the policies of the Qing and Tokugawa successful in keeping their realms safe and stable?

▶ For additional resources, including maps, primary sources, visuals, and quizzes, please go to www.oup.com/us/vonsivers. Please see the Further Resources section at the back of the book for additional readings and suggested websites.

Thinking Through Patterns

▶ **Why did late Ming and early Qing China look inward after such a successful period of overseas exploration?**

In some respects the problem is similar to that faced by planners for defense spending in nations today: Why maintain huge, expensive systems when there are no enemies against which to use them? While the commercial prospects for China's fleets grew in prominence, maritime trade was simply not essential to the Chinese economy at that point. Moreover, urgent defense preparations were needed in the overland north against the resurgent Mongols. It is important to remember that the discontinuing of the fleets seems like a mistake in hindsight because of what happened to China hundreds of years later due to a lack of adequate naval defenses. At the time, however, these measures seemed both rational and appropriate to the Chinese and outside observers.

One almost universal pattern of world history among agrarian states is that their governments adopt policies aimed at promoting social stability. The reason for this is that, in short, nearly everything depends on having reliable harvests. Given the agricultural techniques and technology of preindustrial societies, the majority of the population must be engaged in food production to ensure sufficient surpluses to feed the nonproducing classes. If such a society places a premium on change and social mobility, it risks chronic manpower shortages and insufficient harvests. Thus, social classes—whether in feudal Europe, India, China, or Japan—are carefully delineated and the state directs its policies toward eliminating social upheaval.

▶ **How do the goals of social stability drive the policies of agrarian states? How does the history of China and Japan in this period show these policies in action?**

▶ **In what ways did contact with the maritime states of Europe alter the patterns of trade and politics in east Asia?**

In both China and Japan, these connections resulted in severe restrictions regarding the regulation of maritime trade: the Canton system in China and the seclusion policies of the Tokugawa in Japan. Earlier, the Chinese emperor had welcomed Jesuit missionaries for their expertise in mathematics and science and even considered conversion to Catholicism. But the backlash against "subversive" influence induced the Qing to drive Christianity underground. In Japan such contact had earlier injected European influences into Japan's civil wars, and the reaction against this was Tokugawa seclusion.

The fundamental difference was that Japan was a military society, which adopted the forms and structures of Neo-Confucianism to make daimyo and samurai into officials. They therefore were expected to maintain this civil role as bureaucrats but also stand ready to fight if need be. The low esteem in which the military was held in China was just the opposite of that of the martial elites of Japan. Another key difference was that officials in China were selected on the basis of competitive examinations, thus creating some social mobility. In Japan, the social classes were frozen and no exams were offered for potential officials.

▶ **How did Neo-Confucianism in China differ from that of Tokugawa Japan?**

PART FIVE

The Origins of Modernity

1750–1900

What we have termed "modernity" in this section may be said to have begun roughly around 1800 in western Europe and may be characterized as the product of what historian Eric Hobsbawm (b. 1917) called "the twin revolutions" of the late eighteenth century. One of these was the new political landscape brought into being by the trio of constitutional revolutions in North America, France, and Haiti, which dealt a telling blow to the concept of traditional monarchial rule by divine right and introduced popular sovereignty as the new justification for political power. The other was the Industrial Revolution, which began in England with the introduction of steam-driven, machine-produced textiles and other goods. Scientific–industrial modernity, with its developing constellation of values marked by experimentation, political, social, and technological progress, social mobility, and secularism, was thus set on a path to displace the older agrarian–urban order of religious civilizations that had been characterized by hierarchy, natural order, and divinely ordained law and morality. This transition is, in fact, still ongoing. Although the old agrarian–urban *political* order has been almost universally superseded, its values still contend with those of modernity in many parts of the world today.

The Origins of Modernity

The political and industrial revolutions that define modernity have intellectual roots reaching back to the 1500s. As scholars increasingly recognize, the discovery of the Americas, as well as the Copernican revolution in astronomy, provided powerful incentives for the introduction of new patterns of science and political philosophy. For more than two centuries, however, these ideas remained the province of only a small intellectual elite.

Political and Industrial Revolutions

By the 1700s, however, adherents of the new science and philosophy among urban, educated administrators and professionals in northwestern Europe had grown in numbers and began to become influential in society. In Britain, the *theory* of the social contract entered into the *practice* of constitutionalism following the Glorious Revolution of 1688. Both were vastly expanded by thinkers during the

1765
James Watt Perfects
the Steam Engine

1776–1804
American, French,
and Haitian
Revolutions

1798–1801
Napoleon's Occupation
of Egypt

1815
Congress of
Vienna

1832
Greece Wins
Independence from
the Ottomans

1839–1876
Tanzimat
Reforms in
the Ottoman
Empire

1848
Karl Marx and Friedrich
Engels Publish *The
Communist Manifesto*

1853–1854
Commodore Perry Opens
Trade and Diplomatic
Relations with Japan

eighteenth-century Enlightenment and helped to inspire the American, French, and Haitian Revolutions. These were narrow revolutions in the sense of ending monarchial–aristocratic rule—courageous revolts during still deeply religious times. Nonetheless, this era set human emancipation from the confining traditions of the past as a goal to be achieved. And in the case of Haiti, the idea that "all men are created equal" emblazoned earlier in the American Declaration of Independence and the French Declaration of the Rights of Man, formed the basis of a successful slave rebellion against revolutionary France itself.

The Industrial Revolution, beginning around 1800 in Great Britain, was a socially transformative and self-sustaining sequence of technical inventions and commercial applications. Britain industrialized during the first half of the 1800s through steam-driven iron foundries, textile factories, overland transportation, and ocean travel. In a second wave, Germany and the United States industrialized, with the introduction of chemicals, electricity, and motorcars into the factory system. The two waves of industrialization created an unequal class system, with a citizenry composed of both landed aristocrats—fading in power as the old agrarian–urban order decayed—and a new, dynamic urban middle class amassing political and economic power. But the equally new phenomenon of the industrial working class, bidding for political, social, and economic equality, added a volatile social factor to the mix as its members sought to make good on the promises of the constitutional revolutions.

Resistance and Adaptation to the Western Challenge

The twin political–industrial revolutions in Europe were a major factor in the mid-nineteenth-century expansion of the existing seaborne European empires in Asia and Africa. Postrevolutionary France renewed its competition with Britain, and both later used "gunboat diplomacy" to establish favorable commercial conditions and trade outposts. From here, these two and other European nations proceeded to compete in imperial conquests for what they now considered to be strategically important territories across the globe.

The traditional agrarian and religious empires and states of Asia and Africa responded to the increasingly superior military power of the European maritime empires and the United States during the 1800s with both resistance and adaptation. Resisting with traditional armies and weapons, however, became more difficult as the 1800s unfolded and the industrial development of the West spawned new and sophisticated weaponry. "Adaptation," as it occurred under the duress of imperialism, was a creative process in which the states under challenge selected generic elements from the constitutional and industrial revolutions that had made the West powerful and attempted to harmonize them with their inherited traditions.

Thinking Like a World Historian

▶ What were the origins of the "twin revolutions" of the late eighteenth century? How did they combine to create what we call "modernity"?

▶ Why were the values of scientific–industrial society opposed to the older agrarian–urban order? Why does this conflict still persist in many parts of the world today?

▶ What patterns of resistance and adaptation characterized the responses of traditional agrarian and religious empires to European military power and expansion?

1857
Sepoy Mutiny, India

1868–1912
Reign of Emperor Meiji, Japan

1878–1885
Independence of Serbia, Montenegro, Rumania, and Bulgaria

1888
End of Slavery, Brazil

1894–1895
Sino-Japanese War

1904–1905
Russo-Japanese War

1861
Emancipation of Serfs in Russian Empire

1869
Opening of Suez Canal

1884
Hiram Maxim Invents the First Fully Automatic Machine Gun

1900
Boxer Rebellion and Anti-Foreign War

1905
Albert Einstein Publishes Theory of Relativity

1908
Young Turks Rise to Power in Ottoman Empire

Chapter 22

1750-1871

Nation-States and Patterns of Culture in Europe and North America

THE NORTH ATLANTIC, 1750-1900

In a diary entry dated June 4, 1785, George Washington, the hero of the American War for Independence and future first president of the United States, noted that "the celebrated Mrs. Macauly [sic] Graham & Mr. Graham her Husband . . . arrived here." Washington seems to have thoroughly enjoyed the visit, for after their departure he wrote to his friend Richard Henry Lee to express his appreciation for his letter of introduction to this distinguished

Seeing Patterns

▶ How did the pattern of constitutional nationalism, emerging from the American and French Revolutions, affect the course of events in the Western world during the first half of the nineteenth century?

▶ In what ways did ethnolinguistic nationalism differ from constitutional nationalism, and what was its influence on the formation of nation-states in the second half of the nineteenth century?

▶ What were the reactions among thinkers and artists to the developing pattern of nation-state formation? How did they define the intellectual–artistic movements of romanticism and realism?

Constitutional Nationalism in Action, London 1831. This colored lithograph, entitled *Staunch Reformers,* captures the way in which many ordinary Europeans and Americans, such as the rag-tag crew depicted here on a London street corner, saw themselves as part of a wider political reform movement. The drawing makes references to many important political developments and symbols of the era—one man holds a placard that reads, "Tom Paine's *Rights of Man*—one penny!' topped by a red liberty cap, symbol of revolutionary France." In the left background, a sign outside a doorway reads "Support The Crown"—a reminder that in Britain at least, political reform went hand in hand with loyalty to the King.

visitor from England, "whose principles are so much, & so justly admired by the friends of liberty and of Mankind."

Who was this "celebrated" woman, and what had she done to earn the abiding respect of George Washington? Biographical dictionaries of her day called Catharine Macaulay Graham (1731–1791) "the patroness of liberty," for her staunch views on constitutional liberties and rights, including women's rights. But British contemporaries also considered her an eccentric for her flamboyant personal lifestyle: After the death of her husband in 1785, she married William Graham, a medical apprentice—she was 47 and he was 21. Her star dimmed somewhat thereafter in Great Britain, but North Americans continued to admire her, as evidenced by the eager invitation to Washington's Mt. Vernon.

She published her political views on British constitutionalism and the American and French Revolutions in a number of widely read essays and books. For example, in a pamphlet of 1775, Graham expressed her support for the North American colonists, who "year by year [have been] stripped of the most valuable of their rights" and who have suffered under "oppressive taxes," particularly the Stamp Act, "by which they were to be taxed

747

in an arbitrary manner." In 1783 she published the eight-volume *History of England*, which reflected many ideals of the Enlightenment, particularly antimonarchical sentiments, and support for the concept of natural rights and the sovereignty of the people. And in 1791, shortly before her death, she wrote a review of Edmund Burke's *Reflections on the Revolution in France* (1790), in which she issued a strongly worded rebuke of Burke's castigation of the French Revolution. Among other things, she observed "[t]hat the people have often abused their power, it must be granted . . . but *no abuse* of their power *can take away their right*, because their rights exists [sic] *in the very constitution of things.*"

Graham's writings fell into oblivion during the 1800s and through much of the 1900s when the defense of constitutional nationalism no longer aroused the passions of citizens in many nation-states. Indeed, the very fact that such debate no longer seemed fashionable is testimony to the ultimate success of her cause. But like her more famous contemporary, Mary Wollstonecraft, her early advocacy of feminism and views on education attracted attention again during the second half of the twentieth century; and today she is increasingly recognized as a pioneer of gender equality.

The first half of this chapter focuses on this new pattern of state formation that the American and French Revolutions of 1776–1789 introduced into world history—and that was so passionately espoused by Catharine Graham in its time. The revolutionaries in North America and France, and the many other places that followed in their wake, renounced or overthrew traditional divine-right kingdoms and empires and replaced them with the *constitutional nation-state*, that is, a state where all people were citizens with the same constitutional rights and duties and where the borders of the political state corresponded more or less to territories where people had developed a sense of collective identity: the *nation*. The ideology of constitutional nationalism became a powerful driving force in state formation during the 1800s and 1900s.

The constitutional nation-states that emerged after these initial revolutions, however, fell short of the lofty ideals above; and, in a backlash, monarchical and imperial regimes making minimal concessions to constitutional nationalism survived in Europe. Toward the middle of the 1800s, the new ideology of *ethnolinguistic nationalism* arose: the nation consists of people with strong ethnic ties and often sharing a common language, religion, and historical experience. It followed that such nations should also have their own states.

The movement toward ethnolinguistic nationalism was especially strong in central and eastern Europe, which had not had constitutional movements. It also developed in western Europe, where it grew to rival constitutional nationalism as a force within the pattern of nation-state formation. In some cases it led to the unification of ethnically related peoples who lived in smaller states into one large state, as with Italy and Germany. More frequently, it led people who saw themselves as nations governed by large empires to agitate for autonomy or independence in order to form their own ethnic nation-states—as with the many Balkan peoples under control of the Ottomans (see Chapter 25).

To complicate matters further, many people did not draw sharp distinctions between the two nation-state ideologies, especially in the realm of culture, on which the second half of this chapter concentrates. Indeed, ethnolinguistic nation-states that adopted constitutions embodied both trends, though sometimes rather uncomfortably. Moreover, these new patterns of state formation stimulated competition and disputes over national boundaries, which were now more intense because of the ethnic component. All of this would play a large role in the events leading up to World War I. Thus, the new culture of modernity that emerged in the nation-states during the nineteenth century was a complex and often volatile mixture of these two sometimes competing forms of nationalism. But as these forms evolved in the twentieth century, they became the pattern to which more and more states ultimately adhered. Today, the nation-state is not only the dominant form of polity but virtually the only one.

Origins of the Nation-State, 1750–1815

The subject of our vignette, Catharine Macaulay Graham, wrote many of her essays within the tradition of the rights and liberties obtained through the Glorious Revolution of 1688 in England. She was steeped, therefore, in not only the ideas but also the practices of constitutional nationalism that the Glorious Revolution pioneered. In this revolution, for the first time in Europe, the traditional divine rights of a monarch had been curbed through a set of constitutional rights and duties granted to the subjects of the kingdom. The innovative ideas of *subjects* becoming *citizens* with constitutionally guaranteed rights and duties and of the Parliament representing the nation—the people living in England—also became central in the American Revolution and developed close parallels during the French Revolution. Beyond the Glorious Revolution, however, the American and French Revolutions were more radical in the sense that they ended the British compromise of royal and parliamentary power and resulted in republican, middle-class nation-states without traditional divine-right monarchies.

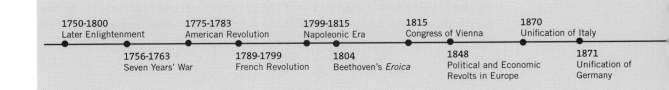

1750-1800 Later Enlightenment	1775-1783 American Revolution	1799-1815 Napoleonic Era	1815 Congress of Vienna	1870 Unification of Italy
1756-1763 Seven Years' War	1789-1799 French Revolution	1804 Beethoven's *Eroica*	1848 Political and Economic Revolts in Europe	1871 Unification of Germany

The American and French Revolutions

The two revolutions were outgrowths of the Seven Years' War, in which Great Britain and France fought for the dominance of their respective seaborne empires in the world. The governments of both kingdoms went deeply into debt to win the war. They owed this debt to their wealthy subjects, many of whom were landowners and administrators forming the ruling class. To pay back the debt, however, the kings had to go to their subjects at large and raise their taxes. The incongruence of monarchs holding the mass of their subjects responsible for their debts to a few wealthy subjects was apparent to a large number of people, who had found the intellectual movement of the Enlightenment congenial and formulated political principles of reform, if not revolution.

Conditions for Revolution in North America

When Britain won the Seven Years' War, it acquired France's trade forts in India as well as French possessions in Canada and the Ohio–Mississippi River valley. France turned Louisiana over to its ally Spain (which had lost Florida to Britain) and retreated entirely from North America. But the British territorial gains came at the price of a huge debt: The payment of the interest alone devoured most of the country's regular annual budget. Taxes had to be raised domestically as well as overseas, and in order to do so the government had to strengthen its administrative hand in an empire that had grown haphazardly and—in North America—without much oversight.

By 1763, the 13 North American colonies had experienced both rapid demographic and powerful economic growth. Opening lands beyond the Appalachian Mountains into the Ohio valley would relieve a growing population pressure on the strip of land along the Atlantic coast that the colonies occupied. Environmental degradation, through overplanting and deforestation, had increased the landless population and contributed to the presence of growing numbers of poor people in the burgeoning cities of Philadelphia, Boston, and New York. The occupation of new land across the Appalachians, on the other hand, increased the administrative challenges for the British. They had to employ large numbers of standing troops to protect not only the settlers from the hostility of the Native Americans but also the native peoples from aggression by settlers. Grain, timber, and tobacco exports from the colonies had made the colonies rich immediately before 1763, but the war boom inevitably gave way to a postwar bust. While new land created new opportunities, the economic slump created hardships (see Map 22.1).

As the government faced the task of strengthening the British administration of the colonies, a young and inexperienced monarch, George III (r. 1760–1820), was determined to increase the influence of the Crown on British politics. Unfortunately, he was not terribly adept at surrounding himself with capable advisors. Furthermore, instead of conceiving a systematic plan for governing the colonies, British politics lurched from one measure to another. The Proclamation of 1763, for example, limited the expansion of settlement to lands east of the Appalachians, to forestall difficulties with England's recent Iroquois allies. In addition to protests from those hoping to open up the new lands acquired from France, it resulted in expanded migrations to the cities and towns.

Settlers could simply ignore the proclamation if they chose to take their chances in the wilderness. The Stamp Act of 1765, however, was much harder to evade. Suddenly, everyone had to pay a tax on the use of paper, whether for legal documents,

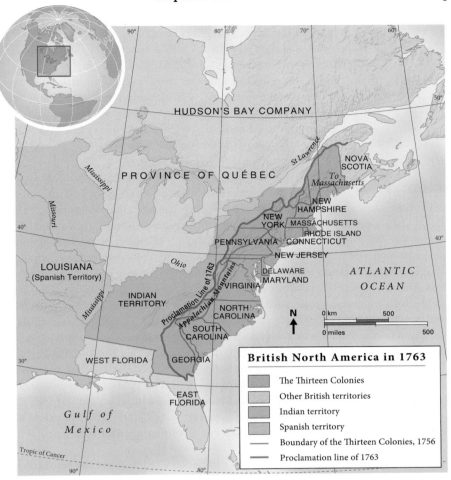

MAP **22.1 British North America in 1763.**

newspapers, or even playing cards. The tax was to be used for the upkeep of the standing troops, many of which were withdrawn from the Ohio valley, ordered to be quartered in the colonies, and intended to be used for the enforcement of increased taxes.

A firestorm of protest against the Stamp Act broke out among the urban lower middle ranks of shopkeepers, small merchants, mechanics, and printers, who organized themselves in groups such as the "Daughters" or "Sons of Liberty." The Daughters declared a highly successful boycott of British goods and promoted the production of homespun textiles. Parliament withdrew the Stamp Act when British exports fell, but the efforts by British troops to suppress the urban riots that continued even after the act's withdrawal only inflamed an increasingly volatile situation. In Boston, one of the flashpoints of unrest, the British administration also managed to offend colonists of the upper urban classes when it dissolved the Massachusetts Assembly.

Two of its members were Samuel Adams and John Hancock, the one a repentant tax collector and son of a brewer-merchant and the other a nephew of a merchant and successful shipping entrepreneur. They became prominent organizers of the opposition to new and less visible indirect taxes, which the British sought to collect in

The Boston Tea Party. This print from the late 1700s is one of dozens of depictions of this famous incident during which a group of Bostonians dumped some 300 chests of tea shipped by the East India Company into the harbor.

place of the direct Stamp Tax. The Parliament in Britain, well aware that the taxes yielded only a fraction of colonial expenditures in North America, canceled all taxes in 1770 except for the tea duty. But since this decision came at the same time as the "Boston Massacre," a particularly incendiary killing by British troops of five Bostonians during a riot, this cancelation turned out to be too little too late: Principles came into play that now hardened the positions of both sides.

Sovereignty versus Independence   Britain retained the tea tax to assert a basic right of sovereignty. This elevation of the tea tax to a matter of principle was particularly galling to the Americans since it was actually a subsidy to keep the near bankrupt East India Company afloat and had nothing to do with America. On the other side, Adams and many others were openly propagating the principle of independence from about 1769 onward: "No Taxation Without Representation" had become one of the main rallying cries of the protestors. The governmental tax subsidy for a private company in India quickly became fodder for a vociferous propaganda campaign against an allegedly arbitrary, corrupt, and tyrannical George III who dared to rule North America from afar. The colonists' propaganda culminated with the symbolic—and rather expensive—dumping of a cargo of tea into Boston Harbor in 1773. In response to this "Boston Tea Party," Britain closed the harbor, demanded restitution, and passed the so-called Coercive Acts (called the "Intolerable Acts" in the colonies), which put Massachusetts into effective bankruptcy. Both sides now moved inexorably toward a showdown in which Thomas Hobbes's principle of indivisible sovereignty and John Locke's principle of equal representation would become locked in a bloody struggle for supremacy.

The War for Independence   Two Continental Congresses of the colonies in 1774–1775 failed to resolve this clash of principles. The colonial assemblies elevated themselves into the Continental Association, which claimed to speak for all the people. But the debate about representation—with one-third of the North American population not sufficiently propertied to have the right to vote for the assemblies—reverberated into the colonial assemblies themselves. Demands for expanded voting rights confronted complaints about "low" people like cobblers, caulkers, blacksmiths, religious dissenters, and non-Christians participating in the debate for independence. As with the French Revolution later on, the leaders needed the masses to support them in their bid for independence but were afraid of the potential violence and momentum of these masses, which might at any time overwhelm them.

While this coalition of leaders and the masses was coming together, Britain seized the initiative. In an effort to isolate the revolutionary hotbed of Massachusetts from the rest of the colonies, British troops ventured out in April 1775 to seize a suspected cache of arms and ammunition in Concord. The silversmith Paul Revere, son of a French Huguenot immigrant, in the midnight ride of later fame, warned Adams and Hancock of the British plans to arrest them and roused a militia of farmers—the famous "Minute Men"—near Concord to arms. War broke out in earnest, and the Second Continental Congress appointed George Washington, a former officer from a wealthy Virginian family of tobacco planters, as commander of the colonists' troops.

Feelings on both sides now ran at a fever pitch, as exemplified by Thomas Paine's widely read pamphlet *Common Sense*. Paine had been a corset maker and tax officer in Britain before emigrating to Pennsylvania in 1774. His plainspoken prose style powerfully appealed to craftspeople and laborers, as did his use of well-known biblical examples and avoidance of high-toned Latin quotes. By contrast, when the Second Continental Congress voted to separate the colonies from Britain on July 4, 1776, the resulting Declaration of Independence was a highly literate document steeped in Enlightenment thought. Its author was Thomas Jefferson, like Washington the son of a Virginian planter with an advanced university education that included the New Sciences. The great majority of the signers were also educated men of means—planters, landowners, merchants, and lawyers. Thus, the American and earlier English Revolutions shared a certain similarity in their leadership.

Although the revolution affirmed the Enlightenment idea that the equality of all "men" was "self-evident," it tacitly excluded the one-fifth of all Americans who were black slaves and the roughly half who were women, not to mention the Native Americans. On the other hand, the signers also excluded Locke's property ownership from what they considered to be the most valuable rights of citizens and rendered these rights as "life, liberty, and the pursuit of happiness." When the colonists eventually won the war of independence in 1783, the founders created a revolutionary federal republic with a Congress that was far more representative of its citizens than the Parliament in Great Britain.

The new republic's initial years, however, were fraught with organizational difficulties. The governing document, the Articles of Confederation, granted so much power to the individual states that the latter operated in effect like separate countries. In 1787 a constitutional convention was called in Philadelphia and a far more effective federal system created. Careful to add checks and balances in the form of a bicameral legislature and separation of powers into legislative, executive, and judicial branches, the new constitution seemed to embody many of the ideals of the Enlightenment—including a set of 10 initial amendments: the Bill of Rights. Though still imperfect—particularly in sidestepping the contentious issue of slavery—it provided a model for nearly all the world's constitutions that followed. A later commentator praised it as "a machine that would go of itself"; another, more critical one called its checks and balances "a harmonious system of mutual frustration." In 1789, under the new system, George Washington was elected the first president of the United States.

Though the new republic fell far short of what we would consider today to be "representative," its abolition of the divine right of monarchial rule and its replacement by the sovereignty of the people was for most people a previously unimaginable reversal of the natural order of things. In this respect, the American and French Revolutions signaled the inauguration of a new pattern of state formation and the advent of modernity.

The French Revolution   King Louis XVI (r. 1774–1792) and the French government had watched the American War for Independence with great sympathy, hoping for an opportunity to avenge the kingdom's defeat in the Seven Years' War. It supplied the Americans with money, arms, and officers and in 1778–1779, in alliance with Spain, declared war on Great Britain. The French–Spanish entry into the war forced Britain into an impossible defense of its entire colonial empire. Although

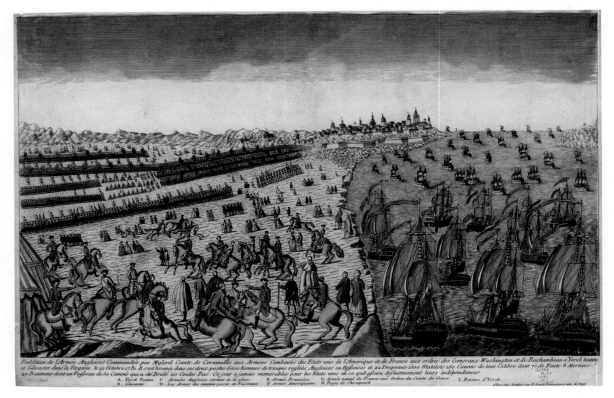

The Battle of Yorktown, 1781. This French engraving emphasizes the key role they played in this decisive battle of the war. A large French army assisted in the siege of Yorktown, visible in the background, while the French fleet cut off British attempts to escape, forcing them to surrender.

mounting a creditable military effort, Britain conceded defeat in 1783 in the hope of escaping with minimal territorial losses, apart from the North American colonies. Indeed, in the peace negotiations France and Spain made few territorial gains. The French government furthermore had to begin exorbitant payments—much higher than what Britain faced after the Seven Years' War—on the interest for the loans to carry out the war. Crippling debt, which the French government was ultimately unable to pay, played a large role in establishing the preconditions underlying the outbreak of the French Revolution.

The Crises of the 1780s

As in America, the French population had increased sharply during the 1700s. Food production could barely keep up, and inflation increased. As recent scholarship has shown, the rural economy responded to the rising demand, though with difficulty; and in the region of Paris, production for the market was highly profitable. Furthermore, colonial trade with the Caribbean colonies boomed. Had it not been for the debt, the government would have been well-financed: It collected direct taxes as well as monies from compulsory loans and the sale of titles and offices to a large upper stratum of ordinary people of means—merchants, lawyers, and administrators. These people were deeply invested in the regime, buying themselves into the ranks of the aristocracy and benefiting from administrative offices handling the kingdom's tax revenue. Although claiming to be absolute, the king in reality shared power and wealth with a large ruling class of old and new aristocrats as well as aspiring ordinary urban people of wealth.

In 1781, suspicions arose about the solvency of the regime when the finance minister, who had kept the extent of the subsidies for the American revolutionaries a secret, quit. But the government continued to borrow, even though bad weather leading to two poor harvests in 1786–1787 diminished tax revenues. The hardship caused by these 2 years became crucial for the eventual revolution in 1789: Without reserves in grain and animals, the peasants suffered severe famine and grew increasingly angry when government imports intended to help ended up in the hands of profiteers and hoarders.

By 1788, the government was unable to make payments on short-term loans and had to hand out promissory notes, with bankruptcy looming in the background. As in Britain in the 1760s, a reform of the tax system became unavoidable. At first, the king sought to initiate this reform with the help of a council of appointed notables. When this failed, he held general elections for a popular assembly to meet in Versailles (called the "Estates-General," last convened in 1614). Voters, defined as males over 25 who were French and paid taxes, met in constituent meetings in their districts across France, according to their "estate" as clergy, aristocrats, or commoners. Peasants met in large numbers in the "Third Estate," or commoner meetings; but the deputies they elected to meet in Paris were overwhelmingly administrators, lawyers, doctors, academics, businessmen, and debt holders. At the request of the king, the deputies composed petitions in which they listed their grievances about taxes, waste, luxury at court, and ministerial "despotism" to form the basis for the reform legislation.

The most famous among the petitions was the pamphlet of the priest (*abbé*) Emmanuel-Joseph Sieyès [See-YES], entitled *What Is the Third Estate?* Sieyès was elected as a commoner from Paris and became one of the leading intellectual figures in the revolution. In his pamphlet he put forward the revolutionary idea that the French nation of 25 million *was* the Third Estate, while the other two estates, totaling 200,000 members, were no more than a tiny fraction. The Third Estate, embodying Rousseau's idea of the "general will" of the nation, should alone form the "National Assembly" and translate this general will into a constitution, fiscal reform, and the abolition of aristocratic privileges.

Outbreak of the Revolution   Amid widespread unrest and rioting among peasants in many places in France and workers in Paris, the Third Estate now outmaneuvered the other estates and the king. In June 1789 they seceded from the Estates-General and relocated to a local tennis court where they swore an oath not to disband until they had formed a constitution. Following this Tennis Court Oath, they declared themselves a National Assembly. Louis XVI had initially been favorably inclined toward the Third Estate since the other two estates had rejected the government's reform plans. But he changed his mind after the Third Estate's declaration. Pressured by the pro-aristocracy faction at court, he issued a veiled threat that if it would not support his reforms, "I alone should consider myself their [the people's] representative." The king then reinforced his troops in and around Paris and Versailles and dismissed his popular finance minister, Jacques Necker (1732–1804), who had brought some famine relief in spring. Parisians, afraid of an imminent military occupation of the city, swarmed through the streets on July 14, 1789, and provisioned themselves with arms and gunpowder from arsenals, gunsmith shops, and the Bastille, the royal fortress and prison inside Paris, which they stormed. Thus,

The French Revolution. The French Revolution began with the storming of the Bastille for weapons and gunpowder on July 14, 1789 (top left). It gained momentum when Parisian women marched to Versailles, demanding that the king reside in Paris and end the famine there (top right). The inevitability of a republic became clear when the king and queen were captured after they attempted to flee (bottom left).

by his vacillation—first inclining to accept the role as a constitutional monarch, then switching to a reassertion of absolutism—Louis XVI lost the initiative.

Three Phases of Revolution   The French Revolution, unfolding from 1789 to 1799, went through three phases: constitutional monarchy (1789–1792), radical republicanism (1792–1795), and military consolidation (1795–1799). The first phase began with the "great fear" of near anarchy, which reigned during July and August 1789. People in the provinces, mostly peasants, chased their aristocratic and commoner landlords from their estates. Paris, too, remained in an uproar since food supplies, in spite of a good harvest, remained spotty. Agitation climaxed in October when thousands of working women, many with arms, marched from Paris to Versailles, forcing the king to move to Paris and concern himself directly with their plight.

No longer threatened by the king, the National Assembly issued the Declaration of the Rights of Man and of the Citizen (1789), subjected the Catholic Church to French civil law (1790), established a constitutional monarchy (1791), and issued laws ending the unequal taxes of the Old Regime (1792). The principal author of the Declaration of the Rights of Man and of the Citizen was Marie-Joseph Gilbert du Motier, Marquis de Lafayette (1757–1834), descendant of an old French aristocratic family but an early joiner of the Third Estate Assembly. Earlier, Lafayette had made major contributions to the American War for Independence as a military officer, and during the French Revolution he was the commander of the fledgling French National Guard, engaged in efforts to protect what was at this point a constitutional revolution favoring an emerging propertied and urban middle class.

The second phase of the revolution, the period of radical republicanism (1792–1795), began when the revolutionaries found themselves unable to establish a stable constitutional regime. After the king tried unsuccessfully to flee with his unpopular Austrian-born, Habsburg wife Marie-Antoinette from Paris to a monarchist stronghold in eastern France in the summer of 1791, Austria and Prussia threatened to intervene if the king and queen were harmed. The idea of preventive war now gained adherents across the political spectrum as patriotic feelings were invoked: Many aristocratic families had fled to their relatives in Austria and Prussia. In April 1792 the prowar party declared war on its eastern neighbors. Then, in September, republicans seized the government, deposed the king, and held elections for a new assembly to draw up a republican constitution. They separately executed the king and queen in 1793, while the huge *levée en masse*, or conscript army, of the republic regained control of the French borders in 1794 after a lengthy and difficult war against its European neighbors.

In the meantime, a Committee of Public Safety had assumed power and launched the "Reign of Terror," in which perhaps 30,000 citizens were executed. One of its leaders was Maximilien Robespierre (1758–1794), a well-educated lawyer from an old administrative family in northern France who prided himself on his alliance with the laborers and craftspeople of Paris. Because they wore no middle-class silk breeches, they were called *sans-culottes* [san-coo-LOTT] and had become the shock troops of the revolution, particularly in Paris. Robespierre's theory of terror held that France needed to be cleansed of "counter-revolutionaries" and that by surmounting this last difficulty, all the benefits of the revolution would then take effect. Thus, he insisted, "there is only one crime, treason; and one punishment, death." At the same time, the new government was enacting laws designed to remake society along Enlightenment ideology in an astonishingly ambitious fashion. Robespierre, for example, promoted the new state Cult of the Supreme Being, a variation on the idea of deism. The Supreme Being was to be celebrated every tenth day of the new 10-day week in the new "rational" republican calendar that was dated to January 2, 1792. 1792 was now to be Year I of the Republic. The names of months were changed to match the seasons: Germinal for March, Floreal for April, Thermidor for July/August. New systems of measurement that culminated in the metric system were also developed. Egalitarianism in everyday life, such as addressing everyone as "Citizen" or "Citizeness," was pressed; and schemes were even proposed to eliminate private property. But such wholesale changes also alienated increasing numbers of people; and thus, the ranks of "counter-revolutionaries" multiplied as the revolution became more and more radical.

The Directory   With the foreign wars ended and the danger of a monarchist counterrevolution diminished, many revolutionaries grew fearful of Robespierre's dictatorial powers and use of terror. Plotters arrested him and had him and many supporters guillotined in July 1794. Since this coincided with the new French month of Thermidor, scholars of revolution sometimes refer to such a retreat from radicalism as a "Thermidorean reaction." With a new constitution and bicameral legislature, the revolution entered its third and final phase (1795–1799) under the so-called Directory. But political and financial stability remained elusive, and the Directory increasingly depended on an army that had become professionalized during the defense of the revolution against Austria and Prussia in 1792–1794. Within the army, a brash young brigadier general named Napoleon Bonaparte (1769–1821), of minor aristocratic Corsican descent, was the most promising person to continue the foreign wars successfully. From 1796 to 1798 Napoleon scored major victories against the Austrians in northern Italy and invaded Egypt, which he occupied in

---

From Declaration of the Rights of Man and of the Citizen

"Article 1. Men are born and remain free and equal in rights. Social distinctions can be based only on public utility.

Article 2. The aim of every political association is the preservation of the natural and imprescriptible rights of man. These rights are liberty, property, security, and resistance to oppression.

Article 3. The source of all sovereignty resides essentially in the nation. No body, no individual can exercise authority that does not explicitly proceed from it."

—Primary Sources of the French Revolution, http://www.thecaveonline.com/APEH/frrevdocuments.html

The Guillotine

It is estimated that during the period of the Terror (June 1793–July 1794) the guillotine was responsible for around 1,000 executions in Paris alone and for perhaps as many as 15,000–30,000 throughout France. This iconic symbol of grisly public executions is attended by many myths. Among these is the idea that the guillotine was invented by—and took its name from—one Dr. Guillotin solely for the purpose of speeding up executions of perceived enemies of the republic during the infamous Reign of Terror. Neither of these notions is true however. Indeed, the actual train of events is far more compelling—and ironic.

Far from appearing for the first time during the French Revolution, the first known model of a "decapitation machine" is probably the "Halifax Gibbet," in use in England from around 1300 until 1650. Another model, the "Scottish Maiden," was derived from the Halifax Gibbet and used in 150 executions from 1565 until 1708. It was subsequently turned over to a museum in Edinburgh in 1797 and may have earlier served as a model for the French machine.

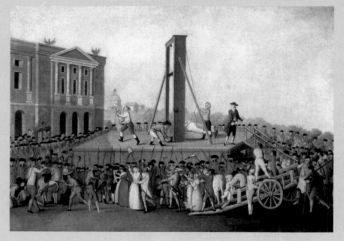

The Execution of Marie-Antoinette. During the radical republican period of the French Revolution, the Committee of Public Safety had Queen Marie-Antoinette condemned to death for treason after a sham trial. She was executed on October 16, 1793, 9 months after the execution of her husband, Louis XVI.

When and how did the instrument first appear in France? Ironically, it came as an indirect result of efforts to end the death penalty. During the early days of the revolution the National Assembly pondered the abolition of the death penalty in France altogether. On October 10, 1789, the Assembly was addressed by Dr. Joseph Ignace Guillotin (1738–1814), founder of the French Academy of Medicine and a staunch opponent of capital punishment, who urged the assembly to at the very least find "a machine that beheads painlessly," if they could not ultimately agree to stop executions altogether. Toward this end Guillotin presented sketches of the kind of machine

preparation for an invasion of British India. But thwarted by a pursuing British fleet, he returned to France. There, the Abbé Sieyès, resurgent as a constitutionalist and worried about continued plots against the government, encouraged Napoleon to take over the weak Directory. But Napoleon outfoxed Sieyès and overthrew the Directory altogether in November 1799, thus ending the revolution.

Revival of Empire Napoleon embarked on sweeping domestic reforms that taken together curtailed much of the revolutionary fervor but restored order and stability in France. His crowning achievement was the reform of the French legal system, promulgated in the Civil Code of 1804, which in theory established the equality of all male citizens before the law but in reality imposed restrictions on many revolutionary freedoms. In 1804 Napoleon sealed his power and cloaked he had in mind, but his initial design was rejected, followed by a second rejection on December 1 of the same year. In 1791 the Assembly finally agreed to retain the death penalty, noting that "every person condemned to the death penalty shall have his head severed." But instead of adopting Dr. Guillotin's design, the Assembly accepted a model designed by Dr. Antoine Louis, secretary of the Academy of Surgery; Dr. Louis then turned to a German engineer, Tobias Schmidt, who constructed the first version of the "painless" decapitation machine. It was not until April 25, 1792, that the guillotine, nicknamed "Louisette" after Dr. Louis, claimed its first victim. It is not clear when the name was changed to "Guillotine" (the final "e" was added later),

but historians speculate that Dr. Guillotin's early advocacy of quick and painless executions was a major factor. As for Dr. Guillotin himself, the crowning irony was that after fighting a losing battle with the government to change the name of the machine because of embarrassment to his family, he changed his own name and retreated to the obscurity he now craved.

Execution by Guillotine in France, 1929. An Enlightenment innovation, the guillotine was intended to execute humans swiftly and humanely. But the mass executions of the French Revolution turned the guillotine into a symbol of barbarism. It was not until 1977 that France executed its last criminal by guillotine. Today, most countries subscribe to the belief that even criminals have inalienable human rights, the most basic being the right to live.

Questions

- Can the guillotine be viewed as a practical adaptation of Enlightenment ideas? If so, how?

- Why do societies, like France in the late eighteenth century, debate the forms of punishment they use to execute prisoners? What are the criteria by which one type of punishment is considered more humane than others?

himself in legitimacy by crowning himself emperor of the French. Secure in his authority at home, he now struck out on a lengthy campaign of conquest in Europe. Victory followed upon victory from 1805 to 1810, resulting in the French domination of most of continental Europe. The goal was the construction of a European empire, by necessity land-based and in the tradition of the Habsburgs, Ottomans, and Russians. With this empire, he planned to challenge the maritime British Empire that had thwarted the French ambitions in the Seven Years' War. As justification for his empire, ironically, he used the constitutional ideas of the French Revolution, allegedly destined to replace the old absolutist regimes of Europe (see Map 22.2).

The failure of Napoleon's Russian campaign in 1812, however, marked the beginning of the end of Napoleon's grand scheme. Sensing his weakness, Great Britain, Austria, Prussia, and Russia formed an alliance that brought about Napoleon's defeat

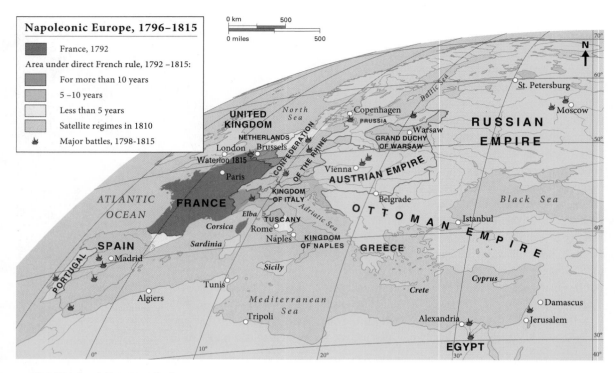

Napoleonic Europe, 1796–1815

France, 1792

Area under direct French rule, 1792–1815:

For more than 10 years

5–10 years

Less than 5 years

Satellite regimes in 1810

Major battles, 1798-1815

MAP **22.2 Napoleonic Europe, 1796–1815.**

at Waterloo in Belgium on June 18, 1815. In exile on the British-controlled island of St. Helena off the west coast of Africa, Napoleon lived until 1821, composing his memoirs. His legacy was equivocal. On the one hand, his revival of traditional imperialism, under the pretense of creating republican nations, only to turn them into vassals of France, discredited constitutionalism. On the other hand, what now could be called a middle class of urban professionals, property owners, and entrepreneurs, liberated by the Napoleonic conquests, was in the process of emerging, which—through the pursuit of constitutional nationalism—began to implement the pattern of modernity that is still with us today.

Enlightenment Culture: Radicalism and Moderation

Enlightenment:
European intellectual movement (1650–1800) growing out of the New Science and based on the ideology of materialism in which matter is considered the basic constituent of reality and mind or reason is a derivative.

The American and French Revolutions flowed out of the culture of the later **Enlightenment** (ca. 1750–1800). This culture both influenced the revolutions and, in turn, was influenced by them. The political heritage of the early Enlightenment (1650–1750), whose twin poles were represented by Thomas Hobbes (1588–1679) and John Locke (1632–1704), had witnessed a new, narrow definition of reality modeled after the New Science (see Chapter 17). The primacy of mathematics as the means to understand nature pioneered by Galileo and the thinkers who championed the New Science had a profound effect on these men—as they did on many of the later Enlightenment *philosophes*. For Hobbes and Locke, reality consisted only of matter detectable by the senses, and mind or reason existed only insofar as it was embodied in matter in the form of consciousness. Hobbes, the more radical thinker and a mathematician himself, viewed consciousness as a kind of bundle in which the passions held reason hostage; Locke, in most ways a more moderate thinker, assumed that reason could dominate the passions. But both radical and moderate strains of these ideas, though undergoing considerable transformation, continued into the later Enlightenment.

Early and Late Enlightenment

The early Enlightenment, of course, embodied modes of thought shared by many other thinkers besides Hobbes and Locke, who are usually categorized as part of a distinct "English Enlightenment." Outstanding figures whose works are still read today include Baruch Spinoza (1632–1677), Gottfried-Wilhelm Leibniz (1646–1716), George Berkeley (1685–1753), and Charles-Louis de Secondat, Baron de Montesquieu (1689–1755), to name just a few. Taken together, the representatives of the early Enlightenment came close to forming a movement in the loose sense of the word: People read each other's works, often corresponded with each other, and sometimes engaged in protracted criticisms of and polemics against each other. What changed in the period after 1750 was not so much the culture; Enlightenment thinkers continued to adhere to the idea of reason or consciousness embedded in the material world as the basic constitution of reality. What gradually grew was the social dimension of the Enlightenment: Thanks to a number of energetic writers popularizing the new ideas, the later eighteenth century saw thousands subscribing to Enlightenment-themed books, pamphlets, and newspapers or attending academies, salons, and lectures. They still were a minority even among the growing middle class of urban administrators, professionals, merchants, and landowners, not to mention the 80 percent of the population engaged in the crafts and in farming. But their voices as radical or moderate "progressives" opposing tradition-bound ministers, aristocrats, or clergy became measurably louder.

It was the late eighteenth-century generation of this vociferous minority that was central to the revolutions in America and France and—a minority within the minority—in the French slave colony Haiti (see Chapter 27). They translated their materialist conception of reality into such "self-evident" ideals as life, liberty, equality, social contract, property, representation, nation, popular sovereignty, and constitution. In the wider, more broadly conceived culture of the Enlightenment, they translated the materialist approach into the creation of new scholarly disciplines and new forms of artistic expression.

Voltaire and Social Criticism   Perhaps the most famous champion of Enlightenment ideas and an accomplished writer, social critic, and *philosophe*, as the French thinkers were known, was François-Marie Arouet, better known by his pen name of Voltaire (1694–1778). He was also the most prolific of the Enlightenment writers, producing more than 2,000 books, articles, and pamphlets during his career. As a young man Voltaire experienced the arbitrary justice of France's absolute monarchy when he was imprisoned in the famous Bastille without trial for insulting a

Napoleon. This dazzling portrait of Napoleon by the French painter Jean Ingres (1780–1867) shows the glitzy majesty of the "Little Corporal" who crowned himself emperor in 1804.

well-connected aristocrat. He managed to have his open-ended sentence commuted to exile in England, where he came away impressed with the balance of the English constitutional monarchy and the findings of the New Science as codified by Isaac Newton. On his return to France he formed a long and fruitful relationship with the Marquise Gabrielle-Emilie du Châtelet (1706–1749), who not only gave him emotional support but was a considerable scholar in her own right. They assembled a library of over 20,000 volumes and produced a formidable array of historical, political, philosophical, and scientific works. Following the death of the marquise, Voltaire accepted an invitation from the "enlightened despot" Frederick the Great of Prussia and moved to his court for a time. His quick temper and outspokenness again landed him in trouble however, and he left Prussia for Geneva and, finally, an estate just inside the French border at Ferney.

The most quotable of the *philosophes*, Voltaire is still remembered today for such sayings as "history is a pack of lies we play on the dead" and "if God did not exist it would be necessary to invent Him." He signed many of the thousands of letters he wrote with the injunction to "crush the infamous thing," by which he meant the Catholic Church. He is also reputed to have come up with the story of Isaac Newton grasping the nature of gravity when an apple fell on his head. But his most famous work was the savagely satirical, picaresque tale *Candide* (1759). As the hero, Candide, lurches from tragic–comic misadventure to misadventure, his experiences lay bare all the venality, corruption, and absurdity of government, religion, and even some Enlightenment ideas themselves. Indeed, Candide's mentor, the thinly disguised figure of Leibniz in the person of Dr. Pangloss, constantly informs anyone who will listen that "all is for the best in this best of all possible worlds"—this while he suffers misfortunes ranging from being hanged to contracting syphilis. Such sunny optimism outraged Voltaire, who wrote the book against the backdrop of the Lisbon earthquake of 1755, which killed perhaps 50,000 people.

Denis Diderot and the *Encyclopédie* The most visible manifestation of the social broadening of the Enlightenment in 1750–1800 was the differentiation of an autonomous, secular realm of material nature into a multiplicity of self-contained scientific and artistic branches. In the following sections we will look at representative figures in the fields of philosophy, economics, literature, and music. Here, Denis Diderot (1713–1784) will be the focus of attention as a man of many philosophical and literary talents whose most important contribution to the Enlightenment proliferation of secular scholarly and artistic knowledge was the assembly of this knowledge into an encyclopedia.

Diderot was a precocious son of a knife maker in northeast France, who had received his education at a religious school. But he abandoned the study first of theology and then of law in favor of becoming an independent writer, a new occupation in the urban world of later Enlightenment modernity. During his early years he was penniless and came into a modest income only when he sold his library to Empress Catherine the Great of Russia, who also gave him a regular stipend. In the course of a long life, he composed a great variety of works, from philosophy to literature and art criticism. As an ardent materialist, he became an atheist and spent time in prison for his radical views, unable to publish many of his writings.

The *Encyclopédie*, originally conceived as the translation of an earlier (1728) English encyclopedia, began as an independent work when the publisher hired Diderot. Under the editorship of Diderot, the first volume appeared in 1751 as a work that would encompass not only the fields covered by the academic disciplines but all fields of knowledge. Not only that, it was also to have the power "to change men's common way of thinking." For the next quarter of a century, Diderot poured all his energy into writing entries and soliciting contributions from the "republic of letters," as the French Enlightenment thinkers were called. Many entries dealt with delicate subjects, such as science, industry, commerce, freedom of thought, slavery, and religious tolerance, sometimes edited by the cautious publisher without Diderot's knowledge. Publication itself was not easy since the Catholic Church and the French crown banned the project for several years and forced its continuation in secret. But the roughly 4,000 subscribers received their twenty-eighth and last volume in 1772, ready and able to assimilate everything modern, urbane gentlemen and gentlewomen should know.

Philosophy: Rousseau and Kant   Diderot and his radical friends contributing to the *Encyclopédie* believed in the primacy of freedom and equality of individuals in their natural state. Political and social institutions, they concluded, should be shaped in such a way that they would guarantee a maximum of freedom and equality for every person. What they brushed aside, however, was the problem that this maximum freedom and its justification could not be inherent in matter; therefore, consciousness would have to come from outside, for example, in the form of morality.

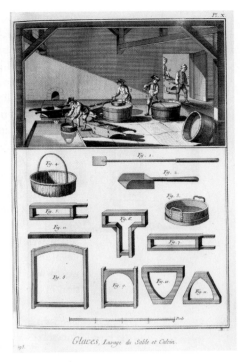

The *Encyclopédie*. Denis Diderot's massive work promoted practical, applied science, such as this illustration showing glass-making.

It was this unwillingness of the radicals to admit the necessity of this external or transcendent morality that was the point of departure for the philosopher Jean-Jacques Rousseau (1712–1778). Rousseau, in contrast to his atheist Enlightenment colleagues, was a firm believer in the existing Protestant and Catholic morality. The son of a cultivated and music-loving Geneva watchmaker, Rousseau was a philosophical moderate. To the consternation of the radicals in France, he espoused in his *Social Contract* (1762) the notion that humans had suffered a steady decline from their "natural" state ever since civilization began and imposed its own external authority on them. The radicals held that even though humans had lost their natural state of freedom and equality and had come under arbitrary authority, they were experiencing a steady progress of civilization toward ever improving degrees of freedom and equality. Rousseau did share with his former friends a low opinion of the absolutist French regime, of which he ran afoul just as much as they did. But he had little faith in such concepts as popular sovereignty, elections, and electoral reforms that they propagated. Instead, he believed that people, rallying in a nation, should express their unity directly through a "general will," a sort of direct democracy—more applicable to his native Geneva than a large nation like France.

Immanuel Kant (1724–1804) lived far away from France in Königsberg, East Prussia, which he never left and from which he was an observer of postrevolutionary France. A much more disciplined philosopher than Rousseau, he was nevertheless also a believer in the progress of civilization and history, as expressed in his *Perpetual Peace* (1795). In fact, he quite immodestly thought of himself as having performed a second "Copernican turn" in modernity with his two main books, *Critique of Pure Reason* (1781, second revised edition 1787) and *Critique of Practical Reason* (1787). As a moderate Enlightenment thinker he made the crucial contribution, through a systematic study of the "antinomies" (internal contradictions) of reason. Pure reason, said Kant, does not reside in material nature and is transcendent; practical reason, which does reside in nature and is immanent, has to be carefully distinguished from pure reason. In contrast to Rousseau, however, with his traditional Christian ethics, Kant sought to build morality on transcendent reason and came to the conclusion that this morality had to be erected on the basis of the *categorical imperative*: Act in such a way that the principle of your action can be a principle for anyone's action. This highly abstract principle entered modern thought as the basis for human rights, with their claim to transcendence or universality, as in the Charter of the United Nations (1945).

Economics   The late Enlightenment saw the birth of the academic discipline of economics. French and British thinkers who were appalled by the inefficient administration of finances, taxes, and trade by the regimes in their countries found the official pursuit of mercantilism wanting. As discussed in previous chapters, mercantilism was the effort to import as little as possible, except from the colonies, and develop domestic crafts so as to export manufactured goods in exchange for the warm-weather commodities of the colonies. Building on the philosophical assumption of the material state of nature, the so-called Physiocrats, most notably François Quesnay (1694–1774) and Anne-Robert-Jacques Turgot (1727–1781), argued that freedom and equality should be the principles of the economy. The state should reduce taxes and other means of control to a minimum so that entrepreneurism in the general population could flourish. It should adopt a policy of *laissez-faire* [les-say-FAIR], that is, "hands-off." The Scottish economist Adam Smith (1723–1790), who spent some time in Paris and was familiar with many of the Physiocrats, developed a British version of laissez-faire economics. In his *Inquiry into the Nature and Causes of the Wealth of Nations* (1776) Smith argued that if the market were largely left to its own devices, without many state regulations and restrictions, it would regulate itself through the forces of supply and demand, appropriate prices, and so forth. It would then move in the direction of increasing efficiency as if guided by "an unseen hand." Like Kant in philosophy, Smith became the founding father of modern economics, whose ideas are still regularly invoked today.

Literature and Music   As in the other fields of modern cultural expression, the Enlightenment also inspired writers, poets, and composers. Noteworthy among the writers and poets were Johann Wolfgang von Goethe (1749–1832) and Friedrich Schiller (1759–1805), sons of a lawyer and a military doctor, respectively. Goethe, a moderate Enlightenment thinker, had a low opinion of his native Lutheranism. He trained as a lawyer but, on the strength of his early writings, found employment under the duke of Weimar in central Germany. Among his numerous poems, novels, plays, and even scientific works (on color), his drama *Faust*, about an ambitious experimenter who sells his soul to the devil to acquire mastery of nature, became a metaphor of modernity—of the technicians and engineers whose dominance of natural forces ran roughshod over environmental concerns.

Schiller, Goethe's younger contemporary, was a trained doctor and later professor of history and philosophy. A moderate Enlightenment thinker, he was greatly disappointed by the violence of the French Revolution. Feeling drawn to Kant's thinking, he strove to harmonize the "sensual passions" and the "formal passions" with which Enlightenment thinkers reflecting on the natural state of humans were wrestling.

Schiller composed major, mostly historical, dramas; and his poem "Ode to Joy" (1785), celebrating the brotherhood and unity of humanity and set to music by Ludwig van Beethoven (1770–1827) in his Ninth Symphony (1824), can be considered the hymn of Enlightenment. As such, it became the anthem of the European Union in 1993.

Wolfgang Amadeus Mozart (1756–1791), son of the music director of the archbishop of Salzburg, was a child prodigy who, as an adult, spent his most productive years at the Habsburg imperial court in Vienna. There, he joined the local lodge of the Freemasons. During the early Enlightenment, Freemasonry had grown from Scottish masonry guilds into one of the many fraternal organizations, friendship circles, salons, and other associations that celebrated sociability. The Freemason slogan was "liberty, fraternity, and equality"—evidently a precursor to the similar slogan of the French Revolution. Toward the end of the 1700s Freemasonry was a substantial organization all across Europe, without, however, being involved in politics. It included many French thinkers, as well as Goethe, the composer Haydn, Benjamin Franklin, and George Washington. Mozart wrote half a dozen pieces for Washington's Masonic lodge, and his opera *The Magic Flute* (1791) is strongly influenced by Masonic concepts and ideas. Together with his older contemporary Franz Joseph Haydn (1732–1809), Mozart was the creator of the classical style, which succeeded the highly complex music of the baroque and was more suited, especially through the new genres of trios and quartets with independent voices, to the cultural sensibilities of the rising urban, educated classes.

Last Movement of Beethoven's Piano Sonata no. 30 in E Major. Composed in 1820 or 1821, this is one of Beethoven's last piano sonatas.

Ludwig van Beethoven, from a family of royal court musicians in Cologne, Germany, was likely also a mason during his time in Vienna. (The Austrian emperor ordered the Vienna lodge to be closed down after the restoration of the monarchy, and the records were destroyed.) Beethoven was perhaps the most revolutionary composer of these revolutionary times: Full of admiration for the French Revolution in 1804, he composed his third symphony, the *Eroica* ("Heroic") for Napoleon, a work in which he broke—or departed—from the Classical style. But when Napoleon crowned himself emperor, Beethoven was so deeply disappointed that he is reported to have exploded in anger, ripping the name "Buonaparte" from the title page.

The imperial turn of the French Revolution may be said to have effectively ended the Enlightenment. A few years later, with the fall of Napoleon and the restoration of monarchies, the European kings actively worked on rescinding its effects; and in the face of overwhelming power, the constitutionalists went either silent or underground.

The Other Enlightenment: The Ideology of Ethnic Nationalism

Most adherents of the Enlightenment in the German-speaking parts of Europe were moderate constitutionalists similar to Rousseau. Like the latter, they sought to combine reason and the "good" passions with tradition. Accordingly, they were constitutionalists but, for the most part, not republicans. In their view, monarchies were part and parcel of a heritage of ethnic, linguistic, and even religious traditions peculiar to a specific nation. They sought to combine the universalism of constitutional nationalism with the ethnic specificity of a people: a *nation*.

Ethnic and Linguistic Traditions
Ethnic and linguistic traditions had existed in Germany for centuries before they became a nationalist ideology. It was not easy to identify these traditions, however, given their great diversity. German thinkers frequently invented traditions and imagined earlier communities, as modern scholars have often charged. But while these charges are often justified, it would be wrong to characterize these traditions as simply fictitious. Aware of the general reality of so many of these traditions, therefore, historians have postulated a "protonationalism," which the German Enlightenment thinkers allegedly turned into an actual **nationalism**. At present, however, both the "imagination" and "protonationalism" interpretations are considered problematic, so historians are again going to the sources in search of more viable interpretations.

> **Nationalism:** Belief that people who share the same language, history, and sense of identity make up a nation and that every nation has the right to pursue its own destiny.

In the case of language barriers to unity we can say that when the revolutions of 1776–1789 occurred in America and France, the constitutional nationalists aspired to universal human rights against a background of monarchical states that had existed for centuries within broadly defined borders. The court and administration in the capital had fostered a culture centered on the specific dialect of English or French spoken and written in London or Paris. But the grammatically complex High French which the revolutionary leaders spoke, for example, was manifestly not shared with the rest of the people living within the borders of the French kingdom. Nearly half of the French spoke dialects; the other half, in the northwest and southwest, spoke no French at all. There is evidence that the French revolutionaries expected everyone to learn "good" French, the "male and sublime" language of French culture. But in 1789 it was clear that plurality was a reality, and uniformity was—at best—a dream.

A similar situation existed concerning ethnicity. The constitutional nationalists took it for granted that there had been kings in the past who represented a population that had a common origin, distinguished between themselves and foreigners, had won and lost battles together, shared the same legal tradition, possessed a central administration, sang the same songs and hymns, and so forth. That all this constituted "Frenchness" was quite clear to the revolutionaries, as is evident in many documents; but it formed the background for, not the conscious content of, a revolution that declared universal human rights. In the American colonies, the "Britishness" of the revolution was more complex since, in pursuit of their struggle for independence, the revolutionaries had to pick and choose what they wanted to retain and what to reject. Here, too, the British character of the United States remained largely unexpressed except for what was to be rejected, as enumerated in the Declaration of Independence. Whatever specific ethnolinguistic character appeared in the two revolutions was not overly emphasized.

Germany displayed ethnolinguistic characteristics very similar to those of Britain and France but, of course, was politically fragmented. Even though it had always possessed a central ruling institution, its imperial, rather than royal, constitution made for a much higher degree of decentralization than in the English and French kingdoms. In addition, many Germans in eastern Europe were widely dispersed among peoples with different ethnic–linguistic–religious heritages, such as Czechs, Slovaks, Hungarians, and Poles, to name only the largest ones. In the west, the Alsatians were ethnolinguistically German but under French royal authority. When the

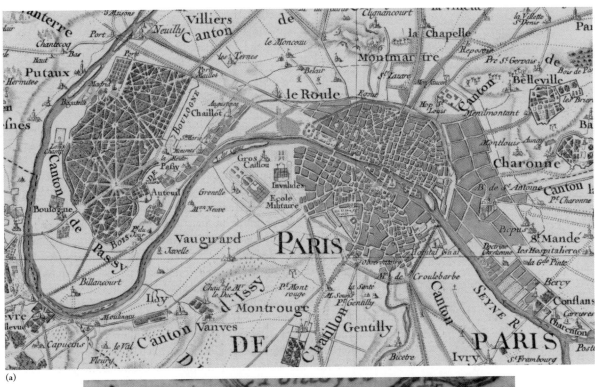

(a)

(b)

Mapping a Nation. Evidence for the emergence of a French national identity can be found by examining two maps that were drawn for the French monarchy at different periods in its history. Commissioned by Louis XIV in 1669, four succeeding generations of the Cassini family produced the first multisheet, topographic map series of an entire country (a). Over 100 years later, in 1789, the Geometric Map of France was finally completed on the eve of the revolution, consisting of 182 sheets that form a 36-foot square when assembled. Shown here is a detail of Paris and its environs. With its recognizable topography and realistic symbols, the map profoundly contributed to the idea of a French nation by articulating a vision of a country whose land was owned by all French citizens. By comparison, a map of France commissioned by King Henry IV in 1594, during a time when France was riven by political and religious strife, shows a completely different spatial geography (b). In contrast to the social patterns of life that can be discerned in the Cassini map, the General Map of France simply concerns itself with depicting the dynastic claims of the monarch. Towns are clearly labeled, but no information is conveyed about the land itself. In the 200 years that separate the two maps, the way the French viewed their land had changed.

In Praise of Language and Heritage

"What a treasure language is when kinship groups grow into tribes and nations! Even the smallest of nations . . . cherishes in and through its language the history, the poetry, and songs about the great deeds of its forefathers. The language is its collective treasure, the source of its social wisdom and communal self-respect. Instruction, games, and dances are connected with it."

—F. M. Barnard, trans. *Johann Gottfried Herder on Social and Political Culture*, p. 165. Cambridge: Cambridge University Press, 1969.

Grimm's Fairy Tales. Perhaps the most famous collection of folktales in the Western tradition, *Children's and Household Stories* (1812) was assembled by Wilhelm and Jakob Grimm as a way to preserve their country's national spirit and to rekindle in their countrymen an appreciation for their Germanic roots. The stories they collected, such as this illustration from *Rapunzel*, were brought together through fieldwork and by peasant women who would visit the brothers and recite stories that awoke "thoughts of the heart."

Enlightenment spread in educated circles, there was clearly an ethnolinguistic background; but in the absence of a central state, the educated urban professionals, administrators, and educators professed a constitutional nationalism tinged with ethnic and linguistic elements.

Herder's Ethnic German Nationalism　A central figure in articulating these ethnolinguistic elements in Germany into what was later to become a German nationalist ideology was Johann Gottfried Herder (1744–1803). Herder's father was an elementary school teacher and Lutheran church warden in eastern Germany. At university, Herder studied with Kant but also with others under whose influence he became familiar with Pietism, a Lutheran version of the medieval Catholic mystical tradition. Employed first as a preacher and then as an administrator at assorted courts in central Germany, he published widely as a literary critic and was on close terms with Goethe and other German Enlightenment figures. Like Locke, he distinguished between negative and positive passions; and like Rousseau, he subverted the exaggerated emphasis on reason by an exploration of aesthetic and emotional "sentiments," as the positive passions were called. When, toward the end of his life, the French Revolution broke out, however, he gave it his full support, to the consternation of the German monarch as well as many of his Enlightenment colleagues who decried the republicanism in the revolution.

In his writings, Herder sought to meld a highly diffuse ethnic heritage into a more or less coherent set of ideas to be preached not only to the educated but to the people in general through school curricula, history, and the arts. His major work, *On the Origin of Language* (1772), contains the core concepts of his new ideology of ethnolinguistic nationalism.

Herder not only focused on the traditions of high culture but also encouraged the collection of folk stories and fairy tales, even though he realized that peasants and laborers were completely outside the nationalism he projected. Similarly, given his interests in mysticism, his extensive references to religion were reflective more of the enlightened but moderate urban, educated population than either the clergy or the Catholic and Lutheran peasants. In principle, however, ethnolinguistic nationalism was open to an incorporation of religion; and thus, this nationalism may be defined as "religio-ethnolinguistic." Finally, while the ethnolinguistic nationalism of Herder's writings centered on "Germanness," it did not exclude pluralism. Far from elevating German culture to the pinnacle of all culture, Herder recognized that other peoples, notably the Slavs, had their own traditions and were therefore entitled to their own nation-states.

Germany's ethnolinguistic version of the Enlightenment received a major boost during the transition from the French Revolution to the Napoleonic wars. The turning point was Napoleon's self-elevation as emperor, as we have already seen in the case of Beethoven. Another influential figure was Johann Gottlieb Fichte

(1762–1814), a student of Kant. In 1806, when the French had defeated Prussia, Fichte turned from his highly abstract Enlightenment
thought in the tradition of Kant to flaming patriotic appeals for the
liberation from French imperialism.

By this time, a German middle class of urban professionals, administrators, and educators was emerging whose members met at
student fraternities, public lectures, salons, musical evenings, and
gymnastics clubs. Aroused for the patriotic liberation of their states
and political unification into a single Germany, they were deeply disappointed by the restoration of the pre-1789 regional monarchies,
which made minimal concessions to constitutionalism. Superior
force for the moment cowed them into reluctant acceptance or underground agitation.

The Growth of the Nation-State, 1815–1871

Napoleon's defeat in Russia in 1812 and the Congress in Vienna of
1815 were major turning points in the political development of Europe. Monarchies and aristocracies reappeared throughout the continent, and the restored kings allowed only for the barest minimum of
popular representation in parliaments, if at all. In France, where republicans were the
most numerous, monarchists and republicans went through several further rounds of
revolution before the republican nation-state emerged supreme. The other countries
of continental Europe did not go that far; here, constitutional monarchies survived,
in spite of a major challenge in 1848. By contrast, in Anglo-America, the supremacy
of constitutionalism was unchallenged during the 1800s. Here, the nation-state grew
with no disruptions, gradually incorporating more citizens into the constitutional
process. The exception in the United States, however, was the Civil War, over the
question of slavery and the incorporation of African-Americans into full citizenship.
The victory of the Union, however, guaranteed and even strengthened the continuation of the pattern of modern nation-state formation.

Restoration Monarchies, 1815–1848

For a full generation, monarchists in Europe sought to return to the politics of absolutism. This return required repression and elaborate political manipulation to keep
the now identifiable middle class of public employees, professionals, schoolteach-
ers, and early factory entrepreneurs away from meaningful political participation. A
"Concert of Europe" emerged in which rulers avoided intervention in the domestic
politics of fellow monarchs, except in cases of internal unrest when they appealed to
their neighbors for support. This was especially the case in Italy, where Austria intervened in several places and at several occasions to suppress nationalist agitation.

The Congress of Vienna   European leaders met in 1815 at Vienna after the
fall of Napoleon in an effort to restore order to a war-torn continent. The driving
principle at the session was monarchical conservatism, articulated mainly by Prince
Klemens von Metternich (1773–1859), Austria's prime minister. An opponent of

---

Germanness

"Thus was the German nation [*Volk*]
placed—sufficiently united within
itself by a common language and
a common way of thinking, and
sharply enough severed from the
other peoples—in the middle of
Europe, as a wall to divide races not
akin.... Only when each people, left
to itself, develops and forms itself
in accordance with its own peculiar
quality ... does the manifestation of
divinity appear in its true mirror as
it ought to be."

—Johann Gottlieb Fichte. *Thirteenth Address,
Addresses to the German Nation.* Edited by
George A. Kelly, p. 190. New York: Harper Torch
Books, 1968.

Contempt for Constitutionalism

"We see this intermediary class abandon itself with a blind fury and animosity ... to all the means which seem proper to assuage its thirst for power, applying itself to the task of persuading kings that their rights are confined to sitting upon a throne, while those of the people are to govern, and to attack all that centuries have bequeathed as holy and worthy of man's respect."

—"Confession of Faith, Metternich's Secret Memorandum to the Emperor Alexander," in Clemens Wenzel Lothar Metternich (Fürst von), *Memoirs of Prince Metternich, 1773–1829*, ed. Prince Richard Metternich and trans. Mrs. Alexander Napier, vol. 3, p. 468 (New York: Charles Scribner's Sons, 1881).

constitutional nationalism, now called "republicanism," Metternich was determined to resist the aspirations of the still struggling middle classes outside France, whose members, as he saw it, were driven by the "evil" of "presumption." Metternich depicted this presumption as a "moral gangrene."

To accomplish his objective of reinstituting kings and emperors ruling by divine grace, Metternich had the congress hammer out two principles: legitimacy and balance of power. The principle of legitimacy was conceived as a way to both recognize exclusive monarchial rule in Europe and to reestablish the borders of France as they were in 1789. The principle of the balance of power involved a basic policy of preventing any one state from rising to dominance over any other. In the case of internal uprisings, member states promised to come to each other's aid. Members agreed to convene at regular intervals in the future in what they called the "Concert," so as to ensure peace and tranquility in Europe. What is remarkable about this is that with only minor exceptions this policy of the balance of power remained intact down to 1914 (see Map 22.3).

As successful as the implementation of these two principles was, the solution devised for the German territories—now no longer with an overall ruler since the Holy Roman Empire was dissolved in 1806—was less satisfactory. The Congress of Vienna created an unwieldy and weak confederation of 39

MAP 22.3 Europe After the Congress of Vienna.

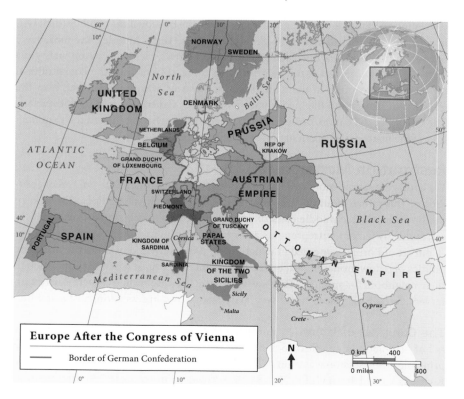

German states, including the empire of Austria and the kingdoms of Prussia, Denmark, and the Netherlands. Prussia and Austria promptly embarked on a collision course over dominance in the confederation, with Prussia keeping the initiative and creating a customs union in 1834. Prussia's main purpose in this was to find outlets for its rising industrial and commercial interests in the northern German Ruhr region. Constitutionalist and republican Germans disliked the confederation as well since they had no meaningful voice in it. Thus, by resolving the overall issue of coexistence among the German states, but not of their fragmentation, the Congress was only partially successful.

Further Revolutions in France

In keeping with the principle of legitimacy, the Congress restored the French Bourbon monarchy with the coronation of King Louis XVIII (r. 1814–1824), a brother of Louis XVI. Louis, even though determined to restore full absolutist powers, was indecisive as to which republican institutions to abolish first. Playing for time, he tolerated the "White Terror," during which the returning aristocracy and other royalists pursued revenge for their sufferings during the revolution. When Louis died in 1824 the conservatives succeeded in putting Charles X (1824–1830), a second brother of Louis XVI, on the throne. Charles took the extreme course of restoring the property of the aristocracy lost during the revolution and reestablishing the crown's ties to the Catholic Church.

Republican reaction to Charles's restoration policy was swift. In two elections, the republicans won a majority and overthrew the king in the 1830 election. But they stopped short of abolishing the monarchy and elevated Louis-Philippe (1830–1848), son of a pro-republican duke who had been guillotined and had fought in the republican guards during 1789–1792, to the throne. Under this "bourgeois king," as he was sometimes caricatured, however, rising income gaps in the middle class as well as difficult living conditions among the nascent industrial working class led to new tensions. In the ensuing revolution of 1848, in which thousands of workers perished, the adherents of restoration and republicanism attempted another compromise: Louis-Philippe went into exile, and the parliament elected Louis-Napoleon Bonaparte (r. 1848–1852; self-declared emperor 1852–1870), a nephew of the former emperor, as president.

Uprisings Across Europe

After the revolution in Paris, uprisings occurred in the spring of 1848 in cities such as Berlin, Vienna, Prague, Budapest, Palermo, and Milan, as well as in three Irish counties. In Prussia the king seemingly bowed to pressure from revolutionaries and promised constitutional reforms. In Austria, hit by uprisings in multiple cities and by multiple nationalities, both the emperor and Metternich, the driving forces of 1815, resigned. The successor

Rebellion. Following the successful revolution of 1848 that ended the monarchy of Louis-Philippe in France, similar uprisings broke out across Europe. This image shows the Berlin Alexander Square barricades of March 1848.

with Russian help slowly regained military control over the Italians, Czechs, and Hungarians, as well as his own Austrians.

In the German Confederation, also hit by uprisings, moderate and republican delegates convened a constitutional assembly in Frankfurt in May 1848. This assembly elaborated the basic law for a new, unified state for German speakers and elected a provisional government. The new hard-line Austrian emperor, however, refused to let go of his non-German subjects. Therefore, the constitution joined only the German Federation and Prussia (also with non-German minorities) into a unitary state, with the provision for a future addition of German-speaking Austria. Against strong resistance by republicans, the delegates offered the Prussian king a new hereditary imperial crown in the name of the German people. But the king, unwilling to accept the principle of popular sovereignty, refused the crown "of clay." This refusal turned the tide against this Frankfurt Assembly. Moderate delegates departed, and radical ones instigated revolts. Prussian troops stepped in and relieved a group of grateful regional monarchs of their insurrectionists. By July 1849, the provisional Frankfurt government had come to an end and Germany's constitutional experiment had ended.

Irish Nationalism   In Ireland, ethnolinguistic nationalism found adherents among groups of urban professionals and educators in the early 1800s. Since they were acutely aware that Ireland did not possess much in terms of a literary-artistic tradition, they sought to position the Catholic tradition as a nationalizing element, around which to center nationalism, while others were more firmly wedded to secularism. In the uprising of 1848 the secularists won out. But the example of Catholicism in Ireland demonstrates that ethnolinguistic nationalism could easily be extended into the religious heritage if desired, foreshadowing trends of the twentieth century.

The events of 1848 had their origins in the Young Irelander opposition movement against the British Union Act of 1800. Through newspapers, lectures, and election campaigns this movement demanded a repeal of the act, frequently invoking Catholic "Irishness." When in 1845 a potato blight broke out on the island (which probably arrived through guano fertilizer imports mined in potato-growing Peru) causing a severe famine, perhaps one-fifth of the population perished. Only mass emigration to the United States alleviated further suffering. The Young Irelanders vehemently (and justifiably) accused the British government of inaction. Groups of Young Irelanders, tenant farmers, and even a few landlords rose in insurrection and battled police forces in three counties. But they were no match for the police, and the revolt quickly collapsed. Ethnolinguistic nationalism with elements of Catholicism had not yet coalesced into a full nationalist ideology.

Ethnolinguistic Nationalism in Italy   Italy was as fragmented politically as Germany, but unlike Germany it was also largely under foreign domination. Austria controlled the north directly and the center indirectly through relatives from the house of Habsburg. The monarchy of Piedmont in the northwest, the Papal States in the center, and the kingdom of Naples and Sicily (the "Two Sicilies") were independent but administratively and financially weak. After the Metternich restoration, the Italian dynasties had made concessions to constitutionalists; but Austria repressed uprisings in 1820–1821 and 1831–1832 without granting liberties. The republican Carbonari inspired both uprisings; they were members of the crafts guild of "charcoal burners" who had formed fraternities similar to the Freemasons during the eighteenth century. After their decisive defeat in 1831, the remnants formed the "Young Italy" movement.

Realistic second-generation politicians of the Restoration recognized that the middle-class ethnolinguistic nationalism coming to the fore in 1848 was a potent force that could be dipped into. By remobilizing this force in the 1860s, they would be able to end state fragmentation and make Italy and Germany serious players in the European Concert. These politicians were more sympathetic toward French-style constitutionalism than the Restoration politicians but still opposed to republicanism. Their pursuit of "Realpolitik"—exploitation of political opportunities—resulted in 1870–1871 in the transformations of the Italian kingdom of Piedmont and the German Empire of Prussia into the nation-states of Italy and Germany.

The Italian politician who did the most to realize Italy's unification was the prime minister of Piedmont-Sardinia, Count Camillo di Cavour (1810–1861). Cavour was the scion of an old aristocratic family in northwestern Italy with training as a military officer. While in the army, he read widely among French and British political philosophers and became a constitutional nationalist. A supporter of Adam Smith's liberal trade economics, he imported guano fertilizer and grew cash crops, like sugar beets, on his estate. As prime minister he was the driving force behind the development of railroads, first in Piedmont and later in Italy. With the backing of his similarly liberal-minded king, Victor Emanuel II (r. 1849–1878), he engineered the unification of most of Italy under decidedly trying circumstances.

Giuseppe Garibaldi. Garibaldi was an Italian nationalist who, in collaboration with Count Cavour, prime minister of the kingdom of Piedmont, contributed decisively to the unification of Italy. Garibaldi and his "Red Shirts" were able to seize Sicily and Naples from its Bourbon-descended monarch in 1860. He then unified his conquests with the constitutional kingdom of Piedmont to form the nucleus of Italy, which was fully unified a decade later.

Cavour began the unification process in 1858 with lukewarm support from Louis Napoleon of France for Piedmontese military action against Austria. When Cavour was victorious, however, France withdrew its support (fearing a powerful Piedmont) and Austria did not budge from its fortifications in northern Italy. Through adroit maneuvering, Cavour was able to arrange for a favorable plebiscite in north-central Tuscany and Emilia in 1859, gaining these two regions from Austria for Piedmont. A year later Cavour occupied the Papal States and accepted the offer of Giuseppe Garibaldi (1807–1882) to add adjoining Naples and Sicily to a now nearly unified Italy.

Garibaldi, a mariner from Nice in the northwest (present-day France), was a Carbonari and Young Italy republican nationalist with a colorful career as a freedom fighter not only in Italy but also in Brazil and Uruguay. Dressed in his trademark red gaucho shirt with poncho and sombrero, the inspiring Garibaldi attracted large numbers of volunteers wherever he went to fight. Despairing of any republican future for Italy, he threw in his lot with Piedmont and, after invading Naples and Sicily and deposing its monarch in 1860, delivered these two regions to Cavour. Cavour died shortly afterward and, thus, did not live to see Piedmont transform itself into Italy in 1870, when it gained Venice from Austria and Rome from France in the wake of the Prussian–Austrian war of 1870–1871. But he clearly was the power politician who laid the decisive groundwork.

Bismarck and Germany

In contrast to Italy, neither King Wilhelm I (r. 1861–1888) nor his chancellor (prime minister) Otto von Bismarck (in office 1862–1890) had deep sympathies for constitutionalism. By combining their antipathies and forming a coalition of convenience, they succeeded in keeping the constitutionalists in the Prussian parliament in check. But they realized they could dip into the ethnolinguistic nationalism that had poured forth in 1848, using it for power politics: Realpolitik.

Bismarck was a Prussian aristocrat with a legal education rather than a military career. He was multilingual, widely read, and experienced in the diplomacy of the European Concert. He realized that Prussia, a weak player in the Concert, had a chance for greater influence only if the kingdom could absorb the German Federation. For Prussia to do so, Bismarck argued, it had to progress from the talk about unification, as in Frankfurt, to military action, using "blood and iron." From the time of his appointment to 1871, he systematically maneuvered Prussia into an internationally favorable position for the coup that would eventually bring unification: war with France.

First, he exploited a succession crisis in Denmark for a combined Prussian–Austrian campaign to annex Denmark's southern province of Schleswig-Holstein in 1865. Then, when Austria objected to the terms of annexation, he declared war on Austria. After Prussia succeeded in defeating Austria, Bismarck dissolved the German Confederation and annexed several German principalities. In France, Louis-Napoleon Bonaparte was greatly concerned about the rising power of Prussia. He had carried out a coup d'état in 1852, ending the Second Republic and declaring himself emperor—an act that prompted the always quotable Karl Marx to claim that "history always repeats itself, the first time as tragedy, the second time as farce." A distraction on his eastern flank was not at all what Emperor Napoleon III desired.

But he carelessly undermined his precarious strength. First, he prevented a relative of King Wilhelm from succeeding to the throne of Spain when it fell vacant. But when he demanded through his minister, then meeting with Wilhelm at the spa in Bad Ems, additional assurances that Prussia would not put forward candidates

Prussian Victory. After Napoleon III's defeat and surrender in the Franco–Prussian War of 1870–1871, French republican politicians declared the Third Republic and continued the war. But in spite of heroic defensive efforts, Prussian troops occupied Paris in January 1871 (the photo shows the victory parade on the Champs-Elysées) and in Versailles declared the unification of Germany and the foundation of the Second German Empire.

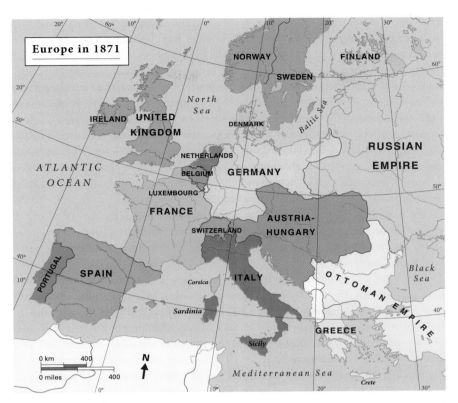

MAP 22.4 **Europe in 1871.**

for any thrones in the future, the canny Bismarck outmaneuvered him. When King Wilhelm politely refused the demand, the chancellor edited the refusal in such a way as to make it insulting to the French. France then declared war on Prussia and was defeated in the crucial battle of Sedan in 1870. Now Bismarck had the upper hand for which he had been diligently working. He used it to annex Alsace-Lorraine from the French, carried out the final unification of Germany, and elevated the new state to the status of an empire in 1871 (see Map 22.4).

Nation-State Building in Anglo-America, 1783–1865

After the independence of the United States in 1783, both the United States and Great Britain were free to pursue their versions of constitutional nation-state development. In the United States, the revolutionaries, as well as subsequent generations, remained faithful to the idea of a republican nation. The restoration of monarchies and ethnolinguistic nationalism that complicated nation-state formation in Europe did not affect the United States and gave rise to a long tradition among American historians of claiming American "exceptionalism." While it is indeed true that the growth of the United States in the 1800s followed its own trajectory, there is also no question that the underlying pattern of modern nation-state formation was very similar to that of Europe. The same conclusion can be drawn concerning Great Britain, which was exceptional in that it became the dominant seaborne world empire but similarly came together as a nation on Atlantic islands subordinating English, Scottish, and Welsh ethnolinguistic traditions to a national constitutionalism.

The United States   During the first half of the nineteenth century the newly independent American states not only prospered but also began a rapid westward expansion. As this process unfolded toward 1850 it became increasingly apparent that sectional differences were developing in the process. Whereas the North developed an industrial and market-driven agricultural economy, the South remained primarily agrarian, relying heavily upon the production of cotton for its economic vitality. Even more, the South relied upon vast numbers of slaves to work the cotton fields of plantations. Cotton was the main fiber for the industrial production of textiles, and it not only defined the wealth of the plantation owners but led them to see chattel slavery as the only viable means to keep the "cotton kingdom" prosperous. In defense of its stance, the South increasingly relied upon the notion of states' rights in opposition to federal control. With the acquisition of new territory extending to the Pacific coast after the war with Mexico from 1846 to 1848 and the constant push of settlement beyond the Mississippi, the vital question of which of the new territories would become "free states" and "slave states" resulted in increasing tensions between North and South.

The result was an attempt by a number of southern states to secede and form a new government, the Confederate States of America. When the new administration of President Abraham Lincoln attempted to suppress this movement, the disastrous American Civil War (1861–1865) began. Resulting in an enormous loss of life—more than 600,000 combatants on both sides were killed—the Civil War finally ended with a northern victory in 1865. There were several major results of the conflict, not least of which was an enhanced unification of the country during the occupation of the southern states by federal troops enforcing the policies of the Reconstruction (1865–1877). First, Lincoln's concept of the primacy of national government over individual assertions of states' rights was now guaranteed. Second, slavery was abolished and slaves were granted full citizenship. Third, rebuilding of the country and opening of the west resulted in a remarkable period of growth, facilitated especially by the expansion of a national network of railroads. By 1900, about 200,000 miles of uniform-gauge track crisscrossed the country and the United States was on its way to becoming the world's predominant industrial power (see Map 22.5). Moreover, there emerged a growing consensus that the American nation had come together after a divisive war, and this was aided by the adoption of signs like the Pledge of Allegiance to the national flag, along with a national anthem, "The Star-Spangled Banner." As a subtle testament to this national unification, historians have noted that before the war people said "the United States *are* . . .; after the war, it became "the United States *is*. . . ."

Despite the new bonds of national unification, the price of reintegrating the old South into the new order was the end of Reconstruction and the reversion over the course of two generations to an imposition of a de facto peonage on its black citizens. Indeed, between 1877 and 1914 state legislatures in the South systematically stripped African Americans of voting rights by means of poll taxes and literacy tests and imposed formal and informal segregation in social and public accommodations. These were enforced by law and all too often by lynchings and other forms of violence. In order to accommodate the sensibilities of white southerners regarding race, most northern policy and opinion makers gradually backed away from the views espoused by the champions of racial equality during Reconstruction and gave tacit acquiescence to southern efforts to retain white hegemony. The drive for full

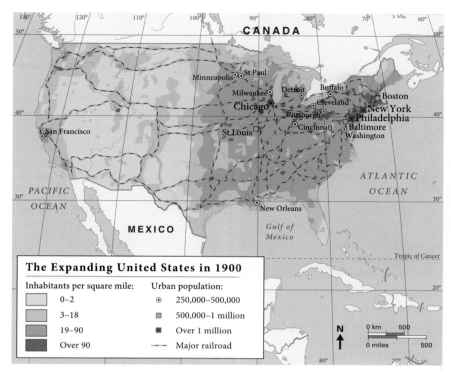

MAP 22.5 **The Expanding United States in 1900.**

civil rights would thus occupy a sizeable share of American domestic policy debates throughout the twentieth century.

Reform Measures   As in other Western nation-states, rapid industrialization produced social and labor unrest, resulting in the reforming initiatives of the Progressive era, which extended from 1890 to 1914. Although the later nineteenth century is referred to as the Gilded Age, epitomized by the staggering wealth of industrial tycoons like Andrew Carnegie (1835–1919) and John D. Rockefeller (1839–1937), all was not well beneath the surface. Big business had grown to such an extent that in the early 1900s a few hundred firms controlled two-fifths of all American manufacturing. The "trust buster" president, Theodore Roosevelt (r. 1901–1909), and Congress ended the monopolies of many firms, Rockefeller's Standard Oil among them, which had to cut itself up into 30 smaller companies. A new Department of Commerce and Labor (1903) and the Pure Food and Drug and Meat Inspection Acts (1906) helped the hard-pressed workers and consumers. With the Federal Reserve Act (1913) and the Federal Trade Commission Act (1914) Congress created an overall framework for the supervision of the financial and business sectors. As many contemporaries realized, a free market prospered only with at least a minimum of regulations.

Great Britain   The pattern of constitutional nation-state construction that Britain pursued in the eighteenth and nineteenth centuries was somewhat steadier. It remained more or less uninterrupted even during the Napoleonic wars, during

Evicted. Demolishing the houses of evicted tenants was ruthlessly practiced by British authorities in Ireland, particularly during the famine years of 1847–50. The wholesale destruction of homes—and livelihoods—horrified many contemporary observers, so much so that when Queen Victoria visited Ireland in 1849 she was publicly rebuked: "Thy royal name must be connected in future history with the astounding record of extermination of our unhappy race." This 1890 painting by Elizabeth Thompson, Lady Butler (1846–1933), one of the most accomplished English women artists of the time, is all the more striking because most of her other works portray the heroism and valor of British soldiers.

which Great Britain was the one enemy Napoleon was unable to harm. As was the Ile de France around Paris during the revolution and throughout the nineteenth century, England remained the core of the nation, to which the other British nationalities had to acculturate culturally if not ethnically. Scotland, traditionally divided between the highlands and lowlands, developed a greater sense of its own identity only slowly. The development began on the level of folklore, with the revival of Scottish dress and music (clan tartans, kilts, and bagpipes). More serious constitutional issues came to the fore in 1853 when the Scots, upset by what they thought was more attention paid by the government to Ireland, founded an association for the vindication of Scottish rights. The Scottish demand for home rule found sympathetic ears in the Liberal Party but not among the Conservatives. In 1885, the government established the position of secretary for Scotland. But home rule would come only after World War I.

The Welsh were even less satisfied with being ruled by London. In part this was due to the relatively early industrialization in Wales and the development of a Welsh working class, which had organized uprisings in the 1830s. Religious issues, mostly related to opposition to the Church of England among nonconformists (e.g., Methodists, Quakers, and Presbyterians), and education issues surrounding the so-called Treachery of the Blue Books added to the unrest. A governmental report of 1847, bound in blue covers, found that education in Wales was substandard: Sunday schools were the only schools offering education in Welsh, while regular schools were based on English for children who spoke only Welsh. Throughout the report ethnic stereotypes proliferated, documenting the fissures in the English-dominated acculturation process. As in Scotland, home rule came only after the Great War.

In Ireland, after the Great Famine of 1845–1849 already discussed in this chapter, rural production and land issues remained the main points of contention around which Irish demands for home rule and independence crystallized. A Protestant Irish landlord class still controlled most of the land in the second half of the nineteenth century. During the worldwide Long Depression of 1873–1896 Irish tenant farmers received low prices for their crops but no reductions in rent. Land reform became a large issue, woven closely into the politics of self-determination. A "land war" ensued between organized tenants and nationalists, on the one hand, and the British Army, on the other. It eventually led in 1898 to local self-rule for the Irish and in 1903–1909 to land reform. Home rule also did not come before World War I.

Apart from the issue of the constitutional nation-state, Britain's Parliament took cognizance of the growing middle class and the need to enact reforms for the working class. A contest between Liberal and Conservative governments ensued over the enactment of increasingly inclusive reforms. For example, the Great Reform Bill of 1832 shifted seats from southern districts to the more industrialized center and north. The result is often called the "victory of the middle classes" because industrial interests now took control of Parliament away from the propertied aristocracy. Further reforms followed: The repeal of the Corn Laws in 1846 liberated imports and made grain cheaper, and the Second Reform Act of 1867 extended the franchise to larger numbers of working-class voters. The end result was not only that Britain escaped the revolutions of 1848 but also that the British electorate was largely united during the Victorian period in its support for British imperialism around the globe.

Romanticism and Realism: Philosophical and Artistic Expression to 1850

The Victorian period, named after the long reign of Queen Victoria of Britain (r. 1837–1901), was a time in which Europeans and Americans alike celebrated the sobriety, frugality, and discipline of the emancipated urban middle class. While the perception of the superficial, extravagant, and dissolute aristocracy had now lost some of its power, the working classes—with their allegedly coarse, violent, and gullible ways—were increasingly seen as a threat to the social stability and moral fiber of the nation. This new "realist" middle class aesthetic at the end of the century was in many ways the opposite of the earlier "romantic" one, which had emerged from the Enlightenment at the beginning of the century. Early on, the liberation from political and artistic absolutism was exhilarating; as time wore on, however, the grim realities of the industrial transformation made this liberty considerably less exciting and more disturbing.

Romanticism: Intellectual and artistic movement that emphasized emotion and imagination over reason and sought the sublime in nature.

Romanticism

As we have seen, Rousseau and Kant had demonstrated the limitations of Enlightenment materialist thought in which *embodied reason*, surrounded by the senses and passions, constituted reality. Kant, therefore, proposed that reason, or mind, is in part independent or transcendent, containing the categories without which any talk about senses and passions would not even be possible. Philosophers, writers, composers, and painters of the period of **romanticism** drew the conclusion that the mind was entirely independent, creating aesthetic categories out of its own powers. Not all romantic thinkers and artists went this far, but for romantics creativity became absolute. Indeed, the stereotype of the creative "genius" heroically attempting to cross imaginative thresholds to grasp at transcendence became firmly implanted in the public imagination during this time.

Dialectic: The investigation of truth by discussion; in the context here, dialectic refers to Hegel's belief that a higher truth is comprehended by a continuous unification of opposites.

Philosophers and Poets
The one philosopher who, building on Kant, postulated the complete freedom of mind or spirit was Georg Wilhelm Friedrich Hegel (1770–1831). The most systematic of the so-called idealist philosophers in Germany, Hegel asserted that all thought proceeded dialectically from the "transcendental ego" to its opposite, matter, and from there to the spiritualized synthesis of nature. This **dialectic** permeates his entire "system" of philosophy.

Nature as Teacher

One impulse from a vernal wood
May teach you more of man,
Of moral evil and of good,
Than all the sages can.

"The Tables Turned; An Evening Scene on the Same Subject," (1798). William Wordsworth, *The Complete Poetical Works*, ed. Henry Reed, p. 393 (Philadelphia: Trautmann & Hayes, 1854).

A parallel "ego-"centered creative poetry burst forth, with William Wordsworth (1770–1850), Samuel Taylor Coleridge (1772–1834), and Percy Bysshe Shelley (1792–1822) in Britain. In America, the "transcendentalist" Ralph Waldo Emerson (1803–1882) was the self-declared prophet of the absolute, imaginative self. Under Emerson's influence, the American Emily Dickinson (1830–1886) wrote poetry welling up "from the interior drama" of imagination. An afterglow of this imaginative absolute was still present in the later French symbolist Arthur Rimbaud (1854–1891), who sought ineffable beauty and pure feeling in the mere evocation by words, rather than formal rhyme.

Composers   While the romantics were struggling to express the sublime, ephemeral evocation of beauty with words that were at least in part concrete, the romantic composers had no such problems. The transitional figure of the German Ludwig van Beethoven, already discussed above, and the Frenchman Hector Berlioz (1803–1869) pioneered the new genre of program music, with the *Pastoral Symphony* (Symphony #6) and the *Symphonie phantastique*, respectively, emphasizing passion and emotional intensity and the freedom of the musical spirit over traditional form. From among the emerging middle class, eager to develop their romantic sensibilities and play music at home, a veritable explosion of composers erupted during the first half of the 1800s, such as Nicolò Paganini (1782–1840), Franz Schubert (1797–1828), Felix Mendelssohn (1809–1847), Frédéric Chopin (1810–1849), Robert Schumann (1810–1856), and Johannes Brahms (1833–1897). Often composing at a furious rate, these musicians were also virtuosi on the violin or piano, playing their own new musical forms and traveling on concert circuits all across Europe.

Painters   Similar to music, the medium of painting also lent itself to the expression of romantic feelings of passion and the mind's overflowing imaginative aesthetics. Not surprisingly, the proliferation of romantic painters numbered in the hundreds, and a small handful will have to suffice for discussion here. The common feature of these painters is that they departed from the established academic practices and styles. They either let nature dictate the direction and extent of their absorption into it or expressed their personal impressions forcefully with new, dramatic topics.

A follower of the first direction was Caspar David Friedrich (1774–1840) in Germany, who drew solitary figures absorbed by and absorbing an all-encompassing nature. Similarly, John Constable (1776–1837) was a British painter of superficially conventional landscapes that dramatically expressed the shapes and forces of nature. The French Théodore Géricault [Ge-ree-CO] (1791–1824) and Eugène Delacroix (1798–1863) followed the second direction and depicted dramatic or unusual scenes, as well as revolutionary gestures. Géricault caused a scandal when he exhibited *Raft of the Medusa* (1819), a float packed with sailors but without a captain: The conventions of traditional society demanded an orderly social hierarchy, even if in distress. Delacroix sought to express the drama of the French revolution of 1830 as well as Orientalist themes, for example, in *The Women of Algiers in Their Apartment* (1834), showing three women in languid poses with a black slave girl. While holding still firmly to the Renaissance style of perspective, light, and shadow, the turn to romantic freedom in these painters is unmistakable.

(a)

(b)

Romantic Art. Romantic painters expressed an absorbing, encompassing nature in their art. Note the barely recognizable steam-powered train in this painting (a) by J. M. W. Turner, *Rain, Steam, and Speed: The Great Western Railway* (1844). Romantic painters also depicted dramatic or exotic scenes relating to revolutions or foreign lands, such as the languid, bored harem scene in *The Women of Algiers in Their Apartment* (1834) by Delacroix (b).

Novels and Stories   As in the other art forms, romanticism in literature appears in heroines or heroes and their passions and sentiments. In the still strongly late Enlightenment-informed prose of the British author Jane Austen (1775–1817), witty and educated urbane society shapes the character and sensibilities of young women and prepares them for their reward, that is, love of the proper gentleman and marriage to him. These plots are developed with great intricacy in, for example, *Pride and Prejudice* (1813) and *Emma* (1816). A generation later, also in Britain, the three Brontë sisters, Charlotte (1816–1855), Emily (1818–1848), and Anne (1820–1849), published novels with equally complex plots but much greater emphasis on romantic passion, on the one hand, and character flaws or social ills, on the other. Charlotte's *Jane Eyre* (1847) and Emily's *Wuthering Heights* (1847) are two examples. Anne's *The Tenant of Wildfell Hall* (1848) goes a step further by including taboo topics such as a sensitive and suffering woman leaving her alcoholic and abusive husband with her son to live in hiding as an artist. The novels also contain mysterious, seemingly inexplicable happenings—artistic devices which the American Edgar Allan Poe (1809–1849) used more explicitly in his thematic Gothic stories and tales, such as "The Fall of the House of Usher" (1839).

Realism

Toward the middle of the 1800s, many artists and writers shifted their focus from the romanticism of the self and its aesthetic or moral sentiments to the **realism** of the middle classes, arranging this new group in an industrializing world. In philosophy, thinkers identified stages leading progressively to the rise of middle classes and industrialism. And in literature, the complex and tangled relationships that characterized the plots of the romantics continued, but now in the more prosaic urban world of factories and working classes.

Histories of Philosophy   One of the works in Hegel's system was *Lectures on the Philosophy of History* (1822–1830). In this work, the philosopher sketches the dialectical progression of the spirit to a progressively more differentiated

Realism: The belief that material reality exists independently of the people who observe it.

Realism. The documentary power of photography spurred the new impulses of realism that emerged around 1850. The photograph here shows the execution of hostages in the Commune of Paris in the spring of 1871 shortly before its final defeat by troops of the provisional French national government. One of the executed hostages was Georges Darboy, archbishop of Paris, a critic of the pope and strong patriot who cared for the wounded of the war against Prussia in 1870.

ASSASSINAT DES OTAGES À LA PRISON DE LA ROQUETTE LE 24 MAI 1871

self-consciousness, until it culminates in his own time with the transcendental ego. The progression was also one from east to west, from India and China via the Middle East to Europe, culminating with the new revolutionary nations of 1776– 1789. The French thinker Auguste Comte (1798–1857) composed a six-volume study entitled *The Positive Philosophy* (1830–1842), in which he arranged world history into the three successive stages of the theological, metaphysical, and scientific. In his view, the scientific advances of the sciences had all but phased out the metaphysical stage and had ushered in the last, scientific era. For Comte this was a sign of Europe's progress and a "positive" stage; his philosophy is therefore labeled "positivism." Comte further argued that the only sure way of arriving at truth was based on scientific facts and knowledge of the world acquired through the senses. Since in Comte's view the laws governing human behavior could be ascertained with the same degree of precision as the laws of nature, he became the founder of the science of sociology. Karl Marx (1818–1883), as we will see in more detail in Chapter 23, equally convinced of the scientific character of his philosophy of history, proposed the stages of slavery, feudalism, capitalism, world revolution, and socialism or communism. Today, these Eurocentric assumptions about Western triumphalism are no longer supportable, given that Enlightenment materialism, constitutionalism, nationalism, and industrialization have become the common, generic property of the contemporary world.

Prose Literature   Prose writers, of course, were for the most part unconcerned about the allegedly scientific character of their writings. On the other hand, as writers of fiction, the move away from sentiments to realistic scenes as they were encountered in middle-class society required new aesthetic experimentation so that the ordinary could be a heightened reflection of the new "reality" of life in the industrial age. William Makepeace Thackeray (1811–1863) in England, for example, was a supreme satirist, as displayed in *Vanity Fair*, a book on human foibles and peccadilloes. His compatriot Charles Dickens (1812–1870) had a similar focus but used working- and lower middle-class characters in his many novels. The English-woman George Eliot, born Mary Ann Evans, (1819–1880) was politically oriented, placing small-town social relations into sets of concrete political events in Great Britain, as in *Middlemarch* (1874). Gustave Flaubert (1821–1880) in France experimented with a variety of styles, among which extremely precise and unadorned description of objects and situations is perhaps the most important, for example, in *Madame Bovary* (1857). Henry James (1843–1916), an American living in Britain, in his self-declared masterpiece, *The Ambassadors* (1903), explored the psychological complexities of individuals whose entwined lives crossed both sides of the Atlantic. In the end, realism, with its individuals firmly anchored in the new class society of the 1800s, had moved far from the freedom and equality celebrated by the romantics.

Putting It All Together

Though the pattern of nation-state building in Europe and North America was relatively slow and, in places, painful, it has become the dominant mode of political organization in the world today. As we will see in subsequent chapters, the aftermath of World War I and the decolonization movement following World War II gave a tremendous boost to the process of nation-state formation around the world. Here, the legacy of European colonialism both planted these ideas among the colonized and, by supplying the Enlightenment ideas of revolution and the radical remaking of society, provided the ideological means of achieving their own liberation from foreign rule. In both cases, the aspirations of peoples to "nationhood" followed older European models as the colonies were either granted independence or fought to gain it from declining empires. But, in many respects, their efforts mirrored the difficulties of the first constitutional nationalist states and, more commonly, the initial ethnolinguistic ones.

Take the example of the United States. Though it achieved world economic leadership by 1914, it had faced an early constitutional crisis, endured a prolonged sectional struggle in which slavery marred the constitutional order for almost three-quarters of a century, fought a bloody civil war for national unification that very nearly destroyed it, and remained united in part by acquiescing in practices of overt segregation and discrimination against the 10 percent of its population that was of African descent. Or take the case of France. Its people adopted constitutional nationalism in 1789, but the monarchy it seemingly replaced bounced back three times. Thus, even in the later nineteenth century, Abraham Lincoln's hope that "government of the people, by the people, for the people shall not perish from the earth" was still very much open to question.

Yet another example is the case of Germany, where ethnolinguistic nationalism diluted the straightforward enthusiasm for the constitution and the symbols accompanying it. Historians continue to argue over whether Germany, and by extension other central and eastern European nations, took a special route (*Sonderweg*) to constitutional normality or whether the path was the same except that the pace slowed at critical times. In retrospect, it is impossible to say which of the speed bumps on the way toward the nation-state—slavery/racism, residual monarchism, or the

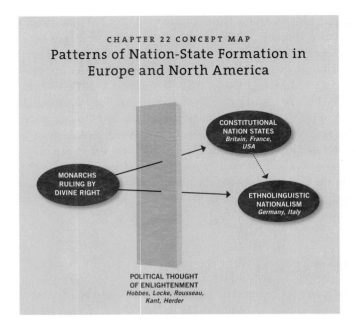

CHAPTER 22 CONCEPT MAP
Patterns of Nation-State Formation in Europe and North America

MONARCHS RULING BY DIVINE RIGHT

CONSTITUTIONAL NATION STATES
Britain, France, USA

ETHNOLINGUISTIC NATIONALISM
Germany, Italy

POLITICAL THOUGHT OF ENLIGHTENMENT
Hobbes, Locke, Rousseau, Kant, Herder

twentieth-century experiments of communism and supremacist nationalism—were responsible for the longest delay. In Part 6 we will consider all of these developments in more detail (see Concept Map).

Review and Respond

1. What were the origins and outcomes of the American Revolution? Of the French Revolution?

2. Why was there a period of monarchical restoration, in Europe in the first half of the nineteenth century?

3. What motivated the successful/abortive revolutions of 1848? Discuss their spread across Europe.

4. Which factors contributed to the unification of Italy and Germany?

5. Which parts of human nature did the romantics glorify and why? With what results?

6. How did realism differ from romanticism?

> For additional resources, including maps, primary sources, visuals, and quizzes, please go to www.oup.com/us/vonsivers. Please see the Further Resources section at the back of the book for additional readings and suggested websites.

Thinking Through Patterns

▶ **How did the pattern of constitutional nationalism, emerging from the American and French Revolutions, affect the course of events in the Western world during the first half of the nineteenth century?**

Constitutional nationalism emerged as a result of the American and French revolutionaries succeeding in overthrowing absolute rule. The constitutional revolutionaries replaced the loyalty of subjects to a monarch with that of free and equal citizens to the national constitution. This form of nationalism called for unity among the citizens regardless of ethnic, linguistic, or religious identity. In the United States, this nationalism had to overcome a conservative adherence to slavery in the South before it gained general recognition after the end of the Civil War. In France, republican nationalists battled conservative monarchists for nearly a century before they were able to finally defeat them in the Third Republic.

Constitutional nationalists emphasized the principles of freedom, equality, constitution, rule of law, elections, and representative assembly regardless of ethnicity, language, or religion. However, nationalists in areas of Europe lacking centralized monarchies sought to first unify what they identified as dispersed members of their nation through ideologies that emphasized common origin, centuries of collective history, and shared literary, artistic, and religious traditions. In these ethnolinguistic (and sometimes religious) ideologies constitutional principles were secondary. Only once unification in a nation-state was achieved, the form of government—monarchist, constitutional-monarchist, republican—would then be chosen.

▶ **In what ways did ethnolinguistic nationalism differ from constitutional nationalism, and what was its influence on the formation of nation-states in the second half of the nineteenth century?**

▶ **What were the reactions among thinkers and artists to the developing pattern of nation-state formation? How did they define the intellectual-artistic movements of romanticism and realism?**

Philosophers and artists in the romantic period put a strong emphasis on individual creativity. They either viewed this creativity as an upwelling of impulses and sentiments pouring forth with little intellectual control or, conversely, considered their creativity as the result of an absolute or transcendent mind working through them as individuals. As middle classes emerged toward the mid-1800s, individual creativity gave way to a greater awareness, called "realism," of the social environment with its class structure and industrial characteristics.

Chapter 23

1750–1914

Industrialization and Its Discontents

In the late summer of 1845, Mary Paul, age 15, came to a decision that would alter her life forever. Already at this tender age she had begun to realize just how limited her prospects were in the hardscrabble farm country of rural Vermont, so she decided to head for Massachusetts and stake her future on finding a job in the newly expanding textile industry.

Exactly how that future would unfold can be seen in numerous letters she wrote to her widowed father, Bela, over the coming years. As her correspondence reveals, the primary reason behind her dramatic decision to uproot herself was simply to make steady wages, rather than rely on the uncertainties and drudgery of farm work. On September 13, 1845, Mary

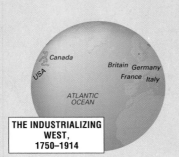

THE INDUSTRIALIZING WEST, 1750–1914

Seeing Patterns

▶ Where and when did the Industrial Revolution originate?

▶ What were some effects of industrialization on Western society? How did social patterns change?

▶ In what ways did industrialization contribute to innovations in technology? How did these technological advances contribute to Western imperialism in the late nineteenth century?

▶ What new directions in science, philosophy, religion, and the arts did industrialism generate? What kind of responses did it provoke?

wrote for her father's consent to leave her nearby domestic job and seek employment in the booming mill town of Lowell, Massachusetts. On November 20, Mary wrote that she had already "found a place in a spinning room and the next morning I went to work." She continued, "I like very well have [sic] 50cts first payment increasing every payment as I get along in work. [I] have a first rate overseer and a very good boarding place." Shortly before Christmas, Mary reported that her wages had increased: "Last Tuesday we were paid. In all I had six dollars and sixty cents paid $4.68 for board. With the rest I got me a pair of rubbers and a pair of 50.cts shoes. Next payment I am to have a dollar a week beside my board." She then went on to offer her father some insights into her daily routine in the mill, one with which millions of workers around the world would soon grow quite familiar: "At 5 o'clock in the morning the bell rings for the folks to get up and get breakfast. At half past six it rings for the girls to get up and at seven they are called into the mill. At half past 12 we have dinner are called back again at one and stay till half past seven." Mary closes by pointing out that "I think that the factory is the best place for me and if any girl wants employment I advise them to come to Lowell."

Child Workers, North Carolina, 1910. The American photojournalist, sociologist, and reformer Lewis Hine (1874–1940) was hired by The National Child Labor Committee in 1908 to document the prevalence of underage boys and girls working in mills and factories throughout the rapidly industrializing United States. The young "spinners" in this North Carolina textile mill smile shyly, even proudly, but they cannot hide their disheveled appearance, visible signs of fatigue, and the psychological stress they endured working long hours for little pay in dangerous conditions.

After working for 4 years in the mill at Lowell, Mary moved to Claremont, New Hampshire, to be with her aging father. Two years later, however, she relocated to Brattleboro, Vermont, where she and another woman started a coat-making business. On November 27, 1853, Mary's letter to her father reveals her guilt about a conflict that would become all too familiar to workers in this new age: how to balance the need to earn a living with the obligation to take care of one's family: "It troubles me very much, the thought of your being lame so much and alone too. If there were any way that I could make it expedient I would go back to Claremont myself and I sometimes think I ought to do so but the chance for one there is so *small* [sic]."

Things apparently did not work out in Brattleboro, and 2 years later Mary's search for better employment led her to one of the many experimental communities that had sprung up in the United States during the first half of the nineteenth century. In this case it was the North American Phalanx, a utopian agricultural community in Red Bank, New Jersey, based on the socialist ideas of the Frenchman Charles Fourier. A little over a year later, however, the Phalanx dissolved, forcing Mary to move back to New Hampshire, where she found work as a housekeeper. Finally, at the age of 27, Mary married and moved to Lynn, Massachusetts, where she and her husband settled down to raise a family.

Mary Paul's experiences, reflecting those of thousands of other young, single women in rural farming regions, signaled a momentous change in the patterns of American and world history. Like Great Britain and areas throughout northern Europe, the northeastern United States was now in the initial stages of what we have termed "scientific–industrial society." The agrarian–urban model, which had lasted for millennia on every inhabited continent except Australia, was now slowly giving way to a society based on machine-made goods, large-scale factories, regimented work hours, and wage labor. Moreover, the economies of the industrializing states would increasingly be dominated by the developing practices of capitalism. An ideology of progress, backed by the acceleration of technology and science, along with the legacy of the Enlightenment, would constitute an important step toward creating what we term in this section "the challenge of modernity." That challenge was already being spread throughout the world, backed by the revolutions in transportation, communications, and weaponry produced by this Industrial Revolution.

For Mary Paul and her fellow mill hands, however, their primary concerns were much closer to home. They saw clearly that the rapid growth of textile factories rendered obsolete the home spinning and weaving of cloth and cottage occupations of farming communities. By migrating to industrial centers in New England like Lowell, where textile mills offered employment opportunities, they could attain economic independence by working for cash wages. In many cases, however, they also witnessed epic and sometimes bloody struggles between management and labor as the laws, institutions, and social norms of this new society were being painfully worked out. And amid the countless interactions and adaptations in which Mary and her fellow workers engaged, the modern world we live in today began to take shape.

Origins and Growth of Industrialism, 1750–1914

Like the agricultural revolution of the Neolithic age, which resulted in humankind's transition from foragers to food producers and made possible urbanization, the Industrial Revolution forever altered the lives of tens of millions around the globe. Whether or not this movement was in fact a "revolution," however, is a matter of some debate. It is perhaps more accurate to say that the process of industrialization evolved over time, originating in Britain in the eighteenth century, then spreading to the European continent and North America in the nineteenth century and subsequently around the globe, interacting with and adapting to local circumstances and cultures along the way. But there is no question that the transition from manual labor and natural sources of power to the implementation of mechanical forms of power and machine-driven production resulted in a vast increase in the production of goods and new modes of transportation, as well as new economic policies and business procedures. In the process the lives of untold numbers of people were forever transformed.

Early Industrialism, 1750–1870

The industrialization of western Europe began in Britain. As with all transformative events in history, however, a number of important questions arise. Why did the industrial movement begin in Britain? Why not, say, in China in the Song or Ming period? Why in the eighteenth century? Why in such areas as textiles, iron, mining, and transport? How did these changes become not only self-sustaining but also able to transform so many other manufacturing processes? And was this process "inevitable," as some have claimed, or was it contingent on a myriad of complex interactions that we are still struggling to comprehend?

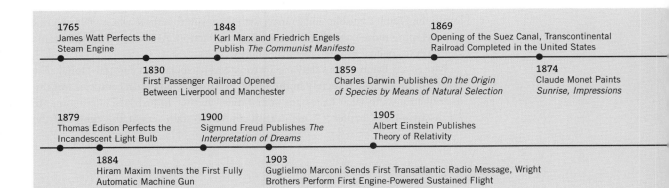

1765
James Watt Perfects the Steam Engine

1848
Karl Marx and Friedrich Engels Publish *The Communist Manifesto*

1869
Opening of the Suez Canal, Transcontinental Railroad Completed in the United States

1830
First Passenger Railroad Opened Between Liverpool and Manchester

1859
Charles Darwin Publishes *On the Origin of Species by Means of Natural Selection*

1874
Claude Monet Paints *Sunrise, Impressions*

1879
Thomas Edison Perfects the Incandescent Light Bulb

1900
Sigmund Freud Publishes *The Interpretation of Dreams*

1905
Albert Einstein Publishes Theory of Relativity

1884
Hiram Maxim Invents the First Fully Automatic Machine Gun

1903
Guglielmo Marconi Sends First Transatlantic Radio Message, Wright Brothers Perform First Engine-Powered Sustained Flight

Preconditions   Although there are no simple answers to these questions, it is possible to cite several conditions enjoyed by the British Isles that rendered them especially suitable for launching the industrial movement. Among other things, Britain benefited from what historians sometimes refer to as the "coal and colonies" theory. Britain has been described as "an island floating on a sea of coal." Large reserves of coal and iron ore, combined with the establishment of overseas colonies and subsequent global trading networks, provided a foundation for commercial expansion, which in turn would help provide capital to fund the new enterprises. In addition, a thriving merchant class, empowered by the Glorious Revolution of 1688, grew in significance in the House of Commons of the British Parliament and supported legislation aimed at economic development. At the same time, Britain developed a flourishing banking system; the Bank of England (1694) provided needed funds to entrepreneurs willing to make risky investments in new ventures.

Thanks to agricultural improvements, due in part to the introduction of new crops from the Americas such as potatoes and new fodder crops for livestock such as clover and turnips, Britain experienced a surge in population. Whereas in 1600 Britain's population amounted to no more than around 5 million, by 1700 it had nearly doubled to around 9 million. At the same time there was a demographic shift, in which displaced tenant farmers migrated to towns and cities, causing a rapid increase in urban growth and creating greater demand for food and consumer goods. In addition, urban dwellers began to crave more exotic consumer products now available from Britain's warm-weather colonies.

One of the first areas in which we see the effects of these changes was the textile industry. Although woolen cloth had long been the staple of the British textile industry, the introduction of new fabrics from Asia, such as silk and cotton, began to gain in popularity among consumers. Cotton's advantages of light weight and ease of cleaning resulted in a growing demand for the domestic production of affordable cotton clothing, or "calicoes." At first, the demand for finished cloth goods was satisfied by weavers working in the older, domestic cottage industries, a system known as "proto-industrialism." Due in large part to concerns for the woolen industry, however, Parliament enacted the protectionist Calico Acts of 1700 and 1720, which prohibited the importation of cotton goods from India. But this legislation had the unintended consequence of increasing domestic demand for English-made cotton textiles, which quickly outstripped available supplies. Given soaring demand, it was apparent that some sort of means was needed to speed up production.

British Resources   The impasse was resolved by a combination of factors peculiar to Britain at this time, which taken together made the use of machines more practical and cost-efficient than it might have been somewhere else. Since wages for workers in rural industries were high, the use of labor-saving machinery was increasingly seen as a means to help firms be profitable. By contrast, wages were relatively low in the Dutch Republic and France, with the result that there was no felt urgency in developing more cost-effective means of production. At the same time, Britain's vast reserves of coal resulted in cheap energy.

Moreover, Britain was singularly fortunate in its social and cultural capital. The composition of British society in the seventeenth and eighteenth centuries was unusually attuned to what historians sometimes call the "Industrial Enlightenment." As discussed in Chapter 17, eighteenth-century Britain was at the center of the

European scientific revolution. From Bacon to Boyle and from Harvey to Newton, the scientific revolution—particularly in its practical and empirical areas—was realized in a more widespread fashion in Britain than elsewhere. Here, too, was a flourishing group of scientific societies—for example, the Lunar Society in Birmingham and the Royal Society, founded in 1660—and the majority of British inventors had interests in and ties to societies aligned with scientific aspects of the Enlightenment. These groups served as centers of discourse and exchange between leading scientists and more down-to-earth men of a practical bent, including inventors, experimenters, and mechanics, who were not only often highly literate but also frequently educated in mathematics.

New Technologies and Sources of Power   These factors produced an explosion of technological innovation in Britain. From 1700 to 1800 over 1,000 inventions were developed, most of which were related to the textile industry. Among the most prominent were the flying shuttle (1733), the spinning jenny (1764), the water frame (1769), and the spinning mule (1779). Each of these devices greatly increased the speed and quality of spinning or weaving; the mule combined both operations into one machine. The power loom (1787) then set the technological stage for full-scale machine production of textiles.

Even these improvements were not enough, however, to supply both domestic and colonial markets with sufficient quantities of textiles. What was needed in order to speed up production was some sort of reliable mechanical power, instead of human, animal, wind, or water to drive the looms. The solution was provided by the development of the steam engine, easily the most important—and iconic—innovation produced during the industrial era.

The Factory System   The growing dependence on large machinery, the necessity of transporting fuel and raw materials to centers of production, and the increased efficiency of housing a multitude of machines under one roof necessitated the construction of large manufacturing buildings. These facilities were initially located near sources of running water in order to provide the necessary power to run mechanical looms. The implementation of steam power to drive machinery allowed entrepreneurs to move mills and production centers away from water sources in rural areas to urban settings, where there were large pools of cheap labor. Another attraction of urban areas was their greater accessibility to roads, canals, and, later, railroads. Once established, these factories in their turn drew larger and larger numbers of workers, contributing to population surges, particularly in the cities of the north and Midlands of England. Manchester, for instance, the leading textile manufacturing center, grew nearly 10-fold from 1750 to 1830. By the 1830s over 1 million people drew wages from textile factories and close to 25 percent of Britain's industrial production came from factories (see Map 23.1).

Railroads   While steam-powered factories provided much of the muscle of the Industrial Revolution, it was the steam railroad that captivated the imagination of the public. The spectacle of great locomotives pulling long trains of cars at previously unheard-of speeds, their pistons panting like the breath of giants, their plaintive whistles haunting the night, all became fixtures of the romance of rail travel. Their origins, like those of the earlier stationary pumping engines, began at the

Patterns Up Close | "The Age of Steam"

More than any other innovation of the industrial age, the advent of practical steam power revolutionized manufacturing, transportation, communications, economics, and even politics and military matters. Indeed, at the height of steam's dominance, many people saw its ability to move freight and people and to run myriad kinds of machines as close to divine. As Frederic A. Bartholdi, builder of the Statue of Liberty, rhapsodized at the American Centennial Exhibition in 1876, the mammoth Corliss steam engine dominating the Machinery Hall there had "the beauty, and almost the grace of human form" in its operation. Even today, one sees a particular kind of avant-garde science fiction based on fanciful nineteenth-century contraptions labeled as "steam-punk."

The origins of the steam age lie in an environmental crisis. A growing shortage of wood for fuel and charcoal making in Britain in the early 1700s forced manufacturers to turn to another fuel source: coal. As we have seen, Britain was blessed with vast amounts of coal, but getting to it was difficult because of a high water table: Mineshafts often flooded after only a few feet and had to be abandoned. Early methods of water extraction featured pumps operated by either human or animal power; but these were inefficient, expensive, and limited in power.

Corliss Steam Engine. A tribute to the new power of the steam engine was this huge power plant in the Machinery Hall of the American Centennial Exposition in 1876. The Corliss engine pictured here developed over 1,400 horsepower and drove nearly all the machines in the exhibition hall—with the distinct exception of those in the British display. Along with the arm of the Statue of Liberty, also on exhibition there, it became the most recognized symbol of America's first world's fair.

The first steam-driven piston engine based on experimentation with vacuum chambers and condensing steam came from the French Huguenot Denis Papin (1647–ca. 1712), who spent his later career in England. Thomas Savery (ca. 1650–1715), also taking up the idea of condensing steam and vacuum power, built a system of pipes employing the suction produced by this process dubbed the "Miner's Friend" that was able to extract water from shallow shafts but was useless for the deeper mines that were more common in rural Britain.

This drawback was partially addressed by Thomas Newcomen (1663–1729). In 1712 Newcomen took Papin's piston-and-cylinder design and vastly improved its practicality. Newcomen's model featured a large wooden rocking beam, weighted on one end, to operate the pump. When the weighted beam was pulled down by the force of gravity, steam was drawn into a cylinder and then condensed by a spray of cold water. The resulting partial vacuum below the piston, augmented by atmospheric pressure above, pulled it downward, forcing the weighted end of the beam upward. The beam was in turn connected to another piston in the mineshaft, which sucked water in and drew it up a pipe.

Though over 100 Newcomen engines were in place throughout Britain and Europe at the time of Newcomen's death in 1729, a number of flaws still rendered them very slow and energy-inefficient, suitable only for places like coal mines, where abundant fuel was available. It remained for James Watt (1736–1819), a Scottish engineer, to make the final changes needed to create the prototype for fast engines sufficiently efficient and versatile to drive factory machinery. Watt had been engaged in repairing Newcomen engines and quickly realized their limitations. To correct them he developed a separate condensing chamber, which allowed the piston cylinder to remain constantly hot; he also added a valve to eliminate the condensed steam after the piston stroke. The newly refined model, completed in 1765 and patented in 1769, was five times as efficient as Newcomen's engine and used 75 percent less coal.

After making several refinements Watt introduced a further improved model in 1783 that incorporated more advances. First, by injecting steam into both the top and bottom of the piston cylinder, its motion was converted to double action, making it more powerful and efficient. Second, through a system of "planetary gearing"—in which the piston shaft was connected by a circular gear to the hub of a flywheel—the back-and-forth rhythm of the piston was converted to smooth, rotary motion, suitable for driving machines in factories and mills. Watt's steam engines proved so popular that by 1790 they had replaced all of the Newcomen engines and by 1800 nearly 500 Watt engines were in operation in mines and factories.

Within a few decades, adaptations of this design were being used not just for stationary engines to run machinery but also to move vehicles along tracks and turn paddle wheels and screw propellers on boats—the first railroad engines and steamships. Both of these innovations soon provided the muscle and sinew of enhanced commerce and empire building among the newly industrializing nations. They were also among the most attractive as well as troublesome innovations for other countries around the globe to adopt. The Japanese fascination with the railroad can be said to date from its first demonstration by Commodore Perry's men in 1853 (see Chapter 24). Settlement of the United States was enormously accelerated by the advent of the railroad and river steamer. Indeed, by 1914, there was scarcely a place on the globe not accessible by either railroad or steamship. Yet, for societies seeking to protect themselves from outside influence, the railroad and steamer were seen as forces of chaos. The first railroad built in China, for example, was purchased by Qing officials and destroyed lest it upset the local economy and facilitate further foreign penetration of the empire. Nevertheless, as the web of railroad lines grew denser on every inhabited continent and the continents themselves were connected by the tissue of shipping lines, steam may indeed be said to be the power behind the creation of modern global society.

The Tools of Empire. Steam power allowed European colonizers and explorers to penetrate into the heart of hitherto inaccessible regions, such as this paddle steamer, the *Ma Roberts*, chugging up the Lower Zambezi in southern Africa in 1859. The bull elephant in the foreground roars in defiance, and while it appears the shooters on deck have missed their mark, the mood of the painting suggests that time is on their side.

Questions

- How does the innovation of steam power show the culmination of a pattern that began with the rise of the New Science in western Europe in the sixteenth and seventeenth centuries?

- Does Frederic A. Bartholdi's statement in 1876 that the Corliss steam engine "had the beauty and almost the grace of the human form" reflect a romantic outlook? If so, how?

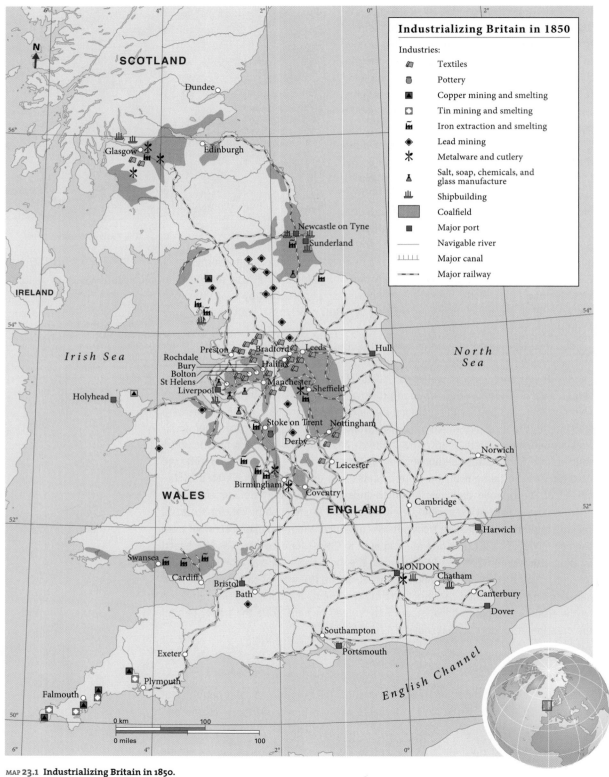

MAP **23.1** **Industrializing Britain in 1850.**

mines. For more than a century, miners had used track-mounted cars to pull loads of coal and iron out of mines. By the 1820s experiments were already under way to attach Watt-type engines to moving carriages. In 1825, under the guidance of British engineer and inventor George Stephenson (1781–1848), the first freight line, the Darlington–Stockton, and in 1829–1830 the first passenger line, the Manchester–Liverpool, were opened; and travelers thrilled to the astonishing speeds of 15–20 miles per hour. This newfound speed, efficiency, and capability of moving passengers and freight resulted in a British railroad boom. Whereas in 1840 Great Britain counted only 1,800 miles of rail, by 1870 the figure had jumped nearly ninefold to 15,600 miles. Railroads not only vastly improved the shipping of coal and other bulk commodities but also greatly enhanced the sale and distribution of manufactures of all kinds. The railroad itself developed into a self-sustaining industry, employing thousands in all sorts of related jobs and spurring further investment by wealthy entrepreneurs.

Steamships   Although their impact was realized somewhat later, the application of steam to ships had far-reaching ramifications, especially in the second half of the nineteenth century. Credit for the first practical steam-powered riverboat goes to the American engineer and inventor Robert Fulton (1765–1815). Fulton's *Clermont*, constructed in 1807, plied the Hudson River from New York to Albany. English engineers were quick to copy Fulton's lead; by 1815 there were 10 steamboats busy hauling coal across the Clyde River in Scotland. In 1816 a steamship sailed from Liverpool to Boston in 17 days, cutting the transatlantic journey to one-half the time taken by sailing ships. In 1838 the *Great Western* began regular transatlantic service; its initial crossing from Bristol to New York took only 19 days. During the 1820s and 1830s steamboats were in regular use on Europe's principal rivers: the Rhine, the Danube, the Rhône, the Seine, and others. During the same time they played a vital role in opening up the Great Lakes and the Ohio and Mississippi Rivers to commerce in the United States. The year 1839 saw the inauguration of regular transatlantic steamship service from England to New York; 2 years later the famous Cunard line was founded. Then, during the 1830s and 1840s the British East India Company used iron-hulled steamers to facilitate maritime trade with its markets in India. Military uses soon presented themselves as well: as we will see in Chapter 24, the innovative iron-clad steam gunboat *Nemesis* shocked its opponents with its durability, mobility, and firepower during the Anglo–Chinese Opium War of 1839–1842.

An important innovation in maritime steam navigation was the development of the screw propeller in the late 1830s. Paddle-wheeled oceangoing ships tended to be top-heavy, and their "walking-beam" drive mechanisms and the paddle wheels themselves were vulnerable to damage in bad weather or, in the case of warships, to hits from enemy fire. The fast-turning screw propeller, in line with the ship's keel and rudder below the water line, proved far less troublesome and allowed all the moving parts of the engine and power train to be enclosed and protected. Still, paddle steamers remained in wide use until the latter part of the century and were the preferred system in shallow-draft river steamers.

The Spread of Early Industrialism

By the 1830s, in Belgium, northern France, and the northern German states—all of which had coal reserves—conditions had grown more suitable for industrialization than earlier when wages were low. More settled political conditions after the Napoleonic Wars led to population increases, contributing to higher consumer demand. At the same time, larger urban areas provided greater pools of available workers for factories. Moreover, within these regions improved networks of roads, canals, and now railways facilitated the movement of both raw materials to industrial centers and manufactured goods to markets. For example, in 1840 only 400 miles of rail were in existence in German territories, but that figure soared to 3,500 in 1850 and then to 11,150 in 1870. In addition, governmental involvement greatly enhanced the investment climate; protective tariffs for manufactures and the gradual removal of internal toll restrictions, particularly in the northern German states, opened up the trading industry.

The United States   Industrialism was imported to the United States toward the end of the eighteenth century by Samuel Slater (1768–1835), a British engineer. Known as the "father of the American Industrial Revolution," Slater established the first water-powered textile factory, in Rhode Island in 1793. By 1825 factories in the northeastern section of the country were producing vast quantities of textile goods on mechanically powered looms.

After a brief interruption during the American Civil War—during which the majority of factories on both sides were engaged in producing munitions and war materiel—industrialization in America resumed at a greatly accelerated pace. As production data indicate, by 1870 America was producing far more spindles of cotton than Great Britain, and its production of iron ingots was swiftly catching up to that of British and European producers. By 1914 the United States had become the world's single largest industrial economy.

In addition to manufacturing, trade and commerce across the vast span of the American continent were facilitated by a national network of railroads, which swiftly took over the carrying trade from the canal networks created in the early nineteenth century. Data for US rail construction show this astonishing growth: only 2,800 miles of rail in 1840 but 9,000 in 1850. At the conclusion of the Civil War there were already about 35,000 miles of railroads in the country—more than the rest of the world combined—though many were still of different gauges. By 1869 the first transcontinental single-gauge railroad was joined with a final golden spike at Promontory Point, Utah, resulting in an astonishing total of 53,000 rail miles by 1870.

Later Industrialism, 1871–1914

In many ways the next stage of industrialism, often referred to as "the second Industrial Revolution," grew out of the first phase. Perhaps the best measure of the difference in the two periods, however, is that while the first stage relied upon steam power, the second introduced several high-technology innovations that taken together altered the course not only of the Industrial Revolution but also of world history. Among the most significant of these were three major innovations: steel, electricity, and chemicals (see Map 23.2).

New Materials: Steel   A significant element in the second Industrial Revolution was the increasing use of steel instead of iron. Refined techniques of making steel had existed for many hundreds of years in different parts of the world but were largely the province of highly skilled craftspeople such as swordsmiths. New

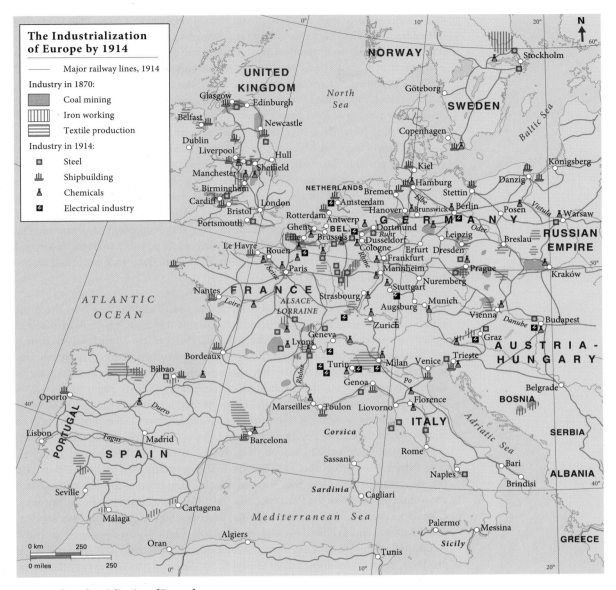

MAP 23.2 **The Industrialization of Europe by 1914.**

technical advances, however, now made it possible to produce large quantities of high-grade *cheap* steel. The first of these was made in Britain by Henry Bessemer (1813–1898) in 1856, who devised a way to increase its carbon content in his "Bessemer Converter." Subsequent improvements in production soon followed in the 1860s and 1870s with the advent of the blast furnace and the open-hearth smelting method.

Following the conclusion of the Franco–Prussian war, Germany's annexation of the ore-rich regions of Alsace-Lorraine led to a dramatic increase in industrial production. Starting with almost no measurable steel production in the 1870s, Germany managed to catch up to British annual steel production in 1893 and then went on to surge far ahead: By 1914 its annual tonnage of steel was more than twice that of Britain. One advantage enjoyed by Germany was that it was able to model its new industrial facilities on those of its most modern competitors, saving substantial time and investment capital and resulting in newer and more efficient equipment and business methods. Yet another advantage was Germany's development of sophisticated research capabilities at universities, particularly in the sciences.

The advantages of steel over iron were that it was lighter, harder, and more durable. Thus, it provided better rails for railroads and, increasingly, girders for the construction of high-rise buildings. Indeed, structural steel and steel-reinforced concrete made possible the construction of high-rise "skyscrapers," which by the turn of the century were soaring past the tallest masonry buildings. The switch from iron to steel construction of ships also marked a significant advance in steamship technology during the third quarter of the nineteenth century. Steel ships greatly improved the travel time between far-flung continents. By 1900, 95 percent of all commercial ocean liners were being constructed of steel. Steel made possible stronger, faster, and roomier ships, while steel warships also proved far more durable in battle and set the tone for naval construction to this day.

Chemicals   Advances were also made in the use of chemicals. Here, the most significant developments were initiated by academic scientists, whose work resulted in later advances in the chemical industry. In 1856 the first synthetic dye, mauveine, was created, which initiated the synthetic dyestuffs industry. The result was not only a wider array of textiles but also new chemical compounds important in the refinement of wood pulp products, ranging from cheaper paper in the 1870s to artificial silk, referred to as "rayon." Later discoveries, such as the synthesizing of ammonia and its conversion to nitrates for use in fertilizers and explosives, were to have far-reaching effects during World War I. Associated with advances in chemical experimentation was the invention of dynamite by the Swedish chemist and engineer Alfred Bernhard Nobel (1833–1896). This powerful new explosive provided the means to blast through rock formations, resulting in great tunnels and massive excavation projects like the Panama Canal (1914). In yet another chemical advance, Charles Goodyear (1800-1860) invented a process in 1839 that produced vulcanized rubber; and celluloid—the first synthetic plastic—was developed in 1869. Additional offshoots, ranging from pharmaceuticals and drugs like aspirin to soap products, contributed to healthier lifestyles. By the early part of the twentieth century, these developments had led to a "hygiene revolution" among the industrialized countries.

New Energies: Electricity   Although electricity had been in use during the first period of industrialization, its development and application were greatly advanced after 1850, especially in the generation of electrical power. The first step came with Michael Faraday (1791–1867) patenting the electromagnetic generator in 1861. But large-scale electrical generation would require a number of other innovations before it became a reality. Perhaps the most important devices in this regard were developed by a relatively obscure engineer, Nikola Tesla (1856–1943). Among Tesla's inventions were alternating current (AC), the Tesla Coil (1891) for the more efficient transmission of electricity, and a host of generators, motors, and transformers. In 1888 the introduction of Tesla's "electric induction engine" led to the widespread adoption of electricity-generating power plants throughout industrialized Europe.

The first widespread use of electricity, however, had come earlier, in the realm of communications. Although electric telegraph messages were transmitted as early as the 1840s with the advent of Samuel F. B. Morse's (1791-1872) devices and code, it was only in the 1860s and 1870s that major continental landmasses were linked by submarine transoceanic cables. The first successful link from Britain to India was installed in 1865. The first transatlantic cable from Britain to America was laid as early as 1858, though it was only in 1866 that the cable was deemed operationally successful. By the latter part of the nineteenth century, telegraphic communication was a worldwide phenomenon, which has been likened to the Internet in its impact on human contact. This was vastly augmented with Alexander Graham Bell's (1847–1922) telephone in 1876, which made voice contact possible by wire.

But perhaps most revolutionary of all was the advent of wireless communication. The theoretical groundwork for this had been laid by James Clerk Maxwell (1831–1879), a Scottish physicist researching the theoretical properties of electromagnetism, and Heinrich Rudolf Hertz (1857–1894). In 1885 Hertz—whose name was later given to the units of measurement for radio wave cycles—discovered that electromagnetic radiation actually produces unseen waves that emanate through the universe. In the later 1890s, Guglielmo Marconi (1874–1937) developed a device using these radio waves generated by electric sparks controlled by a telegraph key to send and receive messages over several miles. By 1903 Marconi had enhanced the power and range of the device enough to send the first transatlantic radio message from Cape Cod in the United States to Cornwall in England. The "wireless telegraph" was quickly adopted by ships for reliable communication at sea. Subsequent improvements, such as the development of the vacuum tube amplifier and oscillator, resulted in greater power and reliability and, within a few years, the ability to transmit sound wirelessly.

New Energies: The Internal Combustion Engine

When oil, or liquid petroleum, was commercially developed in the 1860s and 1870s, it was at first refined into kerosene and used for illumination. One of the by-products of this process, gasoline, however, soon revealed its potential as a new fuel source. The first experimental internal combustion engines utilizing the new fuel appeared in the 1860s. Their light weight relative to their power was superior to steam engines of comparable size, and the first practical attempts to use them in powering vehicles came along in the next decade.

Who invented the automobile? Although it is usual to credit two Germans, Gottlieb Daimler (1834-1900) and Karl Benz (1844-1929), with the invention, the first true automobile was invented by an unheralded Austrian mechanic and inventor named Siegfried Marcus (1831–1898). As early as 1864 Marcus harnessed his own experimental internal combustion engine to a cart, which moved under its own power for over 200 yards. Over the next several years Marcus tinkered with several gadgets and devices in order to perfect his self-propelled contraption. Among these were the carburetor, the magneto ignition, various gears, the clutch, a steering mechanism, and a braking system. All of these inventions were incorporated in the first real combustion-engine automobile, which Marcus drove through the streets of Vienna in 1874.

Hiram Maxim. In this photo, taken in 1900, the proud inventor of the machine gun looks on with self-satisfied pride as Albert Edward, prince of Wales (the future King Edward VII), experiences for himself the awesome firepower of Maxim's "little daisy of a gun." In 1885 Maxim put on a similar demonstration for Lord Wolseley, commander-in-chief of the British Army. The British War Office adopted the gun 3 years later. The lethal power of the machine was first put to use in Africa at the Battle of Omdurman in 1898, where 20,000 Sudanese cavalrymen were slaughtered in fruitless charges against a line of 20 Maxim guns.

Internal combustion engines were also applied to early attempts at sustained flight. In 1900 Ferdinand von Zeppelin (1838–1917) constructed a rigid airship—a *dirigible*—consisting of a fabric-covered aluminum frame that was kept aloft by the incorporation of bags filled with hydrogen gas and powered by two 16-horsepower engines. Zeppelin's airships thus became the ancestors of the blimps that even today still ply the airways. Perhaps more momentous was the marriage of the gasoline engine to the glider, thus creating the first airplanes. Though there were several claimants to this honor, the Wright brothers in Kitty Hawk, North Carolina, on December 17, 1903, are usually credited with the first sustained engine-powered flight. By 1909, the first flight across the English Channel had been completed; in 1911 the first transcontinental airplane flight across the United States took place, though by taking 82 hours of flight time within a span of 2 months it could scarcely compete with railroad travel. Still, the potential of both the automobile and the airplane were to be starkly revealed within a few years during the Great War.

The Weapons Revolution   The advances in chemistry and explosives, metallurgy, and machine tooling during the second half of the nineteenth century also contributed to a vastly enhanced lethality among weapons. The earlier advances from the 1830s to the early 1860s that had included the percussion cap, the conical bullet, the revolver, and the rifled musket—all of which had made the American Civil War so deadly—now provided the base for the next generation of ever more sophisticated firearms. Breech-loading weapons, in their infancy during the early 1860s, rapidly came of age with the advent of the brass cartridge. By 1865, a number of manufacturers were marketing repeating rifles, some of whose designs, like the famous Winchester lever-action models, are still popular today. Rifles designed by the German firms of Krupp and Mauser pioneered the bolt-action, magazine, and clip-fed rifles that remained the staple of infantry weapons through two world wars.

Artillery went through a similar transformation. Breech-loading artillery, made possible by precision machining of breech-locks and the introduction of metallic cartridges for artillery shells, made loading and firing large guns far easier, faster, and more efficient. By the early 1880s the invention of the recoil cylinder—a spring or hydraulic device like an automobile shock absorber—to cushion the force of the gun's recoil eliminated the necessity of reaiming the piece after every shot. Field artillery could now be anchored, aimed, and fired continuously with enhanced accuracy: It had become "rapid-fire artillery." Its effectiveness was enhanced further by the new explosives like guncotton, dynamite, and later TNT, available for use in its shells. Another innovation in this regard was the development of smokeless powder, or *cordite*, which, in addition to eliminating much of the battlefield smoke generated by black powder, was three times more powerful as a propellant. Thus, the range and accuracy of small arms and artillery were pushed even further.

By far, the most significant—and lethal—advance in weaponry during the later nineteenth century, however, was the invention of the machine gun, the deadliest weapon ever developed, responsible for more deaths than any other device in history. Though many quick-firing weapons had been developed with varying degrees of success during these years—the most famous being the Gatling Gun (1861)—the first fully automatic machine gun was conceived by Hiram Maxim (1840–1916), an American inventor and dabbler in electricity. How he designed and manufactured the gun, first fired in 1884, along with how it was received and adopted by European states is recounted in Maxim's autobiography, *My Life* (1915), from which the accompanying excerpt is taken. Near the end of his memoir Maxim also recounts, somewhat ruefully, that he was applauded more highly for inventing his "killing machine" than for inventing a steam inhaler for those suffering from bronchitis.

By the outbreak of World War I, every major army in the world was equipping itself with Maxim's guns, now manufactured in licensed factories in Europe and the United States. Perhaps more than any other single weapon, the machine gun made the western front in Europe from 1914 to 1918 the most devastating killing field in human history.

> **Hiram Maxim on the Mechanics of His Machine Gun**
>
> "I first made an apparatus that enabled me to determine the force and character of the recoil, and find out the distance that the barrel ought to be allowed to recoil in order to do the necessary work. All the parts were adjustable, and when I had moved everything about so as to produce the maximum result, I placed six cartridges in the apparatus, pulled the trigger, and they all went off in about half a second. I was delighted. . . . I had made an automatic machine gun with a single barrel, using service cartridges, that would load and fire itself by energy derived from the recoil over six hundred rounds in a minute."
>
> —Hiram Maxim. *My Life* (London: Methuen, 1915), p. 170.

The Social and Economic Impact of Industrialism, 1750–1914

All of these changes in modes of production, particularly the emergence of the factory system, resulted in wholesale transformations in the daily lives of millions around the globe. Along with new networks of transportation, new materials, and new sources of energy, the industrialized nations underwent significant changes in the way they viewed politics, social institutions, and economic relationships across the period of industrialization.

Demographic Changes

Changes in the demographics of industrialized nations followed the development of new industries and consequent transformations in the lives of millions. Perhaps most significantly, the populations of these countries grew at unprecedented rates and became increasingly urbanized. Indeed, Great Britain became by the latter half of the nineteenth century the first country to have more urban dwellers than rural inhabitants. This trend would continue among the industrialized nations through the twentieth century.

Population Surge and Urbanization   As data from 1700 to around 1914 reveal, the industrialized nations experienced a significant population explosion (see Map 23.3). Advances in industrial production, expansion of factories, and improved agriculture during the first industrial revolution combined to produce increasing

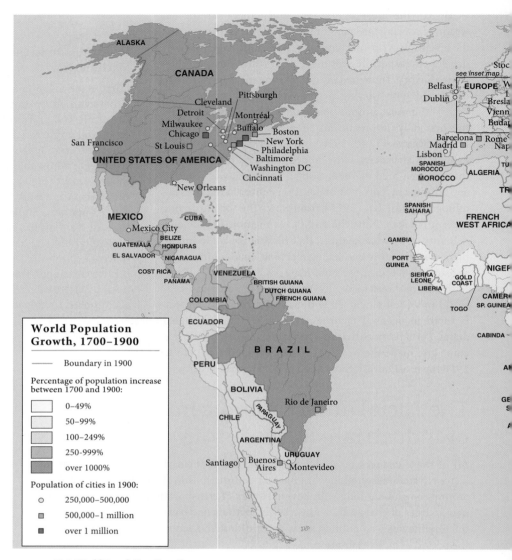

MAP **23.3** **World Population Growth, 1700–1900.**

opportunities for jobs as well as more plentiful and nutritious food in order to sustain a larger population. In the second Industrial Revolution scientific advances in medicine, including medications and vaccinations, and notions of sanitation contributed to a declining mortality rate. For example, the population of Britain grew from around 9 million in 1700 to around 20 million in 1850. Then from 1871 to 1914 Britain's population soared from 31 million to nearly 50 million. Other industrialized states experienced similar population increases. In Germany much the same occurred: around 41 million in 1871 versus 58 million in 1914.

More revealing than overall population figures is the shift of populations away from rural areas and into urban areas. For example, in Great Britain in 1800 around 60 percent of the population lived in rural areas. By 1850, however, about

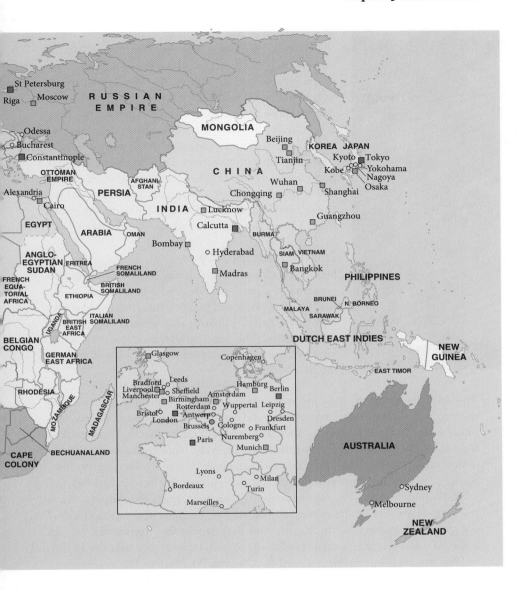

50 percent of the population lived in cities. In numerical terms, the population of London amounted to around 1 million in 1800, but by 1850 that figure had more than doubled to around 2.5 million. Moreover, in 1801 only 21 cities in Europe (including London) could boast of populations over 100,000. By 1850, this had more than doubled to 42. Significant in this respect were the appearance of new industrial and commercial centers such as Manchester, Liverpool, Birmingham, and Glasgow, as well as vast increases in the size of older capital cities such as Paris, Berlin, and St. Petersburg.

European Migrations   Another social change during the industrial era concerns emigrations of Europeans to foreign lands. In part, this movement was sparked

Italian Family at Ellis Island, New York, ca. 1905. This iconic photo of an Italian mother and her three children, taken by the photojournalist Lewis Hine and later hand colored, has come to portray the dreams of peace and prosperity that millions of immigrants to America brought with them in the late nineteenth and early twentieth centuries. The mother and her girls stare at the camera with dazed looks, but with a sack thrown jauntily on his back, the boy looks ready to explore his new world.

by the dramatic rise in population figures in industrialized areas of Europe. Another contributing factor, however, was the desire to escape the grinding poverty of underdeveloped regions of the West—particularly Ireland and southeast Europe—in order to seek better opportunities in developing industrial parts of the West. It should also be noted that advances in transportation, such as railroads and steamships, made it easier for Europeans to emigrate to foreign lands. In all, some 60 million Europeans left for other parts of the world (North and South America, Australia, and Asiatic Russia) between 1800 and 1914. Of these, the majority emigrated to the United States and Canada (see Map 23.4).

Industrial Society

Significant changes in the lower levels of society also occurred as a result of industrialization. Although the landed elites continued to enjoy their privileged status, they nevertheless began to lose ground to the rising middle classes. The principal alteration in social classes, however, was the appearance of a new class: the working class.

The Middle Classes   The prosperous middle classes, which included those in professional, administrative, educational, and commercial jobs, rose to prominence in the new age, thanks largely to their acquisition of liquid wealth. Distinguished from the landed aristocracy above them and from the working classes below, the middle classes themselves were divided into an upper class of wealthy industrialists, bankers, lawyers, and doctors at the top and tradespeople and handcrafters below.

These middle classes constituted around 15 percent of Europe's total population. It was this class that set the cultural and moral tone for most of the second half of the nineteenth century. What counted most in their eyes was "respectability"; not a hint of impropriety or sexual scandal was to be tolerated. As a measure of this, in 1867 the English Parliament passed the Obscene Publications Bill in an attempt to crack down on pornographic literature. The middle classes set themselves apart from the elites above and especially from those below by emphasizing what they considered their respectability, frugality, and industry. Indeed, with their emphasis on family and respectability, the morality of the middle classes during the reign of Britain's Queen Victoria inspired the adjective "Victorian" to describe a particular kind of prudish, self-disciplined—"earnest"—code of behavior. Determined to succeed at all costs, the middle classes eagerly consumed numerous self-improvement books, of which the most famous was Samuel Smiles's *Self Help* (1859). The book went through multiple editions in succeeding years and emerged as the most popular work on self-improvement in the Victorian era.

The Working Class   Urban factory workers were distinguished from farmers and workers in rural areas by their daily routine of regulation by the factory time clock and by selling their labor in return for cash wages. Among the working classes,

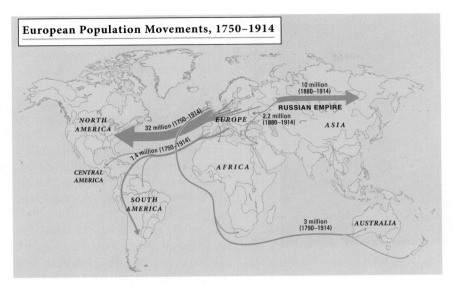

MAP 23.4 **European Population Movements, 1750–1914.**

divisions applied between skilled and unskilled workers, largely determined by familiarity with the intricacies of industrial machinery and its maintenance.

What were typical working conditions in British textile mills in the early 1800s? In a word, deplorable. In a new age when there were no traditional protective guilds or associations, workers were at the mercy of factory owners. The factory clock and the pace of factory machinery determined the day's work; the work was repetitive, dirty, and dangerous, not to mention dehumanizing. This was especially the case with young children—some as young 7 years—who either worked in factories alongside their parents as family units or had been orphaned or turned over to local parishes by parents who could no longer provide for their care. Working long hours—12- to 14-hour days were common in the early 1800s—children were constantly urged to speed up production and severely disciplined for "idling." Indeed, they were commonly beaten for falling asleep and to keep them from falling into the machinery, which, because of the lack of protection from its moving parts, could easily maim or kill them. In fact, until the 1840s in Britain, the majority of "hands," or factory workers, were women and children, who, by virtue of their inexperience and expendability, could be paid less than their male counterparts.

Conditions were often even worse in the mines. Children frequently began work in mines as early as age 6 or 7, most often as "trappers," responsible for opening and shutting ventilation doors in mineshafts. As they continued, they often moved up to "hurrying," or lugging newly dug coal along long, low underground passageways for conveyance to the surface. Girls were especially victimized in underground mines, where they not only had to drag heavy coal-filled carts by chains fixed to leather belts around their waists but also were frequently sexually abused by their supervisors.

Factory Towns   Because industrial cities expanded close to factories and mills, conditions there generally mirrored those of the factories themselves. Clouds of coal smoke tended to hang over them, blackening buildings, acidifying the rain and soil, and often causing respiratory ailments among the citizens—prompting William

Working-Class Tenements in English Industrial Cities. In this engraving, entitled *Over London by Rail*, the celebrated engraver Gustave Doré (1832–1883) depicts the overcrowded and squalid living conditions in working-class tenements during the early years of the Industrial Revolution. Notice the long rows of houses separated by walls and arranged in back-to-back fashion. Notice also the stretched lines for drying clothes, as well as the large number of occupants in each outdoor area.

Blake's famous allusion to "dark Satanic Mills." In addition to the acrid smell of coal, there were usually a variety of other stenches assaulting the nostrils of the inhabitants. Piles of coal ash and clinkers, pungent waste materials from coking or from gas works, and vile outpourings from tanneries and dye-works all lent their smells to the more prosaic ones of household waste, sewage, and horse manure. With the population exploding and only rudimentary waste disposal and access to clean water, it was little wonder that diseases like cholera, typhus, and tuberculosis were rampant.

Adding to the miseries of the inhabitants were their wretched living conditions. The working classes lived in crowded tenements consisting of row after row of shoddily built houses packed together in narrow, dark streets. One social activist, Friedrich Engels (1820–1895), the son of a wealthy mill owner and later collaborator with Karl Marx, was determined to call attention to such abysmal conditions. As a young man Engels was sent to his father's cotton-producing factory in Manchester, England, to learn the factory system. What Engels observed there compelled him to write a scathing attack on the industrial movement, *The Condition of the Working-Class in England in 1844* (1845), in which he described what he perceived as the horrors of workers' lives.

Critics of Industrialism

It was not long before the criticisms of Engels and other socially conscious observers began to draw attention to the obvious abuses of the industrial movement and to stimulate reform of working conditions. Efforts to improve these sordid conditions were launched in Great Britain in the 1820s and 1830s and carried over into the 1870s.

The Laboring Quarters

"[R]ight and left a multitude of covered passages lead from the street into numerous courts, and he who turns in thither gets into a filth and disgusting grime.... In one of these courts there stands directly at the entrance, at the end of the covered passage, a privy without a door, so dirty that the inhabitants can pass into and out of the court only by passing through foul pools of stagnant urine and excrement."

—Friedrich Engels. *The Condition of the Working-Class in England in 1844* (London: Allen Unwin, 1943) p. 37

Socialists   The plight of the working classes caught the attention of a variety of social activists who determined to take up the fight for reform. Into the fray stepped several French and English "utopian socialists"—a term originally used derisively to describe the presumed impracticality of their schemes. One of the earliest of these activists was Henri de Saint-Simon (1760–1825), who presented a view of humanity that flew in the face of industrial society's competition for individual wealth. In Saint-Simon's view, private property should be more equally distributed, according to the notion that "from each according to his abilities, to each according to his works." Louis Blanc (1811-1882) criticized the capitalist system in his *The Organization of Work* (1839). In the book Blanc urged workers to agitate for voting rights, called for radical ideas like the right to work, and reconfigured Saint-Simon's memorable phrase to read "from each according to his abilities, to each according to his needs." Charles Fourier (1772–1837) advocated the founding of self-sustaining model communities in which jobs were apportioned according to ability and interest, with a sliding scale of wages tailored to highly compensate those doing the most dangerous or unattractive jobs. Fourier's concept of such "phalanxes" was the one adopted by the North American Phalanx, in which Mary Paul spent time (see the vignette to this chapter).

Robert Owen (1771–1858), a factory owner in the north of England, led a movement to establish the Grand National Consolidated Trades Union. Its objective was to call for a national strike of all trade unions, but owing to a lack of participation among workers, the movement was disbanded. Owen had previously established a model community in Scotland called "New Lanark," where more humane living and working conditions for workers resulted in greater profits. After campaigning for the formation of workers' unions, Owen left for America, where he set up a model socialist community in Indiana called "New Harmony," which eventually dissolved amid internal quarrels when he returned to England.

Chartism was another organized labor movement in Britain. Taking its name from the Peoples Charter (1838), chartism was formed by the London Working Men's Association; and its purpose was, among other issues, to call for universal male suffrage. Millions of workers signed petitions, which were presented to Parliament in 1839 and 1842; both were rejected. Nevertheless, the chartist movement galvanized for the first time workers' sentiments and aspirations, and it served as a model for future attempts at labor reform.

Karl Marx

By far the most famous of the social reformers was Karl Marx (1818–1883). The son of a prosperous German attorney, Marx proved a brilliant student, eventually earning a PhD in philosophy from the University of Berlin. Marx's activities, however, resulted in his being exiled from Germany and then from France. During a visit to the industrial center of Manchester, where he met and befriended Friedrich Engels, Marx observed both the miserable lives of factory workers and the patent inequities of industrialism. From this, Marx developed his theory, which he termed "scientific socialism," that all of history involved class struggles. Borrowing the dialectical schema of the German philosopher Georg Wilhelm Friedrich Hegel (1770–1831), Marx replaced its idealism with his own materialist concept based on economic class struggle: *dialectical materialism*. Moreover, Marx saw revolution as the means by which the industrial working classes will ultimately topple the capitalist order: Just as the Third Estate and bourgeoisie had overthrown the aristocracy during the French Revolution, the current struggle between the working classes and the capitalist entrepreneurs would ultimately result in the demise of capitalism.

Convinced of the need for the overthrow of the capitalist system, Marx and Engels joined the nascent Communist Party in London. In preparation for a meeting in 1848, the two collaborators dashed off a pamphlet entitled *The Communist Manifesto* (1848), a book that later on emerged as the bible for worldwide communism. The slender work is really a propaganda piece designed to rally support among the working classes, or *proletariat*, and to encourage them to rise up and overthrow the capitalist factory owners, or *bourgeoisie*. Compiled from a variety of

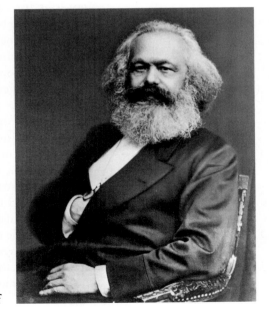

Karl Marx. In this photo, taken in London in 1875, Marx displays many of the character traits for which he is best known. Following the publication of his *Das Kapital* in 1871, Marx had established his reputation as a scholar of economic theory. Notice his self-satisfied and confident demeanor as he stares at the camera in an almost defiant manner. Notice as well his attire, ironically suggestive of a successful member of the bourgeoisie. After Marx's death, his longtime friend Friedrich Engels distributed 1,200 copies of this photo to communists around the world.

French socialist, German philosophical, and personal interpretations of past history, the *Manifesto* reflects Marx's vision that "the history of all hitherto existing society is the history of class struggle" and that the time had come for the working classes to follow earlier examples and to overthrow the capitalists: "The proletarians have nothing to lose but their chains. They have a world to win. WORKING MEN OF ALL COUNTRIES, UNITE!"

Inquiries and Reforms   As critics of industrialism began to cry out against obvious abuses of the industrial movement, many called for government efforts and programs for the reform of working conditions. Efforts to improve these horrid conditions were launched in Great Britain in the 1820s and 1830s. In 1832 Parliament launched an inquiry into abuses within factories. In 1833 the Factory Act was passed, which set a minimum age of 9 for child employees and limited the workday to 8 hours for children between the ages of 9 and 13 and to 12 hours for those aged 13–18. Similar inquiries were conducted concerning working conditions within mines. As a result, the Mines Act of 1842 forbade the underground employment of all girls and women and set a minimum age of 10 for child laborers.

Improved Standards of Living

Although still a matter of debate among historians, contemporary data suggest that in overall terms living and working conditions began to improve in Britain from around the 1830s to the end of the century. Thanks to the series of reforms already mentioned, conditions in factories and mines were substantially better than at the beginning of the century. Textile factories were now located in urban areas, and housing conditions for workers were more amenable. Most important, wage levels increased across the nineteenth century for industrial workers. For example, from 1850 to 1875 wages of British workers increased by around one-third and by nearly one-half by 1900.

New Jobs for Women   As a result of the second Industrial Revolution, many women fared far better in terms of employment. In overall terms, women represented around one-third of the workers in later nineteenth-century industrial jobs. Mary Paul's experience, discussed in the vignette at the beginning of this chapter, is one example of opportunities for women. Again, the data from these textile mills offer supporting evidence. While fewer than 2,000 women were employed in the mills in 1837, that figure nearly doubled by 1865; and by around 1900 the number of female textile workers had increased to nearly 6,000. But factory work in textile mills was not the only avenue opened to women as the industrial era unfolded in the later years of the nineteenth century.

When new technologies and social trends created new employment possibilities, women constituted a readily available pool of workers. Inventions like the typewriter (perfected in the 1870s), the telephone (invented by Alexander Graham Bell in 1876), and calculating machines (in use in the 1890s), for instance, required workers to handle related jobs, the majority of which went mostly to single women and widows. As a result, women became particularly prominent in secretarial office jobs. In addition, the explosion of business firms created countless jobs for secretaries, while department stores opened up jobs for women as clerks.

Women Working as Telephone Operators. The first telephone exchange appeared in 1879. In this image from 1881, women operators are shown at work at an early pyramidal switchboard. Women were selected as operators because their voices were considered pleasing to the ear and because they were considered more polite than men.

Women's Suffrage Movement   Although many women were afforded new opportunities in business and in professions like nursing and education after 1871, in many other areas women remained second-class citizens. Women in both the United States and Europe did not begin to gain the right to own property or to sue for divorce until the third quarter of the nineteenth century, as exemplified by the passage of the English Married Woman's Property Act in 1882.

More pressing in the eyes of many female reformers was the right to vote. Throughout Europe during the late nineteenth and early twentieth centuries, women formed political activist groups to press for the vote. The most active of these groups was in Britain, where in 1867 the National Society for Women's Suffrage was founded. The most famous—and most radical—of British political feminists was Emmeline Pankhurst (1858–1928), who together with her daughters formed the Women's Social and Political Union in 1903. They and their supporters, known as *suffragettes*, resorted to public acts of protest and civil disobedience in order to call attention to their cause. Although these tactics were of no avail prior to 1914, the right to vote was extended to some British women after the war (taken over from the British colony of New Zealand, which granted the right in 1893).

Political feminists were also active on the Continent. The French League of Women's Rights was founded in the 1870s, and the Union of German Women's Organizations was formed in 1894; in neither country was the right to vote granted women until after World War I. Women in the United States pursued a parallel course with similar results: After decades of lobbying before the war, women's suffrage was finally granted by constitutional amendment in 1920.

Emmeline Pankhurst. Pankhurst was arrested numerous times for her militancy and aggressive actions against the British government and its refusal to extend the suffrage to women. In this photo, taken on May 21, 1914, Pankhurst is shown being arrested outside Buckingham Palace after attempting to present a petition to King George V.

Improved Urban Living

Living conditions within the major urban areas in industrialized nations underwent significant improvements during the late nineteenth and early twentieth centuries. Largely the result of the application of new technologies emerging from the industrial movement, there is no question that the lives of urban dwellers were improved in the second half of the nineteenth century.

Sanitation and Electricity   One measure of improved living conditions was in the provision of better sanitation. A first of its kind was the Public Health Bill (1848) in Britain, followed by a further measure in 1875. Beginning in the 1860s and 1870s large cities in Britain and Europe established public water services and began to construct underground sewage systems to carry waste from houses, outfitted with running water, to rivers and other locations beyond urban areas. By the latter part of the nineteenth century, the widespread use of gas lighting gradually began to give way to electrical varieties. Thomas Edison (1847–1931) perfected the incandescent lightbulb in 1879, making the lighting of homes and business interiors more affordable and practical and gradually replacing gas lighting.

Paris represents a good example of the implementation of these reforms. In the 1850s and 1860s Napoleon III (r. 1852–1870) appointed the urban planner Georges Haussmann (1809–1891) to begin a massive reconstruction of the city. Haussmann tore down close-packed tenements in order to provide modernized buildings for residential and commercial use and to construct wide boulevards. This was in part driven by a desire to beautify the city, but it was also driven by the necessity of providing better access for government troops in the event of public demonstrations; barricaded streets, a feature of the revolutions of 1830 and 1848, thus became a thing of the past. And, like most cities of the industrialized West by the turn of the

The Great Stink. In the summer of 1858 the combination of a heat wave and unusually slow flow in the Thames resulted in one of London's worst modern health threats. The smell was so vile that shades treated with carbolic acid had to be mounted in the Houses of Parliament. The situation was also fair game for cartoonists, as depicted here. Beyond this, the incidence of waterborne diseases skyrocketed. The result was the building of a new citywide sewer and treatment system that vastly reduced the amount of raw sewage in the river.

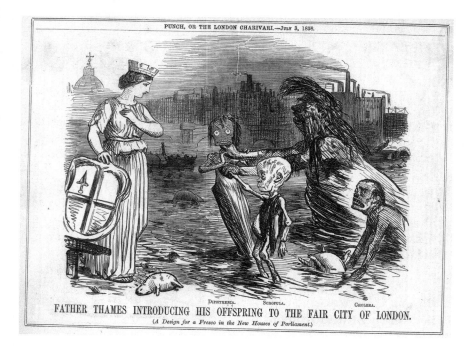

PUNCH, OR THE LONDON CHARIVARI.—July 3, 1858.

DIPHTHERIA.   SCROFULA.   CHOLERA.

FATHER THAMES INTRODUCING HIS OFFSPRING TO THE FAIR CITY OF LONDON.
(A Design for a Fresco in the New Houses of Parliament.)

twentieth century, Paris featured lighted and paved streets, public water systems, parks, hospitals, and police.

A dramatic symbol of both the newly redesigned city of Paris and the triumph of industry and science during the second Industrial Revolution was the Eiffel Tower, designed and erected by Alexandre Gustave Eiffel (1832–1923). Constructed for the Paris Exposition of 1889, the tower took years to construct and, at nearly 1,000 feet in height, was the tallest structure in the world until the construction of the Empire State Building in New York in 1931.

Big Business

As the scale of urban planning and renewal increased toward the end of the nineteenth century, together with the size of buildings and other constructions, so did business. As manufacturing, transportation, and financing matured, entrepreneurs and businessmen became concerned about competition and falling profit rates. Since governments generally pursued hands-off liberalism (*laissez-faire*, see Chapter 22) in the economy, except for protective tariffs, entrepreneurs sought to establish cartels and monopolies, creating big business enterprises in the process.

Eiffel Tower and Paris Exposition, 1900. Although it was reviled as an eyesore by many when it was first constructed, the Eiffel Tower emerged as one of the world's great symbols of industrial elegance. It was the centerpiece—along with the great globe next to it and the Palace of Electricity—of the Great Exhibition in Paris in 1900, pictured above.

Large Firms When Britain industrialized, it gradually shifted from a closed mercantilist economy to the liberal free-trade policy Adam Smith advocated (see Chapter 22). Britain's competitors, especially Germany and the United States, by contrast, erected high tariff walls around their borders in order to help their fledgling industries. After the second wave of steel, chemical, and electricity industrialization in the second half of the nineteenth century, the scale of industrial investments rose exponentially. On domestic markets, governments did not interfere with business organization and practice, except for labor protection in Europe. As a result, in several branches of the economy, big businesses emerged during the second half of the nineteenth century that protected their profit rates through *cartels* (market-sharing agreements) or strove altogether for monopolies.

Large firms typically developed in Germany and the United States, the leaders of the second wave of industrialization. Corporations like the Krupp steelworks in Germany and Standard Oil Company in the United States had evolved by the 1890s, controlling large shares of their markets. Standard Oil at its height, for example, produced over 90 percent of the country's petroleum. Another example is the United States Steel Company, founded in 1901 by Andrew Carnegie (1835–1919), which dominated the production of American steel. Carnegie himself amassed a huge personal fortune of almost $250 million, making him the richest man in the world.

New Management Styles In addition, new technologies in all industrial sectors offered more efficient means of production; the result was a series of significant changes in production processes during the second phase of European industrialism. One example is the implementation of the so-called American System, incorporating the use of interchangeable parts, which greatly enhanced mass production. A related development was the appearance of "continuous-flow production," wherein workers

The Assembly Line. The American System of interchangeable parts for muskets of the early nineteenth century had evolved into the assembly line by the early twentieth. Here, Ford Model T automobiles are moved along a conveyor to different stations, where workers assemble them in simple, repetitive steps, resulting in production efficiency and low prices for the cars.

performed specialized tasks at stationary positions along an assembly line. In addition, new "scientific management" tactics were employed in mass-production assembly plants. Since no more than basic skills were required on many assembly lines, labor costs could be kept low.

The best known of the new management systems was "Taylorism," named after Frederick W. Taylor (1856–1915), an American engineer. The objective was to measure each factory worker's production based on how many units were completed in an hour's time. The result was that workers were not only more carefully managed by their superiors but also paid in accordance with their productivity. The combined result was a rapid escalation in the speed of production, which in turn contributed to a marked increase in the production of goods for daily consumption and, therefore, in the development of a consumer market at the turn of the twentieth century.

Intellectual and Cultural Responses to Industrialism

The new society that industrialism was creating not surprisingly spawned entirely new directions in science, philosophy, religion, and the creative fields such as literature and art. It generated new kinds of popular expression, from dime novels to photography. The advent of *mass society* also led to the beginnings of a mass culture, in which widespread literacy and public education allowed a far greater percentage of the populace access to what had largely been the province of elites. It allowed artists, writers, composers, and musicians to have mass followings for the first time. Men and women like Charles Dickens, Harriet Beecher Stowe, and Richard Wagner, to name only three, were the popular equivalent of today's "superstars" in their own time. Yet, there was also a profound disquiet among scientists, intellectuals, and artists. With so many of the old standards falling by the wayside, tremendous uncertainty was present just underneath the surface of material progress. This disquiet would come to the surface with a vengeance in the immediate years after World War I.

Scientific and Intellectual Developments

The latter half of the nineteenth century saw advances in both theoretical and empirical sciences that laid the basis for many of the staples of the twentieth century. Among the most far-reaching were atomic physics and relativity theory, Darwinism and evolution, and the foundations of modern psychology. Scientists also laid the foundations for medicine, although here the most important breakthroughs had to await the twentieth century.

New Theories of Matter   Quests for understanding the nature of matter, under way since Galileo (see Chapter 17), became systematic with the foundation of technical universities and science faculties in existing universities in the second half of the 1800s. Researchers carried out extensive experiments and made important discoveries in the 1890s that would have far-reaching consequences in defining atomic physics and theories of relativity. In 1892 the Dutch physicist Hendrik Lorentz (1853–1928) demonstrated that the atom, far from being a solid billiard ball, actually contained smaller particles, which he named "corpuscles"; these were later renamed "electrons." A few years later, Wilhelm Roentgen (1845–1923) discovered a mysterious form of emission he called "X-rays." The ability to generate these rays would shortly lead to using them in medical diagnoses and creating the modern X-ray machine. The following year, 1896, saw the first experiments in assessing radioactivity in uranium and radium by Antoine Becquerel (1852–1908) and Marie Curie (1867–1934).

As a result of these experimental findings, theoretical physics advanced new theories on the nature of light and energy. In 1900 Max Planck (1858–1947) proposed that instead of the accepted notion that energy is emitted in steady streams or waves, it is issued in bursts, or what he termed "quanta." This idea, later developed into quantum theory, suggested that matter and energy might be interchangeable. Ernest Rutherford (1871–1937), interested in this interchangeability, demonstrated in 1911 that radioactive atoms release a form of energy in the process of their disintegration. Thus, nearly three centuries of speculation about atoms as the building blocks of nature led to experimentally verified theories of subatomic particles.

Albert Einstein   These discoveries in the physical sciences set the stage for the appearance of perhaps the most sensational of the turn-of-the-century scientific theories: Albert Einstein's (1879–1955) theory of relativity. In 1905 and then again in 1915 Einstein published papers in which he destroyed the Newtonian notion of a certain, absolute, and mechanistic universe that obeys unvarying and objectively verifiable laws. Instead, Einstein argued that there are no absolutes of time, space, and motion; rather, these are relative to each other and depend on the position of the observer.

Moreover, Einstein demonstrated that Newton was incorrect in thinking that matter and energy were separate entities; they were, in fact, equivalent and he developed the corresponding mathematical formula. In his equation $E = mc^2$, Einstein theorized that the atom contains an amount of energy equal to its mass multiplied by the square of the speed of light. In other words, relatively small amounts of matter could convert into massive amounts of energy. This discovery, developed further in the twentieth century, provided the foundation for a full understanding of the forces among subatomic particles and the construction of nuclear weapons.

Charles Darwin   The basis of modern theories of evolution was laid by Charles Darwin (1809–1882). Darwin's *On the Origin of Species by Means of Natural Selection* (1859) argued that in nature species gradually evolved from lower to higher forms. As a young man Darwin sailed on an exploratory mission on the H.M.S. *Beagle* from 1831 to 1836 to the waters off the South American coast in the Pacific. Observing the tremendous variability of species in the string of the isolated Galapagos Islands, he found himself at a loss to explain why so many different species cohabited within such close geographical areas.

It occurred to Darwin—and independently to another English naturalist, Alfred Russell Wallace (1823–1913)—that an explanation for the appearance of new

Charles Darwin as Ape.
Darwin's theories about the evolution of humankind aroused enormous scorn. In this scathing 1861 cartoon, Darwin, with the body of a monkey, holds a mirror to a simian-looking creature. The original caption quoted a line from Shakespeare's *Love's Labor Lost*: "This is the ape of form."

species in nature might lie in the struggle for food: Only those species equipped with the tools to survive in their environments would win out; those without these characteristics would become extinct.

In its essence, therefore, the Darwinian theory of evolution as spelled out in the *Origin* boils down to three main elements: (1) in nature more species appear than can be supported by existing food supplies, (2) there is a resultant struggle among species to survive, and (3) through inheritance subtle mutations within species are transmitted that render some more able than others to survive in the struggle for food. The most controversial part of this theory rests in the notion that characteristics are passed on by means of "natural selection." In other words, there is no intelligence or plan in the universe—only random chance and haphazard process, resulting in a pessimistic view of "nature red in tooth and claw."

Although the *Origin* said nothing about the theory of evolution as applied to humankind—this appeared later in the *Descent of Man* (1871)—there were those who quickly applied it to society and nations. As noted in other chapters in this section, the work of Herbert Spencer (1820–1903) was instrumental in proposing a theory that came to be called "social Darwinism," which sought to apply ideas of natural selection to races, ethnicities, and peoples. Spencer's ideas were frequently used to support imperial ventures aimed at the conquest and sometimes the "uplift" of non-European or American peoples as well as to justify increasingly virulent nationalism in the years leading to World War I.

Developments in Psychology   The first scientist to separate psychology from philosophy and to make it a serious scientific discipline was Wilhelm Wundt (1832–1920). A German physiologist and student of human behavior, Wundt established the first psychology laboratory in 1879, where he conducted early experiments on aspects of human behavior.

Increasingly important among psychologists was the topic of insanity. What especially concerned Victorians were apparently unconscious impulses for actions not subject to human will. The best known of the early psychologists was Sigmund Freud (1856–1939), an Austrian physician. After obtaining a degree in medicine in Vienna, Freud studied cases of emotionally disturbed patients in Paris, and then in 1886 he set up his own practice in Vienna. Freud specialized in treating patients suffering from what was then called "hysteria," which he treated using a technique he labeled "psychoanalysis." In 1900 Freud published his highly influential *The Interpretation of Dreams*, in which he drew connections between dreams and the unconscious in humans. Although controversial, and today largely discarded, Freud's theories stressed the dominance of unconscious urges and motivations—mostly sexual in nature—in determining human behavior. The sum total of Freudian psychological theories is that humans, so far from being rational creatures, are in fact irrational creatures, driven by subconscious, and not conscious, urges. Today, it no longer enjoys the unquestioned dominance it once did in the field and has largely become a branch of medicine and, in particular, the study of brain chemicals. But it still survives on the practical level in the form of lifestyle counseling and behavior modification.

The Meaning of the New Scientific Discoveries   Physics, biology, and psychology were not the only sciences contributing fundamentally to the emergence of scientific–industrial society at the end of the nineteenth century. Medicine began to acquire a scientific character, for example, with the discoveries of vaccines by Louis Pasteur (1822–1895). But it had to await the twentieth century before it reached maturity. With the arrival of the theories of relativity, Darwinian selection, and the psychological unconscious, however, enough of a transition toward the scientific–industrial age had occurred to throw people into deep philosophical and religious confusion.

In a sense, the path of reductionism begun in the seventeenth century and discussed in Chapter 17 was being reached. In previous centuries, the Hobbesian embodied mind, fear of death, "war of all against all," and the religious skepticism, secularism, and atheism of the Enlightenment were merely speculations that remained ultimately unproved. Now, the specter of a meaningless universe inhabited by beings devoid of free will and driven by biological forces over which they have no control seemed to many to be inescapable. Thus, the new era seemed to usher in a profoundly disturbing devil's bargain: The sciences had created so many useful things to ease the burdens of human life but had taken away the sense of purpose that made that life worth living. It was left to philosophers, religious leaders, intellectuals, and artists to wrestle with the implications of this central problem of scientific–industrial society.

Toward Modernity in Philosophy and Religion

Despite the impressive achievements of Western industrialized society during the late nineteenth century, there were many who felt uneasy about the results. Scores of detractors—mostly in the intellectual community of western Europe—decried the boastful claims of a "superior" scientific civilization. These voices ridiculed Western bourgeois values and advocated alternative approaches to personal fulfillment.

Friedrich Nietzsche   Easily the most celebrated of these detractors was the German philosopher Friedrich Nietzsche (1844–1900). A brilliant, but increasingly mentally unstable, professor at the University of Basel, Nietzsche railed against the conventions of Western civilization and criticized the perceived decadence of modern culture. Nietzsche represents a growing trend toward pessimism and doubt about the progress of Western culture near the end of the nineteenth century.

Nietzsche began his assault on Western culture in 1872 with the publication of *The Birth of Tragedy*, which was followed in later years by works like *Beyond Good and Evil* (1886) and *On the Genealogy of Morals* (1887). One object of derision for Nietzsche was the entire notion of scientific, rational thought as the best path toward intellectual truth. For Nietzsche, and for others of like mind, rational thought will not improve either the individual or the welfare of humankind; only recourse to "will" instead of intellect—what Nietzsche called the "will to power"—will suffice.

The individual who follows this path will become a "Superman" and will lead others toward truth.

Another target of Nietzsche's wrath was Christianity, which in his eyes led its believers into a "slave morality"; and in a famous quote, he declared that "God is dead."

Roman Catholicism   As might be expected, the various religious establishments of the West were forced into a defensive position by the growing prestige and influence of the sciences. Although mainstream Protestant leaders tended to urge accommodation with scientific progress—though they struggled considerably with the implications of Darwinism—the Catholic Church was more inclined to resist both the allure of science and the appeal of materialism and capitalism. Pope Pius IX for example, staunchly resisted the drift toward modernism by issuing the encyclical entitled "Syllabus of Errors" in 1864 and by convening the First Vatican Council in 1871.

With the death of Pius IX in 1878, however, the church adopted a new position under the leadership of Pope Leo XIII (r. 1878–1903). On the one hand, Leo mounted a full-scale offensive against what he considered an alarming trend toward secular materialism by urging Catholic workers to form socialist unions and workers' parties. In 1891 Leo XIII issued "De Rerum Novarum" ("On Modern Things"), in which he criticized capitalism for widening the gulf between the haves and the have-nots in the age of industrialism. On the other hand, Leo made slight concessions to science and the study of the sciences by Catholics and by establishing a Vatican office to look into scientific advances. Leo XIII's successor, Pope Pius X (r. 1903–1914), reversed these moves of moderation and criticized those who supported the church's reconciliation with science.

Toward Modernity in Literature and the Arts

As we have seen throughout this chapter, the creation of scientific–industrial society—modernity—was a slow and excruciatingly traumatic process. The social

Kulturkampf. The "conflict of cultures" between church and state in Germany reached its peak in the 1870s. In this cartoon from the period, the German chancellor Otto von Bismarck appears to have the upper hand in a game of political chess against Pope Pius IX.

realities of interacting and adapting to the new order were already on painful display in the post-romantic period of realism in the arts and literature that marked the second third of the nineteenth century (see Chapter 22). The succeeding decades were to yield what in many ways was an even grimmer and more disjointed view of the new scientific–industrial society. On the one hand, many artists sought to combat what they perceived as the ugliness and shoddiness of the machine age by returning to handcrafting furniture and decorative items. In this arts and crafts movement, which thrived from the 1880s until the outbreak of World War I, William Morris (1834–1896) and John Ruskin (1819–1900) championed an idealized nostalgia for medieval motifs and techniques as the high point of European art. But a much darker and more despairing critique of the period was also present among writers and artists, which set the foundation for many of the movements that would emerge in the 1910s and 1920s.

Literature   Literary expression was generally negative toward the popularization of "soulless" science and the materialism of the second half of the industrial revolution. Thomas Hardy (1840–1928), for example, in his *Far from the Madding Crowd* (1874) emphasized the despair resulting from the futility of fighting against the grinding forces of modernity. The plays of George Bernard Shaw (1856–1950) reflect the influence of Darwin, Nietzsche, and others and mock the shallowness and pretension of urban, bourgeois *fin de siècle* ("end of the century") society. Around the mid-1880s two new genres in literature, decadence and symbolism, made their appearance. The decadents registered disgust with prevailing bourgeois conventions and pretensions. A good example is the French novelist J. K. Huysmans (1848-1907), whose *A Rebours* (*Against the Grain*, 1884) shocked the literary world with its unsettling, bizarre allusions to the weird and mysterious. Huysmans himself had flirted with Satanism before taking up Catholicism. For their part, symbolists preferred to revert to a form of the earlier romantic era and in the process to emphasize the ideal, the aesthetic, and the beautiful side of life. Symbolist poets of note are the Irishman William Butler Yeats (1865–1939) and the American T. S. Eliot (1888–1965), whose early works capture the essence of symbolist representation.

Modernism in Art   Like their counterparts in literature, artists in the period 1871–1914 were similarly confronted by the sweeping changes in life brought on by industrialism and science. Artists during the latter part of the nineteenth and early twentieth centuries were seldom content with the world around them and sought novel ways to express their often hostile attitudes. The world of artistic expression in this period, often grouped together under the heading "modernism," in fact consisted of a great variety of successive movements, all of them skeptical of accepted middle-class conventions and truths; and they became more and more abstract and "avant-garde" as the Great War approached.

The first group of painters was known as the "impressionists," and their style dominated from the 1870s until around 1890. The movement takes it name from a painting by Claude Monet (1840–1926) entitled *Impression, Sunrise* (1874). By around 1890 the impressionist school had been superseded by a more freewheeling style known as postimpressionism, which ran into the new century. The driving force of the new school of artists was to depict particularly subjective interpretations of things from the mind's eye of the artist. Perhaps the most famous of the postimpressionists was the

(b)

Modernism in Art. Perhaps the most iconic artwork of the new age of anxiety at the end of the nineteenth century is the painting by Norwegian artist Edvard Munch, *The Scream* (1893). Munch himself described it as deriving from an incident in which he was walking with friends when the sky turned "blood red" and he was overcome with feelings of exhaustion and "sensed an infinite scream passing through nature." It has come to represent everything from mental illness to the unbearable crises of meaning in the industrial age (*a*). Fourteen years later, Pablo Picasso's *Les Demoiselles d'Avignon* generated similar anxieties when it was unveiled in Paris in 1907 (*b*). Its distorted and broken forms of expression set in a fractured and flattened space mark a conscious break with the Western artistic tradition. The painting's borrowing from "primitivist" African and ancient Iberian sources, and its forceful and unsettling depiction of *demoiselles*, a euphemism for prostitutes, unsettle the viewer.

Dutch painter Vincent Van Gogh (1853–1890), whose lurid anti-realist colors and twisted forms were intended as expressions of his mind. His life, ending in suicide, reflects the often tormented sensibilities of the modernists' reaction to scientific–industrial modernity.

The period of art history from 1905 to 1914 saw numerous offshoots of the postimpressionists, each one more revolutionary and experimental than the last. These various artistic "schools" truly represent the beginnings of twentieth-century avant-garde art. Perhaps the best known of these, cubism, is represented in the works of Pablo Picasso (1881–1973). Picasso stretched fascination with geometrical forms to their limits to deliberately fly in the face of accepted artistic conventions. In such works as *Les Demoiselles d'Avignon* (1907), for example, often considered the first of the cubist paintings, Picasso reveals his interest in African masks as an alternative to conventional European motifs.

Modernism in Music

The musical arts departed from other forms of expression in their development during the second half of the nineteenth century. The compositions of Liszt, Brahms, and Wagner were in many respects extensions of the early romantics and adhered to classical forms. During the 1870s, however, and especially after the death of Wagner in 1883, musical expression followed two separate tracks until 1914. One of these tracks is known as "modernism," which was more attuned to cultural developments evolving in other fields during the waning years of the nineteenth century and early years of the twentieth. Some musicians fell in line with the experiments of the impressionists. As might be expected, many of these were Frenchmen, including Claude Debussy (1862–1918) and Maurice Ravel (1875–1937). Debussy, for example, sought to establish a misty mood and dreamy atmosphere in his compositions.

More in line with emerging modernist trends in the period 1905–1914 was a movement in music often labeled "primitivism." Here, a series of composers set out to abandon the constraints of formal structure and convention and to express their personal musical perceptions. Perhaps best known of this school is the Russian composer Igor Stravinsky (1882–1971). Stravinsky's most famous—if not notorious—work was *Le Sacre du printemps* (*The Rite of Spring*), first performed in Paris on May 29, 1913. The work was so unconventional and dissonant that its first performance in Paris touched off 3 days of rioting in the streets.

Other musicians were even more outrageous and unconventional—and more typical of avant-garde rejections of Western musical conventions. In 1908 the Austrian composer and theoretician Arnold Schoenberg (1874–1951) deliberately began to compose pieces that abandoned the traditional tonal system of Western music in favor of atonality. In his *Theory of Harmony* (1911), Schoenberg proudly announced the inauguration of a new, modern style of musical composition, in which themes reflecting Freudian theories of the unconscious along with the noises and dissonances of engines, machines, and urban life would now dominate musical composition.

Putting It All Together

The series of dramatic and sweeping changes associated with the Industrial Revolution had profound implications for both the industrializing countries and the nonindustrialized world. Thanks in large part to new technologies and facilitated by advances in transportation and communication, the period from 1871 to 1914 saw world trade networks and empires dominated by the newly industrialized nations.

The Industrial Revolution began in Britain in the early eighteenth century and eventually spread to Europe and North America during the nineteenth century. Britain began the revolution when it harnessed steam engines to the rapid production of textiles. The subsequent development of the factory system along with more efficient transportation systems facilitated by railroads greatly expanded British manufacturing. Not everyone benefited, however, from the emergence of the factory system; capitalist entrepreneurs were reluctant to share with workers their slice of the economic pie, which in turn led to social unrest and calls for reform.

During the second Industrial Revolution in the later nineteenth century, advanced technologies led to the development of steel, electricity, and chemicals, which in turn greatly expanded the industrial economies of highly industrialized countries beyond Britain, including those of America and Germany. The daily lives of most citizens in industrialized nations were also improved by the application of industrial technologies to advances in transportation, communication, and even safety and sanitation.

These same advances also contributed to a new and greatly expanded surge of European imperialism. The explosive growth of industry and commerce, aided and abetted by new technologies and inventions, resulted in a quest among highly industrialized nations for raw materials, cheap labor, and new markets in order to sustain and expand their developing industries (see Concept Map). Moreover, Western industrial nations soon discovered that new needs forced the importation of not only raw materials but also foodstuffs. It is important to point out that nineteenth-century imperialism was made possible in the first place by technological innovations associated with advances in science and industrialism. Quinine prophylaxis, steam-powered gunboats, rapid-firing breechloaders, and the machine gun provided the overwhelming firepower to subdue nonindustrial societies and to open up interior regions of continents to Western colonialism. By the 1880s sailing ships were eclipsed by faster oceangoing ships powered by much more efficient compound engines and submarine cables provided for more efficient overseas communications and for the setting of more exact timetables. After 1871, the world's economy was increasingly divided into those who produced the world's manufactured products and those who both supplied the requisite raw materials and made up the growing pool of consumers.

Amid this process the basis for many of the patterns of twentieth-century modernity was being laid, as well as the foundations of its opposition. With the coming of World War I, and its aftermath, many of the cleavages created by modernity and its scientific–technological underpinnings were laid bare. Yet, as a new form of society,

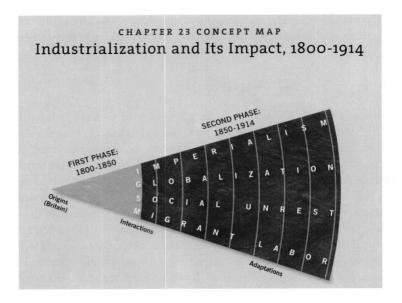

CHAPTER 23 CONCEPT MAP
Industrialization and Its Impact, 1800-1914

its interaction and adaptation with older forms continued unabated. Today, the two places that contain the largest number of "Mary Pauls" in world history—young women migrating from their farms to find work in urban factories—are the successors to the agrarian–urban religious civilizations that held out against the new order most tenaciously: India and China, both of whose economies now increasingly set the pace for twenty-first century industrial development. It is the story of the impact of modernity on these societies and others around the globe to which we now turn (see Concept Map).

Review and Respond

1. How was the steam engine originally used in the Industrial Revolution, and with what results?

2. How did industrialization improve daily life in Europe and the United States during the nineteenth century? What were the negative effects of industrialization?

3. Discuss the origin and development of negative reactions to the industrial movement.

4. Do you agree or disagree with the following statement: The expansion of Western imperialism in the nineteenth century reflects the positive contributions of inventions and technological advances emanating from industrialism.

5. Discuss and analyze ways in which the steady advance of industrialism during the second Industrial Revolution provoked responses from the scientific, intellectual, and cultural communities toward the turn of the twentieth century.

▶ For additional resources, including maps, primary sources, visuals, and quizzes, please go to www.oup.com/us/vonsivers. Please see the Further Resources section at the back of the book for additional readings and suggested websites.

Thinking Through Patterns

▶ **Where and when did the Industrial Revolution originate?**

Because of several advantageous factors, the Industrial Revolution began in Britain in the early eighteenth century. Among these were an earlier political revolution that empowered the merchant classes over the landed aristocracy, along with a prior agricultural revolution, and abundance of raw materials like coal.

Industrialization resulted in several social changes and adjustments. The capitalist middle classes were enriched and empowered by the growth of industrialism, as were the working classes, which did not exist as a group prior to industrialism. The benefits of industrialism were not evenly distributed across social strata; factory and mine workers were frequently exploited by the entrepreneurial and prosperous middle classes.

▶ **What were some effects of industrialization on Western society? How did social patterns change?**

▶ **In what ways did industrialization contribute to innovations in technology? How did these technological advances contribute to Western imperialism in the late nineteenth century?**

With the invention and perfection of the steam engine, capitalist entrepreneurs were able to substitute mechanical power for natural power and, thus, to develop the factory system. The factory system spread to the Continent and America as middle-class capitalism eclipsed mercantilism. Further advances contributed to a second Industrial Revolution after ca. 1850 that emphasized steel, chemistry, and electricity.

Progress in industrial technology during the second Industrial Revolution led to innovations ranging from practical inventions like the lightbulb to advances in communication and transportation. Inventions developed from industrial advances included the machine gun, new medicines, and startling developments in communications, to name a few. These tools facilitated the expansion of Western imperialism in Africa and Asia during the closing years of the nineteenth century

The new society that industrialism was creating not surprisingly spawned entirely new directions in science, philosophy, religion, and the creative fields such as literature and art. It generated new kinds of popular expression, from dime novels to photography. The advent of *mass society* also led to the beginnings of a mass culture, in which widespread literacy and public education allowed a far greater percentage of the populace access to what had largely been the province of elites. Yet, there was also a profound disquiet among scientists, intellectuals, and artists. With so many of the old standards falling by the wayside, tremendous uncertainty was present just underneath the surface of material progress. This disquiet would come to the surface with a vengeance in the immediate years after World War I.

▶ **What new directions in science, philosophy, religion, and the arts did industrialism generate? What kind of responses did it provoke?**

Chapter 24 | The Challenge of Modernity

1750-1910

EAST ASIA

In Asia, our two countries, China and Japan, are the closest neighbors, and moreover have the same [written] language. How could we be enemies? Now for the time being we are fighting each other, but eventually we should work for permanent friendship . . . so that our Asiatic yellow race will not be encroached upon by the white race of Europe.

So commented Chinese statesman Li Hongzhang to his Japanese counterpart, Ito Hirobumi, as they discussed terms to end the Sino–Japanese War at the Japanese town of Shimonoseki in the spring of 1895. For Li it was the culmination of more than three decades of frustration as China's most powerful advocate of *self-strengthening*—using new foreign

Seeing Patterns

▶ What was the impact of Western imperialism on the "regulated societies" of China and Japan?

▶ Why did European empire building in Asia have such dramatically different effects on China and Japan?

▶ How have historians seen the nature of these outside forces and their influences in east Asia?

technologies and concepts to preserve China's Confucian society in the face of European and American intrusion. During Li's lifetime such intrusions had come with alarming frequency. Now, at 71, he was forced to go to Japan to sue for peace as Japanese troops occupied Korea and southern Manchuria. To add injury to insult, he had just narrowly survived being shot in the face by a Japanese fanatic while en route to the peace talks.

For Ito, one of the architects of Japan's astonishing rise to power, the victory over China was tinged with sadness and puzzlement as he responded: "Ten years ago when I was at Tientsin (Tianjin), I talked about reform with [you]. . . . Why is it that up to now not a single thing has been changed or reformed? This I deeply regret." As did Li, whose reply betrays a weary bitterness at China's deteriorating position: "At that time when I heard you . . . I was overcome with admiration . . . [at] your having vigorously changed your customs in Japan so as to reach the present stage. Affairs in my country have been so confined by tradition that I could not accomplish what I desired . . . I am ashamed of having excessive wishes and lacking the power to fulfill them."

The significance of this rueful exchange was not lost on the other countries with interests in east Asia, who viewed the war's outcome with a

Li Hongzhang and Ito at Shimonoseki. In this ukiyo-e print of the peace negotiations held in the Shunpanro Restaurant in the Japanese town of Shimonoseki in early 1895, Li Hongzhang, the chief Chinese diplomat is dressed in the reddish brown gown at the right side of the table. His Japanese counterpart, Ito Hirobumi, sits opposite him and wears a sash; to his left is the Japanese foreign minister Mutsu Munemitsu, also wearing a sash. John W. Foster, former U.S. Secretary of State and advisor to the Chinese during the negotiations, stands at the head of the table close to Li. Interestingly, the negotiations were conducted in English through interpreters.

mixture of fascination and alarm. Japan's surprisingly complete victory over China was cited as proof that it was now ready to join the ranks of the great powers. It also upset a shaky balance of power that required China's feeble Qing dynasty to not collapse altogether. Now Japan had dramatically raised the stakes. In addition to imposing a crippling indemnity on the Qing, reducing Korea to a client state, and annexing the island of Taiwan, the new Treaty of Shimonoseki called for the occupation by Japan of Manchuria's Liaodong Peninsula, which guarded the approaches to Beijing.

For Russia, France, and Germany, who saw their own interests threatened by this move, it was time to act. In what became known as the Triple Intervention, they threatened Japan with joint action if it did not abandon its claims to Liaodong. Unable to take on all three powers, the Japanese bitterly acquiesced. They grew more bitter the following year when the Qing secretly leased the territory to Russia in a desperate attempt to counter Japanese expansion. For the Japanese, this began a decade-long state of tension with Russia that would culminate in the Russo–Japanese War of 1904–1905. For the other powers in east Asia, it began a "race for concessions" in China that stopped just short of dismembering the empire.

For the Chinese, however, it marked the most dramatic and humiliating role reversal of the past 1,500 years. China had always viewed Japan in Confucian terms as a "younger brother." Like Korea and Vietnam, Japan was considered to be on the cultural periphery of the Chinese world, acculturating to Chinese institutions and following Chinese examples in those things considered "civilized." Now, after barely a generation of exposure to Euro-American influence, Japan had eclipsed China as a military power and threatened to extend its sway throughout the region.

This new east Asian order also pointed up the larger effects of one of the most momentous patterns of world history: the phenomenon of imperialism growing from the innovations that created scientific–industrial society—one of the foundations of modernity that we have examined in this part of the text. As we began to see in the previous two chapters, in less than a century, European countries and their offshoots—and now Japan—expanded their power so rapidly and completely that on the eve of World War I in 1914 more than 85 percent of the world's people were under their control or influence. How were a very few countries like Japan able to resist and adapt to the broad forces of modernity, while China struggled to cope with its effects through most of the nineteenth and twentieth centuries?

China and Japan in the Age of Imperialism

As we saw in Chapter 21, the reign of the Qing emperor Qianlong (r. 1736–1795) marked perhaps the high point of China's power in the early modern world and the period in which the first hints began to appear of trouble to come. Some of the problems facing the Qing began to emerge within a year after Qianlong stepped down from the throne in 1795. A Buddhist sect with secret-society connections called the White Lotus sparked a smoldering rebellion, which took years to suppress, while at the same time highlighting the limitations of the Manchu bannermen as a military force. Less obvious, but perhaps more debilitating for the agrarian imperial order as a whole, were the new directions in economics. China was steadily drawn into the emerging European global commercial system, but the increasing forces of free trade were eroding its tried and true systems of exchange control. Specifically, China's efforts to retain close control over its export trade in tea, porcelain, silk, and other luxury goods coupled with action to stamp out the new, lucrative, and illegal opium trade created a crisis with Great Britain in the summer of 1839, which led to the First Opium War, China's first military encounter with the industrializing West.

China and Maritime Trade, 1750–1839

By the 1790s, with the China trade at record levels and the French Revolution making European trade increasingly problematic, the British government sought to establish diplomatic relations with the Qing. In the summer of 1793, they dispatched Lord George Macartney, an experienced diplomat and colonial governor, to Beijing with a sizeable entourage and boatloads of presents. His mission was to persuade the Qianlong emperor to allow the stationing of diplomatic personnel in the Chinese capital and the creation of a system for the separate handling of ordinary commercial matters and diplomacy along the lines of European practices. Qianlong, however, politely but firmly rebuffed Macartney's attempts to establish a British embassy. In addition to observing that China really had "no need of your country's ingenious manufactures," Qianlong stated bluntly that permanent foreign embassies were contrary to the tradition of tribute missions and would "most definitely not be permitted." A second British mission in 1816 met with similar results.

> ### Possessing All Things
>
> "As your Ambassador can see for himself we possess all things ... this then is my answer to your request to appoint a representative at my Court; a request that is contrary to our dynastic usage, which would only result in inconvenience to yourself. I have expounded my wishes in detail and have commanded your tribute Envoys to leave in peace on their homeward journey ..."
>
> —The Qianlong emperor's rebuff of the Macartney Mission, *in* H.F. MacNair, *Modern Chinese History, Selected Readings*, Shanghai: Commercial Press, 1923, p. 2.

China

| 1736–1795 Reign of Qianlong Emperor | 1839–1842 First Opium War with Great Britain | 1860–1895 Self-Strengthening Era | 1898 Hundred Days of Reform, Emperor Placed Under House Arrest |

1793 Macartney Mission to Beijing · 1851–1864 Taiping Rebellion · 1894–1895 Sino–Japanese War · 1900 Boxer Rebellion and Anti-Foreign War

Japan

1853–1854 Perry Mission Opens Trade and Diplomatic Relations with Japan · 1868–1912 Reign of Emperor Meiji · 1900 Seiyukai (Constitutional Government Party) Founded

1863–1867 Restoration War · 1899–1902 Japan Abrogates Unequal Treaties and Negotiates Alliance with Great Britain

The Imbalance of Trade?   One important reason that Europeans and Americans were anxious to bring the Chinese into their diplomatic system was the widespread perception that China was benefiting from a huge trade imbalance. Though recent scholarship has shown that China's economy actually supported much of the interconnected Eurasian commercial system, contemporary merchants and political economists were convinced that China's control of trade functioned in the same way as did European mercantilism. Thus, they believed that the money paid to Chinese merchants essentially stayed in the "closed" economy of the Qing Empire, draining the West of its stocks of silver. However, as Qianlong's reply to Macartney noted, European merchants offered little that the Chinese needed or wanted.

Thus, by the end of the eighteenth century, European and American traders had become increasingly anxious to find something that Chinese merchants would buy in sufficient quantities to stem the flow of Western silver into China. By the beginning of the nineteenth century, a growing number of merchants were clandestinely turning to a lucrative new commodity, with tragic consequences. When tobacco was introduced into China from the Americas, the innovation of smoking quickly spread. In southwestern China, tribesmen living in remote mountain villages began combining small quantities of powdered opium with tobacco. The Dutch, who briefly maintained bases on Taiwan, also introduced the practice there, from which it spread gradually to the maritime provinces of south China. Disturbed by the growing use of opium beyond normal medicinal practice in the area, the Qing banned the smoking of the substance as early as 1729. For the rest of the century opium use remained a strictly local problem in China's south.

Smugglers, Pirates, and "Foreign Mud"   By the end of the eighteenth century, the British East India Company's territory in Bengal had come to include the area around Patna, historically a center of medicinal opium production. While company traders were strictly prohibited from carrying opium to China as contraband, an increasing number of noncompany merchants willing to take the risk discovered that they could circumvent Chinese regulations and sell small quantities of the drug for a tidy profit. Initially, their customers were the wealthy of Canton society; and the exotic "foreign mud," as opium was nicknamed, soon became a favorite local diversion. With success came increased demand, and by the early decades of the nineteenth century, an elaborate illicit system of delivery had been set up along the south China coast. Heavily armed ships unloaded their cargo of opium on small, sparsely inhabited offshore islands, from which Chinese middlemen picked up the drug and made their rounds on the mainland (see Map 24.1). The ever-rising profits from this illegal enterprise encouraged piracy and lawlessness along the coast, and the opium trade soon became a major irritant in relations between China and the West.

The relationship that the British East India Company and the government-licensed Chinese merchant guild, or *Cohong* had so carefully developed over the previous century was now being rapidly undermined by the new commerce. Moreover, growing free trade agitation in England put an end to the East India Company's monopoly on the China trade in 1833. With the monopoly lifted, the number of entrepreneurs seeking quick riches in the opium trade exploded. With wealth came power, and in the foreign trading "factories" in Canton, newcomers engaged in the opium trade vied for prestige with older firms involved in legitimate goods.

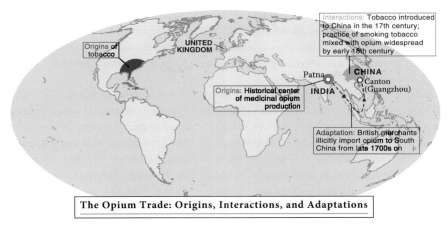

MAP **24.1** **The Opium Trade: Origins, Interactions, Adaptations.**

The push for legitimacy among the opium merchants coincided with an aggressive attempt by Westerners to force China to open additional trading ports for legal items. Chinese authorities, however, viewed this Western assertiveness as driven primarily by opium and Christian evangelism. The East India Company itself was now fatally compromised as well since an estimated one-quarter of its revenues in India were directly tied to opium production.

Far worse, however, were the effects on the ordinary inhabitants of south China. The huge rise in availability and consequent plunge in prices increased opium usage to catastrophic levels. Its power to suppress pain and hunger made it attractive to the

Commissioner Lin Destroys the Opium. This drawing depicts Lin Zexu burning 20,000 chests of opium surrendered by the foreign merchants. Because of the potency of the drug, Lin not only burned it but mixed the ashes with lime and flushed them in sluiceways out to sea. He then offered prayers to the spirits of the sea asking forgiveness for burdening them with this noxious poison.

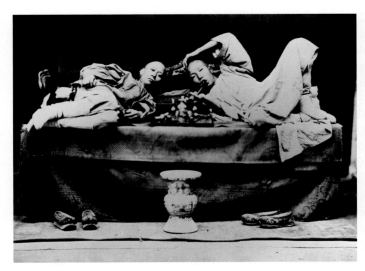

Chinese Opium Smoker. This photograph, taken in the early 1870s, shows the pervasiveness of the opium habit among ordinary Chinese. These men are smoking in the back room of a restaurant, a common practice, even here in British-controlled Hong Kong.

poor engaged in physical labor, though the dream-like state it induced often made it dangerous to work under its influence. Its addictive properties led people to seek it even at the expense of food, thus creating a health crisis for tens of thousands, made infinitely worse by the drug's notoriously difficult withdrawal symptoms.

Commissioner Lin Zexu   Matters came to a head in the spring of 1839. The Daoguang emperor sent Lin Zexu (1785–1850), a widely respected official with a reputation for courage and honesty, to Canton as an imperial commissioner. Lin's task was to cut off the opium trade at its source, and he was given wide-ranging powers to deal with both Chinese and foreign traffickers. In addition to setting up facilities for the recovery of addicts, he demanded that all foreign merchants surrender their opium stocks and sign an agreement that they would not, under penalty of death, deal in the drug anymore. When the foreign community balked at surrendering the goods, Lin blockaded the port and withdrew all Chinese personnel from Western firms. His determined stance finally cracked the stalemate, and the dealers eventually surrendered 20,000 chests of opium, with most also signing the pledge. Lin then publicly burned the surrendered opium and flushed the ashes into the sea. Following Lin's actions, however, the dealers appealed to the British government for compensation.

The British government decided to use the incident to settle the long-standing diplomatic impasse with the Qing over foreign representation and open ports. In a show of force, the British sent a fleet of warships to Canton to demand reparations for the burned opium, pressure the Qing to establish diplomatic relations, and open more ports. In sad contrast to the days four centuries earlier when Zheng He commanded his great fleets, the Chinese now had no real naval forces to contest the British. What vessels they had were modestly armed with seventeenth-century cannon and used for customs collection. The British fleet, on the other hand, was the most powerful in the world and in a high state of readiness. When negotiations broke down, a small Chinese squadron sailed out to confront the British men-o'-war. By an incredible chance, a rocket from a British ship hit the Chinese flagship in its powder magazine and blew it up. Such inauspicious circumstances marked the beginning of the First Opium War (1839–1842) and, with it, a long, painful century of foreign intrusion, domination, and ultimately revolution for China.

The Opium Wars and the Treaty Port Era

The hostilities that began in the fall of 1839 between China and Great Britain exposed the growing gap between the military capabilities of industrializing countries and those, like China, whose armed forces had fallen into disuse. The military had never been an honored profession in China, and the consequences of maintaining scattered Manchu banner garrisons, discouraging militia recruiting, and underfunding the Chinese regular forces (Armies of the Green Standard) were immediately put on painful display. The massive English ships of the line, mounting as many as 128 guns, moved with impunity among the small Chinese fleets of coastal vessels frantically sent to oppose them. The armored steam gunboat *Nemesis*, whose heavy pivot gun allowed it to dominate riverside batteries, landed the British expeditionary forces wherever they pleased.

Over the next 2 years, with a brief truce called in 1841, the British methodically attacked and occupied ports along the Chinese coast from Canton (Guangzhou)

Extraterritoriality: The immunity of a country's nationals from the laws of their host country.

Steam Power Comes to China. The new technologies of the Industrial Revolution were on painful display in China in 1840 as the British gunboat H.M.S. *Nemesis* took on provincial warships down the river from Guangzhou (Canton). The *Nemesis* featured an armored hull put together in detachable sections, shallow draft and steam–powered paddle wheel propulsion for river fighting, and a large pivot gun to take on shore batteries. Its power and versatility convinced Lin Zexu and a growing number of Chinese officials over the coming decades that China needed, at the very least, the same kinds of "strong ships and effective cannon" if they were to defend their coasts and rivers. By the 1860s the first attempts at such craft were finally under way.

to Shanghai at the mouth of the Yangzi River, for the most part without serious opposition. As the British planned to move north to put pressure on Beijing, Chinese officials opened negotiations in August 1842. The resulting Treaty of Nanjing (Nanking) marked the first of the century's "unequal treaties" that would be imposed throughout east Asia by European powers.

The Treaty of Nanjing   Curiously, the treaty ending the First Opium War did not mention opium. In the final agreement, the British claimed the island of Hong Kong, with its excellent deep-water harbor; levied an indemnity on the Chinese to pay the costs of the war; and forced the Chinese to open the ports of Shanghai, Ningbo, Fuzhou, and Xiamen (Amoy), in addition to Guangzhou (Canton). The Chinese were also confronted with British insistence on **non-tariff autonomy**: By treaty they could now charge no more than a 5 percent tariff on British goods. Taking a page from arrangements in the Ottoman Empire, whereby merchants of particular countries were the responsibility of their respective consuls, the British also imposed the policy of **extraterritoriality** in the newly open ports: British subjects who violated Chinese laws would be tried and punished by British consuls.

Over the next several years, the Chinese signed similar treaties with France and the United States. An important addition in these later treaties was the *most-favored nation* clause: Any new concessions granted to one country automatically reverted to those who by treaty were "most-favored nations." Thus, the time-honored Chinese diplomatic strategy of "using barbarians to check barbarians" was dealt a near fatal blow (see Map 24.2).

Non-tariff autonomy: The loss by a country of its right to set its own tariffs.

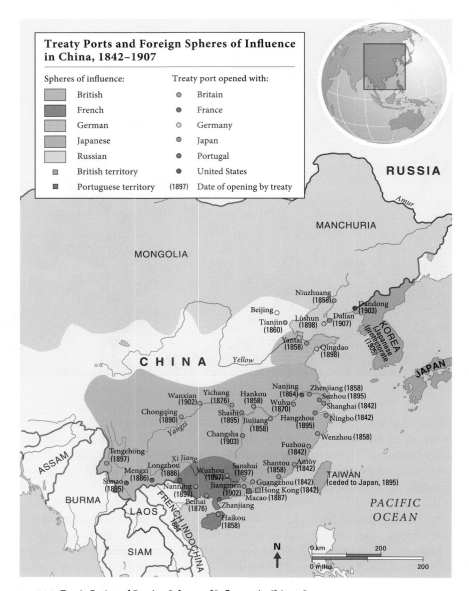

MAP 24.2 **Treaty Ports and Foreign Spheres of Influence in China, 1842–1907.**

The Taiping Movement, 1851–1864   In addition to the spread of the opium trade to the newly opened ports, long-established trade routes for more legitimate items swiftly shifted from Guangzhou to more convenient outlets. The growth of Shanghai was especially important in this regard because it served the Yangzi River, the greatest highway through China's heartland. Coastal trade also increased, while Hong Kong grew as the primary point of opium transfer to small smuggling vessels. The swiftness of all of these changes and their accompanying economic dislocation, along with smoldering discontent at the inability of the Qing government to resist foreign demands, made south China particularly volatile. In 1851 the region exploded in rebellion. Before it was over, this largest civil war in world history and its related conflicts would claim as many as 30 million lives.

The catalyst for revolt was in many ways symbolic of the diverse cultural influences penetrating the area. Though Christian proselytizing had been banned by the Qing since the early eighteenth century, missionary activity was protected in the foreign enclaves and now increased dramatically with the enactment of the new treaties. A candidate for the local Confucian examinations, Hong Xiuquan [HUNG SHIOO-chwahn] (1813–1864), had come upon some Christian missionary tracts passed on by a colleague. Not long after, he failed the examination for the third time and lapsed into a nervous breakdown. When he eventually recovered, Hong gradually came to believe that the Christian God had taken him up to heaven and informed him that he was in fact Christ's younger brother. Hong told his startled listeners that it had been revealed to him that he must now work to bring about the Heavenly Kingdom of Great Peace (*taiping tianguo*) on earth. The movement became known as the "Taiping Rebellion" and lasted from 1851 until 1864.

Hounded from their community, Hong and his group moved into a mountain stronghold and began to gather followers from the disillusioned and unemployed, anti-Manchu elements, religious dissidents, secret societies, and fellow members of south China's Hakka minority. By 1851 they had created a society based on Protestant Christian theology, Chinese traditions, and a vision of equality in which all goods were held in common; women worked, fought, and prayed alongside men; and foot binding, opium smoking, and gambling were forbidden. As a sign that they were no longer loyal to the Qing, the men cut their queues and let the hair grow in on their foreheads, prompting the Qing to refer to them as "the long-haired rebels." Repudiating Confucian tradition, the rebels targeted the scholar-gentry in their land seizures and executions.

By late 1851, the movement had gathered enough strength to stand against local government forces and began an advance to the north. By 1853 they had captured the city of Nanjing and made it their capital. That winter they were narrowly thwarted from driving the Qing from Beijing and pushed back to central China. For the next decade they would remain in control of the Chinese heartland, and the long, bloody contest to subdue them would leave thousands of towns and villages devastated for decades to come.

For the foreigners in China, the prospect of a Christian movement taking power seemed like a cherished dream about to come true. As time went on, however, missionaries and diplomats became less sure of where the movement was heading. On the one hand, Hong and his advisors talked about instituting Western-style administrative reforms and building a modern industrial base—something Western wellwishers had continually urged on Chinese officials. On the other hand, a powerful Taiping China might repudiate the unequal treaties and throw the new trade arrangements into disarray. Thus, the foreign powers in the end grudgingly elected to continue recognizing the Qing as China's legitimate rulers (see Map 24.3).

The Second Opium War, 1856–1860

At the height of the rebellion in 1856, a new dispute arose between the Qing and the British and French. After 4 years of intermittent fighting, it produced the next round of "unequal treaties" that greatly expanded foreign interests and control in the empire. Britain, France, and the United

The Taiping Rebellion, 1851–1864

Area controlled by rebels, ca.1861

Nanjing

Shanghai

Wuhan

Hangzhou

Nanchang

Wenzhou

GUANGXI
PROVINCE

Xiamen
(Amoy)

Guangzhou

TAIWAN

0 km   200

0 miles   200

N

Hong Kong

MAP **24.3 The Taiping
Rebellion 1851–1864.**

States all felt by the mid-1850s that the vastly expanded trade in China—and now Japan—called for the opening of still more ports, an end to Qing prohibitions on missionary activity, and diplomatic relations along Western lines.

The catalyst came in late 1856. A Chinese customs patrol in Canton hauled down the British flag on the *Arrow*, a Chinese vessel whose registry had been falsified to take advantage of British trading privileges. The British seized upon this purported insult to their flag as an opportunity to force treaty revision. The French, who considered themselves the protectors of Catholic missionaries and their converts, saw an excellent opening to pressure China on the missionary issue and so joined the British.

The war itself was fought intermittently in a highly localized fashion. The British seized the walled city of Canton, captured the governor-general of the region's two provinces, and sent him into exile in India. As the conflict moved into 1857, however, the Great Rebellion in India consumed British attention through much of the year, while in China negotiations dragged on intermittently and the Qing remained preoccupied with the Taipings. In 1858, a draft treaty was worked out, but the Qing court refused it. Returning in 1860 with a large expeditionary force, British and French troops advanced to Beijing, drove the emperor from the city, and burned and looted his summer palace. The final treaty stipulated that a dozen ports be opened to foreign trade, that opium be recognized as a legal commodity, that extraterritoriality be expanded, and that foreign embassies be set up in the capital. A newly created Chinese board, the Zongli Yamen, was to handle Qing foreign relations; and the Chinese were invited to send their own ambassadors abroad.

Self-Strengthening   The end of the Second Opium War began a period lasting through the early 1870s sometimes referred to by historians as the "cooperative era." There were few major disputes between the foreign powers and the Qing; indeed, in several instances, foreigners worked closely with Chinese officials to help them in assessing ways to upgrade their defenses, lay the foundations of modern industrial concerns, and start programs that signaled institutional change. The motives of these men ranged from simple altruism to missionary devotion to what might be called "enlightened self-interest": the belief that a strong, modern China would be a more stable trade and diplomatic partner.

For their part, Chinese officials, desperate to roll back the foreign threat and suppress the Taipings, favored a diverse array of strategies. Few advocated simply fighting the foreigners with whatever means were at hand. Most, like the emperor's brother, Prince Gong, felt that over time these new peoples would be assimilated to Chinese norms, like invaders and border peoples of the past. In the meantime, however, they should be "soothed and pacified" but not unconditionally. As the prince later remarked to the British Ambassador, "Take away your opium and your missionaries and you will be welcome."

In order to do this, however, China needed to be able to halt further encroachments by the powers. Toward this end, a growing number of prominent officials advocated a policy that came to be called "self-strengthening." During the 1860s, the two most prominent were Li Hongzhang (1823–1901) and his senior colleague Zeng Guofan (1811–1872). Both men had distinguished themselves as Confucian scholars and as leaders of militia armies during the Taiping years. In 1864, their combined forces finally captured the Taiping capital at Nanjing and forced the suicide of Hong Xiuquan, bringing the movement to an end.

Like a number of leaders during these desperate times, Li and Zeng were also distinguished by the flexibility of their thinking and, increasingly, by their growing familiarity with the new weapons and techniques brought to China by foreign forces. By the end of the rebellion, they had begun to move toward a strategy of what a later slogan called "Chinese studies for the essence; Western studies for practical application." They sponsored an impressive array of projects in the 1860s and early 1870s: a foreign language and technical school, modern arsenals and factories at Nanjing and Jiangnan (Kiangnan), a modern navy yard at Fuzhou, initiatives to send Chinese students to the United States and Europe, a modern shipping concern (The China Merchants' Steam Navigation Company), and the first moves toward sending representatives abroad.

Opposition to such programs also mounted during the period and continued throughout the century. These were the people Li Hongzhang had cited as being "confined by tradition" in the vignette beginning this chapter. Often highly placed—including, ultimately, the Empress Dowager Cixi [SIH-shee] (1835–1908) herself—these opponents felt that any and all reforms of the kind advocated by Li and Zeng would bring down China's Confucian society. For them, the kind of change necessary to create an industrial base in China would erode the social, cultural, and economic ties that held that society together. In the end, they said, the people would cease to be Chinese in any meaningful sense and become like Europeans and Americans. As much as anything else, the lack of a clear strategy at the top and the ferocity of these debates among Chinese officials worked to frustrate the hopes of the "self-strengtheners" through the turn of the century.

Self-Straighteners. Two of the key figures in China's Self-Strengthening Movement were Zeng Guofan (top) and Li Hongzhang (bottom). The two men began working together during the last years of the Taiping Rebellion, both having formed and led militia armies in their home provinces of Hunan (Zeng) and Anhui (Li). Both men also pioneered the use of modern weapons by their troops. After Zeng's death in 1872, Li emerged as the most active proponent of self-strengthening and China's most powerful official.

Toward Revolution: Reform and Reaction to 1900

While China's efforts at self-strengthening seemed promising to contemporaries during the 1870s, the signs of their underlying weakness were already present for those who cared to look. As we have seen, the architect of many of these efforts, Li Hongzhang, was all too aware of the political constraints he faced. With the ascension of the infant Guangxu as emperor in 1874 came the regency of the Empress Dowager Cixi. Desperate to preserve Manchu power, Cixi constantly manipulated factions at court and among the high officials to avoid concentration of power in any particular area. Such maneuverings, sometimes favoring Li's colleagues and as often opposing them, severely hampered the long-term health of many self-strengthening

Interaction and Adaptation: "Self-Strengthening" and "Western Science and Eastern Ethics"

Most of the important technical innovations taking place in China and Japan during the late eighteenth and early nineteenth centuries came from outside east Asia. This, of course, is not surprising since the Scientific and Industrial Revolutions were largely focused on developing labor-saving machinery, weaponry, and improving the speed and efficiency of transportation—things of lesser priority in these labor-rich societies. Confronted by the expansive, newly industrialized countries of Europe and America, their possible responses were largely confined to what might be called the "three R's"—Reaction, Reform, and Revolution. Perhaps most interesting in this regard is the middle path of reform taken by both countries in attempting to create a synthesis of tried and true Confucian social structures and what were considered to be the best of the new technologies and institutions.

As we have seen in past chapters, Chinese philosophical concepts tended toward the desire for correlation and the reconciliation of opposites. In this tradition, *ti* and *yong*, or "essence" and "function/application," became the two key terms in the popular self-strengthening formulation, *Zhongxue wei ti; Xixue wei yong* ("Chinese

Interaction and Adaptation in China and Japan Weapons on display at the Nanjing Arsenal in 1868 include an early Gatling-type rotary machine gun, a Congreve rocket, and a pyramid of round explosive shells. (*a*), while an 1890 lithograph of a Japanese seamstress (*b*) shows the delicate balance between "essence" and "function" that Japan has tried to maintain since the middle of the nineteenth century. The woman is attired in Western dress and she works a Western-style sewing machine. Has the "function" degraded the essence of what she is doing? It is a question that many in Japan still ask today.

studies for the essence; Western studies for the practical application"). Thus, Chinese thinkers were able to accommodate the need for new foreign technologies within historically and philosophically acceptable terminology. Similarly, the Japanese, also schooled in Neo-Confucianism, were able to justify an even more thoroughgoing transformation of society by means of the balanced formula they called "Western science and Eastern ethics."

(b)

However, the two sides of the concept were not equally balanced. As with many Neo-Confucian formulae, the "essence" and "ethics" elements were considered to be primary and the method of implementation—"function"—secondary. Thus, their proponents could argue that their chief aim was the preservation of the fundamentals of Confucian society, while being flexible about the appropriate means of attaining their goals. Opponents, however, argued that the formula could—and eventually would—be reversed: that "function" would eventually degrade the "essence." Here, they pointed to the alleged Westernization of students sent abroad and the wearing of Western clothes in Japan as examples of the dangers of this approach.

Yet, in both countries, one can argue that this has remained a favored approach, even through war and revolution. Though societal and generational tensions over "tradition" and "modernity" have been present for nearly a century and a half in Japan, the Japanese have made foreign technologies and institutions their own, while retaining some of their most cherished Shinto and Buddhist practices alongside social customs still tinged with Neo-Confucianism. Similarly, in China, since the beginning of the Four Modernizations in 1978, coupling technological and institutional modernization with an effort to rediscover and preserve what is considered to be the best of traditional Chinese civilization has been the dominant approach. Thus, the present regime pursues a policy of "socialism with Chinese characteristics" and supports the founding of Confucian institutes alongside computer factories—all in the service of creating what the Communist Party calls "the harmonious society."

Questions

- How were the Chinese and Japanese adaptations to Western innovations similar? How were they different? What do these similarities and differences say about the cultures of these two countries?

- Do you believe that, over the course of time, the "function" of foreign innovations has degraded the "essence" in China and Japan?

measures. In addition, the new programs were costly, usually requiring foreign experts, and China's finances were continually strained by the artificially low treaty tariffs and the obligation to pay old indemnities.

China and Imperialism in Southeast Asia and Korea

By the 1880s foreign tensions exposed more problems. France had been steadily encroaching upon southeast Asia since the late 1850s. By the early 1880s, however, Vietnamese resistance led by a force called the Black Flags was on the verge of rolling back the French. Li Hongzhang supported the Black Flags, and in order to preempt outright Chinese intervention, the French launched a surprise attack on the modern Chinese naval facilities at Fuzhou, sinking the cream of China's steam fleet. Though Chinese forces gave a better account of themselves in other engagements, the French emerged from this conflict with control of the whole of Vietnam, which they promptly combined with Cambodia and Laos into the colony of French Indochina in 1885.

In 1885, as China was still involved with France, tensions with Japan over Korea threatened to dislodge that kingdom as a Qing client state. Japanese diplomats had exerted influence over the Korean court as it sought to deal with the smoldering Tonghak Rebellion (see later, "Creating an Empire"). China sent its own team of officials to keep watch on Qing interests, and both sides quickly threatened to send troops. In the agreement between Li Hongzhang and Ito Hirobumi at Tianjin (Tientsin) that year, both sides agreed not to take any action in the future without informing the other.

By the early 1890s, however, rising tensions surrounding the Korean court and intrigues by Japanese and Chinese agents involving various factions threatened war once again. Japan sent a force which was claimed to be diplomatic; troops of a Chinese counterforce were killed when a Japanese warship sunk their transport. By the fall of 1894, both sides were sending troops and naval forces to Korea and a full-scale war over the fate of Korea and northeast Asia was under way.

The Sino–Japanese War

As we noted at the beginning of this chapter, the war between China and Japan over control of Korea graphically exposed the problems of China's "self-strengthening" efforts. China's arms procurement, for example, was not carried out under a centralized program, as was Japan's. The result was that different Chinese military units were armed with a wide variety of noninterchangeable weapons and ammunition, making it difficult for them to support each other. China's rebuilt fleet, though impressive in size and armament, faced similar problems. Unlike the Japanese ships, China's largest warships had their components separately built at various shipyards in Europe. In one memorable incident during the Battle of the Yellow Sea in 1894, the recoil from the mismatched, oversized guns aboard the Chinese flagship destroyed its own captain's bridge. Worse still, Chinese gunners found to their dismay that many of the shells they were firing were filled with sand rather than explosive—the result of the empress dowager's diversion of naval funds to rebuild the summer palace destroyed in 1860.

While many of the land battles were hotly contested, superior Japanese organization and morale enabled them to drive steadily through Korea. A second force landed in southern Manchuria to secure the territory around the approaches to Beijing, while Japanese naval forces reduced the fortress across from it at Weihaiwei. By spring 1895, after some preliminary negotiations, Li made his humiliating trip to

(a)

(b)

Scenes from the Sino–Japanese War.
News accounts of the Sino–Japanese
War aroused great interest and an
unprecedented wave of nationalism
in Japan. They also marked the last
extensive use of ukiyo-e woodblock
printing in the news media as the
technology of reproducing photos in
newspapers was introduced to Japan
shortly after the conflict. Because few
of the artists actually traveled with
the troops, the great majority of these
works came from reporters' dispatches
and the artists' imaginations. In these
representative samples from the assault
on Pyongyang and the use of the new
technology of the electric searchlight to
illuminate an enemy fort (a), the pride in
Japan's modernization and the disdain
for China's "backwardness" are all too
evident. Note the almost demon-like
faces and garish uniforms of the Chinese
as they are invariably depicted as being
killed or cowering before the Japanese;
note, too, the modern, Western uniforms
and beards and mustaches of the
Japanese (b).

Shimonoseki and was forced to agree to Japan's terms. The severity of the provisions, especially the annexation of Taiwan, the control of Korea, and, temporarily at least, the seizure of Liaodong, signaled to the Western powers in east Asia that China was now weak enough to have massive economic and territorial demands forced on it.

Thus, a "race for concessions" began in which France demanded economic and territorial rights in south China adjacent to Indochina; Great Britain did the same in the Yangzi River valley; Russia and Japan made demands in the north for rights in Manchuria; and a newcomer, Germany, demanded naval bases and rights at Qingdao [Ching-DOW] (Tsingtao) on the Shandong Peninsula. China's total dismemberment was avoided in 1899 when John Hay, the US secretary of state, circulated a note with British backing suggesting that all powers refrain from securing exclusive concessions and instead maintain an "open door" for all to trade in China.

The Hundred Days of Reform   Amid this growing foreign crisis, the aftermath of the war produced a domestic crisis as well. The terms of the Shimonoseki treaty had prompted patriotic demonstrations in Beijing and raised levels of discussion about reform to new levels of urgency. A group of younger officials headed by Kang Youwei (1858–1927) petitioned Emperor Guangxu, now ruling in his own right, to implement a list of widespread reforms, many modeled on those recently enacted in Japan. Guangxu issued a flurry of edicts from June through September 1898, attempting to completely revamp China's government and many of its leading institutions. Resistance to this "hundred days' reform" program, however, was

EN CHINE
Le gâteau des Rois et... des Empereurs

Dismembering China. The weakness of the Qing during the final years of the nineteenth century prompted the so-called Race for Concessions among the imperial powers in east Asia. In this French cartoon, China is depicted as a flatbread or pizza around which caricatures of the monarchs and national symbols of the various powers sit with their knives poised arguing over who should get the best pieces. A desperate Chinese official—perhaps Li Hongzhang himself—with his long fingernails and flapping queue, holds up his hands imploring them to stop. The French caption says roughly, "In China: The cake of kings and emperors."

extensive, and much of it was centered on the emperor's aunt, the empress dowager. With support from her inner circle at court, she had the young emperor placed under house arrest and rounded up and executed those of Kang's supporters who could be found. Kang and his junior colleague, the writer and political theorist Li-ang Qichao [LEEAHNG chee-CHOW] (1873–1929) managed to escape to the treaty ports. For the next decade they traveled to overseas Chinese communities attempting to gather support for their Constitutional Monarchy Party.

The Boxer Rebellion and War   The turmoil set off by the "race for concessions" among the imperial powers was particularly intense in north China, where the ambitions of Russia, Japan, and Germany clashed. With the stepped-up activity of German missionaries on the Shandong Peninsula came a new wave of antiforeign sentiment, increasingly centered on a group called the Society of the Harmonious Fists. Anti-Qing as well as antiforeign, the members' ritual exercises and name prompted the foreign community to refer to them as the "Boxers." By late 1899 the Boxers were regularly provoking the foreign and Christian communities with the aim of pushing their governments to pressure the Qing to suppress the movement, by which they hoped to stir up rebellion against them.

In the spring of 1900 matters came to a head. Boxers assassinated the German ambassador, and the Germans demanded that the Qing crush the movement once and for all, pay a huge indemnity, and erect a statue to their ambassador as a public apology. In the midst of this crisis, the empress dowager, who had been negotiating in secret with the Boxers, declared war on all the foreign powers in China and openly threw the court's support behind the movement. The result was civil war across northern China as Boxer units hunted down missionaries and Chinese Christians, many Chinese army units aided the Boxers in attacking foreigners, and the foreign diplomatic quarter in Beijing was besieged from June until August.

The foreign governments quickly put together a multinational relief force led by the Germans and British and largely manned by the Japanese but including units of nearly all the countries with interests in China. By August they had fought their way to the capital and chased the imperial court nearly to Xi'an. Amid considerable carnage in the mopping up of Boxer sympathizers, Li Hongzhang, in his last official duty before his death, was commissioned to negotiate the end of the conflict for the court. With Qing power utterly routed, the foreign governments were able to impose the most severe "unequal treaty" yet: They extracted the right to post troops in major Chinese cities, they demanded the total suppression of any antiforeign movements, and they received such a huge indemnity that China had to borrow money from foreign banks in order to service the interest on the payments. The only bright point in the Boxer Protocols of 1901 was that the United States agreed to return its share of the indemnity money to China on the condition that it would be used to send Chinese students to study in American institutions.

Toward Revolution   With the return of the imperial court to Beijing and the enhanced foreign presence in the capital, the Qing finally turned to institutional reform. During the first decade of the twentieth century, the old Confucian examination system was abolished and new curricula—including science and technology—were created. Similarly, the army was overhauled and modernized. Perhaps most dramatically, the government itself was to be restructured more or less along the lines envisioned by Kang Youwei and Emperor Guangxu—who was still under house arrest. An imperial commission was sent abroad to study the constitutional systems of the great powers, and upon its return a plan to turn the Qing into a constitutional monarchy was created. By 1910, 2 years after the deaths of both the empress dowager and Guangxu, the first limited elections were being held for a planned legislative body.

The Empress Dowager Cixi. Following the rout of the Qing and Boxer forces in the fall of 1900, the empress dowager made herself more accessible to Western diplomats and photographers. There are numerous pictures of her in various royal poses; here, she sits with her court ladies-in-waiting. The legend above her throne reads from right to left: "The reigning Saintly Mother, Empress Dowager of the Great Qing, (may she rule) 10,000 years! 10,000 years! 10,000, 10,000 years!"—the last exhortation (*wan sui, wan sui, wan wan sui*) the Chinese rendering of the more familiar Japanese "Banzai."

While Qing reform efforts were proceeding apace, however, the plans of revolutionaries were moving even more rapidly. As we will see in Chapter 28, the central figure in this regard was Sun Yat-sen (1866–1925), a man in many ways emblematic of the changes in China during the nineteenth century. Born near Canton, Sun received the fundamentals of classical education but then undertook Western training in medicine in Hong Kong and developed a thriving medical practice in Canton. A student of European and American history, his political ideas were already germinating by the time of the Sino–Japanese War. Like growing numbers of Chinese, the war convinced Sun that the feeble and increasingly corrupt Manchu government was the biggest obstacle to China's regeneration. In the end, his movement would play the leading role in forcing it out.

In Search of Security Through Empire: Japan in the Meiji Era

As we have just seen, the close of the nineteenth century saw Japan looming larger and larger as China's chief threat. Yet, they both faced similar pressures and, as Li Hongzhang observed, shared a common culture and in many ways a common cause. How, then, was Japan, with only a fraction of China's population and resources, able to not only survive in the face of foreign pressure but join the imperial powers itself?

The Decline of Tokugawa Seclusion   Though the eighteenth century saw occasional attempts by foreign ships to put in at Japanese ports, Europeans generally honored Japan's seclusion policies. Moreover, since all maritime trade with China took ships along a southerly route to Canton, the opportunity to go to Japan seldom presented itself. By the first decades of the nineteenth century, however, the situation was changing. The vastly expanded legitimate trade with China and the development of the opium trade increased the volume of shipping closer to Japanese waters. Moreover, the rapid growth of the whaling industry in the northern Pacific increasingly brought European and American ships into waters adjacent to

Japan. From their perspective, the need for establishing relations for the disposition of shipwreck survivors and perhaps trade was therefore becoming ever more urgent.

By the 1840s the pressure to establish relations with the Tokugawa shogunate became even more intense for the Western powers with interests in China. The treaty ports created in the wake of the First Opium War included Shanghai, which was rapidly becoming east Asia's chief commercial enclave. Because of its geographical position, major shipping routes to Shanghai now ran directly adjacent to southern Japan. Moreover, the Mexican War (1846–1848) brought the Pacific coast of North America under the control of the United States. At the same time, the discovery of gold in California made boomtown San Francisco the premier port for all American transpacific trade. In addition, increasing numbers of Chinese sought passage to the gold fields and the promise of employment in the American West, while the infamous "**coolie** trade" continually increased human traffic to Cuba and Peru. Plans to open steamship service along the great circle route from San Francisco to Shanghai, and the need for coaling stations to supply it, now threatened to place Japan squarely across the path of maritime traffic (see Map 24.4).

Coolies: Poor migrant laborers from China and India who performed menial work in other parts of the world in the nineteenth century.

The Coming of the "Black Ships"   The Tokugawa were well aware of the humiliation of the Qing at the hands of the British in 1842 and watched nervously as foreign commerce mounted in the Chinese treaty ports. As pressure increased on Japan to open its ports, divided counsels plagued the shogunate. The influential Mito School, long exposed to "Dutch learning" (see Chapter 21), feared the growing military and technological power of the Europeans and Americans and advocated a military response to any attempt at opening the country. Others looking at the situation in China felt that negotiation was the only possible way for Japan to avoid invasion.

MAP 24.4 **Steamship Routes and Underwater Telegraph Cables, ca. 1880.**

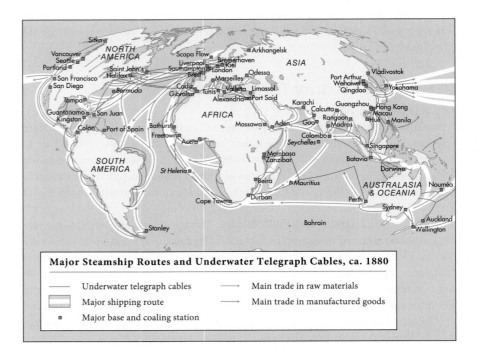

Major Steamship Routes and Underwater Telegraph Cables, ca. 1880

———   Underwater telegraph cables   ⟶   Main trade in raw materials

▭   Major shipping route   ⟶   Main trade in manufactured goods

▪   Major base and coaling station

The Americans, taking the lead in seeking diplomatic and commercial relations, put together a fleet of their newest and most powerful warships in arriving in July, 1853. Their commander, Matthew C. Perry, assembled multiracial and -ethnic crews for them in order to impress his Japanese hosts with the reach and power of the United States. Anxious to awe them as well with the new technologies available, he brought along as presents a telegraph set and a model railroad, both of which proved immediately popular. When negotiations flagged, the shogun's men gleefully amused themselves aboard the miniature train, smacking the engine and its operator with their fans to make it go faster.

On Perry's return trip in 1854 with even more of the "black ships," as the Japanese dubbed them, the Treaty of Kanagawa was signed, Japan's first with an outside power. Like China, Japan had now entered the treaty port era.

"Honor the Emperor and Expel the Barbarian!" The widely differing attitudes toward foreign contact expressed within the shogunate were reflected among the daimyo and samurai as well. The treaty with the Americans, and the rapid conclusion of treaties with other foreigners, tended to reinforce antiforeignism among many of the warrior elite, while emphasizing the weakness of the Tokugawa to resist further demands. Moreover, the new cultural contacts taking place in treaty ports like Yokohama and Nagasaki hardened positions and raised tensions further. Many samurai felt that dramatic gestures were called for to rouse the country to action. Hence, as with the Boxers later in China, they attacked foreigners and even assassinated Tokugawa officials in an effort to precipitate antiforeign conflict. By 1863, a movement aimed at driving out the Tokugawa and restoring imperial rule had coalesced around the samurai of two southern domains, Satsuma and Choshu. Taking the slogan *sonno joi* ("Honor the emperor, expel the barbarian!") members of this "Satcho" (*Satsuma* and *Choshu*) clique challenged the shogunate and fought the smoldering Restoration War, which by the end of 1867 forced the Tokugawa to capitulate. In short order, the new regime moved to the Tokugawa capital of Edo and renamed it "Tokyo" (Eastern Capital).

The new emperor, 15-year-old Mutsuhito, took the reign name of Meiji (Enlightened Rule) and quickly moved to make good on its promise. As proof that the new regime would adopt progressive measures, the throne issued a charter oath in April 1868. A constitution was also promulgated, which spelled out in more detail how the new government was to be set up.

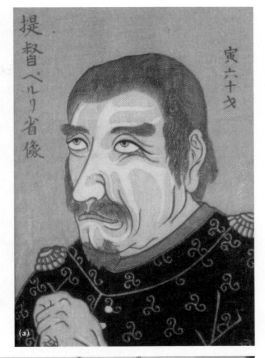

"Blue-eyed Barbarians." Japanese commonly referred to Westerners as "blue-eyed barbarians." In these sketches, part of a long series that artists made after Commodore Perry's four heavily-armed steamships sailed into Tokyo Bay in July 1853, Perry's son Oliver, who served as his father's personal secretary, is portrayed as jowly and slightly demonic looking *(a)*, while a group of US Marines are portrayed as both menacing and ridiculous at the same time *(b)*.

Emperor Meiji. A number of portraits and photographs of Emperor Meiji were done during his lifetime, particularly in his twenties and thirties. Here, in a portrait probably done in the late 1870s or early 1880s, he is shown as a vigorous and decisive man at the height of his powers. Note the European-style military uniform and Van Dyke beard of the kind frequently sported by Western monarchs and leaders.

Creating a Nation-State   While the Tokugawa had created an efficient warrior bureaucracy based on Neo-Confucianism, Japan was still dominated by regional loyalties and fealty to the daimyo of one's *han*, or feudal domain. The foreign threat and restoration of the emperor provided the opportunity as well as the necessity to forge a more thoroughgoing national unification. Thus, the new government quickly set about dismantling the feudal han and replacing them with a centralized provincial structure; the daimyo were replaced by governors, and the samurai were disbanded, given stipends, and encouraged to form business enterprises or to teach. In their place, a new conscript army modeled after that of Germany was created and a navy modeled on Great Britain's was established. In addition, the new order was to be held together by a national system of compulsory education in which loyalty to the emperor and state was carefully nurtured at every level.

The 1870s also marked the flourishing of government-managed social experimentation. Like the Chinese "self-strengtheners," Japanese senior advisors, or *genro* [hard "g": GEN-row], to the emperor sought to use new foreign technologies and institutions to strengthen the state against further foreign intrusion. Japan's planners, however, proved more systematic and determined in their efforts and, unlike their Chinese counterparts, had the full backing of the imperial court. Thus, Japan's proclaimed goals of using "Western science and Eastern ethics" in the service of "civilization and enlightenment" were seen as the primary tools in asserting eventual equality with the Western imperial powers and rolling back Japan's unequal treaties.

Adventures Abroad and Revolt at Home   Amid these dizzying changes, some senior advisors advocated an aggressive foreign policy in order to create a buffer zone around Japan. For these men, most prominently former samurai Saigo Takamori (1827–1877), Korea, which so far had resisted Western attempts to end its seclusion, was the obvious place to start. Saigo offered to sacrifice himself in order to create an incident in Korea that would justify Japanese action to "open" the so-called Hermit Kingdom. The Meiji court and inner circle, however, favored restraint. Instead, Japan contented itself with the expedition against Taiwan in 1874 and the purchase of the Ryukyu Islands in 1879.

The social turmoil at home and the tempering of Japan's ambitions abroad stirred discontent among many former samurai. In their view, Japan had abandoned its true character and was rapidly becoming a second-rate copy of the Western countries, fueled by greed, lack of honor, and international cowardice. In 1876, such sentiments helped spark a revolt among dissident samurai. Saigo, an imposing giant of a man much admired by the samurai, was persuaded to join them. Their movement, however, was crushed with brutal efficiency by the modern conscript army of Yamagata Aritomo (1838–1922), and Saigo himself committed suicide in April 1877. Though discontent at the direction of Japanese modernization continued to fester throughout the nineteenth century, it never again reached the level of open rebellion.

Creating an Empire   As we saw earlier in this chapter, rising tensions between Japan and China over the disposition of Korea ultimately led to the Sino–Japanese War of 1894–1895. The issue was temporarily held in abeyance by the Treaty of Tianjin of 1885, but continuing difficulties arising from the instability of the Korean government, feuding pro-Chinese and pro-Japanese factions within it, and the *Tonghak*, or "Eastern learning," movement, kept the region a volatile one. Combining elements of Confucianism, Buddhism, and a pronounced strain of antiforeignism, Tonghak-led peasant rebellions had erupted in 1810 and 1860. Though the rebellion had been suppressed in the 1860s, the forced opening of Korea to trade in the following decade and the constant intrigues of the Qing and the Japanese surrounding the Yi court in succeeding decades brought about the movement's revival in the 1890s.

As we have seen, Japan's successful showing in the war surprised and alarmed the Western powers in the region. The Triple Intervention, in which Russia, Germany, and France forced Japan to return the Liaodong Peninsula to China, only to have them lease it to Russia the following year, put that empire on a collision course with Japanese aspirations on the Asian mainland. Japan's control of Korea made it intensely interested in acquiring concessions in Manchuria. For Russia, it was vital to build rail links from the Trans-Siberian Railway to their new outposts of Port Arthur and Dairen (Dalian) in Liaodong and to extend the line across Manchuria to Vladivostok on the Pacific. As the twentieth century began, they pressured the Chinese into allowing them the rights to build the Chinese Eastern Railway across Manchuria and the South Manchurian Railway to Port Arthur, with a vital junction at Mukden, known today as Shenyang. Japan and Russia would shortly fight a war that would secure Japan's dominant position in northeast Asia and begin a long train of events that would end in revolution for Russia (see Map 24.5).

> ### Enlightened Rule
>
> "All matters [would be] decided by public discussion . . . evil customs of the past shall be broken off . . . [and] knowledge shall be sought throughout the world so as to strengthen the foundations of imperial rule."
>
> —From *Meiji boshin*, pp. 81–82. Quoted in Ryusaku Tsunoda, William T. De Bary, and Donald Keene, eds. *Sources of Japanese Tradition*, vol. 2, p. 137. New York: Columbia University Press, 1964.

Economics and Society in Late Qing China

The century and a half from 1750 to 1900 marked the structural, cultural, and economic decline of the great agrarian empires. Nowhere was this more evident than in Qing China. By 1900, China's treasury was bankrupt; its finances increasingly were controlled by foreign concerns; its export trade was outstripped by European and Japanese competitors; its domestic markets turned to factory-produced foreign commodities; and its land, ravaged by war, eroded by declining productivity, and squeezed by the world's largest population, grew less and less capable of sustaining its society.

The Seeds of Modernity and the New Economic Order

As we have seen a number of times in this chapter, the economic policies of late imperial China were increasingly at odds with those of the industrializing and

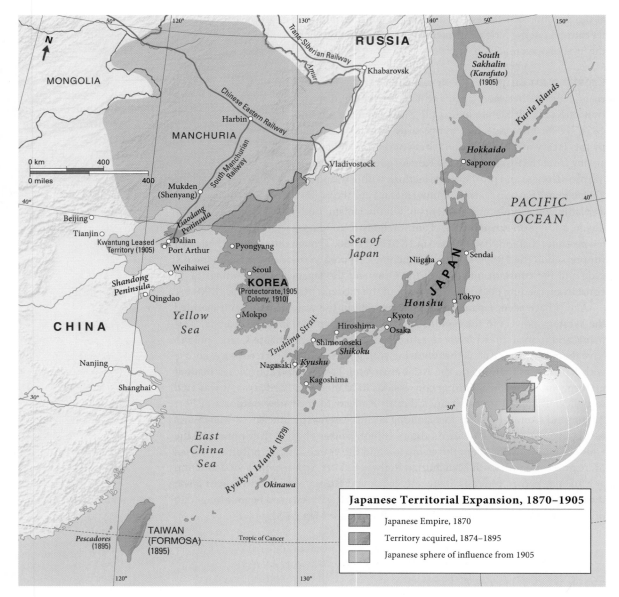

MAP 24.5 **Japanese Territorial Expansion, 1870–1905.**

commercially expanding West. For Chinese thinkers, this was considered sound in both ideological and economic terms. Confucianism held that agriculture was China's primary concern; that the values of humanity, loyalty, and filial piety were tied to agrarian society; and that the values of the merchant—particularly the drive for profit—were in direct opposition to these agrarian values. As the nineteenth century advanced, the opium trade provided ample evidence to Confucian officials of the correctness of this stance.

While opium was the great entering wedge, the building pressures on China and other regulated societies to lower their barriers to legitimate trade and the steps taken by those countries exerting the pressure to safeguard their own markets had equally severe long-term effects. Briefly, China was squeezed both ways in terms of trade. That is, the unequal treaties imposed artificially low tariff rates on the empire, making it increasingly difficult to protect its markets; at the same time, trading nations in the West increased tariffs on their own imports and, in some cases, developed their own substitutes for Chinese products.

Self-Strengthening and Economics   The programs to improve China's economics and trade were set up as "government-sponsored/merchant-operated" enterprises. One of the most initially promising of these was the China Merchants Steam Navigation Company, founded in 1873. The company's purpose was to recapture the carrying trade on China's rivers from foreign operators. With key purchases of foreign steamers and dock facilities during the early and mid-1870s, the company had gone far toward reclaiming a significant percentage of China's river traffic by 1880. However, renewed foreign competition, lackluster governmental support, and traditional avenues of graft eroded the company's position until it folded later in the decade. In many respects, the company's experience marked a crucial tension between the entrepreneurial instincts of the merchants and the expectations of officials in regulation and receiving regular payoff income. The government itself and officials critical of self-strengthening were quick to point out the high cost of such programs, their potential for corruption, and the futility of attempting to beat the Westerners at their own game.

Amid the halting attempts at government-sponsored innovation, however, other economic forces at work would also have a profound effect on China's later economic development. The first is that in the treaty ports themselves the economic climate created by the Western powers for their own benefit exposed much of China's urban population to aspects of modern industrial and commercial society. A substantial class of Chinese people who made a living mediating between Westerners and Chinese interests had developed by the end of the nineteenth century.

The other long-term process at work was the growing influx and popularity of European, Japanese, and American consumer goods diffused from the treaty ports to the interior. While foreign curiosities had been popular with Chinese elites since the eighteenth century, Qing efforts to safeguard domestic markets through the Canton system and internal transit taxes had been steadily beaten down. By the end of the nineteenth century, foreign machine-made cotton cloth dominated the Chinese interior, John D. Rockefeller's Standard Oil Company was giving away kerosene lamps to market their fuel, the British–American Tobacco Company had established its products in the empire, and even the Japanese invention of the rickshaw had become a popular mode of transport in China's cities. With the Qing finally committed to railroad and telegraph construction and modern deep mining and with China's commercial ports resembling more and more their foreign counterparts, the seeds of economic modernity had been at least fitfully planted.

Rural Economics and Society   While about 80–85 percent of China's population remained rural, the old structures of the empire's peasant-based society were slowly beginning to crumble. As we saw during the Taiping era, tensions among peasants, village headmen, scholar-gentry, and local officials were never far from the surface. Landlordism, especially the growing incidence of absentee landlordism, tended to stretch these tensions further. As some controversial economic studies of rural Qing society have suggested, even with the most advanced intensive farming techniques available and the introduction of better crops for marginal areas like corn, peanuts, and potatoes, the land was approaching the limits of its ability to support the population without the widespread introduction of power-driven machinery. Living on the edge of poverty in many areas, with old trade routes and handicrafts disrupted by the treaty ports, many peasants saw in the Taipings, the Nian, and other local rebellions a desperate way to change their situations. But in the end, the radical ideologies and ruthlessness of the rebels disillusioned the peasantry, while in many places their poverty increased due to the immense destruction caused by rebel clashes and the flight of many wealthy scholar-gentry to the treaty ports. As a result, by the beginning of the twentieth century, absentee landlordism had become an increasingly acute problem. As some scholars have noted, the land problems of China—and their parallels in India and the Ottoman Empire—were an important impediment to an effective response to the scientific–industrial challenge of Europe and America.

Chinese Family, ca. 1873. While the later nineteenth century marked changes on a number of fronts, the centrality of the family and its Confucian hierarchy remained largely intact. In the portrait here of the Yang family of Beijing, the father and eldest son occupy the places of honor under the central window of the ground floor, while the wives, concubines, infants, and servants are arrayed on the upper veranda. In most cases, the seclusion of such wealthy women was nearly complete. The photographer reported, however, that these women frequently moistened their fingertips and rubbed them on the paper windowpanes to make them transparent so they could secretly watch events outside.

Social Trends While changes were certainly noticeable in the family, in relationships between men and women, and in the confidence the Chinese displayed in the Confucian system—particularly among urban Chinese—the durability of long-standing traditions is probably far more striking. As we have seen in every chapter on China, the family remained the central Chinese institution. Within it, the father continued to be the most powerful figure and the Confucian ideal of hierarchical relationships between husband and wife, father and son, and elder brother and younger brother remained in force. Daughters, though most often treated with affection, were also considered a net drain on family resources because they would marry outside the family. Thus, the education they received was generally aimed at fostering the skills the family of their husbands-to-be would consider valuable—cooking, sewing, running a household, and perhaps singing and poetry. Enough literacy was also desirable for girls to read such classics as "Admonitions for Women," the "Classic of Filial Piety," and other guides to proper behavior. But the proverbial wisdom remained that "a woman with talent is without virtue." Hence, the daughters of the wealthy were kept secluded in the home, and most—with the exception of certain minorities like south China's Hakkas—continued the practice of foot binding.

The disruptions of the nineteenth century began to have some effect on this situation. Though there had been a slow trickle of foreign influence into China, particularly in the treaty ports, for much of the nineteenth century, the decade following the Sino–Japanese War saw an upsurge in it, particularly as the Qing moved belatedly toward reform and underground revolutionary movements began to gain adherents. Women in Taiping areas had had a brief taste of equality, though it had been undermined by Taiping excesses and the Confucian revival afterward. With wealthier Chinese beginning to send daughters abroad to be educated, the impressions they returned with began to erode some Chinese customs, though the full impact of this would not be felt until the 1920s and 1930s. Meanwhile, such customs as the selling of young girls and female infanticide continued to be common, particularly in economically hard-pressed areas.

Culture, Arts, and Science

Though the late Qing period is often seen by scholars as one more concerned with cataloging and preserving older literary works than innovation, there was nevertheless considerable invigoration due to foreign influences toward the end of the dynasty. Indeed, one could say that the era begins with one of China's great literary masterpieces and ends with China's first modern writers pointing toward a vernacular-language "literary renaissance" starting around 1915. Reversing the trend of thousands of years, the most significant Chinese developments in science and technology were those arriving from the West as products of the Industrial Revolution and the new kind of society emerging there.

The Dream of the Red Chamber   Though the novel during Ming and Qing times was not considered high literary work by Chinese scholars, the form, as with Europeans in the eighteenth and nineteenth centuries, proved immensely popular. During the mid-eighteenth century, what many consider to be China's greatest novel, *Hong Lou Meng* (*The Dream of the Red Chamber*) was written by the shadowy Cao Xueqin [SOW shway-CHIN] (ca. 1715–ca. 1764). Almost nothing is known of Cao, including exactly when he was born and who his actual father was. The novel itself chronicles the decline and fall of a powerful family over 120 chapters. Some scholars see in it a loose autobiography of Cao's own family and a thinly veiled account of events in the early days of the Qing. In fact, the novel has been so closely studied and analyzed that there is an entire field called "red studies" or "redology" (*hong xue*) devoted to examination of the work.

Poetry, Travel Accounts, and Newspapers   While the form of the interlocking "three excellences"—painting, poetry, and calligraphy—remained largely unchanged, their content increasingly treated subjects related to China's new position in the age of imperialism. Though sometimes confining himself to more traditional fare, Huang Zunxian (1848–1905), for example, wrote many poems based on his experience as a diplomat in Japan and the United States.

China's increasing need to understand the nature of the threat confronting it prompted a greater number of atlases, gazetteers of foreign lands, and by the 1860s the first eyewitness travel accounts. Many of the early attempts at compiling information about foreign countries were copies of Western works, whose sophistication gradually increased as the century wore on. The most significant of these were Wei Yuan's (1794–1856) *Illustrated Gazetteer of the Maritime Countries* of 1844 and Xu Jiyu's (1795–1873) *Record of the World* of 1848. These accounts, especially Xu's, formed the backbone of what Chinese officials knew about the outside world until the first eyewitness accounts of travelers and diplomats began to arrive in the late 1860s.

Though hundreds of thousands of Chinese had emigrated to various parts of the world by the mid-1860s, it was only in 1866 that the first authorized officials began to visit foreign countries and not until 1876 that diplomats began to take up their posts in foreign capitals and ports. All of these men, however, were required to keep

Li Gui (1842–1903) on the Philadelphia Exposition in 1876

"Considering that the intent of countries in holding expositions is primarily to display friendship and extend human talent, particular emphasis is placed on the four words 'expand and strengthen commerce.' For the most part, though, we Chinese have not seen this as advantageous nor, since so few of us have gone abroad, have we fully grasped its implications. Still, can it be the case that others do their utmost to understand the precise thoughts of foreigners and eagerly spend hundreds, thousands, tens, or even hundreds of thousands of dollars of their capital competing in enterprises that are not advantageous? We Chinese alone seem capable of thinking that the intent of the Westerners in undertaking these exhibitions rests on principles against which we should guard at any cost. Yet as a means of enriching the country on the one hand, and benefiting the people on the other, how could this ... exposition attendance be considered wasteful?"

—Li Gui, *Huan you diqiu xin lu*, 10a; translated by Charles Desnoyers, in *A Journey to the East*. Ann Arbor: University of Michigan Press, 2004, p. 100.

journals of their experiences, and by the later part of the century China began to acquire a far more complete sense of what the outside world was like. The diaries of the diplomats Zhang Deyi (1847–1919) and Guo Songtao (1818–1891) were particularly significant in this regard.

A new popular medium also emerged in the treaty ports and eventually in most Chinese cities as well—the newspaper. For centuries newsletters tracking official doings at the capital had been circulated among the elites. However, the 1860s saw the first popular Chinese-language papers, the most prominent of which was *Shenbao*. By the turn of the century, Liang Qichao had emerged as China's most influential journalist and scholar, having started and edited five newspapers, each heavily influenced by his views on reform. Such publications and the growing numbers of journals and popular magazines, many started by missionaries anxious to use science and Western material culture as a vehicle for their work, were vitally important in the transfer of ideas between Chinese and foreigners.

Science and Technology   As we have seen, the most pressing need for China during the early nineteenth century was considered to be military technology. During the period between the Opium Wars, Chinese officials attempted with some success to purchase guns and cannon from European and American manufacturers to bolster their coastal defenses. It was quickly apparent to the self-strengtheners, however, that China must understand the basic principles behind these revolutionary weapons and begin to manufacture them on their own. Moreover, this would be impossible to do unless the infrastructure was in place and such supporting industries as mining, railroads, and telegraphy were also established. One early move in this regard was the founding of the All-Languages Institute (*Tongwen Guan*) in 1861. Founded to provide interpreters for the newly arriving diplomats in Beijing, the foreign experts employed soon allowed the school to become a kind of all-purpose science and technology academy as well. With the founding of arsenals and dockyards and their supporting infrastructures, the need for technical knowledge accelerated. Here, the Chinese Education Mission to the United States, as well as later student missions to England and Germany, was meant to create a nucleus of trained personnel to modernize Chinese industry and defense.

Despite the general animosity directed against them by Chinese officials, missionaries ironically were key players in science and technology transfers. Unlike the Jesuit missionaries of the seventeenth century, Protestant missionaries in the nineteenth century directed their efforts at ordinary Chinese but often did so by attracting them with the new advantages of science. Central to their efforts was the role of medical missionaries in setting up clinics and using their presence in the community to foster conversion. The missionary community was also active in popularizing developments in Western science and technology through journals like *The Globe Magazine*.

By the latter part of the century, increasing numbers of Chinese scholars were becoming involved in the study of foreign subjects, going abroad for education, and in the translation of Western works into Chinese. The Chinese mathematician Li Shanlan (1810–1882), for example, collaborated with Shanghai missionaries in translating works on algebra, calculus, and analytical geometry. Later, Liang Qichao and Yan Fu (1854–1921) studied and translated a wide range of foreign scientific and social science works by John Stuart Mill, Thomas Huxley, Herbert Spencer, and Charles Darwin, as well as such Enlightenment authors as Hobbes, Locke, Hume, Rousseau, and Bentham.

Thus, while China had not yet completed its move to the new scientific–industrial society, the momentum had already begun among the empire's intellectual leaders. Even so, nearly all agreed that the future would not lie in slavish imitation of the West. In the meantime, however, the example of Japan confronted them only a short distance away.

Zaibatsu and Political Parties: Economics and Society in Meiji Japan

Scholars of Japan's economic history have often pointed out that the commercial environment developing through the Tokugawa period was well suited to the nurturing of capitalism and industrialism in the nineteenth century. As we saw in Chapter 21, for example, the imposition of the law of "alternate attendance" created a great deal of traffic to and from Edo as daimyo processions made their biannual trips to the capital. This guaranteed traffic supported numerous hostels, restaurants, stables, supply stores, theaters, and all the other commercial establishments necessary to maintain the travelers in safety and comfort. The infrastructure of the major roads also required constant tending and improvement, as did the port facilities for coastal shipping and fishing industries. Towns and cities along the routes also grew, as did the regionally specialized crafts and industries they supported. By 1850, for example, Edo had well over 1 million inhabitants, while Osaka and Kyoto both had about 375,000. Finally, commercial credit establishments, craft guilds, and large-scale industries in ceramics, sake brewing, fine arts, fishing, and coastal shipping—all intensified by being compressed into a relatively small area—had already regularized many of the institutions characteristic of the development of a modern economy.

Commerce and Cartels

Perhaps because of the urgency of their situation following Perry's visits, the Japanese were quicker to go abroad to study the industrially advanced countries of Europe and the United States. In 1860, for example, they sent an embassy to America in which the participants—including the future journalist Fukuzawa Yukichi (1835–1901)—were expected to keep diaries of everything they saw. Even during the last days of the Tokugawa regime, Japanese entrepreneurs were already experimenting with Western steamships and production techniques.

Cooperation and Capitalism   When the Meiji government began its economic reforms, its overall strategy combined elements that still mark Japanese policy today. The first was to make sure that ownership, insofar as possible, would

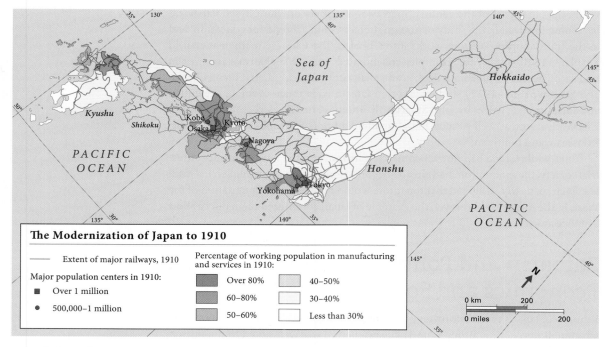

MAP 24.6 **The Modernization of Japan to 1910.**

remain in Japanese hands. The second was that, taking its cue from the success of the leading commercial nations of the West, Japan would develop its exports to the utmost while attempting to keep imports to a minimum. Japanese entrepreneurship also received an enormous boost from the cashing out of the samurai. While many of the former warriors found anything to do with commerce distasteful, some took to heart the government's injunction that starting economic enterprises was a patriotic duty. By the end of the century, Japan's industrial statistics were impressive by any standards: Coal production had increased to six times its 1860 base, and iron, copper, and other mining industries expanded at a similar rate—but still could not keep pace with Japan's industrial needs. By the turn of the century Japan needed to import much of its raw material, a situation that has continued to this day.

Not surprisingly, families with long-standing connections to capital swiftly moved to unite their enterprises to gain market share. The Mitsui Company, for example, used its extensive brewing profits to fund a host of other enterprises, soon becoming one of Japan's largest industrial concerns. Similarly, the Mitsubishi Company expanded from coastal shipping to manufacturing—later creating military vehicles and famous aircraft during World War II as well as popular cars today. The encouragement of the government and the cooperation of social networks among elites in finance and industry led to the creation of a number of **cartels** called *zaibatsu*. By the end of the nineteenth century, the zaibatsu would control nearly all major Japanese industries.

Cartel: A group of domestic or international businesses that form a group to control or monopolize an industry.

The Transportation and Communications Revolutions

The rapid development of railroads and telegraphs was one of the most stunning transformations of the Meiji era. The Japanese pursued these devices with an enthusiasm scarcely paralleled anywhere else in the world. Even today, Japan's fabled "Bullet Train" remains the standard for high-speed ground transportation, while companies such as Sony and Motorola continue to dominate electronic communications markets. By the mid-1870s Japan had in place a trunk railroad line paralleling the main coastal road and several branches to major cities in the interior. Though Westerners found Japanese trains quaint—along with the custom of leaving one's clogs on the platform before boarding the cars—they were efficient and marked a trend for railroad building wherever the Japanese went. Similarly, telegraph—and, by the end of the century, telephone—lines were swiftly strung between the major cities and towns, followed by undersea cables to the Asian mainland and North America. By 1895, Japan was estimated to have over 2,000 miles of private and government railroads in operation and over 4,000 miles of telegraph wires in place (see Map 24.6).

The Meiji Constitution and Political Life   While the Charter Oath and Constitution of 1868 were instituted with considerable success, a debate had already begun among the genro concerning the liberalization of representative government in Japan. In 1881 the emperor approved a plan whereby Ito Hirobumi (1841–1909) and several senior colleagues would launch a painstaking study of the constitutional governments of the United States, Great Britain, France, Germany, and other countries, to see what aspects of them might be suitable for Japan's needs. The Meiji Constitution, as it came to be called, was promulgated in 1889 and remained in force until it was supplanted by the constitution composed during the Allied occupation of Japan after World War II.

While borrowing elements from the US and British models, Ito's constitution drew most heavily from that of Germany. Much of it was also aimed at preserving the traditions of Japan's Confucian society that Ito and the genro most valued. Chief among these was the concept of *kokutai*, the "national polity." In this view, Japan was unique among nations because of its unbroken line of emperors and the singular familial and spiritual relationship between the emperor and his people. Thus, the Meiji Constitution is presented, in Ito's words, as "the gift of a benevolent and charitable emperor to the people of his country." The sovereignty of the country is placed in the person of the emperor as the embodiment of kokutai; the emperor's Privy Council, the army and navy, and the ministers of state are answerable directly to him. There is also a bicameral parliamentary body called the

Visions of the New Railroads. The marvels of the new systems of railroads and telegraphs springing up in Japan provided practitioners of ukiyo-e woodblock art a host of new subjects to depict in the 1870s and 1880s. Here is one of a number of views of new stations, in this case, Ueno on the Ueno–Nakasendo–Tokyo Railway, with small commuter trains arriving and departing.

Progress and Reform

"Political reform and progress is the unanimous wish of our party and has ever been my abiding purpose. It must, however, be achieved by sound and proper means. . . . We differ categorically from those parties which fail to act when the occasion demands it, and which under the guise of working for gradual progress seek private advantage through deliberate procrastination."

—Okuma Shigenobu from Watanabe Ikujiro, *Okuma Shigenobu*, pp. 92–95; quoted in Tsunoda, DeBary, Keene, *Sources of Japanese Tradition*, vol. !!, p.187.

Diet, with an upper House of Peers and a lower House of Representatives. Like the House of Lords in Great Britain, Japan's House of Peers consisted of members of the nobility; the representatives were elected by the people. The primary purpose of the Diet in this arrangement is to vote on financing, deliberate on the everyday items of governance, and provide advice and consent to the Privy Council, Ministry of State, and Imperial Court.

As for the people themselves, 15 articles spell out "The Rights and Duties of Subjects." Duties include liability for taxes and service in the military, while the rights enumerated are similar to those found in European and American constitutions: the right to hold office, guarantees against search and seizure, the right to trial, the right to property, and freedoms of religion, speech, and petition. All of these, however, are qualified by such phrases as "unless provided by law," leaving the door open for the government to invoke extraordinary powers during national emergencies.

Political Parties   As constitutional government began to be enacted in the 1890s, the factional debates among senior advisors naturally began to attract followers among the Diet members and their supporters. In the preceding decades there had been political parties; but their membership was limited, and they were seen by many as illegitimate because of their potential opposition to the government. Now, two major parties came to the fore by the turn of the century. The Kenseito [KEN-say-toe], or Liberal, Party had its roots in the work of Itagaki Taisuke (1837–1919) and his political opponent, Okuma Shigenobu [OH-ku-ma SHIH-geh-no-bu]. The two merged their followers but later split into factions at the turn of the century. It later was reestablished as the Minseito.

The more powerful party during this time was the Seiyukai, or Constitutional Government Party, founded by Ito and his followers in 1900. Generally associated with the government and the zaibatsu, the Seiyukai dominated Japanese politics in the era before World War I; after World War II, its adherents coalesced into Japan's present Liberal Democratic Party.

Social Experiments   In addition to creating an industrial base and a constitutional government, Japan's rulers attempted to curb practices in Japan that were believed to offend foreign sensibilities as part of its program of "civilization and enlightenment." Bathhouses, for example, were now required to have separate entrances for men and women, and pleasure quarters were restricted in areas near foreign enclaves; meat eating was even encouraged in largely Buddhist Japan, resulting in the new dish *sukiyaki*. In the boldest experiment of all, the government mandated the use of Western dress for men and women, accompanied by a propaganda campaign depicting the advantages of this "modern" and "civilized" clothing. Criticism from a variety of quarters, however, including many Westerners, ultimately forced the government to relent and make the new dress optional.

In the same vein, traditional restrictions on women were altered. Though the home remained the primary domain for women, as it does even today, women were far more often seen in public. Concubines were now accorded the same rights as wives. Courtesans and prostitutes were no longer legally considered servants. Among elites, the fad of following all things Western established to some degree Victorian European standards of family decorum. More far-reaching, however, was the role of the new education system. Even before the Meiji Restoration, Japan had one of the highest levels of preindustrial literacy in the world—40 percent for males and 15 percent for females. With the introduction of compulsory public education, literacy would become nearly universal; and the upsurge in specialized women's education created entire new avenues of employment for women.

This same trend toward emancipation was evident among the rural population. The formal class barriers between peasants and samurai were eliminated, though informal deference to elites continued. In addition, some barriers between ordinary Japanese and outcast groups, such as the Eta, were also reduced. During the latter part of the nineteenth century, aided by better transportation, improved crops, maximum utilization of marginal lands, and the opening up of Hokkaido for development, Japan became the most intensely farmed nation in the world. Japan's already well-developed fishing industry contributed mightily by introducing commercial fish-based fertilizers that boosted yields enormously. The result was that although Japan's population increased to 40 million by 1890, it was a net exporter of food until the turn of the century.

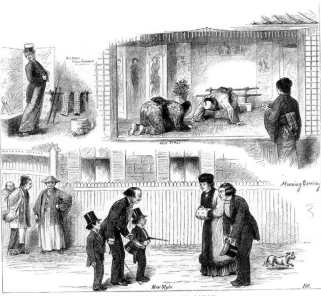

NEW YEAR'S DAY IN JAPAN

New Year's Day in Japan, ca. 1905. An important part of Japan's strategy to roll back its unequal treaties with the West was the campaign of *bunmei kaika*, or "civilization and enlightenment." The idea of this policy was to show Western observers in concrete terms that Japan accepted Western notions of what it meant to be a "civilized" nation. In this cartoon the contrast between the old Japan of the Tokugawa days and the new Japan of the "enlightenment and civilization" is graphically depicted. The upper panel, labeled "Old Style" shows two samurai bowing in greeting in a traditional room replete with screens and scrolls marking the occasion, and the wife of the host entertains the men. The lower panel shows the "new style," in which men and women wear Western fashions, with families greeting each other together on the street in front a Western house surrounded by a picket fence, while a pet dog romps nearby.

"Enlightenment and Progress": Science, Culture, and the Arts

As we saw in Chapter 21, while the Tokugawa sought seclusion, they were by no means cut off entirely from developments in other nations. Of particular importance in this regard was the requirement imposed on the Dutch merchants at Deshima to make their annual reports to the Shogun on the state of the world. By the time of Commodore Perry's visit the accumulated amount of "Dutch learning" was impressive. Much of it consisted of notes on scientific and technical developments.

Engaging "Western Science"   Nevertheless, at the time of their initial contact with the Western powers, the Tokugawa were stunned at the degree to which the accelerating technologies of the Industrial Revolution had armed their adversaries. During Perry's visits Japanese sketch artists frantically sought to capture the details of the ships' gun ports and cannon and the outward signs of their steam power. As we have seen, the Japanese were immediately engaged with the notion of the railroad; just as quickly they sought to create oceangoing steamships. By 1860, they had built and manned steamers and insisted that their embassy to the United States travel aboard one the Japanese had built themselves.

Western Science. The Japanese were fascinated by the new and strange technology they found on Perry's ships, including the paddle wheel from one of his steamships, which they drew with scientific precision.

Journalism in Modern Society

"In editing the paper [*Jiji-shimpo*] I encouraged the reporters to write bravely and freely. I have no objection to any severe criticism or extreme statements, but I warned them that they must limit their statements to what they would be willing to say to the victim face to face. Otherwise, they are what I would call *kage-benkei* [shadow fighters] attacking from the security of their columns. It is very easy for *kage-benkei* to fall into mean abuses and irresponsible invectives which are the eternal shame of the writer's profession."

—Fukuzawa Yukichi. *The Autobiography of Fukuzawa Yukichi*, Kiyooka Eikichi, trans., Tokyo, 1934. Quoted in Tsunoda, DeBary, Keene, *Sources of Japanese Tradition*, p. 129.

The demand for industrial and military technology required large numbers of Japanese to seek technical education. During the initial stages of the Meiji era, thousands of Japanese students studied in Europe and the United States, and the Japanese government and private concerns hired hundreds of foreign advisors to aid in science and technical training. By the 1880s a university system anchored by Tokyo Imperial University and including Keio, Waseda, and Doshisha was offering courses in medicine, physics, chemistry, engineering, and geology, among other advanced disciplines. By the turn of the century, Japan's Institute for Infectious Diseases had become world famous for its pathbreaking work in microbiology. On the whole, however, the bulk of the nation's efforts went into the practical application of science to technology and agriculture in order to support the government's modernization efforts.

Culture and the Arts   As was the case a decade later in China, Japanese intellectuals eagerly absorbed copies of Western Enlightenment, philosophical, and social science works in translation—including Locke, Hobbes, Spencer, Darwin, and Comte, to name but a few. As was also true in China, journalism played a dominant role as a disseminator of information to the public. Here, Fukuzawa Yukichi, like Liang Qichao in China, held a central place both in fostering the growth of newspapers and in articulating the role of journalists in a modern society.

As were nearly all the arts in late nineteenth-century Japan, the novel was also heavily influenced by Western examples. In some respects, the culmination of this trend was *Kokoro*, by Natsume Soseki, (1867–1916) published in 1914. Soseki utilizes the wrenching changes in Meiji Japan set against traditional and generational values to create the tension and ultimate tragic end of the central character in his work.

More traditional arts such as Noh and kabuki theater and ukiyo-e printing survived but often in a somewhat altered state. Updated kabuki variations now featured contemporary themes and often had female actors playing female parts.

In addition, European plays such as Ibsen's *A Doll's House* enjoyed considerable vogue. As for ukiyo-e, it remained the cheapest and most popular outlet for depictions of contemporary events until the development of newspaper photography. Especially telling in this regard are ukiyo-e artist's interpretations of the Sino–Japanese War.

Putting It All Together

Scholars of China and Japan have long debated the reasons for the apparent success of Japan and failure of China. One school of thought sees the fundamental reasons growing from the cultural outlooks of the two countries. China, it is argued, assumed that outsiders would simply be won over to Confucian norms and modes of behavior because this is what China's historical experience had been for the last 2,000 years. When it became apparent that defensive measures were necessary, it was still assumed that China's superior culture would win out. Japan, on the other hand, because of its long history of cultural borrowing and its much smaller size, assumed a more urgent defensive posture. In addition, the Japanese had the advantage of watching events unfold in China before the threat reached their own shores. This allowed them to act in a more united and pragmatic fashion when resisting the Western threat.

Some historians, however, disagree with this approach. They argue instead that the cultural differences between China and Japan were secondary in the face of the foreign threat. According to this school of thought, the primary cause of the radically different outcomes for China and Japan was that China was victimized by foreign imperialism much earlier and much more thoroughly than Japan. Once Japanese modernization efforts were under way, they won for themselves a breathing spell with which to keep imperialism at bay and ultimately fought their way into the great power club themselves (see Concept Map).

Both China and Japan were to continue their relative trajectories for decades to come. Japan would achieve its ultimate military power in early 1942. At that point, during World War II, the Japanese Empire encompassed Korea, Manchuria, much of China, the Philippines, Indonesia, most of southeast Asia, and hundreds of Pacific Islands. In a little over 3 years, however, the empire was gone, the home islands were in ruins, and for the first time in its history Japan was under occupation. Since that time, however, its economic development has resumed with even more vigor, and is today the third largest economy in the world.

China's troubles would, despite a few bright points along the way, multiply. Throwing off the Qing, the Chinese republic would be plagued by warlordism, civil war, and invasion, until the triumph of the Communist Party and founding of the People's Republic of China in 1949. Yet, it is only since 1978 that its most significant progress in industrial and economic development has taken place. Ironically, much of China's newfound economic might was inspired by the approaches employed in Japan's postwar recovery. In the long sweep of China's history, however, this resurgence is seen with growing confidence by the Chinese as marking a return to their accustomed place and in 2010 it passed Japan to become the world's second largest economy.

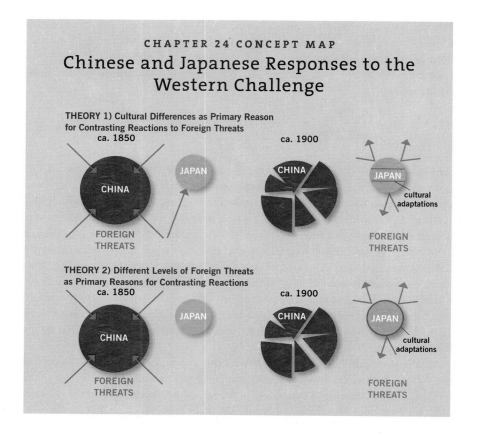

CHAPTER 24 CONCEPT MAP

Chinese and Japanese Responses to the Western Challenge

THEORY 1) Cultural Differences as Primary Reason for Contrasting Reactions to Foreign Threats
ca. 1850

CHINA

JAPAN

FOREIGN THREATS

ca. 1900

CHINA

JAPAN

cultural adaptations

FOREIGN THREATS

THEORY 2) Different Levels of Foreign Threats as Primary Reasons for Contrasting Reactions
ca. 1850

CHINA

JAPAN

FOREIGN THREATS

ca. 1900

CHINA

JAPAN

cultural adaptations

FOREIGN THREATS

Review and Respond

1. How would you characterize the Western maritime countries' economic relationship with China during this period?

2. How did opium become such a problem between Britain and China? Was opium the real cause of the First Opium War? Why or why not?

3. Why did "self-strengthening" produce China and "Western science and Eastern ethics" in Japan as adaptations to modernity have such different results?

4. What do you see as the major strengths and weaknesses of the Meiji response to Western imperialism?

5. Why did Japan become an imperial power instead of simply strengthening its home islands?

▶ For additional resources, including maps, primary sources, visuals, and quizzes, please go to www.oup.com/us/vonsivers. Please see the Further Resources section at the back of the book for additional readings and suggested websites.

Thinking Through Patterns

▶ **What was the impact of Western imperialism on the "regulated societies" of China and Japan?**

The impact of the intrusion of Great Britain, France, the United States, and later Germany and Russia forced both China and Japan into defensive postures. Both countries had sought to keep out what they considered subversive foreign influences after an earlier period of exposure to Western traders and missionaries. China had created a tightly controlled system of overseas trade based in Guangzhou (Canton); Japan allowed only the Dutch to trade with them. But the expansion of trade in both legitimate goods and opium and the need of the British for regularization of diplomatic practices pushed Britain and China into a cycle of war and "unequal treaties" under which China was at an increasing disadvantage. Japan, suddenly thrust into international commerce and diplomacy by the young United States, now sought to protect its borders without pushing the Western powers into seizing any of its territory.

China's long history of absorbing and acculturating outside invaders to Confucian norms encouraged its leaders to assume that the Westerners would be no different. Though many officials realized the qualitative difference between the industrializing Euro-American countries and invaders from the Chinese past, they were of divided opinion about what to do. Thus, attempts at reform were often undercut by political infighting at court and in the bureaucracy. The Taiping Rebellion also played a central role in further depleting China's strength and resources. As time went on, increasing Western control of China's ports and tariffs, absentee landlordism, and declining agricultural productivity also played a role.

▶ **Why did European empire building in Asia have such dramatically different effects on China and Japan?**

For Japan, after a decade of indecision about how to handle the foreign intrusion, a civil war ended in the dismantling of the shogunate and the unification of the country under Emperor Meiji. With remarkable unity born of a deep sense of urgency, Japan embarked upon a thoroughgoing reform program aimed at remaking the country along avowedly Western lines. The focus and consistency displayed by Meiji and his advisors avoided many of the problems China experienced, and Japan's late Tokugawa economics to some degree had predisposed the country toward a smoother transition into that of scientific–industrial society.

▶ **How have historians seen the nature of these outside forces and their influences in east Asia?**

Historians have long debated the relative weight that should be assigned to cultural and material reasons for the differing paths of China and Japan. China's long history as the region's cultural leader, some have argued, made it difficult for the empire to remake itself to face the Western challenge; Japan, on the other hand, has a long history of cultural borrowing and, thus, found it easier to borrow from the Euro-American world. Some historians have argued that China's earlier experience with imperialism stunted the modernizing tendencies within the empire and kept it from responding; they argue that Japan had the advantage of being "opened" later and so could respond more effectively. Others have argued that Japan's tradition of military prowess played a role, still others that China's more complete incorporation into the modern "world system" crippled its ability to respond more independently.

Chapter 25

1683-1908

Adaptation and Resistance

THE OTTOMAN AND RUSSIAN EMPIRES

RUSSIAN AND OTTOMAN EMPIRES, 1683-1908

October 13, 1824, marked a most unusual event in Russia. On this date, Aleksander Nikitenko, born into serfdom, received his freedom at the young age of 20 from his lord, a fabulously wealthy landowning count. Even more remarkable is the subsequent course of Nikitenko's life and career. After earning a university degree, he went on to become a professor of literature at St. Petersburg University, a member of the distinguished Academy of Sciences, and a censor in the Ministry of Education.

▶ Which new models did the Ottomans adopt during the nineteenth century to adapt themselves to the Western challenge?

▶ Why did the tsars and landholding aristocracy fear Western constitutionalism? Why did the Russian constitutionalists eventually lose out to the revolutionaries?

▶ How did the agrarian Ottoman and Russian Empires, both with large landholding ruling classes, respond to the western European industrial challenge during the 1800s?

▶ Why did large, well-established empires like the Russian and the Ottoman struggle with the forces of modernity, while a small, secluded island nation like Japan seemed to adapt so quickly and successfully?

Beginning in 1818 at the age of 14, the bright and precocious Nikitenko kept a diary. The account of events from this date until his emancipation in 1824 at the age of 20 was written as a retrospective memoir. The most important entries refer to the role of the European Enlightenment thinkers in shaping changing intellectual attitudes in Russia. For example, Nikitenko makes repeated reference to the works of Montesquieu, particularly *The Spirit of Laws*, which inspired the so-called Decembrists, leaders of an abortive proconstitutional uprising in 1825, with whom Nikitenko was in touch.

Nikitenko's diary provides deep insights into the role of **serfdom** in the Russian Empire. We are told that "when the inevitable happened," the errant serfs were turned over to a lackey in charge of meting out punishment in the form of flogging with birch rods: "Woe to the unfortunates who fell into [his] hands! He was a master and enthusiast of flogging, especially of girls, and they were terrified by the mere sight of him." Nikitenko also tells of his sadness when he had to part with his classmates upon graduating at age 13 from his country school: "But more painful than anything else was the knowledge that I would not be allowed to join the boys who were preparing to enter high school. For me its doors were inexorably closed.

Auction of Serfs. In this painting, *Auction of Serfs* (1910), the well-known Russian realist painter Klavdiy Vasilievich Lebedev (1852–1916) depicted the room of a Russian aristocratic landowning family as it auctioned off valuables as well as serfs (standing on the right). The 1861 decree ending serfdom in Russia was far less than what its name suggested since the peasants had to buy their land from the nonfarming landowners.

Chapter Outline

- Decentralization and Reforms in the Ottoman Empire

- Westernization, Reforms, and Industrialization in Russia

- Putting It All Together

Serfdom: Legal and cultural institution in which peasants are bound to the land.

Here, for the first time, I had to face the terrible curse that hung over me because of my social status, which later caused me so much suffering and almost drove me to suicide." Nikitenko's curse, Russian serfdom, was scarcely different from plantation slavery in the Americas or from the status of untouchables in India. Slavery was also the common lot of many in the neighboring Ottoman Empire and, though limited to households, was no less demeaning. The end of serfdom in Russia would not come until 1861 and that of slavery in the Ottoman Empire not until 1890.

Serfdom and slavery were dramatic examples of the kinds of practices that the new Enlightenment constitutionalism, in theory at least, stood firmly against. As such, they were among the first of many challenges the world outside western Europe and North America faced from the West in the nineteenth century. Russia was an empire that had inherited Byzantine Christian civilization but had not adopted the New Science and its offspring, the twin revolutions of the Enlightenment and Industrial Revolution. For its part, the Ottoman Empire was heir to both Islamic and Byzantine traditions but had also not participated in the transition to the New Science, Enlightenment, and industrialization. Even though Enlightenment thought had produced and elaborated the political theories of the social contract and popular sovereignty, which were realized in the American, French, and Haitian Revolutions, shortly before the onset of the Industrial Revolution in Great Britain, it would be the campaigns of Napoleon in the early nineteenth century that sowed these ideas throughout Europe.

They also would fling these seeds at the initially unpromising soil of the Russian and Ottoman Empires. Napoleon's invasions of Ottoman Egypt in 1798 and Russia in 1812 drove home to their rulers that his new armies of mass conscripts, equipped with flintlock muskets and light, mobile artillery and drilled to fight in flexible formations, were superior to their own military forces. It became inevitable for the Ottomans and Russians, short of losing their independence, to update their armies and training and to respond somehow to the constitutional nationalism arising from the French Revolution and carried by Napoleon's armies, which now attracted rising numbers of adherents among their subjects.

At the same time, the two empires became mortal enemies: An expanding eastern [Orthodox] Christian Russia declared its goal to be conquest of the former eastern Christian capital Istanbul (Constantinople) and to drive a shrinking Ottoman Empire from Europe back into "Asia" (Asia Minor or Anatolia). Since both empires were members of the Concert of Europe, their profound conflict involved the other European powers as well. These powers found themselves increasingly drawn into a conflict, culminating in the Crimean War of 1853–1856, that was only partially European and increasingly involved Russia and the Ottomans in Asia. For the monarchs, politicians, and diplomats focused after 1815 on the balance of power in western and central Europe, such a power struggle between the Russians and Ottomans held little interest: For them, this contest was "Oriental" and therefore alien.

It is important that we keep this partially non-Western identity of the Russian and Ottoman Empires in mind for this chapter: As forcefully as Russia asserted itself in the European Concert in the early years after 1815 and again at the end of the nineteenth century, it was in reality—despite its Christian character—not any more or less "European" than the increasingly harried Muslim Ottoman Empire. Indeed, as we will see, both empires had far more in common with each other, and to some degree with the empire of the Qing in China, than they did with the evolving nation-states of western Europe. Furthermore, their reactions to the challenges posed by the new nation-states paralleled each other to a degree not often appreciated by students and scholars studying them outside of a world context. Therefore, we consider them together here as their own case studies in the overall patterns of constitutionalism, nation-state formation, and the challenge of modernity.

Decentralization and Reforms in the Ottoman Empire

Prior to the Russian–Ottoman rivalry in the 1800s, the traditional enemies of the Ottomans were the Austrian Habsburgs. This enmity had reached its climax in the second half of the 1600s. The Habsburgs ultimately won but in the course of the 1700s were increasingly sidelined by the rise of Russia as a new, Orthodox Christian empire, whose rulers, the tsars, saw themselves as representatives of the "third Rome," that is, Moscow as the successor of Rome and Constantinople. After consolidating itself on the fertile northeast European plains, Russia expanded eastward and southward, clashing with the Muslim Ottomans, conquerors of Constantinople. Because the Russians adapted themselves earlier than the Ottomans to new western European military tactics, the Ottomans found it increasingly difficult to defend themselves in the later 1700s. They

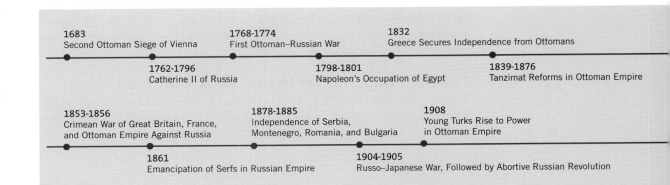

1683
Second Ottoman Siege of Vienna

1768-1774
First Ottoman–Russian War

1832
Greece Secures Independence from Ottomans

1762-1796
Catherine II of Russia

1798-1801
Napoleon's Occupation of Egypt

1839-1876
Tanzimat Reforms in Ottoman Empire

1853-1856
Crimean War of Great Britain, France, and Ottoman Empire Against Russia

1878-1885
Independence of Serbia, Montenegro, Romania, and Bulgaria

1908
Young Turks Rise to Power in Ottoman Empire

1861
Emancipation of Serfs in Russian Empire

1904-1905
Russo–Japanese War, Followed by Abortive Russian Revolution

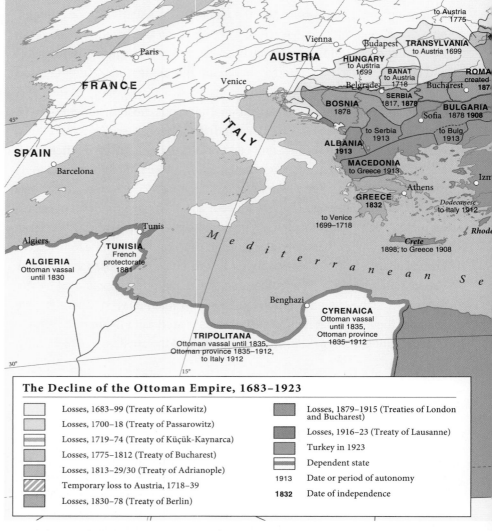

MAP 25.1 **The Decline of the Ottoman Empire, 1683–1923.**

sought to improve their defenses through military and constitutional–nationalist reforms in the mid-1800s but were only half successful. Russia became the patron of nationalist movements among the Slavic populations in the European provinces of the Ottoman Empire. Although they strengthened themselves through reforms, the Ottomans were no match for the combined Russian–southern Slavic aggression. At the end of the Second Balkan War of 1913, they had lost nearly the entire European part of their empire to ethnic–nationalist liberation movements and were barely able to hang on to Istanbul (see Map 25.1).

Ottoman Imperialism in the 1600s and 1700s

In the period from 1500 to 1700 the Ottoman Empire was the dominant political power in the Middle East and North Africa, flanked by the two lesser realms

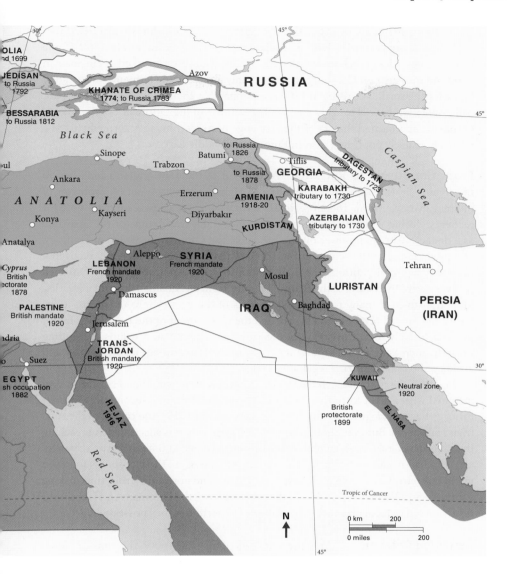

of Persia in the east and Morocco in the west. At that time, as we noted, the main enemy of the Ottomans was not yet Russia but the Habsburg Empire in Spain, Germany, and Austria. The two were fighting each other on dual fronts, the Balkans in the east and North Africa in the western Mediterranean, each gaining and losing in the process and eventually establishing a more or less stable disengagement. It was during this disengagement period that Russia began its expansion southward at the increasing expense of the Ottomans.

Demographic Considerations   As with the other agrarian–urban regions of Asia and Europe, the Middle East had experienced a sustained recovery of population figures after the Black Death of the mid-1400s. This recovery came to an end around 1600, with 25 million inhabitants, though with slow increases to 27 million by 1700 and to about 30 million by 1800. The population figures were thus smaller than those of the Habsburg countries, with 37 million in 1700 and 42 million in 1800. If one takes into consideration, however, that the Spanish Habsburg line died out in Spain in 1700 and the Austrian Habsburgs governed only indirectly in Germany, the resulting figure for the smaller territory in 1800 is a comparable 25 million. Russia, for its part, had population figures roughly comparable to those of the Ottoman Empire. As the Ottomans approached the era of the challenge of modernity, they formed part of a relatively sparsely populated eastern Europe and Middle East.

From Conquests to Retreats   At the end of the 1500s, after a long period of military showdowns, the Ottomans and Habsburgs were beset by problems of military overextension. Therefore, in 1606 they concluded a peace to gain time for recovery, during which the Ottomans recognized the Habsburgs for the first time as a de facto Christian power on the border of the Ottoman province of Hungary. The peace lasted until the end of the 1600s when both were sufficiently recovered to renew their competition. The main administrators responsible for the Ottoman recovery were the viziers of the Köprülü family, from an Albanian line of Janissaries. They transformed many military assignments of the cavalry into tax farms, to increase the flow of revenue, and broadened the recruitment of the Janissary infantry from exclusively rural Christian boys to young, mostly urban Muslims. By shifting from the increasingly less important cavalry to their firearm-equipped infantry and artillery, the Ottoman army regained its edge.

In 1683 the Ottomans renewed their competition with the Habsburgs and marched with a giant force to their northwestern border. For a second time in their history, they laid siege to Vienna (the first siege was in 1529), the capital of the Austrian Habsburgs. But even though sappers and siege cannons succeeded in breaching the walls in several places, a Polish relief army arrived just in time to drive the besiegers, who had neglected to fortify their camp, into a retreat. The Habsburgs followed up on this retreat by seizing Hungary, Transylvania, and northern Serbia, thus making a third siege of Vienna impossible. In the peace of 1699, the Ottomans and Habsburgs finally agreed to recognize each other fully in the territories they possessed.

Renewed Reforms   During the war years of the later 1600s, the Janissary force had swelled to some 70,000 soldiers. In the end, however, only about 10,000 were on active duty. Since they were all on the payroll and given renewed fiscal shortfalls, the money was often debased or in arrears, forcing them to earn a living as craftspeople. A brisk trade developed in which Janissaries and non-Janissaries alike exchanged pay tickets that entitled the holders not only to wages but also to fiscal and juridical exemptions. Coffeehouses near Janissary barracks became flourishing trade centers for pay tickets, food rations, and military supplies. In short, the Janissary force was in the process of becoming a collection of crafts guilds on a kind of government welfare.

New reforms were clearly necessary. In the early 1700s the sultan's government cut the Janissary rolls by half and enlisted Anatolian farmers to supplement the active Janissaries. In order to improve revenues with which to pay the Janissaries, the reformers introduced the new institution of the lifetime tax farm, or **life lease**, for agricultural rents from village farmers. As in France, which developed a similar tax farm regime at the time, the idea was to diminish the temptation—endemic among

Life lease: Lifelong tax farm, awarded to a wealthy member of the ruling class, in return for advances to the central imperial treasury on the taxes to be collected from village farmers.

the annual tax farmers—to squeeze farmers dry so that they would flee from the countryside to the cities. Wealthy and high-ranking courtiers, officers, administrators, and Islamic clerics in Istanbul bought these life leases. They numbered about 2,000, shifting the weight in the ruling class increasingly from the military to civilians. The large cash outlays necessary for the purchase of these life leases required access to liquid capital, which Armenian merchants with European connections provided. Thus, here in the early 1700s was the beginning of a development parallel to similar developments in France and England, with efforts to organize a kind of capital market. As a result of the reforms, in 1720, for the first time in a century and a half, the central budget was balanced again.

(a)

The Tulip Era

The new ruling class, holding life leases, was less connected to the Topkapı, the sultan's palace, and its administrative quarters and invested its wealth in new constructions. A building boom ensued in the early 1700s, expressing itself in the erection of numerous office buildings and mansions in town as well as palaces and gardens along Istanbul's waterfront. Other construction included renovations, aqueducts, mosques, colleges, libraries, public baths, and fountains. In addition, villages in the provinces benefited from construction projects. Ruling-class members who remembered their modest rural origins competed in the capital and countryside for philanthropic recognition.

The new palaces and mansions were architecturally inspired by the long tradition of pre-Islamic Middle Eastern royal residences and parks, especially in Iran. In the salons of these residences, poets and musicians presented their compositions. Books, for the first time printed in Ottoman Turkish, became available: One of these books contained a summary of Copernicus's New Science, although there is no evidence of any intellectual impact made by helio-

(b)

The Tulip Period. During the "Tulip period," the Ottoman ruling class not only prided itself on its ability to breed ever new varieties of tulips, hyacinths, and roses (a) but also frequented coffeehouses and public parks for picnics (b).

centrism in the empire. The gardens of the residences featured hundreds of varieties of flowers, plants, shrubs, and trees. (Many of these varieties, including tulips, had made their way earlier to Europe; and ever since the mid-1600s the Dutch have been *the* tulip specialists of the world.) Modern Turkish writers dubbed the time of cultural efflorescence in the first half of the 1700s the Ottoman "Tulip period."

Decentralization

During the Tulip period, an accelerating transformation of cavalry-held lands into tax farms started a pattern of political decentralization in the Ottoman Empire. Agents responsible for the collection of taxes for their superiors succeeded in withholding increasing amounts from the treasury in Istanbul. By the mid-1700s, these agents were in positions of considerable provincial power as "notables" (*ayan*) in the Balkans or "valley lords" (*derebeys*) in western Anatolia. Starved for funds, the sultan and central administration were no longer able to support a large standing army of infantry and cavalry in the capital.

In 1768–1774 the notables and valley lords played a crucial role not only in financing a major war against Russia but also in recruiting troops—untrained and underarmed peasants—since the numbers of government forces in fighting order had shrunk to minimal levels. The war was the first in which the Russian tsars exploited Ottoman decentralization for a systematic expansion southward. When the sultan promptly lost the war, he was more or less at the mercy of these notables and lords in the provinces.

The Western Challenge and Ottoman Responses

Soon after this Ottoman–Russian war, the Ottoman Empire began to face the challenge of Western modernity. As with China and Japan, the increasing military, political, and economic strength of the West allowed it to force the traditional Asian empires to adapt to its challenges. This adaptation was extremely difficult and entailed severe territorial losses for the Ottoman Empire. But after initial humiliations, the ruling class was able to develop a pattern of responses to the Western challenge, by reducing the power of the provincial magnates, modernizing the army, introducing constitutional reforms, and eventually transforming its manufacturing sector.

External and Internal Blows   During the period 1774–1808, the Ottoman central government suffered a series of humiliations which were comparable in their destabilizing effects to those in the later Opium Wars and the Taiping and Boxer Rebellions in China. Russia gained the north coast of the Black Sea and Georgia in the Caucasus. Napoleon invaded Egypt and destroyed the local regime of Ottoman Mamluk vassals in 1798. But a British fleet sent after him succeeded in destroying his navy, and a subsequent land campaign forced him to return to France in 1801. As he was victimizing the Ottoman Empire, Napoleon apparently wanted to demonstrate the ineffectiveness of Great Britain's European continental blockade and teach it a lesson about the vulnerability of its control of India. Napoleon's sudden imperialist venture produced a deep shock in the Middle East: For the first time a Western ruler had penetrated deeply into the Ottoman Empire, cutting it effectively in half.

Internally, the lessening of central control in the second half of the 1700s left the provinces in virtual independence. Most notables and lords were satisfied with local autonomy, but a few became warlords, engaging in campaigns to become regional leaders. In other cases, especially in Egypt, Syria, and Iraq, *Mamluks*, that is, military slaves from the northern Caucasus whom Ottoman governors had previously employed as auxiliaries in the military, seized power. In eastern Arabia, a local Sunni cleric, Muhammad Ibn Abd al-Wahhab [Wah-HAHB], exploited Ottoman decentralization to ally himself with the head of a powerful family in command of a number of oases, Ibn Saud [Sa-OOD], to establish an autonomous polity in the desert, which today is the most powerful oil state in the world—Saudi Arabia. None of these ambitious leaders, however, renounced allegiance to the sultan, who at least remained a figurehead.

To take power back, the sultan and his viziers once more sought for ways to reform the empire. In 1792, they proclaimed a "new order" (*Nizam-i Cedid* [Nee-ZAHM-ee Jay-DEED]), defined as a reorganization of the army with the creation of a new, separate artillery and flintlock musket corps of some 22,000 soldiers alongside the Janissaries. The new corps was recruited from among Anatolian farmers, with the help of willing notables and lords, and financed through ad hoc measures, such as property confiscations, currency debasements, and tax increases. European officers trained these soldiers in drills, line fighting, bayonet combat, and formation marching. Officers received their education at the newly founded Land Engineering School. The corps underwent its baptism by fire when it defended Acre in Syria successfully against Napoleon.

The ad hoc financing of the new order, however, came to haunt the reformers. During a severe fiscal crisis in 1807, auxiliary Janissaries, refusing to wear new uniforms, assassinated a new order officer. Inept handling of this incident resulted in a quickly mushrooming, full-scale revolt of Janissaries as well as religious scholars and students, costing the sultan his life and ushering in the dissolution of the new troops. In a counterrevolt, thanks to the timely arrival of a Ukrainian-born notable from northern Bulgaria with his private army, a new sultan came to power in 1808. As a price for his accession, the sultan had to agree to power sharing with the provincial lords.

Renewed Difficulties

After a dozen years of careful maneuvering, during which the sultan reconstituted the nucleus for another new army and neutralized many notables and valley lords, he was able to crush the Janissaries in a bloody massacre (1826). But the new corps was in no shape yet to provide the backbone for a sustained recentralization of the empire. New internal enemies arose, in the form of Greek ethnic nationalists, whom the Ottomans would have defeated had it not been for the military intervention of the European powers. As a result, Greece became independent in a war of liberation (1821–1832). It was the first country, prior to Italy and Germany, in which ethnic nationalism was central to its foundation.

Russia, providing support for its fellow Orthodox Christian Greeks, acquired new territories from the Ottomans around the Black Sea. Several Balkan provinces achieved administrative autonomy. Algiers in North Africa was lost in 1830, falling to an invading French force. Worst of all, in 1831, the new Ottoman vassal in Egypt, the Albanian-born officer Muhammad Ali (r. 1805–1848), seeking greater influence within the empire, rose in rebellion. After occupying Syria (1831–1840), he would have conquered Istanbul had he not been stopped by Russian, British, and French intervention. Without the diplomacy of Great Britain, which carefully sought to balance the European powers after the end of the Napoleonic empire, the Ottoman Empire would not have survived the 1830s.

Life, Honor, and Property

The cumulative effect of these setbacks was a realization among Ottoman administrators that only a serious effort at recentralization would save the empire. In 1839, with a change of sultans, the government issued the Rose Garden Edict, the first of three reform edicts, plus more specific additional ones in between, which are collectively known as

Muhammad Ali. Muhammad Ali transformed Egypt during the first half of the nineteenth century more thoroughly than the Ottoman overlord sultan could in his far-flung empire. He astutely realized that long-staple cotton, bred first in Egypt, could make Egypt a wealthy state in the beginning industrial transformation of the world.

Tanzimat: Ottoman reforms inspired by constitutional nationalism in Europe, covering the adoption of basic rights, a legal reform, and a land code.

Tanzimat ("Reorganizations"). In the Rose Garden Edict, the government bound itself to three basic principles: the guarantee of life, honor, and property of all subjects regardless of religion; the replacement of tax farms and life leases with an equitable tax system; and the introduction of a military conscription system, all in accordance with the Shari`a, the compendium of Islamic morality and law. The edict carefully avoided a definition of the position of the Christians and Jews in the empire before the law, offering them the rights of life, honor, and property while maintaining their inequality vis-à-vis the Muslims proclaimed in Islamic law.

The edict addressed the two fundamental problems of the empire, that is, taxes and the military, carefully emphasizing the Islamic justification. It also enumerated basic human rights, inspired by the American Declaration of Independence and the French Rights of Man. Here, we can see a first adaptation of the Ottoman Empire to the Western challenge: The Ottoman Empire adapted, at least in an initial and partial way, to constitutional nationalism, the outgrowth of Enlightenment thought.

Further Reforms   As these reforms were being implemented, a new European political initiative challenged the Ottoman Empire. The aggressively imperialistic Napoleon III (1848-1852 president, 1852-1870 emperor), self-declared emperor of France, challenged the Russian tsar's claim to be the protector of the Christian holy places in Palestine, a claim which the Ottoman sultan had granted after his defeat in 1774. As we saw in Chapter 24, the French joined the British during the Second Opium War for much the same reason: protection of Catholics and French missionaries in China. While the French and Russian diplomats sought to pull a vacillating sultan back and forth toward their respective claims, the political situation turned increasingly tense. Through careful maneuvering, Ottoman diplomats were able to strengthen themselves in a coalition with Great Britain and France. In the Crimean War of 1853–1856 this coalition was victorious against an isolated Russia. It forced Russia in the subsequent peace to recognize the Ottoman Empire's right to full integrity, provided the latter would continue the reforms announced in 1839.

Accordingly, the sultan promulgated the "Fortunate Edict" of 1856, in which he clarified the question of equality left open in the earlier edict: Regardless of religion, all subjects had the right to education, employment, and administration of justice. A number of subsequent measures spelled out this right and the earlier edicts in greater detail. To begin with, the reformers reorganized the judiciary by establishing law courts for the application of newly introduced commercial, maritime, and criminal legal codes, based on European models. Muslim law was collected in the 16 volumes of the *Mecelle* (Arabic "Code"), containing the Hanafi Islamic legal tradition that was constitutive for the empire since its foundation in 1300. Family law remained in the hands of the traditional Islamic judges as well as the heads of the Christian and Jewish communities (called *millets*). Since Muslims were obliged to a 5-year military service in the new army, the edict extended this obligation to Christians and Jews as well. Ironically, however, this extension was subsequently undercut by a regulation which exempted Christians and Jews from the service with the payment of a fee. Hence, de facto equality remained an ambiguous concept in the empire.

A further reform measure was the introduction of a system of secular schools, initially for males, beginning with age 10 and culminating with high schools. But a lack of funds delayed building this system, which at the end of the 1800s still lagged far behind the traditional religious primary schools (*mekteps*) and colleges (*medreses*) as well as the more rapidly expanding Christian, Jewish, and foreign missionary schools. Literacy in the general population hovered around 10 percent in 1900, and thus, the edict had little to show even after half a century of efforts.

A measure that worked out quite differently from what was intended was the Land Code of 1858. The code reaffirmed the sultan as the owner of all land unless subjects or religious foundations possessed title to specific parcels of private property, such as urban real estate, suburban gardens, and endowments. But it also confirmed all users of the sultan's land, that is, farmers who produced harvests on family plots as well landowners collecting rents from the farmers of entire villages. Theoretically, the code subjected all users, family farmers as well as landowners, to taxation. But in practice the central administration had no money to appoint tax collectors (or even establish a land registry prior to 1908). It could not do without tax farmers, who still collected what they could get and transmitted to the government as little as they were able to get away with.

Highly uneven forms of landownership thus developed. In central and coastal Anatolia, as well as in the hill country of Palestine, family farmers received title to their individual plots. In Anatolian swamplands, tribal Kurdish steppe ranges, and Palestinian coastal strips large absentee landownership appeared. Syrian life leaseholders bribed officials to acquire a title to entire village districts. Similarly, Iraqi sheikhs succeeded in registering tribal lands in their name. Overall, tax yields remained as low as ever, improving only toward the end of the nineteenth century, long after the introduction of the Tanzimat. The much needed land reform remained incomplete.

> **Prohibition of Owning an Entire Village and Exemptions**
>
> "The land of an inhabited village cannot be given to one person independently in order to make a *çiftlik* [family plot]; but, as stated in Art. 72, if all the inhabitants of a village are scattered, and the *Tapu* [sovereign as supreme landowner] has acquired the right to its lands, if it is not possible to bring back that village to its original state by bringing fresh agriculturists to live there, and conferring on them the land separately, the land can be given in lots to one, two, or three persons . . ."
>
> —F. Ongley, trans., with revisions by Horace E. Miller. *The Ottoman Land Code.* London: William Clowes and Sons, 1892. Article 130, Internet Archive, http://www.archive.org/details/ottomanlandcodeooturkuoft.

Constitution and War

Seen in the context of the centralization reforms in previous centuries, the Tanzimat decrees of 1839 and 1856 were little more than enactments of traditional policies. In the context of nineteenth-century constitutional nationalism, however, they appeared like autocratic dictates from above, lacking popular approval. In the 1860s, younger Tanzimat bureaucrats and journalists working for the first Ottoman newspapers, meeting in loose circles in Istanbul and Paris under the name of "Young Ottomans," became advocates for the introduction of a constitution as the crowning element of the Tanzimat, to end the autocracy of the sultan.

The idea of a constitution became reality in the midst of a deep crisis in which the empire found itself embroiled from 1873 to 1878. The crisis began when the Ottoman government defaulted on its foreign loans. In order to service the renegotiated loans, it had to increase taxes.

Ottoman Parliament. The constitutional reforms (Tanzimat) of the Ottoman Empire culminated in elections for a parliament and two sessions, uniting deputies from a multiplicity of ethnic backgrounds (1876–1878). It met during the Russian–Ottoman War of 1877–1878, which the Ottomans lost. The newly installed Sultan Abdülhamit used the war as an excuse for ending constitutional rule and governing by decree.

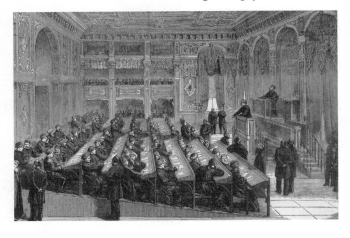

Patterns Up Close | From Constitutional to Ethnic Nationalism

The constitutional revolutions in the United States, France, and Haiti from 1776 to 1804 helped usher in the modern period of world history. They were rooted in two crucial developments in the preceding two centuries.

First, they were intellectually based on the concept of a fictive original state of individuals in nature giving up their independence in return for the establishment of a civilized state with a constitution. According to this constitution, individuals had rights and obligations resulting in elections of deputies, representation in a parliament, and an elected ruler under popular sovereignty.

Second, this intellectual constitutionalism did not remain on paper. It became a revolutionary reality thanks to the existing constitutional practice of England (later Great Britain), which in the Glorious Revolution of 1688 formalized the earlier constitutional practices of shared sovereignty between king and Parliament. In other words, because constitutionalism was functional in England/Great Britain, it became *the* aspirational model in the American colonies of Britain and later France.

As we saw in Chapter 22, however, in the course of the nineteenth century many constitutional nationalists began to add embellishments to the fundamental ideas of liberty, equality, and fraternity that had inspired the revolutions. Romantic thinkers in Germany, such as Johann Gottfried Herder (1744-1803), had already written voluminously on the concept of the "people" (*Volk*) prior to the revolutions. In their writings, the romantics assumed that there were ethnic, linguistic, literary, historical, and religious bonds that predated the formation of constitutional nations.

Visions of a New Order. The stirring events of 1848 produced visions of a new political order in which the peoples of Europe would form a "holy alliance" and a new "universal and social democratic republic," as shown in this lithograph where representatives from each nation march in solidarity with flags aloft past the rubble of toppled monarchs. In reality, the impulses of ethnic-linguistic nationalism sowed deep divisions among the very people depicted here.

This romantic thinking was highly speculative and largely undocumented. Above all, the requirement that a people—often dispersed and living among other peoples—should become a nation (requiring borders for the constitution) was often highly unrealistic. Ethnic–linguistic–religious nationalism was just as fictional as the assumption of an original state of individuals in nature.

As vague as it was, ethnic nationalism attracted groups of followers among many Europeans on the continent during the nineteenth century. They were typically students at the premier universities, graduating as lawyers, journalists, doctors, pharmacists, and other

Byron Dressed as an Albanian. The famous Romantic English poet, George Gordon, Lord Byron (1788–1824) was one of many European intellectuals who came to the assistance of Greece and other Balkan countries in their liberation movements against the perceived tyranny of the Ottoman Empire. In this painting, Byron appears dressed as an Albanian—a backward corner of the Balkans that was then under Ottoman rule. His exotic dress shows his support for the ethnic-nationalist movements that were then bubbling up across the Balkans. Byron, in fact, died in Greece of 1824 of a fever, just a few years before Greece formally achieved independence.

professionals. Much of the scholarship that university professors produced concerned the historical origins of European "peoples," their heroes, literary creations, and enemies against which they had to prevail. Many students, especially from eastern Europe, engaged in highly imaginative ethnic–linguistic–religious identity creation and, in the process, became nationalists who literally created the peoples whom they then wished to liberate from the yoke of their alien monarchs. Not surprisingly, the forces of ethnic-linguistic-religious nationalism would be particularly active within the large, multi-ethnic, multi-linguistic, and multi-religious empires of the Habsburgs, Ottomans, and Russia (see Map 25.2).

MAP 25.2 **Ethnolinguistic Composition of Central Europe, ca. 1900.**

The first to proclaim a people entitled to become a nation under a constitution were the Greeks, who in 1821–1833 waged a war of liberation against the Ottoman sultan. They invoked a "Greekness" that was rooted in the assumption of a common Greek language, the history of the Greek city-states, Alexander the Great, the intellectual achievements of Plato and Aristotle, and a host of other real or imagined precedents. When it came to adopting constitutions, however, the liberators did not aim to create of republics, as the Americans and French had done. They opted for constitutional monarchies, thereby revealing what subsequently became a trademark of ethnic–linguistic–religious nationalism (or, for short, "ethnolinguistic nationalism"): that culture, including that of kings, was more important than the principle of popular sovereignty.

This remains true today. "Peoples" who are supposed to be or become "nations" often seem to tolerate autocrats or dictators who hold constitutions in low regard. Conversely, constitutionally unified "nation-states" encompass ethnic groups which are unwilling to curb their identities and strive for secession. In short, many people in the world have yet to find a balance between the two types of constitutional and ethnic nationalism. Yet, the nation-state, as we have seen, has become nearly the only form of political organization in the world today.

Questions

- How do the origins of ethnic nationalism show the power of an imagined past in shaping people's group identity?

- In which places in the world today is this process still a force in shaping people's national consciousness?

This increase triggered ethnic–nationalist uprisings in Montenegro, Serbia, and Romania in the Balkans in 1875. The heavy-handed repression of these uprisings resulted in a political crisis, with a palace coup d'état by the Young Ottomans, during which a new sultan, Abdülhamit II (r. 1876–1909), ascended the throne and a constitution was adopted. Finally, in this sequence of events, the Russians exploited the perceived political weakness of the new constitutional Ottoman regime for a new Russo–Ottoman war in support of the Balkan nationalist uprisings.

Amid a rapid advance of Russian troops against a crumbling Ottoman army, the Ottomans held elections for the constitutionally decreed parliament between December 1876 and January 1877. Provincial and county councils elected 130 deputies to meet for two sessions in Istanbul. With the invading Russian forces practically at the gates of Istanbul in February 1878, the deputies engaged in a spirited criticism of the government. Irritated, the sultan dismissed the parliament and ruled by decree.

A few months later, at the Congress of Berlin, the sultan had to accept the loss of two-thirds of the empire's European provinces. Montenegro, Serbia, Romania, and (after a delay of 7 years) Bulgaria gained their independence. Bosnia-Herzegovina and Cyprus, although still Ottoman, received an Austrian administration and a British administration, respectively. Sultan Abdülhamit never reconvened the parliament, and the empire reverted back to autocratic rule.

Autocracy Sultan Abdülhamit surrounded himself with capable second-generation Tanzimat bureaucrats who did not have the constitutionalist leanings of the Young Ottomans. He had very little financial leeway since the Public Debt Administration, imposed by the European powers in 1881, collected about one-third of the empire's income to pay for its accumulated foreign debt. Furthermore, the European price depression in the second half of the nineteenth century (1873–1896) was not favorable to foreign investments in the empire. Nevertheless, a few short-distance railroads connecting the fertile Anatolian valleys and their agricultural exports with Mediterranean ports were built thanks to French capital. A postal service and telegraph system connected all provinces, and steamship lines connected the ports. Once the depression was over, foreign investors enabled the government to build long-distance railroads across Anatolia (see Map 25.3). By the early 1900s, a basic communication infrastructure was in place in the Ottoman Empire.

MAP 25.3 **Railways in the Ottoman Empire, 1914.**

Railways in the Ottoman Empire, 1914

Given his fiscal limits, the sultan was all the more active as a propagandist, burnishing his credentials as the pan-Islamic caliph of Muslims in Eurasia, from Austrian Bosnia and Russian Asia to British India. He astutely sensed that the Balkan events of 1878 and subsequent Congress of Berlin had been a watershed in European politics. The Concert of Europe, with its Britain-supported concept of a balance of power, was no more. It was being replaced by the beginning of an imperial rivalry between Germany and Great Britain. France, Austria-Hungary, and Russia played their own subsidiary imperial roles. Since France and Great Britain, furthermore, carried out their imperialism against the Ottoman

Empire, with the conquests of Tunisia in 1881 and Egypt in 1882, respectively, Abdülhamit was particularly affected. His pan-Islamism was therefore a carefully executed effort to instill the fear of jihad in the European politicians and their publics.

Although most of the Ottoman Balkan provinces had become independent nations by 1878, three ethnic–nationalist movements were still left inside the empire. Abdülhamit met them with an iron fist. The first movement consisted of Serb, Bulgarian, Vlah, and Greek nationalists agitating in Macedonia during 1893–1895. Without outside support, none of these feuding groups could impose itself on the province; and Ottoman troops were therefore able to repress them.

The next were the Armenians, who formed sizeable minorities in the six eastern provinces of Anatolia. Most Armenian farmers and craftspeople in these provinces were politically quiet, but urban-based and secularized Armenian ethnic nationalists organized terrorist incidents. In reaction, the sultan armed Kurdish tribal units, which massacred thousands of Anatolian Armenian villagers from 1894 to 1896. Finally, the Ottomans met a revolt in Crete in 1897, in favor of union with Greece, with an invasion and defeat of Greece itself, which had to pay an indemnity. Europe, busy with its imperialist competition in Africa and Asia, had no time to help the remaining ethnic–nationalist stirrings of the Macedonians and Armenians in the Ottoman Empire.

In the later years of his rule, Abdülhamit increasingly failed to suppress dissatisfaction with the lack of political freedom among the graduates from the elite administrative and military academies. As so often prior to revolts or revolutions, improved economic conditions—as they materialized after the end of the worldwide recession of 1893—stoked political ambitions to create a condition social scientists sometimes call a "revolution of rising expectations." In a pattern similar to that unfolding in Qing China at the same time, oppositional circles among Ottoman intellectuals abroad merged with secret junior officer groups in Macedonia and Thrace in 1907. Barely one step ahead of the sultan's secret service, the officers launched a coup d'état in 1908, which urban Ottomans generally received with great relief. The officers forced the sultan to reinstate the constitution of 1878 and, after elections, accept a new parliament.

The Young Turks   The officers, organized as the Committee of Union and Progress (CUP) and colloquially referred to as "Young Turks," did not initially force Abdülhamit from office. They did so in part because the wily sultan presented himself to the public as having engineered the reinstatement of the constitution, blaming his bureaucrats for not having done so earlier. Behind the scene, he did everything to get rid of the Young Turks. He had his courtiers arouse military and government employees, religious students, and religious brotherhood leaders into a countercoup in April 1909. The rebels demanded the reinstatement of the Sharia, which actually had never been suspended, as mentioned earlier. The government gave in to the demand, and the CUP leaders, unsure of army support in the capital, headed for the provinces to find more reliable troops. In short order, they returned at the head of trustworthy soldiers and this time deposed Abdülhamit, enthroning one of his brothers as his successor.

As the CUP consolidated its power against the conservative religious opposition, a weak imperial government fell into disarray. Members of the increasingly marginal (even if CUP-dominated) parliament as well as an array of provincial notables exploited the deposition of Abdülhamit for their own gains. Austria-Hungary and Bulgaria formally annexed Bosnia-Herzegovina and northern Rumelia, respectively, in 1908. Albania revolted in 1910 and Italy invaded Tripolitania in 1911, triggering a nearly 20-year guerilla war of resistance by members of the Sanusiyya brotherhood against the invaders. The CUP found itself in a near desperate position.

Even worse, the newly independent Balkan states of Serbia, Montenegro, Greece, and Bulgaria unified behind the Russian imperial idea of driving the Ottomans once and for all out of Europe. In 1912, they demanded sweeping reforms in Macedonia (where uprisings had been suppressed in 1895). When the Ottoman government rejected these demands, the four countries declared war against the empire. In response, the Ottoman general staff made the mistake of attacking the Balkan states on several fronts, instead of fighting a defensive war. Bulgarian troops broke through the Ottoman defenses, occupied Macedonia and Thrace, and advanced dangerously close to Istanbul. Once more, the survival of the empire hung in the balance.

In this extremely critical situation, the government was willing to give up on besieged Edirne, the second capital of the empire. Infuriated by this defeatism, a triumvirate of CUP officers staged another coup and assumed direct ruling responsibilities. Step by step, power had been narrowed, from the broad parliamentary coalition that had reinstated the constitution in 1908 to the CUP operating behind the scenes in 1909 to now three powerful men within the CUP supported by a cast of about 50 officers. Try as it might, however, the triumvirate was unable to prevent the fall of Edirne. At the subsequent conference in London, it had no choice but to accept the independence of Albania, the loss of Macedonia (with the city of Salonica, the birthplace of the CUP), Thrace, and nearly all of southern Rumelia, including Edirne.

Fortunately for the CUP, the four victorious Balkan states were unable to agree on the division of the spoils. The Ottomans exploited the disagreements and retook Edirne, succeeding in a new peace settlement to push the imperial border westward into Thrace. Nevertheless, the overall losses were horrendous: Except for a rump Rumelia, the Ottoman Empire had now been driven out of Europe, ending more than half a millennium of rule in the Balkans.

Economic Development   While the empire was disintegrating politically, the economic situation improved. The main factor was the end of the depression of 1873–1896 and a renewed interest among European investors in creating industrial enterprises in the agrarian but export-oriented independent and colonial countries of the Middle East, Asia, and South America. When Abdülhamit II was at the peak of his power in the 1890s and early 1900s, investors perceived the Ottoman Empire as sufficiently stable for the creation of industrial enterprises.

New research since the 1980s has considerably refined the concepts of less developed agriculture-based economies and industrialization during the 1800s. Prior to that time, scholars often compared the Ottoman Empire unfavorably to Japan, the only non-Western country that was successful in adopting the British model of industrialization. By 1900, Japan was essentially industrialized, producing its own iron and steel, heavy machinery, and machine-produced textiles. Historians had to free themselves from the fixation on the British and Japanese models and concede that more circuitous paths toward industrialization merited the same serious attention. For example, the Netherlands did not industrialize until the 1890s, and France continued to industrialize slowly from industrial "islands" in certain urban areas out

Silk Manufacture, Turkey, ca. 1892. Small textile factories were able to flourish in the nineteenth century, in spite of cheap English cotton goods. They did so on the basis of lowly paid workers and relatively coarse, low-quality goods affordable to the poor in cities, towns, and villages. Industrialization expanded in the 1890s with the foundation of textile factories, such as the silk manufacture in Bursa depicted here.

into the surrounding countryside and provincial centers until well into the twentieth century. Until the 1890s Latin American countries achieved high economic growth rates through commodity exports, without its leaders feeling a strong urge to industrialize. Thus, these countries all possessed viable economies in the second half of the nineteenth century even though their industries were still comparatively light.

With this notion of viable nonindustrial economies in the 1800s in mind, the Ottoman Empire in the 1800s can be described as a state in which the traditional crafts-based textile industry initially suffered under the invasion of cheap industrially produced English cottons in the period 1820–1850. But a recovery took place in the second half of the 1800s, both in the crafts sector and in a newly mechanized small factory sector of textile manufacturing, producing cottons, woolens, silks, and rugs. This recovery was driven largely by domestic demand and investments because the European price depression of 1873–1896 was not conducive to much foreign capital inflow. Operating with low wages and even more lowly paid female labor, domestic small-scale manufacturing was able to hold foreign factory–produced goods at bay.

Throughout the 1800s, the empire was also an exporter of agricultural commodities, particularly cotton, dried fruit, and nuts. But the recovery of the domestic textile production demonstrates that the Ottomans did not succumb completely to the British free market system. When foreign investments resumed in the 1890s and early 1900s, there was a base for industrialization to build on, similar to what people in the Netherlands, France, and Latin America had when they industrialized.

Iran's Effort to Cope with the Western Challenge

Iran (also called "Persia," in recognition of its long heritage) had risen in the 1500s as the Shiite alternative to the Sunni Ottomans. The two dynasties of kings (*shahs*) who ruled Iran, the Safavids (1501–1722) and Qajars (1795–1925), nurtured a hierarchy of Shiite clerics who formed an autonomous religious institution in their state. While

Isfahan, Ali Qapu (High Gate).
Entrance to the Qajar palace (*a*) from a large rectangular square around which major mosques and bazaars are also located (*b*). The palace contains rooms on several floors with richly plastered and decorated walls and ceilings such as the music room, with instrument motifs set in the plaster (*c*).

the Ottoman sultans always kept their leading Sunni religious leaders under firm control, the Iranian rulers had to respect a careful balance of power with their Shiite leaders. Therefore, when Iran in the 1800s faced the Western challenges, reformers had to establish an alliance with the Shiite clerics to bring about constitutional reforms.

Safavid and Qajar Kings The Safavid Empire was a less powerful state than that of the Ottomans. It comprised Shiite Iran, the Caucasus, Sunni Afghanistan, and parts of Sunni central Asia. The Safavid kings, whose lands were limited in most provinces to oasis agriculture, were not wealthy enough to recruit a large firearm infantry to match the Janissaries. As a result, for most of the time the Ottomans were able to keep the Safavid rivalry within manageable proportions, especially from the mid-1600s onward.

At this time, the Safavids ruled Iran from their newly founded capital of Isfahan in the center of the country, which they embellished with palaces and mosques. One of its suburbs was inhabited by a group of Armenian merchants who controlled silk production along the warm and humid Black Sea coast. Safavid Iran was a major exporter of silk yarn and clothes, second in quality only to Chinese wares, and thus supplemented its limited agrarian revenues with an international trade of silk.

The Safavids were vulnerable not only to the military challenges of their Ottoman neighbors to the west but also to those of tribal federations in the Sunni provinces to the east. In Afghanistan, one of the two major Pashtu tribal federations revolted repeatedly against the efforts of the Safavids to convert them to Shiite Islam. Eventually, in 1722, this federation succeeded in conquering Iran and ending Safavid rule, at a time of advanced decentralization in the empire. The Afghanis, however, were unable to establish a stable new regime. Instead, provincial Iranian rulers reunified and even expanded the empire for short periods during the 1700s. Stabilization finally occurred in 1796, with the accession of the new Qajar dynasty.

The Qajars had been among the founding Shiite Turkic tribal federation of the Safavids, but in contrast to their brethren, they had no Shiite aspirations of their own. Instead, they paid respect to the clerical hierarchy that had become powerful in the aftermath of the Afghani conquest in the 1700s. The clerics supported themselves through their own independent revenues from landholdings in the vicinity of their mosques and colleges, and the Qajars were not powerful enough to interfere.

During the 1800s, two developments dominated Iran's historical evolution. First, like the Ottoman Empire, primarily agrarian Iran was subject to oscillating periods of decentralization and recentralization, following the decline or rise of tax revenues from the countryside. Second, the increasingly hierarchical and theologically rigid Shiite clerics were challenged by the popular, theologically less tradition-bound Babi movement. This movement, begun in 1844, rallied around a figure who claimed to be the promised returned Twelfth Imam or Mahdi (Messiah) with a new law superseding the body of legal interpretations of the Shiite clergy. A combination of Qajar troops and clerically organized mobs succeeded in suppressing this widespread movement, which subsequently evolved into the Baha'i faith.

The Qajars not only faced an unstable internal situation but also suffered from Russian imperialism. The declared Russian goal of liberating Constantinople implied the conquest of the central Asian Turkic sultanates as well as the north face of the Caucasus Mountains astride the land bridge between the Black and Caspian Seas. Accordingly, Russian armies sought to drive the Qajars from their Caucasus provinces. In response, the Qajar kings embarked on centralizing military and

In the Gardens of the Caucasus. Tiflis (modern-day Tbilisi), the capital of Georgia, was the crossroads of the contested and strategically vital Caucasus region that Persia, the Ottomans, and Russia all fought over incessantly for centuries. Though today we tend to think of Georgia as a "post-Soviet" state and part of Russia's "near abroad," for millennia Georgia and its neighboring countries of Armenia and Azerbaijan looked southward toward the Middle East, as reflected in the dress of the Georgian ladies and the musical instruments seen in this lithograph from 1847. But while the Georgian language contains many loan words from Persian, Arabic, and Turkish that reflect this long association with the Middle East, it has always retained deep and ancient Christian roots, as evidenced by the thirteenth-century church perched on a high cliff in the background.

administrative reforms, which were similar to those of the Ottomans though less pervasive. In the absence of sizeable groups of reformers of their own and bowing to Russian pressures, they hired Russian officers to train a small corps of new troops, the Cossack Brigade. (The tsar, although bent on expanding into the Caucasus, did not want Iran to collapse as a counterweight to the Ottomans.) Swedish advisors trained the police force, in an effort to improve civil peace. British subjects acquired economic concessions, such as monopolies for minerals and telegraph connections or the manufacture of tobacco. The increasing foreign influence in Iran aroused the ire of the conservative clerical hierarchy, and the kings had to withdraw the concessions. The Qajar ruling class was acutely aware of the Western challenge, but its reformist power vis-à-vis the clerical establishment was limited.

Perceptive Iranian constitutional nationalists from among the educated younger ruling class were less numerous than their Young Ottoman colleagues. They therefore founded a tactical alliance toward the end of the 1800s with conservative clerics and merchants. In 1906, after widespread revolts against tax increases to cover a lavish European trip by the shah, this alliance mounted a successful constitutional revolution, imposing parliamentary limits on the Qajar regime. The constitutional-nationalist alliance with the clerics was, however, inherently unstable and parliamentary rule failed to become a reality. As World War I drew near, Iran reverted to autocratic rule by the shahs. Nevertheless, the memory of the abortive Constitutional Revolution of 1906 lived on, becoming decisive in the later twentieth century with the formation of the Islamic Republic in 1979 and the enactment of a hybrid Islamic–democratic constitution.

Westernization, Reforms, and Industrialization in Russia

The Russian Empire that expanded during the 1800s southward at the expense of the Qajar and Ottoman Empires had arisen in 1547 as a tsardom in Moscow, succeeding the Byzantine eastern Christian "caesars" (from which the Russian term "tsar" or "czar" is derived). It was a relatively late empire, succeeding that of the Mongols; and it spanned eastern Europe as well as Asia. Given this geographical location at the eastern edge of Europe and outside western Christian civilization, Russia developed along an uneven pattern of relations with western Europe. The western European Renaissance and Enlightenment did not spread to Russia. Western culture became a force only around 1700 when the tsar Peter the Great (r. 1682–1725) became its advocate. The idea of constitutionalism arrived in the wake of the French Revolution and Napoleon's failed invasion of Russia (1812). But it remained weak and was diluted by pan-Slavic ethnic nationalism, an ideology whereby Russians sought unification with the Slavic peoples of the Balkans. Multiple small political groups competed with each other, with no single united reformist force emerging. These groups rose amid the social dislocations that followed the Russian industrialization effort at the end of the nineteenth century, but none was able to take over leadership in the abortive revolution following the disastrous defeat at the hands of a modernizing Japan in 1905. Although this uprising produced a weak Russian parliament, the Duma, the autocratic tsarist regime tottered on until collapsing under the unbearable strain of World War I.

Russia and Westernization

In 1768 George Macartney, British envoy to Russia (whom we met as the leader of Britain's attempted diplomatic overture to Qing China in Chapter 24 and the man generally credited with saying that Britain had an empire on which "the sun never sets"), observed that Russia was "a great planet that has obtruded itself into our system, whose place is yet undetermined, but whose motions most powerfully affect those of every other orb." The states of western Europe were, of course, aware of a large empire on their eastern flank but did not consider it fully European. Indeed, at a time when feudal practices were dying in western Europe, Russia under the Romanov dynasty *institutionalized* serfdom. Half a century earlier, Tsar Peter the Great, attempting to travel incognito—despite his six-foot eight-inch frame—went on a mission of investigation to western Europe and began a reform and urbanization process from the top, against an often fierce resistance in both the ruling class and the population at large, to bring Russia closer to the western European norms. His legacy was the new capital of St. Petersburg, extensive military reorganization, and concerted attempts to reign in the power of Russia's high nobility, the *boyars*—including physically cutting off their beards so that they would be clean-shaven like their Western counterparts. But another legacy was a deep-set resistance on a political and cultural level to any such measures coming from outside Russia, not unlike the cultural resistance that would plague Chinese reformers in the nineteenth century.

The German-born "enlightened despot" Tsarina Catherine II, the Great (r. 1762–1796), continued the reform process from the top, which by its very nature, however, was slow to trickle down. When the constitutional-nationalist revolutions broke out in the United States, France, and Haiti, the Russian Empire was an autocratic, fiscal–military state that had expanded in all directions. And its expansion did, indeed, affect many other "orbs."

Aristocratic Charter. The charter that Empress Catherine II of Russia granted to the Russian nobility in 1785 consolidated the Russian aristocracy as a class with its own set of rights and privileges. The charter also contained ideas of liberty that later were interpreted as extending to the other ranks of society as well. Shown here is frontispiece, with the coats of arms of the various provinces of the Russian Empire extending along the edge of the document, while the empress's official title is handwritten in gold in the center.

Catherine II's Reforms

Catherine the Great was the dominant figure of tsarist Russia during the eighteenth century. By origin, she was the princess of a minor German family in the service of Prussia. Early on she learned the art of aristocratic discretion and later in life set a record with her string of lovers in the recesses of her palace in St. Petersburg. Also early in life she developed an abiding intellectual engagement with the Enlightenment trends that proliferated not only in academies and salons but also among the European courts. According to the courtly version of this thought, called "the royal thesis (*thèse*)," rulers were to remain firmly committed to absolute rule but should also pursue administrative, judicial, and educational reforms in order to increase the welfare of their subjects. Catherine subscribed to a digest reporting on the latest trends in Parisian Enlightenment thought. In correspondence with Voltaire, a supporter of the royal thesis, and even Diderot, whom she subsidized (ignoring his atheism and antimonarchical impulses), she kept abreast of who was in and who was out of fashion among the leading *philosophes*. With her Enlightenment engagement,

Catherine was far ahead of the Russian aristocracy, not to mention the small urban educated upper strata, both of which were still much beholden to eastern Christian traditions.

As much an activist as Peter the Great but more subtle, the energetic Catherine pushed through a number of major reforms. Urban manufactures, especially of linen and woolen cloth, had greatly expanded in the early 1700s; and Catherine strengthened urban development with a provincial reform in 1775 and a town reform in 1785 that allowed local nonaristocratic participation. But in 1785 she also strengthened the aristocracy with a charter that exempted its members from the poll tax and increased their property rights, including the purchase of serfs. This was largely a measure to head off a repetition of the terrible peasant rebellions of 1762–1775, which had culminated with Pugachev's Cossack revolt. In a reform of the educational system (1782), the government set up a free, mostly clergy-staffed educational system, from urban primary schools to high schools. Catherine's legal reform project, however, apart from a police ordinance issued in 1782, remained incomplete; and the codification and humanization of Russia's laws had to wait for another 80 years.

In foreign affairs, Catherine was determined to revive Peter the Great's expansionism. She first undertook the dismemberment of the kingdom of Poland, accomplished together with Prussia and the Austrian Habsburgs in three stages, from 1772 to 1795. Then, in two wars with the Ottoman Empire (1768–1792), Catherine waged a successful campaign to end the Ottoman alliance with the Tatars, a Turkic-speaking population of mixed ethnic descent that had succeeded the Mongols of the Golden Horde (ca. 1240–1502) in Crimea and adjacent northern Black Sea lands. Catherine's modernized infantry forces were successful in humbling the considerably larger but disorganized Ottoman army and navy. In the first war, Russia gained access to the Black Sea, ending the Tatar–Ottoman alliance and gaining free access for Russian ships to the Mediterranean. In the second war, Russia absorbed the Tatars within its imperial borders, which now advanced to the northern coast of the Black Sea.

Russia in the Early Nineteenth Century

The ideas of the French Revolution made their first fleeting mark on Russia in the form of the Decembrist Revolt in 1825, several decades before they did in the Ottoman Empire. But since in the pattern of traditional empire formation the personality of the ruler still counted more than the continuity of the administration, the reign of the deeply monarchical Nicholas I for a generation in mid-1800 Russia meant that whatever the Decembrists had set in motion could only spread under the surface. Above the ground, Nicholas pursued an aggressive foreign policy of expansion, in the tradition of Catherine the Great (see Map 25.4).

Russia and the French Revolution   In her old age, Catherine was aghast at the monarchical constitutionalism of the French Revolution, not to mention its republicanism and radicalism. In an abrupt about-face, her government had Voltaire's books burned and other Enlightenment books banned. Alexander Radishchev (1749–1802), a Russian landed aristocrat and prominent author with sympathies for the revolution, was forced into exile in Siberia. The situation eased under Catherine's grandson, Alexander I (r. 1801–1825), who was educated in Enlightenment ideas. He initially showed inclinations toward constitutionalism, coaxed by his

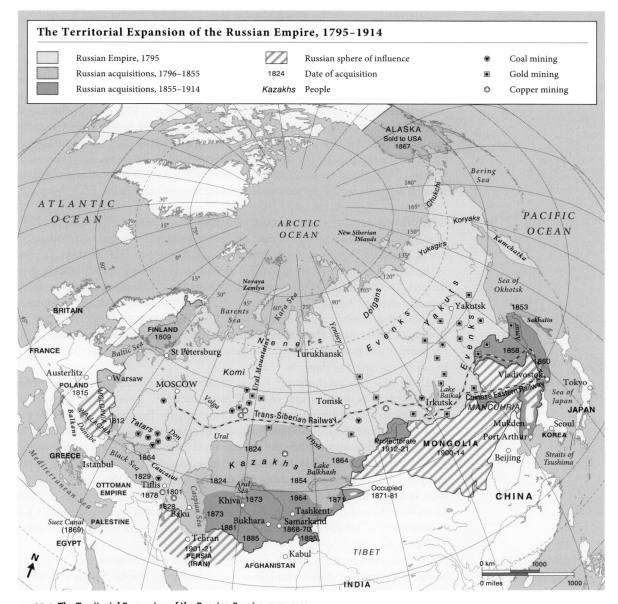

The Territorial Expansion of the Russian Empire, 1795–1914

	Russian Empire, 1795
	Russian acquisitions, 1796–1855
	Russian acquisitions, 1855–1914

Russian sphere of influence

1824 Date of acquisition

Kazakhs People

● Coal mining

■ Gold mining

○ Copper mining

MAP 25.4 **The Territorial Expansion of the Russian Empire, 1795–1914.**

discreetly constitutionalist minister Mikhail Speranskii (1772–1839); but Napoleon's imperial designs interrupted any idea of implementation.

Russia emerged as a key power in efforts to prevent Napoleon's takeover of Europe. In 1805 Russia joined Britain and Austria in the Third Coalition against France; but Napoleon's smashing victory at Austerlitz in December 1805—where Alexander personally commanded the Russian troops—doomed the coalition. Napoleon followed up on his victorious campaigns by defeating Russian forces in June 1807. This was followed by a dramatic meeting between Napoleon and Alexander on a raft anchored in the River Niemen on July 27, 1807. Napoleon forced

Alexander into an agreement of mutual aid and the recognition of French conquests on the European continent.

However, after the defeat of Napoleon during his disastrous Russian campaign of 1812, Alexander rebounded. At the Congress of Vienna in 1815 he assumed a prominent role in the negotiations for the territorial settlements and reestablishment of peace, advocating a "holy alliance" of monarchs to be its guarantors. As a result, Napoleon's duchy of Warsaw became the kingdom of Poland, with the Russian tsar as its king. In contrast to his monarchical colleagues in Europe, however, Alexander remained open to Enlightenment reforms, initiating the liberation of serfs in Russia's Baltic provinces, pursuing constitutional reform in Finland and Poland, and mapping out a new status for eastern Christianity. But Russia also experienced unrest, so Alexander gradually lost interest in the continuation of his reforms.

Orthodoxy, Autocracy, and Nationality   No sooner did Nicholas I (1825–1855) ascend the throne in 1825 than a bloody revolt broke out, led by a small number of Russian officers exposed to the ideas of constitutional nationalism. Known as the Decembrist Revolt, the uprising was quickly suppressed and its leaders were hanged. The revolt had few connections with civilians and was furthermore intellectually divided between federalists and unionists. The former serf Nikitenko, introduced at the beginning of this chapter, was fortunate to escape with his life from his contacts with Decembrists. Despite this relative lack of impact, the revolt represented the first anti-tsarist, constitutional-revolutionary movement and, thus, became a harbinger of things to come.

Determined to preclude any future constitutional revolts, in 1833 Nicholas implemented the doctrine known as "official nationality," aimed particularly at the suppression of constitutional movements sweeping the European continent in the early1830s. According to this new formulation of tsarist policy, three fundamental theories would in future guide the government: *orthodoxy*, reaffirming the adherence to eastern Christianity and rejection of secularist notions originating in the Enlightenment; *autocracy*, meaning the absolute authority of the tsar; and *nationality*, or the equivalent of something like the "spirit" of Russian identity. In order to enforce these directives, Nicholas created a secret police agency known as the "Third Section," which vigorously suppressed dissidence against the government in any form.

Nicholas also carried through on his conservative policies by joining other conservative European rulers in suppressing constitutional revolts. When a revolt in Poland in 1830 threatened to topple the viceroy (meaning ultimately the tsar himself as overlord), Nicholas intervened by suppressing it and abolishing the country's autonomy. Then, during the widespread agitation of revolutionary constitutional movements across Europe in 1848, Nicholas supported the Austrian emperor in suppressing the Hungarian nationalists. The failure of the attempted constitutional revolutions of 1848 was largely attributable to Nicholas's determined intervention.

In larger terms, Nicholas was determined to continue Russia's drive toward Constantinople (Istanbul). In the Russo–Ottoman War of 1828–1829 Russia succeeded in helping the Greeks achieve independence. With Russian help Serbia attained autonomy, while Moldavia and Wallachia—technically still within the Ottoman Empire—became protectorates of Russia. However, when Napoleon III of France in 1853 demanded recognition as protector of the Christians in Palestine under Ottoman rule, Russia did not fare as well. After Nicholas responded by insisting that the Ottomans honor their agreement with the Russian tsars as the actual protectors, the ensuing diplomatic wrangling ended in the outbreak of the Crimean War between Britain, France, and the Ottoman Empire, on one side, and Russia, on the other.

Poor planning, missed opportunities, language barriers, and a lack of coordination between soldiers and officers plagued both sides in the Crimean War. One of the first products of the mid-nineteenth century industrial weapons revolution, the French Minié ball, whose hollow expanding base allowed for ease of ramming in muzzle-loading rifles, quadrupled the effective range of infantry weapons and vastly increased their accuracy. As they would a few years later during the American Civil War, armies fighting with increasingly obsolescent tactics would suffer fearful losses from these new weapons. French steam-powered and iron-hulled floating batteries inaugurated the age of ironclad navies. Telegraph lines permitted correspondents to send frontline reports to their London newspapers. And the nascent technology of photography was there to document the conflict. To lessen the sufferings of the wounded, doctors and nurses on both sides staffed field hospitals—including the English nurse Florence Nightingale (1820–1910), the founder of modern medical care on battlefields and the first prominent advocate of nursing as a profession for women. The new scientific–industrial age had manifested itself for the first time in war.

The Ottomans, still in the initial stages of their military reform, did not acquit themselves well, suffering from a weak officer corps and the absence of noncommissioned officers. They would have been defeated, had it not been for allied participation. The Russians did not perform well either, except for their navy with its superior shells. The Russian army suffered from overextending its battle lines on too many fronts, from the Danube and Crimea to the Caucasus. Thus, as far as the two imperial foes, the Russian and Ottoman Empires, were concerned, the war was a setback for both in their effort to meet the challenges of the West. Like their counterparts in China during the Second Opium War, also fought in the mid-1850s, however, they did receive a renewed taste of the state of the art in military technology and usage. This would mark many of the reform efforts of all three empires in the coming decades.

Hospital Ward, Scutari, Ottoman Empire, 1856. This airy, uncluttered, warm hospital room shows injured and recovering soldiers. Florence Nightingale is depicted in the middle ground, in conversation with an officer.

The Golden Age   During the period 1810–1853, in spite of times of censorship and repression, Russia enjoyed an outburst of intellectual and cultural activity. Taken as a whole, this period was considered the golden age of Russian culture. Inspired by European romantics, a Russian *intelligentsia*—Western-educated intellectuals predominantly from the ranks of the landowner nobility—met in the salons of Moscow and St. Petersburg, where they considered and debated issues related to religion and philosophy, as well as Russian history. A significant development was the appearance of literary journals, which spread the ideas and appeal of new literary forms as well as new ideas. Many of these ideas were potentially seditious since they concerned ways to end the autocracy of the tsars and to reform serfdom. More importantly, the first stirrings of reform movements emanated from these circles.

Alexander Sergeyevich Pushkin (1799–1837) stood at the forefront of the new intellectual movement. His lineage included old aristocratic forebears and an African-descended servant of Peter the Great, and he committed himself early on to the cause of reform with his poems, novels, as well as political activism, which brought him into conflict with the authorities. Best known among his works are his fairy tale poem "Ruslan and Lyudmila" (1820), the historical drama *Boris Godunov* (1825), and the novel in verse *Eugene Onegin* (1837) about a St. Petersburg dandy. Another prominent figure was Pyotr Chaadayev (1794–1856), also of aristocratic parentage. His sharply critical *Philosophical Letters* (1836) began the debate between constitutionalist "Westernizers" and conservative "Slavophiles." Westernizers considered Western models of governance, exemplified by constitutional government, along with industrial development and urbanism, as good models for progress in Russia. Slavophiles, by contrast, clung to traditional Russian institutions like the eastern Christian Church and the village commune. Nikolai Gogol (1809–1852), of Ukrainian Cossack descent, for example, felt that the distinguishing feature of Russia was its devotion to the Russian Orthodox Church, which served as the focal point of existence for the peasantry. With their determined opposition to Westernization, Slavophiles developed an early form of Russian ethnic nationalism that later evolved into the movement of pan-Slavism.

The Great Reforms

The Russian defeat in the Crimean War convinced the newly enthroned Alexander II (r. 1855–1881) of the need for reforms. Russia, so he believed, lost the war because of a technologically inferior army, a lack of infrastructure, and the unwillingness of the serf-owning aristocracy to shift from subsistence to market agriculture. He implemented major reforms, which, however, took time to produce the intended effects. Many Russians did not want to wait, and the empire entered a time of social destabilization, balanced abroad to a degree by successes against the Ottoman Empire.

The Emancipation of Serfs   Nicholas tackled serfdom first. In 1861, Alexander (the "tsar liberator") issued the Emancipation Edict, in which peasants were ostensibly freed from their bondage to their villages and their dues and labor services to the Russian landowning aristocracy. The traditionally unfree status of the serfs is usually explained on the one hand by the sparse population of the empire, with few cities and poor communication, and on the other hand by the relatively high level of fertility of Russia's humus-rich "black soil" (*chernozem*). On the face of it, the edict ended the centuries-old system of serfdom, affecting some 50 million serfs. But the edict fell far short of liberating the peasantry and satisfying critics. For one thing the decree of emancipation did not go into effect immediately but took 2 years to be fully enacted. For another, peasants were not given land titles per se; the land was turned over to the control of local communities (*mirs*), which then in turn allocated parcels to individual serfs. Finally, serfs had to redeem their new holdings by making annual payments to the state in the form of long-term government loans, the proceeds from which were then used to compensate the landowning nobility. Even worse, these payments were often higher than the former dues which serfs had owed the aristocracy. In effect, then, tens of millions of farmers remained mired in poverty-stricken agricultural self-sufficiency.

Following Western models, Alexander enacted further reforms. For example, in 1864 the administration of government at the local level was reorganized by the establishment of regional councils known as *zemstva*. Each zemstvo was in reality controlled by the local aristocracy, although peasants had a say in their election. Whatever their drawbacks, it must be said that zemstva achieved advances in education, health, and the maintenance of roads within their regions. Legal reforms were enacted shortly afterward; these provided all Russians access to courts, trial by jury, and especially the concept of equality before the law. Then, in 1874, a series of reforms aimed at modernizing the military and bringing it closer to Western standards was enacted. Among these was the reduction of active duty service in the military from 25 to 6 years, followed by several years of service in the reserves, along with an overall improvement in the quality of life in the ranks. Planned infrastructural reforms, however, remained limited for lack of funds. As in the Ottoman Empire, the reforms brought important changes to Russia; but in many cases, their effects would not be known until years later. Yet, just as the Ottoman Empire was increasingly called, after the example of Nicholas, the "Sick Man of Europe," it remained an article of faith among many in the West that, despite its reforms, "Russia could always be beaten for her backwardness."

Radicalization Among Intellectuals   The incompleteness of the reforms and the glaring absence of constitutionalism among what reforms did come expressed itself in a transition from peaceful demands to radicalism. Many Russians perceived this transition as a generational change. The aristocrat turned liberal Ivan Turgenev (1818–1883) observed this transition most astutely. In his aptly named *Fathers and Sons* (1862), a novel still widely read today, he declared that the new generation was dominated by "nihilists" (from the Latin *nihil*, meaning "nothing").

Nihilism: Intellectual and political movement of the late nineteenth century that rejected the institutions and morality of society.

The term **nihilism**, coined in Germany a century earlier and popularized by Turgenev, was meant to signify the inevitable end result of Enlightenment thought, if driven to its extremes. Nihilists, forming small underground circles, were devoted to individual freedom above all else, rejecting society's institutions and morality.

Other circles of radical intellectuals espoused *populism*, an ideology that romanticized rural peasant communities and their allegedly thriving autonomy. Members of these circles demanded that intellectuals go to the villages and stir them up into a socialist revolution from which the empire would be overthrown. In reality, however, the years after 1861 saw tensions arising between more well-to-do villagers able to buy their lands (called *kulaks*) and poor villagers unable to do so. The urban populists, unable to relate to these tensions, found few followers in the countryside, from either the kulaks or the poor.

The New Generation of Nihilists

"Well," replied Pavel Petrovich, "very well. You have discovered all that and you are not less decided not to undertake anything seriously."

"Yes, we have decided not to undertake anything seriously," replied Bazarov in a brusque tone. He reproached himself all at once for having said so much before that gentleman.

"And you confine yourself to insult."

"We insult at need."

"And this is called nihilism."

"This is what is called nihilism," repeated Bazarov, but this time in a tone peculiarly provoking.

Pavel Petrovich winced a little.

"Very well!" he said with a forced calm that was rather strange.

—Ivan Serghéïevich Turgenev. *Fathers and Sons: A Novel*, trans. Eugene Schuyler, p. 61. New York: Leypoldt & Holt, 1867.

Later groups, inspired by the writings of the aristocrat turned anarchist Mikhail Bakunin (1814–1876) and seeking to learn from the failures of the populists, sought to bring together the urban and rural poor for the organization of small, self-administering communities without the need for a state with a central government and bureaucracy. Action-oriented splinter groups among these anarchists devoted themselves to bringing the state down through terrorism, trying to assassinate Alexander II seven times before finally succeeding in 1881. No spontaneous revolutions from below, however, materialized; and the tsar's secret service found it relatively easy to keep the small revolutionary circles under surveillance, except for its final fatal lapse.

Pan-Slavism: Ideology that espoused the brotherhood of all Slavic peoples and gave Russia the mission to aid Slavs in the Balkans suffering from alleged Ottoman misrule.

Pan-Slavism   Concurrently with the appearance of radical ideologies on the left, a new right-wing ideology known as **pan-Slavism** emerged in the 1870s. Pan-Slavism proclaimed the brotherhood of all Slavic peoples and gave Russia the mission to aid Slavs in the Balkan territories who were suffering from alleged Ottoman misrule. Pan-Slavism took on a religious identity, that is, a commitment to Russian eastern Christianity. One of the best-known proponents of this ideology was the novelist Fyodor Dostoyevsky (1821–1881), son of a military surgeon. Dostoyevsky advocated the idea of a Russian "spiritual community" (*sobornost*), whose members would devote themselves to bringing about the unity of all humankind in the name of Christianity. As a writer, he transcended his Russian environment and became one of the most outstanding nineteenth-century authors on the Eurasian continent, with such psychologically refined novels as *Crime and Punishment* (1866) and *The Brothers Karamazov* (1879–1880).

Balkan Affairs   Two issues contributed to mounting Russian pan-Slavic engagement in the Balkans. First, across the nineteenth century the Ottomans had been forced to relinquish control of large areas of their empire in the Balkans, and an end was not in sight. Second, the increasingly popular appeal of ethnolinguistic nationalism in Europe—Italian unification in 1870, followed by German unification in 1871—strengthened the assertiveness of the Balkan nationalities. In 1875 Bosnia-Herzegovina revolted against the Ottomans, and the rebellion then spread to Bulgaria, Serbia, and Montenegro. What would happen if these provinces did in fact break away from the Ottoman Empire? Which of the European powers might then take them over and, thus, increase its presence in this vital region? Thus, the Balkans became an area of increasing attention for the leading powers, while at the same time representing a powder keg ready to ignite.

The Russo–Ottoman War   Encouraged by Russian popular pan-Slavic support and sensing an opportunity to exploit rising anti-Ottoman sentiments among ethnic national movements in the Balkans, the tsar reopened the war front against the Ottomans in July 1877. The pretext was the Ottoman repression of tax revolts in Bosnia-Herzegovina and Bulgaria, which had led to a declaration of war by neighboring Montenegro and Serbia in June 1876 and a call for Russian military aid. The Russians invaded across the Danube and by December had advanced as far as Rumelia. Serbia, claiming complete independence, and Bulgaria, under Russian tutelage, were now poised to gain control of Istanbul. The other European powers stood by, anxiously waiting to see whether Russia would advance on the Ottoman capital.

In 1878, alarmed over what appeared to be an imminent Russian occupation of Istanbul, Austria and Britain persuaded Germany to convene the Congress of Berlin. In order to preserve peace among the great powers and to diffuse rising tensions over this "eastern question," the Congress decided to amputate from the Ottoman Empire most of its European provinces. For its part, Russia agreed to give up its designs on Istanbul in return for maintaining control over lands it had secured in the Caucasus Mountains. Serbia, Romania, and Montenegro became independent states. Austria acquired the right to "occupy and administer" the provinces of Bosnia and Herzegovina. There things stood for the rest of the nineteenth century, as the European powers began their imperial scramble; and Russia, forced to deal with renewed internal unrest, turned its attention away from the Balkans.

Russian Industrialization

Following the assassination of Alexander II in 1881, the next Romanov tsars reaffirmed autocratic authority and exercised tight political control, harkening back to the policies of Nicholas I. They surrounded themselves with conservative advisors and buttressed their hold on absolute rule by connecting loyalty to the state with adherence to eastern Christianity. These tsarist policies provoked renewed calls for constitutional reforms and generated new movements opposed to the autocracy of the regime. At the same time, when the depression of 1873–1896 began to ease in the 1890s, the country enjoyed a surge in industrialization, aggravating the political and social contradictions in Russia.

The Reassertion of Tsarist Authority In the face of increasing demands by constitutionalists and social reformers, Alexander III (r. 1881–1894) unleashed a broad program of "counterreforms" in order to shore up autocratic control over the country. These actions turned Russia into a police state, in which political trials

Aristocratic Splendor. This oil painting of the wedding of Nicholas II in 1894, by the Danish painter Laurits Regner Tuxen (1853–1927), completed in 1898, shows the rich glory of the eastern Christian Church and the empire in ascendancy, with their iconic art, ermine furs, veiled ladies in waiting, and decorated officers.

before military courts were commonplace. Anyone who opposed Alexander's policies was subjected to intimidation at best, exile or death at worst; revolutionaries, terrorists, and opponents among the intelligentsia were especially targeted. Outside Russia, Alexander insisted on a program of *Russification*, or forced assimilation to Russian culture, especially language, by Poles, Ukrainians, and the Muslim populations of central Asia. For the time being, the regime maintained its grip on power.

Nicholas II (r. 1894–1917), a narrow-minded, unimaginative, and ultimately tragic figure, followed in his father's footsteps. Nicholas's paramount concern was loyalty not only to the state but also to the church. Any deviations were considered treasonous. He held a special contempt for revolutionary groups and individuals, who therefore retaliated with increasingly strident demands for the overthrow of the tsarist government. In addition to continuing the repressive policies of his father, Nicholas held an enduring distrust of Russian Jews as unpatriotic, which climaxed in the pogroms of 1903–1906. These pogroms, a repetition of earlier ones in 1881–1884 following the assassination of Alexander II, triggered mass emigrations to the United States and smaller ones to Britain, South America, South Africa, and Palestine as Russian Jews sought to escape persecution (see Map 25.5).

Industrialization   Industrial development was as slow in Russia as in the Ottoman Empire and for many of the same reasons. For one thing, the empire suffered from a poor transportation infrastructure. Although canal construction had started under Peter the Great, road construction did not follow until the early 1800s. Railroad construction was even slower, owing to the great distances in the empire which made large capital investments from abroad necessary. The first line, from St. Petersburg to Moscow, opened in 1851; but only a few thousand miles of track were laid until 1890 when the European depression of the previous three decades lifted. A major reason for the defeat in the Crimean War was the absence of railroad connections from Moscow

MAP 25.5 **Jewish Emigration from Russia, 1880–1914.**

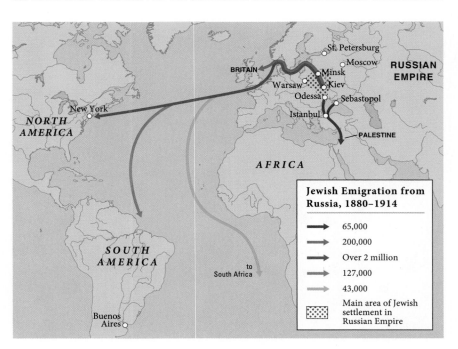

Jewish Emigration from Russia, 1880–1914

→	65,000
→	200,000
→	Over 2 million
→	127,000
→	43,000
▦	Main area of Jewish settlement in Russian Empire

to the Black Sea, forcing the army to rely on water transport and horse-drawn carts. Moreover, even into the twentieth century, Russian railroads never adopted the standard gauge of their Western counterparts, necessitating costly and time-consuming changes of carriages and rolling stock at border crossings.

Still, in the 1890s, British, French, and Belgian capital poured into the empire and helped in building railroads, mining ventures, iron smelters, and textile factories. It is estimated that during this decade Russia's industrial output increased at an annual rate of nearly 8 percent. Among other factors driving the push toward accelerated industrialization was the dawning recognition of the regime that Russia was falling behind the industrialized nations of Europe in the race for economic—and thus political—global political influence.

The driving force in Russia's push for industrialization in the 1890s was the minister of finance, Sergei Witte (1849–1915, in office 1892–1903). Of German–Baltic descent from the Russian province of Estonia, Witte held a degree in mathematics and was a railroad official before becoming responsible for the Russian finances. His "Witte system" included an acceleration of heavy industrial output, the erection of import tariffs, increased taxes on the peasantry, and conversion to the gold standard in order to stabilize the currency. Although historians debate the overall success of Witte's reforms, there is no question that Russia made tremendous progress in heavy industrialization during the late nineteenth century. Dramatic increases in the miles of rail laid, tons of coal and steel produced, and square yards of textiles woven attest to Witte's vigor.

Witte's crowning achievement was the Trans-Siberian Railroad, built during 1891–1905 and connecting Moscow with Vladivostok on the Pacific coast. During Catherine's time, it took 3 years for communications to be sent to and from Vladivostok; now, the distance was covered in 8 days. Witte's objective was not only to make Russia more competitive but also to extend Russia's reach into the rich agricultural and mineral resources of Siberia, while at the same time extending Russia's influence in east Asia. Russia's policy of opening east Asia was the equivalent of Western imperialism in Asia and Africa and designed to ensure that Russia enjoyed a share of the global race for empire.

The Russo–Japanese War   The dramatic surge in industrialization, in conjunction with imperial ambitions in east Asia, brought Russia into conflict with Japan. As we saw in Chapter 24, with the Meiji Restoration in 1867–8, Japan had embarked on a concerted and systematic program of modernization and industrialization. Like western Europe and Russia, it developed imperial ambitions in the 1890s, seeking to replace China as the dominant power in east Asia. To this end Japan provoked war with China and in the Sino–Japanese War (1894–1895) occupied Taiwan and the Liaodong Peninsula of Manchuria. Although successful in defeating China and replacing it as the protector of Korea, the European powers forced Japan to give up the Liaodong Peninsula in the Triple Intervention (1895), which was in turn leased to Russia the following year. Determined to continue Russian expansion in east Asia, Witte completed the construction of a railway spur from the Trans-Siberian Railroad through Manchuria to the warm-water fortress city of Port Arthur on the southern tip of Liaodong.

The construction of this spur was the final straw for Japan, whose imperial goals seemed suddenly threatened by Russian expansion. Already smarting from what they considered Russia's double-dealing in helping to engineer the Triple Intervention and leasing the naval base at Port Arthur from the Qing, in early 1904 Japanese naval forces suddenly attacked the Russian fleet moored at Port Arthur, destroying several of its ships and laying siege to the fortress. The Japanese had had the foresight several years before of signing a treaty with Great Britain of "benign neutrality" in which the British agreed passively to help Japan in the event of war with a third party. They thus refused the Russian Baltic fleet passage through the Suez Canal on its voyage to raise the Japanese siege of Port Arthur. Following a decisive Japanese victory over Russian forces at Mukden in March 1905, Japanese forces finally cracked the stalemate at Port Arthur just as the Russian fleet, forced to sail around South Africa and across the Indian Ocean, attempted to run the narrow Straits of Tsushima. Here, the Japanese fleet was waiting for them and annihilated them in one of the most lopsided naval victories of the modern era. In the peace settlement, Japan gained control of the Liaodong Peninsula and southern Manchuria, as well as increased influence over Korea, which it finally annexed in 1910.

The Abortive Russian Revolution of 1905

In addition to Russia's mauling by the Japanese in the war of 1904–1905, a variety of factors coalesced in the early 1900s that sparked the first revolution against tsarist rule. One of these was a rising discontent among the peasantry, who continued to chafe under injustices such as the redemption payments for landownership. Another was the demand from factory workers for reform of working conditions: The workday ran to 11.5 hours and wages were pitifully low. Although the government had allowed for the formation of labor unions, their grievances fell on deaf ears. In response, workers in major manufacturing centers across the country, especially in St. Petersburg, mounted massive protests and occasional strikes.

Revolutionary Parties   The discontent among workers and peasants pumped new life into calls for reforms, resulting in the creation of two new political parties. One of these was the Social Democratic Labor Party, formed in 1898 by Vladimir Ilyich Lenin (1870–1924), a staunch adherent of Marxism (discussed in Chapter 23). This group sought support from workers, whom they urged to stage a socialist revolution by rising up and overthrowing the bourgeois capitalist tsarist government. The other group, the Social Revolutionary Party, was formed in 1901. Comprised mostly of liberal reformers among the intelligentsia, the Social Revolutionary Party advocated populism as a way to energize the peasantry, upon which they counted to lead the revolutionary effort.

During its meeting in London in 1903 the Social Democratic Labor Party split into two competing factions. The more moderate group, the Mensheviks ("minority," though they were actually numerically in the majority), was willing to follow classical Marxism, which allowed for an evolutionary process from fully evolved capitalism to social revolution and then on to the eventual overthrow of capitalism and tsarist rule. The more radical faction, known as Bolsheviks ("majority"), led by Lenin, was unwilling to wait for the evolutionary process to unfold and instead called for revolution in the near term. In 1902 Lenin had sketched out his agenda in *What Is to Be Done?* which laid out the principal Bolshevik aims. Foremost among these was a demand for the overthrow of the tsar, which could be accomplished only by relying on a highly disciplined core of dedicated revolutionaries leading the masses, whom Lenin distrusted as unwieldy and potentially unreliable. Even after the split in the Social Democratic Labor Party, however, the Bolsheviks were still a long way away from the kind of elite "vanguard of the revolution" party Lenin envisaged.

The Revolution of 1905   Events moved toward a violent climax in the Revolution of 1905. Amid mounting calls for political and economic reforms during the early 1900s, two concurrent events in 1904 shook the government to its foundations. First, reports of the humiliating defeats during the ongoing Russo–Japanese War began to filter to the home front. These made apparent the government's mismanagement of the war. Second, in January 1905, 100,000 workers went on strike in St. Petersburg, resulting in massive disruptions and loss of life commemorated later by Lenin.

The events of Bloody Sunday triggered further protests across the country during the spring and summer of 1905 (see Map 25.6). Then, from September to October, workers in all the major industrial centers staged a general strike, which brought the country to a stand-

> **Lenin on Bloody Sunday**
>
> "Today is the twelfth anniversary of 'Bloody Sunday,' [January 9 or 22, 1905, depending on different calendars] which is rightly regarded as the beginning of the Russian revolution.
>
> "Thousands of workers—not Social-Democrats, but loyal God-fearing subjects—led by the priest Gapon, streamed from all parts of the capital to its centre, to the square in front of the Winter Palace, to submit a petition to the tsar. The workers carried icons. In a letter to the tsar their then leader, Gapon, had guaranteed his personal safety and had asked him to appear before the people.
>
> "Troops were called out. Uhlans [Polish light cavalry] and Cossacks [southern Russian regiments] attacked the crowd with drawn swords. They fired on the unarmed workers, who on their bended knees implored the Cossacks to allow them to go to the tsar. The indignation of the workers was indescribable . . ."
>
> —Vladimir I. Lenin. *Collected Works*, vol. 23, p. 236. Moscow: Progress Publishers, 1964. Accessible through http://www.marxists.org/archive/lenin/works/1917/jan/09.htm.

still. Finally forced to make concessions, Nicholas issued the "October Manifesto," in which he promised to establish a constitutional government. Among other things, the Manifesto guaranteed individual civil liberties, universal suffrage, and the creation of a representative assembly, the Duma. During 1905–1907, however, Nicholas repudiated the concessions granted in the Manifesto, especially an independent Duma, which remained a rubber stamp parliament until Nicholas abdicated in 1917. Its momentum sapped, the revolution petered out.

What factors account for this deflation of revolutionary fervor? One event that enabled Nicholas to renege on his earlier promises was disagreement among the opposition parties; each had its own goals and ambitions, resulting in disagreement on how to bring down the tsarist government. More than that, each of the major political factions was unable to convince its followers among the workers and the peasants that its plans would in the end really address their specific concerns. Nicholas was therefore able to play off one group against the other and to reverse the reforms.

The revolution showed that the generational shift from constitutionalists to revolutionaries seeking to overturn the existing social order, which Turgenev had observed in the 1860s, was nearly complete. This shift made the formation of broader reformist coalitions, perhaps even with military participation, as in the Ottoman Empire, impossible. The tsarist regime, though humbled by Japan, still had enough military resources to wear down the combination of small groups of Marxist revolutionaries and street demonstrators. Without sympathizers in the army, a determined tsarist regime was impossible to bring down. But like Qing China during these years, whatever belated

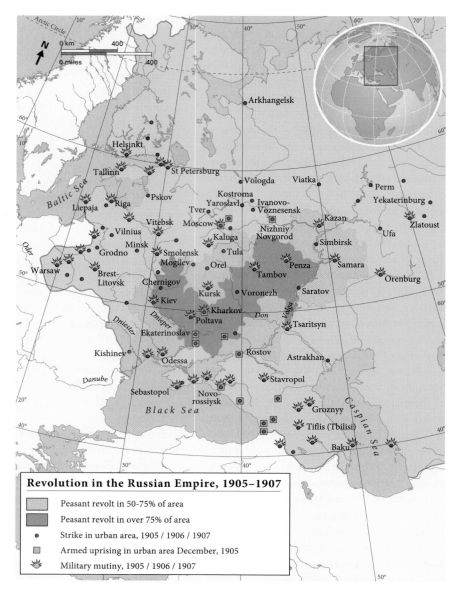

Revolution in the Russian Empire, 1905–1907

- Peasant revolt in 50–75% of area
- Peasant revolt in over 75% of area
- Strike in urban area, 1905 / 1906 / 1907
- Armed uprising in urban area December, 1905
- Military mutiny, 1905 / 1906 / 1907

MAP **25.6 Revolution in the Russian Empire, 1905–1907.**

reforms were initiated by the government would increasingly be seen as irrelevant. It was now perceived that nothing short of changing the system would be effective. For both empires, the revolutionaries would now dominate the scene.

Putting It All Together

Both the Ottoman and Russian Empires faced the initial Western military and constitutional challenges directly on their doorsteps, not from across the ocean, as China and Japan did. Of course, once military technology had undergone its own industrial transformation in Europe during the first half of the 1800s, China was no longer too far away for British steam-powered gunboats and rifled breech-loading weapons. The Ottoman Empire, as a mature empire struggling to regain its traditional centralism, fought largely defensive wars. Russia, still a young empire, expanded aggressively against the defensive Ottomans and its weaker Asian neighbors (except Japan), all the while suffering occasional military and diplomatic setbacks. India failed to master the Western military challenge altogether. China, the Ottoman Empire, and Qajar Iran survived it at the price of diminished territories. The Western challenge was pervasive across the world.

Western constitutional nationalism was another powerful and corrosive pattern. The transformation of kingdoms or colonies into nations in which subjects would become citizens, regardless of language or dialect, social rank, or religion, was difficult enough in Europe. France, with its uneasy shift between monarchy and republic during the 1800s, demonstrated this difficulty. In the Ottoman Empire, a wide gap existed between constitutional theory and practice, especially as far as religion was concerned. Russia, plagued by the reluctance of its aristocracy to give up serfdom even after emancipation, left its constitutionalists out in the cold. Japan created a constitutional state but, like Germany, left the great majority of real power in the hands of its emperor and advisors. China's bid for a constitutional monarchy died once in 1898 and was never fully reborn before its revolution in 1911. Sultans, emperors, and kings knew well that none of their constitutions would fully satisfy the demands for liberty, equality, and fraternity.

To complicate matters for both the Ottoman and Russian Empires, in the second half of the 1800s, many members of the rising educated urban middle class deserted constitutional nationalism and turned to ethnic nationalism (in the Ottoman Empire) or to pan-Slavism, revolutionary socialism, and Marxism (in the Russian Empire). Marxism would eventually carry the day in Russia in the course of World War I. By contrast, both the Ottoman and Russian Empires met the Western *industrial* challenge—cheap, factory-produced cotton textiles—without completely surrendering their markets. Once they were able to attract foreign capital for the construction of expensive railroads and factories at the end of the 1800s, they even started on their own paths to industrialization—the seemingly stable Russia faster than the apparently sick Ottoman Empire. In spite of wrenching transformations, the two were still empires in control of themselves when World War I broke out. Neither would survive the war. Instead, they would be transformed by the forces that had beset them throughout the nineteenth century: Turkey would become a modern, secular nation-state, though always running somewhat behind its European contemporaries in economic development. Russia would be transformed into the world's first Marxist state, pursue breakneck industrial and economic development at a tragic cost, and emerge after World War II as one of two "superpowers" with the United States (see Concept Map).

Vladimir Egorovic Makovsky (1846–1920), *Death in the Snow* (1905). This dramatic oil painting of the crowd protesting against the tsarist regime during the abortive revolution of 1905 is one of the greatest realist paintings. Makovsky was one of the founders of the Moscow Art School and continued to paint after the Russian Revolution of 1917.

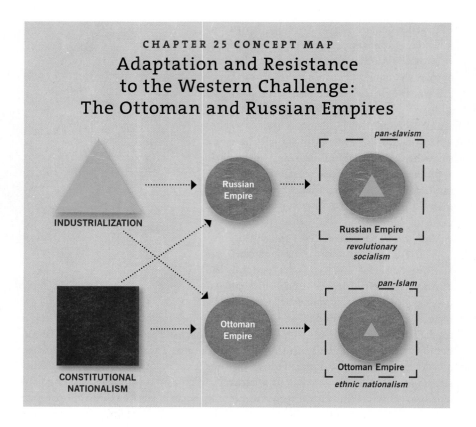

CHAPTER 25 CONCEPT MAP

Adaptation and Resistance to the Western Challenge: The Ottoman and Russian Empires

Review and Respond

1. What was the significance of Napoleon's invasion of Egypt in 1798?

2. How would you summarize the Tanzimat decrees in the Ottoman Empire.

3. What did the Committee of Union and Progress in the Ottoman Empire stand for, and what did it accomplish between 1908 and 1914?

4. Which features characterized Iran in this period, and how did the country adapt to the Western challenge?

5. What were the patterns of agrarian life in Russia during the nineteenth century?

6. Why did the tsars in Russia face a fractured opposition to their autocratic rule?

> For additional resources, including maps, primary sources, visuals, and quizzes, please go to www.oup.com/us/vonsivers. Please see the Further Resources section at the back of the book for additional readings and suggested websites.

Thinking Through Patterns

▶ **Which new models did the Ottomans adopt during the nineteenth century to adapt themselves to the Western challenge?**

The traditional model for reform in the Ottoman Empire was based on the Islamic concept of the divinely sanctioned, absolute authority of the sultan: Officials could be appointed or dismissed at will. The later history of the Ottoman Empire is significant in world history because it shows the *adaptation pattern* to the Western challenge, in this case, the borrowing of constitutional nationalism and modern military technology from Europe.

As agrarian polities with large landowning classes collecting rents from tenant farmers or serfs, the Ottoman and Russian Empires found it difficult to respond to the European industrial challenge. Large foreign investments were necessary for the building of steelworks, factories, and railroads. Given the long economic recession of the last quarter of the 1800s, these investments—coming from France and Germany—went to expanding Russia, more than the shrinking Ottoman Empire, as the safer bet.

▶ **How did the agrarian Ottoman and Russian Empires, both with large landholding ruling classes, respond to the western European industrial challenge during the 1800s?**

▶ **Why did large, well-established empires like the Russian and the Ottoman Empires struggle with the forces of modernity, while a small, secluded island nation like Japan seemed to adapt so quickly and successfully to them?**

This is in many respects a tantalizing question for world historians. Aside from philosophical debates about what actually constitutes "success," one avenue of inquiry is cultural: How receptive were the Russians and Ottomans—or the Qing, for that matter—toward the ideas of the Enlightenment? The short answer must be, "not very." Even the most willing leaders in these empires risked alienating a host of entrenched interests by attempting the most modest reforms. They therefore walked a very fine political line in what they attempted and often found that the reforms disrupted traditional routines but left little or nothing to replace them effectively. In addition, such large multiethnic empires as those of Russia and the Ottomans found it difficult to rally subjects around a distinct "nationality" since they encompassed so many divergent ones. In contrast, the Meiji reformers had the advantage of a unity derived from outside pressures. With the old shogunate gone, the emperor could formulate completely new institutions and count on the loyalty of subjects who had seen him as a semidivine figure. Moreover, the new regime commenced immediately in creating an ideology of Japaneseness—a form of ethnic nationalism—and institutionalized it in education and national policy. There was, to be sure, opposition; but it was scattered, class-based, and not effective against the modern army and industrial power the new regime created. Japan's legacy of cultural borrowing may also have been an advantage, as well as a nascent capitalist system developing in the late Tokugawa era. Finally, the goal of using its progress toward "enlightenment and civilization" according to Western standards could be measured along the way, as were the power and prestige of its new programs.

Riz: Mise en terre des plantes

2

Riz:
Fleur et fruit

Tabac: Mise en terre

Germany

Tabac: Plante de tabac

10

9

Chapter 26 | The New Imperialism in the Nineteenth Century

1750-1914

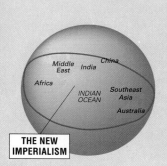

THE NEW
IMPERIALISM

At the end of the Muslim month-long observance of Ramadan in 1827, Hussein (1815–1830), the ruler (*dey*) of the autonomous Ottoman province of Algeria in North Africa, held a celebratory reception for the diplomatic corps of consuls at his palace in the capital, the port city of Algiers. When he saw the French consul, Pierre Deval, Hussein signaled him to come up to the throne. In a quite undiplomatic harangue, the dey accused the consul of deliberately defrauding him of a large sum of money owed him by France for wheat deliveries between 1793 and 1798. He then demanded immediate payment of this long overdue debt. To emphasize his demand, the dey struck the consul with his fan and declared him *persona*

Riz: Battage par

Tabac: Indigène brésilien, fumant

Seeing Patterns

▶ What new patterns emerged in the transition from trade-fort imperialism to the new imperialism?

▶ How did European colonizers develop their colonies economically, given that they were industrializing themselves at the same time?

▶ What were the experiences of the indigenous people under the new imperialism? How did they adapt to colonialism? How did they resist?

non grata, which, in terms of diplomatic protocol, meant that he had to leave the country immediately.

France's restored Bourbon king, Charles X (r. 1824–1830), found this insult by the Algerian dey to an appointee of the French court intolerably injurious to his own divinely-ordained dignity. He dispatched a naval detachment to Algiers in 1828, demanding an apology, declaring the debt liquidated, and asking for reparations for a number of piracy depredations that had occurred in the preceding years. When the dey rejected the demands, the French mounted a blockade of the port. In 1830, they followed up on this blockade with an expeditionary force that conquered Algiers, deposed the dey, and sent him into exile. Less than two decades later Algeria became a colony of France.

The events that preceded the "fan slap," as it became known, were rooted in a drought in southern France toward the end of the French Revolution. The government at the time, the Directory, was chronically short of finances and received the Algerian relief shipments without having to pay immediately. They were made on trust, thanks to the services of a

Imperial Bounty. The material benefits of empire—at least for the colonizer—are colorfully illustrated in these panels from a 1910 French school textbook. The stages of cultivation for rice and tobacco are graphically illustrated, from first planting to taking to market. No white people toil in the fields, but the scenes nonetheless exude an idyllic sense of peace and prosperity under the "civilizing" effects of Western rule.

Colonialism: A system in which people from one country settle in another, ruling it and maintaining connections to the mother country; term now used most often to describe the contemporary exploitation of weaker countries by imperial powers.

prominent Italian–Algerian Jewish banking business, Bacri Brothers and Busnach [Boos-NASH].

Repayment was delayed by Napoleon's Mediterranean campaign. Napoleon had toyed with a conquest of Algeria but then decided to go for Egypt instead (1798–1801), possibly to frighten the British in India. After Napoleon fell from power, France made two payments, which were sufficient to satisfy some creditors of Bacri-Busnach but not Hussein—hence the fan slap nearly 30 years after the wheat shipments.

Among other things, the incident illustrates the changing fortunes of those countries that were the beneficiaries of the new forces of modernity—in this case, France—and those like the Ottoman Empire and its territories in Algeria that largely were not. In this chapter, our focus will be on those parts of the world outside east Asia (see Chapter 24) that were unable to preserve, even in a tenuous fashion, their political independence while adapting to the colonial challenge through military, constitutional, and economic reforms. Here, we will study the victims of conquest and occupation in south and southeast Asia, the Middle East, Africa, and the Pacific Ocean that most clearly make visible the underlying patterns of imperialism and colonialism.

Two patterns characterize the evolution of imperialism–colonialism in the period 1750–1900. The first was a shift from coastal trade forts under chartered companies—the old imperialism on the cheap—to government takeover, territorial conquest, and **colonialism**. Great Britain pioneered this "new imperialism" in India but also prevented the other European countries for a century from following in its footsteps.

The second pattern was the rise of direct territorial imperialism–colonialism by European countries in the course of the disintegration of the Ottoman Empire, under assault by Russia since the end of the eighteenth century and, in the course of the nineteenth century, in Asia and Africa. The Europeans first protected the Ottomans from Russia, only later to help themselves to Ottoman provinces, beginning with the capture of Algeria by France. Thus the dey's fan slap in Algeria may be viewed as the unlikely catalyst that set in motion competitive European imperialism–colonialism in Asia and Africa that characterized the remainder of the nineteenth century.

The British Colonies of India, Australia, and New Zealand

The transition in India from European trade-fort activities to governmental colonialism coincided with the decline of the Mughal dynasty (see Chapter 20). The British East India Company exploited the Mughal decline to evolve into a government in all but name. Its notorious corruption and ultimate inability to conduct military affairs, however, forced the British government to assume direct control. As a result, Britain became a colonial power in the Eastern Hemisphere, making India its center for the delivery of the cotton on which early British industrialization depended. Later on, sparsely inhabited Australia and New Zealand began as small British settler colonies, the former as a penal colony and the latter against fierce indigenous resistance.

The British East India Company

As with so many developments that helped to shape the later eighteenth century and its legacy, an important factor in the rise of British power in India was the Seven Years' War. As we have seen, the Seven Years' War resembled in many respects a kind of "first" world war in that fighting took place in Europe, in the Americas, on the high seas, and in India. It was the result of the war in India, along with the deepening political difficulties of the Mughals, that enabled the rise of the British to supremacy not only on the subcontinent but later in Burma and Malaya as well.

The Seven Years' War   The seeds had long been planted for a vibrant British commercial community among the European trading companies by the early eighteenth century. As we saw in Chapter 20, the British had joined forces at Surat on the west coast of India with the Dutch in the lucrative spice trade. But they had also established their own posts in provincial cities that would over time be transformed into India's greatest metropolises: Madras (Chennai), Bombay (Mumbai), and one created from scratch: Calcutta (Kolkata). By 1750 their chief commercial competitors were the French, who were aggressively building up both trade and political power from a base in Pondicherry in the southern part of peninsular India.

For the British East India Company, its evolution into a kind of shadow government in the area around Calcutta in Bengal on the northeast coast would now bear dividends. The decline of Mughal central power meant that regional leaders were being enlisted as French or British allies. If they were more powerful, they sought to use the Sepoy (from Persian *sipahi* [see-pa-HEE], "soldier") armies of the European companies as support in their own struggles. Out of this confused political and volatile military situation, the East India Company leader, Robert Clive (1725–1774), who

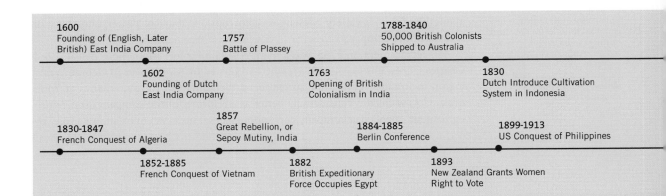

1600		1757		1788-1840	
Founding of (English, Later British) East India Company		Battle of Plassey		50,000 British Colonists Shipped to Australia	

	1602		1763		1830
	Founding of Dutch East India Company		Opening of British Colonialism in India		Dutch Introduce Cultivation System in Indonesia

1830-1847		1857		1884-1885		1899-1913
French Conquest of Algeria		Great Rebellion, or Sepoy Mutiny, India		Berlin Conference		US Conquest of Philippines

	1852-1885		1882		1893
	French Conquest of Vietnam		British Expeditionary Force Occupies Egypt		New Zealand Grants Women Right to Vote

Nabob: A person who acquired a large fortune in India during the period of British rule.

was ambitious, ruthless, and finely attuned to the vagaries of the shifting political landscape, won a signal victory over the Indian French allies at Plassey in 1757 and soon eliminated the French from power in the subcontinent. By the terms of the treaty ending the war in 1763, the East India Company ended up as the sole European power of consequence in India; and Clive set about consolidating his position from Calcutta.

Perceptions of Empire. The British East India Company's real ascent to power in India began with Robert Clive's victory at Plassey in 1757, the symbolism of which is depicted here. Note the deference with which the assorted Indian princes treat the conqueror (*a*). Below, the second from last Mughal emperor, Akbar Shah II (r. 1806–1837), receives the British resident, ca. 1815 (*b*). Despite the fact that the British East India Company had extended its sway over much of northern India by this time, the Indian artist depicts the British government official in a pose of supplication to Akbar Shah—in almost a mirror image of the imagined Indian princes in the painting of Clive.

Going Native—the Nabobs   Clive's aggressive style of economic aggrandizement set the style for what Indian scholars have often called "the Rape of Bengal" in the latter eighteenth century. The East India Company set about expanding its holdings across northern India, dealing, plundering, and extorting funds from pliant local princes. The company men had no interest in changing India or reforming Indian institutions. Indeed, many, inspired by Enlightenment ideals of cosmopolitanism, became great admirers of Indian culture. Some took this to the point of what became known as "going native": After gathering their fortunes, they took Indian wives, dressed as Indian princes, and on occasion wielded power as local magnates or **nabobs** (from Urdu *nawwab* [naw-WAHB], "deputy," "viceroy").

The period of the nabobs perhaps reached its height under the company directorship of Warren Hastings (1732-1818), Clive's successor. Where Clive was brutal and aggressive, Hastings, though acquiring immense wealth, developed an intense scholarly interest in Indian culture. The first translations into English of many of the classics of Indian literature took place during his governor-generalship from 1773 to 1785. Moreover, the first exposure of the Vedas to European scholars yielded the earliest hints that Sanskrit was a branch of the family of languages that came to be called "Indo-European." Over the coming decades additional scholarship on the Vedas contributed mightily to the first linguistic theories on the origins of some of Eurasia's earliest peoples—work that continues today.

The vast distances separating the company's London directors from operations in India, southeast Asia, and China tended to make its local activities more or less autonomous. Its power, organization, and, most importantly, army increasingly became the determining factors in local disputes across northern India, while its attractiveness to ambitious young men on the margins of British society—particularly among the Scots and Irish—wishing to "make their pile" in a few short years, left it vulnerable to corruption on a grand scale. This was particularly true because of the company's policy of paying low wages but winking at employees trading locally on their own behalf. Thus, Hastings was called back to London and subjected to a lengthy trial on a variety of charges of corruption, abuse of power, and abuse of Indians under company rule.

His replacement, in 1785, was a man most famous for ignominious defeat: Lord Charles Cornwallis (1738–1805), who had turned his sword over to George Washington in Britain's humiliating surrender to the American Revolutionaries at Yorktown. Cornwallis did considerably better as a reformer of the company. The British Parliament, appalled at company corruption, had set up a system of "indirect rule" by which the company's actions were to be supervised by a governor-general selected by the British government, rather than by the East India Company directors in London. Cornwallis labored to curb the worst excesses of private trading by increasing salaries and attempted to unify and rationalize the tax structure of the company's holdings.

By 1800, through the company's efforts to pacify turbulent territories adjacent to its holdings, British possessions extended across most of northern India (see Map 26.1). The irregular manner in which this was accomplished prompted many to say that the British Indian empire was created "in a fit of absence of mind." This extension also prompted a shift in the variety of trading goods as the eighteenth century wore on and as the new century dawned. Spices had been replaced by cotton goods as the most lucrative commodity and increasingly by raw cotton to be processed in Britain's mechanized textile revolution. Indian cotton would later be supplemented and eventually supplanted by cotton from the American South, Egypt, and Sudan.

The Perils of Reform   While we have become accustomed to seeing the nineteenth century as the period marking the beginning of Western supremacy, it is well

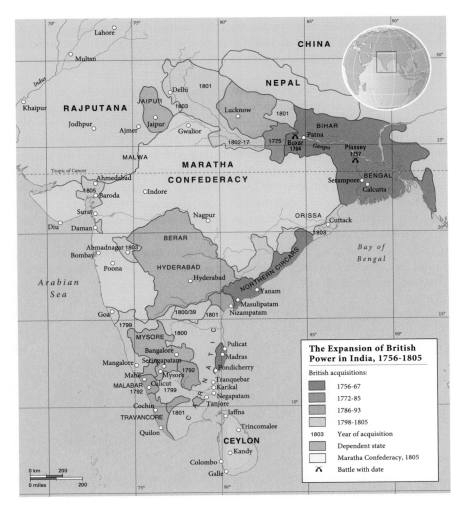

MAP 26.1 **The Expansion of British Power in India, 1756–1805.**

to remember—as we have noted in previous chapters—that even at this late date India and China were still the primary economic engines of Eurasia. As late as 1800, for example, Indian goods and services (what we call today the "GDP" or gross domestic product) accounted for perhaps 20 percent of the world's output, while Britain's came to only 3 percent. As the Industrial Revolution kicked into high gear by the mid-1800s, however, these numbers began to reverse (see Figure 26.1). As Britain's share of India's economy grew, moreover, the British increasingly sought to create markets for their own goods there and to shunt Indian exports toward the exclusive use of the British domestic market. As we saw in Chapter 24, the early acquisition of Patna by the British enabled the creation of the Chinese opium trade, which by 1830 accounted for nearly one-quarter of company revenues in India. In addition, the officials of "John Company," as the East India Company was nicknamed, were busily arbitrating disputes among Indian rulers, taking over their lands as payment for loans, and strong-arming many into becoming wards of the British. Because of this continuous attrition, by the end of the Napoleonic Wars, the Mughal emperor's lands had been reduced to the region immediately surrounding Delhi and Agra.

India's history, however, had long been marked by outsiders conquering large parts of the subcontinent, and while many chafed at company rule, its policy of non-interference with Indian customs and institutions softened the conquest somewhat. The period following the Napoleonic Wars, however, saw changes in this regard that had far-reaching consequences, by bringing the British government into a more direct role.

The economic slowdown, clashes between factory owners and labor, and drive for political reform in Britain during the period following the Napoleonic Wars found echoes in policy toward India. From the opening decades of the century, increasing numbers of Protestant missionaries, especially those of the new Evangelical denominations, saw India as promising missionary ground. As was the case in China, many missionaries brought with them practical skills, particularly in medicine, education, and engineering. Many of those active in mission-based reform in India had also been involved with the abolition of slavery, industrial workers' rights, and electoral reform movements in Britain. By 1830 many of these individuals were driving the agenda on British policy in India, which increasingly asserted that India should be reformed along the lines they envisioned for Britain: better working conditions for the poor, free trade, the abolition of "barbaric" customs, and a vigorous Christian missionary effort.

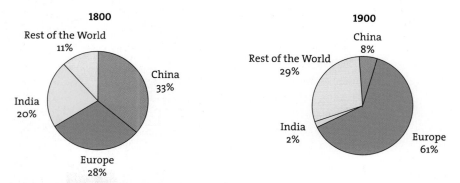

Figure 26.1 Share of World Manufacturing Output, 1800 and 1900.

Their opponents, many of them longtime company veterans, saw the pushing of such policies in India as unwarranted interference in their territory and largely unneeded as far as the Indians themselves were concerned. Nonetheless, missionaries mounted successful campaigns against female infanticide; against *sati*, the self-immolation of widows on their husbands' funeral pyres; and *thugee*, real or (many suggested) imagined ritual murders of travelers on Indian roads. Missionary efforts also increasingly used medicine and education as wedges for the introduction of Christianity to the Indian populace.

In addition, the company reformed the tax system into a money-based land fee for greater efficiency of collection. At the same time, new industrial enterprises and transport and communication advances—steamboats, railroads, and telegraph lines—were being constructed, benefiting the economy at large but also disrupting the livelihoods of many. Coupled with these changes was a perception on the part of opponents, and even some supporters, of these efforts in both India and England as characterized by smug righteousness—the clichéd and often caricatured middle-class "earnestness"—and arrogance of the English toward Indian society. Perhaps the most famous expression of this was found in the parliamentary reformer and historian Thomas B. Macaulay's 1835 "Minute on Education in India," where he asserted that "a single shelf of European books is worth more than all the literatures of Asia and Arabia."

Christian Missionary. The diverse crowd gathered around the young Christian preacher, who is most likely a Methodist, includes Muslims, Hindus, women, a mendicant, and at least one child. But the spectators all share one thing in common: they regard the preacher with a mixture of curiosity and amazement.

The Great Mutiny

The grim result of several decades of such wholesale change exploded in northern India in 1857. General disillusionment with the pace of change and the fear that British missionaries were, with government connivance, attempting to Christianize India came to a head among the company's Sepoy troops. With the introduction of the new Enfield rifle, which required its operator to bite the end off of a greased paper cartridge to pour the powder down its muzzle and ram the new conical bullet home, a rumor started that the grease had been concocted of cow and pig fat. Since this would violate the food restrictions of both Hindus and Muslims, the troops saw this as a plot to leave the followers of both religions ritually unclean and thus open to conversion to Christianity. Though the rumors proved untrue, a revolt raced through many of the Sepoy barracks and in short order became a wholesale rebellion aimed at throwing the British out of India and restoring the aged Mughal emperor, Bahadur Shah Zafar (r. 1837–1857), to full power. The accumulated rage against the perceived insults to Indian religions and culture pushed the troops and their allies to frightful atrocities, with even more that were rumored but never substantiated.

Execution of Indian Rebels. After British troops and loyalist Indian Sepoys had restored order in northern India, retribution was unleashed on the rebels. Here, the most spectacular mode of execution is being carried out. Mutineers are tied across the mouths of cannons and blown to pieces while the troops stand in formation and are forced to watch.

The Great Mutiny (also known by the British as the Sepoy Mutiny and by the Indians as the Great Rebellion, or First War of Independence) swiftly turned into a civil war as pro- and anti-British Indian forces clashed. The British frantically shipped troops just sent to China for the Second Opium War back to India in a desperate attempt to crush the insurgency. Through a number of hard-fought engagements they were ultimately able to reassert control but not without conducting frightful atrocities of their own in retribution for the rebels' excesses. The occupation of many towns was accompanied by mass hangings and indiscriminate shootings of suspected rebels and collaborators. In other areas, British commanders revived the old Mughal punishment of tying the victims to cannons and blowing them to bits in front of the assembled troops. Since this was thought to scatter the karmic "soul" of the victim as well as his body, it was meant to deprive the offender of his next life as well as his present one.

Direct British Rule

After assuming direct rule (Hindi *raj*, hence the term "Raj" for the colonial government), the British were crucially concerned to keep their apparatus of civilian administrators as small as possible but maintain an army large enough to avoid a repeat of 1857. These administrators made use of Indian administrators who, however, did not have any real decision-making powers. The raj functioned because of a "divide and rule" policy that exploited the many divisions existing in Indian society, which prevented the Indians from making common cause and challenging British rule.

Creation of the Civil Service   Even as the pacification was winding down, the British government, stunned by the course of events, conducted an investigation which led to sweeping reforms in 1858. The East India Company was dismantled, and the British government itself took up the task of governing India. In a proclamation to England and India, Queen Victoria announced that British policy would no longer attempt to "impose Our convictions on any of Our subjects." An Indian civil service was created and made open to British and Indians alike to administer the subcontinent's affairs. The incorporation of India as the linchpin of the British Empire was completed when Queen Victoria assumed, among her many titles, that of "Empress of India" in 1877. India had now become, it was said, "the jewel in the crown" of the empire (see Map 26.2).

Less than a decade later, the fruits of the new civil service and the Indian schools feeding it were already evident, though perhaps not in the way its creators envisioned or desired. In 1885, Indians first convened the National Congress, the ancestor of India's present Congress Party. The Congress's ongoing mission was to win greater autonomy for India within the structure of the British Empire and, by the opening decades of the twentieth century, to push for Indian independence.

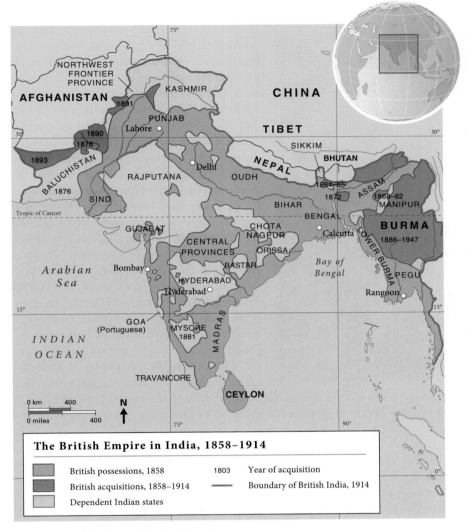

MAP **26.2** **The British Empire in India, 1858–1914.**

Already by the early 1890s, a young British-trained lawyer named Mohandas K. Gandhi (1869–1948) was actively campaigning for the rights of Indians in British-controlled South Africa. There, he honed the skills and developed the techniques that would make him among the most recognized world figures of the twentieth century as he pursued his quest to oust the British from India through nonviolence and noncooperation.

The Civil Service Caste   In the final decades of the nineteenth century the British community in India, rarely more than about 100,000 at any given time (in a population of some 270 million in 1900), increasingly set itself up as a caste and race apart. During the heyday of company rule, few wives and families moved from England to what was considered a hardship post. India's unrelenting summer heat and constant rain during the monsoon season took a considerable toll on those not fully acclimated, as did its array of tropical diseases, particularly malaria. One of the

Lord Curzon. Following the Great Rebellion, the British government dissolved the East India Company and inaugurated direct rule of the subcontinent through a civil service. Here, Lord Curzon, the British resident, or governor-general, and Lady Curzon preside over a tiger they bagged during a hunting trip. Curzon was famous for mounting flamboyant spectacles to enhance British prestige during government-sponsored durbars and was responsible for building the modern Indian capital of New Delhi.

reasons young company men were so eager to "make their pile" in a hurry was the knowledge that their life expectancy in India was rather low.

With the coming of reformers and missionaries in the 1820s and 1830s, the number of English families and dependents grew rapidly, and this increased further with the assumption of direct British rule at the end of the 1850s. The older practice of company men marrying Indian women and leaving them and their children behind when they left for home was now replaced by the professional bureaucrat or businessman and his proper Victorian family living in India for long stretches of time. This was made less physically arduous by the widespread use of quinine to treat the fevers of malaria—and popularizing the famous drink gin and tonic (the "tonic" including quinine water). In places where there were concentrations of Europeans, they tended increasingly to mingle almost exclusively among themselves, setting up their own social circuits, clubs, literary and theatrical societies, and other activities and groups. Many vacationed together during the hot months at the "hill stations" in the cooler upland areas. Thus, with the exception of their servants and civil service subordinates, European families had little contact with ordinary Indians.

"Never the Twain Shall Meet"

This, of course, was by now a familiar pattern at other outposts in European colonial empires. But this social segregation also coincided with the rise of social Darwinism and pseudoscientific theories of race that increasingly encouraged the British to see the Indians as inferior and became an additional inducement toward segregation. These attitudes can be seen in bold relief in much of Rudyard Kipling's literary work, in which, although there is much he finds admirable about things Indian, in the end concedes that "East is East and West is West and never the twain shall meet." For Kipling, the inability of these two peoples to connect suggests the superiority of the white Europeans over their Indian "charges."

Divide and Rule

The Indian civil service, among the most difficult bureaucracies in the world in which to gain admission, seldom had more than 1,000 "Anglo-Indian" (ethnically British subjects who were either born in India or longtime residents there) and Indian officials to govern a quarter of a billion people. The civil service was intended as a showpiece of British incorruptibility and professionalism, in stark contrast to the perception of endemic graft and petty bribery customary among the Indian princes. Some of the ablest men in the British Empire, particularly those whose class or ethnic background might have proven a hindrance at home, passed the grueling examinations and entered the service as "readers." With so few officials, the workload was very heavy and demanded a sophisticated understanding of local conditions and sensibilities. The numbers of civil service members increased markedly in the twentieth century as Britain began to implement a gradual devolution to a kind of federated Indian autonomy. Even at this point, however, the numbers were only slightly above 3,000.

How did such a small government apparatus and expatriate population control such a large and populous country? In many respects it was done by bluff and artifice. The Indian Army of Great Britain, "the thin red line" as it was called in the days before the uniforms were khaki, was small, well trained, but made up mostly of Indians. The British officers and noncommissioned officers included substantial numbers of Scots and Irish, themselves minorities often subject to discrimination at home. But the incipient threat of the army to suppress rebellion and the fruits of the weapons revolution of the late nineteenth century—machine guns, rapid-fire artillery, repeating rifles—made any small revolt unthinkable, while the tactics of British divide and rule made large-scale organization across caste, religious, ethnic, and linguistic lines extremely problematic.

> ### Kipling on the Indian Civil Service
>
> "Until steam replaces manual power in the working of the Empire, there must always be the men who are used up, expended, in the mere mechanical routine. For these promotion is far off and the mill-grind of every day very instant. . . . The older ones have lost their aspirations; the younger are putting theirs aside with a sigh. Both learn to endure patiently until the end of the day. Twelve years in the rank and file, men say, will sap the hearts of the bravest and dull the wits of the most keen."
>
> —Rudyard, Kipling. "The Education of Otis Yeere." In: *Under the Deodars, The Phantom Rickshaw, Wee Willie Winkie*, p. 16. Garden City, NY.: Doubleday, 1911.

Though the bureaucracy and political structure of British India served to unite the country for administrative purposes, the British secured their rule locally and regionally by "divide and rule" tactics. A key divide they utilized was the obvious one between Hindus and Muslims. British policy had encouraged Muslims to see the British as their protectors, while also often leaning toward them in matters contested with the Hindus. Thus, Muslims often felt they had a stake in the Raj, particularly when the alternative that presented itself was a Hindu-controlled India should independence from Britain ever come. In the end, this fear translated itself into the partition of India into India and West and East Pakistan—as Muslim-dominated territories. East Pakistan later became Bangladesh.

Other divides exploited differences among the Hindus. Rajputs and Gurkhas, for example, as military castes, were widely employed in the army in areas away from their home regions; this was also true of the Sikhs. In order to undermine the power bases of local Brahmins, lower castes were sometimes subtly given favorable treatment. Depending on the circumstances, different regions might be given preferential treatment as well.

One other area that the British exploited with success was to appeal to the sense of grandeur of the Indian elites by staging elaborate durbars (see Chapter 20) at the Raj's showpiece capital of New Delhi, built during the early twentieth century under the aegis of the British Resident, Lord Curzon (1859–1925). His vision was to use these occasions to bolster the prestige, if not the actual power, of the Indian maharajas, who held about one-third of the country, and to reinforce traditional notions of deference and hierarchy.

The British administration created new systems of honorary ranks and revived older ones, all in the service of what some British jokingly called "Tory-entalism" because of Curzon's Conservative ("Tory") Party ties. By identifying British rule

Patterns Up Close | Military Transformations and the New Imperialism

French Defeat of the Mamluks at the Battle of the Pyramids, 1798. This painting shows the clear advantage of the military innovation of the line-drill. The orderly French forces on the right, commanded by officers on horseback, mow down the cavalry charges of the Mamluks.

As we have seen in earlier chapters, between 1450–1750 firearm-equipped infantries rose to prominence throughout Eurasia. Many rulers throughout Eurasia even reconstituted their states as *fiscal–military* polities in order to pay either mercenaries or standing infantries under their command, ready to march in short order. Recently, scholars have hotly debated the significance of the differences among the infantries and military organization more generally during this age of empire.

An answer to this question is important because historians believed for a long time that western Europeans had superior firearms, cannons, and cannon-equipped ships that enabled them to embark on overseas expansion, establish trade-fort mercantile empires, and eventually achieve imperial conquest and colonization of the Middle East, Africa, and southeast Asia. (The Americas were a different case since here the superiority of European arms is beyond doubt, even if their importance during the conquest is questionable.)

The debate is unresolved, although most scholars are now of the opinion that, beginning in the late seventeenth century, the flintlock muskets, bayonets, and line drill that distinguished western European infantries from other armies in Asia and Africa gave the Europeans an advantage. (*Line drill* was the Swedish-introduced innovation of training infantry soldiers stretched out in long lines five or six deep to fire, step back, allow the next line to fire, reload their muzzle-loaded flintlock muskets, and so on with the third to sixth lines.) These advantages were manifested in the Ottoman–Russian War of 1768–1774 and in Napoleon's invasion of Egypt in 1798.

In the early 1730s, the Ottomans realized that they could not match other powers with their matchlock muskets and that their infantry, the Janissaries, lacked sufficient discipline. Although their gunsmiths switched to flintlocks, the largely

Ethiopian Forces Defeating an Italian Army at Adowa, 1896. A hundred years after Napoleon's victory, the tables were turned when an Ethiopian army equipped with repeating rifles, machine guns, and cannon routed an Italian invasion force. In response to the defeat, the *Times* of London bemoaned that "the prestige of European arms as a whole is considerably impaired."

part-time and lowly paid Janissaries resisted all efforts at drills. Lack of finances caused these military reforms to grind to a halt. The Russian military, by contrast, learned much from the Seven Years' War (1756–1763), in which it was allied with Austria and France against Prussia and Great Britain. Its sizeable line infantries were of great importance during the war of 1768–1774 against the Ottomans. The victory was not easy, given the long supply lines south to the Black Sea and Danube. But in the end the sizeable Russian line infantry regiments prevailed over the uncoordinated and untrained Ottoman foot soldiers. Similarly, Napoleon successfully employed his small, highly mobile, and flexible units (composed of mixed infantry, cavalry, and artillery) in his victory against the lopsidedly cavalry-dominated Egyptian Mamluks in 1798.

The Mughals in India and the Qing in China did not have to worry about flintlock, bayonet, and line infantry attacks in the eighteenth century, either from their neighbors or from the far-away Europeans. Like the Ottomans, who continued to maintain large cavalry forces against their nomadic neighbors in the Middle East and central Asia, the Mughals and Qing privileged their cavalries and treated their ethnically indigenous and not very mobile firearm-equipped infantries as secondary. However, once British East India Company officers elevated indigenous infantry soldiers to the privileged ranks of the Sepoy regiments, as Karl Marx astutely observed, their discipline ultimately created such problems for the company that the British Crown had to take over the governance of India in 1858.

When European innovators introduced workable breech-loading rifles and artillery in the late 1850s, the technological balance shifted decisively toward Europe. The addition of rapid-firing mechanisms in the second half of the 1800s to these improved weapons further cemented Europe's technological superiority. They amplified western Europe's ability to subdue and colonize all but the largest states of the Middle East, Africa, and Asia by World War I. In addition to infantries, cavalries could be equipped with rapid-fire rifles and pistols, enabling detachments to land on Middle Eastern, African, and Asian coasts and quickly sweep through the interior. The French in particular made use of this improved cavalry capability in their conquests of Africa south of the Sahara.

Thus, in this shift from an initially slight to an eventually pronounced superiority of European arms during this period, the new imperialism and the Industrial Revolution were parallel developments engendered by the same modernity that also saw the rise of constitutional nationalism and the formation of a new type of polity, the nation-state. Certainly, industrially produced weapons in the later nineteenth century greatly enhanced Europe's ability to dominate much of the Middle East, Africa, and Asia. But modernity is a complex bundle of many different interacting elements. In short, there is—if you will excuse the pun—no "smoking gun."

Questions

- Examine the photo showing French forces defeating the Mamluk cavalry. Are the military advantages of the line drill evident? If so, what are they?

- Does the photo of Ethiopian forces defeating an Italian army in 1896 show that indigenous peoples could adapt Western innovations to their own purposes? If so, how?

Subaltern: A person or thing considered subordinate to another.

with India's historic past, it was hoped that the perception of strength and legitimacy would be enhanced. This effort to co-opt local rulers into upholding the British government as the historically destined status quo is sometimes called by historians a **subaltern** relationship. Yet, a small but growing elite of Western-educated, often accomplished, Indian leaders began to use the arguments of empire against their occupiers. By the 1920s many of these people would make up the burgeoning national movement associated with Gandhi's strategy of noncooperation and the Indian National Congress's outlines for government when Britain was finally forced to "quit India."

The British Settler Colonies of Australia and New Zealand

India was merely one area in Asia and the Pacific where the British advanced from exploration and trade forts to imperial expansion and colonial settlement. In the continent of Australia and on the islands of New Zealand they colonized indigenous forager and agrarian populations as well as—in contrast to India—encouraged large-scale immigration of European settlers.

White Settlement in Australia and New Zealand

Dutch navigators, blown off course on their way to Indonesia, initially discovered the western coast of Australia in 1606; but when profitable trade opportunities with the forager Aborigines (the name given to the indigenous Australians) failed to materialize, they did not pursue any further contacts. The British navigator James Cook (1728–1779), during one of his many exploratory journeys in the Pacific, landed in 1770 on the Australian east coast and claimed it for Great Britain. After the United States wrested its independence from Britain in 1783, the British government looked to Australia as a place where it could ship convicts. Between 1788 and 1840, some 50,000 British convicts were shipped to the penal colony.

The Making of Australia. British Army redcoats register convicts disembarking in Australia at Sydney Cove. As a result of poverty and crime accompanying the early industrialization in Britain, prisons were so overcrowded that the authorities sought relief by sending prisoners to penal colonies overseas. About 25 percent of the prisoners were Irish, mostly arrested on political charges.

Immigration by free British subjects, begun a decade before the end of convict shipments, led to a pastoral and agricultural boom. Settlers pioneered agriculture in south Australia where rainfall, fluctuating according to dry and wet *El Niño/La Niña* cycles, was relatively reliable and provided the population with most of its cereal needs. Sugar and rice cultivation, introduced to the tropical northeast in the 1860s, was performed with indentured labor recruited from Pacific islands. Even during penal colony times, sheep ranching in the east and the exportation of wool developed into an early thriving business, with half of the wool needed by the British textile industry being supplied from Australia. Even more important for the evolution of the Australian colony was the mining of gold and silver, beginning in the east in 1851 and continuing thereafter in nearly all parts of the continent. Although a colony, Australia was very similar to independent Latin America (see Chapter 27) in that it was a labor-poor but commodity-rich region, seeking its wealth through export-led growth (see Map 26.3).

Mining generated several gold rush immigration waves, not only from Britain but also from China, as well as internal migrations from mining towns to cities when the gold rushes ended. Cities like Sydney and Melbourne expanded continuously during the 1800s and encompassed more than two-thirds of the total white population of about 5 million by 1914. The indigenous population of Aborigines, who had inhabited the continent since 65,000 BCE, shrank during the same time from several hundred thousand to 67,000, mostly as a result of diseases but also after confrontations with

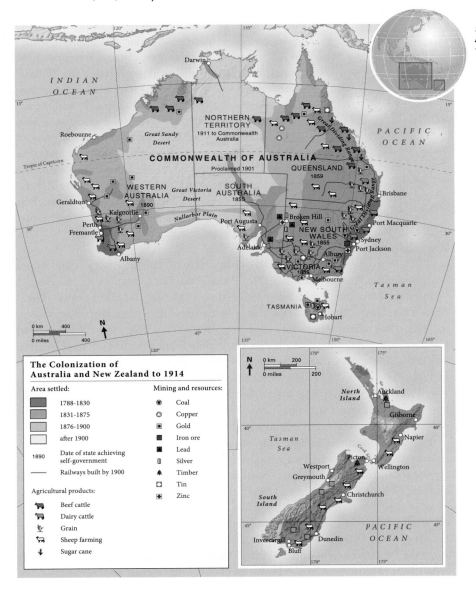

MAP **26.3** **The Colonization of Australia and New Zealand to 1914.**

The Colonization of
Australia and New Zealand to 1914

Area settled:

▓	1788-1830
▒	1831-1875
░	1876-1900
□	after 1900

1890   Date of state achieving
self-government

———   Railways built by 1900

Mining and resources:

◓	Coal
○	Copper
◙	Gold
■	Iron ore
■	Lead
▯	Silver
♣	Timber
▢	Tin
◈	Zinc

Agricultural products:

Beef cattle
Dairy cattle
Grain
Sheep farming
Sugar cane

GOVERNOR DAVEY'S
PROCLAMATION
TO THE ABORIGINES
1816

Racial Harmony in Australia.
The government's attempts to encourage cooperation between natives and settlers found little success, as shown in this 1816 oil painting. At top, whites and Aborigines, dressed in European clothing, mingle harmoniously. Harmony prevails in the second panel from the top, in which uniformed soldiers and a government official greet the Aborigines courteously. Things begin to deteriorate in the third panel, however, as an Aborigine spears a white man and is hung for his infraction. A cycle of violence takes over in the bottom panel as a white man shoots an Aborigine and is in turn hung by soldiers.

ranchers intruding on their hunting and gathering lands. As in North America, whites were relentless in taking an allegedly empty—or expected soon to be empty—continent into their possession.

The Long Boom   As it did in Latin America, a long boom favored Australia in the second half of the nineteenth century, up until the 1880s. A wet La Niña cycle, strong wool and gold exports, and the inflow of investments for the construction of railroads supported growth. An Australian-born generation of whites came into its own during this boom, which, on the one hand, was still strongly colonial in outlook, cherishing the metropolitan ties, but, on the other hand, was proud of its Australian pioneer differences. In early stirrings of Australian literature and art, these differences stood out. The writers of the weekly magazine the *Bulletin*, founded in 1880, discussed the harshness of farming in the bush and the virtues of republicanism; and the so-called Heidelberg painters (after their camp near Melbourne) in the 1880s developed their own version of impressionism, emphasizing shades of ochre and olive green. The legislative councils of the colonies became veritable battlegrounds between native white Australians and the colonial government over issues such as "free selection" (the Australian equivalent of homesteading), land-squatting, and tariffs.

The Difficult Turn of the Century   The boom years ended for Australia around 1890. During the last quarter of the nineteenth century, the economies of the three leading industrial countries of the world—Great Britain, the United States, and Germany—slowed, with first a financial depression in 1873–1879 and another more economy-wide one in 1890–1896. Australia had been able to ride out the first depression, mainly thanks to continuing gold finds. But in the 1890s, construction as well as banking collapsed and factories closed. Coincidentally, a dry El Niño cycle devastated free selection farming. Labor unrest followed: Although widespread strikes failed, the newly founded Labor Party (1891) immediately became a major political force. The country adopted labor reforms, an old-age pension, fiscal reforms, and a white-only immigration policy. The discovery of huge gold deposits in western Australia in 1892–1894 helped to redress the economy. In 1900, Australia finally adopted a federal constitution, which made the country the second fully autonomous "dominion," after Canada (1867) but before New Zealand (1907), Newfoundland (1907), South Africa (1910), and Ireland (1922).

New Zealand   Fourteen hundred miles southeast of Australia lies the archipelago of New Zealand. Both the north and south islands had been settled around 1200 CE by Polynesians called "Maori," farmers who brought along yams, sweet potatoes, and taro. Most of their settlements were on or close to the coasts on the northern island, where agriculture was most productive. After initial hostile and even bloody encounters between Maoris, numbering about 100,000, and Europeans, the British negotiated a controversial treaty in 1840, which entitled the Maoris to their land and status as British subjects. The governor, however, disregarded the treaty; and white settlements proceeded apace, with Maoris pushed off their land. In a series of clashes from 1860 to 1872, a number of Maori groups retaliated with violence, slowing down white settlement severely but also eventually ending Maori independence. Disease reduced Maori numbers to a low of 40,000 in the 1890s.

Large-scale immigration began only in 1870, and within a decade the white population doubled to 200,000. As in Australia, wheat farming made New Zealand self-sufficient and wool and gold sustained export-led growth. High-quality coal, mined from 1873, added to the exports. Refrigeration (introduced in 1882) initiated New Zealand's specialization in lamb meat and butter production for export. In the wake of rapid urbanization and the rise of a textile industry, far-reaching social legislation was set in motion, which culminated in 1893 with New Zealand becoming the first country in the world to grant voting rights to women. Thus, a small British settler colony far away from either Europe or the United States set the pace for women's emancipation at the end of the nineteenth century.

Maori Meeting House. Shown here is the entrance, made of carved wood, to the oldest tribal meeting house of the Maori, built in 1842. The chief carver, Raharuhi Rukupo, portrayed himself on the right. When the British colonial government proceeded with its land confiscations in 1860–1872, it transferred the house from the tribe to what is today the Museum of New Zealand. After lengthy litigations by the Maori, the government admitted in the 1990s to the illegality of the seizure.

European Imperialism in the Middle East and Africa

The British role in the Middle East during the eighteenth and early nineteenth centuries was much more modest, as was that of Europeans in general. Their function was limited to that of merchants, diplomats, or military advisors in an Ottoman Empire with a long tradition of conquering European lands. The situation changed at the end of the eighteenth century when Russia adopted a plan of southern expansion designed to drive the Ottomans back into Asia, take Istanbul, and convert it back into an eastern Christian capital. The other European powers sought to slow the Russian advances, with Great Britain assuming the lead role in protecting the Ottomans. In the long run, this policy of containment failed. Under Russian pressure, Ottoman territory shrank, the Europeans joined Russia in dismembering the Ottoman Empire, and a general imperialist competition for carving up other parts of the world—notably south and east Asia as well as Africa—ensued.

The Rising Appeal of Imperialism in the West

Empires (multiethnic, multi-linguistic, and multi-religious polities) were, as we have repeatedly seen in this book, of old lineage in world history. Their current embodiments were the Ottoman, Habsburg, and Russian Empires. The Russian Empire, a latecomer, saw its mission as replacing the Ottoman Empire as the dominant eastern

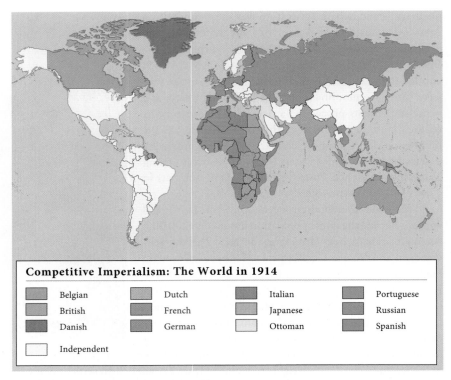

Competitive Imperialism: The World in 1914

▢	Belgian	▢	Dutch	▢	Italian	▢	Portuguese
▢	British	▢	French	▢	Japanese	▢	Russian
▢	Danish	▢	German	▢	Ottoman	▢	Spanish
▢	Independent						

MAP 26.4 **Competitive Imperialism: The World in 1914.**

European power and, by expanding eastward across the steppe, the leading Asian power. Its ambition became the catalyst for France, Great Britain, Belgium, Germany, and even late-industrializing Italy to embark on competitive imperialism in other parts of the world (see Map 26.4).

The Ottoman, Russian, and British Empires   After the failure in 1815 of Napoleon's imperial schemes in both Egypt and Europe, Great Britain was the undisputed leading empire in the world. No country had a navy that could rival it, British trade posts and colonies were widely distributed over the world, and British colonialism in India was geared toward growing and exporting Indian cotton to fuel British industrialization. On the European continent, Britain worked to restore the monarchies of France, Austria, Prussia, and Russia so that they would balance each other as "great powers" in a **Concert of Europe**. Under no circumstances would Britain tolerate any renewed European imperialism of the kind that Napoleon had pursued. Meeting more or less regularly in congresses, the great powers were actually remarkably successful at maintaining peace in Europe. For an entire century not a single war engulfed the continent as a whole, throwing Europe into turmoil as had happened during the Napoleonic era.

The Concert of Europe, however, was less successful with curbing the imperial ambitions of its members reaching for lands outside the western European core. Russia did not hide its goal of throwing the Ottoman Empire (admitted to the Concert

Concert of Europe: International political system that dominated Europe from 1815 to 1914 and which advocated a balance of power among states.

for better protection of its integrity in 1856) back into "Asia," that is, Asia Minor or Anatolia. Great Britain, although it made itself the protector of the integrity of the Ottoman Empire, could at best only slow the ambitions of Russia. The movement to secure the independence of Greece (1821–1832) is a good example of this pattern. Russia, as the Greeks' coreligionist and protector, was centrally involved in initiating a pattern of ethno-linguistic nationalism that replaced constitutional nationalism as the organizing ideology for many Europeans in the nineteenth century.

The French Conquest of Algeria   Britain, unable to prevent an early spark of renewed French imperialism, directed outside Europe against Ottoman Algiers. The French naval expedition—the circumstances of which were described at the beginning of this chapter—conveniently took place in 1830 while British attention was still focused on the negotiations for Greece's independence. In its North African expedition, France followed an earlier short-lived blueprint of Napoleon's, which envisaged the creation of a Mediterranean empire encompassing Algeria and/or Egypt, prior to his lightning imperialism in Europe, possibly to signal to Britain the ease of reaching India via the Mediterranean.

Algeria was the crucial first step of a European power toward seizing provinces of the Ottoman Empire in competition with the Russians, while officially protecting its integrity. This first step was still full of hesitations and counter maneuvers. At first, the French stayed on a small coastal strip around Algiers and other places, encouraging the rise of indigenous leaders to take over from the Ottoman corsairs and Janissaries and share the country with the French. The British discreetly supported Algerian leaders with weapons to be used against the French.

In the longer run, however, coexistence proved impossible and the French military—against strong Algerian resistance—undertook an all-out conquest. The civilian colonial administration after 1870 encouraged large-scale immigration of French and Spanish farmers, who settled on small plots, as well as French corporate investments in vineyards and citrus plantations on the coast. The indigenous population of Arabs and Berbers, decimated by cholera epidemics in the 1860s, found itself largely reduced to less fertile lands in the interior.

The Conquest of Algiers. Algiers fell to France in 1830, a development driven in part by the efforts of King Charles X (1824–1830) to salvage his regime. Charles, a younger brother of Louis XVI (executed in the French Revolution), had sought a restoration of absolutist rule. Although Napoleon had fleetingly thought of conquering Algeria, Charles had no plans beyond the defeat of the Algerian dey. In spite of the French victory, republican revolutionaries overthrew Charles and established the constitutional monarchy of Louis-Philippe (r. 1830–1848).

The Great Game:
Competition between
Great Britain and Russia
for conquest or control of
Asian countries north of
India and south of Russia,
principally Afghanistan.

Britain's Containment Policy   Great Britain adhered longer to the policy of protecting what remained of the Ottoman Empire. It also opposed Russia in its own backyard of central Asia, inaugurating what was called the **Great Game** against Russia in Asia with the first Anglo–Afghan war in 1838. Although Great Britain failed to occupy Afghanistan and make it an advance protectorate against the approaching Russians, it eventually succeeded in turning Afghanistan into a buffer state, keeping Russia one country away from India. A little later, in 1853–1856, Britain and France teamed up in the Crimean War to stop Russia from renewing its drive for Istanbul. This defeat, demonstrating the superiority of industrially produced new rifles and breech-loading artillery, chastened Russia for the next two decades.

In the second half of the nineteenth century, however, the ethnic–nationalist unification of Germany in 1870–1871, engineered by Prussia through a successful war against France (the Franco–Prussian War), destroyed the balance of the European Concert. Germany, much larger than Prussia and strengthened further through the annexation of the French industrializing region of Alsace-Lorraine, was now the dominant power in western Europe. Russia promptly exploited the new imbalance in Europe during anti-Ottoman uprisings in the Balkans in 1876. Leaving the humiliation of the Crimean War behind, Russian troops broke through Ottoman lines of defense and marched within a few miles of Istanbul. However, Great Britain, although no longer the arbiter of the European Concert, still had enough clout to force Russia into retreating.

British Imperialism in Egypt and Sudan   To prevent a repeat of the Russian invasion, Britain and the Ottomans agreed in 1878 to turn the island of Cyprus (off the Syrian coast) over to the British as a protectorate. This protectorate would have British advisors and troops, ready to defend Istanbul against a renewed Russian invasion. Thus, in the name of curbing Russian imperialism, Great Britain became an imperial power itself in the Mediterranean.

Events after the occupation of Cyprus, however, followed a dramatically different course. Instead of watching Russia, the commanders of the British navy squadron in Cyprus had to turn their attention to Egypt. This province was the wealthiest part of the Ottoman Empire. It was governed by a dynasty of autonomous rulers, beginning with Muhammad Ali (r. 1805–1848), an Albanian officer in the Ottoman army who assumed political control after Napoleon's troops had evacuated Egypt. An energetic statesman, Muhammad Ali reorganized the Nile-irrigated agricultural lands into large estates, producing Egyptian-bred long-staple cotton, and created his own independent army of conscripted Egyptians. Efforts to create a textile industry failed because he was unable (as an Ottoman governor) to establish high tariff barriers against British imports. Similarly, efforts to use his new army for a conquest of Istanbul and take over the Ottoman Empire were thwarted by a Great Britain anxious to protect the sultans. Even in failure, however, Muhammad Ali had a huge impact on Egypt. In a major cultural renewal, similar to the Tanzimat constitutional reforms in Istanbul, Cairo and Alexandria became centers of adaptation to European arts and letters as well as a reformed Islam.

Muhammad Ali's successors were less able rulers who incurred considerable debts, in part for the French-led construction of the Suez Canal in 1869. Britain took over a large part of the canal shares from the debt-ridden Egyptian ruler in 1857. A year later, Britain and France imposed a joint debt commission that garnished a portion of Egyptian tax revenue. Opposition in Egypt to this foreign interference grew in the following years, both inside and outside the Egyptian government. It culminated in 1881 with a revolt in the Egyptian army, endangering the continuation of the debt repayments.

British-initiated negotiations between the Ottoman sultan and the leader of the army revolt, Col. Ahmad Urabi (1841–1911, an early Egyptian—as opposed to foreign-descended—officer), over the issue of the debt collapsed after riots in Alexandria and a careless British bombardment of the port in response to Egyptian fortification efforts. Interventionists in London, fearing for their bonds and eager for more cotton imports from Egypt for the British textile industry, gained the upper hand. Overcoming the fiercely resisting Egyptian army, a British expeditionary force occupied Egypt in 1882.

The Ottoman sultan acquiesced to the occupation because the appointment of a British-appointed high commissioner, charged with the reorganization of the Egyptian finances, was announced to be only temporary. Costly campaigns by British-led Egyptian troops in Sudan during 1883–1885, however, derailed any early departure plans. Egypt had occupied Sudan in the 1820s and, as in Egypt, had made cotton a major export crop for the British textile industry. Sudanese resentment over the occupation and anxiety over the accompanying social changes became focused when Britain occupied Egypt and were expressed in a religiously inspired uprising in Khartoum in 1883.

> ### Strengthening the Empire
>
> "I have always, and do now recommend it [the purchase of the Suez Canal shares] to the country as a political transaction, and one which I believe is calculated to strengthen the Empire. That is the spirit in which it has been accepted by the country, which understands it though the two right honourable critics may not."
>
> —Benjamin Disraeli, Prime Minister of Britain (in office 1874–1880) addressing Parliament. In *The Nation. A Weekly Journal Devoted to Politics, Literature, Science and the Arts*, 22 (1876), p. 193.

Scottish Troops at the Sphinx, 1882. The British occupied Egypt as a means to secure the Suez Canal and guarantee the repayment of Egyptian debts. Subsequent negotiations with the Ottoman sultan for the status of Egypt failed, and the province became an unofficial protectorate of Britain. Although granted internal independence in 1922, Egypt remained in a semi-colonial relationship with Britain until 1956.

The leader of the uprising was Muhammad Ahmad Ibn Abdallah (1844–1885), head of an Islamic Sufi brotherhood and self-styled Mahdi ("rightly guided" or "Messiah"), sent to establish a realm of justice. After the Mahdi succeeded in driving the British–Egyptian forces from Sudan and establishing an independent state, he was left alone for the next decade.

Until the British slaughtered his forces at the Battle of Omdurman in 1898, Egypt's finances, aggravated by problems in Sudan, were sufficiently in disarray to keep the British focused on Egypt. On the one hand, the British wanted to put the Egyptian finances on a sound footing again, but, on the other hand, they wanted out so as to not be responsible for the country's governance. They had no plans yet for a full-fledged Mediterranean imperialism. As a compromise, they conceived of a conditional departure, with the right of return at times of internal unrest or external danger. The Ottoman sultan, however, refused to sign this compromise. He was grateful to Britain for recognizing Ottoman sovereignty but sought to avoid the responsibility of governance. A veritable dance around the question of governance developed. The two sides exchanged notes concerning the issue no fewer than 66 times, with neither side budging. In the end, Britain stayed for almost three-quarters of a century, running Egypt as an undeclared colony for the first 40 years. Without a clear plan, Britain had nonetheless transplanted the pattern of imperialism–colonialism it had first experimented with in India.

France's Tunisian Protectorate   The quid pro quo for Britain's acquisition of Cyprus in 1878 was for France to gain title to Tunisia. Similar to Algeria and Egypt, Tunisia was an autonomous Ottoman province, ruled by its own dynasty of *beys*. The dynasty had been founded by a Janissary officer in 1705 when the military ruling class began to shift from corsair raids against Christian shipping to the fiscal exploitation of the villages and nomadic tribes of the interior. Fertile northern Tunisia provided limited but fairly reliable tax revenues from olive oil, barley, wheat, fruits, and nuts. Annual tax expeditions to the south among the semi-nomadic sheep and camel tribes usually yielded few taxes and served mostly to demonstrate the dynasty's sovereignty.

The beys responded to the Western challenge early, being the first in the Muslim Middle East and North Africa to modernize their military and adopt a constitution (1857). With their more limited revenues, they hit the debt ceiling already in 1869, much earlier than the Ottomans and Egyptians, and had to accept a British–French–Italian debt commission for the reorganization of the country's revenues. When the French took over in 1881, they began with the same thankless task of balancing the budget as the British had in Egypt. Only later did they benefit from the French and Italian settlers they called in to the protectorate to intensify agriculture.

The Scramble for Africa

Competitive European imperialism exploded beyond the Mediterranean in early 1884 as Germany claimed its first protectorates in Africa. Conveniently, after having secured lands for his country, the German chancellor Otto von Bismarck (in various offices 1862–1890) called a conference in Berlin, which met from late 1884 to early 1885. The main agenda of the Berlin conference was a discussion on how the 14 invited European countries and the United States should "define the conditions under which future territorial annexations in Africa might be recognized." Bismarck's proposal of the main condition was "effective occupation," with the creation of "spheres of influence" around the occupied places. The first "protectorates," confirmed at the conference, were Cameroon in west central Africa for Germany and Congo as a private possession of King Leopold II of Belgium. The **scramble for Africa** was on (see Map 26.5).

Explorers, Missionaries, and the Civilizing Mission
Sub-Saharan Africa was still little known in Europe and poorly misunderstood to most Europeans in 1880. The Enlightenment had instilled curiosity about the geography, flora, fauna, and ethnology of Africa among the European reading public. But to endure the hardships of traveling in the savanna, rain forest, and desert required strong commitment. David

Scramble for Africa: Competition among European powers from 1884 to 1912 to acquire African colonies.

MAP **26.5** The Scramble for Africa.

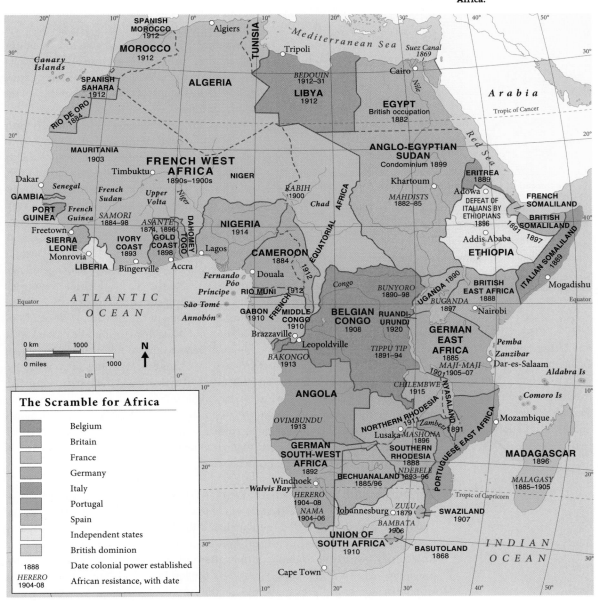

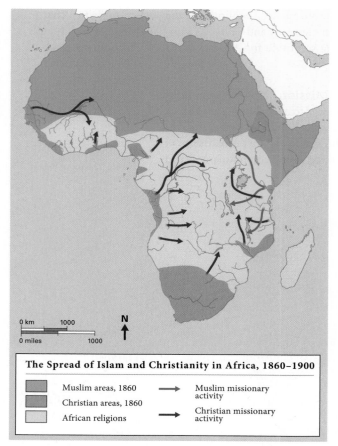

The Spread of Islam and Christianity in Africa, 1860–1900

■	Muslim areas, 1860	→	Muslim missionary activity
■	Christian areas, 1860		
■	African religions	→	Christian missionary activity

MAP 26.6 **The Spread of Islam and Christianity in Africa, 1860–1900.**

Civilizing mission:
Belief that European colonizers had a duty to extend the benefits of European civilization to "backward" peoples.

Livingstone (1813–1873), a tireless missionary and passionate opponent of slavery, was the best known among the pioneers who explored much of south central Africa. The European middle class was fascinated with the early explorers' tales of exotic and mysterious lands and peoples.

The generation of explorers after Livingstone was better equipped, led larger expeditions, and composed more precise accounts. Here, the outstanding figure was Henry Morton Stanley (1841–1904), a Welsh journalist who worked in the United States and became famous for his encounter with Livingstone ("Dr. Livingstone, I presume?") at Lake Tanganyika in east central Africa. Still, in spite of extensive explorations, European politicians at the end of the century had only the vaguest idea of the geography of the "dark continent."

Christian missionaries contributed little to the knowledge of Africa but through their preaching shaped a sense of both responsibility for and superiority to the Africans in the European public. They were at the forefront of the **civilizing mission**, the belief prevalent in the West in the nineteenth century that colonists had a duty to extend the benefits of civilization, that is, European civilization, to the "backward" people they ruled. In the earlier 1800s, the danger of malaria and yellow fever still confined missionaries to the coasts of Africa. Supported by missionary societies in Europe, they trained indigenous missionaries to translate tracts and scriptures for the conversion of Africans in the interior. When quinine (made from the bark of a Brazilian tree) became available in the middle of the 1800s, allowing for treatment of malaria, missionaries were able to follow their indigenous colleagues into the interior (see Map 26.6). At that time, tensions often arose between the two groups. African converts preached the gospel in the spirit of Christian equality, as did the former slave and later Anglican bishop Samuel Adjai Crowther (ca. 1809–1891); but many Western missionaries considered African Christianity to be contaminated by animist "superstitions" and did not accept Africans as equal. Malaria was one infectious disease that could be overcome, but the rising racism of the Victorian period went largely unchecked.

Conquest and Resistance in West Africa   Colonialism on the coast of West Africa after 1885 was an outgrowth of the traditional trade-fort system. By the 1800s, the British had ousted the Dutch and the French from most of the trading forts and had become the dominant European presence in the region. Ghana is a particularly instructive example of the pattern of conquest and resistance. Ghana, previously known as the Gold Coast, was the land of the Ashante kingdom. The Ashante had emerged back in the time of the empire of Songhay, when they mined the gold of the Alkan fields that caravans carried across the Sahara. When gold declined in importance, the kingdom turned to the Atlantic slave trade and benefited handsomely from it. After the 1807 British prohibition of slavery, Ashante merchants switched to commodities, especially palm oil, used for the greasing of machinery and for making soap, that were in great demand in industrializing Europe.

But the Ashante and British traders were in constant conflict over the terms of trade in the forts. Disciplined and well-armed Ashante troops defeated the British repeatedly. Only in 1896, when the British sent regular troops with breech-loader rifles and machine guns to put down the Ashante with their now antiquated muskets, was Ghana finally turned into a protectorate. Later on, after well over a half-century of colonialism, the memory of Ashante nineteenth-century prowess was an important factor in the Ghanaian struggle for independence.

France lost its West African trade forts after the Seven Years' War (1756–1763) to Britain but later received one of them back, a fortified island at the mouth of the River Senegal. It was from this base that career-hungry French officers after 1850 carried out expeditions into the interior of the river rain forest, for alliances and trade purposes. In 1857 they came into conflict with Al-Hajj Umar (ca. 1791–1864), an Islamic reformer in the interior savanna who was in the process of building a state in what are today Guinea, Senegal, and Mali. The French barely survived a siege in a border fort and for decades were in no state to advance any further. Once the scramble was on, however, the West African Islamic state was doomed. In 1891, in the teeth of stiff resistance from the Islamists, the French began to carve out their huge colony in the steppe and savanna of West Africa that formed the core of their colonial empire.

Al-Hajj Umar was one of several West African Muslim religious scholars who became holy warriors (jihadists). Like other Middle Eastern and North African reformers, Umar was dismayed by the decline of Ottoman power. The reformers sought to rejuvenate Islam through a return to the study of the original Islamic sources. In the footsteps of what they perceived as the Prophet Muhammad's original state in Mecca, rising among the defeated unbelievers, the West African reformers forcibly converted black animists to Islam. In contrast to the Islamic kings and emperors of the previous centuries who made no efforts to convert their subjects, the jihadists of the 1800s succeeded in making Islam the dominant religion of West Africa.

A Slave Who Became Bishop. The remarkable life of Samuel Adjai Crowther (ca. 1809–1891) shows that Africans and Asians also participated in the "civilizing mission." Born in Yorubaland in present-day West Africa, Crowther was enslaved as a young man but was rescued by the British navy and freed in 1821. He then converted to Christianity, and after training in London he was ordained an Anglican priest in 1841. He was appointed the first African Anglican bishop in 1864 and went on to produce Yoruba translations of the Bible and the Book of Common Prayer.

Conquest and Resistance in East Africa

The arrival of colonialism in East Africa differed from the pattern in West Africa. Here, as early as the sixteenth century, the Portuguese had established trade forts in the south to acquire gold and ivory for their spice purchases in India. When Swahili patricians in the city-states

Ivory Merchants. Besides slaves, Zanzibar imported elephant tusks from the interior to be marketed for the carving of ivory jewelry and art objects. Principal buyers of the tusks were British, German, and Arab traders.

farther north resisted this intrusion into their traditional Indian Ocean trade, the Portuguese responded with piracy and the construction of coastal forts in their midst. But the arrival of the Dutch with more powerful and numerous ships in the 1630s to take over the spice trade forced the Portuguese to curtail their East African engagement. An Omani Arab expeditionary force exploited the reduced Portuguese presence in 1698 by conquering the Swahili city-state of Mombasa after a 2-year siege. Oman had long-standing trade relations with East Africa and seized its opportunity to expand its limited domestic agricultural base on the Arabian peninsula. Once in control, the Omanis developed a flourishing plantation system for sugar, rice, grain, and cotton on the coastal islands, along with slaves imported from the African interior. In the 1820s, the Omanis—by now under their separate sultan residing on the island of Zanzibar—began to specialize in cloves, becoming the main exporters of this precious spice on the world market. Thanks to the Omanis, the Swahili coast was prosperous again.

Zanzibar was the staging ground for adventurers, explorers, and missionaries in the nineteenth century to enter the African interior. It was here that they vied for places to occupy and spheres of influence to declare. Accordingly, in 1886 Germany received the lion's share on the coast and in the interior, Belgium gave up its claims in return for being recognized in the Congo, and Zanzibar somewhat later became a British protectorate. In its colony of Tanganyika (in current Tanzania), Germany used forced labor for the growing of cotton, provoking the fierce but in the end brutally suppressed Maji Maji rebellion of 1905–1907.

Atrocities and Genocides   Similar atrocities stalked the European civilizing mission. As Germany was quelling rebellion in Tanganyika, it led a ferocious campaign on the other side of the continent against the Herero and Nama people of southwest Africa (modern Namibia). In their determination to establish colonial rule in the region, the German general staff ordered the extermination of the Herero in terms that can be described only as genocide: "I believe that the nation as such must be destroyed," commented General Lothar von Trotha (1848–1920 [TROW-tah]). From 1904 to 1908 the war on the Herero resulted in 80,000 deaths. North of Namibia, King Leopold II (r. 1865–1909) of Belgium turned his personal colony of the Congo into a vast forced-labor camp for the production of rubber. The rubber tree, native to South America, gained great importance in Europe for a variety of industrial applications. Leopold was particularly sadistic in his exploitation of the native workforce, using beatings and mutilations if collection quotas were not filled. An astonishing 3,000,000 Congolese were either killed or starved to death. The horror of the Belgian Congo was the setting for Joseph Conrad's *Heart of Darkness* (1902), perhaps the most powerful anti-imperialist novel of the time and still widely read today. It was also the catalyst for Mark Twain's virulently satirical attack on the Belgian exploitation of the Congolese, *King Leopold's Soliloquy* (1905).

Colonial Atrocities. The German garrison at Windhoek, in present-day Namibia, was besieged by the native Herero people in 1904. Retaliation was swift and violent, with the colonial authorities encaging prisoners in concentration camps, which in turn led to reprisals, such as the massacre of railroad workers shown here.

The scramble finally ended in 1912 with the French declaration of a protectorate over Morocco. By this time, the political competition in Europe had narrowed to the struggle between Germany and Great Britain for political predominance in western Europe. Italy's imperialist dreams were stymied by its crushing defeat at the battle of Adowa in 1896, in which one-third of its army was killed by Ethiopian forces (see Patterns Up Close). Ethiopia emerged from the scramble as the only non-colonized state in Africa. French and British rivalry in Africa, which had cropped up during the scramble and had even led to a confrontation at Fashoda over the control of Sudan in 1898, ended between 1905 and 1911, when Britain allied with France to counter-balance Germany. As a result of this alliance, Britain recognized France's interests in Morocco, adjacent to the two French territories of Algeria and Tunisia, over protests by Germany.

Western Imperialism and Colonialism in Southeast Asia

Parallel to developments in Africa, the new imperialism made its appearance also in southeast Asia, specifically Indonesia, the Philippines, Vietnam, Cambodia, and Laos. While the new imperialism in southeast Asia was an outgrowth of the earlier trade-fort presence of Portugal, Spain, and the Netherlands, it also included the return of France to imperial glory.

The Dutch in Indonesia

The Dutch were heirs of the Portuguese, who had set up forts that traded for spices in Indonesia during the sixteenth century. For 100 years, they were the middlemen for the distribution of spices from Portugal to northern Europe. But after liberating themselves from Habsburg–Spanish rule, the Netherlands displaced Portugal from its dominant position as a spice importer to Europe. From 1650 to 1750, the Netherlands was the leading naval power in the world. After 1750, they shifted from the trade of spices in their trade forts in Indonesia to the planting of cash crops, such as sugar, cacao, coffee, and tobacco—the mild warm weather commodities to which Europeans were addicted and which they consumed in ever larger quantities. The aim of the full colonization of Indonesia during the nineteenth century was to profit from European industrial demand for agricultural and mineral commodities.

Early Indonesia   The western part of southeast Asia, comprising today's Indonesia, is a complex of well over 17,000 islands, fewer than half of which are inhabited. The term "Indonesia" dates to the eighteenth century, denoting sparsely inhabited large and small tropical islands to the southeast of India. The five largest and today most densely populated islands are, from west to east, Sumatra, Java, Borneo, Sulawesi (Celebes), and New Guinea. The earliest inhabitants were prehistoric foragers; the first agrarian–urban settlers were speakers of Austronesian languages. The Austronesians were intrepid sailors across the Pacific and Indian Oceans who settled islands as far away as Hawaii off the Americas and Madagascar off of Africa.

In Sumatra and the Malay Peninsula, chieftainships gave way to a first kingdom around 700 CE, organized around Buddhist religion and law. The kingdom was mostly coastal and commercial, trading pepper, nutmeg, cinnamon, cardamom, cloves, ivory, gold, and tin to the Middle East and China. In the following centuries, it extended its influence to islands as far as the Philippines in the east and the mainland in the north.

Islam gained converts in Indonesia only slowly in the face of stiff Buddhist opposition, but from about 1300, indigenous Indonesian rulers began to convert to Islam. The leading Islamic sultanate was Aceh [AT-shay] (1496–1903) on the western island of Sumatra, a major producer of pepper. In the sixteenth century, when the Portuguese rose to dominance in the Indian Ocean, the Ottomans supported it with firearms.

Portuguese and Dutch Trade Forts   Portuguese sailors arrived in the strategic Strait of Malacca (separating Sumatra from the Malay Peninsula and dividing the Indian Ocean from the Chinese Sea) in 1511, defeating the local sultanate and establishing a fort in the Malaysian capital, Malacca. Their main interest, however, given the power of Aceh on Sumatra, was to push onward to the spice islands of Maluku (today the Maluccas) in eastern Indonesia (between Sulawesi and New Guinea), where they established a trade fort in 1522, amid several Islamic island lords. From there, the Portuguese pushed on to China and Japan, where they arrived in the mid-1500s. Overall, their role in the Indonesian spice trade remained small, and indigenous Islamic merchants maintained their dominance.

After declaring their independence from Spain in 1581, the northern provinces of the Netherlands formed the Republic of the United Netherlands and pushed for their own overseas network of trade forts. In 1602, the Dutch government chartered the Dutch United East India Company (VOC), which spearheaded the expansion of Dutch possessions in India and southeast Asia. After a slow start, the company erected outposts on many Indonesian islands and in the mid-1600s founded Batavia (today Jakarta) on the island of Java as its main southeast Asian center. The VOC was by far the largest and wealthiest commercial company in the world during the seventeenth century, with a fleet consisting of nearly 5,000 merchant ships supported by large naval and land forces.

When the Dutch *stadhouder* (ruler) of the Netherlands, William of Orange (1650–1702), became king of England after the English Glorious Revolution of 1688 that imposed constitutional limits on monarchical rule, the Dutch and English overseas trade interests were pooled. Great Britain (as the country was known after

England's union with Scotland in 1707) deepened its Indian interests through the English East India Company, and the Dutch pursued their engagements in Indonesia. Like the British Company in India, the VOC was increasingly drawn during the early 1700s into dynastic wars. Supported by some 1,000 Dutch soldiers and 3,000 indigenous auxiliaries, the VOC established peace in 1755 in the fragmenting Islamic sultanate of Banten (1527–1808). Thereafter, it became the de facto government on the island of Java over a set of pacified Islamic protectorates.

Several decades earlier than its British counterpart in India, the VOC fell on hard times. Governing and maintaining troops was expensive. VOC employees often paid their expenses out of their own pockets since contact with the Netherlands in pretelegraph times was slow and sporadic. In the late eighteenth century, trade shifted from spices to bulk commodities, such as sugar, cacao, coffee, tobacco, indigo, and cotton. The inability of the VOC to shift from spices to commodities, requiring investments in plantations and accompanying transportation infrastructures, was the decisive factor which led, in 1799, to the liquidation of the VOC. Similar to the British experience in India, the government of the Netherlands then became the ruler of Indonesian possessions that had grown from trade forts into small colonies, surrounded by dependent indigenous principalities as well as independent sultanates.

Dutch Colonialism   The Dutch government took the decisive step toward investments in 1830 when Belgium separated from the large Dutch kingdom created after the Napoleonic Wars to form an independent Catholic monarchy. Faced with severe budgetary constraints and cut off from industrializing Belgium, the Dutch government adopted the **cultivation system** in Indonesia. According to this system, indigenous Indonesian subsistence farmers were forced into compulsory planting and labor schemes which required them to either grow government crops on

Cultivation system: Dutch colonial scheme of compulsory labor and plantation of crops imposed on indigenous Indonesian self-sufficiency farmers.

Indonesia in the Nineteenth Century. A traditional house in north Sumatra, with animal stables in the bottom and human living quarters on top. (*a*) Dutch judges meting out harsh sentences, including death by hanging, against Indonesians. (*b*) Workers in Batavia (today Jakarta), ca. 1830, stacking tropical wood for export in the harbor. (*c*)

20 percent of their land or work for 60 days on Dutch plantations. Overnight, the Dutch and collaborating Indonesian ruling classes turned into landowners. They reaped huge profits while Indonesian subsistence farmers, having to replace many of their rice paddies with commercial crops, suffered in many places from famines. In the course of the nineteenth century, Indonesia became a major or even the largest exporter of sugar, tea, coffee, palm oil, coconut products, tropical hardwoods, rubber, quinine, and pepper to the industrial nations.

To keep pace with demand, the Dutch pursued a program of systematic conquest and colonization. In a half-dozen campaigns, they conquered the Indonesian archipelago, finally subduing the most stubborn opponents, the Muslim guerillas of Aceh, in 1903 (see Map 26.7). Even then, the conquest was incomplete and inland rain forests remained outside Dutch government control. Conquered lands were turned over to private investors who established plantations. To deflect criticism at home and abroad, the Dutch government also introduced some reform measures. In 1870 they liberated farmers from the compulsory planting of government crops, and in 1901 they issued an "ethical policy," announcing measures such as land distribution, irrigation, and education. Severe underfunding, however, kept these measures largely on paper; and it was clear that the profits from colonialism were more important than investment for indigenous people.

Spain in the Philippines

Adjacent to the Indonesian islands in the northeast were the Philippines. Here, the Spanish had built their first trade fort of Manila shortly after conquering Mexico from the Aztecs. Manila served as a port from which to trade with China. Using

MAP **26.7** **Western Imperialism in Southeast Asia, 1870–1914.**

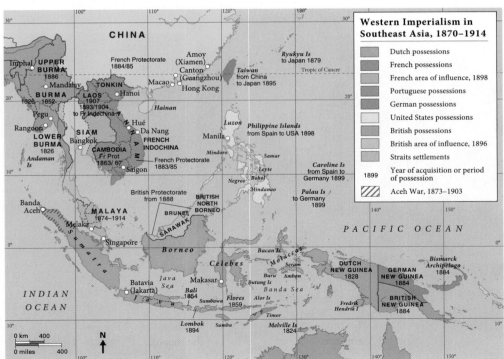

Mexican silver, Spanish merchants bought Chinese luxury manufactures. Manila expanded only slowly, suffering from constant raids by indigenous highlanders from the interior, Islamic rulers from the southern islands, and Dutch interlopers. Imperial conquest had to await the later eighteenth century, and colonization followed in the middle of the nineteenth century with the introduction of sugarcane.

Galleons and Trade with China   Spain expanded early on from the Americas farther west in order to prevent Portugal from claiming all the lucrative spice islands of Indonesia. A Portuguese explorer in Spanish service, Ferdinand Magellan (d. ca. 1480–1521), successfully crossed the sea channels at the southern tip of South America in 1520 and, on a journey that took his fleet eventually around the entire globe, discovered what later became known as the "Philippines," in honor of King Phillip II of Spain. It took another half-century, however, before Spain could spare ships and men for the implantation of a first trade fort and small colony. This fort, Manila, became the base for subsequent biannual silver fleets from Mexico. Spanish merchants based in Mexico, from where Manila was administered, benefited greatly from the trade of silver for Chinese silk, porcelain, and lacquerware. Thus, Manila began as a small sub-colony of the large Spanish colony of Mexico or New Spain.

The Philippines are a collection of some 7,000 islands, with the four largest, from north to south, being Luzon, Visaya, Mindanao, and Sulu. The earliest inhabitants were prehistoric islanders, followed ca. 2000 BCE by Austronesians who settled mostly on the coasts, growing rice and exploiting maritime resources. Similar to the inhabitants of the Indonesian islands, the Filipinos were animists influenced to varying degrees by Indian and Chinese cultures. As the Spanish gradually expanded their hold on the coastal lowlands outside Manila on Luzon and Visaya (where the local king had converted to Christianity), they established estates, thus advancing from trade-fort imperialism to the beginnings of territorial expansion.

Incipient Colonialism   The indigenous farmers on the Philippine estates were obliged to deliver rents, paid in kind, in the form of rice and animals, to ensure the food supply for some 30,000 inhabitants of Manila, mostly merchants of Spanish, Chinese, and Japanese origin. Warrior chieftains outside Spanish lands who converted were confirmed as owners on their lands and transformed themselves into a Hispanicized landowner class. By the early eighteenth century, the Spanish controlled enough of a critical mass on the two islands of Luzon and Visaya that they were able to establish a regular administration for fiscal and juridical matters. The beginnings of colonialism in the Philippines had emerged.

The balance sheet for the colonial administration was always in the red, however, since the fiscal revenue did not yield surpluses and villagers produced only small quantities of exportable ginger, cinnamon, and gold. Much money had to be invested in defending the Spanish-controlled territory from attacks by independent Filipinos in the mountainous upland interiors of Luzon and Visaya who resisted conquest and conversion. Even more vexing were raids supported by Islamic sultanates which had formed in the south on the basis of trading hardwoods for luxuries with China.

To make matters worse, a brief British occupation of Manila during the Seven Years' War (1756–1763) demonstrated that Spain lacked the means to protect itself against the rising naval and merchant power of Great Britain in the China trade.

On Filipino Ethnic Nationalism

"Does your Excellency know the spirit of (my) country? If you did, you would not say that I am 'a spirit twisted by a German education,' for the spirit that animates me I already had since childhood, before I learned a word of German. My spirit is 'twisted' because I have been reared among injustices and abuses which I saw everywhere, because since a child I have seen many suffer stupidly and because I also have suffered. . . . And 'twisted' like my spirit is that of hundreds of thousands of Filipinos who have not yet left their miserable homes, who speak no other language except their own, and who, if they could write or express their thoughts, would make my *Noli me tangere* [one of Rizal's novels] very tiny indeed, and with their volumes there would be enough to build pyramids for the corpses of all the tyrants . . ."

—José Rizal. *La Solidaridad*, a newsletter published by the Propaganda Movement, February 15, 1890. In Diosdado G. Capino, Minerva A. Gonzalez, and Filipinas A. Piñeda, *Rizal's Life, Works and Writings: Their Impact on Our National Identity*, p. 104. Quezon City, Philippines: Publisher's Association of the Philippines, 1977.

Using Indian cottons and Chinese middlemen, the British diverted much of the American silver trade to India, calling into question the entire rationale for Spanish trade-fort commerce and limited colonialism in the Philippines. The last galleon bringing silver from Mexico sailed in 1815.

Full Colonialism   Major reforms, shifting the economy from silver to commodity exports, began at the same time, motivated by the Spanish loss of Mexico to independence. These reforms resulted in the liberalization of trade and the beginnings of commercial agriculture for export. Ports were opened to ships from all countries, discrimination against Chinese settlements ended, and Spanish administrators and churchmen lost their trade privileges. Foreign entrepreneurs cleared rain forests and exported hardwoods. On the new land they grew cash crops, such as sugar, tobacco, hemp (for ropes and sacks), indigo (as a dye), coffee, and cotton. Large-scale rice farms replaced a great number of small-scale village self-sufficiency plots, and thus, commercialization even invaded subsistence agriculture.

Strong resistance by landowners against a reform of the land regime and tax system until the very end of the nineteenth century, however, assured that Spain did not benefit much from the liberalization of trade. Additionally, Philippine society stratified rapidly into a wealthy minority and a large mass of landless rural workers and urban day laborers. Manila had over 100,000 inhabitants in the early nineteenth century. This stratification, however, was very different from that in the Americas. There was no real Creole class, that is, a Spanish–Philippine upper stratum of landowners and urban people. Although the French Revolution and subsequent Napoleonic upheavals in Spain had their impact on the islands, agitation for independence and constitutionalism was largely limited to urban intellectuals. The Philippines remained a colony, producing no revenue and still demanding costly administrative—especially fiscal—reforms and infrastructural investments, both of which Spain was unable to afford.

The first stirrings of Filipino nationalism, primarily among Hispanicized Filipinos of mixed Spanish and indigenous or Chinese descent, made themselves felt in the second half of the nineteenth century. The principal spokesman was José Rizal (1861–1896), whose subversive novels were a response to the Spanish justification of continued colonialism.

Colonial authorities promptly arrested Rizal for his activities, banishing him to Hong Kong; but he returned to Manila in 1892, inspiring both overt and underground resistance groups. One of these groups, Katipunan, operated in secret, advocating Filipino independence through armed struggle. In 1896 the government discovered the existence of the organization in Manila and executed hundreds of revolutionaries, including Rizal, before firing squads. But it was unable to destroy Katipunan in the provinces, and the two sides agreed in 1897 to a truce which included the end of armed revolt in return for exile of the leadership in Hong Kong.

Philippine–American War Although it appeared that the colonial government was successful in suppressing the Filipino revolt for independence, events took a dramatic turn when the Spanish–American War broke out in 1898. A mysterious explosion of an American warship in Cuba—newly autonomous under Spanish suzerainty—had led to mutual declarations of war. The two sides fought their first battle in Manila Bay, where the United States routed a Spanish squadron. An American ship fetched the exiled Filipino rebel Emilio Aguinaldo (1869–1964) from Hong Kong, and he quickly defeated the Spanish and declared independence. Over four centuries of Spanish colonialism in the Pacific had come to an end.

American Soldiers in the Philippines. The victory of the United States over Spain in 1898 and its decision to annex the Philippines created for the first time an American overseas empire. Resistance was immediate, and a brutal war against Philippine fighters lasted from 1902 until 1913, with isolated outbreaks continuing until Philippine independence in 1946. Here, American troops dig in and fortify an outpost in Luzon.

After 4 months of fighting, Spain was defeated not only in Cuba, Puerto Rico, and Guam but also in the Philippines. The United States and Spain made peace at the end of 1898, ignoring the independent Philippine government in their agreement. Accordingly, US forces took possession of Manila in 1899 and within a year defeated the troops of the protesting Filipino government under the elected president, Emilio Aguinaldo. The Filipinos shifted to guerilla war, but US troops were able to capture Aguinaldo in 1901. The United States declared the war over in 1902 but had to fight remnants of the guerillas as well as southern rebels until 1913. Thus, the United States had joined the European race for imperial and colonial control of the non-Western world.

The French in Vietnam

North of Indonesia and west of the Philippines is Vietnam. Indochina, the peninsula on which Vietnam is located, also includes Cambodia, Laos, and Thailand. Portuguese monks were the first western Europeans to go to Indochina in the sixteenth century, seeking converts among the Buddhist, neo-Confucian, and animist indigenous inhabitants. French imperial and colonial involvement began in 1858, a time when Europe was industrializing and competition in the Concert of Europe was beginning to spill over from the Balkans and Middle East into Africa. At first focusing on the south of Indochina, France gradually expanded northward, establishing protectorates over the Nguyen royal dynasty, which was the last of a succession of kingdoms that had begun in the third century CE.

French Interests in Vietnam As discussed in earlier chapters, in the later first and early second millennia CE Vietnam was intermittently part of China, from where the country received strong Buddhist, Confucian, and Daoist cultural impulses. Independent dynasties reemerged after 1400, and by the later eighteenth century a royally sponsored Vietnamese culture developed, replacing the original

Saigon Street Scene, 1915.
As they did in other areas
in their empire, the French
pursued what they termed
their "civilizing mission." What
this meant in practical terms
was the importation of French
culture, and urban planning
including architecture as
well as language, education,
and literature. The French
increasingly looked at their
empire as "overseas France" and
took it for granted that their
subjects would want to adopt
French culture and practices.

Chinese script with its own reformed script. French royal efforts in the seventeenth and early eighteenth centuries to sponsor Catholic missions and trading companies were largely unsuccessful and ended altogether after the lost Seven Years' War (1756–1763). When France renewed these efforts after the French Revolution and Napoleon, it was rebuffed by the Vietnamese kings, who shared Chinese concerns about the Western challenge. Both China and Vietnam adopted a policy of isolationism as their first answer to Western patterns of challenge.

The French, however, were not deterred. Napoleon had toyed with the idea of a Mediterranean empire that included either Algeria or Egypt before embarking on his campaign of European imperialism. The French then actually conquered Algeria in 1830–1847, as we have seen earlier in this chapter. The ruler who was subsequently most active in pushing for the renewal of Napoleon's imperialism outside Europe was his nephew, Napoleon III (r. 1848–1870). This self-styled emperor involved himself in a variety of short-lived ventures in Mexico, China, and Japan. His one enduring conquest was that of "Cochinchina," that is, southern Vietnam, in 1858–1862. Taking as a pretext the renewed torture and execution of French missionaries and Vietnamese converts, the French dispatched a squadron that occupied the sparsely inhabited Mekong River delta in 1858–1862, annexing it as a protectorate.

Conquest and Colonialism   Serious colonization efforts by the French had to await the scramble for the division of Africa and what remained of Asia in the mid-1880s. After Napoleon III's fall from power as a result of the lost war against Prussia and the establishment of the Third Republic, opinions among politicians about the wisdom of a French empire were divided. But when pro-imperialists came to power in 1883, the French challenged China a year later in a successful war for the control of northern Vietnam. In contrast to the thinly settled south, the Red River estuary with the capital of the kingdom, Hanoi, in the north was densely populated. When the imperialist frenzy was at its peak during the Berlin conference of 1884–1885 for the partition of Africa, the French conquerors united southern and northern Vietnam into the French colony of Indochina. Two members of the deposed Vietnamese dynasty took to the mountains and waged a guerilla war against the occupation, called the Black Flag Revolt. But by the early twentieth century the French had captured both and were in full control.

The French government and French entrepreneurs invested substantial sums in the Mekong delta. They established plantations for the production of coffee, tea, and rubber. Indigenous rice farmers had to deliver 40 percent of their crops to the colonial government. Hanoi was made the seat of the colonial administration in 1902 and was enlarged as an architecturally French city. The port of Haiphong, downriver from Hanoi, became the main entry point for ships to load agricultural commodities for export. The commodities for the world market, which French West Africa largely lacked, existed in Vietnam, Cambodia, and Laos (the latter two added in 1893–1904).

Early Nationalism   Given Vietnam's long tradition of Confucian scholar-administrators, it was only a question of time before the pre-1858 spirit of anti-foreign Vietnamese patriotism reasserted itself. The driving force in this reassertion was Phan Boi Chau (1867–1940), trained by his father and other scholars and an eyewitness of the crushing by the French of a protest by scholars in 1885. Initially a royalist harking back to the glory of the last dynasty, in 1904 Phan Boi Chau founded the first of a number of small groups, mostly abroad, devoted to driving out the French. He spent some time in Japan, where he was active among Vietnamese students for a number of years, buoyed by the Japanese victory over Russia in 1904–1905 and seeking support from Japanese politicians.

Phan Boi Chau's activities and writings inspired antitax demonstrations and a provincial uprising in Vietnam in 1908–1909, which the French suppressed harshly. Under French pressure, the Japanese expelled Phan Boi Chau from Japan in 1909. By 1912, he had given up his royalism, and from then on a newly formed nationalist grouping favored the expulsion of the French and the formation of a Vietnamese democratic republic.

> **Creating a Revolutionary Party**
>
> "Inukai [Inukai Tsuyoshi, leader of the Progressive Party in Japan] went on to ask me: 'Have you organized a revolutionary party?' At that moment I felt so ashamed I wished to die, knowing that there was not yet any real revolutionary party in our country. Reluctantly, however, I replied: 'An organization there is, but its influence is negligible, as if it did not exist.'"
>
> —Phan Boi Chau. *Overturned Chariot: The Autobiography of Phan-Boi-Chau.* Translated by Vinh Sinh and Nicholas Wickenden, SHAPS Library of Translations, p. 89. Honolulu: University of Hawaii Press, 1999.

Putting It All Together

Ever since Vladimir Lenin, the founder of the Soviet Union, declared in his famous 1916 work that imperialism was "the highest stage of capitalism" (adopting a similar thesis first suggested by the English historian John A. Hobson in 1902), scholars have hotly debated the topic of whether or not the capitalist industrialization process in Europe, North America, and Japan needed colonies to sustain its growth. Most recent historians, beginning with David K. Fieldhouse in 1984, have come to the conclusion that imperialism and colonialism were not needed and that all the mineral and agrarian commodities crucial for industrialization during the first and second Industrial Revolutions could have been bought from independent countries on the world market. It so happened, of course, that Great Britain had transformed India from trade-fort imperialism to territorial imperialism just prior to its industrialization and used Indian cotton as raw material for its textile factories. But this raises the reverse question: Would industrialization have happened had Great Britain not conquered India? This counterfactual question has no easy answer.

Perhaps a better approach to finding an answer is to think of trade-fort and territorial imperialism as world-historical patterns of long standing. By contrast, industrialization was a much later phenomenon that arose out of the application of the New Science to practical mechanical uses, of which steam engines and textile factories were the first examples, appearing around 1800. Thus, old patterns of imperialism continued to exist during the rise of the new pattern of industrialization. These old patterns received a tremendous amplification as a result of the new power that industrialization bestowed on the European countries. Therefore, the new imperialism of

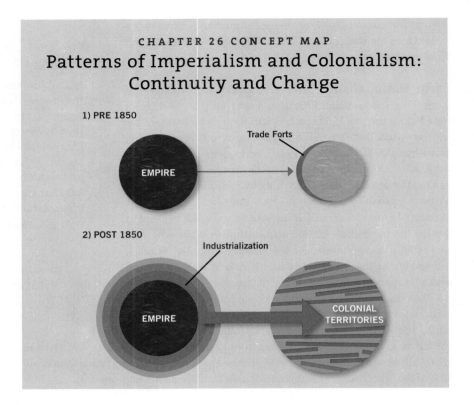

CHAPTER 26 CONCEPT MAP

Patterns of Imperialism and Colonialism: Continuity and Change

1) PRE 1850

Trade Forts

EMPIRE

2) POST 1850

Industrialization

EMPIRE

COLONIAL TERRITORIES

the nineteenth century and the colonialism which followed in its wake can be seen as phenomena in which old patterns continued but were superimposed on and enlarged by the patterns of industrial power (see Concept Map).

Review and Respond

1. What were the role and activities of the British East India Company, and why was this company important in the rise of British imperialism?

2. How did Australia and New Zealand evolve as British settler colonies?

3. What was the European Concert, and how did it affect the new imperialism?

4. How did the "scramble for Africa" originate, how did it evolve, and what were its results?

5. Compare and contrast Dutch, Spanish, and French imperialism and colonialism in southeast Asia.

▶ For additional resources, including maps, primary sources, visuals, and quizzes, please go to www.oup.com/us/vonsivers. Please see the Further Resources section at the back of the book for additional readings and suggested websites.

Thinking Through Patterns

▶ **What new patterns emerged in the transition from trade-fort imperialism to the new imperialism?**

During the early modern period, European monarchs commissioned merchant marine companies, such as the British East India Company and the Dutch United East India Company (VOC), to avoid military expeditions of their own but still receive a share of the profits of trade. The mariner-merchants built coastal forts for storage and protection, granted to them by the local rulers with whom they traded. In the seventeenth and eighteenth centuries, much larger trading companies were formed, in which investors pooled their resources and large numbers of mariner-merchants now served in dozens of trade forts overseas. In India and Indonesia, these companies became too big to fail and resorted to their governments in England and the Netherlands to rescue them. Thus, through the back door, governments found themselves forced to conquer and to colonize—they had become imperialist-colonizers.

Great Britain was the pioneer in the development of exportable agricultural and mineral commodities in its colonies for the support of its expanding industries. By the middle of the nineteenth century, other industrializing countries either embarked on imperial conquests or shifted to full colonialism in order to obtain necessary commodities. As a rule, labor for the production of these commodities was scarce. Workers had to be recruited forcibly and were routinely paid low wages.

▶ **How did European colonizers develop their colonies economically, given that they were industrializing themselves at the same time?**

▶ **What were the experiences of the indigenous people under the new imperialism? How did they adapt to colonialism? How did they resist?**

Many imperial conquests involved protracted campaigns that claimed many indigenous victims. If one of the goals of the ensuing colonization was commodity production, the indigenous population was recruited, often forcibly and with low wages. Resistance to European colonialism manifested itself in ethnic nationalism, as demonstrated by the examples of José Rizal, Phan Boi Chau, and Emilio Aguinaldo discussed in this chapter. In Australia and New Zealand and other colonies where European settlement was encouraged, colonial governments or settlers ousted the indigenous population from the most fertile lands, often in the face of fierce resistance.

Chapter 27 | Creoles and Caudillos

1790-1917 | LATIN AMERICA AND THE CARIBBEAN
IN THE NINETEENTH CENTURY

When the French Revolution broke out in 1789 a young Caribbean mulatto named Vincent Ogé (ca. 1755–1791) was on business in France. His extended family of free *Creoles*—inhabitants born in the Caribbean or Louisiana—owned a coffee plantation and a commercial business with slaves on Saint-Domingue [SAN-dow-MANG] (later Haiti). Caught up in the excitement of 1789, Ogé embraced the French revolutionary principles of liberty, equality, and fraternity with great enthusiasm and quickly became an adherent of French constitutional nationalism: As we saw in Chapter 22, the former absolute monarchy in France was swiftly

Seeing Patterns

▶ Which factors in the complex ethnic and social structures of Latin America were responsible for the emergence of authoritarian politicians or caudillos?

▶ Why did Latin American countries, after achieving independence, opt for a continuation of mineral and agricultural commodity exports?

▶ How do the social and economic structures of this period continue to affect the course of Latin America today?

reorganized to incorporate a written constitution and an elected National Assembly. As part of the general atmosphere of emancipation so prevalent during the early part of the revolution, he joined the antislavery Society of the Friends of Blacks in Paris and demanded that French constitutionalism be extended to Saint-Domingue.

In a short time the society's efforts appeared to bear fruit. In March 1790, the National Assembly granted self-administration to the colonies, and Ogé returned to Saint-Domingue full of hope that he would be able to participate as a free citizen in the island's governance. But the governor stubbornly refused to admit mulattoes as citizens of the new order. Ogé and a group of friends therefore joined a band of 250–300 freedmen and took up arms to carve out a stronghold for themselves in the north of the island by arresting plantation owners and occupying their properties. One plantation owner later testified that the rebels looted and killed during their uprising but that Ogé himself was a man of honor who treated his prisoners fairly and even left him in the possession of his personal arms.

After only a few weeks of fighting, however, government troops pushed the rebels into the Spanish part of the island. Ogé and his followers

To Preserve Their Freedom. The great African American painter Jacob Lawrence (1917–2000) depicted the Haitian Revolution in a series of 41 paintings between 1937–1938. The painting here shows the defeat of Napoleon's efforts to restore slavery by force in 1802.

surrendered after being guaranteed their safety. But the Spanish governor, washing his hands of his prisoners, turned them over to the French. After a trial for insurrection in February 1791, Ogé and 19 followers were condemned to death. Ogé suffered particularly barbaric tortures before expiring: He was condemned to perhaps the old French regime's most painful mode of public execution: being broken on the wheel. Executioners strapped him spread-eagle on a wagon wheel and systematically broke his bones with an iron bar until he was dead.

The Ogé insurrection was the opening chapter of the Haitian Revolution, which began in August 1791 and culminated with the achievement of independence under a black government in 1804. It was the third of the great constitutional-nationalist revolutions—after the American and French Revolutions—that inaugurated, with the Industrial Revolution, the modern period of world history. While the other two revolutions were events in which aristocratic rule ended and the middle classes assumed power, the Haitian Revolution was a much more radical movement in which the underclass of slaves liberated itself from both aristocratic and middle-class control. Indeed, the presence of a free, black republic in the New World both haunted slave owners in the Americas and lent itself to strengthening abolitionist sentiment. Thus, it presaged the eventual arrival of full emancipation of blacks in the United States and other states in the region.

After Haiti, Latin America followed with its own wars of independence, which took place during and immediately after the Napoleonic era and also produced constitutional revolutions. In some Spanish colonies Creoles and mulattoes collaborated, but in most colonies the Creoles—like the white colonists in the North American colonies—were by far the chief beneficiaries of the fruits of independence. Given their European cultural and intellectual connections, many Creoles found it relatively easy to adapt to the new challenges of modernity. After independence, wealthy Creoles often traveled to Europe, sent their children to France or England for education, and imported industrial consumer goods from Great Britain. Moreover, most of the Latin American regimes—with the prominent exception of Brazil—abolished slavery before mid-century. As in the United States, however, the lower classes of *mestizos* (mixed Native Americans and Europeans) and mulattoes and the underclasses of Native Americans and blacks were for the most part excluded from the benefits of modernization. For much of the nineteenth century, too, authoritarian **caudillo** regimes allied with landowners and army generals governed under the pretense of constitutional nationalism.

In the economy, the Creole landowners themselves had little interest in industrialization, which would have meant a shifting of scarce labor from

Caudillo: Latin American strongman or dictator.

the estates to factories in cities. They found it much more profitable instead to adopt the role of suppliers to the industrial states through mineral and agricultural exports until the very end of the nineteenth century. Latin America thus took a path of development that diverged substantially from that of Europe and most of North America after the initial constitutional-nationalist revolutions.

Independence, Authoritarianism, and Political Instability

As in the United States and France, the growth pattern of constitutional nationalism in Latin America was slow, full of reverses, and uneven. Historians now give greater weight to the participation of urban craftspeople, of both Iberian and African descent, in the independence movements; but it is generally agreed that the leadership was for the most part in the hands of the Creole landowning class. The revolutionary potential of urban mass participation, so visible in the United States and France, was relatively weak in Latin America. No changes in social structures occurred except in Haiti, from which the white Creole settlers had largely fled after the revolution. The outcome of the independence movements in Latin America was not a single federal or central, constitutionally defined *nation* but a multiplicity of states defined by more or less the same constitutional nationalism of the Creoles, unwilling to share power very broadly.

Independence and Political Development in the North: Haiti and Mexico

The French Revolution in 1789 had two very different consequences for Latin America. In Saint-Domingue, or Haiti, the revolution triggered a direct and immediate adaptation process among the large majority of slaves, who quickly embraced the radical concept of *égalité* for acquiring their freedom. They eliminated their competitors, the white Creoles, and pushed the adaptation process to its ultimate conclusion, independence and constitutionalism for what was now fundamentally a nation of blacks. By contrast, in Mexico, the adaptation to the French Revolution was indirect, limited largely to the Creoles, and never broadened to include much of the non-Creole population prior to the twentieth century. It was indirect insofar as it came only by way of Napoleon's invasion of Iberia and its consequences. And it

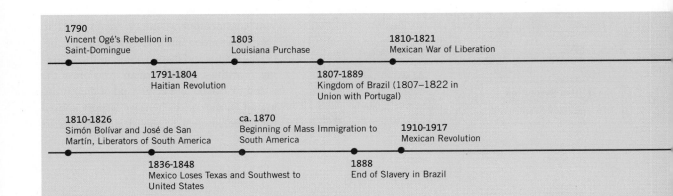

1790
Vincent Ogé's Rebellion in
Saint-Domingue

1803
Louisiana Purchase

1810-1821
Mexican War of Liberation

1791-1804
Haitian Revolution

1807-1889
Kingdom of Brazil (1807–1822 in
Union with Portugal)

1810-1826
Simón Bolívar and José de San
Martín, Liberators of South America

ca. 1870
Beginning of Mass Immigration to
South America

1910-1917
Mexican Revolution

1836-1848
Mexico Loses Texas and Southwest to
United States

1888
End of Slavery in Brazil

remained a stunted revolution, in part because the urban, small-propertied, entrepreneurial, and professional classes that provided so much of the momentum of the American and French Revolutions were much smaller than in the United States and France. Thus, the impulse toward radicalism and social leveling characteristic of France in early 1790 never really took deep roots during the independence movement in Mexico.

Sugar and Coffee in Haiti The Caribbean island of Hispaniola, today Haiti and Santo Domingo, was one of the earliest and richest European colonies, based on plantations that produced vast amounts of sugar, coffee, and cotton for export to the Old World from the 1700s onward. At the time of the French Revolution, the French part of the island produced half of the world's sugar and coffee. Originally, the entire island had been a Spanish colony. But as Spain's power slipped during the seventeenth and eighteenth centuries, France took advantage of the situation and assumed control of the western end of the island in 1697. In the following century, settlers enjoyed French mercantilist protectionism for splendid profits from their slave plantations. By 1789, some 30,000 white settlers, 28,000 mulattoes (holding about one-third of the slaves), and about 500,000 black plantation and household slaves formed an extremely unequal colonial society in which fear and violence reigned supreme.

Revolt of the Slaves After the failure of Ogé's uprising, discussed in the vignette that opens this chapter, resentment continued to simmer among the mulattoes and blacks in the north of Saint-Domingue. Resentment turned into fury, however, when the French revolutionary Constitutive Assembly in May 1791 began to debate the issue of citizen rights for propertied mulattoes (for which Ogé had been fighting), while the settlers in Saint-Domingue continued to refuse any debate. Plantation slaves chafing under a dehumanizing regime of exploitative owners and managers exploded in August 1791 with a collective rage not previously seen in an American colony. Within weeks, the slave rebellion numbered 100,000 followers and encompassed the entire northern province of the island. The settlers were well-armed but suffered heavy casualties under the onslaught of overwhelming numbers.

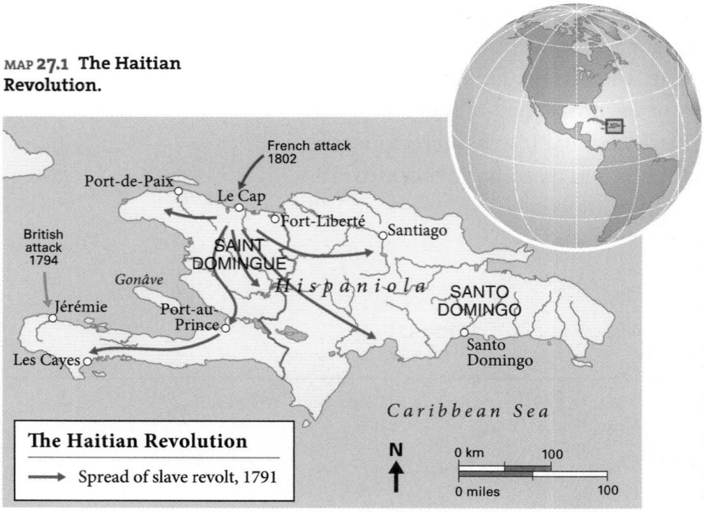

With the rebellion taking an increasingly severe toll on the economy, the Legislative Assembly of the new French Republic sent commissioners and troops in 1792 to reestablish order. But when war broke out between France and its neighbors in the following year, the possibility of an invasion of the island by Britain and Spain, and of their forming an alliance with the slave leaders, caused the commissioners to abolish slavery. This act

MAP 27.1 **The Haitian Revolution.**

The Haitian Revolution

→ Spread of slave revolt, 1791

of abolition, confirmed in France by February 1794, enabled the most powerful slave leader, François-Dominique Toussaint Louverture (ca. 1743–1803), to end foreign interference and make peace with the few thousand remaining French forces and settlers (see Map 27.1).

Nation-State Building To repair the plantation economy—sugar production, for example, had fallen by 75 percent—Louverture dispatched his officers, who forced former slaves to resume production. In 1801, Louverture was sufficiently strong to assume the governorship of Saint-Domingue and proclaim a constitution that incorporated the basic principles of French-inspired constitutional nationalism. Napoleon Bonaparte, in control of France since 1799, however, was determined to rebuild the French overseas empire and now revoked the abolition of slavery. He dispatched a military force to the island, which succeeded in capturing Louverture in 1802. Louverture died shortly thereafter in 1803.

His deputy, the former slave Jean-Jacques Dessalines (r. 1802–1806), was able to defeat Napoleon's troops and in 1804 declared the colony an independent nation. Subsequently, Dessalines made himself emperor and renamed the country "Haiti," its supposed original Native American name. When he changed the constitution in favor of autocratic rule, he provoked a conspiracy against him, which culminated in his assassination in 1806. In the aftermath, the state split into an autocratically ruled north with a state-run plantation economy and a democratic south with a small-farm privatized economy (1806–1821).

A subsequently reunified state annexed neighboring Spanish Santo Domingo for a short time (1822–1842) before losing it again. This loss touched off a period of political instability in the middle of the century before constitutional rule and the agricultural commodity economy were stabilized (1874–1911). Despite all its difficulties, Haiti entered the twentieth century as the first successful black constitutional state—and one with nearly one hundred years of independence behind it. Together with the United States and France, Haiti created the pattern of constitutional nationalism in the nineteenth century, which became part of the modern challenge to the traditional kingdoms and empires of the world.

Defending the Revolution. When Poland ceased to exist after the Third Partition of the Polish Commonwealth (1795) between Russia and Prussia, thousands of Polish soldiers joined Napoleon's forces. Napoleon sent some of the Polish soldiers to Haiti in 1802 to reconquer it; but even though the soldiers fought bravely, as depicted in *Battle on Santo Domingo* by the Polish painter January Sucholdoski (1797–1875), the Haitian Republic defeated Napoleon's troops and gained full independence in 1804.

Napoleon's Conquest of Iberia and Its Impact on the Americas

Napoleon's defeat in Haiti ended France's efforts to rebuild its overseas empire. Instead, the French embarked on the conquest of Europe for the end of absolutism and a new revolutionary empire from Portugal to Russia. The effect of this policy of European conquest, however, was a decisive weakening of Iberian colonialism in the Americas. Ironically, the first step in this weakening was unintended. In the Battle of Trafalgar off the southwestern coast of Spain in 1805 France and Spain lost a substantial part of their combined sea power. Great Britain, the victor, entered the nineteenth century as the unchallenged maritime power in the world.

Then, during the Peninsular War in 1807–1808, Napoleon Bonaparte conquered Portugal and Spain in a bid to put his brother on the Spanish throne. The Portuguese

Land and Liberty. This enormous mural by Diego Rivera (1886–1957), in the National Palace in Mexico City, shows Father Hidalgo above the Mexican eagle, flanked by other independence fighters. Above them are Emiliano Zapata and Pancho Villa, the heroes of the Revolution of 1910, holding a banner, "Tierra y Libertad." The other parts of the mural show historical scenes from the Spanish conquest to the twentieth century.

heir apparent, Prince João (later João VI of Brazil and Portugal, r. 1816–1826), and his family fled to Brazil; and the French ruled by military decree. In Spain, Napoleon forced the king, Fernando VII (r. 1808 and 1813–1829), to abdicate and placed his own brother, Joseph Bonaparte (r. 1808–1813), on the throne. Joseph ruled tenuously, dependent on generals under his brother's command as the Spanish mounted a determined guerilla campaign against their occupiers, and eventually abdicated with alacrity. An interesting legacy of this struggle is that the Spanish term *guerilla* for this kind of irregular warfare stuck and is the name we still use today for popular insurgencies against larger conventional forces.

As a consequence of Napoleon's conquest of Iberia, the Creoles of the Spanish colonies rejected Joseph Bonaparte's rule and declared their loyalty to the deposed king Fernando. But since Napoleon held the king captive in France, this declaration meant for all practical purposes independence for the American colonies. Once the Spanish had chased the French army out of Iberia and King Fernando returned to his throne in 1813, however, the American colonies had to fight in order to remain independent.

Mexican Independence

In New Spain (modern Mexico), Miguel Hidalgo y Costilla (1753–1811), son of a Creole hacienda estate administrator, launched his movement for independence from Bonapartist Spain in 1810. A churchman since his youth, Hidalgo was broadly educated, well versed in Enlightenment literature, and on the margins of strict Catholicism. Later in his life he became a parish priest and devoted himself to creating employment opportunities for native Americans or Amerindians in a province southeast of Mexico City. He had earlier participated in a conspiracy of Creoles, some of them members of the military, to overthrow a group of Spanish colonial military officers who had staged a successful coup d'état against the civilian colonial administration in 1808. On the point of being discovered, the conspiracy launched a popular rebellion in 1810, declaring itself in favor of Fernando VII, whom they considered to be Spain's legitimate ruler, as opposed to Joseph Bonaparte.

Under the leadership of Hidalgo, tens of thousands of poor Creoles, mestizos, and Amerindians who had suffered in a drought marched on Guanajuato, looting and killing *peninsulares* (Spaniards from Europe) and Creoles without distinction. They were initially successful in defeating the Spanish troops marching against them. When Hidalgo, shocked by the violence, avoided an attack on Mexico City, however, the rebellion began to sputter and was eventually defeated in 1811. Spanish forces ultimately captured and executed Hidalgo.

Under militarily experienced mestizo and Creole leaders, the war of independence continued in several southwestern provinces of Mexico but failed to make a comeback in the heartland around Mexico City. Here, monarchists intent on retaining the union between Spain and Mexico appeared to retain the upper hand. But during a constitutionalist uprising in Spain (1820–1823) King Fernando VII came close to defeat. The Mexican Creole monarchists, not wishing to submit to a Spanish republic, made the colony a regency ready to receive Fernando in order for him to continue Spanish colonial rule. Fernando, however, overcame the uprising in Spain. When he then declined to take up his American regency, the Creoles made Mexico an independent empire of its own in 1821, thereby provoking declarations of independence from Mexico in the southern provinces of El Salvador, Nicaragua, Costa Rica, and Honduras. Mestizo and Creole independence fighters in Mexico redoubled their efforts for an independent republic as well. In 1824, they succeeded with the declaration of the Republic of Mexico and a constitution broadly following the US and French models (see Map 27.2).

Early Independence   Initially, Mexico had a number of advantages as an independent nation. It had abundant natural resources, and its northern territories—Texas, Colorado, and California—contained much valuable pasture and agricultural

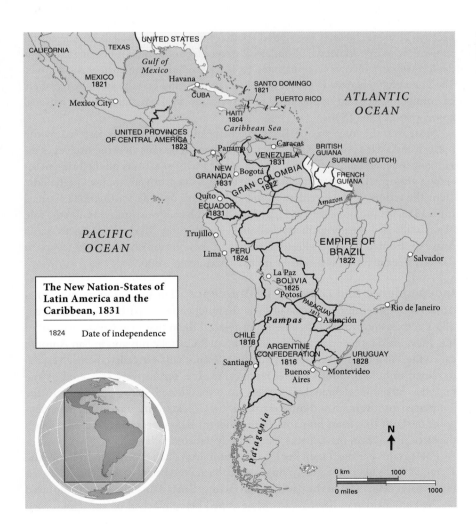

MAP **27.2 The New Nation-States of Latin America and the Caribbean, 1831.**

land. The great dying of the indigenous population of Amerindians from European mass diseases in the sixteenth and early seventeenth centuries, however, had radically depopulated much of the land. Thus, while Mexico's territory was vast, it was doomed to stay largely undeveloped unless a policy of open immigration was encouraged.

From the early 1820s, Mexico therefore encouraged immigration, gave generous terms for the purchase of land to settlers, and allowed them to be largely self-governing as long as taxes were duly paid. At the same time, Mexico's rapidly expanding northern neighbor, the United States, went through a protracted period of growth. Settlement of the rich agricultural areas of the formerly French Ohio and Mississippi valleys moved with astonishing speed. The new demand for American cotton in British and American factories drove a frenetic expansion into Alabama, Mississippi, Louisiana, and Arkansas. Cotton exhausted the soil quickly, and the availability of cheap land made it more efficient to abandon the depleted lands and keep pushing the realm of "King Cotton" ever westward.

As North American settlement drew closer to Mexico's territories, many North Americans emigrated to Mexico to take advantage of its land policies and autonomy. The Mexican province of Texas was particularly attractive, especially to southerners, because of its nearness to the settled southern states and its suitability for cotton cultivation. While Mexico had outlawed slavery from the time it became independent, most slave owners who migrated to Texas tended to ignore these restrictions. The increasingly blatant violation of the antislavery laws and the swelling numbers of immigrants seeking opportunity in Texas came to alarm the Mexican national government by the 1830s.

Moreover, the huge size of Texas, the habit of local autonomy fostered by the settlers, and their ties to the United States made many Texans view themselves as essentially independent. The perception in Mexico City of a Texas on the brink of seceding prompted the government to send the army to crush any incipient rebellion. Here, the actions of the president, General Antonio López de Santa Anna (in office from 1833, off and on, until 1855), in dissolving the congress and assuming the role of a caudillo had already sparked rebellion in several other Mexican provinces. Santa Anna confronted these rebellions in turn, and then personally led 4,000 troops to deal with Texan pro-independence militias in March of 1836.

Independence and Growing US Influence

For the Texan militias Santa Anna's actions became the cause of a war for independence, particularly as the caudillo's ruthlessness toward the militias convinced them that negotiation was out of the question. Santa Anna's men besieged a small Catholic mission in San Antonio called the "Alamo" in which several hundred Texans had barricaded themselves, determined to hold out until a relief force came. The Texans were bolstered by the presence of some celebrated volunteers from the United States, among them the Tennessee frontiersman and congressman Davy Crockett, and Jim Bowie, the inventor of the knife that bears his name. In the end, the defenders were all killed, though the circumstances of their deaths are still hotly debated today.

For Texans, the dead men became instant martyrs and the Alamo became "the shrine of Texas liberty." Santa Anna's army had suffered heavy casualties, and Texan forces soon defeated it in the battle of San Jacinto. Santa Anna himself was captured on the battlefield and, having narrowly escaped being lynched on the spot, ceded

Texas to the insurgents. Mexico's largest province now became an independent state. Santa Anna, after being taken to the United States and meeting with President Andrew Jackson (in office 1829–1837), was repatriated to Mexico and served as president six more times in his long career as that nation's most famous caudillo.

Mexico's Dismemberment   After some 30 years of not doing much with its right to govern Louisiana—the huge land on both sides of the Mississippi in the center of today's United States—Spain had returned its territorial rights there to France. Napoleon, for his part, sold the rights to the United States in 1803, in the hope of strengthening the latter against Great Britain, his main opponent in his European imperial conquests. By the early 1840s, American settlement of the territory of this so-called Louisiana Purchase on both sides of the Mississippi was proceeding rapidly. Settlers bought some land from the indigenous Amerindians, whose opinions had not been consulted during the purchase, and gained even more land from wars against them. Moving farther west, American settlers made claims on the Oregon Territory along the northern Pacific Coast. These claims now meant that the young US republic's ambitions were swiftly making it a continental power.

During the administration of President James K. Polk (1845–1849), the idea of "Manifest Destiny"—that it was the evident fate of the United States to be the dominant power of the North American continent, with territory stretching from the Atlantic to the Pacific—was becoming an article of faith. Both the British in Canada and the Mexican government were increasingly alarmed by this new aggressive US posture. Moreover, Texas, insecure as an independent republic between the United States and Mexico and dominated by Americans, now applied for annexation to the United States.

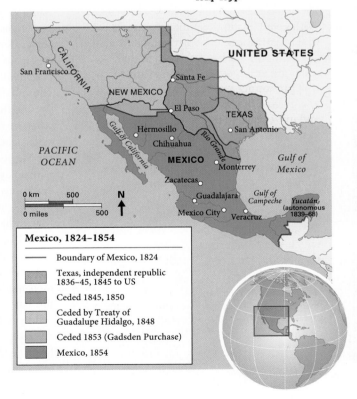

MAP 27.3 **Mexico's Loss of Territory to the United States, 1824–1854.**

For Santa Anna, president once again of Mexico, such a move meant a war for survival; for Polk and many Americans, it meant a potential opportunity to expand the republic's borders directly to the Pacific. When Texas was admitted to the union, therefore, the United States and Mexico went to war. Despite vigorous protests against this war as one of conquest—including a spirited condemnation by a young Illinois congressman named Abraham Lincoln—the war was prosecuted by the United States with vigor. A small but well-trained expeditionary force, launching a seaborne invasion of central Mexico, fought its way to Mexico City. Other American troops fought in what were to become New Mexico and California. By 1848 Mexico sued for peace and gave up most of what is now the southwestern and western United States: Texas, New Mexico, Arizona, Colorado, Nevada, and California (see Map 27.3).

To make the territorial losses even harder to swallow for Mexico, the richest gold strike in the continent's history began almost immediately in California. The boomtown of San Francisco attracted tens of thousands of newcomers—"Forty-Niners"—seeking riches, and California entered the union as a state in 1850. Santa Anna stayed on in Mexico as caudillo until 1855. Then, even his supporters could no longer take his lavish crony-ism and payoffs to the military and deposed him. In a strange historical footnote, Santa Anna spent his last years of exile in the United States, where his efforts at im-porting *chicle*, the base for modern chewing gum, ultimately led to one of his associ-ates starting the Chiclets Chewing Gum company. In 1876, under a general amnesty, Santa Anna went back to Mexico and soon after passed away.

The French Interlude in Mexico   The Latin American independence move-ments had inspired the declaration of the US Monroe Doctrine in 1823. According to this policy, the US government would not tolerate European attempts to recolo-nize the new republics of the Western Hemisphere. For four decades the doctrine had been remarkably successful at deterring the European powers, largely because it suited British policy as well. Mexico easily beat back two attempts by small ex-peditionary forces at invasion, one from Spain in 1829 and another from France in 1838. With the American Civil War raging in the mid-1860s, however, the tempta-tion to create an empire in Mexico proved too much for Louis-Napoleon Bonaparte (in office 1848–1852 as president; r. 1852–1870 as emperor) of France to resist. As a nephew of Napoleon, he yearned to return France to imperial glory.

After staging a coup d'état in 1852 and becoming Emperor Napoleon III, he pursued imperial campaigns in North Africa, West Africa (Senegal), and In-dochina (Vietnam), apart from flexing France's military muscle in Russia, Italy, China, and Korea. His opportunity to intervene in Mexican affairs came after the downfall of Santa Anna in 1855 and the subsequent uprising of con-servatives against the liberal constitution of 1857, with its separation of church and state. The liberals under the lead-ership of Benito Juárez, the first Amerindian to become president (1861–1864, 1867–1872), thus defeated the conservatives.

But the state that Juárez inherited was bankrupt, and when he found himself forced to suspend payments on the state debt, the international repercussions were disastrous for Mexico. Napoleon III seized on the payment issue and, with an eye on the Mexican silver mines, set into motion an ambitious plan of imposing a pliable ruler from the outside. In 1862, he provided military backing to the Austrian prince Maximilian, well liked by Mexican conservatives, to install himself as the emperor of Mexico (1864–1867).

With the defeat of the Confederate states in April 1865, however, and the Union army ballooning to over a million men, many of whom had just been sent to Texas to suppress the last Confederate holdouts, Maximilian's position was suddenly in grave danger. In the following year, after some discreet aid from the US government under the aegis of the Monroe Doctrine, an uprising broke out in Mexico. Cut off from any hope of effective support from France, Mexican

---

Birth and Death of Constitutions

"With good reason the public now feels that constitutions are born and die, that governments succeed each other, that codes are enlarged and made intricate, that pronouncements and plans come and go, and that after so many mutations and upheavals, so much inquietude and so many sacrifices, nothing positive has been done for the people, nothing advantageous for these unhappy classes, from which always emerge those who shed their blood in civil wars, those who give their quota for armies, who populate the jails and labor in public works, and for which were made, finally, all the evils of society, and none of its goods."

— Special vote (report) of Ponciano Arriaga in the Mexican Assembly, June 23, 1856. In Kenneth L. Karst and Keith S. Rosenn. *Law and Development in Latin America: A Case Book*. UCLA Latin American Studies Series, vol. 28, p. 275. Berkeley: University of California Press, 1975.

liberal forces defeated Maximilian, captured him, and executed him by firing squad in 1867.

Porfirio Díaz's Long Peace   With the withdrawal of most US government troops from Texas at the end of Reconstruction—ending the potential threat of invasion or border incursions—and the rise of Mexico's next conservative caudillo, Porfirio Díaz (in office 1876–1880 and 1884–1911), a period of relative peace came at last. Díaz's lengthy hold on power allowed a degree of conservative stability to settle in on Mexico's turbulent politics. Moreover, the period also coincided with the defeat of

The Execution of Emperor Maximilian of Mexico, June 19, 1867. Édouard Manet has been characterized as the "inventor of modernity" not only for his technique, but for the way he portrayed events, even significant political events, in a calm and composed manner. The soldiers who dispatch the hapless Emperor come across as cool and professional—what they are doing is all in a day's work.

the last Amerindians north of the border and the settlement and development of the American West. In addition, Díaz, like his contemporary, President José Balmaceda (1886–1891) of Chile, favored some initial industrial and infrastructural development in Mexico. The basic lines of Mexico's major rail, telegraph, and telephone systems were laid during this time; textile factories and some basic heavy industry were set up; and modest agricultural improvements were made.

Most of this investment, however, came from British and American firms in return for Mexican mineral, precious metal, and fruit and vegetable exports. Toward the end of Díaz's dictatorship, the first petroleum drilling enterprises were set up, an industry that, although nationalized today, still has proved disappointing at consistently generating revenue. In assessing Mexico's relative lack of economic development since the late 1800s, poverty, and ongoing tensions with the industrial colossus to the north, it is no wonder that he once exclaimed so poignantly, "Alas, poor Mexico! So far from God, so close to the United States!"

The Mexican Revolution   Díaz's long presidency and Mexico's halting development tended to foster discontent, particularly among the poor urban workers and *peons*—agricultural laborers on large estates, who were held in conditions of virtual serfdom. In 1910, half of the Mexican population worked on estates and 20 percent of the farmland was foreign-owned. The reform-minded Francisco Madero, from a wealthy northern family, drove Díaz from power and through elections legitimized his own presidency (1911–1913); but he was unable to gain control over the country. Two additional movements now vied for power in different parts of Mexico: Emiliano Zapata (1879–1919) advocated for plantation land reform in the south and Pancho Villa (José Doroteo Arango Arámbula, 1878–1923) for hacienda land reform in the north. In addition, a seesaw struggle for the presidency erupted between reformers from wealthy backgrounds and conservative pro-Díaz officers, each seeking to gain a grip on the movements by Zapata and Villa as well as other provincial rebels.

During a short-lived interval in the middle of this struggle, a group of reformers were able to convene a constitutional congress, which passed a new, revolutionary

constitution with paragraphs establishing land reform, limits to foreign ownership of resources, a labor code, and a secular, compulsory educational system (1917). It took altogether at least 2 million and possibly in the vicinity of 3.5 million victims in the struggle for and against the revolution, as well as one more military coup, before a moderate general, Álvaro Obregón (in office 1920–1924), was able to stabilize the presidency and begin the implementation of the constitution. In contrast to the 1824 and 1857 constitutions, the new one of 1917 stood out for its socialist programs, creating greater equality in the distribution of farmland and ending the grip of the Catholic Church on land as well as education.

Mexican Oil Boom. After drilling at El Baño in 1904, the pressure of the gas and petroleum in the ground resulted in a blowout (*a*). The blowout was easily plugged. This was not the case at the Dos Bocas well in 1911, which resulted in an environmental disaster, producing a lake 1,000 feet in diameter, dead vegetation, and hot gases and water seeping to the surface (*b*). Apart from producing environmental problems, oil in Mexico during the Díaz regime benefited only the US investors and the Mexican oligarchy.

Independence and Development in Northern South America

The viceroyalty of New Granada in northern South America, with today's countries of Venezuela, Colombia, Ecuador, and Panama, had far fewer Creoles than that of New Spain, from which independent Mexico issued. For its struggle for independence to succeed, leaders had to seek support from the *pardos*, as the majority population of free black and mulatto craftspeople in the cities was called. Independence eventually came through the building of strong armies from these diverse elements, mostly by Simón Bolívar, the liberator of northern South America from renewed Spanish colonialism. After independence, however, the Creoles quickly moved to dissolve their coalitions with the lower classes and embraced the same conservative caudillo politics that Mexico practiced for most of the nineteenth century.

Comuneros and Pardos   In contrast to New Spain, with its relatively large Creole and mestizo populations in the cities and countryside, New Granada's Creole population was small in relation to mestizos and pardos. The latter constituted over half of the urban and two-thirds of the rural people. Unrest began early, expressing itself in loyalty to the Spanish king but also in fury against the high taxes collected by the peninsular administrators: The *comunero* revolt of 1781–1782—together with the Túpac Amaru revolt of 1780–1781 in Peru—was a harbinger of things to come during the independence struggle a generation later. The comuneros were urban and

Revolutionary Women.
Women, such as these
soldaderas taking rifle practice,
played many significant roles
in the Mexican Revolution,
1910–1920.

rural Creoles and mestizos whom the hard-pressed authorities placated with promises, only to renege once their assemblies dissipated.

In 1810, the battle cry was again loyalty to the Spanish king, the deposed Fernando VII, and outrage against the peninsulars, although this time it was more
massive, bringing together Creoles and pardos. In 1810 they created *juntas*, or committees, among which the junta of Cartagena in what was to become Colombia was
the most important, and drove the peninsulars from their administrative positions.
Initially, they agreed on the equality of all ethnicities and worked on constitutions
that provided for elections by all free men. But they were also suspicious of each
other, denouncing their allegedly aristocratic versus democratic aspirations.

In 1811, cooperation broke down and the pardos assumed power in a coup. The
Creoles struck back a year later when they declared the First Republic of Cartagena.
Their power was limited by the pardo-dominated militias however, and in a compromise they agreed on the continuation of full voting rights. In the long run, during the
1800s, this revolutionary achievement did not last and the Creoles established oligarchic rule. But Cartagena, together with Mexico under Hidalgo, proved that Latin
American independence was not exclusively the work of a conservative Creole class
consolidating its privileges.

Bolívar the Liberator   The junta of Cartagena, together with other juntas,
formed the federation of the United Provinces of New Granada in 1811, with a
weak executive unable to prevent squabbling among the juntas. Fernando VII, after returning to Spain in 1813, was determined to reestablish colonial control by
dispatching armies to Latin America. The largest forces, comprising some 10,000
troops, landed in the United Provinces in 1814, taking Cartagena after a siege, and
resurrected the viceroyalty of New Granada.

The eventual liberator of northern South America from renewed Spanish rule in
1819 was Simón Bolívar (1783–1830). Bolívar was born in Venezuela, into a wealthy
Creole background; his family owned cacao plantations worked by slaves and was

engaged in colonial trade. Venezuela, like Colombia, was a part of New Granada. Although lacking a formal education, thanks to his tutor Bolívar was familiar with Enlightenment literature. In 1799, he visited Spain, where he met his future wife; and he later returned to Europe after her death. In 1804, he was deeply impressed when he watched Napoleon's lavish spectacle of crowning himself emperor in Paris. These European visits instilled in Bolívar a lasting admiration for European ideals of liberty and popular sovereignty, and he longed to create a constitutional republic in his homeland.

In 1810, as in Cartagena, Venezuelan cities formed Creole-led juntas with pardo participation. A young Bolívar participated in the congress of juntas that declared outright independence for Venezuela in 1812, against the resistance of royalists who remained faithful to Fernando VII. A civil war ensued, which made Bolívar's tenure in Venezuela insecure and, after the arrival of the Spanish expeditionary force of 1815, impossible. He went into exile first to British Jamaica and then to revolutionary Haiti. In 1816 Bolívar returned from exile to Venezuela with a military force, partly supplied by Haiti. After some initial difficulties, he succeeded in defeating the Spanish troops. In 1822, he assumed the presidency of "Gran Colombia," an independent republic comprising the later states of Colombia, Venezuela, Ecuador, and Panama.

The Bolívar–San Martín Encounter   After their defeat in Gran Colombia, Spanish troops continued to occupy Peru in the Andes, where an independence movement supported by Argentina was active but made little progress against Spanish and royalist Creole troops. In the face of this situation, the Argentinian general and liberator José de San Martín (ca. 1778–1850) and Bolívar met in 1822 to deliberate on how to get rid of the Spanish and to shape the future of an independent Latin America. As for fighting Spain, they agreed that Bolívar was in a better geographical position than San Martín to send military forces to Peru. But even for Bolívar that task was daunting. His troops were unaccustomed to high-altitude fighting and were hindered as much by mountain sickness as by enemy resistance. One of Bolívar's lieutenants finally got the better of the fiercely resisting Spanish in 1824. Two years later, Spanish colonialism in Latin America finally ended when the last troops surrendered on the Peruvian coast.

The content of the discussion for the future of Latin America between San Martín and Bolívar never became public and has remained a bone of contention among historians. San Martín, bitterly disappointed by endless disputes among liberal constitutionalists and royalists, federalists and centralists, as well as Creole elitists and mestizo and mulatto populists, favored monarchical rule to bring stability to Latin America. Bolívar preferred republicanism and Creole oligarchical rule, although he always sought limited pardo and mestizo collaboration, especially in his armies. Clearly, there was not much common ground between the two independence leaders.

San Martín's sudden withdrawal from the Andes after the meeting and his subsequent resignation from politics, however, can be taken as an indication of his realization that the chances for a South American monarchy were small indeed. Bolívar, also acutely aware of the multiple cleavages in Latin American politics, more realistically envisioned the future of Latin America as that of relatively small independent republics, held together by strong, lifelong presidencies and hereditary senates. He actually implemented this vision in the 1825 constitution of independent upper Peru, renamed after him "Bolivia." Ironically, in his own country Bolívar was denied the role of strong president. Although he made himself a caudillo, he was unable to coax his recalcitrant politicians into an agreement on a constitution for Gran Colombia similar to that of Bolivia. Eventually, in 1830 Bolívar resigned, dying shortly after of tuberculosis. In 1831 Gran Colombia fell apart into its component parts of Colombia, Venezuela, Ecuador, and (later) Panama.

Revolving-Door Caudillos Independent Venezuela, as perhaps the poorest and most underpopulated of northern South America's newly independent countries, acquired the dubious distinction of being among its most politically turbulent. In Carácas, the capital, caudillos displaced each other at an astonishing rate. By one estimate, there were 41 presidencies and 30 insurrections in the period 1830–1899. Although many of these presidents sought foreign financial support for development, little was accomplished and much of the money went into the private coffers of the leaders. The main issue that kept rival factions at odds was federalism versus tighter central control, with at least one all-out war being fought over the issue during the 1860s. Following this so-called War of the Caudillos, the official name of the country was changed from the "Republic of Venezuela" to the "United States of Venezuela," a name which it retained into the middle of the twentieth century.

Venezuela's neighboring countries traversed a similar pattern of caudillo politics. Though enjoying longer periods of stability, Colombia—the name adopted in 1861 to replace that of New Granada—also saw a continuing struggle between federalists and centralizers, liberals and conservatives, with each party seeking the support of the Catholic Church. From 1899 until 1902, the "War of a Thousand Days" was conducted, leaving the country sufficiently weak for Panamanian rebels to establish an independent state of Panama, supported by the United States. After independence, the administration of Theodore Roosevelt (1901–1909) swiftly concluded a treaty with the new country to control a 10-mile-wide strip bisecting the narrow isthmus and began the construction of the Panama Canal, completed in 1914.

Machines in the Garden. The first railroads in Latin America were constructed in Mexico in 1836. Initially, construction was supported by state funds, with private and foreign participation. A railway bridge spans the Rio Grande River in Costa Rica, 1902 (a). In the 1870s and 1880s, once profitable railroads were privatized and expanded. The United States built the 51-mile Panama Canal in 1904–1914 with Treasury bonds, after encouraging Panama to secede from Colombia and appropriating the land for construction (b).

Independence and Development in Southern and Western South America

Independence movements also began in 1810 farther south in South America. Under the guise of remaining loyal to the deposed Fernando VII of Spain, Creoles in Buenos Aires seized the initiative to establish a junta rejecting the viceregal peninsular authorities. By contrast, Creoles along the Andes similarly avoided declarations of loyalty to Napoleon but supported the existing colonial administration, even after 1814 when fresh Spanish troops arrived. The figure who eventually broke the logjam between the two sides of pro- and antipeninsular Creole parties in 1816–1822 was José de San Martín.

Independence in Argentina

The viceroyalty of La Plata, comprising the modern countries of Argentina, Uruguay, Paraguay, and Bolivia, was the youngest of Spain's colonial units. In the course of the Bourbon reforms, Spain decided in 1776 to separate it from the viceroyalty of Peru, where declining silver exports diminished the importance of the port of Lima. La Plata, with the rising port of Buenos Aires, had grown through contraband trade with Great Britain; and the Bourbon reformers wanted to redirect its trade more firmly back to Spain. Buenos Aires was so important to the British even after the reform of 1776, however, that a naval commander and British merchants exploited the destruction of the Spanish navy by Britain in the battle off Trafalgar in southwestern Spain (1805) to occupy Buenos Aires in 1806–1807, until they were driven out by Spanish colonial forces.

Creoles in La Plata had far fewer Amerindians, African slaves, mestizos, and mulattoes to deal with—or fear—than in any of the other viceroyalties. But in 1810, when the first independence movements formed, there was a clear distinction between the proindependence Creoles of Buenos Aires, or *porteños*, and the Creoles of the *pampas*, or grasslands of the temperate interior of Argentina and Uruguay, and the subtropical plains and hills of Paraguay favoring continued colonialism. The latter either were royalists or strove for separate independence. Uruguay, furthermore, was initially claimed by Brazil and eventually achieved its own independence only in 1828. Upper Peru, or modern Bolivia, with its high-elevation plains, lowland Amazon basin rain forest, large Amerindian population, and Potosí silver mines, was heavily defended by colonial and peninsular Spanish troops. Given these various urban–rural and geographical circumstances, the porteño independence movement fought to no more than a standstill during the initial period 1810–1816.

As in the northern tier, the breakthrough eventually came via an experienced military figure, the highly popular José de San Martín. San Martín was a Creole from northeastern Argentina. His father, an immigrant from Spain, was a military officer and administrator of a Jesuit-founded Amerindian mission district. The son, educated from an early age in a Spanish military academy, began service in the porteño independence movement in 1812, where he distinguished himself in the Argentinian independence struggle.

During his service, San Martín realized that the final success for independence in the south also required the liberation of the Andes provinces. Accordingly, he trained the Army of the Andes, which included mulatto and black volunteers, with which he crossed the mountains to Chile in 1818, liberating the country from royalist forces. With the help of a newly established navy composed of ships acquired from the United States and Britain, he conquered Lima in Peru but was defied by the local Creoles when he sought to introduce social reforms, such as an end to the Amerindian tribute system, the *mit'a*, and the emancipation of the children of black slaves. When he was also unable to dislodge Spanish troops near the city, he traveled north for his meeting with Bolívar. As discussed, it was Bolívar who completed the liberation of the Andes lands and, thereby, also helped Argentina to defeat the peninsulars and royalist Creoles in the south.

Independent Peru Peru's independence came following the defeat of Spanish forces in 1824–1826. As with the other new states in South America, it took decades for Peru, Chile, and Bolivia to work out territorial disputes. The most serious of these by far was the War of the Pacific from 1879 to 1884, resulting in a victorious Chile annexing Peruvian and Bolivian lands. Most devastating for Peru was the destruction that Chilean troops wrought in southern Peru. The economy, which had made modest progress by using nitrate exports in the form of guano to fund railroad building and mining, was only painfully rebuilt after the destruction of war. Political stability for several decades returned under the presidency of Nicolás de Piérola, who introduced a number of belated reforms during his terms (1879–1881 and 1895–1899). As the presidency from this time until the 1920s was held by men from the upper landowning Creole class, it is sometimes called the period of the "Aristocratic Republic."

Caudillos and Oligarchic Rule During the later 1820s the independence junta in Buenos Aires solidified into an oligarchy of the city's wealthy Creole elite, but the vast, largely undeveloped areas of the pampas with their small floating population of Amerindian peoples and Creole *gauchos*, or cowboys, remained largely outside the new state. A war with Brazil drained the country of much of its manpower and resources. The political circles in Buenos Aires began to solidify around those favoring a strong central government to conduct a strong foreign policy and exercise control over the provinces, which advocated a looser federal system. By the 1830s these unsettled conditions gave rise to the first of many Argentine caudillos, Juán Manuel de Rosas (in office 1829–1852).

De Rosas was descended from a wealthy ranching family and tended to identify with the gauchos. But he saw himself as a champion of national unity rather than one who sought to limit the role of the government in regional affairs. After becoming governor of Buenos Aires in 1829, he systematically extended his personal influence (*personalismo*) over his fellow governors until he was named caudillo in 1835, imposing a severe and fundamentally conservative brand of autocratic rule on the country.

Ultimately, his centralism and appetite for expansion helped in his downfall. Fierce in his opposition to British annexation of the Malvinas Islands—or Falklands, as the British called them—though frustrated by not being able to reverse it, he unwisely intervened in a civil war in Uruguay in 1843. His popularity flagged as the war dragged on for 9 years. Finally, the unsuccessful war, coupled with his unwillingness to lend his support to a constitution favorable to the provinces, led to his ouster in 1852.

The Settling of the Pampas The victor was a provincial governor named Justo José de Urquisa, who became the new caudillo. Urquisa swiftly extricated Argentina from Uruguay, defeated an army of de Rosas loyalists, and successfully sponsored a constitutional convention in 1853, lessening political centralism. In 1854 he

> **"In My Country I Am Like a Princess"**
>
> "Marriages were made among a small number of families, **endogamously**. Their children's education began in exclusive schools. Playmates continued as schoolmates and as classmates in the universities. . . . Families were generally large with an abundance of servants, who were sometimes treated as if they belonged to the same family circle. There were drawing rooms where only those with certain surnames could enter and which were closed to those who had only the power of money; there were families before which one knelt with respect, awe, and adulation. The daughter of one of these once said in Europe, 'In my country I am like a princess.'"
>
> —Peter F. Klarén, trans. "The Origins of Modern Peru, 1880–1930." In *The Cambridge History of Latin America*, vol. 5, *c. 1870 to 1930*. Edited by Leslie Bethell, p. 613. Cambridge: Cambridge University Press, 1986.

Endogamy: Custom of restricting marriage to a local community, clan, or tribe.

was elected president, and it seemed for the moment that Argentina was on the road to a more open, representative government. But the presidency remained the property of a small Creole oligarchy from the provincial elite. Not surprisingly, renewed conflict broke out with Buenos Aires over the issue of a strong centralized regime versus a projected new federal arrangement. In 1861, the forces of Buenos Aires defeated Urquisa's provincial forces and the country was reintegrated, with Buenos Aires as the national capital.

In the following years, many of the same forces that were shaping the North American West were also actively transforming the pampas. The land was opened to settlement, driving the gauchos from their independent existence into becoming hired hands. The railroad was spurring settlement, and the remaining Amerindians were driven south to Patagonia or exterminated. In contrast to the homesteading policies in the United States, however, the pampas were divided up into huge *estancias*, or estates, of tens of thousands of acres, aided by the introduction of barbed wire to fence in the ranges. Thus, the old system of rounding up essentially wild livestock and driving it to market now gave way to the ranching of cattle, sheep, and goats. As in other areas of South America, the new landed Creole elites dominated politics and economics long into the twentieth century.

Toward Party Politics   Despite the cozy arrangement of nineteenth-century Argentine politics, the growing urban center of Buenos Aires and the waves of Spanish and Italian immigrants grew restless under the rotating presidency that characterized the period 1880–1900. Spurred by the development of radical politics in Europe, especially those adopting versions of Marxism and socialism, two major urban opposition parties took shape in the 1890s: the Radical Party and the Socialists. As the influence of these parties grew, electoral reforms were forced on an unwilling landed oligarchy. In 1912, universal male suffrage was passed, and voting would take place by secret ballot. By 1916, the closed oligarchy was at last cracked open by the arrival of a new president, Hipólito Yrigoyen (1916–1922, 1928–1930). He relied for support mostly on an urban constituency, which dominated politics in the early twentieth century.

Brazil: From Kingdom to Republic

During the late colonial period, Brazil underwent the same centralizing administrative, fiscal, and trade reforms as the Spanish possessions. These reforms were resented as much by the Brazilian planter and urban Creoles as by their Spanish counterparts, but their fear of rebellion among the huge population of black slaves held them back from openly demanding independence. As it happened, independence arrived without bloody internecine wars, through the relocation of the monarchy from Portugal to Brazil in the wake of Napoleon's invasion of Iberia in 1807. Brazil had since become an empire and when the second emperor, Dom Pedro II (r. 1831–1889), under pressure from Britain, finally abolished slavery in 1888, the politically abandoned plantation oligarchy avenged itself by deposing him and switching to a republican regime under the military in 1889. Given the enormous size of the country, as well as the split of the Creole oligarchy into mining, sugar, and coffee interests, the regime became solidly federal, making it difficult for caudillos to succeed and allowing eventually for the rise of civilian presidents.

Transfer of the Crown from Portugal to Brazil   Portugal's royal family fled the country in advance of Napoleon's armies in 1807. Escorted by British ships, it took refuge in Brazil and elevated the colony to the status of a coequal kingdom in union with Portugal but governed from Brazil after Napoleon's defeat in 1815. The arrival of some 15,000 Portuguese together with the dynasty, however, created resentment among the Brazilian Creoles, sharpening the traditional tension between Creoles and Portuguese-born reformers. A crisis point was reached in 1820 when rebels in Portugal adopted a liberal constitution, which demanded the return of Brazil to colonial status as well as the transfer of the dynasty back to Portugal. The reigning king returned but left his son, Pedro I (r. 1822–1831), behind in Brazil. On the advice of both his father and courtiers, Pedro uttered in 1822 his famous *"fico"* ("I remain"), and proclaimed "Independence or Death!" thereby making Brazil an independent kingdom.

Pedro I's Authoritarianism   On acceding to the throne, Pedro declared Brazil an empire because of its size and diversity. His rule, however, embodied many of the same characteristics as that of the caudillos in the Spanish-speaking South American countries. In addition, like the restoration monarchs of Europe in the early 1800s, he firmly adhered to his belief in divine right, which was incompatible with more than token constitutionalism. Consequently, he rejected an attempt by the landed Creole oligarchy to introduce limited monarchical rule. Instead, he issued his own constitution in 1823 that concentrated most powers in his hands as well as a council of state, with a weak lifetime senate and a legislative chamber based on severely limited voting rights. Since he also reserved to himself the nomination and dismissal of ministers, the dissolution of the chamber, and, above all, the appointment of provincial governors, his rule was far too authoritarian even for the conservative planter elite.

In reaction, in 1824 six northeastern provinces attempted to secede. They proclaimed the republican Federation of the Equator and, somewhat illogically, demanded more central government support for the traditional northern sugar and cotton plantations, neglected by a rising emphasis on south-central coffee plantations. Increased British patrols in the Atlantic to suppress the slave trade had increased the price for slaves. The sugar planters could ill afford the increased prices, but the expanding coffee market enabled its planters to pay (see "Patterns Up Close").

Given the close ties between Britain and Brazil, Pedro found it difficult to resist mounting British demands for the abolition of slavery. As a result, early signs of alienation between the crown and the Creole planter elite crept in. It also did not help that Pedro supported the open immigration to Brazil of skilled foreigners, as well as foreign loans and investments for development. Like their counterparts in the American South, the plantation elites sought to limit immigration except for servile labor and control the courts to assure severe punishments for infractions by slaves; and they voiced their opposition to internal improvements like railroads, for fear of disrupting the stability of the plantation system. Ultimately, a succession crisis in Portugal in 1830 led to a conservative revolt against Pedro. In 1831, he lost his nerve and abdicated, sailing back to Portugal. He left the throne for his 5-year-old son, Pedro II (r. 1831–1889), who required a regent. Given a temporarily weak monarchy, the plantation oligarchy exploited the situation by renewing its demands for federalism.

Slave Rebellions in Cuba and Brazil

The successful slave revolt in Haiti was the most inspiring event for blacks in the first half of the nineteenth century. Blacks had gained little from the American and French Revolutions, and the pattern of brutal exploitation continued in many parts of the Americas. Not surprisingly, therefore, blacks sought to emulate the example of Haiti during the first half of the 1800s. Through careful and systematic preparation, they sought to tap into the repressed fury of the plantation slaves. However, none of the subsequent Haiti-inspired revolts was any more successful against the well-prepared authorities than previous revolts had been in the 1700s, as a look at rebellions in Cuba and Brazil during the first half of the nineteenth century shows.

In Cuba, the decline of sugar production in Haiti during the revolution encouraged a rapid expansion of plantations and the importation of African slaves. As previously in Haiti, a relatively diversified eighteenth-century society of whites, free mulattoes, and blacks, as well as urban and rural black slaves, was transformed into a heavily African-born plantation slave society, forming a large majority in many rural districts. The black freedman José Antonio Aponte (ca. 1756–1812), militiaman and head of the Yoruba confraternity (*cabilde*) in Havana, led an abortive revolt in 1812 that drew support from both sectors. In the subsequent revolts of 1825, 1835, and 1843, the urban element was less evident. Authorities and planters, invested heavily in new industrial equipment for sugar production and railroads, and exhausted by the unending sequence of uprisings, unleashed a campaign of sweeping arrests of free blacks and mulattoes that cut the urban–rural link once and for all.

Brazil, like Cuba, also benefited from the collapse of sugar production on Haiti in the 1790s and the first half of the 1800s. It expanded its plantation sector,

Slave Revolt Aboard Ship. Rebellions aboard ship, such as the famous 1839 mutiny aboard the *Amistad* shown here, were common occurrences. The *Amistad* was engaged in intra-American slave trafficking, and the slaves overpowered the crew shortly after embarkation in Cuba. After protracted legal negotiations, the slaves were eventually freed and retuned to Africa.

particularly in the province of Bahia, and imported large numbers of slaves from Africa. But here distrust divided African-born from Brazilian slaves, freedmen, and mulattoes. Many freedmen and mulattoes served in the militias that the authorities used to suppress the revolts. Furthermore, in contrast to the narrow island of Cuba, plantation slaves could run away more easily to independent settlements (called *quilombos*) in the wide-open Brazilian interior, from where revolts were more easily organized than either in cities or on plantations. In fact, no fewer than a dozen quilombo revolts extending into plantations occurred in Bahia during 1807–1828, revolts which the militias found difficult to crush, having to march into often remote areas.

Two urban revolts of the period were remarkable for their exceptional mix of insurgents, unparalleled in Cuba or elsewhere in Latin America. The first was the Tailor's Rebellion of 1798 in Salvador, Bahia's capital. Freedmen, mulattoes, and white craftspeople cooperated in the name of freedom and equality against the Creole oligarchy. The second was the Muslim uprising of 1835, also in Bahia, organized by African-born freedmen as well as slaves with Islamic clerical educations that they had received in West Africa before their enslavement.

The impact of Islam on African American slave societies has not been sufficiently studied. West African Muslims, including clerics, were frequently enslaved in the early 1800s during the many conflicts and the civil wars in what is today coastal Nigeria. These clerics represented an African strand of Islam that was tolerant of West African animism, to which the majority of slaves in Salvador adhered. Distinguished by their knowledge of Arabic, white gowns, and protective amulet necklaces, the clerics converted slaves in Salvador and surrounding areas to Islam and took up arms as freedom fighters during the short-lived rebellion in 1835. The role of Islam as an alternate ideology to that of constitutionalism, as symbolized by the Haitian Revolution, is an important reminder that American slaves, far from being culturally dependent, had the freedom to carve out their own unique identities.

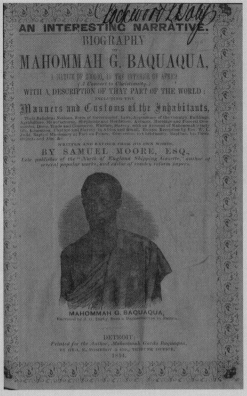

Man of Many Worlds. The life of Mahommah G. Baquaqua demonstrates the way in which some enslaved Africans could forge their own identities in the New World despite the daunting obstacles they faced. Captured and enslaved in West Africa in 1845 at about the age of 20, Baquaqua was taken to Pernambuco, Brazil, and then later to Rio de Janeiro, where a ship's captain bought him. He eventually escaped, made his way to New York City and then Haiti and then back to New York and finally on to Canada where he wrote his autobiography, the cover of which is shown here. He last shows up in the historical record in Britain, where seems to have lived out his remaining days.

Questions

- Do the slave rebellions in Cuba and Brazil in the early nineteenth century confirm or complicate the pattern of slave revolution that was first manifested first in Haiti?

- Why would Islam be attractive to many slaves in the Americas?

The Federalist Interlude   After lengthy debates, in 1834 the government granted the provinces their own legislative assemblies with strong tax and budget powers, effectively strengthening the provincial landholding elites with their various regional interests. It also abolished the council of state but created a national guard to suppress slave revolts and urban mobs. This mixed bag of reforms was not enough for some provinces. The most dangerous one was that of 1835 in Rio Grande do Sul, a southern province led by cattle owners who commanded military forces composed of gauchos. These owners established an independent republic that attracted many domestic and foreign radicals opposed to slavery, including Giuseppe Garibaldi, the Italian nationalist who played a crucial role in the unification of Italy. In reaction to the coexistence of a now weak and decentralized monarchy with an antislavery republic offering a refuge to runaways on Brazilian soil, the centralists reasserted themselves. In 1840 they proclaimed the 14-year-old Pedro II king and curbed the powers of the provincial assemblies, and in 1845 they negotiated a return of Rio Grande do Sul to Brazil.

The End of Slavery   The 1830s and 1840s coincided with a transition in Brazil from sugar to coffee as a major export commodity on the world market. The old sugar plantation elite lost clout, and a newer coffee planter oligarchy ascended to prominence. Both needed slaves, and as long as the crown did not seriously fulfill its promises of 1831 to the British to curb the importation of slaves, there was no more than unease about the mutual dependence of the king and the oligarchy on the continued existence of slave labor. But when the British in 1849 authorized warships to enter Brazilian waters to intercept slave ships, the importation of slaves virtually ceased. A serious labor shortage ensued, leading to a movement of slaves from the north to the center. For different reasons, sugar, cotton, and coffee plantation owners began to think of ridding themselves of a monarchy that was unable to maintain the flow of slaves from overseas.

In the 1860s and 1870s, anti-monarchy agitation gathered speed. Brazilians, especially professionals and intellectuals in the cities, became sensitive to their country being isolated in the world on the issue of slavery. After the United States, the Spanish colonies of Puerto Rico and Cuba ended slavery for all aged slaves and newborn children. Brazil was now left as the only unreformed slave-holding country in the Western Hemisphere. In the following decade and a half, as the antislavery chorus increased in volume, the government introduced a few cosmetic changes and it fell on the provinces to take more serious steps. Planters began to see the demise of the system on the horizon and encouraged their provinces to increase the flow of foreign immigrants, to be employed as wage labor on the coffee plantations. The political situation neared the point of anarchy in 1885, with mass flights of slaves from plantations and armed clashes to keep them there. Only then, in 1888, did the central government finally end slavery.

The Coffee Boom   Predictably, given the grip of the planter oligarchy on the labor force, little changed in social relations after the abolition of slavery. The coffee growers, enjoying high international coffee prices and the benefits of infrastructure improvements, through railroads and telegraph lines since the 1850s, could afford low-wage hired labor. The now free blacks received no land, education, or urban jobs, scraping by with low wages on the coffee and sugar plantations. Economically, however, after freeing itself from the burdens of slavery, Brazil expanded its economy in the 5 years following 1888 as much as in the 70 years of slavery since independence.

The monarchy, having dragged its feet for half a century on the slavery issue, was thoroughly discredited among the plantation elite and its offshoot, the officer corps in the military. By the 1880s, officers were also drawn from professional and intellectual urban circles. Increasingly, they subscribed to the ideology of *positivism* coming from France, which celebrated secular scientific and technological progress (see Chapter 22). Positivists, almost by definition, were liberal and republican in political orientation. In 1889, a revolt in the military supported by the Creole plantation oligarchy resulted in the abolition of the monarchy and proclamation of a republic, with practically no resistance from any quarter.

Two political tendencies emerged in the constituent assembly 2 years after the proclamation of the republic. The coffee interests of the south-central states favored federalism, with the right of the provinces to collect export taxes and maintain militias. The urban professional and intellectual interests, especially lawyers, supported a strong presidency with control over tariffs and import taxes as well as powers to use the federal military against provinces in cases of national emergency. The two tendencies were embodied in a compromise with a tilt toward federalism, which produced provincial caudillos, on the one hand, but regularly elected presidents, on the other.

Following this tilt, in the 1890s the government was strongly supportive of agricultural commodity exports. Coffee, rubber, and sugar exports yielded high profits and taxes until 1896, when overproduction of coffee resulted in diminishing returns. The State of São Paulo then regulated the sale of coffee on the world market through a state purchase scheme, which brought some stabilization to coffee production. At the same time and continuing into the early twentieth century (and without much state or central government support), immigrants and foreign investors laid the foundation for **import-substitution industrialization**, beginning with textile and food-processing factories. The comparative advantage from commodity exports had run its course by the late 1800s and early 1900s and now had to be supplemented with industrialization.

Children Picking Coffee in Brazil, ca. 1900. The first coffee bush was planted in Brazil in 1727. With the decline of the slave trade in the late nineteenth century, Brazil increasingly had to rely on immigrants—such as the children shown here—to provide labor for its booming coffee industry, which was centered in the hilly region near Rio de Janeiro and in the Paraíba Valley in the state of São Paulo.

Import-substitution industrialization: The practice by which countries protect their economies by setting high tariffs, and construct factories for the production of consumer goods (textiles, furniture, shoes; followed later by appliances, automobiles, electronics), and/or capital goods (steel, chemicals, machinery).

Latin American Society and Economy in the Nineteenth Century

Independence brought both disruptions and continuities in the economy as well as in politics. In Spanish America, four colonial regions broke apart into eventually 21 independent republics, organized around the pattern of constitutional nationalism. Trade with Europe was thus radically altered. What continued were deep divisions between the small landowning elites and the urban masses of officials, professionals, craftspeople, and laborers. Although many members of the elites and urban lower classes had collaborated in the drive for independence, afterward they broke apart into conservative and liberal wings, unable to establish a consensus and stable state institutions. When trade with Europe resumed, a lowest-denominator pattern of export-led growth based on mineral and agricultural commodities evolved (see Map 27.4).

MAP 27.4 **The Economy of Latin America and the Caribbean, ca. 1900.**

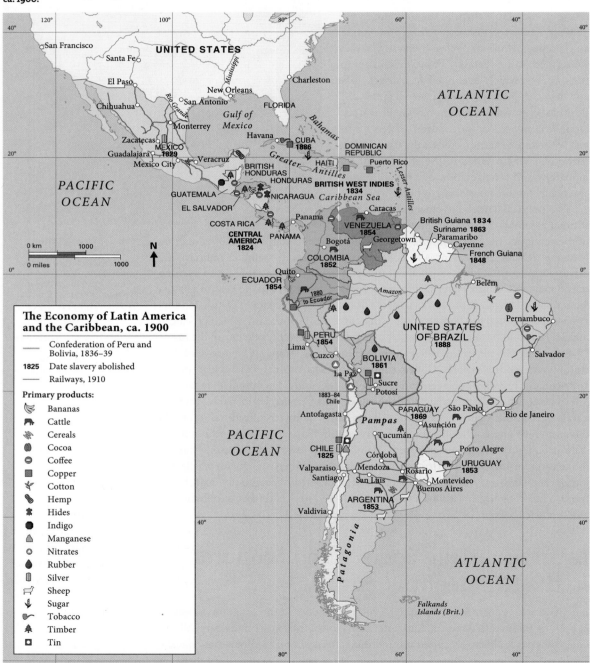

The Economy of Latin America and the Caribbean, ca. 1900

— Confederation of Peru and Bolivia, 1836–39

1825 Date slavery abolished

— Railways, 1910

Primary products:

- Bananas
- Cattle
- Cereals
- Cocoa
- Coffee
- Copper
- Cotton
- Hemp
- Hides
- Indigo
- Manganese
- Nitrates
- Rubber
- Silver
- Sheep
- Sugar
- Tobacco
- Timber
- Tin

Rebuilding Societies and Economies

Reconstruction in the independent republics and the Brazilian monarchy took several decades. Mercantilist trade was gone, and in its place, free trade had to be built. Social structures changed little, and constitutional disagreements took some time to be settled. Production in the mines and on the estates had to be restarted with fresh capital. All this took time, and it was only by mid-century that Latin America had overcome the aftereffects of the wars of independence.

On the Eve of Independence   During the colonial period, the economies of Spain and Portugal in the Americas followed a pattern of mercantilism. In mercantilist theory, as we have seen a number of times, the Spanish and Portuguese colonies could purchase only goods manufactured in Iberia and had to pay with gold, silver, sugar, cocoa, indigo, or other goods from the colonies. In practice, as Spain and Portugal reformed colonial administration and trade in the 1700s, it became easier for the colonies to buy from European countries via transit through Iberia. Contraband trade similarly mitigated and undercut Iberian mercantilism. Interregional trade increased during the reform period, especially for foodstuffs and cattle, Mexican and Ecuadorian textiles, and Argentinean and Chilean wine. Overall, however, interregional trade remained a poor cousin of the export trade.

Taxes were considerably higher in the Americas than in Iberia, with estimates of a 40–70 percent differential. But since tax surpluses from rich regions, such as Mexico, had to subsidize poor regions for administrative, judicial, and military costs, Spain did not earn much from its American colonies. Portugal was luckier with its colony of Brazil, which more or less consistently yielded a tribute. But, in contrast to earlier centuries, during the 1700s Iberia as a whole did not earn much from its American conquests.

After Independence   The achievement of independence in the 1820s, after lengthy struggles with Spain and local and internal conflicts, had a number of far-reaching consequences. The most important result was the end of Spain's mercantilist monopoly. The Latin American republics were free to buy or sell and to borrow money anywhere in the world. Among trading partners, this freedom benefited Great Britain most directly. Its merchants had already established themselves in several Latin American cities during the continental boycott of Napoleon, which had shut out Great Britain from trade with the European continent.

Initially, however, for Latin Americans the freedom to trade was more hope than reality. Dislocations from the struggle of independence were considerable. Capital had fled the continent and left behind uncultivated estates and flooded mines. The Catholic Church held huge, uncollectable debts. In many areas taxes could not be collected. Troops helped themselves to payment through plunder. In Mexico, where the struggle between republicans and royalists was the fiercest, the disruptions were worst and reconstruction took longest. Chile also experienced violent struggles but stabilized itself relatively quickly. On average, though, it took until about 1850 for Latin America to fully recover.

Constitutional Nationalism and Society   The Creoles were everywhere the winners in the wars of independence. Many were ardent constitutional nationalists, finding it easy to adapt to conservative versions of this form of the Western challenge of modernity. The most powerful among them were large landowners, that is, owners of grain-farming self-sufficiency estates, cattle ranches, and sugar, indigo, cacao, coffee, or cotton plantations. Independence did not produce much change in agrarian relations: Landowners of self-sufficient estates and plantations in many parts of Latin America continued to employ tenant farmers and slaves.

The large majority of the Creoles were urban administrators, professionals, craftspeople, and laborers. Their leaders, ardent constitutional nationalists, tended toward political and economic liberalism. In many areas they were joined by mestizos, mulattoes, and black freedmen, also largely craftspeople and laborers. The main issue dividing the liberals and conservatives, as in the French Revolution, was the extent of voting rights: Liberals wanted to extend it to all males, while conservatives sought to limit it through literacy and property requirements to a minority of males. No influential group at this point considered extending voting rights to women.

Deep Political Divisions   Once independence was won, distrust between the two groups with very different property interests set in and the political consensus fell apart. Accordingly, landed constitutional conservatives restricted voting rights, to the detriment of the urban constitutional liberals. The exceptions were Argentina and, for a time during the mid-century, Peru: The one had few mestizos and mulattoes but a relatively large urban Creole population that gained the upper hand, and the other had large numbers of urban mestizos and Amerindians who could not be ignored. Nevertheless, even if constitutionalism was submerged for periods of time under caudillo authoritarianism, as we have seen, adaptation to constitutionalism, in its conservative or liberal variation, remained a permanent fixture. It was this early adoption of constitutionalism which distinguished Latin America from the Ottoman Empire, Russia, China, and Japan.

Split Over State–Church Relations   Among the many issues over which conservatives and liberals split, the relationship between state and church was the deepest. Initially, given the more or less close collaboration between republicans and conservatives during the struggle for independence, Catholicism remained the national religion for all. Accordingly, education and much property remained under church control.

But the new republics ended the powers of the Inquisition and claimed the right of *patronato*, that is, of naming bishops. At the behest of Spain, however, the pope left bishoprics empty rather than agree to this new form of lay investiture. In fact, Rome would not even recognize the independence of the Latin American nations until the mid-1830s. The conflict was aggravated by the church's focus on its institutional rather than pastoral role. The Catholic clergy provided little guidance at a time when industrial modernity, even if only indirectly via urbanization, was crying out for spiritual reorientation. At the same time, papal pronouncements made plain the church's hostility toward the developing capitalist industrial order.

This hostility of the church was thus one of the factors that in the mid-1800s contributed to a swing back to liberalism, beginning with Colombia in 1849. Many countries adopted a formal separation between church and state and introduced secular educational systems. But the state–church issue remained bitter, especially in Mexico, Guatemala, Ecuador, and Venezuela, where it was often at the center of political shifts between liberals and conservatives. In Colombia, for example, it even led to a complete reversal of liberal trends in the mid-1880s, with the reintroduction of Catholicism as the state religion.

Economic Weakness   Given the difficulties of arriving at a political and cultural consensus during the period of recovery after independence (ca. 1820–1850), the reconstruction of a fiscal system to support the governments remained contradictory and problematic. For example, governments resorted to taxation of trade, even if this interfered with declared policies of free trade. The yields on tariffs and export taxes, however, were inevitably low and made the financing of strong central governments difficult. Consequently, maneuvering for the most productive mix of the two taxes trumped official pronouncements in favor of free trade and often eroded confidence among trade partners.

This maneuvering had little effect on the domestic economy—self-sufficiency agriculture and urban crafts production—which represented the great bulk of economic activities in Latin America. Grain production on large estates and small farms, especially in Brazil where gold production declined in late colonial times, had escaped the turbulence of the independence war and recovery periods relatively unscathed. Land remained plentiful, and the main bottleneck continued to be labor. The distribution of marketable surpluses declined, however, given the new internal borders in Latin America with their accompanying tariffs and export taxes. Self-sufficiency agriculture and local economies relying on it thus remained largely unchanged throughout the 1800s.

The crafts workshops, especially for textiles, suffered from the arrival of cheap British factory-produced cottons, which represented the majority of imports by the mid-1800s. Their impact, however, remained relatively limited, mostly to the coasts, since in the absence of railroads transportation costs to the interior were prohibitively expensive. Only Mexico encouraged the financing of machine-driven textile factories, but the failure of its state bank in 1842—from issuing too many loans—ended this policy for a number of decades. On the one hand, there was a definite awareness in most countries of the benefits of factories, using domestic resources, and linking the self-sufficiency agricultural sector to modern industrial development. On the other hand, its necessity in the face of traditional opposition was not demonstrated until later in the nineteenth century.

Export-Led Growth

The pursuit of a policy of commodity exports—export-led growth—from about 1850 led to expanding rates in the standard of living for many Latin Americans. The industrializing countries in Europe and North America were voracious consumers of the minerals and materials that Latin America had in abundance and of its tropical agricultural products. More could have been sold, had there not been a chronic labor shortage.

Raw Materials and Cash Crops   Mining and agricultural cash crop production recovered gradually so that by the 1850s, nearly all Latin American governments had adopted export-led economic growth as their basic policy. This was about

Loading Nitrate into Rail Cars, Chile, 1915. In the 1830s, farmers realized the value of nitrate as a fertilizer and an export boom to industrializing Europe ensued. Most of the deposits were located in what were then coastal lands of Peru and Bolivia. In 1879, Bolivia raised its taxes on nitrate mining, and in response Chile declared war on Bolivia. Chile won the war against Bolivia (and Peru, which sided with the latter) in 1884; as a result, Bolivia became landlocked. The nitrate boom eventually collapsed in World War I when Germany began making synthetic fertilizer.

all the conservatives and liberals were able to agree on since land distribution to poor farmers and a system of income taxes were beyond any consensus. Mexican and Peruvian silver production, the mainstay of the colonial mercantilist economy, became strong again, although the British adoption of the gold standard in 1821 imposed limits on silver exports. Peru found a partial replacement for silver with guano mining. Guano, seabird excrement accumulated over the millennia and fossilized, was mined by laborers using simple implements, such as pickaxes and shovels. It was exported for use as an organic fertilizer and as a source of nitrates for explosives. Chile hit the jackpot with guano, nitrate, and copper exports, of crucial importance during the chemical- and electricity-driven second Industrial Revolution.

In other Latin American countries, tropical and subtropical cash crops defined export-led economic growth during the mid-1800s. In Brazil, Colombia, and Costa Rica, labor-intensive coffee growing redefined the agricultural sector. In Argentina, the production of jerked (dried) beef, similarly labor-intensive, refashioned the ranching economy. The main importers of this beef were regions in the Americas where plantation slavery continued into the second half of the 1800s, especially the United States, Brazil, and Cuba. The latter, which remained a Spanish colony until 1895, profited from the relocation of sugarcane plantations from the mainland and a number of Caribbean islands after the British outlawing of the slave trade (1807) and slavery itself (1834) and the Latin American wars of independence (1810–1826).

In the long run, however, like silver, cane sugar had a limited future, given the rise of beet sugar production in Europe. Minerals and cash crops were excellent for export-led economic growth, especially if they required secondary activities such as the processing of meat or the use of mining machinery. But competition on the world market increased during the 1800s, and thus, there was ultimately a ceiling, reached in the 1890s.

Broadening of Exports With their eyes increasingly focused on exports, Latin American governments responded quickly to the increased market opportunities resulting from the Industrial Revolution in Great Britain, the European continent, and the United States. Peru broadened its mineral exports with copper, Bolivia with tin, and Chile with nitrates. Brazil and Peru added rubber, Argentina and Uruguay wool, and Mexico *henequen* (a fiber for ropes and sacks) to its traditional exports. Luxuries from tropical Latin America, like coffee, cacao (for chocolate bars, invented in 1847), vanilla, and bananas, joined sugar after 1850 in becoming affordable mass consumer items in the industrialized countries. Argentina, with investments in refrigeration made by Britain, added frozen meat to this list in 1883. This commodity diversification met not only the broadened demand of the second Industrial Revolution, with its demand for chemicals and electricity, but also the demand for consumer goods among the newly affluent middle classes.

Since the choice among minerals and crops was limited, however, most nations remained wedded to one commodity only (50 percent of exports or more). Only two, Argentina and Peru, were able to diversify (exports of less than 25 percent for the leading commodity). They were more successful at distributing their exports over the four main industrial markets of Great Britain, Germany, France, and the United States. On the eve of World War I the United States had grown to be the most important trading partner in 11 of the 21 Latin American countries. Given its own endowments and under the conditions of world trade in the second half of the nineteenth century, the continent's trade was relatively well diversified.

The prices of all Latin American commodities gyrated substantially up and down during the second half of the nineteenth century. This fluctuation was in contrast to the imported manufactured goods, primarily textiles, metal utensils, and implements, which became cheaper over time. In fact, Brazil's government was so concerned about fluctuating coffee prices in the 1890s that it introduced the Taubaté coffee valorization scheme in 1906. As the largest producer, it regulated the amount of coffee offered on the world market, carefully adjusting production to keep market prices relatively stable in much the same way that oil-producing countries would later do with petroleum. Since coffee trees need 5 years to mature, Brazil was largely successful with its scheme until World War I, when worldwide conditions changed. An American oligopoly (the United and Standard Fruit Companies) in control of banana production in Central America from the 1890s similarly controlled prices. A careful investigation of commodity prices by economic historians has resulted in the conclusion that in spite of all fluctuations commodity prices rose overall during 1850–1914.

Rising Living Standards   From all evidence, in the period from the middle of the 1800s to the eve of World War I, the governments can be judged as having been successful with their choice of export-led growth as their consensus policy. Living standards rose, as measured in gross domestic product (GDP). At various times during 1850–1900, between five and eight Latin American countries kept pace with the living standards in the industrialized countries. Argentina and Chile were the most consistent leaders throughout the period. Thus, although many politicians were aware that at some point their countries would have to industrialize in addition to relying on commodity export growth, they can perhaps be forgiven for keeping their faith in exports as the engine for improved living standards right up to World War I.

Labor and Immigrants   As in the industrialized countries, the profitable exports were achieved through low wages. Together with the rest of the world, Latin America experienced high population increases during the 1800s. The population grew sevenfold, to 74 million, although it remained small in comparison to the populations of Europe, which doubled to 408 million, and Africa and Asia, which each grew by one-third to 113 and 947 million, respectively. The increases were not large enough to dent the favorable land–person ratio, so it is not surprising that the high demand for labor continued during the 1800s. This demand, of course, was the reason the institution of forced labor—revolving labor duties (mit'a) among Amerindians in the Andes and slavery—had come into existence in the first place.

Not surprisingly, mit'a and slavery continued during the 1800s, liberal constitutionalism notwithstanding, in a number of countries. Even where forced labor was abolished early, however, low wages continued. One would have expected wages to rise rapidly, given the continuing conditions of labor shortage and land availability. Mine operators and landowners, however, were reluctant to raise wages because they feared for the competitiveness of their commodities on the world market. Governments, doing their bidding, preferred to resort to selective and mass immigration from overseas to enlarge the labor pool.

Typical selective immigration examples were *coolies* (from Urdu *kuli*, hireling), that is, "indentured" laborers recruited from India and China on 5- or 10-year contracts and working off the costs of their transportation. During 1847–1874, nearly half a million East Indians traveled to various European colonies in the Caribbean. Similarly, 235,000 Chinese came to Peru, Cuba, and Costa Rica, working in guano pits and silver mines, on sugar and cotton plantations, and later on railroads. If the experience of five Caribbean islands can be taken as a guide, only about 10 percent of the coolies returned home. Coolie migration to Latin America, therefore, can be described as a major part of the pattern of massive migration streams across the world that typified the nineteenth century (see Map 27.5).

Immigration to Latin America from Europe was on an even bigger scale. In Argentina, Uruguay, Brazil, and Chile, Italians and Spaniards settled in large numbers from around 1870 on. In Argentina, nearly one-third of the population consisted of immigrants, a share much higher than at any time in the United States. The Italian population of Argentina numbered close to 1 million by the turn of the century. Most immigrants settled in cities, and Buenos Aires became the first city on the continent with more than a million people. Only here did a semi-regular labor market develop, with rising urban and rural wages prior to World War I. Elsewhere in Latin America, governments, beholden to large landowners, feared the rise of cities with immigrant laborers who did not share their interests. They, therefore, opposed mass immigration.

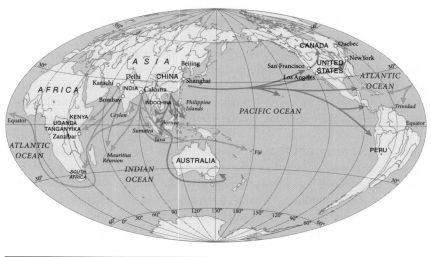

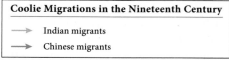

Coolie Migrations in the Nineteenth Century

→ Indian migrants

→ Chinese migrants

MAP 27.5 **Coolie Migrations in the Nineteenth Century.**

Dining Hall for Recently Arrived Immigrants, Buenos Aires. Immigrants, all male, and more than likely all Italian, rub shoulders sometime around 1900 in a dining hall in Buenos Aires set up for newly arrived immigrants. By 1914, 2 percent of the population of Buenos Aires—about 300,000 people—had been born in Italy, most from the poor southern regions of Campania, Calabria, and Sicily.

Self-Sufficiency Agriculture   Except for Argentina, Chile, and Uruguay, the levels of commodity exports did not rise sufficiently to reduce the size of the rural labor force not working for exports, a major condition for improved living standards across the board. On the eve of World War I, two-thirds to half of the laborers in most Latin American countries were still employed as tenant farmers or farmhands on large estates. In much smaller numbers, they were indigenous villagers who owned their small farmsteads. Their contribution to the national GDP, for example, in Brazil and Mexico was less than one-quarter. Toward the end of the century, observers began to realize that export-led growth—even though it looked like an effective economic driver—did not have much of a transformative effect on the rural masses in most countries.

The absence of such transformative effects was visible, for example, in the high levels of illiteracy among rural inhabitants. Adult illiteracy rates of up to 80 percent were not uncommon, even in relatively diversified countries, such as Brazil and Mexico. Only Argentina and Chile after 1860 invested heavily in primary education, on levels similar to the United States and Britain, followed by Costa Rica in the 1890s. Literate self-sufficiency farmers, knowledgeable in plant and animal selection as well as fertilizers, were practically nonexistent north of the southern end of Latin America.

Governments paid greater attention to the improvement of rural infrastructures from about 1870 onward, with the development of railroads. Almost everywhere, they looked to direct foreign investment, given the low-yielding and highly regressive trade taxes on which the relatively slim central domestic revenues depended. The foreign investors or consortiums built these railroads primarily for the transportation of commodities to ports. Many self-sufficiency farmers or even landlords, therefore, received little encouragement to produce more food staples for urban markets. Argentina and Chile, followed by Costa Rica and Uruguay, built the most railroads, with between 2.8 and 1.5 miles per 1,000 heads of population. Correspondingly, with fertilizers and better implements available via railroads, corn yields quintupled

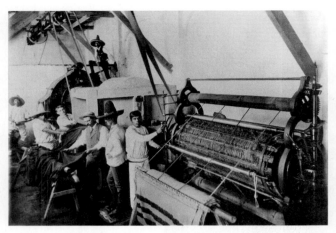

Mexican Textile Factory. Cocolapam in the state of Veracruz was the site of the first Mexican cotton textile factory, founded in 1836 by Lucas Alamán, a Mexican government minister and investment banker. Its machinery, imported from Great Britain, was water-driven. The textiles it produced remained inferior to imports, but they were cheap and satisfied the needs of most Mexicans.

in Argentina. Conversely, these yields changed little in Mexico, which had only 1.2 miles per 1,000 heads. Overall, the Latin American railroad network represented only about one-fifth to one-third of that in other Western developing settler countries, such as Australia, Canada, and New Zealand.

Factories   Until about 1870, the handicrafts sector met the demands of the rural as well as low-earning urban population. It produced cheap, low-quality textiles, shoes, soap, candles, tools, implements, cutlery, and horse tack. As is well known, this sector failed in most parts of the world during the 1800s or 1900s to mechanize itself and establish a modern factory system. Latin America was no exception. Most crafts shops were based on family labor, with a high degree of self-exploitation, unconnected to the landowning elite and deemed too small by lending banks. There was no path from workshops to factories.

However, even entrepreneurial investors interested in building factories for the manufacture of yarn or textiles were hampered in their efforts. They had little chance for success prior to the appearance of public utilities in the 1880s, providing water during the dry season and electricity as an energy source, in the absence of high-quality coal in most parts of Latin America. Even then, the risk of engaging in manufacturing, requiring long-term strategies with no or low profits, was so great that the typical founders of factories were not Creoles but European immigrants.

In Argentina and Chile these immigrants labored hard during their first years after arrival and saved the start-up capital necessary to launch small but modern textile, food-processing, and beverage factories. Argentina, Chile, Mexico, and Peru made the greatest advances toward factory industrialization, producing import-substituting consumer goods to the tune of 50–80 percent. Prior to World War I, the only country that took the step from consumer goods to capital goods (goods for factories) was Mexico, with the foundation of the Fundidora Iron and Steel Mill in 1910 in Monterrey, which, however, was unprofitable for a long time. Full capital goods industrialization had to await the postwar period.

Culture, Family, and the Status of Women

Economic growth and urbanization added considerably to the growth of constitutional-nationalist modernity in Latin America. But the absence of industrialization until the end of the nineteenth century impeded the transformation of society and its cultural institutions. The law and custom represented by the Catholic Church remained pervasive. In the second half of the nineteenth century, however, the idea of separating church and state gained adherents, with some major legal consequences for social institutions.

Legal Changes   In most countries, repeated attempts by governments after independence to reduce the role of the Catholic church in society remained unsuccessful. The church resisted the efforts of the constitutional nationalists to carry out land expropriations and to separate state and church in social legislation. In a number of civil codes women's rights in inheritance and property control improved, but overall husbands retained their patriarchal rights over their families. Typically, they were entitled to the control over the family budget, contractual engagements, choice of husbands for their daughters (up to age 25 in some countries), or residence of unmarried daughters (at home, up to age 30). Only from the middle of the nineteenth century did the influence of the Catholic Church diminish sufficiently to allow legislation for secular marriages and divorce in a number of countries. Catholicism remained doctrinally unchanged.

"Men in the Street and Women at Home"   As it also developed in the Euro-American Victorian world, on the cultural level there was a popular ideal in nineteenth-century Latin America of nuclear family domesticity. But, as research has also shown, in both places this was often honored more in the breach than in the observance. That is to say, in Mexico and South America, despite the long-standing proverb *El hombre en la calle, la mujer en la casa* ("Men in the street, women in the home"), it was often the case that the two roles were intermingled. In urban areas, women frequently ran shops, managed markets, were proprietors of *cantinas*, and performed a host of skilled and unskilled jobs, particularly in the textile and food trades. In rural areas, farm work on small holdings and peonages was often shared by men and women, though a number of individual tasks—plowing, for example—were most frequently done by men.

As in Europe and North America, too, there was a remarkably high level of widowhood and spinsterhood. In areas where the predominant form of employment was dangerous—mining, for example—the incidence of widowhood was very high. Widows often could not or chose not to remarry, especially if they had relatives to fall back on or were left an income. The stereotype of the stern patriarchal husband was also pervasive enough so that many middle-class women, often to the consternation of their families, chose not to marry at all. Both of these conditions were common enough so that by one estimate one-third of all the households in Mexico City in the early nineteenth century were headed by women. Widows were entitled to their dowries and half of the community property, while boys and girls received equal portions of the inheritance. Thus, despite society's pressures to marry and raise children, many women did not marry or, after becoming widowed, remained single. In this sense, they achieved a considerable degree of autonomy in a male-dominated society. Thus social realities and legal rights diverged in early independent Latin America, even before legal reform.

The Visual and Literary Arts   To try to encapsulate the culture and arts of more than a continent—and one so vast and diverse as Latin America—is far beyond the scope of this textbook. In general terms, the legacy of European baroque and romantic-era paintings remained alive throughout the nineteenth century as a background current until giving way to the influences of European impressionists and painters.

The trend in all of Latin America colonial-era high culture under the aegis of Spanish and Portuguese influences after independence was toward "indigenization": Much like the way the United States attempted during this time to break away from European art and literary influences, a similar movement pervaded the Latin American world. Along with attempts to form national and regional styles of their own, many countries also engaged in art as a nation-building exercise—artistic and literary celebrations of new national heroes or famous historic instances through portraiture and landscape painting. Finally, there were also periodic engagements with the popular or folk arts of Amerindian peoples, mulattoes, mestizos, and Africans in celebration of regional uniqueness.

Literature to some extent paralleled the trajectory of the other arts. In the latter eighteenth and early nineteenth centuries, a style had developed called *criollo* (Creole), for its inception and popularity among that class. The most famous of work in this style was José Joaquin Fernández Lizardi's *The Mangy Parrot* (*El Periquillo Samiento*), published in 1816. Though ostensibly a tale of children's stories, it is more in the vein of Voltaire's *Candide* in lampooning the venality, corruption, and incompetence of the late colonial world. Initially, there was little nostalgia for the pre-independence years.

Following independence, as in painting, literature often turned to themes befitting countries trying to establish themselves as nations with distinct historic pasts and great future potential. In some cases, as with sometime newspaper crusader and later Argentine president Domingo Faustino Sarmiento (in office 1868–1874), critique of the present was the order of the day. Sarmiento relentlessly criticized the authoritarian rule and arbitrary ways of the caudillo Juán Manuel de Rosas in his book *Facundo: Civilization and Barbarism*. The book, written while Sarmiento had been forced into exile by Rosas in 1845, is an indictment of Rosas thinly disguised as a biography of the brutal gaucho leader Juán Facundo Quiroga. It is also, however, a meditation on the meaning of "civilization" and "barbarism" as exemplified by Europe, Asia, Africa, and Latin America. As such, it has been called by some the most important book to be published in the nineteenth century in Latin America.

The themes of the social sciences and reportage merged in much of the work of the Brazilian writer Euclides da Cunha (1866–1909). In his most famous work, *Os Sertões* (*The Rebellion in the Backlands*, 1902), he examines with a critical eye the social demography of Brazil, its racial composition and conflicts, and weighs them against the claims of the new Brazilian Republic. The vehicle for this is the attempt by the government to crush a rebellion of isolated settler outcasts in Bahia, during the 1890s, who, despite the odds against them, repeatedly defeat the government forces and become regional heroes. The book acquired considerable popularity in Brazil and was also championed by a number of leading writers in Europe and the United States. In Brazil as in the Spanish-speaking Americas, authors in the nineteenth century had a keen eye for society caught between tradition and modernity.

Civilization and Barbarism

"No, we are not the lowest among Americans. Something is to result from this chaos; either something surpassing the government of the United States of North America, or something a thousand times worse than that of Russia—the Dark Ages returned, or political institutions, superior to any yet known."

—Domingo F. Sarmiento. *Life in the Argentine Republic in the Days of the Tyrants: Or Civilization and Barbarism*, p. 247. New York: Hurd and Houghton, 1868.

Putting It All Together

The term "banana republic" appeared for the first time in 1904. The American humorist O. Henry (1862–1910) coined it to represent politically unstable and economically poor Latin American countries, governed by small elites and relying on tropical exports, such as bananas. O. Henry had spent several years at the end of the nineteenth century in Honduras, hiding from US authorities. Thus he knew whereof he spoke.

Today, political stability is much greater; but many parts of Latin America are still poor and underindustrialized. Consequently, banana republics still resonates. Were Latin American elites, therefore, wrong to engage in a pattern of export-led growth, and did they collude with elites in the industrial countries to maneuver the continent into permanent dependence on the latter? Indeed, an entire generation of scholars in the second half of the twentieth century answered the question in the affirmative and wrote the history of the 1800s in gloomy and condemnatory tones. They called their analysis "dependency theory."

Contemporary historians are less certain about many of these conclusions. They compare Latin America not with the United States or western Europe but with the settler colonies of South Africa, Australia, and New Zealand or the old empires of the Middle East and Asia. In these comparisons, Latin America did very well and was not any more dependent on the industrializing countries than the latter were on Latin America.

Dependence increased only at the very end of the 1800s when industrial countries like the United States and Britain began to make significant capital investments. It was then that foreign companies, such as those that owned railroads in Nicaragua and Honduras, succeeded in exploiting and controlling production and export. The question we may need to ask then is not why Latin America failed to industrialize in the 1800s but, rather, did Latin America, choosing from the available choices, make

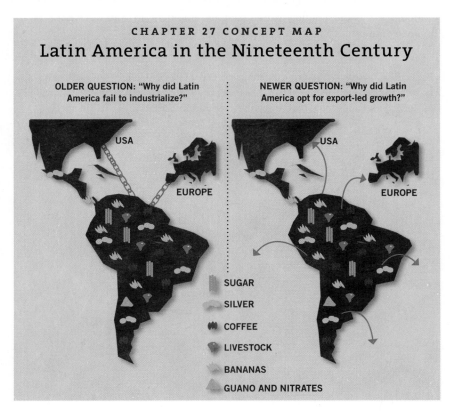

CHAPTER 27 CONCEPT MAP
Latin America in the Nineteenth Century

OLDER QUESTION: "Why did Latin America fail to industrialize?"

NEWER QUESTION: "Why did Latin America opt for export-led growth?"

USA

EUROPE

USA

EUROPE

SUGAR

SILVER

COFFEE

LIVESTOCK

BANANAS

GUANO AND NITRATES

the right decision when it opted for export-led growth up to about 1890? Did such a choice represent a "third way" toward economic growth, separate from industrial capitalism and tenacious attempts to keep economies closed off from the vagaries of world trade? Perhaps it did (see Concept Map).

Review and Respond

1. Define the concept of constitutional nationalism, and explain how and why it became a pattern of state formation in Latin America in the nineteenth century.

2. Compare Vincent Ogé and Toussaint Louverture. How are these two revolutionaries similar? How are they different?

3. Compare the political development of Haiti and Mexico in the early nineteenth century.

4. Why did the Creoles not become radical constitutional nationalists? Which kind of constitutionalism did they espouse?

5. Why did slavery persist for so long in Brazil? How is Brazilian slavery an example of the origins-interactions-adaptations model that informs this book?

6. Who were Simón Bolívar and José de San Martín, and what brought them together?

7. What distinguished the political development of Brazil from a colony to an independent country in Latin America?

8. Compare and contrast the dependency theory model and the export-led growth model for understanding patterns of development in Latin America in the nineteenth century.

▶ For additional resources, including maps, primary sources, visuals, and quizzes, please go to www.oup.com/us/vonsivers. Please see the Further Resources section at the back of the book for additional readings and suggested websites.

Thinking Through Patterns

▶ **Which factors in the complex ethnic and social structures of Latin America were responsible for the emergence of authoritarian politicians or caudillos?**

Similar to the United States and France, which also underwent revolutions in the late 1700s and early 1800s, Latin America's independence movements (1810–1824) did not extend the constitutional revolution beyond a small number of property owners who inhabited the highest levels of the social strata. The dominant class of large landlords and plantation owners was conservative and did not favor land reform for the benefit of small farmers. Urban professionals and craftspeople, divided in many places by ethnicity, did not share common interests that allowed them to provide an effective opposition to the landed class. Landowning and plantation interests thus protected themselves through authoritarian caudillo politics and sought to keep the opposition weak.

In colonial times, Latin America was the warm-weather extension of Europe, sending its mineral and agricultural commodities to Europe. When it acquired its independence and Europe industrialized during the 1800s, these commodities became even more important and the continent opted for a pattern of export-led development. This meant the systematic increase of mineral and agricultural commodity exports, with rising living standards not only for those who profited directly from the exports but also for many in the urban centers. Even with rising living standards it became clear by the turn of the century that a supplementary policy of industrialization had to be pursued.

▶ **Why did Latin American countries, after achieving independence, opt for a continuation of mineral and agricultural commodity exports?**

▶ **How do the social and economic structures of this period continue to affect the course of Latin America today?**

Many countries in Latin America are barely richer than they were in the 1800s. Even though industry, mineral, and commodity exports, as well as services, expanded in urban centers in the early part of the twentieth century, poor farmers with low incomes continued to be a drag on development. This phenomenon still characterizes many parts of Latin America today.

From Three Modernities to One

1914–PRESENT

World War I and the Interwar Period

The first great crisis in the evolution of modern scientific–industrial society was World War I (1914–1918). Although imperial competition in the Balkans indirectly triggered the war, there were even stronger forces playing their part in the background, together with other reasons still hotly contested by historians today.

For our purposes, the most dramatic effect of the war was that the single nineteenth-century pattern of modernity—constitutional and ethnic–linguistic nationalism and scientific–industrial society—splintered into the three subpatterns: capitalism–democracy, socialism–communism, and supremacist nationalism. The countries representing these subpatterns of modernity formed camps that were bitterly hostile to each other:

- Capitalist democracy (most notably the United States, Britain, France, and parts of Latin America): support for the concepts of freedom (especially the free market), capitalism, and international institutions for maintaining peace.

- Communism–socialism (the Soviet Union): professed support for equality over freedom and a command economy originating from the top.

- Supremacist nationalism (Italy, Germany, and Japan): contempt for both democracy and communism, the celebration of racial supremacy and authoritarian/dictatorial rule, a state-controlled economy, and territorial expansion through military conquest.

In the period after World War I, the countries representing these three modernities moved in very different directions:

- The democratic victors, Great Britain and France, expanded their colonial empires by acquiring, under the rubric of "mandates," new territories taken from the liquidated Ottoman Empire in the Middle East and German possessions in Africa. Since a variety of ethno–linguistic nationalisms in these territories were forming at the same time, future conflicts were inevitable.

1908
Oil Discovered in the Middle East

1911–1912
Revolution in China, Fall of Qing Dynasty

1914–1918
World War I

1917
Bolshevik Revolution

1919
Versailles Treaty, Founding of League of Nations

1929–1933
Stock Market Crash and Great Depression

1937–1945
World War II in China and the Pacific

1942
Nazis Implement the Final Solution

1947
Indian and Pakistani Independence

1948
State of Israel Founded, First Arab–Israeli War

1950–1953
Korean War

1957
Soviet Union's Launch of Sputnik Satellite, Decolonization Begins in Africa

1958
Great Leap Forward in China

1962
Cuban Missile C

- In Russia, a small but highly disciplined communist party managed to engineer a political takeover, withdraw from the war, and build a communist state: the Union of Socialist Soviet Republics (USSR or Soviet Union). The Soviet Union acquired full industrial strength in the 1930s.

- The loser of World War I, Germany, together with Italy and Japan (both of which had joined the Allies in hopes of territorial gains), turned toward supremacist nationalism.

World War II and the Rise of New Nations

In contrast to World War I, the Second World War was actively planned by the supremacist nationalists and was far less avoidable. Both World War I and the Great Depression effectively ended the global free trade that had characterized the nineteenth century. All countries, including the capitalist democracies, now subscribed to the idea that the future of industry lay in economic "spheres" each dominated by one *autarkic*—that is, self-sufficient—industrial power. With the victory of the Allies, the United States and Soviet Union emerged after World War II as the leading examples of the two surviving patterns of modernity: capitalist democracy and socialism–communism. The proponents of each of these patterns competed with the other during the Cold War (1945–1991):

- The first, or "hot," phase, 1945–1962: The United States and Soviet Union surrounded themselves with allies in Europe and Asia and fought one another militarily through proxies, that is, smaller allied states. They also sought to align the new nations, emerging in the wake of decolonization, into their respective camps. The Cold War climaxed during the Cuban Missile Crisis of 1962.

- The second, "cooling" phase, 1962–1991: During this time, the two nuclear powers reduced tensions ("détente") and agreed on a mechanism to limit, and then to reduce, their nuclear arsenals. But they continued their proxy wars, in particular in Vietnam and Afghanistan.

Capitalist-Democratic Modernity

Perhaps the most significant event that put the United States on course for eventual victory over the Soviet Union in 1991 was the computer revolution—the third industrial revolution after the steam engine (ca. 1800) and steel, electricity, and chemicals (ca. 1865). After fully adapting itself to this revolution, the United States became the unrivaled superpower, deriving its strength from its advanced computer technology, powerful financial services, and unmatched military strength.

Thinking Like a World Historian

▶ How are the three patterns that emerged after World War I different adaptations to modernity? Despite their marked differences, what common features do they share?

▶ Why, after World War II, was socialism–communism in many ways a more attractive pattern to decolonizing countries than capitalism–democracy?

▶ Why was the United States better able to adapt to technological innovation than the Soviet Union?

▶ How do consumerism and the widespread use of social networking show the emergence of a global culture in the twenty-first century? Can we predict what future patterns will look like?

63	1966–1969	1968–Present		1979		1989		1989–1991
uclear Test an Treaty	Cultural Revolution in China	Rise of "Women's Liberation" and Modern Feminism		Shah of Iran Overthrown, Soviet Union Invades Afghanistan		Tiananmen Square Demonstrations in China, Berlin Wall Torn Down, and German Unification		Collapse of Communism in Soviet Bloc

	1965–1973	1968		1978		1985–1989	1991		1990–2000
	Vietnam War	Massive Student Demonstrations in Europe, the United States, and Mexico		Deng Xiaoping Announces "Four Modernizations" in China		Perestroika and Glasnost in the Soviet Union	Collapse of the Soviet Union and End of the Cold War		Civil War and Ethnic Cleansing in Former Yugoslavia

	2001		2007-2011		2010		2011
f Apartheid and Election of Nelson ela as President in South Africa, Genocide Against Tutsis in Rwanda	Al-Qaeda Attack on United States		Global Financial Crisis and Economic Recession		Number of Cell Phones Reaches 5 Billion Worldwide		"Arab Spring," Nuclear Crisis in Japan, World Population 7 Billion

Chapter 28

1900-1945

World War and Competing Visions of Modernity

A WORLD AT WAR,
1900–1945

Professor Minobe seemed clearly rattled. For 30 years he had been Japan's leading jurist and constitutional theorist. His decades of work in the law school of Japan's leading academic institution, Tokyo Imperial University, were celebrated not just in Japan but among scholars throughout the world. Indeed, such was his prestige that he had received a noble rank and occupied an honored place in Japan's House of Peers, the upper chamber of its Diet, or

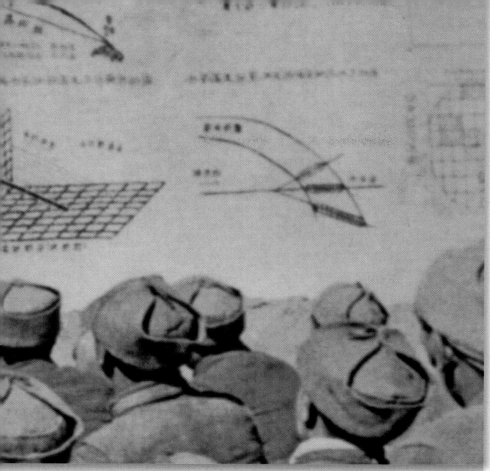

Seeing Patterns

▶ Which three patterns of modernity emerged after World War I? How and why did these patterns form?

▶ What were the strengths and flaws of each of the three visions of modernity?

▶ Why did supremacist nationalism disappear in the ashes of World War II?

parliament. A self-confident, even combative, man, he was not ordinarily given to suffering fools or meekly taking a dressing down.

But today was different, and only later would Minobe Tatsukichi (1873–1948) realize what a dramatic turning point it was for him and for the direction of Japanese law and politics. On this bleak February day in 1934, his fellow peer, Baron Takeo Kikuchi, had taken the floor and publicly denounced Minobe's most famous legal theory. Decades earlier, Minobe had posited that the relationship of the emperor to the constitution was one in which the emperor was an "organ" of the state. More than a generation of Japanese lawyers and scholars had internalized and practiced law according to this "organ theory." But now, the baron had accused Minobe of belittling the emperor's role in Japan's unique *kokutai*, or "national polity/ essence." This concept, as we shall see, played a key role in Japanese supremacist nationalism during the 1930s.

Though Minobe defended his position skillfully, reminding his colleagues that to say the emperor was an organ of the state simply means that he rules for the state and not for himself, the damage had been done.

Tracing Modernity's Path. Members of the People's Liberation Army undergo artillery training during the civil war between the Nationalists and Communists, which ended with Communist victory in 1949.

Following more attacks in the Diet, Minobe resigned from his position, narrowly escaped being tried for his views, and was nearly assassinated in 1936. Already, however, in their drive to "clarify" the meaning of the "national essence," the cabinet had eliminated all of Minobe's writings and banned his works from study or circulation.

Minobe's experience personalizes a struggle to come to grips with new visions of modernity not only in Japan but in much of the world as well. By the 1930s, the liberal principles of modernity—constitutionalism, capitalism, science, and industry—were being tested in the crucible of the Great Depression and increasingly found wanting. In Japan, these values were already giving way to what we call "supremacist nationalism," offering close parallels to the ideologies of Nazism in Germany and fascism in Italy. In Russia, Communism represented another new subpattern of modernity. Other nations—Spain, Portugal, and China, for example—struggled with variations of one or more these competing ideologies.

In this chapter we will explore how the conflicts of spreading modernity spawned these new visions and how each fared through two world wars and the largest economic depression in history. We will also see how the supremacist nationalism that haunted Minobe, as embodied in the Axis powers, was utterly destroyed by the alliance of Communism and capitalist democracy. Their interlude of victory, however, was destined to be short-lived. Within a few years the remaining two divisions of modernity renewed the struggle for supremacy against each other under the shadow of potential nuclear annihilation.

The Great War and Its Aftermath

On July 27, 1914, the nations about to plunge into the abyss of total war the following day represented a host of different conditions with regard to modernity. As we saw in the preceding chapters, some, like Great Britain, Germany, and France, were, along with the United States, among the world leaders in the development of what we call "scientific–industrial society." Others, like Austria-Hungary, Ottoman Turkey, the newly independent Balkan nations, Russia, and even Japan, were at various stages of industrialization, more or less along the lines of the leading powers. In most cases, this latter group had come to this condition somewhat reluctantly, often after violent interactions with the new industrial powers. In terms of political modernity, all of these initial members of what would shortly be known as the Allies and Central powers—with the exception of France—were monarchies, though a number had become modified over the course of the nineteenth century with the addition of constitutions and legislative assemblies. The larger powers were also imperial powers which, collectively, had reduced much of Asia and effectively the entire continent of Africa to the status of colonies. Over the next 4 years, this picture would change so completely that the old order would be dimly glimpsed only through the fog of memory of the diminished numbers who could recall it.

Once the war was on, science and industry made it far more lethal than any previous conflict had ever been; and when it ended, peace turned out to be elusive. Though the old empires of Germany, Austria-Hungary, and Ottoman Turkey were broken up, the new nations that arose from their wreckage emerged with their own sets of problems. Moreover, the new international order embodied by the League of Nations lacked the power to resolve conflicts and enforce its sanctions. Finally, the contradictions inherent in modernity between constitutionalism, imperialism, and emancipation were powerfully brought home to inhabitants of the colonial empires of the victors. For many, it meant using the ideas of nationalism—both ethnolinguistic and constitutional—and those of the new subpattern of communism as tools to achieve autonomy or independence.

Total War. By 1918, large swaths of northern France and Belgium resembled moonscapes from four years of destruction and carnage. One of the unluckiest places was the Belgian city of Ypres, which suffered three battles and was all but completely obliterated by war's end.

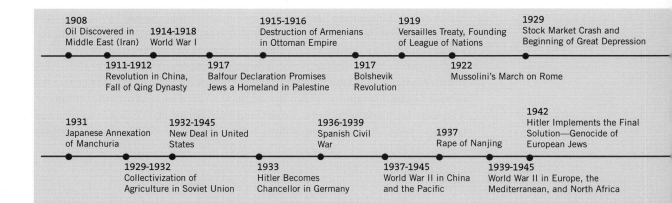

1908 Oil Discovered in Middle East (Iran)	1914-1918 World War I	1915-1916 Destruction of Armenians in Ottoman Empire	1919 Versailles Treaty, Founding of League of Nations	1929 Stock Market Crash and Beginning of Great Depression
	1911-1912 Revolution in China, Fall of Qing Dynasty	1917 Balfour Declaration Promises Jews a Homeland in Palestine	1917 Bolshevik Revolution	1922 Mussolini's March on Rome
1931 Japanese Annexation of Manchuria	1932-1945 New Deal in United States	1936-1939 Spanish Civil War	1937 Rape of Nanjing	1942 Hitler Implements the Final Solution—Genocide of European Jews
	1929-1932 Collectivization of Agriculture in Soviet Union	1933 Hitler Becomes Chancellor in Germany	1937-1945 World War II in China and the Pacific	1939-1945 World War II in Europe, the Mediterranean, and North Africa

A Savage War and a Flawed Peace

Time-honored imperial politics, tempered by the need for a balance of power among the major states, dominated Europe during the century following the Napoleonic Wars. This intersected with the two trends of nineteenth-century modernity we have identified in the last several chapters: the political patterns of constitutional nationalism and ethnolinguistic nationalism and the pattern of industrialization. The rise of the new imperialism in the nineteenth century, itself part of the growth of nationalism and industrialism accompanying modernity, carried a logic of its own that seemed destined to disrupt the ongoing efforts of statesmen to adjust the balance of power to ever-shifting political conditions. Here was the desire for naked conquest for a variety of reasons: markets, raw materials, strategic advantage, and national prestige, to name only the most prominent. For the moment, the victims of these conquests were the peoples of Africa, Asia, and Oceania, though the lesser European powers saw that they could be victims as well. Hence, as nationalism, imperialism, and industrialization moved forward, powers great and small sought alliances for protection and maintenance of the balance of power.

Empires and Nations in the Balkans   The causes of World War I have been endlessly debated from the moment the first shot was fired. Indeed, the role of Germany, rightly or wrongly, was enshrined in the Versailles Treaty ending the war as the famous "war guilt" clause. After decades of consensus and revision, modern scholars have begun to emphasize German aspirations for expansion into Eastern Europe as one of the prime catalysts for its support of Austria against Serbia in 1914. For its part, France had sought at various times *revanche*—revenge—for Germany's annexing of its "amputated provinces" of Alsace and Lorraine in 1870, though this was tempered by the painful awareness of Germany's superior might. In the first decade of the twentieth century, however, the key to the preservation of peace in Europe was seen as maintaining the balance among the three unequal empires that met in the Balkans.

The shrinking Ottoman Empire, beset by continuing demands from ethnic-nationalist minorities for independence, struggled to survive. The expanding Russian Empire, despite having suffered a defeat at the hands of Japan and an abortive revolution in 1904–1905, was rapidly recovering its aggressiveness, if not its military strength. For its part, the opportunistic Habsburg Empire of Austria-Hungary opposed Russian expansionism but also sought to benefit from Ottoman weakness. Germany had largely replaced Great Britain as the protector of the Ottomans and assisted the latter in strengthening their army. Though it had taken Mediterranean territories from the Ottomans, Britain still had a stake in keeping the rest of the Ottoman Empire in existence, as did the other powers, all of whom feared the results of a territorial scramble if the Ottoman Empire collapsed altogether. Hence, as there had been in China during the scramble for concessions of the late 1890s, there was also a rough community of interest aimed at strengthening the Ottoman Empire, whose leaders were themselves seeking to improve their military posture.

One unresolved ethnic-nationalist issue of concern to the three empires was Bosnia-Herzegovina. After the Balkan war of 1878, Austria-Hungary had become the territory's administrator—but not sovereign—as a compromise with the Ottomans, who were unable to keep Serbs, Croats, and Muslims apart. When Russia renewed its support for Serb ethnic nationalism in the Balkans after 1905, Austria-Hungary felt compelled to assume sovereignty of Bosnia-Herzegovina in a protective move in 1908. This in return offered Russia support for its demand for open shipping through the Bosporus. Britain and Germany, however, forced Russia to withdraw this demand. Russia, committed to a policy of pan-Slavism—support for the aspirations of Slavs everywhere—avenged itself by stirring up Serb nationalists. On June 28, 1914, members of a Bosnian Serb nationalist group assassinated the Austrian heir to the throne, Franz Ferdinand, and his wife while they toured the Bosnian city of Sarajevo. This assassination began the tragic slide of the two rival alliances that maintained the balance of power into the cataclysm of World War I. Yet even this occurred only after a month of intense diplomacy and increasing desperation among most of the politicians involved. In the end, each country's perceived military necessities were invoked to trump any diplomatic solution to the crisis.

Total war: A type of warfare in which all the resources of the nation—including all or most of the civilian population—are marshaled for the war effort. As total war became elaborated, all segments of society were increasingly seen as legitimate targets for the combatants.

The Early Course of the War   In contrast with past conflicts, this war was no longer limited and localized but comprehensive from the start: **total war**. In addition, the contingency plans of the combatants' general staffs in many cases relied on precise timing and speedy mobilization of their forces. Here, the most dramatic example was that of Germany. In order to avoid a two-front war, Germany, with its allies Austria-Hungary and the Ottoman Empire (the Central powers), had to defeat France before Russia's massive army was fully mobilized. The German Schlieffen Plan therefore called for a massive assault on northern France through Belgium that would take Paris in 6 weeks, while trapping and isolating the Allied armies aimed at invading Alsace and Lorraine, taken by Germany after the Franco–Prussian War of 1870.

Though the German plan came close to succeeding, it ultimately failed after the desperate French–British victory in the first Battle of the Marne in early September 1914, a more rapid Russian mobilization than expected, and a poor showing of the Austrians against Russia. After several months of seesaw fighting along the lines of the initial German advance into France, the Germans and the French and British dug in. By 1915 the two sides were forced to conduct grinding trench warfare in northeastern France and an inconclusive war in the east. The Germans, with superior firepower and mobility, were able to keep the Russians at bay and inflicted heavy losses on their troops—many of whom marched into battle without weapons, being expected to pick them up off their dead comrades. For its part, the Ottoman Empire suffered a crushing Russian invasion in the Caucasus, prompting it to carry out a wholesale massacre of its Armenian minority, which was alleged to have helped in the invasion. From official Turkish documents published in 2005 it can be concluded that the number of Armenians killed was close to 1 million. This planned

War of Annihilation

"I got to my position and looked over the top. The first thing I saw in the space of a tennis court in front of me was the bodies of 100 dead or severely wounded men lying there in our own wire . . . I sent my runner 200 yards on my right to get into touch with our right company, who should have been close beside me. He came back and reported he could find nothing of them. It subsequently transpired that they never reached the front line as their communication trenches had caught it so much worse than mine, and the communication trench was so full of dead and dying, that they could not get over them. . . . Those three battalions [2,500 men] who went over were practically annihilated. Every man went to his death or got wounded without flinching. Yet in this war, nothing will be heard about it, the papers have glowing accounts of great British success . . . 60 officers went out, lots of whom I knew. I believe 2 got back without being wounded . . ."

—Quoted in Michael Kernan. "Day of Slaughter on the Somme." *Washington Post*, June 27, 1976. From the diary of Captain Reginald Leetham, a British soldier who fought in the Battle of the Somme, July–November 1916. Nearly 60,000 British soldiers were killed in the first day of battle.

massacre, the one large-scale atrocity of the war, still requires a full accounting today and is hotly debated by scholars, lawyers, and politicians.

As the war dragged on, both camps sought to recruit new countries to their sides. Italy, Greece, and Romania entered on the Allied side with the hope of gaining territory from Austria-Hungary and the Ottomans; Bulgaria joined the Central powers in the service of its own territorial ambitions. Japan declared war on Germany in 1914 as part of a previous alliance with Britain but used its occupation of German territories in the Pacific and China as a step toward expanding its own empire. The Allies also recruited volunteers from among their dominions and colonies in considerable numbers, some 800,000 from India alone. Thus, with soldiers from the mostly white dominions of Australia and New Zealand, as well as the African and Asian colonies of Britain and France fighting and dying in the trenches, the war became a true world war. With the token entrance of China in 1917 and the pivotal entrance of the United States that same year the war now involved every major state in the world.

The Turning Point: 1917   By early 1917 the ever-intensifying slaughter took its first toll. In March 1917, tsarist Russia collapsed in the face of horrendous casualties, crippled industry, extensive labor unrest, government ineptitude, and general internal weakness. This February Revolution (actually in March, so called because it took place during February in the old-style Julian calendar still in use in Russia at the time) forced Tsar Nicholas II to abdicate and created a provisional government. The new social-democratic government committed itself to carrying on the war, which now grew even more unpopular and untenable for Russia to manage. The communist Bolshevik Party of Vladimir Lenin (1870–1924), now liberated from persecution by the provisional government, steadily campaigned against continuing the war and in early November (October in the Julian calendar) launched a takeover of the government in the capital of Petrograd—as St. Petersburg had been renamed

Supporting the Empire. The colonies were drawn into the conflicts of their rulers. One million Indian troops, such as the ones shown here, fought with the British during World War I.

at the beginning of the war. Capturing the reins of government, the Bolsheviks began tortuous negotiations with the Germans, which resulted in the disastrous Treaty of Brest-Litovsk in March 1918. Roughly one-third of the Russian Empire's population, territory, and resources were handed over to the Germans in return for Russia's peaceful withdrawal from the conflict. They had now come close to what the Supreme Army Command (*Oberste Heeresleitung*, OHL) had secretly declared as its war goal: the creation of *Lebensraum* (living space) for Germany in the industrialized European part of Russia.

The United States had declared neutrality at the outset of the war, but despite President Woodrow Wilson's plea to Americans to stay "neutral in thought" as well as action, the course of the war had shifted US opinion decidedly toward the Allied side. The German violation of Belgian neutrality in the opening days of the war and extensive German use of the new technology of the submarine swung Americans toward a profound distaste for German actions. The German torpedoing and sinking of the British liner *Lusitania* on May 7, 1915, cost the lives of more than 100 Americans and brought the United States to the brink of war. German guarantees to abandon their policy of "unrestricted" submarine warfare contained the crisis for the time being. Still, the ties of American banks and industries to France and Britain continued to tilt the United States increasingly toward the Allies.

Several key decisions prompted the Germans to risk and ultimately bring on war with the United States. With each side increasingly desperate to gain a decisive advantage over the other and the British naval blockade of Germany wreaking increasing hardships on their economy and populace, the German naval staff calculated that they could starve England into submission with an all-out campaign of submarine warfare. Knowing this would bring the United States into the war, they concluded that they could accomplish their task before the Americans could draft and train a large army. They also felt that their submarines could sink many American troop ships and stifle any US efforts to bolster the Allies. However, they then made a singularly clumsy diplomatic overture to Mexico to join the Central powers if the United States declared war on Germany. The British intercepted this so-called Zimmerman note and gleefully passed it on to the Americans. When Germany announced resumption of unrestricted submarine warfare, Wilson had no choice but to ask Congress to declare war, which it did on April 6, 1917.

The entrance of the United States added the critical resources needed by the Allies to ultimately win the war. More importantly, Wilson's war aims, embodied in his Fourteen Points, sought to transform the conflict from one of failed diplomacy and territorial gain to a war "to make the world safe for democracy." He called for freedom of the seas, the rights of neutral powers, self-determination for all peoples, and peace "without annexations or indemnities." These new causes represented not only American war aims but now were presented as the Allies' war aims as well. For peoples in all the world's empires yearning for independence and self-determination, it appeared, briefly at least, that one side decisively championed their desires.

It was not until early 1918, however, that American troops began to land in France in appreciable numbers. This coincided with the last spring offensive mounted by Germany. Bolstered by the addition of troops from the now peaceful Russian front, the Germans threw everything they had at the Allies and once again came close to seizing Paris. But the new American troops in France gave the Allies the advantage they needed to stop the German effort, and it soon collapsed. By June, more than 1 million Americans had arrived; by September, nearly 2 million; by the end of fighting in November, 4 million more Americans were in various stages of progress to the western front. Faced with these new conditions and reeling from the Allies' September counteroffensive that now threatened to advance into Germany, the Germans agreed to an armistice on November 11, 1918.

The Versailles Peace   As the staggering war toll sank in, the Allies settled down to make peace. About 20 million soldiers and civilians were dead, and 21 million were wounded. Military deaths were 5 million for the Allies and 4 million for the Central powers. Many more millions perished in the world's worst influenza pandemic, abetted by the massive transportation of goods and soldiers at war's end. The settlement, signed at Versailles on June 28, 1919—the fifth anniversary of the assassination of Franz Ferdinand—has been described unflatteringly as a "victor's peace."

In the peace treaty, the German, Austro-Hungarian, and Ottoman Empires were all dismantled and new nation-states were created in their stead. Germany lost its overseas colonies, Alsace-Lorraine, and East Prussia. The Allies declared Germany responsible for the war and condemned it to substantial military restrictions and huge reparation payments. France did not prevail with plans to divide Germany again into its pre-1871 components but succeeded in acquiring temporary custody of the Saar province with its coal reserves and steel factories as a guarantee for the payment of war reparations. For a long time, historians considered the Allied-imposed reparations excessive but more recent research has come to the conclusion that Germany, not destroyed by war, had the industrial-financial capacity to pay. A new supranational **League of Nations** was entrusted with the maintenance of peace. But since one of its clauses required collective military action in case of aggression, the US Senate refused ratification, rejecting this infringement on American sovereignty. Altogether, the Versailles peace was deeply flawed. Instead of binding a Germany that could not be diminished economically into a common western European framework, the Allies actually encouraged it to go it alone by flanking it in the east with small and weak countries that could be dominated in the future (see Map 28.1).

League of Nations:
An international body ultimately numbering 58 states created as part of the Versailles Treaty and functioning between 1919 and 1946 that sought to ensure world peace by curbing secret diplomacy, settling international disputes through negotiation, supervising colonial dependencies under a mandate system, and punishing aggressor nations through the practice of "collective security."

America First: The Beginnings of a Consumer Culture and the Great Depression

The United States emerged from the war as by far the strongest among the Allied democracies. From a debtor country, it had turned into a creditor country; a majority of Americans now lived in nonrural environments; and the war economy shifted relatively easily into a sustained peacetime expansion. Far less hampered by old traditions than its European counterparts, it espoused modernity with a brusque enthusiasm, although its writers and intellectuals were often all too aware of modernity's contradictions.

Modernity Unfolding in the United States   Increased mechanization in industries such as construction materials, automobile assembly lines, and electrical appliance manufacturing spurred the economic expansion. A new dream arose among Americans: to move from countryside to city and to own a house (with running water and sewage), car, refrigerator, radio, and telephone. Once in the city, during the "Roaring Twenties," as the decade came to be called, Americans wanted

MAP 28.1 Europe, the Middle East, and North America in 1914 and 1923.

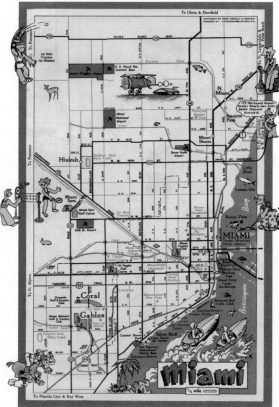

A Vision of American Modernity. This detail from a ca. 1930 Gulf Gasoline "Florida Info Map" vividly captures the American pattern of modernity—miles of roads and highways stretching in all directions, ample leisure opportunities, and a natural environment where the sun always shines.

to be entertained. A remarkable efflorescence of popular culture accompanied the rising urban prosperity. City and small-town dwellers alike were caught up in the mania of the movies, which, after 1927, came with sound. Americans frequented ballrooms to experiment with a large variety of dance steps and to listen to bands playing popular tunes. Jazz music with a large variety of styles found avid listeners. One could now listen to recorded sound on convenient 78-rpm records played on gramophones. The film industry of Hollywood and a recording industry came into being, churning out "hit" after "hit" as their popular products came to be called.

As far-reaching as both of these were, the growth of radio went one step further. From a primitive system of sending Morse-code messages via electrical "spark–gap" transmissions at the turn of the century, radio received vacuum tube amplification and by the time of the war was capable of sending sound and voice messages. In 1919, the first commercial radio station in the United States began broadcasting; by 1930, the number of radios was in the tens of millions. Moreover, experimental work on an even more advanced technology was also under way during the 1920s, though its impact would not come for nearly 30 years: television.

The New Woman   The Nineteenth Amendment of 1920 gave American women the right to vote, enormously expanding the promise of constitutional nationalism by half the population. In addition to winning political rights, American women heightened their social profile. Many colleges and universities went co-ed, although women often majored in education to become teachers, or home economics to become good housewives for the husbands they met at school. Alternatively, they became secretaries skilled in shorthand and typing or nurses in hospitals. Indeed, the typewriter, developed in the latter nineteenth century, directly contributed to the shift from employing mostly men as secretaries to making it an overwhelmingly female profession. Its ease of operation and speed of copying and reproduction (through the use of carbon paper) was ideally suited to what were perceived to be "women's skills" and abilities. Similarly, women swiftly dominated the new occupations of telephone operator and switchboard operator as the new century advanced. By the 1920s it was rare indeed if one picked up the telephone to make a call in the United States and did not hear a female voice ask, "Number please?"

For people of color, however, the situation was far different. Black women, if they were not agricultural laborers, rarely were able to become more than domestic servants or laundry workers in the growing urban economy. In larger segregated areas with more diversified economies, however, African American women often found similar kinds of opportunities as white women, though far more limited in scope and availability. Hence, although emancipation was real for white women, it clearly remained gendered, while the situation for black women continued to be additionally hampered by racism.

Nevertheless, women on the whole became consumers and participants in pop culture in their own right. The new female ideal—or troubling stereotype, depending on your perspective—for many young women was the "flapper." Wearing lipstick and other cosmetics (which were no longer considered signs of being "of ill repute"), having her hair "bobbed" under her cloche hat, wearing dresses above the knee, and throwing away her corset, she drank and smoked cigarettes—and might even drive her own car. She might go to jazz clubs and indulge in such daring dances as the Charleston or the Black Bottom. Sex was also becoming something that she might openly talk about in public, and sexual satisfaction was no longer an emotion to be suppressed. One can still see this contemporary vision of the flapper and her successors in the cartoon series *Betty Boop* from the early 1930s. Liberal social values, as they were called, including premarital sex, divorce, and tolerance for homosexuality, made inroads, although mostly among the relatively small number of white-collar, educated people in the cities.

Inevitably, there was also a conservative backlash, expressing itself most directly in the ratification of the Eighteenth Amendment. From 1920 to 1933, the commercial production of alcohol was prohibited in the United States, primarily for the purpose of reducing public drunkenness among the largely immigrant working classes. Since it did not outlaw noncommercial home brewing or bars, however, widespread production of "moonshine," "bathtub gin" and other "bootleg liquor" and discreet sale of liquor in "speakeasies" (bars where one spoke softly so as not to draw attention) made Prohibition the subject of ridicule and impossible to enforce effectively. The rise of organized crime in America was greatly abetted by its domination of the illegal alcohol industry in the 1920s and 1930s.

High Artistic Creativity American intellectuals, writers, and artists viewed consumer and pop culture modernity with mixed feelings. On the one hand, they hailed what they viewed as the progress of liberal values. But, on the other hand, they were often uneasy about what they perceived as an increasing superficiality and materialism in modernity, furthered by ads, fashions, and fads. Prior to World War I, Europeans continued to consider themselves culturally superior, as reflected in a quip from Oscar Wilde's play *A Woman of No Importance*, where one character remarks that when good Americans die they go to Paris and another character replies that when bad Americans die they go to America. But after World War I, the ambiguities of modernity engendered a veritable explosion of creativity in American culture.

The shattered illusions of the pre–world war era and search for a new beginning in modernity fueled much of this creativity. An entire cohort of artists and intellectuals viewed themselves as belonging to a "lost generation," a term referring to the generation that had lost its best years of life, or even life altogether, to a senseless world war. Such figures as Gertrude Stein (1874–1946), a writer and poet who coined the term, and Wallace Stevens (1879–1955), Sinclair Lewis (1885–1951), Ezra Pound (1885–1972), T. S. Eliot (1888–1965), Eugene O'Neill (1888–1953), F. Scott Fitzgerald (1896–1940), Thornton Wilder (1897–1975), William Faulkner (1897–1962), and Ernest Hemingway (1899–1961)—five among them recipients of the Nobel Prize in Literature—defined the new American style of "modernism" and are still widely read and taught today. For African Americans, a new cultural touchstone was the Harlem Renaissance, featuring the leading innovators in jazz and the writers Claude McKay (1889–1948), Langston Hughes (1902–1967), James Weldon Johnson (1871–1938), and Zora Neale Hurston (1891–1960).

Few later authors plumbed modernity with the breadth of education as these "modernists" did, analyzing its contradictions, exposing its follies, articulating its inner emotional tensions in a "stream of consciousness," or offering countermodels of spirituality, naturalness, Greek classicism, or Chinese monism. Not only did the United States give mass culture to the world; it also provided many of the literary tools to grapple with modernity and attempt to understand it, either by loathing it or by living with it critically.

Business and Labor   Just as much energy characterized American business. Business tycoons and probusiness politicians were integral parts of the Roaring Twenties. Presidents Harding, Coolidge, and Hoover along with the Congress exercised a minimum of political control, illustrated by the slogan "Less government in business and more business in government." President Calvin Coolidge (in office 1923–1929), legendary as "Silent Cal" for his taciturn manner—when the famous wit Dorothy Parker (1893-1967) told him of a bet she had made that she could make him say more than two words, his reply was "You lose"—expressed the spirit of the day with characteristic succinctness: "The business of America is business."

While business boomed, trade and industrial unions stagnated. The American Federation of Labor (AFL), founded in 1886, was the largest trade union pushing for improved labor conditions. But, in contrast to European labor unions, it was always hampered by the problem that its members were unskilled workers of many ethnic, linguistic, and religious backgrounds and, therefore, difficult to organize. Business easily squashed widespread strikes for the right to unionize in 1919. An anti-immigration hysteria followed, with laws that cut immigration by half. The hysteria, mixed with anticommunism, climaxed in 1927 with the trial of Ferdinando

A Klan Lynching. Outside the South, Indiana was the state that experienced the greatest surge in Klan activities in the period immediately after World War I. In 1925, the governor and half the state assembly were Klansmen and about 30 percent of the state's white population were members. In this photo from August 1930, a crowd gathers to gawk at Tom Shipp and Abram Smith, two African American men who were lynched by a mob for allegedly committing robbery and rape.

Nicola Sacco and Bartolomeo Vanzetti, two Italian anarchist immigrants who were convicted and executed for murder on contradictory evidence.

The Backlash   The antiforeigner and anticommunist hysteria was part of a larger unease with modernism. Fundamentalist religion, intolerance toward Catholics and Jews, and fear and violence directed at African Americans rose visibly. The revival of the Ku Klux Klan was at the center of repeated waves of lynchings in the South and attempts to control the local politics of a number of states, most prominently Indiana. The Klan remained a powerful force in the South and Midwest until World War II.

The most startling offenses against the modern principles of liberty and equality, however, came from ideologues wrapping themselves in the mantle of modern science. Researchers at the leading private universities lent respectability to the pseudoscience of **eugenics**, conceptualizing an ideal of a "Nordic" race and searching for ways to produce more athletic, blond, and blue-eyed Americans. Foundations such as the Carnegie Endowment and businessmen such as Henry Ford financed research on how to prevent the reproduction of genetically "inferior" races. California and other states passed laws that allowed for the sterilization of nearly 10,000 patients—mostly women (black and white)—in state mental hospitals, and the Supreme Court in 1927 upheld these laws. Ironically, some of the practices that would inspire Hitler and the Nazis were already quietly in place during the 1920s in the United States and actually seen by many as progressive.

Eugenics: The supposed study of hereditary breeding of better human beings by genetic control. Beginning in the 1920s, a well-financed social movement in the US succeeded in sterilizing thousands of women considered to be mentally and/or racially inferior.

The Great Depression   The Roaring Twenties came to a screeching halt in 1929, when saturation of the market for consumer goods behind high tariff walls during the later 1920s led to falling profit rates. Many of the wealthy had begun to shift their money from investments in manufacturing to speculation on the stock market. In addition, stocks began to be seen as a viable outlet for ordinary investors due to widespread margin borrowing with little money down. As long as the market boomed, investors made money; but if stocks went down, the margin calls went out, and investors could be wiped out. By the late 1920s, a general slowdown in production shifted attention to unsustainable debt levels. Farmers were particularly deep in debt, having borrowed to mechanize while speculating wrongly on a continuation of high prices for commodities. In October 1929, the speculators panicked, selling their stock for pennies on the dollar. The panic rippled through both the finance and manufacturing sectors until it burst into a full-blown cascade. As banks began calling in loans at home and abroad, the panic swiftly became a worldwide crisis: the Great Depression of 1929–1933. Harrowing scenes of unemployment and poverty put the American system of capitalist democratic modernity to a severe test.

Americans largely blamed their probusiness president, Herbert Hoover (in office 1929–1933), for failing to manage the crisis and in 1932 elected Franklin D. Roosevelt (in office 1933–1945). Hoover's approach had been one that previous administrations had turned to in times of economic crisis: cut government spending, raise tariffs to protect US industries, and let market forces correct themselves. But such measures seemed only to make things worse, while the Smoot-Hawley Tariff of 1930—with the highest tariff rates in American history—encouraged retaliatory tariffs in other countries and discouraged world commerce, thus contributing to a world-wide economic collapse. Under Roosevelt's prodding, Congress immediately enacted what he called the "New Deal," in which the government engaged in deficit spending to enact measures designed to help the unemployed and revive business and agriculture. Among the most ambitious of these were the National Recovery Act (1933) aimed at fostering competition, safeguarding the rights of labor, and discouraging monopoly practices; and the Agricultural Adjustment Act (1933), which began the use of subsidies to stabilize the prices of farm commodities Other notable programs included the Civilian Conservation Corps (CCC) in 1933, which enlisted large numbers of the unemployed to conduct improvements in the country's national parks and nature preserves; and the Works Progress Administration (WPA) in 1935, which utilized the talents of the nation's creative community by subsidizing the arts and literature.

One showpiece of the New Deal was the Tennessee Valley Authority, a government-owned corporation for the economic development of large parts of the southeastern United States particularly hard hit by the Depression. In addition, a social safety net was created for the first time, with unemployment benefits and the Social Security Act. Finally, a Securities and Exchange Commission (SEC) was created in 1934 to supervise and enforce regulations governing the stock market in order to prevent a number of the practices that had led to the collapse of 1929.

To finance the New Deal, Roosevelt took the United States off the gold standard, a monetary system that linked currencies to the value of gold, and went deep into deficit spending. In 1937, however, a Congress frightened by the deficit slackened efforts to reduce unemployment, while the Supreme Court declared several of the new programs unconstitutional. The result was a new slump, from which the economy finally recovered only with America's entry into World War II.

Great Britain and France: Slow Recovery and Troubled Empires

While the impact of World War I on the United States was relatively slight, Britain and France suffered severely (see Map 28.2). A lack of finances hampered the recovery, as did the enormous debt both countries contracted during the war. Conservative politicians relinquished the state capitalism of the war period and returned to politics favorable to private investors, without, however, allowing for the same uncontrolled speculations as in the United States. Although socialist politicians gained in importance, they did not succeed in improving working-class conditions or the safety net. Britain benefited from the discovery of oil in its mandates in the Middle East, and the demands of the League of Nations mandate system, in which the colonies were to be prepared for future independence, were not pursued vigorously by either France or Britain.

Weak British Recovery   As the economy shifted from state control during the war back to free enterprise, industry was still in a leading role; but Britain was also heavily dependent on world trade, carried by its merchant fleet. Unfortunately for Britain, world trade declined dramatically after the war. In addition, the country owed a war debt of $4.3 billion to the United States for war materiel, which the United States insisted on receiving back (relenting only during the Depression). Since much of Britain's ability to repay these debts rested upon Germany's ability to pay its reparations, the entire European economic system remained problematic throughout the 1920s.

MAP **28.2 The Great Depression in Europe.**

With the restructuring of Germany's debts under the Dawes Plan in 1924, some stability finally came to the international capital markets. Still, close to half of the annual British budgets in the interwar period went into paying off the war debt. In this situation, industrial investments were low and unemployment was high, dipping below 10 percent of the workforce only once during the 1920s. In addition, business lowered wages, causing labor to respond with a massive general strike in 1926. The strike collapsed after only 9 days, but business, without capital to make industry competitive again, did not benefit either. The British economy remained stagnant.

The dominant conservatives in the government could not bring themselves in the 1930s to accept deficit spending. At a minimum, however, they went off the gold standard and devalued the currency to make exports competitive again. World trade, of course, had declined; but by lowering tariffs within the empire, Britain created the equivalent of the **autarky** that Nazi Germany and militaristic Japan were dreaming of with their planned conquests. A semblance of prosperity returned to the country in the 1930s.

Autarky: The maintenance of a self-supporting state economic system.

France: Moderate Recovery   Together with Russia, France suffered devastating human losses and destruction of property during the war. For every 10 men of

Down and Out in Wales. The 1930s' prosperity was largely limited to southern England. Most of the rest of the British Isles, such as this unemployed miner in Wales, who totters from either drink or depression and is consoled by his two children, were largely left out. George Orwell (1903–1950) published his investigations of British poverty in *The Road to Wigan Pier* (1937), a widely read essay in which he castigated the Conservatives for their lack of a job-creating policy. A strong advocate for social democracy, he became well known after World War II for his opposition to antidemocratic regimes, expressed in his novels *Animal Farm* (1945) and *Nineteen Eighty-Four* (1949).

working age, two were dead, one was an invalid, and three were recuperating from their wounds. The population drop and consequent lack of replacement during the interwar period prompted some French observers to talk about the "hollow years." Alsace-Lorraine, the most important industrial region and the territory that France desperately wanted to recover from the Germans, was now a wasteland. The war had been fought with war materiel borrowed from the United States and Great Britain ($5 billion), to be paid for after the war. Some money for the reconstruction of industry and housing came from increased taxes, German reparations, and taxes from German provinces occupied after the war. But reconstruction could be completed only in 1926–1929, when taxes were once more increased and Germany finally made full reparation payments.

Although French governments were more dependent on coalitions among parties and, therefore, less stable, labor was more often than not represented in the governments. France did not suffer a traumatic general strike like England did, and even though it also returned to the gold standard (1928–1936), it wisely avoided the prewar parity, thereby making the low wages for its workers a bit more bearable. Since it had to reconstruct so much from the ground up, France modernized more successfully in many ways than Britain in the interwar period.

Thanks to its successful reconstruction, France weathered the Depression until 1931. Even then, conservative politicians found the idea of deficit spending as a way to get out of the Depression too counterintuitive. Instead, like the Hoover administration in America, they slashed government spending and refused to devalue the currency. Unrest in the population and rapidly changing governments were the consequences which, in 1933–1934, made supremacist-nationalism an attractive model, especially for business, which was afraid of labor strife. When fascist–communist street fighting broke out in Paris, the Communist Party initiated the formation of a Popular Front coalition with the Socialist Party and others (1936–1938). Although this coalition prevented a further slide into supremacist nationalism, it was too short-lived to allow for the centrist middle-class core to broaden, with disastrous consequences for France's ability to resist Hitler in World War II.

"The Crazy Years"   American pop culture, with its music, dance, movies, and fashions, swept both Britain and France during the 1920s. As in the United States, the ambiguities of modernity also provoked a burst of artistic creativity. The *années folles* ("crazy years") produced in Britain the Bloomsbury Group (after a district in London), a loose collection of modernist writers, such as Virginia Woolf (1882–1941) and E. M. Forster (1879–1970), intellectuals, philosophers, and the economist John Maynard Keynes (1883–1946). Woolf is remembered for her interests in the literary tool of inner monologue, parallel to Faulkner. In addition, the Irishman James Joyce (1882–1941) and D. H. Lawrence (1885–1930) left their permanent imprint on modernity. Joyce employed the stream-of-consciousness approach with extreme formal variations and precision of description. Lawrence became notorious among conservatives for his modernist interests in human intimacy while endearing himself to them with his doubts about the blessings of democracy. A majority of these modernists, reflective of the contradictions of modernity, practiced liberal ethics and expressed socialist leanings.

In France, the 1920s produced *surrealism*, an artistic movement that took its inspiration from the theory of the subconscious popularized by the contemporary Austrian psychiatrist Sigmund Freud. Prominent surrealist painters in Paris were the German Max Ernst (1891–1976) and the Spanish Salvador Dalí (1904–1989). Surrealist poets were André Breton (1896–1966) and Louis Aragon (1897–1982). Ernst famously declared himself dead in 1914 and resuscitated in 1918, a declaration reminiscent of Gertrude Stein's

Surrealism. Surrealist painters allowed their Freudian subconscious to flow into their creations. (*a*) Marcel Duchamp, *Fresh Window* (1920). (*b*) Max Ernst, *Two Children Are Threatened by a Nightingale* (1924). (*c*) Salvador Dalí, *Ghost of Two Automobiles* (1929).

term the "lost generation." Both followed Freud's assertion that the unconscious dominates the artist's creativity: Dreams and myths are stronger influences than reality. Many members, coming originally from the earlier movement of Dadaism in Zurich, also celebrated accident and coincidence as elements in their work, especially in poetry. *An Andalusian Dog* (*Un chien andalou*, 1929) by the Spanish director Luis Buñuel (1900–1983) was a stunning short movie, a visual companion to the surrealist game of "exquisite corpse," the sequential utterance of sentences in free association. In the view of surrealists, the Freudian subconscious typically produced spontaneous, uncontrolled creations. With their playful and often ironic stances, often disdainful of the modernists' adherence to "rational" form, the surrealists anticipated postmodernism, which dominated the arts and humanities during the last quarter of the century.

Colonies and Mandates   The carefree consumer modernity in France and Britain during the 1920s contrasted sharply with the harsh reality of sustaining expensive colonial empires covering much of the world's land mass. After World War I, the British Empire grew by 2 million square miles to 14 million, or one-quarter of the earth's surface, adding 13 million to its 458 million subjects, or one-quarter of the world population. The French Empire at the same time measured 5 million square miles, with a population of 113 million. Although the wisdom of maintaining empires was widely debated in the interwar period, in view of increased subsidies that had to be given many of the colonies, conservatives held fast to the prestige that square mileage was presumed to bestow on their holders. Defense of these far-flung empires, interpreted as the "strategic interest" of the colonial powers, dominated the policies of Britain and France toward their dependencies and mandates during the interwar period (see Map 28.3).

The most important area strategically for both the British and the French after World War I was the Middle East. Under the postwar peace terms, the British and

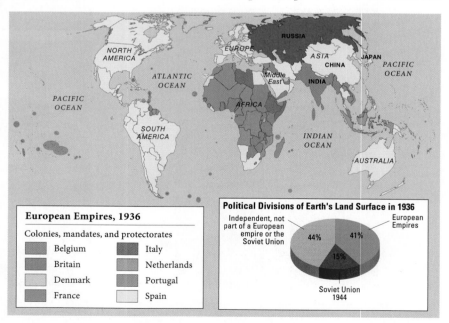

MAP 28.3 **European Empires, 1936.**

French had received the Arab provinces of the former Ottoman Empire (other than Egypt and Sudan, acquired in 1881) as *mandates*—that is, as territories to be prepared for independence. Since a British geologist had in 1908 discovered oil in southwestern Iran, however, Britain and France put a high premium on their new Middle Eastern imperial possessions. Neither was in a hurry to guide its mandates to independent nationhood.

Twice-Promised Lands   As would be expected, Arab leaders were strongly opposed to the British and French mandates. Nationalism was on the rise, ironically encouraged by the British during the war as they were searching for regional allies against the Ottomans. Their agent, T. E. Lawrence (1888–1935), the famous "Lawrence of Arabia," fluent in Arabic and Islamic customs, helped the members of a prominent family, the Hashemites from Mecca in western Arabia, to assume leadership of the Arabs for a promised national kingdom in Syria and Palestine in the so-called McMahon–Sharif Hussein correspondence of 1915–1916.

Since the British, to rally support among Jews in Britain as well as Germany, Poland, and Russia, also promised the Jews a "national home" in Palestine in the Balfour Declaration of 1917, Arab nationalism was stymied even before it could unfold. The French ended a short-lived Arab-declared kingdom in 1920 in Damascus, and the British moved the Hashemites into their mandates of Iraq and Transjordan in 1921, in accordance with the Sykes–Picot agreement (1916) concerning the imperial division of the Middle East between the Allies. As Iraq was divided by majority Shiites and minority Sunnis, the British inaugurated a policy of divide and rule in their Middle Eastern mandates, while dangling the prospect of eventual independence in front of their populations.

In Palestine, the contradiction between the promises to Arabs and Jews during the war forced Britain to build an expensive direct administration under a high commissioner. In 1920, Palestine was inhabited by nearly 670,000 Arabs and 65,000 Jews. Many religious Jews had arrived as refugees from anti-Semitic riots or pogroms in Russia in the early 1880s and 1890s and the difficult postwar years in eastern Europe. When the Austrian Jewish journalist Theodor Herzl (1860–1904) made ethnic nationalism the ideology of secular Jews, early pioneers of **Zionism**, as secular Jewish nationalism was called, began to arrive as well. A Jewish National Fund collected money from Jews worldwide to buy land from willing Palestinian absentee landlords residing in Beirut and Jerusalem. As a consequence, Jewish settlers evicted the landlords' Palestinian tenant farmers. These evictions were the root cause of two Palestinian–Arab nationalist uprisings, in 1929 and 1936–1939, for which the British had no real answer except force and belated efforts in 1939 to limit Jewish immigration.

> **The Balfour Declaration**
>
> Foreign Office
> November 2nd, 1917
>
> Dear Lord Rothschild:
>
> I have much pleasure in conveying to you, on behalf of His Majesty's Government, the following declaration of sympathy with Jewish Zionist aspirations which has been submitted to, and approved by, the Cabinet:
>
> His Majesty's Government view with favor the establishment in Palestine of a national home for the Jewish people, and will use their best endeavors to facilitate the achievement of this object, it being clearly understood that nothing shall be done which may prejudice the civil and religious rights of existing non-Jewish communities in Palestine, or the rights and political status enjoyed by Jews in any other country.
>
> I should be grateful if you would bring this declaration to the knowledge of the Zionist Federation.
>
> Yours,
> Arthur James Balfour
>
> —*The Times* (London), November 9, 1917. Arthur James Balfour was the British foreign secretary; Lionel Walter de Rothschild (1868–1937) was the leader of the Jewish community in Britain.

Zionism: The belief, based on the writings of Theodor Herzl, that European Jews—and by extension all Jews everywhere—were entitled to a national homeland corresponding to the territory of Biblical Israel. It grew into a form of ethnolinguistic-religious nationalism and ultimately led to the formation of the state of Israel in 1948.

Arab–Jewish Violence. British police step in to separate Palestinians and Jewish immigrants fighting each other in November 1933 in Jaffa. Continued unrest led to the Palestinian Arab Revolt of 1936–1939, a nationalist uprising confined initially to urban areas and later spreading to the countryside. The British authorities suppressed the revolt brutally, by most estimates killing perhaps as many as 5,000 Arab Palestinians. Jews aided the British through self-defense forces, both the official Haganah and the clandestine Irgun. In 1939 the British issued a white paper that deplored the hostilities between the two national communities and restricted Jewish immigration.

Egypt and Turkey   After 1882, the Suez Canal acquired vital importance for the British in India and relinquishing it was unthinkable. They rejected a demand in 1919 by a delegation of Egyptian nationalists for independence out of hand and exiled its leader, Saad Zaghlul (ca. 1859–1927). After deadly riots and strikes, the British relented and invited Zaghlul to the peace negotiations in Paris. But the independence the British granted in 1923 was of modest proportions: Both military defense and control of the Suez Canal were withheld from Egypt. A year later, Zaghlul and the Wafd Party won the first independent elections with 90 percent of the vote. The ruling class, as in Iraq, was composed of landlords and urban professionals and, with few exceptions, was uninterested in industrial development. Thus, at the onset of World War II, Egypt was still entirely dependent on agricultural production and exports, though its strategic position was absolutely vital to the British Empire.

The severe punishment meted out to the Ottoman Empire by the Allies provoked the rise of local grassroots resistance groups in Anatolia. These groups merged under the leadership of General Mustafa Kemal "Atatürk" ("Father of the Turks," 1881–1938) into a national liberation movement, driving out the Greeks from western Anatolia, occupying one-half of Armenia (the other half was taken by the new Soviet Union), and ending the Ottoman sultanate (1921–1923) altogether. Atatürk, son of an Ottoman customs official in Salonika, was among the few militarily successful officers in World War I, most notably in his defense of Gallipoli against the British. Atatürk was the driving force behind the creation of a modern, secular Turkey that was able to stand up against the European powers.

Although he was authoritarian, Atatürk saw to it that the new Turkish parliament remained open to pluralism. Parliament adopted the French model of *laicism* (separation of state and religion), European family law, the Latin alphabet, the Western calendar, metric weights and measures, modern clothing, and women's suffrage. During the Depression, Atatürk's economic advisors launched *étatism*, the Turkish version of deficit spending. State capitalism, rather than private domestic or foreign capital, provided for the construction of steel and con-sumer good factories, including textile plants. Both modernism and étatism showed only modest successes by 1939, and the rural masses in Anatolia remained mired in small-scale self-sufficiency farming and wed-ded to religious tradition. But the foundation was laid in Turkey not only for a Westernized ruling class but also for a much larger urbanized middle class.

Indian Demands for Independence

The com-promises negotiated during the Versailles Peace Con-ference, as we have seen, had a profound effect on the colonial world. Nowhere was this truer than in India. In April 1919, frustrated by a British crackdown on politi-cal protest, a large crowd gathered in a walled square in the Sikhs' sacred city of Amritsar. The British responded with a wholesale slaughter of the assembled men, women, and children by an elite unit of Gurkha troops. As the international furor over this "Amritsar Massacre" raged, the British, giving in to the inevitable, reformed the Indian Legislative Assembly by enlarging the por-tion of elected members to nearly three-quarters and the property-based franchise to 5 million, out of a popula-tion of 250 million. The Indian National Congress was infuriated by this minimal improvement and called for full self-rule (Hindi **swaraj**), urging nonviolent nonco-operation, which, among other measures, called for a refusal to pay the land tax, for a boycott of British goods, and for people to spin and weave textiles at home.

Inevitably, civil disturbances accompanied the congress' push for self-rule. Mo-handas Gandhi (1869–1948), a trained lawyer and the most prominent advocate of nonviolence, suspended the push in 1921. The leaders—lawyers, doctors, jour-nalists, and teachers—exited the cities and, with the help of a large influx of party workers, scoured the countryside preaching renunciation. It was during the 1920s and 1930s that the National Congress transformed itself from a small Westernized elite into a broad urban as well as rural mass party.

In Britain, the Labour Party attained a majority of seats in Parliament for the first time in 1929. The Labour government explored the possibility of changing India to dominion status, but there was strong opposition from the other parties. When Labour could not deliver, Gandhi responded with the demand for complete inde-pendence and, on March 12, 1930, embarked on his famous 24-day Salt March to the sea in order for his followers to pan their own salt, which the government refused to free from taxation. Crowds in other places also marched to the sea. Disturbances accompanied the marches, and in a massive crackdown, with 100,000 arrests, the government succeeded in repressing the National Congress.

Nevertheless, after lengthy discussions in three roundtables during the following years—accompanied by much unrest, many jailings (including that of Gandhi), and a rising split with unsupportive Muslims—the British government in 1935 passed the Government of India Act, which devolved all political functions except defense

Secularizing Turkey. Atatürk was a committed educational reformer who sought to create a "public culture," and he was advised by the famous American philosopher of education, John Dewey (1859–1952). Here, in 1928, dressed in a Western-style suit and necktie he gives a lesson on the new Turkish alphabet, a variant of the Latin alphabet, whose use was mandated throughout the Republic.

Swaraj: Literally, "self-rule" (*swa-raj*). Gandhi interpreted this term as meaning "direct democracy" while the Congress Party identified it with complete independence from Great Britain.

Gandhi Leading the Salt March. Perhaps the most famous act of civil disobedience in Gandhi's career was the Salt March in 1930 to protest the British salt monopoly in India. It was a perfect embodiment of Gandhi's belief in nonviolent civil disobedience, which he called *satyagraha*, "soul-" or "truth-force." Though it failed to win major concessions from the British, it focused worldwide attention on the Indian independence movement.

and foreign affairs to India. The members of the National Congress were unhappy, however, because of the decentralized structure of the reformed Indian government and particularly because the act recognized the Muslim League of Muhammad Ali Jinnah (1876–1948), not the congress, as the representative of the Muslims. The British viceroy further inflamed matters in 1939 when he declared India in support of the British World War II effort, without even asking the congress. As in Egypt and Iraq, with their similar forms of "independence," there was a profound reluctance by the Western colonial powers to relinquish colonialism. The legacy of this unwillingness would haunt the capitalist democracies well into the later twentieth century.

Latin America: Independent Democracies and Authoritarian Regimes

Like Britain and France, Latin America remained faithful to its constitutional-nationalist heritage throughout the nineteenth century, though with a preference for strong authoritarian rule. In addition, a pattern of narrow elite rule had evolved in which large estate owners controlled the elections and politics of their countries and, through the military, kept rural black and indigenous Amerindian peoples, as well as the mixed urban populations, in check. Politicians in some countries realized the voting potential of the urban populations after World War I and pursued a new type of autocratic politics, called "populism," in conjunction with more or less extensive industrialization programs. Estate owner politics and populism, together with industrialization programs, characterized Latin America during the later interwar period.

Postwar Recovery   At the beginning of the 1900s, Mexico had enjoyed a long period of political stability and economic growth. It had a relatively diversified array of mineral and agricultural export commodities and began to exploit its mineral wealth in the early 1900s to set up an iron and steel industry. But no change had taken place in agriculture, where the traditional oligarchy of rich ranching and plantation landowners continued to keep wages low. Thanks to American investments, railroad construction had progressed but more to support mining interests than agriculture as there was no desire to improve the mobility of either the landless workers on landlord properties or the indigenous Native American population engaged in subsistence farming.

Latin America During the Depression   In Mexico, a rapid urbanization process, begun in the late 1800s, continued during the interwar period. Immigration from overseas, mostly southern and eastern Europe, as well as rural–urban migration fueled this process. In 1929 the newly created Institutional Revolutionary Party (Partido Revolucionario Institucional, PRI) brought the revolution of 1910–1917 to an end. A sufficiently strong government was in place again to complete land distribution to poor farmers, expand education, and begin social legislation. The PRI weathered the Depression with some difficulty, but thanks to increased state control of economic investments, it was able to maintain its footing until European and east Asian war preparations increased demand for commodities again.

Like Mexico, the countries with the largest internal markets, such as Argentina and Brazil, rode out the Depression more successfully than others. Nevertheless, overall the impact was substantial, with a reduction of commodity exports by over 50 percent (see Map 28.4). Luckily, the countries which were unable to pay back their foreign loans no longer had to fear gunboats and debt commissions but could make more equitable arrangements. Still, the Depression resulted in urban unrest, especially in countries with newly expanded mines or oil wells, such as Chile, Peru, and Venezuela, or expanded administrative bureaucracies, as in Brazil. At no time except the period of independence were there more coups, attempted coups, and uprisings than during 1930–1933.

Thereafter, the political situation remained unstable, except for Argentina and Uruguay under a tenuous constitutionalism. But an important shift away from landed oligarchies began to appear in the ruling classes. Millions of people now lived in urban environments, although in the absence of sizeable import-substitution industries, they did not have the clearly delineated social classes of workers and the nonindustrial lower classes that could be organized by communists, socialists, fascists, and militarists. Instead, a new generation of military officers, with urban backgrounds and no longer tied to the traditional oligarchy, appeared. They offered populist authoritarian programs that mixed elements from the prevailing European ideologies.

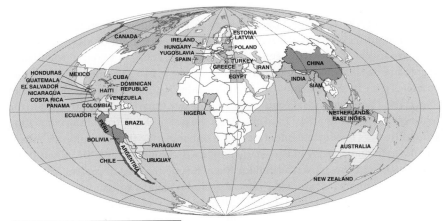

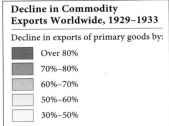

Decline in Commodity Exports Worldwide, 1929–1933

Decline in exports of primary goods by:

Over 80%

70%–80%

60%–70%

50%–60%

30%–50%

MAP **28.4** Decline in Commodity Exports Worldwide, 1929–1933.

New Variations on Modernity I: The Soviet Union and Communism

After capitalist democracy, communism was the second pattern of modernity that arose out of the ashes of World War I. Following their communist coup in November 1917, the Bolsheviks under Lenin overcame a debilitating civil war and established the Union of Soviet Socialist Republics. Lenin's successor, Joseph Stalin (1879–1953), built the Communist Party into an all-powerful apparatus that violently shifted resources from agriculture into industry and dealt ruthlessly with opposition to its policies. By World War II, Stalin's brutal policies had lifted the Soviet Union into the ranks of the industrialized powers.

The Communist Party and Regime in the Soviet Union

As we saw in Chapter 23, Karl Marx (1818–1883), the leading ideologue of communism—which he also referred to as "scientific socialism" or simply "socialism"—believed that capitalist democracy would ultimately be overthrown by an ever-expanding working class—the **proletariat**. For this to happen, however, countries had to be in an advanced stage of industrialization. He did not think that the underdeveloped Russian Empire, with its large majority of peasants, would be ready for a communist revolution for a long time to come. It was the achievement of Vladimir Lenin, however, as the leader of the Bolsheviks, the Russian Communist Party, to adapt communism to his circumstances. For him, the party was the disciplined, militarily armed vanguard that ruled with monopoly power and instilled the ideology of communism in a gradually expanding working class.

Proletariat: A term for the industrial working classes popularized by Marx and Engels in the *Communist Manifesto* and other works.

The Bolshevik Regime

Lenin was from a well-educated middle-class family with Swedish, German, Russian, and Jewish ancestry. Both of his parents were teachers, and his father had been given a patent of nobility; Lenin himself had a degree in law. The execution of his brother by the tsarist government for alleged complicity in the assassination of Tsar Alexander II (1881) imbued him with an implacable hatred for Russian autocracy. At the same time, he became steeped in the writings of Marx and radical thinkers across the political spectrum then circulating around Russia's intellectual underground. Contemplating the revolutionary potential of a communist party in Russia, he published a pamphlet in 1903, called *What Is To Be Done?* Here, he articulated for the first time the idea of professional revolutionaries forming an elite strike force. By eliminating the tsar and seizing control of the government, he argued, Russia's highly centralized political structure would make it possible for an ideologically trained mass communist party to implement its program of equality and industrialization from the top down.

The fall of the tsar's government in the spring of 1917 allowed Lenin and his fellow Bolsheviks to return from political exile, including Leon Trotsky (1879–1940), the well-educated son of an affluent Ukrainian Jewish family, and Joseph Stalin, the hardnosed son of an impoverished Georgian cobbler who had escaped exile in Siberia seven times before the outbreak of World War I. Well aware of Lenin's subversive potential, the German government provided Lenin safe passage from Switzerland to Petrograd. In the words of Winston Churchill, Lenin emerged "like a bacillus" from his special passenger car. By the summer of 1917, the Bolsheviks were mounting massive demonstrations with the slogans "Land, Peace, Bread" and "All Power to the Soviets" (councils of workers and soldiers that helped maintain order as the nation struggled to create a constitution). The collapse of a disastrous Russian summer offensive emboldened the Bolsheviks, who controlled the Petrograd Soviet, which included a "Red Guard" that consisted of some 20,000 armed factory workers in the capital, to make a bid for power. In early November 1917, the Bolsheviks staged a successful coup d'état in Petrograd.

Civil War and Reconstruction   The takeover of Russia by a tiny radical minority unleashed a storm of competing factions all across the political spectrum. For the Bolsheviks the first necessity became building an army from scratch. Here, Trotsky proved a genius at inspiration and ruthless organization. From his armored train flying the new "hammer and sickle" red flag, he continually rallied his forces against the far more numerous but utterly disunited "White" armies arrayed against his "Red" forces. From 1918 to 1921, the Ukraine, Georgia, Armenia, and Azerbaijan were each forced back into the new Bolshevik state. The price for communist victory in the civil war was a complete collapse of the economy, amid a coincidental harvest failure. Lenin had initiated a policy of "war communism"—sending the Red Army into the countryside to requisition food, often with unrestrained brutality. Peasants fought back, and by 1922 a second civil war threatened. Only then did Lenin relent by inaugurating the temporary New Economic Policy (NEP), with a mixture of private and state investment in factories and small-scale food marketing by peasants. At the same time, however, the party—now several hundred thousand members strong—established an iron grip, with no deviation allowed. By 1928, a successful NEP had helped the Soviet Union to return to prewar levels of industrial production.

The Collectivization of Agriculture and Industrialization

Lenin suffered a stroke in 1922 and recovered only for short periods before he died in 1924. His successor was Joseph Stalin, who had garnered the key position of general secretary of the Communist Party in 1922. He had to fight a long struggle, from 1924 to 1930, to overcome potential or imagined rivals, a struggle which left him with a deep reservoir of permanent suspicion. His chief victim was Trotsky, whom he outmaneuvered, forced into exile, and removed altogether by ordering hitmen to assassinate him in Mexico in1940.

"Liquidation of the Kulaks as a Class"   When Stalin finally felt more secure, he decided that industrialization through the NEP was advancing too slowly. The most valuable source of funds to finance industrialization came from the sale of grain on the world market. But farmers had lost all trust in the communist regime after the forcible requisitions during the civil war and hoarded their grain. Grain production had fallen off from predictions and created a so-called "Crisis of 1928." In November, 1929, therefore, the party Central Committee officially decreed the collectivization of agriculture as the necessary step for an accelerated industrialization. Over the next two years , in a carefully laid out plan, 3–5 percent of the "wealthiest" farmers on grain-producing lands, called *kulaks* (Russian for "fist," meaning tightfistedness of wealthier farmers vis-à-vis poor indebted ones) were "liquidated"—selected for

Marching for Modernity. Farmers of a *kolkhoz* behind their party boss prepare to march with their rakes to their fields in May 1931, under a banner propagandizing their success. In reality, Russian peasants experienced the collectivization program of 1929–1940 as a second serfdom, especially in the Ukraine, where private rather than collective village farming was widespread. They resisted it both passively and actively, through arson, theft, and especially the slaughtering of livestock.

execution, removal to labor camps, or resettlement on inferior soils. Their properties were confiscated and the remaining peasant masses were regrouped as employees either of state farms (*sovkhozy*) or of poorer collective farms (*kolkhozy*). Animals were declared collective property, with the result that farmers slaughtered their cherished livestock rather than turn them over to the collectives. Altogether, it is estimated, that between 6 and 14 million farmers were forcibly removed, with the majority killed outright or worked and starved to death.

Stalinism   The impact on agriculture was appalling. Grain, meat, and dairy production plummeted and failed to regain 1927 levels during the remainder of the interwar period. Food requisitions had to be resumed, bread had to be rationed on farms as well as in cities, and real wages on farms and in factories sank. On the other hand, the one-time transfer of confiscated wealth from the kulaks to industry was substantial. Income from accelerated oil exports and renewed grain exports from state farms in the 1930s was similarly plowed into factory construction. By 1939, the rural population was down from 85 to 52 percent and, for all practical purposes, industrialization had been accomplished, though at an unparalleled human cost (see Map 28.5).

The industrial and urban modernity which the Soviet Union reached was one of enforced solidarity without private enterprises and markets. The communist prestige objects were huge plant complexes producing the industrial basics of oil, coal, steel, cement, fertilizer, tractors, and farm combines (see Patterns Up Close). Little investment was left over for textiles, shoes, furniture, and household articles, not to mention cars, radios, and appliances. Consumers had to make do with shoddy goods, delivered irregularly to government outlets and requiring patient waiting in long lines.

The disaster of collectivization had made Stalin even more concerned about any hidden pockets of potential resistance in the country. Regular party and army purges decimated the top echelons of the communist ruling apparatus. In 1937

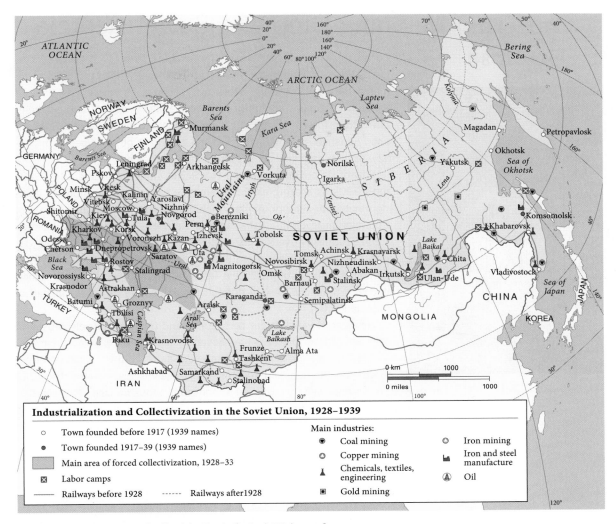

MAP **28.5** **Industrialization and Collectivization in the Soviet Union, 1928–1939.**

alone, Stalin had 35,000 high-ranking officers shot, with disastrous effects for the conduct of World War II a few years later. Thus, in view of the enormity of Stalin's policies, scholars have since wondered about the viability of this attempt at accelerated modernity.

New Variations on Modernity II: Supremacist Nationalism in Italy, Germany, and Japan

The third vision of modernity, underlying the development of the three countries of Italy, Germany, and Japan, was an ideology of nationalist supremacism. In contrast to communism, which was a relatively coherent ideology, the systems of fascism,

Patterns Up Close | Mapping Utopia in Soviet Georgia

When most of us think of "utopias" we tend to imagine far-off or fictional places, such as Thomas More's sixteenth-century island community for which he first invented the word (from the Greek for "not place"). Or we may think of social or religious communities whose members seek to seclude themselves from the corrupting influences of the outside world: the Shakers, who flourished in New England in the early part of the nineteenth century, may immediately come to mind.

Few of us probably consider the Soviet state during the late 1920s and 1930s as sharing anything remotely similar to the impulses guiding nineteenth-century utopias (including Marx's own original utopia of a proletarian revolution ushering in a state-less and class-less society). Stalin's ruthless drive to industrialize was accompanied by extreme violence. Millions perished from hunger, and thousands lost their lives in the political purges of the "Great Terror." Certainly, the upheavals associated with Stalinism make it difficult for us today to view them as part of a utopian enterprise.

However, if we shift our perspective and transport ourselves back in time, we can begin to see how Soviet policymakers regarded their mission as the creation of a type of utopia. Central to this "revolution from above" was the transformation of space. The vast expanses of the Soviet Union were to be improved, civilized, and, above all, industrialized. "We conquer space and time/We are young masters of the land" was a popular refrain from the 1930s. On the right, a map of the Soviet republic of Georgia, from *The Great Soviet*

Utopian Paradise. The Georgian city of Batumi, located on the Black Sea, was developed by the Soviets into a subtropical vacation resort, famed for its tea, citrus, and pleasure beaches.

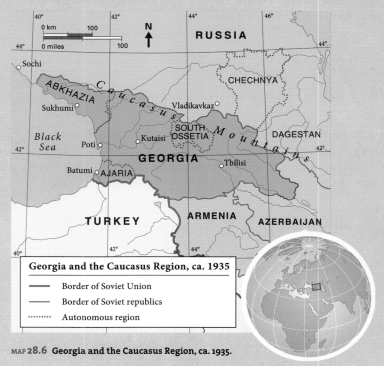

Georgia and the Caucasus Region, ca. 1935

——— Border of Soviet Union

——— Border of Soviet republics

·········· Autonomous region

MAP 28.6 Georgia and the Caucasus Region, ca. 1935.

The civilizing effects of socialism are brought to the Georgian people by the Georgian-Military Highway, which runs through the Caucasus Mountains and connects the country with Russia.

Georgia's strides toward utopia are charted by the number of automobiles it produces each year, as well as the level of production of its petroleum, timber, manganese, cement, and silk and wool industries.

Energy production is a key metric for determining conformity with the socialist pattern of modernity. The colored stars stand for different types of energy sources.

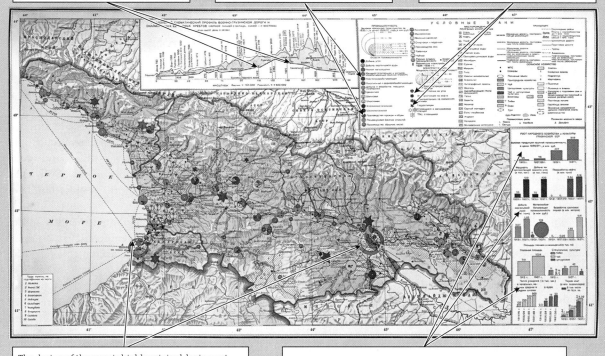

The design of the map is highly original, laying out industrial production in giant circles, subdivided by color according to the type of industry, with the size indicating the amount of the output. For the power needed to run various industries, the map designers employed a six-sided star whose size corresponded to an exact amount of output. Different color stars correspond to the type of energy--coal, petroleum, or hydroelectric.

The map celebrates Soviet agricultural and industrial successes through a "Growth Chart." Each row of graphs is devoted to an area of success: The top row shows increased agricultural output, the second and third improved industrial production, and the fourth and fifth rows the increase in the number of people attending school as well as the growing number of books printed. Just like agriculture or industry, the progress of human culture can be scientifically and precisely graphed.

World Atlas of 1937–1939, provides a vivid demonstration of this utopian impetus. Through its innovative use of symbols, the map shows how Soviet technocrats visualized their socialist utopia—literally, on paper.

Questions

- Does the map above confirm or alter the way you think about the goals that animated the socialist–communist pattern of modernity? Do you believe that the term "utopian" can also be applied to those who strove to implement the democratic-capitalist and nationalist-supremacist patterns of modernity? If so, why?

- What does this map say about the Soviet Union as an empire? What dynamics between the center (Russia) and the periphery (Georgia) can you see revealed in this map?

Nazism, and Japanese militarism were far more diffuse, and cobbled together from a wide variety of nineteenth-century intellectual sources. Fascism became a persuasive alternative to democracy and communism in Italy right after World War I. The much more brutal German Nazi and Japanese militarist ideologies became acceptable only once the Depression hit and discredited capitalist democracy as being capable of weathering the crisis.

From Fascism in Italy to Nazism in the Third Reich

Benito Mussolini (1883–1945), son of a blacksmith with anarchist leanings and a teacher, was well read in nineteenth-century philosophy and held positions as a journalist at various socialist newspapers. His support for the war as an instrument of radical change brought him into conflict with the majority of socialists, who bitterly opposed the war. As a result, he grew disillusioned with Marxism and founded the "Italian Combat Squad" (*Fasci italiani di combattimento*). War veterans, dressed in black shirts and organized in paramilitary units, roamed the streets and broke up communist labor rallies and strikes. The symbol of the movement was the *fasces* [FAS-sees]—derived from the old Roman emblem of authority with a bundle of sticks and an ax, tied with a ribbon.

With their street brawls, the fascist "Blackshirts" contributed mightily to the impression of a breakdown of law and order, which the democratic government allegedly was unable to control. Anticommunism thus was accompanied by denunciations of democracy as a chaotic form of government incapable of decisive action. Although Mussolini's party was still woefully behind the Socialist, Christian Democrat, and Conservative Parties in the parliament, he demanded and received the premiership by threatening a march on Rome by 10,000 Blackshirts. This turned into a victory parade, with the king acquiescing to the fascists' "third way" between democracy and socialism.

Mussolini's Dictatorship   Once given his chance, Mussolini transformed the Blackshirts into a militia for national security, paid for by the state. In 1923 he used the threat of their violence again when he led his coalition government in the passing of a law that gave two-thirds of the seats in parliament to the party that garnered the most votes (at least 25 percent). A year later, "Il Duce" ("The Leader"), as he now styled himself, won his two-thirds and began to implement his fascist **corporate state**.

By 1926, elections were abolished, strict censorship of the press was in place, and the secret police kept a close eye on the population. Fascist party officials, provincial governorships, and mayors were appointed from above and labor unions closed down. In the Ministry of Corporations, industrialists and bureaucrats, representing labor, met and sharply curtailed wages and labor conditions. The Lateran Accords of 1926–1929 made Catholicism the Italian state religion in return for full support by the Vatican. Youth and women's organizations instilled authoritarian behavior. The new vision of Italian efficiency prompted observers to say admiringly of Mussolini that "he made the trains run on time." In architecture and art, as well as the new technologies of automobiles and aircraft, Italy, long seen as backward, now became a world pacesetter.

Depression and Conquests   Italy weathered the Depression through deficit spending and state investments. In 1933, Mussolini formed the Industrial

---

What Was Fascism?

"Fascism replaces ... the old atomistic and mechanistic state theory that was at the basis of the liberal and democratic state theory with an organic and historical concept ... Instead of the liberal and democratic formula, 'society for the individual,' we have 'individuals for society,' with this difference, however: that while the liberal doctrines eliminated society, fascism does not submerge the individual in the group. It subordinates him but does not eliminate him, the individual as part of his generation ever remaining an element of society however transient and insignificant he may be."

—Alfredo Rocco, "The Political Doctrine of Fascism," *International Conciliation* 223 (October 1926): 393-415. Reprinted in Schnapp, Jeffrey Thompson, Olivia E. Sears, and Maria G. Stampino, ed. and trans. *A Primer of Italian Fascism*, p. 111. Lincoln, NE: University of Nebraska Press, 2000. Rocco was minister of justice (1925–1932) under Mussolini.

Reconstruction Institute, which took over the industrial and commercial holdings of the banks that had failed earlier. This institute was crucial in efforts to revive the Italian industrial sector, which was still much smaller than elsewhere in Europe. Only in the mid-1930s did the urban population, concentrated mostly in the north, acquire majority status. In spite of a few swamp-reclamation and grain-procurement reforms, the fascists had no answer for the endemic underdevelopment of southern Italy, which remained profoundly rural and poor.

Nevertheless, Italy's military industry was sufficiently advanced for Mussolini to proclaim a policy of autarky with the help of overseas territories. First, the conquest of formerly Ottoman Libya was completed with utmost brutality in 1931. Declaring Libya to be the "Fourth Shore," the fascists encouraged emigration into the largely infertile Sahara colony, which eventually numbered some 100,000 settlers. The other major colony was the proud Christian kingdom of Ethiopia, conquered by Italy in 1935–1936 and merged thereafter with the earlier territories of Italian Eritrea and Somalia into Italian East Africa. Eager to avenge Italy's defeat by the Ethiopians forty years before, Mussolini's forces invaded with airplanes, tanks, and poison gas and, after crushing Ethiopian resistance, pacified the new colony with the settlement of 200,000 Italians.

The Ethiopian conquest prompted protests by the League of Nations. Although these were ineffective, Mussolini felt sufficiently isolated to seek closer relations with Adolf Hitler and the Nazis. He had formerly treated Hitler as a junior colleague but now found him to be a useful counterweight against international isolation. An increasingly close cooperation began between the two dictators, who formed the nucleus of the later Axis powers, joined in 1941 by Japan.

The Foundation of the Weimar Republic In September 1918, the German Supreme Army Command came to the conclusion that Germany had lost World War I. In the subsequent 2 months unrest broke out in the navy and among workers. German soldiers melted away from the western front, and communist worker councils formed in a number of major cities. Alarmed civilian politicians in Berlin did everything in their power to bring about a peaceful transition from empire to republic. When the emperor eventually abdicated, his last chancellor (head of the government) appointed Friedrich Ebert (1871–1925), a prominent member of the German Social Democratic Party, on November 9, 1918, as his successor. This appointment was not quite legal, but Ebert immediately contacted the OHL for armed support; and in the following months the two cooperated in crushing well-organized and armed communist workers' councils.

The first test for the new republic (founded in nearby Weimar during the height of communist unrest in Berlin) came in the summer of 1919 when the Allies presented their peace settlement. The French, concerned about both their military security and the future economic power of their more populous and industrially advanced German neighbor, would have liked to have Germany divided again, as it was before 1871. The British and Americans, however, were opposed to such a drastic settlement. Germany was let off with what historians now see in retrospect as relatively moderate reparations for civilian casualties and the loss of two western provinces, although it was also forced to accept responsibility for the beginning of the war. The compromise settlement was satisfactory to no one: France's security remained unresolved, German conservatives and nationalists screamed defiance, and

Corporate state: Sometimes called an "organic state"; a philosophy of government that sees all sectors of society contributing in a systematic, orderly, and hierarchical fashion to the health of the state, the way that the parts of the body do to a human being. In practice, it was a polity in which a dictator or an authoritarian leader orchestrated the single state party and all ministries, business corporations, associations, and clubs, while other parties and organizations such as labor unions were outlawed.

Play Money. German children in 1923 playing with bundles of money in the streets. Hyperinflation had made money in the Weimar Republic worthless: Printed overnight, it was practically worthless before it even hit the market in the morning. At the height of inflation, $1 US was worth 4.2 million reichsmark.

the democrats of Weimar who accepted the settlement were embittered by its immediate consequence: inflation.

Asked to begin the payments immediately, Germany was unable to correct the general inflation which also occurred in other countries in 1918–1919, when pent-up consumer demand exploded with the onset of peace. Instead, the inflation accelerated to a hyperinflation in which the German mark became virtually worthless and Germany had to suspend payments. France and Belgium responded by occupying the industrial Ruhr province in 1923. German workers in the Ruhr retaliated with passive resistance, and a deadlock was the result.

Faced with this crisis, the new Weimar Republic made peace with the French by recognizing the new borders. Recognizing, too, the dire financial implications of an economically crippled Germany, the American-crafted Dawes Plan of 1924 had US banks advance credits to European banks to refinance the now considerably reduced German reparation payments. France and Belgium withdrew from the Ruhr, inflation was curtailed, and the currency stabilized. The newly solvent Weimar Republic then experienced a considerable economic and cultural efflorescence during the rest of the decade.

The Golden Twenties   In these years, Germany produced more movies than the rest of Europe combined, with such classics as *Metropolis*, by the director Fritz Lang (1890–1976). Sports fans followed the career of the boxer Max Schmeling (1905-2005), world champion in 1930, and watched car races on the Avus in Berlin, the first freeway (*Autobahn*). The *Kabarett* ("cabaret"), with its biting political satire, attracted major literary figures who wrote sketches for this new popular art form. Playwrights probed the conflicts of social class, which were more pronounced in Germany than elsewhere. Perhaps best known was *The Threepenny Opera* of 1928, with lyrics by Bertolt Brecht (1898–1956) and music by Kurt Weill (1900–1950).

Painters and architects probed the geometrical and detached style they assumed was the essence of modernity at the Bauhaus school in Weimar, which became an international trendsetter for art, architecture, and design. The Russian Wassily Kandinsky (1866–1944) and the Swiss Paul Klee (1879–1940) taught the new style of abstract painting, which they had pioneered at the school. Similarly, the pioneer of modern glass, steel, and concrete architecture, Ludwig Mies van der Rohe (1886–1969), began his career at the Bauhaus, before he designed some of the best-known skyscrapers of the Chicago cityscape.

The Rise of the Nazis   The Golden Twenties disintegrated quickly in the months after the US stock market crash of 1929. American banks, desperate for cash, began to recall their loans made to Europe. Beginning in 1931 in Austria, European banks began to fail; and in the following 2 years world trade shrank by two-thirds, hitting an exporting nation like Germany particularly hard. Unemployment soared at the same time to 30 percent of the workforce. Once more, as during the hyperinflation of 1923, millions of Germans were cast into misery. The number of people voting for extremist opponents of democracy—communists and nationalist supremacists—rose from marginal to more than half of the electorate by July 1932. Among them, the National Socialist German Workers' Party (NSDAP), or Nazi Party, achieved 38 percent, becoming the largest party in parliament.

In early 1933, the Nazi leader, Adolf Hitler (1889–1945), a failed artist and son of an Austrian customs official, could look back on a checkered postwar political career. He had led a failed uprising in 1923, done time in prison, and in *Mein Kampf* (*My Struggle*), a book published in 1925, openly announced a frightening political program. Hitler advocated ridding Germany of its Jews, whom he blamed for World War I, and communists, whom he blamed for losing the war, and sought to punish the Allies for the peace settlement they had imposed on Germany. In its most grandiose sections he supported the German conquest of a "living space" (*Lebensraum*) in Russia and eastern Europe for the superior "Aryan" (German) race, with the "inferior" Slavs reduced to forced labor. No one who followed politics in Germany during the 1920s could be in doubt about Hitler's unrestrained and violent supremacist nationalism. Throughout the decade, however, he remained marginalized and ridiculed for his extreme views.

Function and Simplicity. The architect Walter Gropius (1883–1969) founded the Bauhaus movement. Its emphasis on function and simplicity still exerts great influence.

The Nazis in Power   When the Nazis won a plurality in parliament, however, not only in spring 1932 but again in the fall (albeit with a loss of 4 percent, while the communists gained nearly 3 for a total of nearly 17 percent), Hitler demanded the chancellorship. Upon the advice of his counselors, President Paul von Hindenburg (in office 1925–1934), one of Germany's heroes as a leading general during World War I, nominated Hitler to the post on January 30, 1933, in an effort to neutralize Nazism and keep Hitler under control. Hitler, however, wasted no time in escaping all restraints. Following a major fire in the Reichstag (German parliament) building in February 1933, the causes of which have never been fully explained, but which Hitler blamed on the communists, the president allowed his new chancellor the right to declare martial law for a limited time. Two months later, the Nazi Party in parliament passed the Enabling Act with the votes of the mostly Catholic Centrist Party: Its leaders calculated that they could control Hitler while receiving a much desired agreement between the Vatican and Germany parallel to the one of Mussolini. According to the constitution, Hitler now had the power to rule by emergency decree for 4 years.

Taking their cue from Mussolini's policies, the Nazis abolished the federalist structure of the Weimar Republic, purged the civil service of Jews, closed down all parties except the NSDAP, enacted censorship laws, and sent communists to newly constructed concentration camps. Other inmates of these camps were Roma (Gypsies), homosexuals, and religious minorities. In order to gain the support of Germany's professional army, Hitler replaced his *Sturmabteilung* (SA) militias of thugs with the smartly outfitted *Schutzstaffel* (SS). A new secret police force (abbreviated *Gestapo*) established a pervasive surveillance system in what was now called the Third Empire (*Drittes Reich*), following that of the Holy Roman Empire and Germany after its unification in 1871.

At the same time, Hitler succeeded in gaining enthusiastic support from among the population. Aided by a general recovery of the economy, within 1 year of coming to power he lowered unemployment to 10 percent. He had the support of able economists who advised him to reduce unemployment through deficit spending and build a mixed economy of state-subsidized private industrial cartels. Enthusiastic Germans built freeways, cleared slums, constructed housing, and, above all, made arms, for minimal wages. A once mediocre artist and aspiring architect, Hitler also pronounced upon the "decadence" of modern art and pushed his planners to create monumental buildings in older neoclassical or art-deco styles. In all of these endeavors he advocated a personal vision of a stridently "nationalist" German art. In his appeal to the patriotic and economic aspirations of so many Germans, Hitler thus succeeded in making himself a genuinely popular leader (*Führer*) among the great majority of Germans.

German rearmament was initially secret but, after 1935, public knowledge, with the introduction of the draft and the repudiation of the peace settlement cap on troop numbers. During 1935–1939, the army grew from 100,000 to 950,000 men, warships from 30 to 95, and, most startling of all, the air force from 36 to over 8,000 planes. France, realizing the danger this rearmament signified for its security, signed a treaty of mutual military assistance with the Soviet Union, which Hitler took as a pretext for the remilitarization of the Rhineland (one of the German provinces temporarily occupied by France after World War I) in 1936.

This first step of German military assertion was followed with the unofficial air force support of General Francisco Franco (1892-1975) who rose against the legitimate Republican government in the Spanish Civil War (1936–1939) and incorporation of Austria in 1938. Now alarmed at Germany's growing appetite for expansion and committed by treaty to defend the eastern European states created after the war, the heads of state of Britain and France met with Hitler and Mussolini in Munich in the summer of 1938 to hammer out a general agreement on German and Italian territorial claims. In the Munich Agreement, Hitler was allowed to occupy the Sudetenland, an area largely inhabited by ethnic Germans in Czechoslovakia, with the understanding that it represented his final territorial demand. The British prime minister, Neville Chamberlain, (in office 1937–1940) seeking to mediate between the less compromising France and Hitler, claimed that this appeasement of Germany represented "peace in our time." Hitler went to war, however, in little more than a year.

World War II in Poland and France

In 1939 Hitler decided that the German armed forces were ready to begin the quest for Lebensraum in eastern Europe. In a first step, Poland needed to be taken; and in order to do so, Stalin had to be led to believe that it was in the best interest of the Soviet Union and Germany to share in the division of eastern Europe. Stalin, of course, was under no illusions about Hitler's plans but needed time to rebuild his army after the purges of 1937 and found the idea of a Russian-dominated Polish buffer against Germany appealing. Accordingly, the two signed a nonaggression pact on August 23, 1939; and German troops invaded Poland on September 1, triggering declarations of war by Poland's allies Britain and France 2 days later. World War II had begun in Europe.

Having removed the two-front problem that had plagued Germany in World War I, Hitler had to eliminate Britain and France before turning to the next phase in the east. This he did by attacking France on May 10, 1940. The German army in Poland had pioneered a new kind of warfare: "lightning war," or *Blitzkrieg*. Using aircraft to cripple rear area defenses and harass enemy troops, while smashing enemy lines with tanks and motorized infantry, the Germans turned warfare from the stagnant defensive posture of World War I into a fast, highly mobile form of conflict. The French, bled dry of manpower in the previous war, had since relied largely on the highly elaborate but fixed defenses of their Maginot Line. Now, the German troops simply went around these fortifications on a broad front, from the Netherlands and Belgium to Luxemburg. After breaking through the thick unprotected Ardennes Forest in southern Belgium, to the great surprise of the French and British, the German troops turned northward, driving the Allies toward the Atlantic coast. Establishing a desperate defensive perimeter at Dunkirk, the encircled French and British troops used every available vessel to escape across the English Channel to Britain as the Germans regrouped for their final thrust.

France had no choice but to agree to an armistice. Hitler divided the country into a German-occupied part, consisting of Paris and the Atlantic coast, and a small unoccupied territory under German control, with its capital in Vichy. The German follow-up effort of an invasion of Britain failed when the air force, having suffered more losses than anticipated in the invasion of France, was unable to deliver the final blow. During the worst air raids the conservative politician Winston Churchill (in office 1940–1945) replaced Neville Chamberlain as prime minister. Churchill's inspirational and unbending will during the aerial Battle of Britain proved to be a turning point in rallying the Allied cause.

The Eastern Front   A year after finishing with France, and with Britain only desperately hanging on, Hitler launched an invasion of the Soviet Union on June 22, 1941, to the surprise of an unprepared Stalin. Although the Soviet forces were initially severely beaten, they did not disintegrate, thanks in part to a force of new T-34 tanks that proved superior to German models and were four times more numerous than the Germans expected. The Soviets held out against the German attacks on Leningrad (the renamed St. Petersburg/Petrograd), Moscow, and the Ukraine. Neither side made much progress in 1942, until the Soviets succeeded in trapping a large force of Germans in Stalingrad on the lower Volga, near the vital Caspian oil fields. The Soviet victory on February 2, 1943, became the turning point in the European war. Thereafter, it was an almost relentless and increasingly desperate retreat for the Germans, particularly after the western Allies invaded the continent in Italy and France.

The Final Solution   As Hitler's *Mein Kampf* foretold, the war in the east became an ideological war of annihilation: Either the supremacist or the communist vision of modernity would prevail. The Soviets began early with their killings, when they massacred nearly 22,000 Polish prisoners of war in the forest of Katyn and sent hundreds of thousands of eastern Europeans to their eventual deaths in labor camps. The German SS and army, driven by their racism against Slavs, murdered soldiers and civilians alike; and German business tycoons worked their Slavic slave laborers to death. The so-called **Final Solution** (*Endlösung*), the genocide of the European Jews, was the horrendous culmination of this struggle. After Poland and the western Soviet Union were conquered, the number of Jews under

Genocide. The specters of the Holocaust that haunt us usually involve the infamous extermination camps—Auschwitz, Treblinka, Majdanek, Sobibor—but millions of Jews and other "undesirables"—Slavs, gypsies (Roma), and homosexuals—were shot, such as this man calmly waiting for the bullet to penetrate his brain while SS stooges accomplices look blithely on.

Final Solution: German nationalist-supremacist plan formulated in 1942 by Adolf Hitler and leading Nazis to annihilate Jews through factory-style mass extermination in concentration camps; resulting in the death of about 6 million Jews or roughly two-thirds of European Jewry.

German authority increased by several million. The Final Solution, set in motion in January 1942, entailed transporting Jews to eight extermination camps, the most infamous of which was at Auschwitz, in Poland, to be gassed in simulated shower stalls and their corpses burned in specially constructed ovens. In its technological sophistication in creating a kind of assembly line of death and the calm, bureaucratic efficiency with which its operators went about their business, the Holocaust (Hebrew *Shoa*) marks a milestone in twentieth-century inhumanity. It has since become the standard of genocide against which other planned mass murders are measured.

The Turn of the Tide in the West   The first counteroffensives of the Allies in the west after their defeat in 1940 came in November 1942. After fighting a desperate rearguard action against the German general Erwin Rommel (1891–1944), "The Desert Fox," British forces in Egypt and American forces landing in occupied French North Africa launched a combined offensive, capturing Rommel's forces in a pincer movement and driving them to capitulate 6 months later. But it took another 2.5 years of long campaigning to grind down the forces of the Axis powers. Here, the industrial capacity of the United States proved to be the determining factor. For example, between 1942 and 1945 American factories produced 41,000 Sherman M4 tanks alone, which was more than the production of all German tank types taken together. German aircraft production peaked in 1944 at 44,000 planes; US manufacturers produced more than 100,000 the same year. The United States enjoyed similar advantages in manpower. By war's end, over 16 million American men and women, or 10 percent of the entire population, had served in the armed forces. Finally, the natural barriers of the Atlantic and Pacific Oceans and American naval power ensured against invasion, while the lack of a long-range strategic bombing force prevented Axis air attacks on North America.

Furthermore, starting in 1943, the US Army Air Force and Britain's Royal Air Force began a furious campaign of "around-the-clock" bombing of military and civilian targets in Germany. Despite heavy Allied losses in planes and men, by war's end, there was scarcely a German city of any size or industrial center that had not been reduced to rubble by air attack—quite a contrast to World War I, when Germany's interior was unscathed. With the landing of troops in Sicily in July 1943 and Normandy in June 1944, combined with the steady advance of Soviet forces in the east, the eventual unconditional German surrender on May 8, 1945 ("Victory in Europe," or "VE," Day) was inevitable (see Map 28.7).

Japan's "Greater East Asia Co-Prosperity Sphere" and China's Struggle for Unity

The Japanese ruling class that implemented the Meiji industrialization consisted for the most part of lower-ranking samurai "oligarchs." After World War I, this generation retired and for the first time commoners entered politics. These commoners formed two unstable conservative party coalitions, representing small-business and landowner interests, but were financed by big-business cartels, the zaibatsus (see Chapter 24) By the mid-1920s Japan's interwar liberalizing era had reached perhaps its high point, with universal male suffrage for all over the age of 25. Thereafter, however, and at an accelerated pace during the Depression of 1929–1933, the military increased its power and ended the liberalizing era.

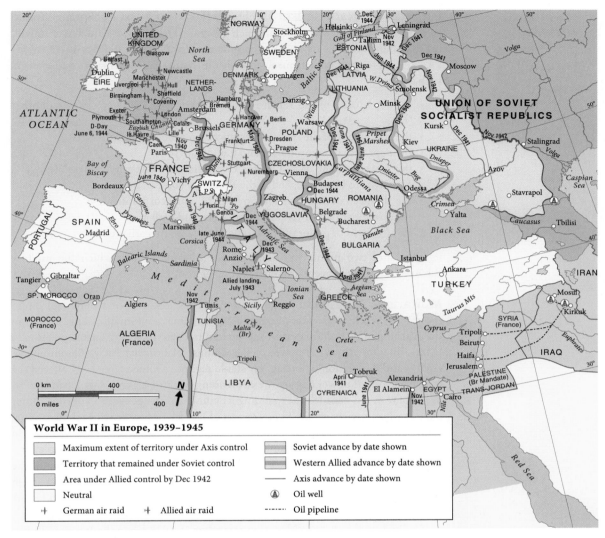

MAP 28.7 **World War II in Europe, 1939–1945.**

Liberalism and Military Assertion

In the midst of the middle-class ferment of "Taisho Democracy," as Japan's politics during the reign of Emperor Taisho (r. 1912–1926) was known, the government not only broadened the suffrage but also enacted the first of what would be a long line of security laws. Worried about communist influence, the Peace Preservation Law of 1925 drew a line against frequent labor strikes and general leftist agitation. Anyone violating the "national essence" (*kokutai*) not only through action but also thought could be arrested. A branch of the secret services, the *Tokko*, made widespread use of this law, with some 70,000 mostly arbitrary arrests during 1925–1945. The law was a turning point as Western-inspired liberalism began to swing toward militarism. Nowhere was this more dramatically on display than in the saga of Professor Minobe, described at the beginning of this chapter, who would go in a few short years from being Japan's leading legal theorist to being denounced as a traitor.

Supremacist Nationalism Military officers of modest rural origin, trained prior to World War I and without much general education, were unable or unwilling to comprehend the democracy, cultural transformation, and labor strikes of the 1920s. They intoxicated themselves with the staples of supremacist nationalism, such as

- the superiority of the Yamato "race" of Japan and the inferiority of all other "races" in Asia;
- the supremacy of the "national essence" over the individual;
- the depravity of communism and democracy;
- the establishment of a "Greater East Asia Co-Prosperity Sphere" (*Dai-to-a Kyoeiken*) to be established in the Pacific by conquest;
- the abolition of class divisions in favor of social corporatism;
- the absolutism of the emperor, above law and parliament;
- and the right of junior officers to refuse to execute parliamentary laws.

The latter two points were decisive for actions through which the military achieved dominance over parliament in the 1930s.

Militaristic Expansion The early 1930s saw the end of a period of diplomacy by which Japan sought to consolidate its gains in international prestige from the Washington Naval Treaty and subsequent treaties stabilizing Japan's position in China. The growth of the power of the Chinese Nationalist Party (Guomindang, GMD) and its creation of a relatively stable regime in China after 1927 altered the fragile balance of power among the contending warlord regimes that Japan had exploited for over a decade for expanding its influence. The generation of rural junior officers who frowned on the liberalization of Japan and hearkened back to samurai values also found a home and opportunity in the colonial armies of Manchuria. In addition, nationalist radicals like Kita Ikki (1883–1937) expounded a complete reorganization of Japan based on a stricter interpretation of the kokutai. Finally, the long-standing maneuverings of semimilitary groups advocating further expansion in the Asian heartland, such as the Black Dragon Society, kept the situation in Japan's Asian possessions in turmoil.

The first step in this new direction was taken in 1928 when the Japanese Kwantung Army (the name for Japan's force in Manchuria) blew up the train of Chinese warlord Zhang Zuolin because of his leanings toward the GMD. This was followed by the Mukden Incident of 1931, in which the Japanese military engineered another railroad bombing, which was blamed on local warlords and used as the pretext for the annexation of Manchuria. Politicians in Tokyo, cowed by the aggressiveness of supremacist nationalist ideologues, and by the select assassinations of political opponents of Japan's expansion, acquiesced. By way of making it a puppet state, they installed the last Manchu Qing Chinese emperor (Henry) Pu-Yi (r. 1908–1912; 1932–45), deposed in the Chinese Republican Revolution of 1911–1912. Over the next several years, the Japanese army in Manchuria systematically moved into northern China. In July 1937, after a clash between Chinese and Japanese forces near the Marco Polo Bridge outside Beijing, Japan launched a full-scale invasion of China.

The Republican Revolution in China The Qing dynasty had failed to develop a sustained effort at reform in response to the Western challenge during the

1800s. Following belated attempts at institutional reform in the wake of the Boxer uprising in 1900, a variety of radical groups, aided by the growing numbers of overseas Chinese, began to work for the overthrow of the Qing. The most important figure among these groups was Sun Yat-sen (1866–1925), a medical doctor and son of peasants in south China, with his Revolutionary Alliance of 1905. Making common cause with a number of local revolutionary groups and Chinese secret societies, Sun's group formed an umbrella organization for a wide array of political ideas. Sun's core ideas, however, were relatively straightforward and given as the Three Principles of the People (*san min zhuyi*):

- Nationalism: Expulsion of the Manchus and later all Western interests.
- Democracy: Representative institutions based on a constitution. One-party tutelage until the Chinese people grow used to the new forms of democratic institutions.
- "People's livelihood": Sometimes rendered as "socialism," this principle called for comprehensive land reform and a government commitment to safeguard the economic well-being of the people.

On October 10, 1911, an explosion in a Wuhan barracks signaled a takeover of the base. The movement quickly spread, and by the end of the year three groups of Qing opponents—provincial warlords, scholar-gentry, and nationalists—staged separate uprisings which reduced the Qing to a small territory in the north. The Qing commander, Yuan Shikai (1859–1916), struck a deal with the insurgents whereby he came over to them in return for the presidency of the new republic, formed upon the abdication of the Qing in February 1912. Sun was thus elbowed aside by the revolution he had done so much to begin. With Yuan's death in 1916, the remaining warlords feuded with each other for control of the country for the next decade.

Reemergence of Nationalism   Sun Yat-sen, however, was not quite finished. With the republic in shambles and the provinces hijacked by the warlords, Sun remained a profoundly inspirational figure for Chinese nationalists, mostly through his numerous publications issued from exile in the Western treaty port of Canton (Guangzhou). Meanwhile, the decision announced on May 4, 1919, by the Allies at Versailles to allow Japan to keep the German territory in China it had seized at the beginning of the war set off mass demonstrations and a boycott of foreign businesses. This May Fourth Movement, as it came to be called, is often cited as the modern beginning of Chinese nationalism. Shortly thereafter, inspired by the Bolshevik Revolution in Russia, the Chinese Communist Party (CCP) was founded in 1921.

By 1923, encouraged by support from the Third Communist International (Comintern), Sun's Nationalist Party was being reorganized and supplied with Russian help, in return for which the party agreed to allow members of the CCP to join with them to form what became known as the First United Front (1924–1927). The Nationalist Party organized the National Revolutionary Army in the south, and the CCP fomented communist-inspired strikes in the industrial cities of the Yangtze delta, including Shanghai. Sun died in 1925, and a year later Chiang K'ai-shek (1887–1975) ascended to the leadership of the army. Chiang came from a wealthy salt merchant family and was a military officer trained in the Nationalist Party academy and in Moscow. The most pressing objective in 1926 was the unification of China. The two parties mobilized an army of some 85,000 men, and the so-called

Mao. The images of Mao that dominate our consciousness are usually the old Mao, when his health was failing, his youthful vigor was long gone, and his political power diminished. But it is in the young Mao, such as this photo from 1938, that we can best see his leadership skills in action. As Mao's longtime associate Zhou Enlai (1898–1976) observed in 1943, "The Comrade's style of work incorporates the modesty and pragmatism of the Chinese people; the simplicity and diligence of the Chinese peasants; the love of study and profound thinking of an intellectual; the efficiency and steadfastness of a revolutionary soldier; and the persistence and indomitability of a Bolshevik."

Northern Expedition of 1926–1927 became a remarkably successful effort which brought about the unification of southern China as far north as the Yangzi River.

In the middle of the campaign, however, the bonds between the GMD and CCP ruptured. The socialist wing of the GMD and the CCP had taken the important industrial centers of Wuhan and Shanghai in the Yangtze delta from warlords, setting the stage for a showdown with the nationalist wing. Though he had been trained in Moscow, Chiang had grown intensely suspicious of Comintern and CCP motives and, thus launched a preemptive purge of communists in nationalist-held areas. Though much of the leftist opposition was eliminated, a remnant under Mao Zedong (1893–1976) fled to the remote province of Jiangxi in the south to regroup and create their own socialist state. Mao, a librarian by training from a wealthy peasant family, was an inspiring rural organizer; and he set about developing his ideas of Marxist revolution with the heretical idea of having peasants in the vanguard.

By the early 1930s Mao's Chinese communists had developed this crucial variant of rural communism, which Marx and Lenin had found impossible to envisage. Mao replaced the capitalists with the landlords as the class enemy and promised a much needed land reform to the downtrodden peasants. Moreover, the peasants would be the leading participants in the "People's War"—a three-stage guerilla conflict involving the entire populace and borrowing from sources as diverse as Sun Zi's *Art of War* and American tactics against the British in the War for Independence.

Believing the communist threat to be effectively eliminated, Chiang resumed his Northern Expedition in 1928, submitting Beijing to his control but failing to eliminate the strongest northern warlords. Nevertheless, China was now at least nominally unified, with the capital in Nanjing, the National Party Congress functioning as a parliament, and Chiang as president. Chiang made substantial progress with railroad and road construction as well as cotton and silk textile exports. Thanks to the silver standard of its money, rather than the fatal gold standard of most other countries, the financial consequences of the Depression of 1929–1933 remained relatively mild. Chiang made little headway, however, with land reform. Furthermore, the volatile relations with the remaining warlords made the government vulnerable to border violence and corruption. Hovering above all after 1931 was the Japanese annexation of Manchuria and creeping encroachment on northern China.

The Long March and the Rape of Nanjing   In the early 1930s, Chiang knew that Japan was the enemy to watch, but he was painfully aware of the need to completely eliminate his internal opponents. Following the old proverbial advice of "disorder within, disaster without" he resolved to eliminate the remaining threat from Mao's "Jiangxi Soviet." He mounted increasingly massive "bandit extermination" campaigns from 1931 to 1934, but each one was defeated by the superior mobility, local loyalty, and guerilla tactics of Mao's growing People's Liberation Army. With the help of German advisors, Chiang turned to encircling the CCP areas with a ring of trenches and blockhouses to eliminate the mobility of his opponents. By the fall of 1934 he had tightened the noose around the communists and almost succeeded in destroying their army.

But Mao and about 100,000 soldiers broke out in October 1934, thanks to the negligence of one of the warlords entrusted with the encirclement. Once free, the majority of the Red Army embarked on its epic Long March of 6,000 miles, describing a semicircle from the south through the far west and then northeast toward Beijing. Along the way harassment by nationalist troops, warlords, and local people as well as hunger, famine, heat, swamps, bridgeless rivers, and desertion decimated the bedraggled marchers. In the fall of 1935 some 10,000 communists eventually straggled into the small enclave of Yan'an (Yenan), out of Chiang's reach. Living in caves cut into the loess soil, they set up communes and concentrated on agricultural production and reconstituting their forces.

The communists had seized upon Japan's aggression as a valuable propaganda tool and declared war against Japan in 1932. Chiang's obsession with eliminating his internal enemies increasingly made him subject to criticism of appeasement toward Japan. By 1936, a group of warlords and dissident nationalist generals arrested Chiang outside the city of Xi'an and spirited him off to CCP headquarters at Yan'an. After weeks of fraught negotiations, Chiang was released as the leader of a China now brought together under a Second United Front, this time against Japan.

Seeing their prospects for gradual encroachment quickly fading, Japan seized on the so-called Marco Polo Bridge Incident and launched an all-out assault on China. The bridge was a key point along the frontier between Japanese and Chinese forces just outside Beijing, and on the night of July 7, 1937, a brief exchange of fire accidentally took place between the two sides. When a Japanese soldier seeking to relieve himself during the exchange did not return to post, the Japanese used this as a pretext to move against the Chinese. Though Chinese resistance was stiff in the opening months, the Japanese were able to use their superior mobility and airpower to flank the Chinese forces and take the capital of Nanjing (Nanking) by December 1937. Realizing the need to defeat China as quickly as possible in order to avoid a war of attrition, they subjected the capital to the first major atrocity of World War II: "the Rape of Nanjing." Though scholars are still debating the exact number of casualties, it is estimated that between 200,000 and 300,000 people were slaughtered in deliberately gruesome ways: hacked to death, burned alive, buried alive, and beheaded. Over and above this brutality, however, rape was systematically used as a means of terror and subjugation.

The direct message of all of this was that other Chinese cities could expect similar treatment if surrender was not swiftly forthcoming. Like the British and Germans under aerial bombardment a few years later, however, the destruction only stiffened the will to resist of the Chinese. Continually harassed as they retreated from Nanjing, the Chinese adopted the strategy of trading space for time to regroup, as did the Soviets a few years later. In an epic mass migration, Chinese soldiers and civilians stripped every usable article possible and moved it to the region of the remote city of Chongqing (Chungking), which became the wartime capital of China until 1945. Thereafter, both nationalists and communists used the vast interior for hit-and-run tactics, effectively limiting Japan to the northeast and coastal urban centers but themselves incapable of mounting large offensives.

The Rape of Nanjing. Of the many horrors of the twentieth century, few can match the Rape of Nanjing for its sadistic brutality, in which perhaps as many as 300,000 people lost their lives in a killing orgy.

World War II in the Pacific   While Japan had used its control of Manchuria, Korea, and Taiwan in its support of autarky and economic stability in the 1930s, its bid for empire in the Pacific was portrayed as the construction of "The Greater East Asia Co-Prosperity Sphere." This expansion was considered essential because oil, metals, rubber, and other raw materials were still imported in large quantities from the United States and the Dutch and British possessions in southeast Asia. After Hitler invaded the Netherlands and France in 1940, the moment arrived when the Japanese could plan for extending their power and removing the United States from the Pacific. Moreover, the stalemate in China was increasingly bleeding Japan of vital resources, while mounting tensions with the United States over China were already resulting in economic sanctions. Accordingly, in the summer of 1941, the Japanese government decided on the extension of the empire into the Dutch East Indies and southeast Asia, even if this meant war with the United States. Under the premiership of General Tojo Hideki (in office 1941–1944), Japan attacked Pearl Harbor, Hawaii; the Philippines; and Dutch and British territories on December 7–8, 1941. Within a few months, the Japanese completed the occupation of all the important southeast Asian and Pacific territories they had sought (see Map 28.8).

Japan's newfound autarky did not last long however. Within 6 months, in the naval and air battle of Midway, American forces regained the initiative. The Japanese now

MAP **28.8** **World War II in the Pacific, 1937–1945.**

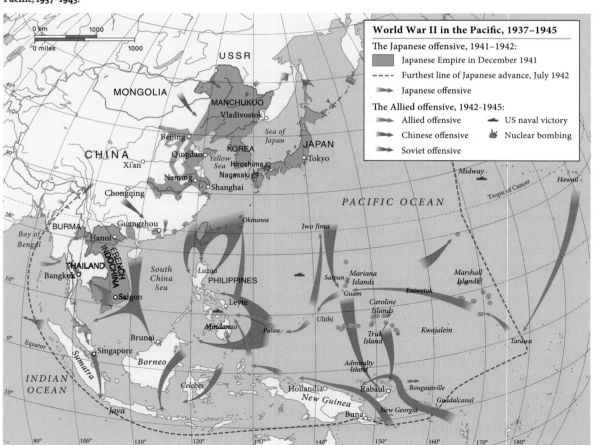

exploited the populations of their new territories for their raw materials with increasing urgency. As the American forces slowly deprived the Japanese of these resources through their highly effective "island-hopping" strategy, they came within bombing range of the Japanese home islands by late 1944. Starting in March 1945, they subjected Japan to the most devastating firebomb attacks ever mounted. Finally, President Harry S Truman (in office 1945–1953) made the fateful decision to have two experimental atomic bombs dropped on Hiroshima and Nagasaki (August 6 and 9, 1945), effectively obliterating both cities. With the Soviets declaring war against Japan on August 8 and advancing into Manchuria, the Japanese were finally convinced that the war was lost and surrendered on August 14, 1945, with the final ceremony taking place aboard the US battleship *Missouri* on September 2, 1945.

Putting It All Together

As discussed in previous chapters, the patterns of constitutional nationalism and industrialization in the late eighteenth and early nineteenth centuries were most visibly manifested in Great Britain, the United States, and France. Subsequently, two further patterns complicated the evolution of nations joining in the pursuit of modernity: ethnolinguistic nationalism and the rise of the industrial working class. Abetted by the imperialistic tendencies inherited from before 1800, all of these patterns collided in the First World War. After the war, they recombined into the three ideologies of modernity analyzed in this chapter: capitalist democracy, communism, and supremacist nationalism (see Concept Map).

For the most part, only democracy and communism are considered to be genuine ideologies of modernity, in the sense of being based on relatively coherent programs. More recent historians, however, have come to the conclusion that nationalist supremacism was a genuine variety of modernity as well, though one defined more by what it opposed than by what it supported. The adherents of the three modernities bitterly denounced the ideologies of their rivals. All three considered themselves to be genuinely "progressive" or modern.

What is very difficult to understand in a country like the United States, still deeply loyal to its foundational national constitutionalism, is that someone could be an ardent ethnic nationalist, have little faith in constitutional liberties, find the conquest of a large and completely self-sufficient empire perfectly logical, and think of all this as the wave of a future modernity. Indeed, historians have customarily thought of these views as revolts *against* modernity. Yet, as we have seen so often, innovations frequently create a "gelling" effect in which opposition to the new clarifies and solidifies, often in unexpected ways. The "modern" notion of ethnolinguistic nationalism thus created

---

Emperor Hirohito's (r. 1926–1989) Surrender Message to the Japanese People, August 14, 1945

"We declared war on America and Britain out of Our sincere desire to ensure Japan's self-preservation and the stabilization of East Asia, it being far from Our thought either to infringe upon the sovereignty of other nations or to embark upon territorial aggrandisement. But now the war has lasted for nearly four years. Despite the best that has been done by everyone—the gallant fighting of the military and naval forces, the diligence and assiduity of Our servants of the State and the devoted service of Our one hundred million people, the war situation has developed not necessarily to Japan's advantage, while the general trends of the world have all turned against her interest. Moreover, the enemy has begun to employ a new and most cruel bomb, the power of which to damage is indeed incalculable, taking the toll of many innocent lives. Should We continue to fight, it would not only result in an ultimate collapse and obliteration of the Japanese nation, but also it would lead to the total extinction of human civilization. Such being the case, how are We to save the millions of Our subjects; or to atone Ourselves before the hallowed spirits of Our Imperial Ancestors? This is the reason why We have ordered the Acceptance of the provisions of the Joint Declaration of the Powers."

—Transmitted by Domei Tsushinsha (Japanese Federated News Agency) and recorded by the US Federal Communications Commission, August 14, 1945

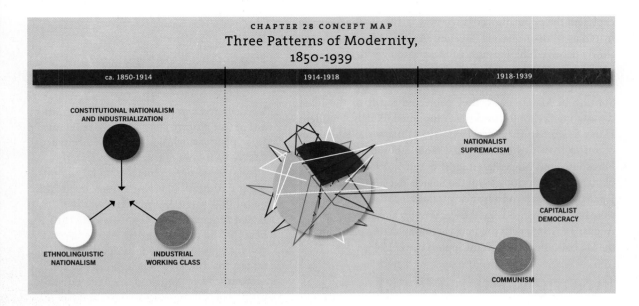

**Three Patterns of Modernity,
1850-1939**

ways of opposing other modern innovations such as constitutionalism and industrialism—with their messy uncertainties and feelings of rootlessness—by insisting on a purer, more mystical bond for the modern nation-state that, ironically, hearkened back to a simpler, reimagined past. But Mussolini, Hitler, and the Japanese generals all aspired to the same scientific–industrial future as Roosevelt, Churchill, Stalin, Chiang K'ai-shek, and Mao Zedong.

Review and Respond

1. How did the Allies deal with Germany after its defeat in 1918, and how did it recover?

2. Explain the shift from capital goods to consumer goods investment in the capitalist economies after World War I. How did this shift express itself?

3. Which factors contributed to the Great Depression of 1929–1933?

4. What role did the protagonist play in the communist vision of modernity? Why was industrialization central to the Soviet communist pattern of modernity?

5. Trace the steps through which Hitler advanced from prisoner to dictator.

6. How did a version of constitutionalist modernity arrive in Japan, and which factors limited its impact?

7. What reasons limited constitutional nationalism in China after the creation of the republic in 1912?

8. What were some of the artistic responses to modernity? How did they reflect the anxiety of the period?

▶ For additional resources, including maps, primary sources, visuals, and quizzes, please go to www.oup.com/us/vonsivers. Please see the Further Resources section at the back of the book for additional readings and suggested websites.

Thinking Through Patterns

▶ **Which three patterns of modernity emerged after World War I? How and why did these patterns form?**

Ethnic nationalism was difficult to accommodate in the nineteenth century, which began with the more inclusive constitutional nationalism of Great Britain, the United States, and France. New nations like Italy, Germany, and Japan were formed on the basis of an ethnic nationalism that in a sense created nations but not necessarily ones with the ideals of equality embodied in constitutional nation-states. World War I set back Germany, Italy, and Japan, but afterward they inflated their ethnic nationalism into supremacist nationalism and adopted imperialism, all under the banner of modernity. In Russia, communists seized the opportunity offered by the turmoil of World War I to turn a constitutionally as well as industrially underdeveloped empire into a communist one-party, industrial empire. The United States, Britain, and France, each based on variations of constitutionalism, industry, and smaller or larger empires, became advocates of a capitalist democratic modernity.

Capitalist democracy was a modernity that upheld free enterprise, the market, and consumerism. It succeeded in providing the modern items of daily life, but it suffered a major setback in the Depression and had to be reined in through tightened political controls. It also withheld freedom, equality, and the staples of daily life from minorities and the colonized. Communism succeeded in industrializing an underdeveloped empire and providing the bare necessities for modern life; it did so with untold human sacrifices. Supremacist nationalism was attractive to nationalists who were not workers and therefore afraid of communism. Supremacist nationalists held democracies in disdain because they considered constitutions meaningless pieces of paper.

▶ **What were the strengths and flaws of each of the three visions of modernity?**

▶ **Why did supremacist nationalism disappear in the ashes of World War II?**

Supremacist nationalism was a modernity that failed because the conquest of new, self-sufficient empires proved to be an impossible goal. The advocates of democratic capitalist and communist modernity—most notably the United States, Great Britain, France, and the Soviet Union—were dangerously threatened by Germany, Italy, and Japan and came together to destroy these supremacist national countries.

Chapter 29

1945-1962

Reconstruction, Cold War, and Decolonization

By any standard the event seemed symbolic of a new world order, one in which the emerging nonaligned nations would set the pace of innovation. Appropriately enough, it also marked the beginning of a new decade, one that would begin full of promise and peril and end in conflict and confusion for much of the world. The event was the 1960 election of the world's first female prime minister, Sirimavo Bandaranaike (1916–2000), of what was then called Ceylon (renamed Sri Lanka in 1972), a large island off the southeastern coast of India.

Her country had achieved independence from Great Britain only a dozen years before and had maintained close ties to its former colonial

THE COLD WAR AND DECOLONIZATION

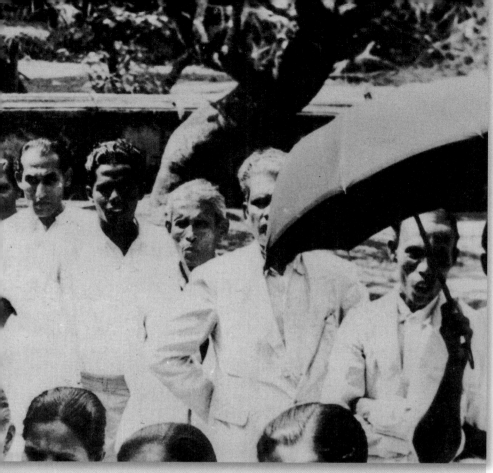

Seeing Patterns

▶ **Why did the pattern of unfolding modernity, which offered three choices after World War I, shrink to just capitalist democracy and socialism–communism in 1945? How did each of these two patterns evolve between 1945 and 1962?**

▶ **What are the cultural premises of modernity?**

▶ **How did the newly independent countries of the Middle East, Asia, and Africa adapt to the divided world of the Cold War?**

overlord. In 1956, however, Bandaranaike's husband Solomon was elected prime minister with a pronounced nationalist and socialist platform, in the newly assertive spirit of the nonaligned nations reflected in the Bandung Conference the year before. As prime minister, he replaced English with Sinhalese as the country's language and evicted the British military from its bases. When a Buddhist monk opposed to Western medicine assassinated him in 1959, she succeeded her husband, winning an election in 1960, becoming prime minister in her own right, and serving her first term from 1960 to 1965.

Coming from a prominent Buddhist family, she held the same deep political convictions as her husband, believing in a strong national foundation for her country as an independent nation beholden to neither West nor East. As a socialist, she continued the nationalization of the banking, insurance, and petroleum sectors begun by her husband; ordered the state to take over all Catholic schools; and joined the Nonalignment Movement in 1961. The movement sought to bring India, Egypt, Yugoslavia, Indonesia, and a number of other states together as a bloc to retain their independence from the pressures of the Cold War between the two superpowers of the United

Democracy in Action. One important element in the spread of representative government in Asia was the right of women to vote and hold office. Here, in a remote village on the island of Ceylon (now Sri Lanka) men and women line up separately to cast their votes in the general election of March 22, 1960. The victor in the race for prime minister, Sirimavo Bandaranaike, became the world's first woman prime minister.

United Nations: Successor of the League of Nations, founded in 1945 and comprising today about 200 countries; with a Secretary General, a General Assembly meeting annually, and a standing Security Council composed of permanent members (United States, China, Russia, Great Britain, and France) as well as 5 rotating temporary members.

States and the Soviet Union and their allies. Her strong commitment to a Sinhalese-only language policy, however, aroused considerable resistance in the country, especially from the Tamil minority in the north. The Theraveda Buddhist Sinhalese comprise about 74 percent and the Hindu Tamils 17 percent of the population. Only 2 years into Bandaranaike's tenure, the country was gripped by a Tamil civil disobedience campaign and it rapidly became apparent that Ceylon was entering a time of political turbulence. Ultimately, anti-Tamil discrimination led to the abortive Tamil Tiger liberation war (1976–2009), pursued on both sides with the utmost brutality.

During her four terms as prime minister (1960–1965, 1970–1972, 1972–1977, and 1994–2000), Bandaranaike was a prominent leader on the world stage. Like her fellow female prime ministers Benazir Bhutto in Pakistan and Indira Gandhi in India and first-generation nonaligned leaders like Jawaharlal Nehru of India, Sukarno of Indonesia, and Gamal Abdel Nasser of Egypt—Bandaranaike spent much of her time and scarce resources trying to navigate the turbulent waters of ethnic and religious conflict, superpower pressure, and nation-building in an increasingly competitive economic arena. The backdrop against which all these nonaligned nations acted was woven from two main developments in the unfolding pattern of scientific–industrial modernity: the Cold War and decolonization. The capitalist–democratic and the socialist–communist spheres competed with each other for political, military, and economic dominance; at the same time, the West rid itself of what was now seen as its biggest curse— colonialism—which bedeviled it and had severely detracted from its appeal during the interwar and early postwar periods.

The early Cold War, discussed in the first half of this chapter, dominated world politics during this time because the contest between the two superpowers allowed practically no escape. The one partial exception was China, which presented itself as a nonaligned country as it distanced itself from the Soviet Union but was viewed with ambivalence by its nonaligned colleagues. Decolonization, discussed in the second half of this chapter, was a subsidiary political process; but it nevertheless played a major role in the dynamics of the Cold War because it created many of the new nations over which both superpower blocs sought influence and so many tried to escape. By the 1962 Cuban Missile Crisis, during which the superpower confrontation reached its climax, the configuration of the two superpower blocs and the camp of the nonaligned nations was still in flux. Over the coming years, the tilting to one camp or another of India, Pakistan, Indonesia, and ultimately China, to name only a few, would loom large in the superpower struggle. And the role of Bandaranaike and other nonaligned leaders as spoilers between the superpowers, for a time at least, was secure.

Superpower Confrontation: Capitalist Democracy and Communism

World War II was the most destructive war in human history. Nearly 6 years of fighting in Europe and 9 years in Asia resulted in casualties on a scale scarcely conceivable in the past. The total loss of life, including combatants, civilians, and victims of the Holocaust, is estimated at over 50 million, three times as many as in World War I. With the exception of the continental United States, which was unreachable by enemy aircraft, all combatant countries in World War II suffered widespread destruction. Most ominous was that the final days of the war also ushered in the nuclear age. The use of the first atomic weapons by the United States against Japan meant that future general wars would almost certainly be nuclear ones. Yet, while the war was still on, the foundations of a new world organization to replace and fix the shortcomings of the old League of Nations—the **United Nations**, whose charter was later signed by 51 nations in October 1945—were being laid in San Francisco. Thus, the year 1945 was simultaneously one of hope that the war's end might result in a better world and one of grim assessment as the full extent of the global damage began to be understood. Remarkably, within a few years, out of the ruins, the world's remaining strains of modernity—capitalism–democracy and socialism–communism—would reemerge stronger than ever, each according to its own vision.

Destruction and Despair in the Nuclear Age. World War II was the most destructive human conflict in history, far exceeding the damage of what had only a short time before been considered to be "the war to end all wars"--World War I. Nowhere was the damage more complete than in Japan, where an aerial campaign of firebombing Japanese cities by American B-29s had destroyed nearly every major Japanese center. The culmination of this campaign was the first—and to date, last—use of nuclear weapons in warfare on the Japanese cities of Hiroshima and Nagasaki in August, 1945. Here, a mother and child who survived the nuclear destruction of Hiroshima sit plaintively amid the utter devastation of their city in December, 1945.

The Cold War Era, 1945–1962

As the world rebuilt, the United States and the Soviet Union promoted their contrasting visions of modernity—capitalist-democratic and communist—with deep missionary fervor. For the next 45 years the two powers were locked in a prolonged struggle to determine which approach would eventually prevail in the world. While each on occasion engaged in brinkmanship—pushing crises to the edge of nuclear war—as a rule both sought to avoid direct confrontation. Instead, they pursued their aims of expanding and consolidating their respective systems, dubbed the "Cold War," through ideological struggle and proxy states (that is, states acting as substitutes against each other). Two phases can be discerned in the early Cold War. The first lasted from 1945 to 1956, when the Soviet Union continued to pursue Stalin's prewar policy of "socialism in one country," which was now extended to include Eastern Europe. The second comprised the years 1956–1962, when Stalin's

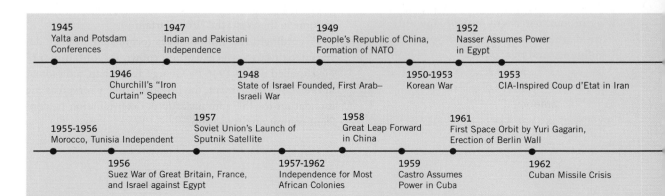

| 1945 | 1947 | 1949 | 1952 |
| Yalta and Potsdam Conferences | Indian and Pakistani Independence | People's Republic of China, Formation of NATO | Nasser Assumes Power in Egypt |

| 1946 | 1948 | 1950-1953 | 1953 |
| Churchill's "Iron Curtain" Speech | State of Israel Founded, First Arab–Israeli War | Korean War | CIA-Inspired Coup d'Etat in Iran |

| 1955-1956 | 1957 | 1958 | 1961 |
| Morocco, Tunisia Independent | Soviet Union's Launch of Sputnik Satellite | Great Leap Forward in China | First Space Orbit by Yuri Gagarin, Erection of Berlin Wall |

| 1956 | 1957-1962 | 1959 | 1962 |
| Suez War of Great Britain, France, and Israel against Egypt | Independence for Most African Colonies | Castro Assumes Power in Cuba | Cuban Missile Crisis |

Cold War: Ideological struggle between the United States and its allies and the Soviet Union and its allies that lasted from 1945 to 1989.

Containment: U.S. foreign policy doctrine formulated in 1946 to limit as much as possible the spread of communism.

successor Nikita Khrushchev (1894–1971, in office 1953–1964) reformulated the policy to include spreading aid and influence to new nationalist regimes in Asia and Africa that had won their independence from Western colonialism, even if these regimes were not (yet) communist. This new policy, applied to Cuba, produced the near disaster of the Cuban Missile Crisis in 1962 during which the United States and the Soviet Union almost came to blows (see Map 29.1).

Cold War Origins   The origins of the **Cold War** have been bitterly debated and minutely studied since the 1940s, with apologists for each side tending to see its inception in the actions of the other. While it may not be possible at this point to establish an exact time or event for the beginning of the Cold War, we can point to certain mileposts in its development. One such milepost that most scholars point to came in the spring of 1945, when the Soviet Red Army occupied German-held territories in Eastern Europe and communist guerillas made rapid advances in the Balkans. In a secret deal between British Prime Minister Churchill and Soviet leader Josef Stalin in May 1944, Greece became part of the British sphere, in return for Romania and Bulgaria being apportioned to the Soviet sphere of responsibility for occupation at war's end.

Later, at the Yalta Conference in February 1945, Churchill, Stalin, and a haggard and ill American president Franklin Roosevelt agreed that the armies of the Allies would each undertake the occupation of the territories they held at war's end and hold free elections in those areas as soon as possible. Stalin also agreed that the Soviet Union would enter the war with Japan after the surrender of Germany. At the Potsdam Conference in July 1945, American interests were represented by Roosevelt's former vice president, Harry S Truman, who had assumed the office of president following Roosevelt's death in April.

Truman (in office 1945–1953) was more openly skeptical of Stalin's motives than Roosevelt, and he now had an edge that his predecessor lacked: On July 16, scientists at the "Manhattan Project," the US effort to develop an atomic weapon, had succeeded in detonating a plutonium test device in New Mexico. Armed with the astonishing results of the device's power and the knowledge that bombs were already being constructed for use against Japan, Truman felt confident he could deal firmly with Stalin's demands. His assessment of Stalin's motives was not reassuring; he felt the Russians had no intention of either withdrawing from Eastern Europe or allowing for democratic elections. By early 1946, Churchill, in a speech at Fulton, Missouri, coined the phrase that would define the communist sphere for decades to come in the West: the "Iron Curtain."

Accordingly, the United States formulated a policy designed to thwart Soviet expansion known as "**containment**." First spelled out in 1946 by George F. Kennan, a diplomat in the State Department, the proposed policy served as the foundation for the administration's determination to confront communist expansion.

Containing the Soviet Threat

"It is clear that the main element of any United States policy toward the Soviet Union must be that of long-term, patient but firm and vigilant containment of Russian expansive tendencies. . . . It is clear that the United States cannot expect in the foreseeable future to enjoy political intimacy with the Soviet regime. It must continue to regard the Soviet Union as a rival, not a partner, in the political arena. It must continue to expect that Soviet policies will reflect no abstract love of peace and stability, no real faith in the possibility of a permanent happy coexistence of the Socialist and capitalist worlds, but rather a cautious, persistent pressure toward the disruption and weakening of all rival influence and rival power."

—George F. Kennan. "The Sources of Soviet Conduct." *Foreign Affairs* 24, no. 4 (1947): 566–582. www .historyguide.org/europe/kennan.html.

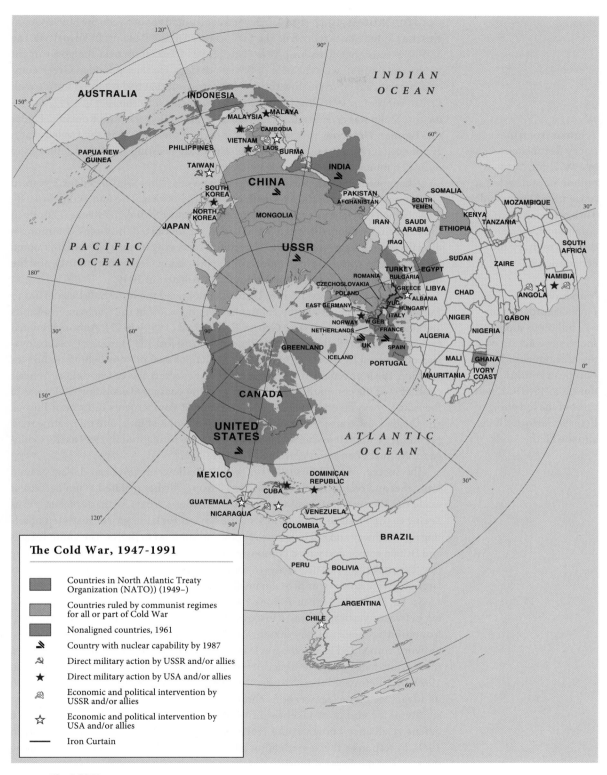

The Cold War, 1947-1991

	Countries in North Atlantic Treaty Organization (NATO)) (1949–)
	Countries ruled by communist regimes for all or part of Cold War
	Nonaligned countries, 1961
⚔	Country with nuclear capability by 1987
☭	Direct military action by USSR and/or allies
★	Direct military action by USA and/or allies
☭	Economic and political intervention by USSR and/or allies
☆	Economic and political intervention by USA and/or allies
—	Iron Curtain

MAP **29.1 The Cold War, 1947–1991.**

Truman Doctrine:
Policy formulated
in 1947, initially to
outline steps directed at
preventing Greece and
Turkey from becoming
communist, mostly
through military and
economic aid.

Marshall Plan:
Financial program of
$13 billion to support
the reconstruction of
the economies of 17
European countries
during 1948–1952, with
most of the aid going to
France, Germany, Italy,
and the Netherlands.

Confrontations, 1947–1949   Several confrontations between the Soviet Union and the United States followed. The first occurred in the Balkans. In Yugoslavia, the anti-Nazi resistance hero Josip Broz Tito (1892–1980) took over the government in November 1945 with the help of Soviet advisors. He then provided Greek communists with aid, to overthrow the royal government that had returned to rule with British support in 1946. The United States stepped in with supplies in 1947, assuming that Stalin was orchestrating aid from Yugoslavia, Bulgaria, and Romania. Under the **Truman Doctrine**, proclaimed in a speech of the same year, the United States announced its support of all "free peoples who are resisting attempted subjugation by armed minorities or by outside pressures."

What appeared like a proxy civil war between East and West raged for 2 years in Greece until it ended in the aftermath of the split between Tito and Stalin. In 1948, Tito claimed his right to regional communism, against Stalin's insistence on unity in the Communist Bloc. Although Stalin had never supported the Greek communists directly, given his agreement with Churchill, a surprising majority of the latter opted for Stalin. Tito withdrew his support for the pro-Stalin Greek communists, and the bid for communism in Greece was doomed to collapse in 1949.

Following up on his doctrine, Truman announced the **Marshall Plan** of aid to Europe, for the recovery of the continent from the ruins of the war, named after its architect, the secretary of state George C. Marshall (1880–1959). Although invited to take part, Stalin flatly rejected American aid and forbade Hungary, Czechoslovakia, and Poland to ask for it. In addition to the political reasons behind Stalin's injunction, the Marshall Plan's requirement of free markets and convertible currencies contradicted the communist ideology of a central command economy. Stalin was in the midst of engineering his fledgling communist governments in Eastern Europe and the Balkans, transforming them into the Communist Bloc, and integrating their economies with that of the Soviet Union. This was formalized in 1949 as the Council for Mutual Economic Assistance (COMECON).

The success of the Marshall Plan, with its billions of American dollars poured into relief and reconstruction in Western Europe, further irritated Stalin because it made the Western sectors of Germany and Berlin magnets for Eastern Europeans fleeing to the West. In 1948, therefore, the Soviets took the provocative step of setting up a highway and rail blockade of food and supplies to Berlin. The United States and Britain responded with a demonstration of technological prowess by mounting the "Berlin Airlift." For nearly a year, food, fuel, and other supplies required by this large city were flown in until Stalin finally gave up the blockade.

So far, the Cold War in Europe had been confined to diplomatic maneuvering between Washington and Moscow. During the Berlin crisis, however, the confrontation assumed military dimensions. Thanks in part to an elaborate espionage network embedded inside the nuclear programs of Britain and the United States, the Soviets had been able to accelerate their efforts to build a nuclear bomb. In 1949, they detonated their first device 4 years earlier than anticipated. Now, with its advantage in nuclear weapons eliminated and concern increasing over the possibility of a communist takeover in Western Europe, the United States formed a defensive alliance known as the North Atlantic Treaty Organization (NATO) in 1949. In response, the Soviet Union later formed the Warsaw Pact in 1955 among the states of the Eastern Bloc.

The Berlin Airlift. During nearly 1 year from June 1948 to May 1949 US, British, and British Commonwealth airplanes delivered more than 2 million tons of food and supplies to Berlin after Stalin had blocked all land access to the city. Berlin children eagerly await the next delivery of supplies.

Hot War in Korea   Emboldened by the development of the nuclear bomb and the victory of the Chinese communists over the nationalists in October 1949, Stalin ratcheted up the Cold War. After a series of raids and counterraids between communist North Korea and nationalist South Korea and Stalin's blessing for an invasion by the north, the Cold War turned hot. In June 1950, large numbers of communist troops crossed over into South Korea in an attempt at forcible unification. South Korean troops fought a desperate rearguard action at the southern end of the peninsula. Under US pressure and despite a Soviet boycott, the United Nations (UN) Security Council branded North Korea as the aggressor, entitling South Korea to UN intervention. At first, in July 1950, the North Korean invaders trapped US troops arriving from Japan and what remained of the South Korean defense forces in the southeast. But by October US troops, augmented by troops from a number of UN members, had mounted a surprise amphibious invasion and fought their way into North Korea, occupied the capital (Pyongyang), and advanced to the Chinese border.

In the meantime, the United States had sent a fleet to the remnant of the Chinese nationalists who had formed the Republic of China on the southern island of Taiwan, to protect it from a threatened invasion by a newly communist China. Thwarted in the south at Taiwan, Mao Zedong took the pronouncements of General Douglas MacArthur, the commander of the UN forces in Korea, about raiding Chinese supply bases on the North Korean border seriously. Stalin, on the other hand, opposed an escalation and gave Mao only token support.

Secretly marching to the border in October 1950, communist Chinese troops launched a massive surprise offensive into the peninsula, pushing the UN forces back deep into South Korea. Over the next 3 years, the war seesawed back and forth over the old border of the 38th parallel, while negotiations dragged on. Unwilling to expand the war further or use nuclear weapons, the new Eisenhower administration and the North Koreans agreed to an armistice in 1953. The armistice has endured from that date, and no official peace treaty was ever signed. For more than half a century, the border between the two Koreas has remained a volatile flashpoint, with provocative incidents repeatedly threatening to reopen the conflict.

McCarthyism in the United States   The strains of a "hot war" in Korea produced troubling domestic fallout in the United States as well. Amid the general atmosphere of anticommunism, Joseph McCarthy (1908–1957), a Republican senator from Wisconsin, rose to prominence almost overnight when he revealed in a 1950 speech that he had a lengthy list of members of the Communist Party employed by the State Department. Though he never produced the list, his smear tactics, together with denunciations made by the House Committee on Un-American Activities, ruined the careers of hundreds of government employees, movie actors and writers, and private persons in many walks of life. McCarthy went as far as accusing Presidents Truman and Eisenhower of tolerating communist "fellow travelers" in their administrations. For 4 years hysteria reigned until finally enough voices of reason arose in the Senate to censure McCarthy and relegate him to obscurity in 1954. The legacy of bitterness engendered by the "McCarthy era" remained for decades and generated abundant political accusations on both sides.

Revolt in East Germany   As the McCarthy drama unfolded in the United States and the frustrating Korean armistice negotiations at Panmunjom dragged on, Stalin died of a stroke in April 1953. The death of this all-powerful, inscrutable, and paranoid dictator was profoundly unsettling for the governments of the Eastern Bloc. This was especially the case in the German Democratic Republic (East Germany), where the government was nervously watching the rising wave of defections to the Federal Republic (West Germany)—nearly a million persons during 1949–1953. It had sealed off the border through a system of fences and watchtowers, but Berlin—also divided into East and West sectors—was still a gaping hole. The population was seething over rising production quotas, shortages resulting from the shipment of industrial goods to the Soviet Union (in the name of reparations), and the beginnings of a West German economic boom in which it could not share.

In June 1953, a strike among East Berlin workers quickly grew into a general uprising, encompassing some 500 cities and towns. East German police and Soviet troops, stunned at first, quickly moved to suppress the revolt. The Politburo (the Communist Party's Central Committee Political Bureau) in Moscow, still trying to determine Stalin's succession, refused any concessions, except for a few cosmetic changes in the reparations. The German Stalinist government obediently went along.

Stalin's eventual successor in the fall of 1953 was Nikita Khrushchev, a metalworker from a poor farmer's family on the Russian–Ukrainian border who had worked his way up through the party hierarchy during the war years. It took Khrushchev a year and a half to consolidate his power as party secretary and premier, during which he made substantial investments in agriculture, housing, and consumer goods. In February 1956 he gave a much-noted speech in which he denounced Stalin's "excesses" during collectivization and the purges of the 1930s. Thousands were released from prisons and the labor camps in Siberia (*gulags*) and other remote areas. In the Communist Bloc Khrushchev pushed for the removal of Stalinist hard-liners and the arrival of new faces willing to improve general living conditions for the population. To balance the new flexibility within the Soviet Bloc, Khrushchev was careful to maintain toughness toward the West. He alarmed leaders of the West when he announced that he was abandoning Stalin's doctrine of socialism in one country for a new policy that supported anticolonial nationalist independence movements around the globe even if the movements were not communist. The policy sent shivers down the spines of the cold warriors in the West.

Revolt in Poland and Hungary   Khrushchev's speech and reforms awakened hopes in Eastern Europe that new leaders would bring change there as well. In Poland, where collectivization and the command economy had progressed only slowly and the Catholic Church could not be intimidated, Khrushchev's speech resulted in workers' unrest similar to East Germany 3 years earlier. Nationalist reformists gained the upper hand over Stalinists in the Polish Politburo, and Khrushchev realized that he had to avoid another Tito-style secession at all costs. After a few tense days in mid-October, pitting Soviet troops and an angry population against each other, Poland received its limited autonomy.

In Hungary, the Politburo was similarly divided between reformers and Stalinists. People in Budapest and other cities, watching events in Poland with intense interest, took to the streets. The Politburo lost control and the man appointed to lead the country to a national communist solution similar to that of Poland, Imre Nagy [Noj] (1896–1958), felt emboldened by popular support to go further by announcing a multiparty system and the withdrawal of Hungary from the Warsaw Pact. These announcements were too much for Khrushchev, who unleashed the Soviet troops stationed in Hungary to repress the by now fully blossoming grassroots revolution.

Aware of British, French, and American preoccupation with the Suez Crisis, the Soviets crushed the uprising in November 1956. Nagy, finding sanctuary in the Yugoslav Embassy and promised safe conduct out of the country, was duped and found

Unrest in the Soviet Bloc. In the Hungarian uprising from October to November 1956, some 2,500 Hungarians and 700 Soviet troops were killed, while 200,000 fled to neighboring Austria and the West. Here, a young boy and older man watch with a surprising degree of nonchalance while a Soviet tank rumbles through an intersection with barricades set up by Hungarian "freedom fighters."

Aiming for the Stars. New scholarship sheds light on Sputnik's role in Russian cultural history. As this commemorative postcard from 1958 reveals, the connection between the technological achievement of Sputnik and popular interest in space travel was strong. The legend reads in Russian: "4 October, the USSR launched Earth's first artificial satellite; 3 November, the USSR launched Earth's second artificial satellite."

himself arrested. The new pro-Moscow government executed him in 1958. During the brief uprising, perhaps a quarter of a million Hungarian citizens escaped to the West. For those who stayed, in the hopes of experiencing greater freedom, the events were a crushing blow.

ICBMs and Sputniks   The suppression of anticommunist unrest in the Eastern Bloc decreased the appeal of communism among many Marxists and revolutionary socialists in the West. But steady advancement in weapons technologies and by extension in missiles and space flight, revealed that there was a powerful military punch behind Soviet repression. In 1957 the Soviet Union announced the development of the world's first intercontinental ballistic missile (ICBM), with a range of around 3,500 miles, making it capable of reaching America's East Coast. In the same year, the Soviet Union launched the world's first orbiting satellite, named "Sputnik," into space. Then, in 1961, Russian scientists sent the world's first cosmonaut, Yuri Gagarin (1934–1968), into space, followed 2 years later by Valentina Tereshkova (b. 1937), the world's first female cosmonaut.

These Soviet achievements duly frightened the Eisenhower administration and Congress as the implications of nuclear weapons falling from space with no practicable defense against them began to set in. Politicians played up the apparent technological leadership of the Soviet Union to goad Congress into accelerating the US missile and space program even at the risk of reheating the Cold War with the Soviet Union. Thus, in 1958 the United States successfully launched its first satellite, Explorer I, and the following year its first ICBM, the Atlas. The space and missile races were now fully under way.

Communism in Cuba   In 1959, Fidel Castro (b. 1926), a nationalist guerilla fighter opposed to the influence of American companies over a government generally perceived as corrupt, succeeded in seizing power in Cuba. A trained lawyer, Castro was the son of a Spanish immigrant who had become a wealthy planter. About 6 months after the coup, Cuba was the new symbol of the Khrushchev government's widely hailed openness toward national liberation movements worthy of communist largesse. The Soviet Union lavished huge sums on the development of the economy of the island. Khrushchev's instincts were proven right when Castro openly embraced communism in 1960.

To counter Khrushchev's overtures to national liberation movements, President Eisenhower and the head of the American Central Intelligence Agency (CIA), Allen Dulles (1893–1969), secretly supported and trained anticommunist dissidents in the Middle East, Africa, and Latin America. In the case of Latin America, a group of Cuban anticommunists trained in Guatemala with CIA support for an invasion and overthrow of Castro in Cuba. President John F. Kennedy (in office 1961–1963) inherited the initiative and, against his better judgment, decided to steer a middle course, sanctioning an invasion of Cuba by seemingly independent freedom fighters with no direct US armed forces support. The so-called Bay of Pigs invasion in April

1961 (named for the small bay in southern Cuba where the anticommunist invasion began) was promptly intercepted and easily defeated by Castro's forces, to the great embarrassment of Kennedy.

The Berlin Wall   Fortunately for the United States, Khrushchev suffered a severe embarrassment of his own. East Germany, which retained its Stalinist leadership, pressured Khrushchev to close the last loophole in Berlin through which its citizens could escape to West Germany. Between 1953 and 1961, the East German "brain drain" reached 3 million defectors or nearly one-fifth of the population, most of them young and ambitious people whose talent and skills the regime coveted. The East German Stalinists, allied with a few remaining Stalinists in the Politburo, prevailed over Khrushchev's opposition and built the Berlin Wall in 1961, effectively turning the German Democratic Republic into a prison.

The playing field between East and West was now level, with setbacks on both sides, when the two reached the climax of the Cold War: the first direct confrontation between the Soviet Union and the United States nearly two decades after the end of World War II. In October 1962 US spy planes discovered the presence of missile launching pads in Cuba. In October 1962 President Kennedy demanded their immediate destruction and then followed up with a naval blockade of the island to prevent the arrival of Russian missiles. In defiance, Khrushchev dispatched Russian ships to Cuba; when it was discovered that they were bearing missiles, President Kennedy demanded that Khrushchev recall the ships. The world held its breath for several days as the ships headed steadily for Cuba, raising the very real possibility of a nuclear exchange between the world's superpowers (see Map 29.2).

In the face of American determination, Khrushchev recalled the ships at the last minute. Kennedy, for his part, agreed to remove American missiles from Turkey. Realizing just how close the world had come to World War III, Kennedy and Khrushchev signed the Nuclear Test Ban Treaty in 1963, an agreement banning the aboveground testing and development of nuclear weapons. The treaty also sought to prevent the spread of these technologies to other countries. After this dramatic climax in the Cold War, relations gradually thawed.

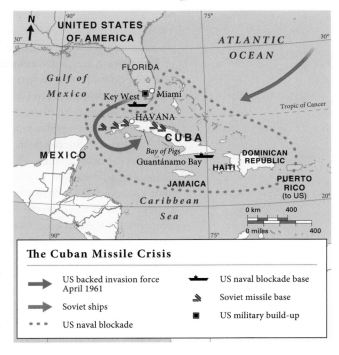

MAP **29.2 The Cuban Missile Crisis.**

Society and Culture in Postwar North America, Europe, and Japan

As in many other wars, World War II was followed by years of conservatism during which the generation of war veterans, deprived of some of their best years because of military service, sought to pursue civilian lives of normalcy and comfort. Intellectuals and artists again cast a critical eye on the modernity that was relentlessly evolving around them, not unlike the previous generation had after World War I. Now, however,

The G.I. Bill for African Americans. Staff Sergeant Herbert Ellison explains the G.I. Bill to members of his company. The bill, enacted in 1944, provided soldiers returning from the war with support for training and education as well as subsidized home loans. Some 7.8 million veterans benefited from the training and education it provided.

the political and ideological options were narrower. Supremacist nationalism in the form of fascism, Nazism, or militarism had been thoroughly bankrupted; and choices had shrunk to communism and capitalist democracy. Still, among the emerging nations, artists and intellectuals struggled to forge new paths, often with attempts at synthesis among indigenous culture and socialist and democratic ideas.

Mass Consumption Culture As discharged American soldiers returned to civilian life, they married and had children. The "baby-boomer" generation appeared on the scene between 1945 and 1961. Families with four to six children were almost the norm. Medical advances and improved diet and nutrition helped in the health and survival of parents and children. The growing population triggered increased consumer demand, not only for the basics of living, such as food, clothes, shoes, and shelter, but also for consumer durables which increased the comfort of living, such as refrigerators, dishwashers, vacuum cleaners, radios, televisions, telephones, and cars. In the United States, the G.I. Bill supported not only the middle-class lifestyle but also university studies for better-paying jobs. In Europe, the Marshall Plan helped to provide Europeans with similar, if still somewhat lower, living standards. Americans increasingly took on credit to move into their middle-class lives, while Europeans tended to save first before spending their money on consumer goods.

One convenience symbolic of the new era was the innovative plastic container with a tight-fitting lid to keep food fresh in the refrigerator. Earl Tupper (1907–1983), a subcontractor of the chemicals conglomerate DuPont during the war, experimented with the plastic compound polyethylene and in 1947 launched his line of Tupperware, inexpensive containers of all sizes and shapes. Sales began to pick up, however, only after the Tupperware company hired Brownie Wise (1913–1992), an eighth-grade dropout from Georgia who sold household products through a home party plan which she had developed. This plan provided suburban housewives with the motivation to organize neighbors at parties where they could demonstrate and sell Tupperware. Successful housewives rose in the sales-force hierarchy, and annual jubilees celebrated the champion saleswomen of the year at the "Tupperware College of Knowledge" in Kissimmee, Florida. Tupperware sales took off, and a highly accomplished Wise went on to become vice president and the first female entrepreneur featured on the cover of *Business Weekly*. Wise and a half-dozen other women were the first executives to break into the male-dominated corporate structure of American business, pioneers of a trend that is only now becoming more commonplace.

In addition to the Tupperware parties, the Avon lady and the encyclopedia man were fixtures of American suburban life. In the idealized family of the 1950s and early 1960s, husbands worked downtown from 9:00 to 5:00, while mothers and grandmothers were responsible for the household and children. Shopping was done in the new suburban mall, and everybody went to church or synagogue on weekends

Suburban Convenience. Three suburban housewives examine the latest in food container design and utility at what had become a fixture in the postwar landscape—the Tupperware party. Tupperware sparked and reinivigorated a host of other women-dominated, door-to-door businesses like Avon, Amway, Herbalife, and Mary Kay Cosmetics. Note that while middle-class hair styles and clothing have undergone fashion cycles over the intervening decades, the differences between the styles of these women from the early 1960s is not dramatically different from styles of the early 2000s.

and occasionally treated themselves with a trip to the downtown department store and movie theater. This gendered and spatially segregated life was highly structured, corresponding to the yearning of the expanding middle classes for regularity and order after the years of economic depression and war. In Europe and Japan, with variations due to cultural differences and a later suburbanization process, similar changes in consumer culture took place. An important minority of baby boomers found this middle-class life eventually so stultifying that they revolted in the 1960s, as we will see in Chapter 30.

American Popular Culture Dominates the World   Thanks to US leadership in the entertainment industry first established during the Roaring Twenties, American pop culture spread again across the world. American shows produced for television in the 1950s were wildly popular and constituted over one-half of televised shows played in British and Western European homes. Westerns were exemplified by the long-running success of *The Lone Ranger*, which was broadcast from 1949 to 1957. Some of the most successful film directors were John Ford (1894–1973), Alfred Hitchcock (1899–1980), and Joseph Losey (1909–1984), who recruited internationally known stars such as Marlene Dietrich (1901–1992), Clark Gable (1901–1960), James Stewart (1908–1997), Marilyn Monroe (1926–1962), and Elizabeth Taylor (1932–2011) to their productions. American music had a similar influence in shaping the development of popular culture on both sides of the Atlantic. Blues and, especially, jazz resumed their pre-1930s dominance of

Popular Culture and Rock and Roll

Perhaps the most successful musical genre and export of twentieth-century popular culture was rock and roll. Today, rock and roll and its descendents—disco, rap, and hip-hop, among many—are all-pervasive on the world scene, appearing in tiny cafes in Congo and remote villages in South America and spawning a host of local artists and imitators worldwide. As part of an identifiable global youth culture, it has also inspired most of the fashions associated with youth and rebellion since the mid-1950s.

Music scholars avidly debate who actually "created" the music, and a host of pioneers have been cited. The origins of the music may be found in blues, rhythm and blues, and jazz. By the late 1940s many African American musicians were performing in small groups featuring combinations of recently developed electrically amplified guitars and basses, drums, horns, and keyboard instruments. This kind of group allowed for a loud, hard-driving music with a more economical configuration than the large jazz groups that dominated the war years. Some scholars have cited Ike Turner's 1951 "Rocket 88" as the first rock and roll record; more conventionally, Bill Haley and the Comets' "Rock Around the Clock" (1954) is considered to be the breakout song that took African American musical forms and made them accepted by a larger—and mostly white—teenage audience.

Rock Around the Clock. The breakthrough success of the new form of popular music called "Rock and Roll" by the mid-1950s was unmistakable, though its origins in African American music forms led many conservative white parents to view it as dangerous and subversive—while their sons and daughters took to it with enthusiasm. Here, the first rock-and-roll group with cross-over success, Bill Haley and the Comets, wails away with exuberance.

Within short order, Elvis Presley, Buddy Holly, Little Richard, Jerry Lee Lewis, and a host of other performers also came to dominate the charts; their recordings sold in the millions from the mid-1950s onward. By the early 1960s the influence of this music in Great Britain led to the famous "British Invasion" of the United States by such groups as the Beatles, the Rolling Stones, the Yardbirds, the Kinks, the Who, and others. By the late 1960s the international appeal of what was now being called "rock music" or simply "rock" and its successful transplantation far and wide had created rock culture throughout Europe, Latin America, and Asia. Despite vigorous efforts to ban it or create substitutes for it in Soviet-Bloc nations, it also achieved major cult status as underground music for a variety of political and lifestyle dissidents. Since the 1950s, each successive generation has sought to use a variation of the music to push its own ideas of rebellion and outrageousness in distancing itself from its predecessors. But in the end, they all seem to agree with the Rolling Stones, who sang "It's only rock and roll but I like it!"

Questions

• How is rock and roll a cultural expression of the capitalist-democratic pattern of modernity?

• Does rock's global impact show that cultural forms of expression are in many ways more enduring than political ones?

Rock Around the World. Over the succeeding decades, rock-and-roll—later shortened to simply "rock"—became a kind of world music, with local variants. By the end of the twentieth century there was probably no place on earth where the music had not become established. In this startling scene an image of the wildly successful performer Madonna graces a van door window in the city of Jenné-Jeno, in Mali in West Africa.

European popular music. A new musical form, rock and roll, arose from the older musical forms and appealed to the baby-boom generation as it entered its teenage years in the later 1950s. Parents were generally aghast at this "noise," but the teenagers prevailed—and rock and roll conquered the world (see "Patterns Up Close").

Existentialism   Consumerism was a central element in the capitalist-democratic order and was based on the belief in the autonomous individual as the basic component of society. The Enlightenment ideas of materialism and the social contract continued to dominate the Anglo-American cultural sphere, but their reductionist vision, which diminished everything to nature and atoms, had prompted Kant and Hegel to reintroduce the transcendence of mind into continental European thought in the early nineteenth century.

The effect of these different orientations was that when the broad nineteenth-century movements of early modernity—first romanticism and then realism—gave way to the twentieth-century **modernism**, the great majority of Anglo-American thinkers and artists continued their broad modernist approaches. By contrast, European thinkers and artists, dissatisfied with the nineteenth-century solutions to modernity's materialist shortcomings, remained more strongly committed to finding new ideological solutions to materialism. In philosophy, the most important modernist thinker was Martin Heidegger (1889–1976), who saw himself as a prophet offering a non-materialist future in his work *Being and Time* (1927). His ideas became constitutive not only for the ideology of existentialism, which swept continental Europe in the 1950s and early 1960s, but also for the ideologies of poststructuralism and postmodernism which became dominant in the world after the mid-1970s.

In Germany, Heidegger was tainted by his support for the Nazis. But in France, his castigation of what he viewed as a modernity of meaningless materialism exerted a powerful attraction on intellectuals, such as Jean-Paul Sartre (1905–1980) and Albert Camus (1913–1960). Sartre was a communist enthralled by the egalitarian core of socialism; Camus was an anticommunist who was appalled at the barbarity of Stalin as revealed by Khrushchev after Stalin's death in 1953. Sartre, in *Being and Nothingness* (1943) and other essays and plays, described life as a material existence without God amid the horrors of a gaping nothingness in space and time. For him, the only way of living in such a bleak reality was to espouse the absurdity of existence in the here and now as intensively as possible, choosing whatever would give one authenticity from among equally relative possibilities.

For Camus, who rejected the label of **existentialism**, the absurdity of life in a purely material universe without God was nevertheless also a point of departure. He pinned his hope not on socialist egalitarianism but on rebellion against the denial of human rights in any form of mass politics. His novel *The Stranger*, essay *The Rebel* (1951), and other essays and plays were pleas for a spirited engagement of the individual in an existence of honesty and justice as a way out of modernity's materialist absurdity. The Irish playwright Samuel Beckett (1906–1989) and the Romanian playwright Eugène Ionesco (1909–1994), both writing in French, were less optimistic about humanity's ability to escape absurdity. For them, even more than Sartre and Camus, the only point of one's existence was to uncover modern life's abundant moments of pointlessness, often presented in a hilarious way in their scripts, so as to make existence less hypocritical and more honest.

Modernism: Any of various movements in philosophy and the arts characterized by a deliberate break with classical or traditional forms of thought or expression.

Existentialism: A form of thought built on the assumption that the scientific–industrial society of modernity is without intrinsic meaning unless an answer to the question of what constitutes authentic existence is found; in the later 1970s this question was renewed in the intellectual movement known as postmodernism.

Poetry and Literature   Not surprisingly, the basic materialist problem of modernity was fertile ground not only for existentialists in philosophy and the theater but in a more generalized form also for writers and film directors, the two often collaborating. With cultural variations, typically modern themes (individualism, loneliness, and alienation; conformism, freedom, and personal fulfillment; family bonds and parental relations; class, race, and gender sensibilities; political persecution, torture, and mass murder), all provided fodder for rich national literary and cinematographic post–World War II cultures in Western countries. As culture-specific as many authors and filmmakers were, by not merely dwelling on the reductionism of modernity but rather confronting it with their rich inherited premodern traditions, they created works that could be understood across cultures. In many cases, they created classics that are today as fresh and relevant as they were then.

A few representative examples illustrate the breadth of global culture in 1945–1962. In the United States it was the rich premodern culture of the South which produced figures such as William Faulkner (1897–1962) and Tennessee Williams (1911–1983), who explored in different ways the complexities of southern family life. The influential southern journal *New Criticism* revolutionized the understanding of literary works on their own formal and substantive merits, without recourse to biography and social environment. The poets Wallace Stevens (1879–1955) and Elizabeth Bishop (1911–1979) emerged from interwar modernism with fresh approaches. Stevens focused his attention on the autonomy and depth of modern imagination, while Bishop wrote a carefully crafted formal poetry that obscured more than it revealed about her search for belonging in the modern world.

Poetry in Great Britain was similarly oriented toward personal struggles with the emotional effects of modernity, as in the work of the Englishman (later American citizen) W. H. Auden (1907–1973) and the Welshman Dylan Thomas (1914–1953). By contrast, German-language authors, such as the Swiss playwright Max Frisch (1911–1991), the Romanian-born Jewish poet–essayist Paul Celan (1920–1970), the Austrian Ingeborg Bachmann (1926–1973), and the German Günter Grass (b. 1927)—albeit in their own different ways—focused on social themes such as identity, suffering, guilt, and the truth of language. Similar social themes within different cultural contexts are found in the works of the Italian Alberto Moravia (1907–1990), the Japanese Shohei Ooka [OH-kah] (1909–1988), the Russian Aleksandr Solzhenitsyn (1918–2008), and the Spaniard Jorge Semprún (1923–2011). Latin America was a microcosm of the varieties of modernism, coming to the fore in such different authors as the Argentine Jorge Luís Borges (1899–1986), the Chilean Pablo Neruda (1904–1973), and the Mexican Octavio Paz (1914–1998). Strikingly, in all of these authors the ebullient and often strident modernism of the early twentieth century gives way to a more reflective, sometimes distant, and always more personal encounter with the ambiguities and contradictions of modernity.

Sartre on Consciousness

"Thus it amounts to the same thing whether one gets drunk alone or is a leader of nations. If one of these activities takes precedence over the other, this will not be because of its real goal but because of the degree of consciousness which it possesses of its real goal; and in this case it will be the quietism of the solitary drunkard which will take precedence over the vain agitation of the leader of nations."

—Jean-Paul Sartre. *Being and Nothingness*. Translated by Hazel E. Barnes, p. 797. New York: Philosophical Library, 1956.

Abstract Expressionism. (*a*) Hans Hofmann (1880–1966), *Delight*, 1947. (*b*) Willem de Kooning (1904–1997), *Montauk Highway*, 1958. Abstract expressionism was a New York–centered artistic movement that combined the strong colors of World War I German expressionism with the abstract art pioneered by the Russian-born Wassiliy Kandinsky and the artists of the Bauhaus school. Before and during the Nazi period, many European artists had flocked to New York, including Hofmann and de Kooning. The movement caught the public eye when Jackson Pollock, following the surrealists, made the creation of a work of art—painting a large canvas on the floor through the dripping of paint—an art in itself.

Film, Painting, and Music   Many literary works, including some by the afore-mentioned authors, made their way into film, in the hands of directors who elevated the pop-culture entertainment movie into an art that sought to visualize the multi-faceted literary modernity of 1945–1962. The pioneers of the "art flick" were Erich von Stroheim (1885–1957) and Jean Renoir (1894–1979, son of the impression-ist painter Pierre-Auguste Renoir), who made their main contributions during the modernist interwar period. After World War II, two broad movements emerged: the neorealist school of Italian filmmakers that dealt with the harsh life in post–World War II Italy and the related New Wave (*Nouvelle vague*) in France, beginning in the late 1950s, that featured free-wheeling baby boomers breaking loose from the regi-mented post-war life.

Similar to the movements in film, two artistic developments swept through painting and music in the post–World War II period: abstract expressionism and serialism. The proponents of these two movements presented their works as existen-tialist reflections of conflicted emotions, expressed in art as pure color without form and in music as sound without harmony or traditional form. Abstract expressionism began in the United States with Mark Rothko (1903–1970) and Jackson Pollock (1912–1956) and swiftly spread across the world.

Latin America, by contrast, continued to follow social realism, a version of early twentieth-century modernism which, especially in Mexico, fit well within the cul-tural approach of the dominant revolutionary party. Here, the outstanding represen-tatives were the Mexican husband and wife team Diego Rivera (1889–1957) and Frida Kahlo (1907–1954). Rivera executed many commissioned murals celebrat-ing important historical episodes from the Aztec and early independence periods. Kahlo's folk art approach masks a deep and often troubled self-exploration, which has had a strong impact both in Mexico and the world.

Serialism, based on the pioneering "atonal" music of the Austrian American composer Arnold Schoenberg (1874–1951), was international from the start, with such representatives as the Italian Luigi Nono (1924–1990), the French Pierre Boulez [Boo-LEZ] (b. 1925), and the Germans Werner Henze (b. 1926) and Karlheinz Stockhausen (1928–2007). The 12–tone octave allows for 66 pitches, or sound frequencies, and is no longer organized around a key, or central tone, characteristic of all music from the Renaissance to Romanticism. Compositions after the middle of the twentieth century were, typically, mathematically related series of pitches (hence "serialism"). The works of both abstract expressionism and serialism require considerable understanding to be enjoyable, and for many people they remain unknown cultural territory.

Populism and Industrialization in Latin America

Given its large Creole and European immigrant populations, Latin America's dominant social classes had participated since the time of the constitutionalist revolutions in the pattern of unfolding cultural modernity. But Latin America also had a large population of Amerindians and blacks, who participated only marginally in this modernity and large majorities of whom were mired in rural subsistence. Since these populations increased rapidly after World War II, the region faced problems that did not exist in North America or Europe, where industry and its related service sector employed an overwhelmingly urban society. Latin America began to resemble Asia and Africa, which also had massive rural populations, small middle classes, and limited industrial sectors. Populist leaders relying on the urban poor thus sought to steer their countries toward greater industrialization, although with limited success.

Slow Social Change

Latin America had stayed out of World War II. The postwar aftermath therefore neither disrupted nor offered new opportunities to the pattern of social and economic development. The region had suffered from the disappearance of commodity export markets during the Depression of the 1930s, and politicians realized that import-substitution industrialization, replacing imported manufactures with domestically produced ones, had to be seriously taken up as a postwar policy. Tackling industrialization, however, was not easy since landowners opposed it and the great majority of rural and urban Latin Americans were too poor to become consumers.

Rural and Urban Society   Prior to 1945, the rural population had been decreasing, though very slowly. It still comprised about two-thirds of the total population. But during 1945–1962, the pace of urbanization picked up, with the proportions nearly reversed (see Map 29.3). Overall population growth during this period accelerated, but the poverty rates remained the same or even increased, making Latin America the one world region with the greatest income disparities. The inequalities were exacerbated by the continuation of sizeable indigenous Amerindian farming populations in Guatemala, Ecuador, Peru, Bolivia, and parts of Mexico, as well as blacks in Brazil. Landowners continued to thwart efforts at land reform: Except for Mexico (in spurts after 1915) and Bolivia (1952) no country abolished landlordism

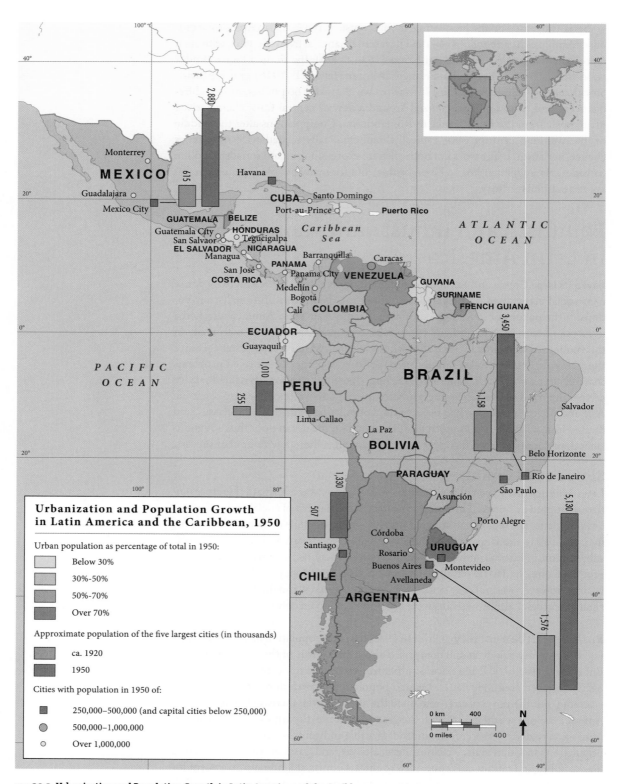

Urbanization and Population Growth in Latin America and the Caribbean, 1950

Urban population as percentage of total in 1950:

- Below 30%
- 30%–50%
- 50%–70%
- Over 70%

Approximate population of the five largest cities (in thousands)

- ca. 1920
- 1950

Cities with population in 1950 of:

- 250,000–500,000 (and capital cities below 250,000)
- 500,000–1,000,000
- Over 1,000,000

MAP 29.3 **Urbanization and Population Growth in Latin America and the Caribbean, ca. 1950.**

prior to 1962. Cuba's land reform (1959) and the threat of local peasant revolutions made the issue urgent again, but agrarian reforms picked up only in the 1960s.

Much of the landless population migrated to the cities, making up nearly half of the arrivals. They settled in sprawling shantytowns with no urban services. Some migrants found employment in the expanding industrial sector, but more often than not they survived through occasional labor in the so-called informal sector, a new phenomenon of peddling, repairing, and recycling which comprised about one-third of the urban population. In contrast to the villages, rural–urban migrants benefited at least marginally from the health and education benefits which populist politicians introduced. The industrial labor force grew to about one-quarter of the total labor force, a growth that was far behind that of the East Asian "Tigers" or "Little Dragons" of Korea, Taiwan, and Hong Kong in the 1950s and reflected the hesitant attitude of the politicians toward industrialization in view of rebounding commodity exports in the 1950s.

At the end of World War II, industrialism was still confined mainly to food-processing and textile manufacturing; only Mexico and Brazil had moved into basic goods, such as steel and chemicals. In the later 1940s and early 1950s, the larger Latin American countries moved to capital goods and consumer durables, such as machinery, tools, cars, and refrigerators. Smaller countries, like Bolivia, Peru, and Paraguay, overextended themselves with industrial import substitution and, after a few years of trying, had to return in the early 1950s to a primacy of commodity exports. Very little private capital was available on the domestic market for risky industrialization ventures, and therefore, the state jumped into the fray to allocate the necessary funds.

Populist Guided Democracy

As we have seen, the period 1945–1962 was the time when the siren songs of fascism and Nazism faded and only democracy and communism remained as political and ideological choices. The attraction of democracy in its constitutional-nationalist North American and European forms, however, was limited since the United States, in the grip of the Cold War, was primarily interested in the professed loyalty of autocratic rulers in its Latin American backyard. Communism was initially also of limited appeal, given Stalin's preference for large, obedient communist parties that toed his line, and flourished only once Khrushchev supported national liberation movements, as in Cuba. **Populism** was an intermediate form of governance that found strong, albeit brief, support in Latin America from 1945–1962.

The Populist Wave Democracy in Latin America during this time was represented by the three countries of Venezuela (1958), Colombia (1953–1964), and Costa Rica (1953–). Democratic politicians, however, were unable to put Venezuela's oil to productive use or bring about land reform in Colombia, resulting eventually in the formation of a communist guerilla underground in the latter country in 1964. Eight Latin American countries had populist regimes for varying periods from the mid-1940s onward: Guatemala (1944–1954), Argentina (1946–1955), Brazil (1946–1954), Venezuela (1945–1948), Peru (1945–1948), Chile (1946–1952), Costa Rica (1948–1953), and Ecuador (1948–1961). In Guatemala, the Cold War and the banana plantation interests of the United Fruit Company formed the background for a CIA-fomented military coup d'état which ended the rule of the elected populist Jacobo Arbenz and was the prelude to a vicious civil war (1960–1996). The

Populism: Type of governance in which rulers seek support directly from the population, through organizing mass rallies, manipulating elections, and intimidating or bypassing parliament.

remaining countries similarly moved in and out of coups d'état and authoritarian or dictatorial regimes from 1945 to 1962.

Peronism is the best-known form of the populist interlude in Latin America that characterized the period of 1945–1962. Colonel Juan Perón (1895–1974), of modest rural background, was a member of a group of officers who staged a coup in 1943 against the traditional landowners and their conservative military allies. They sympathized with the urban population of workers in the nascent food-processing industries as well as the poor in the traditional crafts, service employments, and the informal sector of street vending, repairing, mending, and trash collecting. Perón became minister of labor in the junta. In this position, he entered into an alliance with labor unions and improved wages, set a minimum wage, and increased pensions. After an earthquake, as the junta solicited donations from celebrities, Perón met Eva Duarte (1919–1952), a movie actress. An attractive, popular person in her own right, she headed a variety of social organizations and charities; and the two together became the symbol of Peronism. In elections in 1946, at the head of a fractious coalition of nationalists, socialists, and communists, Perón gained a legitimate mandate as president.

After the elections he started a 5-year plan of nationalization and industrialization—the characteristic state socialism pursued also in Asia and Africa. Banks, phone companies, railroads, and streetcars, mostly in the hands of British and French capital, were nationalized, as was the entire export of agricultural commodities. A year later, construction of plants for the production of primary and intermediate industrial goods, such as iron, steel, farm machinery, ships, and airplanes, got under way. Interestingly, Perón's state socialism stopped short of the automobile sector in order to avoid a confrontation with US investors. During Perón's tenure, the economy expanded by 40 percent.

To get the national factories going, however, they had to be equipped with imported machinery. Initially, Perón paid for these imports with reserves accumulated from commodity exports during World War II. But soon the costs for the imported machinery exceeded the internal reserves and revenues of Argentina. Inflation and strikes plagued the country. What eventually derailed Perón, however, was the Cold War. President Truman refused to include Argentina in the list of recipients for Marshall Plan aid. He disliked a populist regime in his own hemisphere that strove to leap into full industrialization through state socialism. Plagued by chronic deficits and unable to pay its foreign debts, Perón was overthrown by a conservative-led coup against him in 1955. Thus, Argentina, instead of leaping into industrialization, stumbled—not unlike China in the later 1950s.

The End of Colonialism and the Rise of New Nations

Like Latin America, Asia and Africa also experienced rapid population growth and urbanization in the period 1945–1962. But in contrast to the politically independent American continent, colonialism was still dominant in Asia and Africa at the end of World War II. The governments of Great Britain and France had no inclination to relinquish their empires at this point, but both were too exhausted by the war to hold them completely. Thus, in a first wave after the end of war, a few independence movements succeeded in more or less forcibly prying themselves loose, notably in the Middle East and Asia. A major shift in the perception of the benefits of colonialism during the mid-1950s, however, had to take place before Britain and France were willing to relinquish their colonial grip in Africa.

"China Has Stood Up"

Japan maintained a short and brutal colonial regime from 1937 to 1945 in China. Given Japan's defeat in World War II by the Allies, the Chinese did not have to fight for their independence; but they were not spared conflict. In 1949 the communists finally prevailed over the nationalists after 4 more years of a civil war that had begun over a decade earlier. China was still fundamentally a peasant-based economy with scant industrial resources. Mao's theories of revolution had adopted Marxist principles to put peasants instead of industrial workers at the forefront of the movement toward socialism. For Mao, this reinterpretation of Marxism opened up fresh possibilities of development, with the expropriation of landlords, the construction of communal farms, and the eventual leap into decentralized village industrialization. During the Stalin years, China depended heavily on Soviet material aid and advisors. After Khrushchev introduced his consumer-oriented reforms in the mid-1950s and refused to share nuclear and space technology, estrangement set in, culminating in the Soviet Union's withdrawal of all advisors from China in 1960.

Victory of the Communists   China emerged from World War II on the winning side but was severely battered militarily, economically, and politically. The brutal war with Japan had taken 10–20 million lives, according to various estimates. Moreover, the shaky wartime alliance between the communists under Mao Zedong and the nationalists under Chiang K'ai-shek unraveled in the later civil war. The communists, who had entrenched themselves deeply in the countryside, were at a strategic advantage in China's overwhelmingly rural society. Despite the nationalists' superiority, resulting from modern arms and American support, the communists were able to systematically choke the cities, causing hyperinflation in Shanghai and other urban centers in 1947.

By 1948 the size of the two armies had reached parity; but Mao's People's Liberation Army had unstoppable popular momentum, and the United States cut back on its aid to Chiang as he faced imminent defeat. By 1949, Chiang and most of his forces had fled to Taiwan, Mao's forces took Beijing, and the new People's Republic of China set about reshaping the country according to the Maoist vision of the communist pattern of collectivist modernity. For millions of Chinese Mao's pronouncement on October 1, 1949, from atop the Gate of Heavenly Peace in Beijing that "China has stood up" and would never be a victim of imperialism again was a source of enormous pride. What would follow in the next decade, however, would be welcomed with more selective enthusiasm.

Land Reform   During the 1950s, a central aspect of Mao's thinking was the idea that Chinese peasants were the only reliable resource the country possessed. Lacking a workable industrial and transportation base, the early Maoist years thus were

Land Reform with a Vengeance, 1952. A Chinese farmer kneels at gunpoint before a Communist court enforcing land redistribution policies. Like thousands of others, the landowner was convicted of being a "class enemy" and was executed.

marked by repeated mass mobilization campaigns. Aside from the "Resist America/Aid Korea" campaign in support of Chinese intervention in Korea, the most important of these was the national effort at land reform. Party cadres moved into the remaining untouched rural areas and proceeded to expropriate land and divide it among the local peasants. Landlords who resisted were "struggled"—abused by tenants who were egged on by party cadres—and often lynched. By some estimates, land reform between 1950 and 1955 took as many as 2 million lives. As hoped for, peasant landownership caused agricultural productivity to increase.

Several years into the land reform program, party leaders decided it was time to take the next step toward socialized agriculture. Mao desperately wanted to avoid the mass chaos and bloodletting that had accompanied Soviet collectivization of agriculture in 1930–1932. The party leadership felt that by going slowly they could greatly ease the transition. Thus, in 1953 peasants were encouraged to form "agricultural producers' cooperatives" in which villages would share scarce tools and machinery. Those who joined were given incentives in the form of better prices and tax breaks. By 1956, agricultural production had recovered to pre–World War II levels and was registering impressive gains.

"Let a Hundred Flowers Bloom" By 1957, Mao was ready to take the temperature of the nation's intellectuals. Many had been initially enthusiastic about the reforms, but Mao was not sure whether these people were really behind the programs or simply being circumspect. The party therefore invited intellectuals to submit their criticisms and suggestions. Adopting a slogan from China's philosophically rich late Zhou period, "Let a hundred flowers bloom, let a hundred schools of thought contend," officials threw open the door to public criticism of the party's record, assuring the intellectuals that offering their critique was patriotic.

By mid-1957 the trickle of criticisms had become a torrent, but when some critics suggested forming an opposition party, Mao acted swiftly. The "Hundred Flowers" campaign was terminated and the "Anti-Rightist" campaign was launched. Calls for an opposition party were denounced as the worst kind of right-wing thinking—as opposed to the "correct" left-wing thinking of the monopoly Communist Party. Those accused of "rightism" were rounded up and subjected to "reeducation." Even Deng Xiaoping (1904–1997), an old companion of Mao's and later the architect of China's present market economy, was forced to endure 5 years on a hog farm. In addition to being imprisoned and made to endure endless "self-criticism" sessions, many intellectuals were sentenced to long stretches of "reform through labor" in remote peasant villages.

The Great Leap Forward   At about the same time, Mao was growing impatient with the pace of Chinese agricultural collectivization. If production could be ramped up sufficiently, the surplus agricultural funds could then be used to fund 5-year plans for industrial development along the lines of those in the Soviet Union. Moreover, China had been borrowing heavily from the Soviet Union through the 1950s and had availed itself of Soviet technicians and engineers. All of the progress of the decade might be radically slowed or halted if agricultural revenues could not keep pace.

Mao therefore prodded the Communist Party into its most colossal mass mobilization project yet: the Great Leap Forward (1958–1961). The entire population of the country was to be pushed into a campaign to communalize agriculture into self-sustaining units that would function like factories in the fields. Men and women would work in shifts and live in barracks on enormous collective farms. Peasants were to surrender all their iron implements to be melted down and made into steel to build the new infrastructure of these "communes." The most recognizable symbol of the campaign was the backyard steel furnace, which commune members were to build and run for their own needs. Technical problems were to be solved by the "wisdom of the masses" through politically correct "red" (revolutionary) thinking. The entire country would therefore modernize its rural areas and infrastructure in one grand campaign.

Predictably, the Great Leap was the most catastrophic policy failure in the history of the People's Republic. Knowledgeable critics had been cowed into silence

Great Leap Backward. Workers at the Shin Chiao (Xin Jiao) Hotel in Beijing, in the process of constructing a small steel furnace in October 1958, during the Great Leap Forward. Mao Zedong's plan was to transform China within 15 years and 600,000 furnaces from an agrarian–urban into a scientific–industrial country. Instead, the policy became a total disaster, costing China some 30 million deaths.

by the anti-rightist campaign, and the initial wave of enthusiasm that greeted the mobilization swiftly ground to a halt as peasants began to actively resist the seizure of their land and implements. So many were forced into building the communal structures and making useless steel that by 1959 agricultural production in China had plummeted and the country experienced its worst famine in modern times over the next several years. By 1962 an estimated 30 million people had died in its wake.

Conditions became so bleak that Mao stepped down from his party chairmanship in favor of "expert" Liu Shaoqi (1898–1969) and retreated into semiretirement. Liu, from a well-off peasant background in south-central China, and the rehabilitated Deng Xiaoping were now reinstated. Together they tackled the task of rebuilding the shattered economy and political structures, made worse by the Soviet withdrawal of its advisors, who had become useless during the Great Leap. The next 5 years saw impressive gains in China's technical, health, and education sectors as the country returned to something like normalcy. But Mao was soon plotting his return.

Decolonization, Israel, and Arab Nationalism in the Middle East

Parallel to China ridding itself of Japanese colonialism after World War II, independence movements arose in the Middle East and North Africa against the British and French colonial regimes. Here, countries achieved their independence in two waves, the first following World War II and the second during 1956–1970 (see Map 29.4).

MAP 29.4 Decolonization in Africa, the Middle East, and Asia Since 1945.

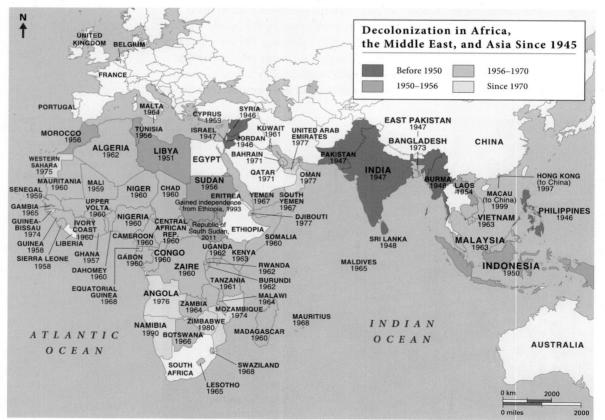

The first wave was the result of local pressures, which colonial authorities found too costly to resist, as in the cases of Syria, Lebanon, Iraq, Jordan, and Israel. The second wave had to await the realization of the British and French governments that they were no longer powerful enough in a world dominated by the United States and the Soviet Union to maintain their empires.

Palestine and Israel   As World War II ended, Britain found itself in a tight spot in Palestine. After the suppression of the uprising of 1936–1939, the Arab Palestinians were relatively quiet; but Zionist guerilla action protesting the restrictions on Jewish immigration and land acquisitions had begun in the middle of the war. Sooner or later some form of transition to self-rule had to be offered, but British politicians and the top military were determined to hold on to the empire's strategic interests (oil and the Suez Canal), especially once the Cold War heated up in 1946.

When it became impossible to find a formula for a transition acceptable to the Arabs,

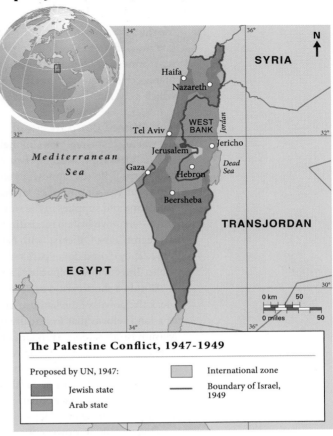

The Palestine Conflict, 1947–1949

Proposed by UN, 1947:
- Jewish state
- Arab state
- International zone
- Boundary of Israel, 1949

MAP **29.5** **The Palestine Conflict, 1947–1949.**

in February 1947 Britain turned the question of Palestinian independence over to the United Nations. After the collapse of the Soviet Union in 1991, documents surfaced showing that—interestingly, given the Soviet Union's later animosity toward the Jewish state and support of the Arabs—during the 1940s Stalin had used the United Nations to push for a weakening of the British imperial position in the Middle East by favoring the creation of the state of Israel. Accordingly, the United Nations adopted a partition plan worked out with American assistance in November and Israel declared its independence on May 14, 1947 (see Map 29.5).

The Soviet Union backed up its tactical, Cold War–motivated support for Israel to release 200,000 Jewish emigrants from the Soviet Bloc and have Czechoslovakia deliver rifles, machine guns, and World War II vintage planes to Israel. Israel was victorious against the Arab armies that invaded from surrounding countries, which, although determined to contest the new state, were unable to obtain weapons as the result of British and American embargoes. Only Jordan was successful, conquering the West Bank and Old Jerusalem. Between November 1947 and the end of fighting in January 1949, the territory in and around the new state experienced, albeit on a smaller scale, the same kind of tragic and chaotic population shift that took place at about the same time in India and Pakistan. Some three-quarters of a million Palestinians were either forced from their villages or fled, leaving only 150,000 in an Israeli territory now substantially larger than that of the original partition plan. In response, the Arab countries expelled about half a million Jews during the next decade from their countries. In the end, Stalin's early Cold War tactics were a grave miscalculation: Israel became a staunch Western ally. But the Western camp did not fare much better: The Arab "catastrophe" (Arabic *nakba*), as it was called, led to the replacement of liberal, landowning Arab nationalists by ardent military hard-liners of refugee background determined to end what remained of Western colonialism—which now, in their eyes, included the state of Israel.

The Officer Coup in Egypt   One Egyptian officer serving with distinction in the war against Israel was Colonel Gamal Abdel Nasser (1918–1970), eldest son of a postal clerk from southern Egypt. Nasser had benefited from the opening of the officer corps from the landowner elite to commoners. He was bitter toward the Egyptian royalty—supported by landowners who had done little to support the country with arms and supplies in the war. In the middle of a declining internal security situation—massive British retaliation against acts of sabotage in the Suez Canal Zone—the secret "Free Officers," with Nasser at their head, assumed power in a coup in July 1952. They closed down parliament and sent the king into exile on his private luxury yacht. The coup was bloodless, and there was little reaction in the streets.

Within a short period of time, Nasser tightened the rule of his military regime. To break the power of the landowners, the Free Officers in 1952 initiated the first round of a land reform that eventually eliminated large estates. A rival for power was the Muslim Brotherhood, a militant organization founded in 1928 by the preacher Hasan al-Banna (1906–1949), who propagated a reformed Islam in place of the traditional Sufi Islam to poor and rural–urban migrants in the cities with some success and advocated the establishment of an Islamic regime. Accusing the Brotherhood of an assassination attempt, Nasser outlawed it in 1954, driving it underground. In a plebiscite in 1956, Nasser made himself president, with a largely rubber-stamp parliament.

Once firmly in power, Nasser espoused the Arab nationalist cause. Palestinian Arab "freedom fighters" carried out raids against Israel from refugee camps in the Arab countries, which inevitably provoked Israeli reprisals. After the first raid and reprisal involving Egypt in February 1955, Nasser realized that the Egyptian military needed urgent improvements. When the United States would not sell weapons readily, Khrushchev jumped in 6 months later, based on his new Soviet strategy of supporting anticolonial nationalists. Where Stalin had failed, Khrushchev succeeded: After its failure in Israel, the Soviet Union was in the Middle Eastern Cold War struggle again.

At the same time, Nasser laid early plans for infrastructural improvements in advance of a later state-industrialization plan: He asked the World Bank for a loan to finance the Aswan High Dam. Initially, the United States and Britain, main underwriters of the World Bank, were in support. But they withdrew this support in spring 1956 when Nasser pressured his neighbor, Jordan, into dismissing the British commander of its crack troops, the Arab Legion. Now the gloves were off: Nasser responded with the nationalization of the Suez Canal (but with compensation of the shareholders) and closure of the Strait of Tiran (used by Israel for Indian Ocean shipping) in July 1956. Without the necessary loans, Nasser had to put the construction of the High Dam on hold.

Israel considered the closure of the Strait of Tiran an act of war and, with French participation, prepared for a campaign to reopen the straits. France, anxious to punish Nasser for weapons deliveries to the Algerian war of liberation that had begun in 1954, persuaded Britain to join in a plan that would be initiated with an attack on Egypt by Israel. If Nasser would close the Suez Canal, France and Britain would occupy it, ostensibly to separate the combatants but actually to reestablish Western control. The plan was hatched in secret because of US opposition to the use of force against Nasser. It unraveled badly when Israel ended its canal campaign victoriously on November 2 but the British and French troops were unable to complete the occupation of the Canal Zone before November 4, the day of the ceasefire called by the UN General Assembly and the United States. Although defeated militarily, Nasser scored a resounding diplomatic victory, effectively ending the last remnants of British and French imperialism in the Middle East.

After the Suez War, Nasser rode high on waves of pan-Arabism, nonalignment, and Arab socialism. The monarchical regimes in Arabia were on the defensive and maintained themselves only thanks to the United States, heir of the strategic oil interests of Britain after the demise of the latter's empire. Although unification with Syria as the United Arab Republic (1958–1961) did not work out, Egypt succeeded in establishing a cultural hegemony from North Africa to Yemen based on propaganda, movies, and music. The relationship with the Soviet Union

Contrasting British and US Votes in the UN Security Council on the Suez Crisis. Although the Western powers agreed to keep the Soviet Union out of the Middle East, the United States viewed a Suez Canal under Egyptian control as the lesser evil. In spite of having been defeated in the war, Nasser emerged as the diplomatic victor. He kept his distance from the United States and became a leader of the Nonalignment Movement. This photo starkly contrasts the different votes of the British and American ambassadors during the UN Security Council session on the crisis.

Non-alignment movement: An international, anti-colonialist movement of state leaders that promoted the interests of countries not aligned with the superpowers.

deepened: Thanks to the Soviets, the Aswan Dam was completed, Soviet military and technical support grew, and Egyptian students received advanced educations in the Eastern Bloc. In 1961, the regime cofounded the **Non-Alignment Movement**, together with Indonesia's Sukarno, India's Nehru, Yugoslavia's Tito, and Ceylon's Bandaranaike. In the same year, Nasser announced his first 5-year plan, which included the nationalization of all large businesses and the construction of heavy steel, aluminum, cement, and chemical plants. Egypt espoused industrial modernity but under the aegis of state investments similar to what Stalin had originally pioneered in 1930. Nasser called this "Arab socialism."

Decolonization and the Cold War in Asia

Nationalist forces similar to those in the Middle East arose also in south and east Asia as a consequence of World War II. The war had either thoroughly destroyed or considerably diminished the colonial holdings of Great Britain, France, the Netherlands, and Japan in Asia. With the destruction of Japan, the Greater East Asia Co-Prosperity Sphere around the Pacific Rim and its islands dissolved. In several colonies, existing independence movements established nationalist governments or fought against the attempted reimposition of European rule. In quick succession India and Pakistan (1947), Burma (1948), Malaysia (1948), Ceylon (1948), Indonesia (1950), and Vietnam (1954) achieved independence from the British and French. India and Vietnam merit a closer look as countries that played important roles during the Cold War competition between the two modernities of communism and capitalist democracy on which this chapter focuses.

Independence and Partition on the Subcontinent   India, Pakistan, and Bangladesh form a prime example of the trials and tribulations encountered by the newly independent ethnic–religious nations in Asia. As the Indian crown colony emerged from the war, to which it had once again contributed huge numbers of volunteer soldiers, nationalists demanded nothing less than full independence. Gandhi, Nehru, and the majority of the Indian National Congress envisaged an Indian nation on the entire subcontinent in which a constitution, patterned after that of Britain, would trump any ethnic, linguistic, and/or religious identities, of which there were literally hundreds. For the congress, to be an Indian meant adherence to the constitutional principles of equality before the law, due process, and freedom from oppression.

The Muslim minority, however, beginning in the 1930s, had drifted increasingly toward religious nationalism, demanding a separate state for themselves in regions where they formed a majority. The main advocate for this separatism was the Muslim League, led by Muhammad Ali Jinnah (1876–1948). Not surprisingly, there was also a small minority of Hindu religious nationalists who had already in the 1920s published pamphlets advocating independence under the banner of "Hindu-ness" (*hindutva*). To the dismay of the Indian National Congress, the British negotiators lent an ear to the demands of the Islamic religious nationalists and prevailed on Gandhi and Nehru to accept independence with partition—and the possibility of widespread disruption, given that even the northwest and northeast, with their Muslim majorities, were home to sizeable minorities of millions of Hindus.

When, on August 15, 1947, the two nations of India and Pakistan ("Land of the Pure") became independent, the jubilation for being free at last was immediately mixed with the horrors of a population exchange on a scale never seen before. Desperate to save themselves and a few belongings, more than 2 million panicked people fled hundreds of miles on foot, by cart, or by railroad to settle in their respective countries. More than 100,000 Indians died in the accompanying communal violence. Gandhi himself fell victim 5 months later to an assassin from the hindutva supremacist-nationalist minority who was enraged by both the partition and Gandhi's principled adherence to constitutional nationalism, to which Hindu nationalism was to be subordinated.

Srinagar. This 1948 color photo shows Srinagar on the Jelhum River in Kashmir, a northern province disputed between Pakistan and India. The river, flowing in and out of a chain of lakes, is surrounded by the Himalayas and empties into the Indus. The majority population of Kashmir is Muslim, but its former Hindu prince inclined in 1947 toward Indian sovereignty, thereby touching off a conflict that has yet to be resolved.

Predictably, while India settled into a freewheeling, boisterous, and rough-edged federal parliamentary democracy, Pakistan's constitution became disposable and the regime authoritarian. From the start, it was clear that religious nationalism was insufficient to define the identity of Pakistanis, distributed over two physically separated regions of the nation, Punjab in the west and East Bengal in the east. The capital, Islamabad, was in the west and Urdu became the national language, relegating Bengali in the east to secondary status (to the dismay of its speakers, who eventually seceded in a bloody civil war and formed the nation of Bangladesh in 1971).

A decade into independence, a military officer, Field Marshal Ayub Khan (1907–1974) from the Pashtu minority in Waziristan on the western border, assumed power in a bloodless coup. Subsequently, he abrogated the 1948 British-style constitution and in 1962 imposed a new constitution, providing for a "guided democracy" of elected village councilors who voted for the president and the members of the national assembly. The constitution's definition of Islam as a national identity and its relationship to subsidiary ethnic and linguistic identities in the country, however, were so contentious that they remained unresolved in the constitution.

Worst of all, given the role of Islam as the religious–nationalist foundation principle, Pakistan was in conflict with India over Kashmir, a province lying in the north between India and Pakistan. In 1947, its Hindu prince hesitated to join Pakistan, while its majority Muslim population demanded incorporation. In the ensuing first war between Indian and Pakistan, India succeeded in conquering most of the province, with Pakistan holding on to only a small sliver, but Kashmiri Muslims remained restive. As in so many other postcolonial territorial disputes, clashes between constitutional and ethnic–linguistic–religious nationalism became irresolvable.

Independent India   As a newly independent India embraced its "tryst with destiny," as its first prime minister, Jawaharlal Nehru (in office 1947–1964), called it, his powers of negotiation and firmness served him well. Tying the subcontinent's disparate constituencies together into a united government was a formidable task. Within the British system, perhaps one-quarter of the territory had remained under the nominal rule of local princes, who now had to surrender their realms to the national government. The bewildering array of castes and the social inequalities built into the system also posed a powerful obstacle, especially since the British had, in many cases, played upon these inequalities to divide and rule. The new government was itself in the uncomfortable situation of constitutionally mandating equality for women and outlawing caste discrimination, while being forced to acquiesce to the de facto absence of the former and continuation of the latter. In the end, the British parliamentary and court systems were adopted and the old civil service was retained, while the economy of the new government would officially be a modified, nonrevolutionary kind of socialism. Nehru's admiration for Soviet successes persuaded him to adopt the 5-year plan system of development. Not surprisingly, India's first 5-year plan (1951–1955), like the early efforts in the Soviet Union and China, was geared toward raising agricultural productivity as a precondition for industrial development.

The most formidable problem was poverty. Though the cities were rapidly expanding beyond the ability of their local governments to keep pace with services, India, like China at the same time, was still fundamentally rural. The new nation's village population was second only to China's in size. The strains upon the land and reliance on the monsoon cycle could spell famine at any time. In the 1950s, India launched a family planning program, to encourage a slowing of the demographic expansion. As a democratic country, however, India had to rely on the voluntary cooperation of the villagers, a cooperation which was difficult to achieve as long as urbanization and industrialization were in their initial stages. For poor families, children were either important laborers in agriculture or, among the landless and the poor in city slums, crucial additional breadwinners as soon as they were old enough to work.

Political and Economic Nonalignment

Similar to the governments of the Soviet Union, China, and Egypt, Nehru and the Congress Party argued that the pressing rural poverty could be overcome only through rapid industrialization undertaken by the state. A hybrid regime of capitalist-democratic constitutionalism with private property (on a small scale) and guided "socialist" state investments came into being, which was officially aligned with neither the West nor the East. This nonalignment (Nehru coined this term in 1954) became the official policy of India and under its initiative also the founding principle of an entire organization, the Non-Alignment Movement, informally established in Bandung, Indonesia, in 1955, and formally inaugurated in 1961. The Nonaligned Movement, still in existence today, sought to maintain neutrality in the Cold War. It predictably incurred the wrath of Western Cold War warriors but was generally successful in maintaining its own course independent from the Western and Soviet Blocs.

Indian state socialism began with the state's second 5-year plan (1956–1961), which focused on state investments in heavy industry. Existing private enterprises were nationalized, and an immense hydroelectric complex and five steel plants were built, along with numerous cement works and an ambitious expansion of coal mines and railroads. In 1958, the Atomic Energy Commission was formed, to pursue both peaceful and military applications of nuclear fission. With the iron, aluminum, cement, and chemicals from heavy industry, so the planners

The Strains of Nonalignment. India's determined stance to navigate its own course between the superpowers was a difficult one, especially during the height of the Cold War. Here, however, a degree of diplomatic warmth appears to pervade the proceedings in Geneva, Switzerland, as People's Republic of China Foreign Minister Chen Yi (left) toasts his Indian colleague, Defense Minister V.K. Krishna Menon (right), and Soviet Foreign Minister Andrei Gromyko (center background) smiles on them both. The date of this conference, however, formally convened to discuss issues between the Soviet and American sides over influence in the Southeast Asian nation of Laos in July, 1962, also coincided with rising border tensions between India and China. This photo was specifically released to show that both sides were still on friendly terms. Within a few months, however, they were shooting at each other.

hoped, private Indian investors, still minute in number but recipients of compensation for factories lost to nationalization, would buy the heavy industrial goods—iron, aluminum, and chemicals—to construct housing and build factories for the production of basic consumer goods, such as textiles, shoes, soap, and toothpaste. The giant domestic market of India was to become fully self-sufficient and independent of imports.

Though begun with much hope at a time of prosperity, the second plan failed to reach its goals. The government debt, owed both to domestic banks and to foreign lending institutions, grew astronomically. Tax collection was notoriously difficult and unproductive, and chronic national and federal budget deficits drove up inflation. Bad monsoon seasons caused food shortages. In democratic India it was not possible to use the draconian dictatorial powers a Stalin had employed. India ran into difficulties that were experienced time and again in other countries after independence.

Southeast Asia   In contrast to India, where the postwar British imperialists gave in to the inevitable, the French under Charles de Gaulle (1890–1970) in 1944–1946 were determined to reconstitute their empire. De Gaulle and a majority of French politicians found it inconceivable that this new republic would be anything less than the imperially glorious Third Republic. To de Gaulle's chagrin, military efforts to hold on to Lebanon and Syria failed against discreet British support for independence and the unilateral establishment of national governments by the Lebanese and Syrians in 1943–1944. After these losses, the politicians of the Fourth Republic were determined not to lose more colonies.

Unfortunately for the French, however, when they returned to Indochina (composed of Vietnam, Laos, and Cambodia) in the fall of 1945, the prewar independence communist movement had already taken over. With covert American assistance, the communists had fought the Japanese occupiers in a guerilla war; and on September 2, 1945, the day of Japan's surrender to the United States, Ho Chi Minh, the leader, read a Vietnamese declaration of independence to half a million people in Hanoi.

Following protracted negotiations in early 1946 between Ho and the French, a stalemate ensued. Ho did not budge from independence, while the French insisted on returning to their "colony." The Vietminh promptly relaunched their guerilla war. Because of the rapid escalation of the Cold War, particularly the communist victory in China, the Soviet atomic bomb, and the Korean War, the French were successful at persuading the American administration that a victory of the Vietminh was tantamount to an expansion of communism in the world. By the early 1950s, the United States was providing much of the funding and the French and allied Vietnamese troops did the actual fighting.

In May 1954, however, the Vietminh defeated the French decisively. Having created an isolated base at Dien Bien Phu in the northwest, the French allowed Vietminh forces to encircle them and pound them with heavy artillery from surrounding hills in their now indefensible

Undeniable Truths

"The Declaration of the French Revolution made in 1791 on the Rights of Man and the Citizen also states: 'All men are born free and with equal rights, and must always remain free and have equal rights.' Those are undeniable truths. Nevertheless, for more than eighty years, the French imperialists, abusing the standard of Liberty, Equality, and Fraternity, have violated our Fatherland and oppressed our fellow citizens. They have acted contrary to the ideals of humanity and justice . . ."

—Ho Chi Minh. *On Revolution: Selected Writings, 1920–1966.* Translated by Bernard B. Fall, p. 143. New York: Praeger, 1967.

camp beneath. Resupply through airdrops eventually became impossible. During the Geneva negotiations carried out later that year, the French surrender resulted in a division of Vietnam into north and south along the 17th parallel, pending national elections, and the creation of the new nations of Laos and Cambodia.

The elections, however, never took place and instead Ngo Dinh Diem [No Deen Jem, in office 1955–1963], an authoritarian politician with a limited power base primarily composed of Catholics, emerged in the south. He legitimized his rule in 1955 through a fraudulent plebiscite. Although the new Kennedy administration (1961) was well aware of Diem's shaky and unscrupulous rule, concerns about military successes being achieved by Laotian and South Vietnamese communists receiving North Vietnamese support, led to the fateful American decision to carry the Western Cold War into Indochina. President Eisenhower had already sent several hundred military advisors to Diem but President Kennedy, faced with the Bay of Pigs disaster in Cuba (April 1961) and the East German wall in Berlin (August 1961), increased the military to 16,000 personnel by 1963. Since Diem was corrupt and unwilling to carry out much-needed land reforms, the United States engineered a coup in November 1963 that put a military government in place. This proxy regime was soon propped up by a growing American military presence that would reach a half-million men by 1967.

Decolonization and Cold War in Africa

Only 7 months after their defeat at Dien Bien Phu, the French had to face the declaration of a war of independence by the Algerian Front of National Liberation (November 1, 1954). Algeria, a French colony of 10 million Muslim Arabs and Berbers, had a European settler population of nearly 1 million. The French army was determined to prevent a repeat of the humiliation it had suffered in Indochina. But that is precisely what happened only 2 years later in the Suez war of 1956, and British and French politicians began to realize that the maintenance of colonies was becoming too costly. France hung on to Algeria and was even able to largely repress the liberation war by the later 1950s. But in the long run, Algerian independence (in 1962) could not be prevented, even though French military elements and settlers did everything (including two revolts in 1958 and 1961 against Paris) to keep the country French. France's colonial interests were too costly to be maintained and the United States took over the West's strategic interests in the world. Since the colonies required immense expenditures to support newly burgeoning populations, and the reconstruction of Europe was still far from complete, both Britain and France were forced to rethink the idea of colonialism.

Amid much soul-searching, European governments began to liquidate their empires, beginning in 1957. Only Portugal and Spain continued to maintain their colonies of Angola, Mozambique, and Rio de Oro. South Africa introduced its apartheid regime (1948–1994), designed to segregate the white Afrikaaner (Dutch-descended) ruling class from the black majority. As the British, French, and Belgians decolonized, however, they ensured that the governments of the newly independent African countries would remain their loyal subalterns. For them, African independence would be an exchange for support in the Cold War and continued economic dependence.

The Legacy of Colonialism   Between 1918 and 1957, even though the governments of Britain, France, Belgium, and Portugal had invested little state money in their colonies, vast changes had occurred in sub-Saharan Africa. For one thing, the population had more than doubled from 142 to 300 million, mostly as a result of the reduction of tropical diseases through better medicine. Urbanization was accelerating, reliance on commodity exports alone was becoming too narrow, and an emerging small middle class of merchants, lawyers, doctors, pharmacists, and journalists was becoming restless. Heavy investments were required, not merely in mining and agriculture but also in social services to improve the lot of the growing African population. Faced with this financial burden, most of the colonial powers decided to grant independence rather than divert investments badly needed at home.

Ghana, the African Pioneer   Once Britain had decided to decolonize, the governmental strategy toward African independence was to support nationalist groups or parties that adopted British-inspired constitutions and the rule of law, guaranteed existing British economic interests, and abided by the rules of the British Commonwealth of Nations. The first of these to fit the criteria was Ghana in 1957. Its leader was Kwame Nkrumah (1909–1972), a graduate with a master's degree in education from the University of Pennsylvania who appeared to be a sound choice.

Ghana made an initial bid to be the pioneer of sub-Saharan independence and development. It had a healthy economy based on cocoa production as well as some mineral wealth. Its middle class was perhaps the most vital of any African colony. Nkrumah had had a long career as an activist for African independence and a leading advocate of pan-African unity. Jailed during the 1950s for his activism in the Convention People's Party and therefore viewed with some concern, the British nevertheless also realized that Nkrumah wielded genuine authority among a majority of politically inexperienced Ghanaians.

Only 2 years into his rule, however, Nkrumah discarded the independence constitution. Exploiting ethnic tensions among Ashante groups, where an emerging opposition to his rule was concentrated, he promulgated a new republican constitution, removing the country from the British Commonwealth. A year later, he turned to socialist state planning, similar to that of Egypt and India.

The construction of a massive hydroelectric dam on the Volta River, begun in 1961, was supposed to be the starting point of a heavy industrialization program, including aluminum, steel, glass, and consumer goods factories. But the country soon ran into financing problems since cocoa, the main export commodity, was fetching declining prices on the world market and large foreign loans were required to continue the program. On the political front, Nkrumah in 1964 amended the already once-changed constitution by making Ghana a one-party state with himself as leader for life. An unmanageable foreign debt eventually stalled development, and an army coup, supported by the CIA in the name of Cold War anticommunism, ousted Nkrumah in 1966.

> **True Freedom**
>
> "Capitalism is too complicated a system for a newly independent nation. Hence the need for a socialistic society. But even a system based on social justice and a democratic constitution may need backing up, during the period of independence, by emergency measures of a totalitarian kind. Without discipline true freedom cannot survive."
>
> —Kwame Nkrumah. *Ghana: The Autobiography of Kwame Nkrumah*, p. XVI. London: Panaf Books, 2002.

The Struggle for the Congo's Independence   Among the large group of sub-Saharan colonies achieving independence between 1957 and 1960, the Belgian Congo is an important case study because, like Vietnam, it became a battleground of the Cold War. The Belgian Congo had been under the authority of the Belgian government since the beginning of the century, when it took over from the king, who had exploited the colony as his personal property with scandalous brutality. During the interwar period, concession companies invested in mining, especially in the southern and central provinces of Katanga and Kisaï, where huge deposits of copper, cobalt, iron, uranium, and diamonds were discovered. Little money went into human development until after World War II when Catholic mission schools, with state support, expanded the health and the primary school systems. The urban and mine worker populations expanded considerably, but no commercial or professional middle classes to speak of existed.

Serious demands for independence arose in the Congo only after Ghana became independent in 1957. Several groups of nationalists, some advocating a federation and others a centralized state, competed with each other. The urban and mine worker–based National Congolese Movement (*Mouvement National Congolais*, MNC), founded in 1958 by the former postal clerk and salesman Patrice Lumumba (1925–1961), was the most popular group, favoring a centralized constitutional nationalism that transcended ethnicity, language, and religion. After riots in 1959 and the arrest of Lumumba, accused of stirring up the riots, Belgian authorities decided to act quickly so as not to lose control over events: They needed compliant nationalists who would continue existing economic arrangements. A Brussels conference with all nationalists—including Lumumba, freed from prison—decided to hold local and national elections in early 1960. To the dismay of Belgium, the centralists led by the gifted firebrand orator Lumumba won. On June 30, 1960, the Congo became independent, with Lumumba as prime minister and the federalist Joseph Kasa-Vubu (ca. 1910–1969) from Katanga as president.

Lumumba's first political act was the announcement of a general pay raise for state employees, which the Belgian army commander countermanded by spreading the rumor that the Congolese foot soldiers would be left out. Outraged, the soldiers mutinied; and amid a general breakdown of public order, Katanga declared its independence. Lumumba fired the Belgian officers, but for the restoration of order he had to ask for help from the United Nations. Order was indeed restored by the United Nations, but Belgium made sure that Katanga did not rejoin the Congo. To force Katanga, Lumumba turned for support to the Soviet Union, which airlifted advisors and equipment into the country. The Cold War had arrived in Africa.

Kasa-Vubu and Lumumba dismissed each other from the government on September 5, giving the new Congolese army chief, Mobutu Sese Seko (1930–1997), the opportunity to seize power on September 14. Mobutu was a soldier turned journalist and member of the MNC whom Lumumba had appointed as army chief, even though it was general knowledge that he was in the pay of the Belgians and the CIA. (Mobutu went on to become the dictator of the Congo, renamed "Zaire," and was a close ally of the United States during the period he held power, 1965–1996.) He promptly had Lumumba arrested. Eventually, Belgian agents took Lumumba to Katanga, where they executed him on January 17, 1961.

At the time, as it is now known from documents studied in the 1990s, the Belgian government and the Eisenhower White House were deeply convinced that Lumumba was another Castro in the making, a nationalist who would soon become a communist, falling prey to Khrushchev's charm offensive among the African nationalists about to achieve independence. In the Cold War between the United

States and the Soviet Union the fierce but inexperienced Lumumba was given no chance by the Belgian and American governments acting with mutual consultation. At all costs, the Congo had to remain in the Western camp as a strategic, mineral-rich linchpin in central Africa.

Putting It All Together

Rapid, dizzying change characterized the pattern of modernity as it unfolded in the middle of the twentieth century. After only 150 years of constitutionalism and industry, 75 years of worldwide imperialism, and 15 years of a three-sided competition among the modernist ideologies of capitalist democracy, communism, and supremacist nationalism, the world changed drastically once more. An intense Cold War competition between the proponents of the ideologies of capitalist democracy and communism ensued. Imperialism and colonialism collapsed within a mere 17 years. And nearly 200 nations came to share the globe in the United Nations. Compared to the slow pace of the agrarian–urban period of world history for 5,300 years, the speed of development during a mere 145 years of scientific–industrial modernity was dizzying (see Concept Map).

Perhaps the most noteworthy series of events characterizing the 17 years of the early and intense Cold War between capitalist democracy and communism in 1945–1962 was the sad fate of many countries as they emerged into independence or as they struggled to accommodate themselves as best they could in the Western camp, Eastern Bloc, or Non-Aligned Movement. As we have seen in this chapter, US and Soviet leaders were ruthless wherever they perceived communists, communist fellow travelers, or heretics of the Communist Party line in their ranks. But even when new nations could not easily be brought into line and instead pursued a policy of nonalignment, there were subtler ways through which both West and East could apply financial pressures with devastating consequences: Egypt lost its finances for the Aswan Dam, and China lost its Soviet advisors during the Great Leap Forward.

Not that capitalist democracy and communism were on the same plane: The former, even if it did not readily offer meaning or equality to its adherents, provided greater political participation than the latter, which paid only lip service to its notions of equality, as became obvious by 1991. But the period of the early, active Cold War and decolonization from 1945 to 1962 was far less brutal than the preceding interwar period. Although several confrontations between East and West were hot, and nuclear war on one occasion posed a serious threat, humanity was spared the cataclysms of World War II. Change was rapid but less horrific.

Review and Respond

1. What was the Cold War? Sketch the salient moments in its evolution.

2. Describe the differences in Stalin's and Khrushchev's approaches to communism.

3. Why did the United States issue the Marshall Plan, who benefited, and what were the results?

4. Why was the Cuban Missile Crisis the major turning point in world history during the second half of the twentieth century?

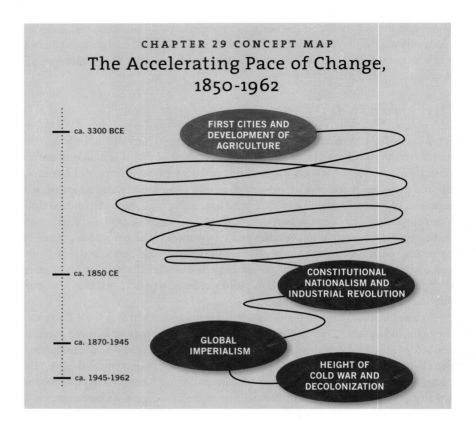

5. Discuss the basic tenets of existentialism, and explain why understanding this philosophy is important for modernity during the middle of the twentieth century.

6. Explain the different paths of evolution between India and Pakistan after independence in 1947.

7. Why was populism such an attractive mode of governance in Latin America after 1945?

8. Outline the sequence of policies which Mao Zedong pursued in communist China after 1949.

9. Discuss the significance of Ghana and the Congo for understanding decolonization in Africa.

▶ For additional resources, including maps, primary sources, visuals, and quizzes, please go to www.oup.com/us/vonsivers. Please see the Further Resources section at the back of the book for additional readings and suggested websites.

Thinking Through Patterns

▶ **Why did the pattern of unfolding modernity, which offered three choices in 1918 after World War I, shrink to just capitalist democracy and communism in 1945? How did each of these two patterns evolve between 1945 and 1962?**

The pattern of modernity evolved in the nineteenth century with four major ingredients: constitutional nationalism, ethnic–linguistic–religious nationalism, industrialism, and communism. However, traditional institutions such as monarchies and empires from times prior to 1800 continued to flourish. World War I wiped out most monarchies, but capitalist democracy continued, communism came into its own in the Soviet Union, imperialism and colonialism survived, and supremacist nationalism attracted all those who found democracy and communism wanting. World War II eliminated supremacist nationalism and, after a delay of 17 years, also imperialism and colonialism. The remaining choices of capitalist democracy and communism were divided between two power blocs, which during the early Cold War period of 1945–1962 almost evenly shared the world among themselves.

Modernity grew out of the philosophy of the New Science in the 1600s, with its assumptions of materialism and the social contract. After acquiring mass support, modernity with its twin ideologies of constitutional nationalism and industrialism evolved into scientific–industrial modernity with profound cultural consequences. On the one hand, wave after wave of ever more modern ideologies and artistic movements appeared, from early nineteenth-century romanticism to mid-twentieth-century existentialism. On the other hand, these consecutive waves of newness could at best only paper over the basic materialist flaw of modernity, which in each generation gave rise to the question of the meaning of it all. Did a modern world without transcendence, rampant consumer choices, and gaping social inequities have intrinsic meaning even if people continued to find ever new and thrilling possibilities in material and intellectual–artistic life? The question still haunts us today.

▶ **What are the cultural premises of modernity?**

▶ **How did the newly independent countries of the Middle East, Asia, and Africa adapt to the divided world of the Cold War?**

During 1945–1962 the number of nations on earth quadrupled to eventually (in 2011) comprise about 200. The new nations, emerging from colonialism, were in theory, like the older nations of early modernity in the nineteenth century, countries with ethnic–linguistic–religious cores and functioning constitutional institutions. In fact, many were not. Since most, furthermore, were still overwhelmingly agrarian, industrialism was beyond reach. With great hope, the ruling elites in a number of large new nations embraced a mixed capitalist-democratic and socialist regime, with heavy state investments in basic industries, such as textiles, steel, chemicals, cement, and fertilizer. However, in contrast to Stalin, who first introduced these type of investments under the label of state-guided socialism, none of the elites in the new nations had the will to collect the money for these investments from their rural population. Instead, they borrowed heavily from the capitalist-democratic countries. True independence remained an elusive goal.

Chapter 30

1963-1991

The End of the Cold War, Western Social Transformation, and the Developing World

THE WORLD, 1963–1991

North America

Europe

Asia

Africa

South America

Australia

The machine made an aggressive, rapid thudding sound as it slowly worked its way through the air by the dun-colored, snow-capped mountain. The fighter recognized it immediately, and his stomach tightened on seeing what it was: *Shaitan Arba*—"Satan's Chariot," the Soviet MI-5 "Hind" attack helicopter. This new, heavily

Seeing Patterns

▶ How did the political landscape of the Cold War change from 1963 to 1991?

▶ Why did such radically different lifestyles emerge in the United States and the West during the 1960s and 1970s? What is their legacy today?

▶ Why did some nations that had emerged from colonialism and war make great strides in their development while others seemed to stagnate?

armed, and armored helicopter gunship was more like a flying tank and had proven largely impervious to the rifle and small arms fire the fighter and his *mujahideen* Afghan warriors had used in their usually vain attempts to down it. Worse still, it carried a devastating array of rockets and machine cannon; the fighter had seen these gunships wipe out entire squads of his comrades. In this desperate fight in the Afghan high country, the Soviets, it appeared, had acquired a decisive technological edge as they sought to eliminate resistance to the client regime they had installed in the capital of Kabul nearly 8 years before, in 1979.

Just as he took a last look before seeking cover, he heard a peculiar sound, a kind of *whoosh*. He raised his eyes just in time to see the machine explode into a lurid red and orange fireball and plummet swiftly into the mountainside, its rotor blades windmilling helplessly without lift. A rapidly dissolving vapor trail marked a spot about 200 meters away from where it appeared a rocket had been fired. A small group of men shouted "God is great!" and cheered lustily at their victory.

This scene was to be repeated more than 300 times during the coming years. The weapon that had downed the helicopter was a new American

Mujahideen Soldiers Standing on a Destroyed Soviet Helicopter. The determination of Afghan resistance to secularism and Soviet-style communism is vividly portrayed in this photograph of the momentary triumph of a small unit of fighters celebrating the downing of a Russian helicopter. The technological disparity between the sides is clear as well: Note that all of the Afghan fighters hold long-obsolescent bolt-action rifles, many of them British models dating from before World War I. The arrival and capture of large quantities of automatic weapons and the secret supplying of American shoulder fired antiaircraft missiles would soon decisively change this situation.

"Stinger" shoulder-fired missile, which the United States was now clandestinely supplying to the Afghan Muslim fighters attempting to expel the Soviet forces occupying their country. Perhaps more than any other weapon, the Stinger neutralized the Soviet technological advantage in airpower and enabled an international force of mujahideen to ultimately push the Soviets out of Afghanistan in this last contest of the Cold War, in much the same way that the United States had been forced from South Vietnam. In fact, as we will see in more detail in this chapter, the immense cost of the Soviet–Afghan War, added to the even higher price of trying to match the American effort to create a missile defense system against intercontinental ballistic missiles (ICBMs), helped to grind the Soviet economy into a state of collapse by the end of the 1980s and led to the end of the Eastern Bloc and the Soviet Union itself. It thus appeared that the West and its version of modernity—capitalist democracy—had convincingly won both the physical and ideological contests of the Cold War.

In this chapter we will trace the progress of this struggle and the immense social changes associated with the period from 1963 to 1991 in the West and the progress of the struggle in the developing world. Although the end result was an apparent victory for democracy and capitalism—both of which were to be introduced into the successor states of the Soviet Union in the 1990s—the contest in the developing world was still active even beyond this time. From the seedbed of Muslim resistance to the secular communist vision of modernity in Afghanistan would sprout a new worldwide movement of resistance to the secular West, democratic capitalism, and the sole remaining vision of modernity itself: al-Qaeda and its affiliates.

The Climax of the Cold War

The Cold War continued through several phases into the 1980s when the power of the Soviet Union began to markedly ebb. During the 1960s, despite the progress of the Nuclear Test Ban Treaty, the United States and the Soviet Union remained bitter ideological enemies and both the Soviet Union and the People's Republic of China sent aid to Ho Chi Minh's forces fighting the Americans in Vietnam. The Soviets also supported the Arab efforts against United States–backed Israel in 1967 and 1973. Moreover, both sides continually upgraded and expanded their nuclear arsenals. Despite this continuing hostility, the late 1960s and early 1970s also witnessed the era of *détente*: a downplaying of overt aggression toward one another and the pursuit of competition through diplomatic, social, and cultural means. The Soviet invasion of Afghanistan in 1979, however, ushered in a final phase of openly hostile competition and covert warfare. In the end, the Soviet Union's resources were simply not sufficient to outlast those of the West in the struggle.

The Soviet Superpower in Slow Decline

In 1963, only a few months after the Cuban Missile Crisis, it still appeared that the Soviet Union was an adversary more or less equal to the United States. In fact, in many respects, it seemed to have the momentum of history on its side. Marxism and socialism more broadly were gaining popularity in the world as means of rapid development; the United States did not seem particularly successful at stopping the expansion of Soviet influence in Southeast Asia, Latin America, or Africa; and the Soviet Union still seemed to be setting the technological pace in the "space race." Yet, in less than 30 years the Soviet Union would fall apart, to be replaced by its core political unit of Russia and a host of newly independent former Soviet republics. What forces were at work in setting this unexpected course of events in motion?

From the Brink of War to Détente   While Nikita S. Khrushchev had developed an earthy, peasant-flavored popularity in the Soviet Union and, to some extent, on the international stage, his initial success in rolling back some of the worst abuses of Stalinism had been overshadowed by two signal failures during the early 1960s. The first was allowing the Sino–Soviet split of 1960 to become a complete break. By 1963, the Soviet response to Chinese displeasure with Khrushchev's lack of notice prior to his denunciation of Stalin and Chinese criticism of Khrushchev's more temperate approach toward the United States and the West were met by the wholesale withdrawal of Soviet advisors from China. Moreover, Khrushchev's building of the Berlin Wall, though largely effective in its immediate objective of stopping the flood of refugees from East Berlin, had been a propaganda failure. His American

1963 Nuclear Test Ban Treaty	**1965-1973** Vietnam War	**1967** Arab–Israeli War ("Six-Day War")	**1968-1973** Era of Détente Between United States and Soviet Union
	1964 Soviet Premier Khrushchev Steps Down	**1966-1969** Cultural Revolution in China	**1968** Assassination of Martin Luther King Jr., Massive Student Demonstrations in Europe, United States, and Mexico
1973 Arab–Israeli War ("Yom Kippur/Ramadan" War)	**1978** Deng Xiaoping Announces "Four Modernizations" in China	**1985-1989** *Perestroika* and *Glasnost* in Soviet Union	**1991** Collapse of Soviet Union and End of Cold War
	1968-Present Rise of "Women's Liberation" and Modern Feminism	**1979** Shah of Iran Overthrown, Soviet Union Invades Afghanistan	**1989** Tiananmen Square Demonstrations in China, Berlin Wall Torn Down and German Unification

Soviet N-1 Being Rolled Out to Its Launching Pad. The power of Soviet rocket boosters and ICBMs was a source of great anxiety to American military planners and those in NASA involved in US space initiatives. In this rare photograph, a Soviet booster developed specifically for the Russian manned lunar program is wheeled out to its launching area in the 1960s.

counterpart, the youthful, charismatic President John F. Kennedy (in office 1961–1963), had rallied world support against the wall when he proclaimed before it, "Ich bin ein Berliner" ("I am a Berliner")!

But Khrushchev's key blunder had been in appearing to back down during the Cuban Missile Crisis in October 1962. Seeking to test the resolve of the young American president by installing nuclear missiles on America's doorstep, the premier instead was forced to dismantle their bases in Cuba. Though the United States also agreed to the face-saving gesture of dismantling its own medium-range missiles in Turkey, the Soviet Politburo shortly acted to oust Khrushchev, who duly resigned in October 1964. The succession was remarkably smooth for the Soviet system, which tended toward intrigue and occasional violence when leaders left. Into the position of power stepped Leonid Brezhnev (in office 1960–1964, 1977–1982), who would preside over the Soviet Union as first secretary of the Communist Party until 1982, with Aleksey Kosygin (1964–1980) as premier.

The Brezhnev years were noteworthy in a number of areas. Both the United States and the Soviet Union had been shaken by how close they had come to all-out nuclear war in October 1962. One way that this danger had been partially defused was by the Nuclear Test Ban Treaty, signed in October 1963. Alert to the toxic effects of nuclear fallout and the possibility that tests may raise false alarms about attacks, the signatories agreed to abandon all aboveground nuclear testing. Nonnuclear nations were severely discouraged from developing their own weapons in subsequent "nonproliferation" treaties. Additional safeguards were built into the detection and early warning systems both sides used as part of missile defense. The last, and most famous, link in this chain was the installation of the Hot Line—a direct telephone link between the White House and the Kremlin—for American and Soviet leaders to alert each other if an accident or false attack signal had been issued. Nonetheless, the mood of the 1960s remained one of nuclear tension on both sides, and American popular culture was rife with doomsday fantasies of the catastrophic effects of nuclear war. Moreover, new types of weapons systems, such as submarine-based ICBMs that could be launched close to enemy shores and independently guided multiwarhead ICBMs (multiple independent reentry vehicles, or MIRVs) that could hit several targets simultaneously, raised tensions on both sides. Not surprisingly, from the early 1970s on, the two sides engaged in a series of Strategic Arms Limitation Treaty (SALT) talks.

By the late 1960s, the United States and the Soviet Union had entered into a period of relatively tranquil relations often referred to by historians as "détente," from the French term for "release of tension." Because a principal goal of the administration of President Richard M. Nixon (in office 1969–1974) was to achieve "peace with honor"—that is, a viable way for the United States to withdraw its forces while somehow avoiding the stigma of defeat—in Vietnam, the Americans sought Russian support for peace talks with North Vietnam. For the Soviets, tensions were

Détente. Following closer diplomatic contact between the United States and the Soviet Union in the wake of the Arab–Israeli War in the beginning of June 1967, President Lyndon Johnson and Soviet Premier Aleksey Kosygin met at Glassboro State College (now Rowan University). The talks centered around the US position in Vietnam and the possibility of opening talks on lessening nuclear tensions. Here, President Johnson and Soviet foreign minister Andrei Gromyko are engaged in a frank discussion.

swiftly mounting with the People's Republic of China over disputed borders along the Amur River and the rising chaos of the Cultural Revolution. At several points, military engagements took place; and at least once, the Americans were approached by the Soviets about the possibility of a preemptive nuclear strike against China.

The era of détente abruptly ended in the fall of 1973, however, with the Egyptian and Syrian surprise attack on Israel, which coincided with both the Jewish holy day of Yom Kippur and the Muslim month of Ramadan and sparked the largest Arab–Israeli conflict to date. While the Soviets had been supplying equipment and advisors to Arab countries during the earlier "Six-Day War" in 1967, that conflict had ended too quickly for either the US or USSR to contemplate intervention. The more protracted fighting of the 1973 war and the support of the United States for Israel, which finally defeated its opponents, raised superpower tensions for the next several years. The Soviets actively supported the largely Arab Organization of Petroleum Exporting Countries (OPEC) boycott of oil shipments to the United States during the mid-1970s and resumed support for North Vietnam's final drive to conquer South Vietnam after the American withdrawal in 1973.

"Prague Spring" and "Solidarity" in Poland   The Brezhnev years were also marked by a growing incidence of dissent, both in the Soviet Union and, even more markedly, in its Eastern European client states (see Map 30.1). Since the uprising in Hungary in 1956, for example, the government efforts to stifle dissent and reform had been increasingly difficult and threatened to stir up latent nationalistic feeling. One result was the evolution under János Kádár (in office 1956–1988), Hungarian party secretary, of what came to be called "goulash communism": a relatively relaxed attitude toward criticism of the regime, the introduction of limited market reforms, some attention to consumer demands, and limited trade with the West.

In 1968, dissent took a more direct course in Czechoslovakia, in what came to be called the "Prague Spring." With the rise to power of Alexander Dubček (in office

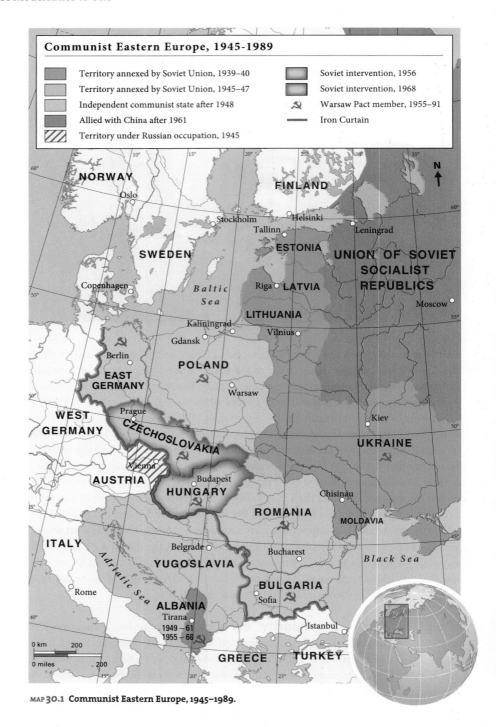

Communist Eastern Europe, 1945-1989

- Territory annexed by Soviet Union, 1939–40
- Territory annexed by Soviet Union, 1945–47
- Independent communist state after 1948
- Allied with China after 1961
- Territory under Russian occupation, 1945
- Soviet intervention, 1956
- Soviet intervention, 1968
- Warsaw Pact member, 1955–91
- Iron Curtain

MAP 30.1 Communist Eastern Europe, 1945–1989.

1968–1969) in January 1968, a sweeping set of reforms, more extensive than those by Kádár in Hungary, was introduced. Calls for a new decentralized administrative structure, relaxation of censorship, free speech, and opposition political parties were voiced; and an atmosphere of excitement and expectation prevailed in the capital of Prague. Brezhnev's government, however, saw this as evidence of the Czech Communist Party slipping in power and entered into negotiations in order to bring the country back into line. By August, as the push for reform became more and more persistent, the Soviets sent Warsaw Pact forces into Czechoslovakia, where they ousted Dubček, installed Gustáv Husák (1913–1991), and promptly dismantled the reforms of the previous 7 months. The Soviet move became known as the "Brezhnev Doctrine"—the right of the Soviets and Warsaw Pact to forcibly hold in line any member country attempting to abandon socialism and the alliance with the Soviet Union.

With the shadow cast by the Brezhnev Doctrine, dissent once again went underground. In 1980, however, it reemerged in Poland, this time with more lasting results. Several factors were at work. One of these was the still prominent position of the Roman Catholic Church in Poland, which the local Communist Party was never able to totally suppress. The election of a Polish pope, John Paul II, in 1978 galvanized Polish Catholics even further. In addition, Poland had been undergoing a long economic crisis in the late 1970s, with consumer goods reduced to a minimum and many workers laid off. In 1980, a strike by electrical workers at the Lenin Shipyard in Gdansk was called, which quickly spread to other port cities. A labor union was formed called "Solidarity," led by an electrician named Lech Walesa (b. 1943), which called for an end to censorship, the lifting of economic restrictions, and the right of workers to organize outside of the Communist Party. Despite numerous arrests and government threats, by the end of 1980 one-fourth of Poland's population had joined the movement, including 80 percent of the country's workers.

The Polish government declared martial law in an attempt to stave off Soviet invocation of the Brezhnev Doctrine. Still, a massive general strike crippled the country, while international sympathy for the movement increased. This became even more intense after a visit by the pope and Walesa's selection for the Nobel Peace Prize in 1983. With the installation of Mikhail Gorbachev as the new Soviet leader in 1985, and his liberalizing policies of *glasnost* and *perestroika* in the Soviet Union, the future of Solidarity as a political movement became more assured. In 1989 Solidarity was finally relegalized, and it became the largest political party in Poland during the 1990s. Not surprisingly, Walesa was elected president of Poland, serving from 1991 to 1995.

Lech Walesa and Solidarity. The strike at the Gdansk shipyard in Poland in 1980 brought to the fore an obscure electrician but able leader named Lech Walesa. Here, he is shown at a 1981 meeting of the organization he helped found, Solidarity, which ultimately helped topple Poland's communist government. Walesa himself went on to win the Nobel Peace Prize and was elected president of Poland in 1991.

The 1980s: Afghanistan and "Star Wars" Despite the tensions following the collapse of détente and the Brezhnev Doctrine, some genuine progress on strategic arms limitation was achieved between the superpowers. During the late 1970s, the

United States sought to counter the overwhelming conventional power of the Soviet ground forces in Europe with medium-range ballistic missiles armed with the new technology of the "neutron bomb"—a nuclear weapon designed for minimal blast damage but maximal radiation lethality. The idea was that such weapons would leave many structures intact but devastate the personnel of an invading army. During the on-going SALT II talks from 1977 to 1979, a historic agreement was reached in 1979 that would, for the first time, require the United States and the Soviet Union to limit certain types of nuclear weapons and begin a process of actually reducing them—a process that would later be known as START (Strategic Arms Reduction Talks/Treaty).

Much of the feeling of progress achieved by this breakthrough was checked, however, by the Soviet invasion of Afghanistan in December 1979. The Egyptian–Israeli treaty of 1979, the tilting of Saudi Arabia and Iraq toward the United States, and the Iranian Revolution had altered the Middle Eastern landscape radically in favor of the West. Fearful of having a weak, nominally communist Afghan government on its flank, adjacent to pro-American Pakistan and a China that appeared to have shifted toward the United States, the Soviets launched a swift coup in Afghanistan and installed a strong communist leader with a massive military force to back him up. The Soviets were immediately subjected to international condemnation, and the United States announced that it would boycott the 1980 Summer Olympics, scheduled to take place in Moscow.

More concretely, the resistance to Afghan communism, led chiefly by idealistic Afghan Muslims and an increasingly large volunteer force of mujahideen, armed with small arms funneled through North Atlantic Treaty Organization (NATO) countries, battled the Soviets for a decade. As the fight wore on, Soviet morale deteriorated, especially with the introduction of more sophisticated weapons capable of countering the immense Russian advantage in armor and airpower. The key weapon is this regard was the shoulder-fired antiaircraft missile we encountered in the vignette at the beginning of this chapter.

At the same time, the new administration of President Ronald Reagan (in office 1981–1989) in the United States sought to adopt a more assertive policy toward the Soviet Union. The administration felt that the previous president, Jimmy Carter (in office 1977–1981), had been somewhat soft toward both the Iranian taking of American hostages and the Soviet invasion of Afghanistan. At the same time, breakthrough technologies in computers and satellite communications made it theoretically possible for the United States to create an antiballistic missile system in outer space. Such a system was in violation of the antiballistic missile provisions of the 1969 SALT I accords, but the advantages of having a reliable missile defense hundreds of miles in space—while at the same time retaining "first strike capability"—were overwhelming to American defense planners. Thus, over Soviet protests, the United States began to develop its Strategic Defense Initiative (SDI), nicknamed "Star Wars" from the popular movie of the same name.

From the mid-1980s, both superpowers thus began an enormously expensive strategic arms development race. For the Soviets, however, the drain of this new arms race, combined with the increasingly expensive and unpopular war in Afghanistan, was simply unsustainable for very long. As we will also see in the next chapter, the Soviet Union's increasing inability to reap the advantages of the computer revolution, and American economic dominance of the world economy through the "dollar regime" proved to be central factors in the decline of the USSR. By 1985, moreover, a new factor was also at work to undermine the old order.

Glasnost and Perestroika   The death of Leonid Brezhnev in 1982 ushered in two short-lived successors before the relatively young Mikhail Gorbachev (b. 1931) took office as first secretary in the Politburo in 1985. Faced with growing dissent in Poland and other Eastern Bloc countries, an increasingly inefficient economy (the problems of which seemed highlighted by successful Chinese experiments with market economics), the endless war in Afghanistan, and now the expensive arms race with the United States, Gorbachev called for large-scale structural reforms in the Soviet system.

What's for Dinner? Not much, if you are one of the miserable-looking shoppers eyeing the meager selection of meat at a Moscow market in early December 1991, just a few weeks before the dissolution of the Soviet Union. By the final days of the Soviet Union, consumer goods and food had become so scarce that many items had to be imported from abroad.

Up until the 1980s, the Soviet economy had functioned as a giant command economic pyramid. Some 100 ministries in Moscow and 800 in the provinces oversaw some 50,000 enterprises, which produced some 24 million individual products. At that time, the Soviet Union had some 200,000 computers compared to the United States with 25 million. With entire roomfuls of computers, the army of ministerial bureaucrats crunched every figure connected with the production and distribution process, figured out prices and wages, and saw to it that the books were balanced at the end of the budget year. The bureaucrats could never count on accurate figures, however, since both workers and managers had every incentive to overreport production figures and produce shoddy consumer goods manufactured as cheaply as possible. Periodic shortages were inevitable, and at any given time a percentage of workers were out in the streets with shopping bags, searching for stores where rumor had it that a fresh consignment of goods had arrived. As the saying on factory floors went, "They pretend to pay us and we pretend to work."

By the mid-1980s, however, Soviet planners had realized that their command system was delivering diminishing returns. Overall growth rates—in the 1950s and 1960s ranging around an impressive 10 percent—had declined to 3 percent. Several factors were responsible for the decline: fewer people were migrating to the factories, lack of investment in new technologies and labor-saving machinery meant that factories were becoming less productive, and the percentage of people over 60 years of age had doubled between World War II and the mid-1980s, requiring the increasingly unproductive labor force to support more and more retirees. In addition, raw materials were less abundant and had to be shipped in from farther away, on top of which bad weather in the later 1970s and early 1980s kept agricultural production low and required large purchases, with dollars, of foodstuffs on the world market. Soviet economic planners therefore asked themselves with increasing urgency how they could return to high growth rates and find the finances to do so.

Two years after becoming secretary of the Politburo in 1985, Gorbachev launched his two trademark economic and political programs, "restructuring" (**perestroika**)

Perestroika: "Restructuring" of the Soviet bureaucracy and economic structure in an attempt to make it more efficient and responsive to market demand.

Glasnost: "Openness"; an attempt to loosen restrictions on media in the Soviet Union with an aim at more accurate reporting of events and the creation of "socialist pluralism."

and "openness" (**glasnost**), which were intended to revitalize communism. Restructuring entailed the partial dismantling of the command economy. Gorbachev drastically reduced the Politburo's oversight function. He slashed the planning bureaucracy by nearly half. Partially freed from the planners' oversight, managers could sell up to one-third of what their factories produced on the market, instead of delivering everything to the state. Citizens were free to establish "cooperatives," the communist euphemism for private business enterprises. By the end of the 1980s, the law permitted co-ops in practically all branches of the economy, including agriculture. Gorbachev sold the new mixed command and market economy as a "socialist" or "regulated" system, advertising it as the same order once pursued by Lenin (then called the New Economic Policy, or NEP).

In practice, perestroika did not work out as intended. Market production rose to a meager 5 percent of total production. Many managers were stuck with the manufacture of unprofitable goods, such as soap, toothpaste, matches, and children's clothes. Consumers complained about continued or even worse shortages in the stores. Other managers, eager to increase production, granted irresponsible wage increases to their workers as incentives. People of modest means founded stores, restaurants, repair shops, construction firms, and software and engineering offices. They charged outrageous prices and did everything to evade paying taxes. Support structures for the co-ops, such as credit, banking, contract law, wholesale distribution centers, and wage bargaining mechanisms, were lacking. Gorbachev's measures, therefore, did little to get the state factories out of stagnation and encouraged the rise of wild "carpetbagger" capitalism.

Parallel to economic restructuring, Gorbachev introduced political "openness," or glasnost. The catalyst for glasnost was the nuclear accident at Chernobyl in the Ukraine in April 1986. When it became impossible to conceal the magnitude of the disaster, reporting in the media became remarkably frank, quickly turning to other hitherto suppressed topics. Journalists, writers, filmmakers, historians, and social scientists proceeded to unmask the taboos and hypocrisies of the previous decades. Gorbachev's glasnost was supposed to produce a "socialist pluralism," but the unintended result was a more genuine pluralism, reducing communism to just one of many competing ideologies in the rapidly evolving Soviet political scene.

Transformations in the Soviet Bloc   The countries of the Soviet Bloc, which were not oil producers, had borrowed heavily from the West in the 1970s and early 1980s for their costly oil imports and the renewal of their industrial base at the beginning of the electronic revolution. Others borrowed to build oil and gas pipelines from Russia via their territories to Western Europe. But the oil price collapse of 1985–1986 forced all Soviet Bloc countries to reschedule their debts and cut their budgets, especially expenditures for their social safety nets and subsidies for basic consumer goods. Popular protests against these cuts rose up from the grass roots in 1989 and 1990 in Poland, Hungary, and Czechoslovakia, accompanied by demands for power sharing.

In the German Democratic Republic (GDR, East Germany), a particularly dramatic shift occurred. Germans, at the end of their summer vacations at the Black Sea in 1989, refused to return home. They massed at the Hungarian border with Austria in hopes of being permitted to leave. Hungary, at that moment in search of its own reforms, including the introduction of democracy, let the vacationers cross the border. Back in the GDR, massive demonstrations led to the fall first of the communist government and then of the infamous Berlin Wall on the night of November 9, 1989. A year later, with Gorbachev's blessing, the two Germanys united, ending nearly a half-century of division.

Communist governments now fell in other Soviet Bloc countries as well (see Map 30.2). Before too much pressure built up from below, the governments of the Baltic states of Estonia, Latvia, and Lithuania, as well as that of Bulgaria, gave way

MAP **30.2** **The Fall of Communism in Eastern Europe and the Soviet Union.**

The Fall of Communism in Eastern Europe and the Soviet Union

- Former republics of the Soviet Union gaining independence in 1991
- Boundary of Russian Federation after December 1991
- Independence from Soviet Union declared 1991; at war with Russia, 1994-2000
- Former Warsaw Pact country holding free elections, 1990-1992
- —— Boundary of the former Soviet Union to 1991
- ☙ Violent ethnic conflicts

more or less voluntarily to democracy. Albania followed suit in 1992. The only exception was Romania, where Nicolae Ceauşescu [Chow-CHESS-coo] (in office 1974–1989) had built a strong personality cult and had put family members into key party and government offices. The botched eviction by the police of a protestant Hungarian minority pastor from his parish in western Romania in November 1989 resulted in scores of deaths. Following a mass demonstration in Bucharest protesting the deaths, portions of the army defected and arrested the fleeing Ceauşescu and his wife Elena. Army elements assembled a tribunal, sentenced the two to death, and summarily executed them on December 25, 1989. Subsequently, however, the army and the Communist Party reconciled and the country returned to a dictatorship. It was not until 1996 that Romania adopted a democratic system.

The dissolution of communism in the Eastern Bloc eventually caught up with the 15 states making up the Soviet Union. Most of these states declared their sovereignty or even independence in the course of 1990. Gorbachev alienated his supporters by allowing the Soviet army to harass or even kill demonstrators in Georgia and Lithuania, in a vain attempt to salvage the Soviet Union. Meanwhile, elections in several Soviet states brought legitimate presidents to power. One of the presidents was Boris Yeltsin (in office 1991–1999), who was elected in Russia, the largest of the union states. As the president elected by a newly created but feeble Soviet Union parliament, Gorbachev did not have the popular mandate Yeltsin had within Russia and he resented the latter's grassroots support.

After arduous negotiations, Gorbachev agreed with Yeltsin and the other state presidents to a new federal union treaty for the Soviet Union in spring 1991, to be signed in August. This treaty triggered an abortive plot by eight communist hardliners who briefly succeeded in arresting Gorbachev as he was vacationing for a few days in his dacha on the Black Sea. The conspirators, however, showed thier ineptitude by failing to arrest Yeltsin. In a tense showdown with troops sent to occupy the Russian parliament, Yeltsin and a large crowd of Muscovites forced the hardliners to blink. Officially, the Soviet Union ended on Christmas Day, 1991, replaced by the Commonwealth of Independent States with a democratic Russia under Yeltsin at its center.

With the establishment of the new commonwealth, the Cold War and the epic struggle of competing modernities that had colored so much of the twentieth century quickly and quietly faded away. Russia's transformation to capitalism and democracy, however, was destined to be fraught with corruption, false starts, tension with former enemies, and pressure to return to a more authoritarian ethnolinguistic nationalist system.

Transforming the West

While North America and Western Europe certainly enjoyed an era of impressive growth and social change from the late 1940s through the early 1960s, scholars of popular culture have singled out the period from 1963 through the early 1970s as particularly intensive. Social movements that had long been germinating, such as the African American civil rights movement in the United States, moved to the center of the national agenda; the long-term drive for equal rights for women similarly moved into prominence, as did those of other historically marginalized groups such as the disabled, gays and lesbians, and a host of ethnic groups. Nearly all of these movements borrowed strategies and tactics from the movement for African American civil rights. Most of them also involved peaceful protests and civil disobedience, some borrowing directly from the strategies and philosophy of Gandhi. Some, however, advocated violent confrontation.

Civil Rights Movements

As we saw in Chapters 22 and 29, the story of African Americans since the end of the American Civil War had been one of emancipation from slavery and acquisition of the formal rights of citizenship in the constitutional order, but considerable opposition to their social integration, especially in the southern states. Indeed, by the time of World War II, all of the southern states had laws mandating segregation, and even some northern states and cities had formal and informal restrictions on such things as where African Americans could live and work. The "great migration" of blacks from the rural south to the industrial north during this time and the lobbying by such organizations as the National Association for the Advancement of Colored People (NAACP; founded 1909) increased the pressure for more civil rights for black people. In this respect, the war proved a decisive turning point in their struggle.

The Postwar Drive for Civil Rights   The massive mobilization during World War II began the process of greatly accelerating civil rights efforts on a number of fronts. The vast numbers of African Americans serving in the armed forces, along with professed US and Allied war aims regarding Nazi racial policies, made segregation in the military increasingly untenable. In 1947, therefore, President Truman signed an executive order desegregating the American armed forces. Repeated antilynching and civil rights bills now began to appear before Congress. In 1954, the Supreme Court reversed its earlier stand on segregation in education in the momentous *Brown v. Board of Education* ruling. Overturning the 1896 *Plessey v. Fergusson* decision that "separate but equal" facilities were constitutional, the court now ruled that the "separate" facilities were by definition not equal. Schools were therefore ordered to desegregate "with all deliberate speed." This met with determined resistance in many communities; in 1957, President Dwight D. Eisenhower (in office 1953–1961) was compelled to send in the military to Little Rock, Arkansas, to enforce the ruling. Still, by the early 1960s there was a dramatic movement under way for civil rights and equal treatment for African Americans in the American south.

In addition to the new domestic sense of urgency that desegregation was long overdue, international conditions played a role in pushing it forward. One of these conditions was postwar anticolonialism, particularly in Africa, where former European colonies (e.g., Ghana in 1957) secured their independence. The Cold War also played a vital role. Soviet propaganda had long played up the discrepancies between American claims of freedom and equality and its treatment of black people. Thus, the argument was increasingly made that desegregation and civil rights would give the lie to Soviet claims and thus be patriotic. When the accelerating pressure of civil rights marches and protests resulted in violence against the protesters in the early 1960s, President John F. Kennedy sponsored civil rights legislation to end discrimination.

A high point occurred in August of 1963 when the Reverend Martin Luther King Jr. (1929–1968) delivered his electrifying "I Have a Dream" speech before a huge crowd at the Lincoln Memorial in Washington, D.C. After the assassination of Kennedy that November, his successor, Lyndon B. Johnson (in office 1963–1969),

(a)

(b)

(c)

The Civil Rights Struggle. One of the first major contests for desegregation of public transportation in the American South was the Montgomery, Alabama, bus boycott of 1955. Here, Rosa Parks, by refusing to sit in the back of the bus in the area reserved for African Americans, sparked the boycott of Montgomery's bus lines by people of color (a). As the 1960s began the further desegregation of public areas, in this case, lunch counters were taken over by students "sitting in" and refusing to leave. (b) The career of the charismatic minister Dr. Martin Luther King Jr. was launched during the Montgomery bus boycott. By the early 1960s he had emerged as America's preeminent civil rights leader. Here, he is shown at the peak of his influence, delivering his famous "I Have a Dream" speech on the Capital Mall in Washington, D.C., in August 1963 (c).

secured the passage of the Civil Rights Act of 1964, which provided significant protections for African Americans, not least of which was the prohibition of segregation in public places. This was followed by the 1965 Voting Rights Act, aimed at outlawing the poll taxes, literacy tests, and other means by which states attempted to limit their citizens' ability to vote.

With many legal remedies now in place for past discrimination, civil rights leaders increasingly turned their attention to economic and social justice. The Johnson administration had created a comprehensive program, called "The Great Society," aimed at eliminating poverty in America. Civil rights advocates lobbied vigorously to make sure the proper proportion of jobs and poverty-relief programs were aimed at their constituents. Since that time, the emphasis has been largely on job equity, affirmative action (weighing one's minority status in hiring to make up for past group injustices), and ongoing efforts to improve education in largely African American or minority inner-city areas.

While the drive for African American civil rights was perhaps the most sweeping movement of the 1960s and early 1970s, it also generated many others. Taking their cue from the prominence and media attention of African American efforts, a host of ethnic groups facing discrimination of various kinds mounted their own drives for recognition and rights. Mexican Americans, Asian Americans, Puerto Ricans, the disabled, and gays and lesbians all borrowed heavily from the methods of the African American and the women's movements. In all of these cases, their drives resulted in legislation and social changes aimed at making up for past discrimination and protection from future reversals.

The Antiwar Movement For many of the thousands of idealistic students who had taken part in civil rights demonstrations and programs to register African American voters in southern states in the early 1960s, it seemed to be a natural transition from political activism in favor of civil rights to activism for other causes. By 1965, the building American military effort in Vietnam began to attract protests against US involvement in southeast Asia. This was particularly true for young people of draft age, whether they had college deferments or not. The antiwar movement, initially limited to college campuses and other centers of left or liberal political leaning, increasingly became more mainstream over the next several years. At the same time, the movement generated considerable hostility among the previous generation, who had fought in World War II and felt that the protesters were shirking their duty to defend the country against communist expansionism.

By 1968 an additional factor adding to tensions on both sides was the assassinations of civil rights leaders Martin Luther King Jr. and antiwar presidential candidate Robert Kennedy in the spring of that year. In addition to anger and despair about creating change in the United States, student demonstrations now shook much of the Western world. The most serious of these took place in Paris, where rioting students calling for major education reforms at the University of Paris took to the streets, a movement that spread beyond the students to the laboring sector and threatened the downfall of the French government. Massive demonstrations also took place in Mexico City in advance of the Olympic Games there that summer. In the wake of the quelling of these riots in Europe and the frustration felt by American radicals at their failures in stopping the war, many now called for revolutionary violence directed against the government and programs funded by the military.

Groups like the Weather Underground staged robberies, planted bombs, and prodded demonstrators to be more aggressive in their protests in the belief that the United States and the West more generally were on the brink of revolution and required only some well-placed acts of violence to make it happen. In Italy and West Germany, some students joined violent revolutionary organizations such the Red Brigades and the Baader-Meinhof Gang. Along the way the most radical students expressed solidarity with Third World revolutionary efforts and such as colorful revolutionaries as Ernesto "Che" Guevara (1928–1967), Ho Chi Minh and the Vietnamese communists, and Mao Zedong and the Cultural Revolution in China. With the end of American involvement in the war and the draft in the early 1970s, however, most of these groups broke up, went totally underground, or were dismantled by the authorities.

Women's Rights and the Sexual Revolution   Encouraged by the success of the strategy and tactics of the civil rights and antiwar movements, a new assertiveness also marked the drive for women's rights. While suffragist agitation and mobilization during World War I had led to voting rights for women in both Great Britain and the United States, the more sweeping social changes brought on by World War II and the Cold War pushed the movement for equality in gender relations even further. A leading voice was that of Simone de Beauvoir (1908–1986), whose work *The Second Sex* (1949) challenged women to take more self-assertive actions in order to gain full equality with their male counterparts. De Beauvoir and other influential feminists also contributed to the so-called sexual revolution of the 1960s. European and American women now openly demanded changes in restrictions placed upon their reproductive and sexual freedoms. Laws prohibiting contraception and abortion were overturned in several Western countries during the 1960s and 1970s. The development and widespread use of oral contraceptives became commonplace, and the 1973 Supreme Court decision in *Roe v. Wade* protected a woman's right to have an abortion. The loosening of postwar moral standards, along with relaxed censorship in the media as well as its

As we have seen in this chapter and several previous ones, the emancipation of women, the acquisition of rights in civil society, and changing mores in the family and in the workplace have all been part of a long and difficult process in Europe and America. While the nineteenth and early twentieth centuries witnessed vitally important benchmarks in this regard—the Seneca Falls Convention of 1848, the suffrage movements in the United States and Britain, and the movement of women into the workforce in World War I and World War II—historians often single out the 1960s and 1970s as particularly important. Indeed, the period is often considered to mark the beginning of "second-wave feminism," a renewal of the push that crested with "first-wave feminism's" achievement of suffrage and full political rights (see Map 30.3).

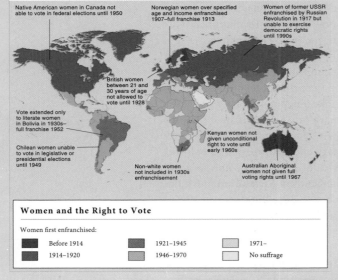

Native American women in Canada not able to vote in federal elections until 1950

Norwegian women over specified age and income enfranchised 1907–full franchise 1913

Women of former USSR enfranchised by Russian Revolution in 1917 but unable to exercise democratic rights until 1990s

British women between 21 and 30 years of age not allowed to vote until 1928

Vote extended only to literate women in Bolivia in 1930s–full franchise 1952

Kenyan women not given unconditional right to vote until early 1960s

Chilean women unable to vote in legislative or presidential elections until 1949

Non-white women not included in 1930s enfranchisement

Australian Aboriginal women not given full voting rights until 1967

Women and the Right to Vote

Women first enfranchised:

Before 1914	1921–1945	1971–
1914–1920	1946–1970	No suffrage

MAP 30.3 **Women and the Right to Vote.**

In addition to the work of Simone de Beauvoir, one reason for this is the influence of such theorists as Betty Friedan (1921–2006), whose 1963 book *The Feminine Mystique* applied many of the same critiques cited by de Beauvoir to a postwar America that treasured a return to home and hearth for women after they had played such a vital role in the workforce during World War II. Another key reason for the importance of the period is that women seeking change had the examples of the African American civil rights movement and the growing antiwar movement on which to draw. Within both of these movements some attention was given to women's rights as part of a larger rubric of emancipation, but it remained largely a secondary issue.

By the mid-1960s growing numbers of women were becoming dissatisfied with what they perceived as the latent *sexism*—the gender equivalent of racism—of other progressive organizations. In response, they founded the National Organization for Women (NOW) in 1966. At about this time the term "women's liberation" began to appear, first in the radical media and shortly thereafter in more mainstream publications and on television and radio. As leaders of the movement like Friedan, Gloria Steinem, and Kate Millett became nationally recognized spokespeople, they agitated for such things as equity in the workplace. In the cultural realm, they led the call for women's studies, "herstory" (instead of the perceived bias of "*his*tory"), and less gendered forms of address like "Mrs." and "Miss" in favor of the more neutral "Ms." As time went on and the stakes of the movement turned toward more personal issues in women's lives, these became political issues as well. The availability of birth control and abortion and laws governing marriage, for example, all became hot-button issues, reflected in the movement's motto claiming that "the personal is political!" Numerous demonstrations calling for everything from legalization of abortion to protesting the Miss America pageant demonstrated the widespread political agenda of this diverse movement.

By the 1970s the women's liberation movement had become firmly anchored in the national consciousness and had inspired similar movements in Europe and many other areas around the world. A new, more radical edge within the movement began to advocate increasingly extreme positions. For example, some argued that marriage itself was essentially sexist and should not be pursued by women; others went so far as to characterize all heterosexual activity as rape under a different name; still others argued for "cultural lesbianism" for women—proposing that women form a distinct community from men and pursue activities within that culture as exclusively as possible.

Although a "third wave" of feminism has taken hold from the 1990s in coexistence with the older ones and often projects a less restrictive attitude toward sexuality of all types than much second-wave feminism, all three waves have become part of the ordinary political landscape of many countries. Indeed, "feminism" has completely supplanted "women's liberation" as the term for a constellation of values and causes that includes equal pay in the workplace, free and full reproductive rights, greater sexual freedom for women, and a thoroughgoing lack of discrimination in society on the basis of gender. In many places, there are still quite specific causes that women seek to champion: an end to female genital mutilation, the abolition of "honor killings" of rape victims, an end to the total domination of males in marriages and arranged marriages, the elimination of female bond slavery, outlawing selective abortion of female fetuses, ending female infanticide, greater emphasis on the prevention of HIV/AIDS transmission, and so on. During the 1980s an evolving movement among scholars from India, Africa, and Southeast Asia (including Gayatri Spivak, Gloria Anzaldua, Chandra Talpade Mohanty, and Trinh Minh-ha), called "postcolonial feminism," explicitly linked sexism and patriarchy to latent colonial racism and its effects among its indigenous "subalterns." During this period, too, there was much theoretical groundwork laid for the problem of the "feminization of poverty" in the developing world: According to a recent United Nations report, women do 66 percent of the world's work, produce at least half of the food, but make only 10 percent of the income and own a scant 1 percent of the property. Thus, female poverty is intricately linked with the patriarchy embedded in long-standing cultural practices.

As the 1990s dawned and the Soviet Bloc collapsed, the problems of women in those countries were also brought to the fore. Thus, feminism as a worldwide movement, despite the many institutional, cultural, and religious obstacles facing it, has grown into perhaps the world's most widespread and influential phenomenon. It promises to be the great emancipation movement of the twenty-first century.

Women's Liberation in the US and India. Taking a page from the success of demonstrations for African American civil rights and the anti–Vietnam War movements, various women's activist organizations mounted their own marches to protest discrimination based on patriarchy and male domination. In this demonstration from 1968 the focus is on eliminating gender discrimination and artificial, male-dictated standards of beauty (*top*). Post-colonial feminism in action: members of the National Federation of Dalit Women demonstrate in support of rights for women of the Dalit ("untouchables") caste in New Delhi, India in 2008 (*bottom*). While discrimination against Dalit is proscribed by law in India, bias against Dalit women is still widespread.

Questions

- How does the women's liberation movement demonstrate many of the characteristics of evolving modernity?

- Why does feminism promise to be the great emancipation movement of the twenty-first century?

Woodstock. The iconic event of the "hippie" or "counterculture" era of the late 1960s was the Woodstock music and art festival held in August 1969 in upstate New York. It was a massive event, attended by perhaps as many as 400,000 people—as this aerial photo dramatically shows (a). Of the dozens of performers playing over the 3 days of the event, one of the most electrifying was the guitarist Jimi Hendrix. Hendrix pioneered a wild, free-form, jazz-inflected style that is still widely admired and imitated today (b).

increased emphasis on sex and eroticism, also played a part in new attitudes toward female sexuality. By the late 1960s, a "women's liberation" movement aimed at such things as equal pay for equal work, more social freedom for women to pursue careers outside the home, and, among the most radical, the pursuit of woman-centered values had come to the fore.

"Tune In, Turn On, Drop Out" At the same time as this political transformation was taking place, students were increasingly engaged in protest against what they perceived as the excessive materialism, conformism, and sexual prudishness of the previous generation. Many of this "permissive generation" of "baby boomers" (those born during the postwar "baby boom" between 1945 and 1961) repudiated the rigidity of their parents by growing their hair long—in imitation of the Beatles and other rock bands—wearing jeans, T-shirts, and "workers'" clothing; dabbling in Asian philosophies; taking drugs and engaging in a variety of forms of sexual experimentation.

The early center for this movement of "hippies" was San Francisco, in which 1967 was proclaimed the "summer of love." The growing popularity of drugs like marijuana and the hallucinogenic compound lysergic acid diethylamide (LSD) encouraged many to experiment with mind-altering substances. Perhaps the most famous advocate of these allegedly "mind-expanding" drugs was Timothy Leary (1920–1996), a former Harvard University psychologist who advised people to "tune in, turn on [i.e., take LSD], and drop out [of society]." Musical groups espousing hippie values—often crudely summed up as "sex, drugs, and rock and roll"— also arose and dominated much of the popular music scene during this time. Among the most influential were The Grateful Dead, Jefferson Airplane, and, from England, Pink Floyd. Perhaps the peak of this movement came in August 1969, when the Woodstock Festival in New York State drew an estimated 300,000–500,000 attendees and sparked a decade of giant music and culture festivals attempting to capture the spirit of what became known as the "Woodstock generation." Though the hippie movement as a force for "liberation" from mainstream values had largely spent itself by the early 1970s, its influence in fashion, sexual attitudes, music, and drug use continues to some extent even today.

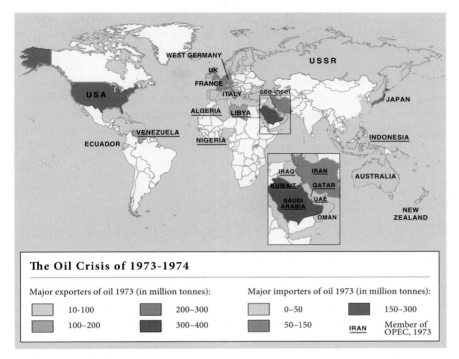

MAP 30.4 The Oil Crisis of 1973–1974.

Economics and Politics in the 1970s and 1980s

Whereas the 1950s and 1960s represented unprecedented growth and prosperity, a sudden economic downturn in the early 1970s initiated a prolonged period of economic stagnation. Several factors were at work here. One cause was the ramping down of the Vietnam War effort, which had driven the US defense industry. Another cause stemmed from renewed hostilities between Arab and Israeli factions in 1973. In retaliation against American support of Israel, the newly formed OPEC, led by Arab states, dramatically increased the price of oil for export to America. The price per barrel of oil rose dramatically from $1.73 in 1973 to nearly $35 in 1981 (see Map 30.4). The consequences of these economic downturns were at first inflation and then by the late 1970s **stagflation**. The emergence of developing economies in Asia and South America also began to lure American manufacturers to relocate to these countries in order to take advantage of lower labor costs, resulting in the decline of major industries in the United States.

The combined effect of these economic fluctuations and restrictions caused corresponding realignments in politics in the 1970s and 1980s. In many Western countries—the United States, Britain, and Germany—the trend shifted toward the adoption of more conservative policies. The most notable examples of what has been termed the "New Conservatism" were the policies of the American president Ronald Reagan and Britain's prime minister Margaret Thatcher (in office 1979–1990). Reagan's fiscal policies, by way of example (sometimes termed "Reaganomics") featured lower taxes as a way to increase jobs, lower interest rates, and offset deficit spending. Although the subject of considerable debate, these policies have been credited with producing a sustained period of economic growth during his presidency. Both leaders orchestrated cutbacks in governmental spending for

Stagflation: Increased prices and record high interest rates but a stagnant economy overall.

social services and welfare programs, and in both countries industrial strikes and the power of labor unions were restricted and the nationalization of major industries was replaced by privatization.

Other countries, like France, took an opposite approach. They rejected conservatism as a way to solve economic problems. The election of François Mitterand (in office 1981–1995) resulted in the adoption of socialist policies like nationalization of banks and industries, increases in wages, and increased spending on social welfare programs. Instead of improving the French economy, however, Mitterand's policies created an economic downturn, resulting in the election of a more conservative leader, Jacques Chirac (in office 1995–2007) at the end of his term.

From "Underdeveloped" to "Developing" World, 1963–1991

As the Cold War reached it peak in the 1960s, the drive for independence in Africa also crested, with the last colonies finally achieving nationhood in the 1970s. At the same time the drive for economic development, national prestige, and national power continued to grow among all of the newly independent nations everywhere. The 1960s through the 1980s marked in many ways the height of the contest among the nonaligned nations for preeminence between our two competing modernisms: market capitalism with democratic governments and variants of communism, based on the Soviet or Chinese model. Some newly independent governments attempted assorted combinations of both forms of modernity as paths to development. Although many countries remained in dire poverty and scarred by internal and external wars, the period also witnessed many more moving from the catchall category of "underdeveloped" to the more optimistic one of "developing."

While the unsurpassed prosperity of the West in this period mightily impressed leaders in the developing world, many, if not most, continued to question whether capitalism was appropriate for their nations as an economic basis. There were several reasons for this, both practical and historical. On a practical level it was considered that capitalism had developed in the West over a long time and with great suffering among the working classes. Putting a newly independent nation into competition with developed nations thus placed the latter at an unfair advantage. Additionally, capitalism encouraged continued economic dominance of the former colonial powers and thus skewed the economies of developing nations toward supporting the economies of their former occupiers. Moreover, the perceived connection between capitalism and imperialism was distasteful to many who had fought to rid their countries of colonialism. Finally, for decades after the end of imperial rule, the legacy of imperialism was blamed for many of the remaining problems of struggling developing countries.

As we saw in Chapter 29, the socialist road for many of these same reasons had a powerful theoretical appeal to many leaders in these emerging nations. The examples of the Soviet Union and China, and implicitly the "Communist Bloc" countries, appeared to show that formerly poor countries could become rich and powerful— even to the point of being superpowers. Moreover, they appeared to be able to do it far more quickly than capitalist countries. Finally, they were without the fatal stain of having been colonialists—at least in the sense that they had not created overseas empires—and thus could be perceived to be without a long-standing ulterior motive.

One key development that is worth considering in this regard revolves around the ideological approaches of the rival camps. Marxist theorists had long argued that underdevelopment was *caused* by capitalism and imperialism. That is, by taking control of the economy of a new colony, imperialism plugged it into the world capitalist system and shunted its products into areas useful to the mother country rather than the people of the colony. This disturbed the natural balance of the colony's economic life and retarded its further development according to its own needs. When the colony becomes independent, therefore, it remains at a disadvantage because its economy still depends on that of the mother country and has no way of breaking away cleanly and reestablishing an independent economy. The only way this can be done, said the theorists, was through a thoroughgoing political and social revolution.

> ### Germs of Rot
>
> "Violence is man re-creating himself.... Imperialism leaves behind germs of rot, which we must clinically detect and remove from our land, but from our minds as well.... The starving peasant ... is the first among the exploited to discover that only violence pays. For him there is no compromise, no possible coming to terms; colonization and decolonization are simply a question of relative strength."
>
> —Frantz Fanon. *The Wretched of the Earth*, p. 71. New York: Grove Press, 1961.

Economists and political thinkers in the West eager to combat this Marxist view asserted that underdevelopment was caused by a lack of modern institutions, basic industries, and infrastructure that would support a market economy. Their *modernization theory* argued that, although the modern elements in the former colonies had certainly not been set up for the benefit of the colonized, they were precisely those needed for survival in the modern world and should therefore be used as the modern base upon which new nations should build. Thus, instead of imperialism being seen as creating underdevelopment, it was viewed as the force that, however grudgingly, created the basis for modern development.

China: Cultural Revolution to Four Modernizations

Of all the major world powers, the People's Republic of China experienced perhaps the most wrenching policy changes during the period 1963–1991. Having just emerged from the first Maoist era of the 1950s, it entered into a less frenetic few years of more Soviet-style socialist development, only to be catapulted into the frenzy of the Cultural Revolution in the late 1960s. The death of Mao in 1976, however, ushered in a complete reversal of economic course. In 1978, the Four Modernizations of Deng Xiaoping called for opening the country to foreign experts, aid and investment, and creating a market economy—that is, to introduce capitalism. To this day, China's economic policy is officially called "Socialism with Chinese characteristics."

China's "Thermidorean Reaction," 1960–1966   The turbulence of the first round of the Maoist years ebbed considerably under the leadership of Liu Shaoqi. The decade began, however, with the "Sino–Soviet split," in which Soviet apprehensiveness about China's radical programs and Mao's distrust of Soviet policy changes under Khrushchev led to a complete withdrawal of Soviet aid and advisors in 1960. For Western observers accustomed to seeing the communist world as a "monolith," this was the first real divide among ideological allies since Tito's independent stance in Yugoslavia in 1948. By the end of the decade, Chinese and Soviet forces would be exchanging fire along several disputed border crossings.

Nonetheless, the early 1960s saw a reassertion of the need for education and technical training in China under Liu, and China made several important technological advances. Chief among these was the detonation of China's first nuclear device in October 1964. This was quickly followed by the testing of a thermonuclear (hydrogen) device in 1966. Chinese scientists also synthesized insulin and made advances in missile technology that would yield the first Chinese satellites in the following decade. Extensive studies of China's natural resources also disclosed large coal deposits and led to the discovery of oil fields at Daqing and in the extreme west. In addition, Liu's regime engaged in a more assertive policy of border rectification. Chinese forces had entered Tibet in 1959 to suppress an independence movement, resulting in the flight of the Dalai Lama to India. In securing Tibet, however, disputes arose regarding the actual border with India. In 1962, Chinese forces moved into the disputed regions and fought a brief undeclared war until withdrawing and submitting the issue to negotiation. This kind of display of force in order to make a point would be seen again in China's attack on Vietnam in 1979, though with far less effectiveness.

The Cultural Revolution   As China's Communist Party and government assumed a more Soviet-style approach to running the People's Republic, Mao Zedong grew increasingly uneasy about the direction of policy. For Mao, the party was reverting to a bureaucracy, increasingly unresponsive to the needs of pushing the revolution forward toward a pure communism. Mao's position of politics taking command was in direct opposition to the increasingly technocratic stance he saw in Liu Shaoqi's policies. Thus, Mao spent several years writing widely circulated essays extolling the virtues of devoted communists and plotting his comeback. An important step along the way was the publication of his famous "little red book," *Quotations from Chairman Mao Zedong*, in 1964. His ideological ally, Lin Biao (in office 1954–1971), as Vice-Premier and head of the People's Liberation Army, made it required reading for the troops and helped Mao establish an important power base.

In the spring of 1966, Mao launched a violent critique of the new direction of the party and called on the nation's youth to rededicate themselves to "continuous revolution." They were encouraged to criticize their elders and form their own pure "red" ideological path to socialism. Mao announced the launching of the Great Proletarian Cultural Revolution, the purpose of which was to stamp out the last vestiges of "bourgeois" and "feudal" Chinese society. Students formed themselves into squads of "Red Guards" with red armbands and attacked their teachers and elders. By August, millions of Red Guards converged on Beijing, where Mao addressed over 1 million of them in Tiananmen Square and symbolically donned their red armband as a show of solidarity.

From 1966 until 1969, when the Cultural Revolution was officially declared over, millions of people were hounded, tortured, killed, or driven to suicide by Red Guards and

---

A Revolution Is Not a Dinner Party

"People of the world unite and defeat the U.S. aggressors and their running dogs!"

"Every Communist must grasp the truth, 'Political power grows out of the barrel of a gun . . .'"

"A revolution is not a dinner party, or writing an essay, or painting a picture, or doing embroidery; it cannot be so refined, so leisurely and gentle, so temperate, so kind, courteous, restrained and magnanimous. A revolution is an insurrection, an act of violence by which one class overthrows another . . ."

—Mao Zedong. *Quotations from Chairman Mao Zedong.* Mao zhuxi yulu, 1964. English language version by Foreign Languages Press, Quotations from Chairman Mao Tsetung (Peking: 1972), pp. 82, 11, 59.

Red Guards on the March.
Mao Zedong's injunction to the youth of China to question the authority of party bureaucrats had swift effects on everything from the school system to factory production. The students banded together into Red Guard units and challenged their elders, often violently, on their adherence to Mao's thought as expressed in the famous "little red book," *Quotations from Chairman Mao Zedong*. In this photo from 1967, Red Guards parade with a portrait of Mao, while many carry the red book in their hands.

their allies. The "little red book" became the talisman of the movement, with people struggling to interpret it correctly to prove their ideological fitness. China's official ideology was now listed as "Marxism–Leninism–Mao Zedong Thought." A cult of personality surrounding Mao and the book sprang up as people waved it at mass rallies and even attributed magical powers to it. By 1968 the country was in complete chaos as pro– and anti–Cultural Revolution factions battled each other in several regions. It was chiefly to end this endemic civil war that Mao declared the Cultural Revolution over in 1969. Its aftermath, however, continued until Mao's death in 1976.

"To Get Rich Is Glorious": China's Four Modernizations   The final years of Mao's tenure as party chair saw at least one important change in policy. Despite the Sino–Soviet split, the People's Republic had maintained a strong anti-American posture in its domestic and foreign policy. This was matched by American Cold War antipathy toward "Red China" as a linchpin of the communist bloc. By the early 1970s, however, with the Vietnam War winding down and Soviet–Chinese tensions still high, President Nixon made a bold visit to the People's Republic, which resulted in the Shanghai communiqué of 1972. In this document, the United States and the People's Republic of China announced plans to begin formal diplomatic and cultural relations (which went into effect in 1979), the United States pledged to no longer block the People's Republic's bid for a seat in the United Nations, and the United States agreed to downgrade its diplomatic presence in Taiwan.

The death of Mao Zedong in September 1976 opened the way for a new generation of Communist Party leadership in China. The end result was a repudiation of the Cultural Revolution and those who promoted it and an entirely different direction in strategy for building a new China. After some jostling among the party factions, the hardy Deng Xiaoping (in office 1978–1992) emerged on the scene in 1978 with the title of "vice premier" but, in fact, held the real power in the regime. The ascendancy of the pragmatic Deng, whose motto was "It doesn't matter whether the cat is black or white, as long as it catches mice," swiftly led to the unveiling of the fundamental policies that remain in force in China to the present: the Four Modernizations.

Painfully aware of the difficulties of pursuing socialism in a country with little wealth to share, Deng's strategy was bent on upgrading the quality of agriculture, industry, science, technology, and the military. China would pursue a new "open-door" policy with regard to foreign expertise from the West; it would allow its own students to study abroad and, most tellingly, allow the market forces of capitalism to

MAP 30.5 **Open Cities and Special Economic Zones in China, 1980–2000.**

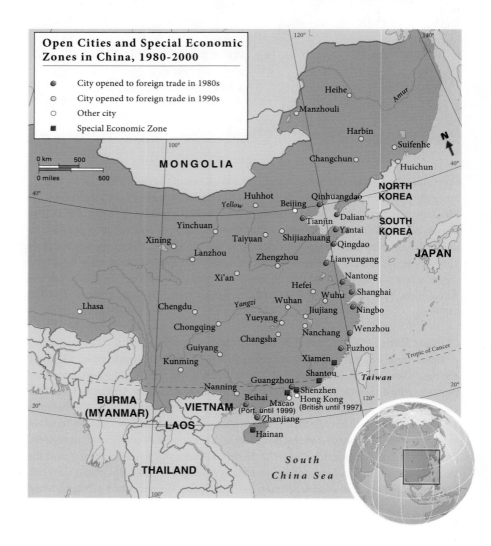

create incentives for innovation in all sectors of the economy. The new motto thus became "To get rich is glorious!"

The "responsibility system," as it was called, was introduced in a special economic zone set up in south China at Shenzhen to take advantage of capital and expertise from Hong Kong. The experiments in capitalism would then be expanded to the country at large once the flaws had been worked out. Peasants were among the first beneficiaries as the communes were disbanded, individual plots assigned, and market incentives introduced. By the mid-1980s China, which had long been a byword in the West for hunger, was rapidly approaching self-sufficiency in food production and, by the 1990s, would register surpluses (see Map 30.5). Through the 1980s and 1990s China's gross domestic product (GDP) would grow at an astonishing double-digit rate. In 2010 it surpassed Japan as the second largest economy in the world, after the United States.

Another more controversial innovation was the "one-child policy." Mao felt that China's huge and growing population was an advantage because of its potential manpower and as a hedge against catastrophic losses from nuclear war. But population pressures were also a powerful brake on China's development. Thus, a policy was inaugurated in 1979 mandating that families (excluding those of most minorities) were to have only one child. A second child would result in loss of subsidies for childrearing; a third pregnancy would result in mandatory abortion. Despite the many problems in enforcing such a policy, and its severe cultural impact on the male-centered traditional Chinese family structure, China's population has remained remarkably stable since the 1980s at around 1.3–1.5 billion. It has, however, abetted problems of selective female abortion, giving up girl babies for adoption, and even, in extreme cases, female infanticide. Moreover, all of these conditions have lent themselves to a large and growing gender imbalance: China currently has 117 male births for every 100 female births.

The "Fifth Modernization" and Tiananmen Square

The heady atmosphere of the early days of these sweeping changes brought political reformers temporarily out of hiding. In the so-called Peking Spring of 1979, thousands of demonstrators called for a wide array of democratic reforms by hanging "big-character" posters on the walls near Tiananmen Square, the site of China's most important government buildings and Mao's mausoleum. This "democracy" movement calling for a "fifth modernization: democracy" was shortly suppressed, but political agitation calling for a more open society, crackdowns on corruption, and even a multiparty system continued in muted form throughout the decade.

For its part, the government managed a delicate balance between allowing foreign technology to come into China while preventing cultural items "injurious to public morals" to enter. Hence, IBM computers were welcome, but MTV was not. Repeated campaigns against such "spiritual pollution" were conducted throughout the 1980s, though with less and less effect. Prodemocracy protests again took place in Beijing following the death of the popular moderate leader Hu Yaobang in 1989. The gatherings grew in size and force as the seventieth anniversary of the May Fourth nationalist movement grew closer. At one point students even constructed a large statue they called "the Goddess of Democracy," which dominated the center of the square near the Monument to the People's Revolutionary Martyrs. By the beginning of June the movement had turned into generalized protest of workers and

Tiananmen Square Demonstrations. At their peak in May 1989, the demonstrations by students seeking greater government accountability and a more open political system were joined by workers and people from all walks of life. Here are two memorable images from this event: (*a*) the "goddess of democracy," taken from behind in a pose that seems to confront the portrait of Mao Zedong on the Gate of Heavenly Peace, and (*b*) the suppression of the demonstration—a lone man confronting a tank. The driver of the tank tried to get around the man and eventually stopped, together with the other tanks. At that point, demonstrators pulled the man back to safety. His subsequent fate is unknown. Both images were widely broadcast throughout the world.

ordinary citizens in addition to students. When they refused to disperse, the government sent in the army on June 4 to crush what to many in the party had become incipient rebellion. One arresting image was flashed in various media around the world and became an instant icon of the movement: television footage of a lone man attempting to stare down an approaching tank. To this day, the number of killed and injured is unknown.

Vietnam: War and Unification

As we noted in Chapter 29, by the early 1960s Vietnam, having finally thrown off French colonialism in the 1950s, had failed to achieve final unification because of Cold War politics and remained divided into North and South Vietnam. The development of communist guerrilla fighters, the Vietcong, in South Vietnam and similar guerrilla threats in Laos had prompted the United States to send aid and military advisors to the shaky government of the Republic of Vietnam (South Vietnam) through the late 1950s. Rocked by clashes between Catholics and Buddhists, the government of South Vietnam was ousted in a coup with help from the American Central Intelligence Agency (CIA) in late 1963. Several weak governments took its place until a more stable one under Nguyen Van Thieu emerged and lasted from 1965 to 1975.

The American War   In the summer of 1964 several alleged attacks on American ships in the Gulf of Tonkin (the authenticity of these allegations is still murky today) resulted in the United States radically ramping up its presence in Southeast Asia, effectively beginning what became known in Vietnam as the American War and in the United States as the Vietnam War. In retaliation for the attacks, American planes bombed sites in North Vietnam. By 1965 tens of thousands of American combat troops were being sent to support the South Vietnamese against the Vietcong. But, as in Korea, the Americans and their allies were plagued by unclear goals and the impatience of a public hoping for quick, decisive results. The task of "winning the hearts and minds of the people," as the slogan went, however, was a long and torturous one at best and always vulnerable to the problem of being a foreign presence in someone else's land. Thus, American forces were increased until they reached a high of over a half-million by 1967. Despite official optimism, there was little evidence that the war was being won (see Map 30.6).

In February 1968, during the Vietnamese lunar new year (*Tet*), the Vietcong, supported by North Vietnamese forces, launched an all-out assault on the South Vietnamese capital of Saigon and a number of other cities. American and Army of the Republic of Vietnam (South Vietnam) forces reeled for several days but launched a successful counterattack, finally destroying the Vietcong as an effective fighting force. In the United States, however, the "Tet Offensive," as it came to be called, was seen as an American defeat. In the wake of massive protests against the war, President Johnson announced he would not seek reelection; and the way was clear for the United States to begin negotiations to end the war by political means. With the election of Richard Nixon in 1968, a combination of massive bombings of North Vietnam and Cambodian supply lines for North Vietnamese forces and peace talks in Paris over the next 5 years finally brought the war to an end.

Though South Vietnam survived the peace treaty in 1973, the American withdrawal spelled its demise within 2 years. Though the country was now finally united, much of Vietnam, Cambodia, and Laos lay devastated from fighting and bombing. Over the next 2 years a Cambodian revolutionary group, the Khmer Rouge (Red Khmers), launched a radical program of depopulating the cities, forced labor, and genocide against religious and political opponents that killed perhaps one-third of the country's population. The ideas and practices of the Khmer Rouge leader Pol Pot (1925–1998) were so radical and brutal that in 1977 Vietnam invaded the state and initiated his overthrow in favor of a more moderate and pliable candidate. In response, China briefly invaded northern Vietnam in 1979 but was soon repulsed by Vietnamese forces, the last and least successful of the many Chinese invasion attempts launched over two millennia.

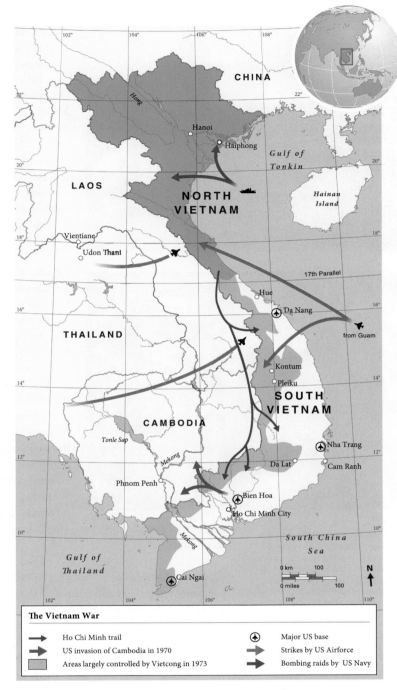

MAP **30.6 The Vietnam War.**

(a)

(b)

The Arab-Israeli War of June 1967. The stunning victory of Israel over the combined armies of Syria and Egypt generated both admiration in the West and consternation in the Arab world and the Soviet Bloc. The Israelis' preemptive use of air power against Egyptian and Syrian tank and troop concentrations and their expert use of armor proved the deciding factors in the conflict. Here, Egyptian prisoners (in white underclothes in the truck to the right) are being transferred to holding camps (a). The war also led to a dramatic rise in the popularity of the Palestinian cause in the Arab and communist spheres. Here, Yassir Arafat marches with members of Al Fatah in 1970 (b).

The Middle East

One of the most troubled areas of the world during the twentieth century was also one that, as we have seen over the course of this book, has been perhaps the most prolific producer of influential religions: the Middle East. Since 1945, the area encompassing the Arabian Peninsula, Iran, Iraq, and the eastern shores of the Mediterranean has seen a number of major wars and minor conflicts; innumerable guerilla raids and assaults; and attacks directed against the religious symbols of Judaism, Christianity, and Islam. As of this writing, despite peace talks that have been conducted over the course of decades, no comprehensive settlement has been reached.

Israeli and Arab Conflict   In addition to competition arising from the increasing demand for petroleum as a strategic commodity, and Shia–Sunni conflict within the context of Persian–Arab competition, by far the most contentious issue in the Middle East has been the presence of the Jewish state of Israel. Israel during the 1950s and 1960s was largely seen in the West as a plucky young country fighting democracy's battles against a vast array of Arab states supported by the Soviet Union. The number of highly educated immigrants in the postwar decades helped the new state immensely in building an efficient agriculture—often through the socialist device of the communal farm, or *kibbutz*—and an increasingly sophisticated manufacturing sector. Mandatory military service and generous American support also contributed to the creation of top-notch armed forces equipped with the latest military technology.

The "Six-Day War"   For the Palestinian Arabs and their allies, however, the perspective was very different. For them it was "the disaster." Hundreds of thousands displaced since 1948 awaited their return in surrounding countries—often in camps—for decades, a situation that grew worse when new refugees arrived after every Arab–Israeli conflict. In the polarized Cold War climate, the Arab states viewed Israel as simply a new Western imperial outpost in what was rightfully Arab territory. Consequently, many subsequent attempts at Arab unity were premised on war with Israel. While Arab nationalism was largely secular, and often socialist-leaning with Soviet support, Muslim fundamentalist groups such as Egypt's Muslim Brotherhood gained adherence, despite government repression, as Western secular values came to be seen as causes of Muslim difficulties.

In 1964, Yassir Arafat (1929–2004) and other like-minded Palestinian nationalists formed the Palestinian Liberation Organization (PLO), whose militant wing, Al Fatah, began a guerilla war against Israel and its backers. Matters soon came to a head in June 1967. Following an Egyptian military buildup along the Sinai border and the expulsion of UN forces there, Iraq sent troops to Jordan at its invitation and local Muslim leaders began to call for holy war against Israel. The Israelis launched a massive preemptive air assault to neutralize the Egyptian and Syrian air forces. With an overwhelming advantage in number and quality of aircraft, Israel took out the Arab armor and ground troops with astonishing skill. The Six-Day War, as it came to be called, established Israel's reputation for military prowess and enlarged the state by the annexing of territories on the eastern side of the Jordan River, known since that time as the Occupied Territories. For many observers, Israel had now moved from a state simply fighting for its existence to one bent on expansion.

The Yom Kippur/Ramadan War   For the two superpowers, the Arab–Israeli conflict provided valuable data on the performance of the weapons systems they supplied to their respective allies. Thus far in these "proxy wars" (as they were sometimes called), American and European weapons—and increasingly, Israeli-made arms like the famous Uzi submachine gun—had tended to outperform the Soviet ordnance supplied to the Arab states. This was almost reversed in 1973 however. In early October

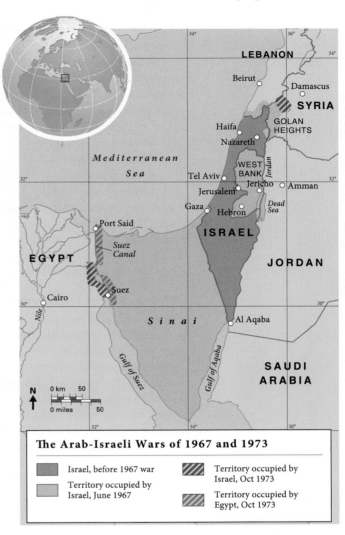

The Arab-Israeli Wars of 1967 and 1973

- ▨ Israel, before 1967 war
- ▢ Territory occupied by Israel, June 1967
- ▨ Territory occupied by Israel, Oct 1973
- ▨ Territory occupied by Egypt, Oct 1973

MAP 30.7 **The Arab–Israeli Wars, 1967 and 1973.**

1973, Egypt, Syria, and a coalition of Arab states, stung by their defeat in 1967, launched a massive attack during the Jewish holy day of Yom Kippur, which in 1973 coincided with the Muslim holy month of Ramadan. This time, with Israel, the United States, and the Soviet Union caught unawares, Egyptian tanks crossed the Suez Canal on pontoon bridges and attacked Israel (see Map 30.7). Syria attacked the Golan Heights and put pressure on Israeli forces at the other end of the state. After taking severe losses and giving ground for a week, Israeli forces managed to take the initiative and ultimately defeat the combined Arab armies once again. Having trapped Egyptian forces along the Suez Canal, Israeli units occupied the west bank of the Canal, pushing within 63 miles of Cairo. Other units drove 25 miles into Syria. A ceasefire was brokered by the United Nations, but the intensity of the fighting and the resupply efforts by the United States and Soviet Union moved both countries dangerously close to direct confrontation. For their part, the Arab oil producers and Iran immediately launched an oil boycott of the United States. Stringent measures and a degree of rationing and vastly higher gasoline prices drove home to Americans how dependent they had now become on foreign oil. (Much of the interest in solar and other alternative energy thus stems from this period.)

For Egypt, the defeat resulted in a transformation of policy toward Israel. Under President Anwar el-Sadat (in office 1970–1981), Egypt took the initiative in undertaking peace talks by visiting Israel in 1977. The following year, the two sides reached an understanding about a basic framework for peace; and with the backing of the American president Jimmy Carter, Egypt and Israel signed the first treaty between an Arab country and the Jewish state at Camp David, Maryland, in 1979. Egypt and Jordan are the only Arab states to date to maintain diplomatic and cultural relations with Israel. While Egyptian–Israeli relations remained relatively cordial on the surface, no other Arab countries followed suit. Syria remained hostile, having lost the Golan Heights, while the PLO stepped up its efforts throughout the 1980s. Profound resentment against Sadat for signing the treaty festered among many Egyptians. Despite some concessions to increasingly vocal fundamentalist Muslim groups—for example, agreeing to base Egyptian legislation on Islamic Shari`a law—Sadat was killed by assassins in 1981.

Africa: From Independence to Development

During the period 1963–1991, the main struggles in Africa moved from those mainly concerned with independence to those revolving around development. As with other parts of the postcolonial world, vigorous internal debates were conducted about strategies for economic development, how best to deploy scarce resources, and the relative merits of a planned economy versus one centered on market forces. But in nearly all cases, the economies of the newly independent states, regardless of which economic system they favored, were problematic. In most cases they were tied to their former colonial regimes by means of the same raw materials—minerals, petroleum, agricultural or forest products—that had been exploitatively extracted during their colonial days. Moreover, they were more frequently than not competing in these products with other former colonies. Thus, they were at the mercy of world commodity prices but not insulated from the worst ups and downs by their former colonial regimes.

In addition, the newly independent states now had to use the revenues generated to support governmental, transport, and military infrastructures, whose costs had formerly been underwritten by the colonial governments. Since many of the new countries, acculturating to the norms of ethnolinguistic nationalism, also wanted to rectify border problems or expand their borders to include ethnic regions ignored by the colonists, their militaries often consumed substantial portions of their budgets. In many cases, too, the first and second generations of government officials and business leaders, smarting from decades of colonial exploitation, felt entitled to reap the benefits of their new status and simply skim the profits from their new positions. Such regimes were often derisively referred to as "kleptocracies." As some scholars have also pointed out, instead of fostering an entrepreneurial middle class, opening up new and innovative areas of investment, all too many members of this "caretaker bourgeoisie" were simply content to milk the enterprises they had to their maximum capacity. Hence, they became far more reliant on foreign aid and investment, which all too often the volatile political environments of their countries made unattractive. For those countries trying to mount socialist policies of land reform and nationalization of businesses, corruption of this type was also an ongoing problem, coupled with little real wealth to share among their growing populations.

As in Chapter 29, far too many new nations emerged in Africa during this period for this chapter to cover them all. Therefore, we will center our examination on Nigeria, Zimbabwe, and South Africa as representative of the problems and prospects of the era.

Nigeria: Civil War and Troubled Legacies

While in the Congo the Cold War played out in fairly dramatic fashion with the United States supporting the overthrow of Patrice Lumumba in favor of Mobutu Sese Seko in the early 1960s, Nigeria's independence started in more promising fashion. With a large and fairly prosperous population, sound agriculture, and abundant resources, it started its postcolonial era as a republic with a British parliamentary system, commonwealth membership, and a federal-style constitution. Like many former African colonies, however, it soon became apparent that Nigeria was also saddled with ethnic and religious conflicts that were its legacy from the old colonial divisions in the continent. Thus, its growing pains were marked by clashes between its established system of constitutional nationalism and the desires of its major constituent groups for their own nation-states more reflective of Nigeria's ethnic, linguistic, and religious makeup.

The new nation brought together three major antagonistic groups, the Yoruba, Igbo, and Hausa, divided by history, culture, religion, and language. The largest, the Yoruba, who controlled most of the national offices, were predominantly Muslim. The Igbo, mostly living in the eastern region where valuable oil deposits had been recently discovered, were predominantly Christian or animist. Starting in 1966, the central government under strongman Yakubu Gowon (in office 1966–1975) had authorized raids to bring Igbo areas under greater control. In 1967, the eastern Igbo region declared itself independent as the state of Biafra under Colonel Chukwuemeka Odumegwu Ojukwu (b. 1933). What followed was perhaps the bloodiest civil war of the era. Both sides fought determinedly, and when a military stalemate was reached the Nigerian forces attempted to starve Biafra into submission. More than 1 million Biafrans died, mostly of starvation and malnutrition, before Biafra surrendered in early 1970. In the remainder of the period to 1991, Nigeria was ruled by a series of military strongmen, each in turn attempting to stabilize the volatile political situation of the central government. By 1991, the prosperity that seemed so promising in 1960 had vanished as a probability to all but the most optimistic observers.

Nigerian Civil War. The attempt by the region of Biafra to secede from Nigeria resulted in one of the bloodiest and most desperate confrontations of the 1960s. In its attempt to starve the Biafrans into surrender, Nigeria blockaded food supplies to the breakaway region with the result of mass malnutrition, starvation, and, ultimately, a sizeable UN relief effort. In this picture relief workers dish out scarce rations to Biafran women and children.

Zimbabwe: The Revolution Continued

Some of the former European colonies in Africa came to independence with substantial populations of white settlers, some of whose families had been there for several generations. Accustomed to a life of relative privilege, they had, in many cases, opposed independence; and when it came, they sought guarantees from the new governments against expropriation of land, discrimination, and reprisals. In 1964 the old colony of Northern Rhodesia gained independence as Zambia, breaking up a federation of the two colonies and Nyasaland, which subsequently became independent as Malawi.

Threatened by the independence of nearby black African nations and confident of support from apartheid-based South Africa, the white leaders of what now called itself simply "Rhodesia" declared unilateral independence in 1965 and set up a government in the colonial capital of Salisbury under Ian Smith (in office 1965–1970). Distressed at this move, Britain refused to recognize the new government and expelled Rhodesia from the commonwealth. Few countries outside of South Africa recognized the regime, which now faced international sanctions and a guerilla movement from within.

Two rival groups, the Zimbabwe African National Union (ZANU) under Robert Mugabe (b. 1924) and the Zimbabwe African People's Union (ZAPU) led by Joshua Nkomo (1917–1999) struggled to bring Smith's regime down and create a majority rule state. The war was a long and bitter one, lasting throughout the 1960s and 1970s, until Mugabe and ZANU finally triumphed and created a new state called "Zimbabwe" in 1980. Mugabe's regime pledged fairness to the remaining white settlers and, after changing the name of the capital to Harare, set about creating a socialist state. In this sense, despite constant condemnation of Africa's imperial legacy, Mugabe has been in constant need of the economic power of the country's white minority and, thus, initially trod fairly lightly on their rights. By the 1990s, however, vigilante seizures of white lands by "revolutionary veterans" became a regular occurrence. By the early-2000s, the chaotic agricultural sector combined with repression of challenges to ZANU one-party rule had plunged the country into a serious economic crisis.

South Africa: From Apartheid to "Rainbow Nation"   South Africa, the richest of the continent's countries, was also the one with the most complex and restrictive racial relations. From the seventeenth century, first Dutch, then English, settlers came to service the maritime traffic around the Cape of Good Hope. By the nineteenth century, the Dutch-descended *boers* had moved inland from Cape Town and begun setting up farms, ranches, and vineyards, pushing the local people before them. The expansion of Zulu power at roughly the same time forced the British

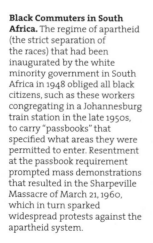

Black Commuters in South Africa. The regime of apartheid (the strict separation of the races) that had been inaugurated by the white minority government in South Africa in 1948 obliged all black citizens, such as these workers congregating in a Johannesburg train station in the late 1950s, to carry "passbooks" that specified what areas they were permitted to enter. Resentment at the passbook requirement prompted mass demonstrations that resulted in the Sharpeville Massacre of March 21, 1960, which in turn sparked widespread protests against the apartheid system.

rulers and Dutch settlers into protracted Zulu wars that, climaxing in 1879, broke the last black empire in the region. By the end of the nineteenth century, the discovery of vast mineral wealth in gold and diamonds led to both the expansion of the colony's holdings and an influx of immigrants, including Chinese and Indians.

By the early twentieth century, the social divisions among whites, Africans, and "coloreds"—south and east Asians and peoples of mixed descent—were hardening into legal classifications. The Indian nationalist leader Mohandas Gandhi, for example, developed his successful nonviolent strategies leading protests in South Africa for Indian rights. After 1910, immigration restrictions on Asians went into effect along with ever more restrictive laws governing relations between whites and Africans. The climax of this trend was the creation of the institution of **apartheid** (Afrikaans, "apartness") in 1948. Africans were relegated to a legal second-class status, they were to live in designated "townships" and tribal "homelands" or "Bantustans," they were required to carry passes when traveling, those commuting to work in white urban areas had to leave by sunset, and even in the townships they were subject to curfew regulations.

Through the 1950s South Africa faced international criticism for its policies, which the white government justified as necessary to maintain its rule, since whites made up less than one-sixth of the population. Moreover, as newly independent black majority countries came into being, the white government felt itself increasingly besieged. It pointed with some justification to a number of these emerging states as Marxist and, thus, claimed that it was fighting the free world's battle against the expansion of the Soviet Bloc in Africa. Nonetheless, it withdrew from the British Commonwealth in 1961, and a number of black political organizations—most prominently the African National Congress (ANC)—campaigned for the dismantling of apartheid. The brutality of the white armed forces and police and the constant harassment of dissenters, both white and black, added to the oppressive atmosphere.

By the 1980s it was clear that events on the continent would sooner or later force the breaking up of apartheid. International boycotts of South Africa had gained momentum, particularly after the public calling for sanctions by the African Episcopal bishop Desmond Tutu (b. 1931), who was awarded the Nobel Peace Prize in 1984. In the townships, the ANC, through a political and guerilla campaign, was making gradual gains. Massive strikes by black workers in 1987 and 1988 also led to increasing paralysis of the government. Finally, in 1990, the newly elected president, F. W. de Klerk (b. 1936), began a sweeping set of reforms aimed ultimately at dismantling apartheid. In quick succession, the ANC was legalized and became South Africa's largest political party; its leader—soon to be the country's president—Nelson Mandela (b. 1918) was released from prison; in 1991 all of the apartheid laws were repealed; and finally, in 1992 white voters elected to amend the constitution to mandate racial equality among all citizens. By 1994, the first multiracial elections were held, and Mandela became the first president of the new South Africa, which Archbishop Tutu dubbed the "Rainbow Nation" in its newly recognized diversity.

Apartheid: System of social and legal segregation by race enforced by the government of South Africa from 1948 until 1994.

Latin America: Proxy Wars

The 1960s in Latin American politics were marked in many ways by the forces contending for dominance against the backdrop of the Cold War. Here, however, because the countries in question had long since achieved their independence—if not yet long-term stability in government—the issues guiding the respective sides were largely ideological and economic, as well as centering around revolutionary politics. This was particularly true for the rural poor, who in many cases continued to live in virtual peonage on large estates, with little hope for economic advancement and little effort on the part of their landlords to improve their lot. In this respect, the appeal of a Marxist movement drawing on such diverse sources as Maoism—with its emphasis on peasants as a revolutionary force—and the recent example of Cuba standing up to the United States and pursuing its own brand of land reforms were often attractive. Cuba, particularly its most visible and charismatic exponent of Latin American revolution Che Guevara, was active throughout this era, though Guevara's execution in Bolivia set the Cuban efforts back somewhat.

By the 1970s, dissatisfaction with the authoritarian regimes of the region, particularly in Central America, resulted in several revolutionary efforts, the most notable being in Nicaragua and El Salvador. Since the mid-1930s, the United States had supported the family of the authoritarian strongman Anastasio Somoza Garcia (collectively in office from 1936–1979). Landlordism and rural poverty had been particularly acute problems in Nicaragua, and from the early 1960s a guerilla insurgency called the Sandinista National Liberation Front (FSLN) had sought to overthrow the Somozas and mount a socialist land-reform scheme. The Somoza regime fell in 1979, and a new government under the Sandinistas (so-called to invoke the name of Emilio Sandino, one of the original Somoza opponents) was formed led by Daniel Ortega (in office 1979–1990; 2007–). The socialist direction of the new regime prompted the American administration of President Ronald Reagan to cut off aid to Nicaragua, begin a covert operation to destabilize Ortega through funding and arming of opposition groups know collectively as the "Contras," and boycott trade with the regime. With US support and fading aid from Cuba and the Soviet Bloc in the late 1980s, the two sides agreed to elections in 1990. These resulted in the presidency of the conservative opposition candidate, Violeta Barrios de Chamorro (in office 1990–1997). In similar fashion, guerilla groups in El Salvador fought United States–backed government forces, whose actions were sometimes directed against Catholic clergy believed to support the insurgents, in a bloody conflict throughout the 1980s, until elections were finally held in 1992. The death toll in this tiny country is estimated to be as high as 75,000. By the early 1990s, however, the two sides, as in Nicaragua, had resolved to work within the new political system.

The commitment of the United States to oppose any groups espousing Marxist or communist aims in Latin America also revealed itself in covert policy toward governments recognized as legitimate. As we saw in Chapter 29, for example, the CIA helped engineer a coup against Guatemalan leader Jacobo Arbenz (in office 1951–1954) in 1954 because he allowed a communist labor union to exist in his country. The most spectacular instance of American Cold War covert action, however, was directed at Chilean President Salvador Allende (in office 1970–1973) in 1973. Allende had led a coalition of socialists, communists, and liberal Christian Democrats to a plurality win in 1970. Many of his policies met opposition within Chile, while his ideology and nationalization of American interests in Chile's mines pushed the Nixon administration to back his opposition. With American blessings and CIA help, Allende was overthrown and the repressive but friendlier regime of General Augusto Pinochet (in office 1973–1990) installed. After Pinochet's term of 16 years in power, his rule remained repressive; but Chile also became increasingly economically vibrant and slowly began to move toward a more open and democratic government. In 1998 Pinochet was arrested in London on charges of human rights violations and torture. After a lengthy court battle, he was ultimately released and returned to Chile, where he died in 2006.

Liberation Theology   In addition to the Marxist-inspired revolutionary movements in Latin America during this period, there were religiously based, activist ideologies animating a host of issues from land reform to protest against human rights violations. These are usually lumped under the heading of "liberation theology." The idea itself is an old one dating back to the Catholic Church's frequent role as champion of the Amerindians and the poor during the colonial and national periods. The calls during the Vatican II Council for a more activist and relevant place for the church resonated with many clergy—Catholic and Protestant—who had formed a vision of Christ's historical and religious role as one of social change. Though particularly active in Latin America, by the early 1970s it had become a worldwide movement within Catholicism and received cautious endorsement of the papacy, though with the caveat that the liberation of the poor and oppressed should not be seen as an endorsement of Marxism. Still, as the decade wore on, increasing numbers of clergy became involved in grassroots organizing, in preaching and pastoral care aimed at propagating a socially active Christianity, and in denouncing the inequities of the economics and politics of authoritarian regimes. The line between such activism and revolutionary work could be thin indeed—Daniel Ortega and his wife, for example, were married by a priest who had become a Sandinista guerilla. The regimes and local elites that were the targets of liberation theology advocates thus often struck back with violence against outspoken priests and nuns. But with the demise of many of these regimes in the 1980s and 1990s and the end of the Cold War, much of the momentum ebbed from the movement, though it is still directed against inequity and poverty among the rural poor even today.

Liberation Theology Service. The historical role of the Catholic Church at various times as advocate for the poor and oppressed in Latin America reemerged with vigor in the 1960s and 1970s against the backdrop of revolutionary turmoil and a new emphasis emanating from the Vatican on social activism. In the accompanying photo, a Mass is being celebrated in Brazil in the 1970s with a distinct message embodying themes associated with Liberation Theology: The banner reads in Portuguese, "The Church of Maranhao prays and fasts for peace and justice in the countryside."

"The Dirty War" and the "Disappeared"   As we have seen in this section, the damage inflicted by the Cold War and the actions of its combatants, real and proxy, upon Latin America was considerable. One of the most tragic and internationally condemned episodes of this struggle was the "Dirty War" (*Guerra Sucia*) carried out in Argentina from 1976 to 1983. The tangled politics of the post-Perón era resulted in a series of guerilla groups ranging from Peronists to radical communists conducting a smoldering guerilla war against various regimes from the 1960s onward. By the early 1970s, many of these groups had coalesced into the Peronist Montoneros and the Marxist People's Revolutionary Army (ERP). While the Montoneros were essentially crushed in 1977, the ERP remained active; and under the cover of "Operation Condor" pursued by the juntas of Jorge Raphael Videla, Roberto Viola, and Leopoldo Galtieri, tens of thousands of Argentinians were kidnapped, imprisoned, and killed. Many, if not most, of these men and women were not guerillas but writers, editors, labor organizers, teachers, and others suspected of having left-wing leanings or whom the government sought to eliminate for other reasons.

These victims became know as the "disappeared." Their plight is still poignantly brought to light by the Mothers of Plaza de Mayo, a group of women who have kept vigil for lost friends and relatives in that plaza in Buenos Aires since 1977 and whose movement has grown into an internationally recognized human rights organization. Already by 1979 the wholesale imprisonments prompted US President Carter to offer asylum to those languishing in Argentine jails.

In 1983, having deeply miscalculated in provoking and losing the Falklands War with Great Britain, the junta stepped down, elections were held, and a National Commission of the Disappearance of Persons (CONADEP) was established in December. While the figures vary greatly, from 15,000 to perhaps 30,000 "disappeared," the progress of the commission and its findings of torture, killing, and indefinite incarceration caused an international sensation. Today, most of the surviving military and political leaders held responsible are in prison themselves or have already served lengthy terms. As with so many other aspects of the Cold War era, the consequences for those involved have far outlived the conflict itself.

Putting It All Together

During the years 1962 to 1991, from the Cuban Missile Crisis to the dissolution of the Soviet Union, the Cold War contest between the two remaining twentieth-century versions of modernity—capitalist democracy and the different varieties of communism-socialism—reached its climax. At the beginning of the period it seemed at the very least that communism was competing evenly, perhaps even winning, in its appeal to so many developing nations and their leaders. But in the end, the wealth and power of the West, particularly the United States, ultimately wore the Soviet Bloc down. Along the way, the most populous communist state, China, abruptly changed from extreme radical leftist programs during its Cultural Revolution to a very capitalist style of market economics by 1991. Many other countries were now looking for some mixture of the two systems or a third way between the two for their own development. As the period drew to a close, it was, ironically, the two iconic communist regimes, the Soviet Union and the People's Republic of China, that were pioneering the way *out* of Marxist socialism. The Chinese sought to do this by retaining a powerful authoritarian government while embracing market economics.

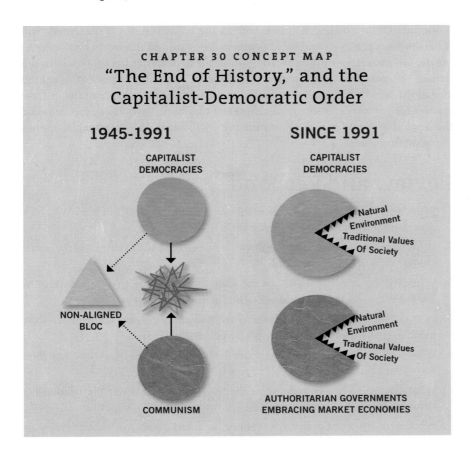

CHAPTER 30 CONCEPT MAP
"The End of History," and the Capitalist-Democratic Order

The former Soviet Union adopted democratic political values and guardedly introduced capitalism.

For the people of the world observing these changes it might indeed have seemed as if the triumphant words of Francis Fukuyama's 1989 essay "The End of History?" actually did sum up the age:

> a remarkable consensus concerning the legitimacy of liberal democracy as a system of government had emerged throughout the world over the past few years, as it conquered rival ideologies like hereditary monarchy, fascism, and most recently communism. More than that, however . . . liberal democracy may constitute the "end point of mankind's ideological evolution" . . . and as such . . . the end of history.

The next two decades, however, would see the emergence of new and unanticipated challenges to the domination of the capitalist-democratic order. For many, its secular character and its breaking down of traditional norms of family, gender, and sexuality in the West convinced them that the evolving culture of this surviving version of modernity would undermine the core values of their own societies. Hence, like the reformers in many of the old empires of the nineteenth century, they engaged in an erratic struggle to acquire the material advantages of modernity while isolating themselves from the cultural threat it presented. Still others in both the West and various other places around the world had come to see the forces of modernity as breaking down the delicate natural balance between human beings and the environment (see Concept Map). They therefore sought to curtail the rapacity of capitalist-democratic countries and corporations in their contest for resources. In the final chapter of this book, both these trends—and the devil's bargain they present to so many—will occupy a considerable amount of our attention.

Review and Respond

1. What were some of the most important turning points of the Cold War? Why have historians designated these as important?

2. What factors ushered in the era of *détente* between the United States and the Soviet Union? Why did this period end?

3. What are the principal causes of the Cultural Revolution in China during the 1960s? What was the role of Mao Zedong in inaugurating it and ending it?

4. Why did the Soviet leadership launch their policies of glasnost and perestroika in the mid-1980s? Did these programs help or hurt the USSR?

5. What is meant by feminism? How do we distinguish among first, second, and third wave feminism?

6. What causes led to the collapse of the Soviet bloc? How did the relationship between the Soviet Union and its allies contribute to this collapse?

7. What were the main political, economic, and social patterns in the developing world from 1963 to 1991? How does the Marxist theory of underdevelopment differ from the modernization theory?

8. Some have claimed that the end of the Cold War spelled the end of ideological struggle—even the "end of history." Do you think this argument has merit on its own terms? Why or why not?

▶ For additional resources, including maps, primary sources, visuals, and quizzes, please go to www.oup.com/us/vonsivers. Please see the Further Resources section at the back of the book for additional readings and suggested websites.

Thinking Through Patterns

▶ **How did the political landscape of the Cold War change from 1963 to 1991?**

Perhaps the biggest changes came in the 1980s. Though the United States had been defeated politically in Vietnam and was facing a recession at home, it still was the world's largest economy and could weather a protracted arms race. Though it was not fully perceived at the time, the Soviet Union was far more economically fragile—which ultimately made it ideologically fragile as well. The strains of Polish dissent, the Afghan War, and a renewed arms race with the United States simply wore the Soviet state down.

The unprecedented prosperity of the United States and the West more generally allowed younger people to attend universities in record numbers, experiment with new ideas of living, and simply indulge their desires for fun and new experiences. The idealism of the era also played a role, as did the threat of the draft and the larger threat of nuclear war. For many, the materialism of the age repelled them and made them long for a simpler, more "authentic" existence. Thus, a popular motto from the time was "turn on, tune in, drop out."

▶ **Why did such radically different lifestyles emerge in the United States and the West during the 1960s and 1970s? What is their legacy today?**

▶ **Why did some nations that had emerged from colonialism and war make great strides in their development while others seemed to stagnate?**

By and large, the nations that prospered were the ones that had already achieved self-sufficiency in agriculture, had at least the basic of a transportation and communications infrastructure, and were resourceful in adopting policies that maximized their labor force. Taiwan, South Korea, and Singapore are good examples of countries that made great strides in their development during this period. China, under Deng Xiaoping, followed a modified version of this strategy and was already growing at record levels by 1991. In the following decades, nearly all Asian countries (an exception being North Korea) would follow suit, with India moving into the top ranks of development and growth. Many Latin American countries—in particular, Brazil—also make great strides, and the drive to follow the example of using cheap labor to create a successful export manufacturing base was also took hold in Africa.

In all cases, culture and ideology could and did play a powerful role in setting the psychological conditions for citizens to believe that progress was possible. Peace and stability also played, for obvious reasons, an important role. he many internal conflicts that pockmarked Latin America and Africa held back development during this period.

Chapter 31

1991-2011

A Fragile Capitalist-Democratic World Order

It was a scene that had been repeated hundreds of times across North Africa and the Middle East during the winter of 2010 and the early spring of 2011. First in Tunisia in December, then with daily regularity in Egypt, Libya, Bahrain, Yemen, and Syria, growing crowds gathered to remonstrate with authoritarian governments over a wide range of issues that had marked the process of modernity for two centuries: the constitutional rights of life, liberty, security, economic opportunity, emancipation of minorities and women, and freedom of expression; the rights of ethnic and religious groups to nationhood, autonomy, or even mere existence.

Seeing Patterns

▶ How did the United States acquire its dominant economic position toward the end of the twentieth century? How did it accelerate the process of globalization?

▶ What made capitalist democracy so attractive toward the end of the twentieth century that it became a generic model for many countries around the world to strive for?

▶ Which policies did China and India pursue so that they became the fastest industrializing countries in the early twenty-first century?

▶ How have information technology and social networking altered cultural, political, and economic interactions around the world?

▶ What is global warming, and why is it a source of grave concern for the future?

The Arab Spring. Tawakkol Karman, a religiously conservative journalist and mother of three, received the 2011 Nobel Peace Prize for her nonviolent struggle for democracy and the safety of women. Throughout the year, she remained steadfastly devoted to a democratic future for Yemen even as the country descended into civil war. Here she leads a rally in Sana, the capital.

The governments challenged by these movements had long been entrenched behind brutal and repressive security services. Unable or unwilling to broaden political participation, aging authoritarian rulers had groomed their sons or favorites to succeed them. The rulers pretended to have liberalized the economies of their countries, but instead "crony capitalism" benefited their relatives and followers and discouraged entrepreneurial innovation. Chronic unemployment and underemployment left both the poor and the middle class in despair over their future. For many years, the unemployed youth of the Middle East had found solace in an Islamism whose preachers promised it would be the solution for all ills. But the ability of these preachers to deliver had turned out not to be any better than that of the increasingly despised rulers. A general stagnation had set in throughout the region.

By mid-spring 2011 the relentlessly repeated, massive, and unarmed street protests had toppled the governments of Tunisia and Egypt. Crowds massed as well in Syria, Bahrain, Libya, and Yemen. Syria and Bahrain sought to suppress the democracy movements while in Libya and Yemen civil wars tore the populations apart. More remarkably, however, was that here in this male-dominated bastion of conservative Islam, the movement was being led by that most "modern" of world personalities, a charismatic female journalist and grassroots organizer. Armed with computers, smart cell phones burgeoning with apps, Twitter, Facebook, and all the latest tools of social networking, Tawakkol Karman, 32, leader of "Women Journalists Without Chains" and mother of three, harangued mostly male crowds of thousands with calls for revolution. "We will make our revolution or we will die trying," she thundered, her words echoing those of so many insurgents of the recent past. "We are in need of heroes," said one Yemeni observer. "She manages to do what most men cannot do in a society that is highly prejudiced against women." But with her personal role models including Nelson Mandela of South Africa, Mohandas Gandhi of India, and Martin Luther King Jr. and Hillary Clinton of the United States, Karman as much as any woman of her time embodied the choices and challenges marking the patterns of world history in the rapidly globalizing early twenty-first century.

Many of the challenges faced by Yemen today are shared by many small, poor, largely traditional societies confronting the growing momentum of capitalist-democratic modernity. Its authoritarian government, for all its faults, has maintained a fragile balance among Yemen's many feuding tribes and religious groups; if and when it falls, what will take its place? Will its tribal groups unite or "balkanize?" As the war on terror continues, will the United States and the West risk chaos in the region as a magnet for such opponents of secular culture as al-Qaeda? What prospects are there for emancipation of women in such a traditional society, especially if economic development in this harsh land stays problematic? How will the continued progress of environmental degradation affect a new regime's approach to economic modernization? Little grows in many parts in the best of times; moreover, like many peoples in the region, Yemenis have traditionally enjoyed chewing *qat*, a mildly narcotic shrub leaf. But the plants themselves and the water needed to process them take up precious resources. Will a future government act to curtail the practice? At what cost? And perhaps the most immediate question: Will political empowerment along constitutional lines resulting from a revolution be sufficient to satisfy the aspirations of the Yemenis who took to the streets?

In the largest sense, then, achieving modernity through the surviving route of urbanization, science, industrialization, the accumulation of capital, and grassroots participation in political pluralism has become close to a universal goal in the world. Where it will lead is anyone's guess. But the story of how this pattern of modernity has grown to become nearly universal—and the old and new forces that oppose it—is the focus of this final chapter in our survey of world history.

Capitalist Democracy: The Dominant Pattern of Modernity

With the demise of communism, the struggle among the three ideologies of modernity that had characterized much of the twentieth century now was over. In the first flush of enthusiasm, some Western observers declared history to have ended, henceforth to be written merely as a series of footnotes to the triumph of capitalism and democracy in the world. Others prophesized soon after that culture would replace ideology as the basis for world competition. More sober observers expressed the hope that capitalist modernity in the coming decades would become an increasingly generic pattern, adoptable in non-Western cultures. But they also realized that democracy would not spread rapidly as long as countries remained poor and stuck in inherited forms of authoritarianism or even autocracy. History continued, the nation-state (as problematic as it was in many parts of Africa and Asia) became standard across the world, and its citizens strove for adaptation to the now dominant pattern of modernity: capitalism, democracy, and consumerism.

A Decade of Global Expansion: The United States and the World in the 1990s

In the aftermath of the oil crisis of 1985–1986, and with even greater vigor after the collapse of communism in 1991, the United States advocated free trade, fiscal discipline, and transnational economic integration as the proper course for world development. It did so as the most economically and politically powerful country. Two characteristics made the United States the sole superpower it currently is. First, the United States dominated the so-called dollar regime—that is, dollars functioned as the currency for all oil sales and purchases. In fact, despite the growth in popularity of the European Union's euro, and other major currencies like the English pound, Swiss franc, and Japanese yen, the dollar remained in a very real sense the world's currency. Second, with its giant consumer economy, the United States functioned as the world's favored destination for manufactured goods, particularly from East Asia. The leverage which the United States gained from these two economic functions was bolstered by overwhelming military force, which made the United States the principal enforcer of peace in the world.

A Hierarchy of Nations   During the 1990s, there were some 190 sovereign countries in the world, forming a three-tier hierarchy. At the top of the first tier, almost in a category of its own, was the United States. It was the richest, most evolved constitutional nation-state, based on a mature scientific–industrial society,

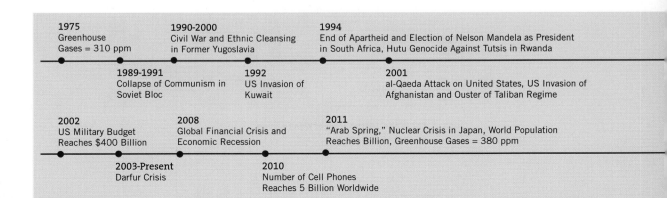

1975
Greenhouse
Gases = 310 ppm

1990-2000
Civil War and Ethnic Cleansing
in Former Yugoslavia

1994
End of Apartheid and Election of Nelson Mandela as President
in South Africa, Hutu Genocide Against Tutsis in Rwanda

1989-1991
Collapse of Communism in
Soviet Bloc

1992
US Invasion of
Kuwait

2001
al-Qaeda Attack on United States, US Invasion of
Afghanistan and Ouster of Taliban Regime

2002
US Military Budget
Reaches $400 Billion

2008
Global Financial Crisis and
Economic Recession

2011
"Arab Spring," Nuclear Crisis in Japan, World Population
Reaches Billion, Greenhouse Gases = 380 ppm

2003-Present
Darfur Crisis

2010
Number of Cell Phones
Reaches 5 Billion Worldwide

sophisticated financial institutions, and by far the most powerful military. In addition, it could boast the densest infrastructure of universities, colleges, public libraries, museums, theaters, and other cultural institutions. Below the United States, the fully industrialized democracies in Europe, North America, and Australia occupied the rest of the first tier. In the course of the 1990s, four "newly industrialized countries" joined this tier, the Asian "Tigers" or "Dragons:" Taiwan, South Korea, Hong Kong, and Singapore. Such was the economic power of the 30 fully industrialized and largely democratic countries in the top tier that they alone conducted nearly three-quarters of all world trade in goods and services.

In the second tier of the world hierarchy were 88 "middle-income countries," according to the United Nations' definition. These were developing countries in economic and democratic "transition." They were either industrializing states in the Middle East, South Asia, East Asia, and Latin America or reindustrializing states located in the former Communist Bloc. The reindustrializing states were replacing their obsolete communist-era manufacturing infrastructures with modern systems. In the broad bottom tier were 66 countries defined as "low-income" or "poor," located for the most part in sub-Saharan Africa and Southeast Asia. Many of these countries were in early stages of economic development, with little or no democratization (see Map 31.1).

In 2000, about one-fifth of the world's population of 6 billion lived in fully industrialized countries, two-thirds in middle-income countries, and 15 percent in poor countries. The world population was still expanding, but the pace of the expansion was slowing, largely as a result of improved female education and contraceptives. The dominance of scientific–industrial society was such that only two centuries after

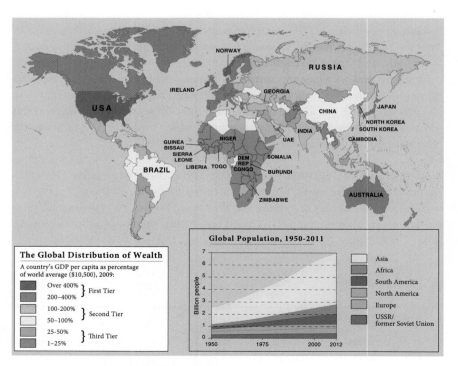

MAP **31.1** **The Global Distribution of Wealth, 2009.**

its beginnings 90 percent of the world population was more or less integrated into the pattern of capitalist modernity characterized by market exchange and consumerism and no longer by traditional agrarian–urban subsistence agriculture.

The Dollar Regime   The United States stood at the top of the world hierarchy thanks largely to the power of its financial system. The beginnings of this system date back to the years following 1971 when President Richard Nixon took the dollar off the gold standard. At that time, in a period of war expenditures in Vietnam and high inflation, the United States was running out of gold payable for dollars at the internationally agreed price of $35 an ounce. Two years later, Nixon persuaded the Middle East–dominated Organization of Oil-Producing Export Countries (OPEC) to accept only dollars as means of payment for oil. In support of Egypt and Syria against Israel in the October War of 1973, OPEC had just quadrupled oil prices. Despite American support for Israel, however, OPEC was anxious to remain in the good graces of the United States as its largest buyer. As a result of the Nixon–OPEC deal, the dollar took over from gold as the acknowledged international standard of exchange.

Under the **dollar regime**, all oil-importing countries, except for the United States, had to manage two currencies. One, denominated in dollars, was for energy purchases; the other, in domestic currencies, was for the internal market of oil consumption. Countries had to carefully look after the strength of their domestic currency as rising dollar prices could lead to severe crises in efforts to control inflationary domestic prices and pay back foreign, dollar-denominated loans. OPEC countries on their part invested their "petrodollars" in US Treasury bills ("T-bills"), as well as in American stocks and bonds. There were repeated grumblings among the non-oil producers of the world, both developed and developing, about being cheated by the dollar regime. But the US–OPEC deal did endure, backed up by a gigantic American financial system that emerged as a result of the dollar regime.

Dollar regime: A system maintained by the United States whereby dollars are the sole currency in which the price of oil and most other commodities and goods in the world are denominated; the regime forces most countries to maintain two currencies, with consequent financial constraints.

The United States as an Import Sinkhole   In a parallel development, the United States tied the industrial countries of the world to itself by becoming the country to which everyone wanted to export. Building these ties was particularly important in East Asia. During the Cold War, the United States had encouraged import substitution industrialization along the lines of Japan in Korea, Taiwan, Hong Kong, Thailand, and Southeast Asian countries. By becoming prosperous, so it was assumed, these countries would be less susceptible to the expansion of communism. Although uneven, the industrialization process advanced apace in most East Asian countries. In the 1990s, it reached levels where the United States began to pressure the Asia Tigers to reduce import substitution protectionism and replace it with free trade. In return for the United States buying their industrial goods, the countries of East Asia agreed to give free access to American financial institutions, such as banks and hedge funds.

In the meantime, communism collapsed and China, pushing its own import substitution industrialization, began to export cheap industrial goods as well to the United States. In the 1990s, aided by abundant cheap labor, these goods undercut those produced by the Asian Tigers and the United States became an even deeper "sinkhole," this time for textiles, toys, and simple electrical and electronic devices made in the People's Republic of China. The United States in effect underwrote China's industrialization, binding the country's economic interests closely to its own financial interests within the dollar regime (see Map 31.2).

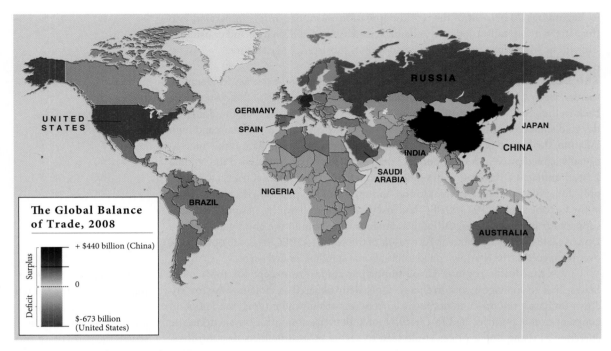

**The Global Balance
of Trade, 2008**

Surplus

+ $440 billion (China)

0

Deficit

$-673 billion
(United States)

MAP 31.2 **The Global Blance of Trade, 2008.**

US Technological Renewal and Globalization   Communism had collapsed in part because the Soviet Union had been unwilling or unable to leap into the new industrial age of consumer electronics. The United States, by contrast, transformed itself thoroughly in the 1990s. Electronics was one of those periodic new technologies with which capitalism, always threatened by falling profit rates in maturing industries, became more profitable again. By computerizing industrial processes, businesses saved on labor. Personal computers in offices made bureaucratic procedures more efficient. A fledgling Internet speeded up communication. An entirely new branch of industry, **information technology (IT)**, put cell phones, online delivery of music and entertainment, and a vast array of other services into the hands of consumers. In the phrase of the Nobel Prize Laureate in economics, Joseph Stiglitz, the United States had entered the "roaring nineties."

During this decade, the national budget was balanced; America became the leader in what was now called the "high-tech industry" of electronics, microbiology, and pharmacology; unemployment shrank; inflation remained low; and the foreign debt was moderate. Worldwide, the volume of trade goods doubled and the volume of capital flows quadrupled. The US Federal Reserve kept up with demand and printed more than half as many dollars in the course of the 1990s as were already in circulation. The domestic economy was humming, and the dollar was literally as good as gold even in remote corners of the world.

The only blemish in the **globalization** process, from an American perspective, was continued protectionism and low consumption in many Asian countries. President Bill Clinton's (in office 1993–2000) closest economic advisors were bankers and investors who had greatly expanded the size and influence of the financial services sector since the Nixon years. This sector handled the spectacularly enlarged

**Information
technology:** The
array of computers,
information, electronic
services, entertainment,
and storage available to
business and consumers;
with information
increasingly stored in
"the cloud," that is,
storage centers rather
than individual computer
hard drives.

volume of dollars floating around in the world. Alongside the traditional means of investment—stocks and bonds—new, more speculative instruments called "derivatives" gained in popularity. Derivatives were complex bets on higher or lower future prices of stocks, bonds, commodities, currencies, or anything else traded on the world market. The US globalization offensive in the 1990s was thus in large part an effort to open protected foreign markets to American financial institutions.

Globalization: The ongoing process of integrating the norms of market economies throughout the world and binding the economies of the world into a single uniform system.

Globalization and Its Critics   In many ways, the dollar and sinkhole regimes were so complex that they attracted critics from the entire political spectrum dissatisfied with one or another specific aspect of the evolving system. Conservative critics were appalled that the United States no longer adhered to the gold standard and sacrificed its sovereignty to oil sheikhs trading oil for dollars. They furthermore bemoaned the disappearance of the traditional manufacturing sector and its replacement by financial institutions and Internet start-ups that produced nothing tangible. In their judgment, the United States could be held hostage to policy dictates by the foreign holders of T-bills.

Progressive critics accused the United States of using its arrangements with OPEC and the East Asian countries to exclude the poorer countries in the world that had little to offer. In their opinion, the United States pursued the establishment of an imperialist capitalist system that limited wealth to a minority of industrialized and industrializing countries and refused to share it with the have-nots. Progressive criticisms were expressed in vociferous protests and occasionally even riots, accompanying meetings among the leaders of the industrial nations, usually in posh resorts around the world. Overall, however, both conservative and progressive criticisms remained marginal during the 1990s, given the general prosperity of the industrial countries.

US Military Dominance   Parallel to pursuing global economic integration, the United States emphasized a number of basic political principles in the 1990s. A first principle was that America was and must continue to be the unchallenged military power in all regions of the world. It defined itself as the guarantor of last resort for the maintenance of world peace. Accordingly, in the year 2002, the US military budget amounted to $400 billion. This astronomical sum was considerably smaller than during the Cold War but still larger than the defense budgets of the next eight countries combined. On the basis of this military machine, President Bill Clinton operated from a position of de facto world dominance. His successor, George W. Bush (in office 2001–2009), articulated this dominance in an official doctrine, the "national security strategy" of 2002. American might was highly visible in all parts of the world, generating considerable resentment among those for whom the combined economic–military power of the United States amounted to a new kind of world dominance (see Map 31.3)

Intervention in Iraq   The national security strategy elevated two policies already in practice into doctrine: prevent countries from establishing dominance in a region and destroy terror organizations bent on destruction in the United States. The first policy was enacted after Saddam Hussein (1937–2006) and his Baath regime occupied Kuwait (1990–1991). President George H. W. Bush (in office 1989–1993) intervened when it became clear that Saddam Hussein, by invading

MAP **31.3** **US Security Commitments Since 1945.**

Kuwait, wanted dominance over Middle Eastern oil exports from Saudi Arabia and the region was unable or unwilling to prevent him from achieving it. At the head of a coalition force and with UN backing, in 1992 Bush ordered US troops to evict the Iraqis from Kuwait in Operation Desert Storm. In a devastating combined air and ground war of 6 weeks the coalition force drove the Iraqi occupiers from Kuwait.

In the following decade, the United States and United Nations subjected Iraq to a stringent military inspection regimen to end Saddam Hussein's ambitions for acquiring nuclear and chemical weapons. The inspectors discovered large quantities

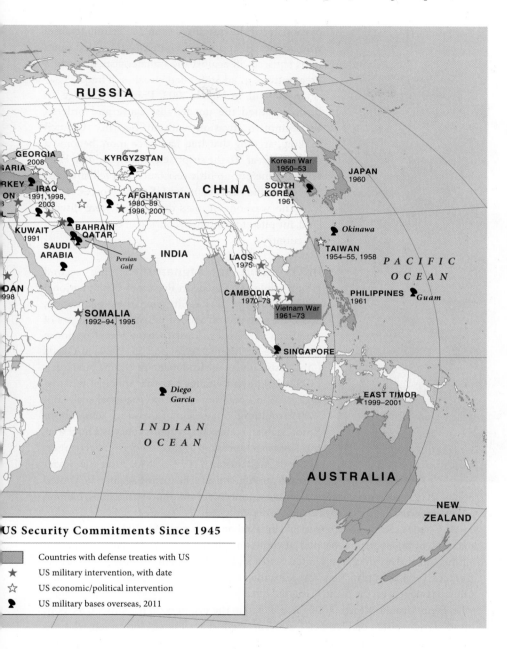

RUSSIA

GEORGIA
2008
GARIA
RKEY
ON
IRAQ
1991, 1998,
2003

KYRGYZSTAN

Korean War
1950–53

JAPAN
1960

CHINA

SOUTH
KOREA
1961

AFGHANISTAN
1980–89
1998, 2001

KUWAIT
1991

BAHRAIN
QATAR

SAUDI
ARABIA

INDIA

Persian
Gulf

Okinawa

TAIWAN
1954–55, 1958

PACIFIC

OCEAN

DAN
1998

SOMALIA
1992–94, 1995

LAOS
1975

CAMBODIA
1970–73

PHILIPPINES
1961

Guam

Vietnam War
1961–73

SINGAPORE

Diego
Garcia

EAST TIMOR
1999–2001

INDIAN
OCEAN

AUSTRALIA

NEW
ZEALAND

US Security Commitments Since 1945

- Countries with defense treaties with US
- ★ US military intervention, with date
- ☆ US economic/political intervention
- ♟ US military bases overseas, 2011

of weapons and supervised their destruction. But in the face of massive Iraqi efforts at obstruction, the inspectors eventually left. Their departure was followed by a retaliatory US bombardment of Baghdad in 1998. After the US invasion of Afghanistan in 2001, a chastened Saddam Hussein readmitted the inspectors. Their inability to find anything significant touched off an intense debate among the members of the UN Security Council. The United States and Great Britain considered further inspections worthless, while France, Russia, and China argued that these inspections should be given more time. A stalemate ensued, and in an extraordinarily

Day of Infamy. Smoke billowing from the north tower of the World Trade Center in New York on September 11, 2001. The south tower had already collapsed. Nearly 3,000 people died in the inferno, in which the heat of the exploding commercial airplanes in the interior of the high rises melted the steel girders supporting the buildings.

passionate worldwide discussion the multilateralists who advocated continued United Nations–led sanctions squared off against the unilateralists favoring a preemptive United States–led invasion of Iraq.

In the end, in March 2003, President George W. Bush espoused the unilateralist cause and ordered a preemptive invasion without Security Council backing, arguing that Iraq had once more become a regional threat. To the surprise of many, Saddam Hussein's regime put up little resistance and fell after just 3 weeks to the vastly superior US armed forces. Afterward, no weapons of mass destruction were discovered, in spite of an intense scouring of every corner of the country.

Intervention in Afghanistan The second US principle announced in President Bush's national security strategy was swift retaliation, prevention, and even preemption against nonstate challengers of American supremacy. This doctrine was a response to the rise of Islamic terrorism. In 1992, al-Qaeda ("the base") under the leadership of Osama bin Laden (1957–2011) had emerged as the principal terrorist organization operating on an international scale. Bin Laden, multimillionaire son of a wealthy Yemen-born Saudi Arabian contractor, won his spurs as a holy warrior (*mujahid*) for Islam against the Soviet occupation forces in Afghanistan (1979–1989). After the Soviet retreat from Afghanistan, he turned against the United States. In his eyes, America was a godless country without moral principles, bent on a Western crusade to destroy Muslim independence.

Al-Qaeda's campaign of terrorism climaxed on September 11, 2001. Suicide commandos, in an operation beyond anyone's imagination, hijacked four commercial airliners in the northeastern United States and crashed them into the World Trade Center's Twin Towers in New York City, the Pentagon outside Washington, D.C., and (after passengers on the plane disrupted the attempted hijacking) a field near Shanksville, Pennsylvania. Nearly 3,000 people died in the disasters. In response, US troops invaded Afghanistan on October 7, 2001, in an effort to eliminate bin Laden, who was protected by the regime in power. They destroyed the pro-al-Qaeda government of the Taliban, receiving support from anti-Taliban Afghans, and drove the al-Qaeda terrorists to western Pakistan. It took another decade for the United States to track down and assassinate bin Laden (May 2011) and several of his close collaborators and to come to grips with the resurgent Taliban terrorists in its ongoing war in Afghanistan.

The United Nations and Regional Peace Even though it was the United States and sometimes the North Atlantic Treaty Organization (NATO) that guaranteed peace in the 1990s and early 2000s and not the United Nations, the UN nevertheless fulfilled vital, if not always successful, peace missions in regional conflicts.

An important example of a failure in this regard was the Rwandan civil war of 1994, in which mostly French peacekeeping troops serving under UN auspices looked the other way as the Hutu ethnic majority massacred the Tutsi ethnic minority by the hundreds of thousands. On the other hand, despite the bloodshed on both sides, the crisis in the Sudan saw the United Nations fare somewhat better. Two vicious civil wars raged between Arab Muslim northern Sudan, on the one hand, and Christian and animist southern Sudan (1983–2005) and the African Muslim region of Darfur in western Sudan (2003–present), on the other. After lengthy efforts under UN mediation, the two sides in the first conflict agreed to the secession of South Sudan as an independent country in 2011. The second conflict continued to smolder, with the United Nations pursuing criminal charges against the president of Sudan and an African Union force seeking to protect the refugees from Arab-inspired attacks. First steps toward settling the ethnic–religious conflicts in Sudan were taken, but much more needed to follow.

American Finances Go Global: Crisis and Recovery   Under the umbrella of world peace maintained by the United States and United Nations, the world economy dominated by the dollar regime expanded during the early 2000s. In the so-called Washington Consensus, lasting a little more than a decade (1989–2002), Western economists and foreign aid officers preached "stabilize, privatize, and liberalize" to the governments of the emerging nations. To receive investments, foreign aid, or emergency loans to overcome recurrent economic crises, recipient countries had to submit to stringent rules concerning balanced budgets, the privatization of state firms, and the opening of protected branches of the economy. Submission to the Washington consensus, however, in many cases had unforeseen consequences.

Spurred by the consensus in the 1990s, private US investors had nearly tripled the value of their assets abroad, to a total of over $6.5 trillion. On the other hand, the now more accessible public and private financial systems in many newly industrialized and developing countries were often not sufficiently robust to respond adequately. In a first crisis, the Mexican government—pressured in 1994 by inflation, budget deficits, and political instability—could not avoid devaluing the peso. It promptly ran out of pesos to service its short-term, dollar-denominated debt. Fortunately, President Clinton was at that time anxious to complete the North American Free Trade Agreement (NAFTA) with Canada and Mexico. He had Congress and the International Monetary Fund (IMF) bail out Mexico with a massive infusion of loans. (The IMF is an international bank, with the US government as the largest shareholder, that provides emergency loans to countries in sudden financial distress.) With the help of this loan, the Mexican government paid off the foreign lenders and steadied its financial system.

The next crisis began in 1997 in Thailand. Here, the state finances were more solid than in Mexico. The liberalized private banking sector was still in its infancy however, with huge unpaid loans on its books. When many private banks could not pay back their American creditors, the latter began withdrawing what they could from Thailand. American funds for derivatives moved in to speculate on the distress. Derivative managers specializing in currency bets sensed an imminent devaluation of the Thai currency, the *baht*. Since they bet with hundreds of billions of dollars, their speculation became a self-fulfilling prophecy. Accordingly, when the devaluation of the baht finally happened, it stripped Thailand of its currency reserves.

Thailand—in good times one of the world's leading tourist destinations—scraped along the edge of bankruptcy, recovered in 1999, but was thrown again into turmoil in 2010–2011 in a near-civil war over allegations of corruption in the government.

From Thailand the crisis expanded in 1998 quickly to Malaysia, Indonesia, and finally even the newly industrialized Korea, Singapore, and Taiwan. These countries suffered from variations of the same problem of overcommitted banks with nonperforming portfolios. They thereby made themselves also vulnerable to American derivatives speculators invading their financial markets. The IMF had to move in with massive loans to the Southeast and East Asian countries. In return, these countries had to tighten credit, close unprofitable banks and factories, tolerate higher unemployment, and promote increased exporting.

Newly industrialized South Korea was relatively successful with its reforms and quickly cranked up its exports again. Less developed Indonesia, however, was singularly unsuccessful. Large-scale demonstrations forced President Mohammed Suharto (in office 1967–1998) from office. Under weak successors and a slow recovery beginning in 2000, enraged Indonesian Muslims turned to militant Islamism or even terrorism as their solution for the country's persistent poverty. Thanks to the majority of moderate Muslims firmly opposed to terrorism and supportive of the new democratic process, however, an Islamic war of secession in Aceh ended in 2005 and politics entered regular democratic channels.

Russia's Crisis and Recovery   Russia defaulted in 1998 on its internal bonds and from 1999 to 2001 on several of its external loans. These defaults were a culmination of the disastrous postcommunist economic free fall. In the decade after 1991, Russia's gross domestic product (GDP) dropped by nearly half, a decline far worse than that experienced by the United States during the Great Depression of the 1930s. Ordinary Russians had to reduce their already minimal consumption by half of what they had been used to under communism. Moreover, the government had yet to dismantle the system of unproductive former state enterprises financing themselves through local tax collection. Consequently, the state was periodically starved of funds needed for the repayment of its external loans. Fortunately, higher oil prices after 2001 eased the debt situation of Russia somewhat.

The oil and gas revenues from state firms available directly to the government, however, strengthened its autocratic tendencies. The former KGB officer Vladimir Putin, president of Russia 2000–2008, was the principal engineer of this autocracy. He eliminated independent television and had state prosecutors go after potential political rivals. Pervasive corruption and obedience to state directives undermined the rule of law so severely that it was no longer possible to speak of the rule of law in Russia. Politically motivated assassinations of journalists, carried out by secret operatives suspected of enjoying government protection, went unpunished. Rival political parties were intimidated and elections manipulated. An obedient parliament changed the federal constitution so that presidents in the republics of the Russian Union were no longer elected but appointed. Given the small size of the private sector in the early 2000s, the country was still years away from subjecting its state enterprises to market rules and creating a comprehensive market economy.

After the Mexican, Asian, and Russian debt crises, private investors began to lose interest in the emerging markets of developing countries. With funds drying up, debt-ridden Latin American states became vulnerable. Thanks to an emergency IMF loan in 1999, Brazil narrowly avoided a financial meltdown. Argentina, however, in 2002 was less fortunate. Here, the government imprudently prolonged a recession with a tax hike. A yawning budget deficit remained unbalanced, high foreign debts were unpaid, and the peso had to be devalued. This time, however, the IMF did not bail out the government with an emergency loan, arguing that Argentina had been reckless with its finances. Without a loan, the government fell, the middle class was virtually wiped out, and the country—like Russia—limped in the next few years from one loan default to another. Recovery set in only toward the end of the decade.

Globalization and Poor Countries The mixed record of development in the middle-income countries was mirrored in the bottom tier of poor countries. Even the World Bank had to admit in a 2000 report that the 1990s expansion with its freewheeling financial sector had brought little improvement to many countries in the bottom tier. Since these countries still had weak manufacturing bases, their governments relied on the export of mineral or agricultural commodities to finance development. Apart from the oil-rich desert states of the Middle East, some 50 poor states depended on three or fewer commodities for over half of their export earnings. In about 20 of these states, these commodities even made up over 90 percent of export earnings. As a result of overproduction on the world market, commodity prices were depressed through most of the 1990s. The price depression imposed severe budget cutbacks on many poor countries, with consequent unemployment, middle-class shrinkage, reduction in education, and a rise in AIDS cases.

Sex and Violence in the New Russia. An often lurid mixture of sex and violence has been a defining feature of post-Soviet popular culture and a source of much public concern. The illustration above shows the cover of a popular detective novel by Alexandra Marinina, *Death and a Little Love*, in 1995. Note the provocative positioning of the automatic pistol jutting at the face of the women in a way both startling and demeaning.

In a global view, however, the developing world benefited from the globalization of the 1990s. Poverty declined up until the recession of 2007, although this decline was unevenly distributed among the regions of the world. The World Bank defines as "absolutely poor" a man or woman who has to live on less than $1.25 a day. According to statistics compiled during 1990–2000, the total number of the poor went down from 29 to 24 percent, even though the world population grew by nearly 1 billion. As encouraging as this figure was, the gains were concentrated almost exclusively in East and South Asia, particularly China, Vietnam, and India. The number of the absolute poor actually increased in sub-Saharan Africa, Southeast Asia (except Vietnam), Russia and central Asia, and Latin America. Thus, while globalization benefited an absolute majority of humans, its uneven geographical distribution made the benefits look substantially smaller in many regions.

Contrasting Worlds. A quiet street early in the morning in Havana, with an old American car parked on the curb. The American embargo, together with a still dominant command economy prohibiting imports, forces most car owners in Cuba to hold on to their clunkers, repairing them over and over (a). A Vietnamese woman in a traditional straw hat and with two baskets, balanced on a pole, passing by a French luxury goods store in Hanoi, the capital of Vietnam. The country enjoyed near double-digit growth rates in its economy during the first decade of the 2000s (b).

The Communist Holdouts: North Korea, Cuba, China, and Vietnam

Communism as an official ideology survived in North Korea, Cuba, China, and Vietnam. North Korea and Cuba stubbornly continued to cling to both the command system and party control. China and Vietnam opened their command economies to the market but maintained single-party control and some large state firms. In both cases, the parties remained communist in name but became in fact ordinary autocracies presiding over capitalist economies.

North Korea and Cuba After the death of North Korea's founding leader, Kim Il-Sung (b. 1912), in 1994, his son Kim Jong-il (b. 1941) became the Communist Party secretary and, thereby, the head of North Korea's government. He inherited a command economy in free fall, with Soviet subsidies having ended and strained relations with China after that country's normalization of relations with South Korea. Several years of floods and drought in the 1990s had accelerated the economic breakdown, culminating with a colossal famine, which killed some 2.5 million people—nearly one-fifth of the population. A moderate turnaround finally began in 1998 with the inauguration of an industrial zone with foreign investments and a limited free market. Kim Jong-il, the army, and the party remained unified during the catastrophic 1990s and continued their iron grip even through 2008 when the leader allegedly suffered a stroke. Since North Korea was a highly armed nuclear country asserting itself regularly through military provocations against South Korea, the political situation on the Korean peninsula continued to be unstable.

Cuba, too, suffered a severe setback when Soviet communism collapsed. Without Soviet subsidies and the ability to continue its sugar exports, the Cuban GDP shrank by one-third, imposing severe hardship on the population. President Fidel Castro (b. 1926) and the Communist Party were forced to reduce their reliance on the command economy. They allowed farmers to exceed their state quotas and grow fruits and vegetables for the open market, and a limited number of urban workers were allowed to open their own shops. Tourism was opened up, catering mostly to Europeans and East Asians since the long-standing US embargo continued almost unchanged. Thanks to a highly developed health sector, Cuba also built export-oriented pharmaceutical and biotechnological industries. During the early 2000s, the government was able to turn the economy around and achieve high growth rates. The hope of discovering substantial offshore oil fields even injected excitement into the country. Castro's resignation from the presidency for health reasons in 2008, however, raised questions of transitional politics similar to those concerning North Korea. In both countries communism remained outwardly as unreconstructed as ever.

The Chinese New Middle Class   After the crushing experience of Tiananmen Square, the new Chinese middle class benefiting from the economic reforms of the Open Door and Four Modernizations had to accommodate itself as best it could to a repressive top layer and a corrosively corrupt bottom layer of a monopoly party that was communist in name but autocratic in practice. The basic characteristics of the middle class were remarkably similar to those of India and Turkey, discussed later in this chapter. Socially conservative migrants from the provinces to the cities found unskilled jobs in the early 1980s. They acquired skills and earned enough to send their children to school. From around 2005, the children, now with college degrees, took jobs as managers, technicians, professionals, and entrepreneurs in state companies, private firms, and Chinese branches of foreign firms. They began to flex their muscles as consumers.

Two Views of China Today. Despite recent attempts to regulate its pace, China's economic acceleration continues at or near double digits. In 2010, its GDP surpassed that of Japan to become second only to that of the United States. The new prosperity has created startling contrasts and a growing diversity of lifestyles in the PRC. In the image above, young Chinese hipsters sport T-shirts harkening back with purposeful irony to revolutionary leaders Mao Zedong and Cuba's romantic figure of Che Guevara. In the lower panel, China's current leadership—smartly decked out in Western suits and "power ties"—strive to steer the country toward continued growth as the means to preserve the ascendancy of the Chinese Communist Party.

The social conservatism of the middle class was rooted in rural popular religious practices, such as ancestral offerings and funeral rituals, blessings, or birthday festivals of gods that involved processions and pilgrimages to and from temples under the leadership of local Daoist priests. During the Maoist period, many temples were destroyed and practices outlawed, disrupting for nearly a generation the transmission of traditional customs. Since the mid-1990s, however, the government authorized or tolerated the reconstruction of temples and resumption of practices, while at the same time regulating the training and accreditation of Daoist and Buddhist ritual specialists. In villages, retired folk who remembered the customs participated in the reconstitution of temple committees, the collection of funds, and the staging of operas, marionette and puppet shows, or movies. In cities, the merged rural and urban scriptural traditions expressed themselves in a standardized Confucianism–Daoism–Buddhism under government control.

To keep the middle class from demanding political participation outside the Communist Party, the government pursued accelerated annual GDP growth, which in some years went into double digits. Wages rose beyond those paid in Vietnam,

Bangladesh, India, and Pakistan. Instead of spending its earnings, however, the middle class saved at rates double those in Japan or Europe prior to the recession of 2007. The only partially subsidized new health-care and education systems consumed much of those savings, even though the payments were bearable under the continued conditions of the one-child law. In addition, urban real estate and rental apartments became increasingly unaffordable in many Chinese cities during the early 2000s. Under the slogan of the "harmonious society"—in which all segments of the populace worked together with no toleration for "disruptive elements," or those advocating independence for Tibet or Uighur regions in Xinjiang—the government and party staked its continued legitimacy on ongoing economic progress.

The Chinese Countryside   This high-wire act was even more pronounced in the countryside. The government maintained the Maoist-era *hukou* registration system, which did not allow farmers to move to cities and find work without a permit, even though this system was largely ignored. The government reformed the system marginally but still refused to grant amnesty to some 100 million migrants working illegally in cities or allow their children access to urban schools. An equal number of farmers were pushed off their lands by authorities eager to make room for businesses, roads, and railroads. Since land continued to be state-owned and farmers were merely leaseholders, corrupt local authorities found it easy to cheat the farmers out of their land. The value of *guanxi* ("connections") thus continued more or less unabated. Tens of thousands of local protests annually in the early 2000s attested to a smoldering resentment in the villages, no matter how loudly the government touted its success in reducing the poverty rate.

The Transformation of Vietnam   As a country that looked to the Soviet Union for leadership, Vietnam was as surprised as Cuba when Soviet-style communism collapsed in 1991. Like the Soviet Union, Vietnam had begun economic liberalization reforms in 1986, especially in agriculture where farmers were permitted to sell above-quota harvests on the open market. Vietnam quickly became the world's third largest rice exporter, after the United States and Thailand, and reduced its poverty rate as drastically as China. But vehement ideological struggles over political liberalization did not end until a decade later with the decision to avoid a multiparty system, as did China a little later. Now the path to a full commitment to economic liberalization was open. In 1995–1996 Vietnam normalized relations with the United States, took out a large World Bank loan, revitalized foreign investment, and began reforming its unprofitable state firms by encouraging the participation of private domestic capital.

With stellar double-digit growth rates in the 1990s, Vietnam outpaced other poor Asian neighbors, such as Cambodia and Bangladesh, diversifying its manufacturing sector from textiles to footwear and electronics. Hong Kong, Taiwanese, and Korean companies, the principal foreign investors, showed a strong preference for Vietnam, on account of its advanced literacy rate and lower wages compared to China. A major new export sector from the later 1990s onward was *aquaculture*, the farming of shrimp, catfish, and tilapia. Vietnam was poised at the beginning of the second decade of the 2000s to move from the poor to the intermediate countries on the world list of nations moving to modernity.

A Decade of Global Shifts: Twenty-First Century Currents and Cross-Currents

In the first decade of the 2000s, there was a palpable swing toward pessimism in the West. Two recessions framed the decade, the Washington consensus fell apart over protests from borrower countries, and the problematic postwar settlement in Iraq demonstrated the limits of US power. The Middle East fared even worse, with terrorism, suicide bombings, no Arab–Israeli peace, and a potential Iranian nuclear bomb. By contrast, China and India, with strong economic growth rates, expanded their educated and entrepreneurial middle classes. Africa and Latin America, benefiting from the voracious demand for oil and minerals in China and India, experienced similarly strong growth. By the second decade of the 2000s, it was clear that, while there might be doubts about the course of modernity in the West, the commitment to it was growing everywhere else.

Unease in the West   Two recessions in the first decade of the 2000s in the United States sapped much of the enthusiasm about the future of modernity that had begun so optimistically after the fall of communism. The first recession, of 2001–2003, was the so-called dot.com crisis, which had its origins in uncontrolled speculation about the expansion of the new medium of the Internet and the World Wide Web. The second recession, of 2007–2011, was rooted in private and public overspending (housing and credit). By 2011, US debts reached the astronomical sum of nearly $14.6 trillion (for comparison, the US GDP was $14.5 trillion).

The recession of 2001–2003 hit the African American and Hispanic working class particularly hard; in the following recession of 2007–2011 many white workers lost their jobs. An unraveling of the credit markets built on speculation on financial derivatives and "credit default swaps" in the mortgage sector spurred a cascade of financial failures in 2008. Only massive intervention by the federal government prevented a general financial panic. As anger over corporate greed, government bailouts, massive federal economic stimulus packages, and health-care reform grew among largely white, middle-class, older, and evangelical voters, a new "Tea Party" movement ("Taxed Enough Already") introduced radically populist antiestablishment and antiforeigner agendas into the political debate. The largely conservative middle classes of self-employed small businesspeople and professionals found themselves squeezed between unskilled and low-earning workers on the bottom and an expanding, increasingly rich upper middle class of corporate officers and Internet entrepreneurs on top, causing no small amount of unease.

The campaign and eventual election of Barack Obama (b. 1961, in office beginning 2009), a law professor and the first African American president of the nation, provided much optimism to a majority of Americans. At first, it appeared that the president's deficit-spending helped in steadying the recession of 2007–2011. But

Edge People

"Being 'Danish' or 'Italian,' 'American' or 'European' won't just be an identity; it will be a rebuff and a reproof to those whom it excludes. The state, far from disappearing, may be about to come into its own: the privileges of citizenship, the protections of card-holding residency rights, will be wielded as political trumps. Intolerant demagogues in established democracies will demand 'tests'—of knowledge, of language, of attitude—to determine whether desperate newcomers are deserving of British or Dutch or French 'identity.' They are already doing so. In this brave new century we shall miss the tolerant, the marginals: the edge people."

—Tony Judt. "Edge People." *The New York Review of Books*, March 25, 2010. Judt, who died in 2010, was one of the leading critics of capitalist democracy.

soon this spending turned out to be insufficient, and the grind of the 2007–2011 recession soon dragged the ebullient mood down again. Meanwhile, conservatives and Tea Party activists relentlessly targeted government spending, health-care reform, illegal immigrants, and especially the slow economic recovery. In the 2010 elections, the Republicans regained the House and rejected tax increases to offset budget deficits out of hand.

A year later the Tea Party wing of the Republican Party held the nation hostage in the negotiations for an increase of the national debt ceiling. It nearly drove the country into default and the credit worthiness of the United States was damaged. Given the unwillingness of lawmakers to reform the tax code, the gap between the wealthy and poor—beginning with the electronic revolution and apparent opportunities for new wealth—continued to widen. This gap increasingly threatened the ability of middle-class Americans to consume and thereby sustain the capitalist system, given that 45–70 percent (depending on conservative or liberal calculations) of the GDP was consumer-generated.

Europe saw a similar trend of rising income disparities, although it was mitigated by a stronger manufacturing sector (around 20 percent of GDP vs. 11 percent in the United States in 2010) and a more generous social safety net. But the costs of this net weighed heavily on the budgets of many countries, seriously imperiling the future not only of, for example, Greece, Portugal, and Ireland (which fell into near bankruptcy in 2008–2011) but also of the European Union (1992) itself, as well as the euro, which was launched with great fanfare in 1999. Since the unemployed were entitled to long-term support in most European countries, the angry populist debate was more muted. Nevertheless, the rise of anti-Muslim immigrant political parties in Scandinavia and the Netherlands and the spectacle of unemployed youth in Portugal and Spain (up to 40 percent) setting up makeshift camps in major cities were stark reminders of the lack of confidence in the future of many young Europeans. As in the United States, optimism about the future of modernity was at a low ebb by the start of the new decade.

On the other hand, given the still comparatively strong, export-oriented manufacturing sector, Europe was years ahead of the United States in industrial innovation. In the first decade of the 2000s, European countries became the leading producers of renewable energy technologies, such as wind turbines, solar cells, and batteries. A study, carried out in Germany in 2010, suggested that it would be feasible for the country to shift entirely from fossil fuels to green energy by 2050. Europe also had an edge in the manufacture of fuel-efficient or electric cars and the exploration of hydrogen propulsion. Though nuclear energy was widely used, particularly in France, its future was open to question after the earthquake, tsunami, and partial nuclear power plant meltdown in Sendai, Japan, in the spring of 2011. The commitment to environmentalism in the early 2000s was much stronger in Europe than in the United States and in this sector at least, gloom is tempered with considerable hope.

A Bloody Civil War in Yugoslavia   Eastern Europe and the Balkans went through an economic collapse and political restructuring similar to Russia, Ukraine, Belarus, and the other republics after the end of communism in 1991. This collapse and restructuring was mostly peaceful except for Yugoslavia, where a civil war raged from 1990 to 1995. Until the 1980s, communism was the main ideology in Yugoslavia through which the country's ethnic nationalisms of the Orthodox Christian Serbs (one-third of the population), Catholic Croats (20 percent), Muslim Bosnians (9 percent), Catholic Slovenes (8 percent), and mostly Muslim Kosovo Albanians (8 percent) were kept under the mantle of a federal constitution granting these ethnic groups a degree of autonomy. The main enforcer of communist unity, through carrot and stick, was President Josip Tito (1892–1980), a Croat whose authority—based on his legitimacy as an underground fighter against the Nazi occupation during World War II—was unimpeachable. After his death, however, the Serb president Slobodan Milošević (1941–2006) exploited the demographic superiority of his ethnic community for the establishment of political dominance while holding on to communism as the pro forma ideology.

Yugoslavia, like many Eastern European communist states, had borrowed heavily from Western countries to keep its industries from collapsing during the oil price slump of 1985–1986. At the end of the 1980s it was practically bankrupt, with hundreds of thousands of unemployed workers carrying their dashed hopes for the good life of consumerism in the city back to their native villages. This disappointment exploded in 1990 with extraordinary fury into deadly religious–nationalist hatred, led by the smaller ethnic groups against Serbs on their territories. The Serb supremacist-nationalist backlash, with an effort to "cleanse" minorities from their "greater Serbian" territory, was no less explosive. It took more than a decade for the European Union and the United States to stop the Serbs from murdering Bosnians and Albanians and enforce a semblance of peace in the Balkans.

Since then, the five successor states of Yugoslavia have struggled to adapt to capitalism and democracy. Slovenia did so quite successfully, while others like

Ethnic Cleansing. The upheavals in the wake of the breakup of the former Yugoslavia brought long simmering ethnic and religious tensions to the surface, particularly in the struggles between the Orthodox Serbs seeking to create a "greater Serbia" in Bosnia and Herzegovina and Bosnia's Muslims. In the accompanying photo, a woman, Hajra Eatiae--the president of the Association of Women of Srebenica--takes a poignant private moment in front of a wall of photographs of the 8,000 Bosnian victims of the massacre in the city of Srebenica at the hands of Serbs. Eatiae herself lost her husband and son in this largest European mass murder since World War II.

Bosnia-Herzegovina, Serb-controlled Bosnia, and Kosovo have not yet at all. Serb supremacist nationalism survived the longest and only gradually died down when the democratically elected pro-European government decided to arrest the main perpetrators of ethnic cleansing, Radovan Karadžić (b. 1945) and Ratko Mladić (b. 1943) in 2008 and 2011, respectively. The two had lived more or less openly in Serbia for years, protected by diehard followers. With these arrests and much relief, the Serbian government opened the way toward joining the European Union.

The Middle East: Paralysis, Islamism, and Liberation

As in the United States and Europe, the momentum that was generated after the collapse of communism had largely expired in the Middle East and North Africa by the early 2000s. In fact, with the exception of Turkey, a pall of economic and political paralysis hung over the region. The republics in the 1990s and early 2000s (e.g., Egypt, Syria, Algeria, Tunisia, and Yemen) inched intermittently toward privatization of state-run businesses but not at all toward democratization. Monarchies (Saudi Arabia, Jordan, Oman, and the Gulf sheikhdoms) actively encouraged private investment, especially in the oil sector, but were extremely cautious, if not altogether hostile, toward democratic reforms. Under the impact of the Arab Spring, in 2011 the kingdom of Morocco adopted constitutional reforms allowing for greater democracy. The "rejection front" of autocratic regimes in Iran and Syria, as well as the guerilla terrorist organizations Hezbollah in southern Lebanon and Hamas in the Gaza Strip, opposed Washington and globalization out of hand. Syria did, however, open state-controlled economy ever so cautiously to privatization in the early 2000s.

Islamism: Religious-nationalist ideology in which the reformed Sunni or Shiite Islam of the twentieth century is used to support the institutions of the state.

Islamism was a major factor accounting for the immobility of "republican autocrats" as well as monarchs. Western secular observers often expressed their surprise at the strength of the religious resurgence in the Middle East after watching its apparent demise with the rise of secular Arab nationalism and Arab socialism. In this case, however, while Islam was less visible in the region in the twentieth century when the political elites consisted of secular liberals and nationalists, it had not receded at all from the villages and poor city quarters, where it remained as vital as ever (see Map 31.4).

The key to understanding the rise of Islamism lay in the acceleration of rural–urban migration in the Middle East in the late 1990s and early 2000s. Ever since the 1960s, when Middle Eastern and North African governments built the first large state-run manufacturing plants in their cities, the workers were largely peasants arriving from villages with highly localized cultures of saintly Sufi or mystical Islam. They encountered militant preachers in the cities who—representing a unified, standard, urban Sunni Islam—were appalled by the "un-Islamic" saint cults among the workers. The children of these workers learned a similar standardized Islam in the schools, intended to buttress Arab nationalism, in which the Prophet Muhammad was the first nationalist. Standard Islam and militant urban Islamism gradually crowded out the rural saintly Islam and eventually produced small but potent offshoots of Islamist terrorism, such as al-Qaeda and the Taliban.

In the 1990s and early 2000s Middle Eastern governments essentially barricaded themselves behind their secret services and armies against the onslaughts of these Islamists. Terrorists attacked tourists, as happened periodically in Egypt, seeking to bring down a government that relied heavily on Western tourism. Sometimes they picked weak states such as Yemen, which, relying on dwindling oil revenues began

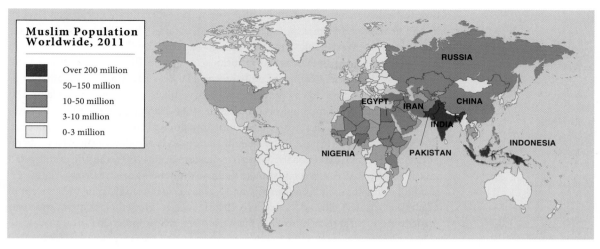

MAP **31.4** **Muslim Population Worldwide, 2011.**

to lose control of its nomadic tribes in the east, agricultural minorities in the north, and urban secessionists in the south, became a haven for al-Qaeda terrorists. Even a stronger state, Algeria, suffered a devastating civil war that claimed 150,000 victims from 1992 to 2002. Under the threat of Islamist terrorism, Middle Eastern and North African governments found it impossible to proclaim bold new initiatives of the kind that China or India advanced (see Map 31.4).

Islamic Terrorism and Israel Two areas where Islamists achieved breakthroughs of sorts were Lebanon and the Gaza Strip. Hezbollah ("Party of God"), an Islamist guerilla organization with attendant social services and recruits from among the Shiite majority of Lebanese Muslims, waged an underground war against Israel and Westerners in Lebanon and abroad. Hezbollah was accused of bombing the US embassy in Beirut in 1983, hijacking an American airliner in 1985, and two bombings against Jews in Argentina in 1992 and 1994. Thereafter, the party changed its tactics, focusing its forces entirely on driving Israel out of southern Lebanon, which it achieved in 2000. Since then, it has steadily increased its role in the Lebanese government and in the Arab–Israeli conflict, regularly firing rockets into northern Israel. After a retaliatory Israeli invasion in 2006, Hezbollah and Israel, kept apart by a contingent of UN soldiers, returned to an uneasy standoff.

Israel successfully transformed itself during the globalization of the 1990s into an advanced economy specializing in high-tech software and microbiology. In 1994, it was officially at peace with two Arab neighbors, Egypt and Jordan. But it continued to face a hostile Arab Middle East and North Africa, in general, and restless Palestinians in the occupied territories on the West Bank and in Gaza, in particular. To protect its citizens from guerilla attacks, the Israeli government began building a border fence in 2002, supplemented in places by a wall of concrete slabs, inside the entire length of the occupied West Bank. In a parallel move it withdrew from the fenced-in Gaza Strip in 2005. Suicide attacks were fewer, but cross-border rocket attacks (from Gaza) increased, trapping Israel in a cat-and-mouse game of low-level cross-border warfare.

After 2006, Israel slid into an even worse trap. The first ever Palestinian elections gave the victory in Gaza to the Islamic guerilla organization Hamas, founded in 1988, over the older, secular, ethnic-nationalist Palestinian Liberation Organization (PLO). The PLO, deprived of its inspiring leader Yasser Arafat (1929–2004), was able to prevail only in the West Bank. The PLO refused to recognize the elections, and a civil war broke out, in which Hamas was victorious, forcing the PLO to retreat to the West Bank. Israel imposed a complete embargo on Hamas-ruled Gaza, in an attempt to bring the organization down. For those in Israel who wished to renew the Camp David peace process, left incomplete in 2000, the PLO–Hamas split was a disaster since it threw the entire idea of a two-state solution into doubt. Hamas was happy to deepen this doubt in the following years by launching thousands of rockets against Israel. In retaliation, Israel invaded Gaza in December–January 2008–2009, causing unmitigated misery for the Palestinian population of Gaza, without being able to defeat Hamas. Efforts at healing the split between PLO and Hamas, crucial for salvaging the concept of a Palestinian state, followed thereafter with little success. Nonetheless, application was made to the UN for recognition of a Palestine state in September 2011.

Israel's Predicament and the Iranian Bomb   Predictably, the failure of the invasion brought a conservative government into power in Israel. The government renewed the open pursuit of Israeli settlement construction on the West Bank while tightening the embargo on Gaza. But neither more Jewish settlements on the West Bank (making the two-state solution illusory) nor punishing Israel's neighbors Hezbollah and Hamas with invasions and/or embargoes brought the country closer to peace. Israel's long dominance over its neighbors, gradually acquired in the last half of the twentieth century, appeared to have reached its limits in the early years of the twenty-first.

Hezbollah and Hamas were able to assert themselves against Israel thanks to Iran, which supplied them with rockets. Iran, a leader of the rejection front against Israel, had experienced a "pragmatic" period after the death of its spiritual guide, Ruhollah Khomeini, in 1989. This pragmatism had raised the hope that the Shiite Islamist regime was lessening its policy of eradicating what it viewed as the "satanic" Western culture of secularism, liberalism, and pop culture. But the reformers were timid, and the still powerful clerics systematically undermined attempts at democratic and cultural reforms.

Any remaining hopes for reform were dashed when Mahmoud Ahmadinejad (b. 1956) [Ah-ma-DEE-nay-jahd], an engineer from a modest rural background, was elected president. He renewed the anti-Western crusade and adopted a policy of populism, with subsidies for food and gas as well as cash distributed by the suitcase on his cross-country trips. Most importantly, under his leadership, the Revolutionary Guard became not only the most effective military organization but, by investing in a wide variety of businesses, also a huge patronage machine. The precipitous decline of revenues from oil exports during the recession of 2008–2011, however, seriously reduced Ahmadinejad's populist largesse. Hence, he needed the Revolutionary Guard commanders to falsify the elections of 2009 to stay in power. Food and gasoline subsidies were cut substantially, but a nuclear program begun three decades earlier continued unabated. Suspected Iranian ambitions for acquiring a nuclear bomb, coupled with North Korea's already existing nuclear arsenal, created recurrent nightmares in the world about nuclear proliferation, "dirty" nuclear material in the hands of terrorists, and the possibility of nuclear war by "rogue" nations.

Guardians of the Revolution. Female Iranian members of parliament listening to Iranian President Mahmoud Ahmadinejad as he presents his annual budget bill in February 2011. Iran follows strict gender segregation, with women required to wear the *chador*, a black cloak that covers the full body, and the *hijab*, a white headdress. Women have, however, full access to education and at present number about 60 percent of all university students.

The Ascent of Turkey   Turkey was the one Middle Eastern country to have largely escaped Islamist militancy and become one of the most dynamic newly industrialized countries in the world. It became the top producer of TV sets in Europe and began the construction of high-speed rail links as well as the world's deepest prefabricated tunnel, under the Bosporus. In contrast to other regimes in the Middle East, Turkish Muslims found access to the political process, thanks to a well established and functioning multiparty system. After many false starts and interruptions by military coups d'état, an Islamic party in 1983 not only captured the premiership of the country but simultaneously implemented bold new initiatives of economic privatization and industrial export orientation. Benefiting from these initiatives, an entire new middle class of socially conservative but economically liberal entrepreneurial businesspeople arose. In an even more effective second wave of middle-class expansion after 2003 under Prime Minister Recep Erdogan [RAY-jep Er-dow-AHN] (b. 1954), Turkey's GDP climbed to become the world's fifteenth largest. Elections in June 2011 enabled Erdogan's party to garner slightly more than half of the vote and, on the basis of this vote, begin constitutional reforms which will rescind the military's role in politics. Thus, Turkey largely completed its arrival in capitalist-democratic modernity.

The Arab Spring of 2011   Turkey was a model example for the compatibility of Islam and democracy. But in spring 2011 Tunisia and Egypt each saw constitutional-nationalist revolutions, which demonstrated that democracy can sprout in Arab countries as well. On December 17, 2010, 26-year-old Mohamed Bouazizi set himself ablaze in a last spectacular act of despair brought about by the humiliations he had suffered at the hands of a Tunisian policewoman. For months she had sought to drive him and his illegal produce cart from the streets of Sidi Bouzid in central Tunisia. In a region plagued by 30 percent unemployment, Bouazizi had become moderately successful selling his produce, which earned him enough to support the university studies of one of his sisters. But on this day he had finally had enough.

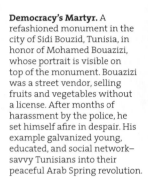

Democracy's Martyr. A refashioned monument in the city of Sidi Bouzid, Tunisia, in honor of Mohamed Bouazizi, whose portrait is visible on top of the monument. Bouazizi was a street vendor, selling fruits and vegetables without a license. After months of harassment by the police, he set himself afire in despair. His example galvanized young, educated, and social network–savvy Tunisians into their peaceful Arab Spring revolution.

Bouazizi's heartbreaking death touched off the mostly peaceful democratic revolutions dubbed the "Arab Spring," on which we centered this chapter's opening vignette. Beginning in Tunisia, they snowballed into Egypt, Libya, Bahrain, Yemen, and Syria in the course of early 2011. In Tunisia and Egypt they ousted longtime and aging autocrats, Tunisia's Zine El Abidine Ben Ali (r. 1987–2011) and Egypt's Hosni Mubarak (r. 1981–2011). After months of fighting, Libya's Muammar el-Qaddafi (r. 1969–Sep. 2011; killed October 20) was finally toppled. Autocratic rulers in countries seeing similar protests held on with iron nerves and unrestrained brutality. Central to the nonviolent daily rallies in Tunisia and Egypt, continuing for days and weeks, were demands for freedom, equality, fair elections, the end of corruption (especially crony capitalism), new democratic constitutions, the rule of law, and, last but not least, jobs.

The demonstrators, for the most part young, Internet-savvy, educated, and fully conversant with international youth culture, documented the events through pictures, videos, and blogs and revealed police violence for the world to instantly see. Social connectedness and the direct transmission of facts on the ground gave these constitutional revolutions a new character. Now a world public watching these events could declare solidarity with the demonstrators and demand action from its own politicians. As these democratic revolutions were beginning to be implemented, they raised the question of how closely the young demonstrators were integrated with the rest of the population—Islamists as well as the poor urban and rural traditional Muslims—to make constitutional and economic reforms meaningful for them as well (see Map 31.5).

The New Middle Class in India The rise of a conservative Islamic middle class in Turkey had its parallel in India in the rise of a religiously conservative Hindu middle class of shopkeepers, traders, merchants, and small manufacturers who had chafed under the tyranny of the petty socialist bureaucrats from the Congress Party in the 1980s. The leading businesspeople in this middle class came from the relatively privileged commercial occupations within the Vaishya stratum of the caste system and were represented by the Indian People's Party (Bharatiya Janata Party, BJP). They demanded the dismantling of the Soviet-style state socialist system,

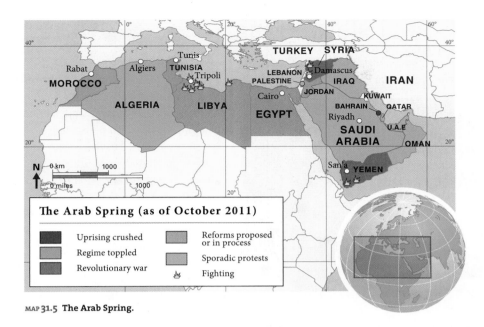

MAP **31.5 The Arab Spring.**

which had dominated India since the 1950s and had run into the same financial difficulties as the Soviet Union in the 1970s. Not surprisingly, the BJP won the 1991 elections on a platform of economic reform and globalization.

The BJP government, however, did not accomplish much. Once in power, it succumbed to its traditional supremacist-nationalist ideology of "Hinduness" (*hindutva*), which the business leaders had sought to tone down. In 1992, the BJP protected radical local hindutva organizations that whipped up a crowd of 150,000 Hindus to raze the Babri Mosque (allegedly founded in the place of a Hindu temple) in the northern Indian state of Uttar Pradesh, home to 31 million Muslims. In the predictable Muslim backlash, some 2,000 Indians died. In the elections of 1998, the BJP played down its hindutva tradition and won again, but its involvement in renewed incidents of communal violence contribtued to an alienation of the voters in 2004. The Congress Party, now also enthusiastically in favor of economic liberalization, returned to power.

The new Indian middle class—defined by a cell phone, motorized transportation, and a color TV—included anywhere between 60 and 300 million Indians, in a population of 1.2 billion in 2010. The most dynamic members of this class lived and worked in the southern heavy industry and high-tech hub of Bangalore. Because the city is 12.5 hours ahead of California, it is perfect for effecting linkages to maintain around-the-clock computing with Silicon Valley. By the second decade of the 2000s, these two leading world centers of information technology on opposite sides of the globe had become closely integrated.

The rapid expansion of urban centers, such as Bangalore, greatly contributed to the decline of the traditional caste divisions in Hinduism within the urban and even, to some degree, rural context. Since descent could be hidden in the cities, even the untouchable caste (*dalit*) began to enter the new middle class. Widespread protests in 2006 against the complex affirmative action system introduced in the 1990s in favor of less privileged social groups indicated the beginning of a dissolution of the caste divisions in the urban environment.

Patterns | Social Networking
Up Close

As we have seen, the Tunisian revolution sparked a wave of revolts across Africa and the Middle East in what has come to be called the "Arab Spring." What makes these movements unique, however, is that they were organized and carried out by means of *social networking sites* (SNSs) like Twitter, Facebook, and YouTube, supported by cell phones and other modern communication technologies. But what are the origins of these devices and how have they developed into such important tools of political and social revolution?

SNSs can ultimately be traced back to the origins of the Internet and the World Wide Web. The Internet is a product of the Cold War. Stunned by the Soviet launch of Sputnik the previous year, in 1958 President Eisenhower called for the creation of a national electronic communication network to help protect the United States from a nuclear attack launched from space. In 1969 the US government initiated the Advanced Research Projects Agency (ARPA), which created a system inking computers at major universities into a network that allowed them to share vital information. From this small, highly classified step the Internet expanded during the 1990s into a global computer network. The World Wide Web (or www) was conceived in 1989 and launched two years later as a part of the Internet. Simply put, the "web" uses the Internet to gain access to categories of data, documents, and other resources found within the larger network.

SNSs sprang up in the 1990s when it was recognized that the Internet and the World Wide Web provided social groups the means to easily communicate with each other and to share information. Among the earliest of these were Classmates.com (1995) and SixDegrees (1997), which enabled users to "network" with each other by means of shared e-mail addresses. The next step allowed users to develop personal sites from which to share information with like-minded readers. The first of these was Friendster in 2002, followed by Linked In and MySpace in 2003, You-Tube in 2004, and Facebook and Twitter by 2006. Along with a welter of personal "blogs" (from "web-logs") these sites represented a global explosion of instantaneously distributed information that revolutionized the nature of communication.

Easily the most recognizable use of SNSs to effect change relates to the recent wave of uprisings in North Africa and the Middle East. An early example of this came in Iran in 2009. Called the "Twitter Revolution," anti-government activists used the full range of SNSs while engaged in an ultimately futile effort to overthrow the Iranian regime. Following the success of the Tunisian revolution, however, an even more spectacular display of the power of SNSs erupted in Egypt on January 25, 2011, when thousands of protesters took to the streets to demand the ouster of

The Face of Revolution.
Perhaps the most novel aspect of the ongoing "Arab Spring" has been the widespread use of electronic media and Social Networking Sites (SNSs) in recruiting, organizing, and popularizing the efforts of activists in various countries. The inventiveness of the participants in avoiding government scrutiny and bypassing restrictions on SNSs by means of proxy servers and third-party connections to outside sites has become legendary. In Syria, the government lifted a ban on these sites in an attempt to stave off unrest in the wake of the successful uprisings in Tunisia and Egypt. Here a Syrian man logs into his Facebook account "legally" for perhaps the first time in February, 2011. Most observers agree, however, that such restrictions have had little effect in blocking access to the most popular SNSs.

authoritarian President Hosni Mubarak. This "Facebook Revolution," was launched by the April 6 Youth Movement, a Facebook group comprised of social and political activists. In 2011 the movement was propelled forward by Wael Ghonim, a young Google marketing executive, who set up a Facebook site to mobilize participants for a rally against harsh governmental policies. Ghonim hoped for a gathering of 50,000 protesters. When, however, over 100,000 showed up, he observed, awe-struck, that "I have never seen a revolution that was preannounced before" [NY Times, February 14, 2011]. Moreover, the Egyptian success was made possible in part by valuable lessons gleaned from SNS exchanges with anti-government coun-terparts in Tunisia. One message, for example, read: "Advice to the youth of Egypt: Put vinegar or onion under your scarf for tear gas" [Ibid.].

For all their success in facilitating uprisings against authoritarian governments, however, SNSs are used with equal effectiveness by extremist terrorist groups. Al Quaeda and the Taliban have learned to take advantage of Facebook and Twitter to broadcast their calls for global *jihad*. SNSs are also used to solicit financial sup-port and share information con_____ ____ s for forthcoming attacks. Moreover, SNS—particu__ _____ _e recruitment tools. The recent death of Anwar al-A____ _____n Laden of the Internet," especially brought into _____ _____ _Tube to inspire *jihad*. The Taliban, too, has esta____ _____s to get out its propaganda and re-cruitment m_____ _____ "Voice of Jihad" proclaims, "Wars today cann_ _____ at the heart rather than the body, [and]if the _____[blog posted by Stephanie Maier, May 15, 2_____site, "Jihadology," which recently lamented t_____ Bin Laden: "Goodbye, Oh Honor-able Shaykh_____Martyr. . . " [Ibid.].

In the or_____sites we are afforded yet another example of _____has altered the course of world history. How _____intended for exchanges among friends have _____d revolution, violence, and ter-rorism. Indeed_____ fervor initiated in Tunisia and Egypt represen_____modern Middle East; on-going revolts have sp_____hmar Gaddafi was overthrown and executed—_____, and Yemen. As one of the organizers of the Egyptian ____ _____ so presciently predicted: "Tunis is the force that pushed Egypt, but what Egypt did will be the force that will push the world" [NY Times, February 14, 2011]. And the sinews binding this force are now electronic.

Questions

- How do SNSs show how an innovation can be adapted for purposes wholly differ-ent from the original purposes for which they were intended?

- Do you believe SNSs have allowed young people around the world to make their wishes and aspirations more powerfully felt? If so, what does this say about the connection between technology and youth?

Driving Toward Prosperity.
The Bajaj scooter was the early status symbol of the emerging Indian middle class. On account of their size, the Indian and Chinese middle classes, numbering perhaps in the hundreds of millions, are a powerful group, representing a huge reservoir of ever more demanding consumers. This picture is from 2010, when the Indian middle class had come of age.

The success of the middle class in India, impressive as it is, must also be measured against conditions in the countryside, much of which is still largely outside the market economy. Almost three-quarters of the population lived in villages with poor water, electricity, and roads during the beginning of the twenty-first century. An overwhelming majority of villagers lived in extreme poverty (less than $1.25 per day), existing completely outside the market circuit and depending on handouts. Although this majority in 2010 was somewhat smaller, perhaps by one-quarter, a birth rate that refused to decline below 2.8 percent did not help much in poverty reduction. A major factor in the persistence of poverty was incomplete land reform. Landlordism and tenancy continued to encompass nearly half of the rural population. Large landholdings had been abolished after independence, but medium and small landlordism persisted undiminished. As a major voting bloc in the Congress Party, the landlords were successful in resisting further land reform.

The unproductive landlord system, providing India with little more than wheat and rice, required enormous state subsidies in seed, fertilizer, and irrigation infrastructures to keep going. These subsidies discouraged investments in a much needed agricultural diversification. The e-Choupal system by the Indian conglomerate ITC was a remarkable exception. ITC developed the system in 2000, about a decade after India had opened its borders to the world market, and used it in its strategy to counter the invading American, European, and Japanese multinationals with competitive Indian exports. Through e-Choupal, Indian soybean farmers were equipped with computers (hooked up to solar panels), through which they could follow soybean prices on the Chicago futures market as well as their nearby ITC station, selling their harvests at the latter instead of in the traditional markets, where brokers collected high fees. A decade later, e-Choupal was a highly successful venture and attracted other private firms. Collectively, its impact was still slight, but every initiative that empowers local farmers to link up with larger markets signifies a gradual improvement.

African Transformations

The half-decade between the oil price slump, debt crisis, and disappearance of communism (1985–1991) was as challenging for sub-Saharan Africa as for India. The continent's GDP in the early 1990s was down by almost half from what it was in 1975 when all main social and economic indicators were at their peak. The decline of living conditions was particularly devastating in the health services, cut back by half in almost all countries, in spite of a steady increase in HIV/AIDS. Many countries expended more hard currency on their debt services than on education. With a doubling of the population at the absolute poverty level ($1.25 per day), sub-Saharan Africa became by far the poorest region in the world.

During this time, the urban population of sub-Saharan Africa increased to almost one-third of the total population, making it more numerous than in India but still smaller than in China, where nearly half of the population was urban. This urbanization process was an important factor in the political consequences of the crisis: Students, civil servants, and journalists became restless and demanded political reforms. Up until the early 1990s, almost everywhere state structures were patronage hierarchies: the civilian or military rulers in power provided cushy government jobs for the ethnic groups from which they hailed. Although all 54 African countries were officially "nations" with seats in the United Nations, none (except South Africa) was either a functionally constitutional or ethnically uniform nation. Urban dwellers, however, were less tied to ethnicity and more committed to constitutionalism. They felt little sympathy for autocratic rulers and their kin running the states into financial ruin and pushed for democratic reforms in the late 1990s and early 2000s.

Freedom, Justice, and Dignity. The end of apartheid in 1994 and the election of Nelson Mandela, seen here visiting his former prison cell, was an inspiring event in Africa and the world. South Africa is the richest and most industrialized country of Africa, with large mineral and agricultural resources. Nearly 80 percent of the population is black, speaking its own languages isiZulu and isiKhosa, but Afrikaans (a Dutch-originated language) remained the dominant media language, with English being only the fifth most spoken language. In spite of South Africa's relative wealth, years of apartheid have resulted in vast income disparities.

Unfortunately, the push for reforms had mixed results. On the one hand, while a majority of rulers in power prior to 1991 had exited office as a result of coups or assassinations, after 1991 they either resigned voluntarily or stepped down after losing elections. On the other hand, incumbents still won more often than not and honest elections were rare. Some regime changes were truly thrilling, notably the end of apartheid and the election of Nelson Mandela (b. 1918, president 1994–1999) in the Republic of South Africa; two cycles (2004 and 2008) of clean multiparty elections in Ghana; the first election of a female president, the Harvard-trained economist Ellen Johnson Sirleaf (b. 1938, in office beginning 2006) in Liberia; and the relatively clean Nigerian presidential elections of 2007 and 2011. African adherence to constitutional politics so painfully fraught in the past was now definitely coming of age.

Ethnic and Constitutional Nationalism   Unfortunately, the beginning of movement away from ethnic nationalism to broader constitutional nationalism was offset by plenty of violence and state instability. The Rwandan Tutsi genocide of 1994 continued on a lower but equally vicious scale in the neighboring Democratic Republic of Congo. This country suffered not only a new military revolution in 1997 but unending military challenges and lootings of mineral resources ever since. Successful coups d'état occurred in no less than eight African countries during the two decades between 1991 and 2010.

A particularly sad case was the political and economic implosion of Zimbabwe, following the expropriation of white farmers in 2000. Here, President Robert Mugabe (b. 1924), in power since overthrowing the white minority regime of Rhodesia (1980), became impatient with the slow process of legal land reform. Mugabe inherited a state whose tiny minority of white farmers controlled 70 percent of all farmland and whose highly productive, modern farms grew most of Zimbabwe's agricultural exports of coffee, tea, and tobacco. In 2000 Mugabe encouraged

A Black American Confronts Africa

"How can anyone talk about democracy and constitutions and the rule of law in places where paramilitary security forces firebomb the offices of opposition newspapers? Where entire villages get burned down and thousands of people are made homeless by competing political loyalties? Where whole chunks of countries are under the sway of armed guerrillas? And where traditional belief runs so deep that a politician can be arrested and charged with casting magic spells over poor villagers to force them to vote for him?"

—Keith B. Richburg. *Out of America: A Black Man Confronts Africa*, pp. 226–227. New York: Basic Books, 1997.

his followers to seize the vast majority of white farms in a violent occupation movement, with the effect that commercial agriculture broke down, the economy collapsed, and hyperinflation ravaged the country. The overall situation in Zimbabwe became so desperate that Mugabe was forced to accept his despised rival Morgan Tsvangirai (b. 1952) as prime minister in 2009 and return to a semblance of constitutionalism. Since then, the economy has begun to improve, with small-plot farmers producing beyond self-sufficiency again, even if overall production was still only one-third of what it was in 2000.

Another example was the corrupt election of 2007 in Kenya, resulting in 1,000 deaths during riots among ethnic groups. When order was reestablished, the two top opponents, incumbent President Mwai Kibaki (b. 1931) and challenger Raila Odinga (b. 1945), came together in a grudging compromise of shared power between them, the former filling the position as president and the latter in the newly created but constitutionally unsanctioned position of prime minister. Odinga, successful in transcending ethnic affiliation for a constitutionalist-nationalist presidential bid, had been widely seen as the winner; and the unrest after the fraud-ridden elections was a regrettable relapse into ethnic nationalism. To repair constitutionalism, it was necessary to make the prime-ministerial arrangement legal, a necessity which was incorporated into a wider constitutional reform. Accordingly, Kenyans adopted a new constitution in 2010, which created a senate in addition to the existing parliament and devolved power from the center to the counties while reverting to a pure presidential system. Endemic corruption, however, continued to accompany the efforts to return to stability (see Map 31.6).

In Ivory Coast, elections in 2010 similarly ended initially in an impasse. President-elect Alassane Ouattara (b. 1942) was able to take office only after a 5-month hiatus (November 2010–April 2011), during which his supporters attempted to depose his defeated predecessor, Laurent Gbagbo (b. 1945) [BAG-bow]. Gbagbo had refused to step down even though the electoral commission had declared Ouattara the winner. The one encouraging note in this continuing cycle of power grabs in the first decade of the 2000s was that there were "only" half as many illegal office seizures in Africa as in 1970–1991. Still, authoritarianism and military rule continued to endure.

Economic Recovery   Similarly spotty was the economic recovery, although it picked up in the early 2000s, mostly because of rising commodity prices. The main oil exporters (Nigeria, Angola, Chad, Sudan, Gabon, Cameroon, Equatorial New Guinea, and the two Republics of Congo) benefited from higher oil prices, as did the mining countries of South Africa, Zambia, both Congos, and Malawi with their diamonds, gold, copper, silver, zinc, lead, and rare metals. In a United Nations–sponsored scheme in 1998, "blood diamonds" mined to finance civil wars, as in Angola, Sierra Leone, Liberia, Ivory Coast, and both Congos, were subjected to certification so as to prevent future wars. (Diamonds mined in Zimbabwe were exempted since Zimbabwe's disintegration into a failed state was not considered to be the effect of a civil

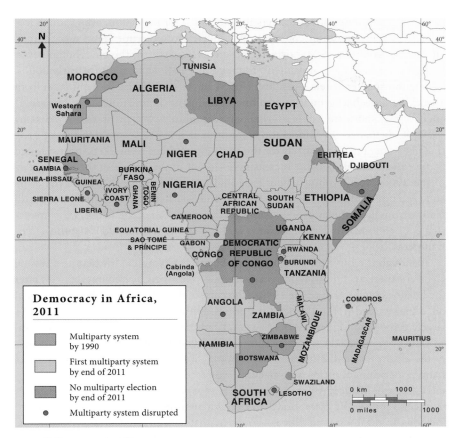

MAP 31.6 **Democracy in Africa, 2011.**

war.) Apart from minerals, agricultural products, such as coffee, cotton, and fresh flowers for the European market, also regained significance in the early 2000s. The recession of 1990–2011 did not have a major impact, largely because of the arrival of China on the scene as a major buyer and investor. Optimism about a sustained recovery and modernity within reach was clearly visible on the continent.

Latin American Expansion   Elections after the scare of the financial meltdowns in the freewheeling 1990s produced more fiscally restrained, socially engaged governments in the large Latin American countries during the early 2000s. Orderly democratic transitions in Mexico, Brazil, Argentina, and Chile (the latter three with socially oriented governments) demonstrated that the unhappy years of military dictatorships in the 1980s had been left behind. In Mexico the long rule of the Institutional Revolutionary Party came to an end in 2000, with an orderly transition to less socially engaged Christian Democratic presidents in the following two elections. Either way, however, the continent enjoyed a sustained economic recovery.

Two extraconstitutional events in smaller Latin American countries, however, demonstrated that authoritarian temptations still survived. The first was an abortive uprising in 2002 of army units in Paraguay, allegedly instigated by a former commander outside the country and wanted for an earlier coup attempt. The second, in Honduras in 2009, was the forcible removal of the president, who intended to hold a referendum on his unconstitutional plan for reelection, even though forbidden by the Honduran constitutional court. More disruptive were continued efforts by revolutionary Marxists in Colombia to overthrow the government, even though their liberation movement, founded in 1964, declined in the early 2000s. In neighboring Venezuela, President Hugo Chávez (b. 1954), a former officer from a working-class background, was alone in mainland Latin America in his adherence to state socialism, encountering periodic middle-class resistance. Mexico, by contrast, deepened its democratic commitment but was severely tested by drug traffickers, organized as cartels for the shipping of drugs to markets in the United States. These cartels became increasingly violent in the course of the first decade of the 2000s, to the point where they infiltrated the police as well as the army and even interfered with elections. Central and South American governments, still reeling from the population explosion of the second half of the 1900s, were not yet rich enough to pay their civil servants well so that the latter could resist the narco-traffickers' bribes.

Although the business of drugs was a blight in Colombia, Mexico, and several Central American countries, the mainstream economy recovered impressively after the financial meltdowns of the 1990s. The countries continued to rely on exports of oil, minerals, and tropical agricultural goods. But industrialization, until the 1990s largely through foreign investments, stimulated state-run firms to become competitive and even private. In some cases, as with Brazilian Embraer commercial airplanes or the electronics and information technology industry of Guadalajara in Mexico, Latin American countries have become world competitors. All four large economies—Brazil, Mexico, Argentina, and Chile—exported more manufactured goods than commodities by 2008. Brazil, in fact, is a member of the "BRIC"—which also includes Russia, India, and China—countries that have attained advanced economic development since the 1990s. As increasingly important trade partners with China and India, these countries clearly demonstrated the features of scientific–industrial modernity by the second decade of the 2000s.

The Environmental Limits of Modernity

What we have defined in the last two parts of this book as *modernity*—the political systems marked by constitutional nationalism and ethnic nationalism and the economic systems propelled by science and industrialism—has now become not simply a regional or "Western" phenomenon but a global one. In the absence of the competing subpatterns of modernity—communism and supremacist nationalism—the systems of capitalism, consumerism, and democracy characterized by the United States, Canada, and Western Europe have increasingly become the ones to emulate. All new nations in the world either are industrializing or want to do so if they have the financial means. The principal obstacle for these nations is the debilitating poverty of the great majority of their inhabitants, who are still mired in either subsistence farming or marginal work in the shantytowns of sprawling cities. The poorest are unskilled and uneducated and, because of high infant mortality rates and the need for farm labor, still view large families as a necessity. Improved public health care is helping to raise life spans for the poorest people, but the combination of modern medicine and the desire for large families has caused a startling increase in the world population since the middle of the twentieth century (see Map 31.7).

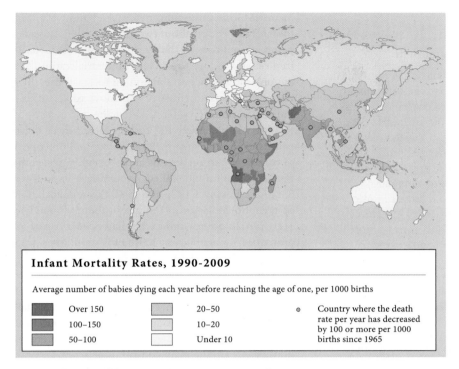

MAP **31.7** **Infant Mortality Rates, 1990–2009.**

Demography and Job Creation   Even though the demographic increase is beginning to slow, there is no question that for the foreseeable future the manufacturing and service sectors of modern industry will not be able to offer enough employment to increase the affluence of the poor and significantly raise their rates of consumption. **Consumerism**, however, is what drives the economics of scientific–industrial modernity; thus, we are dealing with a vicious circle: Without consumers, industry cannot offer sufficient numbers of jobs and the poor cannot become consumers because they are jobless.

As with all vicious circles, this can be overcome only through gradual transformation on both sides of the equation: Scientists, industrialists, and businesspeople have to be innovative and offer new consumer products requiring new jobs; and the poor, through enhanced access to education, need to acquire the resources to motivate them to find their way into modernity. So far, this gradualism appears to be working, albeit slowly. Perhaps the most striking example is the victorious march of the cell phone across the world. In 2010 the world population reached 6.9 billion, the number of cell phones was 5 billion, and the number of computers was close to 1 billion. The e-Choupal example in India is still a drop in the bucket, but it demonstrates how electronics, the most recent industrial innovation, are beginning to make a difference.

Sustainability and Global Warming   The critical factor in this gradualism is modernity's long-term environmental sustainability. In 1800, there was only one country (Great Britain) embarking on industrialization; by 1918, there were about a dozen countries (Europe and Japan); and by 1945, about three dozen

Consumerism: The acquired habit to shop for goods and gadgets (often with built-in obsolescence) beyond the basic needs of food and shelter.

Pope John Paul II on Consumerism

"The historical experience of the West, for its part, shows that even if the Marxist analysis and its foundation of alienation are false, nevertheless alienation—and the loss of the authentic meaning of life—is a reality in Western societies too. This happens in consumerism, when people are ensnared in a web of false and superficial gratifications rather than being helped to experience their personhood in an authentic and concrete way. Alienation is found also in work, when it is organized so as to ensure maximum returns and profits with no concern whether the worker, through his own labor, grows or diminishes as a person, either through increased sharing in a genuinely supportive community or through increased isolation in a maze of relationships marked by destructive competitiveness and estrangement, in which he is considered only a means and not an end."

—Pope John Paul II. "On the Hundredth Anniversary of Rerum Novarum: Centesimus Annus." Encyclical letter of May 1, 1991. Washington, DC: Office for Publishing and Promotion Services, United States Catholic Conference, 1991.

countries (on three continents) had industrialized themselves. Today, about two-thirds of the 194 independent countries of the world are either industrialized or on the way toward full industrialization. We are only now, however, beginning to grasp the environmental consequences of this move to scientific–industrial modernity. Until about the last quarter of the twentieth century the carbon footprint of these countries had risen from 280 parts per million (ppm) of volume of carbon dioxide and other chemical compounds—commonly called "greenhouse gases"—to 330 ppm. Between 1975 and 2010 the concentration of greenhouse gases in the atmosphere climbed to 380 ppm. In other words, what had been a rise of 50 ppm in 175 years became a rise of 70 ppm in only 35 years (see Figure 31.1).

While there has been considerable debate over the last several decades on the nature and degree of global warming—whether it is a natural cyclical phenomenon or human-produced or even if it exists at all—there is a general scientific consensus that greenhouse gases are the main contributors to temperature increases on earth. Scientists generally assume that at current rates of greenhouse gas production the earth will reach a "tipping point" of 450 ppm that will have catastrophic consequences for the planet's climate before the middle of this century.

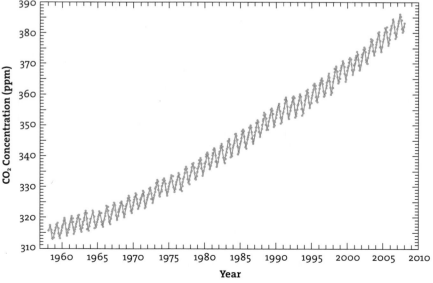

Mauna Loa Observatory, Hawaii
Monthly Average Carbon Dioxide Concentration
Data from Scripps CO_2 Program

Figure 31.1 Greenhouse Gas Emissions Since 1950.

What will happen when this tipping point is reached? If projections hold true, the polar ice caps and high mountain glaciers will have melted. Ocean levels, rising from the melted ice, will have submerged many islands and made inroads on the coasts of all continents. Widespread droughts and violent storms will regularly pound various parts of the earth, eroding by wind and flood what in many places had shortly before been fertile land. The world's tropical forests, already considerably reduced from timber harvesting and agricultural expansion, may well be wiped out, removing the most important agents for cleaning the atmosphere of greenhouse gases. Pollution and overfishing threaten the world's oceans and marine life. The consequence of these grim developments will likely be a severe reduction of the earth's arable land and fisheries needed for the production of food. In addition, biodiversity will be dramatically reduced, further decreasing food supplies (see Map 31.8).

The ultimate outcome of this prospective climate transformation will be much worse for the new countries with less wealth to cushion them than for the older ones that industrialized early and have the resources to adjust. The crushing irony of such projections, therefore, is that the nations which viewed their adaptation to modernity as their salvation may well find themselves among the condemned.

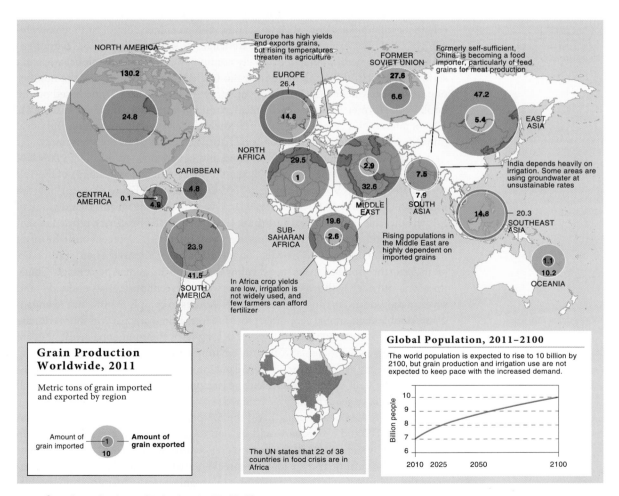

MAP 31.8 **Grain Production and Irrigation Use Worldwide, 2011.**

A Smoggy Future. China, the world's worst emitter of greenhouse gases, has large numbers of coal-fed power plants and factories which continue to belch carbon dioxide as well as toxic substances into the air, with little scrubbing or other devices to clean the emissions before they reach the atmosphere. Here, a power plant on the outskirts of Linfen in Shanxi Province southwest of Beijing fouls the environment in 2009.

Scientific and Political Debate   There is a general consensus among scientists that the warming trend in the world from greenhouse gases is real. Very few scientists still hold a skeptical view—though the prominent physicist Freeman Dyson (b. 1923), for example, remains a trenchant critic and advocate of technological fixes. The general public is gradually coming around to taking global warming seriously, though in Europe more than the United States. To judge by the number of people who watched the 2006 documentary *An Inconvenient Truth*, based on the book by the former American vice president and presidential candidate Al Gore (b. 1948), interest and agreement may have reached their own tipping point. But vocal minorities still vociferously denounce climate warming as a hoax or conspiracy.

So far, political response has been tepid and largely divided. Although two UN conferences have convened since 1992 and the environmental agreements of the 169 participating nations became binding in 2005 in the so-called Kyoto Protocol, only the European Union was on track to meet its provision mandating an annual reduction of 5.2 percent. The United States, during the George W. Bush presidency, refused to sign on to Kyoto and increased its emissions every year by about 1.5 percent until the onset of the recession in late 2007. Sweden, on the other hand, imposed a hefty carbon tax on its industries and has so far stayed below the critical 5.2 annual percentage. China, the worst offender with over half of all the world's greenhouse gases emitted—and seven of the world's ten most polluted cities—refuses to comply in order not to endanger its double-digit annual economic growth. Here, as in many parts of the world, the political risks of curtailing growth in favor of long-term environmental investment are seen as increasingly problematic. But the environmental risks associated with staying the course—such as drilling for oil—were put into stark relief in 2010 when a massive oil spill in the Gulf of Mexico wreaked catastrophic environmental damage, the full effects which have yet to be fully ascertained.

At present, the consensus is that if the 5.2 percent reduction rate were to continue after 2012 and everyone would sign on to reduction, the eventual decline in temperature by the middle of the twenty-first century would be 0.2 degree Fahrenheit below the current average temperature. Whether this would be sufficient to reverse the melting of polar ice and the onset of irregular weather patterns is debatable.

But if present trends continue, the projected temperature increase in 2050 will be more likely in the range of 3–4 degrees Fahrenheit—enough for the projections to indicate the catastrophic consequences we have mentioned, which are widely agreed to be irreversible.

Thus, global warming and its relationship to greenhouse gas emissions remains at present a problem in which some agreement has been achieved as to ends but very little as to means. Its relative imperceptibility makes it difficult to stir people to decisive action on a mass scale. Recessions and economic vitality, the demands of growth, and, at the most basic level, whether one has a job or not—these are all much more immediate problems than small temperature increases or even a few more droughts, storms, and floods, which always seem to hit others and not ourselves. It does seem safe to say, however, that the relationship of all aspects of the patterns of modernity to the environment will be a central problem of the coming decades.

Putting It All Together

The first decade of the twenty-first century witnessed the final transformation of the world from a centuries-old agrarian–urban pattern of life to a new scientific–industrial pattern. All of this was accomplished in the breathtakingly short span of 200 years. What had begun as a culturally specific, western European–pioneered transition, first from descriptive to mathematical science and then from agriculture to industry, had become ubiquitous. Everywhere in the world people have been adapting to a new role as individuals with well-defined "human rights," who aspire to be educated, find fulfilling jobs, become consumers, and achieve a materially secure life—in short, they are becoming *modern*.

The twentieth century also saw the original pattern of modernity split into three. World War I was a cataclysm that produced proponents of a first modernity, who sought to create competitive, capitalist, democratic societies; a second modernity, which sought to collapse power hierarchies and differences of wealth through equality in socialist-communist societies; and a third modernity, in which supremacist-nationalist societies sought to impose the will of allegedly superior races or ethnic groups through conquest (if not complete elimination) of inferior ones. Tremendous suffering and destruction accompanied the struggle among the proponents of these visions of modernity, and in a gradual process of elimination, it was the messiest and most unruly of the three forms of modernity—capitalist democracy—that survived.

Today, the faith in democracy that marked the exuberant beginnings of modernity at the end of the eighteenth century appears to be just as vigorous and unbounded in places far outside its birthplace. People—young, poor, educated, ambitious—continued to be its martyrs (Tiananmen Square, 1989; Tehran, 2009; Arab, Spring 2011) as well as its proud and triumphant flag bearers (Tunisia and Egypt, 2011).

Faith in the future of the environment at this point is a good deal more subdued, however. Here, the devil's bargain of materialism that accompanied the evolution of

---

Rooted in the Earth

"Yes, the only real hope of people today is probably a renewal of our certainty that we are rooted in the earth and, at the same time, the cosmos. This awareness endows us with the capacity for self-transcendence. Politicians at international forums may reiterate a thousand times that the basis of the new world order must be universal respect for human rights, but it will mean nothing as long as this imperative does not derive from the respect of the miracle of Being, the miracle of the universe, the miracle of nature, the miracle of our own existence. Only someone who submits to the authority of the universal order and of creation, who values the right to be a part of it and a participant in it, can genuinely value himself and his neighbors, and thus honor their rights as well."

—Vaclav Havel. "The Need for Transcendence in the Postmodern World." *The Futurist*, July–August 1995.

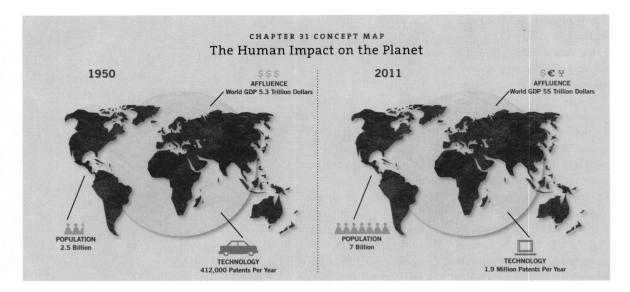

CHAPTER 31 CONCEPT MAP
The Human Impact on the Planet

1950

AFFLUENCE
World GDP 5.3 Trillion Dollars

POPULATION
2.5 Billion

TECHNOLOGY
412,000 Patents Per Year

2011

AFFLUENCE
World GDP 55 Trillion Dollars

POPULATION
7 Billion

TECHNOLOGY
1.9 Million Patents Per Year

modernity continues to haunt us: On the one hand, it gave us the human right to a decent existence in material security; on the other hand, the means of achieving that security through exploitation of the earth's material resources has given us the nightmare prospect of an irreversibly changed nature that may allow for fewer and fewer of the comforts we currently enjoy (see Concept Map). The pattern of modernity and the scientific–industrial society that supports it will no doubt continue, but its future shape will be just as unknowable to us as the patterns of society in the past were to those living through them.

Review and Respond

1. What is the dollar regime? Explain its function in the world.

2. Discuss the two basic principles of the American military posture in the world since 1992.

3. What is IT? How has it transformed cultural interactions? Economic activity?

4. Which countries remained communist after 1991 and in which form?

5. What is globalization? Do the benefits of globalization outweigh its drawbacks? Are the effects of globalization the same throughout the world?

6. Explain the connection in the pattern of modernity between industrialization and consumerism.

7. Is the future of the world environment a grave problem, and if yes, why? Can a balance between the desire to preserve the environment and the need to save jobs be achieved?

▶ For additional resources, including maps, primary sources, visuals, and quizzes, please go to www.oup.com/us/vonsivers. Please see the Further Resources section at the back of the book for additional readings and suggested websites.

Thinking Through Patterns

▶ **How did the United States acquire its dominant economic position toward the end of the twentieth century? How did it accelerate the process of globalization?**

The United States acquired its dominant economic position through the dollar regime and by becoming the sinkhole for industrial exports from developing countries. In compensation for the latter, it expanded the reach of its financial system worldwide. The result was the globalization of the world economy.

Capitalist democracy became the universal model of modernity in part because growing middle classes in cities demanded liberalized markets where they could develop personal initiative and accumulate capital for business ventures. Socially conservative new middle classes became the engines that powered more than half a dozen successful industrialization processes throughout Asia, Latin America, and Africa.

▶ **What made capitalist democracy so attractive toward the end of the twentieth century that it became a generic model for many governments around the world to strive for?**

▶ **Which policies did China and India pursue so that they became the fastest industrializing countries in the early twenty-first century?**

China and India accelerated their industrialization by systematically encouraging the expansion of their middle classes as the engines of investment and innovation. China, however, did not allow the development of a multiparty system, fearing the chaos of popular agitation. India, by contrast, possessed constitutional-nationalist traditions reaching back to the nineteenth century that contained constraints against populism and allowed for peaceful democratic competition.

Perhaps more than any other innovation in the last 20 years, or even the last 200 years, the communications revolution has reshaped the way humans interact with each other. The exponential growth of networking boggles the mind. In 2006, 50 billion e-mails were sent. Just 4 years later, that number had risen to 300 billion. Because of this connectedness, politics, culture, and economic activity now mutate more rapidly--and with more volatility--than ever before.

▶ **How have information technology and social networking altered cultural, political, and economic interactions around the world?**

▶ **What is global warming, and why is it a source of grave concern for the future?**

Global warming is caused by the increase of carbon dioxide and other gases that accumulate in the upper atmosphere and trap the sun's heat in the lower atmosphere. Warming and cooling trends have occurred periodically since the end of the last Ice Age, and for a long time scientists labored to distinguish clearly between a temporary trend toward warmer temperatures and a permanent, greenhouse gas–caused trend toward a catastrophic tipping point that will permanently alter nature as we know it. Today, there is an overwhelming scientific consensus concerning the reality of global warming. But politicians and the general public are not yet entirely convinced that the efforts begun with the Kyoto Protocol of 2005 should be decisively intensified.

Further Resources

Chapter 1

Burroughs, William J. *Climate Change in Prehistory: The End of the Reign of Chaos*. Cambridge: Cambridge University Press, 2005. Very well-researched and up-to-date discussion of climate and human evolution.

Conard, Nicholas J. "Cultural Modernity: Consensus or Conundrum?" *Proceedings of the National Academy of Sciences of the United States of America* 107, no. 17 (2010): 6721–6722, http://www.pnas.org/content/107/17/7621.full. Thoughtful critique, with references, of the out-of-Africa hypothesis of anatomically and culturally modern humans by the archaeologist of Vogelherd in southwestern Germany.

Flood, Josephine. *Archaeology of the Dreamtime: The Story of Prehistoric Australia and Its People*. New Haven, CT: Yale University Press, 1989. Overview of the Australian archaeological record; short on discussion of Aboriginal Dreamtime and myths.

Johanson, Donald, and Kate Wong. *Lucy: The Quest for Human Origins*. New York: Three Rivers, 2009.

McBrearty, Sally, and Allison S. Brooks. "The Revolution that Wasn't: A New Interpretation of the Origin of Modern Human Behavior." *Journal of Human Evolution* 39 (2000): 453–463. Crucial, pioneering article in which the authors grounded anatomically and intellectually fully evolved H. sapiens in Africa.

Stringer, Chris, and Peter Andrews. *The Complete World of Human Evolution*. London: Thames and Hudson, 2005. Clearly organized and richly illustrated summary.

WEBSITES

http://iho.asu.edu/. Arizona State University, Institute of Human Origins, runs the popular but scholarly well-founded website Becoming Human (http://www.becominghuman.org/).

http://www.bradshawfoundation.com/. The Bradshaw Foundation has a large website on human evolution and rock art, with many images, and a link to Stephen Oppenheimer's, *The Journey of Mankind—The Peopling of the World*, an important overview of *Homo sapiens'* migrations.

Chapter 2

Assmann, Jan. *The Search for God in Ancient Egypt*. Ithaca, NY: Cornell University Press, 2001. Reflective investigation of the dimensions of Egyptian polytheism by a leading Egyptologist.

Bottéro, Jean. *Mesopotamia: Writing, Reasoning, and the Gods*. Chicago: University of Chicago Press, 1992. Classic intellectual history of ancient Mesopotamia.

Drews, Robert. *The End of the Bronze Age: Changes in Warfare and the Catastrophe ca. 1200 B.C.* Princeton, NJ: Princeton University Press, 1993. Closely argued essay on the destruction of Mycenaean culture and its consequences for the eastern Mediterranean.

Finkelstein, Israel. *The Archaeology of the Israelite Settlement*. Jerusalem: Israel Exploration Society, 1988. Authoritative presentation of the archaeology of the earliest period of Israelite social formation.

Kuhrt, Amélie. *The Ancient Near East, c. 3000–330 BCE*, 2 vols. London: Routledge, 1994. Comprehensive handbook surveying all regions of the Middle East.

Mithen, Steven. *After the Ice: A Global Human History, 20,000–5000 B.C.* Cambridge, MA: Harvard University Press, 2003. Engagingly written story of humans settling, becoming farmers, and founding villages and towns, as seen through the eyes of a modern time traveler.

Van de Mieroop, Marc. *The Ancient Mesopotamian City*. Oxford: Clarendon Press, 1997. Full examination of Mesopotamian urban institutions, including city assemblies.

WEBSITES

http://mesopotamia.lib.uchicago.edu/. "Ancient Mesopotamia," Website of the Oriental Institute, University of Chicago. A user-friendly portal to the world-renowned Mesopotamia collection of the Oriental Institute.

http://www.ancientegypt.co.uk/menu.html. "Ancient Egypt," website of the British Museum. Pictorial introduction, with short texts.

http://www.livius.org/babylonia.html. "Livius, Articles on Ancient History." A large collection of translated texts and references to philological articles, with portals on Mesopotamia, Egypt, Anatolia, and Greece.

Chapter 3

Bryant, Edwin. *The Quest for the Origins of Vedic Culture: The Indo-Aryan Migration Debate*. Oxford: Oxford University Press, 2001. A scholarly yet readable attempt to address the linguistic and archaeological evidence surrounding the thesis of Aryan migration versus the more recent theory of indigenous Vedic development.

Embree, Ainslee T., ed. *Sources of Indian Tradition*, vol. 1, 2nd ed. New York: Columbia University Press, 1988. Though the language is dated in places, this is still the most comprehensive sourcebook of Indian thought available. Recent additions on women and gender make it even more so. Sophisticated yet readable introductions, glosses, and commentary.

Eraly, Abraham. *Gem in the Lotus: The Seeding of Indian Civilization*. London: Weidenfeld & Nicholson, 2004. Readable, comprehensive survey of recent scholarship from prehistory to the reign of Ashoka during the Mauryan dynasty of the fourth and third centuries BCE. Emphasis on transitional period of sixth-century religious innovations, particularly Buddhism.

Fairservis, Walter A. *The Roots of Ancient India. The Archaeology of Early Indian Civilization*. New York: Macmillan, 1971. Classic, well-detailed, and well-documented treatment of Indian archaeology and history to 500 BCE. Particularly well done on the so-called Vedic dark ages to 800 BCE. More useful in general for experienced students.

Kenoyer, Jonathan Mark. *Ancient Cities of the Indus Valley Civilization*. New York: Oxford University Press, 1998. Comprehensive work by team leader of Harappan Research Project. Particularly good on Lothal.

Kinsley, David R. *Hinduism. A Cultural Perspective*. Englewood Cliffs, NJ: Prentice Hall, 1993. Short, highly accessible overview of the major traditions within the constellation of belief systems called by outsiders "Hinduism." Sound treatment of the formative Vedic and Upanishadic periods.

Possehl, Gregory L., ed. *Harappan Civilization: A Recent Perspective*, 2nd ed. New Delhi: Oxford University Press, 1993. Sound and extensive treatment of recent work and issues in Indus valley archaeology by one of the leading on-site researchers and a former student of Fairservis. Used to best advantage by experienced students.

Trautmann, Thomas. *India: Brief History of a Civilization*. New York: Oxford University Press, 2011. A succinct and lucid account of 4,000 years of Indian history, with particular emphasis on early developments.

Wolpert, Stanley. *A New History of India*, 5th ed. New York: Oxford University Press, 2004. Another extremely useful, readable, one-volume history from Neolithic times to the present. Excellent first work for serious students.

WEBSITES

www.columbia.edu/cu/lweb/indiv/southasia/cuvl/history.html. Run by Columbia University, this site contains links to "WWW.Virtual Library: Indian History"; "Regnal Chronologies"; "Internet Indian History Sourcebook"; and "Medical History of British India."

http://www.harappa.com. Contains a wealth of images of artifacts and other archaeological treasures from the Indus Valley.

Chapter 4

Chang, Kwang-chih. *The Archaeology of Ancient China*, 4th ed. New Haven, CT: Yale University Press, 1986. Sophisticated treatment of archaeology of Shang China. Prime exponent of the view of overlapping periods and territories for the Sandai period. Erudite, yet accessible for experienced students.

Ebrey, Patricia Buckley, ed. *Chinese Civilization: A Sourcebook*, 2nd ed. New York: Free Press, 1993. Wonderful supplement to the preceding volume. Some different classical sources and considerable material on women and social history. Time frame of this work extends to the modern era.

Keightly, David N., ed. *The Origins of Chinese Civilization*. Berkeley: University of California Press, 1983. Symposium volume on a variety of Sandai topics by leading scholars. Some exposure to early Chinese history and archaeology is necessary in order to best appreciate these essays.

Keightly, David N., ed. *Sources of Shang History: The Oracle-Bone Inscriptions of Bronze Age China*. Berkeley: University of California Press, 1978 (2nd ed. 1985). Benchmark in the authoritative interpretation and contextualization of ritual inscriptions. Some grounding in ancient Chinese history helpful.

Lowe, Michael, and Edward L. Shaughnessy, eds. *The Cambridge History of Ancient China. From the Origins of Civilization to 221 B.C.* Cambridge: Cambridge University Press, 1999. The opening volume of the Cambridge History of China series, this is the most complete multiessay volume on all aspects of recent Chinese ancient historical and archaeological work. The place to start for the serious student contemplating in-depth research.

Schirokauer, Conrad. *A Brief History of Chinese Civilization*. New York: Harcourt, Brace Jovanovich, 1991. Readable one-volume text on Chinese history up to the present. More thorough treatment of Sandai period than is generally the case with other one-volume texts.

Thorp, Robert L. *China in the Early Bronze Age: Shang Civilization*. Philadelphia: University of Pennsylvania Press, 2006. Comprehensive yet accessible survey of recent archaeological work on the period 2070–1046 BCE, including traditional Xia and Shang periods under the heading of China's "bronze age."

Wang, Aihe. *Cosmology and Political Culture in Early China*. Cambridge: Cambridge University Press, 2000. Part of the Cambridge Studies in Chinese History, Literature, and Institutions series. Wang argues that control of *cosmology*—how the world and universe operate—was a vital key to the wielding of power among the Shang and Zhou rulers. Recommended for serious students.

Watson, Burton, trans. *The Tso Chuan. Selections from China's Oldest Narrative History*. New York: Columbia University Press, 1989. Elegant translation by one of the most prolific of scholars working today. Excellent introduction to Zhou period and politics. Appropriate for beginning students, though more useful for those with some prior introduction to the period.

WEBSITES

http://lucian.uchicago.edu/blogs/earlychina/ssec/. This is the site of the Society for the Study of Early China. The site is for scholars, and the organization also publishes its own journal, *Early China*, as well as scholarly books.

www.ancientchina.co.uk. This site provides access to the British Museum's ancient Chinese collections and is highly useful for students seeking illustrations of assorted artifacts in a user-friendly environment.

Chapter 5

The Americas

Benson, Sonia, and Deborah J. Baker. *Early Civilizations in the Americas Reference Library*. Farmington Hills, MI: Gale UXL, 2009. Extensive three-volume encyclopedia available as a download or in hard copy. Contains an almanac of historical information and one of biographies and primary sources. Recommended for beginning and experienced students.

Bruhns, Karen Olsen, and Karen E. Stothert. *Women in Ancient America*. Norman: University of Oklahoma Press, 1999. A comprehensive account of women's roles in daily life, religion, politics, and war in foraging and farming as well as urban societies in the Americas.

Burger, Richard L. *Chavín and the Origins of Andean Civilization*. London: Thames and Hudson, 1992. Though somewhat outdated with the work being done on Caral-Supé, this richly illustrated discussion of Andean civilization still has considerable import.

Fiedel, Stuart J., *Prehistory of the Americas*, 2nd ed. Cambridge: Cambridge University Press, 1992. Accessible, detailed survey of the archaeology of the Americas by a leading American scholar.

Thomas, David Hurst. *Exploring Native North America*. Oxford: Oxford University Press, 2000. Selected chapters are useful on the major early North American sites, particularly Adena and Hopewell.

Trigger, Bruce G., Wilcomb E. Washburn, Richard E. W. Adams, Murdo J. MacLeod, Frank Salomon, and Stuart B. Schwartz, eds. *Cambridge History of the Native Peoples of the Americas*, 3 vols. Cambridge: Cambridge University Press, 1996–2000. As with all of the Cambridge histories this is a highly useful set for beginner and accomplished scholar alike. Useful bibliographies with the article entries.

von Hagen, Adriana, and Craig Morris. *The Cities of the Ancient Andes*. Thames and Hudson, 1999. While more geared to later periods, still a useful overview, with illustrations, by specialists on Andean cultures.

Oceania

Bellwood, Peter S. *Man's Conquest of the Pacific: The Prehistory of Southeast Asia and Oceania*. New York: Oxford University Press, 1979. Along with Bellwood's later volume, *The Polynesians*, traces the migrations of succeeding groups through the archipelagoes of the Pacific. Balanced treatment of controversies over gradual versus episodic migrations of Lapita cultures. For advanced students.

Fagan, Brian M., ed. *The Oxford Companion to Archaeology*. New York: Oxford University Press, 1996. Perhaps the best place to start for students interested in archaeological and historical overviews of the peopling of the Pacific. Extensive coverage of Lapita culture and expansion into Micronesia and Polynesia.

Kirch, Patrick V., *The Lapita Peoples: Ancestors of the Oceanic World*. Cambridge, MA.: Blackwell, 1997. Basic introduction by one of the pioneers of Polynesian research.

WEBSITES

http://novaonline.nvcc.edu. Reputable site containing links to online lectures on subjects including "Civilizations in America," "History of the American Indians," "Mesoamerican Civilization," and "Ancient Meso-American Civilizations."

http://www.pbs.org/wayfinders/polynesian2.html. PBS series that examines the Polynesians and their migrations.

Chapter 6

Sub-Saharan Africa

Collins, Robert O., and James M. Burns. *A History of Sub-Saharan Africa*. Cambridge: Cambridge University Press, 2007. Balanced, well-informed textbook with nearly half of its pages on the pre-1450 period.

McIntosh, Roderick J. *Ancient Middle Niger: Urbanism and the Self-Organizing Landscape*. Cambridge: Cambridge University Press, 2005. Important revisionist work on the origins of urbanism and kingship in West Africa.

Vansina, Jan. *Paths in the Rainforests: Toward a History of Political Tradition in Equatorial Africa*. Madison: University of Wisconsin Press, 1990.

Magisterial presentation of the Bantu dispersal and village life in the rain forest.

Mesoamerica and the Andes

Aveni, Anthony F. *Skywatchers*, rev. ed. Austin: University of Texas Press, 2001. Classic study on astronomy and calendars of pre-Columbian Americans, including a discussion of the Nazca lines.

Evans, Susan Tobey. *Ancient Mexico and Central America: Archaeology and Culture History*. London: Thames and Hudson, 2004. Densely but clearly written and detailed, with many sidebars on special topics.

Grube, Nikolai, ed. *Maya: Divine Kings of the Rain Forest*. Cologne, Germany: Könemann, 2001. Lavishly illustrated book with short contributions by many hands.

Schele, Linda, and David Freidel. *A Forest of Kings: The Untold Story of the Ancient Maya*. New York: Quill-William Morrow, 1990. Classic study summarizing the results of the Maya glyph decipherment, by two pioneers.

WEBSITES

http://www-sul.stanford.edu/depts/ssrg/africa/history.html. Africa south of the Sahara: A large, resource-filled website based at Stanford University.

http://www.allempires.com/article/index.php?q=americas_history. Americas: World-historical site with interesting overviews of Pre-Columbian history.

http://www.wsu.edu/~dee/CIVAMRCA/MAYAS.HTM. Washington State University's comprehensive webpage for its studies on Civilizations in America, includes images and information about the Mayans, the Olmecs, the Aztecs, the Incas, and Chavin under headings such as religion, writings, economy, and society.

Chapter 7

Boatwright, Mary, Daniel J. Gargola, and Richard J. A. Talbert. *The Romans: From Village to Empire*. New York: Oxford University Press, 2004. Clearly written, comprehensive introduction to Roman history.

Boyce, Mary. *A History of Zoroastrianism*, vol. 1. *The Early Period*. Handbuch der Orientalistik, second impression, with corrections. Leiden, the Netherlands: E. J. Brill, 1989. Standard work by the leading scholar on the subject.

Briant, Pierre. *From Cyrus to Alexander: A History of the Persian Empire*. Warsaw, Poland: Eisenbrauns, 2000. Monumental work, the most detailed and authoritative study of the topic to date.

Burstein, Stanley M. "The Hellenistic Period in World History." American Historical Association Pamphlets, August 1997, http://www.historians.org/pubs/Free/BURSTEIN.HTM. Comprehensive overview of recent scholarship in Hellenistic studies.

Cameron, Averil. *The Mediterranean World in Late Antiquity, AD 395–600*. London: Routledge, 1993. New perspective on the strengths and weaknesses of the late empire.

Dignas, Beate, and Engelbert Winter. *Rome and Persia in Late Antiquity: Neighbours and Rivals*. Cambridge: Cambridge University Press, 2007. Detailed historical investigation of the rivalry between Rome and Persia.

Shaked, Shaul. *Dualism in Transformation: Varieties of Religion in Sasanian Iran*. London: School of Oriental and African Studies, 1994. Short history of the different religions in Sasanid Persia.

Smith, Mark S. *The Early History of God: Yahweh and the Other Deities in Ancient Israel*. San Francisco: Harper & Row, 1990. Very readable introduction to the problem of early monotheism among Israelites.

WEBSITES

http://www.perseus.tufts.edu/hopper/. Perseus Digital Library, probably the largest website on Greece and Rome, with immense resources, located at Tufts University.

http://darmc.harvard.edu/icb/icb.do?keyword=k40248&pageid=icb.page188868. The University of Harvard allows students to tailor searches in order to access specific geo-political and spatial cartographical representations of the Roman and medieval worlds.

http://www.ancientgreece.co.uk/menu.html. Open the door to the compelling world of Ancient Greece. The British Museum has compiled a collection of images and information on various aspects of Greek History such as the Acropolis, Athens, daily life, festivals and games, Sparta, war, and gods.

Chapter 8

Auboyer, Jeannine. *Daily Life in Ancient India*. London: Phoenix Press, 2002. Overview consisting of sections on social structures/religious principles; individual/collective existence; and royal and administrative existence. Multidisciplinary approach appropriate for most undergraduates.

Chakravarti, Uma. *The Social Dimensions of Early Buddhism*. New Delhi: Oxford University Press, 1987. Thorough analysis, with extensive glossary, of the influence of the north Indian economic transition to peasant market farming on the social milieu of early Buddhism.

Embree, Ainslee T. *Sources of Indian Tradition*, 2nd ed., 2 vols. New York: Columbia University Press, 1988. The latest edition contains a number of new selections useful for the study of social relations in addition to the older religious material. As with all of the works in this series, the level of writing is sophisticated, though accessible; the overviews are masterly; and the works are ably translated.

Keay, John. *India. A History*. New York: Grove Press, 2000. Lively, highly detailed narrative history, with a number of highly useful charts and genealogies of ruling houses. Sympathetic treatment of controversial matters.

Knott, Kim. *Hinduism: A Very Short Introduction*. New York: Oxford University Press, 1998. Sound, brief discussion of modern Hinduism and its formative influences. Asks provocative questions such as "What is a religion?" and "Is Hinduism something more than the Western conception of religion?"

Nikam, N. A., and Richard McKeon, eds. and trans. *The Edicts of Asoka*. Chicago: University of Chicago Press, 1959. Slim but useful volume for those interested in reading the entire collection of Ashoka's Pillar, Cave, and Rock Edicts. Short, accessible introduction.

Pelikan, Jaroslav, ed. *Buddhism: The Dhammapada*. Translated by John Ross Carter and Mahinda Palihawadana. Sacred Writings, vol. 6. New York: Quality Paperback Book Club, 1992. Erudite but accessible translation of one of the key texts in the Buddhist corpus. Students with some exposure to the introductory ideas of Buddhism will find it very useful in its step-by-step elucidation of a number of central concepts.

Willis, Michael. *The Archaeology of Hindu Ritual*. Cambridge: Cambridge University Press, 2009. Best utilized by experienced students, this book uses site archaeology, Sanskrit documents, and studies of ancient astronomy to plot the development of Hinduism under the Guptas and their use of it in statecraft as they created their vision of a universal empire.

Wolpert, Stanley. *A New History of India*, 6th ed. Oxford, New York: Oxford University Press, 2000. The standard introductory work to the long sweep of Indian history. Evenly divided between the period up to and including the Mughals and the modern era. Good coverage of geography, environment, as well as social and gender issues. Good select bibliography arranged by chapter; highly useful glossary of Indian terms.

WEBSITES

www.dli.ernet.in. Digital Library of India. This online resource, hosted by the Indian Institute of Science at Bangalore, contains primary and secondary sources for not only history but also culture, economics, literature, and a host of other subjects.

http://www.pbs.org/thestoryofindia/timeline/1/. Based on P.B.S.'s six part series on the history of India, this colorful website allows you to navigate your way along Ancient India's timeline.

Chapter 9

Ebrey, Patricia Buckley, ed. *Chinese Civilization: A Sourcebook*, 2nd ed. New York: Free Press, 1993. Varied primary sources with an accent on social history material: letters, diary excerpts, etc. Particularly strong on women's history sources.

Hinsch, Bret. *Women in Early Imperial China*. Lanham, MD: Rowman and Littlefield, 2002. Broad examination of the place and transition of the place of women during the crucial early Chinese dynasties.

Huang, Ray. *China: A Macro History*. Armonk, NY: M.E. Sharpe, 1997. Readable, entertaining, and highly useful one-volume history. Particularly good on the complex politics of the post-Han and Song-Yuan periods.

Lewis, Mark Edward. *The Early Chinese Empires: Qin and Han*. Cambridge, MA: Harvard University Press, 2007. Detailed exploration of the rise and adaptations of China's initial empires. Better for advanced students.

Loewe, Michael. *Everyday Life in Early Imperial China During the Han Period, 202 B.C.–A.D. 220*. New York: Harper and Row, 1968. Short, highly useful one-volume survey of Han social history by a preeminent scholar. Especially good on details of peasant and elite daily existence.

Snow, Philip. *The Star Raft: China's Encounter with Africa*. Ithaca, NY: Cornell University Press, 1988. Important, accessible study of the little known area of China's maritime trade with Africa from Han times to the epic fifteenth-century voyages of Zheng He and beyond.

WEBSITES

http://afe.easia.columbia.edu/cosmos/ort/daoism.htm. Defining "Daoism": A Complex History, looks at Daoism as a term, it's use and its practice in terms of morality, society, nature and the self.

http://www.metmuseum.org/explore/china_dawn/index.html. The journey begins with the end of the Han Empire and the arrival of the Xianbei and other Nomads. Packed with interactive features, this site has a fully indexed catalogue of artifacts, maps of historical China and the Silk Road, a chronology and glossary, and even allows you to explore ancient tombs.

http://newton.uor.edu/departments&programs/asianstudiesdept/. *East and Southeast Asia: An Annotated Directory of Internet Resources*. "China," "History." One of the most complete guides to web sites dealing with all manner of Chinese history and society.

Chapter 10

al-Khalili, Jim. *The House of Wisdom*. New York: Penguin, 2010. Elegant and accessible introduction to the golden age of Arabic science.

The Arabian Nights. Translated by Husain Haddawy. New York: Norton, 1990. Translation of the new edition by Muhsin Mahdi, which reconstitutes the original, thirteenth-century text.

Chaudhuri, K. N. *Trade and Civilization in the Indian Ocean*. Cambridge: Cambridge University Press, 1985. Discusses the historical evolution of the trade and its various aspects (sea route, ships, commodities, and capital investments).

Fryde, Edmund. *The Early Palaeologan Renaissance (1261–c. 1360)*. Leiden, the Netherlands: Brill, 2000. Detailed presentation of the main philosophical and scientific figures of Byzantium after the recovery from the Latin interruption.

Laiou, Angeliki E., and Cécile Morrisson. *The Byzantine Economy*. Cambridge: Cambridge University Press, 2007. Comprehensive and well-researched study of ups and downs in the demography, productive capacity, and long-distance trade of Byzantium.

Lapidus, Ira. *Muslim Cities in the Later Middle Ages*. Cambridge: Cambridge University Press, 1984. Seminal work and still the only study of Muslim urban society, although it should be supplemented by Shlomo D. Goitein's monumental study of Jews, *A Mediterranean Society* (1967–1988).

Rippin, Andrew. *Muslims: Their Religious Beliefs and Practices*, 2nd ed. London: Routledge, 2001. One of the best and most accessible introductions to the basic beliefs and practices in Islam, based on the reevaluation of Islamic origins also presented in this chapter.

Tyerman, Christopher. *God's War: A New History of the Crusades*. Cambridge, MA: Belknap Press, 2006. Persuasive revisionist history by a leading Crusade historian.

Whittow, Mark. *The Making of Byzantium, 600–1025*. Berkeley: California University Press, 1996. Revisionist study of the Byzantine struggle for survival in the early years.

WEBSITES

Applied History Research Group, University of Calgary. *The Islamic World to 1600*, http://www.ucalgary.ca/applied_history/tutor/islam/. A multimedia tutorial by a university research group.

University Libraries, University of Washington. "History: Middle East." http://guides.lib.washington.edu/content.php?pid=63215&sid=466019. This website is a comprehensive research guide to primary and secondary sources for Middle Eastern history.

Asia Topics in World History. http://afe.easia.columbia.edu/mongols/. With a timeline spanning 1000-1500 C.E., The Mongols in World History delivers a concise and colorful history of the Mongol's impact on global history.

Chapter 11

Bartlett, Robert. *The Making of Europe: Conquest, Colonization and Cultural Change, 950–1350*. Princeton, NJ: Princeton University Press, 1993. Analyzes the expansion of Europe from a cultural perspective.

Brown, Peter. *The Rise of Western Christendom: Triumph and Diversity, A.D. 200–1000*, 2nd ed. Oxford: Wiley-Blackwell, 2003. Traces the development of Christian Europe from the perspective of the Church.

Grant, Edward. *The Foundation of Modern Science in the Middle Ages*. Cambridge: Cambridge University Press, 1996. Seminal study of the contributions of medieval science to the scientific revolution of the seventeenth century.

Lawrence, C. H. *Medieval Monasticism: Forms of Religious Life in Western Europe in the Middle Ages*, 2nd ed. New York: Longman, 1984. Thorough survey of the development of the Western monastic tradition.

McKitterick, Rosamond. *Charlemagne: The Formation of a European Identity*. Cambridge: Cambridge University Press, 2008. An examination of how Charlemagne's policies contributed to the idea of Europe.

Platt, Colin. *King Death: The Black Death and Its Aftermath in Late-Medieval England*. Toronto: University of Toronto Press, 1997. Riveting analysis of the effects of the Black Death on all aspects of society.

Reynolds, Susan. *Fiefs and Vassals: The Medieval Evidence Reinterpreted*. Oxford: Oxford University Press, 1994. Important revisionist study of medieval feudal institutions.

Riley-Smith, Jonathan, ed. *The Oxford Illustrated History of the Crusades*. New York: Oxford University Press, 1995. A very useful and readable history of the crusading movement.

WEBSITES

http://www.bc.edu/bc_org/avp/cas/fnart/arch/gothic_arch.html. Boston College's Digital Archive of Architecture has a quick index reference guide, which opens up links to images from both early and high Gothic architecture.

http://www.bl.uk/treasures/magnacarta/virtual_curator/vc9.html. An excellent website that makes available a digitized version of the Magna Carta. Audio files answer many FAQ's about the manuscript and its significance.

Chapter 12

DeBary, William T., ed. *Sources of Chinese Tradition*, vol. 1. New York: Columbia University Press, 1960. Excellent introduction to major Chinese philosophical schools. Extensive coverage of Buddhism and Neo-Confucianism with accessible, highly informative introductions to the documents themselves.

Ebrey, Patricia Buckley, ed. *Chinese Civilization: A Sourcebook*, 2nd ed. New York: Free Press, 1993. More varied than DeBary with more social history material: letters, diary excerpts, etc. Particularly strong on women's history sources.

Ebrey, Patricia Buckley, ed. *The Inner Quarters*. Berkeley and Los Angeles: University of California Press, 1993. Perhaps the best scholarly exploration of the roles of women in Song China.

Hansen, Valerie. *The Open Empire: A History of China to 1600*. New York: W. W. Norton, 2000. A fresh and accessible synthesis of pre-modern Chinese history.

Levathes, Louise. *When China Ruled the Seas*. London: Oxford University Press, 1994. Delightful coverage of the voyages of Zheng He from 1405 to 1433. Particularly good on the aftermath of the voyages.

Mujeeb, M. *The Indian Muslims*. London: Allen Unwin, 1967. Thorough historical overview from the eighth century to the twentieth. Especially useful on political and administrative systems of the early and middle periods of Muslim hegemony in north India.

Singh, Patwant. *The Sikhs*. London: John Murray, 1999. Readable popular history of the Sikh experience to the present by an adherent. Especially useful on the years from Guru Nanak to the changes of the early eighteenth century and the transition to a more militant faith.

WEBSITES

http://ngm.nationalgeographic.com/ngm/data/2001/07/01/sights_n_sounds/media.2.2.html. National Geographic traces the journey of Marco Polo from Venice to China to the court of Kublai Khan and back home to his arrest in Genoa.

www.afe.eastasia.columbia.edu. Part of Columbia University's websites on Asia for educators, this segment deals with basic information on China's golden age, 600–1600. Helpful to beginning students and teachers.

Chapter 13

General

Mann, Susan. *East Asia (China, Korea, Japan)*. Washington, DC: American Historical Association, 1999. The second volume in the Women's and Gender History in Global Perspective series. Short, informative volume with historiographic overviews and cross-cultural comparisons among the three title countries. Critical annotated bibliographies on the use of standard texts in integrating women and gender into Asian studies.

Murphey, Rhoads. *East Asia. A New History*. New York: Longman, 1997. One of the few one-volume histories that includes material on China, Japan, Korea, Vietnam, and southeast Asia. Written by a leading scholar of modern China and east Asia. Appropriate for beginning students but more useful for those with some background on the area.

Ramusack, Barbara N., and Sharon Sievers. *Women in Asia*. Bloomington: Indiana University Press, 1999. Part of the series Restoring Women to History. Far-ranging book divided into parts on "Women in South and Southeast Asia" and "Women in East Asia." Coverage of individual countries, extensive chronologies, valuable bibliographies. Most useful for advanced undergraduates.

Korea

DeBary, William T., ed. *Sources of Korean Tradition*, vol. 1. New York: Columbia University Press, 1997. The latest in the renowned Columbia series on the great traditions of east Asia. Perhaps the most complete body of accessible sources for undergraduates.

Korean Overseas Information Service. *A Handbook of Korea*. Seoul: KOIS, 1993. Wonderfully complete history, geography, guidebook, and sociology text. Excellent source, but students should keep in mind its provenance and treat some of its historical claims to uniqueness accordingly.

Japan

DeBary, William T., ed. *Sources of Japanese Tradition*, vol. 1. New York: Columbia University Press, 2002. Like the volume above on Korea, and the others of this series on India and China, the sources are well selected, the glossaries are sound, and the overviews of the material are masterful. As with the other east Asia volumes, the complexities of the various Buddhist schools are especially well drawn. As with the others in the series, students with some previous experience will derive the most benefit from this volume.

Reischauer, Edwin O., and Albert Craig. *Japan. Tradition and Transformation*. Boston: Houghton Mifflin, 1989, and subsequent editions. The companion volume to J. K. Fairbank's *China*, by the leading American scholar of and former US ambassador to Japan. A one-volume history but more emphasis on the more ancient periods.

Totman, Conrad. *A History of Japan*. Oxford: Blackwell, 2000. One of Blackwell's History of the World series. A larger, more balanced, and comprehensive history than the Reischauer volume. More than half of the material is on the pre-1867 period, with extensive coverage of social history and demographics.

Vietnam

Steinberg, Joel David, ed. *In Search of Southeast Asia*, rev. ed. Honolulu: University of Hawaii Press, 1987. Extensive coverage of Vietnam within the context of an area study of southeast Asia. Though weighted toward the modern period, very good coverage of agricultural and religious life in the opening chapters.

Taylor, Keith W. *The Birth of Vietnam*. Berkeley: University of California Press, 1983. Comprehensive, magisterial volume on early Vietnamese history and historical identity amid the long Chinese occupation. Best for students with some background in southeast Asian and Chinese history.

WEBSITES

http://www.britishmuseum.org/the_museum/departments/prints_and_drawings.aspx. Department of Prints and Drawings, British Museum. A comprehensive source for all manner of interests related to Asian studies.

http://digicol.library.wisc.edu/PAIR. Portal to Asian Internet Resources. Extensive list of Internet sources for Asian studies.

Chapter 14

Birmingham, David, and Phyllis M. Martin, eds. *History of Central Africa*, vol. 1. London: Longman, 1983. The first chapter, by Birmingham, provides an excellent summary of the history of Luba prior to 1450.

Crummey, David. *Land and Society in the Christian Kingdom of Ethiopia: From the Thirteenth to the Twentieth Century*. Urbana: University of Illinois Press, 2000. The first book in which the rich land records of the church have been used for a reconstruction of agriculture and land tenure.

Horton, Mark, and John Middleton. *The Swahili: The Social Landscape of a Mercantile Society*. Oxford: Blackwell, 2000. A study that gives full attention to the larger context of East Africa, in which the Swahilis flourished. Middleton is the author of another important study, *The World of the Swahili: An African Mercantile Civilization* (1992, Yale University Press).

Huffman, Thomas N. *Mapungubwe: Ancient African Civilization on the Limpopo*. Johannesburg, South Africa: Witwatersrand University

Press, 2005. Short but illuminating summary of the archaeological record by a leading South African expert, although his interpretation of Zimbabwe in an earlier work (*Snakes and Crocodiles*, 1996, Witwatersrand University Press) is controversial.

Levtzion, Nehemia. *Ancient Ghana and Mali*. New York: Africana Publishing, 1980. Originally published London: Methuen, 1973. Standard history of ancient Ghana, Mali, and Songhay based on a thorough knowledge of the Arabic sources; a revision by David Conrad, Paulo Farias, Roderick J. McIntosh, and Susan McIntosh has been announced but has yet to appear.

Robinson, David. *Muslim Societies in African History*. Cambridge: Cambridge University Press, 2004. Advertised as part of a series of new approaches, this book, nevertheless, presents a conventional view of Islam, albeit in its African context.

Trigger, Bruce. *History and Settlement in Lower Nubia*. Yale University Publications in Anthropology 69. New Haven, CT: Yale University Press, 1965. Chapter 9 is still the best overview of Nubian history, by a scholar with a broad understanding of early civilizations.

WEBSITES

http://www.metmuseum.org/toah/hd/ife/hd_ife.htm. "Heilbrunn Timeline of Art History," "Ife (from ca. 350 B.C.)." An excellent introductory we site can be found at the Metropolitan Museum of Art. It contains many links and presents clear overviews.

Hhttp://apollo5.bournemouth.ac.uk/africanlegacy/index.htm. "Recording West Africa's Visible Archaeology," "Sungbo's Eredu."

For a website by Patrick Darling, the principal archaeological investigator of the Nigerian earthworks see http://cohesion.rice.edu/Centers AndInst/SAFA/emplibrary/49_ch09.pdf for a copy of a 1998 article.

Chapter 15

Bruhns, Karen Olsen, and Karen E. Stothert. *Women in Ancient America*. Norman: University of Oklahoma Press, 1999. Comprehensive account of women's role in the daily life, religion, politics, and war in hunter–gatherer and agrarian–urban societies.

Brumfield, Elizabeth M., and Gary F. Feinman, eds. *The Aztec World*. New York: Abrams, 2008. Collection of expert short chapters on a variety of topics, richly illustrated.

Carrasco, Davíd. *Daily Life of the Aztecs: People of the Sun and Earth*. With Scott Sessions. Westport, CT: Greenwood Press, 1998. Clear, straightforward account by a specialist.

D'Altroy, Terence. *The Incas*. Malden, MA: Blackwell, 2002. Well-organized, comprehensive, and up to-date overview.

Hassig, Ross. *War and Society in Ancient Mesoamerica*. Berkeley: University of California Press, 1992. Best study of the rising importance of militarism in Mesoamerican city-states, up to the Aztec Empire.

Malpass, Michael A. *Daily Life in the Inca Empire*, 2nd ed. Westport, CT: Greenwood Press, 2009. Clear, straightforward, and readable account of ordinary people's lives by a specialist.

WEBSITES

http://www.aztec-history.com/. Aztec-History.com. Introductory website, easily maneuverable, with links.

http://www.discover-peru.org/category/history/history-inca-culture-civilization/. Discover Peru. This website, by the Peru Cultural Society, provides basic articles on aspects of Inca culture.

Chapter 16

Agoston, Gábor. *Guns for the Sultan: Military Power and the Weapons Industry in the Ottoman Empire*. Cambridge: Cambridge University Press, 2005. Thorough study, which is based on newly accessible Ottoman archival materials and emphasizes the technological prowess of Ottoman gunsmiths.

Casale, Giancarlo. *The Ottoman Age of Exploration*. New York: Oxford University Press, 2010. Detailed correction, based on Ottoman and Portuguese archives, of the traditional characterization of the Ottoman Empire as a land-oriented power.

Casey, James. *Early Modern Spain: A Social History*. London: Routledge, 1999. Detailed, well-documented analysis of rural–urban and royal–nobility tensions.

Elliott, John Huxtable. *Spain, Europe, and the Wider World: 1500–1800*. New Haven, CT: Yale University Press, 2009. A comprehensive overview, particularly strong on culture during the 1500s.

Glete, Jan. *War and the State in Early Modern Europe: Spain, the Dutch Republic, and Sweden as Fiscal–Military States, 1500–1660*. London: Routledge, 2002. A complex but persuasive construction of the forerunner model to the absolute state. Unfortunately leaves out the Ottoman Empire.

Murphy, Rhoads. *Ottoman Warfare, 1500–1700*. New Brunswick, NJ: Rutgers University Press, 1999. Author presents a vivid picture of the Janissaries, their discipline, organization, campaigns, and voracious demands for salary increases.

Pamuk, Sevket. *A Monetary History of the Ottoman Empire*. Cambridge: Cambridge University Press, 2000. Superb analysis of Ottoman archival resources on the role and function of American silver in the money economy of the Ottomans.

Ruiz, Teofilo R. *Spanish Society, 1400–1600*. London: Longman, 2001. Richly detailed social studies rewarding anyone interested in changing class structures, rural–urban movement, and extension of the money market into the countryside.

Subrahmanyam, Sanjay. *The Career and Legend of Vasco da Gama*. Cambridge: Cambridge University Press, 1997. Focuses on the religious motivations in Vasco da Gama and the commercial impact of his journey to India.

WEBSITES

http://www.pbs.org/wgbh/pages/frontline/shows/apocalypse/. *Frontline*, "Apocalypse! The Evolution of Apocalyptic Belief and How It Shaped the Western World," PBS, 1995. The contribution by Bernard McGinn, University of Chicago, under the heading of "Apocalypticism," is of particular relevance for the understanding of Christopher Columbus viewing himself as a precursor of Christ's Second Coming.

http://www.pbs.org/empires/islam/timeline.html. Comprehensive and informative, PBS website on the Ottoman Empire examines the various facets of this Islamic culture such as scientific innovations, faith and its leaders.

Chapter 17

Black, Jeremy. *Kings, Nobles, and Commoners: States and Societies in Early Modern Europe—A Revisionist History*. London: Tauris, 2004. Available also electronically on ebrary; persuasive thesis, largely accepted by scholars, of a continuity of institutional practices in Europe across the sixteenth and seventeenth centuries, casting doubt on absolutism as being more than a theory.

Geanakoplos, Deno John. *Constantinople and the West: Essays on the Late Byzantine (Paleologan) and Italian Renaissances and the Byzantine and Roman Churches*. Madison: University of Wisconsin Press, 1989. Fundamental discussion of the extensive transfer of texts and scholars during the 1400s.

Jacob, Margaret C. *Scientific Culture and the Making of the Industrial West*. Oxford: Oxford University Press, 1997. Widely cited short book emphasizing the connections between New Science, scientific societies, and the steam engine.

Margolis, Howard. *It Started with Copernicus: How Turning the World Inside Out Led to the Scientific Revolution*. New York: McGraw-Hill, 2002. Important scholarly study of the connection between the discovery of the Americas and Copernicus' formulation of a sun-centered planetary system.

Nexon, Daniel H. *The Struggle for Power in Early Modern Europe: Religious Conflict, Dynastic Empires & International Change*. Princeton, NJ: Princeton University Press, 2009. Charles Tilly–inspired reevaluation of the changes occurring in sixteenth- and seventeenth-century Europe.

Rublack, Ulinka. *Reformation Europe.* Cambridge: Cambridge University Press, 2006. Cultural history approach to the effects of Luther and Calvin on western Christians.

Schiebinger, Londa. *The Mind Has No Sex? Women in the Origins of Modern Science.* Cambridge, MA: Harvard University Press, 1989. A pioneering study presenting biographies and summaries of scientific contributions. Discusses the importance of Marie Cunitz.

WEBSITES

http://www.earlymodernweb.org.uk/emr/ (http://sharonhoward.org/). "Early Modern Resources." Website with many links on the full range of institutional and cultural change.

http://galileo.rice.edu/index.html. Spanning every facet of the scientist's life, The Galileo Project is both informative and concise in its assessment of Galileo's life work and contribution to modernity and science.

http://kepler.nasa.gov/Mission/JohannesKepler/. NASA's website looks at the life and views of Johannes Kepler. It examines his discoveries, contemporaries and the events that shaped modern science.

Chapter 18

Alchon, Suzanne A. *A Pest in the Land: New World Epidemics in a Global Perspective.* Albuquerque: University of New Mexico Press, 2003. A broad overview, making medical history comprehensible.

Behringer, Wolfgang. *Witches and Witch-Hunts: A Global History.* Cambridge: Polity Press, 2004. A well-grounded overview of the phenomenon of the fear of witches, summarizing the scholarship of the past decades.

Bulmer-Thomas, Victor, John S. Coatsworth, and Roberto Cortés Conde, eds. *The Cambridge Economic History of Latin America.* Vol. 1, *The Colonial Era and the Short Nineteenth Century.* Cambridge: Cambridge University Press, 2006. Collection of specialized summary articles on aspects of Iberian colonialism.

Burkholder, Mark A., and Lyman L. Johnson. *Colonial Latin America,* 6th ed. Oxford: Oxford University Press, 2008. A well-established text, updated multiple times.

Ekberg, Carl J. *French Roots in the Illinois Country: The Mississippi Frontier in Colonial Times.* Urbana: University of Illinois Press, 1998. Detailed, deeply researched historical account.

Socolow, Susan M. *The Women of Latin America.* Cambridge: Cambridge University Press, 2000. Surveys the patriarchal order and the function of women within it.

Stein, Stanley J., and Barbara H. Stein. *Silver, Trade and War: Spain and America in the Making of Early Modern Europe.* Baltimore: Johns Hopkins University Press, 2000. Covers the significance of American silver reaching as far as China.

Taylor, Alan. *American Colonies.* London: Penguin, 2001. History of the English colonies in New England, written from a broad Atlantic perspective.

Wood, Michael. *Conquistadors.* Berkeley: University of California Press, 2000. Accessible, richly illustrated history of the conquest period.

WEBSITES

http://www.pbs.org/conquistadors/. Wonderful interactive website that allows you to track the journy's made by the Conquistadors such as Cortés, Pizzaro, Orellana, and Cabeza De Vaca. Learn more about their conquests in the Americas and the legacy they left behind them.

Chapter 19

Carney, Judith A. *Black Rice: The African Origins of Rice Cultivation in the Americas.* Cambridge, MA: Harvard University Press, 2001. Study which goes a long way toward correcting the stereotype that black slaves were unskilled laborers and carefully documents the transfer of rice-growing culture from West Africa to the Americas.

Dubois, Laurent, and Julius S. Scott. *Origins of the Black Atlantic: Rewriting Histories.* New York: Routledge, 2009. Book that focuses on African slaves in the Americas as they had to arrange themselves in their new lives.

Gray, Richard, and David Birmingham, eds. *Pre-Colonial African Trade.* London: Oxford University Press, 1970. Collective work in which contributors emphasize the growth and intensification of trade in the centuries of 1500–1800.

Hall, Gwendolyn Midlo. *Slavery and African Ethnicities in the Americas: Restoring the Links.* Chapel Hill: University of North Carolina Press, 2005. Study that focuses on slaves in the Americas according to their regions of origin in Africa.

Heywood, Linda M., and John K. Thornton. *Central Africans, Atlantic Creoles, and the Foundation of the Americas.* Cambridge: Cambridge University Press, 2007. Pathbreaking investigation of the creation and role of Creole culture in Africa and the Americas.

Iliffe, John. *Africans: The History of a Continent.* Cambridge: Cambridge University Press, 1995. Standard historical summary by an established African historian.

Kriger, Colleen E. *Cloth in West African History.* Lanham, MD: Altamira, 2006. Detailed investigation of the sophisticated indigenous West African cloth industry.

Oliver, Roland, and Anthony Atmore. *Medieval Africa, 1250–1800.* Cambridge: Cambridge University Press, 2001. Revised and updated historical overview, divided into regions and providing detailed regional histories on the emerging kingdoms.

Thornton, John. *The Kongolese Saint Anthony: Dona Beatriz Kimpa Vita and the Antonian Movement, 1684–1706.* Cambridge: Cambridge University Press, 1998. Detailed biography of Dona Beatriz, from which the vignette at the beginning of the chapter is borrowed; includes a general overview of the history of Kongo during the civil war.

WEBSITES

http://www.slavevoyages.org/tast/index.faces. Atlantic Slave Trade Database. A large electronic website based at Emory University and sponsored by a number of American universities, presenting up-to-date demographic tables.

http://hitchcock.itc.virginia.edu/Slavery/index.php. Described as a visual record, the University of Virginia's website on the Atlantic Slave trade has an extensive collection of images relating to every aspect of slavery from maps of pre and post-colonial Africa, to the slave ships, life in colonies, punishments and emancipation.'

http://www.liverpoolmuseums.org.uk/ism/slavery/americas/abolition_americas.aspx. An amazing and well-planned website that offers students a comprehensive overview of the Atlantic Slave trade from life in Africa before slavery, to the horrific conditions on slave ships, right through to abolition. Students can also listen to extracts depicting the experiences of the enslaved, such as Olaudah Equiano.

www.britishmuseum.org/PDF/british_museum_benin_art.pdf. In addition to offering a brief historical backdrop to the art of the Benin Kingdom, The British Museum's PDF also depicts various artifacts taken by the British from the Royal Palace.

Chapter 20

Bernier, Francois. *Travels in the Mogul Empire, A.D. 1656–1668.* Translated by Archibald Constable. Delhi: S. Chand, 1968. One of many fascinating travel accounts by European diplomats, merchants, and missionaries.

Eaton, Richard M. *Essays on Islam and Indian History.* New York: Oxford University Press, 2002. A compendium of the new scholarly consensus on, among other things, the differences between the clerical view of Islamic observance and its actual impact in rural India. Contains both historiography and material on civilizational and cultural issues.

Nizami, Khaliq A. *Akbar and Religion.* Delhi: IAD, 1989. Extensive treatment of Akbar's evolving move toward devising his Din-i-Ilahi movement, by leading scholar of Indian religious and intellectual history.

Richards, John F. *The Mughal Empire.* Cambridge: Cambridge University Press, 1993. Comprehensive volume in the New Cambridge History of India. Sophisticated treatment; best suited to advanced students. Extensive glossary and useful bibliographic essay.

Schimmel, Annemarie. *The Empire of the Great Mughals: History, Art, and Culture.* London: Reaktion Books, 2004. Revised edition of a volume published in German in 2000. Lavish illustrations, wonderfully drawn portraits of key individuals, and extensive treatment of social, family, and gender relations at the Mughal court.

WEBSITES

http://www.aasianist.org/EAA and http://www.aasianist.org/links/index.htm. As with other Asian topics, two of the most reliable websites are sponsored by the Association for Asian Studies.

http://www.bbc.co.uk/religion/religions/islam/history/mughalempire_1.shtml. The Mughal Empire ruled most of India and Pakistan in the 16th and 17th centuries. Learn more about the religious divides and governance of Muslim Mughals in a country with a majority of Hindi populace.

http://www.pbs.org/treasuresoftheworld/taj_mahal/tlevel_1/t1_mughal.html. PBS's Treasure's of the World series looks at the Mughal dynasty and the art and architecture that flourished under the reign of Babur, Akbar and Shah Jahan. Links allow students to tour the Taj Mahal and Mughal gardens.

Chapter 21

China

DeBary, William T., and Irene Bloom. *Sources of Chinese Tradition*, vols. 1 and 2, 2nd ed. New York: Columbia University Press, 1999. Thoroughgoing update of classic sourcebook for Chinese literature and philosophy, with a considerable amount of social, family, and women's works now included.

Fairbank, John K., and Edwin O. Reischauer. *China: Tradition and Transformation.* Boston: Houghton Mifflin, 1989. A complete textbook on Chinese history, with the majority of the material geared toward the modern era. Emphasis on the "change within tradition" model of Chinese history.

Pomeranz, Kenneth. *The Great Divergence. China, Europe, and the Making of the Modern World Economy.* Princeton, NJ: Princeton University Press, 2001. Pathbreaking work mounting the strongest argument yet in favor of the balance of economic power remaining in east Asia until the Industrial Revolution was well under way.

Spence, Jonathan. *The Memory Palace of Matteo Ricci.* New York: Penguin, 1984. Highly original treatment of Ricci and the beginning of the Jesuit interlude in late Ming and early Qing China. Attempts to penetrate Ricci's world through the missionary's own memory techniques.

Japan

DeBary, William T., ed. *Sources of Japanese Tradition*, vols. 1 and 2. New York: Columbia University Press, 1964. The Tokugawa era spans volumes 1 and 2, with its inception and political and philosophical foundations thoroughly covered in volume 1, while the Shinto revival of national learning, the later Mito school, and various partisans of national unity in the face of foreign intrusion covered in the beginning of volume 2.

Duus, Peter. *Feudalism in Japan*, 3rd ed. New York: McGraw-Hill, 1993. Updated version of short, handy volume spanning all of Japanese history to 1867, with special emphasis on the shogunates. Good introduction on the uses and limitations of the term "feudalism" with reference to Japan within a comparative framework.

Gordon, Andrew. *A Modern History of Japan from Tokugawa Times to the Present.* New York: Oxford University Press, 2009. One of the few treatments of Japanese history that spans both the Tokugawa and the modern eras, rather than making the usual break in either 1853 or 1867/68. Both

the continuity of the past and the novelty of the new era are therefore juxtaposed and highlighted. Most useful for students with a background at least equivalent to that supplied by this text.

WEBSITES

http://ngm.nationalgeographic.com/ngm/0507/feature2/map.html. Track the voyages made by Zheng He to Southeast Asia, India, Arabia and Africa.

http://www.chinaculture.org/library/2008-02/09/content_22914.htm. With some illustrations, ChinaCulture.org offers a short biographical account of the reign of Kangxi, the fourth emperor of the Qing dynasty.

Chapter 22

Israel, Jonathan I. *A Revolution of the Mind: Radical Enlightenment and the Origins of Modern Democracy.* Princeton, NJ: Princeton University Press, 2010. Israel is a pioneer of the contemporary renewal of intellectual history, and his investigations of the Enlightenment tradition are pathbreaking.

Kaiser, Thomas E., and Dale K. Van Kley, eds. *From Deficit to Deluge: The Origins of the French Revolution.* Stanford, CA: Stanford University Press, 2011. Thoughtful reevaluation of the scholarly field that takes into account the latest interpretations.

Kitchen, Martin. *A History of Modern Germany: 1800 to the Present.* Hoboken, NJ: Wiley-Blackwell, 2011. A broadly conceived historical overview, ranging from politics and economics to culture.

Rakove, Jack. *Revolutionaries: A New History of the Invention of America.* Boston: Houghton Mifflin, 2010. A new narrative history focusing on the principal figures in the revolution.

Riall, Lucy. *Risorgimento: The History of Italy from Napoleon to Nation-State.* New York: Palgrave Macmillan, 2009. Historical summary, incorporating the research of the past half-century, presented in a clear overview.

Wood, Gordon S. *The American Revolution: A History.* New York: Modern Library, 2002. A short, readable summary reflective of many decades of revisionism in the discussion of the American Revolution.

WEBSITES

http://www.nationalismproject.org/what.htm. Nationalism Project. A large Website with links to bibliographies, essays, new books, and book reviews.

http://chnm.gmu.edu/revolution/. This website boasts 250 images, 350 text documents, 13 songs, 13 maps and a timeline all focused on the French Revolution.

Chapter 23

Allen, Robert C. *The British Industrial Revolution in Global Perspective.* Cambridge: Cambridge University Press, 2009. An in-depth analysis, well supported by economic data, of not only why the Industrial Revolution occurred first in Britain but also how new British technologies carried industrialism around the world.

Dublin, Thomas, ed. *Farm to Factory: Women's Letters, 1830–1860.* New York: Columbia University Press, 1981. A fascinating collection of correspondence written by women who describe their experiences in moving from rural areas of New England to urban centers in search of work in textile factories.

Headrick, Daniel R. *The Tools of Empire: Technology and European Imperialism in the Nineteenth Century.* Oxford: Oxford University Press, 1981. A fascinating and clearly written analysis of the connections between the development of new technologies and their role in European imperialism.

Hobsbawm, Eric. *The Age of Revolution: 1789–1848.* London: Vintage Books, 1996. A sophisticated analysis of the Industrial Revolution (one element of the "dual revolution," the other being the French Revolution) that examines the effects of industrialism on social and cultural developments from a Marxist perspective.

Mokyr, Joel. "Accounting for the Industrial Revolution." In *The Cambridge Economic History of Modern Britain*, vol. 1. Edited by Roderick Floud and Paul Johnson. Cambridge: Cambridge University Press, 2004. An analysis of the industrial movement that emphasizes its intellectual sources, embraced in the term "Industrial Enlightenment."

More, Charles. *Understanding the Industrial Revolution*. London: Routledge, 2000. A comprehensive explanation of how theories of economic growth account for the development of the industrial movement in Britain.

Stearns, Peter N. *The Industrial Revolution in World History*. Boulder: University of Colorado Press, 1993. A comprehensive study of the origin, spread, and influence of the European industrial revolution and its impact on globalization.

WEBSITES

http://www.thomasedison.org/. Remarkable website that explores Thomas Edison's impact on modernity through his innovations and inventions. This site also reproduces all of Edison's scientific sketches which are available to download as PDF files.

http://www.monetpainting.net/. A visually beautiful website which reproduces many of Monet's masterpieces, this site also includes an extensive biographical account of the famous painter's life and works. It also includes information about his wife Camille, his gardens at Giverny, and a chronology.

http://darwin-online.org.uk/. This website has reproduced, in full, the works of Charles Darwin. In addition to providing digitized facsimiles of his works, private papers and manuscripts it has also added a concise biographical account and numerous images of Darwin throughout his life.

http://www.alberteinstein.info/. Fantastic and informative website that houses digitized manuscripts of Einstein's work. Also includes a gallery of images.

Chapter 24

China

Cohen, Paul. *Discovering History in China*. New York: Columbia University Press, 1984.

Fairbank, John K., and Su-yu Teng. *China's Response to the West*. Cambridge, MA: Harvard University Press, 1954.

Kang, David C. *East Asia Before the West: Five Centuries of Trade and Tribute*. New York: Columbia University Press, 2010.

Spence, Jonathan D. *The Search for Modern China*. New York: Norton, 1990.

Spence, Jonathan D. *God's Chinese Son*. New York: Norton, 1996.

Japan

Beasley, W. G. *The Meiji Restoration*. Stanford, CA: Stanford University Press, 1972.

Reischauer, Edwin O., and Albert M. Craig. *Japan: Tradition and Transformation*. Boston: Houghton Mifflin, 1989.

Totman, Conrad. *Japan Before Perry*. Berkeley: University of California Press, 1981.

Totman, Conrad. *A History of Japan*. Oxford: Blackwell, 2000.

WEBSITES

http://www.asian-studies.org/eaa/. Education About Asia. This site provides the best online sources for modern Chinese and Japanese history.

http://www.asian-studies.org/ This is the site of the Association for Asian Studies, the home page of which has links to sources more suited to advanced term papers and seminar projects.

http://sinojapanesewar.com/. Packed with maps, photographs and movies depicting the conflict between Japan and China at the end of the 19th century, students can learn more about causes and consequences of the Sino-Japanese war.

Chapter 25

Gaudin, Corinne. *Ruling Peasants: Village and State in Later Imperial Russia*. DeKalb: Northern Illinois University Press, 2007. A close and sympathetic analysis of rural Russia.

Inalcik, Halil, and Donald Quataert, eds. *An Economic and Social History of the Ottoman Empire*. Vol. 2, *1600–1914*. Cambridge: Cambridge University Press, 1994. A pioneering work with contributions by leading Ottoman historians on rural structures, monetary developments, and industrialization efforts.

Kasaba, Resat, ed. *The Cambridge History of Turkey*. Vol. 5, *Turkey in the Modern World*. Cambridge: Cambridge University Press, 2008. An ambitious effort to assemble the leading authorities on the Ottoman Empire and provide a comprehensive overview.

Lieven, Dominic. *Empire: The Russian Empire and Its Rivals*. New Haven, CT: Yale University Press, 2002. Broad, comparative history of the Russian Empire, in the context of the Habsburg, Ottoman, and British Empires.

Nikitenko, Aleksandr. *Up from Serfdom: My Childhood and Youth in Russia, 1804–1824*. Translated by Helen Saltz Jacobson. New Haven, CT: Yale University Press, 2001. Touching autobiography summarized at the beginning of the chapter.

Poe, Marshall T. *Russia's Moment in World History*. Princeton, NJ: Princeton University Press, 2003. A superb scholarly overview of Russian history, written from a broad perspective and taking into account a good number of Western stereotypes about Russia, especially in the nineteenth century.

Quataert, Donald. *Manufacturing in the Ottoman Empire and Turkey, 1500–1950*. Albany: State University of New York Press, 1994. The author is still the leading American historian on workers and the early industrialization of the Ottoman Empire.

Riasanovsky, Nicholas, and Mark Steinberg. *A History of Russia*, 8th ed., 2 vols. New York: Oxford University Press, 2011. A comprehensive, fully revised history, ranging from politics and economics to literature and the arts.

Uyar, Mesut, and Edward J. Erickson. *A Military History of the Ottomans: From Osman to Atatürk*. Santa Barbara, CA: Praeger Security International, 2009. A detailed, well-documented history of the Ottoman Empire from the perspective of its imperial designs and military forces, by two military officers in academic positions.

WEBSITES

http://www.paradoxplace.com/Insights/Topkapi/Suleiman%20Topkapi%20Ottomans.htm. A basic web site on the Ottoman Empire at its height, with numerous illustrations.

http://www.russianlegacy.com/en/go_to/history/russian_empire.htm. Russian Legacy, a website devoted to the Russian Empire, organized as a timeline with links.

Chapter 26

Belich, James. *Replenishing the Earth: The Settler Revolution and the Rise of the Anglo-World, 1783–1939*. Oxford: Oxford University Press, 2009. Important study by an Australian historian, focusing on the British settler colonies.

Burbank, Jane, and Frederick Cooper. *Empires in World History: Power and Politics of Difference*. Princeton, NJ: Princeton University Press, 2010. Well-written and remarkably comprehensive comparative work.

Ferguson, Niall. *Empire: The Rise and Demise of the British World Order and the Lessons for Global Power*. New York: Perseus, 2002. Controversial but widely acknowledged analysis of the question of whether imperialism deserves its negative reputation.

Fieldhouse, David K. *Economics and Empire, 1830–1914*. New York: Macmillan, 1984. A classic, profoundly influential study of the economic costs of imperialism, coming to the conclusion that it was not cost-effective.

Hobsbawm, Eric. *The Age of Empire, 1875–1914*. New York: Vintage, 1989. Immensely well-informed investigation of the climactic period of the new imperialism at the end of the nineteenth century.

Jefferies, Matthew. *Contesting the German Empire, 1871–1918*. Malden, MA: Blackwell, 2008. Up-to-date summary of the German historical debate on the colonial period.

Ricklefs, Merle Calvin. *A History of Modern Indonesia Since c. 1200*, 3rd ed. Stanford, CA: Stanford University Press, 2001. Standard history with relevant chapters on Dutch imperialism and colonialism.

Singer, Barnett, John Langdon, and John W. Langdon. *Cultured Force: Makers and Defenders of the French Empire*. Madison: University of Wisconsin Press, 2004. Study of the principal (military) figures who helped create the French nineteenth-century empire.

WEBSITES

http://www.allempires.com/. All Empires Online History Community. Website dedicated to assembling materials on all historical empires, including those of the nineteenth century.

http://www.bbc.co.uk/history/british/empire_seapower/east_india_01.shtml. The BBC looks back at its colonial past and its presence in India. Topics include the East India Company, regional politics, company government and territorial expansion.

Chapter 27

Bulmer-Thomas, Victor. *The Economic History of Latin America Since Independence*, 2nd ed. Cambridge: Cambridge University Press, 2003. A highly analytical and sympathetic investigation of the Latin American export and self-sufficiency economies, calling into question the long dominant dependency theories of Latin America.

Burkholder, Mark, and Lyman Johnson. *Colonial Latin America*, 6th ed. New York: Oxford University Press, 2008. Overview, with focus on social and cultural history.

Dawson, Alexander. *Latin America Since Independence: A History with Primary Sources*. New York: Routledge, 2011. Selection of topics with documentary base; for the nineteenth century on the topics of the nation-state, caudillo politics, race, and the policy of growth through commodity exports.

Drake, Paul W. *Between Tyranny and Anarchy: A History of Democracy in Latin America*. Palo Alto, CA: Stanford University Press, 2009. The author traces the concepts of constitutionalism, autocracy, and voting rights since independence in clear and persuasive strokes.

Eakin, Marshall Craig. *The History of Latin America: Collision of Cultures*. New York: Palgrave Macmillan, 2007. A Brazilianist with a special eye on the ethnic and social class system of Latin America.

Meade, Teresa A. *A History of Modern Latin America: 1800 to the Present*. Chichester, UK: Wiley-Blackwell, 2010. The nineteenth-century portion of this study presents a comprehensive political, social, and economic survey, going more deeply into the details of many aspects discussed in this chapter.

Prados de la Escosura, Leandro. "The Economic Consequences of Independence in Latin America." In: *The Cambridge Economic History of Latin America*. Vol. 1, *The Colonial Era and the Short Nineteenth Century*. Edited by Victor Bulmer-Thomas, John H. Coatsworth, and Roberto Cortés Conde, pp. 463–504. Cambridge: Cambridge University Press, 2006. Superb analysis of the main factors characteristic for Latin America's special path toward economic development without industrialization.

Thurner, Mark, and Andrés Guerrero, eds. *After Spanish Rule: Postcolonial Predicaments of the Americas*. Durham, NC: Duke University Press, 2003. Collection of articles by different authors on the multiple cultural and social challenges which Latin Americans faced after independence.

Wasserman, Mark, and Cheryl English Martin. *Latin America and Its People*, 2nd ed. New York: Pearson Longman, 2007. Thematic approach, drawing general conclusions by comparing and contrasting the individual countries of Latin America.

WEBSITES

http://www.casahistoria.net/latin_american_history19.html. Casahistori.net. Website on nineteenth-century Latin America, for students.

http://www.suite101.com/latinamericanhistory. Suite101.com. A website featuring a long list of short essays on Latin American topics.

http://blpc.bl.uk/onlinegallery/features/spanishamericanind/homepage.html. The British Library looks back at the Spanish-American Independence from the movements origins and key figures to Bolívar's triumphant march. The site has also reproduced extracts from contemporary texts.

Chapter 28

Berend, Ivan T. *An Economic History of Twentieth-Century Europe: Economic Regimes from Laissez-Faire to Globalization*. Cambridge: Cambridge University Press, 2006. Includes Europe-wide, comparative chapters on laissez-faire and state-directed economies, including deficit spending.

Bose-Sugata, and Ayesha Jalal. *Modern South Asia: History, Culture, Political Economy*. New York: Routledge, 2004. Well-informed analyses by two of the foremost South Asia specialists.

Fritzsche, Peter. *Life and Death in the Third Reich*. Cambridge, MA: Harvard University Press, 2008. Book that seeks to understand the German nation's choice of arranging itself to Nazi rule.

Gelvin, James L. *The Modern Middle East: A History*, 3rd ed. Oxford: Oxford University Press, 2011. Contains chapters on Arab nationalism, British and French colonialism, as well as Turkey and Iran in the interwar period.

Gordon, Andrew. *A Modern History of Japan: From Tokugawa Times to the Present*, 2nd ed. Oxford: Oxford University Press, 2009. Detailed overview of Japan's interwar period in the middle chapters.

Grasso, June M., J. P. Corrin, and Michael Kort. *Modernization and Revolution in Modern China: From the Opium Wars to the Olympics*, 4th ed. Armonk, NY: M. E. Sharpe, 2009. General overview with a focus on modernization, in relation to the strong survival of tradition.

Lombardo, Paul A., ed. *A Century of Eugenics in America: From the Indiana Experiment to the Human Genome Era*. Bloomington: Indiana University Press, 2011. Study of a dark chapter in U.S. history.

Martel, Gordon, ed. *A Companion to Europe 1900–1945*. Malden, MA: Wiley-Blackwell, 2010. Collective work covering a large variety of cultural, social, and political European topics in the interwar period.

Meade, Teresa A. *A History of Modern Latin America: 1800 to the Present*. Malden, MA: Wiley-Routledge, 2010. Topical discussion of the major issues in Latin American history, with chapters on the first half of the twentieth century.

Snyder, Timothy. *Bloodlands: Europe Between Hitler and Stalin*. New York: Basic Books, 2010. Book that chronicles the horrific destruction left behind by these two dictators.

WEBSITES

http://www.ushistory.org/us/. Maintained by Independence Hall Association in Philadelphia, it contains many links to topics discussed in this chapter.

http://www.bbc.co.uk/history/worldwars/wwone/ and http://www.bbc.co.uk/history/worldwars/wwtwo/. The BBC's treatment of the causes, course and consequences for both WWI and WWII from an Allied position.

http://www.marxists.org/subject/bolsheviks/index.htm. A complete review of the Bolshevik party members including biographies and links to archives which contain their works.

http://www.ushmm.org/wlc/en/article.php?ModuleId=10005151. The U.S. Holocaust Memorial Museum looks back on one of the darkest times in western history. http://www.nanking-massacre.com/Home.html. A disturbing collection of pictures and articles tell the gruesome history of the Raping of Nanking.

Chapter 29

Baret, Roby Carol. *The Greater Middle East and the Cold War: US Foreign Policy Under Eisenhower and Kennedy*. London: Tauris, 2007. Thoroughly researched analysis of American policies in the Middle East, North Africa, and south Asia.

Birmingham, David. *Kwame Nkrumah: Father of African Nationalism*. Athens: University of Ohio Press, 1998. Short biography by a leading modern African historian.

Conniff, Michael L. *Populism in Latin America*. Tuscaloosa: University of Alabama Press, 1999. The author is a well-published scholar on modern Latin America.

Damrosch, David, David Lawrence Pike, Djelal Kadir, and Ursula K. Heise, eds. *The Longman Anthology of World Literature*. Vol. F, *The Twentieth Century*. New York: Longman/Pearson, 2008. A rich, diverse selection of texts. Alternatively, Norton published a similar, somewhat larger anthology of world literature in 2003.

De Witte, Ludo. *The Assassination of Lumumba*. Translated by Ann Wright and Renée Fenby. London: Verso, 2002. An admirably researched study of the machinations of the Belgian government in protecting its mining interests, with the connivance of CIA director Allen Dulles and President Dwight D. Eisenhower.

Goscha, Christopher E., and Christian F. Ostermann. *Connecting Histories: Decolonization and the Cold War in Southeast Asia, 1945–1962*. Stanford, CA: Stanford University Press, 2009.

Guha, Ramachandra. *India After Gandhi. A History of the World's Largest Democracy*. New York: Harper Collins, 2007. Highly readable, popular history with well-sketched biographical treatments of leading individuals, more obscure cultural figures, and ordinary people. Accessible to even beginning students.

Hasegawa, Tsuyoshi. *The Cold War in East Asia, 1945–1991*. Stanford, CA: Stanford University Press, 2011. A new summary, based on archival research by a leading Japanese historian teaching in the United States. New insights on the Soviet entry into WWII against Japan.

WEBSITES

http://www.economist.com/node/7218678. The Economist Magazine looks back on 'An Affair to Remember, the Suez Crisis and its implications.

http://www.nasa.gov/mission_pages/shuttle/sts1/gagarin_anniversary.html. In addition to providing information and video footage regarding Yuri Gagarin's orbit of the earth, students will also find information on America's space history.

http://www.newseum.org/berlinwall/. The Newseum's interactive website looks at what life was like on both sides of the Berlin Wall.

Chapter 30

Duara, Prasenjit. *Decolonization: Perspectives from Now and Then*. London: Routledge, 2004. A leading scholar of China and postcolonial studies edits essays in this offering in the Rewriting Histories series on the fall of the colonial empires by scholars such as Michael Adas and John Voll and activists and leaders such as Frantz Fanon and Kwame Nkrumah.

Fanon, Frantz. *The Wretched of the Earth*. New York: Grove Press, 1961. One of the most provocative and influential treatments of theoretical and practical issues surrounding decolonization. Fanon champions

violence as an essential part of the decolonization process and advocates a modified Marxist approach that takes into consideration the nuances of race and the legacies of colonialism.

Frieden, Jeffrey. *Global Capitalism: Its Fall and Rise in the Twentieth Century*. New York: W. W. Norton, 2006. Despite the title, a comprehensive history of global networks from the days of mercantilism to the twenty-first century. Predominant emphasis on twentieth century; highly readable, though the material is best suited for the nonbeginning student.

Gaddis, John Lewis. *The Cold War: A New History*. New York: Penguin, 2005. Though criticized by some scholars for his pro-American positions, America's foremost historian of the Cold War produces here a vivid, at times counterintuitive, view of the Cold War and its global impact. Readable even for beginning students.

Gitlin, Todd. *The Sixties: Years of Hope, Days of Rage*, rev. ed. New York: Bantam, 1993. Lively, provocative account of this pivotal decade by the former radical, now sociologist. Especially effective at depicting the personalities of the pivotal period 1967–1969.

Liang Heng and Judith Shapiro. *After the Nightmare: A Survivor of the Cultural Revolution Reports on China Today*. New York: Knopf, 1986. Highly readable, poignant, first-person accounts of people's experiences during the trauma of China's Cultural Revolution by a former husband and wife team. Especially interesting because China was at the beginning of its Four Modernizations and the wounds of the Cultural Revolution were still fresh.

Smith, Bonnie. *Global Feminisms Since 1945*. London: Routledge, 2000. Part of the Rewriting Histories series, this work brings together under the editorship of Smith a host of essays by writers such as Sara Evans, Mary Ann Tetreault, and Miriam Ching Yoon Louie on feminism in Asia, Africa, Latin America, as well as Europe and the United States. Sections are thematically arranged under such topics as "Nationbuilding," "Sources of activism," "Women's liberation," and "New waves in the 1980s and 1990s." Comprehensive and readable, though some background in women's history is recommended.

WEBSITES

www.wilsoncenter.org/program/cold-war-international-history-project. Cold War International History Project of the Woodrow Wilson International Center for Scholars. Rich archival materials including collections on the end of the Cold War, Soviet invasion of Afghanistan, Cuban Missile Crisis, and Chinese foreign policy documents.

Codlibrary.org. College of DuPage Library. Typing in the "search" box "Research guide to 1960s websites" yields a wide-ranging set of relevant topics.

http://news.bbc.co.uk/onthisday/hi/dates/stories/june/4/newsid_2496000/2496277.stm. BBC's archive ON THIS DAY shows video footage from the Tiananmen Square massacre in 1989.

Chapter 31

Béja, Jean-Philippe, ed. *The Impact of China's 1989 Tiananmen Massacre*. New York: Routledge, 2011. Highly diverse contributions on this watershed event and the devastating effect it had on middle-class self-evaluation.

Chau, Adam Yuet, ed. *Religion in Contemporary China*. New York: Routledge, 2011. Collection of fascinating chapters on the revival of Daoist, Confucian, and Buddhist traditions and their adaption to middle-class modernity, with their proponents operating often in a gray zone between official recognition and suppression.

Daniels, Robert V. *The Rise and Fall of Communism in the Soviet Union*. New Haven, CT: Yale University Press, 2010. A magisterial summary of the communist period by a specialist.

Dillon, Michael. *Contemporary China: An Introduction*. New York: Routledge, 2009. Concise yet quite specific overview of the economy, society, and politics of the country.

Eichengreen, Barry. *Exorbitant Privilege: The Rise and Fall of the Dollar and the Future of the Monetary System.* New York: Oxford University Press, 2011. The author is an academic specialist on US monetary policies, writing in an accessible style and presenting a fascinating picture of the role of something as prosaic as greenbacks.

Meade, Teresa A. *A History of Modern Latin America: 1800 to the Present.* Malden, MA: Wiley-Blackwell, 2010. The book is an excellent, comprehensive analysis and has a strong final chapter on recent Latin America.

Saxonberg, Steven. *The Fall: A Comparative Study of the End of Communism in Czechoslovakia, East Germany, Hungary, and Poland.* Amsterdam: Harwood Academic, 2001. A well-informed overview of the different trajectories by an academic teaching in Prague.

Speth, James Gustav. *The Bridge at the Edge of the World: Capitalism, the Environment, and Crossing from Crisis to Sustainability.* New Haven, CT: Yale University Press, 2008. A strong plea to change our capitalist system.

Swanimathan, Jayshankar M. *Indian Economic Superpower: Fact or Fiction?* Singapore: World Scientific Publishing, 2009. A thoughtful evaluation of the pros and cons, in concise overviews.

Wapner, Kevin. *Living through the End of Nature: The Future of American Environmentalism.* Cambridge, MA: MIT Press, 2010. A specialist's look at the vast transformation of nature which is taking place according to the best evidence science can marshal.

WEBSITES

http://sierraclub.org/. Balanced and informative environmental websites.

http://www.bbc.co.uk/history/worldwars/wwone/yugoslavia_01.shtml#four. Tim Judah traces the destruction and violence which led to mass genocide in the conflict known as the Yugoslav Wars.

http://www.epa.gov/climatechange/. The U.S. Environmental Protection Agency's website reviews the threat to the world's climate and the implications of consistent abuse. The site also looks at various initiatives to help reverse some of the damage already done.

http://www.bbc.co.uk/news/world-africa-12305154. The BBC News looks back at the life and career of Nelson Mandela.

Credits and Notes

Credits

Chapter 1: pg. 4–5 © Christoph Hormann; pg. 8 Morton Beebe / Corbis; pg. 12 (top left) akg-images / CDA / Guillemot; pg. 12 (top right) akg-images / CDA / Guillemot; pg. 12 (bottom) National Museum of Tanzania, Dar es Salaam, (c) 1985 David L. Brill; pg. 16 © Kenneth Garrett Photography; pg. 20 Photograph by Chris O'Connell, Bradshaw Foundation, Geneva; pg. 22 (left) © ALEX GRIMM / Reuters / Corbis; pg. 22 (middle) Lion-man", statuette carved of mammouth-tusk, H 296 mm. Site: Hohlenstein-Stadel-cave, community. Asselfingen, Baden-Württemberg, Germany. Upper Paleolithic period (Aurignacien), approx. 32 000 BP. Inv. Ulmer Museum Prä Slg. Wetzel Ho-St. 39 / 88.1. Photo Thomas Stephan, © Ulmer Museum; pg. 22 (right) Foto: Hilde Jensen, copyright University Tübingen; pg. 23 (top) © Walter Geiersperger / Corbis; pg. 23 (bottom) © Charles and Josette Lenars / Corbis; pg. 24 Illustrations used with permission of Michel Lorblanchet and Éditions Sud Ouest; pg. 26 (top) Francesco d'Errico; pg. 26 (bottom) Photo Pierre-Jean Texier; pg. 31 AP Photo / Perfect Image, James Chatters, HO

Chapter 2: pg. 34–35 The Trustees of The British Museum / Art Resource, NY; pg. 39 Courtesy of the Peabody Museum of Archaeology and Ethnology, Harvard University, 61-23-60 / N10296.0 (digital file #98790058); pg. 43 adapted from Gianni Tortoli / Photo Researchers, Inc; pg. 45 Erich Lessing / Art Resource, N.Y.; pg. 48 Réunion des Musées Nationaux / Art Resource, NY; pg. 50 © Copyright Alfred Molon; pg. 52 Nimatallah / Art Resource, NY; pg 55. © Gérard Degeorge / CORBIS; pg. 56 Werner Forman / Art Resource, NY; pg. 59 Réunion des Musées Nationaux / Art Resource, NY; pg. 64 © Nathan Benn / Alamy; pg. 66 (left) akg-images / John Hios; pg. 66 (right) Marie Mauzy / Art Resource, NY.

Chapter 3: pg. 74–75 © DeA Picture Library / Art Resource, NY; pg. 77 (left) © Diego Lezama Orezzoli / CORBIS; pg. 77 (right) © Doranne Jacobson; pg. 78 Photo courtesy of National Museum of Pakistan, Karachi; pg. 79 © Harappa; pg. 80© Harappa; pg. 84 V&A Images, London / Art Resource, NY; pg. 87 bpk, Berlin / Museum fuer Asiatische Kunst, Staatliche Museen / Iris Papadopoulos / Art Resource, NY; pg. 91 Firmin Didot, ~ 1810, Copyright: ImagesofAsia.com; pg. 93 (top left) © Doranne Jacobson; pg. 93 (top right) © Doranne Jacobson; pg. 93 (bottom) © Doranne Jacobson.

Chapter 4: pg. 98–99 © Xiaoyang Liu / Corbis; pg. 104 (top) Photo ChinaStock; pg. 104 (bottom) Photo ChinaStock; pg. 105 (top) Photo ChinaStock; pg. 105 (bottom) Photo ChinaStock; pg. 110 (top) V&A Images, London / Art Resource, NY; pg. 110 (bottom) photo by Gary Lee Todd; pg. 111 photo by Gary Lee Todd; pg. 118 Photo ChinaStock; pg. 120 Photo ChinaStock; pg. 121 (top) © Asian Art & Archaeology, Inc. / CORBIS; pg. 121 (bottom) The Art Archive / Museo Nazionale d'Arte Orientale Rome / Gianni Dagli Orti.

Chapter 5: pg. 128–129 ERNESTO BENAVIDES / AFP / Getty Images / Newscom; pg. 137 (top) © Ricardo Azoury; pg. 137 (bottom) © David Muench / CORBIS; pg. 139 National Geographic; pg. 140 © Sean Sprague / The Image Works; pg. 144 © Charles & Josette Lenars / CORBIS; pg. 145 The Metropolitan Museum of Art / Art Resource, NY; pg. 146 (top) © Charles & Josette Lenars / CORBIS; pg. 146 (bottom) akg-images / Bildarchiv Steffens; pg. 148 Science © 2006; pg. 152 © Caroline Penn / Impact / HIP / The Image Works; pg. 153 © ImageSpan.

Chapter 6: pg. 169 Werner Forman / Art Resource, NY; pg. 171 (top) Roderick J. McIntosh; pg. 171 (bottom) Courtesy Susan McIntosh; pg. 175 Werner Forman / Art Resource, NY; pg. 179 Richard Maschmeyer; pg. 182 bpk, Berlin / Ethnologisches Museum, Staatliche Museen / Art Resource, NY; pg. 184 Photograph K2803© Justin Kerr; pg. 185 Erich Lessing / Art Resource, NY; pg. 188 DEA / G. DAGLI ORTI / Gianni Dagli Orti / CORBIS; pg. 189 © Gianni Dagli Orti / CORBIS; pg. 191 (top) / akg / Bildarchiv Steffens; pg. 191 (bottom left) Bildarchiv Steffens. Henri Stierlin; pg. 191 (bottom right) © Keren Su / CORBIS.

Chapter 7: pg. 196–197 Vanni / Art Resource, NY; pg. 202 SEF / Art Resource, NY; pg. 205 Louis and Nancy Hatch Dupree Collection, Williams Afghan Media Project Archive; pg. 209 Vanni / Art Resource, NY; pg. 214 Scala / Art Resource, NY; pg. 220 © Wolfgang Kaehler / Corbis; pg. 224 (top) Photo © Zev Radovan; pg. 224 (middle) Photo © Zev Radovan; pg. 224 (bottom) Photo © Zev Radovan; pg. 228 akg-images / Gerard Degeorge; pg. 230 Image copyright © The Metropolitan Museum of Art / Art Resource, NY; pg. 232 (top) Erich Lessing / Art Resource, NY; pg. 232 (bottom) Scala / Art Resource, NY.

Chapter 8: pg. 236–237 Courtesy of the Library of Congress; pg. 243 Borromeo / Art Resource, NY; pg. 244 (top) Image copyright © The Metropolitan Museum of Art / Art Resource, NY; pg. 244 (bottom) © Clive Friend; pg. 247 © Lindsay Hebberd / CORBIS; pg. 249 R. u. S. / akg-images; pg. 252 (top) akg-images / A.F.Kersting / ; pg. 252 (bottom) Borromeo / Art Resource, NY; pg. 255 Image copyright © The Metropolitan Museum of Art; pg. 258 (top) Bruno Morandi / Getty Images; pg. 258 (bottom) © The Trustees of the British Museum; pg. 263 (left) Image copyright © The Metropolitan Museum of Art / Art Resource, NY; pg. 263 (right) Image copyright © The Metropolitan Museum of Art / Art Resource, NY.

Chapter 9: pg. 268–269 © The Trustees of the British Museum; pg. 273 © Glow Asia RF / Alamy; pg. 288 akg-images / Laurent Lecat; pg. 279 HIP / Art Resource, NY; pg. 282 photo by Gary Lee Todd; pg. 285 Courtesy of ChinaStock; pg. 287 (all) Courtesy of ChinaStock; pg. 293 Courtesy of the Museum of Fine Arts, Boston. Francis Bartlett Donation of 1912; pg. 294 (top) Image copyright © The Metropolitan Museum of Art / Art Resource, NY; pg 294 (bottom) Marilyn Shea, Ph.D. University of Maine at Farmington.

Chapter 10: pg. 300–301 Library of Congress; pg. 305 © Kazuyoshi Nomachi / Corbis; pg. 307 The Trustees of the British Museum / Art Resource, NY; pg. 310 (right) ALIMDI.NET / Fabian von Poser; pg. 310 (left) bpk, Berlin / Art Resource, NY; pg. 314 (right) © Jon Hicks / Corbis; pg. 314 (left) © Bruno Morandi / SOPA / Corbis; pg. 316 © Steven Vidler / Eurasia Press / Corbis; pg. 321 (left) bpk, Berlin / Staatsbibliothek zu Berlin, Stiftung Preussischer Kulturbesitz, Berlin, Germany / Ruth Schacht / Art Resource, NY; pg. 321 (right) bpk, Berlin / Staatsbibliothek zu Berlin, Stiftung Preussischer Kulturbesitz, Berlin, Germany / Ruth Schacht / Art Resource, NY; pg. 322 © British Library Board. All Rights Reserved; pg. 323 Scala / White Images / Art Resource, NY; pg. 326 bpk, Berlin / Bibliotheque Nationale / Gérard Le Gall / Art Resource, NY; pg. 327 With kind permission of the University of Edinburgh; pg. 330 The Metropolitan Museum of Art / Art Resource, NY; pg. 331 The Metropolitan Museum of Art / Art Resource, NY; pg. 333 Giraudon; pg. 334 V&A Images, London / Art Resource, NY.

Chapter 11: pg. 338–339 Erich Lessing / Art Resource, NY; pg. 344 bpk, Berlin / Cathedral (Palatine Chapel), Aachen, Germany / Stefan

pg. 650 Werner Forman / Art Resource, NY; pg. 652 The Metropolitan Museum of Art / Art Resource, NY; pg. 653 Art Resource; pg. 657 HIP / Art Resource, NY; pg. 661 Art Resource; pg. 664 Bristol Docks and Quay, c.1760 (oil on canvas), English School, (18th century) / © Bristol City Museum and Art Gallery, UK / The Bridgeman Art Library International; pg. 665 © Michael Graham-Stewart; pg. 667 Abby Aldrich Rockefeller Fold Art Museum, The colonial Williamsburg Foundation, Williamsburg, Va; pg. 668 © Robert Holmes / CORBIS; pg. 669 Collection of Herbert M. and Shelley Cole. Photo by Don Cole; pg. 670 (top) Archives Charmet; pg. 670 (bottom) Courtesy of the Library of Congress.

Chapter 20: pg. 674–675 © dbimages / Alamy; pg. 678 (c) The British Library Board, J. 1,2; pg. 679 The Art Archive / Victoria and Albert Museum London / V&A Images; pg. 681 (top) Erich Lessing / Art Resource, NY; pg. 681 (bottom left) Werner Forman / Art Resource, NY; pg. 681 (bottom right) Image copyright © The Metropolitan Museum of Art / Art Resource, NY; pg. 683 (top) Getty Images; pg. 683 (bottom) © Arthur Thévenart / CORBIS; pg. 684 Courtesy of The Chester Beatty Library; pg. 685 The San Diego Museum of Art, Edwin Binney 3rd Collection. 1990.293; pg. 692 Rijksmuseum, Amsterdam; pg. 693 CBL In 03.54 Akbar (r.1556–1605) Receives Gifts from the Ambassadors of Badakhshan, from the 'Akbarnama', c.1605 (gouache on paper), Indian School, (17th century) / © The Trustees of the Chester Beatty Library, Dublin / The Bridgeman Art Library International; pg. 694 The Art Archive / Bodleian Library Oxford / shelf mark MS Pers d43 folio 89v; pg. 697 2009 Museum Associates / LACMA / Art Resource, NY; pg. 701 © Historical Picture Archive / CORBIS; pg. 704 Photograph © 2011 Museum of Fine Arts, Boston.

Chapter 21: pg. 708–709 John C Weber Collection. Photo: John Bigelow Taylor; pg. 714 The Metropolitan Museum of Art / Art Resource, NY; pg. 715 The Metropolitan Museum of Art / Art Resource, NY; pg. 716 Courtesy of the Library of Congress; pg. 717 © Hulton-Deutsch Collection / CORBIS; pg. 719 © CHINASTOCK / QI WEN; pg. 721 © Bettmann / CORBIS; pg. 723 Roy Miles Fine Paintings; pg. 726 Courtesy of the Library of Congress; pg. 728 Réunion des Musées Nationaux / Art Resource, NY; pg. 730 © The Granger Collection, New York; pg. 732 Courtesy of the Library of Congress; pg. 735 (top) University of British Columbia Library, Rare Books and Special Collections; pg. 735 (bottom) Courtesy of the Library of Congress; pg. 737 akg-images; pg. 740 V&A Images, London / Art Resource, NY.

Chapter 22: pg. 746–747 © Trustees of the British Museum; pg. 752 Stock Sales WGBH / Scala / Art Resource, NY; pg. 754 Courtesy of the Library of Congress; pg. 756 (top left) © Bettmann / CORBIS; pg. 756 (bottom left) © Gianni Dagli Orti / CORBIS; pg 756 (right) © Gianni Dagli Orti / CORBIS; pg. 758 © Gianni Dagli Orti / CORBIS; pg. 759 Courtesy of the Library of Congress; pg. 760 Musée de l'Armée / Dist. Réunion des Musées Nationaux / Art Resource, NY; pg. 763 SSPL / Science Museum / Art Resource, NY; pg. 767 (top) Courtesy of the Library of Congress; pg. 767 (bottom) Courtesy of the Library of Congress; pg. 768 bpk, Berlin / Art Resource, N; pg. 771 © Lebrecht Music & Arts / Corbis; pg. 773 © The Print Collector / Corbis; pg. 774 © Hulton-Deutsch Collection / CORBIS; pg. 778 National Folklore Collection, University College Dublin; pg. 781 (top left) National Gallery, London / Art Resource, NY; pg 781 (bottom left) Erich Lessing / Art Resource, NY; pg 781 (right) Saturn Devouring one of his Children, 1821–23 (oil on canvas), Goya y Lucientes, Francisco Jose de (1746–1828) / Prado, Madrid, Spain / The Bridgeman Art Library International; pg. 782 © Hulton-Deutsch Collection / CORBIS.

Chapter 23: pg. 786–787 Courtesy of the Library of Congress; pg. 792 SSPL via Getty Images; pg. 793 The 'Ma Roberts' and an Elephant in the Shallows, Lower Zambezi, 1859, Baines, Thomas (1820–75) / © Royal Geographical Society, London, UK / The Bridgeman Art Library

International; pg. 800 Peter Newark Military Pictures; pg. 804 © Bettmann / CORBIS; pg. 806 The Stapleton Collection; pg. 807 © Bettmann / CORBIS; pg. 809 (top) Archives Charmet; pg. 809 (bottom) © Everett Collection Inc / Alamy; pg. 810 Photo: IAM / akg-images; pg. 811 Archives Charmet; pg. 812 Peter Newark Pictures; pg. 814 Professor Darwin, 'This is the ape of form' Love's Labour's Lost, Act V, scene II, Charles Darwin (1809–72) as an ape, 1861 (colour litho), English School, (19th century) / Natural History Museum, London, UK / The Bridgeman Art Library International; pg. 816 akg-images / ullstein bild; pg. 818 (left) The Scream, 1893 (oil, tempera & pastel on cardboard), Munch, Edvard (1863–1944) / Nasjonalgalleriet, Oslo, Norway / © DACS / The Bridgeman Art Library International; pg. 818 (right) Giraudon.

Chapter 24: pg. 822–823 © Philadelphia Museum of Art / CORBIS; pg. 827 (left) The Art Archive; pg. 827 (right) Courtesy of the Library of Congress; pg. 829 The Art Archive / Eileen Tweedy; pg. 833 (top) National Palace Museum; pg. 833 (bottom) © The Print Collector / Heritage / The Image Works; pg. 834 (left) akg-images / British Library; pg. 834 (right) Peter Newark Pictures; pg. 837 (top left) © Philadelphia Museum of Art / CORBIS; pg. 837 (top right) © Philadelphia Museum of Art / CORBIS; pg 837 (bottom) © Mary Evans Picture Library / The Image Works; pg. 838 Tz'U-Hsi (1835–1908) Empress Dowager of China with ladies of the court, 1903 (b / w photo), Chinese School, (20th century) / Private Collection / The Bridgeman Art Library International; pg. 841 (top) Courtesy of the Library of Congress; pg. 841 (bottom) Courtesy of the Library of Congress; pg. 842 IAM / akg / NA; pg. 851 Courtesy of the Library of Congress; pg. 853 © Mary Evans Picture Library / The Image Works; pg. 854 Courtesy of the Library of Congress.

Chapter 25: pg. 858–859 Auction of Serfs, 1910 (w/c on paper), Lebedev, Klavdiy Vasilievich (1852–1916) / Arkhangelsk Museum, Russia / The Bridgeman Art Library International; pg. 865 (top) Bibliothèque nationale de France or BnF; pg. 865 (middle) Réunion des Musées Nationaux / Art Resource, NY; pg. 865 (bottom) akg-images / British Library; pg. 867 © Bettmann / CORBIS; pg. 869 © Bettmann / CORBIS; pg. 870 (top) Courtesy of the Library of Congress; pg. 870 (bottom) Portrait of George Gordon (1788–1824) 6th Baron Byron of Rochdale in Albanian Dress, 1813 (oil on canvas), Phillips, Thomas (1770–1845) / National Portrait Gallery, London, UK / The Bridgeman Art Library International; pg. 875 © Roger-Viollet / The Image Works; pg. 876 (left) © Diego Lezama Orezzoli / CORBIS; pg. 876 (top right) © Tibor Bognar / Corbis; pg. 876 (bottom right) © Paule Seux / Hemis / Corbis; pg. 877 Courtesy of the New York Public Library; pg. 879 Courtesy of the Library of Congress; pg. 883 © Heritage Images / Corbis; pg.887 © Reproduced by permission of The State Hermitage Museum, St. Petersburg, Russia / CORBIS; pg. 893 RIA Novosti.

Chapter 26: pg. 896–897 Kharbine Tapabor; pg. 900 (top) © National Portrait Gallery, London; pg. 900 (bottom) (c) The British Library Board, Add.Or.3079; pg. 903 (top) The Art Archive / United Society for Propagation of Gospel / Eileen Tweedy; pg. 903 (bottom) © CORBIS; pg. 906 / akg-images / British Library; pg. 908 (top) Réunion des Musées Nationaux / Art Resource, NY; pg. 908 (bottom) Archives Charmet; pg. 910 Dorling Kindersley; pg. 912 National Library of Australia; pg. 913 Werner Forman / Art Resource, NY; pg. 915 Snark / Art Resource, NY; pg. 917 © Hulton-Deutsch Collection / CORBIS; pg. 921 Getty Images; pg. 922 © Bojan Brecelj / CORBIS; pg. 923 ullstein bild / The Granger Collection , New York; pg. 926 (left) Werner Forman / Art Resource, NY; pg. 926 (top right) HIP / Art Resource, NY; pg. 926 (bottom right) © Stapleton Collection / Corbis; pg. 929 Courtesy of the Library of Congress; pg. 930 Courtesy of the Library of Congress.

Chapter 27: pg. 934–935 The Jacob and Gwendolyn Lawrence Foundation / Art Resource, NY; pg. 939 Battle on Santo Domingo, a painting by January Suchodolski; pg. 940 Schalkwijk / Art Resource, NY; pg. 945 Erich Lessing / Art Resource, NY; pg. 946 (left) Published by permission of the Archival Center, Archdiocese of Los Angeles; pg. 946 (right) Ralph Arnold Collection, Huntington Library, San Marino, California; pg. 947 © CORBIS; pg. 949 (top) Rebecca Emery / Getty Images; pg 949 (bottom) Win Initiative (Getty Images); pg. 954 The Granger Collection, New York; pg. 955 Schomburg Center for Research in Black Culture / Manuscripts, Archives and Rare Books Division / New York Public Library; pg. 957 Courtesy of the Library of Congress; pg. 962 © Bettmann / CORBIS; pg. 965 Courtesy of the Library of Congress; pg. 966 © akg-images / The Image Works.

Chapter 28: pg. 974–975 Courtesy of the Library of Congress; pg. 977 © Hulton-Deutsch Collection / CORBIS; pg. 980 Popperfoto / Getty Images; pg. 984 Courtesy of the Library of Congress; pg. 986 Getty Images; pg. 990 The Granger Collection, NYC—All rights reserved; pg. 991 (left) © The Museum of Modern Art / Licensed by SCALA / Art Resource, NY; pg. 991 (top right) © The Museum of Modern Art / Licensed by SCALA / Art Resource, NY; pg. 991 (bottom left) © 2007 Artists Rights Society (ARS), New York / VEGAP, Madrid; pg. 994 © Instructional Resources Corporation; pg. 995 Getty Images; pg. 996 Getty Images; pg. 1000 © Bettmann / CORBIS; pg. 1002 © K.J. Historical / CORBIS; pg. 1006 © Hulton-Deutsch Collection / CORBIS; pg. 1007 © Arcaid / Corbis; pg. 1010 Courtesy of the Library of Congress; pg. 1014 Getty Images; pg. 1016 © Bettmann / CORBIS.

Chapter 29: pg. 1020–1021 Getty Images; pg. 1023 Time & Life Pictures / Getty Images; pg. 1027 Associated Press; pg. 1029 © Bettmann / CORBIS; pg. 1030 © Rykoff Collection / CORBIS; pg. 1032 © CORBIS; pg. 1033 SSPL via Getty Images; pg. 1034 ABC via Getty Images; pg. 1035 Chris Brown; pg. 1038 (left) © The Museum of Modern Art / Licensed by SCALA / Art Resource, NY; pg. 1038 (right) © 2009 Museum Associates / LACMA / Art Resource, NY; pg. 1044 Courtesy of the Library of Congress; pg. 1045 AFP / Getty Images; pg. 1049 Courtesy of the Library of Congress; pg. 1051 © Volkmar K. Wentzel / National Geographic Society / Corbis; pg. 1052 Courtesy of the Library of Congress.

Chapter 30: pg. 1060–1061 © Alain DeJean / Sygma / CORBIS; pg. 1064 Courtesy of Spacephotos.ru; pg. 1065 © CORBIS; pg. 1067 © Robert Maass / CORBIS; pg. 1069 AP Photo / Yuri Romanov; pg. 1074 (top left) © Bettmann / CORBIS; pg 1074 (top right) © Jack Moebes / CORBIS; pg. 1074 (bottom) © Bettmann / CORBIS; pg. 1077 (top) © Bettmann / CORBIS; pg. 1077 (bottom) India Today Group / Getty Images; pg. 1078 (left) © Henry Diltz / CORBIS; pg. 1078 (right) © Bettmann / CORBIS; pg. 1083 © Bettmann / CORBIS; pg. 1086 (left) © Jacques Langevin / Sygma / Corbis; pg. 1086 (right) © Reuters / CORBIS; pg. 1088 (top) © Tim Page / CORBIS; pg. 1088 (bottom) © Bettmann / CORBIS; pg. 1091 © Bettmann / CORBIS; pg. 1092 Courtesy of the Library of Congress; pg. 1095 © Bernard Bisson / Sygma / Corbis.

Chapter 31: pg. 1100–1001 Getty Images Europe; pg. 1110 © Hubert Boesl / dpa / Corbis; pg. 1113 Courtesy of Eliot Borenstein; pg. 1114 (left) © Lee Frost / Robert Harding World Imagery / Corbis; pg. 1114 (right) Getty Images; pg. 1115 (top) ASSOCIATED PRESS; pg. 1115 (bottom) AP Images; pg. 1120 © Manca Juvan / In Pictures / Corbis; pg. 1123 AFP / Getty Images; pg. 1124 © Samuel Aranda / Corbis; pg. 1126 Associated Press; pg. 1128 Associated Press; pg. 1129 © Louise Gubb / CORBIS SABA; pg. 1136 AFP / Getty Images.

Notes

Chapter 3: p. 86 Translated by R. N. Dandekar, in Sources of Indian Tradition, Ainslie T. Emree, ed., 2nd Ed., Vol I (New York: Columbia University Press, 1988) p. 247; p. 88 Translated by Joel Brereton, in Sources [same ed. As above; p. 19; p. 89 Yajnavalkya Smirti, (Code of Vajnavalkya), R.N.Dandekar in Sources, p. 227–8]; p. 89 From Manu Smirti [The Code of Manu], Ibid. [same translator], pp. 228–9.

Chapter 5: p. 140 Greg Borzo, "Anthropologists Establish Date and Importance of the Americas' Oldest City," The Field Musueum, Chicago, Museum Notes, April 26, 2001; http://www.fmnh.org/museum_info/press/press_hass.htm.

Chapter 11: p. 367 *Abbot Suger: On the Abbey Church of St.-Denis and Its Art Treasures,* ed., trans., and annotated by Erwin Panofsky, (Princeton, 1946), pp. 100--01; 375–376 Dante, Monarchia, trans. and ed. By Prue Shaw (Cambridge: Cambridge University Press, 1995), Book One, ch. 5, part 3, p. 15.

Chapter 20: p 688–689 John F. Richards, *The Mughal Empire, in The New Cambridge History of India (Cambridge: Cambridge University Press, 1995), p.105*; p. 688–689 From Muhammad Sadiq, "Shahjahan-Nama," (The autobiography of Shah Jahan) quoted in Richards, *The Mughal Empire,* p. 135.

Chapter 21: p. 714–715 See Kenneth Pomeranz, *The Great Divergence. China, Europe, and the Making of the Modern World Economy,* (Princeton, NJ: Princeton University Press, 2001.)

Chapter 23: p 747 Mary Paul to Bela Paul, September 13, November 20, December 21, 1845, November 27, 1853, in Thomas Dublin, *Farm to Factory: Women's Letters, 1830–1860,* (New York: Columbia University Press, 1993), pp. 124–125, 128, 135; p. 808 Karl Marx, Friedrich Engels, *The Communist Manifesto. A Modern Edition.* With an introduction by Eric Hobsbawm, (London: Verso, 2001) p. 77.

Chapter 24: p. 822–824 All quotes in the vignette are from John K., and Su-yu Teng. *China's Response to the West.* Cambridge, MA: Harvard University Press, 1954. p. 126; p. 832 Prince Gong to Rutherford Alcock, 1869, quoted in Robert Hart, *These From the Land of Sinim* (London: Chapman and Hall,1901), p. 68

Chapter 31: p. 1102 Dexter Filkins, "After the Uprising," *The New Yorker* (online edition) (April, 11, 2011), pp. 5; Sudarsan Raghavan, "In Yemen, Female Activist Struggles for an Egypt-like Revolution," *The Washington Post,* February 15, 2011, Section A, p, 1; p. 1127 NY Times, February 14, 2011. Ibid. "explosives" quote from IPT News, December 10, 2010; p. 1130–1131 NY Times, February 14, 2011.

Index

The letter f following a page number denotes a figure or map.